W9-CCM-493

THIRD EDITION

ESSENTIALS of STRENGTH TRAINING and CONDITIONING

NATIONAL STRENGTH AND CONDITIONING ASSOCIATION

Thomas R. Baechle, EdD; CSCS,*D; NSCA-CPT,*D
Creighton University, Omaha, Nebraska

Roger W. Earle, MA; CSCS,*D; NSCA-CPT,*D
NSCA Certification Commission

EDITORS

Human Kinetics

Library of Congress Cataloging-in-Publication Data

Essentials of strength training and conditioning / National Strength and Conditioning Association ; Thomas R. Baechle, Roger W. Earle, editors. -- 3rd ed.

p. ; cm.

Includes bibliographical references and index.

ISBN-13: 978-0-7360-5803-2 (hard cover)

ISBN-10: 0-7360-5803-6 (hard cover)

1. Physical education and training. 2. Muscle strength. 3. Physical fitness--Physiological aspects. I. Baechle, Thomas R., 1943- II. Earle, Roger W., 1967- III. National Strength & Conditioning Association (U.S.)

[DNLM: 1. Physical Education and Training--methods. 2. Athletic Performance--physiology. 3. Exercise--physiology. 4. Physical Fitness--physiology. QT 255 E78 2008]

GV711.5.E88 2008

613.7'1--dc22

2008001944

ISBN-10: 0-7360-5803-6

ISBN-13: 978-0-7360-5803-2

Acquisitions Editor: Michael S. Bahrke, PhD; **Developmental Editor:** Christine M. Drews; **Assistant Editor:** Katherine Maurer; **Copyeditor:** Joyce Sexton; **Proofreaders:** Erin Cler and Red Inc.; **Indexer:** Susan Danzi Hernandez; **Permission Manager:** Dalene Reeder; **Graphic Designer:** Bob Reuther; **Graphic Artist:** Dawn Sills; **Cover Designer:** Bob Reuther; **Photographer (interior):** Neil Bernstein, except where otherwise noted. Photos on pages 260, 261, 267-269, 302-305, 308-318, 328-330, 419, 424, 428-455, 533-535 by Tom Roberts. Additional photo credits appear on p. xiv; **Photo Asset Manager:** Laura Fitch; **Visual Production Assistant:** Joyce Brumfield; **Photo Office Assistant:** Jason Allen; **Art Manager:** Kelly Hendren; **Associate Art Manager:** Alan L. Wilborn; **Illustrators:** Joanne Brummett; Tim Brummett; Laura Cosner; Jennifer M. Gibas, CMI; Gary Hunt; Gisela Kraus; Gregory Maxson; W. Andrew Recker; Rachel M. Rogge

We thank Creighton University in Omaha, Nebraska, for assistance in providing the location for the photo shoot for this book.

Printed in China 10 9 8 7 6 5 4 3 2 1

Human Kinetics
Web site: www.HumanKinetics.com

United States: Human Kinetics
P.O. Box 5076
Champaign, IL 61825-5076
800-747-4457
e-mail: humank@hkusa.com

Canada: Human Kinetics
475 Devonshire Road Unit 100
Windsor, ON N8Y 2L5
800-465-7301 (in Canada only)
e-mail: info@hkcanada.com

Europe: Human Kinetics
107 Bradford Road
Stanningley
Leeds LS28 6AT, United Kingdom
+44 (0) 113 255 5665
e-mail: hk@hkeurope.com

Australia: Human Kinetics
57A Price Avenue
Lower Mitcham, South Australia 5062
08 8372 0999
e-mail: info@hkaustralia.com

New Zealand: Human Kinetics
Division of Sports Distributors NZ Ltd.
P.O. Box 300 226 Albany
North Shore City
Auckland
0064 9 448 1207
e-mail: info@humankinetics.co.nz

Contents

Section 3 Exercise Techniques 293

Section 4 Program Design 377

Contributors

Thomas R. Baechle, EdD; CSCS,*D; NSCA-CPT,*D
Creighton University, Omaha, NE

Evan B. Brody, PhD
Performance Enhancement Consultants (PEC), Olney, MD

Donald A. Chu, PhD; PT; ATC; CSCS,*D; NSCA-CPT,*D; FNSCA
Athercare Fitness & Rehabilitation, Castro Valley, CA

Joel T. Cramer, PhD; CSCS,*D; NSCA-CPT,*D; FNSCA
University of Oklahoma

Roger W. Earle, MA; CSCS,*D; NSCA-CPT,*D
NSCA Certification Commission

Boyd Epley, MEd, CSCS, FNSCA
National Strength and Conditioning Association

Avery D. Faigenbaum, EdD; CSCS,*D; FNSCA
The College of New Jersey

John Garhammer, PhD, CSCS, NSCA-CPT, FNSCA
California State University, Long Beach

Lori Greenwood, PhD, ATC, LAT
Baylor University, Waco, TX

Michael Greenwood, PhD; CSCS,*D; FACSM; FISSN; FNSCA
Baylor University, Waco, TX

Terry L. Grindstaff, DPT; ATC; SCS; CSCS,*D
University of Virginia, Charlottesville

Patrick S. Hagerman, EdD, CSCS, NSCA-CPT, FNSCA
Quest Personal Training, Inc.

Everett Harman, PhD, CSCS, NSCA-CPT
U.S. Army Research Institute of Environmental Medicine, Natick, MA

Robert T. Harris, PhD
West Virginia State University

Bradley D. Hatfield, PhD, FACSM, FAAKPE
University of Maryland, College Park

Jay R. Hoffman, PhD; CSCS,*D; FACSM; FNSCA
The College of New Jersey

Gary R. Hunter, PhD, CSCS, FNSCA
University of Alabama at Birmingham

Ian Jeffreys, MS; CSCS,*D; NSCA-CPT,*D
University of Glamorgan, United Kingdom

William J. Kraemer, PhD, CSCS, FACSM, FISSN, FNSCA
University of Connecticut

Steven S. Plisk, MS; CSCS,*D
Excelsior Sports, Shelton, CT

David H. Potach, PT; MS; CSCS,*D; NSCA-CPT,*D
Omaha Sports Physical Therapy, Omaha, NE

Nicholas A. Ratamess, PhD; CSCS,*D
The College of New Jersey

Kristin Reimers, PhD, RD
ConAgra Foods, Inc., Omaha, NE

Benjamin H. Reuter, PhD; ATC; CSCS,*D
California University of Pennsylvania

Barry A. Spiering, PhD, CSCS
University of Connecticut

Jeffrey R. Stout, PhD, CSCS, FACSM, FISSN, FNSCA
University of Oklahoma

Ann Swank, PhD, CSCS, FACSM
University of Louisville

John Taylor, MS; CSCS,*D; CP; FNSCA
New Mexico State University

Jakob L. Vingren, PhD, CSCS
University of Connecticut

Dan Wathen, MS; ATC; CSCS,*D; NSCA-CPT,*D; FNSCA
Youngstown State University

Contributors to Previous Editions

William B. Allerheiligen, MS; CSCS,*D; NSCA-CPT,*D; FNSCA

Stephanie Armitage-Kerr, MS, CSCS

Thomas R. Baechle, EdD; CSCS,*D; NSCA-CPT,*D

Richard A. Borden, PhD, PT, CSCS

Evan B. Brody, PhD

Donald A. Chu, PhD; PT; ATC; CSCS,*D; NSCA-CPT,*D; FNSCA

Mike Conley, MD, PhD

Brian Conroy, MD, PhD, CSCS

Gary Dudley, PhD, CSCS, FACSM, FAAKPE

Roger W. Earle, MA; CSCS,*D; NSCA-CPT,*D

Boyd Epley, MEd, CSCS, FNSCA

Avery D. Faigenbaum, EdD; CSCS,*D; FNSCA

Karl E. Friedl, PhD

John Garhammer, PhD, CSCS, NSCA-CPT, FNSCA

Lori Greenwood, PhD, ATC, LAT

Michael Greenwood, PhD; CSCS,*D; FACSM; FISSN; FNSCA

Everett Harman, PhD, CSCS, NSCA-CPT

Robert T. Harris, PhD

Bradley D. Hatfield, PhD, FACSM, FAAKPE

William R. Holcomb, PhD; ATC; CSCS,*D

Jean Barrett Holloway, MA, CSCS

Gary R. Hunter, PhD, CSCS, FNSCA

William J. Kraemer, PhD, CSCS, FACSM, FISSN, FNSCA

Clay Pandorf, BS

Steven S. Plisk, MS; CSCS,*D

David H. Potach, PT; MS; CSCS,*D; NSCA-CPT,*D

Jeffrey A. Potteiger, PhD, FACSM

Kristin Reimers, PhD, RD

Fred Roll, BS

Jaime Ruud, MS, RD

Douglas M. Semenick, EdD

Michael H. Stone, PhD, FNSCA

Dan Wathen, MS; ATC; CSCS,*D; NSCA-CPT,*D; FNSCA

Mark A. Williams, PhD, FACSM, FAACVPR

Preface

In 1994, the first edition of *Essentials of Strength Training and Conditioning* was published. After a second edition (in 2000) and sales of over 100,000 books, this expanded and updated third edition continues the tradition as the most comprehensive reference available for strength and conditioning professionals. In this text, 30 expert contributors further explore the scientific principles, concepts, and theories of strength training and conditioning and their applications to athletic performance.

The first edition grew out of an awareness that there was not a book about strength training and conditioning that captured the views of leading professionals in anatomy, biochemistry, biomechanics, endocrinology, nutrition, exercise physiology, psychology, and the other sciences and related the principles from these disciplines to the design of safe and effective training programs. Also, the lack of relevant and well-conducted research studies had hindered earlier efforts to create an all-inclusive resource. Once it was finally developed, *Essentials of Strength Training and Conditioning* quickly became the definitive textbook on the subject.

The second edition, released six years later, was more than a simple freshening of the content; it was an overhaul of the scope and application of the first edition. Throughout the text and in the additional 100-plus pages, the chapter contributors used updated, relevant, and conclusive research and concepts to turn science into performance. Many learning tools were added, such as chapter objectives, key points, application boxes, and sample resistance training programs for three different sports. These enhancements, plus the addition of a full-color interior and over 300 color photographs, made the second edition truly exceptional.

UPDATES TO THE THIRD EDITION

This third edition expands and applies the most current research and information in a logical format that reaffirms *Essentials of Strength Training and Conditioning* as the most prominent resource for students preparing for careers in strength and conditioning and for sport science professionals involved in training athletes. The enhancements are as follows:

- Restructured information about the body's adaptations to anaerobic and aerobic exercise training (chapters 5 and 6)
- Greatly expanded information about performance-enhancing substances (chapter 9)
- Up-to-date nutritional information, including the new food guide pyramid and recent research-based nutritional guidelines (chapter 10)
- Additional sport-specific testing protocols and comprehensive normative and descriptive data charts (chapter 12)
- New photographs of exercise techniques (chapters 13 and 14)
- New terminology for concepts related to the design of resistance training programs (chapter 15) and periodization (chapter 19)
- Concise explanations of speed and agility training guidelines (chapter 17)
- Step-by-step guidelines on designing aerobic endurance training programs (chapter 18)
- Revised descriptions of strength and conditioning staff duties and checklists for facility maintenance (chapters 21 and 22)

These enhancements, plus the modernized artwork and the addition of instructor and student resources, continue to make this *the* textbook for the study and instruction of strength and conditioning. The third edition retains the study aids that made the second edition so popular. Each chapter begins with objectives and includes key points to guide the reader along the way. Key terms are boldfaced and listed at the end of the chapter, with page numbers indicating where they are explained in the chapter. Chapters include sidebars that apply the content, and later chapters include sample resistance training programs for three different sports. Detailed instructions and photos are provided for testing, stretching, resistance training, and plyometrics. Finally, chapters end with multiple-choice study questions, with an answer key at the end of the book.

INSTRUCTOR RESOURCES

In addition to the updated content, this edition includes newly created instructor resources:

- *Instructor Guide.* The instructor guide contains chapter objectives and outlines, Web sites and resources, definitions of select key terms, application essay questions with suggested answers, and links to the related Lab Activities.
- *Presentation Package and Image Bank.* This comprehensive resource, delivered in Microsoft PowerPoint, offers instructors a Presentation Package containing over 1,000 slides to help augment lectures and class discussions. In addition to outlines and key points, the resource also contains over 450 figures, tables, and photos from the textbook, which can be used as an Image Bank by instructors who need to customize their own presentations. Easy-to-follow instructions help guide instructors on how to reuse the images within their own PowerPoint templates.

These instructor resources can be found at www.HumanKinetics.com/EssentialsOfStrengthTrainingAndConditioning.

STUDENT RESOURCES

Lab Activities are available online to help students practice testing and evaluating athletes. Eleven labs with 20 reproducible sheets are provided. Students can complete the lab forms online and e-mail PDFs of the completed forms to their instructors, or they can print out blank forms and handwrite their findings.

This student resource can be found at www.HumanKinetics.com/EssentialsOfStrengthTrainingAndConditioning.

Full-color art

Key term

Key point

Application sidebars

12 ▪ Essentials of Strength Training and Conditioning

opment of strength early in the range of motion, especially at high velocities (13, 14, 19).

Proprioception

Proprioceptors are specialized sensory receptors located within joints, muscles, and tendons. Because these receptors are sensitive to pressure and tension, they relay information concerning muscle dynamics to the conscious and subconscious parts of the central nervous system. The brain is thus provided with information concerning kinesthetic sense, or conscious appreciation of the position of body parts with respect to gravity. Most of this proprioceptive information, however, is processed at subconscious levels so we do not have to dedicate conscious activity toward tasks such as maintaining posture or position of body parts.

Proprioceptors are specialized sensory receptors that provide the central nervous system with information needed to maintain muscle tone and perform complex coordinated movements.

Muscle Spindles

Muscle spindles are proprioceptors that consist of several modified muscle fibers enclosed in a sheath of connective tissue (figure 1.7). These modified fibers, called **intrafusal fibers**, run parallel to the normal, or **extrafusal**, fibers. Muscle spindles provide information concerning muscle length and the rate of change in length. When the muscle lengthens, spindles are stretched. This deformation acti-

How Can Athletes Improve Force Production?

- Recruit large muscles or muscle groups during an activity.
- Increase the cross-sectional area of muscles involved in the desired activity.
- Preload a muscle just before a concentric action to enhance force production during the subsequent muscle action.
- Use preloading during training to develop strength early in the range of motion. Accommodating-resistance apparatus, such as isokinetic, hydraulic, and friction-modulated systems, do not load the muscle prior to contraction.

Sensory neuron
Intrafusal fiber
Muscle spindle
Motor neuron
Extrafusal fiber

Figure 1.7 Muscle spindle. When a muscle is stretched, deformation of the muscle spindle activates the sensory neuron, which sends an impulse to the spinal cord, where it synapses with a motor neuron, causing the muscle to contract.

vates the sensory neuron of the spindle, which sends an impulse to the spinal cord, where it synapses (connects) with motor neurons. This results in the activation of motor neurons that innervate the same muscle. Spindles thus indicate the degree to which the muscle must be activated in order to overcome a given resistance. As a load increases, the muscle is stretched to a greater extent, and engagement of muscle spindles results in greater activation of the muscle. Muscles that perform precise movements have many spindles per unit of mass to help ensure exact control of their contractile activity. A simple example of muscle spindle activity is the knee jerk reflex. Tapping on the tendon of the knee extensor muscle group below the patella stretches the muscle spindle fibers. This causes activation of extrafusal muscle fibers in the same muscle. There is a knee jerk as these fibers actively shorten. This, in turn, shortens the intrafusal fibers and causes their discharge to cease.

Golgi Tendon Organs

Golgi tendon organs (GTOs) are proprioceptors located in tendons near the myotendinous junction and are in series, that is, attached end to end, with extrafusal muscle fibers (figure 1.8). Golgi tendon organs are activated when the tendon attached to an active muscle is stretched. As tension in the muscle increases, discharge of the GTOs increases. The sensory neuron of the GTO synapses with an

CERTIFICATION EXAMS

Essentials of Strength Training and Conditioning is the primary resource for individuals preparing for the NSCA Certification Commission's Certified Strength and Conditioning Specialist (CSCS) certification exam and serves as a valuable secondary resource for those preparing for the NSCA-Certified Personal Trainer (NSCA-CPT) certification exam.

As a worldwide authority on strength and conditioning, the National Strength and Conditioning Association (NSCA) supports and disseminates research-based knowledge and its practical application to improve athletic performance and fitness. With over 30,000 members in more than 50 countries, including a sister association in Japan, the NSCA has established itself as an international clearinghouse for strength and conditioning research, theories, and practices.

The NSCA Certification Commission, the certifying agency of the NSCA, offers the only fitness-related certification programs that have been nationally accredited since 1993 by the National Commission for Certifying Agencies, a nongovernmental, nonprofit agency in Washington, DC, that sets national standards for certifying agencies. In 2006, both the CSCS and the NSCA-CPT credentials were accredited by the American National Standards Institute (ANSI)/ISO/IEC 17024 Personnel Certification Accreditation Program. The NSCA Certification Commission is the first fitness-related certification organization in the world to offer personnel certifications that are accredited by ANSI. To date, more than 33,000 professionals residing in 59 countries hold one or both of the NSCA Certification Commission's credentials.

Whether used for learning the essentials of strength training and conditioning, for preparing for a certification exam, or as a reference by professionals, *Essentials of Strength Training and Conditioning, Third Edition*, will help practitioners and the scientific community better understand how to develop and administer safe and effective strength training and conditioning programs.

64 • Essentials of Strength Training and Conditioning

CONCLUSION

As we continue to study the endocrine system and its interactions with the nervous system, the immune system, and the musculoskeletal system, we find that the functions of these systems are truly integrated. Communication among systems is accomplished with hormones and other peptides. For years, strength and conditioning professionals and athletes have appreciated the importance of anabolic hormones for mediating changes in the body and helping with the adaptive response to heavy resistance training. Whether trying to optimize a workout or avoid overtraining, the strength and conditioning professional must remember that the endocrine system plays a role. The goal of this chapter is to provide an initial glimpse into this complex but highly organized system that mediates the changes in the body with training.

KEY TERMS

allosteric binding site 46
anabolic hormone 45
catabolic hormone 45
cross-reactivity 46
diurnal variation 54
downregulation 46
endocrine gland 42
myosin heavy-chain (MHC) proteins 45
hormone 42
hormone-receptor complex (H-RC) 47
lock-and-key theory 46
neuroendocrinology 42
polypeptide hormone 47
proteolytic enzymes 61
secondary messenger 48
steroid hormone 43
target tissue 43
thyroid hormone 43

STUDY QUESTIONS

1. After a bout of resistance training, acute hormonal secretions provide all of the following information to the body EXCEPT
   a. amount of physiological stress.
   b. metabolic demands of exercise.
   c. type of physiological stress.
   d. energy expended.
2. Which of the following hormones enhance muscle tissue growth?
   I. growth
4. Which of the following hormones has the greatest influence on neural changes?
   a. growth hormone
   b. testosterone
   c. cortisol
   d. IGF
5. Which of the following hormone levels is higher in women than in men at rest?
   a. cortisol
   b. insulin
   c. testosterone
   d. growth hormone

hat type of resistance training workout promotes the highest growth hormone increases llowing the exercise session?

Rest	Volume	Sets
30 seconds	high	3
0 seconds	low	1
minutes	high	1
minutes	low	3

Learning aids at the end of each chapter include a conclusion, key terms list, and study questions.

Shoulders (CONTINUED)

UPRIGHT ROW

Starting Position
- Grasp the bar with a closed, pronated grip approximately shoulder-width apart or narrower.
- Stand erect with feet shoulder-width apart, knees slightly flexed.
- Rest the bar on the front of the thighs with the elbows fully extended and pointing out to the sides.

Upward Movement Phase
- Pull the bar up along the abdomen and chest toward the chin.
- Keep the elbows pointed out to the sides as the bar brushes against the body.
- Keep the torso and knees in the same position.
- Do not rise up on the toes or swing the bar upward.
- At the highest bar position, the elbows should be level with or slightly higher than the shoulders and wrists.

Downward Movement Phase
- Allow the bar to slowly descend back to the starting position.
- Keep the torso and knees in the same position.

Major Muscles Involved
Deltoids, upper trapezius

Starting position
Upward and downward movements

366

Detailed exercise instructions and photos

Acknowledgments

After completing the second edition of this text and the first edition of *NSCA's Essentials of Personal Training*, we found it difficult to imagine circling the wagons to develop the third edition of this text. Thankfully, we had the assistance of Nolan Harms, MS; CSCS,*D; NSCA-CPT,*D, a staff member at the NSCA Certification Commission who not only has excellent organization and editing abilities but also has valuable content knowledge. With his involvement, this text truly is a step above the second edition. To him, we give a special thanks.

Another boon to the process was the expertise and skills of many people on the Human Kinetics staff, especially Chris Drews, the developmental editor who has been with us for literally *decades*, and a new assistant editor, Kate Maurer, who brought freshness and meticulousness to the project. We recognize and appreciate the efforts of Joyce Sexton, the copyeditor; Dalene Reeder, the permission manager; Bob Reuther, the graphic and cover designer; Dawn Sills, the graphic artist; and Kelly Hendren, the art manager. Their contributions are critical because of the high expectations created as a result of the first and second editions of the text.

We are intensely grateful to the authors and reviewers who contributed to the first and second editions and to the authors and reviewers who provided expert content for this third edition of *Essentials of Strength Training and Conditioning*.

We are also appreciative of Drs. Rainer Martens, president of Human Kinetics, and Mike Bahrke, our long-time acquisitions editor, who have supported this textbook through all of its editions. We want to once again thank John Garhammer, PhD, CSCS, NSCA-CPT, FNSCA, and David H. Potach, PT; MS; CSCS,*D; NSCA-CPT,*D, who contributed in important ways and whose absence would have dulled the edge of quality that this edition provides to readers.

Above all, we thank our wives and children, who sacrificed time and attention and provided us with patience, support, and love. We dedicate this text to them—Susan, Todd, and Clark Baechle and Tonya, Kelsey (KK), Allison (Alli), Natalia (Talia), and Cassandra (Cassie) Earle.

Credits

Figure 3.9 Reprinted from W.J. Kraemer et al., 1990. "Hormonal and growth factor responses to heavy resistance exercise," *Journal of Applied Physiology* 69 (4): 1422-1450. Used with permission.

Figure 3.11 Adapted from W.J. Kraemer et al., 1998, "Hormonal responses to consecutive days of heavy-resistance exercise with or without nutritional supplementation," *Journal of Applied Physiology* 85 (4): 1544-1555. Used with permission.

Figure 4.6 Reprinted, by permission, from B.A. Gowitzke and M. Milner, 1988. *Scientific bases of human movement*, 3rd ed. (Baltimore, MD: Lippincott, Williams & Wilkins), 184-185.

Figure 4.9 Reprinted, by permission, from B.A. Gowitzke and M. Milner, 1988. *Scientific bases of human movement*, 3rd ed. (Baltimore, MD: Williams & Wilkins), 184-185.

Figure 4.13 Reprinted from K. Jorgensen, 1976, "Force-Velocity Relationship in Human Elbow Flexors and Extensors." In *Biomechanics A-V*, edited by P.V. Komi, (Baltimore, MD: University Park Press), 147. By permission of P.V. Komi.

Figure 4.16 Reprinted, by permission, from E.A. Harman, M. Johnson, and P.N. Frykman, 1992. "A movement-oriented approach to exercise prescription," *NSCA Journal* 14 (1): 47-54.

Table 5.3 Reprinted, by permission, from A. Fry, 1993, Physiological responses to short-term high intensity resistance exercise overtraining, Ph.D. Diss., The Pennsylvania State University.

Figure 5.6 Reprinted, by permission, from S.J. Fleck and W.J. Kraemer 2003, *Designing resistance training programs*, 3rd ed. (Champaign, IL: Human Kinetics), 115.

Figure 6.1 This article was published in *Textbook of medical physiology*, 8th ed., A.C. Guyton, pg. 151, Copyright Elsevier 1991.

Figure 6.2 Reprinted, by permission, from W.D. McArdle, F.I. Katch, and V.L. Katch, 1996, *Exercise physiology: Energy, nutrition, and human performance*, 4th ed. (Baltimore, MD: Lippincott, Williams & Wilkins), 230.

Figure 6.3 From E. Fox, R. Bowers and M. Foss, 1993, *The physiological basis for exercise and sport*, 5th ed. (Dubuque, IA: Wm. C. Brown). Reprinted with permission of McGraw-Hill companies.

Figure 7.2 Reprinted, by permission, from W.A. Kraemer et al., 1989, "Resistance training and youth," *Pediatric Exercise Science* 1:336-350.

Figure 8.1 Reprinted with permission from *Research Quarterly for Exercise and Sport*, Vol. 51, No. 1, 82, Copyright 1980 by the American Alliance for Health, Physical Education, Recreation, and Dance, 1900 Association Drive, Reston, VA 20191.

Table 8.2 From R.M. Nideffer, 1976, "Test of attentional and interpersonal style," *Journal of Personality and Social Psychology* 34: 394-404. Copyright © 1976 by the American Psychological Association. Used with permission.

Figure 8.2 Reprinted, by permission, from B.D. Hatfield and G.A. Walford, 1987, "Understanding anxiety: Implications for sport performance," *NSCA Journal* 9(2): 60-61.

Figure 8.3 Adapted, by permission, from G. Martin and D. Hrycaiko, 1983, "Effective behavioral coaching: What's it all about?" *Journal of Sport Psychology* 5(1):13.

Figure 9.2 Reprinted, by permission, from J. Hoffman, 2002, *Physiological aspects of sport training and performance* (Champaign, IL: Human Kinetics), 217.

Figure 9.3 Adapted, by permission, from W.D. Van Marken Lichtenbelt et al., 2004, "Bodybuilders' body composition: Effect of nandrolone decanoate," *Medicine and Science in Sports and Exercise* 36:484-489.

Figure 9.4 Adapted, by permission, from J.R. Hoffman et al., 2006, "Effect of creatine and ß-alanine supplementation on performance and endocrine responses in strength/power athletes," *International Journal of Sport Nutrition and Exercise Metabolism* 16:430-446.

Table 10.3 Adapted, by permission, from K. Foster-Powell, S. Holt, and J.C. Brand-Miller, 2002, "International table of glycemic index and glycemic load values," *American Journal of Clinical Nutition* 76: 5-56. © American Society for Nutrition.

Figure 10.2 Reprinted, by permission, from American Psychiatric Association, 1994, *Diagnostic and statistical manual of mental disorders*, Fourth Edition (Washington, DC: American Psychiatric Press, Inc.) Copyright 1994 American Psychiatric Association.

Figure 10.3 Reprinted, by permission, from American Psychiatric Association, 1994, *Diagnostic and statistical manual of mental disorders*, Fourth Edition (Washington, DC: American Psychiatric Press, Inc.) Copyright 1994 American Psychiatric Association.

Table 11.1 Adapted, by permission, from W.D. McArdle, F.I. Katch, and V.L. Katch, 1996, *Exercise physiology: Energy, nutrition, and human performance*, 4th ed. (Baltimore, MD: Lippincott, Williams & Wilkins), 518.

Figure 12.2 From E. Fox, R. Bowers, and M. Foss, 1993, *The physiological basis for exercise and sport*, 5th ed. (Dubuque, IA: Wm. C. Brown), 675. Reprinted with permission of McGraw-Hill companies.

Figure 12.3 Adapted, by permission, from G.M. Gilliam, 1983, "300 yard shuttle run," *NSCA Journal* 5 (5): 46.

Figure 12.7 Adapted, by permission, from D. Semenick, "Tests and measurements: The T-test," *NSCA Journal* 12(1): 36-37.

Figure 12.8 Adapted, by permission, from K. Pauole et al., 2000, "Reliability and validity of the T-test as a measure of agility, leg power, and leg speed in college age males and females," *Journal of Strength and Conditioning Research* 14.

Table 12.1 Adapted, by permission, from J. Hoffman, 2006, *Norms for fitness, performance, and health* (Champaign, IL: Human Kinetics), 36-37.

Table 12.2 Reprinted, by permission, from J. Hoffman, 2006, *Norms for fitness, performance, and health* (Champaign, IL: Human Kinetics), 36-37.

Table 12.3 Reprinted, by permission, from J. Hoffman, 2006, *Norms for fitness, performance, and health* (Champaign, IL: Human Kinetics), 38.

Table 12.5 Adapted from E. Fox, R. Bowers, and M. Foss, 1993, *The physiological basis for exercise and sport*, 5th ed. (Dubuque, IA: Wm. C. Brown), 676. Reprinted with permission of McGraw-Hill Companies.

Table 12.6 Reprinted, by permission, from J. Hoffman, 2006, *Norms for fitness, performance, and health* (Champaign, IL: Human Kinetics), 58; Adapted, by permission, from D.A. Chu, 1996, *Explosive power and strength* (Champaign, IL: Human Kinetics).

Table 12.7 Reprinted, by permission, from J. Hoffman, 2006, *Norms for fitness, performance, and health* (Champaign, IL: Human Kinetics), 58; Adapted, by permission, from D.A. Chu, 1996, *Explosive power and strength* (Champaign, IL: Human Kinetics).

Table 12.8 Reprinted, by permission, from American College of Sports Medicine, 2000, *ACSM's guidelines for exercise testing and prescription*, 6th ed. (Baltimore, MD: Lippincott, Williams, and Wilkins), 86.

Table 12.9 Source: *Canadian Physical Activity, Fitness & Lifestyle Approach: CSEP-Health & Fitness Program's Health-Related Appraisal & Counseling Strategy, Third Edition*, © 2003. Reprinted with permission from the Canadian Society for Exercise Psychology.

Table 12.17 Reprinted, by permission, from J. Hoffman, 2006, *Norms for fitness, performance, and health* (Champaign, IL: Human Kinetics), 73. Adapted, by permission, from American College of Sports Medicine, 2000, *ACSM's guidelines for exercise testing and prescription*, 6th ed. (Philadelphia, PA: Lippincott, Williams, and Wilkins).

Table 12.18 Reprinted, by permission, from J. Hoffman, 2006, *Norms for fitness, performance, and health* (Champaign, IL: Human Kinetics), 113.

Table 12.19 Adapted, by permission, from V. H. Heyward, 2002, *Advanced fitness assessment and exercise prescription*, 3rd ed. (Champaign, IL: Human Kinetics), 155.

Table 12.20 Adapted, by permission, from V.H. Heyward and L.M. Stolarczyk, 1996, *Applied body composition assessment* (Champaign, IL: Human Kinetics), 12.

Table 12.22 Adapted, by permission, from L.A. Golding, C.R. Myers, and W.E. Sinning, 1989, *Y's way to physical fitness*, 3rd ed. (Champaign, IL : Hùman Kinetics), 125-136.

Figure 15.1 Reprinted, by permission, from R.W. Earle, 2006, Weight training exercise prescription. In: *Essentials of personal training symposium workbook* (Lincoln, NE: NSCA Certification Commission), 2006.

Figure 15.2 Reprinted, by permission, from R.W. Earle, 2006, Weight training exercise prescription. In: *Essentials of personal training symposium workbook* (Lincoln, NE: NSCA Certification Commission).

Figure 16.1 This article was published in *Eccentric muscle training in sports and orthopaedics*, M. Albert, Copyright Elsevier 1995.

Figure 16.2 Adapted from K.E. Wilk, M.L. Voight, M.A. Keirns, V. Gambetta, J.R. Andrews, and C.J. Dillman, "Stretch-shortening drills for the upper extremities: Theory and clinical applications," *Journal of Orthopaedic Sports Physical Therapy* 17 (5): 225-239.

Figure 17.1 Reprinted, by permission, from K. Häkkinen and P.V. Komi, 1985, "The effect of explosive type strength training on electromyographic and force production characteristic of leg extensor muscles during concentric and various stretch-shortening cycle exercises," *Scandinavian Journal of Sports Sciences* 7(2): 65-76. Copyright 1985 Munksgaard International Publishers, Ltd. Copenhagen, Denmark.

Figure 17.2 Adapted, by permission, from J.A. Faulkner, D.R. Claflin, K.K. McCully, 1986, Power output of fast and slow fibers from human skeletal muscles. In *Human muscle power*, edited by N.L. Jones, N. McCarney, and A.J. McComas (Champaign, IL: Human Kinetics), 88.

Figure 17.3 Adapted, by permission, from C.J. Dillman, 1975, "Kinematic analyses of running," *Exercise & Sport Sciences Reviews* 3: 193-218.

Figure 17.4 Reprinted, by permission, from G. Schmolinsky, 2000, *The East German textbook of athletics* (Toronto: Sport Books).

Figure 17.5 Reprinted, by permission, from G. Schmolinsky, 2000, *The East German textbook of athletics* (Toronto: Sport Books).

Figure 17.6 Reprinted, by permission, from G. Schmolinsky, 2000, *The East German textbook of athletics* (Toronto: Sport Books).

Figure 17.10 Reprinted, by permission, from S.S. Plisk, V. Gambetta, 1997, "Tactical metabolic training," *Strength & Conditioning* 19(2): 44-53.

Tactical Modeling and Special Endurance Training Example, p. 483 Reprinted, by permission, from S.S. Plisk, V. Gambetta, 1997, "Tactical metabolic training," *Strength & Conditioning* 19(2): 44-53.

Figure 17.11 Reprinted, by permission, from S.S. Plisk, V. Gambetta, 1997, "Tactical metabolic training," *Strength & Conditioning* 19(2): 44-53.

Table 18.2 Reprinted, by permission, from G.Borg, 1998, *Borg's perceived exertion and pain scales* (Champaign, IL: Human Kinetics), 47. Borg RPE scale © Gunnar Borg, 1970, 1985, 1994, 1998.

Figure 19.1 Reprinted from H. Selye, 1956, *The stress of life* (New York: McGraw-Hill). Reprinted with permission of McGraw-Hill companies.

Figure 19.2 Adapted, by permission, from M.H. Stone and H.S. O'Bryant, 1987, *Weight training: A scientific approach* (Boston, MA: Pearson Custom Publishing), 124.

Figure 19.3 Adapted, by permission, from M.H. Stone and H.S. O'Bryant, 1987, *Weight training: A scientific approach* (Boston, MA: Pearson Custom Publishing), 124.

Figure 19.4 Adapted, by permission, from A. Chargina et al., 1983, "Periodization roundtable, Part 2," *NSCA Journal* 8 (5): 12-23.

Figure 20.4 This article was published in *Clinical Sports Medicine*, Vol. 11(3), W.B. Leadbetter, "Cell-matrix response in tendon injury," pgs. 533-578. Copyright Elsevier, 1992.

Figure 21.1 Reprinted, by permission, from R.W. Patton, et al. 1989, *Developing and managing health fitness facilities* (Champaign, IL: Human Kinetics), 161.

Figure 21.2 Reprinted, by permission, from R.W. Patton, et al. 1989, *Developing and managing health fitness facilities* (Champaign, IL: Human Kinetics), 162-167.

Figure 21.5 Reprinted, by permission, from National Strength and Conditioning Association, 2004, *NSCA's essentials of personal training*, edited by R. W. Earle and T. R. Baechle (Champaign, IL: Human Kinetics), 604-606.

Figure 22.1 Adapted from J.H. Taylor, 2006, *Performance training program manual* (Las Cruces: New Mexico State University).

Figure 22.4 Reprinted, by permission, from B.D. Epley, 1998, *Flight manual* (Lincoln, NE: University of Nebraska Printing).

Figure 22.7 Reprinted, by permission, from R.W. Earle, 1993, *Staff and facility policies and procedures manual*. (Omaha, NE: Creighton University Press), 6.

Photo Credits

page 1 © Visuals Unlimited
page 3 © Dr. Don Fawcett/Getty Images
page 21 © Fotopic International/Camerique Inc./Robertstock
page 41 © Steve Bonini/Getty Images
page 121 © PatitucciPhoto/Aurora Photos
page 141 © Andersen Ross/Age Fotostock
page 159 © Dale Garvey
page 179 © Karlene V. Schwartz
page 201 © Javier Larrea/Age Fotostock
page 457 © PA Wire/PA Photos
page 523 Courtesy of NSCA Certification Commission/Robert Ervin, Photographer

SECTION 1

Concepts and Applications of the Exercise Sciences

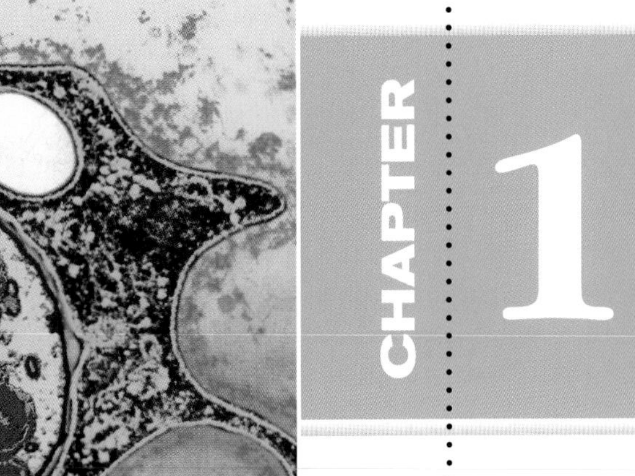

CHAPTER 1

Structure and Function of the Muscular, Neuromuscular, Cardiovascular, and Respiratory Systems

Gary R. Hunter, PhD, and Robert T. Harris, PhD

After completing this chapter, you will be able to

- describe both the macrostructure and microstructure of muscle,
- describe the sliding-filament theory of muscular contraction,
- describe the specific morphological and physiological characteristics of different muscle fiber types and predict their relative involvement in different sport events, and
- describe the anatomical and physiological characteristics of the cardiovascular and respiratory systems.

Physical exercise and sport performance involve effective, purposeful movements of the body. These movements result from the forces developed in muscles, which, acting through lever systems of the skeleton, move the various body parts. These skeletal muscles are under the control of the cerebral cortex, which, working through motor neurons, activates the skeletal muscle cells or fibers. Support for this neuromuscular activity involves continuous delivery of oxygen to and removal of carbon dioxide from working tissues through activities of the respiratory and cardiovascular systems.

At the most basic level, the strength and conditioning professional is concerned with maximizing physical performance and must therefore conduct programs that are designed to increase muscular strength, muscular endurance, and flexibility. However, in addition to being concerned about the function and control of muscle through the motor unit (the basic functional unit of the human neuromuscular system), the professional must be cognizant of how the cardiovascular and respiratory systems interact with the neuromuscular system to provide an optimal environment for sustaining muscular work.

In order to best apply the available scientific knowledge to the training of athletes and the development of effective training programs, strength and conditioning professionals must have a basic understanding of not only skeletal muscle function but also those systems of the body that directly support the work of exercising muscle. Accordingly, this chapter summarizes those aspects of the anatomy and function of the neuromuscular, respiratory, and cardiovascular systems that are essential for developing and maintaining muscular force and power.

MUSCULAR SYSTEM

Each skeletal muscle is an organ that contains muscle tissue, connective tissue, nerves, and blood vessels. Fibrous connective tissue, or epimysium, covers the body's more than 430 skeletal muscles.

Macrostructure and Microstructure

The **epimysium** is continuous with the tendons at the ends of the muscle (figure 1.1). The **tendon** is attached to **bone periosteum**, a specialized connective tissue covering all bones; any contraction of the muscle pulls on the tendon and, in turn, the bone. Limb muscles have two attachments to bone: **proximal** (closer to the trunk) and **distal** (farther from the trunk). The two attachments of trunk muscles are termed **superior** (closer to the head) and **inferior** (closer to the feet). Traditionally, the **origin** of a muscle is defined as its proximal (toward the center of the body) attachment, and the **insertion** is defined as its distal (away from the center of the body) attachment.

Muscle cells, often called **muscle fibers**, are long (sometimes running the entire length of a muscle), cylindrical cells 50 to 100 μm in diameter (about the diameter of a human hair). These fibers have many nuclei situated on the periphery of the cell and have a striated appearance under low magnification. Under the epimysium the muscle fibers are grouped in bundles (**fasciculi**) that may consist of up to 150 fibers, with the bundles surrounded by connective tissue called **perimysium**. Each muscle fiber is surrounded by connective tissue called **endomysium**, which is encircled by and is continuous with the fiber's membrane, or **sarcolemma** (28). All the connective tissue—epimysium, perimysium, and endomysium—is continuous with the tendon, so tension developed in a muscle cell is transmitted to the tendon (see figure 1.1).

The junction between a **motor neuron** (nerve cell) and the muscle fibers it innervates is called the motor end plate, or, more often, the **neuromuscular junction** (figure 1.2). Each muscle cell has only one neuromuscular junction, although a single motor neuron innervates many muscle fibers,

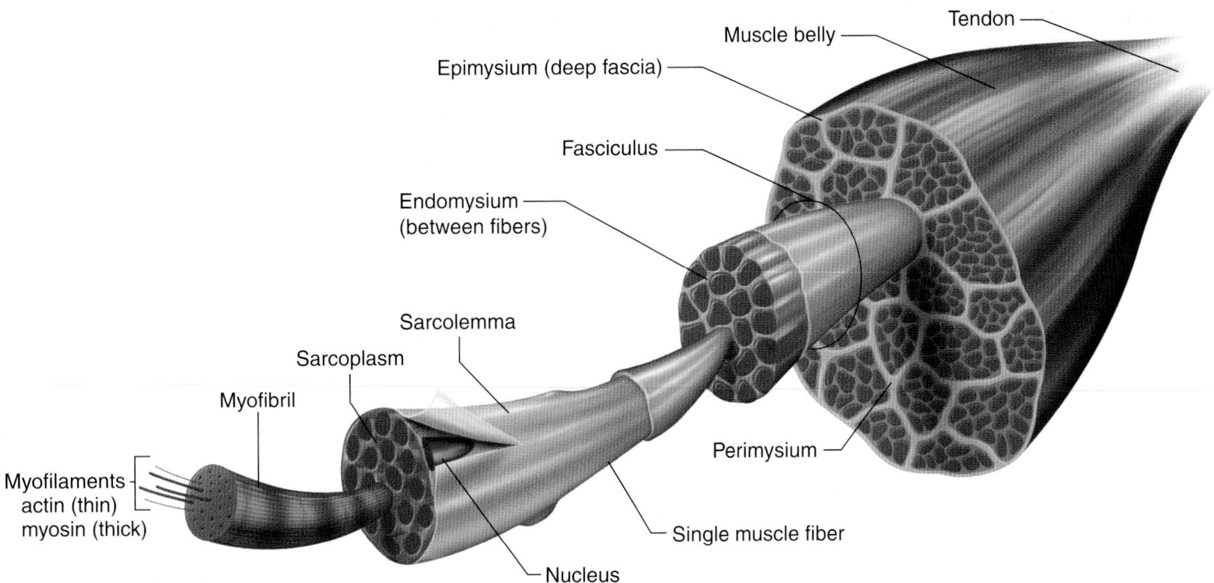

Figure 1.1 Schematic drawing of a muscle illustrating three types of connective tissue: epimysium (the outer layer), perimysium (surrounding each fasciculus, or group of fibers), and endomysium (surrounding individual fibers).

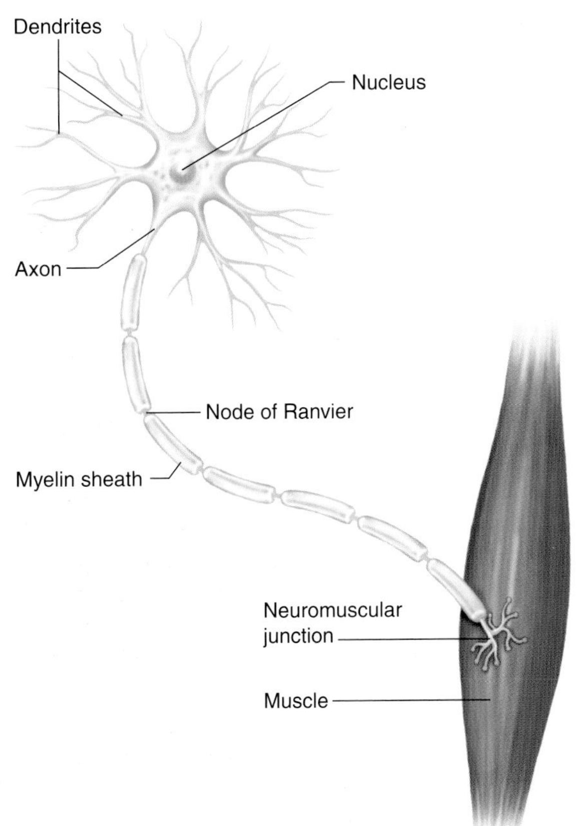

Figure 1.2 A motor unit, consisting of a motor neuron and the muscle fibers it innervates. There are typically several hundred muscle fibers in a single motor unit.

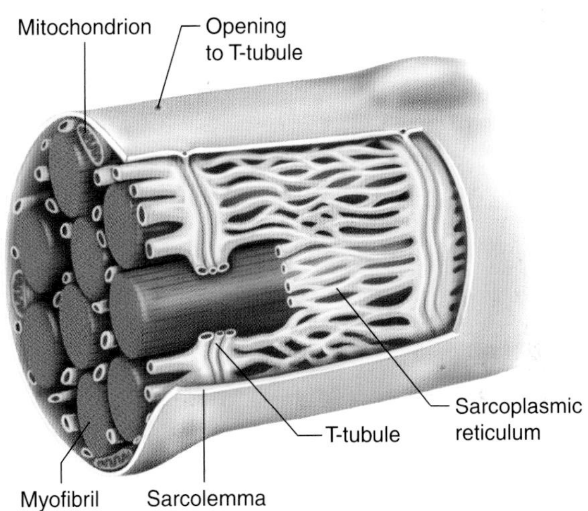

Figure 1.3 Sectional view of a muscle fiber.

sometimes as many as several hundred. A motor neuron and the muscle fibers it innervates are called a **motor unit**. All the muscle fibers of a motor unit contract together when they are stimulated by the motor neuron.

The interior structure of a muscle fiber is depicted in figure 1.3. The **sarcoplasm**—the cytoplasm of a muscle fiber—contains contractile components, which consist of protein filaments, other proteins, stored glycogen and fat particles, enzymes, and specialized organelles such as mitochondria and the sarcoplasmic reticulum.

Hundreds of **myofibrils** (each about 1 µm in diameter, 1/100 the diameter of a hair) dominate the sarcoplasm. Myofibrils contain the apparatus that contracts the muscle cell, which consists primarily of two types of **myofilament**: **myosin** and **actin**.

The myosin filaments (thick filaments about 16 nm in diameter, about 1/10,000 the diameter of a hair) contain up to 200 myosin molecules. Globular heads called **cross-bridges** protrude away from the myosin filament at regular intervals. The actin filaments (thin filaments about 6 nm in diameter) consist of two strands arranged in a double helix. Myosin and actin filaments are organized longitudinally in the smallest contractile unit of skeletal muscle, the **sarcomere**. Sarcomeres average about 2.2 μm in length in a relaxed fiber (approximately 4,500 per centimeter of muscle length) and are repeated the entire length of the muscle fiber (23).

Figure 1.4 shows the structure and orientation of the myosin and actin in the sarcomere. Adjacent myosin filaments anchor to each other at the M-

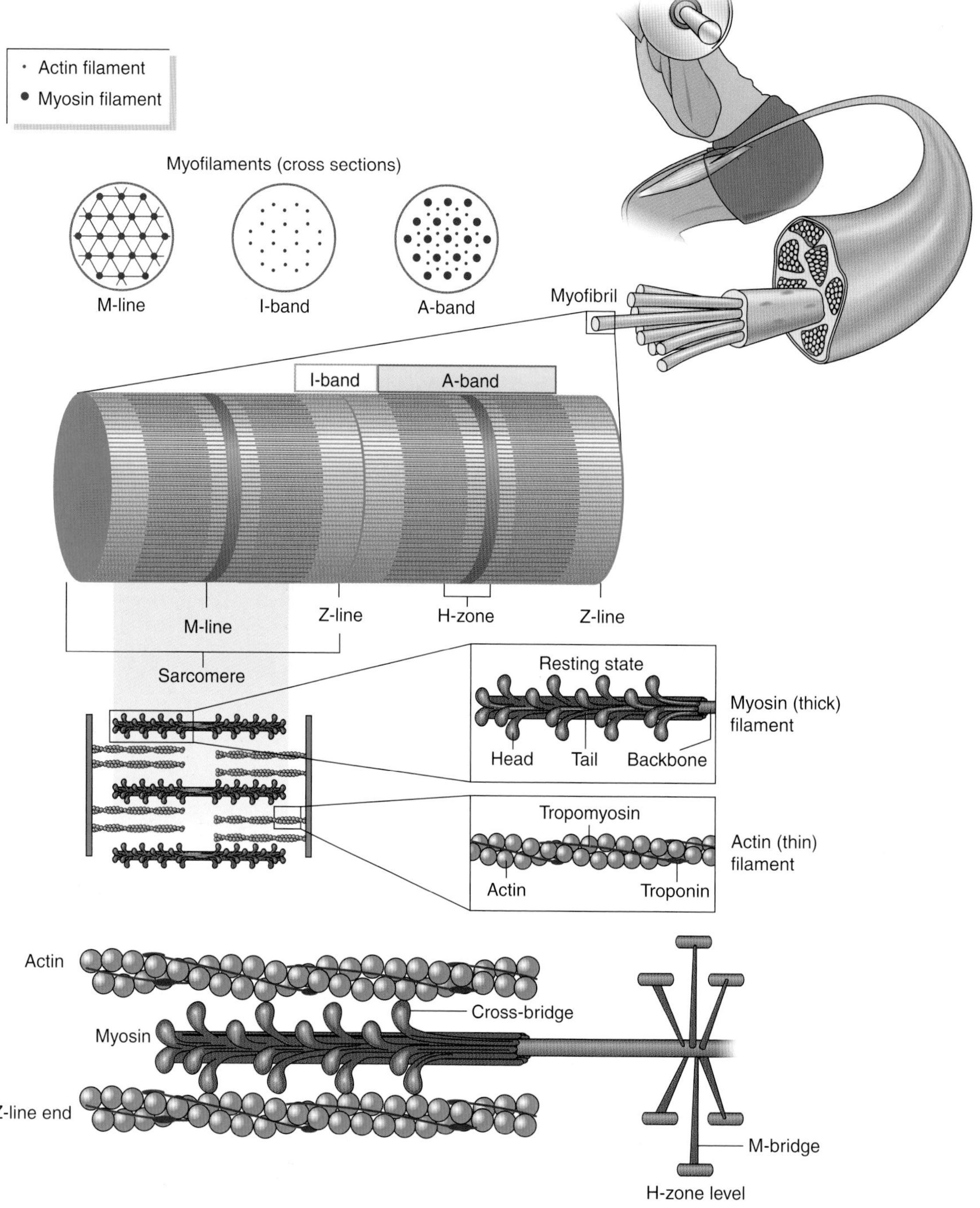

Figure 1.4 Detailed view of the myosin and actin protein filaments in muscle. The arrangement of myosin (thick) and actin (thin) filaments gives skeletal muscle its striated appearance.

bridge in the center of the sarcomere (the center of the H-zone). Actin filaments are aligned at both ends of the sarcomere and are anchored at the Z-line. Z-lines are repeated through the entire myofibril. Six actin filaments surround each myosin filament, and each actin filament is surrounded by three myosin filaments.

It is the arrangement of the myosin and actin filaments and the Z-lines of the sarcomeres that gives skeletal muscle its alternating dark and light pattern—its striated appearance under magnification. The dark **A-band** corresponds with the alignment of the myosin filaments, whereas the light **I-band** corresponds with the areas in two adjacent sarcomeres that contain only actin filaments (2). The **Z-line** is in the middle of the I-band and appears as a thin, dark line running longitudinally through the I-band. The **H-zone** is the area in the center of the sarcomere where only myosin filaments are present. During muscle contraction, the H-zone decreases as the actin slides over the myosin toward the center of the sarcomere. The I-band also decreases as the Z-lines are pulled toward the center of the sarcomere.

Parallel to and surrounding each myofibril is an intricate system of tubules, called the **sarcoplasmic reticulum**, that terminates as vesicles in the vicinity of the Z-lines (see figure 1.3). Calcium ions are stored in the vesicles. The regulation of calcium controls muscular contraction. **T-tubules**, or transverse tubules, run perpendicular to the sarcoplasmic reticulum and terminate in the vicinity of the Z-line between two vesicles. This pattern of a T-tubule spaced between and perpendicular to two sarcoplasmic reticulum vesicles is called a **triad**. Because the T-tubules run between outlying myofibrils and are continuous with the sarcolemma at the surface of the cell, discharge of an **action potential** (an electrical nerve impulse) arrives nearly simultaneously from the surface to all depths of the muscle fiber. Calcium is thus released throughout the muscle, producing a coordinated contraction.

The discharge of an action potential from a motor nerve signals the release of calcium from the sarcoplasmic reticulum into the myofibril, causing tension development in muscle.

Sliding-Filament Theory of Muscular Contraction

In its simplest form, the **sliding-filament theory** states that the actin filaments at each end of the sarcomere slide inward on myosin filaments, pulling the Z-lines toward the center of the sarcomere and thus shortening the muscle fiber (figure 1.5). As actin filaments slide over myosin filaments, both the H-zone and I-band shrink. The flexion of myosin cross-bridges pulling on the actin filaments is responsible for the movement of the actin filament. Because only a very small displacement of the actin filament occurs with each flexion of the

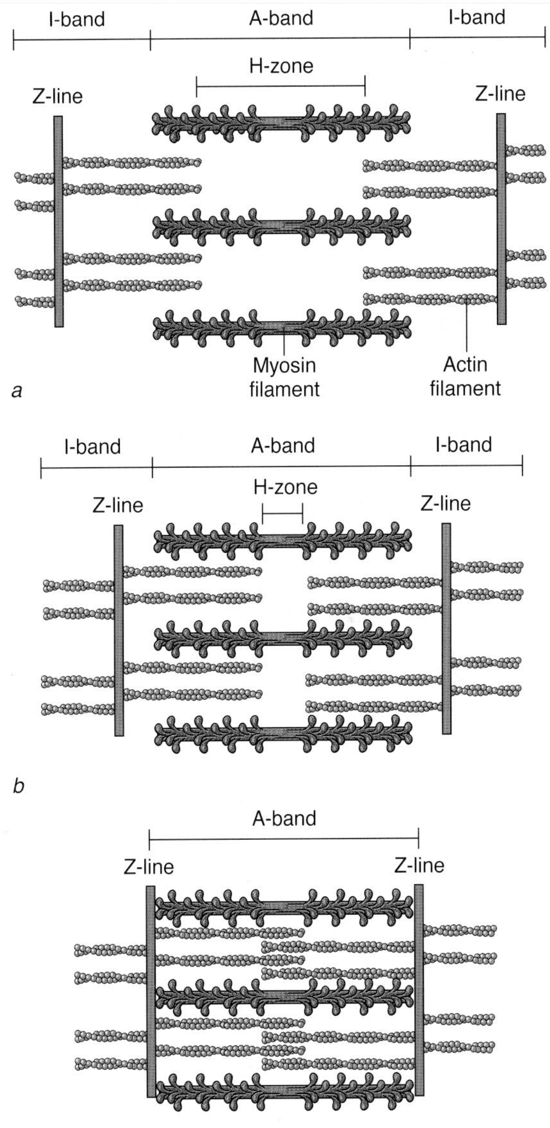

Figure 1.5 Contraction of a myofibril. *(a)* In stretched muscle the I-bands and H-zone are elongated, and there is low force potential due to reduced cross-bridge–actin alignment. *(b)* When muscle contracts (here partially), the I-bands and H-zone are shortened. There is high force potential due to optimal cross-bridge–actin alignment. *(c)* With contracted muscle, there is low force potential because the overlap of actin reduces the potential for cross-bridge–actin alignment.

myosin cross-bridge, very rapid, repeated flexions must occur in many cross-bridges throughout the entire muscle for measurable movement to occur (22).

Resting Phase

Under normal resting conditions, little calcium is present in the myofibril (most of it is stored in the sarcoplasmic reticulum), so very few of the myosin cross-bridges are bound to actin. No tension is developed in the muscle, so the muscle is said to be at rest.

Excitation-Contraction Coupling Phase

Before myosin cross-bridges can flex, they must first attach to the actin filament. When the sarcoplasmic reticulum is stimulated to release calcium ions, the calcium binds with **troponin**, a protein that is situated at regular intervals along the actin filament and has a high affinity for calcium ions (see figure 1.4). This causes a shift to occur in another protein molecule, **tropomyosin**, which runs along the length of the actin filament in the groove of the double helix. The myosin cross-bridge head now attaches much more rapidly to the actin filament, allowing cross-bridge flexion to occur (3). It is important to understand that the amount of force produced by a muscle at any instant in time is directly related to the number of myosin cross-bridge heads bound to actin filaments cross-sectionally at that instant in time (27).

The number of cross-bridges that are attached to actin filaments at any instant in time dictates the force production of a muscle.

Contraction Phase

The energy for cross-bridge flexion comes from hydrolysis (breakdown) of adenosine triphosphate (ATP) to adenosine diphosphate (ADP) and phosphate, a reaction catalyzed by the enzyme myosin adenosine triphosphatase (ATPase). Another molecule of ATP must replace the ADP on the myosin cross-bridge head in order for the head to detach from the active actin site and recock. This allows the contraction process to be continued (if calcium is available to bind to troponin) or relaxation to occur (if calcium is not available). It may be noted that calcium plays a role in regulating a large number of events in skeletal muscle besides contraction. These include glycolytic and oxidative energy metabolism, as well as protein synthesis and degradation (18).

Calcium and ATP are necessary for myosin cross-bridge cycling with actin filaments.

Recharge Phase

Measurable muscle shortening transpires only when this sequence of events—binding of calcium to troponin, coupling of the myosin cross-bridge with actin, cross-bridge flexion, dissociation of actin and myosin, and recocking of the myosin cross-bridge head—is repeated over and over again throughout the muscle fiber. This occurs as long as calcium is available in the myofibril, ATP is available to assist in uncoupling the myosin from the actin, and sufficient active myosin ATPase is available for catalyzing the breakdown of ATP.

Relaxation Phase

Relaxation occurs when the stimulation of the motor nerve stops. Calcium is pumped back into the sarcoplasmic reticulum, which prevents the link between the actin and myosin filaments. Relaxation is brought about by the return of the actin and myosin filaments to their unbound state.

NEUROMUSCULAR SYSTEM

Muscle fibers are innervated by motor neurons that transmit impulses in the form of electrochemical signals from the spinal cord to muscle. A motor neuron generally has numerous terminal branches at the end of its axon and thus innervates many different muscle fibers. The whole structure is what determines the muscle fiber type and its characteristics, function, and involvement in exercise.

Activation of Muscles

When a motor neuron fires an impulse or action potential, all of the fibers that it serves are simultaneously activated and develop force. The extent of control of a muscle depends on the number of muscle fibers within each motor unit. Muscles that must function with great precision, such as eye muscles, may have motor units with as few as one muscle fiber per motor neuron. Changes in the number of active motor units in these small muscles can produce the extremely fine gradations in force that are necessary for precise movements of the eyeball. In contrast, the quadriceps muscle group, which moves the leg with much less precision, may have several hundred fibers served by one motor neuron.

The action potential (electric current) that flows along a motor neuron is not capable of directly exciting muscle fibers. Instead, the motor neuron excites the muscle fiber(s) that it innervates by chemical transmission. Arrival of the action potential at the nerve terminal causes release of a neurotransmitter, **acetylcholine**, which diffuses across the neuromuscular junction, causing excitation of the sarcolemma. Once a sufficient amount of acetylcholine is released, an action potential is generated across the sarcolemma, and the fiber contracts. All of the muscle fibers in the motor unit contract and develop force at the same time. There is no such thing as a motor neuron stimulus that causes only some of the fibers to contract. Similarly, a stronger action potential cannot produce a stronger contraction. This phenomenon is known as the **all-or-none principle** of muscle. It is analogous to the firing of a gun. Once a sufficient amount of pressure is placed on the trigger, the gun fires; however, squeezing the trigger harder will not cause the bullet to go faster.

Each action potential traveling down a motor neuron results in a short period of activation of the muscle fibers within the motor unit. The brief contraction that results is referred to as a **twitch**. Activation of the sarcolemma results in the release of calcium within the fiber, and contraction proceeds as previously described. Force develops if there is resistance to the pulling interaction of actin and myosin filaments. Although calcium release during a twitch is sufficient to allow optimal activation of actin and myosin, and thereby maximal force of the fibers, calcium is removed before force reaches its maximum, and the muscle relaxes (figure 1.6*a*). If a second twitch is elicited from the motor nerve before the fibers completely relax, force from the two twitches summates, and the resulting force is greater than that produced by a single twitch (figure 1.6*b*). Decreasing the time interval between the twitches results in greater summation of myosin cross-bridge binding and force. The stimuli may be delivered at so high a frequency that the twitches begin to merge and eventually completely fuse, a condition called **tetanus** (figure 1.6, *c* and *d*). This is the maximal amount of force the motor unit can develop.

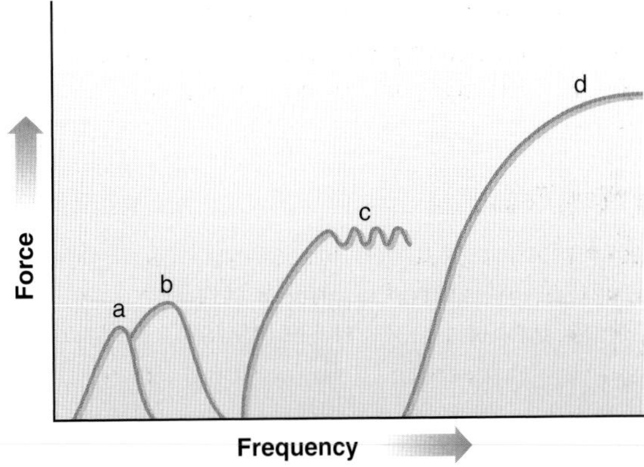

Figure 1.6 Twitch, twitch summation, and tetanus of a motor unit: a = single twitch, b = force resulting from summation of two twitches, c = unfused tetanus, and d = fused tetanus.

Muscle Fiber Types

Skeletal muscles are composed of fibers that have markedly different morphological and physiological characteristics. These differences have led to several different systems of classification, based on a variety of criteria. The most familiar approach is to classify fibers according to twitch time, employing the terms **slow-twitch** and **fast-twitch fiber**. Because a motor unit is composed of muscle fibers that are all of the same type, it also can be designated using the same classification system. A fast-twitch motor unit is one that develops force and also relaxes rapidly and thus has a short twitch time. Slow-twitch motor units, in contrast, develop force and relax slowly and have a long twitch time.

Histochemical staining is often used to classify fibers as slow-twitch or fast-twitch. Although the techniques can stain for multiple fiber types, the commonly identified fibers are **Type I** (slow-twitch), **Type IIa** (fast-twitch), and **Type IIb** (fast-twitch). Traditionally, muscle fibers have been classified according to their myosin heavy chain (MHC) protein complex. Research using gel electrophoresis fiber typing indicates that the muscle fiber previously classified as Type IIb in human skeletal muscle (because it was believed to contain the MHC IIb isoform) actually contains an isoform more closely resembling the MHC IIx isoform (26). Therefore, in this textbook the nomenclature for Type IIb and Type IIab muscle fibers in human skeletal muscle has been changed to **Type IIx** and Type IIax, respectively.

The nomenclature now used for Type IIb and Type IIab muscle fibers in human skeletal muscle is Type IIx and Type IIax, respectively.

The contrast in mechanical characteristics of Type I and Type II fibers is accompanied by a distinct difference in the ability of the fibers to demand and supply energy for contraction and thus to withstand fatigue. Type I fibers are generally efficient and fatigue resistant and have a high capacity for aerobic energy supply, but they have limited potential for rapid force development, as characterized by low actomyosin myofibrillar ATPase activity and low anaerobic power (4, 12).

Type II motor units are essentially the opposite, characterized as inefficient and fatigable and having low aerobic power, rapid force development, high actomyosin myofibrillar ATPase activity, and high anaerobic power (4, 12). Type IIa and Type IIx fibers differ mainly in their capacity for aerobic-oxidative energy supply. Type IIa fibers, for example, have greater capacity for aerobic metabolism and more capillaries surrounding them than Type IIx and therefore show greater resistance to fatigue (5, 11, 17, 25). Based on these differences, it is not surprising that postural muscles, such as the soleus, have a high composition of Type I fibers, whereas large, so-called locomotor muscles, such as the quadriceps group, have a mixture of both Type I and Type II fibers to enable both low- and high-power-output activities (such as jogging and sprinting, respectively). Refer to table 1.1 for a summary of the primary characteristics of fiber types.

Motor units are composed of muscle fibers with specific morphological and physiological characteristics that determine their functional capacity.

Motor Unit Recruitment Patterns During Exercise

Through everyday experiences, we are quite aware that a given muscle can vary its level of force output

TABLE 1.1

Major Characteristics of Muscle Fiber Types

	FIBER TYPES		
Characteristic	**Type I**	**Type IIa**	**Type IIx***
Motor neuron size	Small	Large	Large
Nerve conduction velocity	Slow	Fast	Fast
Contraction speed	Slow	Fast	Fast
Relaxation speed	Slow	Fast	Fast
Fatigue resistance	High	Intermediate/Low	Low
Force production	Low	Intermediate	High
Power output	Low	Intermediate/High	High
Endurance	High	Intermediate/Low	Low
Aerobic enzyme content	High	Intermediate/Low	Low
Anaerobic enzyme content	Low	High	High
Capillary density	High	Intermediate	Low
Myoglobin content	High	Low	Low
Mitochondria size/density	High	Intermediate	Low
Fiber diameter	Small	Intermediate	Large
Color	Red	White/Red	White

*Also termed *Type IIb* in many references. See the section "Muscle Fiber Types" for more information about fiber type nomenclature.

according to the level required by a particular task. This ability to vary or gradate force is essential for performance of smooth, coordinated patterns of movement. Muscular force can be graded in two ways. One is through variation in the frequency at which motor units are activated. If a motor unit is activated once, the twitch that arises does not produce a great deal of force. However, if the frequency of activation is increased so that the forces of the twitches begin to overlap or summate, the resulting force developed by the motor unit is much greater. This method of varying force output is especially important in small muscles, such as those of the hand. Even at low forces, most of the motor units in these muscles are activated, albeit at a low frequency. Force output of the whole muscle is intensified through increase in the frequency of firing of the individual motor units.

The other means of varying skeletal muscle force involves an increase in force through varying the number of motor units activated, a process known as **recruitment**. In large muscles, such as those in the thigh, motor units are activated at near-tetanic frequency when called on. Increases in force output are achieved through recruitment of additional motor units.

The type of motor unit recruited for a given activity is determined by its physiological characteristics (table 1.2). For an activity such as distance running, slow-twitch motor units are engaged to take advantage of their remarkable efficiency, endurance capacity, and resistance to fatigue. If additional force is needed, as in a sprint at the end of a race, the fast-twitch motor units are called into play to increase the pace; unfortunately, exercise at such an intensity cannot be maintained very long. If the activity requires near-maximal performance, as in a power clean, most of the motor units are called into play, with fast-twitch units making the more significant contribution to the effort. Complete activation of the available motor neuron pool is probably not possible in untrained people (6, 7, 10). Although the large fast-twitch units may be recruited if the effort is substantial, under most circumstances it is probably not possible to activate them at a high enough frequency for maximal force to be realized.

The force output of a muscle can be varied through change in the frequency of activation of individual motor units or change in the number of activated motor units.

TABLE 1.2

Relative Involvement of Muscle Fiber Types in Sport Events

Event	Type I	Type II
100 m sprint	Low	High
800 m run	High	High
Marathon	High	Low
Olympic weightlifting	Low	High
Soccer, lacrosse, hockey	High	High
American football wide receiver	Low	High
American football lineman	Low	High
Basketball	Low	High
Distance cycling	High	Low
Baseball pitcher	Low	High
Boxing	High	High
Field events	Low	High
Cross-country skiing	High	Low
Tennis	High	High

Preloading

It should also be understood that even though release of calcium ions and binding of myosin to actin occur very rapidly, the process does not occur instantaneously. It takes time for all of the potential myosin cross-bridge heads to make contact with actin filaments. Consequently, maximal force production does not occur early in the range of motion if the muscle is unloaded prior to muscle action, especially during fast movements. Since human skeletal muscle fibers do not run the entire length of most muscles and it is probable that recruitment patterns will vary depending on the joint position, some of the muscle fibers that are active early in the range of motion will not be fully activated unless the muscle is loaded prior to the muscle action. This **preloading** occurs when weights are lifted, since sufficient force must be developed to overcome the inertia of the weights. However, it will not occur in training systems that do not supply a preload, that is, those using isokinetic, hydraulic, and friction-modulated training apparatus. Research indicates that preloading during training is important in development of strength early in the range of motion, especially at high velocities (13, 14, 19).

Proprioception

Proprioceptors are specialized sensory receptors located within joints, muscles, and tendons. Because these receptors are sensitive to pressure and tension, they relay information concerning muscle dynamics to the conscious and subconscious parts of the central nervous system. The brain is thus provided with information concerning kinesthetic sense, or conscious appreciation of the position of body parts with respect to gravity. Most of this proprioceptive information, however, is processed at subconscious levels so we do not have to dedicate conscious activity toward tasks such as maintaining posture or position of body parts.

Proprioceptors are specialized sensory receptors that provide the central nervous system with information needed to maintain muscle tone and perform complex coordinated movements.

Muscle Spindles

Muscle spindles are proprioceptors that consist of several modified muscle fibers enclosed in a sheath of connective tissue (figure 1.7). These modified fibers, called **intrafusal fibers**, run parallel to the normal, or **extrafusal**, fibers. Muscle spindles provide information concerning muscle length and the rate of change in length. When the muscle lengthens, spindles are stretched. This deformation activates the sensory neuron of the spindle, which sends an impulse to the spinal cord, where it synapses (connects) with motor neurons. This results in the activation of motor neurons that innervate the same muscle. Spindles thus indicate the degree to which the muscle must be activated in order to overcome a given resistance. As a load increases, the muscle is stretched to a greater extent, and engagement of muscle spindles results in greater activation of the muscle. Muscles that perform precise movements have many spindles per unit of mass to help ensure exact control of their contractile activity. A simple example of muscle spindle activity is the knee jerk reflex. Tapping on the tendon of the knee extensor muscle group below the patella stretches the muscle spindle fibers. This causes activation of extrafusal muscle fibers in the same muscle. There is a knee jerk as these fibers actively shorten. This, in turn, shortens the intrafusal fibers and causes their discharge to cease.

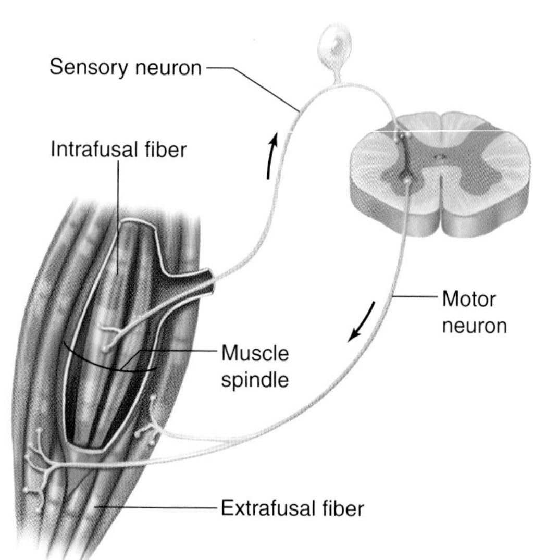

Figure 1.7 Muscle spindle. When a muscle is stretched, deformation of the muscle spindle activates the sensory neuron, which sends an impulse to the spinal cord, where it synapses with a motor neuron, causing the muscle to contract.

How Can Athletes Improve Force Production?

- Recruit large muscles or muscle groups during an activity.
- Increase the cross-sectional area of muscles involved in the desired activity.
- Preload a muscle just before a concentric action to enhance force production during the subsequent muscle action.
- Use preloading during training to develop strength early in the range of motion. Accommodating-resistance apparatus, such as isokinetic, hydraulic, and friction-modulated systems, do not load the muscle prior to contraction.

Golgi Tendon Organs

Golgi tendon organs (GTOs) are proprioceptors located in tendons near the myotendinous junction and are in series, that is, attached end to end, with extrafusal muscle fibers (figure 1.8). Golgi tendon organs are activated when the tendon attached to an active muscle is stretched. As tension in the muscle increases, discharge of the GTOs increases. The sensory neuron of the GTO synapses with an

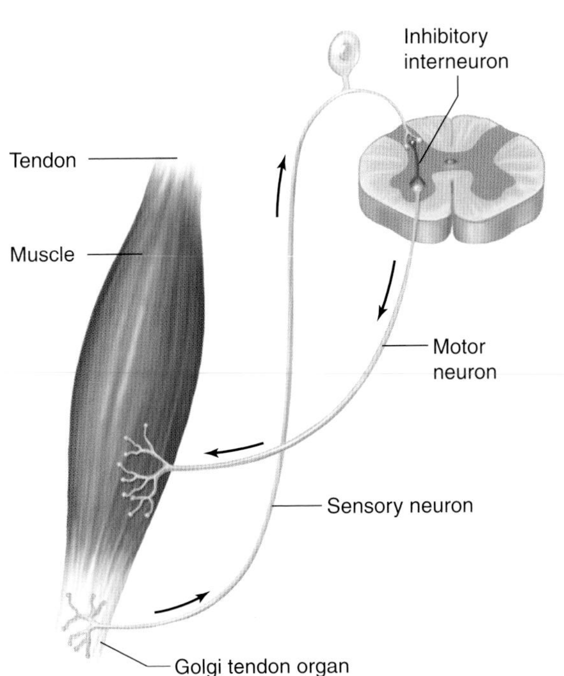

Figure 1.8 Golgi tendon organ (GTO). When an extremely heavy load is placed on the muscle, discharge of the GTO occurs. The sensory neuron of the GTO activates an inhibitory interneuron in the spinal cord, which in turn synapses with and inhibits a motor neuron serving the same muscle.

inhibitory interneuron in the spinal cord, which in turn synapses with and inhibits a motor neuron that serves the same muscle. The result is a reduction in tension within the muscle and tendon. Thus, whereas spindles facilitate activation of the muscle, neural input from GTOs inhibits muscle activation. The GTOs' inhibitory process is thought to provide a mechanism that protects against the development of excessive tension. The effect of GTOs is therefore minimal at low forces; but when an extremely heavy load is placed on the muscle, reflexive inhibition mediated by the GTOs causes the muscle to relax. The ability of the motor cortex to override this inhibition may be one of the fundamental adaptations to heavy resistance training.

Older Muscle

Muscle function is reduced in older adults, and reduced ability to do daily tasks is a large problem in geriatric populations. Skeletal muscle **sarcopenia** (reduced muscle size and strength) as a result of aging or inactivity is amplified in weight-bearing extensor muscles (15). As a result, loss of function appears most pronounced in lower limb and trunk extensors, followed by lower limb flexors, and last, upper limb extensors and flexors. Muscle atrophy with aging results from losses in both number and size of muscle fibers, especially Type II muscle fibers (15). This loss of Type II muscle fiber is accompanied by proportionately larger decreases in power than in strength. Muscle quality (strength relative to muscle mass) also decreases with age. Inactivity plays a major role in sarcopenia, but cannot account for all of the age-related loss of muscle and function (16). Refer to chapter 7 for more detail about neuromuscular differences attributed to age.

CARDIOVASCULAR SYSTEM

The primary roles of the cardiovascular system are to transport nutrients and remove waste products while assisting with maintaining the environment for all the body's functions. The cardiovascular system plays key roles in the regulation of the body's acid-base system, fluids, and temperature, as well as a variety of other physiological functions. This section describes the anatomy and physiology of the heart and the blood vessels.

Heart

The **heart** is a muscular organ comprised of two interconnected but separate pumps; the right side of the heart pumps blood through the lungs, and the left side pumps blood through the rest of the body. Each pump has two chambers: an **atrium** and a **ventricle** (figure 1.9). The right and left atria deliver blood into the right and left ventricles. The right and left ventricles supply the main force for moving blood through the pulmonary and peripheral circulations, respectively (9, 24).

Valves

The **tricuspid valve** and **mitral** (bicuspid) **valve** (collectively called **atrioventricular** [AV] **valves**) prevent the flow of blood from the ventricles back into the atria during ventricular contraction (**systole**). The **aortic valve** and **pulmonary valve** (collectively, the **semilunar valves**) prevent backflow from the aorta and pulmonary arteries into the ventricles during ventricular relaxation (**diastole**). Each valve opens and closes passively; that is, each closes when a backward pressure gradient pushes blood back against it, opening when a forward pressure gradient forces blood in the forward direction (9, 24).

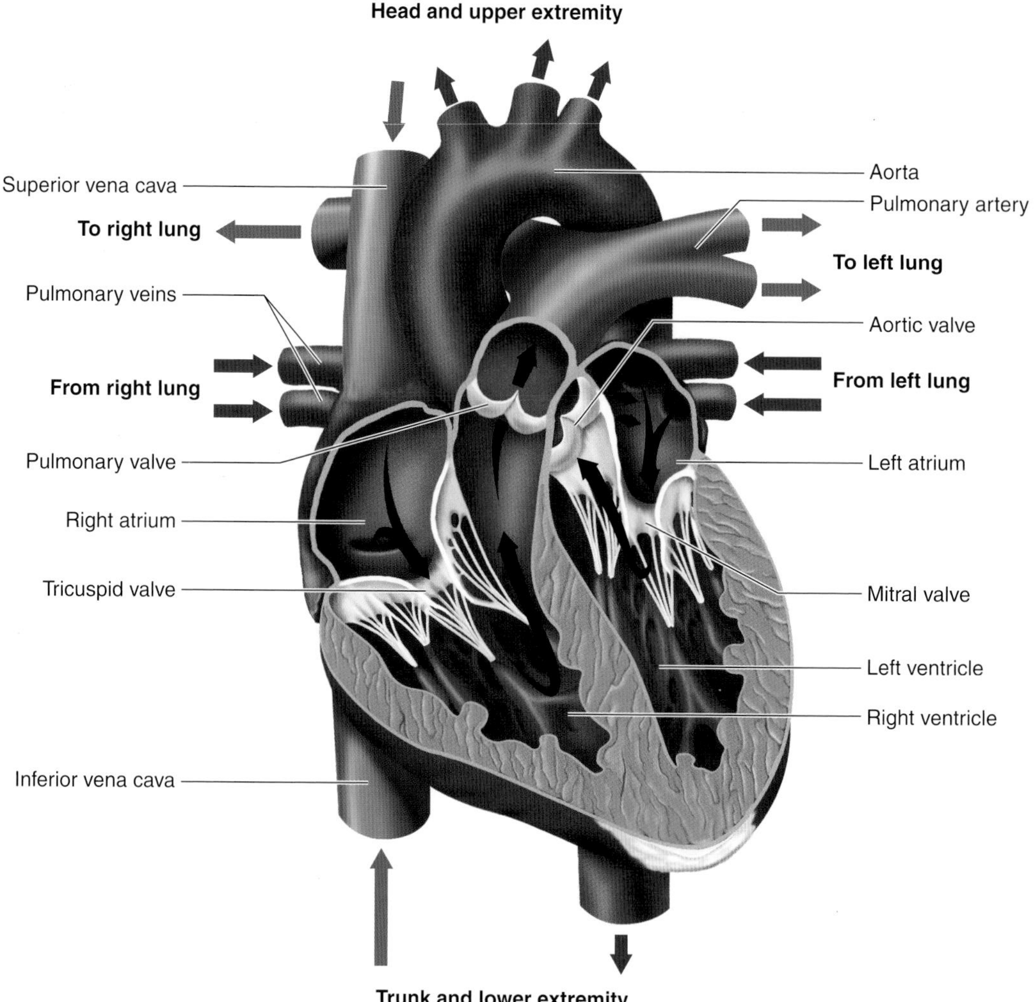

Figure 1.9 Structure of the human heart and course of blood flow through its chambers.

Conduction System

A specialized electrical conduction system (figure 1.10) controls the mechanical contraction of the heart. The conduction system is composed of

- the **sinoatrial (SA) node**—the intrinsic pacemaker—where rhythmic electrical impulses are normally initiated;
- the internodal pathways that conduct the impulse from the SA node to the atrioventricular node;
- the **atrioventricular (AV) node**, where the impulse is delayed slightly before passing into the ventricles;
- the **atrioventricular (AV) bundle**, which conducts the impulse to the ventricles; and
- the **left** and **right bundle branches**, which further divide into the **Purkinje fibers** and conduct impulses to all parts of the ventricles.

The SA node is a small area of specialized muscle tissue located in the upper lateral wall of the right atrium. The fibers of the node are continuous with the muscle fibers of the atrium, with the result that each electrical impulse that begins in the SA node normally spreads immediately into the atria. The conductive system is organized so that the impulse does not travel into the ventricles too rapidly, allowing time for the atria to contract and empty blood into the ventricles before ventricular contraction begins (figure 1.11). It is primarily the AV node and its associated conductive fibers that delay each impulse entering into the ventricles. The AV node is located in the posterior septal wall of the right atrium (9, 24).

The left and right bundle branches lead from the AV bundle into the ventricles. Except for their initial portion, where they penetrate the AV barrier, these conduction fibers have functional characteristics quite opposite those of the AV nodal fibers. They are large and transmit impulses at a much higher

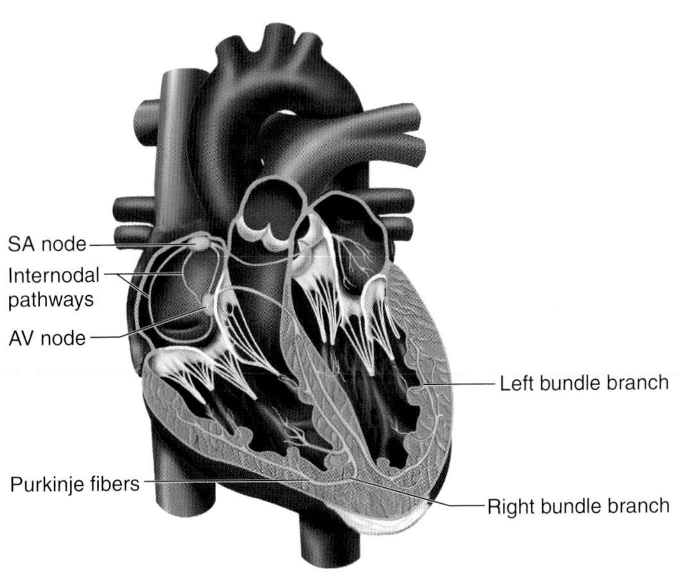

Figure 1.10 The electrical conduction system of the heart.

Figure 1.11 Transmission of the cardiac impulse through the heart, showing the time of appearance (in fractions of a second) of the impulse in different parts of the heart.

velocity than the AV nodal fibers. Because these fibers give way to the Purkinje fibers, which more completely penetrate the ventricles, the impulse travels quickly throughout the entire ventricular system and causes both ventricles to contract at approximately the same time (9, 24).

The SA node normally controls heart rhythmicity because its discharge rate is considerably greater (60-80 times per minute) than that of either the AV node (40-60 times per minute) or the ventricular fibers (15-40 times per minute). Each time the SA node discharges, its impulse is conducted into the AV node and the ventricular fibers, discharging their excitable membranes. Thus, these potentially self-excitatory tissues are discharged before self-excitation can actually occur.

The inherent rhythmicity and conduction properties of the **myocardium** (heart muscle) are influenced by the cardiovascular center of the medulla, which transmits signals to the heart through the **sympathetic** and **parasympathetic nervous systems**, both of which are components of the autonomic nervous system. The atria are supplied with a large number of both sympathetic and parasympathetic neurons, whereas the ventricles receive sympathetic fibers almost exclusively. Stimulation of the sympathetic nerves accelerates depolarization of the SA node (the chronotropic effect), which causes the heart to beat faster. Stimulation of the parasympathetic nervous system slows the rate of SA node discharge, which slows the heart rate. The resting heart rate normally ranges from 60 to 100 beats/min; fewer than 60 beats/min is called **bradycardia**, and more than 100 beats/min is called **tachycardia**.

Electrocardiogram

The electrical activity of the heart can be recorded at the surface of the body; a graphic representation of this activity is called an **electrocardiogram (ECG)**. A normal ECG, seen in figure 1.12, is composed of a **P-wave**, a **QRS complex** (the QRS complex is often three separate waves: a Q wave, an R wave, and an S wave), and a **T-wave**. The P-wave and the QRS complex are recordings of electrical depolarization, that is, the electrical stimulus that

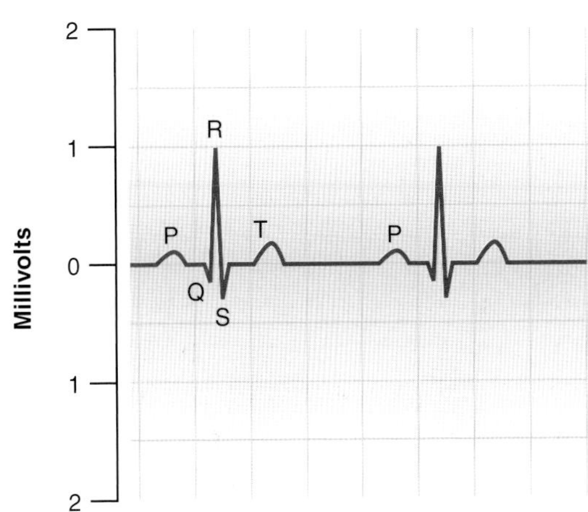

Figure 1.12 Normal electrocardiogram.

leads to mechanical contraction. **Depolarization** is the reversal of the membrane electrical potential, whereby the normally negative potential inside the membrane becomes slightly positive and the outside becomes slightly negative. The P-wave is generated by the changes in the electrical potential of cardiac muscle cells that depolarize the atria and result in atrial contraction. The QRS complex is generated by the electrical potential that depolarizes the ventricles and results in ventricular contraction. In contrast, the T-wave is caused by the electrical potential generated as the ventricles recover from the state of depolarization; this process, called **repolarization**, occurs in ventricular muscle shortly after depolarization. Although atrial repolarization occurs as well, its wave formation usually occurs during the time of ventricular depolarization and is thus masked by the QRS complex (9, 20).

Blood Vessels

The central and peripheral circulation form a single closed-circuit system with two components: an **arterial system**, which carries blood away from the heart, and a **venous system**, which returns blood toward the heart (figure 1.13). The blood vessels of each system are identified here.

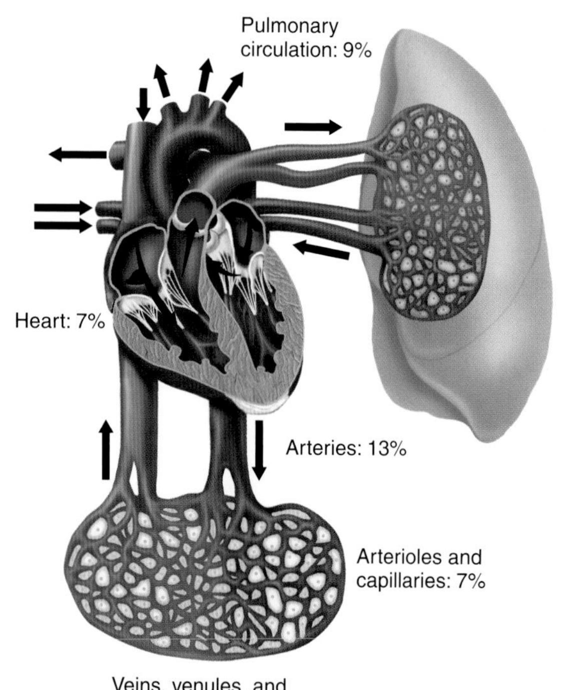

Figure 1.13 The arterial (right) and venous (left) components of the circulatory system. The percent values indicate the distribution of blood volume throughout the circulatory system at rest.

Arteries

The function of **arteries** is to rapidly transport blood pumped from the heart. Because blood pumped from the heart is under relatively high pressure, arteries have strong, muscular walls. Small branches of arteries called **arterioles** act as control vessels through which blood enters the capillaries. Arterioles play a major role in the regulation of blood flow to the capillaries. Arterioles have strong, muscular walls that are capable of closing the arteriole completely or allowing it to be dilated severalfold, thus vastly altering blood flow to the capillaries in response to the needs of the tissues (9, 24).

Capillaries

The function of **capillaries** is to exchange oxygen, fluid, nutrients, electrolytes, hormones, and other substances between the blood and the interstitial fluid in the various tissues of the body. The capillary walls are very thin and are permeable to these substances (9).

Veins

Venules collect blood from the capillaries and gradually converge into the progressively larger **veins**, which transport blood back to the heart. Because the pressure in the venous system is very low, venous walls are thin, although muscular. This allows them to constrict or dilate to a great degree and thereby act as a reservoir for blood, either in small or in large amounts (9, 24). In addition, some veins, such as those in the legs, contain one-way valves that help maintain venous return by preventing retrograde blood flow.

The cardiovascular system transports nutrients and removes waste products while helping to maintain the environment for all the body's functions. The blood transports oxygen from the lungs to the tissues for use in cellular metabolism, and it transports carbon dioxide—the most abundant by-product of metabolism—from the tissues to the lungs, where it is removed from the body.

Blood

Two paramount functions of blood are the transport of oxygen from the lungs to the tissues for use in cellular metabolism and the removal of carbon dioxide, the most abundant by-product of metabolism, from the tissues to the lungs. The transport of oxygen is accomplished by **hemoglobin**, the iron-protein molecule carried by the red blood cells. Hemoglobin also has an additional important role as an acid–base buffer, a regulator of hydrogen ion concentration, which is crucial to the rates of chemical reactions in cells. **Red blood cells**, the major component of blood, have other functions as well. For instance, they contain a large quantity of carbonic anhydrase, which catalyzes the reaction between carbon dioxide and water to facilitate carbon dioxide removal.

RESPIRATORY SYSTEM

The primary function of the respiratory system is the basic exchange of oxygen and carbon dioxide. The anatomy and physiology of the lungs and the control of respiration are discussed in this section.

The anatomy of the human respiratory system is identified in figure 1.14. As air passes through the nose, the nasal cavities perform three distinct functions: warming, humidifying, and purifying the air (9). Air is distributed to the lungs by way of the trachea, bronchi, and bronchioles. The **trachea** is called the first-generation respiratory passage, and the right and left main **bronchi** are the second-generation passages; each division thereafter is an additional generation (**bronchioles**). There are approximately 23 generations before the air finally reaches the **alveoli**, where gases are exchanged in respiration (9).

The primary function of the respiratory system is the basic exchange of oxygen and carbon dioxide.

Exchange of Air

The amount and movement of air and expired gases in and out of the lungs are controlled by expansion and recoil of the lungs. The lungs do not actively expand and recoil themselves but rather are acted upon to do so in two ways: by downward and upward movement of the diaphragm to lengthen and shorten the chest cavity (1) and by elevation and depression of the ribs to increase and decrease the back-to-front diameter of the chest cavity (8) (figure 1.15). Normal, quiet breathing is accomplished almost entirely by movement of the diaphragm. During inspiration, contraction of the diaphragm creates a negative pressure (vacuum) in the chest cavity, and air is drawn into the lungs. During expiration, the diaphragm simply relaxes; the elastic recoil of the lungs, chest wall, and abdominal structures compresses the lungs, and air is expelled.

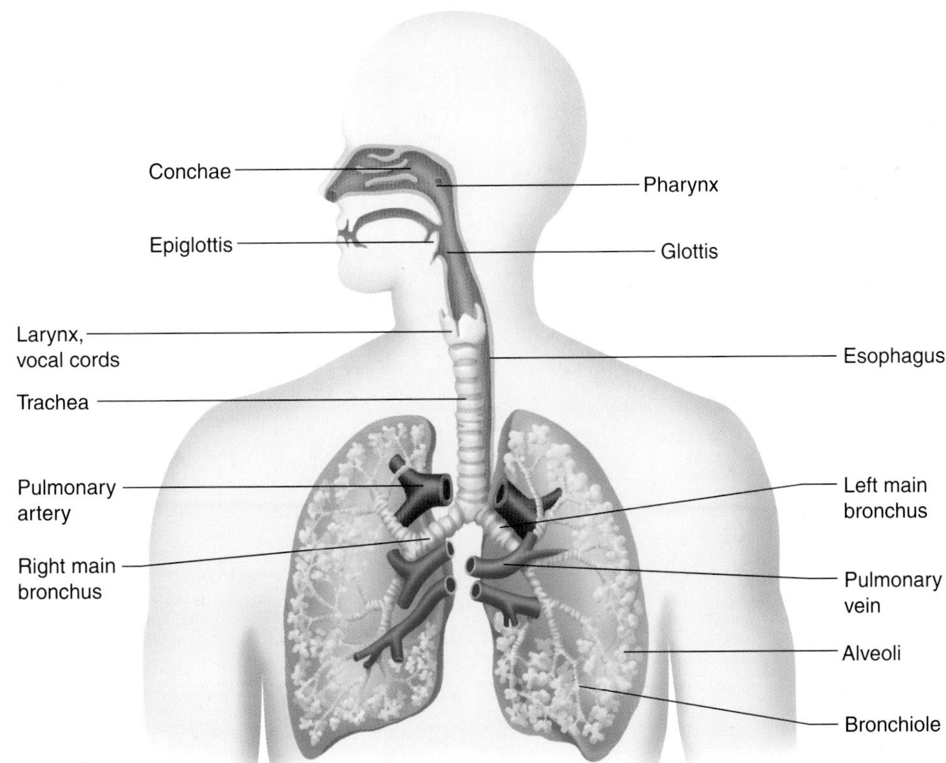

Figure 1.14 Gross anatomy of the human respiratory system.

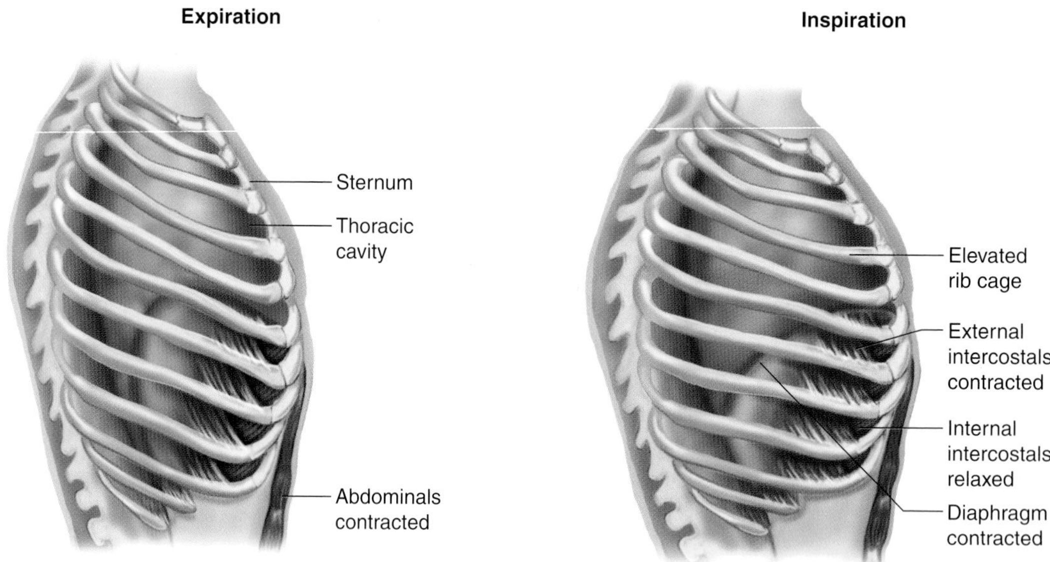

Figure 1.15 Contraction and expansion of the thoracic cage during expiration and inspiration, illustrating diaphragmatic contraction, elevation of the rib cage, and function of the intercostals. The vertical and anteroposterior diameters increase during inspiration.

During heavy breathing, the elastic forces alone are not powerful enough to provide the necessary respiratory response. The extra required force is achieved mainly by contraction of the abdominal muscles, which push the abdomen upward against the bottom of the diaphragm (9).

The second method for expanding the lungs is to raise the rib cage. Because the chest cavity is small and the ribs are slanted downward while in the resting position, elevating the rib cage allows the ribs to project almost directly forward so that the sternum can move forward and away from the spine. The muscles that elevate the rib cage are called muscles of inspiration and include the external intercostals, the sternocleidomastoids, the anterior serrati, and the scaleni. The muscles that depress the chest are muscles of expiration and include the abdominal muscles (rectus abdominis, external and internal obliques, and transversus abdominis) and the internal intercostals (9, 21).

Pleural pressure is the pressure in the narrow space between the lung pleura and the chest wall **pleura** (membranes enveloping the lungs and lining the chest walls). This pressure is normally slightly negative. Because the lung is an elastic structure, during normal inspiration the expansion of the chest cage is able to pull on the surface of the lungs and creates a more negative pressure, thus enhancing inspiration. During expiration, the events are essentially reversed (9).

Alveolar pressure is the pressure inside the alveoli when the glottis is open and no air is flowing into or out of the lungs. In fact, in this instance the pressure in all parts of the respiratory tree is the same all the way to the alveoli and is equal to the atmospheric pressure. To cause inward flow of air during inspiration, the pressure in the alveoli must fall to a value slightly below atmospheric pressure. During expiration, alveolar pressure must rise above atmospheric pressure (9).

During normal respiration at rest, only 3% to 5% of the total energy expended by the body is required for pulmonary ventilation. During very heavy exercise, however, the amount of energy required can increase to as much as 8% to 15% of total body energy expenditure, especially if the person has any degree of increased airway resistance, as occurs with exercise-induced asthma. Precautions, including physician evaluation of the athlete, are often recommended depending on the potential level of impairment.

Exchange of Respiratory Gases

With ventilation, oxygen diffuses from the alveoli into the pulmonary blood, and carbon dioxide diffuses from the blood into the alveoli. The process of **diffusion** is a simple random motion of molecules moving in opposite directions through the alveolar capillary membrane. The energy for diffusion is provided by the kinetic motion of the molecules themselves. Net diffusion of the gas occurs from the region of high concentration to the region of low concentration. The rates of diffusion of the two gases depend on their concentrations in the capillaries and alveoli and the partial pressure of each gas (9, 21).

At rest, the partial pressure of oxygen in the alveoli is about 60 mmHg greater than that in the pulmonary capillaries. Thus, oxygen diffuses into the pulmonary capillary blood. Similarly, carbon dioxide diffuses in the opposite direction. This process of gas exchange is so rapid as to be thought of as instantaneous (9, 22).

CONCLUSION

Knowledge of muscular, neuromuscular, cardiovascular, and respiratory anatomy and physiology is important for the strength and conditioning professional to have in order to understand the scientific basis for conditioning. This includes knowledge of the function of the macrostructure and microstructure of muscle fibers, muscle fiber types, interactions between tendon and muscle and between the motor unit and its activation, as well as the interactions of the heart, vascular system, lungs, and respiratory system. This information is necessary for developing training strategies that will meet the specific needs of the athlete.

KEY TERMS

A-band 7
acetylcholine 9
actin 5
action potential 7
all-or-none principle 9
alveolar pressure 18
alveoli 17
aortic valve 13
arterial system 16
arteriole 16
artery 16
atrioventricular (AV) bundle 14
atrioventricular (AV) node 14
atrioventricular (AV) valves 13
atrium 13
bone periosteum 4
bradycardia 15
bronchi 17
bronchiole 17
capillary 16
cross-bridge 6
depolarization 16
diastole 13
diffusion 18
distal 4
electrocardiogram (ECG) 15
endomysium 4
epimysium 4
extrafusal fibers 12
fasciculus 4
fast-twitch fiber 9
Golgi tendon organ (GTO) 12
heart 13
hemoglobin 16
H-zone 7
I-band 7
inferior 4
insertion 4
intrafusal fibers 12
left bundle branch 14
mitral valve 13
motor neuron 4
motor unit 5
muscle fiber 4
muscle spindle 12
myocardium 15
myofibril 5
myofilament 5
myosin 5
neuromuscular junction 4
origin 4
parasympathetic nervous system 15
perimysium 4
pleura 18
pleural pressure 18
preloading 11
proprioceptor 12
proximal 4
pulmonary valve 13
Purkinje fibers 14
P-wave 15
QRS complex 15
recruitment 11
red blood cell 17
repolarization 16
right bundle branch 14
sarcolemma 4
sarcomere 6
sarcopenia 13
sarcoplasm 5
sarcoplasmic reticulum 7
semilunar valves 13
sinoatrial (SA) node 14
sliding-filament theory 7
slow-twitch fiber 9
superior 4
sympathetic nervous system 15
systole 13
tachycardia 15
tendon 4
tetanus 9
trachea 17
triad 7
tricuspid valve 13
tropomyosin 8
troponin 8
T-tubule 7
T-wave 15
twitch 9
Type I fiber 9
Type IIa fiber 9
Type IIb fiber 9
Type IIx fiber 10
vein 16
venous system 16
ventricle 13
venule 16
Z-line 7

STUDY QUESTIONS

1. To which of the following structures do the cross-bridges attach during muscle action?
   a. actin
   b. myosin
   c. M-bridge
   d. sarcolemma

2. Which of the following substances regulates muscle actions?
   a. potassium
   b. calcium
   c. troponin
   d. tropomyosin

3. Which of the following substances acts at the neuromuscular junction to excite the muscle fibers of a motor unit?
   a. acetylcholine
   b. ATP
   c. creatine phosphate
   d. serotonin

4. Which of the following muscle fiber types is the MOST beneficial for a marathon runner?
   a. Type I
   b. Type IIa
   c. Type IIx
   d. Type IIc

5. When throwing a baseball, an athlete's arm is rapidly stretched just prior to throwing the ball. Which of the following structures detects and responds to that stretch by reflexively increasing muscle activity?
   a. Golgi tendon organ
   b. muscle spindle
   c. extrafusal muscle
   d. Pacinian corpuscle

6. From which of the following is the heart's electrical impulse normally initiated?
   a. AV node
   b. SA node
   c. the brain
   d. the sympathetic nervous system

7. Which of the following occurs during the QRS complex of a typical ECG?
   I. depolarization of the atrium
   II. repolarization of the atrium
   III. repolarization of the ventricle
   IV. depolarization of the ventricle

   a. I and III only
   b. II and IV only
   c. I, II, and III only
   d. II, III, and IV only

CHAPTER 2

Bioenergetics of Exercise and Training

Joel T. Cramer, PhD

After completing this chapter, you will be able to

- understand the basic terminology of human bioenergetics and metabolism related to exercise and training,
- discuss the central role of adenosine triphosphate (ATP) in muscular activity,
- explain the basic energy systems present in human skeletal muscle that supply ATP and the ability of each to supply ATP for various activities,
- recognize the substrates used by each energy system and discuss patterns of substrate depletion and repletion with various types of activities, and
- develop training programs that demonstrate an understanding of human bioenergetics and metabolism, especially the metabolic specificity of training.

Metabolic specificity of exercise and training is based on an understanding of the transfer of energy in biological systems. Efficient and productive training programs can be designed through an understanding of how energy is made available for specific types of exercise and how energy transfer can be modified by specific training regimens. After defining essential bioenergetics terminology and explaining the role of adenosine triphosphate (ATP), this chapter discusses the three basic energy systems that work to replenish ATP in human skeletal muscle. Then we look at substrate depletion and repletion, especially as they relate to fatigue and recovery; bioenergetic factors that limit performance; and aerobic and anaerobic contributions to oxygen uptake. Finally, the metabolic specificity of training is discussed.

ESSENTIAL TERMINOLOGY

Bioenergetics, or the flow of energy in a biological system, concerns primarily the conversion of macronutrients—carbohydrates, proteins, and fats, which contain chemical energy—into biologically usable forms of **energy**, defined as the ability or capacity to perform work. It is the breakdown of the chemical bonds in these macronutrients that provides the energy necessary to perform biological work.

The breakdown of large molecules into smaller molecules, associated with the release of energy, is termed **catabolism**. The synthesis of larger molecules from smaller molecules can be accomplished using the energy released from catabolic reactions; this building-up process is termed **anabolism**. The breakdown of proteins into amino acids is an example of catabolism, while the formation of proteins from amino acids is an anabolic process. **Exergonic reactions** are energy-releasing reactions and are generally catabolic. **Endergonic reactions** require energy and include anabolic processes and the contraction of muscle. **Metabolism** is the total of all the catabolic or exergonic and anabolic or endergonic reactions in a biological system. Energy derived from catabolic or exergonic reactions is used to drive anabolic or endergonic reactions through an intermediate molecule, **adenosine triphosphate (ATP)**. Adenosine triphosphate allows the transfer of energy from exergonic to endergonic reactions. Without an adequate supply of ATP, muscular activity and muscle growth would not be possible. Thus, it is apparent that when designing training programs, strength and conditioning professionals need to have a basic understanding of how exercise affects ATP hydrolysis and resynthesis.

Adenosine triphosphate is composed of adenosine and three phosphate groups (figure 2.1). Adenosine is the combination of adenine (a nitrogen-containing base) and ribose (a five-carbon sugar). The breakdown of one molecule of ATP to yield energy is known as **hydrolysis**, because it requires one molecule of water. The hydrolysis of ATP is catalyzed by the presence of an enzyme called **adenosine triphosphatase (ATPase)**. Specifically, **myosin ATPase** is the enzyme that catalyzes ATP hydrolysis for cross-bridge recycling. Other specific enzymes hydrolyze ATP at other locations, such as **calcium ATPase** for pumping calcium into the sarcoplasmic reticulum and **sodium-potassium ATPase** for maintaining the sarcolemmal concentration gradient after depolarization (43). The following equation depicts the reactants (left), enzyme (middle), and products (right) of ATP hydrolysis:

$$ATP + H_2O \xleftrightarrow{ATPase} ADP + P_i + H^+ + Energy \quad (2.1)$$

where **ADP** represents **adenosine diphosphate** (only two phosphate groups, figure 2.1), P_i is an inorganic phosphate molecule, and H^+ is a hydrogen ion. Further hydrolysis of ADP cleaves the second phosphate group and yields **adenosine monophosphate (AMP)**. The energy released primarily from the hydrolysis of ATP and secondarily from ADP results in biological work.

Adenosine triphosphate is classified as a high-energy molecule because it stores large amounts of energy in the chemical bonds of the two terminal phosphate groups. Because muscle cells store ATP only in limited amounts and activity requires a constant supply of ATP to provide the energy needed for muscle actions, ATP-producing processes must occur in the cell.

BIOLOGICAL ENERGY SYSTEMS

Three basic energy systems exist in mammalian muscle cells to replenish ATP (64, 92):

- The phosphagen system
- Glycolysis
- The oxidative system

In discussion of exercise-related bioenergetics, the terms anaerobic and aerobic metabolism are often used. **Anaerobic** processes do not require the presence of oxygen, whereas **aerobic** mechanisms depend on oxygen. The phosphagen system and the first phase of glycolysis are anaerobic mechanisms that occur in the sarcoplasm of a muscle cell. The Krebs cycle, electron transport, and the rest of the oxidative system are aerobic mechanisms that occur in the mitochondria of muscle cells and require oxygen as the terminal electron receptor.

Of the three main macronutrients—carbohydrates, proteins, and fats—only carbohydrates can be metabolized for energy without the direct involvement of oxygen (11). Therefore, carbohydrates are critical during anaerobic metabolism. All three energy systems are active at any given time; however, the magnitude of the contribution of each system to overall work performance is primarily dependent on the intensity of the activity and secondarily on the duration (31, 64).

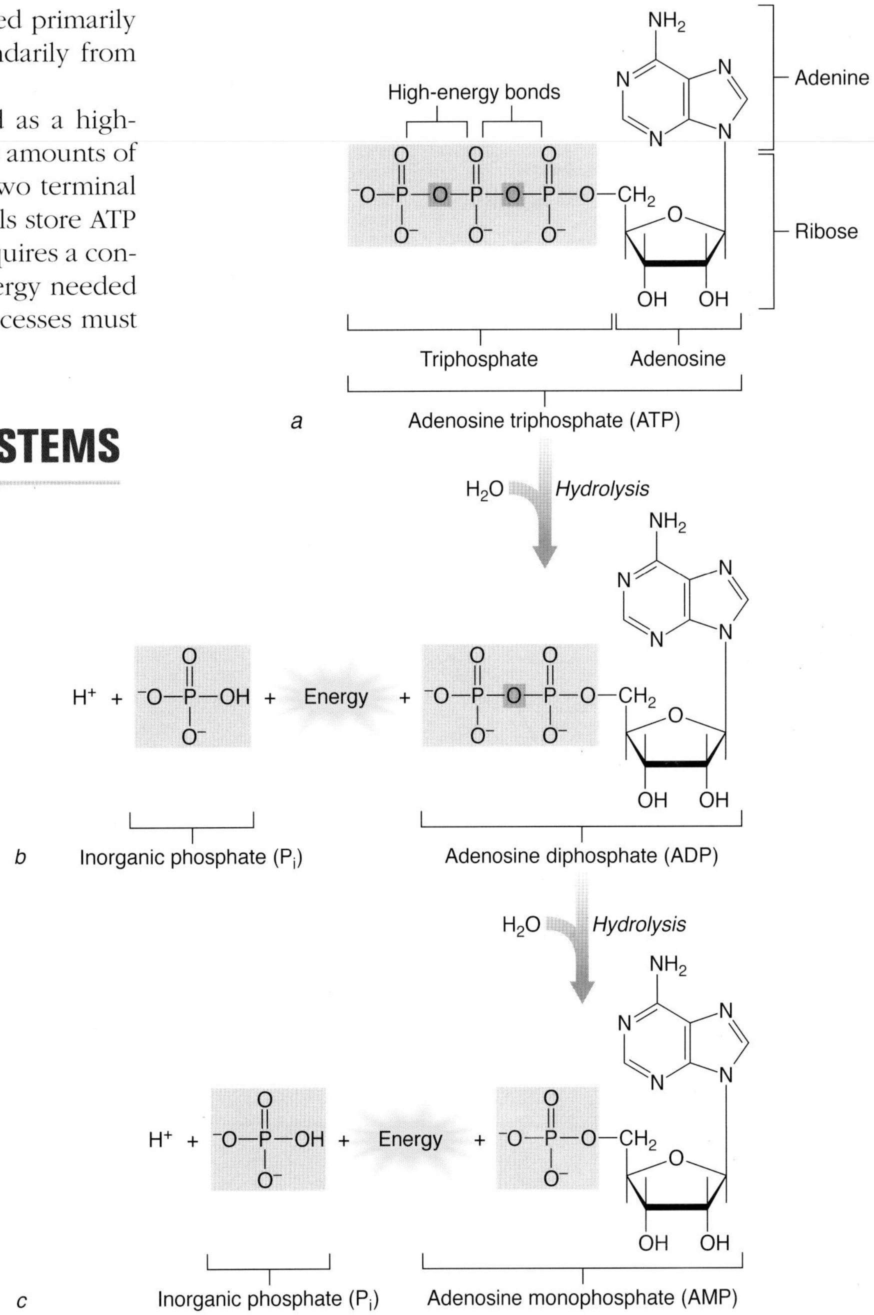

Figure 2.1 *(a)* The chemical structure of an ATP molecule showing adenosine (adenine + ribose), the triphosphate group, and locations of the high-energy chemical bonds. *(b)* The hydrolysis of ATP breaks the terminal phosphate bond, releases energy, and leaves ADP, an inorganic phosphate (P_i), and a hydrogen ion (H^+). *(c)* The hydrolysis of ADP breaks the terminal phosphate bond, releases energy, and leaves AMP, P_i, and H^+.

Energy stored in the chemical bonds of adenosine triphosphate (ATP) is used to power muscular activity. The replenishment of ATP in human skeletal muscle is accomplished by three basic energy systems: (1) phosphagen, (2) glycolytic, and (3) oxidative.

Phosphagen System

The **phosphagen system** provides ATP primarily for short-term, high-intensity activities (e.g., resistance training and sprinting) and is active at the start of all exercise regardless of intensity (45, 53, 117). This energy system relies on the hydrolysis of ATP (Equation 2.1) and breakdown of another high-energy phosphate molecule called **creatine phosphate (CP)**, also called **phosphocreatine (PCr)**. **Creatine kinase** is the enzyme that catalyzes the synthesis of ATP from CP and ADP in the following reaction:

$$\text{ADP} + \text{CP} \xleftrightarrow{\text{Creatine kinase}} \text{ATP} + \text{Creatine} \quad \textbf{(2.2)}$$

Creatine phosphate supplies a phosphate group that combines with ADP to replenish ATP. The creatine kinase reaction provides energy at a high rate; however, because CP is stored in relatively small amounts, the phosphagen system cannot be the primary supplier of energy for continuous, long-duration activities (17).

ATP Stores

The body stores approximately 80 to 100 g (about 3 ounces) of ATP at any given time, which does not represent a significant energy reserve for exercise (85). In addition, ATP stores cannot be completely depleted due to the necessity for basic cellular function. In fact, ATP concentrations may only slightly decrease (21) or may decrease by up to 50% to 60% (109) of the preexercise levels during experimentally induced muscle fatigue. Therefore, the phosphagen system uses the creatine kinase reaction (Equation 2.2) to maintain the concentration of ATP. Under normal circumstances, skeletal muscle concentrations of CP are four to six times higher than ATP concentrations (85). Therefore, the phosphagen system, through CP and the creatine kinase reaction, serves as an energy reserve for rapidly replenishing ATP. In addition, Type II (fast-twitch) muscle fibers contain higher concentrations of CP than Type I (slow-twitch) fibers (73, 100); thus, individuals with higher percentages of Type II fibers may be able to replenish ATP faster through the phosphagen system during anaerobic, explosive exercise.

Another important single-enzyme reaction that can rapidly replenish ATP is the **adenylate kinase** (also called **myokinase) reaction**:

$$2\text{ADP} \xleftrightarrow{\text{Adenylate kinase}} \text{ATP} + \text{AMP} \quad \textbf{(2.3)}$$

This reaction is particularly important because AMP, a product of the adenylate kinase (myokinase) reaction, is a powerful stimulant of glycolysis (12, 15).

Control of the Phosphagen System

The reactions of the phosphagen system (often represented by Equations 2.1, 2.2, and 2.3) are largely controlled by the **law of mass action** or the **mass action effect** (85). The law of mass action states that the concentrations of reactants or products (or both) in solution will drive the direction of the reactions. With enzyme-mediated reactions, such as the reactions of the phosphagen system, the rate of product formation is greatly influenced by the concentrations of the reactants. This is denoted in Equations 2.1, 2.2, and 2.3 by the two-way arrow between reactants and products. For example, as ATP is hydrolyzed to yield the energy necessary for exercise (Equation 2.1), there is a transient increase in ADP concentrations (as well as P_i) in the sarcolemma. This will increase the rate of the creatine kinase and adenylate kinase reactions (Equations 2.2 and 2.3) to replenish the ATP supply. The process will continue until the exercise ceases or the intensity is low enough not to deplete CP stores and allow glycolysis or the oxidative system to supply ATP and rephosphorylate the free creatine (Equation 2.2) (24). At this point, the sarcoplasmic concentration of ATP will remain steady or increase, which will slow down or reverse the directions of the creatine kinase and adenylate kinase reactions. As a result, Equations 2.1, 2.2, and 2.3 are often referred to as **near-equilibrium reactions** that proceed in a direction dictated by the concentrations of the reactants due to the law of mass action.

Glycolysis

Glycolysis is the breakdown of carbohydrates—either glycogen stored in the muscle or glucose delivered in the blood—to resynthesize ATP (12, 64). The process of glycolysis involves multiple enzymatically catalyzed reactions (figure 2.2). As a result, the ATP resynthesis rate during glycolysis is not as rapid as with the phosphagen system; however, the capacity is much higher due to a larger supply of glycogen and glucose compared to CP. As with the phosphagen system, glycolysis occurs in the sarcoplasm.

As depicted in figure 2.2, **pyruvate**, the end result of glycolysis, may proceed in one of two directions:

1. Pyruvate can be converted to lactate.
2. Pyruvate can be shuttled into the mitochondria.

When pyruvate is converted to lactate, ATP resynthesis occurs at a faster rate, but is limited in duration. This process is sometimes called **anaerobic glycolysis** (or **fast glycolysis**). However, when pyruvate is shuttled into the mitochondria to undergo the Krebs cycle, the ATP resynthesis rate

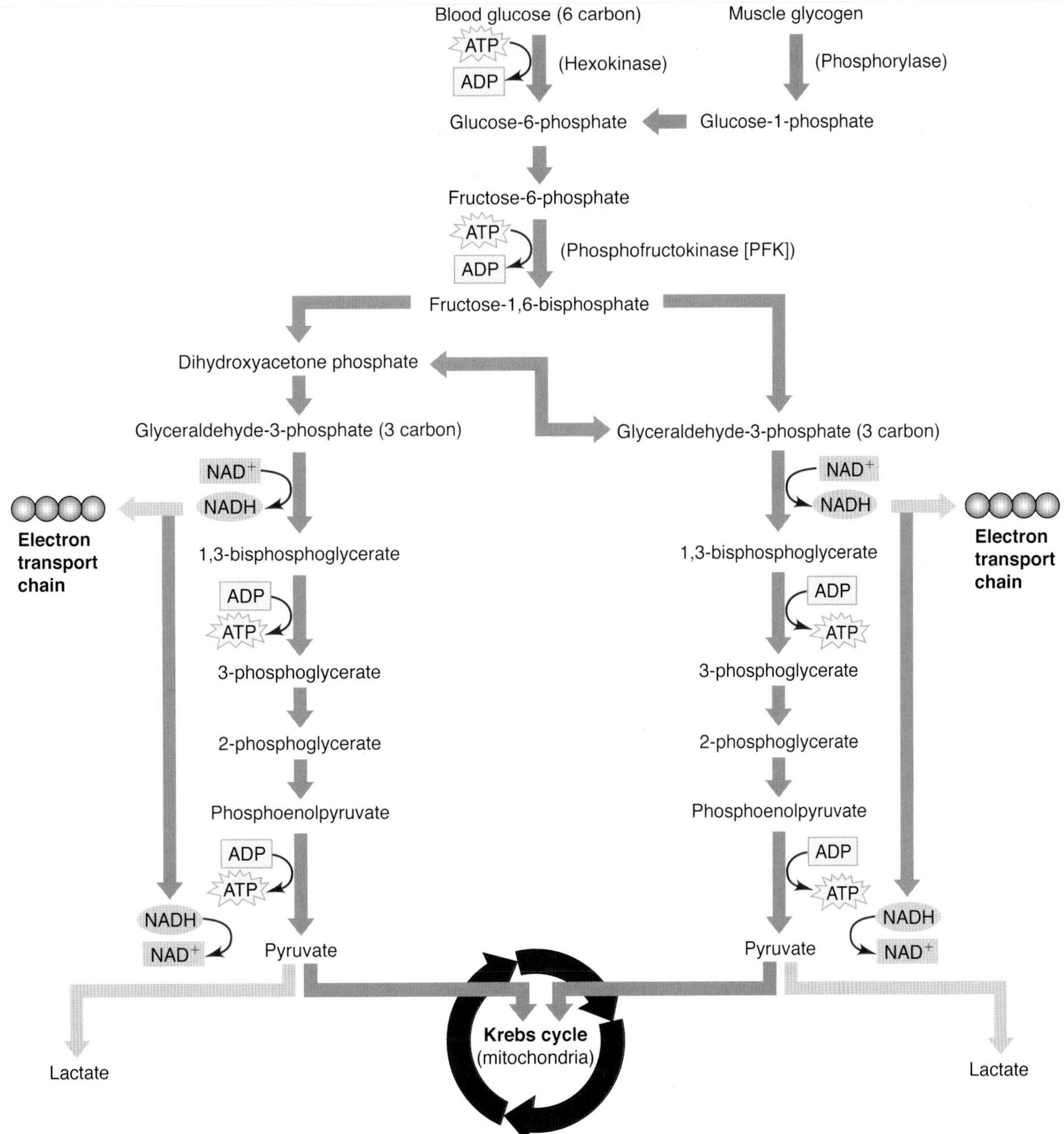

Figure 2.2 Glycolysis. ADP = adenosine diphosphate; ATP = adenosine triphosphate; NAD^+, NADH = nicotinamide adenine dinucleotide.

is slower, but can occur for a longer duration if the exercise intensity is low enough. This process is often referred to as **aerobic glycolysis** (or **slow glycolysis**). Unfortunately, because glycolysis itself does not depend on oxygen, the terms anaerobic and aerobic (or fast and slow, respectively) glycolysis are probably not practical for describing the processes. Nevertheless, the fate of pyruvate is ultimately controlled by the energy demands within the cell. If energy must be transferred at a high rate, such as during resistance training, pyruvate is primarily converted to lactate. If energy demand is not as high and oxygen is present in sufficient quantities in the cell, pyruvate can be further oxidized in the mitochondria.

Glycolysis and the Formation of Lactate

The formation of **lactate** from pyruvate is catalyzed by the enzyme lactate dehydrogenase. Sometimes, mistakenly, the end result of this reaction is said to be the formation of **lactic acid**. However, at physiological pH (i.e., near 7), the lactic acid molecule cannot exist. Instead, its anion lactate$^-$ + H^+ (a hydrogen proton) are the results of the lactate dehydrogenase reaction (12). Therefore, although the muscular fatigue experienced during exercise often correlates with high tissue concentrations of lactate, lactate is not the cause of fatigue (12). It has traditionally been thought that the H^+ accumulation as a result of lactate formation reduces the intracellular pH, inhibits glycolytic reactions, and directly interferes with muscle's excitation-contraction coupling—possibly by inhibiting calcium binding to troponin (42, 89) or by interfering with cross-bridge recycling (37, 42, 57, 89, 110). Also, the decrease in pH inhibits the enzymatic turnover rate of the cell's energy systems (4, 57). Overall, this process of an exercise-induced decrease in pH is referred to as **metabolic acidosis** (93), and may be responsible for much of the peripheral fatigue that occurs during exercise (118). However, recent evidence suggests that other mechanisms, such as the simple hydrolysis of ATP (Equation 2.1), are responsible for most of the H^+ accumulation and that lactate itself actually works to decrease metabolic acidosis rather than accelerate it (93). In fact, lactate is often used as an energy substrate, especially in Type I and cardiac muscle fibers (5, 84, 124). It is also used in gluconeogenesis—the formation of glucose from noncarbohydrate sources—during extended exercise and recovery (10, 84).

Normally there is a low concentration of lactate in blood and muscle. The reported normal range of lactate concentration in blood is 0.5 to 2.2 mmol/L at rest (50) and 0.5 to 2.2 mmol for each kg of **wet muscle** (muscle that has not been desiccated) (50). Lactate production increases with exercise intensity (50, 96) and appears to depend on muscle fiber type. Researchers have reported that the maximal rate of lactate production for Type II muscle fibers is 0.5 mmol $\cdot$ g^{-1} $\cdot$ s^{-1} (32, 83) and for Type I muscle is 0.25 mmol $\cdot$ g^{-1} $\cdot$ s^{-1} (88). The higher rate of lactate production by Type II muscle fibers may reflect a higher concentration or activity of glycolytic enzymes than in Type I muscle fibers (5, 90). Although the highest possible concentration of lactate accumulation is not known, complete fatigue may occur at blood concentrations between 20 and 25 mmol/L (83); one study, however, showed blood lactate concentrations greater than 30 mmol/L following multiple bouts of dynamic exercise (58). Along with exercise intensity and muscle fiber type, exercise duration (50), state of training (49), and initial glycogen levels (50) can also influence lactate accumulation.

Blood lactate concentrations reflect lactate production and clearance. The clearance of lactate from the blood reflects a return to homeostasis and thus a person's ability to recover. Lactate can be cleared by oxidation within the muscle fiber in which it was produced, or it can be transported in the blood to other muscle fibers to be oxidized (84). Lactate can also be transported in the blood to the liver, where it is converted to glucose. This process is referred to as the **Cori cycle** and is depicted in figure 2.3.

Gollnick and colleagues (50) have reported that blood lactate concentrations normally return to preexercise values within an hour after activity.

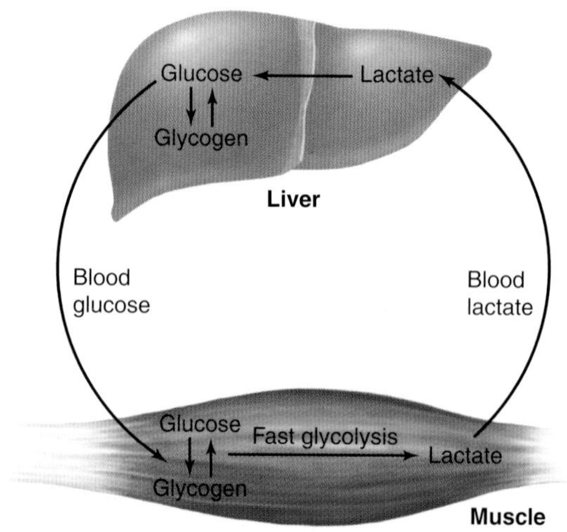

Figure 2.3 The Cori cycle.

Light activity during the postexercise period has been shown to increase lactate clearance rates (40, 50, 58), and both aerobically trained (50) and anaerobically trained (45) athletes have faster lactate clearance rates than untrained people. Peak blood lactate concentrations occur approximately 5 minutes after the cessation of exercise (50), a delay frequently attributed to the time required to buffer and transport lactic acid from the tissue to the blood (72).

Blood lactate accumulation is greater following high-intensity, intermittent exercise (e.g., resistance training and sprints) than following lower-intensity, continuous exercise (58, 79, 115). However, trained people experience lower blood lactate concentrations than untrained people when exercising at an absolute workload (same resistance). This indicates that resistance training results in alterations in lactate response similar to those from aerobic endurance training (50, 68, 107). These alterations include a lower blood lactate concentration at a given workload in trained individuals and higher blood lactate concentrations in trained individuals during maximal exercise (50, 68, 107).

The net reaction for glycolysis when pyruvate is converted to lactate may be summarized as follows:

$$\text{Glucose} + 2P_i + 2\text{ADP} \rightarrow 2\text{Lactate} + 2\text{ATP} + H_2O \quad \textbf{(2.4)}$$

Glycolysis Leading to the Krebs Cycle

If oxygen is present in sufficient quantities in the **mitochondria** (specialized cellular organelles where the reactions of aerobic metabolism occur), the end product of glycolysis, pyruvate, is not converted to lactate but is transported to the mitochondria. Also transported there are two molecules of reduced nicotinamide adenine dinucleotide (NADH) produced during glycolytic reactions (**reduced** refers to the added hydrogen). When pyruvate enters the mitochondria, it is converted to acetyl-CoA (CoA stands for coenzyme A) by the pyruvate dehydrogenase complex. Acetyl-CoA can then enter the Krebs cycle (discussed on p. 29) for further ATP resynthesis. The NADH molecules enter the electron transport system (discussed on p. 30), where they can also be used to resynthesize ATP.

The net reaction for glycolysis when pyruvate is shuttled to the mitochondria may be summarized as follows:

$$\text{Glucose} + 2P_i + 2\text{ADP} + 2\text{NAD}^+ \rightarrow 2\text{Pyruvate} + 2\text{ATP} + 2\text{NADH} + 2H_2O \quad \textbf{(2.5)}$$

Energy Yield of Glycolysis

There are two primary mechanisms for resynthesizing ATP during metabolism:

1. Substrate-level phosphorylation
2. Oxidative phosphorylation

Phosphorylation is the process of adding an inorganic phosphate (P_i) to another molecule. For example, ADP + P_i → ATP is the phosphorylation of ADP to ATP. **Oxidative phosphorylation** refers to the resynthesis of ATP in the electron transport chain (discussed on p. 30). In contrast, **substrate-level phosphorylation** describes the direct resynthesis of ATP from ADP during a single reaction in the metabolic pathways. To illustrate, in glycolysis there are two steps that result in substrate-level phosphorylation of ADP to ATP (64):

$$\text{1,3-bisphosphoglycerate} + \text{ADP} + P_i \xrightarrow{\text{Phosphoglycerate kinase}} \text{3-phosphoglycerate} + \text{ATP} \quad \textbf{(2.6)}$$

$$\text{Phosphoenolpyruvate} + \text{ADP} + P_i \xrightarrow{\text{Pyruvate kinase}} \text{Pyruvate} + \text{ATP} \quad \textbf{(2.7)}$$

The gross number of ATP molecules that are resynthesized as a result of substrate-level phosphorylation during glycolysis is four (figure 2.2). However, the reaction that converts fructose-6-phosphate to fructose-1,6-bisphosphate (catalyzed by the enzyme phosphofructokinase [PFK]) in glycolysis requires the hydrolysis of one ATP molecule. In addition, there are two possible sources of glucose: blood glucose and muscle glycogen. When blood glucose enters the muscle cell, it must be phosphorylated to remain in the cell and to maintain the glucose concentration gradient (85). The phosphorylation of one molecule of blood glucose, which is catalyzed by hexokinase, also requires the hydrolysis of one ATP. In contrast, when muscle glycogen is broken down (i.e., glycogenolysis) to glucose with the help of the enzyme glycogen phosphorylase, the glucose is already phosphorylated, and it does not require the hydrolysis of ATP. Therefore, when glycolysis begins with one molecule of blood glucose, two ATP molecules are used and four ATP are resynthesized, which results in a net resynthesis of two ATP molecules. When glycolysis begins from muscle glycogen, only one ATP is used and four ATP are resynthesized, which yields a net resynthesis of three ATP molecules.

Control of Glycolysis

In general, glycolysis is stimulated during intense muscle actions by high concentrations of ADP, P_i, and ammonia, and by a slight decrease in pH and AMP (12, 44, 106), all of which are signs of increased ATP hydrolysis and a need for energy. In contrast, glycolysis is inhibited by markedly lower pH, ATP, CP, citrate, and free fatty acids (12), which are usually present at rest. However, there are more specific factors that contribute to the regulation of glycolysis (85), such as the concentrations and turnover rates of three important glycolytic enzymes: hexokinase, phosphofructokinase, and pyruvate kinase. All three of these are regulatory enzymes in glycolysis, because each has important *allosteric* (meaning "other site") binding sites. Allosteric regulation occurs when the end product of a reaction or series of reactions feeds back to regulate the turnover rate of key enzymes in the metabolic pathways. Consequently, this process is also called *end product regulation* (64) or *feedback regulation* (44). **Allosteric inhibition** occurs when an end product binds to the regulatory enzyme and decreases its turnover rate and slows product formation. In contrast, **allosteric activation** occurs when an "activator" binds with the enzyme and increases its turnover rate.

Hexokinase, which catalyzes the phosphorylation of glucose to glucose-6-phosphate, is allosterically inhibited by the concentration of glucose-6-phosphate in the sarcoplasm (44). Thus, the higher the concentration of glucose-6-phosphate, the more hexokinase will be inhibited. In addition, the phosphorylation of glucose commits it to the cell so that it cannot leave. Similarly, the phosphofructokinase (PFK) reaction (fructose-6-phosphate → fructose 1,6-bisphosphate) commits the cell to metabolizing glucose rather than storing it as glycogen. In addition, the PFK enzyme is the most important regulator of glycolysis, because it is the **rate-limiting step**. Adenosine triphosphate is an allosteric inhibitor of PFK; therefore, as intracellular ATP concentrations rise, PFK slows down the glycolytic pathway. However, AMP is an allosteric activator and a powerful stimulator of glycolysis. As AMP concentrations rise due to the adenylate kinase reaction (Equation 2.3), glycolysis is stimulated. Moreover, the ammonia produced during high-intensity exercise as a result of AMP or amino acid deamination (removing the amine group from the amino acid molecule) can stimulate PFK. Pyruvate kinase catalyzes the conversion of phosphoenolpyruvate to pyruvate and is the final regulatory enzyme. Pyruvate kinase is allosterically inhibited by ATP and acetyl-CoA (the latter is a Krebs cycle intermediate) and activated by high concentrations of AMP and fructose-1,6-bisphosphate (44).

Lactate Threshold and Onset of Blood Lactate

Recent evidence suggests that there are specific break points in the lactate accumulation curve (figure 2.4) as exercise intensity increases (26, 76). The exercise intensity or relative intensity at which blood lactate begins an abrupt increase above the baseline concentration has been termed the **lactate threshold (LT)** (125). The LT represents an increasing reliance on anaerobic mechanisms; therefore, the LT corresponds well with the ventilatory threshold (breaking point in the relationship between ventilation and $\dot{V}O_2$) and is often used as a marker of the anaerobic threshold.

The LT typically begins at 50% to 60% of maximal oxygen uptake in untrained individuals and at 70% to 80% in trained athletes (16, 38). A second increase in the rate of lactate accumulation has been noted at higher relative intensities of exercise. This second point of inflection has been termed the **onset of blood lactate accumulation (OBLA)** and occurs when the concentration of blood lactate reaches 4 mmol/L (62, 103, 108). The breaks in the lactate accumulation curve may correspond to the points at which intermediate and large motor units are recruited during increasing exercise intensities (71). The muscle cells associated with large motor units are typically Type II fibers, which are particularly suited for anaerobic metabolism and lactate production.

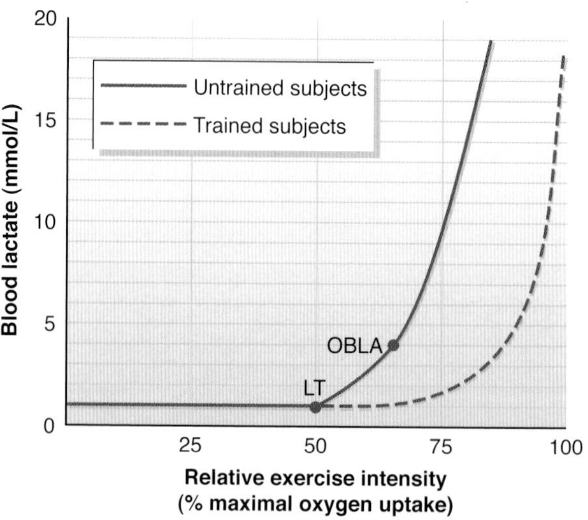

Figure 2.4 Lactate threshold (LT) and onset of blood lactate accumulation (OBLA).

Some studies suggest that training at intensities near or above the LT or OBLA pushes the LT and OBLA to the right (i.e., lactate accumulation occurs later at a higher exercise intensity) (26, 29). This shift probably occurs as a result of changes in hormone release, particularly reduced catecholamine release at high exercise intensities, and increased mitochondrial content that allows for greater production of ATP through aerobic mechanisms. The shift allows the athlete to perform at higher percentages of maximal oxygen uptake without as much lactate accumulation in the blood (12, 26).

The Oxidative (Aerobic) System

The **oxidative system**, the primary source of ATP at rest and during low-intensity activities, uses primarily carbohydrates and fats as substrates (45). Protein is normally not metabolized significantly except during long-term starvation and long bouts (>90 minutes) of exercise (28, 80). At rest, approximately 70% of the ATP produced is derived from fats and 30% from carbohydrates. Following the onset of activity, as the intensity of the exercise increases, there is a shift in substrate preference from fats to carbohydrates. During high-intensity aerobic exercise, almost 100% of the energy is derived from carbohydrates if an adequate supply is available. However, during prolonged, submaximal, steady-state work, there is a gradual shift from carbohydrates back to fats and protein as energy substrates (12).

Glucose and Glycogen Oxidation

The oxidative metabolism of blood glucose and muscle glycogen begins with glycolysis. If oxygen is present in sufficient quantities, the end product of glycolysis, pyruvate, is not converted to lactate but is transported to the mitochondria, where it is taken up and enters the **Krebs cycle**, citric acid cycle, or tricarboxylic acid cycle (3, 44). The Krebs cycle is a series of reactions that continues the oxidation of the substrate begun in glycolysis and produces two ATP indirectly from guanine triphosphate (GTP) via substrate-level phosphorylation for each molecule of glucose (figure 2.5).

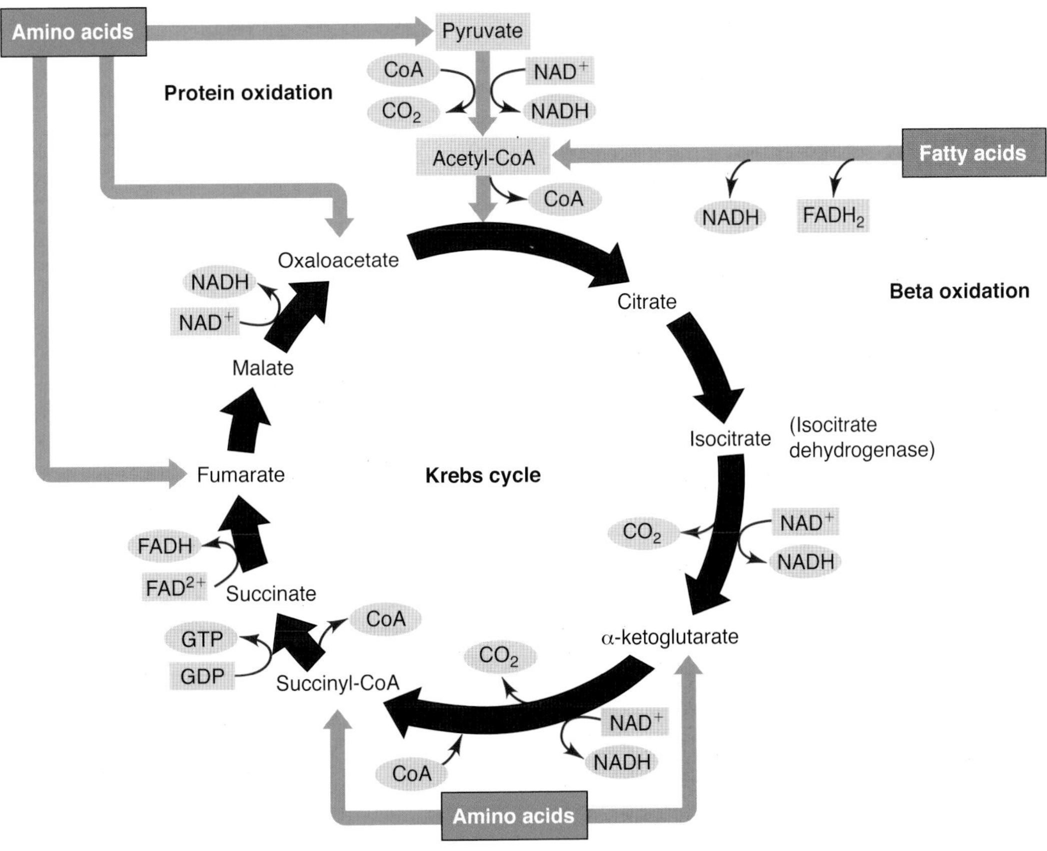

Figure 2.5 The Krebs cycle. CoA = coenzyme A; FAD^{2+}, FADH, $FADH_2$ = flavin adenine dinucleotide; GDP = guanine diphosphate; GTP = guanine triphosphate; NAD^+, NADH = nicotinamide adenine dinucleotide.

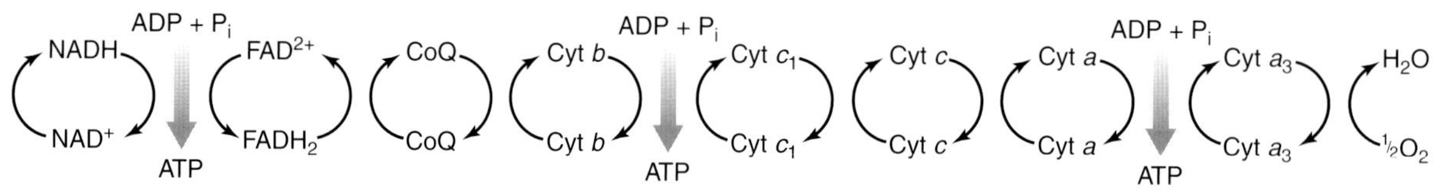

Figure 2.6 The electron transport chain. CoQ = coenzyme Q; Cyt = cytochrome.

Also produced from one molecule of glucose are six molecules of NADH and two molecules of reduced flavin adenine dinucleotide ($FADH_2$). These molecules transport hydrogen atoms to the **electron transport chain (ETC)** to be used to produce ATP from ADP (12, 85). The ETC uses the NADH and $FADH_2$ molecules to rephosphorylate ADP to ATP (figure 2.6).

The hydrogen atoms are passed down the chain (a series of electron carriers known as **cytochromes**) to form a proton concentration gradient to provide energy for ATP production, with oxygen serving as the final electron acceptor (resulting in the formation of water). Because NADH and $FADH_2$ enter the ETC at different sites, they differ in their ability to produce ATP. One molecule of NADH can produce three molecules of ATP, whereas one molecule of $FADH_2$ can produce only two molecules of ATP. The production of ATP during this process is referred to as oxidative phosphorylation. The oxidative system, beginning with glycolysis, results in the production of approximately 38 ATP from the degradation of one molecule of blood glucose (12, 64). However, if the initiation of glycolysis is muscle glycogen, the net ATP production is 39, since the hexokinase reaction is not necessary with muscle glycogenolysis. Nevertheless, oxidative phosphorylation accounts for over 90% of ATP synthesis compared to substrate-level phosphorylation, which demonstrates the capacity of energy transfer by the oxidative system. See table 2.1 for a summary of these processes.

TABLE 2.1

Total Energy Yield From the Oxidation of One Glucose Molecule

Process	ATP production
Slow glycolysis:	
Substrate-level phosphorylation	4
Oxidative phosphorylation: 2 NADH (3 ATP each)	6
Krebs cycle (2 rotations through the Krebs cycle per glucose):	
Substrate-level phosphorylation	2
Oxidative phosphorylation: 8 NADH (3 ATP each)	24
Via GTP: 2 $FADH_2$ (2 ATP each)	4
Total:	40*

*Glycolysis consumes 2 ATP (if starting with blood glucose), so net ATP production is 40 – 2 = 38. This figure may also be reported as 36 ATP depending on which shuttle system is used to transport the NADH to the mitochondria. ATP = adenosine triphosphate; $FADH_2$ = flavin adenine dinucleotide; GTP = guanine triphosphate; NADH = nicotinamide adenine dinucleotide.

Fat Oxidation

Fats can also be used by the oxidative energy system. Triglycerides stored in fat cells can be broken down by an enzyme, hormone-sensitive lipase. This releases free fatty acids from the fat cells into the blood, where they can circulate and enter muscle fibers (12, 67, 91). Additionally, limited quantities of triglycerides are stored within the muscle along with a form of hormone-sensitive lipase to produce an intramuscular source of free fatty acids (12, 33). Free fatty acids enter the mitochondria, where they undergo **beta oxidation**, a series of reactions in which the free fatty acids are broken down, resulting in the formation of acetyl-CoA and hydrogen protons (figure 2.5). The acetyl-CoA enters the Krebs cycle directly, and the hydrogen atoms are carried by NADH and $FADH_2$ to the ETC (12). An example of the ATP produced from a typical triglyceride molecule is shown in table 2.2.

Protein Oxidation

Although not a significant source of energy for most activities, protein can be broken down into its constituent amino acids by various metabolic processes. These amino acids can then be converted into glucose (in a process known as **gluconeogenesis**), pyruvate, or various Krebs cycle intermediates to produce ATP (figure 2.5). The contribution of amino acids to the production of ATP has been estimated to be minimal during short-term exercise but may contribute 3% to 18% of the energy requirements during prolonged activity (9, 104). The major amino acids that are oxidized in skeletal muscle are believed to be the **branched-chain amino acids** (leucine, isoleucine, and valine), although alanine, aspartate, and glutamate may also be used (52). The nitrogenous waste products of amino acid degradation are eliminated through the formation of urea and small amounts of ammonia (12). The elimination through formation of ammonia is significant because ammonia is toxic and is associated with fatigue.

TABLE 2.2

Total Energy Yield From the Oxidation of One (18-Carbon) Triglyceride Molecule

Process	ATP production
1 molecule of glycerol	22
**18-carbon fatty acid metabolism:* 147 ATP per fatty acid × 3 fatty acids per triglyceride molecule	441
	Total: 463

*Other triglycerides that contain a different number of carbons will yield more or less ATP.

Control of the Oxidative (Aerobic) System

The rate-limiting step in the Krebs cycle (see figure 2.5) is the conversion of isocitrate to α-ketoglutarate, a reaction catalyzed by the enzyme isocitrate dehydrogenase. Isocitrate dehydrogenase is stimulated by ADP and allosterically inhibited by ATP. The reactions that produce NADH or $FADH_2$ also influence the regulation of the Krebs cycle. If NAD^+ and FAD^{2+} are not available in sufficient quantities to accept hydrogen, the rate of the Krebs cycle is reduced. Also, when GTP accumulates, the concentration of succinyl CoA increases, which inhibits the initial reaction (oxaloacetate + acetyl-CoA → citrate + CoA) of the Krebs cycle. The ETC is inhibited by ATP and stimulated by ADP (12). A simplified overview of the metabolism of fat, carbohydrate, and protein is presented in figure 2.7.

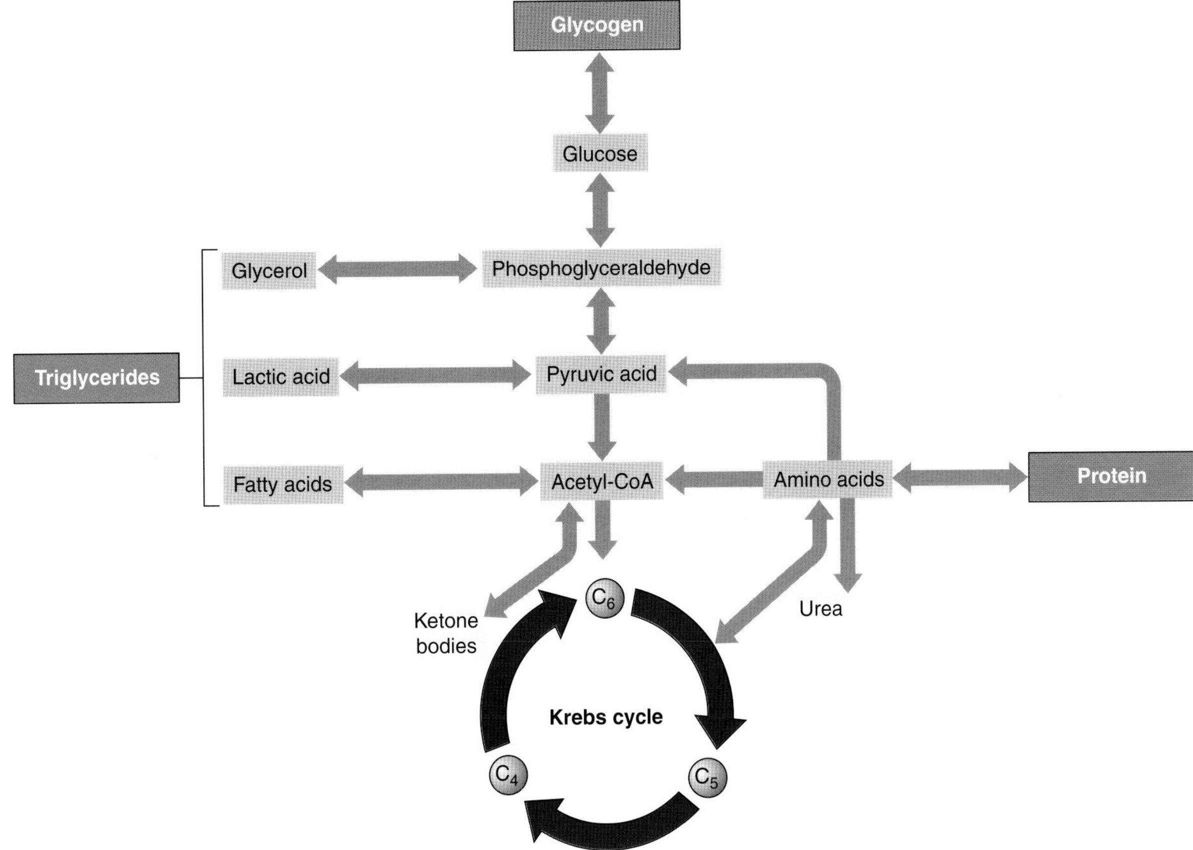

Figure 2.7 The metabolism of fat and that of carbohydrate and protein share some common pathways. Note that all are reduced to acetyl-CoA and enter the Krebs cycle.

Energy Production and Capacity

The phosphagen, glycolytic, and oxidative energy systems differ in their ability to supply energy for activities of various intensities and durations (tables 2.3 and 2.4). **Exercise intensity** is defined as a level of muscular activity that can be quantified in terms of **power** (work performed per unit of time) output (77). Activities such as resistance training that are of high intensity and thus have a high power output require a rapid rate of energy supplied and rely almost entirely on the energy supplied by the phosphagen system. Activities that are of low intensity but long duration, such as marathon running, require a large energy supply and rely on the energy supplied by the oxidative energy system. The primary source of energy for activities between these two extremes shifts, depending on the intensity and duration of the event (table 2.3). In general, short, high-intensity activities (e.g., resistance training and sprinting) rely on the phosphagen energy system and fast glycolysis. As the intensity decreases and the duration increases, the emphasis gradually shifts to slow glycolysis and the oxidative energy system (12, 31, 97).

In general, there is an inverse relationship between a given energy system's maximum rate of ATP production (i.e., ATP produced per unit of time) and the total amount of ATP it is capable of producing over a long period. As a result, the phosphagen energy system primarily supplies ATP for high-intensity activities of short duration (e.g., 100 m dash), the glycolytic system for moderate- to high-intensity activities of short to medium duration (e.g., 400 m dash), and the oxidative system for low-intensity activities of long duration (e.g., marathon).

The duration of the activity also influences which energy system is used. Athletic events range in duration from 1 to 3 seconds (e.g., snatch and shot put) to more than 4 hours (e.g., triathlons and ultramarathons). If an athlete makes a best effort (an effort that results in the best possible performance for a given event), the time considerations shown in table 2.3 are reasonable (12, 34, 57, 94, 110, 112).

At no time, during either exercise or rest, does any single energy system provide the complete supply of energy. During exercise, the degree to which anaerobic and oxidative systems contribute to the energy being produced is determined primarily by the exercise intensity and secondarily by exercise duration (12, 31, 34).

The extent to which each of the three energy systems contributes to ATP production depends primarily on the intensity of muscular activity and secondarily on the duration. At no time, during either exercise or rest, does any single energy system provide the complete supply of energy.

TABLE 2.3

Effect of Event Duration and Intensity on Primary Energy System Used

Duration of event	Intensity of event	Primary energy system(s)
0-6 seconds	Extremely high	Phosphagen
6-30 seconds	Very high	Phosphagen and fast glycolysis
30 seconds to 2 minutes	High	Fast glycolysis
2-3 minutes	Moderate	Fast glycolysis and oxidative system
>3 minutes	Low	Oxidative system

The relationships between duration, intensity, and primary energy systems used assume that the athlete strives to attain the best possible performance for a given event.

TABLE 2.4

Rankings of Rate and Capacity of ATP Production

System	Rate of ATP production	Capacity of ATP production
Phosphagen	1	5
Fast glycolysis	2	4
Slow glycolysis	3	3
Oxidation of carbohydrates	4	2
Oxidation of fats and proteins	5	1

Note: 1 = fastest/greatest; 5 = slowest/least.

SUBSTRATE DEPLETION AND REPLETION

Energy substrates—molecules that provide starting materials for bioenergetic reactions, including phosphagens (ATP and creatine phosphate), glucose, glycogen, lactate, free fatty acids, and amino acids—can be selectively depleted during the performance of activities of various intensities and durations. Subsequently, the energy that can be produced by the bioenergetic systems is reduced. Fatigue experienced during many activities is frequently associated with the depletion of phosphagens (49, 65) and glycogen (11, 12, 57, 69, 99); the depletion of substrates such as free fatty acids, lactate, and amino acids typically does not occur to the extent that performance is limited. Consequently, the depletion and repletion pattern of phosphagens and glycogen following physical activity is important in exercise and sport bioenergetics.

Phosphagens

Fatigue during exercise appears to be at least partially related to the decrease in phosphagens. Phosphagen concentrations in muscle are more rapidly depleted as a result of high-intensity anaerobic exercise compared to aerobic exercise (49, 65). Creatine phosphate can decrease markedly (50-70%) during the first stage (5-30 seconds) of high-intensity exercise and can be almost eliminated as a result of very intense exercise to exhaustion (63, 70, 74, 86). Muscle ATP concentrations may only slightly decrease (21) or may decrease up to 50% to 60% (109) of the preexercise levels during experimentally induced fatigue. It should also be noted that dynamic muscle actions that produce external work use more metabolic energy and typically deplete phosphagens to a greater extent than do isometric muscle actions (8).

The intramuscular ATP concentration is largely spared during exercise as a consequence of creatine phosphate depletion and because of the contribution of additional ATP from the myokinase reaction and other energy sources, such as glycogen and free fatty acids. Postexercise phosphagen repletion can occur in a relatively short period; complete resynthesis of ATP appears to occur within 3 to 5 minutes, and complete creatine phosphate resynthesis can occur within 8 minutes (55, 65). Repletion of phosphagens is largely accomplished as a result of aerobic metabolism (55), although glycolysis can contribute to recovery after high-intensity exercise (16, 27).

The effects of training on concentrations of phosphagens are not well studied or understood. Aerobic endurance training may increase resting concentrations of phosphagens (35, 75) and decrease their rate of depletion at a given absolute submaximal power output (20, 75) but not at a relative (percentage of maximum) submaximal power output (20). Although researchers have noted indications of increased resting concentrations of phosphagens (95), short-term (eight weeks) studies of sprint training have not shown alterations in resting concentrations of phosphagens (7, 113). However, total phosphagen content can be larger following sprint training due to increases in muscle mass (113). Resistance training has been shown to increase the resting concentrations of phosphagens in the triceps brachii after five weeks of training (82). The increases in phosphagen concentration may have occurred due to selective hypertrophy of Type II fibers, which can contain a higher phosphagen concentration than Type I fibers (81).

Glycogen

Limited stores of glycogen are available for exercise. Approximately 300 to 400 g of glycogen are stored in the body's total muscle and about 70 to 100 g in the liver (102). Resting concentrations of liver and muscle glycogen can be influenced by training and dietary manipulations (41, 102). Research suggests that both anaerobic training, including sprinting and resistance training (7, 82), and typical aerobic endurance training (47, 48) can increase resting muscle glycogen concentration.

The rate of glycogen depletion is related to exercise intensity (102). Muscle glycogen is a more important energy source than liver glycogen during moderate- and high-intensity exercise. Liver glycogen appears to be more important during low-intensity exercise, and its contribution to metabolic processes increases with duration of exercise. Increases in relative exercise intensity of 50%, 75%, and 100% of maximal oxygen uptake result in increases in the rate of muscle **glycogenolysis** (the breakdown of glycogen) of 0.7, 1.4, and 3.4 mmol $\cdot$ $kg^{-1} \cdot min^{-1}$, respectively (99). At relative intensities of exercise above 60% of maximal oxygen uptake, muscle glycogen becomes an increasingly important energy substrate; the entire glycogen content of some muscle cells can become depleted during exercise (98).

Relatively constant blood glucose concentrations are maintained at very low exercise intensities (below 50% of maximal oxygen uptake) as a result of low muscle glucose uptake (1); as duration increases beyond 90 minutes, blood glucose concentrations fall, but rarely below 2.8 mmol/L. Long-term exercise (over 90 minutes) at higher intensities (above 50% of maximal oxygen uptake) may result in substantially decreased blood glucose concentrations as a result of liver glycogen depletion. Hypoglycemic reactions may occur in some people with exercise-induced blood glucose values of less than 2.5 mmol/L (2, 22). A decline in blood glucose to around 2.5 to 3.0 mmol/L results from reduced liver carbohydrate stores and causes decreased carbohydrate oxidation and eventual exhaustion (19, 22, 102).

Very high-intensity, intermittent exercise, such as resistance training, can cause substantial depletion of muscle glycogen (decreases of 20% to 60%) with relatively few sets (low total workloads) (78, 94, 110, 111). Although phosphagens may be the primary limiting factor during resistance exercise with few repetitions or few sets, muscle glycogen may become the limiting factor for resistance training with many total sets and larger total amounts of work (94). This type of exercise could cause selective muscle fiber glycogen depletion (more depletion in Type II fibers), which can also limit performance (36, 94). As with other types of dynamic exercise, the rate of muscle glycogenolysis during resistance exercise depends on intensity (i.e., the greater the intensity, the faster the rate of glycogenolysis). However, it appears that when the total work performed was equal, the absolute amount of glycogen depletion was the same, regardless of the intensity of the resistance training session (94).

Repletion of muscle glycogen during recovery is related to postexercise carbohydrate ingestion. Repletion appears to be optimal if 0.7 to 3.0 g of carbohydrate per kg of body weight is ingested every 2 hours following exercise (41, 102). This level of carbohydrate consumption can maximize muscle glycogen repletion at 5 to 6 mmol/g of wet muscle mass per hour during the first 4 to 6 hours following exercise. Muscle glycogen may be completely replenished within 24 hours provided that sufficient carbohydrate is ingested (41, 102). However, if the exercise has a high eccentric component (associated with exercise-induced muscle damage), more time may be required to completely replenish muscle glycogen.

BIOENERGETIC LIMITING FACTORS IN EXERCISE PERFORMANCE

Factors limiting maximal performance (12, 35, 57, 66, 80, 118) must be considered in the mechanisms of fatigue experienced during exercise and training. Understanding the possible limiting factors associated with a particular athletic event is required when one is designing training programs and attempting to delay fatigue and possibly enhance performance. Table 2.5 depicts examples of various limiting factors based on depletion of energy sources and increases in muscle hydrogen ions.

Glycogen depletion can be a limiting factor both for long-duration, low-intensity exercise supported

TABLE 2.5

Ranking of Bioenergetic Limiting Factors

Degree of exercise (example)	ATP and creatine phosphate	Muscle glycogen	Liver glycogen	Fat stores	Lower pH
Light (marathon)	1	5	4-5	2-3	1
Moderate (1,500 m run)	1-2	3	2	1-2	2-3
Heavy (400 m run)	3	3	1	1	4-5
Very intense (discus)	2-3	1	1	1	1
Very intense, repeated (example: sets of 10 repetitions in the snatch exercise with 60% of 1RM)	4-5	4-5	1-2	1-2	4-5

Note: 1 = least probable limiting factor; 5 = most probable limiting factor.

primarily by aerobic metabolism and for repeated, very high-intensity exercise supported primarily by anaerobic mechanisms. Of importance to resistance training, sprinting, and other primarily anaerobic activities is the effect of metabolic acidosis on limiting contractile force (57, 93). Several other factors have been implicated in the development of muscle fatigue and may limit exercise performance, including increased intracellular inorganic phosphate, ammonia accumulation, increased ADP, and impaired calcium release from the sarcoplasmic reticulum (97, 118, 122). Further research is needed to delineate the causes of muscular fatigue and the limiting factors in exercise performance.

OXYGEN UPTAKE AND THE AEROBIC AND ANAEROBIC CONTRIBUTIONS TO EXERCISE

Oxygen uptake (or consumption) is a measure of a person's ability to take in and use oxygen. During low-intensity exercise with a constant power output, oxygen uptake increases for the first few minutes until a steady state of uptake (oxygen demand equals oxygen consumption) is reached (figure 2.8) (3, 62).

At the start of the exercise bout, however, some of the energy must be supplied through anaerobic mechanisms (45, 117). This anaerobic contribution to the total energy cost of exercise is termed the **oxygen deficit** (62, 85). After exercise, oxygen uptake remains above preexercise levels for a period of time that varies according to the intensity and length of the exercise. Postexercise oxygen uptake has been termed the **oxygen debt** (62, 85), recovery O_2 (85), or the **excess postexercise oxygen consumption (EPOC)** (12). The EPOC is the oxygen uptake above resting values used to restore the body to the preexercise condition (105). Only small to moderate relationships have been observed between the oxygen deficit and the EPOC (6, 56); the oxygen deficit may influence the size of the EPOC, but the two are not equal. The possible factors affecting the EPOC are listed in the sidebar (11, 12, 85).

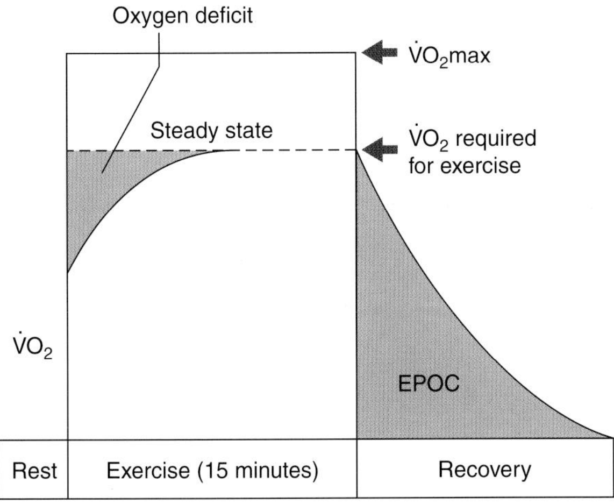

Figure 2.8 Low-intensity, steady-state exercise metabolism: 75% of maximal oxygen uptake ($\dot{V}O_2$max). EPOC = excess postexercise oxygen consumption; $\dot{V}O_2$ = oxygen uptake.

Anaerobic mechanisms provide much of the energy for work if the exercise intensity is above the maximal oxygen uptake that a person can attain (figure 2.9). Generally, as the contribution of anaerobic mechanisms supporting the exercise increases, the exercise duration decreases (3, 51, 120, 121).

The approximate contribution of anaerobic and aerobic mechanisms to maximal sustained efforts on a cycle ergometer is shown in table 2.6 (114, 123). Contributions from anaerobic mechanisms are primary up to 60 seconds, after which aerobic metabolism becomes the primary energy-supplying mechanism. Thus, maximal sustained efforts to exhaustion may depend greatly on aerobic metabolism. The

What Factors Might Increase Excess Postexercise Oxygen Consumption?

- Resynthesis of ATP and creatine phosphate stores
- Resynthesis of glycogen from lactate (20% of lactate accumulation)
- Oxygen resaturation of tissue water
- Oxygen resaturation of venous blood
- Oxygen resaturation of skeletal muscle blood
- Oxygen resaturation of myoglobin
- Redistribution of ions within various body compartments
- Repair of damaged tissue
- Additional cardiorespiratory work
- Residual effects of hormone release and accumulation
- Increased body temperature

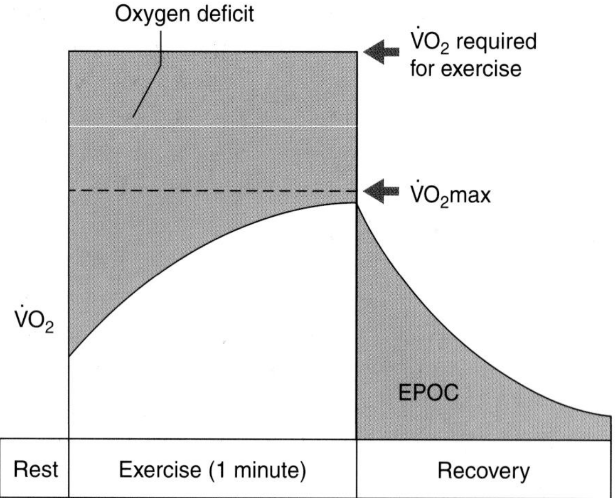

Figure 2.9 High-intensity, non-steady-state exercise metabolism (80% of maximum power output). The required $\dot{V}O_2$ here is the oxygen uptake that would be required to sustain the exercise if such an uptake were possible to attain. Because it is not, the oxygen deficit lasts for the duration of the exercise. EPOC = excess postexercise oxygen consumption; $\dot{V}O_2$max = maximal oxygen uptake.

TABLE 2.6

Contributions of Anaerobic and Aerobic Mechanisms to Maximal Sustained Efforts in Bicycle Ergometry

	0-5 seconds	30 seconds	60 seconds	90 seconds
Exercise intensity (% of maximum power output)	100	55	35	31
Contribution of anaerobic mechanisms (%)	96	75	50	35
Contribution of aerobic mechanisms (%)	4	25	50	65

contribution of anaerobic mechanisms to this type of exercise represents the maximal anaerobic capacity (87, 114).

METABOLIC SPECIFICITY OF TRAINING

Appropriate exercise intensities and rest intervals can permit the "selection" of specific energy systems during training for specific athletic events (12, 85, 119). Few sports or physical activities require maximal sustained-effort exercise to exhaustion or near exhaustion. Most sports and training activities produce metabolic profiles that are very similar to those of a series of high-intensity, constant- or near-constant-effort exercise bouts interspersed with rest periods. In this type of exercise, the required exercise intensity (power output) that must be met during each exercise bout is much greater than the maximal power output that can be sustained using aerobic energy sources. Increasing aerobic power through primarily aerobic endurance training while simultaneously compromising or neglecting anaerobic power and anaerobic capacity training is of little benefit to athletes in these sports (59, 87). (Refer again to the section "Energy Production and Capacity," p. 32.)

The use of appropriate exercise intensities and rest intervals allows for the "selection" of specific energy systems during training and results in more efficient and productive regimens for specific athletic events with various metabolic demands.

Interval Training

Interval training is a method that emphasizes bioenergetic adaptations for a more efficient energy transfer within the metabolic pathways by using predetermined intervals of exercise and rest periods (i.e., work-to-rest ratios). Theoretically, properly spaced work-to-rest intervals allow more work to be accomplished at higher exercise intensities with the same or less fatigue than during continuous training at the same relative intensity. An early paper by Christensen and colleagues (18) compared the total running distance, average oxygen uptake, and blood lactate concentration during continuous running for 5 minutes and interval running with 2:1, 1:1, and 1:2 work-to-rest ratios. Subjects were assigned a continuous running intensity (speed) that would result in fatigue within 5 minutes. At that fast pace during the continuous run, the subjects were able to complete 0.81 mile (1.30 km) before exhaustion. Using 2:1, 1:1, and 1:2 work-to-rest ratios and the same running intensity, however, the subjects were able to complete 4.14 miles (6.66 km), 3.11 miles (5.00 km), and 2.07 miles (3.33 km), respectively. Therefore, much more training can be accomplished at higher intensities with interval training; this concept has been established for over 45 years (18).

Recently, a series of short-term (two-week) interval training studies used six sessions of four to seven 30-second maximum cycling efforts interspaced with 4 minutes of recovery (1:8 work-to-rest ratio). These studies demonstrated improvements in muscle oxidative potential (14, 46), muscle buffering capacity (14, 46), muscle glycogen content (13, 14), and time-trial performance (13), as well as doubled aerobic endurance capacity (14). In addition, a similar four-week interval training program exhibited increases in muscle activation and total work output (25) in trained cyclists. Thus, even the results of recent studies support the use of interval training for metabolic adaptations.

However, few studies provide results that can be used to generate definitive guidelines for choosing specific work-to-rest ratios. Therefore, when one is determining the proper work-to-rest ratio for athletes, knowledge of the time intervals and recovery periods for each of the energy systems is critical to maximizing the amount of work that can be accomplished for a given exercise intensity. For example, after a bout of maximal exercise that depletes CP stores, the complete resynthesis of CP may take up to 8 minutes (55), which suggests that short-duration, high-intensity exercise requires greater work-to-rest ratios due to the aerobic mechanisms that replete phosphagen stores (55).

In contrast, as the goals of training change to longer-duration, lower-intensity tasks, the durations of the work intervals can be longer; this will lengthen the rest periods and decrease the work-to-rest ratios. Table 2.7 provides some general guidelines for work-to-rest ratios that are designed to emphasize the development of specific energy systems based on the theoretical time course for metabolic system involvement and substrate recovery (table 2.3). However, it should be noted that more research is necessary to provide evidence-based recommendations for optimal work-to-rest ratios.

Combination Training

Some authors have suggested that aerobic endurance training should be added to the training of anaerobic athletes (a process that can be termed **combination training** or cross-training) to enhance recovery because recovery relies primarily on aerobic mechanisms. However, aerobic endurance training may reduce anaerobic performance capabilities, particularly for high-strength, high-power performance (59). Aerobic endurance training has been shown to reduce anaerobic energy production capabilities in rats (116). Additionally, combined anaerobic and aerobic endurance training can reduce the gain in muscle girth (23), maximum strength (23, 54, 59), and especially speed- and power-related performance (30), although the exact mechanism is not known (39). It does not appear that the opposite holds true; some studies and reviews suggest that anaerobic training (strength training) can improve low-intensity exercise endurance (60, 61, 39). Although oxidative metabolism is important in recovery from heavy anaerobic exercise (e.g., resistance training and sprint training) (12, 101), care must be used in prescribing aerobic endurance training for anaerobic sports. In this context, it should be noted that specific anaerobic training can stimulate increases in aerobic power and enhance markers of recovery (39). Thus, extensive aerobic endurance training to enhance recovery from anaerobic events is not necessary and may be counterproductive in most strength and power sports.

TABLE 2.7

Using Interval Training to Train Specific Energy Systems

% of maximum power	Primary system stressed	Typical exercise time	Range of work-to-rest period ratios
90-100	Phosphagen	5-10 seconds	1:12 to 1:20
75-90	Fast glycolysis	15-30 seconds	1:3 to 1:5
30-75	Fast glycolysis and oxidative	1-3 minutes	1:3 to 1:4
20-30	Oxidative	>3 minutes	1:1 to 1:3

CONCLUSION

Training programs with increased productivity can be designed through an understanding of how energy is produced during various types of exercise and how energy production can be modified by specific training regimens. Which energy system is used to supply energy for muscular contraction is determined primarily by the intensity of exercise and secondarily by the duration of exercise. Metabolic responses and training adaptations are largely regulated by exercise characteristics (e.g., intensity, duration, and recovery intervals). How these responses and adaptations occur following physical activity forms the basis of metabolic specificity of exercise and training. This principle allows for enhanced athletic performance through the implementation of improved training programs.

KEY TERMS

STUDY QUESTIONS

1. Which of the following is the ultimate source of energy for a muscular contraction?
   a. GTP
   b. oxygen
   c. NADH
   d. ATP

2. Which of the following substances can be metabolized anaerobically?
   a. protein
   b. carbohydrate
   c. fat
   d. glycerol

3. The predominant energy system used during a training session depends primarily on the
   a. session intensity.
   b. session duration.
   c. athlete's training status.
   d. athlete's lean body mass.

4. The production of lactic acid results from the activation of which of the following energy systems?
   a. phosphagen
   b. slow glycolysis
   c. fast glycolysis
   d. fat oxidation

5. Which of the following energy systems has the highest rate of energy production?
   a. phosphagen
   b. fast glycolysis
   c. fat oxidation
   d. carbohydrate oxidation

6. Approximately how many ATP are produced via the oxidative energy system from the degradation of one glucose molecule?
   a. 27
   b. 36
   c. 38
   d. 41

7. Which of the following energy systems is predominantly active at the initiation of all exercise?
   a. oxidative
   b. phosphagen
   c. slow glycolysis
   d. fast glycolysis

8. Which of the following enzymes catalyzes the rate-limiting step of glycolysis?
   a. PFK
   b. isocitrate dehydrogenase
   c. phosphorylase
   d. lactate dehydrogenase

CHAPTER 3

Endocrine Responses to Resistance Exercise

William J. Kraemer, PhD, Jakob L. Vingren, PhD, and Barry A. Spiering, PhD

After completing this chapter, you will be able to

- understand basic concepts of endocrinology, including what hormones are and how they interact with each other and target tissues;
- explain the physiological roles of anabolic hormones;
- describe hormonal responses to resistance exercise; and
- develop training programs that demonstrate an understanding of human endocrine responses.

The endocrine system supports the normal homeostatic function of the human body and helps it respond to external stimuli. Its importance in the field of strength and conditioning is reflected by the critical role it played in the theoretical development of periodization of training (36). Hans Selye, a Canadian endocrinologist, unknowingly provided the theoretical basis for periodization with his work on the adrenal gland and the role of stress hormones in the adaptation to stress, distress, and illness.

Former Eastern Bloc sport scientists and physicians found similarities between the pattern of the training responses in athletes and the stress patterns observed by Selye. Hans Selye coined the term *General Adaptation Syndrome* to describe how the adrenal gland responds with an initial alarm reaction followed by a reduction of an organism's function in response to a noxious stimulus. The key to continued adaptation to the stress is the timely removal of the stimulus so that the organism's function can recover.

It is important for strength and conditioning professionals to have a basic understanding of the hormonal responses to resistance exercise. Such knowledge increases insight into how an exercise prescription can enable hormones to mediate optimal adaptations to resistance training (76, 91). Although resistance training is the only natural stimulus that causes increases in lean tissue mass, dramatic differences exist among resistance training programs in their ability to produce increases in muscle and connective tissue size (35). The type of resistance training workout used dictates the hormonal responses (88, 92, 95, 96, 99, 101). Tissue adaptations are influenced by the changes in circulating hormonal concentrations following exercise (8, 10, 12, 39, 51, 79, 80). Thus, understanding this natural anabolic activity that takes place in the athlete's body is fundamental to successful recovery, adaptation, program design, training progression, and ultimately athletic performance (18, 34, 35, 36, 84, 89, 98, 100).

It has been theorized that the endocrine system can be manipulated naturally with resistance training to enhance the development of various target tissues, thereby improving performance.

SYNTHESIS, STORAGE, AND SECRETION OF HORMONES

Hormones are chemical messengers that are synthesized, stored, and released into the blood by **endocrine glands**—body structures specialized for secretion—and certain other cells (figure 3.1, table 3.1). Similarly, neurons synthesize, store, and secrete neurotransmitters, which may have hormonal functions. The relatively new term **neuroendocrinology** refers to the study of the interactions between the nervous system and the endocrine system. Typically, endocrine glands are stimulated to release hormones by a chemical signal received by receptors on the gland or by neural stimulation. For example, the adrenal medulla (the internal part of the adrenal gland) releases the hormone epinephrine upon neural stimulation from the brain (75, 87, 102, 139). The adrenal cortex (the outer part of the adrenal gland) synthesizes and secretes the hormone cortisol after stimulation by another hor-

I would like to thank all of my current and former students, but especially my graduate students and scientific colleagues, who have made the process of discovery in this field of study exciting and rewarding. The quest for understanding and knowledge is a lifelong pursuit, and you have all helped me in this process. –William J. Kraemer

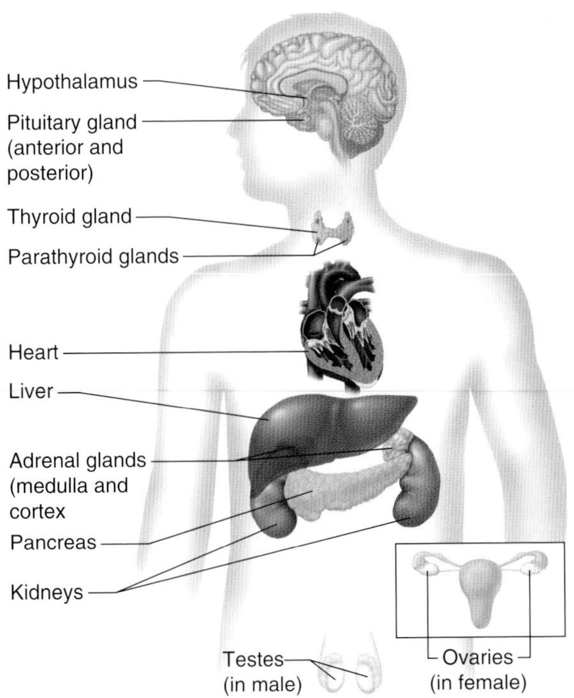

Figure 3.1 The principal endocrine glands of the body along with other glands that secrete hormones.

mone, adrenocorticotropic hormone, released from the pituitary gland (88, 90, 105). Following stimulation, endocrine glands release hormones into the blood, which carries the hormones (and thereby the information) to hormone-specific receptors located on the surface (peptide hormones) or in the nucleus (**steroid hormones** and **thyroid hormones**) of the **target tissue** cells (5, 6, 7, 9, 30, 50).

In addition to endocrine release into blood circulation, hormones can be secreted by autocrine and paracrine mechanisms. Autocrine secretion of a hormone means that the cell releases the hormone inside itself. It may be stimulated to do so via an external stimulus (e.g., another hormone), but the secreted hormone never leaves the cell that produced it. For example, insulin-like growth factor I (IGF-I) could be released inside the muscle fiber when stimulated by mechanical force production or due to growth hormone interactions with muscle. Paracrine secretion of hormones involves the release of a hormone to interact with adjacent cells, without the need for circulation to put the hormone into contact with the target cell. These mechanisms demonstrate the multiple roles that hormones can play in their interactions with a target cell.

A variety of binding proteins that carry hormones are found in the blood (5, 7). These many different binding proteins carry both peptide hormones and steroid hormones. In a sense, these binding proteins act as storage sites within the circulation, help fight degradation of the hormone, and extend its half-life. Most hormones are not active unless they are separated from their specific binding protein. However, some hormone-binding proteins themselves may actually have biological actions. Thus, binding proteins, whether circulating in the blood or bound to a cell, are major players in endocrine function and can be thought of as a type of receptor in some cases (e.g., growth hormone–binding proteins).

Many hormones affect multiple tissues in the body (1, 2, 68, 70, 71, 72). Testosterone or one of its derivatives, for example, interacts with almost every tissue in the body. In this chapter we focus on skeletal muscle tissue as the primary target of hormonal interactions, but many other tissues, such as bone, kidney, and liver, are just as important to the adaptive changes observed with resistance training.

Most hormones play multiple physiological roles. These roles include regulation of reproduction; maintenance of the internal environment; energy production, utilization, and storage; and growth and development. In addition, hormones interact with each other in complex ways. A particular hormone may function in either an independent or dependent manner, depending on its role in a given physiological mechanism. Such complexity and flexibility allow the endocrine system to respond in the proper magnitude to a physiological challenge and to interact differently with various physiological systems or target tissues at the same time.

MUSCLE AS THE TARGET FOR HORMONE INTERACTIONS

Skeletal muscle is somewhat unusual in that it has multinucleated cells. This means that the protein within a muscle fiber is controlled by multiple nuclei. Nuclear domains (figure 3.2) are important in these cells and make possible the differential regulation of protein metabolism along the length of a muscle fiber. This can be observed in the changes in diameter down the length of a long muscle fiber (muscle fibers usually are no longer than 4 to 5 inches, or 10 to 13 cm) which result from differential control of the protein by different nuclear domains.

Hormonal mechanisms that interact with skeletal muscle are a part of an integrated system that mediates the changes made in the metabolic and cellular

TABLE 3.1

Endocrine Glands and Selected Hormones

Endocrine gland	Hormone	Selected physiological actions
Anterior pituitary gland	Growth hormone	Stimulates insulin-like growth factor I, protein synthesis, growth, and metabolism
	Adrenocorticotropic hormone	Stimulates glucocorticoids in the adrenal cortex
	Beta-endorphin	Stimulates analgesia
	Thyroid-stimulating hormone	Stimulates thyroid hormone synthesis and secretion
	Follicle-stimulating hormone	Stimulates growth of follicles in ovary and seminiferous tubules in testes; stimulates ovum and sperm production
	Luteinizing hormone	Stimulates ovulation and secretion of sex hormones in ovaries and testes
	Prolactin	Stimulates milk production in mammary glands; maintains corpora lutea and secretion of progesterone
	Melanocyte-stimulating hormone	Stimulates melanocytes, which contain the dark pigment melanin
Posterior pituitary gland	Antidiuretic hormone	Increases contraction of smooth muscle and reabsorption of water by kidneys
	Oxytocin	Stimulates uterine contractions and release of milk by mammary glands
Thyroid gland	Thyroxine	Stimulates oxidative metabolism in mitochondria and cell growth
	Calcitonin	Reduces calcium phosphate levels in blood
Parathyroid glands	Parathyroid hormone	Increases blood calcium; decreases blood phosphate; stimulates bone formation
Pancreas	Insulin	Stores glycogen and promotes glucose entry into cells; involved in protein synthesis
	Glucagon	Increases blood glucose levels
Adrenal cortex	Glucocorticoids (cortisol, cortisone, etc.)	Inhibit amino acid incorporation into proteins; stimulate conversion of proteins into carbohydrates; maintain normal blood sugar level; conserve glucose; promote use of fat
	Mineralocorticoids (aldosterone, deoxycorticosterone, etc.)	Increase body fluids via sodium-potassium metabolism
Liver	Insulin-like growth factors	Increase protein synthesis in cells
Adrenal medulla	Epinephrine	Increases cardiac output; increases blood sugar and glycogen breakdown and fat metabolism
	Norepinephrine	Has properties of epinephrine; also constricts blood vessels
	Proenkephalin fragments (e.g., peptide F)	Enhance immune cell function, analgesia effects
Ovaries	Estrogens	Stimulate development of female sex characteristics
	Progesterone	Stimulates development of female sex characteristics and mammary glands; maintains pregnancy
Testes	Testosterone	Stimulates growth, increases in protein anabolism, and development and maintenance of male sex characteristics
Heart (atrium)	Atrial peptide	Regulates sodium, potassium, and fluid volume
Kidney	Renin	Regulates kidney function, permeability, solute

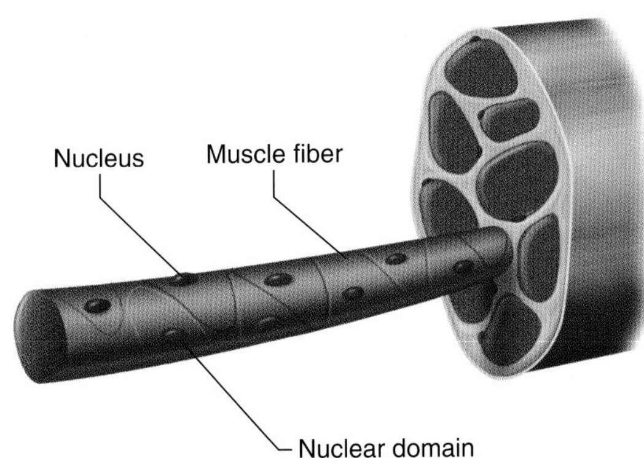

Figure 3.2 The muscle cell is a multinucleated cell in which each nucleus controls a region of the muscle protein, called a *nuclear domain*.

processes of muscle as a result of resistance exercise and training. Muscle remodeling involves the disruption and damage of muscle fibers, an inflammatory response, hormonal interactions, and ultimately the synthesis of new proteins and their orderly incorporation into existing or new sarcomeres (3, 17). The inflammatory process involves the immune system and various immune cells (e.g., T cells), which are under endocrine control. The study of the connection between the neural, endocrine, and immune systems is called *neuroendocrine immunology*. This term demonstrates the interdependence of these systems and the integrative nature of the remodeling process in muscle. We cannot limit our thinking about biological processes to one system.

The most prominent resistance training adaptation in muscle is an increase in the amount of a muscle's contractile proteins: actin and myosin (103, 132). Other changes in these proteins are also significant; for example, **myosin heavy-chain (MHC) proteins** can go through a change in their molecular structure—from Type IIx to IIa heavy-chain proteins. More importantly, the synthesis of noncontractile proteins is needed for structural integrity and orientation of the contractile proteins within the sarcomere. These noncontractile proteins are laid down first in the coordinated physiological development of muscle size.

Stimulation of protein synthesis by heavy resistance training starts at the level of the gene. It allows both the quality and the quantity of muscle to be altered over a period of time, and hormones are involved in this ongoing process of development. In general, the increase in protein synthesis and decrease in protein degradation are the first steps in muscle growth. However, this differs between muscle fiber types. Type I fibers depend more on a reduction in protein degradation, whereas Type II fibers depend on a dramatic increase in protein synthesis to maintain their size or hypertrophy. This difference significantly influences the role that hormones play in the differential regulation of protein metabolism in Type I and Type II muscle fibers.

Hormones are intimately involved with protein synthesis and degradation mechanisms. The production of the contractile proteins, actin and myosin, and their ultimate incorporation into the sarcomere complete the process at the molecular level. A multitude of hormones—including **anabolic hormones** (hormones that promote tissue building) such as insulin, insulin-like growth factors, testosterone, and growth hormone—all contribute to various aspects of this process. Thyroid hormones act as important permissive hormones that allow the actions of other hormones to take place. As another important action in the building of tissue, anabolic hormones also block the negative effects on protein metabolism of **catabolic hormones**, such as cortisol and progesterone, which attempt to degrade cell proteins to support glucose synthesis. The remodeling of a muscle fiber involves changes in protein metabolism and the structural alterations and additions that take place during the recovery period after an exercise stress. The more muscle fibers recruited for the performance of the exercise, the greater the extent of potential remodeling in the whole muscle. The relationship among hormones, muscle fibers, and the subsequent changes in functional capabilities of muscle fibers provide the basis for the adaptive influence of hormones in hypertrophy.

ROLE OF RECEPTORS IN MEDIATING HORMONAL CHANGES

The signal from a hormone (and thereby its effect) is relayed only to cells that express the receptor for that specific hormone. This ensures that the hormone signal affects only the target tissue and not all cells in the body. Typically, the hormone is trying to influence a cellular signal or event that impacts the DNA in the nucleus of the cell, yet direct receptors for all hormones are not found on the DNA. Some hormones have to influence the DNA via secondary reactions. Receptors are found in a mobile form (e.g., binding proteins for growth hormone), integrated into the cell membrane (polypeptide receptors), and on the regulatory elements of the DNA (steroid receptors). Every cell, from muscle fibers to brain cells, has a receptor to mediate the message or the signal from a hormone. One of the basic principles in endocrinology is that a given hormone interacts with a specific receptor. This principle is generally referred to as the **lock-and-key theory** (in which the receptor is the lock and the hormone is the key; figure 3.3); however, it is now known that the hormone–receptor interaction is much more complex than this simple lock-and-key theory conveys. Although only one hormone has exactly the right characteristics to interact with a specific receptor, in cases of **cross-reactivity** a given receptor partially interacts with hormones that are not specifically designed for it (i.e., allosteric binding). When this occurs, the resulting biological actions are different from those induced by the primary hormone.

Receptors can have **allosteric binding sites**, at which substances other than hormones can enhance or reduce the cellular response to the primary hormone. Receptors may also have a number of domains. This means that the receptor may be outside the cell membrane (external), within the cell membrane (internal), or partly inside and partly outside the membrane (integrated). For example, in the case of growth hormone (a polypeptide hormone), the receptor exists in several of these domains. In addition, some hormones may need to be in an aggregated form (several hormones linked together) to produce the optimal signal via the receptor; this is believed to be the case for growth hormone.

Steroid receptors are situated on the nuclear regulatory portion of the cell's DNA (figure 3.4). It is usually the hormone-receptor complex that transmits the message to the nucleus of the cell. The genetic material within the nucleus ultimately translates the hormonal message into either inhibition or facilitation of protein synthesis.

When an adaptation is no longer possible (e.g., the maximal amount of protein has been added to the muscle fiber), receptors can become nonresponsive to a specific hormone, preventing it from stimulating the protein synthesis response in the cell. This inability of a hormone to interact with a receptor is called **downregulation** of receptor function. Receptors have the ability to increase or decrease

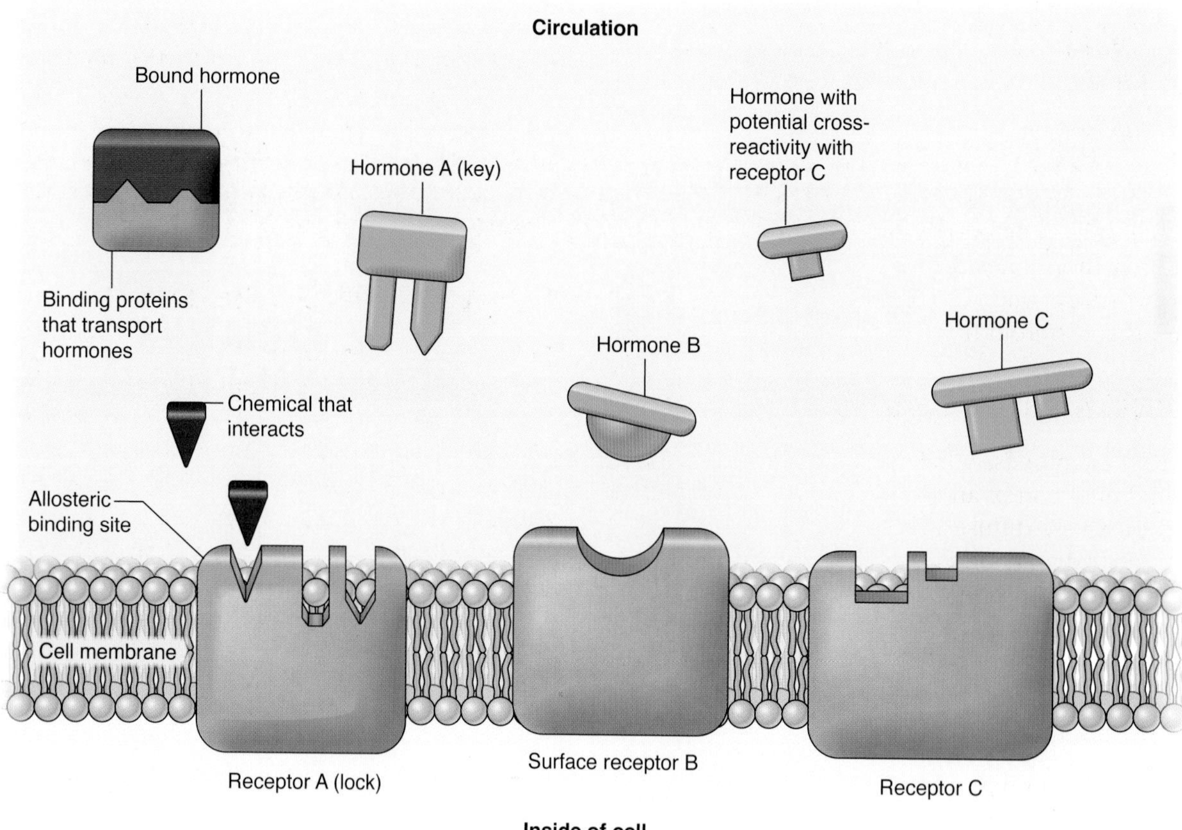

Figure 3.3 A schematic representation of the classic lock-and-key theory for hormonal action at the cell receptor level.

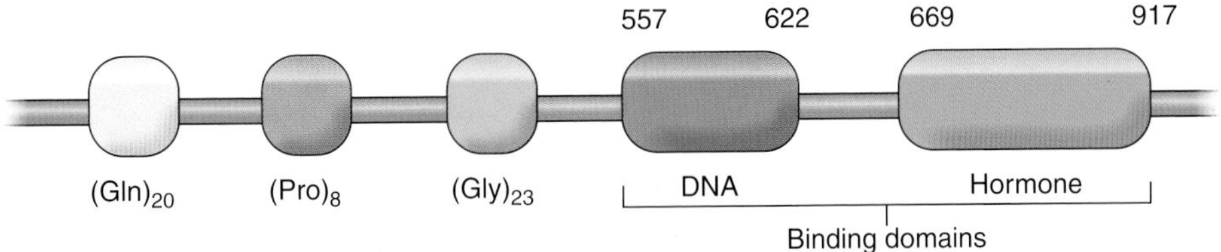

Figure 3.4 Diagram of a typical androgen receptor on the DNA element in the nucleus.

their binding sensitivity, and the actual number of receptors present for binding can also be altered. Alterations in the receptor's binding characteristics or the number of receptors can be as dramatic an adaptation as the release of increased amounts of hormone from an endocrine gland. Obviously, if a receptor is not responsive to the hormone, little or no alteration in cell metabolism will result. For example, it has been shown for the hormone testosterone that exercise training affects only the maximal number of binding sites, not the binding sensitivity of the receptor (24). Scientists are just starting to study and understand the role of receptors in muscle during exercise training.

STEROID HORMONES VERSUS POLYPEPTIDE HORMONES

In terms of molecular structure, there are two main categories of hormones: steroid and polypeptide (or simply peptide) hormones. Each interacts with muscle cells in different ways. Figure 3.5 shows two different hormones: one a polypeptide hormone (growth hormone, 22 kilodalton [kDa] form) and the other a steroid hormone (testosterone).

Steroid Hormone Interactions

Steroid hormones, which include hormones from the adrenal cortex and the gonads, are fat soluble and passively diffuse across the sarcolemma of a muscle fiber, although possible transport mechanisms have been described. Some scientists have hypothesized the presence of transport proteins in the sarcolemma that facilitate this movement. Figure 3.6 shows a typical steroid hormone (testosterone) migrating through the cell membrane into the sarcoplasm of the cell, interacting with the cytosol complex, and binding with the regulatory element on the DNA. The basic series of events is the same for any steroid hormone. After diffusing across the sarcolemma, the hormone binds with its receptor to form a **hormone-receptor complex (H-RC)**, causing a conformational shift in the receptor and activating it. The H-RC arrives at the genetic material in the cell's nucleus and "opens" it in order to expose transcriptional units that code for the synthesis of specific proteins. The H-RC recognizes specific enhancers, or upstream regulatory elements of the genes. Ribonucleic acid (RNA) polymerase II then binds to the promoter that is associated with the specific upstream regulatory elements for the H-RC. The RNA polymerase II then transcribes the gene by coding for the protein dictated by the steroid hormone. Messenger RNA (mRNA) is processed and then moves into the sarcoplasm of the cell, where it is translated into protein. Thus, with its interaction at the genetic level of the cell, the action of the steroid hormone is completed (24, 122). However, the fact that mRNA is produced for a specific protein (e.g., actin) does not mean that that protein is necessarily incorporated into the sarcomere. The hormone message is only one part of the entire process of protein synthesis, which in some cases ends with incorporation of the protein into a cell structure or functional protein (e.g., enzyme).

Polypeptide Hormone Interactions

Polypeptide hormones are made up of amino acids; examples are growth hormone and insulin. Polypeptide hormones can bind to receptors in the blood or to receptors located in the cell membrane of the target tissue. As discussed earlier in this chapter, polypeptide receptors can have different receptor domains where binding and receptor interactions take place (external, integrated, and internal receptor domains). Peptide hormones use three major signaling pathways:

- Cyclic adenosine monophosphate-dependent (cyclic AMP-dependent) signaling pathway
- Cytokine-activated JAK/STAT signaling pathway
- Prototypical growth factor, mitogen-activated signaling pathway

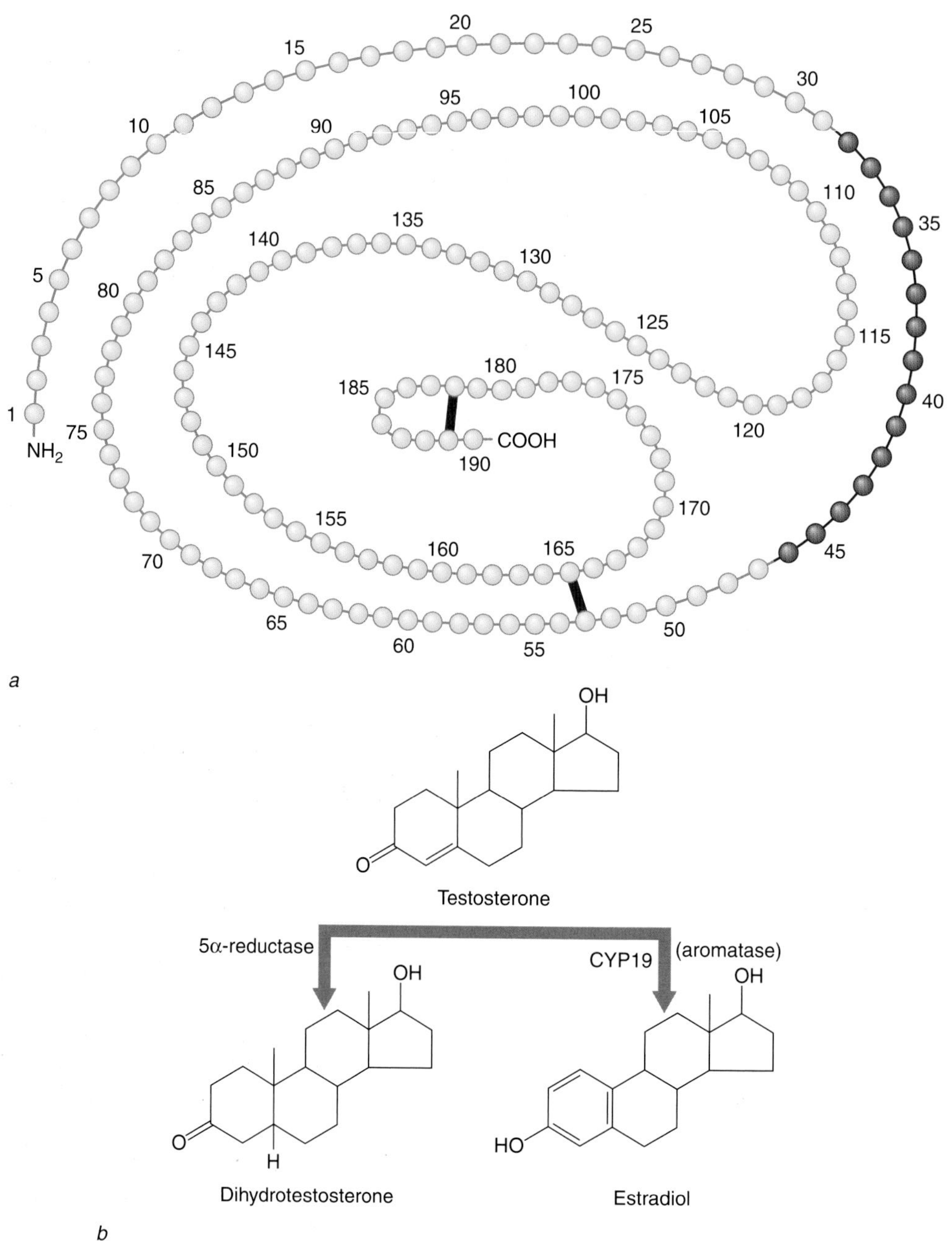

Figure 3.5 Structure of *(a)* a polypeptide hormone (growth hormone, 22 kDa) and *(b)* a steroid hormone (testosterone).

The JAK/STAT pathway involves a family of soluble tyrosine kinases known as the Janus kinases (JAK), which activate transcription factors that are designated STAT, for *s*ignal *t*ransduction *a*ctivating *t*ranscription. Because polypeptide hormones are not fat soluble and thus cannot cross the cell membrane, they rely on **secondary messengers** (STAT) to get their message into the cell. Once inside the cell, the signal can proceed to the cell nucleus and DNA, or affect events in the cytosol, or both. One of the signals from insulin, for example, induces a translocation of glucose transporters from the cytosol to the cell membrane, allowing for increased glucose uptake (57). Secondary messengers inside the cell are activated by the conformational change in the receptor induced by the hormone. The secondary messenger directs its actions to specific areas in the cell, where the hormone's message is amplified. The subsequent cascade of intracellular events eventually leads up to the physiological response ascribed to the specific hormone. Figure 3.7 shows a typical polypeptide hormone interaction with the cell nucleus via the cytokine-activated JAK/STAT signaling pathway.

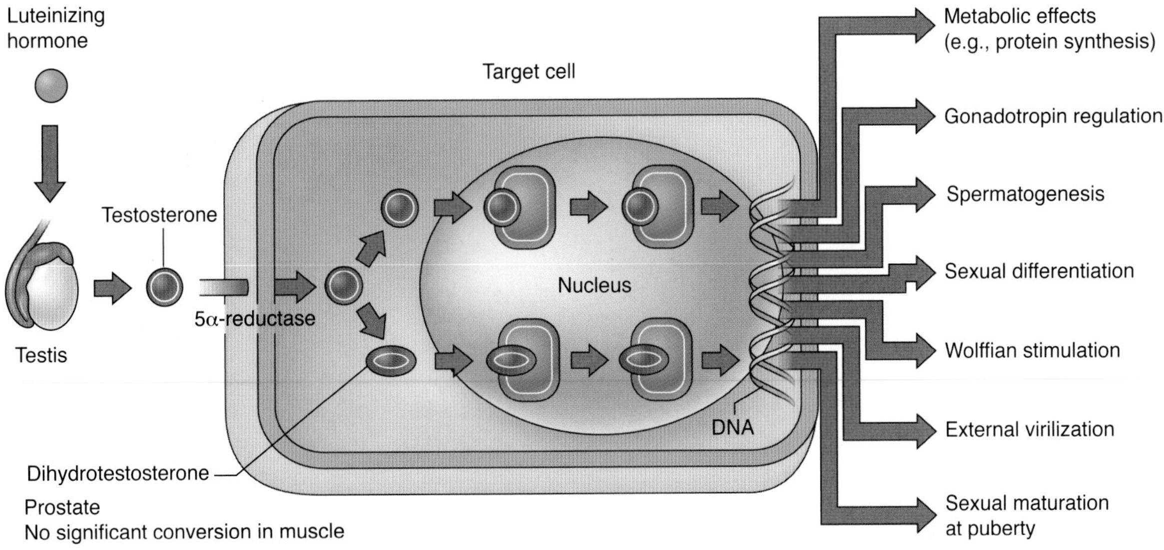

Figure 3.6 Typical steroid migration into a target cell by either testosterone in skeletal muscle or dihydrotestosterone in sex-linked tissues. Only one hormone pathway (testosterone or dihydrotestosterone) is targeted for one cell, but the two are shown together in this diagram. Each has different physiological outcomes.

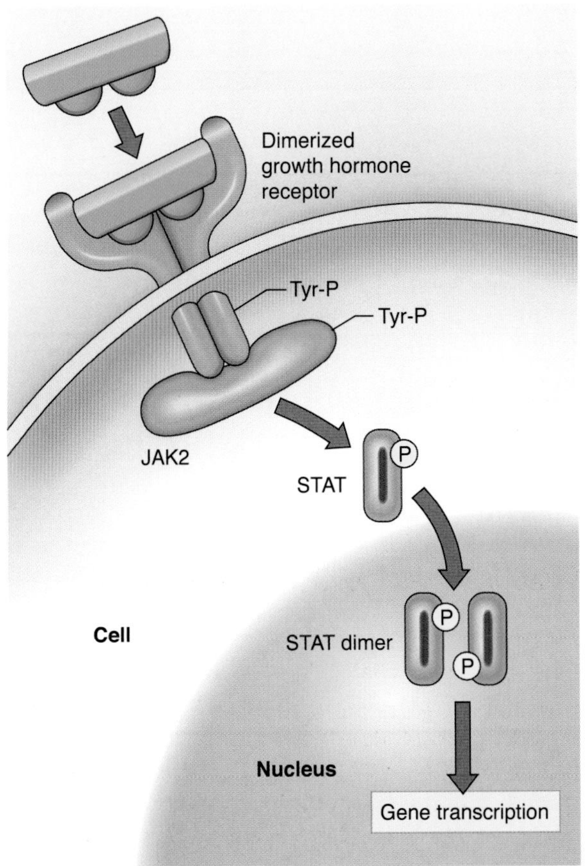

Figure 3.7 Typical polypeptide hormone (growth hormone in this example) interaction with a receptor via the cytokine-activated JAK/STAT signaling pathway. Although the hormone binds to an external receptor, a secondary messenger (STAT) is activated that can enter the cell nucleus. Tyr-P = tyrosinase related protein.

HEAVY RESISTANCE EXERCISE AND HORMONAL INCREASES

Long-term heavy resistance training brings about significant adaptive responses that result in enhanced size, strength, and power of trained musculature (59, 62, 81, 86, 89, 91, 103). The increase in anabolic hormone levels observed consequent to the performance of heavy resistance exercise can increase hormonal interactions with various cellular mechanisms and enhance the development of muscle protein contractile units. On neural stimulation from an alpha motor neuron to initiate a muscle action, various signals (electrical, chemical, and hormonal) are sent from the brain and activated muscles to a number of endocrine glands.

Hormones are secreted during and after the resistance exercise bout due to the physiological stress of resistance exercise (28, 31, 40, 46, 48, 61, 88, 95, 96, 99). Acute hormonal secretion's provide abundant information to the body regarding such things as the amount and type of physiological stress (e.g., epinephrine), the metabolic demands of the exercise (e.g., insulin), and the need for subsequent changes in resting metabolism. Thus, with specific patterns of nervous system stimulation from resistance exercise, certain hormonal changes are simultaneously activated for specific purposes related to recovery and adaptation to the acute exercise stress. The patterns of stress and hormonal responses combine to shape the tissues' adaptive response to a specific training program.

Hormonal increases in response to resistance exercise take place in a physiological environment that is unique to this type of exercise stress. The significant amounts of force that are produced require the activation of high-threshold motor units not typically stimulated by other types of exercise such as aerobic endurance exercise. The muscle fibers of the activated motor units are stimulated and forces are placed on the sarcolemmas of the muscle fibers by the heavy external loads being lifted. Among the many different responses to the force production stress are alterations in the sarcolemma's ability to import nutrients and in the sensitivity and number of hormone receptors in the muscle cells. In addition, local inflammatory processes related to tissue damage and repair mechanisms are activated by stress and run their time course with recovery (17). Ultimately, the specific force produced by the activated muscle fibers determines the alteration in hormone receptor sensitivity to anabolic hormones as well as changes in receptor synthesis. As few as one or two heavy resistance exercise sessions can increase the number of androgen receptors, the receptor for testosterone, in the muscle (107, 148). Combined, these alterations lead to muscle growth and strength increases in the intact muscle.

The specific force produced in activated fibers stimulates receptor and membrane sensitivities to anabolic factors, including hormones, which lead to muscle growth and strength changes.

Following the exercise session, remodeling of the muscle tissue takes place in the environment of hormonal secretions that provide for anabolic actions. Increases in synthesis of actin and myosin and a reduction in protein degradation occur. However, if the stress is too great, catabolic actions in the muscle may exceed anabolic actions as a result of the inability of anabolic hormones to bind to their receptors or the downregulation of receptors in the muscle tissue (24, 110). Thus, hormonal actions are important both during and after an exercise session to respond to the demands of the exercise stress (37, 38, 39). The magnitude of the hormonal response depends on the amount of tissue stimulated, the amount of tissue remodeling, and the amount of tissue repair required consequent to the exercise stress. Thus, the characteristics of the exercise stimulus (i.e., workout) are again paramount to the hormonal response of the body to the exercise protocol (76, 84).

Only muscle fibers that are activated by the resistance training are subject to adaptation. Some fibers may be close to genetic ceilings for cell size, while others may have a great potential for growth. The extent of hormonal interactions in the growth of muscle fibers is directly related to the adapted size of the fibers (i.e., the potential for size increases), which is dictated by the loads and exercise angles used in a resistance training program. Thus, if a specific program uses the same exercise in each training session, only a specific set of muscle fibers associated with that movement will be activated and then stimulated to grow. This could leave many fibers in the muscle unaffected—without any significant interactions with hormonal factors and thus little or no change in size. This dramatic heterogeneity of cross-sectional areas of muscle fibers can be seen even in trained muscle fiber sections (unpublished laboratory observations). All motor units may not be stimulated to the same extent in an exercise protocol. The same can be said of various load patterns and progression schemes. Only the activated fiber directly realizes the benefits of the resistance exercise program and uses physiological mechanisms, including hormonal mechanisms, to adapt to the stress. Studies have demonstrated that the volume of work, rest periods between sets, and the type of protocol are vital to the response pattern and magnitude of hormonal changes in men and women (54, 119).

MECHANISMS OF HORMONAL INTERACTIONS

The mechanisms of hormonal interaction with muscle tissue depend on several factors. First, when exercise acutely increases the blood concentrations of hormones, the probability of interaction with receptors may be greater. If the physiological function to be affected is already close to a genetic maximum (i.e., with little adaptive potential left), however, the receptor is not sensitive to the increased hormonal exposure. For example, a muscle cell that has already reached its maximum size with long-term training may not be sensitive to hormonal signals from the body to stimulate further protein accretion. A similar receptor desensitization (decreased affinity) to a hormone can develop when resting hormone levels are chronically elevated due to disease or exogenous drug use. How and when this reduction in receptor sensitivity to hormonal increases occurs in human muscle is unknown; however, genetic predisposition ultimately limits increases in size. Second, because adaptations to heavy resistance exercise typically are anabolic, the recovery mechanisms involved are related to increases in the size of cells. Third, mistakes in exercise prescriptions can result in a greater catabolic effect or an ineffective exercise program. As a result, hormonal mechanisms either adversely affect cellular development or minimally activate mechanisms that augment hypertrophy.

The combination of many different mechanisms is thought to stimulate exercise-induced hypertrophy. However, not all force production improvements can be explained by muscle mass increases alone. Neural factors affect this process too. The integration of the nervous system and the various hormonal mechanisms is different in trained and untrained people (61, 127). In addition, certain hormonal mechanisms, such as those mediated by testosterone, may not be operational in men or women or fully operational at all ages (31, 94, 95). A wide array of hormonal mechanisms with differential effects based on program design, training level, sex, age, genetic predisposition, and adaptational potential appear to provide myriad possible adaptation strategies for the maintenance or improvement of muscle size and strength (93).

HORMONAL CHANGES IN PERIPHERAL BLOOD

Hormone concentrations can be determined from blood samples drawn from athletes at various stages of training. While interpretation of blood concentrations of hormones can be tricky, as this is only one part of the whole hormonal response puzzle, such data provide an indication of the status or responses of the glands or of the functional status of the mechanisms controlled by the hormone. It should be noted that peripheral concentrations of hormones in the blood do not indicate the status of the various receptor populations or the effects of a hormone within the cell. It is typically assumed, however, that large increases in hormone concentration indicate higher probabilities for interactions with receptors. Decreases in hormonal concentrations indicate several possible fates for the hormone, including higher uptake into the target tissue receptors, greater degradation of the hormone, decreased secretion of the hormone, or some combination of these. Many different physiological mechanisms contribute in varying degrees to the observed changes in peripheral blood concentrations of hormones, including the following:

- *Fluid volume shifts.* Body fluid tends to shift from the blood to the intercellular compartment and the cells as a result of exercise. This shift can increase hormone concentrations in the blood without any change in secretion from endocrine glands. It has been hypothesized that, regardless of the mechanism of increase, such concentration changes increase receptor interaction probabilities.
- *Tissue clearance rates.* Tissue clearance rate is the time it takes a hormone to circulate through the tissue. Hormones circulate through various tissues and organs, with the liver being one of the major processing organs in the body. The time delay as the hormone circulates through the liver and other tissues (e.g., lungs) keeps the hormone out of blood circulation and away from contact with target receptors in other parts of the body, or can degrade it and make it nonfunctional.
- *Hormonal degradation.* The hormone itself can break down.
- *Venous pooling of blood.* Blood flow back to the heart is slowed by pooling of blood in veins; the blood is delayed in the peripheral circulation due to intense muscle activity (muscle contractions greater than 45% of maximum). This pooling of the blood can increase the concentrations of hormones in the venous blood and also increase time of exposure to target tissues.
- *Interactions with binding proteins in the blood.* Hormones bind with specialized proteins in the blood that make it easier for the blood to transport the hormones (5, 7). Free hormones and bound hormones all interact differently with tissue; ultimately, it is the free hormone that interacts with the membrane or other cellular receptors.

All these mechanisms interact to produce a certain concentration of a hormone in the blood, which influences the potential for interaction with the receptors in target tissue and their subsequent secondary effects, leading to the final effect of the hormone on a cell.

Hormone responses are tightly linked to the characteristics of the resistance exercise protocol.

ADAPTATIONS IN THE ENDOCRINE SYSTEM

Although organs such as muscle and connective tissue are the ultimate targets of most resistance training programs, many adaptations occur within the endocrine system as well. These changes are related to changes in the target organs and the toleration of exercise stress. The potential for adaptation in the endocrine system, with so many different sites and mechanisms that can be affected, is great. The following are examples of the potential types of adaptation that are possible:

- Amount of synthesis and storage of hormones
- Transport of hormones via binding proteins
- Time needed for the clearance of hormones through liver and other tissues
- Amount of hormonal degradation that takes place over a given period of time
- How much blood-to-tissue fluid shift occurs with exercise stress
- How tightly the hormone binds to its receptor (receptor affinity); this is an uncommon response to exercise training
- How many receptors are in the tissue
- The magnitude of the signal sent to the cell nucleus by the H-RC or secondary messenger
- The degree of interaction with the cell nucleus (which dictates how much muscle protein to produce)

Hormones are secreted in response to a need for homeostatic control in the body; the endocrine system is part of an overall strategy to bring physiological functions back into normal range (49). These homeostatic mechanisms controlled by the endocrine system can be activated in response to an acute (immediate) resistance exercise stress or can be altered by chronic (over longer periods of time) resistance training (23, 43, 45, 53, 61, 67, 131, 132, 141). The mechanism that mediates acute homeostatic changes to acute resistance exercise stress is typically a sharp increase or decrease in hormonal concentrations to regulate a physiological variable, such as glucose level. A more subtle increase or decrease usually occurs in chronic resting hormonal concentrations in response to resistance training (131). For example, the subtle increases in testosterone over the course of a resistance training program may help to mediate changes in protein synthesis, thus leading to increased muscle fiber size.

PRIMARY ANABOLIC HORMONES

The primary anabolic hormones involved in muscle tissue growth and remodeling are testosterone, growth hormone, and insulin-like growth factors (IGFs), which are discussed here, as well as insulin and the thyroid hormones, which are examined in greater detail in other sources (37, 38, 39, 40, 49).

Testosterone

Testosterone is the primary androgen hormone that interacts with skeletal muscle tissue; dihydrotestosterone is the primary androgen that interacts with sex-linked tissues (e.g., prostate in men). Androgen interactions with specific tissue are determined by enzymes such as 5α-reductase, which converts testosterone to dihydrotestosterone; this enzyme is present in certain sex-linked tissue but not in muscle. Although testosterone affects both men and women, there are differences in the magnitude of responses, and these are clarified throughout this section. Figure 3.8 shows the different processes involved in the biosynthesis of testosterone.

Circulating testosterone was proposed as a physiological marker for both men and women for evaluating the anabolic status of the body (63, 110). The hormonal control of testosterone release has been reviewed in detail (24, 50, 77, 78). The direct effects of testosterone on skeletal muscle growth are probably best gleaned from our experience with anabolic steroids. However, testosterone's effects are not as dramatic in culture as those of IGF-I (37, 38, 39).

Testosterone has both direct and indirect effects on muscle tissue. It can promote growth hormone responses in the pituitary, which can influence protein synthesis in muscle. The potential interac-

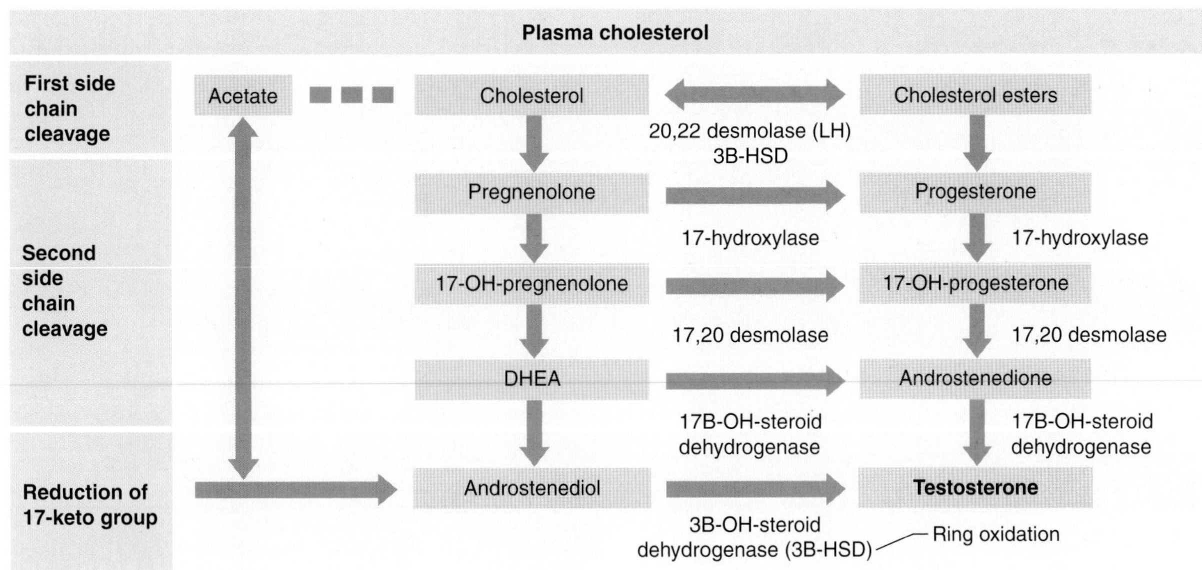

Figure 3.8 Series of chemical reactions in the biosynthesis of testosterone from cholesterol.

tions with other hormones demonstrate the highly interdependent nature of the neuroendocrine-immune system in influencing the strength and size of skeletal muscles. The effects of testosterone on the development of strength and muscle size are also related to the influence of testosterone on the nervous system (10, 74). For example, testosterone can interact with receptors on neurons, increase the amounts of neurotransmitters, and influence structural protein changes. Each of these interactions can enhance the force production potential and mass of the innervated muscle. Finally, testosterone can interact directly with skeletal muscle itself.

Following secretion from the testes in men and the ovaries and adrenal glands in women, testosterone is transported to target tissues by a transport protein (e.g., sex hormone–binding globulin). At the target tissue, testosterone disassociates from the binding protein, crosses the cell membrane, and binds to the nuclear androgen receptor. This testosterone-androgen receptor complex binds to the DNA, causing an increase in DNA transcription, and thus induces protein synthesis (24, 37, 38, 39, 55, 118, 126, 143). Recent discoveries have shown that testosterone also binds to cell membrane receptors. This binding allows a rapid intracellular effect of testosterone, such as calcium release, to occur (29, 144). The knowledge of hormone receptors and their cellular effects is rapidly growing, and the future promises to bring new discoveries that will further elucidate this content area.

Increases in peripheral blood concentrations of testosterone have been observed in men during and following many types of high-intensity aerobic endurance exercise as well as resistance exercise (49). Some preliminary data show small testosterone increases in women after resistance exercise. Variations in testosterone's cellular actions consequent to resistance exercise thus may be attributed to differences in the cell membrane, perhaps because of the forces placed on membranes with resistance exercise, or to different feedback mechanisms sending signals to the higher brain centers (e.g., higher levels of testosterone feeding back in the brain to decrease luteinizing hormone secretion). Furthermore, receptor interactions may be quite different under different exercise conditions due to the differential force on the membrane (24). High-intensity aerobic endurance exercise can cause a dramatic catabolic tissue response, and increases in testosterone may be related to the need for protein synthesis to keep up with protein loss (103, 137, 138). Despite increased testosterone, hypertrophy does not typically take place with aerobic endurance training (103). In fact, oxidative stress may actually promote a decrease in muscle fiber size in order to optimize oxygen transport into the cell (103). Without the proper exercise stimulus, the cellular mechanisms that mediate muscle fiber growth are not activated to the extent that hypertrophy occurs.

In boys and younger men (<18 years), several factors appear to influence acute serum testosterone concentrations and may affect whether significant increases occur during or following exercise. Among these factors is the onset of puberty. Since testosterone production in prepubescent boys is very low, these boys lack sufficient quantities to induce noteworthy hypertrophy. Independently or in various combinations, several exercise variables can increase serum testosterone concentrations in boys and younger men (31, 45, 94, 95):

- Large muscle group exercises (e.g., deadlift, power clean, squats)
- Heavy resistance (85-95% of 1-repetition maximum [1RM])
- Moderate to high volume of exercise, achieved with multiple sets, multiple exercises, or both
- Short rest intervals (30 seconds to 1 minute)
- Two years or more of resistance training experience

Increases in serum total testosterone in men are evident when blood is sampled before and immediately after exercise protocols that use very large muscle groups (e.g., deadlifts but not bench presses) (31, 56, 60, 96, 99, 146). When blood is sampled 4 or more hours after exercise and not immediately following it, other factors, such as **diurnal variations** (normal fluctuations in hormone levels throughout the day) or recovery phenomena, can affect the magnitude or direction of the acute stress response (23). Additionally, possible rebounds or decreases in testosterone blood values over time may reflect augmentation or depression of diurnal variations (100), making interpretation of late blood samples yet more difficult. Recent evidence demonstrates that acute resistance exercise does not appear to affect the diurnal changes in testosterone (unpublished laboratory results). In men, testosterone values are typically highest in the morning and drop with time through the day. This may make increases in the morning easier, but exercise-induced increases later in the day are more effective for increasing overall testosterone concentrations over an entire day. Women appear to have much lower concentrations and little variation during the day (although there are limited data to support the latter contention). Unpublished laboratory results also indicate that increases in testosterone concentrations while sleeping are specific to men; women do not appear to have the same fluctuations at night. This area requires further study, but preliminary data fail to support training theories proposed by the former Eastern Bloc countries alluding to endogenous testosterone as an important effect with multiple training sessions per day (unpublished observations, W.J. Kraemer, S.J. Fleck, and M.H. Stone).

Large muscle group exercises result in acute increased serum total testosterone concentrations in men.

A wide variety of exercise protocols have been shown to elicit increases in men's testosterone in response to the acute exercise stress. Any lack of change can typically be attributed to one of the previously discussed factors (size of muscle group, intensity, etc.). Fahey and colleagues (31) were unable to demonstrate significant increases among high school–aged males in serum concentrations of total testosterone, perhaps due to the nonresponsiveness of cells in testes of young males. A report by Kraemer and colleagues (95) indicates that increases may occur if the resistance training experience of high school–aged males (14-18 years) is two years or more. Another study by Kraemer and colleagues (108) showed that untrained men require a few workouts before they can achieve an exercise-induced increase in testosterone. Such data support the possibility that resistance training may alter the physiological release or concentrating mechanisms (e.g., clearance times and plasma volume shifts) of the hypothalamic-pituitary-testicular axis (hormones from the brain stimulate the testes to produce and secrete testosterone) in younger men and untrained men (95, 108). A recent study with 60 younger women showed a small but significant increase in serum testosterone (unpublished laboratory responses) in response to six sets of 10RM squats. More advanced resistance exercise programs for younger children have become acceptable in both the scientific and medical communities (94). Such programs may be effective in causing changes in testosterone secretion patterns in boys. The consistent use of a wide range of advanced protocols may influence the responses of testosterone even in young boys (>13 and <17 years). Exactly how this finding is related to pubertal growth and development remains to be studied.

Free Testosterone and Sex Hormone–Binding Globulin

The acute exercise responses of free testosterone (testosterone not bound to a protein, such as sex hormone–binding globulin, for transport) are beginning to be understood. A higher total (bound) testosterone level allows for the potential of more free testosterone. Häkkinen and coworkers (59, 60, 62) observed that free testosterone remains unaltered or decreases after resistance exercise sessions. Kraemer and colleagues (97), however, showed that younger men have higher concentrations of free testosterone after a workout than older (i.e., 62-year-old) men, which may indicate greater biological potential for testosterone to interact with the target tissue. The so-called free hormone hypothesis says that it is only the free hormone that interacts with target tissues. Nevertheless, the bound hormone could significantly influence the rate of hormone delivery to a target tissue, such as muscle, and this may be an advantage that younger men have over older men after a workout (27). That is, younger men have more total testosterone and more free testosterone than older men.

The role, regulation, and interaction of binding proteins and their interactions with cells also present interesting possibilities for force production improvements, especially for women, whose total amount of testosterone is very low in comparison with that of men. Muscle cell stimulation of growth keeps testosterone around longer in a bound state. In fact, the binding protein itself may act as a hormone with biological activity (126). The biological role of various binding proteins appears to be an important factor in tissue interactions (58, 59, 62, 126). Häkkinen and coworkers (58, 59, 62) observed that changes in sex hormone–binding globulin and the ratio of this protein to testosterone are correlated with isometric leg strength and reflect the patterns of force production improvements in leg musculature.

Testosterone Responses in Women

Testosterone is the primary male sex hormone. Women have about 15- to 20-fold lower concentrations of testosterone than men do. Most studies have not been able to demonstrate an acute increase in testosterone following a resistance exercise workout for women; recent data show that if increases do occur, they are relatively small (unpublished laboratory data, 20, 31, 64, 67, 92, 96, 146). This may vary with individual women, as some women secrete higher concentrations of adrenal androgens. In one report, changes were observed in baseline concentrations of testosterone in subjects who exercised regularly compared with inactive controls (20). Still, other studies have been unable to demonstrate changes in serum concentrations of testosterone with training (31, 64, 67, 92, 96, 146). Häkkinen and colleagues (64) showed that changes in total and free testosterone levels during strength training were correlated with muscle force production characteristics; yet no significant increases were observed. Responses of testosterone to exercise in women and men are shown in figure 3.9.

Training Adaptations of Testosterone

We are still learning about the responses of testosterone to resistance training (61, 103, 132, 147). It appears that training time and experience may be very important factors in altering the resting and exercise-induced concentrations of this hormone. Its role in skeletal muscle may change, however, as upper limits of muscle cell size increases are achieved. In adult men, acute increases in testosterone are observed if the exercise stimulus is adequate (i.e., multiple sets, 5-10RM, adequate muscle mass used). In a classic study, Häkkinen and colleagues (61) demonstrated that over the course of two years of training, even in elite weightlifters, increases in resting serum testosterone concentrations do occur, concomitant to increases in follicle-stimulating hormone and luteinizing hormone, which are the higher brain regulators of testosterone production and release. Testosterone may have a role in nervous system development in long-term training. Increases in testosterone concentrations may augment the neural adaptations that occur for strength gain in highly trained strength and power athletes.

Research on the effect of resistance exercise and training on the androgen receptor (the receptor for testosterone) is limited; however, recently several studies have been published underscoring the current interest in this topic (107, 123, 145, 148). The findings vary, showing both increases and decreases in androgen receptor content; however, these differences might stem from variations in exercise protocols as well as the time point for tissue sampling. Despite these varying findings, it appears that resistance exercise and training increase the muscle androgen receptor content.

Growth Hormone

One of the most interesting endocrine glands is the pituitary gland, which secretes growth hormone (GH), also called somatotropin. The cybernetic responses of GH are shown in figure 3.10. GH is secreted by the anterior pituitary gland and has many effects on the human body. Specifically, with resistance training it enhances cellular amino acid

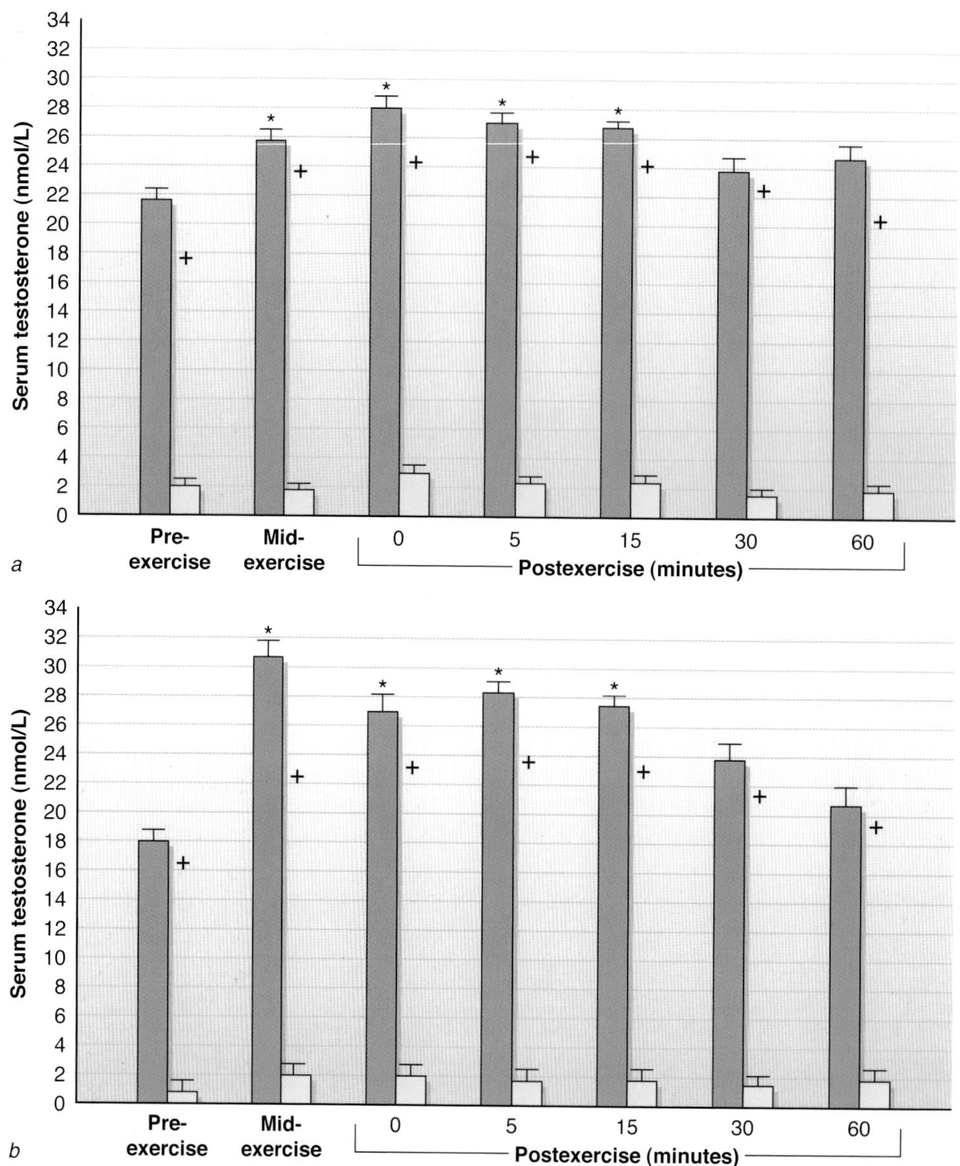

Figure 3.9 Male (blue bars) and female (gold bars) serum testosterone responses to two exercise programs. *(a)* A protocol entailing eight exercises using 5RM and 3-minute rest periods between sets and exercises. *(b)* A program that called for eight exercises using 10RM and 1-minute rest periods between sets and exercises. The total work for the second protocol was higher.

* = Significantly above preexercise levels; + = significantly above the other group.

Reprinted, by permission, from Kraemer et al., 1990 (99).

uptake and protein synthesis in skeletal muscle, resulting in hypertrophy of both Type I and Type II muscle fibers. The anabolic effects of GH on these tissues can be direct as well as mediated through the production of IGF-I by the liver and other cells (e.g., fat cells).

Growth hormone is important for the normal development of a child, but it also appears to play a vital role in adapting to the stress of resistance training. The target tissues for GH are highly variable, and different molecular weight variants have different target tissues, which include bone, immune cells, skeletal muscle, fat cells, and liver tissue. The main physiological roles of GH are these:

- Decreases glucose utilization
- Decreases glycogen synthesis
- Increases amino acid transport across cell membranes
- Increases protein synthesis
- Increases utilization of fatty acids

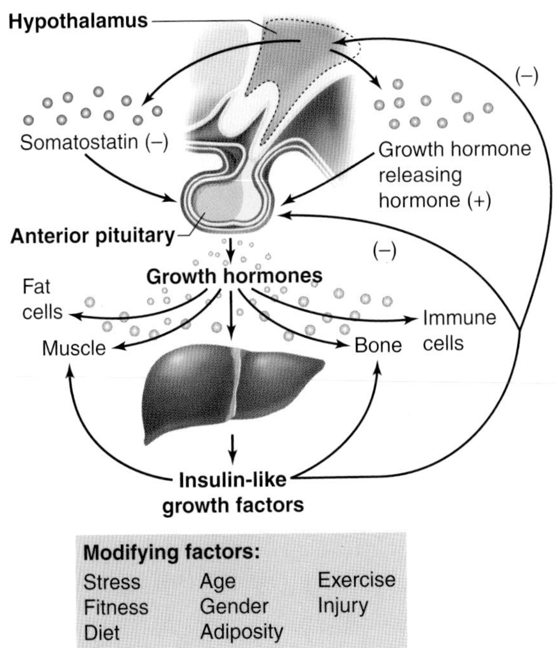

Figure 3.10 Diagram of growth hormone cybernetics and interactions.

- Increases lipolysis (fat breakdown)
- Increases availability of glucose and amino acids
- Increases collagen synthesis
- Stimulates cartilage growth
- Increases retention of nitrogen, sodium, potassium, and phosphorus
- Increases renal plasma flow and filtration
- Promotes compensatory renal hypertrophy
- Enhances immune cell function

The secretion of GH is regulated by a complex system of neuroendocrine feedback mechanisms (18, 19, 32, 114, 125, 130, 149). Many of the hormone's actions may be mediated by a secondary set of hormones, but GH in its many forms interacts directly with target tissues. Growth hormone both stimulates the release of IGFs at the autocrine level of the cell, contributing to the overall changes in IGFs in the body, and increases the availability of amino acids for protein synthesis. This results in conditions that promote tissue repair in general and, perhaps, recovery following resistance exercise. Insulin-like growth factor may be released from nonhepatic tissues (e.g., fat, white blood cells), including muscle itself, which may not produce as much endogenous IGF as other body tissues (22, 38, 65). Nevertheless, GH plays a crucial role in direct cellular interactions as one of the most potent anabolic hormones (115). The secretion of the 22 kDa GH, and thus the amount in the blood, varies according to time of day, with the highest levels observed at night during sleep (33, 80, 130). The 22 kDa form is released in pulsatile, or burstlike, episodes; these pulses also have different amplitudes throughout the day, and exercise appears to increase their amplitude and number. It has been hypothesized that nocturnal increases are involved in various tissue repair mechanisms in the body. Thus, it is possible that GH secretion and release may directly influence adaptations of the contractile unit of muscle and subsequent expression of strength (115). Various external factors, such as age, gender, sleep, nutrition, alcohol consumption, and exercise, all alter GH release patterns (14, 15, 16, 120, 142). Growth hormone is released into the peripheral circulation, where it attaches to specific binding proteins, which represent the extracellular domain of the GH receptor. In general, GH acts by binding to plasma membrane-bound receptors on the target cells.

Efficacy of Pharmacological Growth Hormone

Because GH has so many roles in metabolism, including growth-promoting actions in tissues (18, 37, 38, 39, 115, 125, 130), the pharmacological use of GH has unknown and unpredictable results, especially in people with normal pituitary glands. It appears that the role of GH in muscle tissue is not related to events involving immature muscle fibers, since it has few direct effects on embryonic muscle tissue cultures (38). The enhancement of the contractile unit by GH interactions appears to contribute to the development of the intact muscle, help in metabolic aspects, and affect subsequent force production characteristics. However, further research is needed to clarify exactly how GH is involved with exercise-induced hypertrophy. A review by Rogol (125) showed that GH treatment alone is not effective in causing strength increases and that involvement of the total motor unit is probably necessary. Although size increases are possible, the quality of the muscle may be compromised owing to limitations in activation and control. Any apparent ergogenic effects may be outweighed by a wide variety of secondary effects not related to strength or size changes in muscle tissue (125). It seems plausible that the endogenous mechanisms related to the exercise stimulus have greater specificity and are more effective than GH injections for muscle strength and hypertrophy development. In fact, exercise-induced hypertrophy is apparently quite different from hypertrophy resulting from injections of GH; the force production in muscle fibers consequent to exercise-induced hypertrophy is superior (39, 51, 124, 125). Furthermore, biological timing of cellular events in muscle and release of GH may be crucial for optimal interactions between the exercise-stressed muscle and GH. With the many molecular weight variants involved in the complex picture of GH regulation and interaction, simplistic views of pituitary function are outdated.

Growth hormone is important for the normal development of a child and appears to play a vital role in adapting to the stress of resistance training. However, GH injections result in a wide variety of secondary effects not related to changes in muscle size or strength and can, in fact, result in hypertrophy with less force production than occurs with exercise-induced hypertrophy.

Growth Hormone Responses to Stress

Pituitary hormones (e.g., proopiomelanocortin [POMC], GH, and prolactin) respond to a variety of exercise stressors, including resistance exercise (20, 25, 46, 49, 83, 88, 90, 96, 99, 111, 113). Growth hormone concentrations increase in response to breath holding and hyperventilation alone (26), as well as to hypoxia (136). It appears that a significant stimulus for 22 kDa GH release is increased hydrogen ion and lactate concentrations (53). Not all resistance exercise protocols demonstrate increased serum GH concentration. VanHelder and colleagues (142) observed that when a light load (28% of 7RM) was used with a high number of repetitions in each set, no changes in the serum concentration of GH occurred. It appears that an intensity threshold must be reached in order to elicit a significant GH response to resistance exercise, especially when longer rest periods (>3 minutes) are used (99). This may be due to the metabolic connection with glycolytic metabolism (at least for the 22 kDa variant).

Depending on the load, rest, and exercise volume of a resistance exercise protocol, different GH responses occur (4, 35, 36, 115, 128, 133). In a study designed to sort out the different variables related to GH increases, Kraemer and colleagues (99) found that serum increases in GH are differentially sensitive to the volume of exercise, the amount of rest between sets (less rest, higher GH), and the resistance used (10RM produces higher lactate values and higher GH responses). When the intensity used was 10RM (heavy resistance) with three sets of each exercise (high total work, approximately 60,000 J) and short (1-minute) rest periods, large increases were observed in serum GH concentrations. The most dramatic increases occurred in response to a 1-minute rest period when the duration of exercise was longer (10RM vs. 5RM). Because such differences are related to the configuration of the exercise session (e.g., rest period length), it appears that greater attention needs to be given to program design variables when one is evaluating physiological adaptations to resistance training. A recent study by McCall and colleagues (115) linked GH responses and muscle changes with resistance training. Growth hormone appears to be related to the changes in muscle with training, but it is unclear how the various types of GH are involved in this process. The lack of a high correlation in this study may indicate a need to account for more than one type of GH.

Growth Hormone Responses in Women

Throughout the menstrual cycle, women have higher blood levels of GH than men due to greater frequency and amplitude of secretion. Hormone concentrations and hormone responses to exercise vary with menstrual phase (25), although the mechanisms of this variation are unclear. Kraemer and colleagues (92, 96) found that during the early follicular phase of the menstrual cycle, women had significantly higher GH concentrations at rest compared with men. Furthermore, with use of a heavy resistance exercise protocol characterized by long rest periods (3 minutes) and heavy loads (5RM), GH levels did not increase above resting concentrations. However, when a short-rest (1-minute) and moderate-resistance (10RM) exercise protocol was used, significant increases in serum GH levels were observed. Hormonal response patterns to different resistance exercise routines may vary over the course of the menstrual cycle, owing to alterations in resting levels (92, 96). It is interesting that acute aerobic endurance exercise shows higher post-exercise GH concentrations in women than men, but no differences have been seen in the sexes in response to acute resistance exercise.

The effects of periodizing resistance training over the course of the menstrual cycle remain to be examined, and more research is needed to elucidate any sex-related neuroendocrine adaptational mechanism (36). At present, women's reduced concentrations of testosterone and different resting hormonal concentrations over the course of the menstrual cycle appear to be their most striking neuroendocrine differences from men. How such differences relate to training adaptations, the development of muscle tissue, and expression of strength and power remains to be demonstrated.

Training Adaptations of Growth Hormone

It appears that GH levels need to be measured over longer time periods (2-24 hours) to show whether changes occur with resistance training. The area under the time curve, which includes an array of pulsatile effects, tells whether changes in release have occurred. The responses of GH to resistance training have not been extensively studied, but observations of normal, single measurements of resting GH concentrations in elite lifters suggest little change. It is likely that differences in feedback mechanisms, changes in receptor sensitivities, IGF potentiation, diurnal variations, and maximal exercise concentrations may mediate GH adaptations with resistance training. The typical trends for training-related changes in GH appear to be a reduction in GH response to an absolute exercise stress and alterations in GH pulsatility characteristics. The reduction in the 22 kDa GH exercise-induced responses with training perhaps indicates potential interactions with other molecular weight forms. Individual responses over a nine-month period were highly variable, with no significant group changes over time in a group of elite weightlifters (unpublished observations). We are far from understanding how GH changes with long-term resistance training in athletes.

Insulin-Like Growth Factors

Some of the effects of GH are mediated through small polypeptides called insulin-like growth factors (IGFs), or somatomedins (21, 30, 38). Insulin-like growth factor I is a 70-amino acid polypeptide, and IGF-II is a 67-amino acid polypeptide; the function of the latter is less clear. The liver secretes IGFs after GH stimulates liver cell DNA to synthesize them, a process that takes about 8 to 29 hours. Besides GH, factors such as thyroid hormone and testosterone are also involved in the regulation of IGF synthesis (149, 150, 151, 152). Typical of many polypeptide hormones, both growth factors are synthesized as larger precursor molecules, which then undergo processing to form the hormones themselves. Insulin-like growth factors travel in the blood bound to binding proteins (BP); in the target tissue, IGFs disassociate from the BP and interact with the receptors (1, 134, 135). Blood levels of IGFs are usually measured as either total levels (bound and free) or free IGF concentrations.

Circulating IGFs are associated with BP. At least six circulating BP have been identified that regulate the amount of IGF available for receptor interaction: IGF-I-binding proteins 1 to 6, with BP-1 and BP-3 the most extensively studied in terms of their response to exercise. Each BP responds to exercise stress independently and has its own biological actions.

Binding proteins are important factors in the transport and physiological mechanisms of IGF (18, 19, 41). Insulin-like growth factor has been shown to stimulate the secretion of its own BP from within the muscle cell itself, thus modulating the cell's responsiveness to IGF (116). The circulating IGF-binding proteins play an important role in restricting access of the IGF peptides to receptors and are influenced by GH concentrations. Other factors, such as nutritional status and insulin levels, also have been shown to be important signal mechanisms for IGF release. The nutritional influence on IGF transport, production, and regulatory control is a dramatic variable affecting its cellular interactions. Acute changes in nitrogen balance and protein intake and nutritional status affect a variety of mechanisms (18, 109, 115). It also appears that BP act as a reservoir of IGF, and release from the BP is signaled by the availability of a receptor on the cell (11). This allows IGF to be viable for a longer period of time and could theoretically reduce the amount of degradation of IGF.

In strength training, many of these mechanisms are influenced by the exercise stress; by acute hormonal responses; and by the need for muscle, nerve, and bone tissue remodeling at the cellular level (17, 66, 69, 129). The dramatic interactions of multiple hormones and receptors provide powerful adaptive mechanisms in response to resistance training and can contribute to the subsequent changes in muscular strength and size.

Exercise Responses of Insulin-Like Growth Factors

Insulin-like growth factor I has been the primary IGF studied in the context of exercise because of its prolific role in protein anabolism. The exact reasons for acute increases in blood levels of IGF-I are unknown but are probably related to the disruption of various cells, including fat and muscle cells, because these cells manufacture and store IGF (140). How acute changes occur with exercise is a bit of a mystery. As mentioned previously, it takes 8 to 29 hours for IGF to be produced following stimulation by GH. This seems to indicate that IGF is released from storage sources other than the liver, that release is due to cellular disruption of cells that already contain IGF, or that GH-mediated release of IGF with certain types of exercise has a different time course from that of injection-response studies. Systematic alterations in circulatory concentrations of IGF in response to various types of exercise protocols appear to be closely related to regulatory factors of IGF release and transport (11). Evaluation of serum changes over longer periods is necessary for assessment of specific effects and relationships to GH in the serum (37).

The autocrine and perhaps paracrine release mechanisms of IGF-I may be paramount in the IGF-I influence on muscle. Fat cells contain relatively high concentrations of IGF; skeletal muscle has very little of its own. It is possible that IGF may be released from nonhepatic cells without the mediation of GH (1, 3, 38, 65, 68, 69). In addition, cells may produce and keep IGFs, so that the IGFs exert their effect without entering the peripheral circulation. Although IGF-I has been shown to be responsive to exercise in some studies, this does not follow a classic endocrine response (i.e., stimulus of gland by exercise resulting in hormone release into the blood) in all cases. It was shown that IGF-I was responsive to resistance exercise in men and women, but in those studies the starting concentrations were lower (96, 99). In another study the concentrations were higher and, despite increases in immunoreactive (22 kDa) GH, no increase in IGF-I was observed (83). From these studies it has been theorized that the starting level of IGF-I may be a factor in determining whether an increase is observed with exercise (i.e., no increases if starting concentrations are high, an increase if starting concentrations are low). A study by Kraemer and colleagues (109) supported this theory, but it was also shown that the IGF-I concentrations were more sensitive to acute caloric loads, which included carbohydrate and protein supplementation before and after a workout (figure 3.11).

Training Adaptations of Insulin-Like Growth Factors

Responses of IGF-I to heavy resistance training remain unclear, but recent reports demonstrate that changes are based on the starting concentrations before training (i.e., if basal concentrations are low, IGF-I increases; if high, there is no change or it decreases). It is far too soon to judge what happens to this hormone with resistance training, yet the data for women show little or no change with training. As with GH, training-induced adaptations in IGF-I are probably reflected in a variety of mechanisms related to release, transport, and receptor interaction. Furthermore, the interaction with other ana-

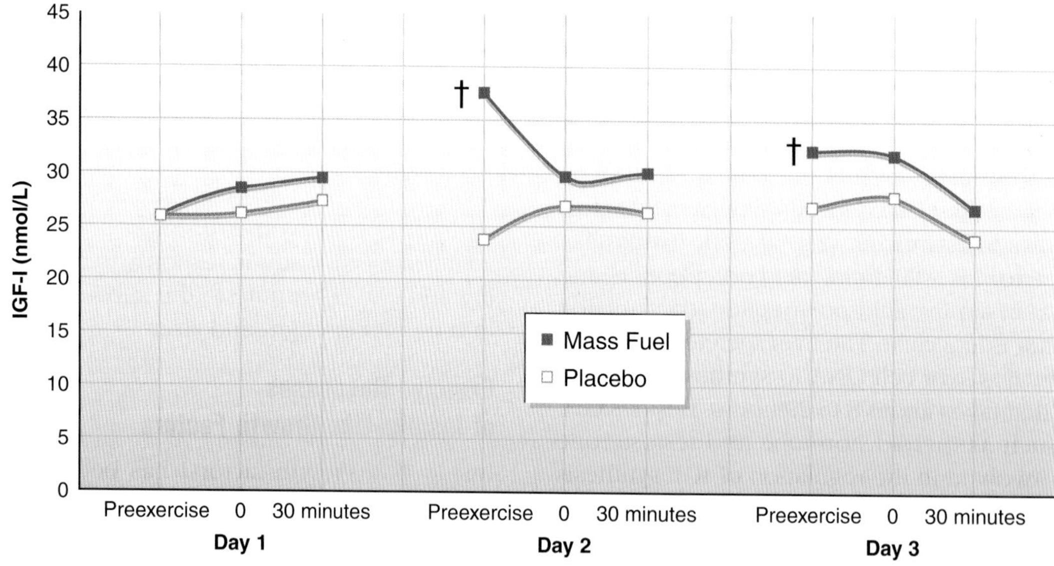

Figure 3.11 Responses of insulin-like growth factor I to a multiple-set, heavy resistance exercise protocol on three consecutive days with and without nutritional supplementation of protein-carbohydrate (i.e., Mass Fuel) before and during the 1-hour recovery period. †$p < .05$ from corresponding placebo value.

Adapted, by permission, from Kraemer et al., 1998 (109).

bolic hormones cannot be ignored, as these often target the same outcome (e.g., protein synthesis). Adaptations to heavy resistance training of IGF-I in the various tissues require further investigation. Insulin-like growth factor I is also produced in the muscles themselves in response to overload and stretch. IGF-I produced in muscle is called mechano growth factor (MGF) and exerts autocrine functions (52, 117). It has been suggested that autocrine actions of MGF are the primary actions of IGF-I in muscle.

ADRENAL HORMONES

The adrenal gland has two major divisions: the cortex and the medulla. Both divisions respond to exercise stress. The adrenal medulla is stimulated by the nervous system and thus provides the faster response; the cortex is stimulated by adrenocorticotropic hormone (ACTH) from the anterior pituitary. The adrenal gland plays a crucial role in the fight-or-flight phenomenon. The adrenal hormones most important to training and conditioning are cortisol, a glucocorticoid from the adrenal cortex; the catecholamines, from the adrenal medulla; and enkephalin-containing polypeptides (e.g., peptide F) (88, 102, 104, 106, 139). Peptide F, a proenkephalin fragment, plays an important role in enhancing immune cell functions (139). Thus, the adrenal medulla also secretes hormones involved in the recovery from stress.

Cortisol

Classically, glucocorticoids, and more specifically cortisol in humans, have been viewed as catabolic hormones in skeletal muscle (38, 39, 110). In reality, however, cortisol is a primary signal hormone for carbohydrate metabolism and is related to the glycogen stores in the muscle. When glycogen concentrations are low, other substrates (proteins) must be catabolized to produce energy.

Role of Cortisol

Cortisol exerts its major catabolic effects by converting amino acids to carbohydrates, increasing the level of **proteolytic enzymes** (enzymes that break down proteins), and inhibiting protein synthesis. It appears that cortisol may have greater catabolic effects on Type II fibers because they have more protein than Type I fibers, but cortisol may be more involved with the control of degradation in Type I fibers. As pointed out earlier in this chapter, Type I fibers rely more on reducing degradation to develop muscle hypertrophy, in contrast to the dramatic increases in synthesis used by Type II fibers to develop hypertrophy.

In situations of disease, joint immobilization, or injury, an elevation in cortisol mediates a nitrogen-wasting effect with a net loss of contractile protein. This results in muscle atrophy, with associated reductions in force production capability (38, 112). In the muscle, the anabolic effects of testosterone and insulin counter cortisol's catabolic effects. If a greater number of receptors are bound with insulin or if testosterone blocks the genetic element in the DNA for cortisol, protein is conserved or enhanced. Conversely, if a greater number of receptors are bound to cortisol, protein is degraded and lost. The balance of anabolic and catabolic activities in the muscle affects the protein contractile unit, directly influencing strength. The acute increases in circulating cortisol following exercise also implicate acute inflammatory response mechanisms in tissue remodeling (85).

Resistance Exercise Responses of Cortisol

As with GH, it appears that cortisol increases with resistance exercise, most dramatically when rest periods are short and the total volume high. As mentioned in the discussion on testosterone, increases may not have negative effects in men after a period of training to which the body has adapted; adaptation "disinhibits" cortisol at the level of the testis, thereby maintaining testosterone concentrations.

Cortisol responds to resistance exercise protocols that create a dramatic stimulus to anaerobic metabolism. It is interesting that the acute exercise protocols that produce the highest catabolic responses in the body also produce the greatest GH response. Thus, though chronic high levels of cortisol may have adverse effects, acute increases may be a part of a larger remodeling process in muscle tissue. Muscle must be disrupted to a certain extent (below injury levels) to remodel itself and enlarge; acute elevations in cortisol would help in this process.

Because of the catabolic role of cortisol, athletes and strength and conditioning professionals have much interest in its potential as a whole-body marker of tissue breakdown. To a certain extent, cortisol is such a marker, but the magnitude of increase may need to be greater than 800 nmol/L to indicate potential overtraining problems (43, 44, 46, 47). The testosterone-to-cortisol ratio also has been used in the attempt to determine the anabolic-catabolic status of the body (63). Although such markers are attractive conceptually, serum cortisol measurements and the testosterone-to-cortisol ratio have met with only limited success in predicting or monitoring changes in strength and power capabilities. Problems with these tests probably have to do with the multiple roles of cortisol and other hormones.

It is probable that vast differences are observed in the physiological role of cortisol in acute versus chronic exercise responses to resistance exercise. Acute cortisol responses may reflect the metabolic stress of the exercise, and chronic aspects may be primarily involved with tissue homeostasis entailing protein metabolism (38). Thus, cortisol's role in overtraining, detraining, or injury may be critical when muscle tissue atrophy and decreases in force production capabilities are observed (112). Such roles remain to be demonstrated; however, cortisol's role in suppressing cells of the immune system (e.g., T cells) has a direct impact on the recovery and remodeling of skeletal muscle tissue. The connection of the endocrine and immune systems is a vital link for resistance exercise adaptations and is just starting to be explored in the laboratory.

Resistance exercise protocols that use high volume, large muscle groups, and short rest periods result in increased serum cortisol values. Though chronic high levels of cortisol may have adverse catabolic effects, acute increases may contribute to the remodeling of muscle tissue.

Catecholamines

The catecholamines—primarily epinephrine but also norepinephrine and dopamine—are secreted by the adrenal medulla and are important for the acute expression of strength and power because the hormones act as central motor stimulators and peripheral vascular dilators and enhance enzyme systems in muscle (104). Thus, the resistance exercise–induced stress leads to events similar to the classic fight-or-flight response. The importance of catecholamines during resistance exercise was recently highlighted by the finding that men who had a higher catecholamine release immediately before and during a heavy resistance exercise session were able to better maintain force output throughout the session (42). The role of catecholamines in growth-promoting actions in muscle tissue is less clear, but they act to stimulate other anabolic hormones.

Role of Catecholamines

The physiological functions of epinephrine and norepinephrine in muscle are these:

- Increase force production via central mechanisms and increased metabolic enzyme activity
- Increase muscle contraction rate
- Increase blood pressure
- Increase energy availability
- Increase blood flow
- Augment secretion rates of other hormones, such as testosterone

Catecholamines appear to reflect the acute demands and physical stress of resistance exercise protocols (101). A high-intensity (10RM), short-rest (10-60 seconds between sets and exercises), heavy resistance exercise routine (10 exercises, three sets) typically used by bodybuilders for development of strength and hypertrophy was shown to maintain increased plasma norepinephrine, epinephrine, and dopamine levels for 5 minutes into recovery (101). In addition, epinephrine has been correlated to lactate concentrations with exercise stress. Adrenal responses are not involved in the recovery responses until the stress is removed. Some specific endogenous opioid peptides (i.e., proenkephalins) are secreted by the adrenal medulla and affect the immune system, which is critical in recovery from exercise stress (139). If training is not varied, continued stress keeps the adrenal gland engaged and recovery is delayed due to the secondary responses of cortisol and its negative effects on immune system cells and protein structures.

Training Adaptations of Catecholamines

Heavy resistance training has been shown to increase the ability of an athlete to secrete greater amounts of epinephrine during maximal exercise (102). It has also been suggested that training reduces epinephrine responses to a single bench press workout (56). Because epinephrine is involved in metabolic control, force production, and the response mechanisms of other hormones (such as testosterone, GH,

How Can Athletes Manipulate the Endocrine System With Resistance Training?

General Concepts

- The more muscle fibers recruited for an exercise, the greater the extent of potential remodeling process in the whole muscle.
- Only muscle fibers activated by resistance training are subject to adaptation, including hormonal adaptations to stress.

To Increase Serum Testosterone Concentrations

Serum testosterone concentrations have been shown to increase by using these methods independently or in various combinations:

- Large muscle group exercises (e.g., deadlift, power clean, squats)
- Heavy resistance (85% to 95% of 1RM)
- Moderate to high volume of exercise, achieved with multiple sets or multiple exercises
- Short rest intervals (30-60 seconds)

To Increase Growth Hormone Levels

Growth hormone levels have been shown to increase by using either of these methods or both in combination:

- Use workouts with higher lactate concentrations and associated acid-base disruptions; that is, use high intensity (10RM, or heavy resistance) with three sets of each exercise (high total work) and short (1-minute) rest periods.
- Supplement diet with carbohydrate and protein before and after workouts.

To Optimize Responses of Adrenal Hormones

- Use high volume, large muscle groups, and short rest periods, but vary the training protocol and the rest period length and volume to allow the adrenal gland to engage in recovery processes (secreting less cortisol) and to prevent chronic catabolic responses of cortisol. This way the stress of the exercises will not result in overuse or overtraining.

and IGFs), stimulation of catecholamines is probably one of the first endocrine mechanisms to occur in response to resistance exercise.

Training protocols must be varied to allow the adrenal gland to engage in recovery processes and to prevent the secondary responses of cortisol, which can have negative effects on the immune system and protein structures.

OTHER HORMONAL CONSIDERATIONS

A host of different hormones are involved in the maintenance of normal body function and in adaptive responses of the body to resistance training (20, 37, 38, 64, 73, 78, 82). Although we might focus on one or two hormones for their roles in a particular physiological function, other hormones actually create an optimal environment in which the primary hormonal actions can take place. Hormones such as insulin, thyroid hormones, and beta-endorphin have been implicated in growth, repair, and exercise stress mechanisms; unfortunately, few data are available concerning their responses and adaptations to resistance exercise or training (40, 88, 97). Owing to the relatively tight homeostatic control of both insulin and thyroid hormone secretion, chronic training adaptations in circulating resting concentrations of these hormones would not be expected. Although improvements in insulin resistance have been observed with resistance training, these changes may reflect only an acute effect from the most recent exercise session (13). It is more likely that longer-term changes such as 24-hour secretion rates, sensitivity of the receptors, and binding interactions would be affected. Pakarinen and colleagues (121) have demonstrated only slight, nonsignificant decreases in serum concentrations of total and free thyroxine (a thyroid hormone) after 20 weeks of strength training. The permissive effects of such hormones in metabolic control, amino acid synthesis, and augmentation of other hormonal release mechanisms are the essence of such interactions with resistance training.

CONCLUSION

As we continue to study the endocrine system and its interactions with the nervous system, the immune system, and the musculoskeletal system, we find that the functions of these systems are truly integrated. Communication among systems is accomplished with hormones and other peptides. For years, strength and conditioning professionals and athletes have appreciated the importance of anabolic hormones for mediating changes in the body and helping with the adaptive response to heavy resistance training. Whether trying to optimize a workout or avoid overtraining, the strength and conditioning professional must remember that the endocrine system plays a role. The goal of this chapter is to provide an initial glimpse into this complex but highly organized system that mediates the changes in the body with training.

KEY TERMS

allosteric binding site 46
anabolic hormone 45
catabolic hormone 45
cross-reactivity 46
diurnal variation 54
downregulation 46
endocrine gland 42
myosin heavy-chain (MHC) proteins 45
hormone 42
hormone-receptor complex (H-RC) 47
lock-and-key theory 46
neuroendocrinology 42
polypeptide hormone 47
proteolytic enzymes 61
secondary messenger 48
steroid hormone 43
target tissue 43
thyroid hormone 43

STUDY QUESTIONS

1. After a bout of resistance training, acute hormonal secretions provide all of the following information to the body EXCEPT
   a. amount of physiological stress.
   b. metabolic demands of exercise.
   c. type of physiological stress.
   d. energy expended. ✓

2. Which of the following hormones enhance muscle tissue growth?
   I. growth hormone
   II. cortisol
   III. IGF-I
   IV. progesterone

   a. I and III only ✓
   b. II and IV only
   c. I, II, and III only
   d. II, III, and IV only

3. All of the following are functions of growth hormone EXCEPT
   a. increase lipolysis.
   b. decrease collagen synthesis. ✓
   c. increase amino acid transport.
   d. decrease glucose utilization.

4. Which of the following hormones has the greatest influence on neural changes?
   a. growth hormone
   b. testosterone ✓
   c. cortisol
   d. IGF

5. Which of the following hormone levels is higher in women than in men at rest?
   a. cortisol
   b. insulin
   c. testosterone
   d. growth hormone

6. What type of resistance training workout promotes the highest growth hormone increases following the exercise session?

	Rest	Volume	Sets
a.	30 seconds	high	3 ✓
b.	30 seconds	low	1
c.	3 minutes	high	1
d.	3 minutes	low	3

CHAPTER 4

Biomechanics of Resistance Exercise

Everett Harman, PhD

After completing this chapter, you will be able to

- identify the major bones and muscles of the human body,
- differentiate among the various types of levers of the musculoskeletal system,
- calculate linear and rotational work and power,
- describe the factors contributing to human strength and power,
- evaluate resistive force and power patterns of exercise devices,
- recommend ways to minimize injury risk during resistance training, and
- analyze sport movements and design movement-oriented exercise prescriptions.

Knowledge of musculoskeletal anatomy and biomechanics is important for understanding human movements, including those involved in sport and resistance exercise. **Anatomy** encompasses the study of components that make up the musculoskeletal "machine," and **biomechanics** focuses on the mechanisms through which these components interact to create movement. By providing insight into how body movements are carried out and the stresses that the movements place on the musculoskeletal system, both areas of study facilitate the design of safe and effective resistance training programs.

This chapter begins with an overview of the musculoskeletal system and body mechanics, followed by biomechanical principles related to the manifestation of human strength and power. Next, the primary sources of resistance to muscle contraction used in exercise devices—including gravity, inertia, friction, fluid resistance, and elasticity—are discussed. Then we turn to concerns in resistance training that relate to joint biomechanics (with special emphasis on the shoulders, back, and knees) and discuss the relationship of biomechanics to movement analysis and exercise prescription. Finally, examples of how biomechanical principles can be applied to training are provided.

MUSCULOSKELETAL SYSTEM

The musculoskeletal system of the human body consists of bones, joints, muscles, and tendons configured to allow the great variety of movements characteristic of human activity. This section describes the various components of the musculoskeletal system, both individually and in the context of how they function together in a system of levers.

Skeleton

The muscles of the body do not act directly to exert force on the ground or other objects. Instead, they function by pulling against bones that rotate about joints and transmit force through the skin to the environment. Muscles can only pull, not push; but through the system of bony levers, muscle pulling forces can be manifested as either pulling or pushing forces against external objects.

There are approximately 206 bones in the body, though the number can vary. This relatively light, strong structure provides leverage, support, and protection. The **axial skeleton** consists of the skull (cranium), vertebral column (vertebra C1 through the coccyx), ribs, and sternum. The **appendicular skeleton** includes the shoulder (or pectoral) girdle (left and right scapula and clavicle); bones of the arms, wrists, and hands (left and right humerus, radius, ulna, carpals, metacarpals, and phalanges); the pelvic girdle (left and right coxal or innominate bones); and the bones of the legs, ankles, and feet (left and right femur, patella, tibia, fibula, tarsals, metatarsals, and phalanges) (24).

Junctions of bones are called **joints**. **Fibrous joints** (e.g., sutures of the skull) allow virtually no movement; **cartilaginous joints** (e.g., intervertebral disks) allow limited movement; and **synovial joints** (e.g., elbow and knee) allow considerable

The opinions or assertions contained herein are the private views of the author and are not to be construed as official or as reflecting the views of the Army or the Department of Defense.

movement. Sport and exercise movements occur mainly about the synovial joints, whose most important features are low friction and large range of motion. Articulating bone ends are covered with smooth **hyaline cartilage**, and the entire joint is enclosed in a capsule filled with **synovial fluid**. There are usually additional supporting structures of ligament and cartilage (36).

Virtually all joint movement consists of rotation about points or axes. Joints can be categorized by the number of directions about which rotation can occur. **Uniaxial joints**, such as the elbow, operate as hinges, essentially rotating about only one axis. The knee is often referred to as a hinge joint, but its axis of rotation actually changes throughout the joint range of motion. **Biaxial joints**, such as the ankle and wrist, allow movement about two perpendicular axes. **Multiaxial joints**, including the shoulder and hip ball-and-socket joints, allow movement about all three perpendicular axes that define space.

The **vertebral column** is made up of several vertebral bones separated by flexible disks that allow movement to occur. The vertebrae are grouped into 7 **cervical vertebrae** in the neck region; 12 **thoracic vertebrae** in the middle to upper back; 5 **lumbar vertebrae**, which make up the lower back; 5 **sacral vertebrae**, which are fused together and make up the rear part of the pelvis; and 3 to 5 **coccygeal vertebrae**, which form a kind of vestigial internal tail extending downward from the pelvis.

Skeletal Musculature

The system of muscles that enables the skeleton to move is depicted in figure 4.1. To cause movement or to generate force against external objects, both ends of each skeletal muscle must be attached to bone by connective tissue. Traditionally, anatomists define the muscle's **origin** as its **proximal** (toward the center of the body) attachment, and its **insertion** as its **distal** (away from the center of the body) attachment. Sometimes the origin is defined as the more stationary structure to which the muscle is attached, and the insertion as the more mobile structure. This definition can lead to a confusing reversal of the origin and insertion (19). For example, during a straight-leg sit-up, the origin of the iliacus muscle would be the femur, because of its relative immobility. The pelvis, being more mobile, would be the insertion. However, during the leg raise exercise, the pelvis is relatively immobile and would therefore become the origin, while the more mobile femur would become the insertion. The traditional definition therefore provides the most consistency.

Muscles are attached to bone in various ways. In **fleshy attachments**, which are most often found at the proximal end of a muscle, muscle fibers are directly affixed to the bone, usually over a wide area so that force is distributed rather than localized. **Fibrous attachments**, such as **tendons**, blend into and are continuous with both the muscle sheaths and the connective tissue surrounding the bone. They have additional fibers that extend into the bone itself, making for a very strong union.

Virtually all body movements involve the action of more than one muscle. The muscle most directly involved in bringing about a movement is called the prime mover, or **agonist**. A muscle that can slow down or stop the movement is called the **antagonist**. The antagonist assists in joint stabilization and in braking the limb toward the end of a fast movement, thereby protecting ligamentous and cartilaginous joint structures from potentially destructive forces. During throwing, for example, the triceps acts as an agonist, extending the elbow to accelerate the ball. As the elbow approaches full extension, the biceps acts as an antagonist to slow down elbow extension and bring it to a stop, thereby protecting elbow structures from internal impact.

A muscle is called a **synergist** when it assists indirectly in a movement. For example, the muscles that stabilize the scapula act as synergists during upper arm movement. Without these synergists, the muscles that move the upper arm (many of which originate on the scapula) would not be effective in bringing about this movement. Synergists are also required to control body motion when the agonist is a muscle that crosses two joints. For example, the rectus femoris muscle crosses the hip and knee, acting to flex the hip and extend the knee when contracting. Rising from a low squat involves both hip and knee extension. If the rectus femoris is to act to extend the knee as a person rises without inclining the trunk forward, then hip extensor muscles such as the gluteus maximus must act synergistically to counteract the hip flexion that would otherwise result from tension in the rectus femoris.

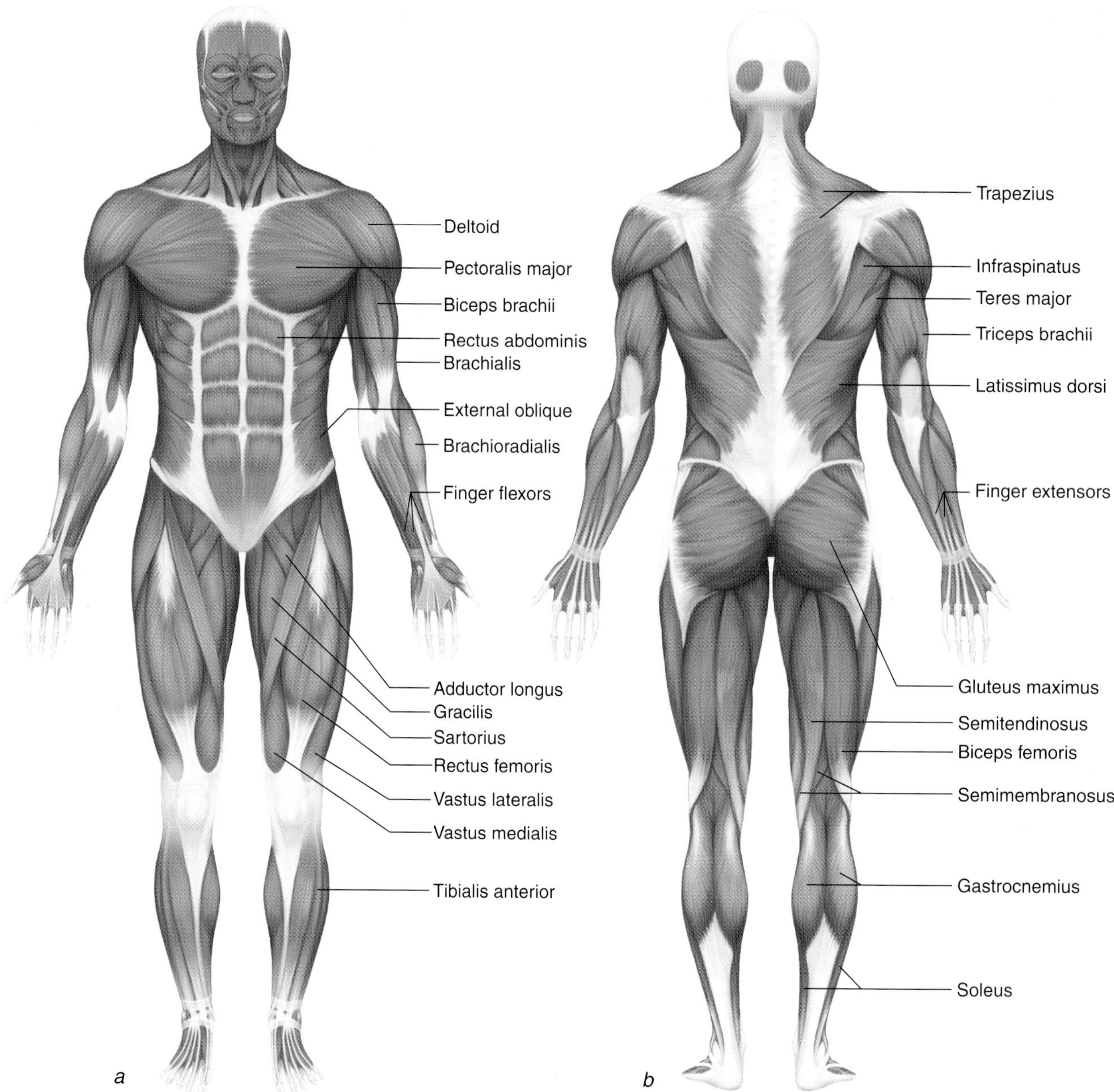

Figure 4.1 *(a)* Front view and *(b)* rear view of adult male human skeletal musculature.

Levers of the Musculoskeletal System

Although there are many muscles in the body that do not act through levers, such as muscles of the face, tongue, heart, arteries, and sphincters, body movements directly involved in sport and exercise primarily act through the bony levers of the skeleton. In order to understand how the body effects such movements, a basic knowledge of levers is required. Several basic definitions follow.

lever—A rigid or semirigid body that, when subjected to a force whose line of action does not pass through its pivot point, exerts force on any object impeding its tendency to rotate (figure 4.2).

fulcrum—The pivot point of a lever.

moment arm (also called force arm, lever arm, or torque arm)—The perpendicular distance from the line of action of the force to the fulcrum. The line of action of a force is an infinitely long line passing through the point of application of the force, oriented in the direction in which the force is exerted.

torque (also called moment)—The degree to which a force tends to rotate an object about a specified fulcrum. It is defined quantitatively as the magnitude of a force times the length of its moment arm.

muscle force—Force generated by biochemical activity, or the stretching of noncontractile tissue, that tends to draw the opposite ends of a muscle toward each other.

resistive force—Force generated by a source external to the body (e.g., gravity, inertia, friction) that acts contrary to muscle force.

mechanical advantage—The ratio of the moment arm through which an applied force acts to that through which a resistive force acts (figure 4.3). For there to be a state of equilibrium between the applied and resistive torques, the product of the muscle force and the moment arm through which it acts must equal the product of the resistive force and the moment arm through which it acts. Therefore, a mechanical advantage greater than 1.0 allows the applied (muscle) force to be less than the resistive force to produce an equal amount of torque. A mechanical advantage of less than 1.0 is a disadvantage in the common sense of the term.

first-class lever—A lever for which the muscle force and resistive force act on opposite sides of the fulcrum (see figure 4.3).

second-class lever—A lever for which the muscle force and resistive force act on the same side of the fulcrum, with the muscle force acting through a moment arm longer than that through which the resistive force acts, as when the calf muscles work to raise the body onto the balls of the feet (figure 4.4). Due to its mechanical advantage (i.e., relatively

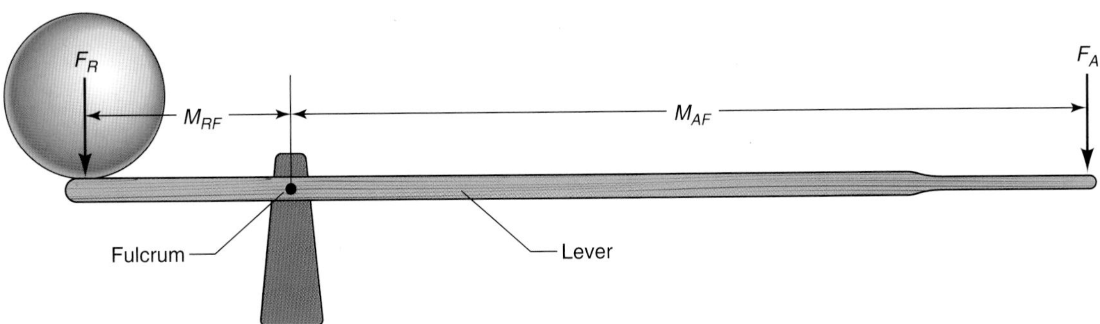

Figure 4.2 A lever. The lever can transmit force tangential to the arc of rotation from one contact point along the object's length to another. F_A = force applied to the lever; M_{AF} = moment arm of the applied force; F_R = force resisting the lever's rotation; M_{RF} = moment arm of the resistive force. The lever applies a force on the object equal in magnitude to but opposite in direction from F_R.

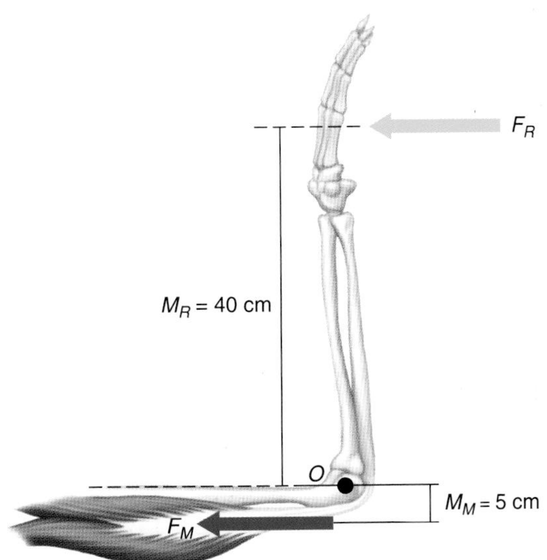

Figure 4.3 A first-class lever (the forearm). Elbow extension against resistance (e.g., a triceps extension exercise). O = fulcrum; F_M = muscle force; F_R = resistive force; M_M = moment arm of the muscle force; M_R = moment arm of the resistive force. Mechanical advantage = M_M/M_R = 5 cm/40 cm = 0.125, which, being less than 1.0, is a disadvantage in the common sense. The depiction is of a first-class lever because muscle force and resistive force act on opposite sides of the fulcrum. During isometric exertion or constant-speed joint rotation, $F_M \cdot M_M = F_R \cdot M_R$. Because M_M is much smaller than M_R, F_M must be much greater than F_R; this illustrates the disadvantageous nature of this arrangement (i.e., a large muscle force is required to push against a relatively small external resistance).

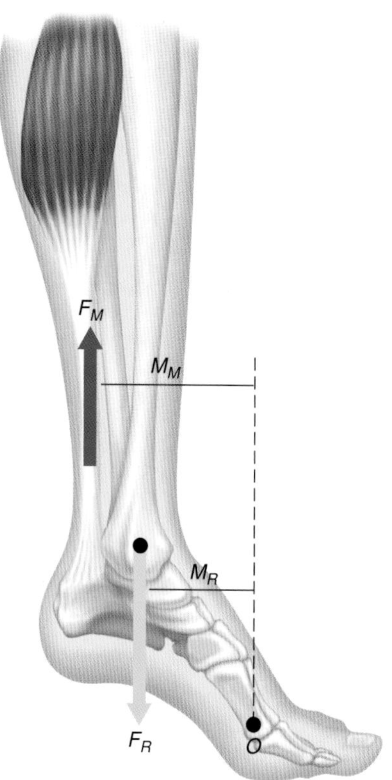

Figure 4.4 A second-class lever (the foot). Plantarflexion against resistance (e.g., a standing heel raise exercise). F_M = muscle force; F_R = resistive force; M_M = moment arm of the muscle force; M_R = moment arm of the resistive force. When the body is raised, the ball of the foot, being the point about which the foot rotates, is the fulcrum (*O*). Because M_M is greater than M_R, F_M is less than F_R.

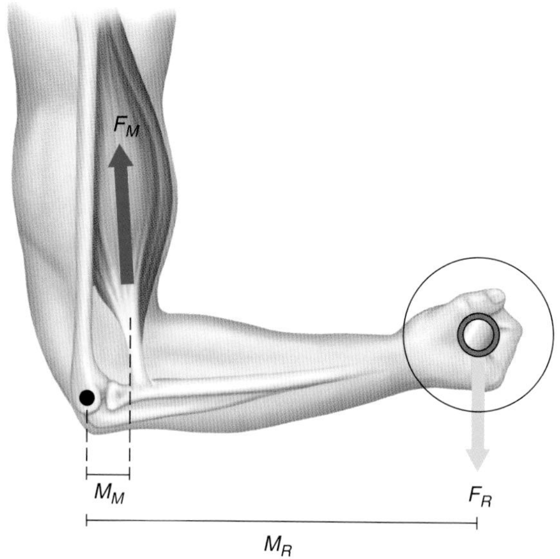

Figure 4.5 A third-class lever (the forearm). Elbow flexion against resistance (e.g., a biceps curl exercise). F_M = muscle force; F_R = resistive force; M_M = moment arm of the muscle force; M_R = moment arm of the resistive force. Because M_M is much smaller than M_R, F_M must be much greater than F_R.

long moment arm), the required muscle force is smaller than the resistive force (body weight).

third-class lever—A lever for which the muscle force and resistive force act on the same side of the fulcrum, with the muscle force acting through a moment arm shorter than that through which the resistive force acts (figure 4.5). The mechanical advantage is thus less than 1.0, so the muscle force has to be greater than the resistive force to produce torque equal to that produced by the resistive force.

Most human muscles that rotate the limbs about body joints operate at a mechanical advantage of less than 1.0 (that is, at a mechanical *dis*advantage). This is why internal muscle forces are much greater than the forces exerted by the body on external objects. For example, in figure 4.3, because the resistance moment arm is eight times longer than the muscle moment arm, muscle force must be eight times the resistive force. The extremely high internal forces experienced by muscles and tendons account in large part for injury to these tissues.

During actual movement, the categorization of a lever as first, second, or third class often depends on the somewhat arbitrary decision of where the fulcrum lies. Therefore, understanding the principle of mechanical advantage is of much greater importance than being able to classify levers. Mechanical advantage often changes continuously during real-world activities. The following are examples of this.

- For movements such as knee extension and flexion, where the joint is not a true hinge, the location of the axis of rotation changes continuously throughout the range of motion, affecting the length of the moment arm through which the quadriceps and hamstrings act. For knee extension, the patella, or kneecap, helps to prevent large changes in the mechanical advantage of the quadriceps muscle by keeping the quadriceps tendon from falling in close to the axis of rotation (figure 4.6).
- For movements such as knee and elbow flexion, there is no structure such as the patella to keep the perpendicular distance from the joint axis of rotation to the tendon's line of action relatively constant (figure 4.7).
- During weightlifting, the moment arm through which the weight acts equals the horizontal distance from a line through the center of mass of the barbell or dumbbell to the body joint about which rotation of the limb occurs; the resistive moment arm thus varies throughout the movement (figure 4.8).

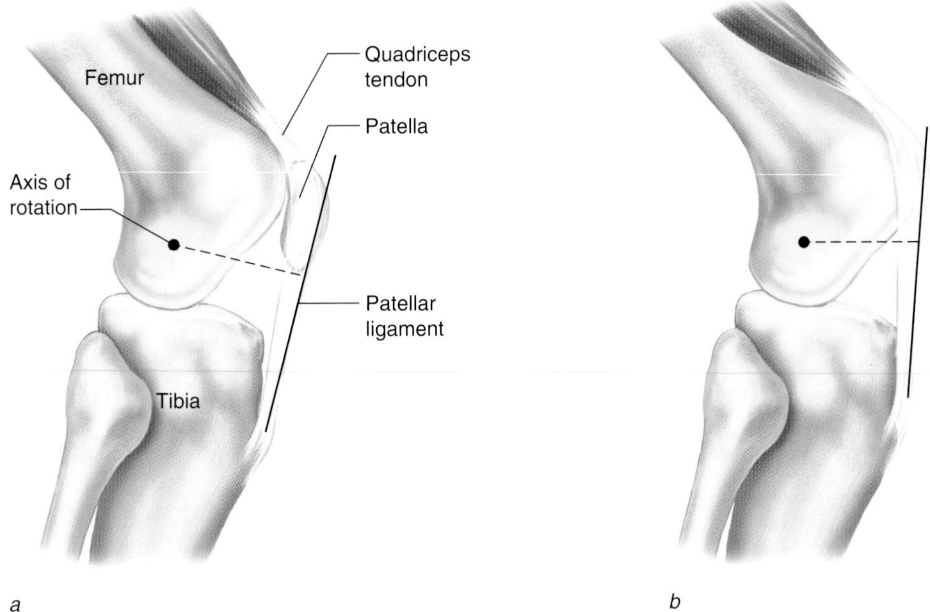

Figure 4.6 *(a)* The patella increases the mechanical advantage of the quadriceps muscle group by maintaining the quadriceps tendon's distance from the knee's axis of rotation. *(b)* Absence of the patella allows the tendon to fall closer to the knee's center of rotation, shortening the moment arm through which the muscle force acts and thereby reducing the muscle's mechanical advantage.

Reprinted, by permission, from Gowitzke and Milner, 1988 (11).

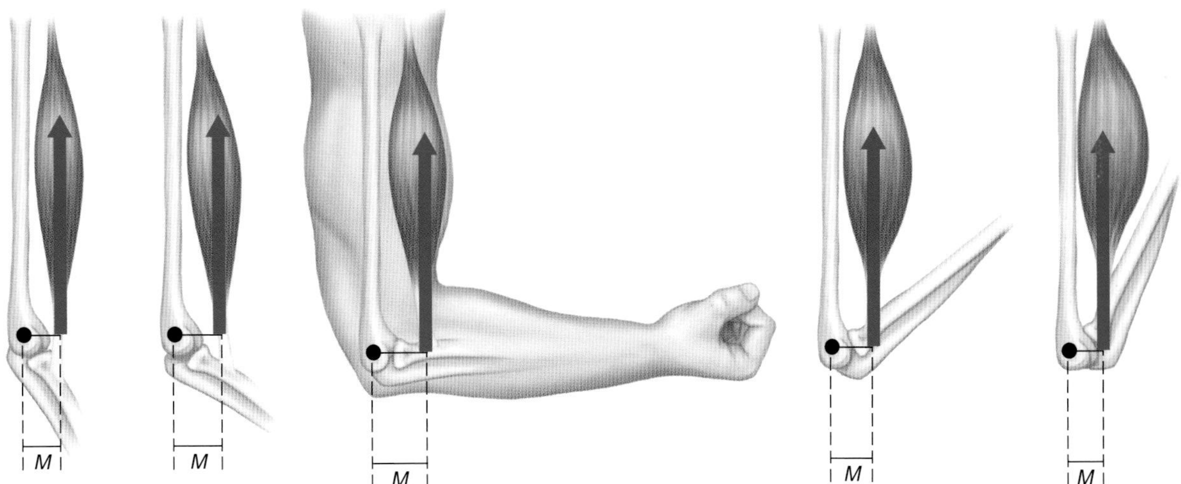

Figure 4.7 During elbow flexion with the biceps muscle, the perpendicular distance from the joint axis of rotation to the tendon's line of action varies throughout the range of joint motion. When the moment arm (*M*) is shorter, there is less mechanical advantage.

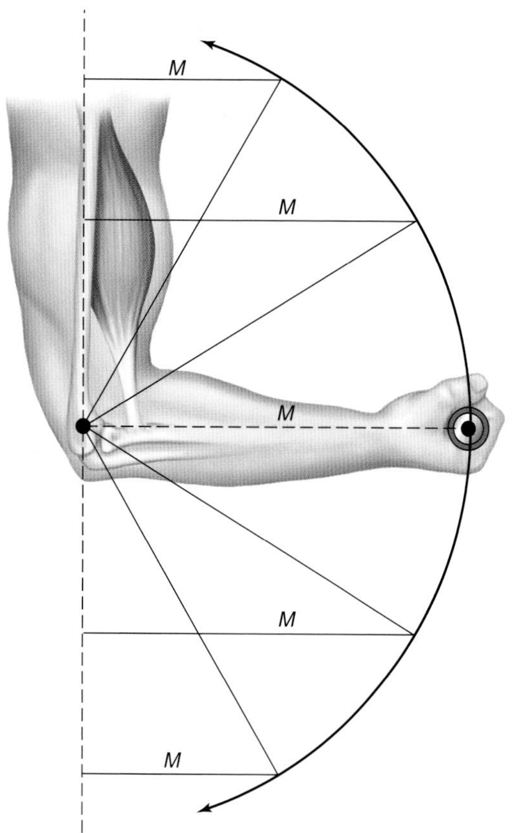

Figure 4.8 As a weight is lifted, the moment arm *(M)* through which the weight acts, and thus the resistive torque, changes with the horizontal distance from the weight to the elbow.

Most of the skeletal muscles operate at a considerable mechanical disadvantage. Thus, during sports and other physical activities, forces in the muscles and tendons are much higher than those exerted by the hands or feet on external objects or the ground.

Variations in Tendon Insertion

Considerable variation in human anatomical structure exists, including the points at which tendons are attached to bone. A person whose tendons are inserted on the bone farther from the joint center should be able to lift heavier weights because muscle force acts through a longer moment arm and thus can produce greater torque around the joint. (In figure 4.7, for example, consider how the moment arm [*M*] would change if the tendon insertion were farther to the right.) It is important, however, to recognize the trade-off involved in tendon insertion. The mechanical advantage gained by having tendons insert farther from the joint center is accompanied by a loss of maximum speed because, with the tendon inserted farther from the joint center, the muscle has to contract more to make the joint move through a given range of motion. In other words, a given amount of muscle shortening results in less rotation of body segments about a joint, which translates into a loss in movement speed. Figure 4.9*a* shows that, starting with the joint extended, when a hypothetical muscle shortens by a given amount, the joint rotates by 37°. However, if the muscle were inserted farther from the joint center, as in figure 4.9*b*, the same amount of muscle shortening would bring about only 34° of joint rotation because of the geometry of the dynamic triangle whose vertices are the muscle insertion and origin and the joint center of rotation.

To produce a given joint rotational velocity, a muscle inserted farther from the joint center must contract at a higher speed, at which it can generate less force due to the inverse force–velocity relationship of muscle (40) described later in this chapter. Therefore, such a tendon arrangement reduces the muscle's force capability during faster movements.

One can see how relatively subtle individual differences in structure can result in various advantages and disadvantages. For slow movements, as in powerlifting, tendon insertion farther from the joint than normal can be advantageous, while for athletic activities occurring at high speeds, such as hitting a tennis ball, such an arrangement can be disadvantageous.

Anatomical Planes of the Human Body

Figure 4.10 depicts a person standing in the standard **anatomical position**. The body is erect, the arms are down at the sides, and the palms face forward. Anatomical views of the body, as in magnetic resonance imaging, are generally shown in the **sagittal**, **frontal**, and **transverse planes**, which slice the body into left-right, front-back, and upper-lower sections respectively, not necessarily at the midpoint. The anatomical planes are also useful for describing the major body movements. Examples of exercise movements that take place in these planes include standing barbell curl (sagittal plane), standing lateral dumbbell raise (frontal plane), and dumbbell fly (transverse plane).

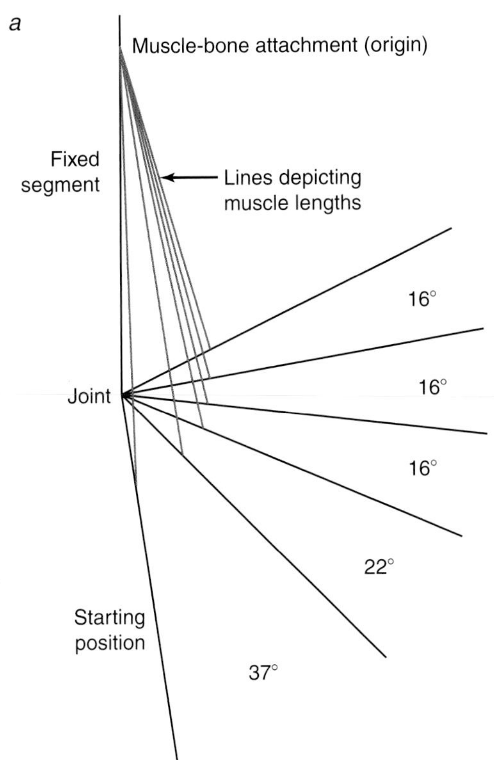

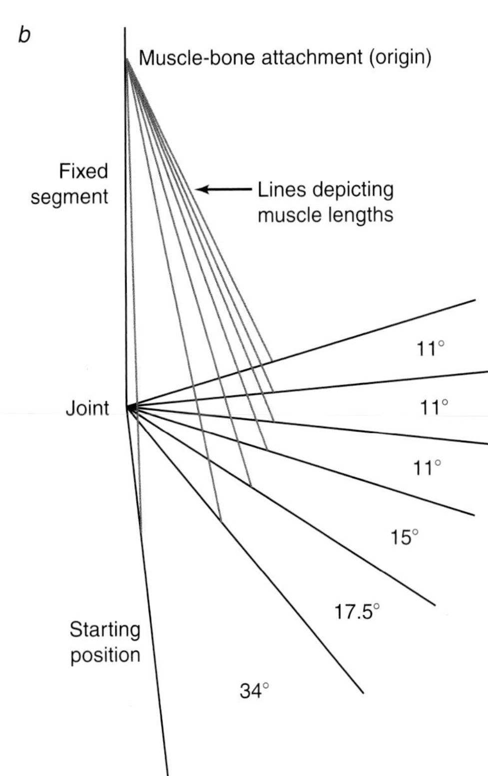

Figure 4.9 Changes in joint angle with equal increments of muscle shortening when the tendon is inserted *(a)* closer to and *(b)* farther from the joint center. Configuration *b* has a larger moment arm and thus greater torque for a given muscle force, but less rotation per unit of muscle contraction and thus slower movement speed.

Reprinted, by permission, from Gowitzke and Milner, 1988 (11).

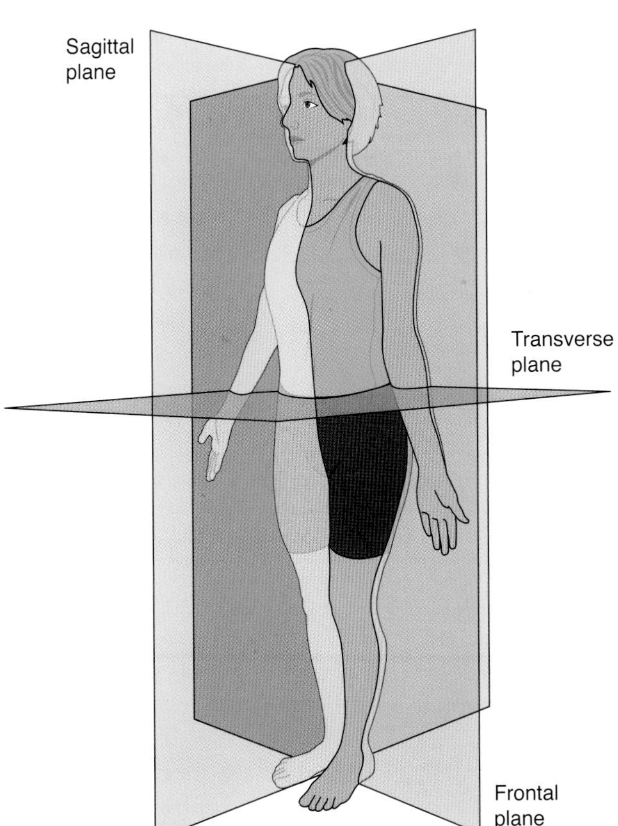

Figure 4.10 The three planes of the human body in the anatomical position.

HUMAN STRENGTH AND POWER

The terms *strength* and *power* are widely used to describe some important abilities that contribute to maximal human efforts in sport and other physical activities. Unfortunately, there is often little consistency in the way the terms are used. This section provides a scientific basis for understanding human strength and power and shows how various factors contribute to their manifestation.

Basic Definitions

Though it is widely accepted that strength is the ability to exert force, there is considerable disagreement as to how strength should be measured. The weight that a person can lift is probably the oldest quantitative measure of strength. Technological developments have popularized the use of isometric strength testing and, more recently, isokinetic strength testing.

All sports involve **acceleration** (change in velocity per unit time) of the body and, for some sports, of an implement as well (e.g., baseball bat, javelin, tennis racket). Acceleration is associated with resistive force according to Isaac Newton's second law:

$$\text{Force} = \text{Mass} \cdot \text{Acceleration} \tag{4.1}$$

Because of individual differences in the ability to exert force at different speeds (27), strength scores obtained from isometric and low-speed resistance tests may have limited value in predicting performance in sports, such as tennis or handball, that involve acceleration at high speed. That is why Knuttgen and Kraemer (29) have suggested a more inclusive definition of **strength**: the maximal force that a muscle or muscle group can generate at a specified velocity. Although controlling and monitoring velocity during strength testing require sophisticated equipment, the resulting strength scores are more meaningfully related to sport ability than are static strength measures or maximum loads lifted.

The limited meaning of isometric and low-speed strength scores has led to a heightened interest in power as a measurement of the ability to exert force at higher speeds. Outside of the scientific realm, power is loosely defined as "strength, might, force" (49). However, in physics, **power** is precisely defined as "the time rate of doing work" (34), where **work** is the product of the force exerted on an object and the distance the object moves in the direction in which the force is exerted. Quantitatively, work and power are defined as follows:

$$\text{Work} = \text{Force} \cdot \text{Distance} \tag{4.2}$$

and

$$\text{Power} = \text{Work} / \text{Time} \tag{4.3}$$

Power can also be calculated as the product of force on an object and the object's velocity in the direction in which the force is exerted, or the product of the object's velocity and the force on the object in the direction in which the object is traveling.

For all the equations in this chapter to work out correctly, consistent units must be used. In the International System of Units (SI, abbreviated from the French) (47), the worldwide standard, force is measured in newtons (N), distance in meters (m), work in joules (J, i.e., newton-meters, or N·m), time in seconds (s), and power in watts (W, i.e., J/s). The appropriate SI units for the equations can be obtained from other common units using the factors listed in table 4.1.

TABLE 4.1

Factors for Conversion of Common Measures to SI Units

To get	Multiply	By
newtons (N)	pounds (lb)	4.448
newtons (N)	kilograms mass (kg)	local acceleration of gravity
newtons (N)	kilograms force (kg)	9.807
meters (m)	feet (ft)	0.3048
meters (m)	inches (in)	0.02540
radians (rad)	degrees (°)	0.01745

As an example of applying equation 4.2, the net work performed when a weight is lifted is equal to the magnitude of the weight multiplied by the vertical distance the weight is lifted, regardless of any horizontal excursion of the weight during its ascent or any variation in the speed at which the weight travels. For example, to calculate the work involved in lifting a 100 kg (220-pound) barbell 2 m (6.6 feet) per repetition for 10 repetitions:

1. Determine the **weight** of the bar in SI units (newtons) by multiplying the mass of the bar in kilograms by the local acceleration due to gravity in meters per second squared. If the local acceleration due to gravity is not available, 9.8 m/s^2 is a good approximation:

   $$\text{Weight} = 9.8\ m/s^2 \cdot 100\ kg = 980\ N$$

2. Apply equation 4.2 to calculate the work for 10 repetitions in joules:

   $$\text{Work} = 980\ N \cdot 2\ m \cdot 10\ \text{reps} = 19{,}600\ J$$

This method of calculating work can be very useful for quantifying the volume of a workout. The work for each set is calculated as shown, and the total work for the whole workout is determined by addition. For free weight exercises, the vertical travel of the bar for one repetition of each exercise is measured for each individual by subtracting the height of the bar relative to the floor at its low position from the height of the bar at its high position. For weight-stack exercises, the vertical travel of the stack is measured. These measurements can be made with an empty bar or the lowest-weight plate on the stack because the vertical distance traveled by the weight during a given exercise for an individual should be about the same regardless of the weight used.

In the previous example, in which work was determined, if it takes 40 seconds to perform the 10 repetitions, the average power output in watts for the set is calculated using equation 4.3:

$$\text{Power} = 19{,}600 \text{ J} / 40 \text{ seconds} = 490 \text{ W}$$

The work and power equations just presented apply to an object moving from one location to another. Work and power are also required to start an object rotating about an axis or to change the velocity at which it rotates, even if the object as a whole does not move through space at all. The angle through which an object rotates is called its **angular displacement**, the SI unit for which is the radian (rad); 1 rad = 180° ÷ π = 57.3°, where π = 3.14. **Angular velocity** is the object's rotational speed, measured in radians per second (rad/s). Torque is expressed in newton-meters (N·m), but should not be confused with work, which is also expressed in newton-meters. The difference is that the distance component of the torque unit refers to the length of the moment arm (which is *perpendicular to* the line of action of the force), while the distance component of the work unit refers to the distance moved *along* the line of action of the force. Just as for movement through space, the work done in rotating an object is measured in joules (J), and power in watts (W) (47).

This equation is used to calculate **rotational work**:

$$\text{Work} = \text{Torque} \cdot \text{Angular Displacement} \quad (4.4)$$

Equation 4.3 is used to calculate **rotational power**, just as it was used to calculate linear power.

The discrepancy between the common and scientific definitions of power has led to misunderstandings. For example, in the sport of powerlifting, which involves high forces but relatively low movement speeds, less mechanical power is produced than in several other sports, including Olympic lifting (10). Despite the discrepancy, the sport of powerlifting is unlikely to be renamed. However, the strength and conditioning professional should use the word *power* only in its scientific sense in all other contexts to avoid ambiguity.

Furthermore, although the word *strength* is often associated with slow speeds and the word *power* with high speeds of movement, both variables reflect the ability to exert force at a given speed. Power is a direct mathematical function of force and velocity. Therefore, if at any instant, any two of the variables force, velocity, and power are known, the third can be calculated. If an individual can generate high force or high power at a particular velocity of movement, precisely the same ability is being described, that is, the ability to accelerate a mass at that particular speed. Therefore, it is not correct to associate strength with low speed and power with high speed. Strength is the capacity to exert force at any given speed, and power is the mathematical product of force and velocity at whatever speed. What is critical is the ability to exert force at speeds characteristic of a given sport to overcome gravity and accelerate the body or an implement. For a sport movement made relatively slow by high resistance, low-speed strength is critical, whereas for a movement that is very fast due to low resistance, high-speed strength is important. For example, when offensive and defensive American football linemen push against each other, their speed of movement is slowed by the muscular force exerted by the opposing player as well as the inertia of the opposing player's body mass. Because the muscles are prevented from contracting at high speed, the ability to exert force and power at low speed is an important component of performance. In contrast, a badminton player's muscles quickly reach high velocity as a result of the minimal inertial resistance of the lightweight racket and the player's arm. Therefore, the ability to exert force and power at high speed is critical to making rapid adjustments in a stroke.

Biomechanical Factors in Human Strength

Several biomechanical factors are involved in the manifestation of human strength, including neural control, muscle cross-sectional area, muscle fiber arrangement, muscle length, joint angle, muscle contraction velocity, joint angular velocity, and body size. These factors are discussed next, as are the three-dimensional strength relationship and the strength-to-mass ratio.

Neural Control

Neural control affects the maximal force output of a muscle by determining which and how many motor units are involved in a muscle contraction (**recruitment**) and the rate at which the motor units are fired (**rate coding**) (8). Generally, muscle force is greater when: (a) more motor units are involved in a contraction, (b) the motor units are greater in size, or (c) the rate of firing is faster. Much of the improvement in strength evidenced in the first few weeks of resistance training is attributable to neural adaptations, as the brain learns how to generate more force from a given amount of contractile tissue (37). It is not unusual for novice resistance trainees to become discouraged when they cannot maintain the rate of increase of the first few training weeks. It is important for them to realize that continued improvement will result if they adhere to the training regimen, although via slower mechanisms.

Muscle Cross-Sectional Area

All else being equal, the force a muscle can exert is related to its cross-sectional area rather than to its volume (25). For example, if two athletes of similar percent body fat but different height have the same biceps circumference, their upper arm muscle cross-sectional areas are about the same. Although the taller (and therefore heavier) athlete's longer muscle makes for greater muscle volume, the strength of the two athletes' biceps should be about the same. With the same strength but greater body weight, the taller athlete has less ability to lift and accelerate his or her own body, as when performing calisthenics or gymnastics. This is why most elite gymnasts are not very tall. As described in chapter 5, resistance training increases both the strength and cross-sectional area of muscle.

Arrangement of Muscle Fibers

Maximally contracting muscles have been found capable of generating forces of 23 to 145 psi (16-100 N/cm^2) of muscle cross-sectional area (1, 18, 19, 33). This wide range can be partially accounted for by the variation in the arrangement and alignment of sarcomeres in relation to the long axis of the muscle (figure 4.11) (13, 19). A **pennate muscle** has fibers that align obliquely with the tendon, creating a featherlike arrangement. The **angle of pennation** is defined as the angle between the muscle fibers and an imaginary line between the muscle's origin and insertion; 0° corresponds to no pennation.

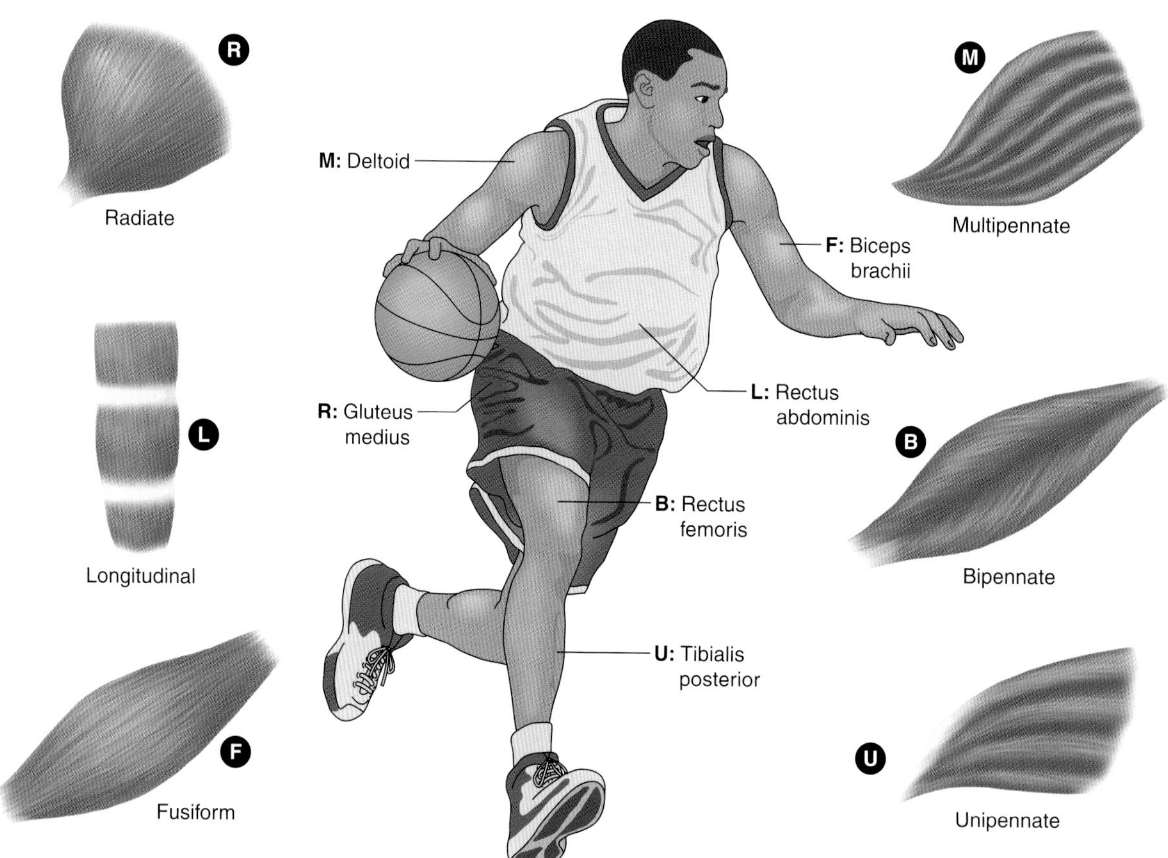

Figure 4.11 Muscle fiber arrangements and an example of each.

Many human muscles are pennated (13), but few have angles of pennation in excess of 15°. Actually, the angle of pennation does not remain constant for a given muscle, but increases as the muscle shortens. Any factor that affects angle of pennation would thus affect strength and velocity of shortening as long as the cross-sectional area remains the same. Muscles with greater pennation have more sarcomeres in parallel and fewer sarcomeres in series; they are therefore better able to generate force but have a lower maximal shortening velocity than nonpennate muscle. Pennation can be somewhat disadvantageous, however, for generating eccentric, isometric, or low-speed concentric force (43). Angle of pennation may vary depending on hereditary factors and even training, which could help account for some of the differences in strength and speed seen in individuals who seem to have muscle of the same size. Although there is a trade-off associated with pennation and it is not the most advantageous arrangement for all muscles, many skeletal muscles are pennate (13).

Muscle Length

When a muscle is at its resting length, the actin and myosin filaments lie next to each other, so that a maximal number of potential cross-bridge sites are available (figure 4.12). Thus, the muscle can generate the greatest force at its resting length. When the muscle is stretched much beyond its resting length, a smaller proportion of the actin and myosin filaments lie next to each other. Because there are fewer potential cross-bridge sites, the muscle cannot generate as much force as it can at its resting length. When the muscle contracts too much below its resting length, the actin filaments overlap and the number of cross-bridge sites is reduced as well, thereby decreasing force generation capability.

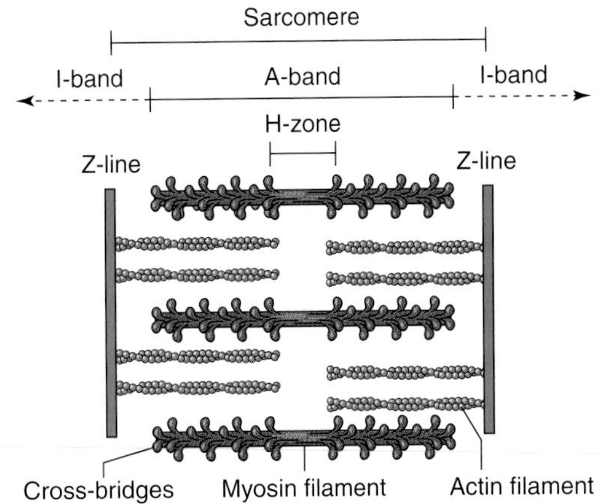

Figure 4.12 A schematic of the interaction between actin and myosin filaments when the muscle is at its resting length and when it is contracted or stretched. Muscle force capability is greatest when the muscle is at its resting length because of increased opportunity for actin-myosin cross-bridges.

Joint Angle

Because all body movements, even those occurring in a straight line, take place by means of rotation about a joint or joints, the forces that muscles produce must be manifested as torques (recall that a higher torque value indicates a greater tendency for the applied force to rotate the limb or body part about a joint); consequently, we speak in terms of torque versus joint angle, rather than force versus joint angle. The amount of torque that can be exerted about a given body joint varies throughout the joint's range of motion largely because of the relationship of force versus muscle length as well as the ever-changing leverage brought about by the dynamic geometry of the muscles, tendons, and internal joint structures. Additional factors include the type of exercise (isotonic, isometric, etc.), the body joint in question, the muscles used at that joint, and the speed of contraction (28).

Muscle Contraction Velocity

Classic experiments by A.V. Hill (23) on isolated animal muscle showed that the force capability of muscle declines as the velocity of contraction increases. The relationship is not linear; the decline in force capability is steepest over the lower range of movement speeds. Human movement technique can make the best of this relationship. For example, as a vertical jump begins, the arms swing upward, thereby exerting downward force on the body at the shoulders, slowing the upward movement of the body, and forcing the hip and knee extensor muscles to contract more slowly than they otherwise would, enabling them to generate higher forces for longer times.

Joint Angular Velocity

There are three basic types of muscle action, during which forces are generated within the muscle that pull the muscle's ends toward each other if not prevented from doing so by external forces. The term *muscle action* is preferable to *contraction*, because the latter means "shortening," which does not accurately describe two of the three muscle actions.

concentric muscle action—A muscle action in which the muscle shortens because the contractile force is greater than the resistive force. The forces generated within the muscle and acting to shorten it are greater than the external forces acting at its tendons to stretch it. Swimming and cycling involve concentric muscle action almost exclusively.

eccentric muscle action—A muscle action in which the muscle lengthens because the contractile force is less than the resistive force. The forces generated within the muscle and acting to shorten it are less than the external forces acting at its tendons to stretch it (which increases the risk of soreness and injury [35]). This occurs during the lowering phase of any resistance exercise. During standard resistance training, the eccentric force exerted by the muscle keeps the weight from being accelerated downward by gravitational force. Thus, the weight moves steadily downward rather than picking up speed and impacting the floor or the athlete's body.

isometric muscle action—A muscle action in which the muscle length does not change because the contractile force is equal to the resistive force. The forces generated within the muscle and acting to shorten it are equal to the external forces acting at its tendons to stretch it. During a sit-up with the trunk held straight, the abdominal muscles act isometrically to maintain the rigidity of the trunk, while the hip flexors carry out the sit-up movement. In contrast, the abdominal muscles act concentrically and eccentrically during the raising and lowering phases of the curl-up exercise, respectively.

Muscle torque varies with joint angular velocity according to the type of muscular action (figure 4.13). Tests have shown that during isokinetic (constant-speed) concentric exercise by human subjects, torque capability declines as angular velocity increases. In contrast, during eccentric exercise, as joint angular velocity increases, maximal torque capability increases until about 90°/s (1.57 rad/s), after which it declines gradually (27, 45). That means that the greatest muscle force can be obtained during eccentric muscle action. Athletes often employ "cheating" movements when a weight cannot be lifted using strict form. For example, an individual who reaches a "sticking point" in the biceps curl exercise due to the limit of concentric elbow flexor strength usually leans the torso back, allowing the elbow flexors to exert increased force by operating isometrically or eccentrically and thereby enabling continued movement of the bar.

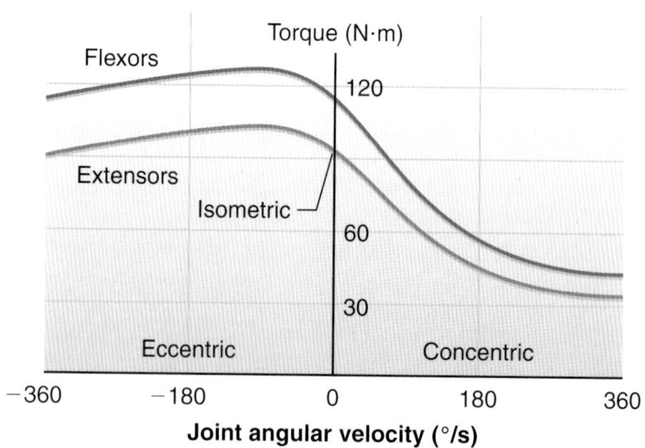

Figure 4.13 Force–velocity curve for eccentric and concentric actions.

Reprinted, by permission, from Jorgensen, 1976 (27).

Strength-to-Mass Ratio

In sport activities such as sprinting and jumping, the ratio of the strength of the muscles involved in the movement to the mass of the body parts being accelerated is critical. Thus, the strength-to-mass ratio directly reflects an athlete's ability to accelerate his or her body. If, after training, an athlete increases body mass by 15% but increases force capability by only 10%, the strength-to-mass ratio, and thus the athlete's ability to accelerate, is reduced. A sprinter or jumper may benefit by experimenting with muscle mass to determine the highest strength-to-mass ratio, which would result in the best possible performance.

In sports involving weight classification, the strength-to-mass ratio is extremely important. If all competitors have the same body mass, the strongest one has a decided advantage. It is normal for the strength-to-mass ratio of larger athletes to be lower than that of smaller athletes because when body size increases, muscle volume (and concomitantly body weight) increases proportionately more than does muscle cross-sectional area (and concomitantly strength) (3). Trial and error can help an athlete determine the weight category in which his or her strength is highest relative to that of other athletes in the weight class. Once an athlete finds his or her most competitive weight class, the object is to become as strong as possible without exceeding the class weight limit.

Body Size

It has long been observed that, all else being equal, smaller athletes are stronger pound for pound than larger athletes. The reason is that a muscle's maximal contractile force is fairly proportional to its cross-sectional area, which is related to the square (second power) of linear body dimensions, whereas a muscle's mass is proportional to its volume, which is related to the cube (third power) of linear body dimensions. Therefore, as body size increases, body mass increases more rapidly than does muscle strength. Given constant body proportions, the smaller athlete has a higher strength-to-mass ratio than does the larger athlete (3).

There has always been interest in comparing the performances of athletes in different weight categories. The most obvious method for doing so is to divide the weight lifted by the athlete's body weight. However, such an adjustment is biased against larger athletes because it does not take into account the expected drop in the strength-to-mass ratio with increasing body size. Various formulas have been derived to compare loads lifted more equitably. In the **classic formula**, the load lifted is divided by body weight to the two-thirds power, thus accounting for the relationship of cross-sectional area versus volume. Other formulas have since been developed because the classic formula seemed to favor athletes of middle body weight over lighter and heavier athletes (21). However, the classic formula's determination that the performances of medium-weight athletes are usually the best may indeed be unbiased. Because of the bell-shaped curve describing the normal distribution of anthropometric characteristics among the population, the body weights of a majority of people are clustered close to the mean. One would expect the weight category with the largest number of competitors to produce the best performers.

SOURCES OF RESISTANCE TO MUSCLE CONTRACTION

The most common sources of resistance for strength training exercises are gravity, inertia, friction, fluid resistance, and elasticity. This section provides information on the force and power required to overcome these forms of resistance. An understanding of the principles behind exercise devices using the various forms of resistance can provide insight into their effectiveness and applicability.

Gravity

The downward force on an object from the pull of gravity, otherwise called the object's weight, is equal to the object's mass times the local acceleration due to gravity:

$$F_g = m \cdot a_g \tag{4.5}$$

where F_g is the force due to gravity (same as the object's weight), m is the object's mass, and a_g is the local acceleration due to gravity.

The acceleration due to gravity can vary by geographic location. Weighing a barbell on a calibrated spring or electronic scale shows its actual weight. A balance scale determines only the object's mass, so its weight (F_g) must be calculated using equation 4.5 if a spring or electronic scale is not available.

Popular terminology for weight and mass is often incorrect. For example, some barbell and stack-machine plates are labeled in pounds. The pound is a unit of force, not mass. In actuality, only the mass of a barbell plate stays constant, while its weight varies according to the local acceleration due to gravity. The kilogram designation on a weight plate refers to its mass. It is not correct to say that an object weighs a certain number of kilograms, since weight refers to force, not mass. Instead, one should say "The mass of the barbell is 85 kg." The amount of mass an individual can lift will be slightly affected by terrestrial location, due to variations in the acceleration due to gravity around the globe.

Applications to Resistance Training

The gravitational force on an object always acts downward. Since, by definition, the moment arm by which a force produces torque is perpendicular to the line of action of the force, the moment arm of a weight is always horizontal. Thus, torque due to an object's weight is the product of the weight and the horizontal distance from the weight to the pivot point (joint). During an exercise, although the weight does not change, its horizontal distance from a given joint axis changes constantly. When the weight is horizontally closer to the joint, it exerts less resistive torque; when it is horizontally farther from a joint, it exerts more resistive torque. For example, in an arm curl, the horizontal distance from the elbow to the barbell is greatest when the forearm is horizontal. Thus, in that position the athlete must exert the greatest muscle torque to support the weight. The moment arm decreases as the forearm rotates either upward or downward away from the horizontal, decreasing the resistive torque arising from the weight. When the weight is directly above or below the elbow pivot point, there is no resistive torque from the weight.

Exercise technique can affect the resistive torque pattern during an exercise and can shift stress among muscle groups. In the back squat, for example, a more forward inclination of the trunk brings the weight horizontally closer to the knees, thus reducing the resistive torque about the knees that the quadriceps must counteract. At the same time, the weight is horizontally farther from the hip, increasing the resistive torque about the hip that the gluteus and hamstring muscles must counteract. When the barbell is positioned as low as possible on the upper back, the athlete must incline the trunk relatively far forward to keep the center of mass of body plus bar over the feet, thereby avoiding a fall. Because the bar is then horizontally far from the hip and close to the knee, stress is focused on the hip extensors and to a lesser extent on the knee extensors.

Weight-Stack Machines

As with free weights, gravity is the source of resistance for weight-stack machines. However, by means of pulleys, cams, cables, and gears, these machines provide increased control over the direction and pattern of resistance. Both free weights and stack machines have advantages and disadvantages. Following are some of the advantages of the stack machine:

- Safety. The likelihood of injury as a result of being hit by, tripping over, or being trapped under a weight is reduced. It requires less skill to maintain control of a weight stack than a free weight.
- Design flexibility. Machines can be designed to provide resistance to body movements that are difficult to resist with free weights (e.g., lat pulldown, hip adduction and abduction, leg curl). To some extent, the pattern of resistance can be engineered into a machine.
- Ease of use. Many people who fear they lack the coordination or technique to safely lift free weights feel confident when using machines. Also, it is quicker and easier to select a weight by inserting a pin in a stack than by mounting plates on a bar.

Advantages of free weights include the following:

- Whole-body training. Free weight exercises are often performed in the standing position with the weight supported by the entire body, taxing a larger portion of the body's musculature and skeleton than a weight-stack machine would. Such weight-bearing exercise promotes bone mineralization, helping to prevent osteoporosis in later life (44). Moreover, the movement of a free weight is constrained by the athlete rather than by a machine, requiring muscles to work in stabilization as well as support. "Structural" exercises, such as the power clean and the snatch, are particularly useful in providing training stimulus for a major portion of the body's musculature.
- Simulation of real-life activities. The lifting and acceleration of objects represent a major part of sport and other physically demanding activities. Machines tend to isolate single muscle groups; the lifting of free weights involves the more natural coordination of several muscle groups.

Nautilus Sports/Medical Industries popularized the concept of tailoring resistive torque through the range of joint motion by creating an exercise machine that uses a cam of variable radius that changes the length of the moment arm through which the weight stack acts (figure 4.14). The rationale was to provide more resistance at points in the range of motion where the muscles could exert greater torque and less resistance where the muscles could apply less torque. For the system to work as planned, however, the athlete has to move at a constant, slow angular velocity, which is difficult to do consistently. Also, cam-based machines

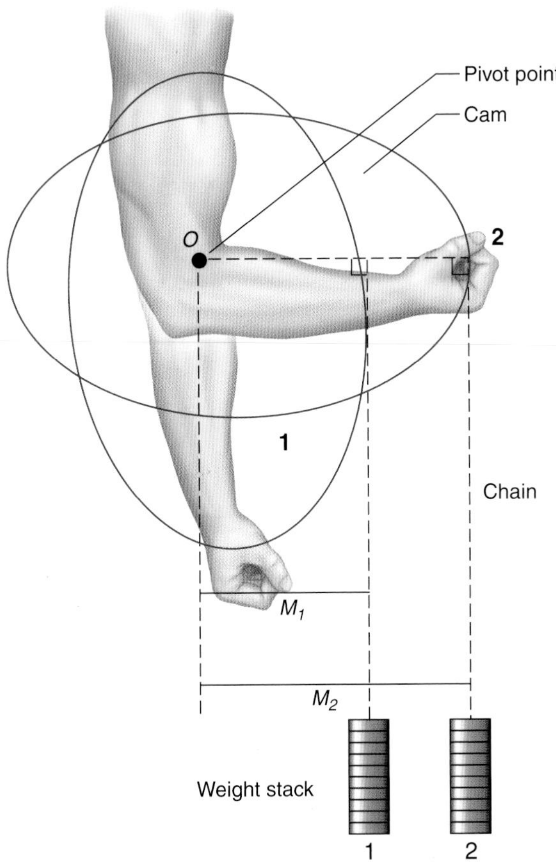

Figure 4.14 In cam-based weight-stack machines, the moment arm *(M)* of the weight stack (horizontal distance from the chain to the cam pivot point) varies during the exercise movement. When the cam is rotated in the direction shown from position 1 to position 2, the moment arm of the weights, and thus the resistive torque, increases.

frequently fail to match normal human torque capability patterns (14, 26).

Inertia

In addition to gravitational force, a barbell or weight stack, when accelerated, exerts **inertial force** on the athlete. Though the force of gravity acts only downward, inertial force can act in any direction. The upward force an athlete exerts equals the weight lifted plus any inertial force, which is the mass times the upward acceleration of the bar. Horizontal bar acceleration occurs if the athlete exerts net force on the bar directed to the front, back, left, or right.

All exercises involve some acceleration at the beginning to bring the bar from a zero to an upward velocity and some deceleration near the top of the exercise to bring the bar's velocity back to zero. With this acceleration pattern, the agonist muscles receive resistance in excess of bar weight early in the range of motion, but resistance less than bar weight toward the end of the range of motion (30). The athlete decelerates the bar by either: (a) reducing upward force on the bar to less than bar weight to let some or all of the bar's weight decelerate it or (b) pushing down against the bar using the antagonist muscles. In either case, the deceleration has the effect of providing less resistance to the agonist muscles late in the range of motion.

Compared to a slow exercise with minimal acceleration of a given weight, an exercise involving higher acceleration (an "explosive" exercise) provides greater resistance to the muscles involved early in the range of motion and less resistance to the muscles involved toward the end of the range of motion. However, heavier weights can be handled in accelerative exercises than in slow exercises, allowing near-maximal resistance to be attained for all muscles involved in the exercise. During a power clean of a heavy weight, for example, the strong leg, hip, and back muscles accelerate the bar vertically to a high enough velocity that, even though the weaker upper body muscles cannot exert vertical force equal to the bar's weight, the bar continues to travel upward until the force of gravity decelerates it to zero velocity at the highest bar position.

Although acceleration changes the nature of an exercise and makes resistance patterns less predictable, acceleration in resistance training is not necessarily undesirable. Because acceleration is characteristic of natural movements in sport and daily life, resistance training exercises involving acceleration probably produce desirable neuromuscular training effects. Olympic lifting exercises such as the snatch and the clean and jerk are effective for improving the ability to produce high accelerations against heavy resistance (10).

Acceleration and deceleration are characteristic of virtually all natural movements. For example, sprinting requires the athlete's arms and legs to go through repeated cycles of acceleration and deceleration. Throwing a baseball, discus, shot, or javelin all involve sequences of body movements that accelerate the objects to high release speeds. Because acceleration is a particular kind of movement pattern, training with accelerative movements can provide specificity of training. That is why explosive exercises, such as the power clean and high pull, are used in training for many different sports in which the leg and hip muscles provide force for accelerating the body. The **bracketing technique**, in which the athlete performs the sport movement with less than normal and greater than normal resistance, is another form of acceleration training. According to the force–velocity relationship of muscle, a shot-putter who trains with an extra-heavy shot develops greater forces during the accelerative movement than when the normal shot is used because the inertia of the heavier implement forces the muscle to contract at relatively low speed. When a relatively light shot is used, the lower inertia of the shot enables the putter to accelerate the shot more rapidly and to reach a higher speed of release, thereby training the neuromuscular system to operate within desired acceleration and speed ranges. The same principle can be applied to sprint training in which the athlete pulls a small parachute for greater resistance at lower speed and is pulled by an elastic cord for lower resistance at greater speed.

When a weight is held in a static position or moved at a constant velocity, it exerts constant resistance only in the downward direction. However, upward or lateral acceleration of the weight requires additional force.

Friction

Friction is the resistive force encountered when one attempts to move an object while it is pressed against another object. Exercise devices that use friction as the main source of resistance include belt- or brake pad–resisted cycle ergometers and wrist curl devices. For such devices,

$$F_R = k \cdot F_N \tag{4.6}$$

where F_R is the resistive force; k is the coefficient of friction for the two particular substances in contact; and F_N is the normal force, which presses the objects against each other.

The coefficients of friction for initiating and for maintaining movement are different. All else being equal, it takes more force to initiate movement between two surfaces in contact than to maintain previously initiated movement. Thus, a friction-resisted exercise device requires a relatively high force to initiate movement and a relatively constant force after movement has begun, no matter what the movement speed. Resistance provided by such devices is sometimes adjusted through a mechanism that alters the normal force that keeps the friction surfaces in contact with each other.

A weighted sled used in training for football or track is an example of a device that is resisted by both friction and inertia. The resistance due to the sled's inertia is directly proportional to both the sled's mass and its acceleration. The resistance due to the friction between the sled's runners and the ground is proportional to both the friction coefficient between surfaces in contact and the net force pressing the sled against the ground, which equals the gravitational force minus any upward force exerted by the individual pushing the sled. Mass can be added to the sled to increase the gravitational force. The friction coefficient varies with the surface on which the sled rests (e.g., sand, bare soil, dry grass, wet grass). Thus, for outdoor training, such devices do not provide consistently repeatable resistance. They are nevertheless useful in providing horizontal resistance, which cannot be directly provided by weights. It takes more force to get the sled moving than to keep it moving, because the coefficient of static friction is always greater than the coefficient of sliding friction. Once the sled is moving, the coefficient of sliding friction stays relatively constant, so that friction resistance does not change as speed increases. However, in keeping with equation 4.3, power output increases with speed. Also, as expressed by equation 4.1, during the transition from a lower to a higher speed there is added resistance due to acceleration.

Fluid Resistance

The resistive force encountered by an object moving through a fluid (liquid or gas), or by a fluid moving past or around an object or through an orifice, is called **fluid resistance**. Fluid resistance is a significant factor in such sport activities as swimming, rowing, golf, sprinting, discus throwing, and baseball pitching. (Except for swimming and rowing, in which the fluid is water, all these involve air resistance.) The phenomenon has become important in resistance training with the advent of hydraulic (liquid) and pneumatic (gas) exercise machines and with the increasing popularity of swimming pool exercise routines, particularly among older people and pregnant women.

The two sources of fluid resistance are **surface drag**, which results from the friction of a fluid passing along the surface of an object, and **form drag**, which results from the way in which a fluid presses against the front or rear of an object passing through it. Cross-sectional (frontal) area has a major effect on form drag.

Fluid-resisted exercise machines most often use cylinders in which a piston forces fluid through an orifice as the exercise movement is performed. The resistive force is greater when the piston is pushed faster, when the orifice is smaller, or when the fluid is more viscous. All else being equal, resistance is roughly proportional to the velocity of piston movement (22):

$$F_R = k \cdot v \tag{4.7}$$

where F_R is the resistive force; k is a constant that reflects the physical characteristics of the cylinder and piston, the viscosity of the fluid, and the number, size, and shape of the orifices; and v is piston velocity relative to the cylinder.

Because fluid cylinders provide resistance that increases with speed, they allow rapid acceleration early in the exercise movement and little acceleration after higher speeds are reached. Movement speed is thus kept within an intermediate range. Although such machines limit changes in velocity to a certain extent, they are not isokinetic (constant speed), as is sometimes claimed. Some machines have adjustment knobs that allow the orifice size to be changed. A larger orifice allows the user to reach a higher movement speed before the fluid resistive force curtails the ability to accelerate.

Fluid-resisted machines do not generally provide an eccentric exercise phase, but they may if they incorporate an internal pump. With a free weight, a muscle group acts concentrically while raising the weight and eccentrically while lowering it. With fluid-resisted machines without eccentric resistance, a muscle group acts concentrically while performing the primary exercise movement, and the antagonist muscle group acts concentrically while returning to the starting position. In other words, whereas free weights or weight machines involve alternate concentric and eccentric actions of the same muscle with little or no rest in between, fluid-resisted machines generally involve alternate concentric actions of antagonistic muscle groups; each muscle group rests while its antagonist works. The lack of eccentric muscle action with fluid-resisted machines means that such exercise probably does not provide optimal training for the many sport movements that involve eccentric muscle actions (e.g., running, jumping, and throwing).

Elasticity

A number of exercise devices, particularly those designed for home use, have elastic components such as springs, bands, bows, or rods as their source of resistance. The resistance provided by a standard elastic component is proportional to the distance it is stretched:

$$F_R = k \cdot x \tag{4.8}$$

where F_R is the resistive force, k is a constant that reflects the physical characteristics of the elastic component, and x is the distance that the elastic component is stretched beyond its resting length.

The most obvious characteristic of elastic resistance is that the more the elastic component is stretched, the greater the resistance. The problem with devices using elastic resistance is that every exercise movement begins with low resistance and ends with high resistance. This is contrary to the force capability patterns of virtually all human muscle groups, which show a substantial drop-off in force capability toward the end of the range of motion. Another problem with elasticity-resisted machines is that the adjustability of resistance is usually limited by the number of elastic components that are available to provide resistance to a movement. An effective resistance exercise device must incorporate enough variation in resistive force that the number of repetitions the trainee can perform is kept within a desirable range.

There are products that provide resistance to vertical jumping with elastic bands as a means of developing jumping power. However, the elastic bands provide little resistance early in the jump when the large gluteus and quadriceps muscles are capable of exerting great force. The bands provide the greatest resistance while the jumper is in the air—serving mainly to pull the jumper back to the ground, rather than resist the muscles, and to increase the speed at which the jumper hits the ground on landing, which may increase injury risk.

Negative Work and Power

Because power equals the product of force and velocity, when force is exerted on a weight in the direction opposite to the one in which the weight is moving (as when a weight is lowered in a controlled manner), calculated power has a negative sign, as does calculated work. All such "negative" power and work occur during eccentric muscle activity, such as lowering a weight or decelerating at the end of a rapid movement.

Strictly speaking, there is no such thing as negative work or power. The term *negative work* really refers to work performed on, rather than by, a muscle. When a weight is lifted, muscles perform work on the weight, increasing the weight's potential energy. When the weight is lowered, its potential energy is used to perform an equal amount of work on the athlete. Thus, while repetitions are performed, the athlete and weight alternately perform work on each other, rather than the athlete alternately performing positive and negative work. The rate at which the repetitions are performed determines the power output.

JOINT BIOMECHANICS: CONCERNS IN RESISTANCE TRAINING

As with any physical activity, there is a degree of risk with resistance training. However, the risks involved are generally lower than for many other sport and physical conditioning activities (42). Rates of injury are the highest for team sports; intermediate for running and aerobics; and lowest for cycling, walking, and resistance training, the latter of which has about four injuries per 1,000 hours of participation. A study of collegiate American football players (50) showed only 0.35 resistance training–related injuries per 100 players per season. Injuries due to resistance training accounted for only 0.74% of the in-season injury-related time loss of the players. Despite the relatively low risk of resistance training, it is desirable to minimize the likelihood of injury through prudent risk management. The following are several factors to consider in avoiding resistance training injuries, with particular attention given to the back, shoulders, and knees.

Back

In contrast to quadrupeds, whose vertebral columns hang like the cables on a suspension bridge, humans normally stand upright, with the vertebral bones stacked one on top of another, separated by rubbery disks. The advantage we gain from our upright posture and free use of the arms and hands is accompanied by the disadvantage of having our intervertebral disks under compressive force even when we are merely standing, sitting, walking, or running, and under even more compressive force when we are lifting and carrying. When we are in a standing position, any force we exert with the upper body must be transmitted through the back to the legs and ground. In addition, the back muscles act at a great mechanical disadvantage and must generate forces much greater than the weight of an object lifted. It is for these reasons that the back is particularly vulnerable to injury.

Back Injury

Back injury can be extremely debilitating, persistent, and difficult to remedy. Thus, every effort should be made to avoid back injury during resistance training. The lower back is particularly vulnerable. It has been observed that 85% to 90% of all intervertebral disk herniations occur at the disk between the lowest two lumbar vertebrae (L4 and L5) or between the lowest lumbar and the top sacral vertebra (L5 and S1) (5). This is not surprising, given the extremely high compressive forces on the disks during lifting. When a weight is supported in the hands or on the shoulders and the trunk is inclined forward, there is great torque about the lower intervertebral disks due to the large horizontal distance between the lower back and the weight. The back muscles operate at an extremely low mechanical advantage because the perpendicular distance from the line of action of the spinal erector muscles to the intervertebral disks is much shorter (about 2 inches, or 5 cm) than the horizontal distance from the weight to the disks. As a result, the muscles must exert forces that frequently exceed 10 times the weight lifted. These forces act to squeeze the intervertebral disks between the adjacent vertebral bodies and can lead to injury.

The flat-back lifting posture has been found to be better overall than a rounded (opposite of arched) back in minimizing L5/S1 compressive forces and ligament strain (2). A normal, slightly arched (**lordotic**) back has been found to be superior to a rounded back for avoiding injury to vertebrae, disks, facet joints, ligaments, and muscles of the back. In addition, the low back muscles are capable of exerting considerably higher forces when the back is arched rather than rounded (20).

The vertebral column is naturally S-shaped, being slightly rounded (**kyphotic**) in the thoracic spine and lordotic in the lumbar spine. The wedged shape of the vertebrae gives the spine its natural curve. However, the intervertebral disks are flat when the back is in its S shape. When the lower back is rounded, the **ventral** (toward the anterior) edges of the vertebral bodies squeeze the front portions of the intervertebral disks. In contrast, extreme arching of the back results in squeezing the **dorsal** (toward the posterior) portions of the disks. Such uneven squeezing of the intervertebral disks likely increases the risk of disk rupture. Thus, resistance training exercises should generally be performed with the lower back in a moderately arched position.

Intra-Abdominal Pressure and Lifting Belts

When the diaphragm and the deep muscles of the torso contract, pressure is generated within the abdominal cavity. Because the abdomen is composed mainly of fluid and normally contains very little gas, it is virtually incompressible. The abdominal fluids and tissue kept under pressure by tensing surrounding muscle (deep abdominal muscles and diaphragm) have been described as a "fluid ball" (figure 4.15) that aids in supporting the vertebral column during resistance training. Such support may significantly reduce both the forces required by the erector spinae muscles to perform an exercise and the associated compressive forces on the disks (4, 38).

It is important to note that the Valsalva maneuver is not necessary for generation of intra-abdominal pressure. In the **Valsalva maneuver**, the glottis is closed, thus keeping air from escaping the lungs, and the muscles of the abdomen and rib cage contract, creating rigid compartments of liquid in the lower torso and air in the upper torso. An advantage of the Valsalva maneuver is that it increases the rigidity of the entire torso, making it easier to support heavy loads. For example, when lifting heavy loads in the back squat exercise, many athletes use the Valsalva maneuver, particularly when the trunk is most inclined forward, near the transition from the eccentric movement phase to the concentric movement phase. However, pressure in the chest associated with the Valsalva maneuver can have the undesirable side effect of exerting compressive force on the heart, making it more difficult for blood to return to the heart. Also, the Valsalva maneuver can transiently elevate blood pressure to high levels, with the potential risk of blackout. The diaphragm and the abdominal muscles can contract *without* the glottis being closed, however, creating the fluid ball in the abdomen without pressurizing the chest compartment. This must be regarded as the safest way to add support to the lower spine without building up pressure in the chest and is the technique that should be used for most resistance training. One can build up intra-abdominal pressure without building up chest pressure by consciously keeping the airway open. During a strenuous repetition, the abdominal muscles and diaphragm contract reflexively, even with the airway open. Athletes, particularly those who compete in Olympic lifting or powerlifting, may choose to use the Valsalva maneuver if they recognize and accept the risks involved and have the experience to avoid increasing pressure to the point of blackout.

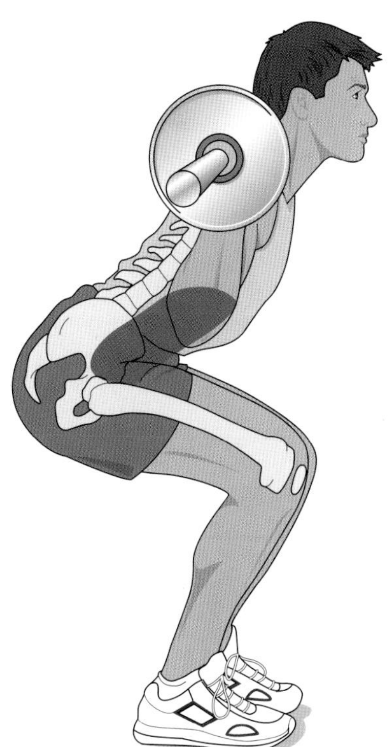

Figure 4.15 The "fluid ball" resulting from contraction of the deep abdominal muscles and the diaphragm.

Weightlifting belts have been shown to increase intra-abdominal pressure during resistance training and are therefore probably effective in improving safety (17, 31, 32). It has been cautioned, however, that if an athlete performs all of the exercises with a belt, the abdominal muscles that produce intra-abdominal pressure might not get enough training stimulus to develop optimally (17). It is particularly risky for an individual who has become accustomed to wearing a belt to suddenly perform an exercise without one, because the abdominal musculature might not be capable of generating enough intra-abdominal pressure to significantly reduce erector spinae muscle forces. The resulting excessive compressive forces on the disks could increase the chance of back injury. Conservative recommendations are as follows:

- A weight belt is not needed for exercises that do not directly affect the lower back.
- For exercises directly stressing the back, an individual should refrain from wearing a belt during lighter sets, but may wear one for near-maximal and maximal sets. The beltless sets allow the deep abdominal muscles, which generate intra-abdominal pressure, to receive a training stimulus without placing excessive compressive forces on the intervertebral disks.
- Individuals may reasonably choose never to wear lifting belts if they build up the strength of their back muscles and the muscles that generate intra-abdominal pressure in a gradual and systematic manner and if they practice safe resistance training exercise techniques. Many world-class Olympic-style weightlifters never wear belts.

Shoulders

The shoulder is particularly prone to injury during resistance training, due to both its structure and the forces to which it is subjected during a training session. Like the hip, the shoulder is capable of rotating in any direction. The hip is a stable ball-and-socket joint, but the glenoid cavity of the shoulder, which holds the head of the humerus, is not a true socket and is significantly less stable.

The shoulder joint has the greatest range of motion of all the joints in the human body (6). It is so mobile that the head of the humerus can actually move 1 inch (2.5 cm) out of the glenoid cavity during normal movement (12); but the joint's excessive mobility contributes to its vulnerability, as does the proximity of the bones, muscles, tendons, ligaments, and bursae in the shoulder. A small degree of swelling in a muscle due to an injury, however minor, can bring about friction with adjacent structures that can worsen the original injury and cause damage to previously uninjured tissue.

The stability of the shoulder largely depends on the glenoid labrum, the joint synovium, and capsules, ligaments, muscles, tendons, and bursae (39). The rotator cuff muscles (supraspinatus, infraspinatus, subscapularis, and teres minor) and the pectorals are particularly instrumental in keeping the ball of the humerus in place (5). With the shoulder's great range of motion, its various structures can easily impinge on one another, causing tendinitis as well as inflammation and degeneration of contiguous tissue. High forces generated during resistance training can result in tearing of ligaments, muscles, and tendons. Athletes must take particular care when performing the various forms of the bench, incline, and shoulder press exercises because of the great stresses these place on the shoulder. For these exercises, it is particularly important to warm up with relatively light weights and to follow a program that exercises the shoulder in a balanced way, using all of its major movements (see the following section on movement-oriented exercise prescription). It is best to exercise at a controlled speed rather than to lower a weight rapidly and decelerate it sharply in the transition from the eccentric to the concentric phase of a repetition.

Knees

The knee is prone to injury because of its location between two long levers (the upper and lower leg). Flexion and extension about the knee occur almost exclusively in the sagittal plane. Rotation in the frontal plane and transverse plane is prevented mainly by ligamentous and cartilaginous stabilizing structures, yet it does not take a great amount of torque about the knee in the frontal plane to cause serious damage. Frontal plane torque on the knee occurs, for example, when a football player is hit at midleg from the side while his foot is planted firmly on the ground. Fortunately, in training, resistive torques occur almost exclusively within the knee's normal plane of rotation.

Of the various components of the knee, the patella and surrounding tissue are most susceptible to the kinds of forces encountered in resistance training (7). The patella's main function is to hold the quadriceps tendon away from the knee axis of rotation, thereby increasing the moment arm of the quadriceps group and its mechanical advantage (see figure 4.6). The high forces encountered by the patellar tendon during resistance training can lead to tendinitis, which is characterized by tenderness and swelling.

It is not unusual for individuals to use knee wraps during training or competition. The wraps vary from the thin, elastic, pull-on variety that can be purchased in drug stores to the heavy, specialized wraps sold only through weightlifting supply houses. The use of knee wraps, particularly the heavy ones, is most prevalent among powerlifters.

Very little research has been done on the efficacy of knee wraps. Detrimental side effects have been reported, however, including skin damage and chondromalacia patellae, the wearing down and roughening of the posterior surface of the patella (15).

Though there is no available evidence that wraps protect the knee against injury, an experiment conducted by Harman and Frykman showed that wraps can improve performance (15). Through a spring effect alone, heavy wraps around the knees added an average of 25 pounds (110 N) to squat lifting force. The notion that wraps work only by stabilizing the knee, lessening the athlete's fear of injury, or providing a kinesthetic cue is incorrect. The wraps actually provide direct help in extending the knee. On the basis of the lack of evidence that knee wraps prevent injury and the opinion of a number of health practitioners who assert that knee wraps can actually cause injury, athletes should probably minimize the use of wraps. If used at all, knee wraps should be limited to the sets with the heaviest loads (48).

How Can Athletes Reduce the Risk of Resistance Training Injuries?

- Perform one or more warm-up sets with relatively light weights, particularly for exercises that involve extensive use of the shoulder or knee.
- Perform basic exercises through a full range of motion. Perform only specialized supplementary exercises through limited ranges of motion.
- Use relatively light weights when introducing new exercises or resuming training after a layoff of two or more weeks.
- Do not ignore pain in or around the joints. Often, an athlete can continue training by using lighter weights with more repetitions, using different exercises, or both.
- Never attempt lifting maximal loads without proper preparation, which includes technique instruction in the exercise movement and practice with lighter weights.
- Performing several variations of an exercise results in more complete muscle development and joint stability (48). Lack of balance between muscles has been cited as a cause of athletic injury. For example, it is recommended that athletes perform exercise routines that maintain a ratio of knee flexion torque to extension torque of 0.67 to 0.77 at slow speed (60°/s), 0.80 to 0.91 at medium speed (180°/s), and 0.95 to 1.11 at fast speed (300°/s), as tested on an isokinetic device (35).
- Take care when incorporating plyometric drills into a training program. It is generally agreed that athletes should be strong in the back squat exercise before beginning a lower body plyometric program (41).

MOVEMENT ANALYSIS AND EXERCISE PRESCRIPTION

The concept of **specificity**, widely recognized in the field of resistance training (9), holds that training is most effective when resistance exercises are similar to the sport activity in which improvement is sought (the target activity). Although all athletes should use well-rounded, whole-body exercise routines, supplementary exercises specific to the sport can provide a training advantage and reduce the likelihood of injury. The simplest and most straightforward way to implement the principle of specificity is to select exercises similar to the target activity with regard to the joints about which movements occur and the directions of movement. In addition, joint ranges of motion in the training exercises should be at least as great as those in the target activity.

Biomechanical analysis of human movement can be used to quantitatively analyze the target activity. In the absence of the requisite equipment and expertise, however, simple visual observation is adequate for identifying the basic features of a sport movement. Exercises can then be selected that involve similar movement around the same joints. Slow-motion videotape can facilitate the observation. Also, moderately priced software is available (e.g., Dartfish) that enables more detailed analysis of sport movements captured in digital video.

Figure 4.16 presents a simple list of possible body movements that provides a manageable framework for a movement-oriented exercise prescription. Only movements in the frontal, sagittal, and transverse planes (see figure 4.10) are considered because, although few body movements occur only in these three major planes, there is enough overlap of training effects that exercising muscles within the planes also strengthens them for movements between the planes.

Wrist—sagittal
Flexion
Exercise: wrist curl
Sport: basketball free throw

Extension
Exercise: wrist extension
Sport: racquetball backhand

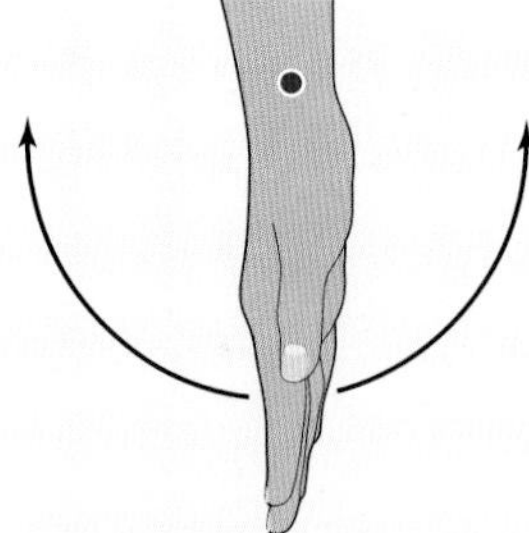

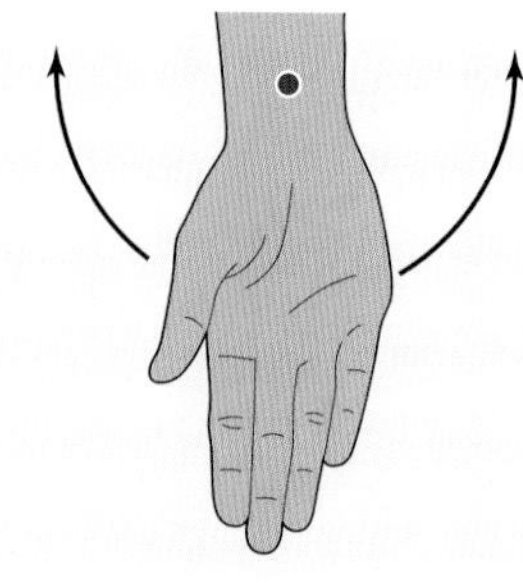

Wrist—frontal
Ulnar deviation
Exercise: specific wrist curl
Sport: baseball bat swing

Radial deviation
Exercise: specific wrist curl
Sport: golf backswing

Elbow—sagittal
Flexion
Exercise: biceps curl
Sport: bowling

Extension
Exercise: triceps pushdown
Sport: shot put

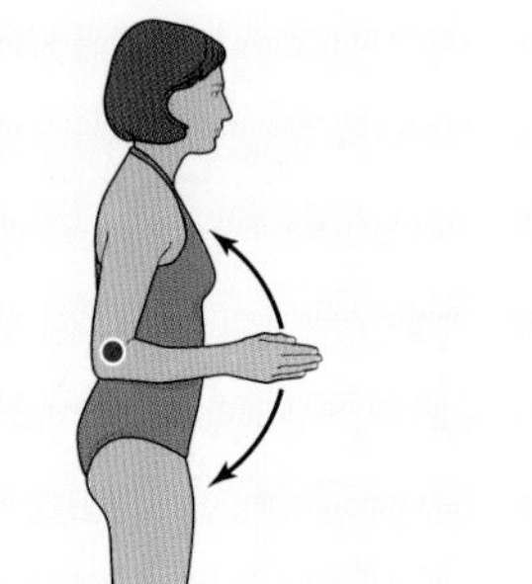

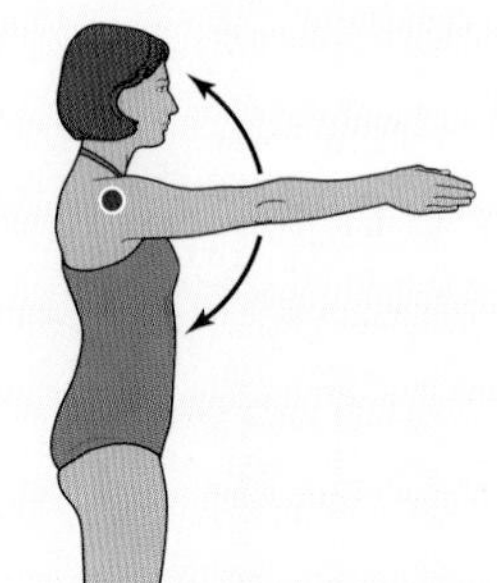

Shoulder—sagittal
Flexion
Exercise: front shoulder raise
Sport: boxing uppercut punch

Extension
Exercise: neutral-grip seated row
Sport: freestyle swimming stroke

Shoulder—frontal
Adduction
Exercise: wide-grip lat pulldown
Sport: swimming breast stroke

Abduction
Exercise: wide-grip shoulder press
Sport: springboard diving

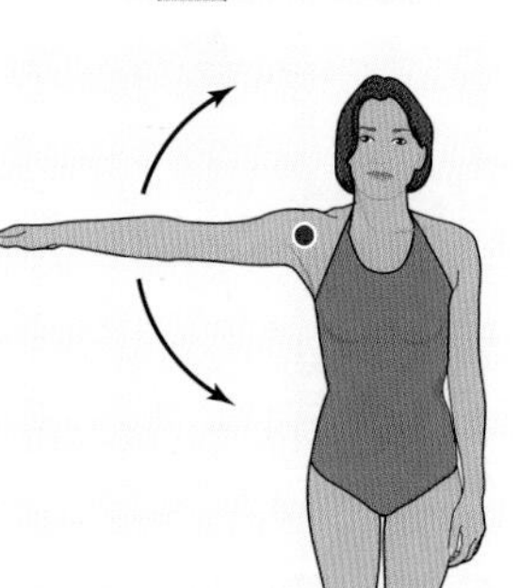

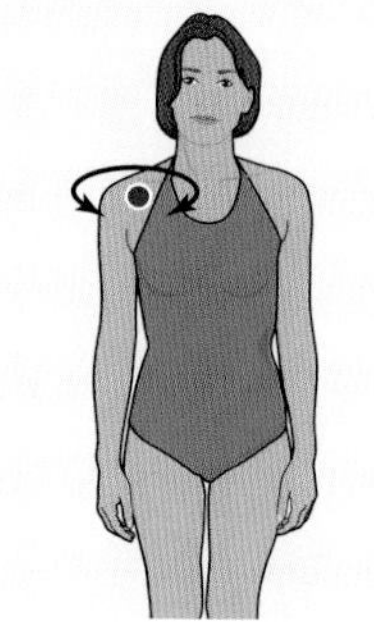

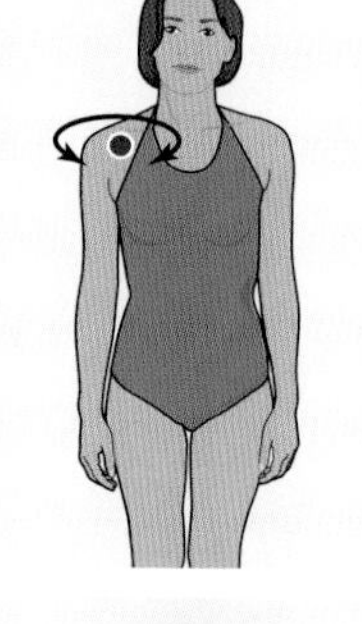

Shoulder—transverse
Internal rotation
Exercise: arm wrestle movement (with dumbbell or cable)
Sport: baseball pitch

External rotation
Exercise: reverse arm wrestle movement
Sport: karate block

Shoulder—transverse
(upper arm to 90° to trunk)
Adduction
Exercise: dumbbell chest fly
Sport: tennis forehand

Abduction
Exercise: bent-over lateral raise
Sport: tennis backhand

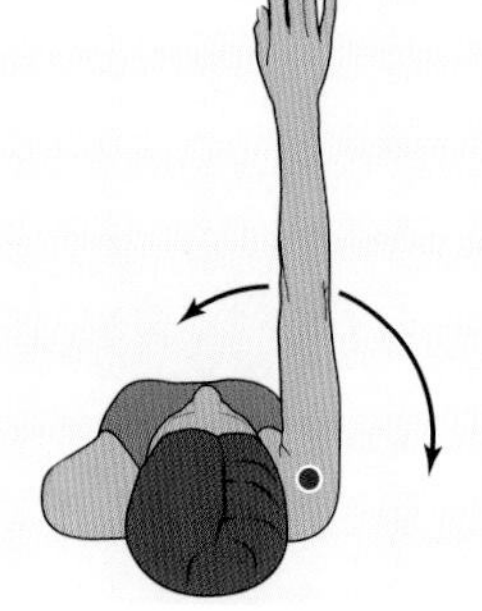

Neck—sagittal
Flexion
Exercise: neck machine
Sport: somersault

Extension
Exercise: dynamic back bridge
Sport: back flip

Neck—transverse
Left rotation
Exercise: manual resistance
Sport: wrestling movement

Right rotation
Exercise: manual resistance
Sport: wrestling movement

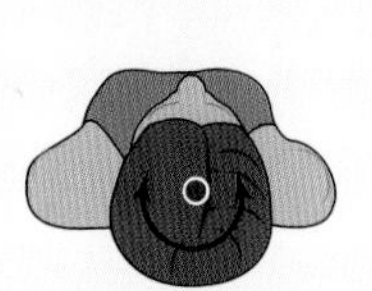

Neck—frontal
Left tilt
Exercise: neck machine
Sport: slalom skiing

Right tilt
Exercise: neck machine
Sport: slalom skiing

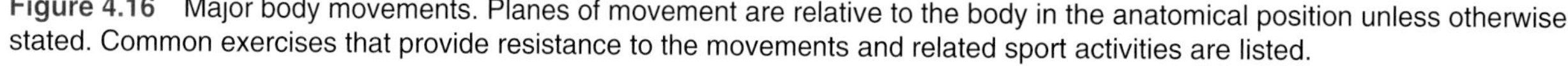

Figure 4.16 Major body movements. Planes of movement are relative to the body in the anatomical position unless otherwise stated. Common exercises that provide resistance to the movements and related sport activities are listed.

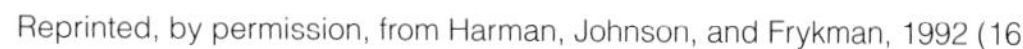

Reprinted, by permission, from Harman, Johnson, and Frykman, 1992 (16).

Lower back—sagittal
Flexion
Exercise: sit-up
Sport: javelin throw follow-through

Extension
Exercise: stiff-leg deadlift
Sport: back flip

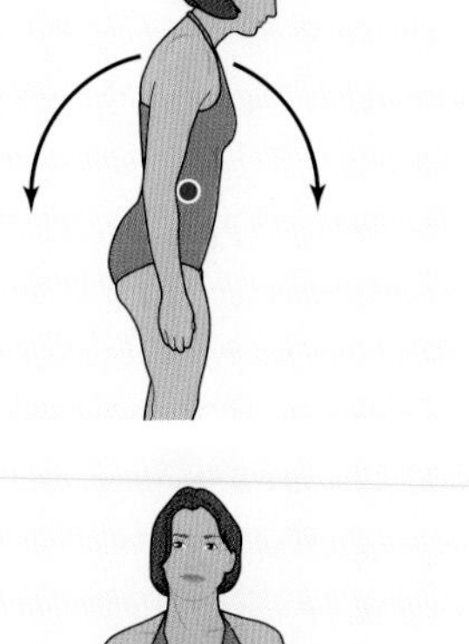

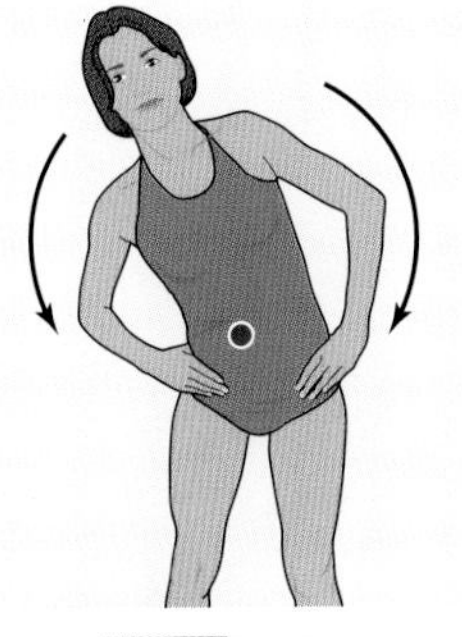

Lower back—frontal
Left tilt
Exercise: medicine ball overhead hook throw
Sport: gymnastics side aerial

Right tilt
Exercise: side bend
Sport: basketball hook shot

Lower back—transverse
Left rotation
Exercise: medicine ball side toss
Sport: baseball batting

Right rotation
Exercise: torso machine
Sport: golf swing

Hip—sagittal
Flexion
Exercise: leg raise
Sport: American football punt

Extension
Exercise: back squat
Sport: long jump take-off

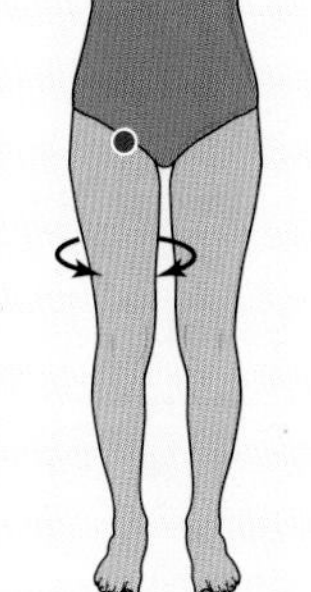

Hip—frontal
Adduction
Exercise: standing adduction machine
Sport: soccer side step

Abduction
Exercise: standing abduction machine
Sport: rollerblading

Hip—transverse
Internal rotation
Exercise: resisted internal rotation
Sport: basketball pivot movement

External rotation
Exercise: resisted external rotation
Sport: figure skating turn

Hip—transverse
(upper leg to 90° to trunk)
Adduction
Exercise: adduction machine
Sport: karate in-sweep

Abduction
Exercise: seated abduction machine
Sport: wrestling escape

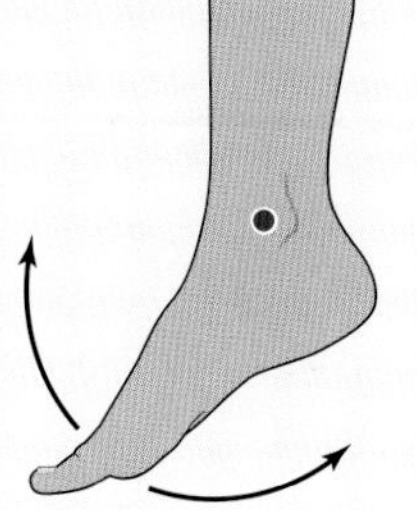

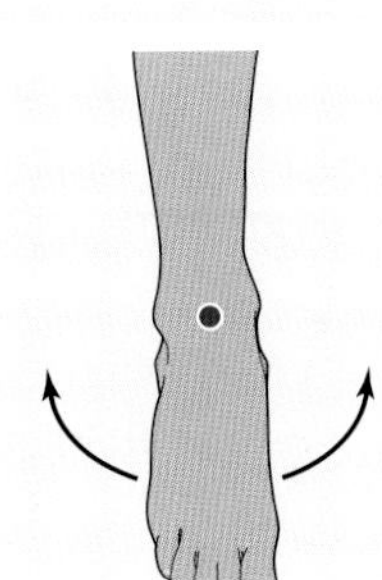

Knee—sagittal
Flexion
Exercise: leg (knee) curl
Sport: diving tuck

Extension
Exercise: leg (knee) extension
Sport: volleyball block

Ankle—sagittal
Dorsiflexion
Exercise: toe raise
Sport: running

Plantar flexion
Exercise: calf (heel) raise
Sport: high jump

Ankle—frontal
Inversion
Exercise: resisted inversion
Sport: soccer dribbling

Eversion
Exercise: resisted eversion
Sport: speed skating

Figure 4.16 *(continued)*

Reprinted, by permission, from Harman, Johnson, and Frykman, 1992 (16).

Specificity is a major consideration when one is designing an exercise program to improve performance in a particular sport activity. The sport movement must be analyzed qualitatively or quantitatively to determine the specific joint movements that contribute to the whole-body movement. Exercises that utilize similar joint movements are then emphasized in the resistance training program.

Although a program providing resistance exercise for all the movements in figure 4.16 would be both comprehensive and balanced, some of the movements are commonly omitted from standard exercise programs whereas others receive particular emphasis. Important sport movements not usually incorporated into standard resistance training programs include shoulder internal and external rotation (throwing, tennis), knee flexion (sprinting), hip flexion (kicking, sprinting), ankle dorsiflexion (running), hip internal and external rotation (pivoting), hip adduction and abduction (lateral cutting), torso rotation (throwing, batting), and the various neck movements (boxing, wrestling). A resistance training program designed around sport-specific exercise movements, however, is important for both improving performance and reducing the likelihood of injury.

Figure 4.16 can assist in the design of comprehensive and balanced training programs, determination of deficiencies in existing programs, and identification of exercises that could improve performance in particular sports. Visual observation of a sport, with or without the assistance of video, allows one to determine the movements that are particularly important to that sport. Sport-specific training exercises can be selected that provide resistance to relevant movements through the appropriate ranges of motion. Not only should the desired movement occur in an exercise, but the movement must be resisted (e.g., the biceps curl exercise involves both flexion and extension of the elbow, but only the flexion is resisted). Specificity of speed is important to consider as well. If a sport involves rapid application of force, then explosive exercises should be incorporated into the training program (46).

As an example of using figure 4.16 to qualitatively analyze a sport activity, we can look at the tennis serve. The following movements in the sagittal plane are key components of the tennis serve: lower back (torso) and hip flexion, shoulder extension, elbow extension, and wrist flexion (19). Thus, a basic resistance training program can include the leg raise, pullover, triceps pushdown, and wrist curl exercises. More specific exercises can include throwing a 4 to 6 pound (1.8 to 2.7 kg) ball forward and downward and executing the serving motion with a weighted racket.

CONCLUSION

It is hoped that readers will apply the biomechanical principles provided in this chapter to the selection of resistance exercise equipment and the design of exercise programs. Knowledge of how different types of exercise provide specific patterns of resistance to the body can aid in developing safe and effective programs to suit the specific needs of both athletes engaged in various sports and others who engage in resistance training for enhancement of physical performance, health, sense of well-being, and self-confidence.

KEY TERMS

acceleration 73
agonist 67
anatomical position 72
anatomy 66
angle of pennation 76
angular displacement 75
angular velocity 75
antagonist 67
appendicular skeleton 66
axial skeleton 66
biaxial joint 67
biomechanics 66
bracketing technique 81
cartilaginous joint 66
cervical vertebra 67
classic formula 79
coccygeal vertebra 67
concentric muscle action 78
distal 67
dorsal 85
eccentric muscle action 78
fibrous attachment 67
fibrous joint 66
first-class lever 69

fleshy attachment 67
fluid resistance 82
form drag 82
friction 82
frontal plane 72
fulcrum 68
hyaline cartilage 67
inertial force 81
insertion 67
isometric muscle action 78
joint 66
kyphotic 84
lever 68
lordotic 84
lumbar vertebra 67
mechanical advantage 69
moment arm 68
multiaxial joint 67
muscle force 69
origin 67
pennate muscle 76
power 74
proximal 67
rate coding 76
recruitment 75
resistive force 69
rotational power 75
rotational work 75
sacral vertebra 67
sagittal plane 72
second-class lever 69
specificity 87
strength 74
surface drag 82
synergist 67
synovial fluid 67
synovial joint 66
tendon 67
third-class lever 70
thoracic vertebra 67
torque 68
transverse plane 72
uniaxial joint 67
Valsalva maneuver 85
ventral 84
vertebral column 67
weight 74
work 74

STUDY QUESTIONS

1. Which of the following describes the knee joint?
    a. cartilaginous
    b. synovial
    c. ball-and-socket
    d. pivot
2. Which of the following is the definition of power?
    a. (mass) · (acceleration)
    b. (force) · (distance)
    c. (force) · (velocity)
    d. (torque) · (time)
3. To compare performances of Olympic weightlifters of different body weights, the classic formula divides the load lifted by the athlete's
    a. body weight.
    b. body weight squared.
    c. lean body weight.
    d. body weight to the two-thirds power.
4. During a free weight exercise, muscle force varies with which of the following?
    I. perpendicular distance from the weight to the body joint
    II. joint angle
    III. movement acceleration
    IV. movement velocity squared
    a. I and III only
    b. II and IV only
    c. I, II, and III only
    d. II, III, and IV only
5. A vertical jump involves knee, hip, and shoulder movement primarily in which of the following anatomical planes?
    a. sagittal
    b. perpendicular
    c. frontal
    d. transverse
6. An athlete is performing a concentric isokinetic elbow flexion and extension exercise. Which of the following types of levers occur at the elbow during this exercise?
    I. first-class
    II. second-class
    III. third-class
    a. I only
    b. II only
    c. I and III only
    d. II and III only

CHAPTER 5

Adaptations to Anaerobic Training Programs

Nicholas A. Ratamess, PhD

After completing this chapter, you will be able to

- discuss the ways in which force output of a muscle can be increased;
- discuss the basic neural adaptations to anaerobic training;
- explain the responses of bone, muscle, and connective tissue to anaerobic training;
- explain the acute responses and chronic adaptations of the endocrine and cardiovascular systems to anaerobic training;
- discuss the potential for enhancement of muscle strength, muscular endurance, power, flexibility, and motor performance during anaerobic training; and
- recognize the causes, signs, symptoms, and effects of overtraining and detraining.

Anaerobic training consists of high-intensity, intermittent bouts of exercise such as weight training; plyometric drills; and speed, agility, and interval training. In certain anaerobic training programs, aerobic metabolism is also highly involved and therefore concurrently trained (114). Performance adaptations to anaerobic training are specific to the training program; as a result, improvements in muscular strength, power, hypertrophy, muscular endurance, and motor skill performance will occur. Some exercises that stress the phosphagen system (e.g., sprints, plyometric drills) are under 10 seconds in duration and provide almost complete recovery between sets (e.g., 5-7 minutes) to enable training at maximal intensities (26). Speed and power training depend greatly on optimal neural recruitment for maximal performance (and high training quality), which requires recovery and minimal fatigue. Glycolytic conditioning uses shorter rest intervals during high-intensity exercise. Integrating these two metabolic demands is vital because many athletes must be able to perform under fatiguing conditions in competition, yet each metabolic component also needs to be trained specifically for optimal results. The aerobic system has limited involvement in high-intensity anaerobic activities but is more involved with recovery of energy stores. In addition to the demands of training, the metabolic demands of each sport (and practices) also contribute to the adaptations accompanying anaerobic training (table 5.1).

Critical physiological adaptations to the nervous, muscular, connective tissue, endocrine, and cardiovascular systems enable an individual to improve athletic performance following anaerobic training (see table 5.2). Adaptations range from those that take place in the early phase of training to those that take place through years of training. The majority of research has typically dealt with adaptations in the early to intermediate stages of training (i.e., 4 to 24 weeks). Understanding how the individual systems of the human body adapt to physical activity provides a knowledge base from which the strength and conditioning professional can predict the outcome of a specific training program.

NEURAL ADAPTATIONS

Anaerobic training may elicit adaptations along the neuromuscular chain beginning in the higher brain centers and continuing down to the level of individual muscle fibers (figure 5.1). An increase in neural drive is critical to the athlete striving to maximize strength and power. The increase in neural drive is thought to occur via increases in *agonist* (i.e., those major muscles involved in a specific movement or exercise) muscle recruitment, firing rate, and the timing and pattern of discharge during high-intensity muscular contractions. A reduction in inhibitory mechanisms (i.e., from Golgi tendon organs) is also thought to occur. Although it is not clear how these mechanisms coexist, it is apparent that neural adaptations are complex and typically occur before structural changes in skeletal muscle occur.

Central Adaptations

The ability to increase motor unit activation begins in the motor cortex with the intent to produce maximal levels of muscular force and power. The primary motor cortex activity increases when the

TABLE 5.1

Primary Metabolic Demands of Various Sports

Sport	Phosphagen system	Anaerobic glycolysis	Aerobic metabolism
Baseball	High	Low	—
Basketball	High	Moderate to high	—
Boxing	High	High	Moderate
Diving	High	Low	—
Fencing	High	Moderate	—
Field events	High	—	—
Field hockey	High	Moderate	Moderate
Football (American)	High	Moderate	Low
Gymnastics	High	Moderate	—
Golf	High	—	—
Ice hockey	High	Moderate	Moderate
Lacrosse	High	Moderate	Moderate
Marathon	Low	Low	High
Mixed martial arts	High	High	Moderate
Powerlifting	High	Low	Low
Skiing:			
Cross-country	Low	Low	High
Downhill	High	High	Moderate
Soccer	High	Moderate	Moderate
Strength competitions	High	Moderate to high	Low
Swimming:			
Short distance	High	Moderate	—
Long distance	—	Moderate	High
Tennis	High	Moderate	—
Track (athletics):			
Short distance	High	Moderate	—
Long distance	—	Moderate	High
Ultra-endurance events	Low	Low	High
Volleyball	High	Moderate	—
Wrestling	High	High	Moderate
Weightlifting	High	Low	Low

Note: All types of metabolism are involved to some extent in all activities.

TABLE 5.2

Physiological Adaptations to Resistance Training

Variable	Resistance training adaptations
Performance	
Muscular strength	Increases
Muscular endurance	Increases for high power output
Aerobic power	No change or increases slightly
Maximal rate of force production	Increases
Vertical jump	Ability increases
Anaerobic power	Increases
Sprint speed	Improves
Muscle fibers	
Fiber size	Increases
Capillary density	No change or decreases
Mitochondrial density	Decreases
Myofibrillar packing density	No change
Myofibrillar volume	Increases
Cytoplasmic density	Increases
Myosin heavy-chain protein	Increases in amount
Enzyme activity	
Creatine phosphokinase	Increases
Myokinase	Increases
Phosphofructokinase	Increases
Lactate dehydrogenase	No change or variable
Sodium-potassium ATPase	Increases
Metabolic energy stores	
Stored ATP	Increases
Stored creatine phosphate	Increases
Stored glycogen	Increases
Stored triglycerides	May increase
Connective tissue	
Ligament strength	May increase
Tendon strength	May increase
Collagen content	May increase
Bone density	No change or increases
Body composition	
% body fat	Decreases
Fat-free mass	Increases

ATP = adenosine triphosphate; ATPase = adenosine triphosphatase.

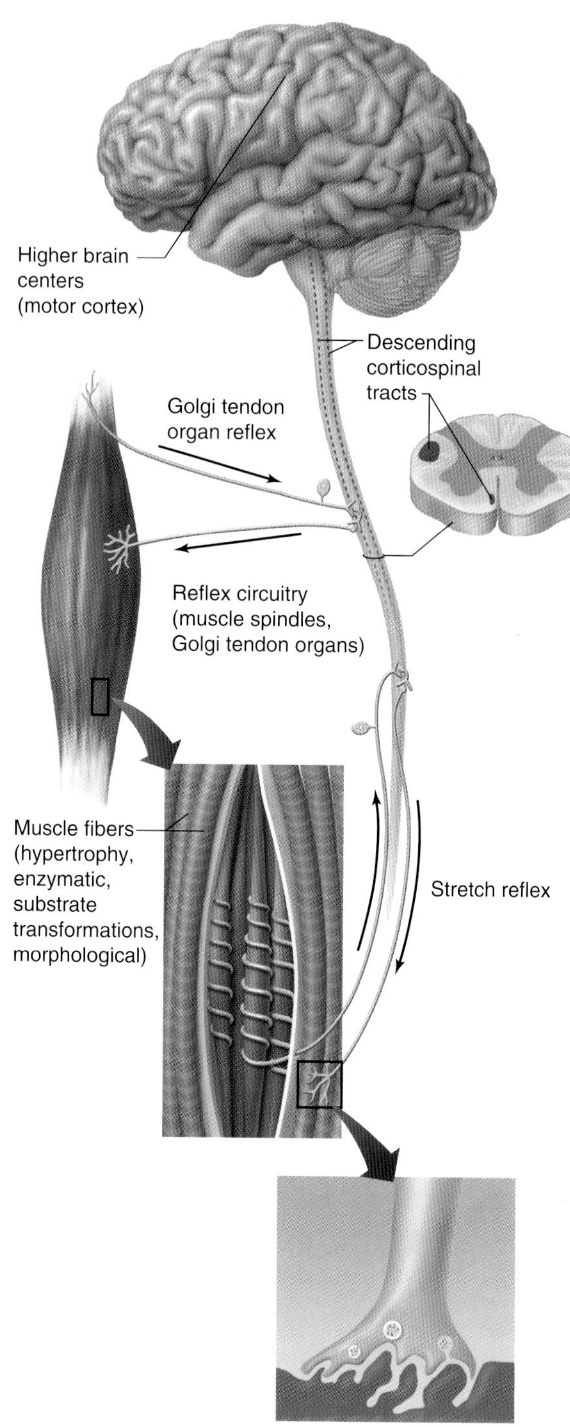

Figure 5.1 Potential sites of adaptation within the neuromuscular system.

level of force developed increases (43) and when new exercises or movements are being learned. A substantial proportion of the neural changes that occur during anaerobic training take place in the spinal cord along the descending corticospinal tracts. Untrained individuals display limited ability to maximally recruit motor units, especially fast-twitch units. Electrical stimulation has been shown to be more effective than voluntary activations in eliciting gains in untrained individuals or in those rehabilitating from injury, further indicating the potential inability to successfully activate all available muscle fibers in certain physiological conditions. A study by Adams and colleagues (7) using magnetic resonance imaging showed that only 71% of muscle tissue was activated during maximal effort in untrained individuals. However, training can greatly reduce this deficit (171), thereby demonstrating a greater potential to recruit fast-twitch motor units.

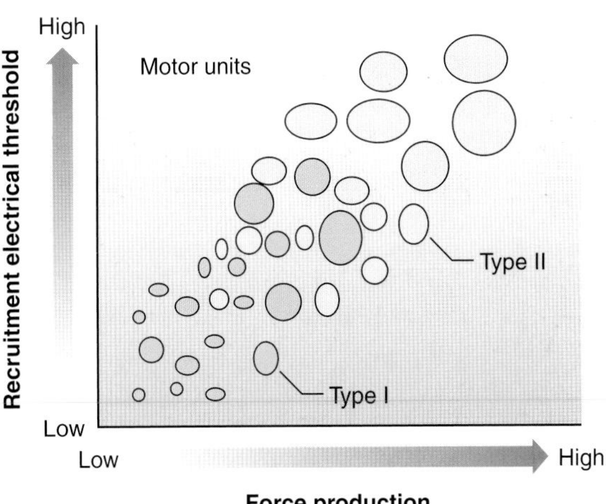

Figure 5.2 Graphic representation of the size principle, according to which motor units that contain Type I (slow-twitch) and Type II (fast-twitch) fibers are organized based on some "size" factor. Low-threshold motor units are recruited first and have lower force capabilities than higher-threshold motor units. Typically, to get to the high-threshold motor units, the body must first recruit the lower-threshold motor units. Exceptions exist, especially with respect to explosive, ballistic contractions that can selectively recruit high-threshold units to rapidly achieve more force and power.

Adaptations of Motor Units

The functional unit of the neuromuscular system is the motor unit (188). A motor unit consists of the alpha motor neuron and the associated muscle fibers that it activates. Motor neurons may innervate <10 muscle fibers for small, intricate muscles yet innervate >100 fibers for large, powerful trunk and limb muscles. When maximal force is desired from a muscle, all the available motor units must be activated. Different types of motor unit firing rates or frequencies affect muscle force. These firing rates are an adaptive mechanism improved by heavy resistance training (187, 188, 189). Maximal strength and power increases of agonist muscles generally result from an increase in recruitment, rate of firing, synchronization of firing, or a combination of these factors.

The recruitment and decruitment of motor units in an orderly manner is governed by the **size principle** (figure 5.2), which is based on the relationship between motor unit twitch force and recruitment threshold (187, 188, 189). Specifically, motor units are recruited in order according to their recruitment thresholds and firing rates, which results in a continuum of voluntary force in the agonist muscle. Because most muscles contain a range of Type I and II muscle fibers (as classified by their motor unit type), force production can range from very low levels to maximum. Before a high-threshold motor unit is recruited, all of the motor units below it are recruited sequentially. Thus, with heavy resistance training, all muscle fibers get larger, because for the most part they are all recruited to produce higher levels of force with heavier weights. Motor units high in the recruitment order are used primarily for high force, speed, or power production. Maximal force production requires not only the recruitment of a maximal percentage of available motor units, including the high-threshold motor units, but also the recruitment of these motor units at very high firing rates (188). Once a motor unit is recruited, less activation is needed in order for it to be rerecruited (78); this may have important ramifications for strength and power training as these high-threshold motor units may be more readily reactivated subsequent to previous recruitment.

With heavy resistance training, all muscle fibers get larger because they are all recruited in consecutive order by their size to produce high levels of force. In advanced lifters, the central nervous system might adapt by allowing these athletes to recruit some motor units not in consecutive order, recruiting larger ones first to help with greater production of power or speed in a movement.

A few exceptions to the size principle exist (59). That is, **selective recruitment** of fast-twitch motor units may occur under certain circumstances that allow an athlete to inhibit lower-threshold motor units and in their place activate the higher-threshold motor units critical to optimal speed and power performance. Rapid changes of direction in force production and ballistic muscular contractions (97, 164, 206), comparable to movements in plyometric, speed, power, and agility training, have been shown to lead to preferential recruitment of fast-twitch motor units. These variations in recruitment order may benefit high-velocity power training in which time of force production is vital to success. For example, it would be very difficult for an athlete to generate enough angular velocity and power to attain maximal height for the vertical jump test if that athlete had to recruit the entire slow-twitch motor unit pool prior to activation of the fast-twitch units. Because the time between the countermovement and the subsequent jump takeoff is often less than 0.4 second, there simply is not enough time to recruit all of the motor units in order and still be able to perform an explosive jump. Thus, selective recruitment appears to be a beneficial intrinsic neural mechanism favoring explosive exercise. In addition, specific training may enhance selective recruitment, which may improve sport performance (165).

Another critical element in recruitment is the level of tissue activation resulting from chronic resistance training for muscular hypertrophy. For example, a muscle does not require as much neural activation to lift a given load after its size increases. This was elegantly shown in a study by Ploutz and colleagues (174), who reported that fewer quadriceps muscle fibers were activated to lift a particular load after nine weeks of resistance training that resulted in a 5% increase in muscle size. These results demonstrate the importance of progressive overload during resistance training for allowing continual recruitment of an optimal amount of muscle tissue.

Other potential motor unit adaptations include changes in the rate and sequence of firing. A positive relationship exists between the amount of force produced and the rate of motor unit firing. The role of increasing firing rate (vs. recruitment) appears to be dependent on muscle size; smaller muscles rely more on an increased firing rate to enhance force production, whereas larger muscles rely more on recruitment. There is evidence to show that anaerobic training can enhance the firing rates of recruited motor units (3, 213). In addition, high firing rates at the onset of ballistic muscle contraction are especially critical to increasing the rate of force development (1). Thus, the ability to increase firing rate appears to be essential to anaerobic training for maximal force and power development. Resistance training may result in a more synchronized pattern (i.e., the firing of two or more motor units at a fixed interval) of activation during the exertion of large forces, rather than the customary asynchronous pattern usually common to motor function (54, 160, 194). Although the specific role played by motor unit synchronization during anaerobic training is unclear, it may be that synchronization is more critical to the *timing* of force production and less significant with regard to the overall level of force developed.

Neuromuscular Junction

The **neuromuscular junction (NMJ)** is the interface between the nerve and skeletal muscle and is another potential site for the occurrence of neural adaptations from anaerobic training (39, 40, 41, 42). The majority of studies on this subject have examined the impact of exercise training on the NMJ in animals and have shown that the NMJ adapts to exercise. Insights into NMJ changes with different intensities of exercise were demonstrated by Deschenes and colleagues (41), who examined the effects of high-intensity versus low-intensity treadmill exercise training on NMJ adaptations in the soleus muscle of rats. Both high- and low-intensity running increased the area of the NMJ. High-intensity training produced more dispersed, irregularly shaped synapses and a greater total length of nerve terminal branching compared to low-intensity training. Another study showed increased end-plate perimeter length and area, as well as greater dispersion of acetylcholine receptors within the end-plate region after seven weeks of resistance training (40). Thus, anaerobic training appears to produce morphological changes in the NMJ that are conducive to enhanced neural transmission.

Neuromuscular Reflex Potentiation

Anaerobic training may enhance the reflex (i.e., muscle spindle or stretch reflex) response, thereby enhancing the magnitude and rate of force development. Resistance training has been shown to increase reflex potentiation by 19% to 55% (4, 182). In addition, resistance-trained athletes (weightlifters, bodybuilders) have greater reflex potentiation in the soleus muscle compared to untrained individuals (192).

Anaerobic Training and Electromyography Studies

Electromyography (EMG) is a common research tool used to examine the magnitude of neural activation following training. An increase in EMG indicates greater neural activation; however, the precise mechanism(s) (i.e., increased recruitment, rate, or synchronization; Golgi tendon inhibition) cannot be determined using surface EMG. Several EMG studies have examined the effects of resistance and power training during periods of at least five weeks to over one year (178). Collectively, these studies have shown strength and power increases of up to 73%.

Approximately 70% of these studies have demonstrated increases in EMG following the training period, whereas the remaining 30% have not shown changes in EMG. An important consideration is the training status of the individual. Neural adaptations (improved motor learning and coordination) predominate early in training without significant increases in muscle hypertrophy (81, 83, 84, 86, 183). The onset of muscle hypertrophy is associated with declines in EMG (162). Thus, with advancement in training it appears that there exists an interplay between neural and hypertrophic mechanisms that contributes to further gains in strength and power.

In studies describing this relationship, Sale (187, 188, 189) reported that dramatic increases in neural adaptations take place early in the training program (6 to 10 weeks). As the duration of training increases (>10 weeks), muscle hypertrophy eventually occurs and contributes more than neural adaptations do to the strength and power gains observed. Although muscle hypertrophy eventually plateaus, if the athlete includes variation and progressive overload in training, neural adaptations will contribute to subsequent performance improvements. This pattern appears to replicate as training continues. As the athlete progresses in training, the type of program used may be one of the most important factors to consider. Neural factors may be especially important for strength gains in programs of very high intensity (>85% of 1-repetition maximum [1RM]) (162). Power training also appears to provide a potent stimulus to the nervous system and results in higher EMG posttraining (85).

Electromyography studies have also yielded some interesting findings regarding neural adaptations to anaerobic training:

- **Cross-education** occurs. That is, training only one limb can result in an increase in strength in the untrained limb. A recent review of the literature has shown that strength in the untrained limb may increase up to 22%, with an average strength increase of about 8% (163). The increase in strength in the untrained limb is accompanied by greater EMG (196), thereby suggesting that a central neural adaptation accounts for most of the strength gain.
- In untrained individuals, a **bilateral deficit** occurs. This means that the force produced when both limbs are contracting together is less than the sum of the forces they produce when contracting unilaterally. Research has shown that the corresponding EMG is lower during bilateral contractions (70, 168); this suggests that neural mechanisms are, at least in part, contributing factors. The bilateral deficit is reduced with bilateral training.
- The muscle activity of the antagonists during agonist movements has been shown to change in response to anaerobic training. Cocontraction of antagonist muscles is a mechanism to increase joint stability and reduce the risk of injury. However, too much antagonist activity can oppose agonist movement and therefore provide resistance to maximal force production. Anaerobic training has produced variable responses in antagonist muscle cocontraction. Some studies have shown reduced antagonist cocontraction following resistance training (28, 84, 171), whereas others do not demonstrate a change (193). In addition, sprint and plyometric training have been shown to change the timing of cocontraction activation (104). Although the specific role of altering antagonist cocontraction patterns is unclear, it does appear that the adaptations enhance force and power production and injury prevention. That is, greater antagonist activity may be seen during ballistic movements in which joint stability is a prime concern, but may be reduced during phases in which force production is needed (and joint stability is sufficient). It does appear that antagonist cocontraction is higher when people are unfamiliar with the task (52).

MUSCULAR ADAPTATIONS

Skeletal muscle adapts to anaerobic training primarily by increasing its size, facilitating fiber type transitions, and enhancing its biochemical and ultrastructural components (i.e., architecture, enzyme activity, and substrate concentrations). Collectively, these changes ultimately result in enhanced muscular strength, power, and muscular endurance, which are critical to athletic success.

Muscular Growth

Muscle **hypertrophy** refers to muscular enlargement resulting from training, primarily owing to an increase in the cross-sectional area (CSA) of the existing fibers (73). There is a positive relationship between muscle CSA and strength. The process of hypertrophy involves an increase in the net accretion (i.e., an increase in synthesis, reduction in degradation, or both) of the contractile proteins actin and myosin within the myofibril (151) and an increase in the number of myofibrils within a muscle fiber (150). The synthesis of other proteins (i.e., structural proteins such as **titin** and **nebulin**) also occurs in proportion to the myofilament changes. The new myofilaments are added to the periphery of the myofibril, resulting in an increase in its diameter. These adaptations create the cumulative effect of enlarging the fiber and, collectively, the associated muscle or muscle group. Mechanical loading leads to a series of intracellular processes that ultimately regulate gene expression and subsequent protein synthesis (186).

Several proteins (e.g., Ankrd2, Smpx, Sehrl) have recently been identified that are responsive to mechanical stress and that increase in activity prior to hypertrophy (105, 109). Recent studies have shown that resistance training has the potential to alter the activity of nearly 70 genes (181). In fact, upregulation of factors (e.g., myogenin and MyoD) involved with muscle regeneration (a process known as **myogenesis**) and downregulation of inhibitory growth factors (e.g., myostatin) have been shown following resistance exercise (18, 106, 111, 182). Further, protein synthesis is elevated after acute resistance exercise and remains elevated for up to 48 hours (146, 173). The magnitude of protein synthesis depends on carbohydrate and protein intake, amino acid availability, timing of nutrient intake, mechanical stress of the weight training workout, muscle cell hydration levels, and the anabolic hormonal and subsequent receptor response (19, 128, 179, 210).

The process of hypertrophy involves both an increase in the synthesis of the contractile proteins actin and myosin within the myofibril and an increase in the number of myofibrils within a muscle fiber. The new myofilaments are added to the external layers of the myofibril, resulting in an increase in its diameter.

Muscle fiber disruption and damage during intense resistance exercise are also a stimulus for muscle growth. The repair process of remodeling the muscle fiber may involve a host of regulatory mechanisms (e.g., hormonal, immune, and metabolic) interacting with the training status of the individual and the availability of protein. The sequence of protein synthesis involves (1) water uptake, (2) noncontractile protein synthesis, and (3) contractile protein synthesis. Reduced degradation maintains the size of fibers by stopping protein loss.

It may take at least a few weeks before muscle hypertrophy becomes evident during resistance training. With the initiation of a heavy resistance training program, changes in the types of muscle proteins (e.g., fast myosin heavy chains) start to take place within several workouts. However, muscle fiber hypertrophy appears to require a longer period of training time (>16 workouts) (201). Similar to power and strength improvements, initial gains in hypertrophy are the greatest, with the rate of muscle growth lessening over time. Athletes studied during two years of heavy resistance training showed increases in strength that paralleled optimization of training intensity, although muscle fiber hypertrophy contributed little to increased lifting performance (89).

The magnitude of hypertrophy ultimately depends on the training stimulus or program prescribed. Optimal muscle growth may result from maximizing the combination of mechanical and metabolic stimuli via training periodization (123). Mechanical factors include the lifting of heavy loads, inclusion of eccentric muscle actions, and low-to-moderate volume (all characteristic of strength training); metabolic factors center around low or moderate to moderately high intensity training with high volume using short rest intervals (characteristic of bodybuilding training) (127). The mechanical factors result in optimal recruitment of muscle fibers (as muscle fibers need to be recruited prior to growth), growth factor expression, and potential disruption to the sarcomeres, all of which increase muscle CSA (48, 75, 178). In addition, the metabolic factors stress the glycolytic energy system and result in increased metabolites that may be involved in muscle growth (197). These programs elicit the most potent anabolic hormonal response (128).

Another mechanism of increasing muscle size that has been debated by exercise scientists for years is hyperplasia. **Hyperplasia** results in an increase in the number of muscle fibers via longitudinal fiber splitting as a response to high-intensity resistance training. Hyperplasia has been shown to occur in animals (76, 77, 95), but the findings are controversial in human studies. Some reject the idea of hyperplasia in humans (144, 147), and other studies provide some support (145, 149, 209). Some cross-sectional studies comparing resistance-trained athletes to untrained individuals showed a greater number of fibers in the trained population. However, it is difficult to determine if this was due to genetics or hyperplasia. A longitudinal study from McCall and colleagues (155) showed indirect evidence for hyperplasia (i.e., a subpopulation of subjects exhibited greater fiber number, although there was no change when all subjects were analyzed) in the biceps brachii muscle following high-intensity resistance training. While hyperplasia cannot be completely ruled out, it does not appear to be a major strategy for muscle tissue adaptation to resistance training and, if it occurs at all, involves only a small amount of the stimulated tissue (maybe less than 10%) if the conditions are optimal (59, 60). One may hypothesize that if hyperplasia occurs, it may be in response to muscle fibers reaching a theoretical upper limit in size, which may occur in athletes using anabolic steroids and other growth agents or undergoing long-term training that produces large to extreme levels of hypertrophy.

Fiber Size Changes

The muscle fiber type is important in any discussion of the magnitude of muscle hypertrophy during anaerobic training. Muscle fibers, especially the high-threshold motor units governed by the size principle, must be activated in order to stimulate hypertrophy. During resistance training, both Type I and II muscle fibers are recruited and are therefore presented with a potent stimulus for adaptation. Resistance training typically results in increases in both Type I and Type II muscle fiber area. This fiber hypertrophy translates into increases in the CSA of the intact muscle after several months of training. However, muscle fiber hypertrophy does not occur uniformly between the two major fiber types. It has been shown that Type II fibers manifest greater increases in size than Type I fibers (92). In fact, it has been argued that the ultimate potential for hypertrophy may reside in the relative proportion of Type II fibers within a given athlete's muscles. That is, athletes who genetically possess a relatively large proportion of fast-twitch fibers may have a greater potential for increasing muscle mass with resistance training than individuals possessing predominately slow-twitch fibers.

Fiber Type Transitions

The pattern of neural stimulation dictates the extent of fiber type adaptations to anaerobic training. Muscle fibers represent a continuum from the most oxidative to the least oxidative type (see figure 5.3 and the description of muscle fiber types in chapter 1). The continuum is as follows: I, Ic, IIc, IIac, IIa, IIax, and IIx, with a concomitant myosin heavy chain (MHC) expression (i.e., MHCI, IIa, and IIx) (200). Although the proportions of Type I and II fibers are genetically determined, changes within each subtype can occur with anaerobic training. The changes in the fast-twitch fiber types have typically not been linked to the rate at which changes in the muscle fiber CSA take place. With training and activation of high-threshold motor units, there is a transition from Type IIx to IIa. In other words, Type IIx muscle fibers change their myosin adenosine triphosphatase (ATPase) isoform content and become progressively more oxidative IIa fibers. While some view the IIx fibers as strength and power fibers, if activated enough they become IIa fibers. Although still powerful, they become more oxidative and fatigue resistant with training. In fact, research has shown nearly full transitions from Type IIx to IIa fiber profiles following the combination of high-intensity resistance and aerobic endurance training (125).

It appears that Type IIx fibers are "reservoir" fibers that, upon consistent activation, change into a more oxidative form along the continuum (i.e., to an intermediate fiber Type IIax to IIa) (27, 215). It has become apparent that changes in the muscle fiber type continuum and associated MHCs occur early in a resistance training program. Staron and colleagues (201) examined the effects of a high-intensity resistance training protocol (multiple sets of the squat, leg press, and knee extension exercises using 6- to 12RM loads and 2-minute rest periods) performed by men and women two times per week

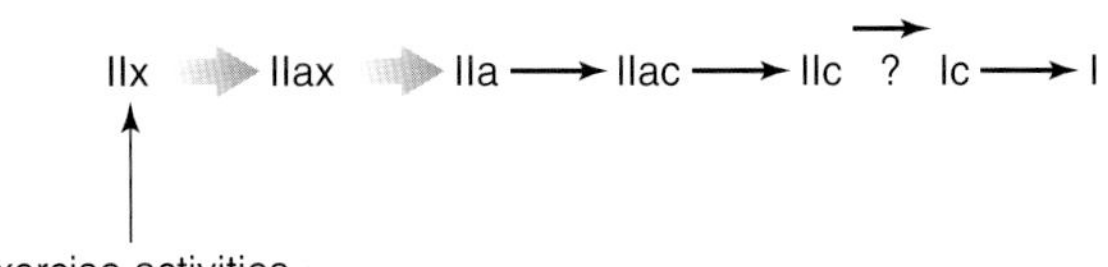

Figure 5.3 Muscle fiber transitions occur during training. This means that a shift of the type of myosin adenosine triphosphatase (ATPase) and heavy chains takes place during training. Transformations from IIx to IIax to IIa can be seen, and then small percentages change to IIac and IIc. Exercise activities that recruit motor units with Type IIx muscle fibers initiate a shift toward IIa fibers.

for eight weeks. They reported a significant decrease in the Type IIx percentage in women after just two weeks of training (four workouts) and in the men after four weeks of training (eight workouts). Over the eight-week training program, Type IIx fiber types decreased to about 7% of the total muscle fibers in both men and women. Analysis of the MHCs showed that in this early phase of training, IIx MHCs were replaced with IIa MHCs. In addition, this study demonstrated that changes in hormonal factors (testosterone and cortisol interactions) correlated with changes in muscle fiber type. Interestingly, detraining has the opposite effect, resulting in an increase in Type IIx fibers and a reduction in Type IIa fibers (172), with a possible overshoot of Type IIx fibers (i.e., higher IIx percentages than observed pretraining [10]). While transformation within the muscle fiber subtypes appears typical, transformation from Type I to Type II or vice versa appears less probable. Whether these transformations are possible remains doubtful at this point, as insufficient evidence is currently available. These possibilities need to be explored in future studies; it is intriguing to consider whether or not the continuum of adaptations extends beyond Type I and II subpopulations, especially during extreme cases in which a marathon runner (high percent of Type I fibers) follows a high-intensity resistance training program or a powerlifter (high percent Type II fibers) begins an extensive aerobic endurance training program.

Structural and Architectural Changes

Resistance training increases myofibrillar volume (143, 151), cytoplasmic density (148), sarcoplasmic reticulum and T-tubule density (8), and sodium-potassium ATPase activity (80, 108). Collectively, these changes accommodate muscle hypertrophy, enhance muscle function, and enable greater expression of strength. Sprint training has been shown to enhance calcium release (170), which assists in increasing speed and power production.

In pennate muscles, resistance training increases the angle of pennation (2). Cross-sectional studies show that strength-trained athletes have larger pennation angles in the triceps brachii and vastus lateralis muscles compared to untrained individuals (102). The increase in pennation angle is augmented by testosterone administration in addition to resistance training (21). Larger pennation angles can then accommodate greater protein deposition that allows greater or further increases in CSA. In addition, fascicle length was greater in the strength-trained athletes (102), and fascicle length of the gastrocnemius and vastus lateralis has been shown to be greater in sprinters compared to distance runners (5). Not all studies have shown an increase in fascicle length following resistance training (101). The combination of resistance, sprint, and jump training has been shown to increase rectus femoris fascicle length, and sprint and jump training have been shown to increase vastus lateralis fascicle length (20). These architectural changes affect the manner in which force is transmitted to tendons and bones.

Other Muscular Adaptations

Heavy resistance training reduces mitochondrial density in the trained muscles, a change that is attributable to increases in muscle size (151). Although the number of mitochondria may remain constant or increase, mitochondrial density is expressed relative to muscle area. Consequently, the density of mitochondria decreases with muscle hypertrophy. Muscle hypertrophy also results in decreased capillary density by similar mechanisms, although the number of capillaries per fiber may increase (202). However, decreases in mitochondrial and capillary densities do not necessarily reduce the ability to perform aerobic exercise (47, 94, 125). Powerlifters and Olympic weightlifters show significantly lower capillary densities than control subjects, whereas bodybuilders have capillary densities similar to those of nonathletes (119). Bodybuilding workouts produce high blood lactate concentrations; having more capillaries per fiber may assist in the clearance of metabolites from exercising muscle (11, 124, 208).

Several mechanisms can increase the buffering capacity of skeletal muscle, that is, increase its acid–base balance during exercise. Anaerobic exercise results in substantial reductions in muscle and blood pH (35). In response to consistent changes in pH via training, buffering capacity can improve. Increasing buffering capacity allows the athlete to tolerate higher concentrations of lactic acid, resulting in delayed fatigue and greater muscular endurance (195). Interval training (sprints, cycling) has been shown to increase buffering capacity significantly—by 16% to 38% (17, 195). The interval training program needs to be performed at a high enough intensity above the lactate threshold (50). Athletes competing in anaerobic team sports have been shown to have higher buffering capacity than endurance athletes and untrained control subjects (51). Thus, improving buffering capacity (in blood and within skeletal muscle) is essential to anaerobic training designed to enhance high-intensity muscular endurance.

Muscle substrate content and enzyme activity may change in response to anaerobic training. Heavy resistance training increases energy substrate levels and their availability in muscle (207). Repeated bouts of intermittent high-intensity contractions that reduce adenosine triphosphate (ATP) and creatine phosphate (CP) concentrations can increase the storage capacity of these high-energy compounds via a "supercompensation" effect (153). MacDougall and colleagues (153) reported a 28% increase in resting CP and an 18% increase in ATP concentrations following five months of resistance training (i.e., three to five sets of 8-10 repetitions with 2-minute rest periods). Increases in glycogen content of up to 112% have been shown following five months of resistance training (153), and it appears that bodybuilding-style programs (stressing anaerobic glycolysis) may be a potent stimulus for glycogen content enhancement.

CONNECTIVE TISSUE ADAPTATIONS

Bone, tendons, ligaments, fascia, and cartilage are examples of connective tissue. Exercise creates mechanical forces that cause deformation of specific regions of the skeleton. These forces, created by muscular actions on the tendinous insertion into bone, can be bending, compressive, or torsional in nature. In response to **mechanical loading**, **osteoblasts** migrate to the bone surface and begin bone modeling (figure 5.4). Osteoblasts manufacture and secrete proteins—primarily collagen molecules—that are deposited in the spaces between bone cells to increase strength. These proteins form the **bone matrix** and eventually become mineralized as calcium phosphate crystals (**hydroxyapatite**). New bone formation occurs predominantly on the outer surface of the bone (**periosteum**), increasing diameter and strength.

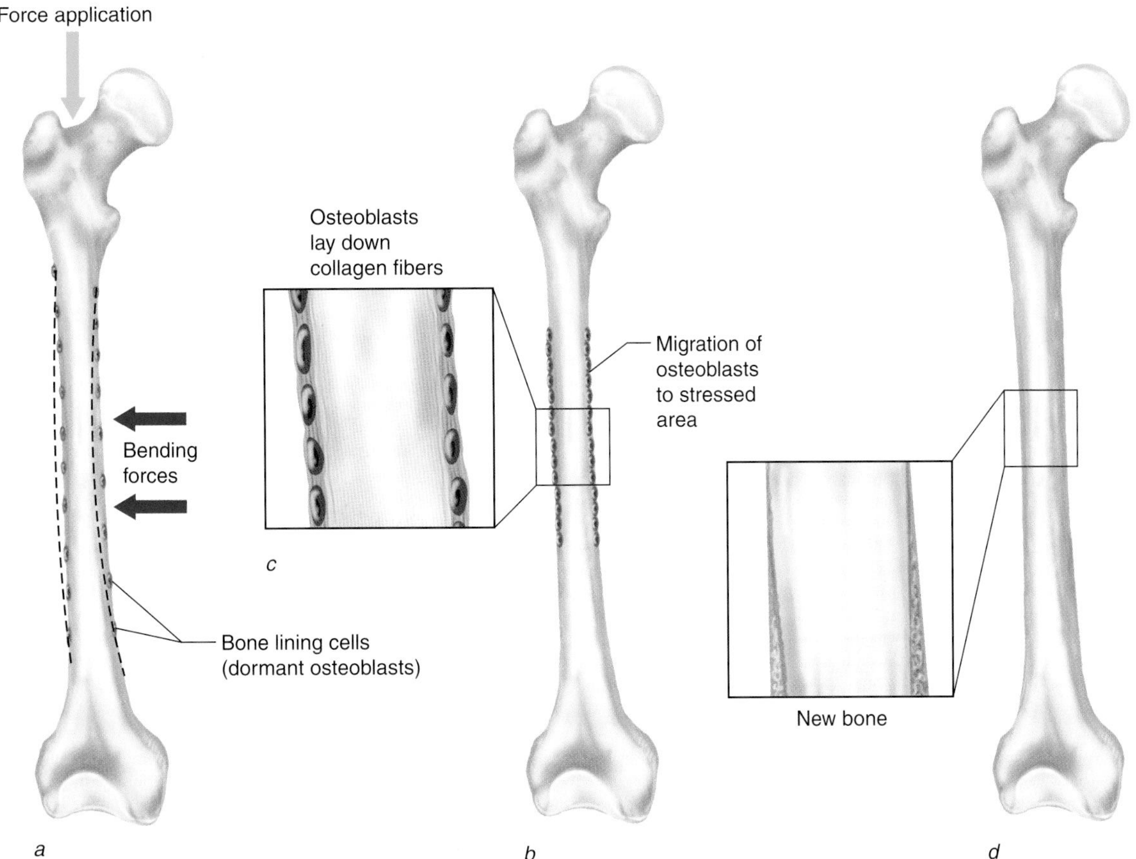

Figure 5.4 Bone modeling in response to mechanical loading. *(a)* Application of a longitudinal weight-bearing force causes the bone to bend (as depicted by the dotted line), creating a stimulus for new bone formation at the regions experiencing the greatest deformation. *(b)* Osteoblasts lay down additional collagen fibers at the site. *(c)* Previously dormant osteoblasts migrate to the area experiencing the strain. *(d)* The collagen fibers become mineralized, and the bone diameter effectively increases.

General Bone Physiology

Bone adaptations occur at different rates in the axial (skull/cranium, vertebral column, ribs, and sternum) and appendicular (shoulder girdle, pelvis, and bones of the upper and lower extremities) skeleton, owing to differing amounts of **trabecular** (spongy) **bone** and **cortical** (compact) **bone**. Cortical bone is dense and forms a compact outer shell that is bridged by trabecular bone. The spaces between the trabecular plates are occupied by bone marrow that consists of adipose tissue and blood products. Blood vessels from the marrow cavity extend into the dense cortical bone through a network of vertical and horizontal canals. Trabecular bone is able to respond more rapidly to stimuli than cortical bone.

✓ The term **minimal essential strain (MES)** refers to the threshold stimulus that initiates new bone formation. Consistently exceeding this threshold signals osteoblasts to migrate to the given region and form bone. Forces that fall below the MES do not present a stimulus for new bone formation. Physical activities that generate forces exceeding the MES are those activities that represent an increase in intensity and are weight bearing; these are most effective for bone formation. Bone cells regulate bone so that forces experienced on a regular basis do not exceed the MES, establishing a margin of safety against fracture. Strain registered by bone is a function of the force per unit area of bone (stress). The MES is thought to be approximately 1/10 of the force required to fracture bone. Increasing the diameter of bone allows the force to be distributed over a larger surface area, thereby decreasing the amount of mechanical stress. Following bone growth, the same force that previously exceeded the MES will now be below the MES threshold—demonstrating the importance of progressive overload for increasing bone size and strength.

> Forces that reach or exceed a threshold stimulus initiate new bone formation in the area experiencing the mechanical strain.

Anaerobic Training and Bone Growth

Muscle strength and hypertrophy gains increase the force exerted on the bones. Stronger forces of muscular contraction increase the mechanical stress on bone, and bone must subsequently increase in mass and strength to provide a sufficient support structure for hypertrophied muscles. Thus, an increase in muscle strength or mass may result in a corresponding increase in **bone mineral density (BMD)**, or the quantity of mineral deposited in a given area of bone (64, 100). Interestingly, inactivity or immobilization has the opposite effect on bone mass, resulting in a more rapid rate of loss of bone matrix and BMD. Numerous studies have shown a positive correlation between BMD and muscle strength and mass (175, 217). Researchers have reported that resistance-trained athletes have higher BMD than age-matched sedentary control subjects (31, 33, 185). In certain populations, physical activity seems to influence bone mass, area, and width more than BMD (22, 217). Thus, exercise that stimulates muscle hypertrophy and strength gains appears to stimulate bone growth.

✓The time course for bone adaptations is rather long. Quantitatively increasing BMD via resistance training is a long-term process—approximately six months or longer (30)—and depends on the structure of the program. However, the process of adaptation begins within the first few workouts. The process of osteogenesis involves secretion of substances into the blood (substances specific to bone only) that can be measured. Thus, an elevation in an osteogenic marker is an early indicator of bone formation and presumably a precursor to increases in BMD, provided that the stimulus is maintained over a long training period.

Principles of Training to Increase Bone Strength

Anaerobic training programs designed to stimulate bone growth need to incorporate specificity of loading, speed and direction of loading, volume, proper exercise selection, progressive overload, and variation (32). **Specificity of loading** entails using exercises that directly load a particular region of the skeleton. If the body interprets these forces as new or unusual, they will stimulate bone growth in the area receiving the strain. As a simple yet practical example, running may be a good stimulus for increasing BMD in the femur but the wrong choice for loading the wrist. The concept of specificity of loading becomes particularly important when a strength and conditioning professional prescribes exercises to increase bone mass in regions of the skeleton most commonly affected by **osteoporosis**—a disease in which BMD and bone mass become reduced to critically low levels. Research indicates that high-impact loading exercises for the lower body, such as gymnastics (204), volleyball, or basketball (44), selectively increase BMD at clinically relevant sites such as the hip and spine more than lower-impact activities do. Additionally, increases in BMD may be seen in highly trained college athletes with already high levels of BMD. These changes in BMD are independent of reproductive hormonal status if the stimulus is sufficient (204).

The selection of appropriate exercises to elicit maximal **osteogenic stimuli** (factors that stimulate new bone formation) is critical to increasing BMD. The exercises should involve multiple joints, should direct the force vectors through the spine and hip (i.e., **structural exercises**), and should apply loads heavier than single-joint assistance exercises. In fact, Cussler and colleagues (37) showed a linear relationship between the amount of weight lifted over the course of one year of training and increases in BMD. In addition, their findings pointed to exercise specificity in that the squat was most effective for increasing BMD of the trochanter of the femur (37). Use of single-joint exercises should be limited because these isolate a single muscle group by stabilizing the body with equipment support rather than skeletal support. Thus, structural exercises such as the back squat, power clean, deadlift, snatch, and push jerk (for the axial skeleton and lower body) and the shoulder press (for the upper body) are recommended for increasing bone strength.

Because bone responds favorably to mechanical forces, the principle of **progressive overload**—progressively placing greater than normal demands on the exercising musculature—applies to training to increase bone mass (79, 214). Although the maximal strength of bone is maintained well above the voluntary force capabilities of the associated musculature, bone responds to higher forces (e.g., 1- to 10RM loads) that are repetitively applied. The adaptive response ensures that forces do not exceed a critical level that increases the risk of **stress fractures** (microfractures in bone due to structural fatigue). Support for progressive overload comes from studies that have compared BMD of various groups of athletes to that of nonathletes (44, 166, 217). In fact, elite adolescent weightlifters have been found to possess levels of bone mineralization that far exceed values found in untrained adults (33, 214). This observation is interesting because it indicates that young bone may be more responsive to osteogenic stimuli than mature bone. Evidence indicates that physical activity during growth modulates the external geometry and trabecular architecture of bone, potentially enhancing skeletal strength (29, 93). These studies have led to the hypothesis that, in order to avoid low bone mass in old age, individuals should train to maximally elevate their **peak bone mass**—the maximum bone mass achieved—during early adulthood.

Another important consideration in the design of programs to stimulate new bone formation is variation. The internal architecture of the human skeleton has a mechanism through which it compensates for new strain patterns experienced by the bone. To optimally dissipate the imposed forces, the direction of the collagen fibers within the bone matrix may change to conform to the lines of stress experienced by the bone. Thus, changing the distribution (and direction) of the force vectors by using a variety of exercises continually presents a unique stimulus for new bone formation within a given region of bone. Overall, if the magnitude of the load, rate of force application, or both are sufficient, it is not typically necessary to perform more than a total of 30 to 35 repetitions, as a greater volume of loading is not likely to provide any additional stimulus for bone growth (63, 198).

The components of mechanical load that stimulate bone growth are the magnitude of the load (intensity), rate (speed) of loading, direction of the forces, and volume of loading (number of repetitions).

How Can Athletes Stimulate Bone Formation?

- Use exercises that directly load particular regions of the skeleton.
- Use structural exercises, that is, exercises that involve many muscle groups at once, direct force vectors through the spine and hip, and apply loads heavier than single-joint assistance exercises.
- Progressively overload the musculoskeletal system, and progressively increase the load as the tissues become accustomed to the stimulus.
- Vary exercise selection, changing the distribution of the force vectors to continually present a unique stimulus for new bone formation.

Programs designed to stimulate new bone formation should incorporate the concepts of specificity of loading, proper exercise selection, progressive overload, and variation. The exercises selected should be structural and weight bearing.

Adaptations of Tendons, Ligaments, and Fascia to Anaerobic Training

Tendons, ligaments, fascia, and cartilage are complex and dynamic structures that are the critical link between muscles and bones. The primary structural component of all connective tissue is the **collagen** fiber (Type I for bone, tendon, and ligaments and Type II for cartilage; figure 5.5) (218). The parent protein, **procollagen**, is synthesized and secreted by fibroblasts. Procollagen molecules consist of three protein strands twisted around each other in a triple helix. Procollagen leaves the cell with protective extensions on the ends to prevent premature collagen formation. Cleavage of the extensions via enzymes results in the formation of active collagen that aligns with other collagen molecules to form a long filament. Measurement of these enzymes provides an indication of collagen metabolism. In fact, enzyme levels increase in response to training, thereby showing increased net Type I collagen synthesis (140). The parallel arrangement of filaments is called a **microfibril**. Collagen has a striated (striped) appearance under a light microscope, somewhat like skeletal muscle, owing to the orderly alignment of the gaps between the collagen molecules within a microfibril. Microfibrils become arranged into fibers, and the fibers into larger bundles. The true strength of collagen comes from the strong chemical bonds (**cross-linking**) that form between adjacent collagen molecules throughout the collagen bundles. Collagen bundles are bunched together longitudinally to form tendons or ligaments, or are arranged into sheets with the layers oriented in different directions, as found in bone, cartilage, and fascia.

Tendons and ligaments are composed primarily of tightly packed, parallel arrangements of collagen bundles. Mature tendons and ligaments contain relatively few cells. The small number of metabolically

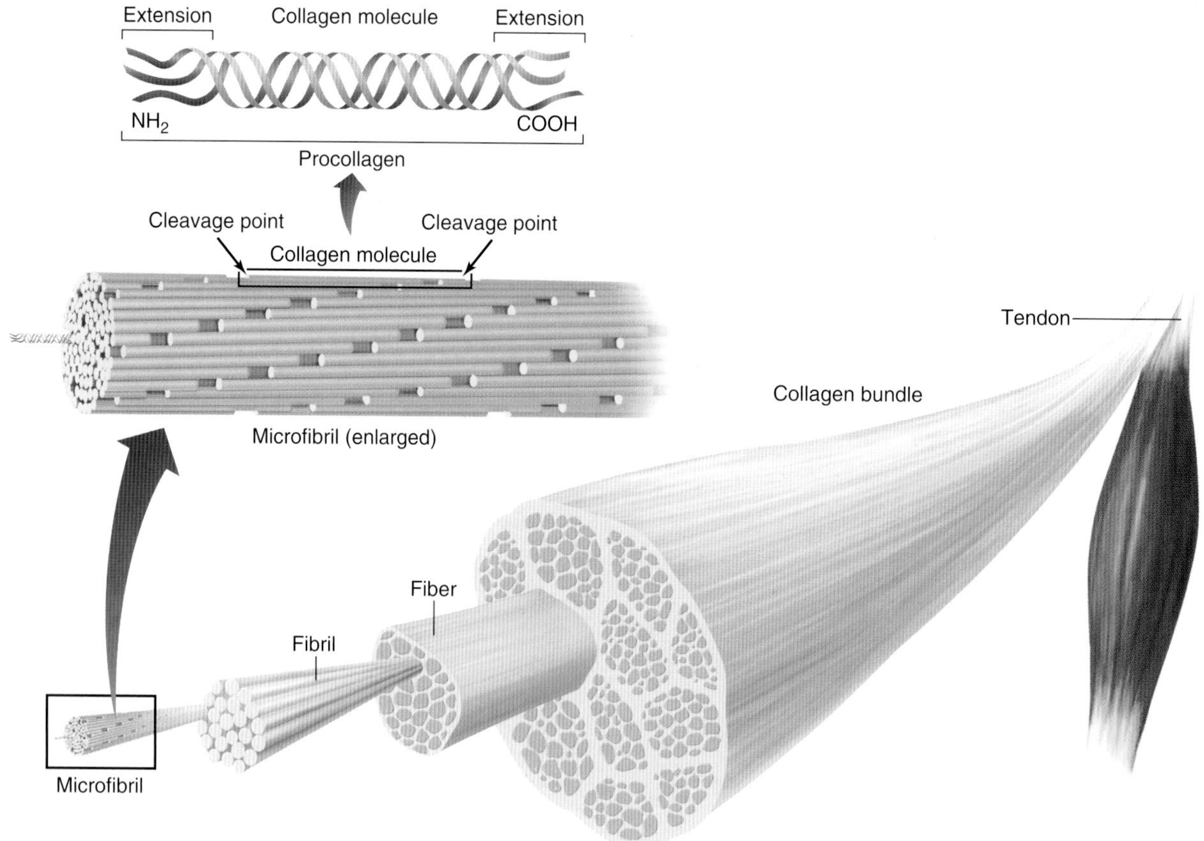

Figure 5.5 Formation of a collagen fiber.

active cells in tendons and ligaments makes the requirement for oxygen and nutrients in these tissues relatively low. Ligaments contain elastic fibers (**elastin**) in addition to collagen. A certain amount of stretch is needed within a ligament to allow normal joint motion. Tendons and ligaments attach to bone with great strength, allowing the maximal transmission of forces. The fibrous connective tissues that surround and separate the different organizational levels within skeletal muscle are referred to as fascia. Fascia have sheets of fibrocollagenous support tissue containing bundles of collagen fibers arranged in different planes to provide resistance to forces from different directions. Fascia within muscles converge together near the end of the muscle to form a tendon through which the force of muscle contraction is transmitted to bone. Compared with that of muscle tissue, tendon metabolism is much slower due to poorer vascularity and circulation (99). In fact, the increase in blood flow to skeletal muscle via exercise is not paralleled by the same flow perfusion in tendons (107).

The primary stimulus for growth of tendons, ligaments, and fascia is the mechanical forces created during exercise. The degree of tissue adaptation appears to be proportional to the intensity of exercise. Consistent anaerobic exercise that exceeds the threshold of strain stimulates connective tissue changes.

Empirical evidence suggests that connective tissues must increase their functional capabilities in response to increased muscle strength and hypertrophy. The sites where connective tissues can increase strength and load-bearing capacity are

- at the junctions between the tendon (and ligament) and bone surface,
- within the body of the tendon or ligament, and
- in the network of fascia within skeletal muscle.

Stronger muscles pull with greater force on their bony attachments and cause an increase in bone mass at the tendon-bone junction and along the line over which the forces are distributed. Such adaptation occurs in the collateral knee ligaments of experimental animals following several weeks of treadmill running (210). Additionally, animals trained on treadmills with uneven surfaces have shown even greater tendon-bone junction strength compared with animals trained on smooth surfaces (6). The adaptation that occurs at the tendon-bone junction is quite effective. The point of ligament rupture in animals moves from the tendon-bone junction in untrained animals to within the body of the tendon or ligament after chronic exercise training (34).

High-intensity anaerobic training results in connective tissue growth and other ultrastructural changes that enhance force transmission. Specific changes within a tendon that contribute to its increase in size and strength include

- an increase in collagen fibril diameter,
- a greater number of covalent cross-links within the hypertrophied fiber,
- an increase in the number of collagen fibrils, and
- an increase in the packing density of collagen fibrils.

Collectively, these adaptations increase the tendon's ability to withstand greater tensional forces (161).

Muscle hypertrophy in animals relates to an increase in the number and size of fibroblasts, thereby resulting in a greater supply of total collagen. Activation of fibroblasts and subsequent growth of the connective tissue network are prerequisites for hypertrophy of active muscle (98, 212). This may explain why biopsies of trained athletes have shown that hypertrophied muscle contains greater total collagen but that the collagen content remains proportional to the existing muscle mass (161). Recent studies indicate that **tendon stiffness** (force transmission per unit of strain, or tendon elongation) increases as a result of resistance training (138). In fact, Kubo and colleagues (136) reported a 15% to 19% increase in Achilles tendon stiffness following eight weeks of resistance training. The intensity is critical, as heavy loads (80% of 1RM) increase tendon stiffness but light loads (20% of 1RM) do not (137).

Adaptations of Cartilage to Anaerobic Training

Cartilage is a dense connective tissue capable of withstanding considerable force without damage to its structure. The main functions of cartilage are to

- provide a smooth joint articulating surface,
- act as a shock absorber for forces directed through the joint, and
- aid in the attachment of connective tissue to the skeleton.

A feature unique to cartilage is that it lacks its own blood supply and must depend on diffusion of oxygen and nutrients from synovial fluid (which is why cartilage does not easily repair itself following injury). Two primary types of cartilage are significant in relation to physical activity. **Hyaline cartilage** (articular cartilage) is found on the articulating surfaces of bones. **Fibrous cartilage** is a very tough form of cartilage found in the intervertebral disks of the spine and at the junctions where tendons attach to bone.

The fact that articular cartilage gets its nutrient supply by diffusion from synovial fluid links joint mobility to joint health. Movement about a joint creates changes in pressure in the joint capsule that drive nutrients from the synovial fluid toward the articular cartilage of the joint (199). Immobilization of a joint prevents proper diffusion of oxygen and essential nutrients throughout the joint, resulting in the death of the chondrocytes and resorption of the cartilage matrix. Further support is evidenced in a knee joint, where the surfaces of the joint that experience the greatest degree of weight bearing are thicker than non-weight-bearing surfaces (169). Animal studies evaluating the effect of chronic aerobic exercise on articular cartilage have shown increased articular cartilage thickness (184). Less is known about chronic anaerobic training and cartilage changes in humans, although it is thought that training has a positive effect on cartilage structure.

How Can Athletes Stimulate Connective Tissue Adaptations?

Tendons, Ligaments, Fascia

- Exercise of low to moderate intensity does not markedly change the collagen content of connective tissue.
- High-intensity loading results in a net growth of the involved connective tissues.

Cartilage

- Weight-bearing forces and complete movement throughout the range of motion seem to be essential to maintaining tissue viability.
- Moderate aerobic exercise seems adequate for increasing cartilage thickness. Strenuous exercise does not appear to cause degenerative joint disease.

ENDOCRINE RESPONSES AND ADAPTATIONS TO ANAEROBIC TRAINING

Hormones play a multitude of important regulatory roles in adaptation to anaerobic training (112, 113). Anabolic hormones such as testosterone, insulin, insulin-like growth factors, and the growth hormone "superfamily" all influence the development of muscle, bone, and connective tissue. Hormones are involved in a wide variety of homeostatic mechanisms that are dedicated to keeping the body's functions within a normal range during rest and exercise (67, 68, 117, 121). As discussed in chapter 3, acute elevations in circulating hormones (resulting from either increased secretion, reduced hepatic clearance, plasma volume reductions, or reduced degradation rates) observed during and immediately following a workout lead to a greater likelihood of interaction either with receptors on target tissue cell membranes (e.g., peptide hormones) or with nuclear or cytoplasmic receptors located within the target tissue (e.g., steroid hormones). Coinciding with blood hormonal concentrations is the number of available receptors for binding. Interaction with the receptor initiates a series of events ultimately leading to muscle size and strength gains (126, 128). Endocrine adaptations and responses to anaerobic training fall within four general classifications: (1) acute changes during and after exercise, (2) chronic changes in resting concentrations, (3) chronic changes in the acute response to a workout, and (4) changes in receptor content.

Acute Anabolic Hormonal Responses

Anaerobic exercise, especially resistance exercise, has been shown to result in elevated testosterone (total and free), growth hormone and its molecular variants, and cortisol for up to 15 to 30 minutes postexercise in men (114, 115, 116, 121, 128, 132). Hormonal fluctuations occur quickly and then stabilize in response to homeostatic challenges both from the initial demands of acute exercise (134, 201) and over longer-term training (156). Testosterone elevations are most prominent in men, although some studies have shown slight testosterone elevations in women (167). Interestingly, the acute elevation in free testosterone has been shown to be greater in resistance-trained men than aerobic endurance-trained men (211). The magnitude of testosterone, cortisol, and growth hormone elevation is greatest when large muscle mass exercises are performed and during workouts with moderate to high intensity and volume and short rest intervals. In fact, high correlations between blood lactate and growth hormone concentrations have been reported (87), and it is thought that hydrogen ion accumulation may be the primary factor influencing growth hormone and cortisol release. When large muscle mass exercises are performed early in a workout, they have a positive effect (i.e., produce greater strength and hypertrophy changes) on smaller muscle mass exercises performed later due, in part, to an enhanced testosterone response (91).

The acute anabolic hormonal response to anaerobic exercise is critical for exercise performance and subsequent training adaptations. Upregulation of anabolic hormone receptors is important for mediating the hormonal effects.

The acute response of circulating IGF-I is often delayed and dependent upon the acute growth hormone response. However, IGF-I has a counterpart produced in skeletal muscle in response to mechanical loading (a *mechano growth factor*), which acts independently of growth hormone and is upregulated following resistance exercise (74). In addition, insulin secretion rates parallel blood glucose and amino acid changes. Thus, insulin is mostly affected by supplementation before, during, or after exercise and not by the anaerobic exercise stimulus. Lastly, catecholamines (epinephrine, norepinephrine, dopamine) reflect the acute demands of anaerobic exercise and are important for increasing force production, muscle contraction rate, energy availability, and augmentation of other hormones such as testosterone. Resistance exercise increases concentrations of epinephrine, norepinephrine, and dopamine (24, 116, 124). The magnitude may be dependent on the force of muscle contraction, amount of muscle stimulated, volume of resistance exercise, and rest period length.

Chronic Changes in the Acute Hormonal Response

As a result of consistent resistance training, the acute hormonal response to an anaerobic workout may improve as the individual is gradually able to exert more effort in successive training sessions. This effect has been shown predominantly with growth hormone. Twelve weeks of resistance training in elderly persons was shown to promote greater acute growth hormone response to a workout (36). The greater hormonal response patterns to maximal exercise appear to augment the individual's ability to tolerate and sustain prolonged high exercise intensities. Thus, progressive overload is a critical training tenet for potentially enhancing the acute hormonal response.

Chronic Changes in Resting Hormonal Concentrations

Consistent chronic changes in resting hormonal concentrations are less likely—as several studies have shown either elevations, reductions, or no change in testosterone, growth hormone, IGF-I, and cortisol over time (128). It appears that resting concentrations reflect the current state of muscle tissue such that short-term elevations or reductions may occur at various stages, depending on substantial changes in the volume and intensity of training or nutritional factors. This may be especially true for testosterone; however, growth hormone overnight pulsatility may be altered as a result of resistance exercise (167). Thus, the elevation during and immediately following a workout may present receptors with enough of a stimulus to affect tissue remodeling without attenuating receptor content or function. It is important to note that chronic elevations in an anabolic hormone may be counterproductive over the long term. For example, receptors tend to downregulate over time when exposed consistently to high levels of hormones. This is why anabolic steroid users repeatedly cycle drug use rather than maintaining consistently high doses. Receptor desensitization reduces the impact of the quantum of hormone released. Therefore, the lack of consistent resting changes, coupled with acute elevations during and following a workout, may be viewed as advantageous for reducing receptor downregulation and optimizing tissue remodeling.

Hormone Receptor Changes

Receptor content is important in mediating the adaptations elicited by the hormonal response. Although glucocorticoid and growth hormone receptors have received some attention, a critical receptor that is often studied is the androgen receptor (AR), as it interacts with testosterone and testosterone derivatives. Androgen receptor content depends on several factors including muscle fiber type, contractile activity, and the concentrations of testosterone. Resistance training has been shown to upregulate AR content within 48 to 72 hours after the workout (14). The resistance exercise stimulus appears to mediate the magnitude of acute AR modifications. Ratamess and colleagues (179) compared one set versus six sets of 10 repetitions of squats and reported no differences in AR content following the single-set protocol; however, the higher-volume protocol elicited significant downregulation of AR content 1 hour after the workout. This study also demonstrated that when sufficient volume is reached, AR protein content may initially downregulate, prior to the upregulation that has been shown in other studies. However, Kraemer and colleagues (133) have shown that consumption of a protein-carbohydrate supplement before and after the workout attenuates this AR downregulation.

CARDIOVASCULAR AND RESPIRATORY RESPONSES TO ACUTE EXERCISE

Acute and chronic anaerobic exercise have a significant impact on cardiovascular and respiratory function. This has been evidenced by enhanced cardiac function and dimensions in anaerobic athletes (55). Acute and chronic responses to heavy-load resistance training are differentiated when possible from responses to more repetitions of light loads with less rest. Resistance training can benefit the cardiovascular system, but in a manner different from conventional aerobic endurance training (56). Improved ability of the heart, lungs, and circulatory system to function under conditions of high pressure and force production can prepare the athlete's body for extreme competitive demands.

Acute Cardiovascular Responses to Anaerobic Exercise

An acute bout of anaerobic exercise significantly increases the cardiovascular responses, especially if the individual uses the Valsalva maneuver (see chapter 4). Heart rate, stroke volume, cardiac output, and blood pressure increase significantly during resistance exercise (57). Peak blood pressures of 320/250 mmHg and a heart rate of 170 beats/min have been reported during a high-intensity (i.e., 95% of 1RM) leg press exercise (152). Generally, the blood pressure response increases nonlinearly with the magnitude of active muscle mass and is higher during the concentric phase of each repetition than during the eccentric phase, especially at the sticking point of an exercise (57). Although large elevations in blood pressure have been shown, no data exist to indicate that resistance training has any negative effects on resting blood pressure. In addition, intrathoracic pressure increases and plasma volume reductions of up to 22% have been reported (174, 179).

Acute anaerobic exercise results in increased cardiac output, stroke volume, heart rate, oxygen uptake, systolic blood pressure, and blood flow to active muscles.

During a set of resistance exercise, stroke volume and cardiac output increase mostly during the eccentric phase of each repetition, especially when the Valsalva maneuver is used (53). Because the concentric phase of a repetition is much more difficult and elevations in intrathoracic and intra-abdominal pressures are more prominent (via the Valsalva maneuver), limiting venous return and reducing end-diastolic volume, the hemodynamic response of resistance exercise is delayed such that cardiac output increases more during the eccentric phase or during the rest period between sets. This is especially true for an individual's heart rate response; during the first 5 seconds after completion of a set, heart rate is higher than during the set (177).

The degree to which blood flow is increased in the working muscles during resistance training depends on intensity of resistance, length of time of effort (i.e., the number of repetitions performed), and size of the muscle mass. Lower resistances lifted for many repetitions produce responses relatively similar to those with aerobic exercise. However, heavy resistance exercise decreases blood flow to the working muscles. Muscular contractions greater than 20% of maximal voluntary contraction impede blood flow during a set, but blood flow increases during the rest period (**reactive hyperemia**) after the set. Interestingly, the lack of blood flow (and subsequent increase in metabolites such as lactic acid and reduction in pH) is a potent stimulus for muscle growth (205). Overall, the magnitude of the acute cardiovascular responses depends on the intensity and volume of exercise, muscle mass involvement, rest period length, and contraction velocity (57, 129, 177).

Chronic Cardiovascular Adaptations at Rest

Resting heart rate may not change significantly in response to anaerobic training. Short-term resistance training has been found to lead to decreases of 5% to 12% in resting heart rate (57). Resistance-trained athletes (bodybuilders, powerlifters, weightlifters) have average or lower than average resting heart rates (60-78 beats/min) compared to untrained individuals (57). Longitudinal studies have shown either no change in resting heart rate or reductions of 4% to 13% (57).

Resting blood pressure may decrease slightly or not change at all. A meta-analysis showed that both systolic and diastolic blood pressure decreased by 2% to 4% as an adaptation to resistance training (103). It appears that the response is greatest in those individuals who initially have a slightly elevated blood pressure. Similarly, the **rate-pressure product** (heart rate × systolic blood pressure; a measure of myocardial work) has been shown to either remain constant or decrease following resistance training (56, 57). Stroke volume has been shown to increase in absolute magnitude, but not relative to body surface area or lean body mass (57). Stroke volume will increase as lean tissue mass increases during long-term resistance training. Lastly, resistance training may either not change or slightly decrease total cholesterol and low-density lipoproteins and increase high-density lipoproteins (96). Therefore, heavy resistance training does little to enhance resting cardiac function, but greater improvements may be caused by adaptations to a high-volume program with short rest periods (i.e., bodybuilding, circuit training) in which the overall continuity of the exercise stress in a workout is much higher.

Chronic resistance training also alters cardiac dimensions. Increased left ventricular wall thickness and mass have been reported, but the increase disappears when expressed relative to body surface area or lean body mass (56, 57). It is thought that this increase may result from exposure to intermittently elevated blood pressures and increases in intrathoracic pressure in addition to accommodating changes from increases in lean body mass and body size. Highly resistance-trained athletes have greater than normal absolute posterior left ventricular and intraventricular septum wall thickness (62). Little or no change in left ventricular chamber size or volume is observed with resistance training; this is a major difference between resistance exercise and aerobic exercise. Greater than normal absolute left and right ventricular end-diastolic and end-systolic volumes have been reported in bodybuilders but not weightlifters (62), which indicates that high-volume training may be more conducive to increasing absolute left ventricular volumes. It is important to note that bodybuilders frequently incorporate aerobic exercise into their training programs; therefore, it is possible that some of these adaptations may have been brought about, in part, by aerobic endurance training. Bodybuilders as well as weightlifters have greater than normal absolute and relative (to lean body mass and body surface) left atrial internal dimensions, with the bodybuilders showing a significantly greater dimension (38).

Chronic Adaptations of the Acute Cardiovasular Response to Anaerobic Exercise

Chronic resistance training reduces the cardiovascular response to an acute bout of resistance exercise of a given absolute intensity or workload. Short-term studies have shown that resistance training results in adaptations that blunt the acute increases in heart rate, blood pressure, and double product caused by the resistance training workout (159, 191). In addition, male bodybuilders have lower systolic and diastolic blood pressures and heart rates during sets of 50% to 100% of 1RM performed to momentary muscular failure than both sedentary and lesser-trained men (58). Bodybuilders' peak cardiac output and stroke volume are significantly greater than those of powerlifters (53), demonstrating that stroke volume and cardiac output may be greater per absolute workload as a result of training. It is thought that these adaptations result from a decreased afterload on the left ventricle that in turn increases cardiac output and decreases myocardial oxygen consumption (59). Lastly, oxygen extraction is generally not improved with resistance training using heavy loads and low volume. It is enhanced to a greater extent with continuous aerobic exercise or perhaps slightly with a resistance training program using high volume and short rest periods.

Ventilatory Response to Anaerobic Exercise

Ventilation generally does not limit resistance exercise and is either unaffected or only moderately improved by anaerobic training (49). During resistance exercise, ventilation is significantly elevated during each set, but this elevation is even greater during the first minute of recovery (177). Ventilations in excess of 60 L/min have been reported (177), and the rest interval length had a large effect such that short rest intervals (30 seconds to 1 minute) produced the most substantial elevation. Training adaptations include increased tidal volume and breathing frequency with maximal exercise. With submaximal activity, however, breathing frequency is often reduced while tidal volume is increased. It appears that such ventilatory adaptations result from local, neural, or chemical adaptations in the specific muscles trained through exercise (15). Additionally, improved ventilation efficiency, as characterized by reduced **ventilation equivalent** for oxygen (the ratio of air ventilated to oxygen used by the tissues, $\dot{V}_E/\dot{V}O_2$), has been observed in trained versus untrained individuals (154).

COMPATIBILITY OF AEROBIC AND ANAEROBIC MODES OF TRAINING

Combining resistance and aerobic endurance training may interfere with strength and power gains primarily if the aerobic endurance training is high in intensity, volume, and frequency (46, 94, 125). Callister and colleagues (26) showed that simultaneous sprint and aerobic endurance training decreased sprint speed and jump power. Possible explanations for this less than optimal power development include adverse neural changes and the alterations of muscle proteins in muscle fibers. In contrast, most studies have shown no adverse effects on aerobic power resulting from heavy resistance exercise despite the expected cellular changes caused by this type of exercise (125), although a recent study has shown that added resistance training can hinder $\dot{V}O_2$max improvements (72). Interestingly, Kraemer and colleagues (135) reported that women who performed both resistance exercise and aerobic endurance training had greater aerobic development than those who performed the aerobic endurance training alone. Such data have encouraged some athletes (e.g., distance runners) to add supplemental sport-specific resistance training to their total training regime.

The physiological mechanisms involved in such responses to simultaneous training remain unclear, but the stimulus to the muscle fiber is related to alterations in neural recruitment patterns and attenuation of muscle hypertrophy (125). Such adaptations may result in overtraining (23). Other potential factors may include inadequate recovery between workouts and residual fatigue from aerobic workouts during resistance exercise.

One study on this potential incompatibility was conducted by Kraemer and colleagues (125). They used three months of simultaneous high-intensity strength and aerobic endurance training under five conditions: with a combination group (C) that performed both resistance and aerobic endurance training, a group (UC) that performed upper body resistance and aerobic endurance training, a resistance training–only group (S), an aerobic endurance training–only group (E), and a control group. The S group increased 1RM strength and rate of strength development more than did the C group. In addition, maximal oxygen consumption improvements were not affected by the simultaneous training (i.e., almost identical improvements in 2-mile run times). Thus, no overtraining state for aerobic endurance was apparent.

A fascinating finding was the changes in the muscle fiber size of the thigh musculature. The transformation of Type IIx to Type IIa fibers was almost complete in the S and C groups. The UC and E groups (who performed only interval training) had about 9% Type IIx fibers after training. This indicates that heavy resistance training recruits more of the Type IIx fibers than high-intensity aerobic endurance interval training. In addition, a small number (<3%) of Type IIa fibers were converted to Type IIc fibers in the aerobic training group. The combined group increased muscle size only in Type IIa fibers, while the S group demonstrated increases in Type I, IIc, and IIa fibers. The lack of change in Type I fiber area and increase in Type IIa fiber area in the C group appear to represent a cellular adaptation that shows the antagonism of simultaneous strength and aerobic endurance stimuli, since strength training alone produced increases in both Type I and II muscle fiber areas. The E group showed decreased size in Type I and IIc fibers, presumably due to higher observed cortisol levels (and reduced testosterone) and their physiological need for shorter distances between capillary and cell to enhance oxygen kinetics. Previous studies have shown decreases in muscle fiber size during aerobic endurance training (59).

The majority of studies used untrained subjects to examine the effects of simultaneous high-intensity resistance training and aerobic endurance training (45, 46, 94). Several studies that have shown an incompatibility used three days a week of resistance training alternating with three days a week of aerobic endurance training (i.e., training on six consecutive days), or four to six days a week of combined high-intensity resistance and aerobic endurance training (16, 46, 125), thereby lending credibility to the suggestion that overtraining could have played a role. When both modalities are performed during the same workout (yielding a frequency of three days a week with at least one day off between workouts), the incompatibility has not been shown as frequently (142, 157, 158). An exception was a study by Sale and colleagues (190), who showed that training four days (two days of

What Are the Improvements in Performance From Anaerobic Exercise?

Muscular Strength

- A review of more than 100 studies showed that mean strength increased approximately 40% in "untrained," 20% in "moderately trained," 16% in "trained," 10% in "advanced," and 2% in "elite" participants over periods ranging from four weeks to two years (9).
- Heavier loads are most effective for fiber recruitment. The effects of training are related to the type of exercise used, its intensity, and its volume. With trained athletes, higher intensity and volume of exercise are needed in order for adaptations to continue (131).

Power

- Heavy resistance training with slow velocities of movement leads primarily to improvements in maximal strength, whereas power training (i.e., lifting light-to-moderate loads at high velocities) increases force output at higher velocities and rate of force development.
- Peak power output is maximized during the jump squat with loads corresponding to 30% to 60% of squat 1RM (13, 216). For the upper body, peak power output can be maximized during the ballistic bench press throw using loads corresponding to 46% to 62% of 1RM bench press (12).

Local Muscular Endurance

- Cross-sectional data in anaerobic athletes have shown enhanced muscular endurance and subsequent muscular adaptations consistent with improved oxidative and buffering capacity (110, 118).
- Skeletal muscle adaptations to anaerobic muscular endurance training include fiber type transitions and increases in mitochondrial and capillary numbers, buffering capacity, resistance to fatigue, and metabolic enzyme activity.

Body Composition

- Resistance training can increase fat-free mass and reduce body fat by 1% to 9% (59).
- Increases in lean tissue mass, daily metabolic rate, and energy expenditure during exercise are outcomes of resistance training.

Flexibility

- Anaerobic training potentially can have a positive impact on flexibility, primarily if the individual has poor flexibility to begin with.
- The combination of resistance training and stretching appears to be the most effective method to improve flexibility with increasing muscle mass.

Aerobic Capacity

- Heavy resistance training does not significantly affect aerobic capacity unless the individual is initially deconditioned. The exception is in relatively untrained people, who can experience increases in $\dot{V}O_2max$ ranging from 5% to 8% as a result of resistance training.
- Circuit training and programs using high volume and short rest periods (i.e., 30 seconds or less) have been shown to improve $\dot{V}O_2max$ (71).

Motor Performance

- Anaerobic training enhances motor performance; the magnitude of change is based on the specificity of the exercises or modalities performed.
- Resistance training has been shown to increase running economy, vertical jump, sprint speed, tennis serve velocity, swinging and throwing velocity, and kicking performance (130).

resistance training and two days of aerobic endurance training) per week was better than training two days (combined resistance training and aerobic endurance training) per week for increasing leg press 1RM (25% vs. 13%). These studies show that increasing the recovery period between workouts may decrease the incompatibility.

Power development appears to be negatively affected more than strength during concurrent high-intensity resistance and aerobic endurance training. Häkkinen and colleagues (82) reported similar dynamic and isometric strength increases following 21 weeks of concurrent training or resistance training only; however, the resistance training–only group showed improvements in the rate of force development whereas concurrent training did not match this increase. Kraemer and colleagues (125) also showed that a resistance training–only group increased muscle power whereas a combined group did not. The resistance training–only group also increased peak power in upper and lower body tests while the combined group did not. It appears that power development is much more susceptible to the antagonistic effects of combined strength and aerobic endurance training than is slow-velocity strength (125). Lastly, the sequence may play a role in the magnitude of adaptation. Leveritt and Abernethy (141) examined lifting performance 30 minutes following a 25-minute aerobic exercise workout and found that the number of repetitions performed during the squat was reduced by 13% to 36% over three sets.

OVERTRAINING

Overtraining has been a topic of great interest (64, 122, 139, 203) and can be defined as excessive frequency, volume, or intensity of training that results in extreme fatigue, illness, or injury (which is often due to a lack of sufficient rest, recovery, and perhaps nutrient intake). Excessive training on a short-term basis is called **overreaching** (65, 180). Recovery from this condition is easily achieved within a few days of rest; consequently, overreaching is often a planned phase of many training programs. The rationale is to overwork (to suppress performance and build up tolerance) and then taper to "rebound" in performance. In fact, it has been shown that short-term overreaching followed by a tapering period can result in substantial strength and power gains (180).

Overreaching can become overtraining syndrome if it continues beyond a reasonable period of time. The **overtraining syndrome** is the condition resulting from overtraining; it is sometimes referred to as staleness. This syndrome may include a plateau or decrease in performance. Many alternative terms have been suggested for overtraining, including *burnout, chronic overwork, physical overstrain,* and *overfatigue.* Some use the term *overtraining* only when a decline in performance occurs (25). The following progression illustrates the overtraining continuum:

Overload stimulus → Acute fatigue
→ Overreaching → Overtraining

The overtraining syndrome can last as long as six months, and recovery may be delayed. In the worst-case scenario, overtraining can ruin an athletic career (122). Long-term decreases in performance have not been demonstrated during resistance overtraining, however, and many athletes rebound after a period of recovery. Because rebounds are possible, it is difficult to determine when overtraining becomes chronically detrimental. In addition, some athletes respond to overreaching (180) whereas others do not. Simply doing too much too soon, or repetitive overuse, may result in overtraining and potentially an injury. Overtraining can cause dramatic performance decreases in athletes of all training levels (122).

Two distinct types of overtraining syndromes have been suggested: sympathetic and parasympathetic syndromes. The **sympathetic overtraining syndrome** includes increased sympathetic activity at rest, whereas the parasympathetic overtraining syndrome includes increased parasympathetic activity at rest and with exercise. Some researchers feel that the sympathetic syndrome develops before the parasympathetic syndrome and predominates in younger athletes who train for speed or power, though few data exist to support this differentiation. All overtraining can eventually result in the parasympathetic syndrome (65).

Strength and power overtraining arises when mistakes are made in the acute training program variables and a plateau below the athlete's potential is observed. A theoretical overview of anaerobic overtraining is shown in table 5.3. Performance reductions may persist for weeks or even months when the overtraining syndrome occurs. A common mistake is a rate of progression that is too high. That is, increasing either the volume or intensity (or both) too rapidly over a period of several weeks or months can result in greater structural damage over time and, potentially, overtraining. Sources of overtraining must be examined—both sport-specific (e.g., in-season practices and competitions) and non-sport-specific training modalities (e.g., resistance training, plyometrics). Only a few studies have examined overtraining models in the laboratory. Purposely causing the overtraining syndrome is not easy in the laboratory setting; therefore, monitoring athletes may be more practical as a way of documenting overtraining physiological responses and performance effects. A study by Callister and colleagues (25) demonstrated that anaerobic overtraining in national-level judo athletes may present a different set of symptoms than aerobic overtraining. Fry and colleagues (66) examined intensity-specific overtraining (eight sets of the machine squat exercise with a 95% 1RM load for six consecutive days) and reported nonspecific performance decreases in isokinetic torque production, longer sprint times, and longer agility times. They also found that 1RM strength was preserved; the one day of rest per week appeared to enhance tolerance to the protocol. Thus, athletes, coaches, and sport scientists need to examine the athlete's peripheral and global performance abilities to ensure that overtraining in one performance parameter does not occur.

In a subsequent study by Fry and colleagues (69), the one day of rest was eliminated in the overtraining protocol so that the subjects performed 10 sets of 1RM over seven days. This resulted in a significant decrease (>9.9 pounds [4.5 kg]) in the 1RM in 73% of the subjects. Interestingly, some subjects made progress and did not reach an overtraining state. This demonstrated that the time course of overtraining greatly depends on individual responses, training status, and genetic endowment. This study showed that an exercise stress that is low in volume but high (100%) in intensity, without a recovery day, can result in dramatic performance decrements in nonspecific variables (e.g., isokinetic knee extension peak torque, sprints) and training-specific variables.

Mistakes That Can Lead to Anaerobic Overtraining

The overtraining state is associated with damage to or negative physiological alterations in the neuromuscular system. A mistake in any acute program variable could theoretically contribute to

TABLE 5.3

Theoretical Development of Anaerobic Overtraining

	ANAEROBIC PERFORMANCE						
Stages of overtraining	**Neural**	**Skeletal muscle**	**Metabolic**	**Cardiovascular**	**Immune**	**Endocrine**	**Psychological**
First (no effect on performance)	Altered neuron function						
Second (probably no effect on performance)	Altered motor unit recruitment					Altered sympathetic activity and hypothalamic control	
Third (probably decreased performance)	Decreased motor coordination	Altered excitation-contraction coupling	Decreased muscle glycogen	Increased resting heart rate and blood pressure	Altered immune function	Altered hormonal concentrations	Mood disturbances
Fourth (decreased performance)		Decreased force production	Decreased glycolytic capacity		Sickness and infection		Emotional and sleep disturbances

Reprinted, by permission, from Fry, 1993 (64).

What Are the Markers of Anaerobic Overtraining?

More research is needed to clarify the monitoring problem. To date, only a few possible markers exist:

- Psychological effects: decreased desire to train, decreased joy from training
- Acute epinephrine and norepinephrine increases beyond normal exercise-induced levels (sympathetic overtraining syndrome)
- Performance decrements, although these occur too late to be a good predictor

Unfortunately, because of the limited markers available for anaerobic overtraining, many athletes and coaches monitor the markers of aerobic overtraining while typically not working to monitor anaerobic overtraining.

overtraining syndrome if it is repeated consistently over time. Overtraining classically was thought to be a function of either chronic use of high intensity or high volume or a combination of the two. Intensity interacts with volume (i.e., sets × reps) to provide a potent stimulus.

Too rapid a rate of progression in the resistance can also result in overtraining. Mistakes in the real world are often due to highly motivated athletes using a high volume of heavy loads with high training frequencies and taking little rest to recover from such workouts. The number of sets is an important factor in the calculation of total work or volume of exercise. Volume has been shown to be important for continued gains in performance. Conversely, an excessively high volume of exercise can create a stimulus that exceeds the athlete's ability to recover from the stress and may result in excessive soreness and residual fatigue. Training periodization consists of careful planning to avoid overtraining.

Hormonal Markers of Anaerobic Overtraining

In addition to simply monitoring performance, some have used other markers to characterize anaerobic overtraining. Many studies have examined hormonal responses to overreaching and overtraining. Overreaching has been shown to decrease resting concentrations of testosterone and IGF-I (88, 176) but to augment the acute testosterone response to resistance exercise in trained individuals with previous exposure to overreaching (68). Volume-related overtraining has been shown to increase cortisol and decrease resting luteinizing hormone and total and free testosterone concentrations (65). In addition, the exercise-induced elevation in total testosterone may be blunted (90).

Intensity-related overtraining, however, does not appear to alter resting concentrations of hormones (65). Fry and colleagues (67) reported no changes in circulating testosterone, free testosterone, cortisol, and growth hormone concentrations during high-intensity overtraining (e.g., 10 1RM sets of the squat exercise each day for two weeks). Endocrine responses appear to require longer than one week of monitoring in order to serve as adequate markers. The most effective markers are those associated with sympathetic overtraining syndrome because this may be the first response to anaerobic overtraining.

Psychological Factors in Overtraining

Mood disturbances, as determined from a profile of mood states, have been associated with increased training volumes. Subscales from this profile have been used successfully to identify athletes who suffer from overtraining syndrome and exhibit the classic "inverted iceberg" profile. Heavy resistance training is accompanied by decreased vigor, motivation, and confidence; raised levels of tension, depression, anger, fatigue, confusion, anxiety, and irritability; and impaired concentration. Altered psychological characteristics are also related to changing endocrine profiles. Many athletes sense overtraining by the associated psychological alterations that are often observed before actual decrements in performance occur. Monitoring the mood and mental state of an athlete is very important to gain insights into overtraining (124).

DETRAINING

Detraining is the cessation of anaerobic training or a substantial reduction in frequency, volume, intensity, or any combination of those three variables that results in decrements in performance and loss of some of the physiological adaptations associated with resistance training. The magnitude of strength loss depends on the length of the detraining period and the training status of the individual. Detraining may occur in as few as two weeks and possibly sooner in well-trained individuals. In recreationally trained men, very little change is seen during the first six weeks of detraining (120). Strength reductions appear related to neural mechanisms initially, with atrophy predominating as the detraining period extends. Interestingly, the amount of muscle strength retained is rarely lower than pretraining values, indicating that resistance training has a residual effect when the stimulus is removed. However, when the athlete returns to training, the rate of strength reattainment is high, suggesting the concept of "muscle memory." Periodization of training is an attempt to provide adequate recovery while preventing detraining (59, 61). Responses of various physiological variables to detraining are shown in figure 5.6.

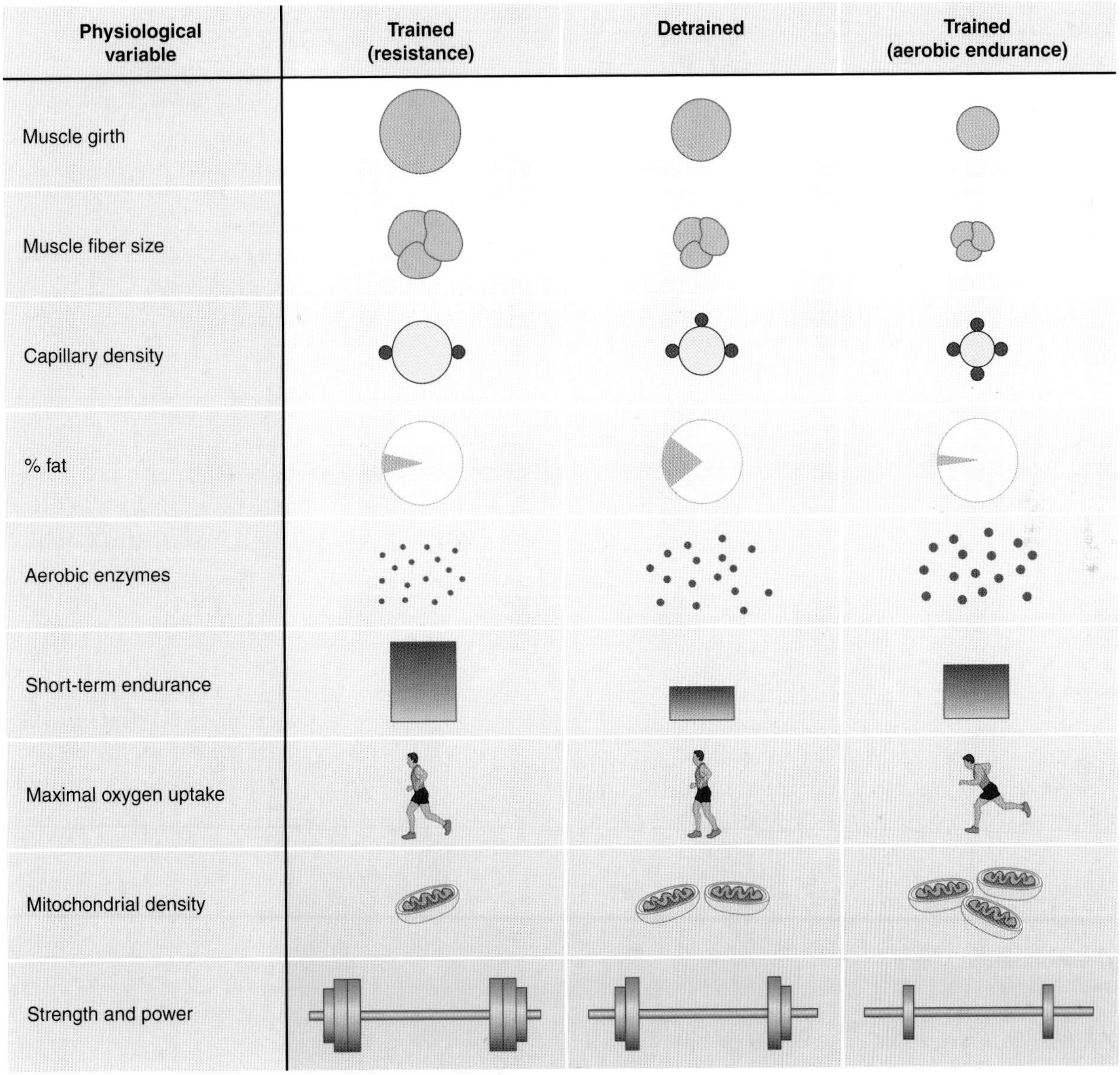

Physiological variable	Trained (resistance)	Detrained	Trained (aerobic endurance)
Muscle girth			
Muscle fiber size			
Capillary density			
% fat			
Aerobic enzymes			
Short-term endurance			
Maximal oxygen uptake			
Mitochondrial density			
Strength and power			

Figure 5.6 Relative responses of physiological variables to training and detraining.

Reprinted, by permission, from Fleck and Kraemer, 2003 (59).

CONCLUSION

Adaptations to anaerobic training are specific to the type of exercise performed. An individual's gender, age, nutrition, prior fitness level, and training motivation affect adaptations. Integration of multiple training programs for an athlete requires careful planning and monitoring to make sure that no incompatibilities or overtraining occur. Explosive training evokes marked increases in muscular power, whereas more conventional heavy resistance training mainly increases muscle size and strength. Anaerobic training (resistance, sprint, plyometric, agility, high-intensity interval training) elicits specific adaptations in the nervous system leading to greater recruitment, rate of firing, synchronization, and enhanced muscle function that enable increases in strength and power.

Anaerobic training also has positive effects on bone, muscle, and the associated connective tissue; the entire musculoskeletal system undergoes a coordinated adaptation to exercise. Athletes undertaking strenuous exercise training experience changes in the force-generating capabilities of muscle, resulting in a coordinated and proportional increase in the load-bearing capacity of bone and other connective tissue. Anaerobic training can increase skeletal muscle mass, force-generating capability, and metabolic capacity and may lead to subtle alterations of the endocrine system that enhance the tissue remodeling process.

Anaerobic training generally results in fewer acute and chronic responses in the cardiovascular and respiratory systems, although low-intensity, high-volume resistance exercise produces some responses that are similar to those with aerobic exercise. Taken together, improved neuromuscular, musculoskeletal, endocrine, and cardiovascular function contribute to enhanced muscle strength, power, hypertrophy, muscular endurance, and motor performance—all of which increase athletic performance. The adaptations observed in athletes are directly related to the quality of the exercise stimulus and accordingly to the levels of progressive overload, specificity, and variation incorporated into program design. The scientific basis of program design is ultimately seen in the effectiveness with which the athlete improves performance.

KEY TERMS

anaerobic training 94
bilateral deficit 99
bone matrix 103
bone mineral density (BMD) 104
collagen 106
cortical bone 104
cross-education 99
cross-linking 106
detraining 116
elastin 107
electromyography (EMG) 98
fibrous cartilage 108
hyaline cartilage 108
hydroxyapatite 103
hyperplasia 100
hypertrophy 100
mechanical load 103
microfibril 106
minimal essential strain (MES) 104
myogenesis 100
nebulin 100
neuromuscular junction (NMJ) 98
osteoblast 103
osteogenic stimulus 105
osteoporosis 104
overreaching 114
overtraining 114
overtraining syndrome 114
peak bone mass 105
periosteum 103
procollagen 106
progressive overload 105
rate-pressure product 111
reactive hyperemia 110
selective recruitment 97
size principle 97
specificity of loading 104
stress fracture 105
structural exercise 105
sympathetic overtraining syndrome 114
tendon stiffness 107
titin 100
trabecular bone 104
ventilation equivalent 112

STUDY QUESTIONS

1. Which of the following muscle fiber types has the GREATEST potential to, when trained in a specific way, CHANGE into a more aerobic or oxidative form?
   a. IIa
   b. IIx
   c. IIc

2. A weightlifter adds 30 minutes of intense (>75% $\dot{V}O_2$max) stationary bicycle riding every other day to her resistance training program. Which of the following describes the GREATEST effect this addition will have on her performance?
   a. power gains will be compromised
   b. power gains will be enhanced
   c. aerobic capacity improvements will be compromised
   d. aerobic capacity improvements will be enhanced

3. A 50-year-old female triathlete is concerned about osteoporosis. Which of the following exercises is the MOST beneficial for improving her bone mineral density?
   a. front squat
   b. leg (knee) extension
   c. bench press
   d. lat pulldown

4. Which of the following muscle fiber types are "bypassed" as a result of selective recruitment that allows an Olympic weightlifter to generate maximum power during a 1RM snatch?
   a. I
   b. IIa
   c. IIx
   d. IIc

5. Which of the following are the MOST effective stimulants of growth hormone production from a resistance training workout?
   I. large muscle mass exercises
   II. small muscle mass exercises
   III. high intensity and volume
   IV. low intensity and volume

   a. I and III only
   b. I and IV only
   c. II and III only
   d. II and IV only

6. The INITIAL decrease in muscular strength caused by detraining is due to undesired changes in which of the following systems?
   a. cardiovascular
   b. connective
   c. muscular
   d. nervous

CHAPTER 6

Adaptations to Aerobic Endurance Training Programs

Ann Swank, PhD

After completing this chapter, you will be able to

- identify and describe the acute responses of the cardiovascular and respiratory systems to aerobic exercise;
- identify and describe the impact of chronic aerobic endurance training on the physiological characteristics of the cardiovascular, respiratory, nervous, muscular, bone and connective tissue, and endocrine systems;
- recognize the interaction between designing aerobic endurance training programs and optimizing physiological responses of all body systems;
- identify and describe external factors that influence adaptations to acute and chronic aerobic exercise; and
- recognize the causes, signs, symptoms, and effects of overtraining and detraining.

An understanding of responses of body systems to both acute and chronic aerobic exercise is crucial to the strength and conditioning professional for providing effective exercise programs. This chapter describes the acute responses of the cardiovascular and respiratory systems to aerobic exercise and the associated physiological variables used to measure these responses. Also presented are chronic adaptations that occur with aerobic endurance training for each of the body systems and a brief discussion of designing an aerobic exercise program. The chapter concludes with discussions of external factors, such as altitude and blood doping, that influence responses to aerobic endurance training, as well as the deleterious impact of overtraining and detraining.

ACUTE RESPONSES TO AEROBIC EXERCISE

A bout of aerobic exercise places a significant metabolic demand on the body (see table 5.1 on p. 95), especially the cardiovascular and respiratory systems. Repeated exposure to the acute stress of exercise results in many changes in the function and responses of all body systems. A basic knowledge of the acute effects of aerobic exercise provides the foundation for an understanding of the chronic adaptations that are discussed in the next section.

Cardiovascular Responses

The primary function of the cardiovascular system during aerobic exercise is to deliver oxygen and other nutrients to the muscles. This section describes the cardiovascular mechanisms of these acute responses.

Cardiac Output

Cardiac output is the amount of blood pumped by the heart in liters per minute and is determined by the quantity of blood ejected with each beat (**stroke volume**) and the heart's rate of pumping (**heart rate**):

$$\dot{Q} = \text{Stroke volume} \times \text{Heart rate} \quad (6.1)$$

where $\dot{Q}$ is the cardiac output. Stroke volume is measured in milliliters of blood per beat, and heart rate is measured in beats (contractions) per minute (33).

In the progression from rest to steady-state aerobic exercise, cardiac output initially increases rapidly, then more gradually, and subsequently reaches a plateau. With maximal exercise, cardiac output may increase to four times the resting level of about 5 L/min to a maximum of 20 to 22 L/min. Stroke volume (see next section) begins to increase at the onset of exercise and continues to rise until the individual's oxygen consumption is at approximately 50% to 60% of maximal oxygen uptake. At that point, stroke volume begins to plateau. College-aged men have maximal stroke volumes averaging between 100 and 115 ml of blood per beat; maximal stroke volumes for college-aged women are approximately 25% less, due to a smaller average body size.

Stroke Volume

Two physiological mechanisms are responsible for the regulation of stroke volume. The first is a result of the **end-diastolic volume**, the volume of blood available to be pumped by the left ventricle at the end of the filling phase, or diastole. The second is due to the action of catecholamines including epinephrine and norepinephrine, which are hormones of the sympathetic nervous system that produce a more forceful ventricular contraction and greater systolic emptying of the heart.

With aerobic exercise, the amount of blood returning to the heart (also called **venous return**) is increased, and thus end-diastolic volume is significantly increased. With the increased volume, the myocardial fibers become more stretched than at rest, resulting in a more forceful contraction and an increase in force of systolic ejection and greater cardiac emptying. This principle, called the **Frank-Starling mechanism**, is related to the concept that the force of contraction is a function of the length of the fibers of the muscle wall. This increase in cardiac emptying is characterized by an increase in the **ejection fraction**, the fraction of the end-diastolic volume ejected from the heart (22, 33). At the onset of exercise, or even with the anticipation of exercise, sympathetic stimulation increases myocardial contractility and consequently increases stroke volume (22, 62).

Heart Rate

Just prior to and at the beginning of an exercise session, a reflex stimulation of the sympathetic nervous system results in an increase in heart rate.

Heart rate increases linearly with increases in intensity during aerobic exercise (22). The rate of increase in heart rate, the actual heart rate response, and the maximal heart rate achieved relate to a variety of individual characteristics of the human system, including fitness and age, in addition to exercise workload.

How Can Athletes Estimate Maximal Heart Rate?

A means of estimating **maximal heart rate** is to subtract one's age from 220; for example, the estimated maximal heart rate for a 47-year-old person is

220 – 47 (age in years) = 173 beats/min.

The variance, or standard deviation, around this estimate is ±10 to 12 beats/min; thus the actual maximal heart rate for this individual could be expected to fall within the range of 161 to 185 beats/min. See chapter 18 for more exercise heart rate calculations.

Oxygen Uptake

Oxygen uptake is the amount of oxygen consumed by the body's tissues. The oxygen demand of working muscles increases during an acute bout of aerobic exercise and is directly related to the mass of exercising muscle, metabolic efficiency, and exercise intensity. Aerobic exercise involving a larger mass of muscle or a greater level of work is likely to be associated with a higher total oxygen uptake. Increased metabolic efficiency allows for an increase in oxygen uptake, especially at maximal exercise.

Maximal oxygen uptake is described as the greatest amount of oxygen that can be used at the cellular level for the entire body. It has been found to correlate well with the degree of physical conditioning and is recognized as the most widely accepted measure of cardiorespiratory fitness (22). The capacity to use oxygen is related primarily to the ability of the heart and circulatory system to transport oxygen and the ability of body tissues to use it. Resting oxygen uptake is estimated at 3.5 ml of oxygen per kilogram of body weight per minute ($ml \cdot kg^{-1} \cdot min^{-1}$); this value is defined as 1 **metabolic equivalent of tasks (MET)**. Maximal oxygen uptake values in normal, healthy individuals generally range from 25 to 80 $ml \cdot kg^{-1} \cdot min^{-1}$, or 7.1 to 22.9 METs, and depend on a variety of physiological parameters, including age and conditioning level (33).

Oxygen uptake ($\dot{V}O_2$) can be calculated with the **Fick equation**, which expresses the relationship of cardiac output, oxygen uptake, and arteriovenous oxygen difference:

$$\dot{V}O_2 = \dot{Q} \times a\text{-}\bar{v}O_2 \text{ difference} \quad (6.2)$$

where $\dot{Q}$ is the cardiac output in milliliters per minute and $a\text{-}\bar{v}O_2$ difference is the **arteriovenous oxygen difference** (the difference in the oxygen content between arterial and venous blood) in milliliters of oxygen per 100 ml of blood. Recalling equation 6.1, we can calculate oxygen uptake as shown in the following example:

$$\dot{V}O_2 = \text{Heart rate} \times \text{Stroke volume} \times a\text{-}\bar{v}O_2 \text{ difference;}$$

$$\dot{V}O_2 = 72 \text{ beats/min} \times 65 \text{ ml blood/beat} \times 6 \text{ ml } O_2/100 \text{ ml blood} = 281 \text{ ml } O_2/\text{min}$$

To express oxygen uptake in its common unit (i.e., $ml \cdot kg^{-1} \cdot min^{-1}$), we would then divide the result by the person's weight in kilograms. For example, for an 80 kg (176-pound) athlete:

$$\dot{V}O_2 = 281 \text{ ml } O_2/\text{min} \div 80 \text{ kg}$$

$$\dot{V}O_2 = 3.5 \text{ ml} \cdot \text{kg}^{-1} \cdot \text{min}^{-1}$$

Blood Pressure

Systolic blood pressure estimates the pressure exerted against the arterial walls as blood is forcefully ejected during ventricular contraction (**systole**) and, when combined with heart rate, can be used to describe the work of the heart. This estimate of the work of the heart is obtained according to the following equation and is referred to as the **rate-pressure product**, or **double product**:

$$\text{Rate-pressure product} = \text{Heart rate} \times \text{Systolic blood pressure} \quad (6.3)$$

Diastolic blood pressure is used to estimate the pressure exerted against the arterial walls when no blood is being forcefully ejected through the vessels (**diastole**). It provides an indication of peripheral resistance and can decrease with aerobic exercise due to vasodilation. In systemic circulation, pressure is highest in the aorta and arteries and rapidly falls off within the venous circulation (figure 6.1). Also, because pumping by the heart is pulsatile, arterial pressure fluctuates between a systolic level of 120 mmHg and a diastolic level of 80 mmHg (approximate values). As the blood flow continues through the systemic circulation, its pressure falls progressively to nearly 0 mmHg (venous pressure) by the time it reaches the termination of the vena cava in the right atrium (33).

The **mean arterial pressure** is the average blood pressure throughout the cardiac cycle (equation 6.4). It is not the average of systolic and diastolic pressures, because the arterial pressure usually remains nearer the diastolic level than the systolic level during a greater portion of the cardiac cycle. Thus, the mean arterial pressure is usually less than the average of the systolic and diastolic pressures.

$$\text{Mean arterial blood pressure} = [(\text{Systolic blood pressure} - \text{Diastolic blood pressure}) \div 3] + \text{Diastolic blood pressure} \quad (6.4)$$

Normal resting blood pressure generally ranges from 110 to 139 mmHg systolic and from 60 to 89 mmHg diastolic. With maximal aerobic exercise, systolic pressure can normally rise to as much as 220 to 260 mmHg, while diastolic pressure remains at the resting level or decreases slightly (33, 62).

Control of Local Circulation

Blood flow is a function of resistance in the blood vessels—as resistance is reduced, blood flow is increased, and as resistance increases, blood flow

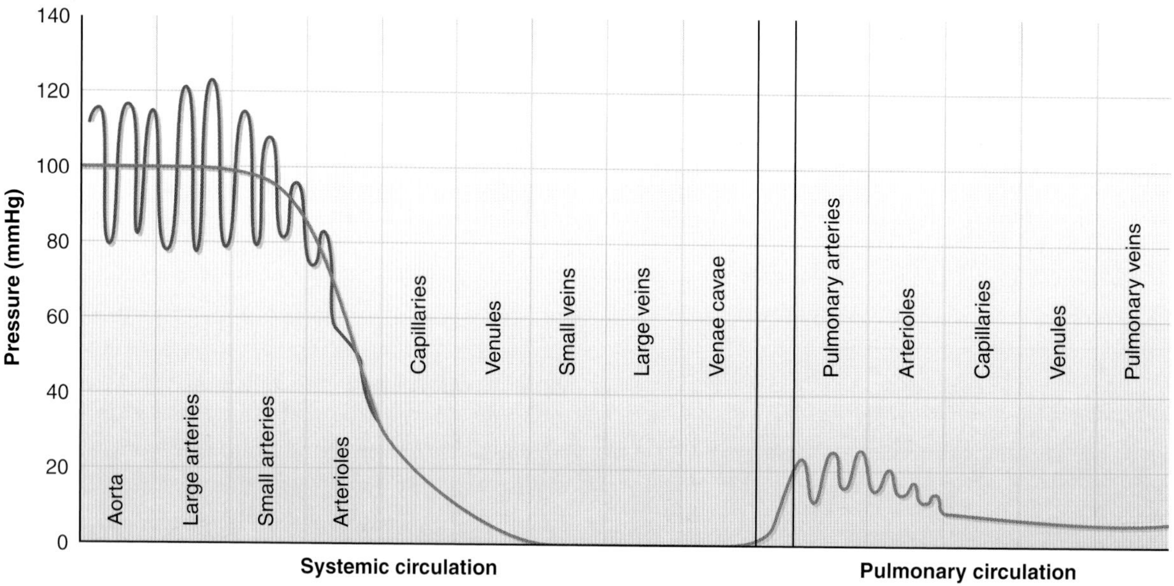

Figure 6.1 Blood pressures in the various portions of the circulatory system.

Repritned, by permission, from Guyton, 1991 (33).

is reduced. The amount of resistance to blood flow is primarily a function of the diameter of the systemic blood vessels. The resistance of the entire systemic circulation is called the **total peripheral resistance**. As blood vessels throughout the body become constricted, total peripheral resistance increases; with dilation, peripheral resistance decreases (33).

Resistance to blood flow is increased with increasing viscosity of the blood and the length of the vessel. However, these factors remain relatively constant under most circumstances. Thus, **vasoconstriction** and **vasodilation** of blood vessels are the primary mechanisms for regulating regional blood flow.

During aerobic exercise, blood flow to active muscles is considerably increased by the dilation of local arterioles; and at the same time, blood flow to other organ systems is reduced by constriction of the arterioles. At rest, 15% to 20% of cardiac output is distributed to skeletal muscle, whereas with vigorous exercise this value may rise to 90% of cardiac output (22, 62).

Acute aerobic exercise results in increased cardiac output, stroke volume, heart rate, oxygen uptake, systolic blood pressure, and blood flow to active muscles and a decrease in diastolic blood pressure.

Respiratory Responses

Aerobic exercise provides for the greatest impact on both oxygen uptake and carbon dioxide production, as compared to other types of exercise. Significant increases in oxygen delivered to the tissue, carbon dioxide returned to the lungs, and **minute ventilation** (the volume of air breathed per minute) provide for appropriate levels of alveolar gas concentrations during aerobic exercise (62).

With aerobic exercise, increased minute ventilation occurs as a result of increases in the depth of breathing, frequency of breathing, or both. During strenuous exercise, the breathing frequency of healthy young adults usually increases from 12 to 15 breaths per minute at rest to 35 to 45 breaths per minute, while **tidal volume** (TV), the amount of air inhaled and exhaled with each breath, increases from resting values (of 0.4 to 1 L) to as much as 3 L or greater. Consequently, the minute ventilation can increase to 15 to 25 times the resting value, or to values of 90 to 150 L of air per minute (22, 33, 62).

During low- to moderate-intensity aerobic exercise, there is an increase in ventilation directly associated with both increased oxygen uptake and carbon dioxide production. In this instance, the increase in ventilation is primarily due to increased tidal volume. The ratio of minute ventilation to oxygen uptake is termed the **ventilatory equivalent** and ranges between 20 and 25 L of air per liter of oxygen consumed. In more intense exercise (generally above 45% to 65% of maximal oxygen uptake in untrained individuals and 70% to 90% in trained athletes), breathing frequency takes on a greater role. At these levels, minute ventilation rises disproportionately to the increases in oxygen uptake and begins to parallel the abrupt rise in blood lactate. At this point, the ventilatory equivalent may increase to 35 or 40 L of air per liter of oxygen consumed with this high-intensity activity (22, 62).

With inspiration, air enters the **alveoli**, the functional unit of the pulmonary system where gas exchange occurs. However, with inspiration, air also occupies areas of the respiratory passages: the nose, mouth, trachea, bronchi, and bronchioles. This area is not useful for gas exchange and is called the **anatomical dead space**. The normal volume of this air space is approximately 150 ml in young adults and increases with age. Because the respiratory passages stretch with deep breathing, the anatomical dead space increases as tidal volume increases (figure 6.2). Nevertheless, the increase in tidal volume with deep breathing is proportionately greater than any increase in anatomical dead space. Thus, increasing tidal volume (deeper breathing) provides for more efficient ventilation than increasing frequency of breathing alone (33, 62).

Physiological dead space refers to alveoli in which poor blood flow, poor ventilation, or other problems with the alveolar surface impair gas exchange. The physiological dead space in the lungs of healthy people is usually negligible because all or nearly all alveoli are functional. Certain types of lung disease such as chronic obstructive lung disease or pneumonia can significantly reduce alveolar function, increasing physiological dead space by as much as 10 times the volume of anatomical dead space (33, 62).

During aerobic exercise, large amounts of oxygen diffuse from the capillaries into the tissues; increased levels of carbon dioxide move from the blood into the alveoli; and minute ventilation increases to maintain appropriate alveolar concentrations of these gases.

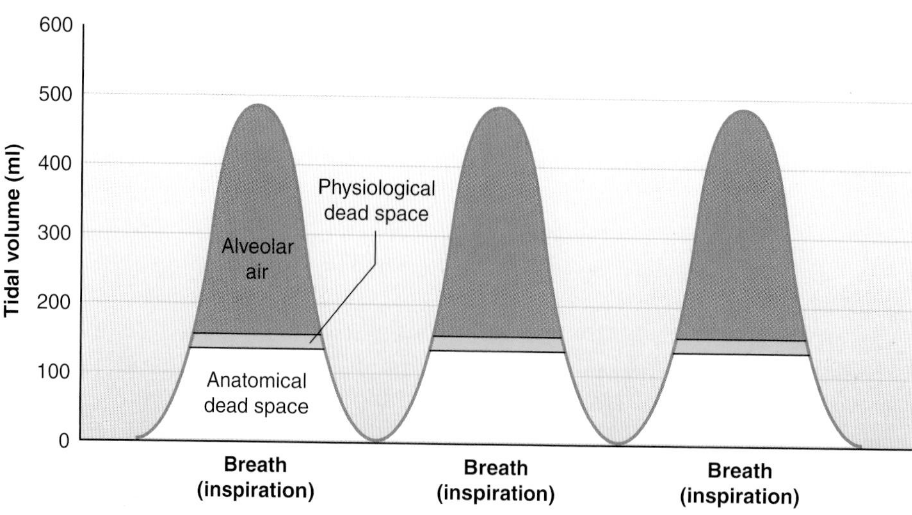

Figure 6.2 Distribution of tidal volume in a healthy athlete at rest. The tidal volume comprises about 350 ml of room air that mixes with alveolar air, about 150 ml of air in the larger passages (anatomical dead space), and a small portion of air distributed to either poorly ventilated or incompletely filled alveoli (physiological dead space).

Reprinted, by permission, from McArdle, Katch, and Katch, 1996 (62).

Gas Responses

Diffusion is the movement of oxygen and carbon dioxide across a cell membrane and is a function of the concentration of each gas and the resulting partial pressure exerted by the molecular motion of each gas. Diffusion results from the movement of gas from high concentration to low concentration. At the tissue level, where oxygen is utilized in metabolism and carbon dioxide is produced, the partial pressures of these gases in some instances differ considerably from those in arterial blood (figure 6.3). At rest, the partial pressure of oxygen in the fluid immediately outside a muscle cell rapidly drops from 100 mmHg in arterial blood to as low as 40 mmHg, while the partial pressure of carbon dioxide is elevated above that of arterial blood to about 46 mmHg. During high-intensity aerobic exercise, the partial pressures of these gases are approximately 3 mmHg for oxygen and 90 mmHg for carbon dioxide. Consequently, these pressure gradients cause the movement of gases across cell membranes. In addition, the diffusing capacities of oxygen and, in particular, carbon dioxide increase dramatically with exercise, which facilitates their exchange (22, 33, 62).

Blood Transport of Gases and Metabolic By-Products

Oxygen is carried in blood either dissolved in the plasma or combined with hemoglobin. Because oxygen is not readily soluble in fluids, only about 3 ml of oxygen can be carried per liter of plasma. Nonetheless, this limited amount of oxygen that is transported in plasma contributes to the partial pressure of oxygen in blood and other body fluids, thus playing a role in the mechanisms that regulate breathing and in the diffusion of oxygen into alveolar blood and the cells of body tissues (33, 62).

Given the limited capacity of plasma to carry oxygen, the majority of oxygen in blood is carried by the hemoglobin. Men have about 15 to 16 g of hemoglobin per 100 ml of blood and women have about 14 g of hemoglobin per 100 ml of blood. One gram of hemoglobin can carry 1.34 ml of oxygen; thus, the oxygen-carrying capacity of 100 ml of blood is about 20 ml of oxygen in men and a little less in women (62).

The way in which carbon dioxide is removed from the system has some similarities to oxygen transport, but the vast amount of carbon dioxide is removed by a more complex process. After carbon dioxide is formed in the cell, it is transported out of the cell by diffusion and subsequently transported to the lungs. As with oxygen, only a limited quantity of carbon dioxide—about 5% of that produced during metabolism—is carried in the plasma; similar to the situation with oxygen, this limited amount of carbon dioxide contributes to establishing the partial pressure of carbon dioxide in blood. Some carbon dioxide is also transported via hemoglobin, but this too is a limited amount (62).

The greatest amount of carbon dioxide removal (approximately 70%) is from its combination with water and delivery to the lungs in the form of bicarbonate (HCO_3^-). The initial step in this reversible reaction is the combination of carbon dioxide in solution with water in the red blood cells to

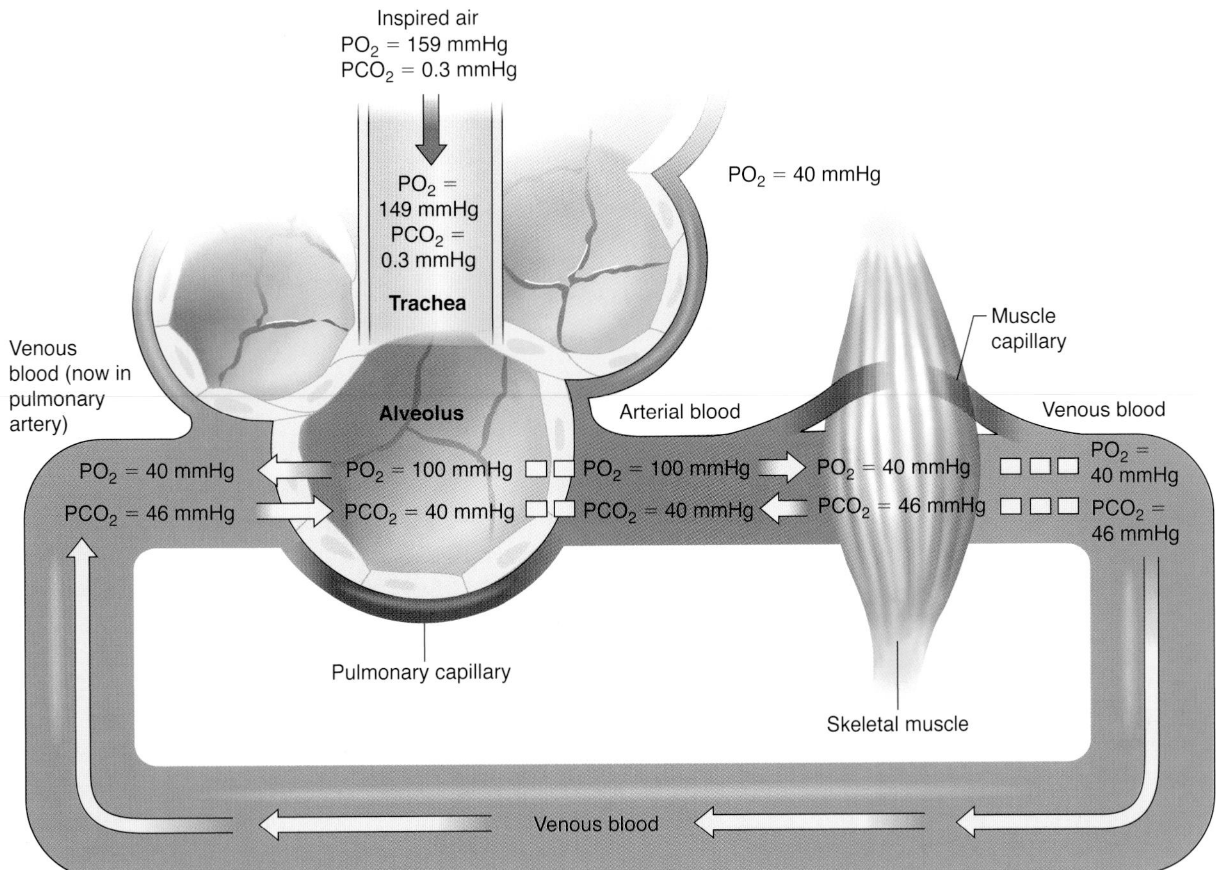

Figure 6.3 Pressure gradients for gas transfer in the body at rest. The pressures of oxygen (PO_2) and carbon dioxide (PCO_2) in ambient air, tracheal air, and alveolar air are shown, as are the gas pressures in venous and arterial blood and muscle tissue.

Reprinted, by permission, from Fox, Bowers, and Foss, 1993 (21).

form carbonic acid. The reaction would normally be quite slow except for the impact of the enzyme carbonic anhydrase, which significantly speeds up this process. Once carbonic acid is formed, it is broken down to hydrogen ions and bicarbonate ions. Because hemoglobin is a significant acid–base buffer, hydrogen ions combine with hemoglobin. This process helps to maintain the pH of the blood. Bicarbonate ions diffuse from the red blood cells out to the plasma while chloride ions diffuse into the blood cells to replace them (33, 62).

Lactic acid is another important metabolic byproduct of exercise. During low- to moderate-intensity exercise, sufficient oxygen is available to the working muscles. Consequently, lactic acid does not accumulate because the removal rate is greater than or equal to the production rate. If, at higher work intensities, aerobic metabolism is not sufficient to keep up with the formation of lactic acid, then the lactic acid level in the blood begins to rise. The aerobic exercise level at which lactic acid (converted to blood lactate at this point) begins to show an increase is termed the onset of blood lactate accumulation or OBLA (see chapter 2).

CHRONIC ADAPTATIONS TO AEROBIC EXERCISE

Understanding the effects of aerobic endurance training on the body systems is important for assessing physical or athletic performance and designing training programs. This section deals with the effects of training on the cardiovascular, respiratory, nervous, muscular, bone and connective tissue, and endocrine systems of the body (see table 6.1).

Cardiovascular Adaptations

Aerobic endurance training results in several changes in cardiovascular function, including increased maximal cardiac output, increased stroke volume, and reduced heart rate at rest and during submaximal

TABLE 6.1

Physiological Adaptations to Aerobic Endurance Training

Variable	Aerobic endurance training adaptations
Performance	
Muscular strength	No change
Muscular endurance	Increases for low power output
Aerobic power	Increases
Maximal rate of force production	No change or decreases
Vertical jump	Ability unchanged
Anaerobic power	No change
Sprint speed	No change
Muscle fibers	
Fiber size	No change or increases slightly
Capillary density	Increases
Mitochondrial density	Increases
Myofibrillar:	
Packing density	No change
Volume	No change
Cytoplasmic density	No change
Myosin heavy-chain protein	No change or decreases in amount
Enzyme activity	
Creatine phosphokinase	Increases
Myokinase	Increases
Phosphofructokinase	Variable
Lactate dehydrogenase	Variable
Sodium-potassium ATPase	May slightly increase
Metabolic energy stores	
Stored ATP	Increases
Stored creatine phosphate	Increases
Stored glycogen	Increases
Stored triglycerides	Increase
Connective tissue	
Ligament strength	Increases
Tendon strength	Increases
Collagen content	Variable
Bone density	No change or increases
Body composition	
% body fat	Decreases
Fat-free mass	No change

ATP = adenosine triphosphate; ATPase = adenosine triphosphatase.

exercise. In addition, capillarization increases as a result of aerobic endurance training.

For optimal aerobic exercise performance, increasing maximal oxygen uptake is of paramount importance. One of the primary mechanisms for increasing maximal oxygen uptake is the enhancement of central cardiovascular function (cardiac output). The normal discharge rate of the sinoatrial (SA) node ranges from 60 to 80 times per minute. Aerobic endurance training results in a significantly slower discharge rate due to an increase in parasympathetic tone. Increased stroke volume also affects the resting heart rate—more blood is pumped per contraction so that the heart contracts less frequently. Aerobic endurance training can increase the heart's ability to pump blood per contraction at rest and thus may account for some of the significant **bradycardia** (slower heart rate) observed in highly conditioned aerobic endurance athletes, whose resting heart rates commonly range from 40 to 60 beats/min (33, 62).

The most significant change in cardiovascular function with long-term (6-12 months) aerobic endurance training is the increase in maximal cardiac output, resulting primarily from improved stroke volume. A significantly lower heart rate in response to a standardized submaximal level of work is another hallmark of aerobic endurance training. Furthermore, the heart rate increases more slowly in trained athletes than in sedentary people for a given workload (23, 62). Because the maximal heart rate may actually decrease slightly with prolonged training, perhaps as a result of increased parasympathetic tone, the size of the left ventricle (both chamber volume and wall thickness) and the strength of contractions (increased contractility) are key to increasing stroke volume with submaximal as well as maximal exercise.

In addition to delivering oxygen, nutrients, and hormones, the capillary circulation provides the means for removing heat and metabolic by-products. Increased capillarization has been observed in response to the increased density of muscle associated with aerobic endurance training and is a function of volume and intensity of training. This increase in capillary density decreases the diffusion distance for oxygen and metabolic substrates (57).

Respiratory Adaptations

Ventilation generally does not limit aerobic exercise and is either unaffected or only moderately affected by training (17). Furthermore, the ventilatory adaptations observed appear to be highly specific to activities that involve the type of exercise used in training; that is, adaptations observed during lower extremity exercise will primarily occur as a result of lower extremity training. If exercise training focuses on the lower extremities, one will not likely observe ventilatory adaptation during upper extremity activities. Training adaptations include increased tidal volume and breathing frequency with maximal exercise. With submaximal activity, breathing frequency is often reduced and tidal volume is increased. Ventilatory adaptations result from local, neural, or chemical adaptations in the specific muscles trained through exercise (5).

Neural Adaptations

Nervous system adaptations play a significant role in the early stages of aerobic endurance training (70). At the outset, efficiency is increased and fatigue of the contractile mechanisms is delayed. Additionally, improved aerobic performance may result in a rotation of neural activity among synergists and among motor units within a muscle. Thus, the athlete produces more efficient locomotion during the activity with lower energy expenditure.

Muscular Adaptations

One of the fundamental adaptive responses to aerobic endurance training is an increase in the aerobic capacity of the trained musculature. This adaptation allows the athlete to perform a given absolute intensity of exercise with greater ease. More impressively, after training, an athlete can exercise at a greater relative intensity of a now-higher maximal aerobic power. Thus, measuring an athlete's maximal oxygen uptake before and after aerobic endurance training may not accurately portray his or her ability to perform during competition. For example, an athlete who can run the marathon at a pace equal to 75% of maximal oxygen uptake may, after training, be able to maintain a pace that is 80% of maximal aerobic power. This adaptation occurs as a result of glycogen sparing (less glycogen use during exercise) and increased fat utilization within the muscle, which prolongs performance (39). Consequently, the OBLA occurs at a higher percentage (up to 80-90%) of the trained athlete's aerobic capacity. This advantageous response may be due to the aerobic endurance athlete's muscle fiber type, specific local adaptations resulting from aerobic endurance training that reduce the production of lactic acid, changes in hormone release (particularly catecholamine release at high-intensity exercise), and a more rapid rate of lactic acid removal (62).

The muscular component of an aerobic endurance training program involves submaximal muscle contractions extended over a large number of repetitions with little recovery. Therefore, the relative intensity is very low, and the overall volume is very high. This manner of training encourages relative increases in aerobic potential that are similar in Type I and Type II fibers. Compared to Type II fibers, Type I fibers have a higher preexisting initial aerobic capacity, to which the increase in aerobic potential from training is added (32). Thus, Type I fibers possess an oxidative capacity greater than that of Type II fibers both before and after training. However, if the intensity is sufficient, as in running repeated 800 m intervals, fast-twitch fibers (especially Type IIx fibers) also make a significant contribution to the effort. Under such conditions, their aerobic capacity also increases with training, but chronic aerobic endurance training reduces the concentration of glycolytic enzymes and can reduce the overall muscle mass of these fibers (59).

Conversely, selective hypertrophy of Type I muscle fibers occurs (14) due to their increased recruitment during aerobic activities, although the resulting cross-sectional diameter is not as great as that seen in Type II fibers adapted to resistance exercise. Also, the change is smaller than the hypertrophy of Type I fibers from a bodybuilding-style resistance training program.

There is little evidence to show that Type II fibers change into Type I fibers as a result of aerobic endurance training, but there may be a gradual conversion within the two major Type II fiber subgroups—of Type IIx fibers to Type IIa fibers (1). This adaptation is significant, in that Type IIa fibers possess a greater oxidative capacity than Type IIx fibers and have functional characteristics more similar to those of Type I fibers. The result of this conversion is a greater number of muscle fibers that can contribute to aerobic endurance performance.

At the cellular level, muscular adaptations to aerobic exercise include an increase in the size and number of mitochondria and increased myoglobin content (21). **Myoglobin** is a protein that transports oxygen within the cell. **Mitochondria** are the organelles in cells that are responsible for aerobically producing adenosine triphosphate (ATP) via oxidation of glycogen. When the larger and more numerous mitochondria are combined with an increase in the quantity of oxygen that can be delivered to mitochondria by the greater concentration of myoglobin, the capacity of the muscle tissue to extract and use oxygen is enhanced. This adaptation is further augmented by increases in the level and activity of the enzymes involved in the aerobic metabolism of glucose (38) and a parallel increase in glycogen (30, 32) and triglyceride (64) stores.

Bone and Connective Tissue Adaptations

The selection of different forms of aerobic exercise has met with some success in bringing about improvements in bone mass. Aerobic programs that are the most successful in stimulating bone growth involve more intense physical activities such as rowing, stair climbing, running, and running with weight packs or vests (15). The key to the success of aerobic exercise in stimulating new bone formation is that the activity be significantly more intense than the normal daily activities the person typically engages in. Thus, brisk walking may stimulate bone growth in previously sedentary individuals who are not accustomed to that level of activity. The intensity of the activity must systematically increase in order to continually overload the bone. Eventually, it may become difficult to overload bone through aerobic exercise when the oxygen transport system rather than limitations of the musculoskeletal system restricts the progression to new exercise intensity. Bone responds to the magnitude and rate of external loading. Therefore, to enhance the stimulus to the musculoskeletal system, it is also necessary to increase the rate of limb movement. Using interval training techniques is one method of providing a greater osteogenic stimulus while still providing the benefits associated with aerobic exercise (24, 79).

In mature adults, the extent to which tendons, ligaments, and cartilage grow and become stronger is proportional to the intensity of the exercise stimulus, especially from weight-bearing activities (66). As with bone and muscle, intensities of exercise that consistently exceed the strain placed on the connective tissues during normal daily activities are what is needed to create connective tissue changes (see chapter 5 for more information).

An example of the positive effects of weight-bearing activity on cartilage is evidenced in a typical knee joint, where the surfaces of the joint that experience the greatest degree of weight bearing are thicker than the non-weight-bearing surfaces (66). Complete movement through a full range of motion during weight bearing seems to be essential to maintain tissue viability (73).

Animal studies to evaluate the potential negative effects of aerobic exercise on cartilage have shown encouraging results. Long-term adherence to treadmill exercise in guinea pigs thickens the cartilage and increases the number of cells (69). Running studies using dogs as subjects demonstrated that a moderate running program (2.5 miles [4 km] per day, five days per week for 40 weeks) increased cartilage thickness and stimulated remodeling of bone tissue. It was also found that more strenuous running (increased to 12.5 miles [20 km] per session) decreased cartilage thickness; but even running 25 miles (40 km) per session for one year, or weighted running (using jackets weighing 130% of the animals' weight) of 2.5 miles (4 km) five days per week for 550 weeks, did not cause degenerative joint disease (9).

Endocrine Adaptations

Similar to what occurs with anaerobic exercise (see chapter 5), changes in hormone production contribute to the body's adaptation to aerobic exercise (28, 29, 43, 49). Not only do testosterone, insulin, insulin-like growth factors (IGF-I), and growth hormone affect the integrity of muscle, bone, and connective tissue; they also help to keep metabolism within a normal range (25, 26, 52, 53, 76). Increases in hormonal circulation and changes at the receptor level are specific responses to aerobic exercise.

High-intensity aerobic endurance training augments the absolute secretion rates of many hormones, including epinephrine, in response to maximal exercise, although trained athletes have blunted responses to submaximal exercise. Their hormone concentrations equal those of their untrained counterparts at the same relative submaximal exercise intensity. The greater hormonal response patterns to maximal exercise appear to augment the athlete's ability to tolerate and sustain prolonged high aerobic exercise intensities. When exercise intensity is very high and exercise duration is very short (from 5 to 10 seconds), only "fight-or-flight" changes in peripheral blood hormone concentrations occur (e.g., epinephrine and norepinephrine concentrations increase) (56).

Aerobic endurance training, especially running, is often associated with protein sloughing from the muscle, brought about in part by stress-induced cortisol secretion that the body attempts to offset by increasing hormonal anabolic responses in testosterone and IGF-I. Chronic, high-volume running creates a catabolic response that can lead to muscle degradation and reduction in power. It is not uncommon for elite aerobic endurance runners who are training with high mileage to be able to jump vertically only several inches.

DESIGNING AEROBIC ENDURANCE PROGRAMS FOR OPTIMIZING ADAPTATIONS

The basis of any adaptation is the exercise stimulus of the training program. Aerobic endurance training provides a continuum of modalities that affect various physiological systems (6, 8, 13, 16, 35, 37, 41, 55, 60, 61, 63, 72). The magnitude of change in response to any program depends on the athlete's pretraining level and the characteristics of the program. Aerobic endurance training requires proper progression, variation, specificity, and overload if physiological adaptations are to take place (18). Many adaptations are needed, from the cellular to the whole-body level (31, 68).

There are a host of different variables that one must consider and ultimately manipulate when designing training programs for different physiological systems (4, 18, 21, 42, 44, 45, 46, 48, 58). Refer to chapter 18 for more detail about how to design an aerobic exercise program. The purpose of this chapter is to emphasize that understanding the responses of the body systems is essential to effective program design.

Volumes of information have been produced on aerobic exercise and subsequent training adaptations. Aerobic metabolism plays a vital role in human performance and is basic to all sports, if for no other reason than recovery. Metabolically, the Krebs cycle and electron transport chain are the main pathways in energy production. Aerobic metabolism produces far more ATP energy than anaerobic metabolism and uses fats, carbohydrates, and proteins. Many sports involve interactions between the aerobic and anaerobic metabolic systems and thus require appropriate training. For example, soccer, lacrosse, basketball, field hockey, and ice hockey involve continuous movement (and thus constant aerobic demand) mixed with bursts of sprint and power activities. Proper conditioning of the aerobic system is vital to the ability of the player to sustain such activity and adequately recover.

It appears that every athlete needs a basic level of cardiovascular endurance, which can be achieved using a wide variety of training modalities and programs. The traditional modality has been the slow, long-distance run. For the strength and power athlete, however, this may be irrelevant or even detrimental to power development. Adequate gains in aerobic fitness can be accomplished with interval training when appropriate and needed (21, 27). The old concept of an "aerobic base" for purposes of recovery in anaerobic sports is somewhat misunderstood; athletes can gain aerobic endurance training adaptations without the use of long-distance running because a variety of alternative training programs exist (e.g., interval training with short rest periods).

One of the most commonly measured adaptations to aerobic endurance training is an increase in maximal oxygen uptake associated with an increase in maximal cardiac output (7, 18, 35, 77). As the intensity of exercise increases, the oxygen consumption rises to maximal levels. When oxygen consumption can no longer increase to meet the demands, maximal oxygen uptake has been achieved. Aerobic endurance training can improve an athlete's aerobic power by 5% to 30%, depending on the starting fitness level (3). Greater improvement can usually be attributed to exceptionally low starting fitness levels. It is interesting that most adaptations in maximal oxygen consumption can be achieved within a 6- to 12-month period. After that, changes in aerobic endurance performance are related more to running efficiency and changes in anaerobic metabolism (e.g., increased lactate threshold). Metabolic changes include increased respiratory capacity, lower blood lactate concentrations at a given submaximal exercise intensity, increased mitochondrial and capillary densities, and improved enzyme activity. Although an athlete's maximal oxygen uptake may not change from year to year with aerobic endurance training, the oxygen cost of running does improve; several studies have shown a progressive improvement in the economy of running in elite aerobic endurance athletes. Long-term aerobic endurance training may improve the athlete's running economy more than the maximal ability to extract and use oxygen (i.e., $\dot{V}O_2max$). Experienced runners may not improve their $\dot{V}O_2max$, but their performance may be better due to enhanced running economy (7, 36).

The intensity of training is one of the most important factors in improving and maintaining aerobic power. Short, high-intensity bouts of interval sprints can improve maximal oxygen uptake if the interim rest period is also short. Callister and colleagues (12) showed that long rest periods used with sprints improve sprint speed without significant increases in maximal aerobic power. Therefore, longer training sessions with higher amounts of rest between exercise bouts result in less improvement in aerobic capacity.

Aerobic endurance training is associated with alterations in body composition. Aerobic endurance training usually decreases the relative percentage of body fat and has little or no significant effect on fat-free mass. Longer-term programs can result in greater decreases in the percentage of body fat (7, 18, 40, 65). When training intensity and volume balance anabolic and catabolic activities in muscle, the optimal exercise prescription depends on the training level of the athlete and the variation in the exercise protocol. Excessive training might lead to a predominance of catabolic activity in the body and cause muscle metabolism not to be able to keep up with the needed amount of protein synthesis.

Aerobic endurance training results in reduced body fat, increased maximal oxygen uptake, increased respiratory capacity, lower blood lactate concentrations, increased mitochondrial and capillary densities, and improved enzyme activity.

Table 6.2 lists the physiological changes that occur with short-term (three- to six-month) aerobic endurance training and compares the results for previously untrained and elite aerobic endurance athletes.

TABLE 6.2

Physiological Variables in Aerobic Endurance Training

	PREVIOUSLY UNTRAINED SUBJECTS*		
Variable	**Before training**	**After training**	**Elite aerobic endurance athletes**
Heart rate:			
Resting (beats/min)	74	61	45
Maximal	194	190	185
Stroke volume:			
Resting (ml)	64	82	127
Maximal	122	142	201
Cardiac output:			
Resting (L/min)	4.5	4.6	4.4
Maximal	22.3	25.8	34.9
Heart volume (ml)	750	823	1,250
Blood volume (L)	4.8	5.2	6.1
Blood pressure:			
Resting (mmHg)	120/80	124/78	105/65
Maximal	206/85	202/82	209/69

	PREVIOUSLY UNTRAINED SUBJECTS*		
Variable	**Before training**	**After training**	**Elite aerobic endurance athletes**
Pulmonary ventilation, BTPS:			
Resting (L/min)	7	6	6
Maximal	123	142	201
Breathing rate:			
Resting (breaths/min)	14	12	11
Maximal	42	47	59
Tidal volume (TV):			
Resting (L)	0.6	0.6	0.6
Maximal	2.8	3.1	3.1
Residual volume (RV) (L)	1.0	1.4	1.4
Arteriovenous oxygen difference:			
Resting (ml/100 ml)	6.1	6.1	6.1
Maximal	14.5	15.2	16.4
Maximal oxygen uptake ($ml \cdot kg^{-1} \cdot min^{-1}$)	47	55	79
Weight (kg)	75	72	62
% Body fat	16.0	14.9	6.7
% Type I fibers	55	55	81
Fiber area:			
Type I (μm^2)	4,730	4,820	4,180
Type IIa	6,860	7,150	4,299
Type IIx	6,167	6,433	3,899
Capillary density:			
Number/mm^2	290	350	460
Number/fiber	1.2	1.4	3.2
Citrate synthetase (activity units)	28	37	78
Hexokinase (activity units)	2.4	2.9	4.2
Lactate dehydrogenase (activity units)	580	654	629
Maximal fiber shortening velocity:			
Type I (fiber lengths/s)	0.86	1.42	1.02
Type II	4.85	5.25	5.77

*These subjects completed a short-term (3- to 6-month) aerobic endurance training program. BTPS = body temperature and pressure, saturated.

EXTERNAL INFLUENCES ON THE CARDIORESPIRATORY RESPONSE

A variety of external factors can influence both the acute response and the chronic adaptation of the cardiovascular and respiratory systems to exercise. The effects of altitude, hyperoxic breathing, smoking, and blood doping are described here.

Altitude

At elevations greater than 3,900 feet (1,200 m), acute physiological adjustments begin to occur to compensate for the reduced partial pressure of oxygen in the atmosphere (34). Two adjustments that occur early in the acclimatization process are particularly important. First, there is an increase in pulmonary ventilation (**hyperventilation**) at rest and during exercise (table 6.3). The increase in ventilation is primarily the result of increased breathing frequency. With longer stays at high elevation, however, increased tidal volume also contributes to augmented ventilation. Stabilization of ventilation is dependent upon level of altitude. Second, in the early stages of altitude exposure, there is an increase in cardiac output at rest and during submaximal exercise, due primarily to increases in heart rate (34, 62). Submaximal heart rate and cardiac output can increase 30% to 50% above sea level values, and stroke volume is constant or slightly reduced. Increased submaximal cardiac output reflects the need for increased blood flow at a time when arterial blood oxygen content is reduced.

Within 10 to 14 days at a given altitude, heart rate and cardiac output begin to return to normal values

TABLE 6.3

Adjustments to Altitude Hypoxia

System	Immediate adjustments	Longer-term adjustments
Pulmonary	Hyperventilation	Increase in ventilation rate stabilizers
Acid-base	Body fluids become more alkaline due to reduction in CO_2 with hyperventilation.	Excretion of HCO_3^- by the kidneys with concomitant reduction in alkaline reserve
Cardiovascular	Cardiac output increases at rest and during submaximal exercise.	Continued elevation in submaximal heart rate
	Submaximal heart rate increases.	
	Stroke volume remains the same or is slightly lowered.	Decreased stroke volume at rest and with submaximal and maximal exercise
	Maximal heart rate remains the same or is slightly lowered.	Lowered maximal heart rate
	Maximal cardiac output remains the same or is slightly lowered.	Lowered maximal cardiac output
Hematologic		Increased red cell production (polycythemia)
		Increased viscosity
		Increased hematocrit
		Decreased plasma volume
Local tissue		Increased capillary density of skeletal muscle
		Increased number of mitochondria
		Increased use of free fatty acids, sparing muscle glycogen

because of the longer-term acclimatization response of increased red blood cell production. Thus, with acute exposure to altitude, hyperventilation and increased submaximal cardiac output are rapid and relatively effective responses to offset the challenges of the reduced partial pressure of oxygen. However, despite these adjustments, arterial oxygen saturation decreases and results in decreases in maximal oxygen uptake and aerobic performance. Changes revert in about one month after return to sea level. Chronic physiological and metabolic adjustments that occur during a prolonged altitude exposure include

- increased formation of hemoglobin (generally 5-15% increase, although higher values have been reported) and red blood cells (30-50% increase),
- increased diffusing capacity of oxygen through the pulmonary membranes,
- the maintenance of the acid–base balance of body fluids by renal excretion of HCO_3^- and through hyperventilation, and
- increased capillarization.

All these adaptations generally improve tolerance of the relative hypoxia at medium and high altitudes (33, 34, 62) and may result in nearly sea level exercise capacities with adequate acclimatization. A minimum of three to six weeks is needed to adapt in moderate altitude. However, reduced performance is generally expected with altitude exposure regardless of the period of acclimatization. Strength and conditioning professionals are encouraged to remind athletes of both expected acute responses and chronic adaptations to altitude so that athletes can maintain appropriate training regimens and a positive mental approach to the impact of altitude.

Hyperoxic Breathing

Breathing oxygen-enriched gas mixtures (**hyperoxic breathing**) during rest periods or following exercise may positively affect some aspects of exercise performance, although the mechanisms for these results are not well understood and the procedure remains controversial. It is suggested that hyperoxic breathing increases the amount of oxygen carried by the blood and therefore increases the supply of oxygen to working muscles. The breathing of ambient air at sea level by healthy people results in arterial hemoglobin oxygen saturation of 95% to 98%. Thus, hyperoxic breathing during rest periods or postexercise has little potential for increasing this value (33, 67). However, psychological (placebo effect) or other physiological advantages may account for the infrequent reports of positive effects.

Smoking

Relatively little research is available regarding smoking and exercise performance, primarily because most regularly active people and athletes avoid smoking for fear of impairing performance or increasing disease risk. Smokers experience impairments in lung function and are at increased risk for obstructive lung diseases. However, these findings are generally seen much later in life. Younger athletes who smoke rarely exhibit significant effects on physical performance. In theory, however, certain acute effects of tobacco smoking could impair exercise performance, particularly when ventilation and aerobic capacity are critical factors in the performance. These effects include

- increased airway resistance due to nicotine-related bronchiole constriction or increased fluid secretion and swelling in the bronchial tree due to the irritation of smoke; and
- the paralysis of the cilia on the surfaces of the respiratory tract by nicotine, which limits the ability to remove excess fluids and foreign particles, causing debris to accumulate in the respiratory passageways and adding to the difficulty of breathing.

Thus, even the light smoker may feel respiratory strain during exercise and a reduction in the level of performance (33, 62).

Carbon monoxide, a component of cigarette smoke, is associated with an impaired hemodynamic response to exercise and increased catecholamine release. Carbon monoxide has a higher affinity for hemoglobin than does oxygen. The resulting carboxyhemoglobin reduces the amount of oxygen that can be carried by hemoglobin and thus reduces the oxygen that can be provided to the working muscles. Hence, maximal exercise capacity may be lowered and submaximal cardiovascular responses may increase in an effort to provide adequate oxygenated blood to the working muscles. In addition, the increased catecholamine release increases heart rate and blood pressure.

Blood Doping

The practice of artificially increasing red blood cell mass (**blood doping**) as a means to improve athletic performance has been criticized as unethical and as posing serious health risks to the athlete. Nonetheless, research has suggested that this practice can improve aerobic exercise performance and may enhance tolerance of certain environmental conditions (71).

Blood doping can be accomplished through infusion of an individual's own red blood cells or those from someone else, or through administration of erythropoietin (EPO), which stimulates red blood cell production. Infusion of red blood cells rapidly increases red blood cell mass, but for just a few weeks, whereas the effects of the drug EPO produce changes over weeks and last as long as EPO continues to be administered. In either case, it is theorized that increasing red blood cell mass increases the blood's ability to carry oxygen and thus increases oxygen availability to working muscles. Maximal oxygen uptake has been demonstrated to increase by up to 10% with either red blood cell infusion or EPO administration. At standardized submaximal workloads, blood doping is associated with decreased heart rate and blood lactate as well as higher pH values. The positive effects on athletic performance have also been substantiated (71).

The effects of blood doping suggest the potential for diminishing the impact of various environmental conditions. The effects of altitude appear to be lessened with blood doping, although as altitude increases, the positive influence of blood doping is reduced. Environmental stressors such as heat and cold exposure may also be affected by blood doping. During heat exposure, a blood-doped athlete will be able to tolerate submaximal exercise stress more easily. The increased blood volume associated with increased red blood cell mass allows the body to shunt more blood to the skin for improved thermoregulation, while still providing sufficient blood to transport oxygen to the working muscles. However, blood doping appears to provide these benefits primarily to individuals who are already acclimatized to heat and provides very little aid in the response to heat of those who are not acclimatized. Much less is known about blood doping with regard to cold stress, and although some theoretical benefit has been suggested, this practice could conceivably increase health risks (71).

The health risks associated with blood doping further complicate the controversy surrounding this practice. Theoretically, high hematocrit levels may increase risks for embolic events such as stroke, myocardial infarction, deep vein thrombosis, or pulmonary embolism. Increased arterial blood pressure, flu-like symptoms, and increased plasma potassium levels may present themselves with EPO use. Finally, there is risk associated with infusion or transfusion, although in most cases the risk is relatively small (71).

INDIVIDUAL FACTORS INFLUENCING ADAPTATIONS TO AEROBIC ENDURANCE TRAINING

Additional factors affect how and how well an athlete responds to chronic aerobic endurance training. These factors influence how nearly all of the body's systems react to training; an athlete's predisposition to adaptation combined with the existing training status has an effect on additional or future improvements in aerobic capacity and performance. Also, an athlete's age, sex, and current training health (i.e., if the athlete is in an overtrained or detrained state) further influence training adaptations.

Genetic Potential

The upper limit of an individual's genetic potential dictates the absolute magnitude of the training adaptation. The magnitude of change also depends, however, on how much potential for adaptation the person undergoing training has, that is, how much adaptation has already occurred within his or her physiological system. Each adaptation has an upper limit, and as the athlete gets closer to that upper limit, smaller and smaller gains are observed. For example, in some elite competitions (e.g., swimming), small gains in performance may be the difference between the gold medal and 26th place. Thus, in an event in which tenths or hundredths of a second make a big difference, it may be worth the extra training time to gain that 0.05% improvement in performance. Because of the small gains possible with training in elite athletes, careful program design and monitoring become even more critical (18, 51, 58, 78). It must be acknowledged that to yield such gains, more time and smarter training programs must be undertaken to fine-tune a specific sport performance capability. At the top levels of competition, the observation that part-time athletes just do not exist supports the notion that improving and maintaining high levels of athletic performance require full-time attention. Here is where training for health and fitness and training for sport performance, as well as the time commitment, dramatically differ (74). Interestingly, for most athletes, sport performance involves the fitness of more than one physiological system. Thus, training involves the careful integration of several different targeted physiological systems (10, 47, 50, 72).

Age and Sex

Physiological adaptations to aerobic endurance training vary according to age and sex (2, 77). Maximal aerobic power decreases with age in adults (2). On the average, when women and men are matched by age, the aerobic power values of women range from 73% to 85% of the values of men (77). However, the general physiological response to training is similar in men and women. The differences in aerobic power may be caused by several factors, including women's higher percentage of body fat and lower blood hemoglobin values and men's larger heart size and blood volume (7, 21).

Overtraining

It has been a long-term priority for athletes to avoid the effects of **overtraining**, which is typically caused by extreme levels of training frequency, volume, intensity, or a combination of these variables without sufficient rest or recovery (10, 11, 24, 54, 58, 75). The result of overtraining is termed the **overtraining syndrome** or, more simply, staleness.

An overtrained state can last for a brief period of time, perhaps a few days; this condition is often called **overreaching** (25) to distinguish it from the overtraining syndrome. Although recovery can occur with several absolute or relative rest days, unplanned overreaching should be considered a warning sign of true overtraining.

An athlete can remain overtrained for an extended period of time and have difficulty recovering quickly, even with what seems to be enough rest (54). This is especially the case for overtraining associated with aerobic endurance training. In resistance training, long-term decrements have not been demonstrated, and many athletes rebound after a period of recovery. With both types of training, however, many athletes train too intensely for too long without proper recovery. Injury or illness also can result from overtraining (25).

Differences exist between aerobic and anaerobic overtraining syndromes. Among aerobic endurance athletes, physiological responses to increased training volume have been monitored in distance runners, swimmers, cyclists, and rowers. Increased training intensity has also been studied in distance runners and swimmers. Increasing the volume of training may produce performance decrements. Body weight may or may not decrease, although lowered body fat percentages may result. Muscle size and strength may not be affected. On the other hand, increased training intensity can improve physical performance.

Overtraining can lead to dramatic performance decreases in athletes of all training levels and is caused by mistakes in the design of the training program.

Cardiovascular Responses

Greater volumes of training affect heart rate. In at least one instance, the decreased resting heart rates were later followed by increased heart rates. Exercise-induced maximum heart rates decrease from overtraining, as have heart rates at absolute submaximal exercise intensities. Increased volumes of training do not generally affect resting blood pressures. However, increased training intensity can produce increased resting diastolic blood pressures without affecting resting systolic pressures.

Biochemical Responses

High training volume results in increased levels of creatine kinase, indicating muscle damage. Lactate concentrations, on the other hand, either decrease or stay the same when training volumes increase. Blood lipids and lipoproteins are not altered by volume overtraining. Muscle glycogen decreases with prolonged periods of overtraining, although this may be largely due to dietary considerations. Decreased glycogen levels may contribute to the lowered lactate responses.

Endocrine Responses

In men, total testosterone decreases after an initial increase in response to the exercise stimuli. Concentrations of free testosterone also decrease in some cases. These changes do not appear to be regulated by the pituitary, since luteinizing hormone levels are not affected. The changes in free testosterone appear to be independent of protein-binding capacity, because concentrations of sex hormone–binding globulin are not altered. Therefore, the decreased ratio of total testosterone to sex hormone–binding globulin that can accompany increased volumes of training seems to be due to altered total testosterone levels.

Cortisol responses to increased volumes of training are variable. Specific responses appear to depend on several variables, including training protocol, diurnal variations, and whether resting or acute responses were measured. Increased cortisol concentrations have been associated with empirically identified overtraining syndromes and decreased aerobic performance. Pituitary regulation of adrenal cortex activity may be an important factor, because decreased levels of adrenocorticotropin have resulted from overtraining protocols, although levels of this hormone may eventually increase.

The anabolic-catabolic state of an organism may be quantified by the testosterone-to-cortisol ratio, which decreases or stays the same with greater training volumes. The free testosterone component may be more influential physiologically. Decreases of 5% to 50% in the ratio of free testosterone to cortisol have also been reported with increased training volumes. A possible marker of an overtraining syndrome is a decrease of 30% or more in this ratio.

Decreased pituitary secretion of growth hormone occurs with overtraining. This and other endocrine responses to an overtraining stimulus appear to be due primarily to impaired hypothalamic function, not pituitary function. Whether these endocrine alterations are responsible for performance decrements is open to debate. Levels of free testosterone, total testosterone, cortisol, and creatine kinase seem to simply reflect training volumes. Actual physical performance is occasionally related to total testosterone concentrations, but not in all cases.

Catecholamines appear very responsive to an overtraining stimulus. Alterations in basal levels of epinephrine, norepinephrine, and dopamine are reported to be significantly related to the severity of self-reported complaints in overtrained runners. Changes in catecholamine and cortisol concentrations may mirror each other during overtraining, although cortisol is not as sensitive to increased training volume as catecholamines are. Severely increased volumes of training can result in decreased nocturnal levels of epinephrine, which indicate basal levels. Preexercise or resting levels of epinephrine and norepinephrine are either unchanged or increased. The same absolute load of exercise results in increased epinephrine and norepinephrine levels in the presence of overtraining compared with before overtraining, although maximum levels of epinephrine and norepinephrine are unchanged. Basal levels of dopamine decrease with volume

What Are the Markers of Aerobic Overtraining?

Many of the previously mentioned physiological variables have been suggested as markers of overtraining syndrome for aerobic endurance athletes because of the responsiveness of these variables to an overtraining stimulus. The following are some of these variables (19):

- Decreased performance
- Decreased percentage of body fat
- Decreased maximal oxygen uptake
- Altered blood pressure
- Increased muscle soreness
- Decreased muscle glycogen
- Altered resting heart rate
- Increased submaximal exercise heart rate
- Decreased lactate
- Increased creatine kinase
- Altered cortisol concentration
- Decreased total testosterone concentration
- Decreased ratio of total testosterone to cortisol
- Decreased ratio of free testosterone to cortisol
- Decreased ratio of total testosterone to sex hormone–binding globulin
- Decreased sympathetic tone (decreased nocturnal and resting catecholamines)
- Increased sympathetic stress response

overtraining, as do dopamine concentrations at the same absolute workload. With submaximal exercise, dopamine responses vary, but appear to counter norepinephrine patterns. Although often difficult to document, severe volume overtraining of aerobic endurance athletes produces characteristics of the parasympathetic overtraining syndrome, including reduced sensitivity to catecholamines, and may result in advanced cases of severe overtraining syndrome.

Detraining

If inactivity, rather than proper recovery, follows exercise, an athlete loses training adaptations; that is, he or she experiences **detraining**. Little is known about detraining following various conditioning protocols. Aerobic endurance adaptations are most sensitive to periods of inactivity because of their enzymatic basis. The exact cellular mechanisms that dictate detraining changes are unknown; further research is needed to clarify the underlying physiological alterations. It appears that when detraining occurs, the individual's physiological function reverts to a normal, untrained state. Proper exercise variation, maintenance programs, and active recovery periods can adequately protect against serious detraining effects (20). Figure 5.6 on page 117 shows the relative responses of physiological variables to training and detraining.

CONCLUSION

Aerobic exercise produces many acute cardiovascular and respiratory responses, and aerobic endurance training produces many chronic adaptations. This information can be of particular value for developing the goals of a conditioning program and can provide a basis for clinical evaluation and the selection of parameters included in such an evaluation process. Knowledge of cardiovascular, respiratory, nervous, muscular, bone and connective tissue, and endocrine system responses to aerobic endurance training can help the strength and conditioning professional understand the scientific basis for aerobic conditioning and the adaptations to expect and monitor during training. Adaptations to specific types of exercise stimuli take place in the body. Properly designing the workout protocol is vitally important to meeting the goals of the program. Optimal adaptations reflect careful design, implementation, and performance of strength and conditioning programs.

KEY TERMS

STUDY QUESTIONS

1. A 17-year-old high school cross-country runner has been training aerobically for six months in preparation for the upcoming season. Which of the following adaptations will occur in the muscles during that time?
   a. increased concentration of glycolytic enzymes
   b. hyperplasia of Type II fibers
   c. transformation from Type I to Type II fibers
   d. hypertrophy of Type I fibers

2. The amount of blood ejected from the left ventricle during each beat is the
   a. cardiac output.
   b. a-$\bar{v}O_2$ difference.
   c. heart rate.
   d. stroke volume.

3. All of the following normally increase during an aerobic exercise session EXCEPT
   a. end-diastolic volume.
   b. cardiac contractility.
   c. cardiac output.
   d. diastolic blood pressure.

4. The mean arterial pressure is defined as the
   a. average blood pressure throughout the cardiac cycle.
   b. average of the systolic and diastolic blood pressures.
   c. average systolic blood pressure during exercise.
   d. average of blood pressure and heart rate.

5. Primary training adaptations of elite aerobically-trained athletes include which of the following?
   I. increased maximal oxygen uptake
   II. decreased blood lactate concentration
   III. increased running economy
   IV. decreased capillary density
   a. I and III only
   b. II and IV only
   c. I, II, and III only
   d. II, III, and IV only

6. Which of the following is an early adaptation to acclimatizing to high altitude?
   a. decreased tidal volume
   b. decreased respiration rate
   c. increased resting cardiac output
   d. increased stroke volume

CHAPTER 7

Age- and Sex-Related Differences and Their Implications for Resistance Exercise

Avery D. Faigenbaum, EdD

After completing this chapter, you will be able to

- evaluate the evidence regarding the safety and effectiveness of resistance exercise for children,
- discuss sex-related differences in muscular function and their implications for female athletes,
- describe the effects of aging on musculoskeletal health and comment on the trainability of older adults, and
- explain why adaptations to resistance exercise can vary greatly among participants.

Resistance exercise has proven to be a safe and effective method of conditioning for individuals with various needs, goals, and abilities. Though much of what we understand about the stimulus of resistance exercise has been gained through examination of the acute and chronic responses of adult men to various training protocols, resistance exercise for children, women, and older people has received increasing public and medical attention in recent years. When designing and evaluating resistance training programs, strength and conditioning professionals need to understand age- and sex-related differences in body composition, muscular performance, and trainability and their implications for each individual.

For the purposes of this chapter, **resistance exercise** is defined as a specialized method of conditioning that involves the progressive use of resistance to increase one's ability to exert or resist force. This term should be distinguished from the sport of weightlifting in which individuals attempt to lift maximal amounts of weight in competition. The term **preadolescence** refers to a period of life before the development of secondary sex characteristics (e.g., pubic hair and reproductive organs), and the term **adolescence** refers to the period between childhood and adulthood. For ease of discussion, the terms *children* and *youth* are broadly defined in this chapter to include the preadolescent and adolescent years. The terms *older* and *senior* have been arbitrarily defined to include men and women over 65 years of age. In this chapter, muscular strength is expressed on an absolute basis (i.e., total force measured in pounds or kilograms) or on a relative basis (i.e., ratio of absolute strength to total body mass, fat-free mass, or muscle cross-sectional area).

CHILDREN

With the growing interest in youth resistance training, it is important for strength and conditioning professionals to understand the fundamental principles of normal growth and development. An understanding of these principles and an appreciation for how they can influence training adaptations and confound interpretation of research data are essential to the development and evaluation of safe and effective resistance training programs. Because the training of young athletes is becoming more intense and complex, anatomical and physiological factors that may be associated with acute and chronic injury also need to be considered.

The Growing Child

In this section, the terms *growth*, *development*, and *maturation* are used to describe changes that occur in the body throughout life. The term *growth* refers to an increase in body size or a particular body part; *development* describes the natural progression from prenatal life to adulthood; and *maturation* refers to the process of becoming mature and fully functional. **Puberty** refers to a period of time in which secondary sex characteristics develop and a child is transformed into a young adult. During puberty, changes also occur in body composition and the performance of physical skills.

Chronological Age Versus Biological Age

Because of considerable variation in the rates of growth and development, it is not particularly accurate to define a stage of maturation or development by age in months or years, which is known as the **chronological age**. Children do not grow at a constant rate, and there are substantial inter-individual differences in physical development at any given chronological age. A group of 14-year-old children can have a height difference as great as 9 inches (23 cm) and a weight difference up to 40 pounds (18 kg). Furthermore, an 11-year-old girl may be taller and more physically skilled than an 11-year-old boy. These differences correspond to variations in the timing and magnitude of growth during puberty. The timing of puberty can vary from 8 to 13 years in girls and from 9 to 15 years in boys, with girls typically beginning puberty about two years before boys.

Stages of maturation, or pubertal development, can be better assessed by the **biological age**, which can be measured in terms of skeletal age, somatic (physique) maturity, or sexual maturation. For example, two girls on a team may have the same chronological age but differ by several years in their biological age. One girl may be sexually mature, whereas the other may not begin the process of sexual maturation for several years. In girls the onset of menstruation (**menarche**) is a marker of sexual maturation, whereas in boys the closest indicators of sexual maturity include the appearance of pubic hair, facial hair, and deepening of the voice. The assessment of maturation in children is important for several reasons. Maturity assessment can be used to evaluate growth and development patterns in children. In addition, since the degree of maturation is related to measures of fitness including muscular strength and motor skills performance (82), techniques used to assess maturation can help ensure that children are fairly matched for fitness testing and athletic competition. Although there has been concern regarding the potential negative consequences of resistance training and weightlifting on growth and maturation, in adequately nourished children there is no scientific evidence that physical training delays or accelerates growth or maturation in boys and girls (54, 94). Physical activity, specifically weight-bearing activity, actually generates compressive forces that are essential for bone formation and growth (136).

A common method of evaluating biological age was devised by Tanner (132) and involves assessing the development of identifiable secondary sex characteristics: breast development in girls, genital development in boys, and pubic hair development in both sexes. The Tanner classification has five stages: Stage 1 represents the immature, preadolescent state, and stage 5 represents full sexual maturation. Even though there can be some variation in the degree of sexual maturity of children and adolescents at a particular stage, this technique for assessing sexual maturation is often used by physicians during physical examinations.

Sensitivity to individual differences in abilities and past experiences is especially important for children in the weight room. An early-maturing 14-year-old girl may be ready to train for a sport such as weightlifting, whereas a late-maturing 14-year-old boy may not be ready for the demands of heavy resistance exercise. In addition, a child's **training age** (i.e., the length of time the child has been resistance training) can influence adaptations to resistance training; the magnitude of gain in any strength-related measure is affected by the amount of adaptation that has already occurred. For example, a 12-year-old with two years of resistance training experience (i.e., a training age of 2 years) may not achieve the same strength gains in a given period of time as a 10-year-old who has no experience resistance training (i.e., a training age of zero). Strength and conditioning professionals must recognize these differences and should individualize the training program based on each child's maturity level, training age, and specific needs.

During the period of **peak height velocity** (pubertal growth spurt), young athletes may be at increased risk for injury (102). Peak height velocity usually occurs about age 12 in females and age 14 in males. The relative weakening of the bone during this stage of growth, muscle imbalances between the flexor and extensor groups around a joint, and the relative tightening of the muscle-tendon units spanning rapidly growing bones are risk factors for overuse injuries in children. Strength and conditioning professionals may need to modify training programs (i.e., emphasize flexibility, correct muscle imbalances, or decrease the volume and intensity of training) during periods of rapid growth. If a young athlete complains of pain or discomfort during a growth spurt, the strength and conditioning professional should be suspicious of an overuse injury rather than labeling these complaints "growing pains."

Muscle and Bone Growth

As children grow, muscle mass steadily increases throughout the developing years. At birth, approximately 25% of a child's body weight is muscle mass, and by adulthood about 40% of a person's total body mass is muscle. During puberty, a 10-fold increase in testosterone production in boys results in a marked increase in muscle mass, whereas in girls an increase in estrogen production causes increased body fat deposition, breast development, and widening of the hips. Although muscle mass in girls continues to increase during adolescence, the increase occurs at a slower rate than in boys due to hormonal differences. Throughout this time period the increase in muscle mass in both sexes is due to the hypertrophy of individual muscle fibers and not hyperplasia. Peak muscle mass occurs between the ages of 16 and 20 years in females and between 18 and 25 years in males unless affected by resistance exercise, diet, or both.

Bone formation occurs in the **diaphysis**, which is the central shaft of a long bone, and in the **growth cartilage**, which is located at three sites in the child: the epiphyseal (growth) plate, the joint surface, and the apophyseal insertions of muscle-tendon units. When the epiphyseal plate becomes completely ossified, the long bones stop growing. Although bones typically begin to fuse during early adolescence, girls generally achieve full bone maturity about two to three years before boys. The actual age varies considerably, but most bones are fused by the early 20s.

A particular concern in children is the vulnerability of the growth cartilage to trauma and overuse (103). Injuries there may disrupt the bone's blood and nutrient supply and result in permanent growth disturbances. Trauma from falls or excessive repetitive stress that may result in a ligament tear in an adult may produce an epiphyseal plate fracture in a child. Because the peak incidence of epiphyseal plate fractures in children occurs at about the time of peak height velocity, it seems that a preadolescent child may be at less risk for an epiphyseal plate fracture than an adolescent child. It has been suggested that the epiphyseal plates of younger children may be stronger and more resistant to shearing-type forces, which may be the cause of injuries to the growth cartilage (105). The potential for injury to the epiphyseal plate during resistance training is discussed later in this chapter.

Growth cartilage in children is located at the epiphyseal plate, the joint surface, and the apophyseal insertions. Damage to the growth cartilage may impair the growth and development of the affected bone.

Developmental Changes in Muscular Strength

As muscle mass increases throughout preadolescence and adolescence, there is an increase in muscular strength. In fact, the growth curves for strength are similar to those for body muscle mass. In boys, peak gains in strength typically occur about 1.2 years after peak height velocity and 0.8 years after peak weight velocity, with body weight being the clearer indicator. This pattern suggests that during periods of rapid growth, muscle increases first in mass and later in its ability to express strength (15). In girls, peak gains in strength also typically occur after peak height velocity, although there is more individual variation in the relationship of strength to height and body weight for girls than for boys (95). Although the strength of boys and girls is essentially equal during preadolescence, hormonal differences during puberty are responsible for an acceleration in the strength development of boys and a continuation at approximately the same rate in the strength development of girls as during the preadolescent years. On average, peak strength is usually attained by age 20 in untrained women and between the ages of 20 and 30 in untrained men.

An important factor related to the expression of muscular strength in children is the development of the nervous system. If myelination of nerve fibers is absent or incomplete, fast reactions and skilled movements cannot be successfully performed, and high levels of strength and power are impossible. As the nervous system develops, children improve their performance in skills that require balance, agility, strength, and power. Since the myelination of many motor nerves is incomplete until sexual maturation, children should not be expected to respond to training in the same way or reach the same skill level as adults until they reach neural maturity (86).

Because physiological functions are more closely related to biological age than to chronological age, at any given time an early-maturing child probably has an advantage in measures of absolute strength when compared with a later-maturing child of the same sex who has less muscle mass. In general, the body type of early-maturing youngsters tends to be mesomorphic (muscular and broader shoulders) or endomorphic (rounder and broader hips), whereas late maturers tend to be ectomorphic (slender and tall) (figure 7.1). Clearly, physical differences in body proportions can affect the execution of resistance exercises. For example, short arms and a large chest cavity are an advantage in bench presses, whereas long legs and a long torso are a disadvantage in squats. These factors have implications for strength and conditioning professionals who are attempting to standardize fitness tests or develop a resistance training program for a group of boys and girls who vary greatly in physical size. The reasons for individualized training programs should be explained to all participants, and special encouragement should be offered to late maturers who may be smaller and weaker than chronological-age peers with more biological maturity and therefore greater height and strength. Although late maturers tend to catch up to the early maturers as they proceed through adolescence, young athletes should realize that many factors—including motivation, coaching, and ability—contribute to success in sport.

Youth Resistance Training

Despite previous concerns that children would not benefit from resistance exercise or that the risk of injury was too great, clinicians, coaches, and exercise scientists now agree that resistance exercise can be a safe and effective method of conditioning for children (10, 41, 56, 86). An increasing number of boys and girls are participating in resistance training activities, and major sports medicine organizations support children's participation in resistance exercise provided that the programs are appropriately designed and competently supervised (1, 2, 5, 13, 42). Comprehensive school-based programs such as Physical Best are specifically designed to enhance health-related fitness components that include muscular strength and muscular endurance (110).

First and foremost, strength and conditioning professionals must remember that children are not miniature adults. No matter how big or strong a child is, children are physically less mature and are often experiencing training activities for the very first time. Children should begin resistance training at a level that is commensurate with their maturity

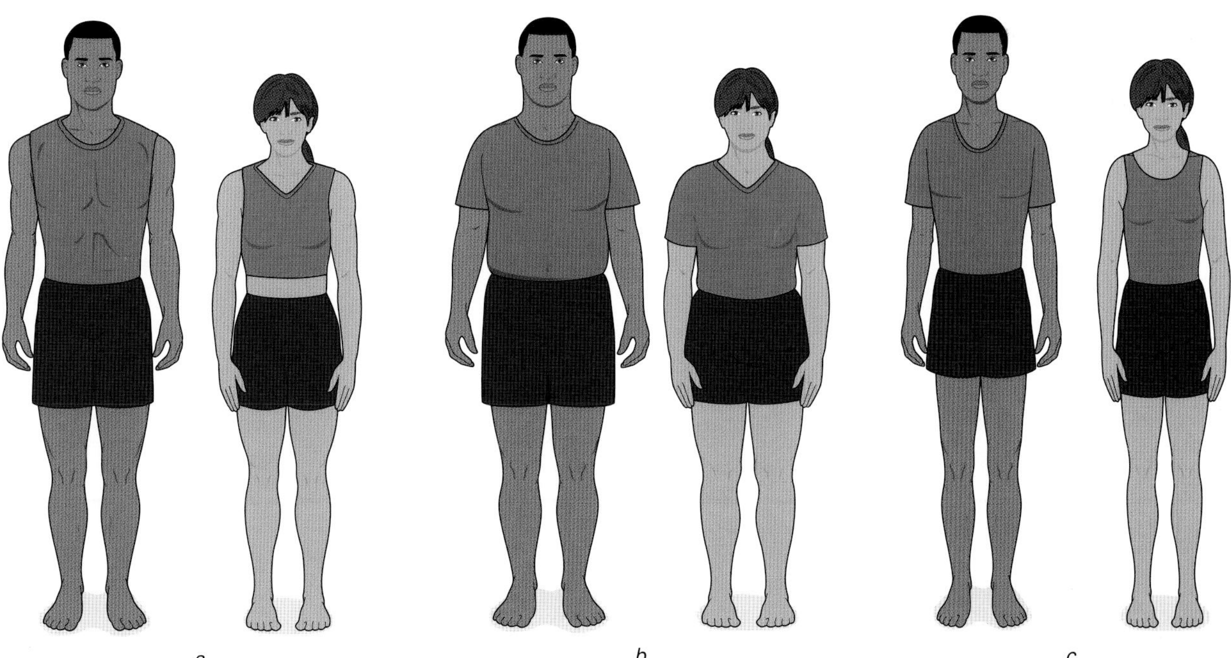

Figure 7.1 General body types: *(a)* mesomorph, *(b)* endomorph, and *(c)* ectomorph.

level, physical abilities, and individual goals. Adult programs and training philosophies are not appropriate for younger populations. Often the intensity and volume of training are too severe, and the recovery periods are inadequate for a child's fitness level. When introducing children to resistance training activities, it is always better to underestimate their physical abilities and gradually increase the volume and intensity of training than to overshoot their abilities and risk an injury.

Trainability of Children

Much of the controversy surrounding youth resistance training stemmed from the issue of children's trainability, that is, children's responsiveness to the stimulus of resistance exercise. The first studies failed to demonstrate a strength increase in preadolescents who participated in a resistance training program (36, 72). Although the lack of significant findings in these studies could be explained by methodological shortcomings, such as short study duration or inadequate training volume, the results from these reports are sometimes cited as proof that resistance training is ineffective for children. As previously discussed, muscular strength normally increases from childhood through the teenage years; thus a more appropriate conclusion from these reports may be that training-induced gains from a short-duration, low-volume training program are not distinguishable from gains attributable to normal growth and maturation.

Other investigations have clearly demonstrated that boys and girls can increase muscular strength above and beyond that accompanying growth and maturation, provided that the intensity and volume of training are adequate (43, 45, 53, 91, 121, 122, 140). Children as young as age 6 have benefited from resistance training (50, 55), and a variety of training modalities—including modified adult-sized weight machines, child-sized weight machines, medicine balls, free weights (barbells and dumbbells), and body weight calisthenics—have proven to be effective (49). Strength gains of roughly 30% to 40% have been typically observed in untrained preadolescent children following short-term (8- to 20-week) resistance training programs, although gains up to 74% have been reported (53). The variability in strength gain may be due to several factors, including the program design, quality of instruction, and background level of physical activity. Overall, it seems that the relative (percentage) improvement in muscular strength in preadolescents is quantitatively similar to, if not greater than, gains made by older populations. Conversely, when strength gains are compared on an absolute basis, preadolescents seem to be less trainable. Whether training-induced strength gains should be compared on a relative or absolute basis is debatable, but it seems unrealistic to expect a child to make the same absolute gains in strength as a larger adult, who probably has more than twice the absolute strength of a child.

Preadolescent boys and girls can significantly improve their strength with resistance training. Neurological factors, as opposed to hypertrophic factors, are primarily responsible for these gains.

Children who participate in resistance training programs are likely to undergo periods of reduced training or inactivity due to program design factors, extended travel plans, busy schedules, or decreased motivation. This temporary or permanent reduction or withdrawal of the training stimulus is called *detraining*. In children, unlike adults, the evaluation of strength changes during the detraining period is complicated by the growth-related strength increases during the same period of time. Nevertheless, data suggest that training-induced strength gains in children are impermanent and tend to return to untrained control group values during the detraining period (52, 78, 134). In one report, participation in physical education classes and organized sports throughout a detraining period did not maintain the preadolescents' training-induced strength gains (52). In another study comparing the effects on children of one and two days per week of resistance training, participants who resistance trained only once per week averaged 67% of the strength gains of participants who resistance trained twice per week (44). Collectively, these findings underscore the importance of continuous training to maintain the strength advantage of exercise-induced adaptations in children. Though the precise mechanisms responsible for the detraining response remain unclear, it seems likely that changes in neuromuscular functioning are at least partly responsible.

Changes in muscle hypertrophy can significantly contribute to training-induced strength gains in adolescents and adults, yet it is unlikely that muscle hypertrophy is primarily responsible for training-induced strength gains (at least up to 20 weeks) in preadolescents (120, 122). Although some findings do not agree with this suggestion (61), preadolescents appear to experience more difficulty increasing their muscle mass through a resistance training program due to inadequate levels of circulating testosterone. In preadolescent boys and girls, testosterone concentration is between 20 and 60 ng/100 ml, whereas during adolescence, testosterone levels in males increase to about 600 ng/100 ml while the levels in females remain unchanged.

It appears that preadolescents have more potential for an increase in strength owing to neural factors, such as increases in motor unit activation and changes in motor unit coordination, recruitment, and firing (120, 122). It has also been suggested that intrinsic muscle adaptations, improvements in motor skill performance, and the coordination of the involved muscle groups could be partly responsible for training-induced strength gains in preadolescents (122). One cannot state without qualification, however, that resistance training does not result in muscle hypertrophy in preadolescents, because it is possible that longer study durations, higher training volumes, and more precise measuring techniques (e.g., computerized imaging) may be needed to uncover potential training-induced muscle hypertrophy in youth who are following a resistance training program. During and after puberty, however, training-induced gains in strength are typically associated with gains in muscle hypertrophy due to hormonal influences. Although lower levels of testosterone in adolescent females limit the magnitude of training-induced increases in muscle hypertrophy, other hormone and growth factors (e.g., growth hormone and insulin-like growth factor) may be at least partly responsible for their muscle development (84). Figure 7.2 highlights the factors that contribute to the development of muscular strength, namely fat-free mass, testosterone concentrations, nervous system development, and the differentiation of fast-twitch and slow-twitch muscle fibers.

Potential Benefits

In addition to increasing muscular strength, power, and muscular endurance, regular participation in a youth resistance training program has the potential to influence many health- and fitness-related measures. Resistance exercise may favorably alter selected anatomic and psychosocial parameters, reduce injuries in sport and recreation activities, and improve motor skills and sport performance (48, 131). More recently, it has been reported that regular participation in a resistance training program can result in a decrease in fatness among obese children and adolescents (139). Although the treatment of childhood obesity is complex, it seems that obese youth enjoy resistance training because it is

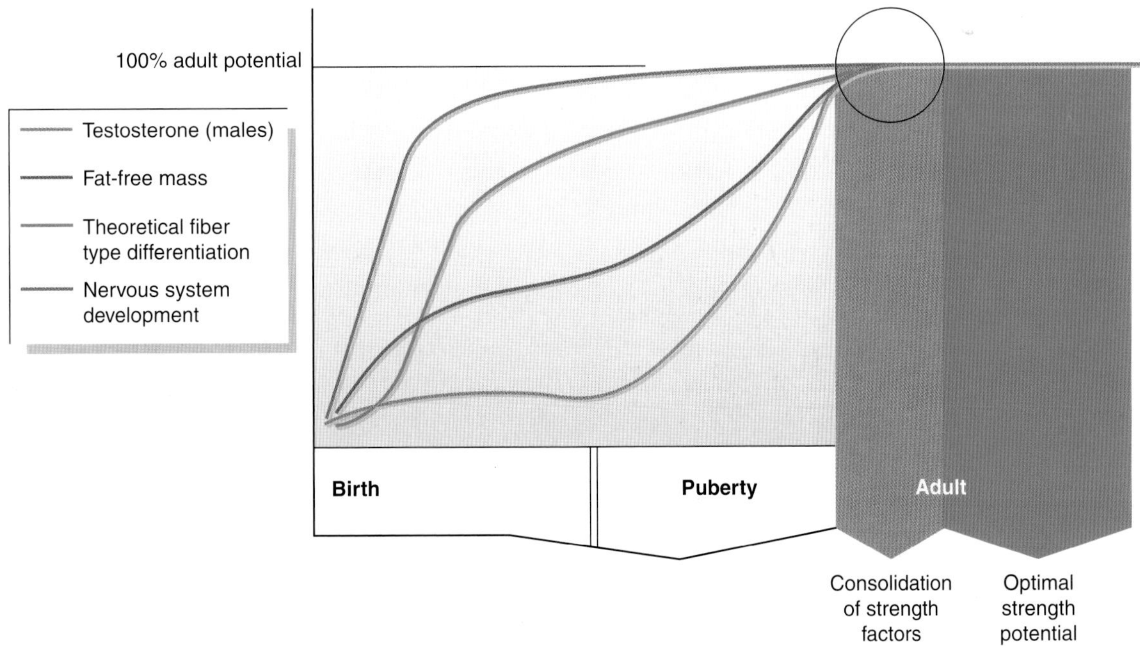

Figure 7.2 Theoretical interactive model for the integration of developmental factors related to the potential for muscular strength adaptations and performance.

Reprinted, by permission, from Kraemer et al., 1989 (86).

not aerobically taxing and provides an opportunity for all participants to experience success and feel good about their performance.

A common misperception is that resistance training will stunt the statural growth of children. While resistance training does not affect the genotypic maximum, it probably has a favorable influence on growth at any stage of development, as long as appropriate guidelines are followed (7, 54). In fact, regular participation in an exercise program that includes resistance training and weight-bearing physical activities has been shown to enhance bone density in children and adolescents (98, 109, 115). In support of these observations, it has been reported that elite adolescent weightlifters who regularly train with heavy weights while performing multijoint exercises display levels of bone density well above values of age-matched controls (29, 137). These findings may be especially important for young women who are at increased risk for developing **osteoporosis**, a clinical condition characterized by low bone mass and an increased susceptibility to fractures.

It has also been suggested that regular participation in a preseason conditioning program that includes resistance training may increase a young athlete's resistance to injury (38, 74). Every year millions of injuries occur during sport participation among children and adolescents in the United States (106), and it has been estimated that 15% to 50% of both acute and overuse injuries sustained by children could be prevented if they were better prepared to play these games (104). Strength and conditioning professionals can play a pivotal role in preparing young athletes for sports and thereby minimize or offset the incidence and severity of sport-related injuries common to young athletes. In many cases, aspiring young athletes who enroll in organized sport programs are unfit and ill prepared to handle the demands of their chosen sport. Children who are obese or those who lead sedentary lives (e.g., who take a bus to school and watch television or play computer games after school and on weekends) are not ready for one to two hours of sport training four or five days a week. Current findings indicate that among American youth aged 2 through 19 years, 33.6% are at risk for becoming obese (≥85% but <95% of the sex-specific body mass index [BMI] for age) and 17.1% are obese (≥95% of the sex-specific BMI for age) (117). Others report that 33.6% of adolescents in the United States have low fitness (<20th percentile for estimated $\dot{V}O_2max$) (20). While all aspiring young athletes will likely benefit from preparatory conditioning that includes resistance training, it seems that those who might benefit the most are the ones who are less fit to begin with.

Even though some coaches may argue that early sport specialization is the key to success, it seems that development of fundamental fitness skills and involvement in a variety of sports and activities may be more related to later sport success than early sport specialization (1, 93). Although the total elimination of youth sport injuries is an unrealistic goal, the addition of resistance training (including plyometric exercises) to a youngster's preseason fitness program may better prepare the young athlete to handle the duration and magnitude of forces that develop during practice and game situations (26, 74). Because of individual differences in stress tolerance, the training intensity, volume, and rate of progression need to be carefully prescribed since resistance training adds to the chronic repetitive stress placed on the young musculoskeletal system. Proper progression and program variation will optimize gains, prevent boredom, and reduce the stress from overtraining. In addition, well-planned recovery strategies (e.g., proper cool-down, postexercise meal or snack, and adequate sleep) can help to maximize training adaptations.

Because many sports have a significant strength or power component, it is attractive to assume that resistance training will enhance athletic performance. Though comments from parents and children support this contention, scientific reports on this issue are limited. Improvements in selected motor performance skills—such as the long jump, vertical jump, 30 m dash time, and agility run time—have been observed in children who participated in a resistance training program (55, 91, 116, 140). Although only a few reports have provided direct evaluations of the effects of youth resistance training on sport performance (9, 16, 59), it appears that a progressive resistance training program will in all likelihood result in some degree of improvement in sport performance in young athletes.

Potential Risks and Concerns

Appropriately prescribed youth resistance training programs are relatively safe when compared with other sports and activities in which children and adolescents regularly participate (70). Paradoxically, it seems that the forces placed on the joints of young athletes during sport participation may be far greater than those generated from resistance training programs. The belief that resistance train-

How Can We Reduce the Risk of Overuse Injuries in Youth?

- Prior to sport participation, young athletes should be evaluated by a sports medicine physician to identify medical problems and musculoskeletal deficits.
- Parents should be educated about the benefits and risks of competitive sports and should understand the importance of preparatory conditioning for aspiring young athletes.
- Children and adolescents should be encouraged to participate in year-round physical activity to enhance health and fitness. Ideally, youth activity programs should vary in type, volume, and intensity throughout the year and meet the specific needs of each child.
- Youth coaches should implement well-planned recovery strategies between hard workouts and competitions in order to maximize recovery and the return to an optimal performance state.
- The nutritional status of young athletes should be monitored to ensure that their diets are adequate.
- Youth sport coaches should participate in educational programs to learn more about conditioning, sport skills, safety rules, equipment, the psychology of children, and the physiology of growth and development. Coaches should support and encourage all children and adolescents to participate but should not excessively pressure them to perform at a level beyond their capabilities.
- Boys and girls should be encouraged to participate in a variety of sports and activities.

ing is dangerous for children is not consistent with the needs of children and the documented risks associated with this type of training. Nevertheless, children have been injured in the weight room, and strength and conditioning professionals therefore need to heed safety guidelines when working with younger populations.

Perhaps the most traditional concern about youth resistance training involves the potential for injury to the epiphyseal plate. As previously mentioned, this area of the bone has not yet ossified and is therefore prone to injury. Although epiphyseal plate fractures have been reported in adolescents who are following a resistance training program, these reports were case studies and typically involved the performance of heavy overhead lifts in unsupervised settings (66, 125, 126). An epiphyseal plate fracture has not been reported in any prospective youth resistance training study that adhered to established training guidelines. Even 1-repetition maximum (1RM) testing in children is safe, provided that appropriate testing guidelines are followed (i.e., adequate warm-up periods, individual progression of loads, and close supervision) (46). It seems that if children are taught how to resistance train properly, the risk of an epiphyseal plate fracture is minimal.

The greatest concern for youth who are following a resistance training program may be the risk for repetitive-use soft tissue injuries (12, 14, 124). In particular, the risks of injury to the lower back (114, 124) and shoulder (91, 123) are noteworthy concerns. Furthermore, a catastrophic injury can result if safety standards for youth resistance training—qualified adult supervision, safe equipment, and age-specific training guidelines—are not followed (65).

Program Design Considerations for Children

Resistance training should be one part of a well-rounded exercise program for children that also addresses other fitness goals. Although there is no minimal age requirement for participation in a youth resistance training program, children should have the emotional maturity to follow directions and should be eager to try this type of activity. A pretraining medical examination is not mandatory for apparently healthy children; however, all participants should be screened for any injury or illness that may limit or prevent safe participation in a resistance training program. The goals of youth resistance training programs should not be limited to increasing muscular strength but should also include teaching children about their bodies, promoting an interest in physical activity, and having fun. It seems likely that children who enjoy participating in physical activities and sports are more likely to be active later in life (133).

Two important areas of concern in the development of youth resistance training programs are the quality of instruction and rate of progression. Strength and conditioning professionals must have a thorough understanding of youth resistance training guidelines, a willingness to demonstrate proper exercise technique, and the ability to speak with children at a level they understand. Professionals should play down competition between participants and focus on proper technique instead of the amount of weight lifted. The use of individualized workout logs can help each child understand the concept of progression. When working with youth it is important to focus on intrinsic factors such as skill improvement, personal successes, and having fun.

Although only limited data are available regarding the relationship between repetitions and selected percentages of the 1RM in children, it appears that the number of repetitions that can be performed at a given percentage of the 1RM are specific to a given exercise (51). Thus, the minimal strength threshold, when expressed as a percentage of 1RM, may vary between muscle groups, possibly due to the amount of muscle mass involved with each exercise. The best approach to prescribing a resistance training program for children may be to first establish the repetition range (e.g., 10 to 12) and then determine by trial and error the maximal load that can be safely handled for the prescribed range. Although increasing the resistance or the number of sets is necessary to make continual gains, this does not mean that every session needs to be more intense or voluminous than the previous one. While it is important to keep the program fresh and challenging, children should be given an opportunity to develop proper form and technique.

Advanced multijoint exercises such as the snatch and clean and jerk can be incorporated into a child's program, but the focus must be on developing proper form and technique (17, 47). Poor technique can put abnormal stress on musculoskeletal tissues and lead to an injury. The resistance must be lowered if proper exercise technique cannot be maintained. When learning new exercises, children should start with an unloaded barbell or even a long wooden stick to learn the correct technique. Strength and conditioning professionals should be aware of the time required to safely and effectively teach advanced multijoint lifts to children. Because of the potential risk of shoulder and lower back injuries, prehabilitation exercises for the shoulder and torso should be incorporated into the training program. In other words, exercises that would be prescribed for the rehabilitation of shoulder injuries and back injuries should be performed beforehand as a preventive health measure. A summary of youth resistance training guidelines is presented in the sidebar.

Youth Resistance Training Guidelines

- Each child should understand the benefits and risks associated with resistance training.
- Competent and caring fitness professionals should supervise training sessions.
- The exercise environment should be safe and free of hazards, and the equipment should be in good repair and properly sized to fit each child.
- Dynamic warm-up exercises should be performed before resistance training.
- Static stretching exercises should be performed after resistance training.
- Carefully monitor each child's tolerance to the exercise stress.
- Begin with light loads to allow appropriate adjustments to be made.
- Increase the resistance gradually (e.g., 5% to 10%) as strength improves.
- Depending on individual needs and goals, one to three sets of 6 to 15 repetitions on a variety of single- and multijoint exercises can be performed.
- Advanced multijoint exercises, such as the snatch and clean and jerk, may be incorporated into the program provided that appropriate loads are used and the focus remains on proper form.
- Two to three nonconsecutive training sessions per week are recommended.
- When necessary, adult spotters should be nearby to actively assist the child in the event of a failed repetition.
- The resistance training program should be systematically varied throughout the year.
- Children should be encouraged to drink plenty of water before, during, and after exercise.

Adapted from Faigenbaum et al., 1996 (52).

FEMALE ATHLETES

Women who regularly participate in resistance training activities can improve their health, develop good feelings about themselves, reduce their risk of degenerative diseases (e.g., osteoporosis), and enhance their sport performance. Whereas in the past some women may have questioned the value of resistance training or even avoided this type of exercise due to social stigmas, evidence clearly indicates that women are capable of tolerating and adapting to the stresses of resistance exercise and that the benefits are substantial (87, 112). The current interest in resistance training by women is evidenced by the great number of women who now resistance train and the growth of female weightlifting contests.

Sex Differences

Strength and conditioning professionals need to understand sex-related differences in physique, body composition, and physiological responses to resistance exercise when designing and evaluating resistance training programs. An understanding of these differences and the areas of concern that are unique to female athletes can help to optimize performance and decrease the risk of sport-related injuries.

Body Size and Composition

Before puberty there are essentially no differences in height, weight, and body size between boys and girls. As puberty begins and progresses, differences in these measurements become more evident, primarily because of hormonal changes. During puberty the production of estrogen in girls increases fat deposition and breast development, whereas testosterone production in boys increases bone formation and protein synthesis. Though estrogen also stimulates bone growth, boys have a longer growth period, and therefore adult men tend to achieve greater stature than adult women. On average, adult women tend to have more body fat and less muscle and bone than adult males. Furthermore, women tend to be lighter in total body weight than men. Although some female athletes may have lower fat percentages than untrained men, extremely low fat percentages in women may be associated with adverse health consequences (119, 141). Anthropometric measurements of adults indicate that men tend to have broader shoulders relative to their hips and women tend to have broader hips relative to their waists and shoulders. The broader shoulders in men can support more muscle tissue and can also provide a mechanical advantage for muscles acting at the shoulder.

Strength and Power Output

When comparing training-induced changes in muscular strength between sexes, it is important to distinguish between absolute and relative measures. In terms of absolute strength, women generally have about two-thirds the strength of men (88). The absolute lower body strength of women is generally closer to male values as compared to the absolute values for upper body strength. Sex-related differences in body composition, anthropometric characteristics, and fat-free mass distribution (women tend to have less muscle mass above the waist) can partly explain these sex-related differences, which are apparent in recreationally trained individuals as well as highly trained athletes.

When considered on a relative basis, sex-related differences in muscular strength are greatly reduced. Because the average man and woman differ considerably in body size, it is useful to compare sex differences in strength relative to body weight, fat-free mass, and muscle cross-sectional area. When expressed relative to body weight, the lower body strength of women is similar to that of men, while the upper body strength of women is still somewhat less. If comparisons are made relative to fat-free mass, differences in strength between men and women tend to disappear (75). Interesting but limited data suggest that eccentric strength may be more similar between men and women than concentric strength when compared relative to fat-free mass (27, 130).

When strength is expressed relative to muscle cross-sectional area, no significant difference exists between sexes, which indicates that muscle quality (peak force per cross-sectional area) is not sex specific (21, 107). Granted that the muscle fibers in men and women are also similar in fiber type distribution and histochemical characteristics, men tend to have a larger muscle fiber cross-sectional area than women. Notwithstanding the importance of these observations, strength and conditioning professionals need to remember that there is a wide range of strength abilities and that in some cases differences between two women may in fact be greater than differences between a man and a woman.

In terms of absolute strength, women are generally weaker than men because of their lower quantity of muscle. Relative to muscle cross-sectional area, no differences in strength exist between the sexes, which indicates that muscle quality is not sex specific.

Sex-related differences in power output are similar to those for muscular strength. Measurements comparing power outputs of competitive lifters revealed that during the entire snatch or clean pulling movements, women's power output relative to total body weight was about 63% of men's (63). Similar findings regarding power output were observed in presumably untrained women (83). Maximal vertical jump and standing long jump scores also tend to be lower in women than in men (28, 33, 96), although when expressed relative to fat-free mass, the gap between sexes tends to narrow. Though men still perform better in general than women, it appears that differences in fat-free mass are not entirely responsible for differences in power output. Although equivocal, sex-related differences in the rate of force development could partly explain these findings (127).

Resistance Training for Female Athletes

Despite sex-related differences, men and women respond to resistance exercise from their pretraining baselines in similar ways. Although the magnitudes of change in selected variables may differ somewhat, the overall trends suggest that the value of resistance exercise for women extends far beyond an increase in muscular strength and includes favorable changes in other important measures of health and fitness.

Trainability of Women

Through participation in a resistance training program, women can apparently increase their strength at the same rate as men or faster. Although absolute gains in strength are often greater for men, relative (percentage) increases are about the same or greater in women. Even though nervous system adaptations clearly contribute to the development of strength, the influence of hypertrophic factors in women should not be overlooked. When sophisticated techniques (e.g., computed tomography) are used to accurately measure changes in muscle cross-sectional area, short-term gains (up to 16 weeks) in muscle hypertrophy are similar between sexes (31, 68).

Judging by the muscular development of female weightlifters, bodybuilders, and track and field athletes who have not used anabolic steroids, it is obvious that substantial muscle hypertrophy is possible in women who regularly participate in high-volume or high-intensity training programs. Although further study is warranted, it is possible that testosterone concentrations in women may vary with training and that women with relatively high levels of testosterone may have more potential for an increase in muscle size and strength (30, 69). Furthermore, it is possible that the complexity of the exercise movement used during training may influence the degree of muscle hypertrophy (24). More complex movements, such as the squat and bench press (as compared with the biceps curl), may require a relatively longer neural adaptation period, thereby delaying muscle hypertrophy in the trunk and legs (24). A genetic disposition to develop a large muscle mass may also be a contributing factor.

Program Design Considerations for Women

Since the physiological characteristics of muscle in the sexes are the same, there is no sensible reason why resistance training programs for women need to be different from those for men. In fact, because the muscle groups involved in a particular sport are obviously the same for men and women, resistance training programs should be designed to improve the performance of the muscles needed for successful sport performance, regardless of sex. It is a misperception that resistance training programs for women should be different from those for men or that women lose flexibility or develop "bulky" muscles if they train with weights. The only real difference between training programs for men and women is generally the amount of resistance used for a given exercise. It is particularly important for young female athletes to perform some type of resistance exercise regularly in order to increase their resistance to injuries and approach their genetic potential in musculoskeletal strength and power during adulthood. The observations that elite female gymnasts are able to perform 40 pull-ups and that competitive female weightlifters can clean and jerk over two times their body weight demonstrate what is possible.

Two areas of concern regarding the prescription of resistance training programs for women relate to the development of upper body strength and the prevention of sport-related injuries, in particular those that involve the knee. Since the upper body strength of women tends to be less than that of men, emphasizing development of the upper body is important for female athletes who play sports that require upper body strength and power. A significant portion of the total training volume of these female athletes should focus on the development of the upper body. The addition of one or two upper body exercises or one or two extra sets may be beneficial for women who have difficulty performing multijoint free weight exercises (e.g., various full and partial snatching and cleaning movements) because of limitations in upper body strength. Female athletes can benefit by incorporating various snatching and cleaning movements into their training programs because adaptations resulting from these large muscle mass, multijoint exercises transfer well to performance in recreational and sport activities. Furthermore, the caloric cost of performing these lifts can be relatively high (64).

It is important for strength and conditioning professionals to be aware of the increasing incidence of knee injuries in female athletes, particularly in sports such as soccer and basketball (6, 34, 73). According to one National Collegiate Athletic Association report, female basketball players were six times more likely to incur an anterior cruciate ligament tear than male players (111). On the basis of these findings, some observers suggest that over 15,000 debilitating knee injuries can be expected to occur in female intercollegiate athletes during any given year (74). Although it is possible that the increasing number of knee injuries simply reflects an increase in participation by women in organized sport, others have suggested causative factors. It is possible that joint laxity, limb alignment, notch dimensions, ligament size, body movement, shoe-surface interaction, skill level, hormonal changes, use of ankle braces, and training deficiencies contribute to the observed difference in the number of knee injuries between male and female athletes (6, 73, 108, 128, 143). Though it is likely that none of the aforementioned factors is solely responsible, increasing the level of physical activity in an attempt to strengthen ligaments and enhance neuromuscular control of the knee joint prior to sport participation merits consideration. Since most anterior cruciate ligament injuries in female athletes occur from noncontact mechanisms (e.g., deceleration, lateral pivoting or landing [11]), regular participation in a conditioning program that is designed to enhance the strength of supporting structures and increase neuromuscular control of the knee joint may reduce the risk of sport-related injuries (38, 74).

With appropriate instruction and progression, a year-round conditioning program that includes lower body resistance exercises and also agility, balance, and plyometric drills to improve muscular strength and power, as well as neuromuscular control of the knee joint, appears to be indicated. Furthermore, it is important that female athletes consume adequate energy and emphasize quality protein and healthy fat consumption to optimize training adaptations (138). Although additional clinical trials are needed to determine the best method for reducing the incidence of sport-related injuries in female athletes, the injury prevention strategies listed in the sidebar will likely help.

How Can Female Athletes Reduce Their Risk of Injury?

- Begin with a preparticipation screening by a sports medicine physician. This should include identification of risk factors for injury along with musculoskeletal testing.
- Participate in a year-round conditioning program that includes resistance training, plyometric training, agility training, and flexibility training. The conditioning program should meet the specific needs of each athlete and should progress in a periodized fashion that allows for proper musculoskeletal adaptation.
- Every exercise session should be preceded by a general dynamic warm-up and a specific warm-up using movements that resemble those involved in the activity.
- Athletes should wear appropriate clothing and footwear during practice and games.
- Athletes should be encouraged to maximize their athletic potential by optimizing their dietary intake.

OLDER ADULTS

The number of men and women over the age of 65 is growing, and it seems that more opportunities for participation in sports ranging from marathoning to weightlifting are available to older athletes. While the cardiovascular endurance and muscular strength of older competitors or masters athletes are truly exceptional, even the most highly trained athletes experience some decline in performance after age 30. For example, Olympic-style weightlifting ability has been shown to decline with age at a rate of approximately 1% to 1.5% per year until approximately age 70, after which a more dramatic decrease occurs (99). Strength and conditioning professionals should understand the physiological changes that occur with aging and the trainability of older individuals. In addition, the potential health risks associated with physical activity in aging athletes need to be considered.

Age-Related Changes in Musculoskeletal Health

Significant changes in body composition with advancing age can lead to the development of physical functional impairments and injury. The well-documented loss of bone and muscle with age not only makes activities of daily life—such as getting out of a chair and opening a window—more difficult, but also increases the risk for falls, hip fractures, and long-term disability (25, 75, 76). Bones become fragile with age because of a decrease in bone mineral content that causes an increase in bone porosity. The bone mineral content and microarchitecture of bone can deteriorate to such an extent that even activities of daily life may cause a bone fracture, particularly of the hip, spine, or wrist. **Osteopenia** is defined by a bone mineral density between –1 and –2.5 standard deviations (SD) of the young adult mean; osteoporosis is defined by a bone mineral density below –2.5 SD of the young adult mean (81). These conditions, which result in bones with less density and strength, are serious concerns in older people, particularly women. The slow but progressive loss of bone with age has been linked to physical inactivity and to hormonal, nutritional, mechanical, and genetic factors (37).

Advancing age is also associated with a loss of muscle mass, which has been termed **sarcopenia** (40). Computed tomography has revealed that after age 30 there is a decrease in the cross-sectional areas of individual muscles, along with a decrease in muscle density and an increase in intramuscular fat. These changes seem to be a predictable consequence of advancing age and seem to be most pronounced in women (77). The observed muscle atrophy with aging appears to result from physical inactivity and a gradual and selective denervation of muscle fibers, most notably the Type II (fast-twitch) fibers (90, 135). Thus, older people have less muscle mass and a higher proportion of Type I (slow-twitch) muscle fibers.

Decreased muscle mass results in a loss of muscle strength. In one report, 40% of women aged 55 to 64 years, 45% of women aged 65 to 74 years, and 65% of women aged 75 to 84 years were unable to lift about 10 pounds (4.5 kg) (80). The reduction in the size or number of muscle fibers, especially the Type II fibers, also leads to a decrease in the ability of a muscle to generate power (i.e., exert force rapidly) (8, 67). Since everyday activities require a certain degree of power development, a decrease in the ability of muscles to produce force rapidly may adversely affect the ability of older adults to safely perform activities such as stair climbing and walking. Since power recedes at a faster rate than muscle strength with age (101), the development of power may be most important for the performance of daily activities as well as the prevention of accidental falls in older adults. Factors that may contribute to the age-related decline in muscle strength and power include reductions in muscle mass, nervous system changes, hormonal changes, poor nutrition, and physical inactivity (35, 71, 118). The functional consequences of these age-related changes are significant because the magnitude and rate of change influence the age at which a person may become functionally dependent (e.g., unable to perform household tasks or rise from a chair) or reach a threshold of disability. A summary of adaptations to aging and resistance training is presented in table 7.1.

Advancing age is associated with a loss of muscle mass, which is due to physical inactivity and the selective loss of Type II (fast-twitch) muscle fibers. A direct result of the reduction in muscle mass is a loss of muscular strength and power.

Resistance Training for Older Adults

Aging does not appear to enhance or reduce the ability of the musculoskeletal system to adapt to resistance exercise. Significant improvements in muscular strength, power, muscle mass, bone mineral density, and functional capabilities (e.g., gait speed) have been observed in older people who participated in progressive resistance training programs (4, 25, 76, 92). For older adults, such improve-

TABLE 7.1

Summary of Adaptations to Aging and Resistance Training

Characteristic	Aging	Resistance training
Muscular strength	Decreases	Increases
Power	Decreases	Increases
Muscular endurance	Decreases	Increases
Muscle mass	Decreases	Increases
Muscle fiber size	Decreases	Increases
Muscular metabolic capacity	Decreases	Increases
Resting metabolic rate	Decreases	Increases
Body fat	Increases	Decreases
Bone mineral density	Decreases	Increases
Physical function	Decreases	Increases

ments enhance exercise performance, decrease the risk for injury, promote independent living, and improve quality of life. Because of the age-related changes in musculoskeletal health, resistance exercise may be one of the most beneficial modes of training for older populations who need to enhance musculoskeletal strength, power, muscle mass, bone mineral density, and functional abilities.

Trainability of Older Adults

A great deal of attention has focused on strategies to improve the musculoskeletal health of older men and women. Because of the deconditioned state of many seniors, desirable changes in muscle strength and function can result from a variety of resistance training protocols, particularly during the first few weeks of training (62). Previously sedentary older men have more than doubled knee extensor strength and tripled knee flexor strength (60), and similar observations have been made in older women (23). In one study the ability of very old men and women (87 to 96 years old) to improve muscular strength was demonstrated following only eight weeks of resistance training (57). Improvements in gait speed, stair climbing ability, balance, and overall spontaneous activity have also been associated with training-induced strength gains in older populations (25, 58, 92). More recent evidence suggests that resistance training specific for power development may help optimize functional abilities in older adults (71, 118). While the optimal training protocol for improving muscular strength and power in seniors is not known, it appears that there is a dose–response relationship between training intensity and improvements in muscular strength and power (35).

Regular participation in a resistance training program also seems to have profound anabolic effects in older populations (23, 57, 60). Computed tomography and muscle biopsy analysis showed evidence of muscle hypertrophy in older men who participated in a high-intensity resistance training program (60), and other investigations involving older adults have shown that resistance training can improve nitrogen retention, which can have a positive effect on muscle protein metabolism (19, 144). Resistance training has also been shown to have an important effect on energy balance in older adults, as evidenced by an increase in the resting metabolic rate of men and women who resistance train (18). It is noteworthy that dietary modifications (a change in total food intake or selected nutrients) in older men who resistance trained had a positive effect on muscle hypertrophy (100).

Although the response of bone to resistance exercise is influenced by a complex interaction of many variables (e.g., hormonal status, activity history, and nutrition), it has been reported that resistance exercise has a positive effect on bone health in older men and women (32, 89, 113). Regularly performed resistance training can offset the age-related declines in bone health by maintaining or increasing bone mineral density. Resistance training may also reduce the risk of osteoporotic fractures by improving dynamic balance, muscle mass, and overall level of physical activity. While there is no doubt that resistance exercise can improve bone health in older adults, the interaction of exercise with hormonal and nutritional factors influences the degree of benefit of the exercise program. Furthermore, bones retain the beneficial effects of exercise only as long as training is continued. During periods of inactivity, bone density tends to revert to preexercise levels (79).

Though aging is associated with a number of undesirable changes in body composition, older men and women maintain their ability to make significant improvements in strength and functional ability. Both aerobic and resistance exercise are beneficial for older adults, but only resistance training can increase muscular strength and muscle mass.

Program Design Considerations for Older Adults

Whereas aerobic exercise has been recommended for many years as a means of increasing cardiovascular fitness, resistance training is currently recognized as an important component of a fitness conditioning program for older adults (4, 25, 62, 85, 142). Because age-related losses of musculoskeletal strength, power, and mass may be almost universal, programs designed to maintain or improve musculoskeletal health in older adults should be implemented. Not only can regular participation in a resistance training program offset some of these age-related losses, but it can help older people maintain an active, high-quality lifestyle.

The fundamental principles of designing a resistance training program for an older person and a younger person are basically the same, but there are several concerns that strength and conditioning professionals need to be aware of when working with seniors. Issues regarding preexisting medical ailments, exercise progression, and nutritional status should be evaluated before the beginning of a resistance training program. Even though older populations retain the capacity to adapt to increased levels of physical activity, safe and effective exercise guidelines must be followed.

Before participation in an exercise program, seniors should complete a medical history and risk factor questionnaire (3). Potential limitations and possible restrictions for physical activity can be ascertained from this information. In some cases physician clearance is required before the initiation of a moderate or vigorous exercise program (3). Any questions regarding a participant's medical status (e.g., heart disease, hypertension, arthritis, osteoporosis, or diabetes mellitus) should be answered by a health professional. After this information is obtained, a preprogram evaluation to document baseline measurements and assess responses to specific exercise modalities should be performed. Although a treadmill exercise test is often used to evaluate cardiovascular responses to aerobic exercise, a strength test (preferably on the equipment used in training) should be used to assess responses to resistance exercise and aid in the exercise prescription. Various methods of assessing muscular strength, including 1RM testing, can be used in senior populations, provided that appropriate testing guidelines are followed (129).

Evidence suggests that resistance training can be safe for seniors if appropriate training guidelines are followed (39, 97, 142). On the other hand, poorly designed programs can be potentially hazardous. Many older men and women have at least one chronic health problem, and therefore proper health screening (and consultation with a physician, if necessary) should be part of senior fitness programs. The risk of injury can be minimized with qualified instruction, sensible progression, program variation, and adequate recovery between training sessions.

Untrained seniors who begin resistance training should start at a relatively low exercise intensity, and therefore the exercise prescription should be individualized. Although higher intensities of resistance exercise can be tolerated by some older men and women who have resistance training experience, the early phase of the training program should be directed toward learning proper exercise technique while minimizing the potential for muscle soreness and injury. Less intense training during the first few weeks of an exercise program may also be beneficial for seniors who are apprehensive about participating in a resistance training program. Following the initial adaptation period, the training program can gradually progress, provided that the program continues to meet the needs and medical concerns of each person. In training older men and women, it is particularly important to focus on the major muscle groups that are used in everyday activities, such as load carrying and climbing stairs.

Once participants master the performance of basic resistance exercises, standing postures with free weights (barbells and dumbbells), multidirectional medicine ball exercises, and balance training (e.g., one-legged stands and circle turns) can be incorporated into the program. Seniors should gradually progress from one set of 8 to 12 repetitions at a relatively low intensity (e.g., 40% to 50% 1RM) to higher training volumes and intensities (e.g., three sets per exercise with 60% to 80% of 1RM) depending on individual needs, goals, and abilities (62, 85). In addition, high-velocity power exercises can be gradually incorporated into the overall training regimen provided that seniors have successfully completed a general strength training program. Current recommendations for increasing power in healthy older adults include the performance of one to three sets per exercise with a light to moderate load (40% to 60% 1RM) for 6 to 10 repetitions with high repetition velocity (85).

A resistance training program for older men and women should vary in volume and intensity throughout the year to lessen the likelihood of overtraining and ensure that progress is made throughout the training period. Because recovery from a training session may take longer in older populations, a training frequency of twice per week is recommended, at least during the initial adaptation period. Strength and conditioning professionals should listen to individual concerns and be able to modify a training program based on the person's health history and individual goals. With competent instruction and support from friends, older men and women can gain confidence in their ability to resistance train, which may be enough to ensure good adherence to the program. However, since a majority of older adults do not currently engage in resistance training activities (22), professionals need to increase awareness of the fitness benefits associated with resistance exercise and address the concerns that seniors may have about participating in a resistance training program.

An additional consideration related to resistance training in older men and women is proper nutrition. The quality and quantity of a person's food intake (or perhaps selected nutrients) may mean the difference between losing and gaining muscle mass. In particular, it seems that adequate amounts of protein are essential for muscle hypertrophy in older people. Furthermore, inadequate intakes of kilocalories, carbohydrates, protein, calcium, and iron are associated with potential health consequences, including fatigue, compromised immune function, and delayed recovery from injury. Improving an older person's food intake not only improves health, but may optimize adaptations to resistance training.

What Are the Safety Recommendations for Resistance Training for Seniors?

- All participants should be prescreened, since many older people suffer from a variety of medical conditions. If necessary, medical advice should be sought concerning the most appropriate type of activity.
- Warm up for 5 to 10 minutes before each exercise session. An acceptable warm-up includes low- to moderate-intensity aerobic activity and calisthenics.
- Perform static stretching exercises before or after, or both before and after, each resistance training session.
- Use a resistance that does not overtax the musculoskeletal system.
- Avoid performing the Valsalva maneuver.
- Allow 48 to 72 hours of recovery between exercise sessions.
- Perform all exercises within a range of motion that is pain free.
- Receive exercise instruction from qualified instructors.

CONCLUSION

Research shows that resistance exercise can be a safe and effective method of conditioning for males and females of all ages and abilities. The potential benefits include improvements in musculoskeletal health and sport performance as well as in self-image and confidence. Moreover, regular participation in a resistance training program can reduce the risk of sport-related injuries in athletes and promote independent living in seniors. Though the fundamental principles of resistance training are similar for people of both sexes and all ages, there are unique concerns specific to each population. Knowledge of age- and sex-related differences is essential to the development and evaluation of safe and effective resistance training programs. Strength and conditioning professionals should be aware that individual responses to resistance exercise may vary greatly and should be sensitive to the individual needs of all participants.

Over the past two decades, coaches, clinicians, and exercise scientists have added to our understanding of age- and sex-related differences and their implications for resistance exercise. Their work has quantified the impact of resistance training on males and females of all ages and has provided the foundation for recommendations about the design of conditioning programs. The information in this chapter and other chapters should help strength and conditioning professionals to understand and appreciate age- and sex-related differences and enhance their ability to develop safe and effective resistance training programs for children, women, and older adults.

KEY TERMS

adolescence 142
biological age 143
chronological age 143
diaphysis 144
growth cartilage 144
menarche 143
osteopenia 154
osteoporosis 148
peak height velocity 143
preadolescence 142
puberty 142
resistance exercise 142
sarcopenia 154
training age 143

STUDY QUESTIONS

1. When males and females are compared relative to muscle cross-sectional area, it appears that the potential for force production is
   a. greater in males.
   b. greater in females.
   c. equal in males and females.
   d. dependent upon body weight.

2. Which of the following is the MOST significant adaptation to chronic resistance training for an older adult?
   a. increased cardiovascular fitness
   b. improved blood lipid profile
   c. increased muscle mass
   d. improved flexibility

3. An eight-year-old boy dramatically increased his upper body strength after following a six-month resistance training program. Which of the following is MOST likely responsible for this gain?
   a. increased number of muscle fibers
   b. enhanced cross-sectional area
   c. greater muscle density
   d. improved neuromuscular functioning

4. Growth cartilage in children is located at all of the following locations EXCEPT the
   a. diaphysis.
   b. epiphyseal plate.
   c. joint surface.
   d. apophyseal insertion.

5. All of the following are likely outcomes of preadolescent resistance training EXCEPT increased
   a. resistance to injury.
   b. strength.
   c. hypertrophy.
   d. bone density.

6. The condition characterized by a bone mineral density more than 2.5 SD below the young adult mean is called
   a. sarcopenia.
   b. osteopenia.
   c. osteoporosis.
   d. scoliosis.

7. Which of the following should be evaluated FIRST when designing a training program for a 68-year-old competitive female tennis player?
   a. cardiovascular fitness
   b. lower body strength
   c. balance and agility
   d. medical history

8. Deconditioned female college athletes who participate in sports such as basketball and soccer appear to be at increased risk for developing injuries to the
   a. back.
   b. knee.
   c. wrist.
   d. neck.

CHAPTER 8

Psychology of Athletic Preparation and Performance

Bradley D. Hatfield, PhD, and Evan B. Brody, PhD

After completing this chapter, you will be able to

- understand the relationship between psychological states, physiological arousal, and physical performance;
- comprehend terms relevant to psychological areas of concern, such as arousal, anxiety, attention, the ideal performance state, motivation, and applied sport psychology;
- design a motivational program based on goal-setting principles; and
- discuss intervention strategies designed to control psychological and physiological arousal.

Excellence in athletic performance is the result of sound skill and physical training accompanied by optimal rest and recovery cycles and appropriate diet. At any particular stage of biological maturity, the phenotypic development of the athlete's genetic potential represents a relatively stable ceiling for performance, but the expression of that skilled performance can vary tremendously from contest to contest and even from moment to moment. The role of sport psychology is to help athletes achieve more consistent levels of performance at or near their physical potential by carefully managing their physical resources through appropriate psychological strategies and techniques. By understanding these strategies and techniques, strength and conditioning professionals can design sport-specific and even position-specific training programs that have the ultimate goal of maximizing performance.

After defining foundational terms, we address how the mind, or psyche, can influence physical performance, and then we describe the **ideal performance state**—the ultimate goal of every athlete. In part, this state is marked by **psychological** and **physiological efficiency** (i.e., employing only the amount of psychic and physical energy required to perform the task). We discuss two primary psychological influences on skill acquisition and performance—motivation and anxiety—citing several theories of how these emotional phenomena can change psychomotor learning and athletic performance. Finally, we discuss techniques, including goal setting, relaxation, mental imagery, and psyching strategies, that can be employed for managing physical resources (i.e., mental training).

DEFINITIONS OF KEY CONCEPTS IN SPORT PSYCHOLOGY

The **athlete** is someone who engages in a social comparison (i.e., competition) involving psychomotor skill or physical prowess (or both) in an institutionalized setting, typically under public scrutiny or evaluation. The essence of athletic competition involves comparing oneself to others and putting ego and self-esteem on the line in a setting that is bound by rules and regulations. No wonder athletes experience anxiety! The psychologically well-prepared athlete is characterized by efficiency of thought and deed. Efficiency is typically associated with skilled performance, when actions are fluid and graceful. The concept can also be extended to psychological activity; an efficient athlete adopts a task-relevant focus, not wasting attention on task-irrelevant processing such as worrying, catastrophizing, and thinking about other things such as a critical audience or coach.

Sport psychology is the subdiscipline of exercise science that seeks to understand the influence of behavioral processes on skilled movement. Exercise science together with various clinical areas of medicine (physical therapy, orthopedics, cardiology, etc.) constitutes the larger field of sports medicine (25); thus, sport psychology is classified as a scientific field of study within sports medicine. Within exercise science, sport psychology has three major goals:

1. Measuring psychological phenomena
2. Investigating the relationships between psychological variables and performance
3. Applying theoretical knowledge to improve athletic performance

By applying the information gained through sport psychology, athletes can manage their physical resources.

Anxiety: State and Trait

Athletes are frequently concerned about anxiety, arousal, and attention. The first two terms are often used interchangeably to mean stress, but this lack of specificity can cause real confusion and poor communication among athletes, coaches, and sport psychologists.

Anxiety, or more specifically **state anxiety**, is a subjective experience of apprehension and uncertainty accompanied by elevated autonomic and voluntary neural outflow and increased endocrine activity. State anxiety is a negative experience, but its effects on athletic performance can be positive, negative, or indifferent, depending on such factors as the athlete's skill level and personality and the complexity of the task to be performed. State anxiety is distinct from but related to **trait anxiety**, a personality variable or disposition relating to the probability that one will perceive an environment as threatening. In essence, trait anxiety acts as a primer for the athlete to experience state anxiety (38).

State anxiety is the actual experience of apprehension and uncontrolled arousal. Trait anxiety is a personality characteristic, which represents a latent disposition to perceive situations as threatening.

Arousal is simply the intensity dimension of behavior and physiology (4). For example, a "psyched-up" athlete may experience tremendous mental activation characterized by positive thoughts and a strong sense of control (in line with Martens' [28] notion of **psychic energy**). In such a state the athlete is not described as anxious. Arousal is always present in an individual to some degree as a continuum ranging from being deeply asleep, or comatose, to highly excited; it can be indexed by such measures as heart rate, blood pressure, electroencephalography (EEG), electromyography (EMG), and catecholamine levels, or with self-report instruments, such as the activation-deactivation checklist (39). The optimal arousal required for efficient performance depends on several factors.

In a nonanxious state, arousal is under the control of the athlete; it can be elevated or lowered as needed. The athlete who is psychologically well prepared knows the appropriate zone for optimal performance and can manage it accordingly. In an anxious state, arousal is relatively uncontrolled. Typically, arousal is too high during state anxiety; the skeletal muscles are tense, the heart is racing, and negative thoughts intrude. This lack of physical and psychological efficiency is typically initiated by uncertainty about a present or anticipated event. At least three important factors are usually present:

- A high degree of ego involvement, in which the athlete may perceive a threat to self-esteem
- A perceived discrepancy between one's ability and the demands for athletic success
- A fear of the consequences of failure (such as a loss of approval from teammates, coach, family, or peers)

State anxiety, then, typically modifies psychological and physical arousal so that it becomes elevated and uncontrolled. Some investigators have advocated using both cognitive and somatic assessments of anxiety because it is a multidimensional, or at least bidimensional, phenomenon (36). **Cognitive anxiety** relates to psychological processes and worrisome thoughts, whereas **somatic anxiety** relates to such physical symptoms as tense muscles, tachycardia (fast heart rate), and the butterflies. Because anxiety and arousal are rather vague terms, table 8.1 includes explanations of more specific terms.

Stress, for our purposes, is considered as any disruption from homeostasis or mental and physical calm. A **stressor** is an environmental or cognitive event that precipitates stress (i.e., the stress response). Stress can be described as a negative (**distress**) or a positive (**eustress**) state. Therefore, distress comprises cognitive and somatic anxiety, whereas eustress comprises psychic energy and physiological arousal.

TABLE 8.1

Specific Components of the Anxiety and Arousal Constructs

Component	Definition
Cognitive anxiety	A psychological state involving task-irrelevant mental processes that are negative in nature, flood attention, and can deter performance proportionally (especially activities requiring high amounts of information processing). That is, the more the athlete experiences cognitive anxiety, the worse the performance, especially when performance depends on complex decision making.
Somatic anxiety	Relatively uncontrolled physiological arousal, which is influenced by cognitive anxiety. Shows an inverted-U relationship to sport performance unless accompanied by significant cognitive anxiety, which causes a sharp decline in performance (i.e., catastrophe theory).
Psychic arousal or energy	A continuum of psychological intensity that is not manifested as apprehension and uncertainty, but rather as a sense of activation and focus. It is usually positively related to sport performance unless complex decision-making tasks are involved that require lower levels of psychological arousal.
Physiological arousal	A psychological neural intensity dimension of physical arousal. Extreme levels aid activities requiring heightened energy metabolism, especially those relying primarily on the ATP-creatine phosphate and glycolytic pathways. Carefully regulated arousal facilitates endurance and predominantly aerobic activity.

Attention and Skill

The athlete's ability to focus can be better understood through the construct of **attention**. Attention is defined as the processing of both environmental and internal cues that come to awareness. The information-processing model views attention as a fixed capacity, like a box with finite volume (21). This fixed capacity (a scarce commodity) is constantly bombarded by externally (e.g., sights and sounds) and internally (e.g., thoughts and afferent stimuli within the body) generated cues.

Conscious attention is continuously bombarded with a variety of stimuli and thoughts to which it can be directed. The ability to inhibit awareness of some stimuli in order to process others is termed **selective attention**, and it suppresses task-irrelevant cues (e.g., people on the sidelines, planes flying over the stadium) in order to process the task-relevant cues in the limited attentional space. For an American football quarterback, task-relevant cues might include wind conditions and a receiver's path and speed. It is important to note that the ability to focus attention on task-relevant cues and to control distraction is a skill that can be learned. Frank Costello (3), formerly a world-class high jump competitor and now a strength and conditioning professional, purposely encouraged people to walk across his approach to the jump during practices while he engaged in mental preparation. The motivation to engage in this attentional training initially stemmed from his experiences with distractions from the media and attendant personnel during a major event at Madison Square Garden in New York City. He believed that if he trained to suppress distraction, the ability would then transfer to competitive situations.

Selective attention is commonly referred to by athletes as their level of focus and refers to the suppression of task-irrelevant stimuli and thoughts.

Kandel and Schwartz (24), in a classic treatise, described fascinating evidence that emotion can alter the neural programming involved in initiating and controlling voluntary movement. In essence, emotion can change the order in which the brain structures and executes commands to the working muscles. Perhaps the frustration incurred by an athlete's inability to block distractions can bring a subcortically controlled movement to a conscious level (i.e., the athlete starts forcing the movement). As the brain changes its programming sequence, the timing and force of the agonistic, antagonistic, and synergistic muscles involved in a particular movement might also be altered. This phenomenon could be relevant particularly to fine motor skills such as golf, placekicking, and high jumping.

American football coaches often exploit the potential for this psychological neuromotor problem in opponents by calling a time-out just before a field goal attempt. During the time-out an athlete might flood his attentional capacity with task-irrelevant self-doubt and thoughts of failure. Placekickers can deal with this anxiety and attentional challenge by adopting a ritual or a mental checklist, commonly referred to as a **preparatory routine**, that consciously directs thoughts to task-relevant and controllable concerns (e.g., breathing, checking the turf, and stretching the hamstrings).

The important underlying principle is that thinking about one set of thoughts actively precludes attending to other worrisome thoughts because of the limited capacity of working memory. This human shortcoming can be used to advantage. Before a lifting performance, for example, the athlete might use key phrases to focus on the task-relevant cues associated with the lift, such as foot placement, back position, point of visual focus, and knee angle during a squat. This strategy can reduce distractions, which often deter optimal effort. Such focusing strategies can promote mental consistency during the preparatory state, which in turn can promote physical consistency—the hallmark of a skilled athlete.

Cue Utilization

Easterbrook's (7) **cue utilization** theory is helpful in explaining the effect of stress or increased levels of physiological arousal on attentional processing of information. Figure 8.1 highlights this phenomenon. In this figure, task-relevant cues are represented by a plus sign (+), while task-irrelevant cues are represented by a zero (0). At low levels of arousal, attentional width is very broad, and both relevant and irrelevant cues can come to the athlete's awareness. The athlete may not concentrate well at these underaroused levels. This may explain why some teams commit mental errors when playing against an easy opponent. As arousal increases up to a moderate level, attentional width progressively decreases, enabling more focus because of the exclusion of task-irrelevant cues (assuming that the athlete has been coached about the proper cues [+] for allocating the narrowed attentional capacity). If arousal is allowed to increase beyond this moderate level, a point of diminishing returns may be reached. At high levels of arousal, so much shrinkage of attentional capacity may occur that task-relevant cues are eliminated. In other words, too much attentional shrinkage occurs.

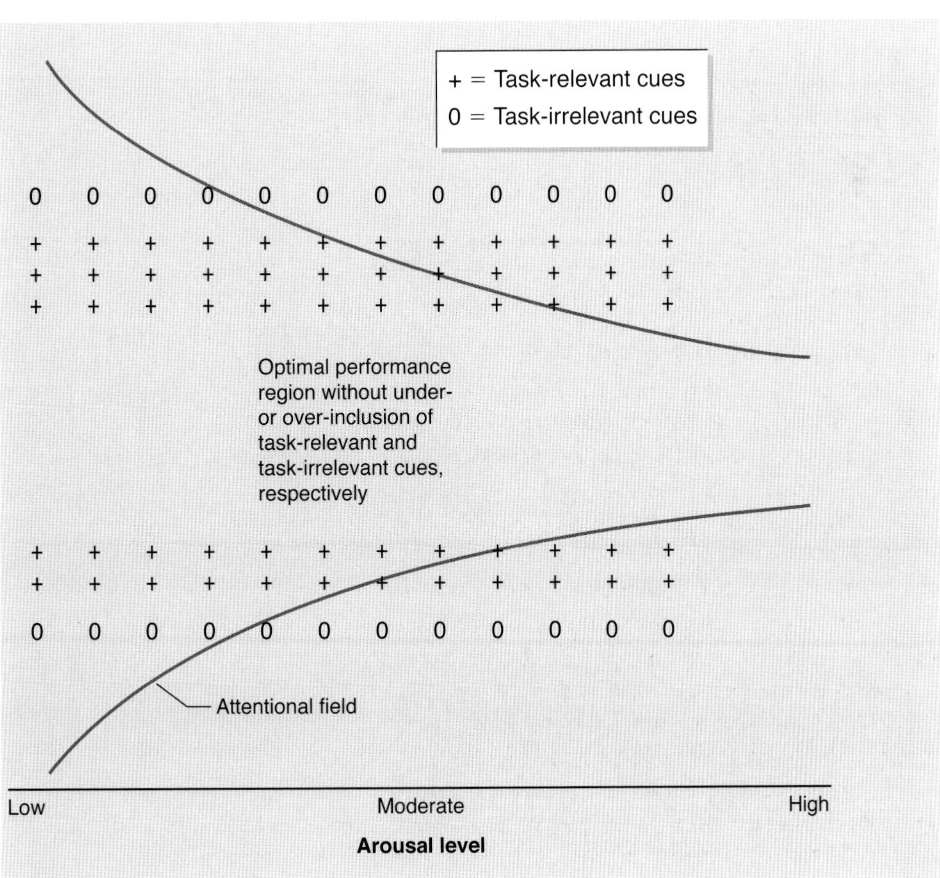

Figure 8.1 Cue utilization.

Reprinted, by permission, from *Research Quarterly for Exercise and Sport*, 1980 (26).

Attentional Style

Nideffer (33) formulated an important concept in sport psychology when he theorized that individuals tend to fall into categories of chronic attentional styles. He developed an instrument to measure these tendencies, the Test of Attentional and Interpersonal Style (TAIS). His studies revealed that attentional style as a personality trait tends to be characterized by two dimensions, internal-external and broad-narrow. The first dimension refers to an introspective versus an externally oriented perspective, whereas the second dimension refers to an integrative (expansive) versus a highly selective orientation. Using these dimensions of attention, he identified six categories of dispositional styles, which are described in table 8.2.

Understanding attentional styles can improve coaching effectiveness. For example, a player who tends to become overloaded with external stimuli might be coached to focus on one important cue, such as an opponent's footwork. Without such coaching, such a player would likely attend to too many cues, becoming confused and reacting slowly.

HOW THE MIND AFFECTS THE ATHLETE'S PHYSICAL PERFORMANCE

Athletes and coaches often think of the mind and body as somewhat distinct, but in fact there are direct physical links between the psyche and the soma, or the mind and the body. This relationship provides the basis for psychosomatic disorders and, more important for our purposes, explains how the athlete's psychological state affects his or her physical state and subsequent performance. There are three pathways leading from the brain and spinal cord—in other words, the central nervous system (CNS)—to the athlete's physical apparatus (bone, muscle, nerves, vasculature, and glands). First, there are connections via the voluntary nervous outflow (i.e., pyramidal and extrapyramidal systems) to the skeletal muscles. In essence, the cerebral cortex, where thought occurs, is "hardwired" to the muscles. Therefore, increased psychological arousal could result in increased muscular activity, as evidenced by additional motor unit recruitment. Second, in concert with the motor efference (i.e., outflow) is the autonomic efference to the various organs and blood vessels that subserve the metabolic needs of the muscles. Finally, by way of the endocrine system, the brain influences the various endocrine glands of the body, which release hormones such as testosterone, cortisol, and thyroxin that can dramatically affect the physiological state via anabolic and catabolic processes.

To illustrate the mind–body influence—the cerebral cortex can be in a state of heightened activity if the athlete is in a highly aroused state (whether anxious or psyched up), which could facilitate efferent neural activation to the involved muscles. In essence, there may be increased neural traffic to the muscles because of heightened cortical activation. Such a state might improve gross motor performance but be debilitating for a fine motor skill (because of excessive tension in the muscles or a lack of inhibition and relaxation in the antagonistic muscles). In fact, Weinberg (41) provided empirical evidence for such an occurrence, finding disruptions in the activation patterns and coordination of the

TABLE 8.2

Attentional Styles

Style	Description
1. Broad external attentional focus	Ability to effectively manage many environmental stimuli simultaneously
2. Overloaded by external stimuli	Tendency to be confused because of the intake of too many stimuli
3. Broad internal attentional focus	Ability to effectively manage many internal stimuli (autonomic responses, covert thoughts, etc.)
4. Overloaded by internal stimuli	Tendency to be confused because of the intake of too many stimuli
5. Narrow attentional focus	Ability to effectively narrow attention
6. Reduced attentional focus	Tendency to reduce attention so that task-relevant information is lost

Adapted, by permission, from Nideffer, 1976 (33).

arm muscles (as measured by EMG) in anxious subjects performing an overhand throw for accuracy.

Tangible physical processes occur in the brain and body as a result of the athlete's thought processes. These changes influence neuromuscular activation, coordination, autonomic arousal, and metabolism, which can cause further changes in motor performance. The resultant changes may be beneficial, detrimental, or neutral, depending on the nature of the task, the athlete's level of skill, and the complexity of the task in terms of decision making. See the section "Influence of Arousal on Performance" on page 168.

IDEAL PERFORMANCE STATE

The ideal performance state has been studied from a number of perspectives. Williams and Krane (44) listed the following characteristics that athletes typically report about this state:

- Absence of fear—no fear of failure
- No thinking about or analysis of performance (related to the motor stage of automaticity)
- A narrow focus of attention concentrated on the activity itself
- A sense of effortlessness—an involuntary experience
- A sense of personal control
- A distortion of time and space, in which time seems to slow

In a sense, this ideal performance state seems to represent everything that applied sport psychology programs attempt to promote. There is an absence of negative self-talk, a strong feeling of efficacy, and an adaptive focus on the task-relevant cues. An important aspect is that the athletes trust in their skill and conditioning levels and just "let it happen," without interference from negative associative processes in the cerebral cortex.

Walter Payton, one of the premier running backs in the history of the National Football League, reported a good example of this state (1):

> I'm Dr. Jekyll and Mr. Hyde when it comes to football. When I'm on the field sometimes I don't know what I am doing out there. People ask me about this move or that move, but I don't know why I did something, I just did it. I am able to focus out the negative things around me and just zero in on what I am doing out there. Off the field I become myself again. (pp. 2-3)

Payton's comments richly reinforce many of the concepts discussed throughout this chapter. It is important to remember that his mental state rested largely on a sound physical training program and on a history of performance success. Payton exhibited phenomenal physical prowess, arduously running sprints, training on hills, and lifting weights in the off-season. Combined with superior performance on the field, such preparatory physical effort contributed greatly to his focused, confident psychological state.

According to Fitts and Posner's (11) classic notion of motor skill learning, the athlete progresses through three stages. The first stage, termed the cognitive stage, is characterized by effortful and conscious regulation of the movement. That is, the athlete has to think about the details of the task. During the second stage, the associative stage, the athlete must focus on the task but is less concerned with the details of the movement. Finally, the athlete achieves the stage of automaticity, during which the mind is relaxed and the skill is executed automatically without thinking. Assuming proper instruction and coaching, the relaxed mind focuses only on what is relevant to the task at that moment and, at the same time, automatically filters out all irrelevant cues.

The mind state associated with automaticity has been investigated by some sport psychologists who have measured regional brain activity in elite athletes during performance. Using EEG technology, Hatfield and colleagues (18) examined left hemispheric and right hemispheric activity in world-class competitive marksmen as they prepared for their shots. These researchers showed that the analytical left hemisphere decreased its activation level during the preparatory sighting phase, whereas the right hemisphere (more involved in visual-spatial processing) relaxed too, but not as much. In essence, these highly skilled and focused athletes experienced an overall quieting of the forebrain accompanied by a shift in relative hemispheric activation. The dynamics and requirements of riflery differ from those of other sports, but rifle shooters provide a nice model for studying skilled attentive states using EEG technology because they are motionless and yet highly engaged psychologically. Accordingly, the relationship between attentional processes and performance examined in such studies may provide valuable information about attention and performance in other sports.

It is risky to extrapolate the findings to other athletes, but Payton's statement, "I don't know why

I did something, I just did it," seems consistent with the hemispheric shift phenomenon. Although it appears on one level that he thought about "nothing" during a given play (in terms of the analytical domain), there may have been a high level of processing in another domain, such as the visual-spatial. A position such as running back in American football requires the ability to allocate fixed attentional resources to process spatial cues. This ability would allow the athlete to react efficiently to changing conditions on the field. If the athlete was highly skilled, he would not need to consciously think about or analyze what he was doing. Such a high degree of skill probably minimizes negative self-talk. It may be that a performance state such as that reported by Payton would also show relative right-brain activation if assessed by psychophysiological technology, such as an EEG.

Again, this attentional allocation or shift in allocation to process only the cues and cognitive activity that relate to the athletic performance nicely represents the concept of **mental-psychological efficiency**. We believe that such a state precipitates the fluid, graceful movements of superior performers, which can be described as physically efficient. Thus, such a state exemplifies the optimal mind–body relationship in sport. A practical point for coaches relates to the kind of advice they give an athlete just prior to performance. It appears to be counterproductive to engage in much analytical thought about the skill to be performed. An analytical approach may be useful for the novice, but a different approach, allowing the athlete to "just let it happen," should be employed as skill develops.

The ideal performance state is characterized by a "quiet mind" that results in less cortical interference with the (subcortical) motor control centers and in consistent and efficient execution of motor performance.

MOTIVATIONAL PHENOMENA

Selected aspects of motivational phenomena are highlighted in the following sections. We first discuss intrinsic motivation, which greatly influences the athlete's desire to train and compete. Then we discuss achievement motivation, which helps to explain individual differences in competitiveness. Finally, positive and negative reinforcement are explained as they apply to skill learning and performance. An important facet of motivation, goal setting, is described in a later section of this chapter.

Intrinsic Motivation

Intrinsic motivation is important for any athlete. Deci (6) defined this construct as a desire to be competent and self-determining. With intrinsic motivation, the athlete is a self-starter because of his or her love of the game. The coach's work of teaching skills and effective strategies with team sports can be much more effective when athletes are self-motivated. Surrounded by such players, a coach can concentrate on task-relevant concerns rather than on encouraging effort by cajoling, punishing, or exhorting. Intrinsically motivated athletes are more likely to maintain effort consistently across practice and competition. How can such a desirable state be maintained or encouraged? The answer lies in Deci's (6) definition, which stresses success (competence) and "pulling one's own strings" (self-determination). Appropriate goals, especially process or performance goals, can increase perceived competence. Additionally, giving the athlete some latitude in decision making increases perceived self-determination. Effective leaders in business and industry know that placing an appropriate degree of responsibility (i.e., latitude in decision making) on their employees is empowering in terms of increasing commitment, effort, and creativity (40). Authoritarian behavior is sometimes warranted in sport, in that clear directives are needed in a stressful and competitive environment; but a total lack of delegated responsibilities could result in a loss of initiative and drive in athletes.

Achievement Motivation

Another desirable construct is **achievement motivation**, which relates to the athlete's wish to engage in competition, or social comparison. All things being equal between two athletes, whoever is higher in achievement motivation will be the better athlete because he or she has an appetite for competition.

McClelland and colleagues (31) theorized that all people have opposing personality traits within themselves: the **motive to achieve success (MAS)** and the **motive to avoid failure (MAF)**. The MAS is self-explanatory; MAF relates to the desire to protect one's ego and self-esteem. The following discussion illustrates the relevance of these traits to the psychology of coaching.

McClelland and colleagues (31) showed, by means of an arithmetically stated theory, that MAS-dominated athletes are most intrigued by situations that are either uncertain or challenging, with a 50% probability of success. On the other hand, MAF-dominated players are comfortable in situations in which it is either very easy to achieve success or extremely difficult (i.e., they would not be expected to win). At a high level of sport involvement, it is unlikely that athletes would be dominated by MAF, but they would certainly show degrees or a range of competitiveness. Confronted by a very challenging goal, such as gaining a significant amount of lean muscle weight during the hypertrophy phase of a periodized cycle, the MAF-dominated individual might reduce effort because he or she fears failure and the threat to self-esteem (and might also claim that the goal is unrealistic), whereas the MAS-dominated individual might heighten effort in response to the challenge and not perceive any threat.

During a tense game the coach should handle these two players' psychological orientations differently to maximize success. Suppose that two defensive backs in an American football game—one dominated by MAS and the other by MAF—are confronted by a situation in which their team, playing defense, has 1 minute left in the game and leads by only 2 points. The opposing team's offense has just crossed midfield. The MAS-dominated player views this scenario as an opportunity to display defensive skills, whereas the MAF-dominated player adopts an avoidance behavior. The coach would not have to issue any motivational instructions to the MAS-dominated player because he perceives the outcome as challenging (i.e., 50% probability of success). But the coach should define the MAF-dominated player's responsibility to make goal attainment relatively easy. For example, this athlete could be told simply to cover his territory while in a zone defense or simply to execute proper footwork during pass coverage. This kind of coaching instruction removes some of the self-induced pressure, allowing the athlete to focus on task-relevant cues. If success is achieved, the MAF-dominated athlete may become more comfortable in highly competitive situations.

Positive and Negative Reinforcement in Coaching

Coaches can benefit from understanding the concepts of positive and negative reinforcement and positive and negative punishment (29). An important behavioral technology can be used to increase a positive, confident psychological outlook. **Positive reinforcement** is the act of increasing the probability of occurrence of a given behavior (a target behavior, such as correct footwork in basketball, is termed an **operant**) by following it with an action, object, or event such as praise, decals on the helmet, or prizes and awards. **Negative reinforcement** also increases the probability of occurrence of a given operant by removing an act, object, or event that is typically aversive (29). For example, if the team particularly hustled in practice (i.e., the operant is enthusiasm and hustle), then the coach could announce that no wind sprints will be required at the session's end. This coaching reinforcement style forces attention on what the athlete is doing correctly.

Punishment, on the other hand, is designed to decrease the occurrence of a given operant, that is, negative behaviors such as mistakes or a lack of effort. **Positive punishment** is the presentation of an act, object, or event following a behavior that could decrease the behavior's occurrence. An example is reprimanding a player after a fumble. **Negative punishment**, or the removal of something valued, could take the form of revoking privileges or playing time, as in benching. Although coaches use a mixture of both reward and punishment, reinforcement (i.e., reward), or a positive approach, is arguably better because it focuses on what athletes should do and what they did right (termed "specific positive feedback"). Reinforcement (both positive and negative) increases task-relevant focus rather than worry focus. A task-relevant focus facilitates reaction time and decision making. With reinforcement, athletes also build long-term memories of success, self-esteem, self-efficacy, and confidence. Successful experiences more likely color the athlete's view of competition as desirable and as an opportunity to perform. Of course, coaches should punish unwarranted lack of effort, but it seems ineffective to punish athletes for mistakes if they are making the effort to perform correctly.

How Should Positive and Negative Reinforcement Be Applied?

- Coaches should generally subscribe to a reinforcement strategy to assist athletes in focusing on what they do correctly.
- Punishment should be used sparingly, as it increases the likelihood that the athlete will focus on what he or she is doing incorrectly.
- Under conditions that promote attentional narrowing, positive reinforcement aids focus on task-relevant cues, while punishment floods attentional capacity with a predominance of task-irrelevant cues.

INFLUENCE OF AROUSAL ON PERFORMANCE

This section explains the basic relationship between arousal and performance in terms of Yerkes and Dodson's (46) inverted-U theory and then describes the mediating influences of skill level, task complexity, and personality. Other related theories that further explain this relationship are outlined, including Hanin's (14) zone of optimal functioning, Fazey and Hardy's (9) catastrophe theory, and Bandura's (2) theory of self-efficacy.

Inverted-U Theory

One of the major tenets of the arousal–performance relationship, derived from the classic work of Yerkes and Dodson (46), is referred to as the **inverted-U theory**. Basically, this theory states that arousal facilitates performance up to an optimal level, beyond which further increases in arousal are associated with reduced performance. Figure 8.2 graphically shows this relationship. A number of revisions have been postulated to improve this predictive model, such as Hanin's (14) zone of optimal performance theory, which we discuss later. The inverted-U concept helps coaches and athletes understand why arousal affects performance and enables them to gain greater control over the appropriate level of arousal for a given athlete within a given sport.

Skill Level

An athlete's skill level can increase the latitude of optimal arousal; that is, the more skill an athlete has developed, the better he or she can perform during states of less or greater than optimal arousal. In the beginning stages of learning a skill, the athlete is in a stage of analysis or cognition (11). This means that he or she has to think about actions. For example, a novice basketball player has to be conscious of the ball while dribbling and needs to devote some attention to the task. At a given level of arousal, worrisome thoughts compete with an attentional capacity already filled by details of motor performance (i.e., dribbling). If a new situation suddenly develops, the novice's mind is already occupied, and he or she may not see it.

The optimal arousal point is lower for less skilled athletes than for more advanced players. Therefore, coaches should lower arousal and decrease the decision-making responsibilities of developing or unseasoned athletes (players who are skilled but lack competitive experience) and have them focus on simple assignments to prevent attentional overload. In coaching Olympic-style lifters during an important meet, instructions to novice competitors should be simple, clear, and direct. When they experience success, the derived self-confidence may reduce negative self-talk and the sense of uncertainty that typically characterizes such performers.

Task Complexity

A second factor that influences the appropriate level of arousal to achieve optimal performance is task complexity (34). Most athletic skills are exceedingly complex from a biomechanical perspective, but the complexity that concerns us relates to conscious decision making. For example, sprinting is a very complex task in terms of motor control and functional anatomy, but athletes fortunately do not have to devote much conscious attention to the coordinated action. In fact, the action becomes altered and inefficient if they think about it, because they change the neural sequences for movement initiation. From an attentional perspective, simple skills can tolerate a higher degree of arousal (and attentional narrowing) because they have few task-relevant cues to monitor. Fortunately, physiological arousal, which typically accompanies psychic arousal, may be beneficial. Any increase in neuromuscular activation enables more powerful and explosive movements.

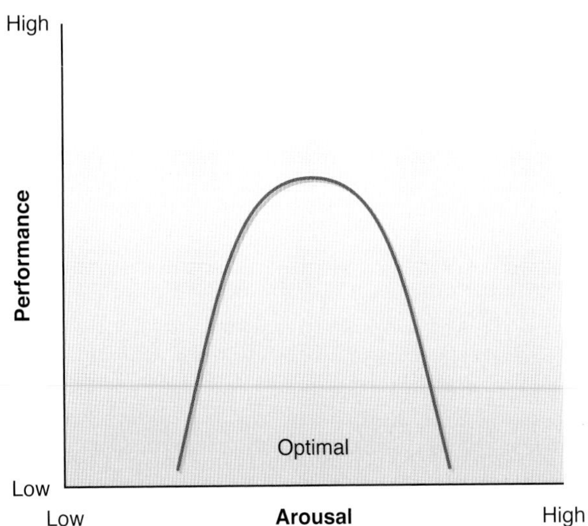

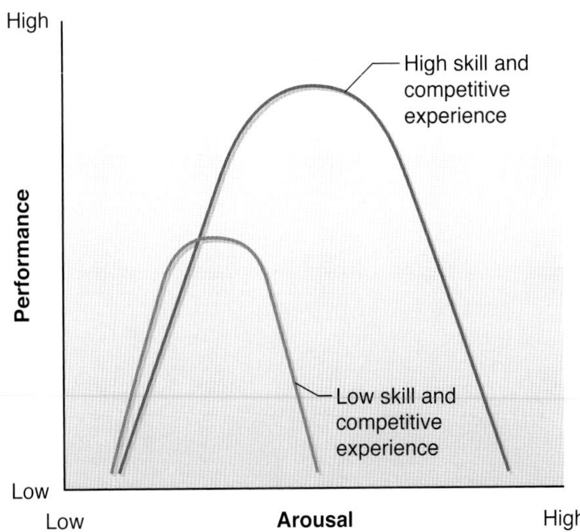

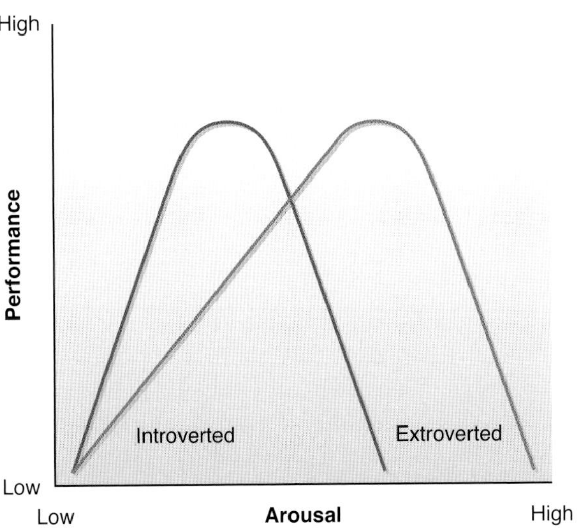

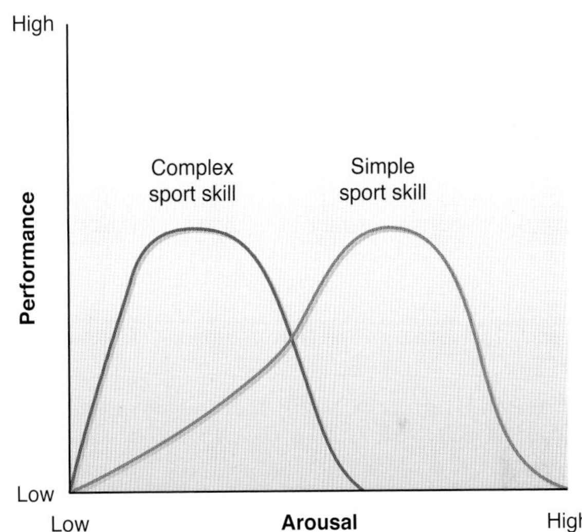

Figure 8.2 Inverted-U theory and its modifications.

Reprinted, by permission, from Hatfield and Walford, 1987 (20).

However, the situation is dramatically reversed for skills that necessitate tremendous decision-making effort, such as those required by a goalie in soccer or a baseball catcher who is facing a critical, bases-loaded pitch. In these instances, arousal must be kept relatively low because of the need to maintain attentional width.

Personality

A third factor, personality, can also influence the appropriate level of arousal. According to Eysenck (8), extroverted individuals differ neurologically from introverts. Extroverts are sensory reducers, whereas introverts are sensory augmenters, or increasers. Accordingly, because people seek an optimal level of arousal, the extrovert requires heightened stimulation (compared with the introvert) because of the tendency to reduce or dampen arousing effects. On the other hand, the introvert requires a lower level of stimulation because of the tendency to increase arousal. All things being equal between two athletes in terms of physical ability and skill level, the extroverted player can better handle the more arousing, or critical, game situation. This is why it is important for coaches to fully understand athletes from both a psychological and physiological perspective and adjust their styles to fit the individual needs of the athlete.

Trait Anxiety

Trait anxiety also affects the appropriate level of arousal for a given individual. People with high levels of trait anxiety tend to flood attentional capacity with task-irrelevant cognitions, such as thoughts of failure, catastrophe, or ego-oriented concerns. During a complex decision-making task, these attentionally demanding cues could compromise a player's selective attention. The athlete with low trait anxiety can handle higher levels of pressure because of the decreased probability of engaging in such personal catastrophizing.

There are probably additional factors that moderate the inverted U of optimal arousal, but the interaction of even the few factors described here can cause tremendous variation in the optimal levels individuals require.

Optimal Functioning Theory

Hanin (14) noted the interactions of factors that affect optimal arousal and developed the zone of **optimal functioning theory**. He basically holds that different people perform best with very different levels of arousal. It is unclear whether the factors discussed earlier fully account for such individual differences; nevertheless, some practical determinations can be made. Athletes can retrospectively recall the arousal associated with several performances that differed in quality. Self-reported arousal can be measured by a standardized psychometric instrument, such as the State Anxiety Inventory (37), which ranges from a low score of 20 to a maximum of 80. An average score is derived from those associated with the best performances. Hanin (14) argues that a deviation of 4 points around this mean generates the optimal zone of self-reported arousal. The athlete can monitor his or her state prior to an important match and make adjustments to fall into this zone. As discussed earlier, the athlete should then be able to concentrate, or allocate attention, appropriately and prepare physically.

Catastrophe Theory

According to Fazey and Hardy (9), assessment of the cognitive and somatic dimensions of arousal can sharpen the ability to predict (and therefore control) their impact on performance. Earlier assumptions associated with the inverted-U theory held that increases in arousal beyond the optimal level resulted in gradual, proportionate declines in performance. However, common observation tells us that this is not always the case—an athlete may suffer a severe and catastrophic decline rather than a gradual quadratic or curvilinear decline in performance, and restoring a degree of calm does not necessarily bring a return to the level of performance exhibited before the decline. In the Fazey and Hardy (9) model, somatic arousal has a curvilinear, inverted-U relationship to athletic performance, whereas cognitive anxiety shows a steady negative relationship to performance. When increases in physiological arousal occur in the presence of cognitive anxiety, a sudden drop—rather than a gradual decline—in performance occurs. The practical implication of **catastrophe theory** is that the arousal construct needs to be more clearly defined. Arousal is a rather vague term, and it would be more precise to use such terms as psychic energy, cognitive anxiety, physiological arousal, and somatic anxiety.

Self-Efficacy

Of course, the main objective for applied sport psychology is generating a psychological perspective that improves performance, and it has been argued that perceived self-confidence, or **self-efficacy** (2), is a better predictor of task execution than either arousal or anxiety. Self-efficacy is perceived self-confidence about a given task in a specific situation (2). It is the sense of success that an athlete feels he or she embodies or can control; someone who is highly self-efficacious does not doubt his or her ability to succeed at a given task, even when failure is experienced. Anxiety and arousal seem to be outcomes, rather than determinants, of this state. Nevertheless, they still are significant, inasmuch as they represent the state of the mind and body. It may be that psychic energy, cognitive anxiety, physiological arousal, and somatic anxiety interface with self-efficacy and physical performance.

MENTAL MANAGEMENT OF PHYSICAL RESOURCES: CONTROLLING PSYCHOLOGICAL PROCESSES

Some time ago, Morgan and Pollock (32) reported that elite American distance runners tend to carefully monitor their efforts, probably in an attempt to optimize pace, whereas nonelite distance runners tend to distract themselves more often in an attempt to reduce the perceived pain and fatigue of their efforts. The monitoring strategy was termed **association**, whereas the distracting strategy was called **dissociation**. Because it was unknown whether the strategy of association causally contributed to superior endurance performance, Hatfield and colleagues (19) examined the effect of the two strategies (i.e., associative and dissociative) on pulmonary activity, oxygen uptake, and muscle tension levels in intercollegiate distance runners during treadmill running. These researchers found that the runners breathed more efficiently when they adopted the associative strategy. In light of Daniels' (5) work on the importance of efficiency for endurance performance, the results of the study illustrate how mental management (i.e., the associative strategy) may affect physical performance.

If self-efficacy and a relaxed, confident mind (i.e., the efficient management of an athlete's mental and physical resources) are critical to sport performance, how can such a state be achieved? We believe that the most powerful determinant of confidence and a sense of preparation is quality physical practice in which a number of positive experiences are stored in long-term memory. In essence, the most powerful psychological skills package is quality practice and successful competitive exposure. Gould and colleagues (13) provided evidence from their national survey of U.S. coaches that this represents a widespread belief and practice. In a sense, coaches act as practicing sport psychologists simply by conditioning and teaching athletes the skills of sport.

Applied sport psychology involves the employment of techniques to gain control over psychological factors, which influence sport performance. The validation of such techniques is one mission of the scientific discipline of sport psychology.

Physical training is rich in psychological effects—the two realms cannot really be separated. This is why many athletes develop a strong sense of confidence and psychological preparedness even though they may never have been exposed to the formal practice of sport psychology in the form of psychological skill techniques such as mental imagery, hypnosis, and progressive muscle relaxation. Moreover, many athletes have a strong social support system as well, which includes family, friends, coaching personnel, teammates, and others who tend to provide positive feedback and emotional nurturance. Equally important, outstanding coaches at all levels of play are excellent communicators who provide very specific, focused instructions for their athletes and give ample feedback about performance quality in practice and during competition. In fact, athletic coaches tend to assume the role of teachers who often find themselves in a very positive emotional environment. That is, their students typically want to be there and have high intrinsic motivation.

Goal Setting

All coaches can probably improve performance quality by directing their athletes' attention to appropriate task-oriented and emotional goals and by instilling a sense of success and self-efficacy through positive and negative reinforcement of desired actions. **Goal setting** can be described as a process whereby progressively challenging standards of performance are pursued with a defined criterion of task performance that increases the likelihood of perceived success (27). For example, a goal for a swimmer may be to execute a technically correct stroke throughout a sanctioned distance, such as the 50 m freestyle. In the beginning, the swimmer's skill level might be so low that such a task would be overwhelming and produce a strong sense of failure and frustration, yet physiological testing may show the coach that the athlete has the physical resources to excel at such an event (i.e., the swimmer has a high degree of fast-twitch, or Type II, muscle fibers, exhibits superior muscular power or speed-strength in the upper and lower body, and seems to have a high capacity for anaerobic metabolism). However, the stroke mechanics are inefficient, and therefore the athlete lacks confidence. First, the coach and athlete can break the skill and conditioning units down into manageable components (the traditional whole-part-whole method of learning). As the athlete focuses on and masters each component, a sense of progress and success is nurtured.

Process Goals

An important distinction, in terms of setting goals, is the process versus the outcome (12). **Process goals** are those over whose achievement the athlete has control. If the effort is expended, success occurs with a relatively high degree of probability. Examples of process goals within the skill domain relate to form and technique, although an individually determined time (in the case of a swimmer or track athlete) could also be considered a process goal. An example of a process goal within strength and conditioning is to have the athlete focus on the strategy for weight reduction (e.g., what the athlete must do on a daily basis, such as aerobic activity and dietary modifications) rather than on the actual result (e.g., a loss of weight), thereby increasing a sense of control over actions. With process goals, success is strongly contingent on effort.

Outcome Goals

On the other hand, **outcome goals** are ones over which the athlete has little control; typically winning is the primary focus. We believe that winning is a sound goal orientation but that, ironically, an athlete can increase the likelihood of its achievement by having both a process and an outcome goal orientation, as opposed to a winning-only attitude. Undue emphasis on winning may occupy such a proportion of fixed attentional capacity that it causes narrowing of attentional focus. Task-relevant cues are missed, reaction time is slowed, and coordination is diminished by forced movements and compromised automaticity, which alter neuromuscular sequencing.

Both process and outcome goals can be applied to conditioning as well. For example, emphasizing arm technique during sprinting illustrates process orientation, whereas focusing only on winning the drill illustrates outcome orientation. An exception to the general caveat about avoiding outcome goals is the situation in which an athlete is extremely confident and undermatched in competition. He or she may then want to focus solely on outcome and a personal best to maximize motivation.

Guidelines for Using Goal Setting

- Long-term goals and short-term goals are interdependent.
- Long-term goals provide a sense of meaningfulness for pursuing short-term goals.
- The attainment of short-term goals provides a hierarchical sense of mastery and success that builds self-confidence.
- Athletes should define process goals to focus on elements of their performance over which they have control.

Short-Term Goals

In addition to the process and outcome distinction, goals can be categorized as short-term and long-term. Short-term goals increase the likelihood of success because, although challenging, they are relatively close to the athlete's present ability level. They increase confidence, self-esteem, and self-efficacy. In this regard, short-term process and outcome goals counteract the boredom and frustration that are potential side effects of long, arduous training regimens.

Long-Term Goals

However, the full meaning of the short-term standards of success is framed by an appropriate long-term goal. The athlete may see more relevance in everyday practice goals if it is apparent how they help attain the ultimate level of performance. For example, a gymnast who has a long-term goal of winning the floor routine for the national championship during her senior year may be much more intense and positive about weight room conditioning exercises when she perceives their relevance to her dream. An athlete may be more aroused psychologically and physiologically during practice by the perception that today's activity is another step on the ladder to a personal, long-term dream.

Effective Behavioral Coaching

Martin and Hrycaiko (30) outlined a very sound program of goal setting in an article discussing the tenets of effective behavioral coaching. In this program a coach specifies the components of a given skill and charts the athlete's success with each part until the whole skill is mastered. Figure 8.3 illustrates this motivational technique for the skill of drive blocking in American football. In behavioral psychology, short-term goals that progressively increase in difficulty are termed **successive approximations**, because they increasingly resemble the long-term goal. Each targeted goal or behavior is termed an operant. Operants are clearly defined standards of performance and derive from the term **operationalize**, which means to concretely specify a behavior so that it can be measured.

The specificity of the goals is important to giving the athlete feedback in effective coaching. Feedback, or the knowledge of success and failure, is more effective in the presence of specific, quantifiable goals—as opposed to vague standards of performance. Feedback is a corrective mechanism, like a thermostat or cybernetic device. Both suc-

EFFECTIVE BEHAVIORAL COACHING CHART TO ASSESS AN AMERICAN FOOTBALL PLAYER PERFORMING THE DRIVE BLOCK

Scoring Key

I = Needs improvement

G = Good

E = Excellent

Date:			
Arms are crossed at the wrists with palms up			
Initial step is taken with foot closest to the defender			
Athlete drives out of stance, with short initial steps toward target			
Arms are brought up and forward on the rotation, aimed at the chest of target			
As rotation of arm starts, the back is arched with the head up—forward thrust is from a low position			
On impact, the block is delivered with the forearms, not the head; side view will reveal that both elbows are ahead of the head			
Both fists (closed) are held against the chest, not away from the body			
Elbows are at blocker's chest level, not above shoulders			
If fists are open, palms should face opponent			
Blow is delivered from a wide base			
Athlete follows through with short, choppy steps (footfire) from a wide stance; takes the defender in the desired offensive direction			

Figure 8.3 Effective behavioral coaching chart to assess an American football player performing the drive block.

From NSCA, 2008, *Essentials of Strength Training and Conditioning*, 3rd ed. (Champaign, IL: Human Kinetics). Adapted, by permission, from G. Martin and D. Hrycaiko, 1983, "Effective behavioral coaching: What's it all about?" *Journal of Sport Psychology* 5(1):13, (30).

cess and failure can help the athlete stay on course toward long-term success. For example, a specific goal of 25 minutes of continuous running in a heart rate range of 160 to 170 beats/min is a much more engaging task than "going out for a run." The vague phrasing may be fine for a recreational participant, but it is not helpful for a competitive cross-country runner, especially when the goal is to develop physiological capacity.

Systematic goal setting can simultaneously increase the psychological development and performance of the athlete. This approach has an abundance of empirical support from research studies that contrast goal setting to relatively vague motivational strategies, such as exhortations to "do your best" (42, 43). A number of reasons explain why goal setting affects performance:

- Goals direct an athlete's attention by prioritizing efforts.
- Goals increase effort because of the contingency of success on goal attainment.
- Goals increase positive reinforcement through the feedback given to athletes.

It seems that the informational nature of thoughtfully derived goals, which increase effort because they are challenging yet attainable, is a powerful ingredient for behavioral change.

Optimal goal setting requires knowledge of the exercise sciences in both the biophysical and behavioral domains. The efficacy of goals for improving athletic performance lies in their relevance to the physical needs of the athlete. For example, formulating a series of appropriate goals to enable a 400 m runner to decrease his or her time in the event rests on understanding the physical profile, relevant metabolic pathways, and biomechanical technique to be developed.

Of course, some goals may be completely psychological and therefore only indirectly performance based. An example of such a goal is to adopt a positive mood state for an entire practice. Although such goals demand less biophysical knowledge, they may be profoundly useful in increasing performance because they are goals that an athlete has tremendous control over and they can facilitate inhibiting habitual negative self-talk. However, the most comprehensive goal-setting programs encompass several areas of exercise science. We believe this requirement uniquely distinguishes sport psychology, or kinesiological psychology, from other behavioral sciences.

Although a scientific and motivationally sound coaching program can greatly help in the development of athletes, several other complementary techniques exist. In reality, most athletes probably have a combination of adaptive and maladaptive experiences during practice and competition, and they may have developed a lack of self-confidence from experiences outside of sport. These people need to exert control over their mental and physical states to improve performance and enjoy competition more fully. Therefore, we turn now to some cognitively and somatically based sport psychology techniques that athletes can use to better manage their physical resources.

Physical Relaxation Techniques

Several physical techniques can help athletes manage their psychological processes through relaxation. Relaxation techniques are designed to reduce physiological arousal and increase task-relevant focus. These techniques are important when people are executing complex tasks or practicing new ones.

Diaphragmatic Breathing

One technique for reaching a higher level of physical and mental relaxation is **diaphragmatic breathing**. Referred to as belly breathing, this form of breathing is a basic stress management technique and a precursor to all other mental training techniques. It focuses thought on breathing (a controllable aspect of physiology) to clear the mind and therefore increase attentional capacity. During any mental training exercise, athletes should attempt to engage in deep, rhythmic breathing in a relaxed, natural manner. They should avoid hyperventilation and breath holding (Valsalva maneuver). Diaphragmatic breathing is a somatopsychic (muscle-to-mind) technique (15). This means that peripheral (muscular) action is the initiator of central (mental) relaxation. Physiologically, this form of breathing has a major influence on heart rate and muscle tension due to feedback mechanisms that link the respiratory and cardiac control centers in the brain stem. The relatively deep inspiration, followed by a controlled expiration, alters autonomic nervous system (ANS) balance so that increased vagal tone or parasympathetic activity can occur (35). The parasympathetic branch of the ANS promotes the effect opposite the sympathetic-mediated fight-or-flight response. Thus, rhythmic breathing can decrease neural stimulation of both the skeletal muscles and organs (e.g., heart, lungs, liver), resulting in a sense of deep relaxation.

Diaphragmatic breathing requires that attention be directed away from the chest as the origin of the conscious control of breathing, and instead to the abdominal region. To accomplish this, the abdominal muscles must first relax. Therefore, it is best to start from a standing position so that breathing is not inhibited. The athlete should let the arms hang loosely and concentrate on relaxing, particularly in the neck and shoulder region, by first taking a couple of deep breaths. Next, the athlete should relax the abdominal muscles so that they appear flaccid. The initiation of each breath should occur simultaneously with the relaxed protrusion of the abdominal muscles; placing a hand on the abdomen gives feedback to ensure that the abdomen protrudes with the initiation of each breath. With each breath the stomach should become naturally distended. When this portion of the technique is performed properly, the diaphragm (a muscle at the base of the lungs) contracts and drops, allowing a deeper breath to occur. This is the first stage of taking a maximal inhalation. The entire process of inhalation takes place in three different areas and stages: the lower abdomen, the midchest, and finally the upper chest. Diaphragmatic breathing can be combined with a more dynamic muscular relaxation technique called progressive muscular relaxation. The discussions by Harris and Harris (16) and Williams and Krane (44) are excellent sources for learning how to apply these and other mental training techniques.

Progressive Muscular Relaxation

To achieve an appropriate level of psychic vigor and physiological arousal before performance, many athletes employ **progressive muscle relaxation (PMR)** (22). Progressive muscle relaxation can be defined as a somatopsychic technique by which psychological and physical arousal are self-regulated through the control of skeletal muscle tension. In essence, by going through a series of alternate muscular tensing and relaxing phases, the athlete learns to become aware of somatic tension and thereby to control it. Theoretically, the technique exerts its effect by means of a process termed **reciprocal inhibition** (45), which reflects the principle that a relaxed body will promote a relaxed mind. In many cases, a positive side effect of the reduced muscle tension may be an increase in smooth, fluid, or efficient movement as well as an increased range of motion around the joint. This can be an effective self-regulation technique for some athletes before practice or competition, or even during an intense moment in a given contest.

A person learns to control the somatic input to the CNS through stages progressing to instant, voluntary, and total body relaxation whenever needed. First, the athlete practices alternate tension and relaxation cycles in several small muscle groups throughout the body. Contraction of a given muscle (e.g., the biceps brachii) may occur for 10 to 15 seconds, during which the person generates excessive and uncomfortable levels of tension. Then tension is released, and a similar amount of time follows during which the person attempts to achieve deep relaxation (i.e., by trying to feel warmth and heaviness in the limbs). Athletes can use tapes of PMR instruction at their own convenience to save valuable practice time. Also, using training tapes at bedtime not only teaches the athlete to relax, but may also ensure increased depth of sleep, an essential component of the rest and recovery cycle of hard-training athletes. Ultimately, through diligent mental relaxation training, athletes learn to reduce whole-body tension at will.

Autogenic Training

For athletes who are injured or who for some reason find it uncomfortable or impractical to experience high muscular tension levels, the PMR cycle for each muscle group can be replaced with an attentional state that simply focuses on the sense of warmth and heaviness for a particular limb or muscle group. This kind of technique is referred to as **autogenic training**. Autogenic training refers to shifting autonomic neural processes from sympathetic to parasympathetic dominance. Because autogenic training eliminates the need for uncomfortable levels of muscle tension in the contraction-relaxation cycles, some older athletes may find this an attractive alternative to PMR.

Relaxation techniques are designed to reduce physiological arousal and increase task-relevant focus. These techniques are of extreme importance when one is executing complex tasks and those not well learned.

Mental Imagery

Mental imagery can be defined as a cognitive psychological skill in which the athlete uses all the senses to create a mental experience of an athletic performance. The athlete simulates reality by mentally rehearsing a movement, imagining visual, auditory, kinesthetic, olfactory, and even exertional cues. Feltz and Landers (10) provided convincing evidence for the effectiveness of mental imagery in the enhancement of sport skill based on a meta-analytic review of the literature. During the initial stages of using imagery, the athlete may start with a relatively simple, visual (i.e., unisensory rather than multisensory) image. This helps successful practice of the technique. As with learning any skill by proceeding from simple to complex, the person starts with static images, such as visualizing a golf ball or mentally examining the visual characteristics of a tennis racket. The vividness or detail of the image should become clearer and clearer with continued practice. Some people have a natural talent for achieving image clarity, but everyone can improve with repeated practice.

The perspective of the image can be internal (first person) or external (third person). Although the research literature is unclear as to whether one is superior, it seems that the image that is more engaging and natural to the athlete is appropriate. Of course, the internal, first-person perspective seems more specific to skill execution, inasmuch as the actual task is performed with such an orientation.

After the athlete successfully visualizes a stationary object with vivid detail, he or she may start to move the object or begin to "walk around" it in the mind, viewing it from a number of different perspectives. For an image such as a basketball, the athlete may attempt to bounce the ball and feel it against the fingertips. In this manner, the athlete increases complexity by controlling the image or moving it with control (e.g., bouncing the ball) and by bringing a multisensory perspective to bear (i.e., using tactile or kinesthetic as well as visual sensation).

Rehearsing successful execution of a skill during imagined competitive conditions can provide the subconscious mind with positive memories, thus increasing the athlete's sense of confidence and preparedness for the particular sport. Of course, mental imaging is not as powerful a determinant of self-efficacy as actual success, but it does offer two potentially potent ingredients. First, successful performance is entirely under the control of the athlete during imaging, whereas a degree of uncertainty is inherent about the outcome in reality. In imagery the athlete has a great opportunity to "experience" success. We believe that athletes should be realistic in the kinds of success they imagine; that is, the mental images should be personally challenging yet within the realm of possibility. Second, the athlete can "experience" competition repeatedly, fostering a sense of familiarity and preparedness.

For some athletes the months of preparation for a season of play—involving off-season, preseason, and in-season conditioning and skill development—may lead to only a few minutes of actual competitive experience. Even for the starters in team sports, actual competitive experience may be infinitely small relative to physical practice time. Mental imagery, however, allows the athlete to get used to this uncertain environment.

Hypnosis

Although hypnosis is misunderstood by much of the general public, it can be an effective tool for psychological arousal and sometimes for behavior or performance change (17). **Hypnosis** can be defined as an induced state of hypersuggestibility in which positive suggestions relating to an athlete's performance potential can be planted in the subconscious mind. Some athletes may not effectively manage their physical resources because of perceived incompetence or lack of self-efficacy. This is particularly unfortunate when physical tests and a coach's judgment indicate superior potential. The athlete seems to have a mental block in terms of rationally and realistically viewing ability, despite receiving positive performance-based feedback. Such a psychological perspective may inhibit muscular effort or decrease coordination because the athlete forces the movement, as described earlier.

To understand the effect of hypnosis on inhibitory processes, consider the case described years ago by Johnson and Kramer (23) in which an athlete under hypnotic suggestion was able to dramatically increase the number of repetitions for a bench press exercise. Did this psychological technique result in improved chronic strength and muscular endurance? Obviously not, but it did result in the increased expression of the athlete's strength and endurance potential. In this case, there may have been an actual neurological disinhibitory process occurring at the spinal motor neuron level. An athlete's realization that he or she can perform at such a high level can profoundly alter his or her self-concept and, indirectly, future performance.

Systematic Desensitization

Sometimes fears are learned by association of previously neutral stimuli with a stressful event. For example, an adult nonswimmer who experienced a threatening event in the water as a child may avoid activities around water because of a learned association. This individual may become fearful and therefore tense doing basic resistance or stretching exercises in a pool, even ones that require no swimming skill. This example illustrates the importance of understanding exercise science. For example, the aquatic environment is a great aid in enhancing flexibility. To benefit maximally from a stretching program, however, a participant must learn to fully relax. If the purpose of the pool session is to enhance flexibility, the inability of a nonswimmer to relax in that environment could easily prevent gains in flexibility.

One technique that helps an athlete initially confront or reduce fear is **systematic desensitization (SD)** (45). Systematic desensitization is a hybrid of cognitive and somatic techniques that allows an athlete to replace a fear response to various cues with a relaxation response. This adaptive, learned replacement process, the principle behind SD, is called **counterconditioning**.

To practice the technique, an athlete should be reasonably skilled at both PMR and mental imagery. The athlete should construct a hierarchy, or progression, of events and situations that he or she specifically perceives as fearful. For example, a competitive gymnast who suffered a serious injury on the balance beam may list a series of fearful scenes proceeding from warming up prior to her event to the actual movement that precipitated her injury. The hierarchy consists of an appropriate number of intervening scenarios, say 10 to 12.

In a relaxed setting the athlete visualizes the first scene and experiences a mild degree of anxiety. At the same time, PMR is instituted, and a strong relaxation response theoretically should overcome the relatively weak fight-or-flight syndrome. This technique is practiced until the athlete can hold the image clearly while maintaining a relaxed state. The athlete progresses through the hierarchy, experiencing conditioned fear in small, manageable doses that are overcome by the relaxation achieved with PMR and rhythmic breathing. This procedure prevents cognitive avoidance and counterconditions a new response (relaxation) to the formerly fear-inducing stimuli.

How Should Athletes Use Arousal Control Techniques?

- An athlete should employ arousal **reduction** techniques when performing a new skill or one that is complex in nature.
- Athletes should employ arousal **enhancement** techniques when executing simple skills or ones that are well learned.
- The purpose of employing such techniques is to allow the athlete to perform with an unburdened mind while matching his or her mental and physical intensity to the demands of the task.

CONCLUSION

The coach and athlete can improve performance outcomes and increase the enjoyment of competition by attending to the psychological aspects of performance. A positive, goal-oriented coaching approach is one of the most powerful contributors to psychological preparation for sport. The physical and nutritional preparation of the athlete represents the foundation on which performance potential is based; the role of psychology is to mentally manage the developed physical resources (i.e., strength, speed, flexibility, and skill), thereby allowing the athlete to achieve his or her potential on a more consistent basis. Additionally, an adequate understanding of the mind–body relationship can facilitate communication between the coach and athlete and aid the athlete in controlling and managing emotion and arousal. Using appropriate psychological techniques can help this self-management process. The experience of success in sport may be important in and of itself, but we believe that the greatest outcome may be the enhanced self-esteem, confidence, and positive self-concept that the athlete achieves.

KEY TERMS

STUDY QUESTIONS

1. During the closing seconds of a basketball game, an athlete's team is down by one point and he has been awarded two free throw shots. The player is apprehensive about the outcome of the game. Which of the following best describes the athlete's situation?
   a. He will not be able to make the free throws.
   b. He is experiencing state anxiety.
   c. He is in control of his arousal.
   d. His anxiety will improve his performance.

2. An Olympic weightlifter attempting a personal record is able to ignore the audience to concentrate solely on her performance. Which of the following abilities is this athlete most likely using to perform the exercise?
   a. selective attention
   b. somatic anxiety
   c. successive approximation
   d. dissociation

3. Prior to performing the long jump, an athlete reviews and concentrates on the technique required to jump as far as possible. Which of the following strategies is the athlete using to prepare for the jump?
   a. focus on task-relevant cues
   b. reliance on experience
   c. association
   d. trait anxiety

4. Which of the following is MOST important to achieve the ideal performance state?
   a. fear of failure
   b. analyzing performance
   c. broad focus on the activity and the environment
   d. personal control

5. An athlete's desire to perform to his or her potential is an example of
   a. the motive to avoid failure.
   b. dissociation.
   c. intrinsic motivation.
   d. achievement motivation.

6. For a high school American football team, if any player squats two times his body weight, his name is placed on the wall. This is an example of
   a. negative reinforcement.
   b. positive reinforcement.
   c. negative punishment.
   d. positive punishment.

7. How does an athlete's optimal level of arousal change with limited skill and ability to perform the activity?
   a. It increases.
   b. It decreases.
   c. It has no effect.
   d. It is not related to the activity.

CHAPTER 9

Performance-Enhancing Substances

Jay R. Hoffman, PhD, and Jeffrey R. Stout, PhD

After completing this chapter, you will be able to

- provide reliable information to athletes on the risks and benefits of performance-enhancing substances, including anabolic steroids;
- evaluate advertising claims for over-the-counter supplements marketed for performance benefits; and
- describe the current status of research on performance-enhancing supplements (e.g., β-alanine and creatine).

Performance-enhancing drugs and dietary supplements have been around since the ancient Olympic Games. Because of the ethical considerations relating to unfair advantage during competition and the potential for adverse events, most athletic governing bodies have generated a list of substances that are banned from national and international competition. Athletes caught using such substances can be suspended or forced to forfeit their medals or both. In situations in which the athlete tests positive for a banned substance on repeated occasions, he or she risks a lifetime ban on participation in the given sport. However, numerous nutritional supplements and ergogenic aids are permissible and are frequently used by athletes to maximize performance enhancement. Often the use of these substances is promoted on the basis of unfounded claims. Thus, it is imperative that the athlete become informed about the legality of these substances, understand the potential risks associated with consumption, and know whether results support the claims (i.e., what the efficacy is). Note that, although an **ergogenic aid** can be any substance, mechanical aid, or training method that improves sport performance, for the purposes of this chapter the term refers specifically to pharmacological aids.

Athletes try to gain a competitive advantage by using supplements that are reputed to be ergogenic but are not banned, or they may use banned substances in the belief that they can stay ahead of the drug testers. The consequence is that athletes who would normally refrain from using these substances may feel pressured to use them just to stay abreast of their competitors. However, athletes who are well informed can confidently ignore useless and possibly harmful products despite what their fellow athletes claim. It may also be possible to steer athletes away from the use of banned drugs if they are aware that competitors who cheat run a high risk of being detected.

Before athletes consider the use of any sport supplement or ergogenic aid, they should first devote themselves to a strength and conditioning program that adheres to the principles of training and should ensure adequate nutrition. Only if they deal with these two issues effectively should they consider using a sport supplement or ergogenic aid. Having made this decision, athletes need to seek guidance to make sure that what they are considering is both legal and efficacious.

An athlete's first priorities should be to apply sound principles of training and to ensure adequate nutrition.

TYPES OF PERFORMANCE-ENHANCING SUBSTANCES

The two principal categories of performance-enhancing substances considered in this chapter are (1) hormones and the drugs that mimic their effects and (2) dietary supplements. The distinction between a drug and a dietary supplement is not intuitively obvious (e.g., the stimulant caffeine, found in coffee, a foodstuff); however, it is important. The separation affects whether or not a product meets United States Food and Drug Administration (FDA) approval for safety and effectiveness. If a product is not classified as a drug or advertised as having therapeutic value, FDA regulations concerning its sale are relatively relaxed. This means that any manufacturer can introduce a new dietary supplement to the market without special approval and that the FDA will not investigate its safety or effectiveness unless a health risk is brought to the agency's attention (118). The FDA's definition of a drug encompasses substances that change the body's structure or function. This includes substances that stimulate hormone secretion. In addition, if a substance looks like a medicine or is administered differently from the way in which foods would be consumed, it may be classified as a drug.

The distinction between a drug and a dietary supplement is linked to FDA approval for safety and effectiveness.

Generally, **dietary supplements** are highly refined products that would not be confused with a food. They may not have any positive nutritional value; hence they are not referred to as nutritional supplements. Carbohydrate loading to bolster glycogen stores before an athletic competition is sport nutrition, but a tablet of a single purified amino acid not promoted for medicinal properties is a dietary supplement.

Until recently, dietary supplements included substances that were not considered "drugs" by the FDA and substances that did not fall into the categories of normal foods or food additives. Dietary supplements were regulated by the FDA, however, to ensure that they were safe and wholesome and that their labeling was truthful and not misleading. These requirements have changed. In 1994, the U.S. Congress passed the Dietary Supplement Health and Education Act (DSHEA). With the new legislation, premarket safety evaluations are no longer required for products falling within this definition, although some other safety provisions are still in effect. Dietary supplements can be sold if they do not present "a significant or unreasonable risk of illness or injury when used as directed on the label or under normal conditions of use (if there are no directions)" (199). Companies can also make claims about effects on the body's structure and function as long as the manufacturers can show that the statements are truthful and not misleading; this is a much less stringent requirement than for effectiveness claims made for drugs.

Ergogenic substances are usually banned from athletic competition when a consensus is reached that they may provide an unfair competitive edge or pose a significant health risk. This prohibition does not need to be based on conclusive proof that a substance does anything advantageous; it simply represents an agreement among administrators or clinicians that this may be the case. Figure 9.1 lists the 2007-2008 National Collegiate Athletic Association banned-drug classes. This list is used by universities in the United States and is subject to change on a yearly basis. As mentioned previously, every sport's governing body publishes its list of banned drugs, as do many national Olympic committees and the International Olympic Committee. The list differs for each organization; thus it is incumbent on the athlete, sport coach, strength and conditioning professional, and all support staff to ensure that they are compliant with their respective organizations.

Some of the substances are illegal under governmental statute as well. Anabolic steroids are a Class III substance, which makes their possession, for other than medical use, punishable by up to five years in jail and a fine of not more than US$250,000 for the first offense, and up to 10 years in jail and a fine of not more than US$500,000 for the second offense. If an athlete or coach provides anabolic steroids to someone, the issue is no longer one of possession; that athlete or coach is now classified as a dealer and the punishments are much greater in scope.

Definition of Products That Can Be Sold as Dietary Supplements

The following points define which products can be sold as dietary supplements in the United States.

1. A product (other than tobacco) intended to supplement the diet that contains one or more of the following dietary ingredients:
   a. A vitamin
   b. A mineral
   c. An herb or other botanical
   d. An amino acid
   e. A dietary substance for use by humans to supplement the diet by increasing the total dietary intake
   f. A concentrate, metabolite, constituent, extract, or combination of any ingredient identified in *a* through *e*
2. The product must also be intended for ingestion and cannot be advertised for use as a conventional food or as the sole item within a meal or diet.

2007-2008 NATIONAL COLLEGIATE ATHLETIC ASSOCIATION BANNED-DRUG CLASSES

A. Stimulants

Amiphenazole, amphetamine, bemigride, benzphetamine, bromantan, caffeine (concentration in urine >15 μ/ml), chlorphentermine, cocaine, cropropamide, crothetamide, diethylpropion, dimethylamphetamine, doxapram, ephedrine (ephedra, ma huang), ethamivan, ethylamphetamine, fencamfamine, meclofenoxate, methamphetamine, methylenedioxymethamphetamine (MDMA, ecstasy), methylphenidate, nikethamide, octopamine, pemoline, pentetrazol, phendimetrazine, phenmetrazine, phentermine, phenylpropanolamine (ppa), picrotoxine, pipradol, prolintane, strychnine, synephrine (citrus aurantium, zhi shi, bitter orange), and related compounds

The following stimulants are *not* banned: phenylephrine and pseudoephedrine

B. Anabolic Agents

Anabolic Steroids

Androstenediol, androstenedione, boldenone, clostebol, dehydrochlormethyltestosterone, dehydroepiandrostenedione (DHEA), dihydrotestosterone (DHT), dromostanolone, epitrenbolone, fluoxymesterone, gestrinone, mesterolone, methandienone, methyltestosterone, nandrolone, norandrostenediol, norandrostenedione, norethandrolone, oxandrolone, oxymesterone, oxymetholone, stanozolol, testosterone (ratio >6:1 testosterone:epitestosterone), tetrahydrogestrinone (THG), trenbolone, and related compounds

Other Anabolic Agents

Clenbuterol

C. Substances Banned for Specific Sports

Rifle: alcohol, atenolol, metoprolol, nadolol, pindolol, propranolol, timolol, and related compounds

D. Diuretics and Other Urine Manipulators

Acetazolamide, bendroflumethiazide, benzhiazide, bumetanide, chlorothiazide, chlorthalidone, ethacrynic acid, finasteride, flumethiazide, furosemide, hydrochlorothiazide, hydromethiazide, methyclothiazide, metolazone, polythiazide, probenecid, spironolactone (canrenone), triamterene, trichlormethiazide, and related compounds

E. Street Drugs

Heroin, marijuana (concentration in urine of THC metabolite >15 nanograms/ml), tetrahydrocannabinol (THC) (concentration in urine of THC metabolite >15 nanograms/ml)

F. Peptide Hormones and Analogs

Corticotrophin (ACTH), growth hormone (HGH, somatotrophin), human chorionic gonadotropin (HCG), insulin-like growth factor (IGF-I), and luteinizing hormone (LH)

All the respective releasing factors of the above-mentioned substances also are banned: darbepoetin, erythropoietin (EPO), and sermorelin

G. Anti-Estrogens

Anastrozole, clomiphene, and tamoxifen

Figure 9.1 The National Collegiate Athletic Association's list of substances banned for athletes at colleges and universities in the United States. Check with your institution or governing body for the list specific to your situation.

HORMONES

A variety of endogenously produced hormones are used to enhance athletic performance. The most commonly used hormone is testosterone, along with its synthetic derivatives. In addition, a variety of other hormones produced by the body have been employed by athletes as ergogenic aids to stimulate the testes to produce testosterone, or have anabolic properties in themselves; growth hormone is an example. Erythropoietin, which is secreted by the kidneys, is used to stimulate red cell production for enhancement of aerobic endurance performance; and **catecholamines** such as adrenaline (or epinephrine), which have metabolic and nervous system effects, are often used to enhance weight loss and to provide greater arousal for performance.

Anabolic Steroids

Anabolic steroids are the synthetic (man-made) derivatives of the male sex hormone, testosterone. Physiologically, elevations in testosterone concentrations stimulate protein synthesis, resulting in improvements in muscle size, body mass, and strength (27, 28). In addition, testosterone and its synthetic derivatives are responsible for the development and maturation of male secondary sex characteristics (i.e., increase in body hair; masculine voice; development of male pattern baldness, libido, sperm production, and aggressiveness). These androgenic properties include the full development of the primary sexual characteristics of the male. As a result, it is more accurate to refer to synthetic derivatives of testosterone as anabolic-androgenic steroids. However, they are also referred to as androgens, androgenic steroids, or simply anabolic steroids.

Secretion of testosterone occurs primarily in the interstitial Leydig cells in the testes. Although several other steroid hormones with anabolic-androgenic properties are produced in the testes (e.g., dihydrotestosterone and androstenedione), testosterone is produced in far greater quantities. Testosterone and these other male sex hormones are also secreted in significantly smaller amounts from the adrenal glands and ovaries. Many of the ergogenic aids on the market today are precursors for testosterone (i.e., androstenedione) and are discussed in further detail later in this chapter.

The physiological changes that testosterone regulates have made it one of the drugs of choice for strength/power athletes or other athletes interested in increasing muscle mass. However, testosterone itself is a very poor ergogenic aid. Rapid degradation occurs when testosterone is given either orally or through injectable administration (212). Thus, chemical modification of testosterone was necessary to retard the degradation process in order to achieve androgenic and anabolic effects at lower concentrations and to provide effective blood concentrations for longer periods of time (212). Once these modifications occurred, anabolic steroid use through either oral or injectable administration became possible. Examples of commonly used oral and injectable anabolic steroids are listed in table 9.1.

Dosing

Athletes typically use anabolic steroids in a "**stacking**" regimen, in which they administer several different drugs simultaneously. The rationale for stacking is to increase the potency of each drug. That is, the potency of one anabolic agent may be enhanced when it is consumed simultaneously with another anabolic agent. Individuals use both oral

TABLE 9.1

Types of Anabolic Steroids Used by Athletes

Generic name or category	Examples of trade names
ORALLY ACTIVE STEROIDS	
Methandrostenolone	Dianabol
Oxandrolone	Anavar
Stanozolol	Winstrol
Oxymetholone	Anadrol
Fluoxymesterone	Halotestin
Methyltestosterone	Oreton-M
Mesterolone	Proviron
INJECTABLE STEROIDS	
Testosterone esters*	Delatestryl, Sustanon
Nandrolone esters*	Deca-Durabolin
Stanozolol	Strombaject
Methenolone enanthate	Primobolan Depot
Boldenone undecylenate	Parenabol
Trenbolone acetate	Parabolan

*These are general categories of substances; many different preparations of each are available.

and injectable compounds. Most users take anabolic steroids in a cyclic pattern, meaning that they use the drugs for several weeks or months and alternate these cycles with periods of discontinued use. Often athletes administer the drugs in a pyramid (step-up) pattern in which dosages are steadily increased over several weeks. Toward the end of the cycle, the athlete "steps down" to reduce the likelihood of negative side effects. At this point, some athletes discontinue the drug use or perhaps initiate another cycle of different drugs (e.g., drugs that may increase endogenous testosterone production, taken to prevent the undesirable drop in testosterone concentrations that follows the removal of the pharmaceutical agents). A recent study showed that the typical steroid regimen involved an average of 3.1 agents, with a typical cycle ranging from 5 to 10 weeks (152). The dose that the athlete administered was reported to vary from between 5 and 29 times greater than physiological replacement doses (152). These higher pharmacological dosages appear necessary to elicit the gains that the athletes desire. In a classic study on the dose–response curve of anabolic steroids, Forbes (68) demonstrated that the total dose of anabolic steroids has a logarithmic relationship to increases in lean body mass; low doses produce only slight effects, but there is a progressive augmentation of lean body mass with increasingly larger doses (figure 9.2). These results reinforce the athlete's philosophy that if a low dose is effective, then more must be better.

Athletes typically use higher doses of the substances than are prescribed for men with low testosterone levels. Methandrostenolone (Dianabol), for example, maintains normal secondary sexual characteristics in hypogonadal men at a replacement dose of approximately 15 mg/day; athletes have reported using up to 300 mg/day (71). This orally active drug has not been available for medical use in the United States for more than a decade but is still available through black market sources. Testosterone enanthate, a testosterone ester and the main injectable steroid used by athletes, is readily available in the United States and is used clinically for some rare diseases and for replacement treatment. A replacement dose is approximately 75 to 100 mg/week administered every one to two weeks. Injectable steroids are administered intramuscularly, typically by deep gluteal injections. They are also more potent than oral steroids because of their route of delivery, and perhaps as well because they do not require additional modification to protect them from immediate metabolism by the liver. The injectable compounds have a wide range of half-lives. Among the testosterone esters, testosterone propionate remains in the circulation for approximately 1.5 days, whereas testosterone buciclate lasts for three months after a single injection (17).

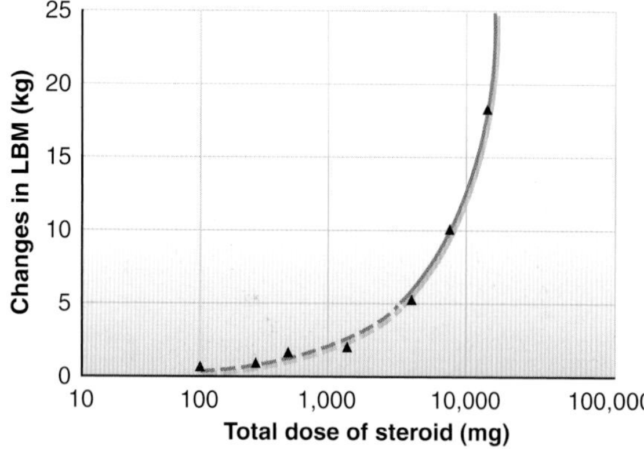

Figure 9.2 Dose–response curve of anabolic steroids and changes in lean body mass. LBM = lean body mass.

Reprinted, by permission, from Hoffman, 2002 (100).

Who Uses Anabolic Steroids?

Boje (32) was the first to suggest that exogenous testosterone administration may enhance athletic performance. By the late 1940s and the 1950s, testosterone compounds were being experimented with by west coast bodybuilders (214). The first dramatic reports of anabolic steroid use circulated following the 1954 world weightlifting championships (214). Use of these drugs spread quickly through the 1960s and became popular among athletes in a variety of Olympic sports (58). In the United States, widespread use has also been reported in powerlifters (206), National Football League players (214), and collegiate athletes (213). Although results of several surveys suggest that anabolic steroid use appears to have been declining over the last 20 years (5, 6, 7, 60, 113), anabolic steroids are among the top sport issues today because of accusations of widespread use in many sports during the past few years.

Strength athletes are not the only users of anabolic steroids. People outside organized sport use steroids to enhance appearance rather than performance. A national survey of male American high school seniors showed that 7% were using, or had used, anabolic steroids (40). One-third of the admitted steroid users were not involved in school-sponsored sports, and more than one-fourth stated that their main reason for using steroids was to improve appearance, as opposed to athletic performance. Pope and his colleagues (155, 159) described a subset of bodybuilders with an altered self-image who believed that they looked small and weak even though they were large and muscular. These individuals used ergogenic substances and weight training to increase their body size. Pope calls this condition "reverse anorexia nervosa"; it is also known as **muscle dysmorphia**. These bodybuilders appear to be substantially different from competitive athletes in terms of their objectives, the substantial health risks that some of them are willing to take, and their strategies of using extremely large doses. This phenomenon suggests why the most serious illnesses associated with steroid use have occurred almost exclusively in bodybuilders and not in other steroid-using athletes (71).

Ergogenic Benefits

The purported ergogenic benefits commonly attributed to anabolic steroid use are increased muscle mass, strength, and athletic performance. The degree and incidence of these changes are variable, depending greatly on the training status of the individual as well as other factors.

Muscle Mass and Strength When anabolic steroids are given in dosages similar to those used by recreationally trained and competitive athletes, increases in muscle protein synthesis are seen (86). These increases are likely responsible for the increases observed in lean body mass in both recreationally trained and competitive athletes taking anabolic steroids (3, 93, 147, 182, 206). Even when anabolic steroids are administered to normal adult men not engaged in intensive resistance training, increases in body mass, including the nonfat component, are observed (27, 69, 71, 208). In a study of competitive powerlifters, body mass increased more than 5 kg (11 pounds) following 26 weeks of anabolic steroid administration (3). In comparison, the control group, consisting of both powerlifters and bodybuilders, did not display any increase in body mass during the same time period.

A dose–response effect resembling a logarithmic relationship (see figure 9.2) is apparent between the concentration of exogenous anabolic steroid used and increases in lean body mass (68). For some time it was postulated that increases in body mass with androgen use came from an increase in body water (93). An increase in total body water is expected with an increase in muscle mass, since water constitutes a majority of the cellular weight; however, anabolic steroids may increase water retention as well by increasing interstitial and extracellular volume. Although water retention may explain why not all of the weight gain is sustained after cessation of anabolic steroid use, this issue is still not well understood. In a study of experienced male bodybuilders, an eight-week cycle of nandrolone decanoate (200 mg/week, intramuscularly) resulted in a significant 2.2 kg (5-pound) increase in body mass (2.6 kg increase in fat-free mass and 0.4 kg decrease in fat mass), with no change in hydration of fat-free mass (200). In addition, the extracellular and intracellular water ratio was unaltered. Even after six weeks of discontinued androgen use, the body mass of the bodybuilders was still significantly greater than baseline levels (1.6 kg [3.5 pounds] greater), yet no hydration changes were seen. The increase in fat-free mass and possible reduction in fat mass may last for several months after cessation of use (69) (figure 9.3). Thus, athletes may derive a benefit from steroid use even if they stop taking the drugs long enough before competition to obtain a negative drug test. This is why unannounced, year-round drug testing of some elite athletes is important for the prevention of unfair drug use.

Athletic Performance Initially, researchers examining the ergogenicity of exogenously administered anabolic steroids were unable to see any significant performance effects (66, 70, 81, 131, 187).

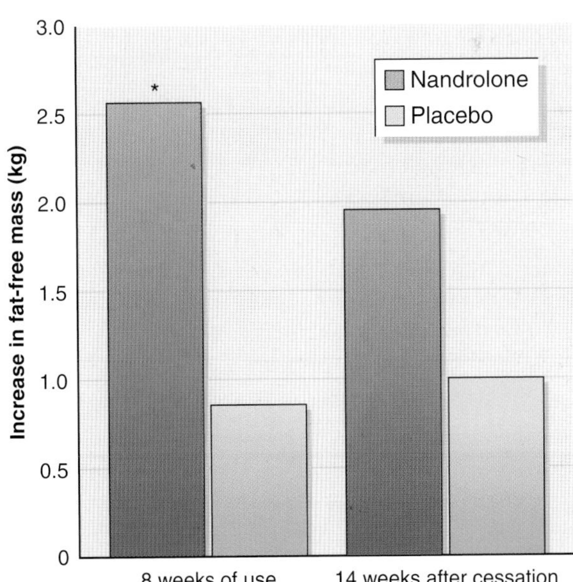

Figure 9.3 Changes in fat-free mass with anabolic steroid administration (200 mg/week nandrolone decanoate for eight weeks) and following drug cessation.

*$p < .05$.

Adapted, by permission, from Van Marken Lichtenbelt et al., 2004 (200).

Consequently, the scientific and medical community suggested that anabolic steroids had little influence on athletic performance. This, however, was contrary to anecdotal reports emanating from gyms that showed large strength improvements in the athletes. Upon further examination of the initial studies, several methodological flaws became apparent. Several of these initial studies used physiological doses, in contrast to the suprapharmacological doses that are typically taken by athletes self-administering androgens. In essence, these subjects were shutting down their own endogenous production and replacing it with an exogenous anabolic steroid. Another flaw was the method of strength assessment. In several studies, strength performance was evaluated using a mode of exercise that was different than the training stimulus. This lack of specificity likely masked any possible training effect. In addition, several studies used subjects who had only minimal resistance training experience. When exogenous androgens have been administered to experienced resistance-trained athletes, significant strength gains have been consistently reported (4, 93, 147, 182, 206).

Strength gains in experienced strength-trained athletes are generally quite small, relative to those seen in novice lifters; but when strength-trained athletes begin to use anabolic steroids, their strength gains may be two- to threefold higher than those typically seen in similarly trained athletes who are not supplementing (93, 200, 206). In a case study of a bodybuilder who was cycling anabolic steroids, strength levels were elevated during the times of the year when the athlete was using anabolic steroids (3). During cycles when the athlete trained drug free, strength levels tended to decline. Although well-controlled studies using similar subject populations are still lacking, the results in this case study are consistent with many of the anecdotal reports from competitive athletes.

The principal mechanisms that appear to be responsible for increasing strength and lean body mass are increases in protein synthesis and inhibition of the catabolic effects resulting from high-intensity training. The anticatabolic activity of androgen administration is reflected by changes in the testosterone-to-cortisol ratio (T/C ratio) (168). A higher T/C ratio may not only give the athlete the ability to maintain a higher intensity and volume of training, but also enhance the recovery processes between exercise sessions. If the athlete can train harder and for a longer duration, the stimulus presented to the muscle will result in a greater physiological adaptation. Thus the androgens may be considered to have an indirect effect on performance and size gains.

The purported ergogenic benefits commonly attributed to anabolic steroid use are increased muscle mass, strength, and athletic performance, but these changes depend on the training status of the individual.

Psychological Effects

Anabolic steroid use is also associated with changes in aggression, arousal, and irritability. The East Germans reportedly used anabolic steroids for this effect, delivering high doses to the central nervous system by taking steroids through the nose. The issue has not been well studied, but anecdotal reports suggest that this practice markedly increased aggressiveness and enhanced performance among athletes (56). Elevations in arousal and self-esteem may be a positive side effect for the anabolic steroid user. Increases in aggressiveness can also be perceived as a benefit, especially for athletes participating in contact sports.

Increased aggressiveness may not be confined to athletic performance, however. Anabolic steroid users experiencing increased aggressiveness may pose a threat both to themselves and to those they come in contact with (156, 157). Anabolic steroids are also associated with mood swings and psychotic episodes. Studies have shown that nearly 60% of anabolic steroid users experience increases in irritability and aggressiveness (158, 176). Pope and colleagues (160) reported significant elevations in aggressiveness and manic scores following 12 weeks of testosterone cypionate injections in a controlled double-blind crossover study. Interestingly, the results of this study were not uniform across the subjects. Most subjects showed little psychological effect, and few developed prominent effects. A cause-and-effect relationship has yet to be identified in anabolic steroid users, but it does appear that individuals who experience psychological or behavioral changes recover when steroid use is discontinued (73). Furthermore, psychosis may occur in some susceptible individuals or perhaps with doses that also activate corticosteroid-specific responses (corticosteroids have been known to produce psychosis).

Adverse Effects

Adverse effects associated with anabolic steroid use are listed in table 9.2. Recent literature has suggested that the medical problems related to anabolic steroids may be somewhat overstated (25, 104, 186), considering that many of the side effects linked to abuse are reversible upon cessation. It is important to note that there are differences between the side effects of anabolic steroid use under medical supervision and those associated with abuse (i.e., consumption of many drugs at high doses).

Most of the information concerning adverse medical events associated with anabolic steroid use has been acquired from athletes self-administering the drugs. Anecdotally, it appears that a disproportionate magnitude of use and incidence of adverse events are evident in bodybuilders (who are also known for consuming several other drugs, such as diuretics, thyroid hormones, insulin, and anti-estrogens, that relieve some side effects but potentiate other risk factors as well) compared to strength/power athletes.

TABLE 9.2

Adverse Effects Associated With Anabolic Steroid Use

Affected system	Adverse effects
Cardiovascular	Lipid profile changes Elevated blood pressure Decreased myocardial function
Endocrine	Gynecomastia Decreased sperm count Testicular atrophy Impotence and transient infertility

Genitourinary	Males
	  Decreased sperm count
	  Decreased testicular size
	Females
	  Menstrual irregularities
	  Clitoromegaly
	  Masculinization
	Males and females
	  Gynecomastia
	  Libido changes

Dermatological	Acne Male pattern baldness
Hepatic	Increased risk of liver tumors and liver damage
Musculoskeletal	Premature epiphyseal plate closure Increased risk of tendon tears Intramuscular abscess
Psychological	Mania Depression Aggression Mood swings

Testosterone Precursors (Prohormones)

The basis for the use of testosterone precursors, also called **prohormones**, as an ergogenic aid evolved from a study showing a threefold increase in testosterone in healthy women who were given 100 mg of either androstenedione or dehydroepiandrosterone (134). Athletes have continued to supplement with these testosterone precursors (androstenedione, androstenediol, and dehydroepiandrosterone [DHEA]) on the premise that they will increase testosterone concentrations and achieve performance changes similar to those experienced by people taking anabolic steroids. However, these precursors have only relatively weak androgenic properties in themselves; androstenedione and DHEA have only 1/5th and 1/10th the biological activity of testosterone, respectively (140). Even if a large dose is ingested, most of these substances (similarly to testosterone) are rapidly eliminated from circulation. Nevertheless, testosterone precursors were officially listed as controlled substances in the 2004 Anabolic Steroid Control Act passed by the U.S. Congress, which mandated a physician's prescription for these substances.

Studies examining the efficacy of testosterone precursors have produced varying results. No significant differences in strength or body composition were seen in middle-aged men performing a resistance training program while supplementing with either DHEA, androstenedione (100 mg), or a placebo for three months (205). When DHEA supplementation (150 mg) was examined in a group of younger males (19-29 years) on a two-weeks-on, one-week-off cycle for eight weeks, there were no gains in strength or lean tissue (38). In addition, the investigators were unable to see any changes in serum testosterone, estrone, estradiol, or lipid concentrations with supplementation. Even in studies using higher dosages (300 mg) of androstenedione for eight weeks, in a similar two-weeks-on, one-week-off protocol, no significant effect was observed in strength, muscle size, or testosterone concentrations (119). However, androstenedione supplementation did cause an increase in serum concentrations of estradiol and estrone and was associated with lower high-density lipoprotein levels. These results suggest that although performance changes may not occur in athletes taking this supplement, they may be at higher risk for some of the side effects that are associated with anabolic steroid use.

Although performance changes may not occur with prohormone use, athletes taking prohormones may be at higher risk for experiencing adverse side effects similar to those associated with anabolic steroid use.

Recently it has been concluded that these prohormones fall far short of providing the anabolic effects generally associated with androgens (37). However, use of the prohormones has not been studied in highly trained athletes. In addition, oral administration has been the primary method of taking prohormones. Leder and colleagues (127) demonstrated that 100 and 300 mg dosages of oral androstenedione did convert to testosterone; however, most of the conversion occurred in the liver, from which 89% of the converted testosterone is excreted without reentry into the circulation. Thus, oral use of prohormones may not be as effective as other means of intake (e.g., injection). All of this suggests that continued study of the efficacy of the testosterone precursors for performance enhancement is still needed; specifically warranted is examination of other routes of ingestion in a trained competitive athletic population.

Human Chorionic Gonadotropin

Human chorionic gonadotropin (HCG) is a hormone obtained from the placenta of pregnant women and is very closely related in structure and function to luteinizing hormone. When injected into men, it can increase testicular testosterone production; testosterone levels can nearly double within four days after a large intramuscular injection (47). Human chorionic gonadotropin is primarily used by athletes who are finishing a cycle of anabolic steroids and are looking to activate their own endogenous testosterone production (165). In addition, because HCG can stimulate endogenous testosterone production, the thinking is that it can help stabilize the testosterone-to-epitestosterone ratio (T/E), which serves as an indicator of anabolic steroid use. However, because HCG can increase testosterone levels, many of the side effects associated with anabolic steroid use may become evident.

Insulin

Insulin is a very potent **anabolic hormone**. It is secreted by the pancreas in response to elevations in blood glucose and amino acid concentrations. Its role is to facilitate the uptake of glucose and amino acids into the cell. Since insulin increases protein synthesis, it is considered an anabolic hormone; and because it is a peptide hormone, its use as an ergogenic aid cannot be detected in the urine. It is taken primarily by bodybuilders to potentiate the effects of growth hormone and insulin-like growth factors. However, use among those who are not bodybuilders appears to be on the rise (165). The use of insulin, though, comes with serious consequences. A major side effect is hypoglycemia (i.e., low blood sugar), which can prove to be fatal.

Human Growth Hormone

Human growth hormone (**HGH**), a protein secreted from the anterior pituitary gland, has several important physiological functions that enhance its ergogenic effect. It is anabolic due to its stimulation of bone and skeletal muscle growth, but it also has important metabolic functions such as maintaining blood glucose levels, increasing the uptake of glucose and amino acids into muscle cells (94), and stimulating release of fatty acids from the fat cells.

The primary source of pharmacological growth hormone is a relatively complicated molecule from which it is synthetically derived using recombinant DNA technology. However, until 1986, the only source of the hormone was the pituitaries of human cadavers. Because HGH receptors are unable to cross-react with growth hormone from animal sources, the financial cost of HGH was very high before 1986. Although the use of cadaver growth hormone did not come without significant health risks, these consequences did not prevent athletes from taking the supplement, but instead only restricted use substantially. The development of recombinant HGH provided clinicians with a relatively low-risk drug at a lower cost with greater availability. Clinicians can now prescribe recombinant HGH to increase stature in normal children and alter body composition in normal adults. However, since the 1980s, athletes have become well aware of the anabolic potential of HGH and its ability to reduce body fat. The use of HGH by competitive athletes appears to be on the rise; it is either taken alone or stacked with anabolic steroids (165). Even though recombinant technology has increased the availability of HGH, its cost, especially on the black market, is extremely high (between US$150 and US$170 per dose). Humatrope, Nutropin, Norditropin, Genotropin, Serostim, Saizen, and Protropin are brand names of HGH commonly used in the United States.

Efficacy

There appear to be no studies on the efficacy of HGH in athletic populations. Most investigations of HGH have focused on HGH as replacement therapy in growth hormone–deficient adults or children. These studies have consistently shown positive alterations in body composition (increases in lean body tissue with decreases in body fat) (1, 54, 99, 170, 171, 198). In men with established growth hormone deficiencies, nightly injections of recombinant HGH for six months resulted in an average increase of 12 pounds (5.4 kg) in lean body mass and a similar amount of fat loss (171). Most studies have not addressed the effect of HGH therapy on muscle strength and performance. One study showed no changes in isokinetic strength following 12 months of therapy (99). However, the subjects in that study did not perform any resistance training during the course of treatment. A study involving trained adults given growth hormone (three days per week for six weeks) showed modest changes in body composition, but no strength assessment was performed (54). Nevertheless, anecdotal reports suggest impressive musculoskeletal performance changes in athletes using HGH. Although the scientific literature does not provide support for the efficacy of HGH use in athletic populations, it is likely the inability to perform such studies (due to ethical constraints) that will limit much of our understanding of HGH and human performance. However, as already noted, the use of HGH by athletes appears to be increasing, owing to its perceived efficacy and the fact that it cannot be detected in random drug tests.

The anabolic potential of human growth hormone (HGH) and its ability to reduce body fat have contributed to the rise in HGH use among athletes.

Growth hormone is a protein molecule. Injection is necessary in order to avoid its complete metabolization and maintain its effectiveness. Oral ingestion does not result in any benefit. As a peptide hormone, HGH is not detected in the urine via a drug test, and many athletes may opt to use it for this reason.

Many of the actions of growth hormone are mediated through insulin-like growth factor I (IGF-I), another peptide hormone, which is produced and secreted from the liver in response to growth hormone stimulation. Insulin-like growth factor I is now being synthesized using recombinant DNA technology and will likely produce the same effects as HGH.

Adverse Effects

The use of HGH does, however, present some potential health risks. Excessive secretion of growth hormone during childhood causes **gigantism**, a condition in which a person becomes abnormally tall. After puberty, once linear growth has stopped, excess secretion of growth hormone causes **acromegaly**, a disfiguring disease characterized by a widening of the bones, arthritis, organ enlargement, and metabolic abnormalities. This is a potential risk for athletes who use HGH as an ergogenic aid. In addition, these side effects may provide some indication that the athlete may be using this drug. In clinical studies in growth hormone–deficient adults, side effects appear to be minimal for even up to two years of replacement therapy (1, 99, 198). However, athletes who supplement with HGH generally use dosages that far exceed the doses commonly administered in replacement treatment. Thus, one should not assume that HGH use is benign with regard to adverse medical events in doses commonly used by an athletic population.

Although growth hormone used as replacement therapy for people with growth hormone or IGF-I deficiency can be effective and can have minimal adverse consequences, the dosages that are likely used by athletes may pose a significant risk for acromegaly.

Erythropoietin

Erythropoietin (EPO) is another protein hormone that can be produced by recombinant DNA techniques and is reportedly being abused by athletes (2). Erythropoietin is produced in the kidneys and stimulates the production of new red blood cells. Its level increases in response to aerobic endurance exercise such as marathon running (174). In certain types of anemia, especially in kidney patients with inadequate EPO production, recombinant human EPO can improve the quality of life. Injections of EPO are generally associated with elevations in both hematocrit and hemoglobin. When EPO was given to normal men during six weeks of treatment, hematocrit levels increased by 44.5% to 50%, hemoglobin concentrations increased by 10%, aerobic capacity increased between 6% and 8%, and the time to exhaustion improved by up to 17% (24, 64). The enhanced oxygen-carrying capacity of the blood makes EPO an effective ergogenic aid for the aerobic endurance athlete. The mechanism for increasing hemoglobin levels has been reported to be related to the elevated hematocrit and a decrease in plasma volume (132). The change in plasma volume is thought to be mediated by a downregulation of the renin-angiotensin-aldosterone axis (132).

The increase in hematocrit presents a significant health risk. Increases in red blood cell number increase blood viscosity. This poses several problems that include increased risk of blood clotting, elevations in systolic blood pressure, and a compromised thermoregulatory system. During aerobic endurance events, the additional problem of dehydration could compound cardiovascular risks by eliminating any safety margin in the balance between performance advantages from artificially increased hematocrit and decrements from increased blood viscosity. The deaths of a number of bike racing cyclists have been related to EPO administration (79). The primary risk associated with EPO is its lack of predictability compared to red blood cell infusion. Once EPO is injected into the body, the stimulus for producing red blood cells is no longer under control. Consequently, aerobic endurance athletes should stay away from this drug because of the significant cardiovascular risk, leading to possible death, associated with its administration.

β-Adrenergic Agonists

Synthetic β-adrenergic agonists, or **β-agonists**, are substances chemically related to epinephrine, a hormone produced in the adrenal medulla that regulates physiological effects, such as **lipolysis** (the breakdown of fat) and **thermogenesis** (increased energy expenditure for heat production). β-Agonists were originally developed for the treatment of asthma and other life-threatening medical conditions. Some of these compounds have been found to have specific effects on body composition, such as increases in lean mass and decreases in stored fat; because of this, these drugs are sometimes referred to as **partitioning agents** (23).

The implicit proof of the effectiveness of β-agonists is demonstrated in their increased use in livestock. Without question, these drugs work in the species for which they are intended, increasing protein synthesis and muscle mass and decreasing fat mass through enhanced lipolysis and lowered **lipogenesis** (fat synthesis and storage) (72). The main drugs used in animals are ractopamine, cimaterol, and clenbuterol.

Clenbuterol is a β_2-agonist that is generally used to reverse bronchial constriction. In recent years athletes have begun to use it as an ergogenic aid to increase lean muscle tissue and reduce subcutaneous fat (161). This has been based on studies in a rodent model demonstrating that clenbuterol can increase muscle protein synthesis (133, 166). Though studies in humans are limited, several findings have indicated an ergogenic potential of β_2-agonists for strength improvements (135, 136). Athletes generally use clenbuterol in doses twice the recommended amounts administered for clinical purposes, in a cyclic fashion (three weeks on alternated with three weeks off, with a two-days-on, two-days-off cycle during the "on" week) (161). It is believed that this cycling regimen avoids β_2-receptor downregulation (57). Athletes consume clenbuterol in a capsule form, in contrast to the inhalation route that is often used for relieving bronchial constriction. Although a number of potential side effects have been suggested (i.e., transient tachycardia, hyperthermia, tremors, dizziness, palpitations, and malaise), actual documented events are quite limited. In addition, the scarcity of data on the ergogenicity of clenbuterol in humans makes determining its efficacy difficult.

β-Blockers

β-Blockers are a class of drugs that block the β-adrenergic receptors, preventing the catecholamines (i.e., norepinephrine and epinephrine) from binding. β-Blockers are generally prescribed by cardiologists for the treatment of a wide variety of cardiovascular diseases, including hypertension. The ergogenic benefit of these drugs may reside in their ability to reduce anxiety and tremors during performance (100). Thus, athletes who rely on steady, controlled movements during performance (i.e., archers or marksmen) would appear to benefit from these drugs. In addition, it has been suggested that β-blockers improve physiological adaptations from aerobic endurance training by causing an upregulation of β-receptors (210). This may result in an exaggerated response to sympathetic discharge during intense exercise upon cessation of supplementation.

Several studies have shown that β-blockers can improve both slow and fast shooting accuracy (9, 125, 191). In addition, the dose taken appears to have significant effects on the magnitude of improvement. In shooters who administered β-blockers in two different doses (80 mg vs. 40 mg of oxprenolol), the group taking the higher dose shot with greater accuracy (9). In certain sports, however, some degree of anxiety may be important. Tesch (191) reported that bowlers whose performance was improved during blockade with oxprenolol had significantly greater heart rates before, during, and after competition than subjects whose performance did not improve while on β-blockers.

β-Blockers may also have an **ergolytic** effect (reduce performance). Studies have shown that β-blockers impair the cardiovascular response to exercise by reducing oxygen and substrate delivery to exercising muscles (210). Risks associated with these drugs include bronchiospasms in individuals with asthma, light-headedness (due to decreases in blood pressure), increased fatigue, and hypoglycemia in type 2 diabetics (β-blockers can increase insulin secretion).

More research is needed to examine the effect of many ergogenic aids in athletic populations. Athletes should not misconstrue a lack of scientific information as an indication of safety.

DIETARY SUPPLEMENTS

The sport supplement industry throughout the world has exploded, with more than 600 sport nutrition companies marketing over 4,000 products that produce annual sales of more than US$4 billion in the United States alone (165). To enhance their marketing potential and compete for sales, many of these companies make unsubstantiated claims concerning the efficacy of their products. At times, unscrupulous companies have knowingly laced their products with banned substances to enhance their effects. As a result, much confusion has been created among athletes regarding appropriate supplements and the ethics of companies. It has become critical for the athlete and coach to make educated choices. This section describes dietary supplements that are commonly used by athletes.

Essential Amino Acids

Essential amino acids (EAA) are not produced in the body and must be obtained through the diet. Essential amino acids include isoleucine, leucine, valine, lysine, methionine, phenylalanine, threonine, and tryptophan. High levels of the EAA can be found in any number of animal-based proteins or as supplements sold over-the-counter.

Recently, scientists have demonstrated that the consumption of EAA can augment muscle protein synthesis in healthy human subjects (164, 193). For example, Tipton and colleagues (193) examined the effects of EAA in six healthy adults, three men and three women. The subjects participated in resistance exercise (eight sets of eight repetitions at 80% of 1-repetition maximum [1RM]) and then consumed either 40 g EAA or a placebo. Investigators then examined the subjects' muscle protein synthesis and found that the acute ingestion of EAA was very effective at stimulating muscle protein anabolism. In a follow-up study, using the same protocol (but with only 6 g EAA and 35 g sugar), Rasmussen and colleagues (164) demonstrated significantly greater anabolic drive—that is, the building of new muscle tissue—with the EAA supplement (when given shortly after resistance exercise) versus the placebo. Subsequently, Tipton and colleagues (194) examined the effects of consuming 6 g EAA plus 36 g of sugar, before or after resistance training, on muscle protein metabolism. They reported that when the EAA plus sugar was consumed 30 minutes before resistance training, the acute (3 hours postexercise) anabolic response was 158% greater than when the EAA and sugar supplement was consumed posttraining. As a result of these acute findings, Tipton and colleagues (194) and Rasmussen and colleagues (164) theorized that a person who consumed EAA before or after (or both before and after) every resistance training session over a period of weeks would experience greater changes in muscle mass than with training only.

Some scientists, however, did not agree that the enhanced acute anabolic response of resistance training from EAA supplementation would chronically translate into greater gains in muscle mass, citing the **Nadir effect** (148). Pacy and colleagues (148) theorized that the acute anabolic stimulus from dietary protein (EAA) intake, resistance exercise during the day, or both would be matched by a negative muscle protein balance equal in magnitude during the night (Nadir effect). If this is true, then EAA supplementation before or after training (or both before and after) would be ineffective at enhancing the rate of muscle synthesis over time. To test this theory, Tipton and colleagues (192) examined the 3-hour and 24-hour response to ingesting 6 g EAA before and after a single session of resistance training. As expected, the acute augmented anabolic effect of resistance exercise from EAA supplementation was similar to previously published findings (193, 194) and reflected the 24-hour response. Therefore, the authors concluded that there was no Nadir effect. Further, Tipton and colleagues (192) indicated that supplementing with EAA either before or after exercise (or both before and after) may indeed enhance the training adaptations usually seen with chronic resistance training.

Very recently, Willoughby and colleagues (211) examined the effects of supplementing with 6 g of EAA plus 14 g of milk proteins, 1 hour before and immediately after resistance training, for 10 weeks in young men. Prior to training, the subjects' body composition, strength, and thigh mass were measured; subjects were then randomly assigned to protein plus EAA or the sugar placebo. The authors reported significant changes in fat mass (–6%), fat-free mass (+8%), thigh mass (+20%), and bench (+34%) and leg (+27%) press strength, which were all greater than the changes seen in the placebo group. In support of these findings, Bird and colleagues (29) demonstrated that a 12-week resistance training program combined with 6% liquid carbohydrate plus 6 g EAA ingested between sets of each exercise session resulted in a 30% greater gain in fat-free mass than consumption of 6% carbohydrates.

There appears to be evidence supporting the use of EAA consumed before or after (or both before and after) a workout to increase the effects (strength and muscle mass) of resistance training in men. While short-term data in women are similar, more research is needed to validate the long-term effects on body composition and strength changes of EAA supplementation in association with resistance training.

β-Hydroxy-β-Methylbutyrate

β-Hydroxy-β-methylbutyrate (HMB) is a derivative of the EAA leucine and its metabolite α-ketoisocaproate. It is believed that HMB has both anabolic and lipolytic effects. However, to date limited research is available to support such claims. In limited studies, significantly greater improvements in strength and lean body mass have been reported in previously untrained subjects following resistance training programs of four to eight weeks after supplementation than in subjects consuming a placebo (77, 116, 144, 150). In addition, no adverse effects on hepatic enzyme function, lipid profile, renal function, or the immune system have been noted following eight weeks of HMB supplementation (78). Studies of HMB administration have also demonstrated possible anticatabolic properties of the supplement (172, 196). This has been attributed to reduced enzyme markers of muscle damage and an enhanced recovery during periods of high muscular stress following HMB administration (120). Specifically, these studies have shown significantly lower creatine kinase and lactate dehydrogenase concentrations following a prolonged run (20 km or 12.4 miles) in aerobic endurance–trained athletes (120) or in the initial weeks of a resistance training program (144). The subjects in these studies supplemented with 3 g/day of HMB for periods lasting three to six weeks. During supplementation schedules of shorter duration (less than one week), the ability to attenuate the catabolic effects of exercise or enhance strength appears to be limited (177).

The ergogenic effects of HMB in trained athletic populations are less clear. Studies using resistance-trained or competitive athletes were unable to duplicate the results seen in a recreationally trained population using similar supplementation schedules (123, 145, 149, 163). In addition, a recent study by Hoffman and colleagues (101) examined the effects of a 10-day supplementation period on collegiate American football players during preseason training camp. No significant differences were noted between subjects supplementing with HMB and subjects consuming a placebo in any performance measure or in any marker of stress and fatigue.

Recent studies of HMB supplementation do not support the efficacy of HMB supplementation in resistance-trained athletes. With only limited research available in trained subject populations, additional study appears warranted to further explore the effects of HMB during prolonged periods of supplementation and during various types of physical stress.

Nutritional Muscle Buffers

During high-intensity anaerobic exercise, a large accumulation of hydrogen ions (H^+) is coupled with a reduction of pH within skeletal muscle and has been shown to adversely affect performance (167). The ability to regulate H^+ concentration in skeletal muscle during high-intensity exercise has been termed **muscle buffering capacity (MBC)** (21, 143). There is a strong positive relationship between MBC and exercise performance (repeated sprint ability, high-intensity exercise capacity, anaerobic threshold, and training volume) (62, 63). In fact, researchers have demonstrated a positive relationship between exercise performance and MBC in athletes who participate in sports like basketball, soccer, hockey, cycling, crew (rowing), triathlons, and sprinting (30, 62, 63). In theory, improving MBC by training or by nutritional means (β-alanine, sodium bicarbonate, and citrate) would improve performance in sports and activities that may be limited by H^+ buildup. Therefore we briefly review the use of β-alanine, sodium bicarbonate, and sodium citrate in relation to high-intensity exercise performance.

β-Alanine

β-Alanine is a nonessential amino acid that is common in many foods that we eat, such as chicken. By itself, β-alanine has limited ergogenic properties. However, when it enters the muscle cell, it becomes the rate-limiting substrate for carnosine synthesis (59). Harris and colleagues (91) reported that four weeks of supplementing with β-alanine (4 to 6 g/day) resulted in a mean increase of 64% in skeletal muscle β-alanine concentrations.

In humans, carnosine is found primarily in fast-twitch skeletal muscle and is estimated to contribute up to 40% of the skeletal MBC of H^+ produced during intense anaerobic exercise, thus encouraging a drop in pH (91, 96). Theoretically, increasing skeletal muscle carnosine levels through chronic training or β-alanine supplementation (or both) would improve MBC and most likely improve anaerobic performance. Interestingly, carnosine concentrations in athletes such as sprinters and bodybuilders appear to be significantly higher than those in marathoners, untrained individuals, and people who are elderly (91, 188).

Suzuki and colleagues (188) recently examined the relationship between skeletal muscle carnosine levels and high-intensity exercise performance in trained cyclists. The authors reported a significant and positive relationship between carnosine concentration and mean power in a 30-second maximal sprint on a cycle ergometer. This finding supported the theory that skeletal muscle carnosine levels have a positive correlation with anaerobic performance because of the relationship between carnosine and MBC.

Hill and colleagues (96) examined the effect of β-alanine supplementation on muscle carnosine levels and exercise performance in untrained subjects. In a double-blind fashion, 25 male subjects (19-31 years) supplemented with either 4.0 g β-alanine or sugar placebo for the first week, then with up to 6.4 g for an additional nine weeks. Muscle carnosine levels (via muscle biopsy) and total work done (kilojoules) were measured at weeks 0, 4, and 10 during cycling to exhaustion at maximal power established from a graded exercise cycle ergometry test. Mean carnosine levels increased by 58% at week 4 and an additional 15% at week 10. Additionally, 13% and 16% increases in total work done during cycle ergometry were seen at weeks 4 and 10, respectively.

In another study, Stout and colleagues (183) examined the effects of β-alanine supplementation on **physical working capacity at fatigue threshold (PWC_{FT})** in untrained young men. In double-blind fashion, subjects consumed either 1.6 g of β-alanine or sugar placebo four times per day for 6 days, then 3.2 g/day for 22 days. Prior to and following supplementation, the subjects performed an incremental cycle ergometry test to determine PWC_{FT}, which was measured from bipolar surface electromyography recorded from the vastus lateralis muscle. In theory, the PWC_{FT} represents the highest exercise intensity a person can maintain without signs of fatigue and has been highly correlated with anaerobic threshold measurements (lactate and ventilatory thresholds). The results revealed a statistically significant increase in PWC_{FT} (9%) in the β-alanine group compared to no change in the placebo group. In a follow-up study, Stout and colleagues (184) examined the effects of β-alanine supplementation in untrained college-aged women and reported significant increases in PWC_{FT} (12.6%), ventilatory threshold (13.9%), and time to exhaustion (2.5%) during a graded exercise cycle ergometry test. The findings suggest that 28 days of β-alanine supplementation may increase the level of intensity that men and women can train or compete at without signs of rapid fatigue. Essentially, performance and quality of training would be augmented as the onset of fatigue threshold is elevated.

β-Alanine supplementation (3.2 to 6.4 g/day) appears to elevate muscle carnosine levels, which may improve exercise performance in untrained men and women by delaying fatigue as a consequence of an improved MBC. Currently, several studies are addressing the effects of β-alanine supplementation on muscle carnosine levels and exercise performance in highly trained athletes. In addition, investigators are examining the combined effect of β-alanine supplementation and training on performance changes.

Sodium Bicarbonate

Sodium bicarbonate (SB) is an antacid (alkalinizing agent), meaning that it counteracts or neutralizes acid (low pH). Sodium bicarbonate is naturally formed in the body and is also found in baking soda. Supplementation with SB has been shown to increase the pH of blood. A pH difference is created between the inside and outside of muscle cells that causes an accelerated movement of H^+ out of the contracting muscle, helping to regulate intramuscular pH (112). Supplementing with SB has been shown to improve MBC and in turn high-intensity exercise performance. McNaughton and colleagues (138, 139) and Coombes and McNaughton (49) have demonstrated improved total work capacity, peak power, peak torque, and strength from acute SB supplementation in men and women. Recently, Edge and colleagues (62) examined the effects of eight weeks of SB ingestion during high-intensity interval training on cycling performance parameters. The results exhibited a significant increase in the effects of high-intensity interval training on anaerobic threshold, time to fatigue, and peak power with SB versus placebo. Edge and colleagues (62) suggested that increasing the ability to regulate H^+, thus maintaining intracellular pH, may be vital to enhancing the benefits of intense training.

It appears that a dosage of 136 to 227 mg/pound of body weight (27-45 g for a 200-pound [91 kg] person) improves short-duration, high-intensity exercise performance and training. However, dosages at this amount have been associated with unpleasant side effects such as diarrhea, cramping, nausea, and vomiting. A more tolerable dose (90 mg/pound of body weight) has been shown to reduce these side effects; however, research has revealed that this dose does not improve exercise performance (129). It appears that a minimum SB dose of 136 mg/pound of body weight, 90 minutes prior to exercise, is needed to improve performance (75, 107, 207). Due to the severity of the side effects, many sport scientists recommend that athletes try SB supplementation during practice before using it as a precompetition aid.

Sodium Citrate

Although sodium citrate (SC) is not actually a base, it can increase blood pH without the gastrointestinal distress that is commonly seen with SB supplementation (201). It is believed that once in the blood, SC actually breaks down into bicarbonate, thus increasing the extracellular pH (195). As a result, SC would help regulate intramuscular pH during high-intensity exercise by the same mechanism as SB. Interestingly, most studies have demonstrated that SC, unlike SB, has no ergogenic effects during short-duration, high-intensity exercise (13, 52, 201). However, improved performance in maximal exercise lasting between 2 and 15 minutes has been suggested (130). A dose of 200 mg/pound of body weight given 60 to 90 minutes before exercise also led to significant improvement (about 20% greater) in leg muscular endurance during maximal isometric knee extensions (92). More research, however, is needed before SC can be recommended before a workout or competition for performance enhancement.

L-Carnitine

L-carnitine is synthesized from the amino acids lysine and methionine and is responsible for the transport of fatty acids from the cytosol into the mitochondria to be oxidized for energy (117). Carnitine's role in lipid oxidation has generated interest in its efficacy as a dietary supplement, primarily to enhance exercise performance by increasing fat utilization and sparing muscle glycogen. However, studies examining L-carnitine's role as an ergogenic aid for increasing lipid oxidation have not shown clear efficacy in either human or rat models (10, 11, 34). Although Bacurau and colleagues (12) have shown enhanced fatty acid oxidation following three weeks of L-carnitine supplementation, which was attributed to a greater carnitine content in the muscle, most studies have been unable to demonstrate elevated muscle carnitine levels following supplementation (11, 16). This may be related to limits in the amount of carnitine that can be absorbed through oral supplementation (110), or potentially related to limits in the amount of fat that can be transported into the mitochondria through the carnitine system due to feedback regulators within the muscle, such as malonyl CoA, which is a product of metabolism.

Interestingly, several studies have suggested that L-carnitine may enhance recovery from exercise (80, 179, 204). Decreases in pain and muscle damage (80), decreases in markers of metabolic stress (179), and enhanced recovery (204) have been demonstrated following high-intensity resistance exercise in untrained or recreationally trained individuals who supplemented with L-carnitine. The mechanisms that have been proposed involve enhancing blood flow regulation through an enhanced vasodilatory effect that reduces the magnitude of exercise-induced hypoxia (108, 109). In addition, Kraemer and colleagues indicated that L-carnitine supplementation (2 g/day for three weeks) upregulates androgen receptors (121) and increases IGF-binding proteins that preserve IGF-I concentrations (122). These endocrine adaptations from the supplement may have an important role in the enhanced recovery seen following high-intensity exercise.

Up to 3 g of daily L-carnitine supplementation (for three weeks) appears to be well tolerated in healthy volunteers, with no adverse subjective, hematological, or metabolic events reported (169). Yet as with most supplements, this information should not be extrapolated to suggest the safety of greater dosing or of use for prolonged supplementation periods.

Creatine

Creatine is a nitrogenous organic compound that is synthesized naturally in the body, primarily in the liver. It can also be synthesized in smaller amounts in both the kidneys and pancreas. The amino acids arginine, glycine, and methionine are the precursors for the synthesis of creatine in those organs. Creatine can also be obtained though dietary sources. It is found in abundance in both meat and fish. Approximately 98% of creatine is stored within skeletal muscle in either its free form (40%) or its phosphorylated form (60%) (95). Smaller amounts of creatine are also stored in the heart, brain, and testes. Creatine is transported from its site of synthesis to the skeletal muscle via circulation.

Importance of Creatine to Exercise

Creatine, in the form of creatine phosphate (CP; also called phosphocreatine [PCr]), has an essential role in energy metabolism as a substrate for the formation of adenosine triphosphate by rephosphorylating adenosine diphosphate (ADP), especially during short-duration, high-intensity exercise. The ability to rapidly rephosphorylate ADP is dependent upon the enzyme creatine kinase and the availability of CP within the muscle. As CP stores become depleted, the ability to perform high-intensity exercise declines. In short-duration sprints (e.g., 100 m sprint), the energy for fueling the activity is derived primarily through the hydrolysis of CP (76, 98). However, as high-intensity exercise increases in duration, the ability of CP to serve as an energy source is drastically reduced.

Depletion of muscle CP during high-intensity exercise is the primary mechanism leading to fatigue in such events. During a 6-second bout of maximal exercise, CP levels within the muscle are reduced 35% to 57% from resting levels (33, 76). As the duration of high-intensity exercise increases to 30 seconds, CP levels in the muscle are further reduced by approximately 64% to 80% from resting levels (31, 33, 44); during bouts of repeated high-intensity exercise, CP levels in the muscle are almost completely depleted (137). As muscle CP concentrations decrease, the ability to perform maximal exercise is reduced. Hirvonen and colleagues (97) demonstrated that sprint times were slower as CP concentrations were reduced. It stands to reason that if muscle CP concentrations could be maintained, the ability to sustain high-intensity exercise would be improved. This is the basis for creatine supplementation in athletes.

Creatine Supplementation

Reports suggest that 48% of male collegiate athletes use, or have used, creatine during their preparation for competition (126). However, the prevalence of use among strength/power athletes may approach more than 80% in certain sports (126). Creatine use has also gained popularity among high school athletes; 90% of athletes who supplement choose creatine (189). As a result of their widespread use, creatine supplements may be the most extensively studied ergogenic aid in recent history.

Creatine supplementation is reported to increase the creatine content of muscles by approximately 20% (67, 111). However, it appears that a saturation limit for creatine exists within muscle. Once creatine concentrations in skeletal muscle reach 150 to 160 mmol/kg dry weight, additional supplementation appears to be unable to further increase muscle creatine concentrations (15, 84). This has important implications for the "more is better" philosophy that governs the thinking of many athletes, and may affect the development of proper and realistic dosing schemes.

A typical creatine supplementation regimen involves a loading dose of 20 to 25 g daily for five days, or 0.3 g/kg body mass if an individual wishes to dose relative to body weight, followed by a maintenance dose of 2 g/day (111). If one ingests creatine without an initial loading dose, muscle creatine content will reach levels similar to those seen in people who do initially use a loading dose, but reaching that muscle creatine concentration will take longer (~30 days vs. 5 days). Muscle creatine levels will remain elevated as long as the maintenance dose is maintained (2 g/day or 0.03 g/kg body mass per day) (111). Once creatine supplementation is stopped, muscle creatine levels will return to baseline levels in approximately four weeks (67, 111).

Ergogenic Benefits

Most studies examining the effect of creatine supplementation on strength performance have been fairly consistent in showing significant ergogenic benefits (22, 35, 61, 88, 105, 124, 128, 151, 202). Strength increases in the bench press, squat, and power clean may be two- to threefold higher in trained athletes (see figure 9.4) supplementing with creatine compared to placebo (105, 151).

These results may highlight the benefit of creatine supplementation in experienced resistance-trained athletes whose potential to improve strength may be limited. In experienced strength athletes, supplementing with creatine may enhance the quality of workouts (less fatigue, enhanced recovery), which may be crucial for providing a greater training stimulus to the muscle.

> Creatine supplementation has been shown to increase strength and improve training by reducing fatigue and enhancing postworkout recovery.

Most studies looking at the effect of creatine supplementation on a single bout of explosive exercise (sprint or jump performance) have not shown any significant performance improvements (48, 55, 141, 146, 178). However, in many of these studies, subjects were supplemented with a loading dose for only three to five days (141, 146, 178). When subjects have supplemented for an extended period of time (28-84 days), significant improvements in jump and power performance have been seen (88, 123, 202). It appears that creatine is more effective as

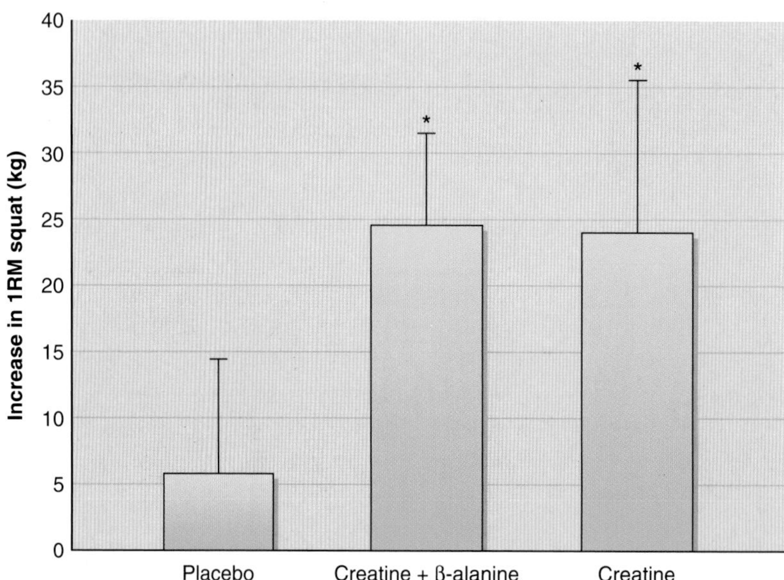

Figure 9.4 Changes in 1RM squat strength in experienced collegiate American football players ingesting creatine, creatine plus β-alanine, or a placebo.

* = Significantly different ($p < 0.05$) compared to placebo.

Adapted, by permission, from Hoffman et al., 2006 (105).

a training supplement than as a direct performance enhancer. Creatine supplementation may improve the quality of each training session, which will result in better performance.

Most studies demonstrating the efficacy of short-term (five to six days) creatine supplementation have used a loading dose (20 g/day) as the supplement regime (51, 53, 142, 162, 185). There appear to be only two investigations that have shown ergogenic benefits of low-dose creatine supplementation (41, 106). However, one study used a dosing scheme of 7.7 g/day (0.1 g/kg) during 28 days of supplementation (41). This was the first study to show efficacy with a low-dose and relatively short-duration supplement regimen, although the supplementation period was much longer than is typically seen during short-term studies. Hoffman and colleagues (106) demonstrated that even a low-dose (6 g/day), short-duration (six days) supplementation regimen in active college-aged men may reduce fatigue.

Body Mass Changes

Prolonged creatine supplementation has been generally associated with increases in body weight. These increases appear to primarily relate to increases in fat-free mass. The increase in body mass is believed to be partly related to an increase in total body water. An increase in creatine content within the muscle is thought to enhance the intracellular osmotic gradient, causing water to fill the cell (203). In addition, increasing the creatine content of muscle appears to be coupled with an increased rate of muscle contractile protein synthesis (14, 26).

Adverse Effects

Increase in body mass has at times been referred to as an unwanted side effect (173). However, in athletes supplementing with creatine, weight gain is often a desired outcome. When people talk about side effects from a drug or supplement, they are generally referring to a potentially debilitating effect. There have been a host of anecdotal reports of gastrointestinal, cardiovascular, and muscular problems, including muscle cramps, in association with creatine ingestion. However, controlled studies have been unable to document any significant side effects from creatine supplementation. Even during prolonged supplementation (10-12 weeks), no increases in reported side effects were noted in subjects supplementing with creatine—either competitive athletes or recreationally trained individuals (105, 123, 204).

Another concern with any supplement is the long-term health effects. A retrospective study on health variables in 26 former or current competitive athletes who had used creatine for up to four years indicated only occasional gastrointestinal upset during the loading phase (173). These disturbances ranged from "gas" to mild diarrhea. Other major concerns during creatine supplementation include a strain on the kidneys due to the high nitrogen content of creatine and increased creatine excretion during short-term ingestion (90). However, no renal dysfunction has been reported in either short-term (five days) or long-term (up to five years) creatine use (153, 154).

Stimulants

There is little question about the usefulness of stimulants to many types of athletic endeavors; the effects of stimulants include reduced fatigue, increased alertness, increased confidence, and even euphoria. Because stimulants have to be used at the time of competition to confer an ergogenic advantage, drug testing performed immediately after the competition can effectively reduce their abuse. However, many stimulants (e.g., caffeine) are also available in food items, while others (e.g., ephedrine) may be found in decongestants and other medications.

Caffeine

Caffeine is one of the most widely used drugs in the world. It is found in coffee, tea, soft drinks, chocolate, and various other foods. It is a central nervous system stimulant and its effects are similar to, yet weaker than, those associated with amphetamines. Caffeine has been used as a performance enhancer for more than 30 years and is one of the few ergogenic aids that may be used to an equal extent by aerobic and anaerobic athletes. For the aerobic athlete, caffeine is thought to prolong aerobic endurance exercise. The mechanisms that have been proposed to cause this effect involve an increase in fat oxidation through the mobilization of free fatty acids from adipose tissue or intramuscular fat stores (180). The greater use of fat as a primary energy source slows glycogen depletion and delays fatigue. During short-duration, high-intensity exercise, the primary ergogenic effect attributed to caffeine supplementation is enhanced power production. This is thought to be the result of an enhanced excitation-contraction coupling, affecting neuromuscular transmission and mobilization of intracellular calcium ions from the sarcoplasmic reticulum (190). In addition, caffeine ingestion is thought to enhance the kinetics of glycolytic regulatory enzymes such as phosphorylase (180).

A central nervous system stimulant, caffeine is an ergogenic aid that may enhance performance in both aerobic and anaerobic athletes.

Efficacy Initial studies dealing with the effect of caffeine supplementation on aerobic endurance performance indicated a 21-minute improvement in the time to exhaustion (from 75 minutes in a placebo trial to 96 minutes in the caffeine trial) during cycling at 80% of $\dot{V}O_2max$ (50). These results were confirmed by a number of additional studies demonstrating the ergogenic effect of caffeine during prolonged aerobic endurance activity (65, 83, 114, 181). These studies showed that caffeine in doses ranging from 3 to 9 mg/kg (equivalent to approximately 1.5 to 3.5 cups of automatic drip coffee in a 70 kg [154-pound] person) produced a significant ergogenic effect. Similar performance effects from caffeine have also been demonstrated during short-duration (approximately 5 minutes), high-intensity exercise (39, 115).

When the effects of caffeine ingestion on sprint or power performance are examined, however, the ergogenic benefits become less clear. Several studies have shown that caffeine ingestion does not improve power performance (45, 85), but those studies used recreational athletes. With competitive swimmers, caffeine ingestion (250 mg) was shown to improve sprint times during repeated 100 m sprints by an average of 3% (46). An additional study demonstrated similar improvements in power performance (7% increase, $p < 0.05$) during a series of 6-second sprints (8). The number of studies on caffeine ingestion and sprint and power performance is limited compared to the number that measured caffeine's effect on aerobic endurance performance by tracking the volume of work completed. The results of the studies on the ergogenic benefit of caffeine for power performance are inconclusive. If there is any performance benefit, it likely occurs in the trained athlete.

Caffeine from a food source (coffee consumption) and anhydrous caffeine have both shown significant performance effects; however, the extent of performance improvements appears to be greater when caffeine is ingested in tablet form (82). When caffeine is provided as a pure caffeine supplement, the ergogenic benefit with respect to improved aerobic endurance performance has been reported to range between 28% and 43% (82, 83). However, when it is provided in a food source such as coffee (either caffeinated coffee or decaffeinated coffee with added caffeine), the ergogenic benefit for aerobic endurance exercise may not be seen (43, 82) or may be seen only at a reduced rate (50, 197, 209). Graham and colleagues (82) suggested that although the bioavailability of caffeine is the same whether it is consumed in a food source or in an anhydrous form, some compound in coffee antagonizes the action of caffeine. A recent study has shown that a coffee product containing 450 mg of caffeine, 1,200 mg of garcinia cambogia (50% hydroxycitric acid), 360 mg of citrus aurantium extract (6%), and 225 µg of chromium polynicotinate can improve aerobic endurance performance 29% in aerobic endurance–trained subjects, but no effects on power performance were seen (102).

Adverse Effects The side effects associated with caffeine include anxiety, gastrointestinal disturbances, restlessness, insomnia, tremors, and heart arrhythmias. In addition, caffeine can act as a diuretic and may increase the risk for heat illness in high-temperature climates. Caffeine is also physically addicting, and discontinuation can result in some withdrawal symptoms. Caffeine intakes greater than 9 mg/kg appear to result in a greater risk for side effects (180).

Ephedrine

Another β-agonist that is reported to be relatively popular, especially among bodybuilders, is ephedrine (87). Ephedrine is thought to have a strong thermogenic quality that bodybuilders desire in order to reduce body fat. It often is used as a stacking agent with caffeine to enhance the thermogenic effect. Similar to caffeine, ephedrine also increases fat oxidation and spares muscle glycogen.

Efficacy Studies examining the ergogenic effect of ephedrine have shown it to be effective only when it is taken in combination with caffeine (20). These results have been quite consistent with respect to improving aerobic endurance performance (18, 19). However, side effects (vomiting and nausea) following exercise have been reported in 25% of the subjects ingesting a caffeine-ephedrine mixture of 5 mg/kg caffeine and 1 mg/kg ephedrine (18). A subsequent study performed by the same investigators showed that at a lower dose (4 mg/kg caffeine and 0.8 mg/kg ephedrine), similar ergogenic benefits are realized with no side effects (19). The caffeine-ephedrine mixture appears to have a greater benefit than either supplement taken alone.

Adverse Effects Ephedra, also called ma huang, is a plant or herb that contains ephedrine. In the United States before 2004, most over-the-counter sport and weight loss products contained ephedra. However, in April 2004, the FDA banned all products containing ephedra after determining that it posed an unreasonable risk to those who used it. The FDA ban was based on a report published by the Rand Institute (175) indicating that 16,000 adverse events were linked to the use of ephedra-containing dietary supplements. Further, Shekelle and colleagues (175) reported that the use of ephedra-containing dietary supplements or ephedrine plus caffeine was associated with an increased incidence of nausea, vomiting, psychiatric symptoms such as anxiety and change in mood, autonomic hyperactivity, palpitations, and in a few cases death. As a result of the many adverse effects, ephedrine use has been banned by most sport governing bodies including the International Olympic Committee.

Citrus Aurantium

Citrus aurantium is from a fruit commonly known as "bitter orange" and is often used as an Asian herbal medicine to treat digestive problems (74). However, it is also a mild stimulant and is thought to contribute to appetite suppression and increased metabolic rate and lipolysis (74). Citrus aurantium contains synephrine, a sympathomimetic agent, which some have suggested stimulates specific adrenergic receptors (β-3, but not β-1, β-2, or α-1) that in turn stimulate fat metabolism without any of the negative side effects generally associated with compounds that stimulate the other adrenergic receptors (42). Synephrine, a known active component of citrus aurantium, is thought to interact with β-3 receptors to increase lipolysis and minimize the cardiovascular effect typical of adrenergic amines (42). Synephrine has been shown to stimulate peripheral α-1 receptors, resulting in vasoconstriction and elevations in blood pressure (36). However, other research has shown that when citrus aurantium is ingested alone, no effect on blood pressure is seen (89), but in combination with other herbal products it may cause significant elevations in systolic blood pressure (89, 103). When citrus aurantium is combined with caffeine and other herbal products, significant improvements in time to fatigue have been reported (103). It should be noted that synephrine has been on the National Collegiate Athletic Association's banned list of performance-enhancing drugs but not those of the World Anti-Doping Association or the U.S. Anti-Doping Association. Synephrine is presently being monitored by these two organizations for potential placement on the banned list of performance enhancement substances.

CONCLUSION

How athletes approach the use of ergogenic aids and sport supplements depends in part on information received from strength and conditioning professionals. Ignorance and exaggeration serve no one, and strength and conditioning professionals should provide accurate information about the risks and benefits of supplements that an athlete may contemplate using.

Athletes are frequently exposed to information about ergogenic aids. Virtually each week, research is presented or published that confirms concerns about efficacy, safety, or other issues related to the use of performance-enhancing substances. Because of this unpredictability, the strength and conditioning professional must stay abreast of the latest research and news regarding the efficacy, safety, and legality of supplements.

KEY TERMS

β-agonist 190
β-blocker 190
acromegaly 189
anabolic hormone 188
anabolic steroid 183
caffeine 197
catecholamine 183
creatine 195
dietary supplement 181
ergogenic aid 180
ergolytic 191
erythropoietin (EPO) 189
essential amino acids (EAA) 191
gigantism 189
human growth hormone (HGH) 188
lipogenesis 190
lipolysis 190
muscle buffering capacity (MBC) 193
muscle dysmorphia 185
Nadir effect 191
partitioning agents 190
physical working capacity at fatigue threshold (PWC_{FT}) 193
prohormone 187
stacking 183
thermogenesis 190

STUDY QUESTIONS

1. All of the following are ingredients that qualify as dietary supplements in the United States EXCEPT

a. EAAs.
b. vitamin C.
c. milk.
d. iodine.

2. All of the following describe caffeine's role in improving athletic performance EXCEPT

a. increased power production.
b. decreased glycogen depletion.
c. increased fat oxidation.
d. decreased urine production.

3. Which of the following are the MOST closely linked in a logarithmic relationship?

I. intake of anabolic steroids
II. intake of androstenedione
III. increase in lean body mass
IV. increase in endogenous androgen production

a. I and III only
b. I and IV only
c. II and III only
d. II and IV only

4. Which of the following substances has been shown by multiple research studies to improve strength performance?

a. androstenedione
b. creatine
c. L-carnitine
d. chromium

5. Which of the following is the BEST reason for aerobic endurance athletes to avoid erythropoietin use?

a. Hematocrit and hemoglobin levels may decrease.
b. It may cause an unregulated increase in RBC production.
c. Resistance to infectious disease may be impaired.
d. It may reduce the ability of blood to carry oxygen.

CHAPTER 10

Nutritional Factors in Health and Performance

Kristin Reimers, PhD

After completing this chapter, you will be able to

- identify the protein, carbohydrate, and fat recommendations for athletes;
- discern between dietary recommendations for disease prevention and recommendations for performance;
- identify and apply appropriate hydration practices for athletes;
- apply precompetition and posttraining eating strategies and advise athletes on guidelines for weight gain and weight loss;
- recognize signs and symptoms of eating disorders;
- understand the importance of having an intervention and referral system in place for athletes suspected of having an eating disorder;
- recognize the prevalence and etiologies of obesity; and
- assist in the assessment process for obese individuals.

Proper nutrition is an important consideration for athletes who seek to maximize their performance. No diet directly increases strength, power, or aerobic endurance, but an adequate diet allows athletes to train and compete to the best of their ability. This chapter focuses on the scientific rationale for performance-enhancing nutritional practices and on practical information concerning the nutritional needs of athletes.

Athletes and professionals who work with athletes are often confused about nutritional guidelines for athletes. Should athletes gorge on carbohydrates? Or should they follow a high-protein diet? Does the timing of food intake matter? Are certain foods detrimental and others helpful? The answer to each of these questions depends on the athlete. Although athletes' diets should follow basic nutritional principles for health and disease prevention, sometimes the common understanding of "good nutrition" does not apply to athletes. The physiological needs of competitive athletes often require diets that are quite different from a sedentary individual's diet. The ideal diet for an athlete depends on many factors: age, body size, sex, genetics, and environmental training conditions, as well as on duration, frequency, and intensity of training. Requirements thus vary greatly between and within athletic groups. The effective strength and conditioning professional does not fall into a "one-size-fits-all" mentality when working with athletes. The best diet for an athlete is one that is individualized.

Although eating disorders are complex, the strength and conditioning professional should recognize signs of eating disorders, provide information on what preventive measures can be put into place, and explain how to deal with the situation when it arises. Additionally, obesity remains a prevalent problem. Strength and conditioning professionals need to understand the assessment and treatment of this complex and resistant condition.

ROLE OF THE NUTRITIONIST

When athletes approach the strength and conditioning professional with complex nutritional issues, it is important to refer them to the proper resources, such as the team physician, a sport nutritionist, or a registered dietitian familiar with sport. The team physician is responsible for decisions related to the athlete's care and medical needs. The nutritionist is responsible for the athlete's dietary needs and works closely with the physician and strength and conditioning professional to communicate the proper messages to the athlete.

Some of the responsibilities of the nutritionist are the following:

- Personalized nutritional counseling: weight loss and weight gain, strategies to improve performance, menu planning, dietary supplements

This chapter is dedicated to honor the memory of Jaime Ruud. Jaime was an accomplished author, expert nutrition consultant, willing volunteer, dedicated community servant, loyal friend, and devoted, loving wife to her husband, Tom, and mother to her children, Barrett, Bo, and Kim. Jaime's outer beauty was surpassed only by her inner beauty. Jaime's can-do attitude, eager work ethic, relentless energy, sincere kindness, and radiant smile remain an inspiration to all who had the privilege of knowing her.

- Dietary analysis of food records
- Nutritional education: presentations and handouts
- Referral and treatment of eating disorders

Designing a nutritional program for an athlete is challenging because no two athletes are alike. Athletes have diverse nutritional goals: to increase energy, to build muscle, to lose fat, to heal injuries, and to speed recovery between training and competition. The first step in nutritional counseling is to define the athlete's goals. Most competitive athletes are interested in developing personal nutritional strategies to improve performance. Weight loss, weight gain, eating while traveling, nutritional supplements, precompetition eating, and improving performance are among the reasons athletes often seek the advice of a nutritionist. Counseling may be as simple as helping the athlete overcome barriers to eating breakfast or as complicated as acquiring a complete nutritional assessment, including analysis of food records, anthropometric measurements, and laboratory tests. It is imperative for the strength and conditioning professional to work closely with other sports medicine personnel who are helping the athlete so that consistent messages are communicated.

HOW TO EVALUATE THE ADEQUACY OF THE DIET

When working with athletes from various backgrounds and cultures, it is important to remember that many different eating styles can equate to an adequate diet; there is no one "right" diet for all athletes. Whether from a vegan diet, a typical Western diet, or any other diet, the human body needs adequate amounts of protein, carbohydrate, fat, vitamins, minerals, and water.

Standard Nutrition Guidelines

Most athletes have two basic dietary goals: eating to maximize performance and eating for optimal body composition. Some athletes also want diets that promote good health, that is, prevent chronic diseases such as heart disease and cancer. Whether the diet is designed to enhance performance, prevent disease, or both, two fundamental components of the diet must be present: (1) appropriate calorie level and (2) appropriate nutrient levels to prevent nutrient deficiency or toxicity. One tool designed to provide guidance for evaluating nutrient adequacy of the diet is the **Food Guide Pyramid**, developed by the U.S. Department of Agriculture in 1992 and updated to **MyPyramid** in 2005 (90).

MyPyramid (www.MyPyramid.gov) has all the food groups from the original Food Guide Pyramid, but it also includes a graphic depiction of physical activity and is based on the latest nutritional science (figure 10.1). After the original Food Guide Pyramid was developed in 1992, new standards for nutrition, the Dietary Reference Intakes (DRIs), were created by the National Academy of Sciences Institute of Medicine (see the next section in this chapter for more information); the 2005 Dietary Guidelines for Americans (from the U.S. Department of Agriculture and the U.S. Department of Health and Human Services) were released; and new information was obtained about typical food consumption and food composition data.

MyPyramid displays recommended types and amounts of food to eat daily. The color bands represent five food groups that are needed each day for health:

1. Grains
2. Vegetables
3. Fruits
4. Milk
5. Meat and beans

The narrow yellow band in the pyramid represents oils. Although they provide essential fatty acids and vitamin E, they are not a food group. When added to a balanced, varied diet, oils can serve as sources of calories for athletes with high caloric needs. For athletes with lower caloric requirements, these foods should be eaten in moderation but not completely omitted from the diet.

MyPyramid is an excellent starting point from which to evaluate the adequacy of an athlete's diet. If a diet provides a variety of foods from each group, it is likely adequate for vitamins and minerals. However, if the diet excludes an entire food group, specific nutrients may be lacking.

The 1992 version of the Food Guide Pyramid recommended a certain number of servings based upon the food group and total daily caloric intake. The concern with this approach was that individuals equated a "serving" with a portion of food that they

MyPyramid

STEPS TO A HEALTHIER YOU

Grains Make half your grains whole	Vegetables Vary your veggies	Fruits Focus on fruits	Milk Get your calcium-rich foods	Meat & Beans Go lean with protein
Eat at least 3 ounces of whole-grain cereals, breads, crackers, rice, or pasta every day 1 ounce is about 1 slice of bread, about 1 cup of breakfast cereal, or 1/2 cup of cooked rice, cereal, or pasta	Eat more dark-green veggies like broccoli, spinach, and other dark leafy greens Eat more orange veggies like carrots and sweet potatoes Eat more dry beans and peas like pinto beans, kidney beans, and lentils	Eat a variety of fruit Choose fresh, frozen, canned, or dried fruit Go easy on fruit juices	Go low-fat or fat-free when you choose milk, yogurt, and other milk products If you don't or can't comsume milk, choose lactose-free products or other calcium sources such as fortified foods and beverages	Choose low-fat or lean meats and poultry Bake it, broil it, or grill it Vary your protein routine—choose more fish, beans, peas, nuts, and seeds
For a 2,000-calorie diet, you need the amounts below from each food group. To find the amounts that are right for you, go to MyPyramid.gov.				
Eat 6 ounces every day	**Eat 2 1/2 cups every day**	**Eat 2 cups every day**	**Get 3 cups every day;** for kids aged 2 to 8, it's 2	**Eat 5 1/2 ounces every day**

Find your balance between food and physical activity

- Be sure to stay within your daily calorie needs.
- Be physically active for at least 30 minutes most days of the week.
- About 60 minutes a day of physical activity may be needed to prevent weight gain.
- For sustaining weight loss, at least 60 to 90 minutes a day of physical activity may be required.
- Children and teenagers should be physically active for 60 minutes every day, or most days.

Know your limits on fats, sugars, and salt (sodium)

- Make most of your fat sources from fish, nuts, and vegetable oils.
- Limit solid fats like butter, margarine, shortening, and lard, as well as foods that contain these.
- Check the Nutrition Facts label to keep saturated fats, *trans* fats, and sodium low.
- Choose food and beverages low in added sugars. Added sugars contribute calories with few, if any, nutrients.

Figure 10.1 MyPyramid. For more information and resources, go to www.mypyramid.gov.

typically consumed, so recommending a specific number of servings implied that they should eat that portion that many times. For those who were used to small portion sizes, this was not a problem. For most individuals, however, the typical portion size is much larger than the standard "serving" size that the Food Guide Pyramid was based on. To remedy this, MyPyramid provides recommendations (with examples) in cups or ounces for the entire day that can be divided into several meals or snacks (90).

Foods within each group share similar nutrient compositions and are considered interchangeable; however, balance and variety within each food group are encouraged. For example, the combination of an orange, an apple, and a pear provides more essential nutrients than three apples. In general, the grains group provides carbohydrates (sugar and starch), as do fruits and vegetables. These foods are also the primary sources of dietary fiber, riboflavin, thiamin, niacin, folate, vitamin C, and beta carotene. Meat, poultry, fish, dry beans, eggs, and nuts are major contributors of protein, iron, zinc, and vitamin B_{12} in the diet. Dairy products are excellent sources of dietary protein, calcium, and riboflavin.

MyPyramid is an excellent starting point from which to evaluate the adequacy of an athlete's diet. As a rule of thumb, if a diet provides a variety of foods from each group, it is likely adequate for vitamins and minerals. However, if the diet excludes an entire food group, specific nutrients may be lacking. For example, exclusion of meat from the diet increases the risk of inadequate protein, iron, zinc, and vitamin B_6 intake; exclusion of milk and dairy products increases the risk of inadequate calcium and riboflavin intake; exclusion of all animal foods means that the diet lacks vitamin B_{12}; exclusion of fruits and vegetables increases the risk of inadequate vitamin C and beta carotene intake; and exclusion of grains increases the risk of inadequate riboflavin, thiamin, and niacin. Each of the food groups provides essential nutrients. If one group is omitted, key nutrients may be missing in the diet.

The frequently seen version of MyPyramid (figure 10.1) is designed for the general population. Although the basic guidelines in the pyramid are universal, athletes, especially elite and professional athletes, have different needs from those of the general population. Thus, the guidelines may need to be adjusted to meet the recommended dietary intakes for a specific athlete (67). For example, consuming the food amounts shown in figure 10.1 provides about 2,000 kcal. For athletes with greater caloric needs, table 10.1 provides the suggested amounts of food to consume from the basic food groups and oils to meet recommended nutrient intakes at 12 different calorie levels.

TABLE 10.1

Recommended Nutrient Intakes at 12 Different Calorie Levels

Calorie level	1,000	1,200	1,400	1,600	1,800	2,000
Grains[1]	3 ounces	4 ounces	5 ounces	5 ounces	6 ounces	6 ounces
Vegetables[2]	1 cup	1.5 cups	1.5 cups	2 cups	2.5 cups	2.5 cups
Fruits[3]	1 cup	1 cup	1.5 cups	1.5 cups	1.5 cups	2 cups
Milk[4]	2 cups	2 cups	2 cups	3 cups	3 cups	3 cups
Meat and beans[5]	2 ounces	3 ounces	4 ounces	5 ounces	5 ounces	5.5 ounces
Oils[6]	3 tsp	4 tsp	4 tsp	5 tsp	5 tsp	6 tsp
Calorie level	**2,200**	**2,400**	**2,600**	**2,800**	**3,000**	**3,200**
Grains[1]	7 ounces	8 ounces	9 ounces	10 ounces	10 ounces	10 ounces
Vegetables[2]	3 cups	3 cups	3.5 cups	3.5 cups	4 cups	4 cups
Fruits[3]	2 cups	2 cups	2 cups	2.5 cups	2.5 cups	2.5 cups
Milk[4]	3 cups	3 cups	3 cups	3 cups	3 cups	3 cups
Meat and beans[5]	6 ounces	6.5 ounces	6.5 ounces	7 ounces	7 ounces	7 ounces
Oils[6]	6 tsp	7 tsp	8 tsp	8 tsp	10 tsp	11 tsp

tsp = teaspoon. See inside back cover for metric conversions.

1. **Grain group**. Includes all foods made from wheat, rice, oats, cornmeal, or barley, such as bread, pasta, oatmeal, breakfast cereals, tortillas, and grits. In general, 1 slice of bread, 1 cup of ready-to-eat cereal, or 1/2 cup of cooked rice, pasta, or cooked cereal can be considered as 1 ounce equivalent from the grains group. At least half of all grains consumed should be whole grains.

2. **Vegetable group**. Includes all fresh, frozen, canned, and dried vegetables and vegetable juices. In general, 1 cup of raw or cooked vegetables or vegetable juice, or 2 cups of raw leafy greens, can be considered as 1 cup from the vegetable group.

3. **Fruit group**. Includes all fresh, frozen, canned, and dried fruits and fruit juices. In general, 1 cup of fruit or 100% fruit juice, or 1/2 cup of dried fruit, can be considered as 1 cup from the fruit group.

4. **Milk group**. Includes all fluid milk products and foods made from milk that retain their calcium content, such as yogurt and cheese. Foods made from milk that have little to no calcium, such as cream cheese, cream, and butter, are not part of the group. Most milk group choices should be fat free or low fat. In general, 1 cup of milk or yogurt, 1 1/2 ounces of natural cheese, or 2 ounces of processed cheese can be considered as 1 cup from the milk group.

5. **Meat and beans group**. In general, 1 ounce of lean meat, poultry, or fish; 1 egg; 1 tablespoon peanut butter; 1/4 cup cooked dry beans; or 1/2 ounce of nuts or seeds can be considered as 1 ounce equivalent from the meat and beans group.

6. **Oils**. Include fats from many different plants, and from fish, that are liquid at room temperature, such as canola, corn, olive, soybean, and sunflower oil. Some foods are naturally high in oils, like nuts, olives, some fish, and avocados. Foods that are mainly oil include mayonnaise, certain salad dressings, and soft margarine.

Adapted from United States Department of Agriculture and the Center for Nutrition Policy and Promotion, 2005 (90).

Dietary Reference Intakes

Because athletes eat food, not individual nutrients, describing dietary changes in terms of foods is the most effective way of helping the athlete achieve an adequate diet. Nonetheless, it is also important to have an understanding of the athlete's basic nutrient requirements from which to make food recommendations. **Dietary Reference Intakes (DRIs)** are recommendations for 50 nutrients (14 vitamins, 18 minerals, and 18 macronutrients and related food components). In 2005, the DRIs replaced the "Recommended Dietary Allowances" guidelines that had been used since 1941.

Between 1997 and 2004, the National Academy of Sciences Institute of Medicine issued eight reports, with six containing information about nutrient recommendations and two containing information about assessment and planning in relation to dietary intakes (57). The DRI report for each nutrient or food component includes the following information:

1. Estimated average requirement and its standard deviation by age and gender
2. Recommended dietary consumption based on the estimated average requirement
3. An adequate intake level when a recommended intake cannot be based on an estimated average requirement
4. Tolerable upper intake levels above which risk of toxicity increases

MACRONUTRIENTS

A macronutrient is a nutrient that is required in significant amounts in the diet. Three important classes of macronutrients are protein, carbohydrates, and lipids (fats and related compounds).

To support training and competition, athletes should consume a balanced diet that provides all the essential nutrients: carbohydrate, protein, fat, water, vitamins, and minerals.

Protein

Athletes and strength and conditioning professionals, particularly those involved in strength and power sports, have an interest in the role of protein in the diet and the use of protein supplementation. This section reviews the function of protein in the body, the effects of exercise on protein metabolism, and dietary requirements of athletes.

Structure and Function of Proteins

Proteins, like carbohydrates and fats, are composed of carbon, hydrogen, and oxygen atoms. Unlike carbohydrates and fats, proteins also contain nitrogen. "Amino" means "nitrogen-containing," and **amino acids** are the molecules that, when joined in groups of a few dozen to hundreds, form the thousands of proteins occurring in nature. Proteins in the human body are composed of 20 amino acids. More than half of these can be synthesized by the human body and are commonly called "nonessential" amino acids because they do not need to be consumed in the diet (table 10.2). Nine of the amino acids are "essential" because the body cannot manufacture them and therefore they must be obtained through the diet (table 10.2).

Amino acids are joined together by peptide bonds. Two amino acids together are referred to as a dipeptide, and several amino acids together are referred to as a **polypeptide**. Polypeptide chains bond together to form a multitude of proteins with

TABLE 10.2

Essential and Nonessential Amino Acids

Essential	Nonessential
Histidine*	Alanine
Isoleucine	Arginine
Leucine	Asparagine
Lysine	Aspartic acid
Methionine	Cysteine (cystine)
Phenylalanine	Glutamic acid
Threonine	Glutamine
Tryptophan	Glycine
Valine	Proline
	Serine
	Tyrosine

*Some adults can synthesize histidine on their own. For other adults and for infants, histidine is an essential amino acid.

various structures and functions. Muscle tissue is often the first bodily structure that comes to mind when one considers protein's existence in the body; and indeed, the majority of the body's protein exists as skeletal muscle, organs, and bone tissue. Although sometimes perceived to be all protein, tissues are mostly water and contain various amounts of protein. For example, protein makes up 20% of the weight of the heart, skeletal muscles, liver, and glands and 10% of brain tissue.

Nonstructural or plasma proteins, such as enzymes, antibodies, lipoproteins, hormones, hemoglobin, albumin, and transferrin, constitute only a small proportion of the body's protein; but they are profoundly powerful and negatively affected by poor nutritional status.

Dietary Protein

The amino acid content of a dietary protein affects its value in supporting growth and tissue maintenance. Whether the protein supplies amino acids in amounts proportionate to the body's needs determines the **protein quality**. *High-quality protein*, protein of *high biological value*, and *complete protein* are synonymous terms used to refer to a protein with an amino acid pattern similar to that needed by the body; high-quality proteins include proteins of animal origin (those in eggs, meat, fish, poultry, and dairy products). Proteins that are deficient in one or more of the essential amino acids (grains, beans, vegetables, and gelatin) are referred to as *low-quality proteins*, proteins of *low biological value*, or *incomplete proteins*. Plant proteins tend to be low in lysine (grains) or methionine and cysteine (beans). Of the plant proteins, soy is the highest in quality.

Protein quality is one of the issues that **vegans** (those who consume only plant proteins—no meat, fish, poultry, eggs, or milk) must consider. When relying on the lower-quality proteins, it is important to consume a variety of plant foods that provide different amino acids, often referred to as **complementary proteins**, so that all essential amino acids are consumed over the course of the day. Common examples of complementary proteins are beans and rice, corn and beans, corn tortillas and refried beans, and peanut butter and bread. As a general rule, combining beans or legumes with grains provides the essential amino acids in appropriate ratios. It was believed for some time that complementary proteins had to be consumed at the same meal. However, it is now known that consumption of a variety of proteins from legumes, seeds, nuts, and grains over the course of the day is adequate (101).

Protein Requirements

Although dietary recommendations are stated as *protein* requirements, the actual requirement is for amino acids. The need for dietary proteins/amino acids in sedentary, healthy adults results from the constant turnover of cells. During **cell turnover**—the constant breakdown and regeneration of cells—the immediate supplier of amino acids is the body's free amino acid pool. The pool is replenished from dietary protein digestion, as well as the amino acids released from tissue turnover. Substantially more protein is turned over daily than is ordinarily consumed, indicating that amino acids are recycled. This process is not completely efficient, however, so dietary amino acid intake is required to replace losses.

General Requirements When estimating the protein requirements for individuals, one must consider two key factors: caloric intake and biological value of the protein. Protein can be metabolized as a source of energy in a state of **negative calorie balance**, in which fewer calories are consumed than are expended. In this case, the protein cannot be used for the intended purpose of replacing the amino acid pool. Thus, an inverse relationship exists between caloric intake and protein requirement. When caloric intake goes down, protein requirement goes up. Dietary protein requirements were derived from research on subjects who were consuming adequate calories. Requirements for individuals who are not consuming adequate calories are higher than the stated requirements. Additionally, approximately 65% to 75% of the protein in those studies was from foods of animal origin (meat, fish, poultry, dairy products, and eggs), proteins of high biological value. The higher the biological value of the protein, the lower the protein requirement. Assuming that caloric intake is adequate and that two-thirds or more of the protein is from animal sources, the recommended intake for protein for adults is 0.8 g/kg (0.36 g/pound) of body weight for both men and women (56). Expressed as a percent of daily caloric intake, a common protein intake recommendation is 10% to 15%. Requirements of individuals who have a negative calorie balance or who consume lower-quality proteins are higher, although these have not been quantified to date.

Recommendations to increase or decrease protein intake should be made on an individual basis after the normal diet has been analyzed and caloric intake considered. A mixed diet is the best source of high-quality protein. Strict vegetarians must plan their diet carefully to ensure an adequate intake of all essential amino acids.

Increased Requirements for Athletes Beyond the maintenance requirement of protein just described, athletes' protein requirements are increased by training. Both aerobic endurance training and resistance training can increase protein need, although the exact mechanisms are unclear and may be different. For aerobic endurance athletes, the underlying mechanisms could include tissue repair and the use of the branched-chain amino acids for auxiliary fuel, whereas for strength and power athletes, the mechanisms are probably tissue repair and the maintenance of a positive nitrogen balance so that the hypertrophic stimulus is maximized (46).

Research indicates that the protein requirement of aerobic endurance athletes is slightly over 0.8 g/kg of body weight and can reach 1.4 g/kg of body weight, due in part to increased use of protein as a fuel source during exercise (46). Research has shown that heavy resistance training can increase requirements to as high as 1.7 g/kg of body weight (46). Because most athletes do not fall neatly into one category (aerobic endurance or resistance trained), a general recommendation of 1.5 to 2.0 g/kg of body weight ensures adequate protein intake, assuming adequate caloric intake and a diet with at least 65% of the protein of high biological value. Athletes consuming a vegan diet or restricting calories may require more than 2.0 g/kg of body weight.

Concerns regarding potential negative effects of protein intakes greater than 0.8 g/kg of body weight have often been expressed. These concerns are unfounded for the most part, especially in healthy individuals. Proteins consumed in excess of the amounts needed for the synthesis of tissue are broken down. The nitrogen is excreted as urea in urine, and the remaining ketoacids are either used directly as sources of energy or converted to carbohydrate (gluconeogenesis) or body fat. The strength and conditioning professional should be aware that excessively high intakes, greater than 4.0 g/kg of body weight per day, are not advisable for athletes with impaired renal function or low calcium intake or those who are restricting fluid intake.

Based on current research, it appears that the protein requirements for athletes are between 1.5 and 2.0 g/kg of body weight, assuming that caloric intake and protein quality are adequate.

Carbohydrates

The primary role of **carbohydrate** in human physiology is to serve as an energy source. The importance of carbohydrates in the diets of athletes and physical laborers was recognized as early as 1901. In 1939, diets high in carbohydrate content were found to enhance subjects' ability to perform prolonged, heavy physical activity (17). Numerous studies have documented an ergogenic effect of carbohydrate intake and elevated muscle glycogen concentration on aerobic endurance performance, work output, and high-intensity intermittent activity (2, 75, 77). Additionally, high muscle glycogen concentrations may be beneficial to high-intensity exercise of short duration (50).

Structure and Sources of Carbohydrates

Carbohydrates are composed of carbon, hydrogen, and oxygen. Carbohydrates can be classified into three groups according to the number of sugar (saccharide) units they contain: monosaccharides, disaccharides, and polysaccharides.

Monosaccharides (glucose, fructose, and galactose) are single-sugar molecules. Glucose is the most common monosaccharide, the building block of many larger sugars. In the body, glucose is present as circulating sugar in the blood; is the primary energy substrate for cells; and composes glycogen, a polysaccharide stored in muscle and liver cells. Glucose in a free form is not sweet. It is not found on the grocery shelf. In foods, it is usually combined with other monosaccharides to form, for example, sucrose. Isolated glucose is used in intravenous fluids and sometimes in sport drinks. In this form, it is referred to as dextrose. Fructose has the same chemical formula as glucose, but because the atoms are arranged differently, it tastes much sweeter and has different properties. Fructose accounts for the sweet taste of honey. Fructose occurs naturally in fruits and vegetables. In the body, fructose causes less insulin secretion than other sugars, which has made it a focus of much research in the area of aerobic endurance performance. However, large doses of fructose have been shown to increase the risk of gastric cramping and diarrhea, so applications of fructose as the primary source of carbohydrate during exercise are limited (31). Galactose, the third monosaccharide, combines with glucose to form lactose, milk sugar.

Disaccharides (sucrose, lactose, and maltose) are composed of two simple sugar units joined together. Sucrose (or table sugar), the most common disaccharide, is a combination of glucose and fructose. Its sweetness is derived from fructose. Sucrose occurs naturally in most fruits and is crystallized from the syrup of sugar cane and sugar beets to make brown, powdered, or white sugar. Lactose (glucose + galactose) is found only in mammalian milk. Maltose (glucose + glucose) occurs primarily when polysaccharides are broken down during digestion. It also occurs in the fermentation process of alcohol and is the primary carbohydrate in beer.

Polysaccharides, also known as complex carbohydrates, contain up to thousands of glucose units. Some of the most common polysaccharides of nutritional importance are starch, fiber, and glycogen. Starch is the storage form of glucose in plants. Grains, nuts, legumes, and vegetables are good sources of starch. Before starch can be used as a source of energy, it must be broken down into glucose components. Dietary fiber, a constituent of the plant cell wall, is also a form of carbohydrate. Cellulose, hemicellulose, beta-glucans, and pectins are fibers; these and noncarbohydrate fibrous materials (lignins) are generally resistant to human digestive enzymes and therefore increase bulk and water content and decrease transit time of feces.

Glycogen is found in small amounts in human and animal tissue as a temporary source of stored energy. It is not present to any large extent in the foods we eat. When glucose enters the muscles and liver, if it is not metabolized for energy it is synthesized to form glycogen. Two-thirds of the glycogen in the body is stored in skeletal muscle; the remaining third is stored in the liver. The process of converting glucose to glycogen is called **glycogenesis**. The liver has the highest glycogen content of all the tissues in the body and, in fact, can convert many of the end products of digestion (i.e., noncarbohydrate sources) into glycogen—a process called *gluconeogenesis*.

Dietary Carbohydrate

Traditionally, breads, cereals, pasta, fruits, and starchy vegetables are promoted to athletes as ideal sources of carbohydrate, and indeed they are. It should be understood, however, that all types of dietary carbohydrate—sugars as well as starches—are effective in supplying the athlete with glucose and glycogen. Consumption of a mix of sugars and starches is desirable.

Athletes typically consume a variety of carbohydrates in their normal diets, but occasionally seasoned athletes reach a point in their training when fine-tuning such details as the metabolic response to carbohydrates and the subsequent effect on performance becomes pertinent. It is this situation that has stimulated interest in and some research on the glycemic index or response of foods (14).

Glycemic Index

The **glycemic index (GI)** has historically been of interest to individuals with diabetes, and much of the research has been conducted in this population. Only recently has the GI become an area of interest for the general population. The GI classifies a food by how high and for how long it raises blood glucose (i.e., the food's glycemic response) (30). The reference food is glucose or white bread, which is given a rating of 100 (42). Foods that are digested quickly and raise blood glucose (and insulin) rapidly have a high GI. Foods that take longer to digest and thus slowly increase blood glucose (and therefore stimulate less insulin) have a low GI.

Table 10.3 summarizes the GI of some common carbohydrate foods. Contrary to previously held assumptions, sugars do not always rank higher than starches. In fact, potatoes and instant rice rank higher than table sugar. At first glance, there appears to be little rhyme or reason to the ranking of foods. Indeed, many factors affect the GI of a food, and this phenomenon limits its application. For example, cooking, processing, eating the food as part of a meal, eating a different amount, and eating at a different time of day all affect the GI of a food in an individual. In fact, what was eaten the day before can have a latent effect on the glycemic response of a food. Thus, although the GI is of interest and can be used for a general understanding of how foods behave when consumed, it is far from an exact science.

If an athlete applies the GI to guide food choices, the selection, for example, of oatmeal or another high-GI food depends on the athlete's goal. If the goal is to quickly replenish glucose and glycogen, foods that rapidly appear as glucose in the blood are desirable (13, 15, 21). On the other hand,

TABLE 10.3

Glycemic Index (GI) of Various Foods*

Bakery products	
Angel food cake	95
Sponge cake	66
Croissant	96
Doughnut (cake type)	108
Muffin (bran)	85
Waffles	109
Breads	
Bagel	103
Hamburger bun	87
Kaiser roll	104
Wheat bread	99
Cereals	
All-Bran	60
Cheerios	106
Cornflakes	116
Oat bran	78
Puffed wheat	105
Rice Krispies	117
Shredded Wheat	107
Cereal grains and pasta	
Barley	36
White rice	91
Brown rice	79
Instant rice	98
Linguine	70
Dairy foods	
Ice cream (regular)	87
Ice cream (low fat)	71
Milk (whole)	38
Milk (skim)	46
Yogurt (low fat with added fruit)	44
Yogurt (low fat with artificial sweetener)	20
Sugars	
Honey	78
Fructose	27
Glucose	141
Sucrose	97
Lactose	66
Maltose	150
Fruit	
Apple	52
Apple juice	57
Banana	74
Cherries	32
Fruit cocktail (canned)	79
Grapefruit	36
Grapefruit juice	69
Grapes	66
Orange	60
Orange juice	74
Pear	54
Pineapple	84
Plum	55
Raisins	91
Watermelon	103
Legumes	
Baked beans	69
Chickpeas	39
Kidney beans	39
Lentils (green)	42
Lima beans	46
Pinto beans	55
Split peas	45
Vegetables	
Potatoes (baked)	121
Sweet potatoes	77
Peas	68
Corn	78
Soups	
Lentil	63
Split pea	86
Tomato	54
Snack foods	
Oatmeal cookies	79
Vanilla wafers	110
Rice cakes	117
Jelly beans	114
Pretzels	119
Popcorn	79
Corn chips	60
Potato chips	77
Peanuts	21

*Using white bread (GI = 100) as a standard. When variations exist in a food item, the mean is reported.

Adapted, by permission, from Foster-Powell, Holt, and Brand-Miller, 2002 (30).

scientists have speculated that low-GI foods may spare carbohydrate by minimizing insulin secretion and increasing fatty acid levels in the blood. Studies have supported that these metabolic changes occur but that the changes do not uniformly result in improved performance. For example, Thomas and colleagues (88) and DeMarco and colleagues (23) noted improved cycling time after low-GI feedings. But Wee and colleagues (98) and Sparks and colleagues (79) reported no difference in the performances of runners and cyclists when low-GI feedings were compared with high-GI feedings. In a later study, Thomas and colleagues (89) did not report differences in cycling times with different GI feedings. Given the lack of agreement in this area, athletes should experiment during training so that food choices can be assessed and gradually incorporated into the diet.

Fiber

Diets low in **fiber** have been associated with several disorders, including diverticulosis, constipation, heart disease, cancer of the colon, and diabetes. Consequently, a high-fiber diet is recommended by many public health organizations. The Dietary Reference Intake for fiber is 38 and 25 g/day for young men and women, respectively, based on the intake level observed to protect against coronary heart disease. Although appropriate for many individuals, this level of fiber may be excessive for some aerobic endurance athletes, specifically runners, who may experience "runner's trots." On the other hand, increasing fiber for athletes who experience irritable bowel syndrome can be effective in normalizing bowel habits. A high fiber intake is often achieved in the typical American diet by a high-fiber cereal or a supplement. Fiber is also found in fruits, vegetables, nuts, seeds, legumes, and whole-grain products such as whole-grain bread, oatmeal, and popcorn.

Carbohydrate Requirements

Roughly 50 to 100 g of carbohydrate per day is needed to prevent **ketosis** (high levels of ketones in the bloodstream) (97). Beyond that need, carbohydrates provide fuel for energy. The Institute of Medicine recommends 45% to 65% of total daily calories as carbohydrate (56).

Because of the relationship of carbohydrate intake to muscle and liver glycogen stores and to the protein-sparing effect of high concentrations of muscle glycogen, a high-carbohydrate diet is commonly recommended for all athletes. However, it is important to note that a variety of diets, with various carbohydrate, protein, and fat mixtures, have been shown to be equally effective in supporting training and performance (55, 62, 64). The notion that all athletes need and should consume diets very high in carbohydrates should be dispelled. Some athletes certainly benefit from a high-carbohydrate diet, but others do not benefit; and in the worst case, some athletes do not perform as well on a high-carbohydrate diet. Individualizing carbohydrate intake based on the training program, sport, and diet history is imperative.

One important factor to consider when determining recommendations for carbohydrate intake is the training program. Aerobic endurance athletes who train for long durations (90 minutes or more daily) should replenish glycogen levels by consuming maximal levels of carbohydrate, approximately 8 to 10 g/kg of body weight (41, 75, 77). This is equivalent to 600 to 750 g of carbohydrate (2,400-3,000 kcal from carbohydrate) per day for an athlete weighing 165 pounds (75 kg). This level has been shown to adequately restore skeletal glycogen within 24 hours (1, 20, 44, 49, 65). Athletes who benefit from this level of carbohydrate intake include those engaged in continuous aerobic activity for more than an hour on most days, such as distance runners, road cyclists, triathletes, and cross-country skiers. More recently, research has shown that athletes engaged in high-intensity, intermittent activities, such as soccer players, also benefit from high-carbohydrate diets (7, 83). (Carbohydrate loading is discussed later in this chapter.) However, the majority of power and sprint athletes do not train *aerobically* for more than an hour each day. Research on the carbohydrate needs of these athletes—such as American football players, sprinters, basketball players, wrestlers, and volleyball players—is limited. Carbohydrate intake and muscle glycogen levels seem to have much less of an impact, if any, on strength performance (53, 86, 91, 100). Intake of approximately half of that recommended for aerobic endurance athletes appears adequate to support training and performance of strength, sprint, and skill athletes, and thus an intake of 5 to 6 g/kg per day is reasonable (12, 76).

Some aerobic endurance athletes have maximal carbohydrate requirements, up to 10 g/kg per day. Most athletes do not deplete muscle glycogen on a daily basis, however, and therefore have lower carbohydrate requirements.

Lipids

Although the terms **fat** and **lipid** are often used interchangeably, lipid is a broader term. Lipids include triglycerides (fats and oils) as well as related fatty compounds, such as sterols and phospholipids. The lipids of greatest significance in nutrition are triglycerides, fatty acids, phospholipids, and cholesterol. Triglycerides are formed by the union of glycerol with three fatty acids. The majority of lipids found in foods and in the body are in the triglyceride form, and within this chapter the term *fat* refers to triglycerides.

Fat in food is often perceived negatively by athletes, but avoidance of dietary fat by athletes is not indicated. To understand the implications of dietary fat, it is important to view fat from two distinct perspectives: One is fat and its role in disease, and the other is fat and its impact on performance. The following discussion of fat covers both perspectives as they apply to athletes.

Structure and Function of Lipids

Like carbohydrate, fat contains carbon, oxygen, and hydrogen atoms; but because the fatty acid chains have more carbon and hydrogen relative to oxygen, they provide more energy per gram. For example, fats provide approximately 9 kcal/g, while carbohydrates and protein provide approximately 4 kcal/g.

Fat's behavior in the body is related in part to the saturation of the fatty acids. The saturation of a fatty acid is related to the amount of hydrogen it contains. Saturated fatty acids contain all the hydrogen they can carry. In unsaturated fatty acids, some of the positions where hydrogen atoms are usually attached are missing, and carbon atoms are joined together by double bonds, which are chemically more reactive. Fatty acids containing no double bonds are **saturated**. Fatty acids containing one double bond are called **monounsaturated**. With two or more double bonds, a fatty acid is **polyunsaturated**. Generally, most dietary fats and oils are a mix of all three types of fatty acids, with one type predominating. Soy, corn, sunflower, and safflower oils are relatively high in polyunsaturated fatty acids; olive, peanut, and canola oils are high in monounsaturated fatty acids; and most animal fats and tropical oils (e.g., coconut, palm kernel) are relatively high in saturated fatty acids.

Fat serves many functions within the body. Energy is stored primarily as adipose tissue in humans. Although commonly considered negatively, body fat is necessary for insulation and protection of organs, and for hormonal regulation. Fat also serves as a carrier for the fat-soluble vitamins A, D, E, and K and supplies the essential fatty acids, linoleic acid (omega-6) and linolenic acid (omega-3). These two essential fatty acids are necessary for the formation of healthy cell membranes, the proper development and functioning of the brain and nervous system, and the production of hormones. In addition to its physiological functions, fat is important because it is responsible for the characteristic flavor, aroma, and texture of many foods. Fat also promotes a feeling of fullness, or satiety, after a meal.

Like fat, **cholesterol** in the body is perceived negatively. However, it too has many essential functions. It is an important structural and functional component of cell membranes. It is necessary for the production of bile salts, vitamin D, and several hormones, including the sex hormones (estrogen, androgen, and progesterone) and cortisol. Cholesterol is synthesized in the liver and intestine.

Fat and Disease

High levels of cholesterol or unfavorable ratios of lipoproteins are associated with increased risk of heart disease. Standardized categories of blood cholesterol levels are shown in table 10.4. High levels of HDLs protect against heart disease, and HDLs can be increased by exercise and weight loss. In patients with heart disease and high total cholesterol levels, a low-fat diet can decrease total cholesterol and decrease the ratio of total cholesterol to HDLs. Refer to the report by the National Heart, Lung, and Blood Institute of the National Institutes of Health (NHLBI-NIH) (59), which provides a standardized protocol for assessment and intervention when various risk factors for cardiovascular disease are present.

Although replacing saturated fat with carbohydrates has been a common public health recommendation, it is increasingly recognized that high carbohydrate intake can have the negative metabolic consequence of increasing triglycerides in some individuals. Scientists are currently examining the use of monounsaturated fats to replace certain saturated fats as an effective alternative to increasing carbohydrate for some individuals. Although a link between high saturated fat intake and disease exists, a more sophisticated understanding of dietary fat and an appreciation of the other important lifestyle and genetic factors in heart disease are unfolding.

TABLE 10.4

Classification of LDL, Total Cholesterol, and HDL Levels

Levels	Classification
LDLs	
<100	Optimal
100-129	Near optimal/Above optimal
130-159	Borderline high
160-189	High
≥190	Very high
Total cholesterol	
<200	Desirable
200-239	Borderline high
≥240	High
HDLs	
<40	Low
≥60	High

LDLs = low-density lipoproteins; HDLs = high-density lipoproteins. Levels are given in mg/dL.

From National Heart, Lung, and Blood Institute of the National Institutes of Health (NHLBI-NIH) (59).

For a complete review of the relationship of fats and oils to health and diseases, refer to Rivlin (68).

Fat Requirements and Recommendations

It is estimated that individuals should consume 5% to 10% of energy from omega-6 (linoleic) fatty acids and 0.6% to 1.2% from omega-3 (linolenic) fatty acids (22). Because of the prevalence of these fatty acids in foods and their low intake requirements, fatty acid deficiency was once of concern only for individuals with malabsorption diseases. The availability of fat-free foods combined with the obsession to cut fat from the diet, however, has made this a real concern for otherwise healthy individuals who overly restrict dietary fat.

Approximately 34% of calories in the typical American diet are from fat (27). The recommendation for the general public from the Institute of Medicine is that fat should constitute 20% to 35% of the total calories consumed, with less than 10% from saturated fats (one-third of total fat intake). The Institute of Medicine also recommends keeping cholesterol as low as possible (56). These recommendations are given primarily to reduce the incidence of cardiovascular disease. It is predicted that reductions of dietary fat from current levels to recommended levels can achieve a reduction in total cholesterol and LDLs of about 5% (39).

Fat guidelines for individual athletes, however, may be higher than standard "heart healthy" guidelines. Research shows that during periods of heavy aerobic endurance training, increasing dietary fat to as high as 50% of calories does not negatively affect plasma lipids (11, 45). Indeed, fat intakes greater than 30% are common in elite athletes (32).

With the emphasis on decreasing fat, a lower limit is often ignored. However, the Institute of Medicine set an acceptable lower limit of 20% of calories from fat, thus recognizing the necessity of eating enough fat for health. Very-low-fat diets, such as those sometimes prescribed for patients with severe heart disease, are not recommended for athletes. In certain populations, reducing dietary fat to 10% of total calories may actually worsen lipid profiles (24). Additionally, diets extremely low in fat (less than 15% of total calories) may decrease testosterone production, thus decreasing metabolism and muscle development (94).

It is, of course, the overconsumption rather than the underconsumption of fat that has held the attention of scientists, health care providers, and the general public. The negative view of fat evolved from research conducted over the past three decades linking excess dietary fat intake to cardiovascular disease, cancer, diabetes, and obesity. Reducing dietary fat to decrease the risk of any of these chronic conditions is obviously not the top goal of most young athletes. Athletes want to eat to improve performance. It is a paradox, then, that there is so much focus on reducing dietary fat, because there are very few performance enhancements from significantly reducing fat in the athlete's diet; in fact, an emphasis on low-fat or no-fat diets may prove negative for many (93). Because of fat's negative image, some athletes overly restrict dietary fat. This fat phobia is unfounded and can lead to diets void of meat and dairy products, which in turn increase the risk of deficiencies of nutrients such as protein, calcium, iron, and zinc.

Fat phobia, or fear of eating fat, can lead to nutrient deficiencies, which harm performance. Athletes who eat very little or no fat should receive nutritional counseling and information.

When Should Athletes Decrease Dietary Fat?

In general, there are three reasons for athletes to reduce dietary fat:

1. *Need to increase carbohydrate intake to support training type.* In this case, to ensure adequate protein provision, fat is the nutrient of choice to decrease so that caloric intake can remain similar while carbohydrate is increased.
2. *Need to reduce total caloric intake to achieve weight loss.* Because fat is dense in calories and is highly palatable, decreasing dietary fat, if the diet has excess fat, can help reduce caloric intake.
3. *Need to decrease elevated blood cholesterol.* Some young athletes are strongly predisposed to heart disease, although this is uncommon. Manipulation of fat and carbohydrate may be necessary if medically indicated for an athlete who has high blood cholesterol levels or a family history of heart disease. This diet therapy should be guided by a registered dietitian.

Fat and Performance

Both intramuscular and circulating fatty acids are potential energy sources during exercise. It appears that intramuscular fatty acids are more important during activity and that circulating fatty acids (from adipose tissue or diet) are more important during recovery (62). Compared with the limited capacity of the body to store carbohydrate, fat stores are large and represent a vast source of fuel for exercise (34). At rest and during low-intensity exercise, a high percentage of the energy produced is derived from fatty acid oxidation (70). With increasing exercise intensities (over 70%-80% $\dot{V}O_2$max), however, there is a gradual shift from fat to carbohydrate as the preferred source of fuel.

In search of techniques to improve athletic performance, researchers have focused on strategies to enhance fat utilization during exercise. Nutritional interventions that may theoretically promote fat oxidation and decrease muscle glycogen depletion include ingestion of caffeine; consumption of medium-chain triglycerides; and exposure to high-fat, low-carbohydrate diets (34). Although consuming caffeine has been shown to improve aerobic endurance capacity in some individuals (19), supplementing with medium-chain triglycerides has been shown to have no effect on performance. Use of medium-chain triglycerides has caused gastric distress, thereby actually diminishing performance (16, 43). Consumption of high-fat diets (38% of calories from fat) in the presence of adequate caloric intake has been shown to enhance performance in trained runners (55). High-fat diets (35% of calories) compared with lower-fat diets (24% of total calories) consumed by female soccer players resulted in longer distance to exhaustion (7.0 miles [11.2 km] on higher fat vs. 6.0 miles [9.7 km] on lower fat) in treadmill tests replicating soccer performance (38). In untrained men, chronic consumption of a high-fat diet resulted in the same improvement in aerobic endurance performance as a high-carbohydrate diet (35). Acute supplementation of fat does not appear to improve performance in those who were not necessarily consuming a high-fat diet previously (60). Because training increases the capacity of the muscle to use fatty acids and because the type of diet to which the body is adapted influences the outcome, the effects of high-fat diets vary, depending on the individual.

MICRONUTRIENTS

A micronutrient is a nutrient that is required in small amounts (typically measured in milligram—or even smaller—quantities) in the diet. Two primary types of micronutrients are vitamins and minerals. Vitamins and minerals are sometimes touted as doing everything from curing diseases to enhancing energy and sexual prowess. The actual role of vitamins and minerals in health promotion and disease prevention continues to be explored. This section briefly reviews the sources and functions of vitamins and minerals as well as athletes' needs for these micronutrients.

Vitamins

Vitamins are organic substances (i.e., containing carbon atoms) that cannot be synthesized by the body. They are needed in very small amounts and perform specific metabolic functions. Table 10.5 describes the functions and some food sources of individual vitamins.

TABLE 10.5

Vitamins

Vitamin	Function	Some good food sources
Vitamin A	Promotes growth and repair of body tissues, bone formation, and healthy skin and hair. Essential for night vision.	Liver (all sources), giblets, some cheese, egg yolk, whole milk, butter
Beta carotene	Serves as an antioxidant.*	Sweet peppers, carrots, grape leaves, pumpkin, sweet potatoes, yams, broccoli, dandelion greens, chili peppers, mustard greens, spinach, kale, turnip greens, apricots, papaya, watermelon, peaches, asparagus, winter squash, cantaloupe, muskmelon, chard
Vitamin D	Aids in the absorption of calcium and helps to build bone mass and prevent bone loss. Helps maintain blood levels of calcium and phosphorus.	Fish (herring, salmon, oysters, catfish, sardines, tuna, shrimp, mackerel), milk, margarine, fortified breakfast cereals, egg yolks, butter
Vitamin E	Serves as an antioxidant.* Needed for normal growth and development.	Oils (wheat germ, vegetable), mayonnaise, fortified breakfast cereals, nuts (almonds, hazelnuts, peanuts, hickory, pistachio), margarine, wheat germ, peanut butter
Vitamin K (phyllo-quinone)	Needed for normal blood clotting and bone health.	Kale, Brussels sprouts, spinach, chard, cauliflower, broccoli, turnip and mustard greens, carrots, asparagus, avocados, bell peppers, strawberries, tomatoes, apples, peaches
Vitamin C	Promotes healthy cell development, wound healing, and resistance to infections. Serves as an antioxidant.* Necessary for conversion of the inactive form of folic acid to the active form. Makes iron available for hemoglobin synthesis.	Sweet peppers, broccoli, Brussels sprouts, cauliflower, strawberries, oranges, orange juice, limes, lemon juice, grapefruit, grapefruit juice, papayas, cantaloupe, tomatoes, tomato juice, asparagus, raw cabbage, spinach, pineapple, raspberries, potatoes, onions
Thiamin (B_1)	Coenzyme for carbohydrate metabolism. Needed for normal functioning of the nervous system and muscles, including the heart.	Fortified breakfast cereals, sunflower seeds, peas, pork, oranges, orange juice, lima beans, pecans, enriched rice
Riboflavin (B_2)	Coenzyme in red blood cell formation, nervous system functioning, and metabolism of carbohydrate, protein, and fat. Needed for vision and may help protect against cataracts.	Liver, wheat germ, brewer's yeast, almonds, cheese, fortified breakfast cereal, whey protein, milk, eggs, lamb, pork, veal, beef, broccoli, yogurt
Niacin	Coenzyme for carbohydrate, protein, and fat metabolism and proper nervous system functioning. High intakes can lower elevated cholesterol.	Soy protein, soy flour, textured vegetable protein, whey protein, beef, peanuts, peanut butter, sunflower seeds, fortified breakfast cereals
Pyridoxine (B_6)	Coenzyme for protein metabolism and nervous and immune system function. Involved in synthesis of hormones and red blood cells.	Liver, bananas, fortified breakfast cereals, soybeans, chicken, tuna, raw carrots, beef, broccoli, spinach, potatoes, alfalfa sprouts, navy beans, peanut butter, garbanzo beans, walnuts, sunflower seeds, avocados, eggs, lima beans, cabbage, salmon
Folic acid	Needed for normal growth and development and red blood cell formation. Reduces risk of neural tube birth defects. May reduce risk of heart disease and cervical dysplasia.	Brewer's yeast, fortified breakfast cereals, liver, black-eyed peas, beans (pinto, black, lima, white, garbanzo, soy), peanuts, peanut butter, spinach, turnip greens, asparagus, mustard greens, seaweed, eggs, enriched bread, oranges, orange juice
Cobalamin (B_{12})	Vital for blood formation and healthy nervous system.	Liver, oysters, lamb, eggs, beef, shellfish, fish, poultry, pork, chicken, fortified breakfast cereals
Biotin	Assists in the metabolism of fatty acids and utilization of B vitamins.	Nuts (peanuts, hazelnuts, almonds, cashews, macadamia), soybeans, peanut butter, black-eyed peas, liver, milk, egg yolks, yeast, cheese, cauliflower, carrots, avocados, sweet potatoes
Pantothenic acid	Aids in normal growth and development.	Liver, sunflower seeds, fortified breakfast cereals, egg yolks, whey protein, soy protein, peanuts, peanut butter, pecans, veal, enriched rice, broccoli, lima beans

*Antioxidants are those substances that protect cells from oxygen singlets (free radicals). Oxidative damage plays a causative role in heart disease, some cancers, and cataracts. Thus, antioxidant vitamins can protect against such diseases.

Minerals

The human body requires various **minerals** for a wide variety of metabolic functions. For example, calcium is needed for bone and tooth formation and function, nerve transmission, and muscle contraction. Iron is necessary for oxygen transport and is also a component of enzymes necessary for energy metabolism. Calcium, phosphorus, magnesium, iron, and the electrolytes sodium, potassium, and chloride are often called the major minerals. For the athlete, the importance of minerals for bone health, oxygen-carrying capacity, and fluid and electrolyte balance is well recognized. Zinc, iodine, selenium, copper, fluoride, and chromium are referred to as trace elements. The minerals, their functions, and some good food sources are given in table 10.6.

TABLE 10.6

Minerals

Mineral	Function	Food sources
Calcium	Essential for developing and maintaining healthy bones and teeth. Assists in blood clotting, muscle contraction, and nerve transmission. Reduces risk of osteoporosis and may also reduce the risk of preeclampsia in pregnant women.	Fruit juices and fruit drinks fortified with calcium, cheese, sardines, milk, cottage cheese, yogurt, ice cream, calcium-set tofu, turnip greens, Chinese cabbage, mustard greens, kale, rutabaga
Phosphorus	Works with calcium to develop and maintain strong bones and teeth. Enhances use of other nutrients. Essential for energy metabolism, DNA structure, and cell membranes.	Cheese, fish, beef, pork, whole-wheat products, cocoa powder, pumpkin seeds, sunflower seeds, almonds
Magnesium	Activates nearly 100 enzymes and helps nerves and muscles function. Constituent of bones and teeth.	Bran (wheat and rice), cocoa powder, fortified breakfast cereals, seeds (pumpkin, sunflower), soybeans, nuts (almonds, pine nuts, hazelnuts, cashews, walnuts, peanuts), spinach
Molybdenum	Needed for metabolism of DNA and ribonucleic acid (RNA) and production of uric acid.	Milk, milk products, peas, beans, liver, whole-grain products
Manganese	Necessary for the normal development of the skeletal and connective tissues. Involved in metabolism of carbohydrates.	Wheat germ, wheat bran, rice bran, fortified breakfast cereals, rice cakes, nuts (peanuts, pecans, pine nuts, walnuts, almonds, hazelnuts), soybeans, mussels, whole-wheat products (pastas, breads, and crackers)
Copper	Involved in iron metabolism, nervous system functioning, bone health, and synthesis of proteins. Plays a role in the pigmentation of skin, hair, and eyes.	Liver, shellfish (especially oysters), lobster, nuts (cashews, Brazil nuts, hazelnuts, walnuts, peanuts, almonds, pecans, pistachios), seeds (sunflower, pumpkin), fortified breakfast cereals, great northern beans
Chromium	Aids in glucose metabolism and may help regulate blood sugar and insulin levels in people with diabetes.	Mushrooms (white), raw oysters, wine, apples, brewer's yeast, beer, pork, chicken
Iodine	Part of the thyroid hormone. Helps regulate growth, development, and energy metabolism.	Iodized salt, saltwater fish and seafood
Iron	Necessary for red blood cell formation and function. Constituent of myoglobin and component of enzyme systems.	Liver, beef, lamb, pork, veal, poultry, clams, oysters, fortified breakfast cereals, enriched bread products, brewer's yeast, nuts (pine nuts, cashews, almonds), beans (kidney, green, garbanzo)
Selenium	Essential component of a key antioxidant enzyme. Necessary for normal growth and development and for use of iodine in thyroid function.	Tenderloin of beef, pollack, trout, tuna, oysters, mackerel, flounder, liver, sunflower seeds, wheat bran, wheat germ, some pork, fortified breakfast cereals, perch, crab, clams, cod, haddock, whole-wheat breads
Zinc	Essential part of more than 100 enzymes involved in digestion, metabolism, reproduction, and wound healing.	Oysters, beef, veal, lamb, pork, chicken, lima beans, black-eyed peas, white beans

Ultratrace minerals are needed in minute amounts, and therefore evidence for their essentiality is often difficult to find. Deficiencies in humans have not been established for any of these ultratrace elements, and no recommended intake for them exists. Ultratrace minerals include arsenic, bromine, cadmium, fluorine, lead, lithium, manganese, molybdenum, nickel, silicon, tin, vanadium, and boron. As early as the 1970s, scientists speculated that deficiencies in one or more of the ultratrace elements contribute to the occurrence of human diseases. Boron, for example, has been linked to bone health. However, research on ultratrace minerals is still in its infancy.

Two minerals—iron and calcium—deserve additional attention. Athletes who do not consume enough dietary iron risk iron depletion and impaired performance. Inadequate dietary calcium can contribute to low bone density and risk for osteoporosis.

Iron

Iron is a mineral that receives a great deal of attention from athletes. Iron is a constituent of hemoglobin and myoglobin and, as such, plays a role in oxygen transport and utilization of energy. Iron deficiency inhibits athletic performance.

Deficiency of most vitamins and minerals is rare in the diets of developed countries; however, iron deficiency leading to anemia is a relatively common nutritional deficiency, especially in women and adolescents. The number of healthy women in the United States who have some degree of iron deficiency has been estimated to be as high as 58%. Iron deficiency also commonly occurs in growing teenage males.

Blood loss is the primary avenue of iron loss from the body. A number of other factors may contribute to low iron stores in athletes, including heavy training, gastrointestinal bleeding, breakdown of red blood cells, increased iron losses through sweating, decreased iron absorption, and inadequate dietary intake. Women who experience heavy menstrual bleeding may be at increased risk for iron deficiency, as may athletes who consume vegetarian diets because of the lower absorption of iron from plant foods. Athletes found to be iron deficient through blood analysis should receive diet counseling and, when indicated, supplemental iron (103).

Just as inadequate iron is problematic, excess iron is also harmful. Some individuals have a silent disease called hemochromatosis, in which the body stores excess iron. Frequently, the first sign of the disease is multiple-organ failure due to excess iron in heart and liver tissue. Men, because they do not lose blood through the menstrual cycle, are more susceptible to the disease. Supplemental iron intake by men should be recommended only after blood analysis showing depleted iron stores.

Calcium

Except for the calcium contributed from maternal stores during fetal development, all calcium in the adult body is derived from external sources. Inadequate calcium intake inhibits bone mineral density. Low calcium intakes have been reported in many female athletes (9, 18, 32). Many women do not consume adequate calcium because of low caloric intake or avoidance of milk and dairy foods, the best sources of calcium (9, 18, 54, 63). Athletes who consume low-calcium diets may be at risk for osteopenia and **osteoporosis**, deterioration of bone tissue leading to increased bone fragility and risk of fracture. Although fracture risk is influenced by genetic, hormonal, and training factors, diet plays an essential role. Athletes should be encouraged to include dairy products and other calcium-rich foods in the diet. Those who are unable to meet calcium requirements via diet may need a calcium supplement.

FLUID AND ELECTROLYTES

Water plays a crucial role in exercise, especially for thermoregulation. **Dehydration** not only affects performance, but also causes serious complications, even death, if not managed properly. Electrolytes play a fundamental role in the regulation of water distribution in various fluid compartments in the body. Sodium in particular has a major influence on fluid regulation. The electrolytes potassium, chloride, and magnesium are essential to muscle contraction and nerve conduction. Any disturbance in the balance of electrolytes in body fluids could interfere with performance. The following sections discuss the role of fluids and electrolytes in athletic performance.

Water

Under optimal conditions, the body can survive 30 days without food but only 4 to 10 days without water. Water is the largest component of the body, representing from 45% to 70% of a person's body weight. Total body water is determined largely by body composition; muscle tissue is approximately 75% water, whereas fat tissue is about 20% water.

Water affects athletic performance more than any other nutrient. Consuming fluids in sufficient amounts is essential for normal cellular function and, of particular importance to athletes, thermal regulation. Ironically, during physiological and thermal stress, humans do not adequately replace sweat losses when fluids are consumed at will. In fact, most athletes replace only about two-thirds of the water they sweat off during exercise. This phenomenon has been called **voluntary dehydration**. Strength and conditioning professionals must be aware of this tendency and make athletes aware of it as well. A systematic approach to water replacement is necessary because thirst is not a reliable indicator of fluid need for athletes who are practicing intensely in hot environmental conditions. This chapter provides a brief overview of fluid and electrolyte balance. The review by Epstein and Armstrong (26) provides further information on fluid and electrolyte balance.

Fluid Balance

Under normal environmental conditions, fluid balance is achieved by regulation of fluid intake through changes in thirst sensations and regulation of loss by the kidneys. An individual's water requirement is the volume needed to replace urine loss, insensible loss from skin and lungs, and loss in feces. The Adequate Intake for water as set by the Food and Nutrition Board for *total* water intake for young men and women (ages 19 to 30 years) is 3.7 L and 2.7 L/day, respectively. It is estimated that fluids (drinking water and beverages) provide about 3.0 L (101 fluid ounces; approximately 13 cups) and 2.2 L (74 fluid ounces; approximately 9 cups) per day for young men and women, respectively (57).

Sweat losses can increase fluid requirements significantly. For example, continuous sweating during prolonged exercise can exceed 1.9 quarts per hour (1.8 L/hour). Athletes sweating profusely for several hours per day may need to consume an extra 3 to 4 gallons (11-15 L) of fluid to replace losses.

Risks of Dehydration

Unless sweat losses are replaced, body temperature rises, leading to heat exhaustion, heatstroke, and even death. Sweat losses are tracked by decreases in body weight. Fluid loss equal to as little as 1% of total body weight can be associated with an elevation in core temperature during exercise. Fluid loss of 3% to 5% of body weight results in cardiovascular strain and impaired ability to dissipate heat. At 7% loss, collapse is likely (33). It is common for athletes to dehydrate 2% to 6% during practice in the heat. For example, in a 220-pound (100 kg) athlete, 5% body weight loss is 11 pounds (5 kg). Although commonplace during practice in the heat, this level of dehydration should be recognized as detrimental to performance and potentially dangerous.

Consuming adequate fluids before, during, and after training and competition is essential to optimal resistance training and aerobic endurance exercise.

Monitoring Hydration Status

A systematic approach to ensuring adequate hydration is to record athletes' body weights immediately before and after a workout. (For accuracy, sweaty clothes should be removed before weighing.) Each pound (0.45 kg) lost during practice represents 1 pint (0.5 L) of fluid loss. This must be replaced before the next training session. In addition to identifying acute dehydration from one workout, the weight chart identifies athletes who are chronically dehydrated—those who lose 5 to 10 pounds (2.3-4.5 kg) over the course of a week, for example. Early in the season, this downward trend in weight can be misidentified as fat loss; however, fat loss does not occur this rapidly. The chronically dehydrated athlete is at increased risk for poor performance and heat illness.

Though it may not be feasible for each team to weigh before and after each training session, implementing this system during early, hot seasons (for example, two-a-day practices during fall American football, volleyball, cross-country, or soccer) helps prevent dehydration and heat illness. It also makes athletes aware of how much water they need to consume to maintain body weight, since athletes' fluid replacement needs vary considerably.

Although not as sensitive as weight change, other indicators of hydration status can be useful monitoring tools. Signs of dehydration include dark yellow, strong-smelling urine; decreased frequency of urination; rapid resting heart rate; and prolonged muscle soreness (5). Normal urine production for adults is about 1.2 quarts (1.1 L) per day, or 8 to 10 fluid ounces (237-296 ml) per urination four times per day. Normal urine is the color of lemon juice, except in athletes who are taking supplemental vitamins, which tend to make the urine bright yellow. Note that urination during the rehydration process does not signal complete rehydration. The kidneys are not completely efficient in the rehydration process (78).

Electrolytes

The major **electrolytes** lost in sweat are sodium chloride, and, to a lesser extent, potassium. Physiological adaptive mechanisms decrease the electrolyte loss in urine and sweat during periods of strenuous exercise; thus, the sweat of a trained athlete is more dilute than the sweat of an untrained individual. The average sodium concentration of sweat is 1.15 g/L, with concentrations ranging from 0.46 to 2.3 g/L. The average daily sodium intake of American adults is approximately 4 to 6 g, usually high enough to replace sodium losses. However, athletes who sweat profusely for a period of days, who are not acclimated to the heat, or who have low sodium intakes can experience heat cramps from sodium depletion. Some athletes may need to increase intake of foods high in salt (pizza, ham, potato chips) or add salt to foods.

Potassium losses in sweat can generally be replaced with a diet providing 2 to 6 g/day. Average potassium intake is 2 to 4 g/day, so some athletes need to be encouraged to consume more potassium-rich foods, such as citrus fruits and juices, melons, strawberries, tomatoes, bananas, potatoes, meat, and milk.

Fluid Replacement

Fluid replacement occurs in three general time frames: before, during, and after exercise. The ultimate goal is to start exercise in a hydrated state, avoid dehydration during exercise, and rehydrate before the next training session.

Before Activity

Consuming at least 1 pint (0.5 L) of fluid 2 hours before activity provides the fluid needed to achieve optimal hydration and allows enough time for urination of excess fluid (3). Because rapid absorption is not critical, athletes can choose to drink water or any other nonalcoholic beverage: milk, juice, carbonated or uncarbonated soft drinks, sport drinks, and so on. The fluid can be consumed with or apart from a meal.

The question whether consuming caffeinated beverages causes dehydration is often asked. Caffeine increases urine production slightly in athletes not accustomed to it, and less in athletes who customarily consume caffeine.

During Activity

As stated previously, athletes may not voluntarily drink enough fluid to replace sweat losses during exercise. Inadequate fluid intake is compounded when athletes are not given time to drink and are not given free access to fluids.

The goal of fluid replacement during exercise is to move the fluid from the mouth, through the gut, and into circulation rapidly and to provide a volume that matches sweat losses. This is achieved by providing fluids that are absorbed rapidly and that the athlete finds palatable, and by providing time for drinking. Athletes should start drinking before sensing thirst and continue to drink at regular intervals. Larger volumes (e.g., 8 fluid ounces, or 237 ml) tend to empty from the stomach more rapidly than small volumes, so chugging is preferred over sipping as long as it does not cause stomach discomfort.

A variety of fluids can serve as effective fluid replacements during exercise (37). Cool water is an ideal fluid replacement. Other options for fluid replacement include commercial sport drinks or homemade sport drinks such as diluted juice or diluted soft drinks. Although plain water can meet fluid requirements in most cases, some athletes find flavored drinks more palatable than water and consequently drink more (99). Aside from promoting water intake, there does not appear to be a physiological benefit from carbohydrate consumption for athletes participating in events less than 1 hour long. However, aerobic endurance athletes, such as distance runners, soccer players, and distance swimmers, can benefit from carbohydrate provision along with water intake during activities lasting more than an hour (8). The beverage choice depends on athlete preference, budget, facilities, and type of event.

Commercial sport drinks contain water, sugars, and electrolytes (usually sodium, chloride, and potassium). The sugar content of sport drinks is slightly less than the amount in most soft drinks and juices. Carbohydrate concentration of commercial sport drinks ranges from 6% to 8%, a solution that tends to be absorbed rapidly. People can make their own sport drink by diluting two parts of a sugared soft drink with one part water and adding salt (1/8 teaspoon [0.7 mg] per quart). Another option is to provide solid food (fruit, sport bars, cereal bars, cookies, etc.) as a carbohydrate source along with plain water. Not all athletes tolerate beverages or foods other than plain water while exercising. If these items are used, tolerance to them should be tested during training, not competition.

After Activity

The goal after a training session is to prepare the body for the next workout. As previously described, monitoring body weight and replacing each pound (0.45 kg) lost with at least 1 pint (0.5 L) of fluid is a helpful guideline to ensure adequate fluid intake. Urination occurs before complete fluid balance is achieved. Thus, total fluid intake will exceed 1 pint per pound lost (0.5 L/0.45 kg).

When significant sweating has occurred, consumption of sodium chloride (salt) in beverages or food minimizes urine output and hastens recovery of water and electrolyte balance (51, 52). In practical terms, this means that the athlete should consume a wide variety of beverages and foods after training. In fact, most fluid consumption occurs during and around mealtimes, and the water comes from both food and beverages. If rapid rehydration without significant food intake is required, as in a tournament situation, consumption of a beverage containing sodium chloride, such as a sport drink, is recommended to reduce urinary output and thereby maximize water retention. The best advice is to drink plenty of fluids, often, between bouts of training or practice, and not to rely on thirst to guide fluid intake.

Fluid Replacement Guidelines

Before a Training Session

- Encourage athletes to hydrate properly before prolonged exercise in a hot environment. Intake should be approximately 16 fluid ounces (0.5 L) of a cool beverage 2 hours before a workout.

During a Training Session

- Provide cool beverages (about 50-70 °F, or 10-21 °C).
- Have fluids readily available, since the thirst mechanism does not function adequately when large volumes of water are lost. Athletes will not seek out water if it is far away. In many cases, they need to be reminded to drink.
- Athletes should drink fluid frequently—for example, 6 to 8 fluid ounces (177-237 ml) every 15 minutes.

After a Training Session

- Athletes should replenish fluids with at least 1 pint (0.5 L) of fluid for every pound (0.45 kg) of body weight lost. Weight should be regained, indicating that rehydration has occurred, before the next workout.
- Water is an ideal fluid replacement, although flavored beverages may be more effective at promoting drinking.
- The ideal fluid replacement beverage depends on the duration and intensity of exercise, environmental temperature, and the athlete.

PRECOMPETITION AND POSTEXERCISE NUTRITION

An athlete's performance depends more on long-term dietary practices than the food consumption just before or after an event. What an athlete eats before and after a training session and a competition, however, can have both physiological and psychological effects on performance.

Precompetition Food Consumption

Although there are few absolute guidelines for the specific foods that should constitute a **precompetition meal**, for many athletes precompetition eating is ritualistic. It is important to appreciate an athlete's concerns and beliefs about precompetition eating while at the same time understanding the physiological aspects. Numerous recommendations on timing, amount, and types of food for precompetition meals appear in sport nutrition publications; however, many of the recommendations are not supported by scientific data and may not be appropriate for all athletes. When advising an athlete about precompetition eating, consider the following points.

Purpose

The primary purpose of the precompetition meal is to provide fluid and energy for the athlete during the performance. Foods and beverages consumed should not interfere with the physiological aspects of athletic performance.

Timing

The most common recommendation is to eat 3 to 4 hours prior to the event to avoid becoming nauseated or uncomfortable during competition. This time frame is probably appropriate for aerobic endurance athletes, such as runners, who often experience abdominal discomfort. Experience shows that the optimal timing of precompetition eating varies greatly from athlete to athlete, however. Some athletes can eat a meal just minutes before an event; others can eat virtually nothing for up to 12 hours before competition.

The following are athletes who should allow at least 3 to 4 hours between a meal and practice or competition:

- Athletes who participate in contact sports with high risk of injury or likelihood of being hit in the stomach.
- Athletes who lose appetite or feel nauseated shortly before training or competition. Eating before gastric distress occurs allows the athlete to get the calories needed and can prevent vomiting related to nervousness.
- Athletes who get diarrhea shortly before or during the event. Anxiety increases gastric peristalsis (contractions that move food through the gastrointestinal tract). Eating can stimulate the bowels even more. Consuming food well ahead of the event helps prevent an untimely trip to the rest room.
- Athletes who exercise in the heat. Dehydration increases the likelihood of stomachaches, gas, or stomach cramping.
- Athletes who participate in a high-intensity sport with a lot of running or jumping, for example, cross-country running, soccer, volleyball, or basketball. While some athletes can handle a full stomach, the jarring taken by the body increases risk of stomach discomfort.

The following athletes should time food consumption to as close as 30 minutes before competition as possible and should eat during competition:

- Athletes who feel uncomfortably hungry during the event. Hunger can be distracting.
- Athletes who have a tendency to feel shaky or weak. These sensations can be symptoms of low blood sugar.
- Athletes who participate in an aerobic endurance event and want to maximize carbohydrate stores.

Some athletes who participate in long events (tournaments, doubleheaders, all-day meets) like to eat shortly beforehand and continue snacking during competition to keep energy high and prevent hunger.

Practical Considerations

Eating foods that the athlete does not like at a time when nervous tension is high can cause nausea and vomiting. Therefore, personal preference and food tolerance must be considered. It is important for athletes to consume food and beverages

- that they like,
- that they tolerate well,
- that they are used to consuming, and
- that they believe result in a winning performance.

Record keeping can be useful in helping athletes determine their best precompetition regimen. Recording the types and amounts of foods eaten, when in relation to competition they were eaten (e.g., 2 hours prior), how the athlete felt at the time of the event, and performance outcome can serve as a guide for fine-tuning the precompetition meal.

The primary goal of the precompetition meal is to provide fluid and energy for the athlete during performance.

Carbohydrate Loading

Carbohydrate loading is a technique used to enhance muscle glycogen prior to long-term aerobic endurance exercise. This technique was developed in 1931 (17). Since then, several variations of carbohydrate loading have been studied. The most effective regimen with the fewest side effects is three days of a high-carbohydrate diet in concert with tapering exercise the week before competition and complete rest the day before the event. The diet should provide adequate calories and approximately 600 g of carbohydrate per day, or 8 to 10 g/kg of body weight. This regimen should increase muscle glycogen stores 20% to 40% above normal (21).

Carbohydrate loading offers potential benefits for distance runners, road cyclists, cross-country skiers, and others who risk depleting glycogen stores. Data indicate that a carbohydrate-loading regimen increases carbohydrate oxidation during submaximal exercise and improves high-intensity, short-duration performance (66).

The degree of benefit derived from carbohydrate loading varies among individuals, even among aerobic endurance athletes, and therefore athletes should determine the value of this regimen before competition. Potential side effects of carbohydrate loading are increased water retention and weight gain. Furthermore, some athletes may experience flatulence and diarrhea on very-high-carbohydrate diets.

Postexercise Food Consumption

Data suggest that high-GI foods consumed after exercise replenish glycogen faster than low-GI foods (12). Initial studies on glycogen repletion after complete depletion emphasized carbohydrate ingestion immediately after exercise, but more recent data show that a delay of 2 hours does not inhibit glycogenesis 8 and 24 hours later, as long as adequate carbohydrate is consumed over the day (61). For athletes who are training two or three times a day or who do not have long periods of time to recover, however, immediate consumption of carbohydrate in the form of foods or supplements may be beneficial. A study by Tarnopolsky and colleagues (87) revealed that as long as adequate calories are consumed, a mixture of carbohydrate, protein, and fat is just as effective as carbohydrate alone at replacing muscle glycogen after an exhaustive run. Although emphasis is usually placed on carbohydrate, in practical terms, consuming a balanced meal ensures the availability of all substrates for adequate recovery, including amino acids (12).

Most research on recovery has focused on glycogen repletion, and since glycogen is usually not depleted during intermittent activities such as many team and skill sports, less is known about recovery in these situations. Two studies (72, 73) revealed that carbohydrate consumption immediately after intense resistance training resulted in a more positive body protein balance and that carbohydrate alone and a mixture of carbohydrate, protein, and fat resulted in similar glycogen synthesis. Again, consumption of foods or meals with mixed nutrient profiles is an effective way to achieve adequate caloric intake and to enhance recovery.

WEIGHT AND BODY COMPOSITION

Knowledge of weight gain and weight loss principles is essential for prescribing training programs that bring about desired results. This section begins with a discussion of energy requirements, which are important to understand in relation to regulating body mass and body composition (i.e., gaining muscle or losing body fat).

Energy Requirements

Energy is commonly measured in kilocalories (kcal or calories). A kilocalorie is the work or energy required to raise the temperature of 1 kg of water 1 °C (or 2.2 pounds of water 1.8 °F). The number of calories an athlete needs depends on body size, demands of the sport, length of training, training conditions, and age. Energy (caloric) requirement is defined as energy intake equal to expenditure, resulting in constant body weight. Maintaining adequate caloric intake to support the athlete's training and competitive schedule is imperative if the athlete is to be successful.

Factors Influencing Energy Requirements

Many researchers have studied dietary intakes of athletes and have found that extremely wide differences exist. There is a wide range of energy expenditures and energy intakes among sports due to differences in body mass, intensity of training, and work efficiency. For example, a weightlifter who weighs 309 pounds (140 kg) expends considerably more energy performing a given training exercise at a given intensity than a 132-pound (60 kg) weightlifter does. Additionally, the size of the muscle mass involved affects the rate of energy use and the total energy used. Large muscle mass resistance training exercises require a greater rate of energy use than small muscle mass exercises. Among groups of athletes, the highest caloric intakes are found in male swimmers, cyclists, triathletes, and basketball players, with average intakes as high as 6,000 kcal/day. Lower intakes are found in female figure skaters, gymnasts, and dancers, who likely consume less than 1,500 kcal/day. Examination of individual athletes shows an even larger range of caloric intakes, from a few hundred kilocalories to over 7,000 kcal (32).

There is a wide range of energy expenditures and energy intakes required by athletes in various sports due to differences in body mass, intensity of training, work efficiency, and the size of the involved muscle mass.

A common assumption is that all athletes have higher than average caloric requirements, but that is not always true. In fact, some athletes may have lower caloric requirements than their nonathlete peers. Research verifies that it is erroneous to make sweeping assumptions about the caloric intakes and requirements of athletes. The best way to know whether the athlete is consuming adequate calories is to monitor body weight. In the absence of dehydration, constant body weight indicates calorie balance. If body weight is decreasing, caloric intake is less than the requirement. If body weight is increasing, caloric intake exceeds the requirement.

The energy requirement of adults is determined by three factors:

1. resting metabolic rate,
2. thermic effect of food, and
3. physical activity.

Each of these factors can be affected directly or indirectly by age, genetics, body size, body composition, environmental temperature, training conditions, nontraining physical activity, and caloric intake. For the adolescent athlete, growth is another variable that increases the energy requirement.

Resting metabolic rate is the largest contributor to total energy expenditure, accounting for approximately 60% to 75% of daily energy expenditure. It is a measure of the calories required for maintaining normal body functions such as respiration, cardiac function, and thermoregulation. Factors that increase resting metabolic rate include increase in lean body tissue, being young, abnormal body temperature, menstrual cycle, and hyperthyroidism. Factors that decrease resting metabolic rate are low caloric intake, loss of lean tissue, and hypothyroidism. Additionally, normal genetic differences in metabolism can account for variations of 10% to 20%.

The thermic effect of food, also known as **diet-induced thermogenesis**, is the increase in energy expenditure above the resting metabolic rate that can be measured for several hours following a meal. The thermic effect of food includes the energy cost of digestion, absorption, metabolism, and storage of food in the body. The thermic effect of food accounts for approximately 7% to 10% of the total energy requirement.

The second largest component of an individual's energy requirement is the energy expended in physical activity. Of all the components, it is the most variable among individuals. The number of calories expended through physical activity increases with the frequency, intensity, and duration of the training program, as well as nontraining physical activity. The highest energy costs are seen in aerobic activities performed by large athletes for long periods of time, whereas lowest energy costs are associated with skill and power sports performed by small athletes.

Estimating Energy Requirements

As previously described, an athlete's energy requirement is the number of calories it takes to maintain his or her ideal competitive weight. Athletes and coaches often desire a more exact number, however. Short of indirect calorimetry, it is difficult to calculate energy needs due to the numerous variables affecting caloric requirements. Guidelines do exist for estimating daily energy needs, however. Table 10.7 provides factors that can be used to loosely estimate the energy needs of an athlete. For example, for a male athlete who weighs 170 pounds (77 kg) and is in heavy training, the requirement would be roughly 3,900 kcal (23 × 170). Remember that these numbers are rough estimates based on averages.

Another, more laborious method that can be used by motivated athletes is to record dietary intake for three consecutive, representative days during a period of stable body weight. The individual's energy requirement can be assumed to equal the number of calories consumed. The pitfall of this method is that recording food intake usually inhibits eating, and recorded intake thus underestimates true intake.

Weight Gain

Athletes attempt to gain weight for two basic reasons: to improve physical appearance or to enhance

TABLE 10.7

Estimated Daily Calorie Needs of Male and Female Athletes by Activity Level

	MALE		FEMALE	
Activity level	**kcal/pound**	**kcal/kg**	**kcal/pound**	**kcal/kg**
Light	17	38	16	35
Moderate	19	41	17	37
Heavy	23	50	20	44

Light activity level: Walking on a level surface at 2.5 to 3.0 miles per hour (4.0 to 4.8 km/h), garage work, electrical trades, carpentry, restaurant trades, housecleaning, child care, golf, sailing, table tennis.

Moderate activity level: Walking 3.5 to 4.0 miles per hour (5.6 to 6.4 km/h), weeding and hoeing, cycling, skiing, tennis, dancing.

Heavy activity level: Walking with load uphill, heavy manual digging, basketball, climbing, football, soccer.

athletic performance. For weight gain in the form of muscle mass, a combination of diet and progressive resistance training is essential. However, genetic predisposition, somatotype, and compliance determine the athlete's progress. Muscle tissue is approximately 70% water, 22% protein, and 8% fatty acids and glycogen. If all the extra calories consumed are used for muscle growth during resistance training, then about 2,500 extra kilocalories are required for each 1-pound (0.45 kg) increase in lean tissue. Thus, 350 to 700 kcal above daily requirements would supply the calories needed to support a 1- to 2-pound (0.45 to 0.9 kg) weekly gain in lean tissue as well as the energy requirements of the training. To accomplish increased caloric intake, it is recommended that athletes eat larger portions of foods at mealtime, eat more items at each meal, eat frequently, choose higher-calorie foods, or use a combination of these strategies. Practical experience shows that it is difficult for athletes to gain weight if they are eating less than five times per day.

Gains in body mass and strength occur when the athlete consumes adequate calories and dietary protein and engages in a progressive resistance training program.

Weight Loss

In sports that have body weight limitations, such as weightlifting, wrestling, boxing, and lightweight crew, it is often necessary to lose body fat to compete in a lower weight class. Even in some sports without weight classes, such as gymnastics, athletes need a low (or a lower) body fat to be competitive. When the athlete begins or follows a fat loss program, a number of facts may be relevant:

- The ability to achieve and maintain minimal body fat is largely genetic. Some athletes are able to do so while maintaining health and performance. Others experience health and performance problems.
- The best dietary plan is a well-balanced diet that achieves a negative calorie balance. Low-fat diets with no specified calorie restriction have been promoted in the scientific and popular press as an effective means of weight loss. Research in the area indicates that eating an at-will diet restricted in fat (e.g., 25 g of fat per day) is one means by which some individuals effectively reduce caloric intake (74). Many individuals are more satisfied eating the higher volume of food allowed on a low-fat diet (36, 85). However, fat restriction alone has left many individuals consuming an excessively high-carbohydrate diet that is depleted of protein but still high in calories.
- Whether athletes can gain muscle and lose body fat simultaneously depends primarily on their level of training. Previously untrained subjects can both lose body fat and gain lean body mass as a result of caloric restriction and training; however, it is unlikely that trained athletes who already possess a relatively low percentage of body fat can achieve body mass reduction without losing some lean body mass.
- People cannot lose substantial amounts of body mass without losing marked amounts of lean body mass, particularly with caloric restriction (95). If all of the expended or dietary-restricted kilocalories apply to body fat loss, then a deficit of 3,500 kcal will result in a 1-pound (0.45 kg) fat loss. The maximal rate of fat loss appears to be approximately 1% of body mass per week. This is an average of 1.1 to 2.2 pounds (0.5-1.0 kg) per week and represents a daily caloric deficit of approximately 500 to 1,000 kcal. Faster rates can lead to dehydration and loss of lean tissue and decrease vitamin and mineral status (29). Fat loss rates vary depending on body size. For example, a 110-pound (50 kg) female weightlifter who wants to reduce body weight should not lose more than 1.1 pounds (0.5 kg) per week, a value that represents 1% of her body weight. In contrast, a 331-pound (150 kg) American football defensive lineman may safely lose 3.3 pounds (1.5 kg) per week, which is 1% of his body weight.
- Gradual weight loss ensures maximum fat loss and preservation of lean tissue. Rapid weight loss can result in the loss of three times more lean tissue (muscle and water) than fat tissue.
- Caloric intake of no less than 1,800 to 2,000 kcal/day can serve as a starting point. Calories should be added or subtracted based on progress. Commonly seen guidelines of 1,000 or 1,200 kcal for women and 1,500 kcal for men are for *sedentary* individuals. For most active people and athletes, these levels are too low. Ideally, caloric level should be individualized.

- The diet should be composed primarily of foods high in nutrient density. **Nutrient density** refers to the nutrients (vitamins, minerals, and protein) present per calorie of food. For example, a plain baked potato is more nutrient dense (has more vitamins and minerals per calorie) than potato chips, and an apple is more nutrient dense than apple pie.
- The diet should be composed of food low in energy density. **Energy density** refers to the calories per weight or volume of food. Examples of foods with low energy density are broth-based soup, salad greens, vegetables, and fruits. In general, foods with low energy density contain a high proportion of water and fiber. These are foods that people can eat in large portions without consuming excess calories. This can help control hunger and can lower caloric intake (69).
- Weight loss is usually best achieved in the off-season or preseason. Hours spent training, traveling, and competing during the season often foil the best weight loss efforts.
- Record keeping, or self-monitoring, is one of the most effective tools for achieving weight loss (81). It increases the individual's awareness of problem areas. Key areas to record include the amount and type of food consumed; feelings, times, and places associated with food intake; and exercise habits. Once problem behaviors or situations have been identified from the records, behavior modification strategies often include limiting exposure to food or high-risk situations (parties, great hunger) to prevent overeating; identifying and modifying triggers that stimulate eating when not hungry (boredom, stress, time of day, being alone); slowing the rate of eating; and scheduling meals and snacks.

The most important goal for weight loss is to achieve a negative calorie balance. Therefore, the types of foods the individual consumes are less important than the portions of those foods. The focus is on calories.

Rapid Weight Loss

Rapid weight loss to compete in a desired weight class, or weight cutting, is very different from gradual weight loss to lose body fat. The two should not be confused. Rapid weight loss is accomplished by restricting food and fluids for 3 to 10 days before competition. Precompetition food and fluid restriction is usually followed by refeeding and rehydrating after weigh-in. Some athletes practice cutting weight with no adverse consequences. However, athletes who attempt to lose too much weight can suffer heat illness, muscle cramping, fatigue, dizziness, weakness, decreased concentration, and even death. There has been a great deal of speculation about growth failure and increased incidence of eating disorders with rapid weight loss. However, few scientific data exist regarding these theories. Most athletes who want to cut weight will do so with or without professional guidance. It is important to recognize that many athletes who cut weight do so because their body fat is already minimal; thus, counseling the athlete to lose weight gradually (i.e., fat loss) is irrelevant. Instead, the strength and conditioning professional can provide information about how the athlete can minimize the time spent at the lower weight and emphasize the importance of staying hydrated at all other times.

For athletes who desire to minimize lean tissue loss, small decreases in caloric intake to achieve gradual weight loss are indicated.

EATING DISORDERS: ANOREXIA NERVOSA AND BULIMIA NERVOSA

Thirty years ago, most laypeople had never heard of **anorexia nervosa** or **bulimia nervosa**. Today, however, awareness and interest are widespread, such that stories about young women with eating disorders make the covers of popular magazines, are highlighted in television news magazines, and are the focus of national efforts aimed at prevention (40). But eating disorders are not a new phenomenon. The first case of anorexia nervosa was described 300 years ago, and by 1874 the disorder was well described (96). Reports of purging after huge meals date back to Roman vomitoriums, sites where vomiting was used as a method of weight control after gorging (10, 82). Some report that the incidence of eating disorders is increasing (48, 84, 92). The reported increases are probably a combination of increased recognition of the problem and more actual incidents of female adolescents practicing the behaviors. Incidence in men is estimated to be one-tenth of that seen in women (84). The reason for the sex disparity is not clear. It may have to do with social factors or biological factors, or it may be that the underlying pathology manifests differently in men. For example, it has been suggested that the same distorted body image issues present in emaciated anorexic women who perceive themselves as fat are present in men who are muscular but perceive themselves as skinny.

Several researchers have asked the question, Is the incidence of eating disorders greater among athletes, and if so, why? Is this a chicken-and-egg situation, or does sport cause the disease? The phenomenon that has most likely spurred this question in the United States is the increasing number of female athletes participating in competitive sport since initiation of Title IX, legislation that mandated equal opportunity for women to participate in interscholastic sport. Because eating disorders have been identified primarily in women, it is no wonder that before women's wide-scale participation in sport, eating disorders were not an issue in athletics. Some studies indicate a high incidence of anorexia nervosa and bulimia nervosa in female athletes, especially in sports that emphasize leanness and aesthetics (25, 47, 71), while others report no difference between athletes and nonathletes (6, 104). It is known that successful athletes and females with eating disorders share several traits such as perfectionism, discipline, and high achievement expectations.

Definitions and Criteria

Eating disorders should never be misunderstood to be purely nutritional problems, that is, problems that can be corrected by normalizing weight or food intake. They are psychological disorders. Malnutrition is secondary to the disease; the root of eating disorders is complex and multifactorial, with the etiology of the problem linked to self-esteem, family dynamics, stress, sense of loss of control, sexual abuse, and other sources.

The two officially recognized eating disorders in the *Diagnostic and Statistical Manual of Mental Disorders* (4) are anorexia nervosa and bulimia nervosa. Anorexia nervosa is self-imposed starvation in an effort to lose weight and achieve thinness. It is characterized by a severe fear of obesity, even when the person is emaciated, and distorted body image. The individual with anorexia nervosa appears very thin, often wears layers of baggy clothing to hide the body and keep warm, and may have a covering of fine white hair on the skin. Figure 10.2 lists the diagnostic criteria for anorexia nervosa.

DIAGNOSTIC CRITERIA FOR ANOREXIA NERVOSA

1. Refusal to maintain body weight at or above a minimally normal weight for age and height (e.g., weight loss leading to maintenance of body weight less than 85% of the expected weight; or failure to gain weight as expected during childhood or teen years, resulting in a body weight less than 85% of that expected).
2. Intense fear of becoming fat or gaining weight, even though underweight.
3. Disturbance in the way in which one's body weight or shape is experienced, undue influence of body weight or shape on self-evaluation, or denial of the seriousness of the current low body weight.
4. In postmenarcheal females, amenorrhea, i.e., the absence of at least three consecutive menstrual cycles. (A woman is considered to have amenorrhea if her periods occur only following hormone, e.g., estrogen, administration.)

Restricting type: During the current episode of Anorexia Nervosa, the person has not regularly engaged in binge-eating or purging behavior (i.e., self-induced vomiting or the misuse of laxatives, diuretics, or enemas).

Binge-eating–purging type: During the current episode of Anorexia Nervosa, the person has regularly engaged in binge-eating or purging behavior (i.e., self-induced vomiting or the misuse of laxatives, diuretics, or enemas).

Figure 10.2 Psychiatrists use these criteria to diagnose anorexia nervosa.

Reprinted, by permission, from American Psychiatric Association, 1994 (4).

DIAGNOSTIC CRITERIA FOR BULIMIA NERVOSA

1. Recurrent binge eating
   - Binge eating is the hurried eating of amounts of food definitely larger than most people would eat under similar situations, in a discrete period of time, e.g., within a 2-hour period.
   - Binge eating includes a sense of lack of control over eating (e.g., fear of not being able to stop eating, not able to control what or how much is eaten).
2. Recurrent inappropriate compensatory behavior in order to prevent weight gain. The individual regularly engages in either self-induced vomiting; misuse of laxatives, diuretics, or enemas; rigorous dieting or fasting; or excessive exercise.
3. At least two binge-eating sessions followed by compensatory behavior (purging) each week for at least 3 months.
4. Self-evaluation is unduly influenced by body shape and weight.
5. The disturbance does not occur exclusively during episodes of Anorexia Nervosa.

Purging type: Regularly engages in self-vomiting or misuse of laxatives, diuretics, or enemas.

Nonpurging type: Uses compensatory behaviors such as fasting or excessive exercise, but does not regularly engage in self-induced vomiting or misuse of laxatives, diuretics, or enemas.

Figure 10.3 Psychiatrists use these criteria to diagnose bulimia nervosa.

Reprinted, by permission, from American Psychiatric Association, 1994 (4).

Bulimia nervosa is characterized by recurrent consumption of food in amounts significantly greater than would customarily be consumed at one sitting, for example, an entire pizza, a half gallon (~2 L) of ice cream, plus a package of cookies. Purging follows this bingeing. The purging is usually one or some combination of the following behaviors: self-induced vomiting, intense exercise, laxatives, or diuretics. Bulimia is more easily hidden than anorexia nervosa because the individual is usually of normal weight; however, frequent weight fluctuations of more than 10 pounds (4.5 kg) are common. Bingeing is a coping response used by the individual to manage stress. The binge–purge cycle can increase in frequency until it occurs many times each day and the individual loses the ability to stop the cycle. The diagnostic criteria for bulimia nervosa are listed in figure 10.3. Quite commonly, anorexia nervosa and bulimia nervosa occur in the same individual, either at the same time or in succession.

Eating and weight control practices lie along a continuum, and in any given collegiate female population, eating behaviors exist all along the continuum. A dilemma for those working with this population is that it is sometimes difficult to discern between quirky eating behaviors that will never become a problem and quirky eating behaviors that will develop into pathogenic eating behaviors. Because a significant and undefined gray area between "normal" and "abnormal" eating exists, for clarity in this chapter the term *eating disorders* refers to anorexia nervosa and bulimia nervosa specifically.

Warning Signs for Anorexia Nervosa

- Commenting repeatedly about being or feeling fat, and asking questions such as "Do you think I'm fat?" when weight is below average
- Dramatic weight loss for no medical reason
- Reaching a weight that is below the ideal competitive weight for the given athlete and continuing to lose weight even during the off-season
- Preoccupation with food, calories, and weight

Warning Signs for Bulimia

- Eating secretively, which may be noted when food wrappers are found in the bedroom or locker or when an athlete is observed sneaking food from the table
- Disappearing repeatedly immediately after eating, especially if a large amount of food was eaten
- Appearing nervous or agitated if something prevents the person from being alone shortly after eating
- Losing or gaining extreme amounts of weight
- Smell or remnants of vomit in the rest room or elsewhere (vomit is sometimes stored in containers to be disposed of later)
- Disappearance of large amounts of food

Warning Signs for Both Disorders

- Complaining frequently of constipation or stomachaches
- Mood swings
- Social withdrawal
- Relentless, excessive exercise
- Excessive concern about weight
- Strict dieting followed by binges
- Increasing criticism of one's body
- Strong denial that a problem exists, even when there is hard evidence

Although an athlete may demonstrate abnormal eating patterns and cease menstruating, these symptoms alone are not sufficient for diagnosis of an eating disorder. Key clues to a serious problem are emotional swings and withdrawal from social relationships. A professional who is experienced and qualified in diagnosing and treating eating disorders should be contacted when an athlete's behavior causes concern.

Management and Care

Recognizing a suspected eating disorder, confronting the athlete, and directing the athlete into treatment very likely make for one of the most uncomfortable situations with which the strength and conditioning professional might be faced. It is a situation wrought with emotion and confusion. Because denial is part of the disease, the professional can begin to second-guess the need for intervention. Coaches and trainers are equipped to deal with physical injuries and illnesses but are not trained to deal with mental illness, nor should they be. It is not the responsibility of the strength and conditioning professional to treat or diagnose an eating disorder. It is his or her ethical responsibility to assist the athlete in attaining diagnosis and treatment. For additional reading on the topic, refer to the work of Faigenbaum and colleagues (28).

Steps in the Management of Eating Disorders

When an athlete is suspected of having an eating disorder, strength and conditioning professionals should know their responsibilities and know when referral is appropriate. The following steps can help the athletic staff establish appropriate policies and procedures for dealing with suspected eating disorders.

1. Fact Finding

Quite often, roommates or teammates observe a food-related problem. These individuals often share the information with the coach, athletic trainer, or strength and conditioning professional. This situation can easily catch sport staff off guard, so having a policy and procedure in place beforehand is imperative. Each facility has different resources and so may handle the management of eating disorders slightly differently. Some athletic departments have the team physician make the first assessment, some refer first to a sport nutritionist, and some refer to a therapist; ideally, the athlete is referred to all three. The goal of this initial assessment is *not* to diagnose an eating disorder but to gather information from which to make the decision whether formal referral for such is necessary. Some warning signs from the initial assessment may include

- lack of menstrual cycle (amenorrhea),
- significant weight loss and refusal to gain weight,
- refusal to make recommended dietary changes,
- reports from the athlete that conflict with what others observe, and
- strong denial that there is a problem or making excuses.

Maintaining athletic performance does not indicate lack of a problem because in many cases performance is not affected until late in the disease, when stress fractures, recurrent illness, and fainting may occur. Ironically, eating-disordered individuals might display improved performance for some time if weight loss allows faster running or higher jumping. In fact, a difficult part of the recovery from an eating disorder for some athletes is a decrease in performance or the inability to make a weight standard. The disease is quite functional for the individual, so one of the greatest difficulties of treatment is finding things about recovery that are more important and rewarding to the individual than the disease itself.

2. Confronting

If the initial assessment warrants, the individual needs to be confronted with the fact that people are worried about his or her health and that it appears he or she needs further assessment. Again, a policy and plan need to be in place so that there is no confusion about what should be said and how the meeting should end. People familiar with the situation and close to the individual should be involved, and they should continue to stress their concern about the individual's health and cite observations and hard data that cause concern. Denial and disdain on the part of the individual are to be expected.

When the person is a minor, a designated athletic staff member should contact the parents to alert them of the situation and discuss insurance. Even if the individual is not a minor, the staff may contact parents if they support the athlete financially and are responsible for insurance.

It is imperative that a plan be in place for managing athletes with suspected eating disorders.

3. Referring

Ideally, as the meeting ends, the athlete schedules an appointment for an assessment at a clinic or hospital (the facility should be contacted beforehand to set up the appointment or admission) or, depending on the severity of the situation, is transported for admission.

Some communities have eating disorder clinics; others do not. The sidebar provides a list of additional resources for those who do not have easy access to community resources.

4. Following Up

Only in the most severe cases is the athlete admitted to a hospital. Some athletes opt to go home to receive treatment if they live locally. Many continue attending school, which brings up the question whether continued sport participation should be allowed. In some cases, if the athlete appears too fragile, an injured status is appropriate. For some athletes, however, taking away their participation on the team can cause even more emotional turmoil. Participation in strength and conditioning activities should be considered separate from competitive participation. Each department, in consultation with the physician, psychologist, nutritionist, and other professionals involved in treatment, must make these determinations based on the situation, considering medical, ethical, and liability concerns.

Eating Disorder Resources

National Eating Disorders Association
3 Stewart St., Ste. 803
Seattle, WA 98101
206-382-3587
800-931-2237
info@NationalEatingDisorders.org
www.edap.org

International Association of Eating Disorders Professionals
P.O. Box 1295
Pekin, IL 61555
309-346-3341
800-800-8126
iaedpmembers@earthlink.net
www.iaedp.com

The Renfrew Center Foundation
475 Spring La.
Philadelphia, PA 19128
877-367-3383
foundation@renfrew.org
www.renfrew.org

National Association of Anorexia Nervosa and Associated Disorders
P.O. Box 7
Highland Park, IL 60035
847-831-3438
www.anad.org

Remuda Ranch Center
1 E. Apache St.
Wickenburg, AZ 85390
928-684-3913
800-445-1900
www.remuda-ranch.com

What Not to Do

Sometimes even the best intentions can make suspected eating problems worse. Common mistakes include trying to help athletes by monitoring their food intake, having them weigh in frequently, giving them nutrition information, or telling them that they look fine. While nutrition information, weighing practices, and careful comments about weight are important in the general prevention of pathological eating, once the problem exists, these measures are futile. When a problem is suspected, avoid stopgap measures. Instead, the individual should be referred for a full assessment.

Eating disorders can never be corrected by simple provision of nutritional information to the individual who is already affected. Any person with an eating disorder is usually already an expert about the nutrient content of food, digestion, and absorption. For example, a young woman in this author's acquaintance who was struggling with bulimia was studying to be an exercise scientist and could recite the Krebs cycle from memory. But even with this knowledge, she could not bring herself to eat fat and could not be convinced that she was not huge, even though she was very lean. The diseases do not have a rational basis, and they do not occur because the individual lacks information. An eating disorder is psychological, and the affected individual is usually not receptive to rational information about healthy eating and weight until the underlying fears, phobias, and insecurities have been addressed.

The strength and conditioning professional's job is not to treat an eating disorder; it is to be aware of warning signs and to refer when a problem is suspected.

OBESITY

Obesity is discussed separately from eating disorders here because it is not typically considered an eating disorder. One syndrome related to eating disorders—**binge-eating disorder**—does lead to obesity. It is estimated that about 30% of those who are severely obese suffer from binge-eating disorder, which is the behavior of ingesting a large amount of food without the purging behavior seen in bulimia nervosa (80, 102).

Aside from being a performance hindrance to athletes, obesity poses serious health problems. Obesity increases the risk of hyperlipidemia (elevated blood lipids), coronary heart disease, stroke, hypertension, glucose intolerance, type 2 diabetes, gallbladder disease, osteoarthritis, sleep apnea, and some types of cancer.

Obesity is a complex, multifactorial condition, with genetic, physiological, metabolic, social, cultural, environmental, and psychological components. Obesity is complex, and the treatment of obesity is equally complex. While great strides have been made in the treatment of heart disease and cancer, no such success story exists for obesity treatment. Unfortunately, maintenance of weight loss for a period longer than three to five years occurs in only a minority of the severely obese population. Obesity is highly resistant to treatment and consequently is one of the most challenging medical and social problems today.

Obesity in athletic populations is, of course, much less prevalent than in the general population. Obesity is seen, however, in sports in which increasing mass, whether fat or lean, is promoted (e.g., American football linemen, throwers). Obesity also manifests in susceptible athletes after their competitive careers are over and physical activity decreases. Strength and conditioning professionals are likely to encounter obese individuals in both the athletic and general populations; therefore, this section addresses both populations.

A thorough assessment of the individual enables the strength and conditioning professional to know whether treatment is appropriate and, if so, to match the best treatment to the individual. **Body mass index (BMI)** is the preferred body composition assessment for obese individuals. Skinfold assessment becomes inaccurate because of the size of the skinfold and the lack of standardized formulas for obese adults. Body mass index is calculated as follows:

$$\text{weight (kilograms)} / \text{height (meters)}^2$$

To estimate BMI using pounds and inches, use this equation:

$$[\text{weight (pounds)} / \text{height (inches)}^2] \times 703$$

Overweight is defined as a BMI of 25 to 29.9 kg/m^2 and *obesity* as a BMI of 30 kg/m^2 or more. Waist circumference, as an indicator of abdominal fat disproportionate to total body fat, can also be assessed and is an additive factor for determining risk. For men, even higher risk of disease is associated with a waist circumference greater than 40 inches (102 cm), and for women, with a waist measurement of more than 35 inches (89 cm). Waist circumferences lose their usefulness in individuals with a BMI exceeding 35.

The range for acceptable, normal, or optimum BMI for Asian populations should be narrowed to 18.5 to 23 kg/m^2. For this group, a BMI of 23 kg/m^2 or higher marks a moderate increase in risk and a BMI of 27.5 kg/m^2 or more represents obesity.

Table 10.8 describes the various classifications of overweight and obesity. For reference, table 10.9 provides the weights and heights that correspond to BMIs of 25, 27, and 30. For more information about the screening process and risk assessment, refer to the summary of the Expert Panel on the Identification, Evaluation, and Treatment of Overweight in Adults (58). Of course, the strength and conditioning professional must remain aware that these BMIs are worthless in athletes who carry higher than average lean body mass. These athletes may appear obese on paper when in reality they have very low body fat.

Although all obese individuals share the trait of excess body fat, they cannot be treated homogeneously. They must be screened for coexisting illnesses such as diabetes, orthopedic problems, cardiac disease, psychological disorders such as binge-eating disorder or depression, social and cultural influences, and readiness. The ultimate question is whether the need for treatment (i.e., weight loss) outweighs the risk of the emotional duress of unsuccessful treatment. Obese athletes who are mandated to lose weight pose a special challenge because losing weight is dictated from an external source and is not an internalized goal. Weight loss takes a great deal of dedication from within the individual. If the assessment suggests that the athlete is not committed to losing weight, the time and resources of the strength and conditioning professional are better spent elsewhere.

Obesity is not the same condition in each individual. Thorough assessment helps determine which treatment is appropriate and, more important, whether the individual is ready for treatment.

TABLE 10.8

Classification of Overweight and Obesity by BMI

Classification	Obesity class	BMI (kg/m)^2
Underweight		<18.5
Normal		18.5-24.9
Overweight		25.0-29.9
Obesity	I	30.0-34.9
	II	35.0-39.9
Extreme obesity	III	≥40

BMI = body mass index. See the chapter text for BMI guidelines for Asian populations.

TABLE 10.9

Selected BMI Units Categorized by Height and Weight

Height in inches (cm)	BMI of 25 kg/m^2	BMI of 27 kg/m^2	BMI of 30 kg/m^2
	BODY WEIGHT IN POUNDS (KG)		
58 (147.32)	119 (53.98)	129 (58.51)	143 (64.86)
59 (149.86)	124 (56.25)	133 (60.33)	148 (67.13)
60 (152.40)	128 (58.06)	138 (62.60)	153 (69.40)
61 (154.94)	132 (59.87)	143 (64.86)	158 (71.67)
62 (157.48)	136 (61.69)	147 (66.68)	164 (74.39)
63 (160.02)	141 (63.96)	152 (68.95)	169 (76.66)
64 (162.56)	145 (65.77)	157 (71.21)	174 (78.93)
65 (165.10)	150 (68.04)	162 (73.48)	180 (81.65)
66 (167.64)	155 (70.31)	167 (75.75)	186 (84.37)
67 (170.18)	159 (72.12)	172 (78.02)	191 (86.64)
68 (172.72)	164 (74.39)	177 (80.29)	197 (89.36)
69 (175.26)	169 (76.66)	182 (82.56)	203 (92.08)
70 (177.80)	174 (78.93)	188 (85.28)	207 (93.89)
71 (180.34)	179 (81.19)	193 (87.54)	215 (97.52)
72 (182.88)	184 (83.46)	199 (90.27)	221 (100.25)
73 (185.42)	189 (85.73)	204 (92.53)	227 (102.97)
74 (187.96)	194 (88.00)	210 (95.26)	233 (105.69)
75 (190.50)	200 (90.72)	216 (97.98)	240 (108.86)
76 (193.04)	205 (92.99)	221 (100.25)	246 (111.58)

BMI = body mass index.

Metric conversion formula = weight/height^2 [kg/m^2].

Example of BMI calculation: A person who weighs 78.93 kg and is 177 cm tall has a BMI of 25: weight/height^2 = 78.93 kg/(1.77 m)^2 = 25.

Nonmetric conversion formula = weight/height^2 × 703 [(pounds/inches^2) × 703].

Example of BMI calculation: A person who weighs 164 pounds and is 68 inches (or 5 feet 8 inches) tall has a BMI of 25: weight/height^2 × 703 = [164 pounds/(68 inches)^2] × 703 = 25.

CONCLUSION

The primary role of nutrition in strength and conditioning enhancement is to support athletic performance. Adequate hydration, appropriate energy intake, and adequate protein, carbohydrate, fat, vitamin, and mineral intakes allow athletes to reap maximal benefits from training, barring injuries and lack of desire. A general understanding of nutrition principles and applications is essential for strength and conditioning professionals, not only to help athletes reach their full potential, but also to help them sort through the confusing information and misinformation so prevalent in sport nutrition.

Eating disorders and obesity are complex, multifactorial diseases and, as such, require a multidisciplinary team approach. The strength and conditioning professional must understand the problems, be aware of how to assess the problems, and know when to refer to experts.

KEY TERMS

amino acid 206
anorexia nervosa 225
binge-eating disorder 230
body mass index (BMI) 230
bulimia nervosa 225
carbohydrate 208
carbohydrate loading 221
cell turnover 207
cholesterol 212
complementary proteins 207
dehydration 217
diet-induced thermogenesis 223
Dietary Reference Intakes (DRIs) 206
disaccharides 209
eating disorder 226
electrolytes 219
energy 222
energy density 225
fat 212
fiber 211
Food Guide Pyramid 203
glycemic index (GI) 209
glycogen 209
glycogenesis 209
ketosis 211
lipid 212
mineral 216
monosaccharides 208
monounsaturated 212
MyPyramid 203
negative calorie balance 207
nutrient density 225
obesity 230
osteoporosis 217
polypeptide 206
polysaccharides 209
polyunsaturated 212
precompetition meal 220
protein 206
protein quality 207
saturated 212
vegan 207
vitamin 214
voluntary dehydration 218

STUDY QUESTIONS

1. Which of the following proteins has an amino acid profile MOST similar to the body's needs?
   a. soy
   b. egg
   c. wheat
   d. rice

2. Which of the following BEST explains the requirement for increased protein intake by athletes?
   a. decreased protein oxidation during aerobic exercise
   b. increased need for tissue repair
   c. restriction of calories to lose weight
   d. the quality of protein consumed

3. Which of the following has the GREATEST influence on an athlete's dietary carbohydrate requirement?
   a. current average daily fat intake
   b. body size and body fat percentage
   c. type, duration, and frequency of exercise
   d. resting blood sugar levels

4. Which of the following BEST describes dietary fat consumption?
   a. It should be less than 15% of total calories for healthy athletes.
   b. It should never be higher than 40% of total calories.
   c. Its restriction can be harmful to health and performance.
   d. It is not an essential nutrient.

5. Which of the following is characteristic of anorexia nervosa?
   a. normal body weight
   b. very low dietary fat intake
   c. preoccupation with food
   d. secretive eating

6. When an eating disorder is suspected, the strength and conditioning professional should
   a. monitor the athlete's daily food intake.
   b. require frequent weigh-ins.
   c. encourage further assessment by an eating disorder specialist.
   d. provide nutritional information.

SECTION 2

Testing and Evaluation

CHAPTER 11

Principles of Test Selection and Administration

Everett Harman, PhD

After completing this chapter, you will be able to

- identify and explain reasons for performing tests,
- understand testing terminology to communicate clearly with athletes and colleagues,
- evaluate a test's validity and reliability,
- select appropriate tests, and
- administer test protocols properly and safely.

The strength and conditioning professional with a broad understanding of exercise science can effectively use tests and measurements to make training decisions that help athletes achieve their goals and maximize their potential. Tests and measurements form the objective core of the evaluation process. This chapter covers the reasons for testing, testing terminology, evaluation of test quality, the selection of appropriate tests, and aspects of proper test administration.

REASONS FOR TESTING

Testing helps athletes and coaches assess athletic talent and identify physical abilities and areas in need of improvement. In addition, test scores can be used in goal setting. Baseline measurements can be used to establish starting points against which achievable goals can be set, and testing at regular intervals can help track an athlete's progress in reaching those goals. Using tests as a basis for goal setting allows coaches to set specific goals for individual athletes that, when taken together, accomplish group or team objectives (see chapter 8 for more information about goal setting).

Assessment of Athletic Talent

It is important for a coach to determine whether an individual has the physical potential to play a sport at the competitive level of the team. That judgment is not difficult if the candidate has already excelled at the sport elsewhere and is of adequate body size. However, in many cases, candidates have not clearly demonstrated their competitive abilities or may lack experience in the sport. The coach then needs some way of determining whether the candidate has the necessary basic physical abilities that, in combination with technique training and practice, could produce a competitive player. Field tests serve as tools for such assessment.

Identification of Physical Abilities in Need of Improvement

While some physical abilities are innate and not amenable to change, other physical abilities can be improved through physical training. Tests can be used by the strength and conditioning professional to determine which deficits of the athletes can be ameliorated by participation in prescribed group or individual exercise programs (2, 21).

Testing can be used to assess athletic talent, identify physical abilities and areas in need of improvement, set goals, and evaluate progress.

TESTING TERMINOLOGY

To communicate clearly with athletes and colleagues, strength and conditioning professionals should use consistent terminology. The following terms and definitions are widely accepted and are used in this text.

test—A procedure for assessing ability in a particular endeavor (1).

field test—A test used to assess ability that is performed away from the laboratory and does not require extensive training or expensive equipment (8).

measurement—The process of collecting test data (5).

evaluation—The process of analyzing test results for the purpose of making decisions. For example, a coach exam-

The opinions or assertions contained herein are the private views of the author and are not to be construed as official or as reflecting the views of the Army or the Department of Defense.

ines the results of physical performance tests to determine whether the athlete's training program is effective in helping achieve the training goals or whether modifications in the program are needed.

pretest—A test administered before the beginning of training to determine the athlete's initial basic ability levels. A pretest allows the coach to design the training program in keeping with the athlete's initial training level and the overall program objectives.

midtest—A test administered one or more times during the training period to assess progress and modify the program as needed to maximize benefit.

formative evaluation—Periodic reevaluation based on midtests administered during the training, usually at regular intervals (6). It enables monitoring of the athlete's progress and adjustment of the training program for the athlete's individual needs. It also allows evaluation of different training methods and collection of normative data. Regular modification of the training program based on formative evaluation keeps the training program fresh and interesting and helps avoid physical and mental staleness.

posttest—Test administered after the training period to determine the success of the training program in achieving the training objectives.

EVALUATION OF TEST QUALITY

Test results are useful only if the test actually measures what it is supposed to measure (validity) and if the measurement is repeatable (reliability). These two characteristics are the key factors in evaluating test quality and must be present in order for the test to be beneficial.

Validity

Validity refers to the degree to which a test or test item measures what it is supposed to measure, and is the most important characteristic of testing (6, 17, 18, 19, 28). For tests of physical properties such as height and weight, validity is easy to establish. For example, close correspondence between the readings on a spring scale and the readings on a calibrated balance scale indicates validity of weighing with the spring scale. The validity of tests of basic sport abilities is more difficult to establish. There are several types of validity, including construct validity, face validity, content validity, and criterion-referenced validity.

Validity is the degree to which a test or test item measures what it is supposed to measure; this is the most important characteristic of testing.

Construct Validity

Construct validity is the ability of a test to represent the underlying construct (the theory developed to organize and explain some aspects of existing knowledge and observations). Construct validity refers to overall validity, or the extent to which the test actually measures what it was designed to measure (27). Face validity, content validity, and criterion-referenced validity, defined next, are secondary to and provide evidence for construct validity.

To be valid, physical performance tests should measure abilities important in the sport, produce repeatable results (see the later section on reliability), measure the performance of one athlete at a time (unless otherwise specified in the protocol), be interesting, appear meaningful, be of suitable difficulty, be able to differentiate between various levels of ability, permit accurate scoring, include a sufficient number of trials, and stand the test of statistical evaluation (1). Given the choice between two valid tests, consideration should be given to simplicity and economy of test administration.

Face Validity

Face validity is the appearance to the athlete and other casual observers that the test measures what it is purported to measure. If a test or test item has face validity, the athlete is more likely to respond to it positively (4). The assessment of face validity is generally informal and nonquantitative. In other fields, such as psychology, tests may be deliberately constructed to have poor face validity because if examinees realize what a test or test item is supposed to measure, they can answer deceptively to manipulate their scores. For tests of basic athletic abilities, however, face validity is desirable based on the assumption that anyone taking a test of physical ability wants to do well and is thus motivated by a test that appears to measure a relevant capability.

Content Validity

Content validity is the assessment by experts that the testing covers all relevant subtopics or component abilities in appropriate proportions (4). For athletic testing, these include all the component abilities needed for a particular sport or sport position. Examples of component abilities in athletics are jumping ability, sprinting ability, and muscular strength of the arms (19). A test battery for potential soccer players should include, at minimum, tests of sprinting speed, agility, coordination, and kicking power. To ensure content validity, the test developer should list the ability components to be assessed and make sure they are all represented on the test. In addition, the proportion of the total score attributable to a particular component ability should be proportional to the importance of that component to total performance. While the terms *face validity* and *content validity* are sometimes used interchangeably, the latter relates to actual validity while the former relates to the appearance of validity to nonexperts (4).

Criterion-Referenced Validity

Criterion-referenced validity is the extent to which test scores are associated with some other measure of the same ability. There are three types of criterion-referenced validity: concurrent, predictive, and discriminant.

Concurrent validity is the extent to which test scores are associated with those of other accepted tests that measure the same ability. Criterion-referenced validity is often estimated statistically. For example, a Pearson product moment correlation coefficient based on the scores on a new body fat assessment device and those from underwater weighing provides a measure of the concurrent validity of the new test. **Convergent validity** is evidenced by high positive correlation between results of the test being assessed and those of the recognized measure of the construct (the "gold standard"). Convergent validity is the type of concurrent validity that field tests used by strength and conditioning professionals should exhibit. A test may be preferable to the "gold standard" if it exhibits convergent validity with the standard but is less demanding in terms of time, equipment, expense, or expertise.

Predictive validity is the extent to which the test score corresponds with future behavior or performance. This can be measured through comparison of a test score with some measure of success in the sport itself. For example, one could calculate the statistical correlation between the overall score on a battery of tests used to assess potential for basketball and a measurement of actual basketball performance as indicated by a composite of such quantities as points scored, rebounds, assists, blocked shots, forced turnovers, and steals.

Discriminant validity is the ability of a test to distinguish between two different constructs and is evidenced by a low correlation between the results of the test and those of tests of a different construct (20). It is best if tests in a battery measure relatively independent ability components (e.g., flexibility, speed, aerobic endurance). Good discriminant validity of tests in a battery avoids unnecessary expenditures of time, energy, and resources in administering tests that correlate very highly with each other.

Reliability

Reliability is a measure of the degree of consistency or repeatability of a test (6, 19, 28). If an athlete whose ability does not change is measured two times with a perfectly reliable test, the same score is obtained both times. On an unreliable test, an individual could obtain a high score on one day and a low score on another. A test must be reliable to be valid, because highly variable results have little meaning. There are several ways to determine the reliability of a test; the most obvious one is to administer the same test twice to the same group of athletes. Statistical correlation of the scores from the two administrations provides a measure of **test-retest reliability**. Any difference between the two sets of scores represents measurement error, which can arise from any of the following factors (6):

- Intrasubject (within subjects) variability
- Lack of interrater (between raters) reliability or agreement
- Intrarater (within raters) variability
- Failure of the test itself to provide consistent results

Reliability is a measure of the degree of consistency or repeatability of a test. A test must be reliable to be valid, because highly variable results have little meaning.

Intrasubject variability is a lack of consistent performance by the person tested. **Interrater reliability**, also referred to as **objectivity** or **interrater agreement** (6, 19, 28), is the degree to which different raters agree. A clearly defined scoring system and competent scorers who are trained and experienced with the test are essential to enhance interrater reliability. For example, even a test that appears simple, such as timing a 40-yard (37 m) dash with a stopwatch, can exhibit both random and systematic error if the timer is not trained and experienced. Sprint times obtained using hand-held stopwatches are typically shorter than those obtained using automatic timers because raters using stopwatches exhibit reaction-time delay when pressing the start button in response to the gun but do not delay in pressing the button at the finish line because they can see the athlete approaching. Interrater reliability is particularly important if different scorers administer tests to different subgroups of athletes. A subgroup with a relatively lenient scorer will have artificially inflated scores. To get an accurate measure of improvement, the same scorer should test a group at the beginning and the end of the training period. If there are two scorers and the scorer at the beginning is more or less lenient than the scorer at the end, the resulting measurements may be worthless for comparative purposes. Consider a situation in which an athlete is tested in the squat. If the pretest scorer is more lenient (requiring less depth on the squat) than the posttest scorer, the athlete may achieve a lower test score on the posttest despite having made significant improvement in strength.

Sources of interrater differences include variations in calibrating testing devices, preparing athletes, and running the test. Different testers may motivate athletes to different degrees, based on factors such as personality, status, physical appearance, demeanor, and sex. A common scenario that increases interrater variability occurs when the coach tests some of the athletes while an assistant tests others. The athletes may be inspired to do better on the tests administered by the coach.

Intrarater variability is the lack of consistent scores by a given tester. For example, a coach eager to see improvement may unintentionally be more lenient on a posttest than on a pretest (10, 18, 22). Other causes of intrarater variability include inadequate training, inattentiveness, lack of concentration, or failure to follow standardized procedures for device calibration, athlete preparation, test administration, or test scoring. To avoid such problems, accurate and consistent athletic testing should be a priority for all strength and conditioning professionals.

Finally, sometimes the test itself might fail to provide consistent results. This may occur if a physical performance test requires a technique in which the athlete has not developed consistency. More technique-intensive tests generally exhibit greater variability in results and require more pretest practice to produce consistency.

For a measure to be valid, it must be reliable; but a reliable test may not be valid because the test may not measure what it is supposed to measure. For example, both the 60 m (66-yard) dash and the 1.5-mile (2.4 km) run are reliable field tests, but only the 1.5-mile run is considered a valid field test for cardiovascular fitness. It is also possible for a test to be highly reliable for one group (e.g., college tennis players) but only moderately reliable for another group (e.g., high school tennis players) because of differences in physical or emotional maturity and skill level, which can affect test performance.

TEST SELECTION

When evaluating tests for high levels of validity and reliability, the strength and conditioning professional must rely on his or her knowledge base and practical experience in the sport. The strength and conditioning professional must consider sport specificity (e.g., metabolic energy systems, biomechanical movement patterns), athlete experience, training status, age, sex, and environmental factors when selecting tests.

Metabolic Energy System Specificity

A valid test must emulate the energy requirements of the sport for which ability is being assessed. Thus, the strength and conditioning professional should have a thorough understanding of the three basic energy systems (phosphagen, glycolytic, and oxidative) and their interrelationships in order to apply the principle of specificity when choosing or designing valid tests to measure athletic ability for specific sports (11, 12, 15, 23, 29, 30, 31). For example, in choosing an appropriate test for running ability in basketball, the strength and conditioning professional must understand that basketball is predominantly an anaerobic running sport (13, 14) and also be familiar with the distances and directions of sprints in a basketball game. It is best for the tests to simulate the physical movements and energy demands of a real game.

Biomechanical Movement Pattern Specificity

All else being equal, the more similar the test is to an important movement in the sport, the better. Sports differ in their physical demands. For example, the vertical jump test is very specific to basketball and volleyball, both of which involve vertical jumping during play, but less specific to hockey, which does not involve vertical jumping. Positions within a sport differ as well. An American football defensive lineman needs pushing strength to move opposing linemen out of the way and 5- to 15-yard (5 to 14 m) sprint speed to reach the opposing quarterback, while a wide receiver depends less on pushing strength but must be able to sprint 30 to 100 yards (27-91 m) quickly. Thus, the bench press and 10-yard (9 m) sprint test would be more relevant to the lineman, while sprint tests of 30 to 100 yards (27-91 m) would be more relevant to the wide receiver.

For a test to be valid, it must emulate the energy requirements and important movements of the sport for which ability is being tested.

Experience and Training Status

For a well-trained, experienced athlete, a technique-intensive test may be appropriate because it can be very sport specific, and one can assume that poor technique will not impair performance of the test. However, this assumption cannot be made for an athlete just learning or trying out for a sport. The number of one-leg hops needed to travel 27 yards (25 m) may represent a valid and reliable test of plyometric strength for an experienced long jumper but not for a novice (8).

Testers must also consider the training status of the athletes being tested. It would not be fair, for example, to ask a baseball player to perform a 3-mile (4.8 km) run test a week before the beginning of fall practice, because the player has probably been doing interval training and relatively short runs (11). A strength test using free weight equipment may not be fair to an athlete who has been training exclusively with isokinetic equipment. A lower body strength test using the parallel squat would not be a fair test for an athlete who has trained using the leg press exclusively.

Age and Sex

Both age and sex can affect the validity and reliability of a test. For example, the 1.5-mile (2.4 km) run may be a valid and reliable field test of aerobic power for college-aged men and women (9) but may not be appropriate for preadolescents because of their probable lack of experience and interest in sustained running (3). A test of the maximum number of chin-ups that can be performed may be a valid test of elbow flexion muscular endurance for male wrestlers, but it is not valid for females because many females lack sufficient upper body strength to complete even one chin-up. The test is thus not capable of differentiating muscular endurance levels among females, for whom a test of maximum pulldown repetitions with a percentage of body weight would be more appropriate.

Environmental Factors

It is necessary to consider the environment when selecting and administering tests of basic athletic ability. High ambient temperature, especially in combination with high humidity, can impair endurance exercise performance, pose health risks, and lower the validity of an aerobic endurance exercise test. Aerobic endurance performance may be impaired when the temperature approaches 80 °F, especially if the humidity exceeds 50% (24). The effects of temperature and humidity on aerobic endurance performance can create problems for comparing the results of tests administered at different times of year, on different days, and even at different times of day. For example, the maximal oxygen uptake of an athlete impaired by the heat is underestimated by the 1.5-mile (2.4 km) run test. Run times can also be impaired by cold temperatures. Thus, outdoor aerobic endurance tests may be inappropriate at locations characterized by wide fluctuations in temperature. In such places, aerobic endurance tests can be administered on an indoor track, if available, or with a treadmill or stationary cycle.

Altitude can also impair performance on aerobic endurance tests, although not on tests of strength and power (16). Norms on aerobic endurance tests should be adjusted when testing at altitudes exceeding 1,900 feet (580 m). Up to about 9,000 feet (2,740 m), maximal oxygen uptake declines by approximately 5% for each 3,000 feet (910 m) of elevation. At even higher altitudes, maximal oxygen uptake declines more sharply. Athletes who arrive at a relatively high altitude after living near sea level for an extended period of time should be given at least 10 days to acclimatize before undergoing aerobic endurance tests (16).

Athletes' experience, training status, age, and sex can affect test performance, so these factors should be considered in test selection. Environmental factors such as temperature, humidity, and altitude can also influence test performance, so testers should try to standardize environmental conditions as much as possible.

TEST ADMINISTRATION

To achieve accurate test results, tests must be administered safely, correctly, and in an organized manner. Staff should ensure the health and safety of athletes, testers should be carefully selected and trained, tests should be well organized and administered efficiently, and athletes should be properly prepared and instructed.

Health and Safety Considerations

Even though all athletes should be medically cleared before being permitted to physically train and compete, the strength and conditioning professional must be aware of testing conditions that can threaten the health of athletes and be observant of signs and symptoms of health problems that warrant exclusion from testing. The strength and conditioning professional must remain attentive to the health status of athletes, especially before, during, and after maximal exertions that occur during training, testing, and competition. Strenuous exercise, such as maximal runs or 1-repetition maximum (1RM) tests, can uncover or worsen existing heart problems, such as impaired blood flow to the heart muscle and irregular heartbeats. Standard medical screening cannot always reveal hidden heart problems, which occasionally result in fatality among young athletes. Heat injury is also a risk during heavy physical exertion in hot environments, especially when humidity is high. Athletes should wear light clothing in warm weather and should be encouraged to drink ample water in the hours before heavy physical exertion in the heat. Musculoskeletal injuries can also be a problem. If symptoms are ignored, recovery can be greatly delayed.

Medical referral may be warranted for an athlete who persistently has any of the following symptoms: chest pressure, pain, or discomfort; listlessness; light-headedness; dizziness; confusion; headache; deeply reddened or cold and clammy skin; irregular pulse; bone or joint pain; blurred vision; nausea; or shortness of breath, rapid pulse, or weakness either not commensurate with the level of exertion or unresponsive to rest. Such symptoms can occur long after exercise is terminated. Even symptoms that occur only once, if severe (such as loss of consciousness), call for immediate medical attention.

When aerobic endurance exercise tests are being administered in a hot environment, caution must be observed to protect both the health and safety of the athlete and the validity of the test. Table 11.1 lists temperature limits at various ranges of relative humidity for strenuous exercise testing, and the sidebar on page 244 lists guidelines from the National Institute of Environmental Health Sciences for aerobic endurance testing in the heat.

Selection and Training of Testers

Test administrators should be well trained and should have a thorough understanding of all testing procedures and protocols. The testing supervisor should make sure that all novice personnel perform and score all tests correctly, as in timing sprint speed with a stopwatch or determining a 1RM back squat. It is essential that all testers have sufficient practice so that the scores they obtain correlate closely with those produced by experienced and reliable personnel. The testers should be trained to explain and administer the tests as consistently as possible. Test reliability is impaired, for example, if one test administrator provides considerable verbal encouragement to a group of athletes while another tester provides no verbal encouragement to another group. Administrators should have a checklist of materials needed for testing and written test protocols to refer to if questions arise during the testing process.

Recording Forms

Scoring forms should be developed before the testing session and should have space for all test results and comments. This allows test time to be used more efficiently and reduces the incidence of recording errors.

TABLE 11.1

Temperature Limits at Various Ranges of Relative Humidity for Strenuous Exercise Testing

Relative humidity (percent)	Temperature limit
0	95 °F (35 °C)
1-20	90 °F (32 °C)
21-50	85 °F (29 °C)
51-90	80 °F (27 °C)
91-100	75 °F (24 °C)

Adapted, by permission, from McArdle, Katch, and Katch, 1996 (26).

Aerobic Endurance Testing in the Heat

Follow these guidelines to minimize health risks and obtain accurate results when testing athletes in hot environments.

1. During the weeks prior to the test, athletes should engage in enough training to establish a baseline of fitness in the activity being tested.
2. Avoid testing under extreme combinations of heat and humidity. Table 11.1 lists the combinations of temperature and humidity at which heat injury risk is present. Using temperature limits at least 5 °F (3 °C) below those listed is recommended, especially on sunny days, to provide a safety margin and enable better test performance. On days when the temperature is expected to or has exceeded the recommended limits, indoor facilities should be used if available, or testing should be conducted during morning or early evening hours when temperatures are acceptable.
3. The athletes, especially those coming from cool climates, should be acclimatized to the heat and humidity for at least one week prior to testing. Start with short workouts and progress to workouts of longer duration.
4. Athletes should make sure they are well hydrated in the 24-hour period preceding aerobic endurance testing in the heat. A good indication of adequate hydration is a plentiful volume of clear urine. Fluid intake should continue until a half hour before testing, at which time athletes should consume about 500 ml (17 fluid ounces). Salt tablets should generally be avoided.
5. Athletes should be encouraged to drink during exercise in the heat, ideally 150 to 250 ml (5-9 fluid ounces) every 15 minutes. Plain water is most appropriate for exercise up to 1 hour in duration, but glucose-electrolyte sport drinks are preferable for longer exercise.
6. Athletes should wear a light-colored, loose-fitting tank top and shorts, preferably of a mesh material. Male athletes may be allowed to go shirtless.
7. Heart rate may be monitored to detect extreme reactions to the heat.
8. Be attentive to possible symptoms of heatstroke or heat exhaustion: cramps, nausea, dizziness, difficulty in walking or standing, faintness, garbled speech, lack of sweat, red or ashen skin, and goose bumps.
9. Be aware of the symptoms of hyponatremia or water intoxication, a potentially fatal condition in which excess water intake reduces blood sodium to dangerously low levels. Symptoms may include extremely dilute urine in combination with bloated skin, altered consciousness, or loss of consciousness, with no increase in body temperature. A victim of hyponatremia should never be given fluid and should be treated by a physician.
10. Athletes should be encouraged to eat foods high in magnesium and potassium, such as cantaloupe, watermelon, tomatoes, carrots, and cucumbers, which are preferable to supplements.
11. Proficient medical coverage should be readily available so that an athlete encountering a test-related health problem can be very rapidly treated or evacuated (or both).

From Brukner and Khan, 2006 (7) and McArdle, Katch, and Katch, 2007 (26).

Test Format

A well-organized testing session, in which the athletes are aware of testing purpose and procedures, usually enhances the reliability of test measures. Reliable measures obtained from valid tests are a great asset in assessing fitness levels and evaluating changes over a period of time.

Test planning must address such issues as whether athletes will be tested all at once or in groups and whether the same person will administer a given test to all athletes. The latter is preferable if time and schedules permit, because it eliminates the issue of interrater reliability. If this is not feasible, the test supervisor can allow simple, well-defined tests (such as counting correct chin-ups) to be administered by different testers and tests requiring schooled judgment (as of proper form in the squat) to be scored by the most skilled personnel. As a rule, each tester should administer only one test at a time, especially when the tests require complex judgments. It is permissible to have one tester alternate between two testing stations to avoid wasting time as athletes get ready.

However, the tester must focus on only one test at a time.

Testing Batteries and Multiple Testing Trials

When time is limited and there is a large group of athletes, duplicate test setups may be employed to make efficient use of testing time. For example, when one is conducting the 300-yard (274 m) shuttle, two test courses can be made available (15). A tester can administer up to two nonfatiguing tests in sequence to an athlete as long as test reliability can be maintained. For example, at a two-test flexibility station staffed by only one tester, the athlete can perform the sit-and-reach test and the shoulder elevation test one right after the other.

When multiple trials of a test (e.g., the repeated trials it takes to find a 1RM) or a battery of tests are performed, allow complete recovery between trials (32). There should be at least 2 to 3 minutes of rest between attempts that are not close to the athlete's maximum and 3 to 5 minutes between attempts that are close to the maximum, as judged by the relative difficulty of the previous trial or testing set. When administering a **test battery** (e.g., one in which wrestlers perform maximal-repetition pull-up and push-up tests for assessment of local muscular endurance), tests should be separated by at least 5 minutes to prevent the effects of fatigue from confounding test results (also see the following section, "Sequence of Tests").

When multiple trials of a test or a battery of tests are performed, allow complete recovery between trials.

Sequence of Tests

Knowledge of exercise science can help determine the proper order of tests and the duration of rest periods between tests to ensure test reliability. For example, a test that maximally taxes the phosphagen energy system requires 3 to 5 minutes of rest for complete recovery (23, 25), whereas a maximal test of the lactic acid energy system requires at least 1 hour for complete recovery (12). Therefore, tests requiring high-skill movements, such as reaction and coordination tests, should be administered before tests that are likely to produce fatigue and confound the results of subsequent tests. A logical sequence, although there are some variations, is to administer tests in this order:

- Nonfatiguing tests (e.g., height, weight, flexibility, skinfold and girth measurements, vertical jump)
- Agility tests (e.g., T-test, pro agility test)
- Maximum power and strength tests (e.g., 1RM power clean, 1RM bench press)
- Sprint tests (e.g., 40-yard [37 m] sprint)
- Local muscular endurance tests (e.g., partial curl-up test)
- Fatiguing anaerobic capacity tests (e.g., 400 m [437-yard] run, 300-yard [275 m] shuttle)
- Aerobic capacity tests (e.g., 1.5-mile [2.4 km] run or 12-minute run)

An effort should be made to administer aerobic tests on a different day than the other tests; but if performed on the same day, aerobic tests should be performed last, after an hour-long rest period.

Preparing Athletes for Testing

The date, time, and purpose of a test battery should be announced in advance to allow athletes to prepare physically and mentally. To maximize test reliability, athletes should be familiar with test content and procedures. A short, supervised pretest practice session one to three days before the test, in which the athletes exert themselves at somewhat less than full intensity, is often beneficial.

The clarity and simplicity of instructions have a direct bearing on the reliability and objectivity of a test (19). The instructions should cover the purpose of the test, how it is to be performed, the amount of warm-up recommended, the number of practice attempts allowed, the number of trials, test scoring, criteria for disallowing attempts, and recommendations for maximizing performance. Viewing a video of the test being performed properly can be a way for athletes to receive consistent instruction before performing a test.

As an important supplement to reading test instructions aloud, the test administrator or a competent assistant should demonstrate proper test performance when possible. The athletes should be given opportunities to ask questions before and after the demonstration. The test administrator should anticipate questions and have answers prepared. It is important to motivate all athletes equally rather than giving special encouragement to only some. Whenever possible, tell athletes their test scores immediately after each trial to motivate them to perform better on subsequent trials (6).

Reliability improves with pretest warm-up (6). An appropriately organized warm-up consists of a general warm-up followed by a specific warm-up. Both types of warm-ups include body movements similar to those involved in the test. An organized, instructor-led general warm-up ensures uniformity. It is acceptable to allow two to three activity-specific warm-up trials, depending on the test protocol, and have subsequent trials actually count toward the score. Depending on the test protocol, the score can be the best or the average of the post-warm-up trials (6).

General and specific warm-ups performed before a test can increase the test's reliability.

Administer a supervised cool-down period to athletes following tests that dramatically increase heart rate and at the completion of the test battery. For example, after the 300-yard (274 m) shuttle, the athlete should not sit or lie down; low-intensity movement and light stretching enhance the recovery process.

CONCLUSION

Tests and measurements can be used to assess athletic talent, identify physical abilities in need of improvement, provide reference values to evaluate the effectiveness of a training program, and set realistic training goals. To evaluate test quality, testers must understand and consider validity and reliability. Test selection involves consideration of the physiological energy systems required by the sport; movement specificity; and the athletes' experience, training status, age, and sex. Testers must also consider environmental factors such as temperature, humidity, and altitude before administering tests. Strength and conditioning professionals must always remain conscious of potential health risks during testing and attentive to signs and symptoms of possible health problems that require medical referral. Testers must be carefully selected and well trained, and the testing session must be well planned and organized using the appropriate testing sequence. Consistent and effective preparation of athletes for testing is essential.

KEY TERMS

STUDY QUESTIONS

1. A college basketball coach would like to know which one of her players has the most muscular power. Which of the following is the MOST valid test for measuring muscular power?
   a. vertical jump
   b. 1RM bench press
   c. 5RM squat
   d. 100 m (109-yard) sprint

2. When measuring maximal strength of an American football lineman, which of the following could potentially adversely affect the test-retest reliability of the results?
   I. using multiple testers
   II. retesting at a different time of day
   III. an athlete's inexperience with the tested exercise
   IV. using an established testing protocol
   a. I and III only
   b. II and IV only
   c. I, II, and III only
   d. II, III, and IV only

3. All of the following procedures should be followed when testing an athlete's cardiovascular fitness in the heat EXCEPT
   a. perform the test in an indoor facility.
   b. use salt tablets to retain water.
   c. schedule the test in the morning.
   d. drink fluids during the test.

4. The bench press, vertical jump, and 10 m (11-yard) sprint are the MOST valid tests for which of the following American football positions?
   a. quarterback
   b. defensive back
   c. wide receiver
   d. defensive lineman

5. Which of the following sequences will produce the MOST reliable results?
   1. T-test
   2. 1RM bench press
   3. 1RM power clean
   4. 1-minute sit-up test
   a. 3, 1, 4, 2
   b. 1, 3, 2, 4
   c. 4, 2, 1, 3
   d. 2, 3, 1, 4

CHAPTER 12

Administration, Scoring, and Interpretation of Selected Tests

Everett Harman, PhD, and John Garhammer, PhD

After completing this chapter, you will be able to

- discern the best ways to measure selected parameters related to athletic performance,
- administer field tests appropriately,
- evaluate and analyze test data and make normative comparisons,
- understand appropriate statistics, and
- combine the results of selected tests to generate an athletic profile.

As discussed in chapter 11, the strength and conditioning professional—often referred to as *tester* in this chapter—who has a broad understanding of exercise science can effectively choose and utilize tests and measurements to make training program decisions that help athletes achieve their goals and maximize their potential. To do this effectively, the tester must administer tests correctly, analyze test data accurately, and then combine the results of selected tests to generate an athletic profile. This chapter covers these basic aspects of testing performance-related parameters and provides comprehensive age- and sport-specific descriptive and normative data for selected tests.

MEASURING PARAMETERS OF ATHLETIC PERFORMANCE

Athleticism incorporates many physical abilities, some of which are much more amenable to training than others. Such abilities may be called components of **athletic performance**, that is, the ability to respond effectively to various physical challenges. This section focuses on how each component can be tested and highlights specific relevant issues.

Maximum Muscular Strength (Low-Speed Strength)

Maximal strength tests usually involve relatively low movement speeds and therefore reflect **low-speed muscular strength**. In this case, muscular strength is related to the force a muscle or muscle group can exert in one maximal effort, and it can be quantified by the maximum weight that can be lifted once (the 1-repetition maximum [1RM]) in exercises such as the bench press or back squat, the maximum force exerted isometrically (against an immovable object) as measured with a transducer, or the maximum force that can be exerted at a particular isokinetic speed (2, 12, 16, 19, 21, 27, 28, 29, 39, 41, 45, 52, 57, 60, 65, 66, 69). Because 1RM tests do not require expensive equipment and reflect the kind of dynamic ability necessary in sport, they are the maximal strength tests of choice for most strength and conditioning professionals.

In general, 1RM tests are administered after the athlete has warmed up by performing a few sets of the test exercise with submaximal loads, beginning with a relatively light one. The first attempt is usually with about 50% of the athlete's estimated 1RM weight. After the athlete has rested enough to feel recovered from the previous attempt (1-5 minutes, depending on the difficulty of the attempt), the strength and conditioning professional increases the weight somewhat, based on the ease with which the previous trial was performed. A skilled strength and conditioning professional should, within three to five attempts following warm-up, be able to find the athlete's 1RM load to within a few percentage points of the true value.

Anaerobic or Maximum Muscular Power (High-Speed Strength)

High-speed muscular strength or **maximal anaerobic muscular power** (or **anaerobic power**) is related to the ability of muscle tissue to exert high force while contracting at a high speed. Tests of such strength and power are of very short

The opinions or assertions contained herein are the private views of the author and are not to be construed as official or as reflecting the views of the Army or the Department of Defense.

duration, are performed at maximal movement speeds, and produce very high power outputs. High-speed maximal muscular power tests are often called (maximal) anaerobic power tests. Scores on high-speed muscular strength tests include the 1RM of explosive exercises (e.g., the power clean, snatch, or push jerk), the height of a vertical jump, and the time to sprint up a staircase (1, 8, 12, 15, 17, 23, 41, 48, 49, 51, 52, 57, 60, 66, 69). As explosive exercise tests take about 1 second while low-speed maximal strength tests generally require 2 to 4 seconds to complete, ATP stored in the active muscle(s) is the primary energy source for both types of tests.

Most maximal muscular strength tests use relatively slow movement speeds and therefore reflect low-speed strength. Conversely, assessment of high-speed muscular strength can involve measuring the 1RM of explosive resistance training exercises, the height of a vertical jump, or the time to sprint up a staircase. ATP is the primary energy source for both low-speed and high-speed muscular strength tests.

Power output reflects both force and velocity. The height of a jump is a function of the velocity at which the athlete leaves the ground. An athlete may not improve in jump height after gaining body weight during a resistance training cycle, making it appear that power output is unchanged. However, because the athlete is heavier and propels the body to the same height, indicating the same takeoff velocity, an increase in power output is evident. This applies to any test in which body weight is manipulated (e.g., running up stairs). Moving a heavier body at the same speed requires a higher power output.

An alternative class of anaerobic power tests involves the use of a cycle ergometer. This type of test can be advantageous for the strength and conditioning professional in some injury situations in which running is restricted or when the athlete participates in a non–body weight support sport such as rowing or cycling. The most commonly used test of this type is the Wingate anaerobic test. A field test protocol involves use of a cycle ergometer with mechanical means of adjusting resistance and measuring pedal revolutions and rate (rpm). In a laboratory setting, an electronically instrumented ergometer can simplify parameter measurement and improve accuracy. Typical protocols involve a basic warm-up followed by a 30-second test interval (9). In this test, resistance is applied quickly after the individual reaches a near-maximal pedaling rate (typically 90 to 110 rpm). The resistance applied is proportional to body weight; the percentage is greater for trained athletes than for individuals with less training. Work performed is determined from the resistance value and number of pedal revolutions. Power is generally calculated as work divided by time for each 5-second time interval during the 30-second test. Parameters typically calculated include peak power, average power, and a fatigue index such as a ratio of maximum to minimum interval power. Norms for cycle ergometer tests are available (32).

Anaerobic Capacity

Anaerobic capacity is the maximal rate of energy production by the combined phosphagen and lactic acid energy systems for moderate-duration activities. It is typically quantified as the maximal power output during muscular activity between 30 and 90 seconds using a variety of tests for the upper and lower body (2, 26, 27, 38, 41, 45, 57, 65, 67), as opposed to maximal anaerobic power tests, which last no longer than a few seconds.

Local Muscular Endurance

Local muscular endurance is the ability of certain muscles or muscle groups to perform repeated contractions against a submaximal resistance (2, 10, 11, 16). A test of local muscular endurance should be performed in a continuous manner for several seconds to several minutes without the advantage of rest periods or extraneous body movements. Examples include performing a maximal number of repetitions in the chin-up, parallel bar dip, or push-up exercises or a resistance training exercise using a fixed load (e.g., a percentage of an athlete's 1RM or body weight) (2, 28, 41, 45).

Aerobic Capacity

Aerobic capacity, also called **aerobic power**, is the maximum rate at which an athlete can produce energy through oxidation of energy resources (carbohydrates, fats, and proteins) and is usually expressed as a volume of oxygen consumed per kg of body weight per minute (i.e., $ml \cdot kg^{-1} \cdot min^{-1}$) (10). Few strength and conditioning professionals have the equipment to measure oxygen consumption directly, so aerobic capacity is generally estimated by performance in aerobic endurance activities such as running 1 mile (1.6 km) or more (2, 6, 27, 28, 29, 33, 40, 48).

Agility

Agility is the ability to stop, start, and change the direction of the body or body parts rapidly and in a controlled manner (7). Tests of agility require proper footwear and a nonslip surface. Electronic timing devices are becoming more accessible to strength and conditioning professionals due to increased ease of use and lower prices; however, many tests of agility and speed are administered using hand timing with a stopwatch, which can be a major source of measurement error, especially if the tester is not sufficiently trained. The most reliable and objective handheld stopwatch times are achieved when the tester starts and stops the stopwatch with the index finger, not the thumb. Even under ideal conditions, stopwatch-measured sprint times are up to 0.24 seconds faster than electronically measured times because of the tester's reaction-time delay in pressing the stopwatch button at the gun and tendency to anticipate and press the button early as the athlete approaches the finish line (2, 8, 17, 44, 45, 50, 52, 54, 59).

Speed

Speed is movement distance per unit time (2) and is typically quantified as the time taken to cover a fixed distance. Tests of speed are not usually conducted over distances greater than 200 m because longer distances reflect anaerobic or aerobic capacity more than absolute ability to move the body at maximal speed (1, 8, 12, 21, 27, 44, 45, 48, 50, 52, 69).

Flexibility

Flexibility can be defined as the range of motion about a body joint (10). Typical devices for measuring flexibility include manual and electric goniometers, which measure joint angle, and the sit-and-reach box, which is used to evaluate the combined flexibility of the lower back and hips. Flexibility measurements are more reliable when standardized warm-up and static stretching precede the flexibility assessment. During a flexibility test, the athlete should move slowly into the fully stretched position and hold this position (7). Ballistic stretching, characterized by bouncing to increase range of motion, should be prohibited during warm-up and cannot be allowed during any flexibility testing (1, 3, 6, 27, 40, 48, 65).

Body Composition

Body composition usually refers to the relative proportions by weight of fat and lean tissue. Although there are sophisticated and expensive devices capable of partitioning the lean component into bone and nonbone lean tissue, the body composition procedures typically performed by strength and conditioning professionals use the basic two-compartment (fat and lean) model. With a trained and competent tester, the skinfold measurement technique provides the most valid and reliable ($r = 0.99$) means for assessing body fatness that is generally available to the strength and conditioning professional and is preferable to body circumference methods (38, 46), although underwater (hydrostatic) weighing and dual x-ray absorptiometry (DEXA) are often labeled as the "gold standards." The skinfold method uses a pincher device that measures the thickness of a double layer of finger-pinched skin and subcutaneous fat. A good skinfold measurement device should squeeze the fold of skin and fat with constant pressure regardless of the amount of tissue being measured (1, 2, 6, 11, 12, 22, 27, 28, 29, 48, 69).

Anthropometry

Anthropometry, which is the science of measurement applied to the human body, generally includes measurements of height, weight, and selected body girths (13). Measurement of height requires a flat wall against which the athlete stands, a measuring tape attached or unattached to the wall, and a rectangular object placed concurrently against both the athlete's head and the wall. Height is usually measured without shoes to the nearest quarter-inch or half-centimeter (37).

The most accurate body mass or body weight measurement is performed with a certified balance scale, which is generally more reliable than a spring scale and should be calibrated on a regular basis (37). A calibrated electronic scale is an acceptable alternative. Athletes should be weighed while wearing minimal dry clothing (e.g., gym shorts and T-shirt, no shoes). For comparison measurements at a later date, they should dress similarly and be weighed at the same time of day. The most reliable body mass (weight) measurements are made in the morning upon rising, after elimination and before ingestion of food or fluids. Level of hydration can result in variability of body mass (weight). Thus, athletes should be encouraged to avoid eating salty food (which increases water retention) the day before weighing and to go to bed normally hydrated.

The most reliable girth measurements are usually obtained with the aid of a flexible measuring tape equipped with a spring-loaded attachment at the end that, when pulled out to a specified mark, exerts a fixed amount of tension on the tape—for example, a Gulich tape (65). Girth measurements should be made at the beginning of a training period for comparison with subsequent measurements (2, 28).

Testing Conditions

In order to maximize the reliability of tests, it is essential that testing conditions be as similar as possible for all the athletes tested and from test to retest of the same athlete. The temperature and humidity should not differ radically from test to test. For any particular test conducted on the ground, the surface—whether gym floor, grass, rubber, or dirt—should always be the same and should not be wet for one test and dry for another. Maximum strength tests should use the same type of racks with the supports set at the same height for a given athlete. For jumping tests, the type of equipment used should be constant.

Athletes should never be tested after fatiguing sport activities or workouts. They should arrive for testing normally hydrated and neither glycogen depleted nor full from eating a large meal. It is best to perform tests and retests at roughly the same time of day. Warm-up for the tests should be standardized and should include both a general warm-up such as jogging or light calisthenics and a specific warm-up that involves movements like those required by the test, such as practice of the test at submaximal intensity. Stretching is appropriate for any test requiring flexibility.

SELECTED TEST PROTOCOLS AND SCORING DATA

1RM BENCH PRESS

Equipment

- A barbell, weight plates, and two safety locks; enough total weight to accommodate the maximum load of the strongest athlete; and a variety of plate sizes to allow for 5-pound (2.5 kg) gradations in weight
- A sturdy bench press bench with integral bar rack (preferably of adjustable height)

Personnel

- One spotter, one recorder

Procedure

1. Instruct the athlete in proper technique for the flat barbell bench press as described in chapter 14 (pp. 342-343).
2. The spotter stands at the head end of the bench throughout the test to help in raising the bar on a failed attempt and to help the athlete place the bar back on the rack.
3. As with any maximal strength test, the athlete first does a specific warm-up of 5 to 10 repetitions with a light-to-moderate load.
4. Usually, at least two heavier warm-up sets of two to five repetitions each are completed before the first actual 1RM attempt.
5. Generally, it is desirable to measure the 1RM within three to five attempts after the warm-up; otherwise fatigue may detract from the final result.
6. A more detailed step-by-step method for the 1RM protocol is shown in figure 15.1 on page 396.

Note: Normative data for the 1RM bench press are presented in tables 12.1, 12.2, and 12.3 on pages 275-277.

1RM BACK SQUAT

Equipment

- A barbell, weight plates, and two safety locks; enough total weight to accommodate the maximum load of the strongest athlete; and a variety of plate sizes to allow for 5-pound (2.5 kg) gradations in weight
- A sturdy squat rack with adjustable spotting bars to support the weight of the bar if the athlete is unable to rise (as an alternative, one spotter can be used at each end of the bar)
- A flat and solid surface to stand on

Personnel

- Two spotters, one recorder

Procedure

1. Instruct the athlete in proper technique for the back squat as described in chapter 14 (pp. 350-351).
2. Warm-up sets are performed as in the 1RM bench press test. However, the loads lifted are typically heavier than in the 1RM bench press test so the load increments will be greater than those of the 1RM bench press.
3. Refer to figure 15.1 (p. 396) for a 1RM testing protocol.

Note: Normative data for the 1RM back squat are presented in tables 12.1, 12.2, and 12.3 on pages 275-277.

1RM POWER CLEAN

Note: Because the power clean exercise is very technique intensive, two athletes with the same muscular power capacity can differ greatly in their tested 1RM, lessening the value of the test for predicting athletic performance.

Equipment

- An Olympic-style barbell with a revolving sleeve, weight plates, and two safety locks; enough total weight to accommodate the maximum load of the strongest athlete; and a variety of plate sizes to allow for 5-pound (2.5 kg) gradations in weight
- A lifting platform or designated area set apart from the rest of the facility for safety

Personnel

- One tester/recorder

Procedure

1. Instruct the athlete in proper technique for the power clean as described in chapter 14 (pp. 372-373).
2. Warm-up sets are performed and load increments are selected as in the 1RM bench press test.
3. Refer to figure 15.1 (p. 396) for a 1RM testing protocol.

Note: Normative data for the 1RM power clean are presented in tables 12.1, 12.2, and 12.3 on pages 275-277.

STANDING LONG JUMP

Equipment

- A flat jumping area at least 20 feet (6 m) in length, which can be a gym floor, artificial turf, grass field, or a track
- A tape measure at least 10 feet (3 m) long
- Duct tape or masking tape
- Permissible alternative: a commercial jumping mat premarked in half-inch (1 cm) increments

Personnel

- One distance judge, one recorder

Procedure (Using a Tape Measure)

1. Place a 2- to 3-foot (0.6-0.9 m) length of tape on the floor to serve as a starting line.
2. The athlete stands with the toes just behind the starting line.
3. The athlete performs a countermovement and jumps forward as far as possible.
4. The athlete must land on the feet for the jump to be scored. Otherwise the trial is repeated.
5. A marker is placed at the back edge of the athlete's rearmost heel, and the tape measure determines the distance between the starting line and the mark.
6. The best of three trials is recorded to the nearest 0.5 inch or 1 cm.

Procedure (Using a Commercial Jump Mat)

1. The athlete stands with the toes just behind the starting line.
2. The athlete performs a countermovement and jumps forward as far as possible.
3. The athlete must land on the feet for the jump to be scored. Otherwise the trial is repeated.
4. The imprinted mat line closest to the back edge of the athlete's rearmost heel indicates the jump distance.
5. The best of three trials is recorded to the nearest 0.5 inch or 1 cm.

Note: Normative data for the standing long jump are presented in tables 12.6 and 12.7 on page 279.

VERTICAL JUMP

Equipment

- A smooth wall with a ceiling higher than the highest jumper's jump height
- A flat floor with good traction
- Chalk of a different color than the wall
- Measuring tape or stick
- Permissible alternative: a commercial device for vertical jump testing (e.g., Vertec)

Personnel

- One tester/recorder

Procedure (Using a Wall and Chalk)

1. The tester rubs chalk on the fingertips of the athlete's dominant hand.
2. The athlete stands with the dominant shoulder about 6 inches (15 cm) from the wall and, with both feet flat on the floor, reaches as high as possible with the dominant hand and makes a chalk mark on the wall.
3. The athlete then lowers the dominant hand and, without a preparatory or stutter step, performs a countermovement by quickly flexing the knees and hips, moving the trunk forward and downward, and swinging the arms backward (figure 12.1*a*). During the jump, the dominant arm reaches upward, while the nondominant arm moves downward relative to the body.
4. At the highest point in the jump, the athlete places a second chalk mark on the wall with the fingers of the dominant hand using a swiping motion of the fingers. The score is the vertical distance between the two chalk marks.
5. The best of three trials is recorded to the nearest 0.5 inches or 1.0 cm.

Figure 12.1 *(a)* Starting position and *(b)* maximum height of the vertical jump.

Procedure (Using a Commercial Vertec Device)

1. The tester adjusts the height of the stack of movable color-coded horizontal plastic vanes to be within the athlete's standing reach height. The highest vane that can be reached and pushed forward with the dominant hand while the athlete stands flat-footed determines the standing touch height.
2. The vane stack is then raised by a measured distance (marked on the shaft holding the vanes) so that the athlete will not jump higher or lower than the set of vanes. This requires a rough estimate of how high the particular athlete will jump, but a correction can be made on the second attempt if necessary.
3. Without a preparatory or stutter step, the athlete performs a countermovement by quickly flexing the knees and hips, moving the trunk forward and downward, and swinging the arms backward (figure 12.1*a*). During the jump, the dominant arm reaches upward while the nondominant arm moves downward relative to the body.
4. At the highest point in the jump, the athlete taps the highest possible vane with the fingers of the dominant hand (figure 12.1*b*). The score is the vertical distance between the height of the highest vane tapped during the standing vertical reach and the vane tapped at the highest point of the jump.
5. The best of three trials is recorded to the nearest 0.5 inches (the distance between adjacent vanes).

Note: Normative data for the vertical jump are presented in table 12.4 on page 278.

MARGARIA-KALAMEN TEST

Equipment

- Staircase with nine or more steps, each about 7 inches (18 cm) high, and a straight and flat lead-up area 20 feet (6 m) or more in length (Figure 12.2)
- Measuring tape or stick
- An electronic timing system with both a start and a stop switch mechanism
- Scale

Personnel

- One tester/recorder

Procedure

1. The height of each step is measured with a ruler or tape measure, and the elevation from the third step to the ninth step is calculated (6 × step height).
2. The timer start switch mechanism is placed on the third step, and the stop switch mechanism is placed on the ninth step.
3. The athlete to be tested is weighed on a scale, warms up, and practices running up the stairs three steps at a time.
4. When ready, the athlete sprints toward the stairs from a standing start 20 feet (6 m) from the base of the stairs and then up the staircase three steps at a time (third step to sixth step to ninth step) as fast as possible.
5. The time from third- to ninth-step contact is determined to the nearest 0.01 second using the timing system.
6. Power in watts is calculated as the athlete's weight (w) in newtons (pounds × 4.45 or kg × 9.807) times height (h) in meters (inches × 0.0254) from the third step to the ninth step divided by the measured time interval (t) in seconds; P (watts) = (w × h) / t.

Note: Normative data for the Margaria-Kalamen test are presented in table 12.5 on page 279.

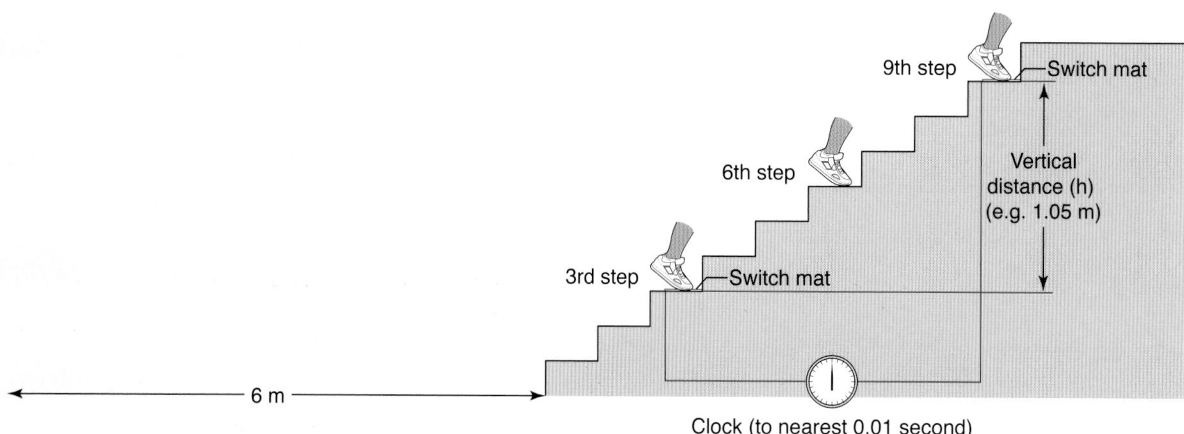

Figure 12.2 Margaria-Kalamen stair sprint test.

Reprinted, by permission, from Fox, Bowers, and Foss, 1993 (23).

300-YARD (274 M) SHUTTLE

Equipment

- A stopwatch with at least 0.1-second resolution
- Two parallel lines 25 yards (22.86 m) apart on a flat surface (figure 12.3)

Personnel

- One timer, two line judges

Procedure

1. Pair off athletes of similar ability.
2. Position two athletes immediately behind one line, facing the other line.
3. On an auditory signal, the athletes sprint to the line 25 yards (22.86 m) away, making foot contact with it, then immediately sprint back to the first line. Six such round trips are made as fast as possible without stopping (6 × 50 yards = 300 yards, or 274 m).
4. On completion of the first trial, record both athletes' times to the nearest 0.1 second and start a clock to time a 5-minute rest interval. As each pair of athletes completes the first trial, they may walk and stretch but must stay alert for the starting time on the second trial.
5. After the rest period, the pair of athletes does another trial.
6. The average of two trials is recorded to the nearest 1.0 second.

Note: Normative data for the 300-yard (274 m) shuttle are presented in table 12.4 on page 278.

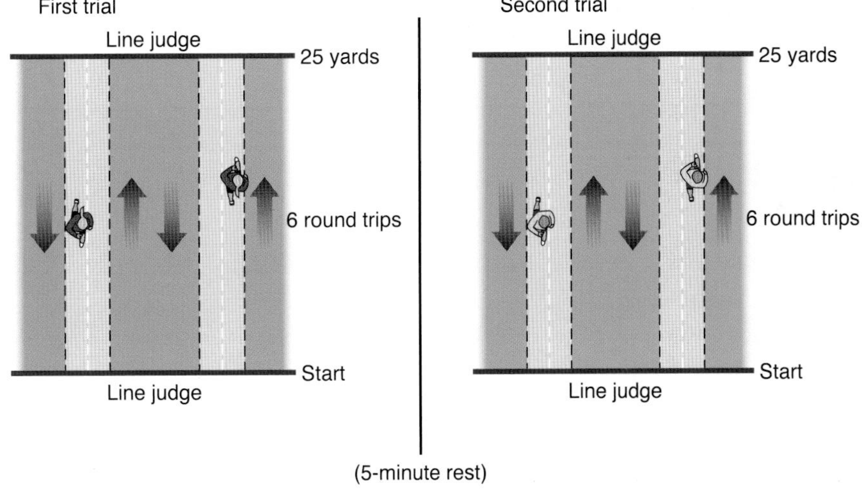

Figure 12.3 Ground layout for 300-yard (274 m) shuttle.

Adapted, by permission, from Gilliam, 1983 (24).

PARTIAL CURL-UP

The partial curl-up test measures the muscular endurance of the abdominal muscles. It is often favored over the sit-up test because it eliminates the use of the hip flexor muscles.

Equipment

- Metronome
- Ruler
- Masking tape
- Mat

Personnel

- One recorder/technique judge

Procedure

1. The athlete assumes a supine position on a mat with a 90° knee angle (figure 12.4*a*). The arms are at the sides, resting on the floor, with the fingers touching a 4-inch (10 cm)-long piece of masking tape positioned perpendicular to the fingers. A second piece of masking tape is situated parallel to the first tape at a distance determined by the age of the athlete (4.7 inches [12 cm] for those younger than 45 and 3.1 inches [8 cm] for those 45 or older).
2. Set a metronome to 40 beats per minute and have the individual do slow, controlled curl-ups to lift the shoulder blades off the mat (trunk makes a 30° angle with the mat; figure 12.4*b*) in time with the metronome (20 curl-ups per minute). The upper back must touch the floor before each curl-up. The athlete should avoid flexing the neck to bring the chin close to the chest.
3. The athlete performs as many curl-ups as possible without pausing, to a maximum of 75.

Note: Normative data for the partial curl-up are presented in table 12.8 on page 280.

Figure 12.4 Curl-up: *(a)* beginning position and *(b)* end position.

PUSH-UP

Equipment

- A 4-inch (10 cm)-diameter foam roller (for female athletes)

Personnel

- One recorder/technique judge

Procedure

1. For both the Army and American College of Sports Medicine (ACSM) standards, men assume the standard push-up starting position with hands shoulder-width apart and elbows and body straight (figure 12.5*a*). For the Army standards, women assume the same position as the men. For the ACSM standards, women start similarly except that the knees rather than the feet contact the ground, with the knees flexed at 90° and the ankles crossed (figure 12.6*a*).
2. For the Army standards, the push-up low position is when the upper arms are parallel to the ground (figure 12.5*b*). For the ACSM standards, the low position for males is when the chest makes contact with the recorder's fist held vertically against the ground. There is no standard criterion for the female low position (23), but it has been suggested that females make torso contact with a foam roller on the ground rather than a fist (figure 12.6*b*). For either standard, repetitions that do not achieve the required low position are not counted.
3. For the Army standard, as many repetitions as possible are done within a timed 2-minute period. The athlete may pause only in the up position. For the ACSM standard, as many repetitions as possible are done continuously until failure.

Note: ACSM normative data for the push-up are presented in table 12.9 on page 280. Army push-up point scores are found in table 12.10 on page 281.

Figure 12.5 Push-up according to Army standard: *(a)* beginning position and *(b)* end position.

Figure 12.6 Push-up according to ACSM standard for females: *(a)* beginning position and *(b)* end position.

YMCA BENCH PRESS TEST

Equipment

- A barbell, weight plates, two safety locks, and enough total weight to assemble an 80-pound (36 kg) or a 35-pound (16 kg) load (including safety locks)
- Flat bench press bench (preferably with an upright rack to hold the barbell)
- Metronome

Personnel

- One spotter/recorder

Procedure

1. Instruct the athlete in proper technique for the flat barbell bench press as described in chapter 14 (pp. 342-343).
2. The spotter/recorder stands at the head end of the bench throughout the test to help in raising the bar on a failed attempt and to help the athlete place the bar back on the rack.
3. Set the resistance at 80 pounds (36 kg) for males and 35 pounds (16 kg) for females.
4. Set the metronome cadence at 60 beats per minute to establish a rate of 30 repetitions per minute (one beat up, one beat down).
5. The athlete grips the bar at shoulder width, lifts the bar off the rack, and extends the elbows. Then, in time with the metronome, the bar is repeatedly lowered to the chest and raised up again, so that the elbows are extended, until the athlete can no longer keep up with the metronome. The movement should be smooth and controlled, with the bar reaching its highest and lowest position with each beat of the metronome.

Note: Normative data for the YMCA bench press test are presented in table 12.11 on page 282.

1.5-MILE (2.4 KM) RUN

Equipment

- Stopwatch
- Quarter-mile running track or measured and marked 1.5-mile (2.4 km) flat course with a good running surface

Personnel

- One tester to call off each athlete's time, one recorder

Procedure

1. Have each athlete warm up and stretch prior to the test.
2. Each athlete should be recognizable to the scorer at the finish line. If that is not possible, numbers should be pinned to the athletes' shirts.
3. At the start, all runners should line up behind the starting line.
4. Instruct the athletes to complete the run as quickly as possible at a steady pace that they can barely maintain over the distance.
5. On an auditory signal, the athletes start running and cover the course as quickly as possible.
6. As the runners cross the finish line, each runner's time is recorded on a form as a timer calls off the time in minutes and seconds (00:00).

Note: Normative data for the 1.5-mile (2.4 km) run are presented in tables 12.12 through 12.15 on pages 282-284. For each 1.5-mile (2.4 km) run time, the tables show an estimated maximal rate of oxygen consumption; the norms for athletes in various sports are shown in table 12.16 on page 285.

12-MINUTE RUN

Equipment

- 400 m (437-yard) track or flat looped course with a marker at each 100 m
- Stopwatch

Personnel

- One tester to call out each athlete's position, one recorder

Procedure

1. Athletes line up at the starting line.
2. On an auditory signal, the athletes travel by foot as far as possible in 12 minutes, preferably by running, but if necessary by walking part or all of the time.
3. At 12 minutes, on an auditory signal, all the athletes stop in place.
4. The distance run by each athlete (laps × 400 m, e.g., 5.25 laps × 400 m = 2,100 m) is calculated and recorded.

Note: Normative data for the 12-minute run are presented in table 12.17 on page 286.

T-TEST

Equipment

- Four cones
- A tape measure at least 5 yards (4.6 m) long
- Stopwatch
- Flat floor with good traction

Personnel

- One tester/recorder, one spotter

Procedure

1. Arrange four cones as seen in figure 12.7 (points A, B, C, and D).
2. Have the athlete warm up and stretch prior to the test. The athlete may run the course with a submaximal effort for practice.
3. The test begins with the athlete standing at point A.
4. On an auditory signal, the athlete sprints forward to point B and touches the *base* of the cone with the right hand.
5. Then, while facing forward and not crossing the feet, the athlete shuffles to the left 5 yards (4.6 m) and touches the *base* of the cone at point C with the left hand.
6. The athlete then shuffles to the right 10 yards (9.1 m) and touches the *base* of the cone at point D with the right hand.
7. The athlete then shuffles to the left 5 yards and touches the *base* of the cone at point B with the left hand, and next runs backward past point A, at which time the watch is stopped.
8. For safety, a spotter and gym mat should be positioned several feet behind point A to catch an athlete who falls while running backward.
9. The best time of two trials is recorded to the nearest 0.1 second.
10. Reasons for disqualification of a trial: The athlete fails to touch the base of any cone, crosses one foot in front of the other instead of shuffling the feet, or fails to face forward for the entire test.

Note: Normative data for the T-test are presented in table 12.4 on page 278.

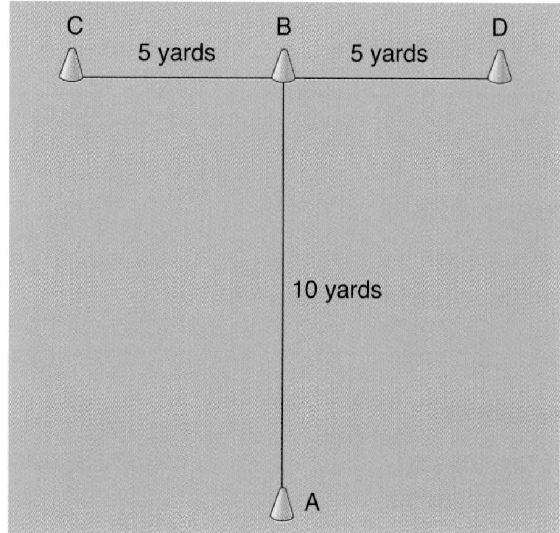

Figure 12.7 Floor layout for the T-test.

Adapted, by permission, from Semenick, 1990 (59).

HEXAGON TEST

Equipment

- Adhesive tape of a color that contrasts with the floor
- Measuring tape or stick
- Stopwatch
- Flat floor with good traction

Personnel

- One timer/recorder, one line judge

Procedure

1. Using the adhesive tape, create a hexagon on the floor with 24-inch (61 cm) sides meeting to form 120° angles (figure 12.8).
2. The athlete warms up and practices performance of the test at submaximal speed.
3. The test begins with the athlete standing in the middle of the hexagon.
4. On an auditory signal, the athlete begins double-leg hopping from the center of the

hexagon over each side and back to the center, starting with the side directly in front of the athlete, in a continuous clockwise sequence until all six sides are covered three times (three revolutions around the hexagon for a total of 18 jumps) and the athlete is again standing at the center. The athlete remains facing the same direction throughout the test.

5. If the athlete lands on a side of the hexagon rather than over it, or loses balance and takes an extra step or changes the direction he or she is facing, the trial is stopped and restarted after the athlete is allowed time for full recovery.
6. The best time of three trials is recorded to the nearest 0.1 second.

Note: Normative data for the hexagon test are presented in table 12.4 on page 278.

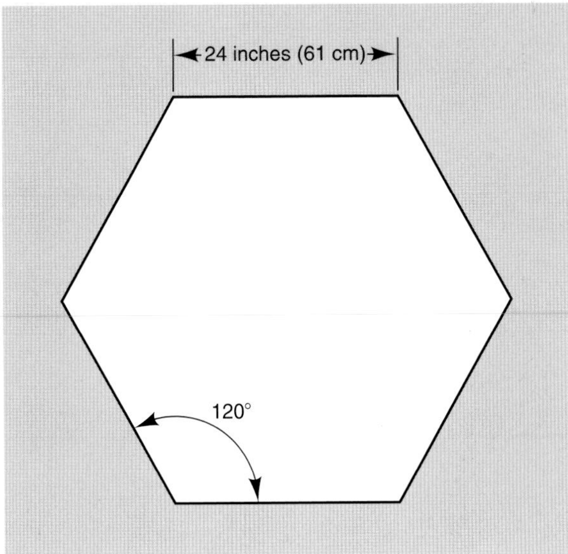

Figure 12.8 Floor layout for the hexagon test.

Adapted, by permission, from Pauole, et al., 2000 (51).

PRO AGILITY TEST (ALSO CALLED THE 20-YARD [18.3 M] SHUTTLE)

Equipment

- An American football field or other field marked with three parallel lines 5 yards (4.6 m) apart (figure 12.9)
- A stopwatch

Personnel

- One timer/recorder, one line judge

Procedure

1. The athlete straddles the centermost of the three parallel lines using a three-point stance.
2. On an auditory signal, the athlete sprints 5 yards (4.6 m) to the line on the left, then changes direction and sprints 10 yards (9.1 m) to the line on the right, then again changes direction and sprints 5 yards (4.6 m) to the center line. Foot contact must be made with all indicated lines.
3. The best time of two trials is recorded to the nearest 0.01 second.

Note: Normative data for the pro agility test are presented in table 12.18 on page 287.

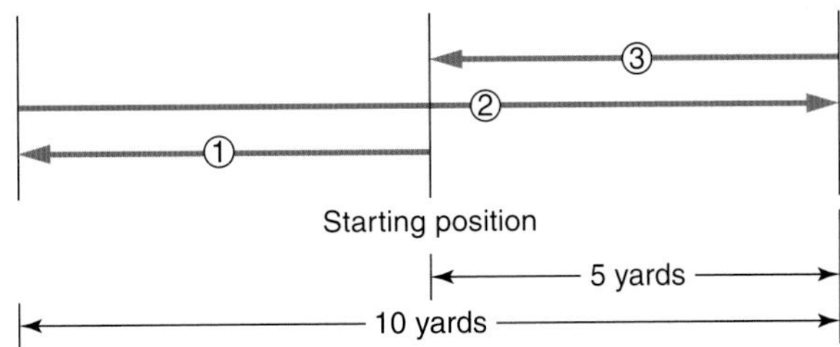

Figure 12.9 Layout for the pro agility test.

40-YARD (37 M) SPRINT

Equipment

- Stopwatch
- Flat running surface with start and finish lines 40 yards (37 m) apart, with at least 20 yards (18 m) after the finish line for deceleration

Personnel

- One timer/recorder

Procedure

1. Have the athlete warm up and stretch for several minutes.
2. Allow at least two practice runs at submaximal speed.
3. The athlete assumes a starting position using a three- or four-point stance.
4. On an auditory signal, the athlete sprints 40 yards (37 m) at maximal speed.
5. The average of two trials is recorded to the nearest 0.1 second.

Note: Normative data for the 40-yard (37 m) sprint are presented in table 12.4 on page 278.

SIT-AND-REACH TEST

Note: A consistent method for the sit-and-reach test should be maintained if the test is done periodically. For example, if the test is performed with a measuring tape or stick during initial testing of the athlete, all subsequent testing of the athlete should be performed with a measuring tape or stick (i.e., a sit-and-reach box should not be used instead).

Equipment

- Measuring tape or stick
- Adhesive tape
- Permissible alternative: a standard sit-and-reach box

Personnel

- One tester/recorder

Procedure

1. Tape the measuring stick or tape measure to the floor. Place one piece of tape about 24 inches (61 cm) long across the measuring stick and at a right angle to it at the 15-inch (38 cm) mark.
2. Have the athlete warm up with nonballistic exercises involving the hamstrings and lower back, for example by walking rapidly for 3 to 5 minutes; performing several repetitions of flexing forward from a standing, knees-straight position, reaching toward the toes, then reaching upward toward the ceiling (all without jerking); jogging in place while trying to kick the heels into the upper thighs from behind; and finishing with standing toe-touching or similar stretching on the floor.
3. Have the athlete sit shoeless with the measuring stick between the legs with its zero end toward the body, the feet 12 inches (30 cm) apart, the toes pointed upward, and the heels nearly touching the edge of the taped line at the 15-inch (38-cm) mark (figure 12.10*a*).
4. Have the athlete slowly reach forward with both hands as far as possible on the measuring stick, holding this position momentarily. To get the best stretch, the athlete should exhale and drop the head between the arms when reaching. Be sure the athlete keeps the hands adjacent to each other and does not lead with one hand. The fingertips should remain in contact with the measuring stick (figure 12.10*b*). The tester may hold the athlete's knees down, if necessary, to keep them straight. A score of less than 15 inches (38 cm) indicates that the athlete could not reach the bottom of the feet.
5. The best of three trials is recorded to the nearest 0.25 inch or 1 cm.

Note: Normative data for the sit-and-reach test are presented in tables 12.12 through 12.15 on pages 282-284.

Figure 12.10 Sit-and-reach: *(a)* starting position and *(b)* final position.

SKINFOLD MEASUREMENTS

Equipment

- Skinfold calipers
- Flexible tape measure
- Marking pen

Personnel

- One tester, one recorder

Procedure (Obtaining a Skinfold Measurement)

1. Skinfold measurements should be made on dry skin, prior to exercise, to ensure maximum validity and reliability (10).
2. Grasp the skin firmly with the thumb and index finger to form a fold of skin and subcutaneous fat.
3. Place the caliper prongs perpendicular to the fold 0.5 inch to 1 inch (approximately 1 to 2 cm) from the thumb and index finger.
4. Release the caliper grip so that its spring tension is exerted on the skinfold.
5. Between 1 and 2 seconds after the grip on the caliper has been released, read the dial on the caliper to the nearest 0.5 mm.
6. Obtain one measurement from each test site, and then repeat all test sites for a second trial. If the measurements do not differ by more than 10%, average the two measurements to the nearest 0.5 mm. Otherwise, take one or more additional measurements until two of the measurements are within 10%, and average those two measurements to the nearest 0.5 mm.

Procedure (Measuring the Selected Site and Calculating the Body Fat Percentage)

1. There are specific equations for estimating body density (Db) (then, in turn, percent body fat [%BF]) for different populations. First, select the equation appropriate for the athlete from table 12.19 on page 288.
2. Refer to the chosen equation and related instructions and mark the skin at the appropriate anatomical sites (6, 29, 53):

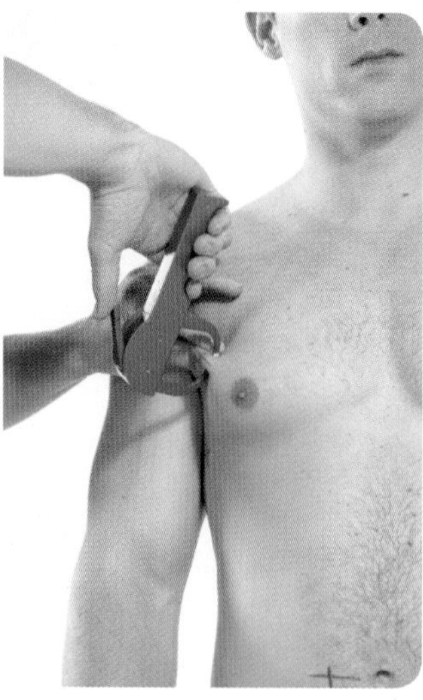

Figure 12.11*a* Chest skinfold.

Figure 12.11*b* Thigh skinfold.

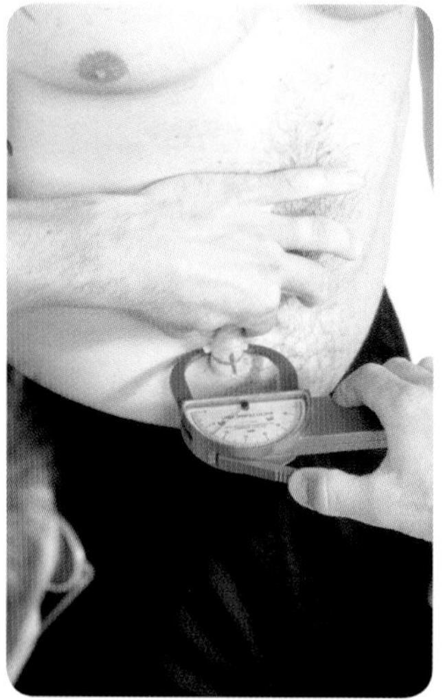

Figure 12.11*c* Abdomen skinfold.

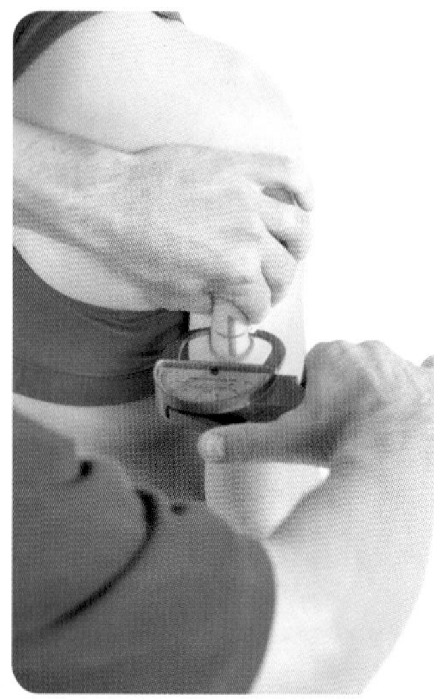

Figure 12.11*d* Triceps skinfold.

- Chest—a diagonal fold one-half the distance between the anterior axillary line and the nipple for men (figure 12.11*a*)
- Thigh—a vertical fold on the anterior aspect of the thigh, midway between the hip and knee joints (figure 12.11*b*)
- Abdomen—a vertical fold 1 inch (2.5 cm) to the right (relative to the athlete) of the umbilicus (figure 12.11*c*)
- Triceps—a vertical fold on the posterior midline of the upper arm (over the triceps muscle), halfway between the acromion and the olecranon processes (the arm should be in anatomical position with the elbow extended and relaxed [figure 12.11*d*])

- Suprailium—a diagonal fold above the crest of the ilium at the spot where an imaginary line would come down from the anterior axillary line (figure 12.11*e*) (some prefer the measure to be taken more laterally, at the midaxillary line [11])
- Midaxilla—a vertical fold on the midaxillary line at the level of the xiphoid process of the sternum (figure 12.11*f*)
- Subscapula—a fold taken on a diagonal line that extends from the vertebral border to a point 0.5 inches to 1 inch (1 to 2 cm) from the inferior angle of the scapula (figure 12.11*g*)
- Calf—a vertical fold along the medial side of the calf, at the level of maximum calf circumference (figure 12.11*h*)

3. Using the appropriate population-specific equation from table 12.19, calculate the estimated body density from the skinfolds (29).
4. Enter the body density into the appropriate population-specific equation from table 12.20 on page 289 to calculate the percent body fat from the body density (29).

Note: Normative data for percent body fat are presented in tables 12.12 through 12.15, 12.21, and 12.22 on pages 282-284 and 290-292.

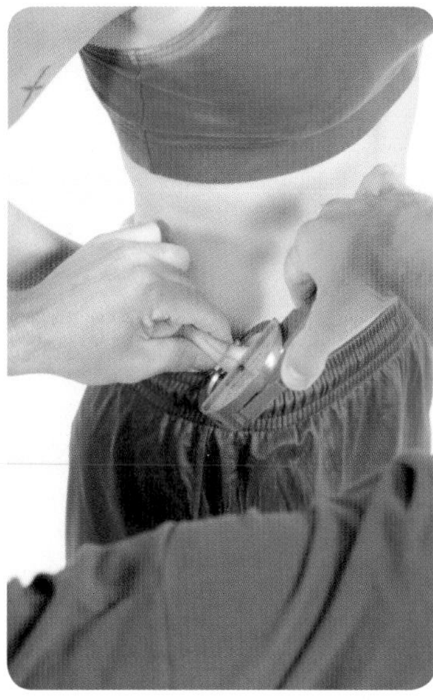

Figure 12.11*e* Suprailium skinfold.

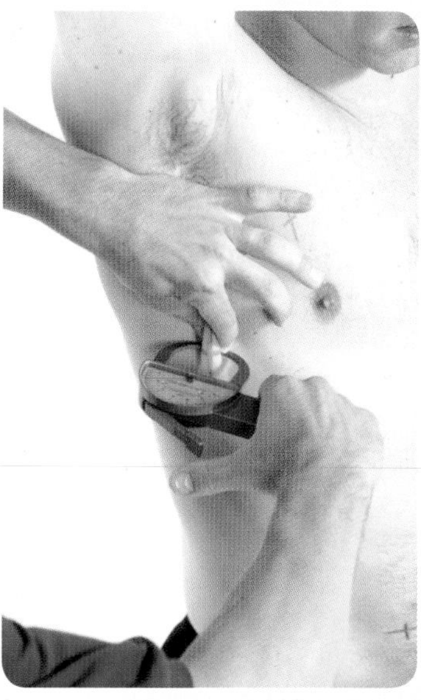

Figure 12.11*f* Midaxilla skinfold.

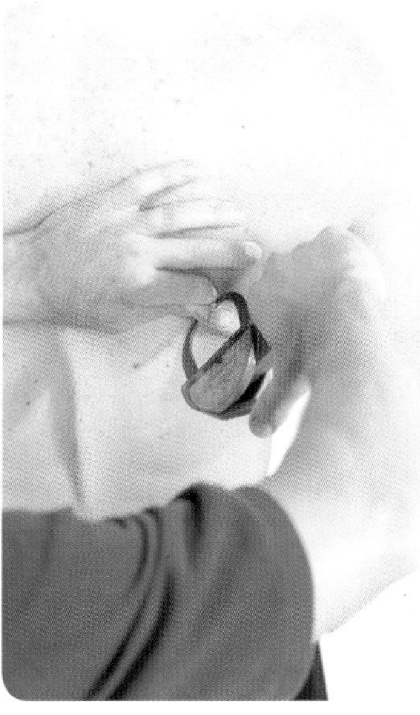

Figure 12.11*g* Subscapula skinfold.

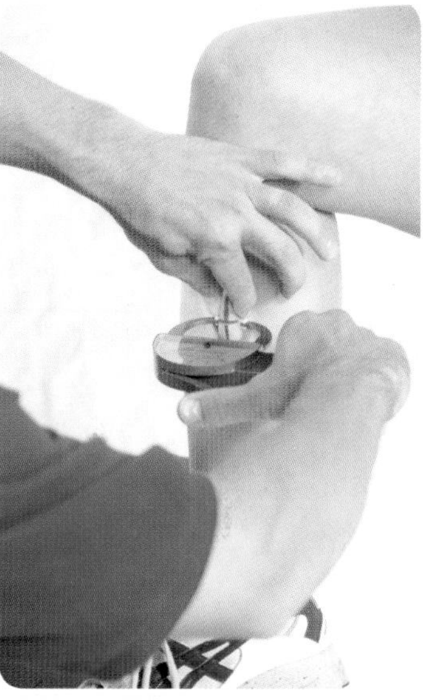

Figure 12.11*h* Calf skinfold.

GIRTH MEASUREMENTS

Equipment

- Flexible, spring-loaded tape measure (e.g., a Gulich tape)

Personnel

- One tester, one recorder

Procedure

1. Position the athlete in a relaxed anatomical position for each measurement (unless otherwise indicated for a particular measurement).
2. Measure the following sites (35, 46):
   - Chest—at nipple level in males and at maximum circumference (above the breasts) in females
   - Right upper arm—at the point of maximal circumference with the elbow fully extended, palm up, and arm abducted to parallel with the floor
   - Right forearm—at the point of maximal circumference with the elbow fully extended, palm up, and arm abducted to parallel with the floor
   - Waist (abdomen)—at the level of the umbilicus
   - Hips (buttocks)—at the maximal protrusion of the buttocks with the heels together
   - Right thigh—at the point of maximal circumference, usually just below the buttocks
   - Right calf—at the point of maximal circumference between the knee and ankle

STATISTICAL EVALUATION OF TEST DATA

Once the proper test or tests have been chosen and administered and the scores collected, the next step may include any or all of the following: (1) analysis of the data to determine the change in performance of the group over the training period (weeks, months, or years); (2) analysis of the group's performance relative to that of similar groups tested in the past; (3) analysis of the relationship of each athlete's scores to those of the group; and (4) comparison of individual scores to local, state, national, or international norms.

An important outcome of repeated performance testing is evaluation of both the improvement of individual athletes and the overall effectiveness of the physical conditioning program as determined by changes in test scores (10). A **difference score** is the difference between an athlete's score at the beginning and end of a training period or between any two separate testing times. However, judging the effectiveness of a training program merely by degree of improvement has two major limitations. First, athletes who begin the training period at a higher training status will not improve as much as untrained athletes who perform poorly at the beginning of training. Second, athletes may deliberately fail to give maximal effort on pretraining tests to inflate their pre- to posttraining improvement scores. It is important to encourage athletes to give maximal effort on both the pre- and posttraining tests.

Types of Statistics

Statistics is the science of collecting, classifying, analyzing, and interpreting numerical data (33, 68). A working knowledge of statistics is helpful in making sound evaluations of test results. There are two main branches of statistics—descriptive and inferential.

Descriptive Statistics

Descriptive statistics summarizes or describes a large group of data. It is used when all the information about a population is known. For example, if all the members of a team are tested, statements can be made about the team with the use of descriptive statistics. There are three categories of numerical measurement in descriptive statistics: central tendency, variability, and percentile rank. In the sections that follow, these terms are defined and examples of how to calculate the values and scores are presented.

Central Tendency Measures of **central tendency** are values about which the data tend to cluster. The three most common measures of central tendency (2, 37, 68) are as follows:

Mean—the average of the scores (i.e., the sum of the scores divided by the number of scores). This is the most commonly used measure of central tendency.

Median—the middlemost score when a set of scores is arranged in order of magnitude. With an even number of scores, the median is the average of the two middlemost scores. Half a group of scores falls above the median and half falls below the median. Depending on the distribution of scores, the median can be a better measure of central tendency than the mean. This is particularly true when very high or very low scores of one or a few members of the group tested raise or lower the group mean to the extent that it does not adequately describe the ability of most group members.

Mode—the score that occurs with the greatest frequency. If each numerical score appears only once, there is no mode. If two or more scores are "tied" for greatest frequency, then all of the similar scores are modes. The mode is generally regarded as the least useful measure of central tendency.

Variability The degree of dispersion of scores within a group is called **variability**. Two common measures of variability are the range and the standard deviation. The **range** is the interval from the lowest to the highest score. The advantage of the range is that it is easy to understand; the disadvantage is that it uses only the two extreme scores and so may not be an accurate measure of variability (2, 68). For example, the range could be the same for a group of widely dispersed scores as for a group of scores that are narrowly dispersed except for one deviant score. The **standard deviation** is a measure of the variability of a set of scores about the mean. The formula for the standard deviation of a sample is as follows:

$$s = \sqrt{\frac{\sum(x - \bar{x})^2}{n-1}} \qquad \textbf{(12.1)}$$

where Σ refers to a summation, x is a score, $\bar{x}$ is the mean of the scores, and n is the sample size (number of scores). A relatively small standard deviation indicates that a set of scores is closely clustered about the mean; a large standard deviation indicates wider dispersion of the scores about the mean. The standard deviation is most useful when the group of scores is "normally distributed," forming the bell-shaped curve shown in figure 12.12 (2, 37, 62, 68).

The z score can be used to express the distance of any individual score in standard deviation units from the mean:

$$z = (x - \bar{x}) / s \quad (12.2)$$

For example, if an athlete runs the 40-yard (37 m) sprint in 4.6 seconds and the mean and standard deviation for the group tested are 5.0 and 0.33 seconds, respectively, equation 12.2 can be applied to determine that the z score for that athlete is –1.2. In other words, the athlete's score is 1.2 standard deviation units below (i.e., faster than) the group mean.

Percentile Rank An individual's **percentile rank** is the percentage of test takers scoring below that individual. As in calculation of the median, percentile ranking requires arranging scores ordinally (lowest to highest). For example, if an athlete is ranked in the 75th percentile, 75% of the group produced scores below that athlete's score. Norms based on large samples are sometimes expressed in evenly spaced percentiles, as in tables 12.12-12.15 on pages 282-284 (2). Several percentile rank tables have been developed for males and females of different age groups for various sports, including American football (10, 20, 42, 45, 57, 58, 70), basketball (31, 56, 57), and volleyball (10, 56), as well as health-related fitness (3, 16, 53, 70).

Inferential Statistics

Inferential statistics allows one to draw general conclusions about a population from information collected in a population sample. For example, if a boys' 9th-grade gym class is put through a battery of tests and it is assumed that the class (sample) is representative of all the 9th-grade boys in the school (the population), then the results of these tests can be used to make inferences about the population as a whole. A basic assumption of inferential statistics is that the sample is truly representative of the population (61). Thus, one might infer that the means and standard deviations of test scores of 200 football players from six different Division I American football programs represent the abilities of all Division I American football players nationwide.

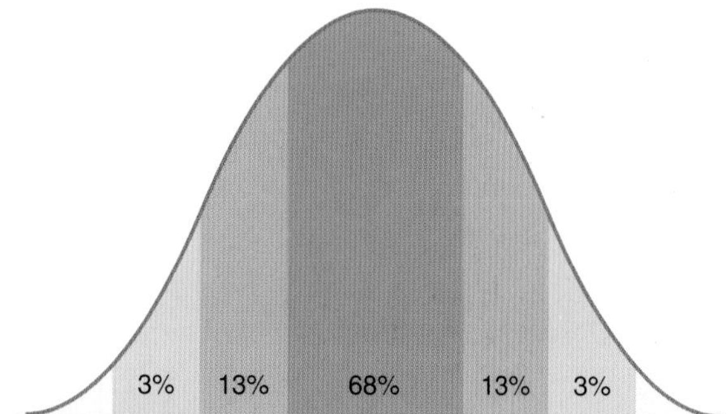

Figure 12.12 Normal bell curve.

Developing an Athletic Profile

To determine the sport-specific training status of an athlete, the strength and conditioning professional can combine the results of selected tests to generate an **athletic profile**, which is a group of test results related to sport-specific abilities that are important for quality performance in a sport or sport position. When evaluating athletes, the strength and conditioning professional should follow these five steps:

1. Select tests that will measure the specific parameters most closely related to the characteristics of the sport or sports in question. For example, a testing battery for wrestlers should include tests for pulling strength, pushing strength, and local muscular endurance.
2. Choose valid and reliable tests to measure these parameters, and arrange the testing battery in an appropriate order with sufficient rest between tests to promote test reliability. For example, appropriate tests for wrestling might include push-ups and sit-ups for maximum repetitions in a given time interval. These two tests should be separated by at least 10 minutes of rest to allow recovery from fatigue and thus promote accurate scores.
3. Administer the test battery to as many athletes as possible.
4. Calculate percentile ranks to present a visual profile.
5. Evaluate the athlete based on percentile rank within the group and against the individual's best performances over previous years, if possible.

CONCLUSION

Motor abilities and body composition variables that can be improved through strength and conditioning programs include maximum muscular strength, maximum muscular power, anaerobic capacity, local muscular endurance, aerobic capacity, agility, speed, flexibility, girths, percent body fat, and lean body mass. Performance testing can be used to evaluate basic motor abilities, as well as the improvement of individual athletes over time and the overall effectiveness of a physical conditioning program. Numerous tests are available to measure sport-specific physical capabilities and training status. Strength and conditioning professionals can either use existing normative data to evaluate athletic performance or develop their own normative data. Statistical measures of central tendency, variability, percentile rank, and standard scores are useful for evaluating physical abilities and the improvement of a group as well as the individuals within the group.

KEY TERMS

aerobic capacity 251
aerobic power 251
agility 252
anaerobic capacity 251
anaerobic power 250
anthropometry 252
athletic performance 250
athletic profile 272
body composition 252
central tendency 271
descriptive statistics 271
difference score 271
flexibility 252
high-speed muscular strength 250
inferential statistics 272
local muscular endurance 251
low-speed muscular strength 250
maximal anaerobic muscular power 250
mean 271
median 271
mode 271
percentile rank 272
range 271
speed 252
standard deviation 271
variability 271

STUDY QUESTIONS

1. Anaerobic capacity is quantified as the maximal power output achieved during activity lasting
   a. less than 10 seconds.
   b. 30 to 90 seconds.
   c. 2 to 3 minutes.
   d. longer than 5 minutes.
2. All of the following tests are used to measure maximum muscular power EXCEPT the
   a. Margaria-Kalamen test.
   b. vertical jump.
   c. 40-yard (37 m) sprint.
   d. 1RM power clean.
3. Flexibility of which of these muscle groups or body areas is assessed during the sit-and-reach test?
   I. hamstrings
   II. erector spinae
   III. lumbar spine
   IV. hip flexors
   a. I and III only
   b. II and IV only
   c. I, II, and III only
   d. II, III, and IV only

4. Which of the following is a reason for a trial of the T-test to be disqualified (see figure 12.7)?
   a. touching the base of cone D
   b. shuffling from cone C to cone D
   c. crossing the feet from cone B to cone C
   d. running forward from cone A to cone B

5. Which of the following is the correct arm position when measuring the girth of the upper arm?
   a. neutral shoulder with elbow flexed to 90 degrees
   b. elbow extended with forearm pronated
   c. shoulder abducted to 90 degrees with elbow extended
   d. elbow flexed to 90 degrees with forearm supinated

6. Of the locations measured in the 3-site skinfold protocols, which of the following are only measured on women?
   I. thigh
   II. suprailiac
   III. abdomen
   IV. triceps
   a. I and III only
   b. I and IV only
   c. II and III only
   d. II and IV only

7. When compiling results from the volleyball team's vertical jump testing, the strength and conditioning professional notices that most scores are similar, but there are three scores that are much higher than the rest. Which of the following measures of central tendency is most appropriate for this group?
   a. mean
   b. median
   c. mode
   d. variance

TABLE 12.1

Percentile Values of the 1RM Bench Press, Squat, and Power Clean in NCAA Division I Female Collegiate Athletes

	BASKETBALL						SOFTBALL					
	1RM bench press		1RM squat		1RM power clean		1RM bench press		1RM squat		1RM power clean	
% rank	lb	kg	lb	kg	lb	kg	lb	kg	lb	kg	lb	kg
90	124	56	178	81	130	59	117	53	184	84	122	55
80	119	54	160	73	124	56	108	49	170	77	115	52
70	115	52	147	67	117	53	104	47	148	67	106	48
60	112	51	135	61	112	51	99	45	139	63	100	45
50	106	48	129	59	110	50	95	43	126	57	94	43
40	102	46	115	52	103	47	90	41	120	55	93	42
30	96	44	112	51	96	44	85	39	112	51	88	40
20	88	40	101	46	88	40	80	36	94	43	80	36
10	82	37	81	37	77	35	69	31	76	35	71	32
$\bar{x}$	105	48	130	59	106	48	94	43	130	59	97	44
SD	18	8	42	19	20	9	18	8	42	19	20	9
n	120		86		85		105		97		80	

	SWIMMING				VOLLEYBALL			
	1RM bench press		1RM squat		1RM bench press		1RM squat	
% rank	lb	kg	lb	kg	lb	kg	lb	kg
90	116	53	145	66	113	51	185	84
80	109	50	135	61	108	49	171	78
70	106	48	129	59	104	47	165	75
60	101	46	120	55	100	45	153	70
50	97	44	116	53	98	45	143	65
40	94	43	112	51	96	44	136	62
30	93	42	104	47	90	41	126	57
20	88	40	101	46	85	39	112	51
10	78	35	97	44	79	36	98	45
$\bar{x}$	98	45	118	54	97	44	144	65
SD	15	7	19	9	14	6	33	15
n	42		35		67		62	

lb = pounds. $\bar{x}$ = mean, SD = standard deviation, *n* = sample size.

Adapted, by permission, from Hoffman, 2006 (32).

TABLE 12.2

Percentile Values of the 1RM Bench Press, Squat, and Power Clean in High School and College American Football Players

	HIGH SCHOOL 14-15 YEARS						HIGH SCHOOL 16-18 YEARS					
	1RM bench press		1RM squat		1RM power clean		1RM bench press		1RM squat		1RM power clean	
% rank	lb	kg	lb	kg	lb	kg	lb	kg	lb	kg	lb	kg
90	243	110	385	175	213	97	275	125	465	211	250	114
80	210	95	344	156	195	89	250	114	425	193	235	107
70	195	89	325	148	190	86	235	107	405	184	225	102
60	185	84	305	139	183	83	225	102	365	166	223	101
50	170	77	295	134	173	79	215	98	335	152	208	95
40	165	75	275	125	165	75	205	93	315	143	200	91
30	155	70	255	116	161	73	195	89	295	134	183	83
20	145	66	236	107	153	70	175	80	275	125	165	75
10	125	57	205	93	141	64	160	73	250	114	145	66
$\bar{x}$	179	81	294	134	176	80	214	97	348	158	204	93
SD	45	20	73	33	32	15	44	20	88	40	43	20
n	214		170		180		339		249		284	

	NCAA DIII				NCAA DI					
	1RM bench press		1RM squat		1RM bench press		1RM squat		1RM power clean	
% rank	lb	kg	lb	kg	lb	kg	lb	kg	lb	kg
90	365	166	470	214	370	168	500	227	300	136
80	325	148	425	193	345	157	455	207	280	127
70	307	140	405	184	325	148	430	195	270	123
60	295	134	385	175	315	143	405	184	261	119
50	280	127	365	166	300	136	395	180	252	115
40	273	124	350*	159*	285	130	375	170	242	110
30	255	116	335	152	270	123	355	161	232	105
20	245	111	315	143	255	116	330	150	220	100
10	225	102	283	129	240	109	300	136	205	93
$\bar{x}$	287	130	375	170	301	137	395	180	252	115
SD	57	26	75	34	53	24	77	35	38	17
n	591		588		1,189		1,074		1,017	

*Hoffman 2006 reported 365 lb, 166 kg, for the 40 percent rank of the NCAA DIII 1RM squat.
lb = pounds. $\bar{x}$ = mean, SD = standard deviation, *n* = sample size.

Reprinted, by permission, from Hoffman, 2006 (32).

TABLE 12.3

Percentile Values of the 1RM Bench Press, Squat, and Power Clean in NCAA Division I Male Baseball and Basketball Athletes

	BASEBALL						BASKETBALL					
	1RM bench press		1RM squat		1RM power clean		1RM bench press		1RM squat		1RM power clean	
% rank	lb	kg	lb	kg	lb	kg	lb	kg	lb	kg	lb	kg
90	273	124	365	166	265	120	269	122	315	143	250	114
80	260	118	324	147	239	109	250	114	305	139	235	107
70	247	112	310	141	225	102	240	109	295	134	230	105
60	239	109	293	133	216	98	230	105	280	127	220	100
50	225	102	270	123	206	94	225	102	265	120	215	98
40	218	99	265	120	200	91	216	98	245	111	205	93
30	203	92	247	112	190	86	210	95	225	102	195	89
20	194	88	237	107	182	83	195	89	195	89	180	82
10	175	80	218	99	162	74	185	84	166	75	162	74
$\bar{x}$	227	103	281	128	210	95	225	102	251	114	209	95
SD	41	19	57	26	36	16	33	15	57	26	34	15
n	170		176		149		142		131		122	

lb = pounds. $\bar{x}$ = mean, SD = standard deviation, n = sample size.

Reprinted, by permission, from Hoffman, 2006 (32).

TABLE 12.4

Vertical Jump, T-Test, 40-Yard (37 m) Sprint, Hexagon Test, and 300-Yard (274 m) Shuttle Descriptive Data* for Various Groups

	Vertical jump		T-test	40-yard (37 m) sprint	Hexagon test	300-yard (274 m) shuttle
Group, sport, or position	inches	cm	seconds	seconds	seconds	seconds
NCAA Division I college American football split ends, strong safeties, offensive and defensive backs	31.5	80		4.6-4.7		<59
NCAA Division I college American football wide receivers and outside linebackers	31	79		4.6-4.7		<59
NCAA Division I college American football linebackers, tight ends, safeties	29.5	75		4.8-4.9		<61
College basketball players (men)	27-29	69-74	8.9			
NCAA Division I college American football quarterbacks	28.5	72		4.8-4.9		
NCAA Division I college American football defensive tackles	28	71		4.9-5.1		<65
NCAA Division I college basketball players (men)	28	71				
NCAA Division I college American football offensive guards	27	69		5.1		<65
Competitive college athletes (men)	25-25.5	64-65	10.0	5.0	12.3	
NCAA Division I college American football offensive tackles	25-26	64-66		5.4		<65
Recreational college athletes (men)	24	61	10.5	5.0	12.3	
High school American football backs and receivers	24	61		5.2		
College baseball players (men)	23	58	9.2			
College tennis players (men)	23	58	9.4			
High school American football linebackers and tight ends	22	56		5.4		
College American football players	21	53		5.35		
College basketball players (women)	21	53	9.9			
17-year-old boys	20	51				
High school American football linemen	20	51		4.9-5.6		
NCAA Division II college basketball guards (women)	19	48				
NCAA Division II college basketball forwards (women)	18	46				
NCAA Division II college basketball centers (women)	17.5	44				
Sedentary college students (men)	16-20.5	41-52	11.1	5.0	14.2	
18- to 34-year-old men	16	41				
Competitive college athletes (women)	16-18.5	41-47	10.8	5.5-5.96	12.9	
College tennis players (women)	15	38	11.1			
Recreational college athletes (women)	15-15.5	38-39	12.5	5.8	13.2	
Sedentary college students (women)	8-14	20-36	13.5	6.4	14.3	
17-year-old girls	13	33				
18- to 34-year-old women	8	20				

*The values listed are either means or 50th percentiles (medians). There was considerable variation in sample size among the groups tested. Thus, the data should be regarded as only descriptive, not normative.

From references 1, 8, 12, 49, 51, 52, 55, 66, and 69.

TABLE 12.5

Margaria-Kalamen Stair Sprint Test Guidelines (Watts)

	MEN'S AGE GROUPS (YEARS)				
Classification	**15-20**	**20-30**	**30-40**	**40-50**	**Over 50**
Excellent	Over 2,197	Over 2,059	Over 1,648	Over 1,226	Over 961
Good	1,844-2,197	1,726-2,059	1,383-1,648	1,040-1,226	814-961
Average	1,471-1,824	1,373-1,716	1,098-1,373	834-1,030	647-804
Fair	1,108-1,461	1,040-1,363	834-1,088	637-824	490-637
Poor	Under 1,108	Under 1,040	Under 834	Under 637	Under 490

	WOMEN'S AGE GROUPS (YEARS)				
Classification	**15-20**	**20-30**	**30-40**	**40-50**	**Over 50**
Excellent	Over 1,785	Over 1,648	Over 1,226	Over 961	Over 736
Good	1,491-1,785	1,383-1,648	1,040-1,226	814-961	608-736
Average	1,187-1,481	1,098-1,373	834-1,030	647-804	481-598
Fair	902-1,177	834-1,089	637-824	490-637	373-471
Poor	Under 902	Under 834	Under 637	Under 490	Under 373

Adapted, by permission, from Fox, Bowers, and Foss, 1993 (23).

TABLE 12.6

Percentile Ranks for Standing Long Jump in Elite Male and Female Athletes

	MALES		FEMALES	
% rank	**inches**	**cm**	**inches**	**cm**
90	148	375	124	315
80	133	339	115	293
70	122	309	110	279
60	116	294	104	264
50	110	279	98	249
40	104	264	92	234
30	98	249	86	219
20	92	234	80	204
10	86	219	74	189

Reprinted, by permission, from Hoffman, 2006 (32).

TABLE 12.7

Rankings for Standing Long Jump in 15- and 16-Year-Old Male and Female Athletes

	MALES		FEMALES	
Category	**inches**	**cm**	**inches**	**cm**
Excellent	79	201	65	166
Above average	73	186	61	156
Average	69	176	57	146
Below average	65	165	53	135
Poor	<65	<165	<53	<135

Reprinted, by permission, from Hoffman, 2006 (32).

TABLE 12.8

Percentiles by Age Groups and Sex for Partial Curl-Up

	AGE AND SEX									
	20-29		30-39		40-49		50-59		60-69	
Percentile*	M	F	M	F	M	F	M	F	M	F
90	75	70	75	55	75	50	74	48	53	50
80	56	45	69	43	75	42	60	30	33	30
70	41	37	46	34	67	33	45	23	26	24
60	31	32	36	28	51	28	35	16	19	19
50	27	27	31	21	39	25	27	9	16	13
40	24	21	26	15	31	20	23	2	9	9
30	20	17	19	12	26	14	19	0	6	3
20	13	12	13	0	21	5	13	0	0	0
10	4	5	0	0	13	0	0	0	0	0

*Descriptors for percentile rankings: 90 = well above average; 70 = above average; 50 = average; 30 = below average; 10 = well below average.

Reprinted, by permission, from American College of Sports Medicine, 2000 (5).

TABLE 12.9

Fitness Categories by Age Groups and Sex for Push-Ups

	AGE AND SEX									
	20-29		30-39		40-49		50-59		60-69	
Category	M	F	M	F	M	F	M	F	M	F
Excellent	36	30	30	27	25	24	21	21	18	17
Very good	35	29	29	26	24	23	20	20	17	16
	29	21	22	20	17	15	13	11	11	12
Good	28	20	21	19	16	14	12	10	10	11
	22	15	17	13	13	11	10	7	8	5
Fair	21	14	16	12	12	10	9	6	7	4
	17	10	12	8	10	5	7	2	5	2
Needs improvement	16	9	11	7	9	4	6	1	4	1

Reprinted, by permission, from Canadian Society for Exercise Physiology, 2003 (14).

TABLE 12.10

Push-Up Standards for U.S. Army Personnel

Male age range	Push-up repetitions in 2 minutes									
17-21	6	13	20	28	35	42	49	57	64	71
22-26	—	5	14	23	31	40	49	58	66	75
27-31	—	1	11	20	30	39	49	58	68	77
32-36	—	—	7	17	26	36	46	56	65	75
37-41	—	—	5	15	24	34	44	54	63	73
42-46	—	—	—	12	21	30	39	48	57	66
47-51	—	—	—	8	17	25	34	42	51	59
52-56	—	—	—	—	11	20	29	38	47	56
57-61	—	—	—	—	9	18	27	36	44	53
62+	—	—	—	—	8	16	25	33	42	50
Points awarded	10	20	30	40	50	60	70	80	90	100
Female age range	**Push-up repetitions in 2 minutes**									
17-21	—	—	2	8	13	19	25	31	36	42
22-26	—	—	—	2	11	17	24	32	39	46
27-31	—	—	—	—	10	17	25	34	42	50
32-36	—	—	—	—	9	15	23	30	38	45
37-41	—	—	—	—	7	13	20	27	33	40
42-46	—	—	—	—	6	12	18	25	31	37
47-51	—	—	—	—	—	10	16	22	28	34
52-56	—	—	—	—	—	9	15	20	26	31
57-61	—	—	—	—	—	8	13	18	23	28
62+	—	—	—	—	—	7	12	16	21	25
Points awarded	10	20	30	40	50	60	70	80	90	100

60 points is passing; 90 points is excellent.

Data from U.S. Department of the Army, 1998 (18).

TABLE 12.11

YMCA Bench Press Norms

	AGE AND SEX											
	18-25		26-35		36-45		46-55		56-65		>65	
Percentile	M	F	M	F	M	F	M	F	M	F	M	F
90	44	42	41	40	36	33	28	29	24	24	20	18
80	37	34	33	32	29	28	22	22	20	20	14	14
70	33	28	29	28	25	24	20	18	14	14	10	10
60	29	25	26	24	22	21	16	14	12	12	10	8
50	26	21	22	21	20	17	13	12	10	9	8	6
40	22	18	20	17	17	14	11	9	8	6	6	4
30	20	16	17	14	14	12	9	7	5	5	4	3
20	16	12	13	12	10	8	6	5	3	3	2	1
10	10	6	9	6	6	4	2	1	1	1	1	0

Score is number of repetitions completed in 1 minute using an 80-pound (36 kg) barbell for men and a 35-pound (16 kg) barbell for women.

Adapted from YMCA, 2000 (71).

TABLE 12.12

Maximal Rate of Oxygen Consumption, 1.5-Mile (2.4 km) Run Time, Sit-and-Reach Test, and Body Composition: Percentile Rankings for 20- to 29-Year-Old Males

	$\dot{V}O_2max$	1.5-mile (2.4 km) run time	Sit-and-reach test		Body fat
Percentile rank	$ml \cdot kg^{-1} \cdot min^{-1}$	minutes:seconds	inches	cm	%
99	>59	<7:29	>23.0	>58	<2.4
90	51	9:09	21.75	55	7.1
80	48	10:16	20.5	52	9.4
70	47	10:47	19.5	50	11.8
60	44	11:41	18.5	47	14.1
50	42	12:18	17.5	44	15.9
40	41	12:51	16.5	42	17.4
30	40	13:22	15.5	39	19.5
20	37	14:13	14.5	37	22.4
10	34	15:10	12.25	31	25.9
01	<27	>17:48	<10.5	<27	>36.4

Adapted from American College of Sports Medicine, 1995 (4).

TABLE 12.13

Maximal Rate of Oxygen Consumption, 1.5-Mile (2.4 km) Run Time, Sit-and-Reach Test, and Body Composition: Percentile Rankings for 20- to 29-Year-Old Females

	$\dot{V}O_2max$	1.5-mile (2.4 km) run time	Sit-and-reach test		Body fat
Percentile rank	ml · kg^{-1} · min^{-1}	minutes:seconds	inches	cm	%
99	>53	<8:33	>24.0	>61	<5.4
90	44	11:43	23.75	60	14.5
80	41	12:51	22.5	57	17.1
70	38	13:53	21.5	55	19.0
60	37	14:24	20.5	52	20.6
50	35	14:55	20.0	51	22.1
40	34	15:26	19.25	49	23.7
30	32	15:57	18.25	46	25.4
20	31	16:33	17.0	43	27.7
10	28	17:21	15.5	39	32.1
01	<23	>19:25	<14.0	<36	>40.5

Adapted from American College of Sports Medicine, 1995 (4).

TABLE 12.14

Maximal Rate of Oxygen Consumption, 1.5-Mile (2.4 km) Run Time, Sit-and-Reach Test, and Body Composition: Percentile Rankings for 30- to 39-Year-Old Males

	$\dot{V}O_2max$	1.5-mile (2.4 km) run time	Sit-and-reach test		Body fat
Percentile rank	ml · kg^{-1} · min^{-1}	minutes:seconds	inches	cm	%
99	>59	<7:11	>22.0	>56	<5.2
90	50	9:30	21.0	53	11.3
80	47	10:47	19.5	50	13.9
70	45	11:34	18.5	47	15.9
60	42	12:20	17.5	44	17.5
50	41	12:51	16.5	42	19.0
40	39	13:36	15.5	39	20.5
30	37	14:08	14.5	37	22.3
20	35	14:52	13.0	33	24.2
10	33	15:52	11.0	28	27.3
01	<27	>18:00	<9.25	<23	>35.6

Adapted from American College of Sports Medicine, 1995 (4).

TABLE 12.15

Maximal Rate of Oxygen Consumption, 1.5-Mile (2.4 km) Run Time, Sit-and-Reach Test, and Body Composition: Percentile Rankings for 30- to 39-Year-Old Females

	$\dot{V}O_2max$	1.5-mile (2.4 km) run time	Sit-and-reach test		Body fat
Percentile rank	$ml \cdot kg^{-1} \cdot min^{-1}$	minutes:seconds	inches	cm	%
99	>49	<10:05	>24.0	>61	<7.3
90	41	12:51	22.5	57	15.5
80	39	13:43	21.5	55	18.0
70	37	14:24	20.5	52	20.0
60	35	15:08	20.0	51	21.6
50	34	15:26	19.0	48	23.1
40	32	15:57	18.25	46	24.9
30	31	16:35	17.25	44	27.0
20	29	17:14	16.5	42	29.3
10	27	18:00	14.5	37	32.8
01	<22	>19:27	<12.0	<30	>40.0

Adapted from American College of Sports Medicine, 1995 (4).

TABLE 12.16

$\dot{V}O_2max$ Descriptive Data for Athletes in Various Sports

Classification and typical $\dot{V}O_2max$ of athletes playing the sport ($ml \cdot kg^{-1} \cdot min^{-1}$)		Sport
Extremely high		
Males	70+	Cross-country skiing
Females	60+	Middle-distance running
		Long-distance running
Very high		
Males	63-69	Bicycling
Females	54-59	Rowing
		Racewalking
High		
Males	57-62	Soccer
Females	49-53	Middle-distance swimming
		Canoe racing
		Handball
		Racquetball
		Speed skating
		Figure skating
		Downhill skiing
		Wrestling
Above average		
Males	52-56	Basketball
Females	44-48	Ballet dancing
		American football (offensive, defensive backs)
		Gymnastics
		Hockey
		Horse racing (jockey)
		Sprint swimming
		Tennis
		Sprint running
		Jumping
Average		
Males	44-51	Baseball, softball
Females	35-43	American football (linemen, quarterbacks)
		Shot put
		Discus throw
		Olympic-style weightlifting
		Bodybuilding

Data from Nieman, 1995 (48).

TABLE 12.17

Percentile Ranks for the 12-Minute Run

	AGE (YEARS) AND DISTANCE									
	20-29		30-39		40-49		50-59		60+	
Percentile	km	miles	km	miles	km	miles	km	miles	km	miles
Men	*n* = 1,675		*n* = 7,095		*n* = 6,837		*n* = 3,808		*n* = 1,005	
90	2.800	1.74	2.752	1.71	2.655	1.65	2.527	1.57	2.398	1.49
80	2.655	1.65	2.591	1.61	2.478	1.54	2.334	1.45	2.205	1.37
70	2.591	1.61	2.494	1.55	2.366	1.47	2.221	1.38	2.076	1.29
60	2.478	1.54	2.398	1.49	2.285	1.42	2.140	1.33	1.996	1.24
50	2.414	1.50	2.334	1.45	2.205	1.37	2.076	1.29	1.915	1.19
40	2.334	1.45	2.237	1.39	2.140	1.33	2.012	1.25	1.851	1.15
30	2.269	1.41	2.173	1.35	2.076	1.29	1.947	1.21	1.786	1.11
20	2.157	1.34	2.076	1.29	1.980	1.23	1.851	1.15	1.690	1.05
10	2.044	1.27	1.947	1.21	1.883	1.17	1.754	1.09	1.529	0.95
Women	*n* = 764		*n* = 2,049		*n* = 1,630		*n* = 878		*n* = 202	
90	2.478	1.54	2.334	1.45	2.269	1.41	2.076	1.29	2.076	1.29
80	2.334	1.45	2.221	1.38	2.124	1.32	1.947	1.21	1.899	1.18
70	2.205	1.37	2.140	1.33	2.012	1.25	1.883	1.17	1.819	1.13
60	2.140	1.33	2.044	1.27	1.947	1.21	1.819	1.13	1.722	1.07
50	2.076	1.29	2.012	1.25	1.883	1.17	1.770	1.10	1.658	1.03
40	2.012	1.25	1.947	1.21	1.819	1.13	1.706	1.06	1.593	0.99
30	1.947	1.21	1.867	1.16	1.770	1.10	1.642	1.02	1.561	0.97
20	1.867	1.16	1.786	1.11	1.690	1.05	1.577	0.98	1.513	0.94
10	1.770	1.10	1.690	1.05	1.625	1.01	1.497	0.93	1.432	0.89

Reprinted, by permission, from Hoffman, 2006 (32).

TABLE 12.18

Percentile Ranks for the Pro Agility Test (Seconds) in NCAA Division I College Athletes

% rank	Women's volleyball	Women's basketball	Women's softball	Men's basketball	Men's baseball	Men's American football
90	4.75	4.65	4.88	4.22	4.25	4.21
80	4.84	4.82	4.96	4.29	4.36	4.31
70	4.91	4.86	5.03	4.35	4.41	4.38
60	4.98	4.94	5.10	4.39	4.46	4.44
50	5.01	5.06	5.17	4.41	4.50	4.52
40	5.08	5.10	5.24	4.44	4.55	4.59
30	5.17	5.14	5.33	4.48	4.61	4.66
20	5.23	5.23	5.40	4.51	4.69	4.76
10	5.32	5.36	5.55	4.61	4.76	4.89
$\bar{x}$	5.03	5.02	5.19	4.41	4.53	4.54
SD	0.20	0.26	0.26	0.18	0.23	0.27
n	81	128	118	97	165	869

Data collected using electronic timing devices. $\bar{x}$ = mean, SD = standard deviation, n = sample size.

Reprinted, by permission, from Hoffman, 2006 (32).

TABLE 12.19

Equations for Calculating Estimated Body Density From Skinfold Measurements Among Various Populations

SKF sites[a]	Population subgroups	Sex	Age	Equation	Reference
Σ7SKF (chest + abdomen + triceps + subscapular + suprailiac + midaxilla + thigh)	Black or Hispanic	Women	18-55 years	Db (g/cc)[b] = 1.0970 − 0.00046971 (Σ7SKF) + 0.00000056 $(\Sigma 7SKF)^2$ − 0.00012828 (Age)	Jackson et al. (36)
Σ7SKF (chest + abdomen + triceps + subscapular + suprailiac + midaxilla + thigh)	Black or athletes	Men	18-61 years	Db (g/cc)[b] = 1.1120 − 0.00043499 (Σ7SKF) + 0.00000055 $(\Sigma 7SKF)^2$ − 0.00028826 (Age)	Jackson and Pollock (34)
Σ4SKF (triceps + anterior suprailiac + abdomen + thigh)	Athletes	Women	18-29 years	Db (g/cc)[b] = 1.096095 − 0.0006952 (Σ4SKF) − 0.0000011 $(\Sigma 4SKF)^2$ − 0.0000714 (Age)	Jackson et al. (36)
Σ3SKF (triceps + suprailiac + thigh)	White or anorexic	Women	18-55 years	Db (g/cc)[b] = 1.0994921 − 0.0009929 (Σ3SKF) + 0.0000023 $(\Sigma 3SKF)^2$ − 0.0001392 (Age)	Jackson et al. (36)
Σ3SKF (chest + abdomen + thigh)	White	Men	18-61 years	Db (g/cc)[b] = 1.109380 − 0.0008267 (Σ3SKF) + 0.0000016 $(\Sigma 3SKF)^2$ − 0.0002574 (Age)	Jackson and Pollock (34)
Σ2SKF (triceps + calf)	Black or white	Boys	6-17 years	% BF = 0.735 (Σ2SKF) + 1.0	Slaughter et al. (63)
Σ2SKF (triceps + calf)	Black or white	Girls	6-17 years	% BF = 0.610 (Σ2SKF) + 5.1	Slaughter et al. (63)
Suprailiac, triceps	Athletes	Women	High school and college age	Db (g/cc)[b] = 1.0764 − (0.00081 × suprailiac) − (0.00088 × triceps)	Sloan and Weir (64)
Thigh, subscapular	Athletes	Men	High school and college age	Db (g/cc)[b] = 1.1043 − (0.00133 × thigh) − (0.00131 × subscapular)	Sloan and Weir (64)

[a]ΣSKF = sum of skinfolds (mm); Db = body density.

[b]Use population-specific conversion formulas (see table 12.20) to calculate %BF from Db.

Adapted, by permission, from Heyward, 2002 (29).

TABLE 12.20

Population-Specific Equations for Calculating Estimated Percent Body Fat From Body Density

Population	Age	Sex	%BF[a]
Race			
American Indian	18-60	Female	(4.81/Db) – 4.34
Black	18-32	Male	(4.37/Db) – 3.93
	24-79	Female	(4.85/Db) – 4.39
Hispanic	20-40	Female	(4.87/Db) – 4.41
Japanese native	18-48	Male	(4.97/Db) – 4.52
		Female	(4.76/Db) – 4.28
	61-78	Male	(4.87/Db) – 4.41
		Female	(4.95/Db) – 4.50
White	7-12	Male	(5.30/Db) – 4.89
		Female	(5.35/Db) – 4.95
	13-16	Male	(5.07/Db) – 4.64
		Female	(5.10/Db) – 4.66
	17-19	Male	(4.99/Db) – 4.55
		Female	(5.05/Db) – 4.62
	20-80	Male	(4.95/Db) – 4.50
		Female	(5.01/Db) – 4.57
Level of body fatness			
Anorexic	15-30	Female	(5.26/Db) – 4.83
Obese	17-62	Female	(5.00/Db) – 4.56
Athletes[b]	High school and college age	Male and female	(4.57/Db) – 4.142

BF = body fat; Db = body density.

[a]Multiply the value from this column's calculations by 100 to yield the percentage value.

[b]Use this formula with the Sloan and Weir formula (64) from table 12.19.

Adapted, by permission, from Heyward and Stolarczyk, 1996 (30).

TABLE 12.21

Percent Body Fat Descriptive Data for Athletes in Various Sports

Classification and typical percent body fat of athletes playing the sport		Sport
Extremely lean		
Males	<7%	Gymnastics
Females	<15%	Bodybuilding (at contest)
		Wrestling (at contest)
		Cross-country
Very lean		
Males	8-10%	Men's basketball
Females	16-18%	Racquetball
		Rowing
		Soccer
		Track and field decathlon (men)
		Track and field heptathlon (women)
Leaner than average		
Males	11-13%	Men's baseball
Females	19-20%	Canoeing
		Downhill skiing
		Speed skating
		Olympic-style weightlifting
Average		
Males	14-17%	Women's basketball
Females	21-25%	American football quarterbacks, kickers, linebackers
		Hockey
		Horse racing (jockey)
		Tennis
		Discus throw
		Volleyball
		Women's softball
		Powerlifting
Fatter than average		
Males	18-22%	American football (linemen)
Females	26-30%	Shot put

Data from Nieman, 1995 (48).

TABLE 12.22

Criterion Scores and Normative Values for Percent Body Fat for Males and Females

	AGE (YEARS)						
Male rating (criterion scores)*	**6-17****	**18-25**	**26-35**	**36-45**	**46-55**	**56-65**	**66+**
Very lean	<5 (not recommended)	4-7	8-12	10-14	12-16	15-18	15-18
Lean (low)	5-10	8-10	13-15	16-18	18-20	19-21	19-21
Leaner than average	—	11-13	16-18	19-21	21-23	22-24	22-23
Average (mid)	11-25	14-16	19-21	22-24	24-25	24-26	24-25
Fatter than average	—	18-20	22-24	25-26	26-28	26-28	25-27
Fat (upper)	26-31	22-26	25-28	27-29	29-31	29-31	28-30
Overfat (obesity)	>31	28-37	30-37	30-38	32-38	32-38	31-38
Male percentiles (normative references)***		**20-29**	**30-39**	**40-49**	**50-59**	**60+**	
90		7.1	11.3	13.6	15.3	15.3	
80		9.4	13.9	16.3	17.9	18.4	
70		11.8	15.9	18.1	19.8	20.3	
60		14.1	17.5	19.6	21.3	22.0	
50		15.9	19.0	21.1	22.7	23.5	
40		17.4	20.5	22.5	24.1	25.0	
30		19.5	22.3	24.1	25.7	26.7	
20		22.4	24.2	26.1	27.5	28.5	
10		25.9	27.3	28.9	30.3	31.2	
Female rating (criterion scores)*	**6-17****	**18-25**	**26-35**	**36-45**	**46-55**	**56-65**	**66+**
Very lean	<12 (not recommended)	13-17	13-18	15-19	18-22	18-23	16-18
Lean (low)	12-15	18-20	19-21	20-23	23-25	24-26	22-25
Leaner than average	—	21-23	22-23	24-26	26-28	28-30	27-29
Average (mid)	16-30	24-25	24-26	27-29	29-31	31-33	30-32
Fatter than average	—	26-28	27-30	30-32	32-34	34-36	33-35
Fat (upper)	31-36	29-31	31-35	33-36	36-38	36-38	36-38
Overfat (obesity)	>36	33-43	36-48	39-48	40-49	39-46	39-40

(continued)

TABLE 12.22 *(continued)*

	AGE (YEARS)				
Female percentiles (normative references)* **	**20-29**	**30-39**	**40-49**	**50-59**	**60+**
90	14.5	15.5	18.5	21.6	21.1
80	17.1	18.0	21.3	25.0	25.1
70	19.0	20.0	23.5	26.6	27.5
60	20.6	21.6	24.9	28.5	29.3
50	22.1	23.1	26.4	30.1	30.9
40	23.7	24.9	28.1	31.6	32.5
30	25.4	27.0	30.1	33.5	34.3
20	27.7	29.3	32.1	35.6	36.6
10	32.1	32.8	35.0	37.9	39.3

When strength and conditioning professionals assess an athlete's body composition, they must account for a standard error of the estimate (SEE) and report a range of percentages that the athlete falls into. Note that the minimum SEE for population-specific skinfold equations is ±3% to ±5%. Therefore, if a 25-year-old male athlete's body fat is measured at 24%, there is a minimum of a 6% range (21-27%) that suggests a criterion reference score of "fat." Note that reporting an athlete's body fat percentage with an SEE range can also cover any gaps and overlaps in the criterion-referenced norms shown. For example, what is the criterion score for a 30-year-old male with 29% body fat? The minimum SEE of ±3% places this athlete between 26% and 32% and therefore would suggest a criterion reference score of "fat-overfat" or "borderline overfat."

*Data for male and female ratings (criterion scores), ages 18-66+, are adapted from Morrow et al., 2005 (47).

**Data for male and female ratings (criterion scores), ages 6-17, are from Lohman, Houtkooper, and Going, 1997 (43).

***Data for male and female percentiles (normative references) are reprinted from ACSM, 2000 (5).

Adapted, by permission, from Golding, Myers, and Sinning, 1989 (25).

SECTION 3

Exercise Techniques

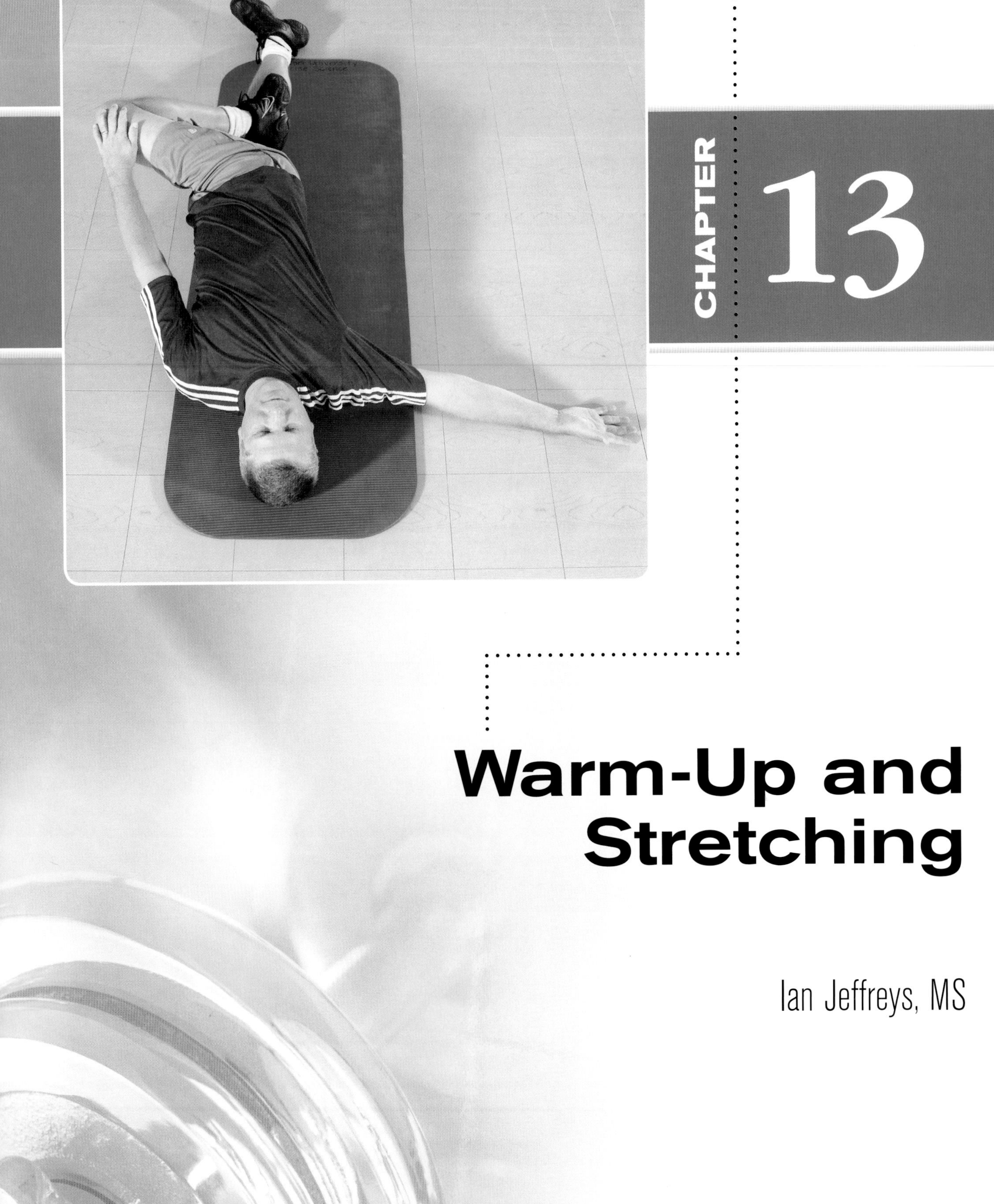

CHAPTER 13

Warm-Up and Stretching

Ian Jeffreys, MS

After completing this chapter, you will be able to

- identify the benefits and components of a preexercise warm-up,
- assess the suitability of performing stretching exercises for a warm-up,
- identify the factors that affect flexibility,
- describe flexibility exercises that take advantage of proprioceptive neuromuscular facilitation,
- explain the mechanisms that cause the muscular inhibition that improves the stretch, and
- select and apply appropriate static and dynamic stretching methods.

This chapter is devoted to two key areas, warm-up and flexibility. While the two are traditionally linked, it is important to differentiate between them as they have different key functions. Warm-up is designed to prepare an athlete for training or competition and can improve subsequent performance and lessen the risk of injury. This chapter discusses the aims of a warm-up and suggests appropriate protocols for designing an effective warm-up. On the other hand, flexibility training, through the use of different forms of stretching, aims to increase the range of motion around a joint. This chapter also looks at the use of different stretching protocols to facilitate this aim.

WARM-UP

A warm-up period is important before any athletic performance, the goal being to prepare the athlete mentally and physically for exercise or competition (45). A well-designed warm-up can increase muscle temperature, core temperature, and blood flow (58) and also disrupt transient connective tissue bonds (29). These effects can have the following positive impacts on performance:

- Faster muscle contraction and relaxation of both agonist and antagonist muscles (45)
- Improvements in the rate of force development and reaction time (4)
- Improvements in muscle strength and power (10, 29)
- Lowered viscous resistance in muscles (29)
- Improved oxygen delivery due to the Bohr effect, whereby higher temperatures facilitate oxygen release from hemoglobin and myoglobin (58)
- Increased blood flow to active muscles (58)
- Enhanced metabolic reactions (29)

While the influence of a warm-up on injury prevention is unclear, the evidence suggests a positive effect (37, 74, 75). For example, increased muscle temperature can increase the resistance to muscle tear (71).

Stretching During Warm-Up

Static stretching has long been used in a warm-up, with the aim of enhancing performance and reducing the risk of injury. Recent reviews of the literature surrounding the role of static stretching question this practice (72, 73, 89). There is little, if any, evidence that stretching pre- or postparticipation prevents injury (44, 65, 74, 75, 77) or subsequent muscle soreness (48). Although static stretching before activity might increase performance in sports that require an increased range of motion, such as gymnastics (77), static stretching can compromise muscle performance (51). In these cases it is important that the strength and conditioning professional perform a benefit–risk analysis when choosing whether or not to include static stretching in a warm-up (56).

Although some studies demonstrated that static stretching had no effect on subsequent performance (53, 79, 87), static stretching has also been shown to lead to a decrease in force production (9, 21, 22, 23, 31, 66), power performance (20, 81, 88), running speed (34), reaction and movement time (8), and strength endurance (63). Additionally, both proprioceptive neuromuscular facilitation (PNF) stretching (14) and ballistic stretching (62) have been shown to be detrimental to subsequent performance.

Dynamic stretching does not seem to elicit the performance reduction effects of static and PNF stretching (34) and has been shown to improve subsequent running performance (34, 53, 87). Given these findings, the use of static, PNF, and ballistic stretching in warm-up needs to be questioned. Based on current evidence, dynamic stretching would be the preferred option for stretching during a warm-up.

The degree of stretching required in the warm-up depends on the type of sport. Sports in which increased flexibility is needed, such as gymnastics or diving, require a greater degree of stretching (41). Additionally, those with high demands for a stretch-shortening cycle of high intensity, as in sprinting and American football, are likely to require more stretching than those with low or medium stretch-shortening cycle activity, as in jogging or cycling (86). Strength and conditioning professionals should look at the specific range of motion and stretch-shortening cycle requirements of the sport or activity and use this information when designing an appropriate warm-up regimen.

Components of a Warm-Up

A total warm-up program includes the following two components:

- A **general warm-up** period (18, 67) may consist of 5 to 10 minutes of slow activity such as jogging or skipping. Alternatively, low-intensity sport-specific actions such as dribbling a soccer ball can be productive at this time. This provides a very sport-specific general warm-up that aids in skill development and raises body temperature. The aim of this period is to increase heart rate, blood flow, deep muscle temperature, respiration rate, and perspiration and to decrease viscosity of joint fluids (26).
- A **specific warm-up** period incorporates movements similar to the movements of the athlete's sport. It involves 8 to 12 minutes of dynamic stretching focusing on movements that work through the range of motion required for the sport, such as the walking knee lift. This is followed by sport-specific movements of increasing intensity such as sprint drills, bounding activities, or jumping. The more power necessary for the sport or activity, the more important the warm-up becomes (35). Including high-intensity dynamic exercises can facilitate subsequent performance (12, 32, 88). This phase should also include rehearsal of the skill to be performed (89).

The warm-up should progress gradually and provide sufficient intensity to increase muscle and core temperatures without causing fatigue or reducing energy stores (58). It is likely that there are optimal levels of warm-up (77) and that these will be related to the sport, the individual, and the environment.

FLEXIBILITY

The degree of movement that occurs at a joint is called the **range of motion (ROM)**. The ROM of a particular joint is determined by a number of factors including connective tissue structure, activity level, age, and sex. Range of motion is specific to each joint's anatomy and the movements required at that joint. It is therefore important to keep the requirements of each sport in mind when assessing ROM.

Flexibility is a measure of ROM and has static and dynamic components. **Static flexibility** is the range of possible movement about a joint (19, 26) and its surrounding muscles during a passive movement (36, 39). Static flexibility requires no voluntary muscular activity; an external force such as gravity, a partner, or a machine provides the force for a stretch. **Dynamic flexibility** refers to the available ROM during active movements and therefore requires voluntary muscular actions. Dynamic ROM is generally greater than static ROM. The relationship between static and dynamic ROM is unresolved (46); therefore, the direct transfer between measures of static flexibility and sport performance cannot be determined.

Flexibility and Performance

Sports and activities have specific requirements for ROM, and it is likely that optimal levels of flexibility exist for each activity, these being related to the movements within the particular sport (40, 77). Therefore there are optimal ranges of flexibility for different sports and activities, and injury risk may be increased when an athlete is outside of this range. It is important to note that both inflexibility and hyperflexibility can result in higher risks of injury (68, 77). In addition, an imbalance in flexibility could predispose the individual to an increased risk of injury (49, 50).

Factors Affecting Flexibility

A number of anatomical and training-related factors affect flexibility. Some factors—such as joint structure, age, and sex—cannot be altered significantly by training. Those activities related to training, including activity level, resistance training, and stretching exercises, can alter flexibility. Strength and conditioning professionals should consider each athlete's unique combination of factors and sport requirements when recommending flexibility exercises.

Joint Structure

The structure of a joint determines its ROM (57). **Ball-and-socket joints**, such as the hip and shoulder, move in all anatomical planes and have the greatest ROM of all joints (2). The wrist is an **ellipsoidal joint** (an oval-shaped condyle that fits into an elliptical cavity) primarily allowing movement in the sagittal and frontal planes; its ROM is significantly less than that of the shoulder or hip (2). In contrast, the knee is a modified **hinge joint**, with movement primarily in the sagittal plane; its ROM is less than that of either a ball-and-socket joint or the ellipsoidal wrist joint. The type of joint, the shapes of the joints' articulating surfaces, and the soft tissues surrounding the joint all affect its ROM.

Age and Sex

Young people tend to be more flexible than older people (84), and females tend to be more flexible than males (39). Differences in flexibility between young men and women may be due in part to structural and anatomical differences and the type and extent of activities performed. Older people undergo a process called **fibrosis**, in which fibrous connective tissue replaces degenerating muscle fibers (2). This is likely due to inactivity and a tendency to use less of the available ROM during movement. Just as older people can improve strength, however, they can improve flexibility with appropriate exercise.

Connective Tissue

Tendons, ligaments, fascial sheaths, joint capsules, and skin may limit ROM (26). **Elasticity** (the ability to return to original resting length after a passive stretch) and **plasticity** (the tendency to assume a new and greater length after a passive stretch) of connective tissue are other factors that determine ROM (35, 85). Stretching exercises can positively affect connective tissues by taking advantage of their plastic potential.

Resistance Training With Limited Range of Motion

Although a comprehensive and proper resistance training program may increase flexibility (52, 76), heavy resistance training with limited ROM during the exercises may decrease ROM (26). To prevent loss of ROM, an athlete should perform exercises that develop both agonist and antagonist muscles (14) and should exercise through the full available ROM of the involved joints.

Muscle Bulk

A large increase in muscle bulk may adversely affect ROM by impeding joint movement. An athlete with large biceps and deltoids, for example, may experience difficulty in stretching the triceps (26), racking a power clean, or holding a bar while performing the front squat. Although altering the training program can decrease the amount of muscle bulk, this may not be advisable for large power athletes such as shot-putters or American football offensive linemen. Strength and conditioning professionals should keep the requirements of the athlete's sport in mind; the need for large muscles may supersede the need for extreme joint mobility.

Activity Level

An active person tends to be more flexible than an inactive one (39). This is particularly true if the activity includes flexibility exercises but is also true if the person performs other activities, such as resistance training and functional activities. Both men and women have successfully increased their flexibility as an outcome of a properly designed resistance training program (83). It is also important to understand that activity level alone will not improve flexibility; stretching exercises are essential if joint flexibility is to be maintained or increased.

Frequency, Duration, and Intensity of Stretching

As with all forms of training, frequency, duration, and intensity are important issues in program design (24). Both static (11) and PNF (30) stretching have been shown to increase joint flexibility around the knee, hip, trunk, shoulder, and ankle joints (77). Despite this, the exact mechanisms responsible for increased flexibility are still unclear. The acute effects of stretching on ROM are transient and are greatest immediately after the stretching session; then they decline, with the duration of significant improvements in flexibility ranging from 3 minutes (25) to 24 hours (27). For longer-lasting effects, a stretching program is required (77). Stretching twice per week for a minimum of five weeks has been shown to significantly improve flexibility (36). Despite this, the literature provides limited guidelines regarding specific stretching parameters, especially for PNF methods (26).

In terms of the appropriate duration for a static stretch, 15 to 30 seconds is generally recommended (68) and has been shown to be more effective than shorter durations (69, 82). Evidence supports the use of 30 seconds (5, 6, 7). Another consideration is the total stretch time throughout a day, which may be as important as the duration of a single stretch (15, 69). When performing static stretches, athletes should hold the stretches at a position of mild discomfort (not pain). Joint integrity should never be compromised in order to increase ROM. All stretching sessions should be preceded by a period of general warm-up to raise muscle temperature. Because neural and vascular structures are stretched during flexibility exercises, athletes should be monitored for a loss of sensation or radiating pain.

When Should an Athlete Stretch?

Stretching should be performed at the following times for optimal benefits:

- *Following practice and competition.* Postpractice stretching facilitates ROM improvements (38) because of increased muscle temperature (35). It should be performed within 5 to 10 minutes after practice. The increased body temperature increases the elastic properties of collagen within muscles and tendons, which allows for a greater stretch magnitude. Postpractice stretching may also decrease muscle soreness (67) although the evidence on this is ambiguous (1, 54).
- *As a separate session.* If increased levels of flexibility are required, additional stretching sessions may be needed. In this case, stretching should be preceded by a thorough warm-up to allow for the increase in muscle temperature necessary for effective stretching. This type of session can be especially useful as a recovery session on the day after a competition.

Proprioceptors and Stretching

Two important proprioceptors should be considered during stretching: **muscle spindles** and **Golgi tendon organs (GTOs)**. Muscle spindles, located within intrafusal muscle fibers that run parallel to extrafusal muscle fibers, monitor changes in muscle length (36). During a rapid stretching movement, a sensory neuron from the muscle spindle innervates a motor neuron in the spine. The motor neuron then causes a muscle action of the previously stretched extrafusal muscle fibers; this is the **stretch reflex**. Stimulation of the muscle spindle and the subsequent activation of the stretch reflex should be avoided during stretching, as motion will be limited by the reflexive muscle action. If the muscle spindles are not stimulated, the muscle relaxes and allows greater stretch. Because of the very slow movement during static stretching (see the next section, "Types of Stretching"), the stretch reflex is not invoked. Rapid (ballistic and dynamic) stretching movements may stimulate the muscle spindles, causing a stretch reflex.

The GTO, a **mechanoreceptor** located near the musculotendinous junction, is sensitive to increases in muscular tension. When stimulated, the GTO causes a muscle to reflexively relax. Relaxation that occurs in the same muscle that is experiencing increased tension is called **autogenic inhibition** (16, 19, 61). Autogenic inhibition is accomplished via active contraction of a muscle immediately before a passive stretch of that same muscle. Tension built up during the active contraction stimulates the GTO, causing a reflexive relaxation of the muscle during the subsequent passive stretch. Relaxation that occurs in the muscle opposing the muscle experiencing the increased tension is called **reciprocal inhibition** (16, 61). This is accomplished when one simultaneously contracts the muscle opposing the muscle that is being passively stretched. Here the tension in the contracting muscle stimulates the GTO and causes a simultaneous reflexive relaxation of the stretched muscle.

TYPES OF STRETCHING

Stretching requires movement of a body segment to a point of resistance in the ROM. At the point of resistance, a force is applied. This stretching movement can be done either actively or passively. An

active stretch occurs when the person stretching supplies the force of the stretch. During the sitting toe touch, for example, the athlete contracts the abdominal muscles and hip flexors to flex the torso forward to stretch the hamstrings and low back. A **passive stretch** occurs when a partner or stretching machine provides external force to cause or enhance a stretch.

Static Stretch

A **static stretch** is slow and constant, with the end position held for 30 seconds (5, 7). A static stretch includes the relaxation and concurrent elongation of the stretched muscle (33). Because it is performed slowly, static stretching does not elicit the stretch reflex of the stretched muscle (17); therefore, the likelihood of injury is less than during ballistic stretching (2, 35, 78). In addition, static stretching is easy to learn and has been shown to effectively improve ROM (11). Although injury to muscles or connective tissue may result if the static stretch is too intense, there are no real disadvantages to static stretching as long as proper technique is used. Static stretching is appropriate for all athletes in a variety of sports for increasing flexibility.

The sitting toe touch is a good example of a static stretch. To perform this stretch statically, the athlete sits on the ground with the lower extremities together and knees extended, leans forward from the waist, and slowly reaches toward the ankles. The athlete gradually increases the intensity of the stretch by leaning forward until he or she feels mild discomfort in the hamstrings or lower back. The athlete holds this position for 30 seconds and then slowly returns to an upright sitting position. The stretch is static because it is performed slowly and the end position is held without movement (refer to figure on p. 316).

Ballistic Stretch

A **ballistic stretch** typically involves active muscular effort and uses a bouncing-type movement in which the end position is not held (60). Ballistic stretching is often used in the preexercise warm-up; however, it may injure muscles or connective tissues, especially when there has been a previous injury (17). Ballistic stretching usually triggers the stretch reflex that does not allow the involved muscles to relax and defeats the purpose of stretching.

As an example, consider the sitting toe touch performed as a ballistic stretch rather than a static stretch. The athlete sits on the ground with knees extended, lower extremities together, and upper body perpendicular to the legs. The athlete reaches quickly toward the ankles, bounces at the end position, and immediately returns to a near-vertical upper body position. With each repetition, the end position extends farther than in the preceding repetition. The ballistic stretch is normally not the preferred technique and should not be used by those with low back or hamstring injuries.

Dynamic Stretch

A **dynamic stretch** is a type of functionally based stretching exercise that uses sport-specific movements to prepare the body for activity (55). Dynamic stretching—also called **mobility drills** (3)—places an emphasis on the movement requirements of the sport or activity rather than on individual muscles. This type of exercise can closely duplicate the movement requirements of a sport or activity (42); for example, a walking knee lift stretch mimics the knee lift of a sprinter. Essentially, one can think of dynamic stretching as actively moving a joint through the ROM required for a sport.

Dynamic and ballistic stretches may appear similar; however, a number of key differences significantly alter the effects of these activities such that dynamic stretching avoids the negative effects associated with ballistic stretching. Dynamic stretching avoids bouncing and is performed in a more controlled manner than ballistic stretching. The result is a controlled ROM that is often smaller than that produced by ballistic stretching.

The ability to actively move a joint through a ROM is generally far more sport specific than the ability to statically hold a stretch. Advantages of dynamic stretching include its ability to promote dynamic flexibility and to replicate the movement patterns and ROM required for sport activities. As a consequence, dynamic stretches are increasingly the preferred method of stretching during warm-up, and ideally match the requirements of the specific warm-up.

The use of dynamic stretches during the specific part of the warm-up provides a number of key advantages. Dynamic stretching helps promote the temperature-related benefits of the general warm-up, unlike static stretching, which can lead to a reduction in temperature. Additionally, a number of joints can be integrated into a single stretch, often including multiplanar movements similar to those that occur in sport. Thus dynamic stretches are extremely time efficient, which can be important where training time is limited (28, 43).

In dynamic stretching, unlike static stretching, the muscle does not relax during the stretch but instead is active through the ROM; this is also more specific to the movements that occur in sport. Even though it is an ideal warm-up activity, dynamic stretching may be less effective than static or PNF stretching at increasing static ROM (6); in situations in which an increased static ROM is needed, static or PNF methods may be preferred.

When one is designing a dynamic stretching program, the starting point should be a careful analysis of the major movement patterns within the given sport and the ROM required for those movements. One can then select exercises that replicate those movements via a series of dynamic stretches. In this way it is possible to achieve a highly specific stretching program.

Dynamic stretching provides the opportunity to combine movements (28). This gives the strength and conditioning professional a large number of combinations that can be used to provide variety in the warm-up. Athletes can perform dynamic stretching exercises either for a series of repetitions in the same place (e.g., 10 lunges) or for a series of repetitions to cover a given distance (e.g., lunge for 15 m). Regardless of the method chosen, each drill should start slowly and gradually increase the ROM, the speed, or both during subsequent repetitions or sets. For example, athletes can perform the knee lift exercise over a distance of 15 m, starting at a walk, and build to a skip over subsequent repetitions. This progression provides for an increase in both speed and ROM. An effective warm-up utilizing dynamic stretching can be achieved in 10 to 15 minutes (55).

In a dynamic stretch that mirrors a sport skill—such as a sprinter's knee lift drill—it is important that the stretch also emphasize the key skill factors required for the movement so that the most important mechanics of the drill are reinforced. For example, if the knee lift drill is used in the warm-up, effective body mechanics should be emphasized along with key joint positions such as dorsiflexion of the ankle of the lifted foot. The use of dynamic stretches must always be coordinated with appropriate sport techniques and never compromise proper technique.

Proprioceptive Neuromuscular Facilitation Stretch

Proprioceptive neuromuscular facilitation (PNF) stretching was originally developed as part of a neuromuscular rehabilitation program designed to relax muscles with increased tone or activity (80). It has since been expanded to athletics as a method of increasing flexibility. Proprioceptive neuromuscular facilitation techniques are usually performed with a partner and involve both passive movement and active (concentric and isometric) muscle actions. Proprioceptive neuromuscular facilitation stretching may be superior to other stretching methods because it facilitates muscular inhibition (18, 30, 47, 64, 70, 76), although evidence for this has not been consistently shown (24). However, PNF stretching is often impractical because most of the stretches require a partner and some expertise. This section serves as an introduction to PNF stretching.

During a PNF stretch, three specific muscle actions are used to facilitate the passive stretch. Both isometric and concentric muscle actions of the antagonist (the muscle being stretched) are used before a passive stretch of the antagonist to achieve autogenic inhibition. The isometric muscle action is referred to as *hold* and the concentric muscle action as *contract*. A concentric muscle action of the agonist, called **agonist contraction**, is used during a passive stretch of the antagonist to achieve reciprocal inhibition. Each technique also involves passive, static stretches that are referred to as *relax*.

There are three basic types of PNF stretching techniques:

- Hold-relax (13, 16, 18, 70, 76)
- Contract-relax (13, 18)
- Hold-relax with agonist contraction (16, 61)

The PNF techniques are completed in three phases. With each of the three techniques, the first phase incorporates a passive prestretch of 10 seconds. The muscle actions used in the second and third phases differ for the three techniques; the second and third phases give each technique its name. A stretch to improve hamstring flexibility provides an illustration (see figures 13.1 through 13.11).

Figure 13.1 Starting position of PNF hamstring stretch.

Figure 13.2 Partner and subject leg and hand positions for PNF hamstring stretch.

Hold-Relax

The **hold-relax** technique begins with a passive prestretch that is held at the point of mild discomfort for 10 seconds (figure 13.3). The partner then applies a hip flexion force and instructs the athlete, "Hold and don't let me move the leg"; the athlete "holds" and resists the movement so that an isometric muscle action occurs and is held for 6 seconds (figure 13.4). The athlete then relaxes, and a passive stretch is performed and held for 30 seconds (figure 13.5). The final stretch should be of greater magnitude due to autogenic inhibition (i.e., activation of the hamstrings).

Contract-Relax

The **contract-relax** technique also begins with a passive prestretch of the hamstrings that is held at the point of mild discomfort for 10 seconds (figure 13.6). The athlete then extends the hip against resistance from the partner so that a concentric muscle action through the full ROM occurs (figure 13.7). The athlete then relaxes, and a passive hip flexion stretch is applied and held for 30 seconds (figure 13.8). The increased ROM is facilitated due to autogenic inhibition (i.e., activation of the hamstrings). In an alternative to this technique, the athlete attempts to extend the hip and the partner does not allow the movement (59). Because this is essentially the same as the hold-relax technique, the contract-relax method described here is preferred.

Hold-Relax With Agonist Contraction

The **hold-relax with agonist contraction** technique is identical to hold-relax in the first two phases (figures 13.9 and 13.10). During the third phase, a concentric action of the agonist is used in addition to the passive stretch to add to the stretch force (figure 13.11). That is, following the isometric hold, the athlete flexes the hip, thereby moving further into the new ROM. With this technique, the final stretch should be greater, primarily because of reciprocal inhibition (i.e., activation of the hip flexors) (59, 61) and secondarily because of autogenic inhibition (i.e., activation of the hamstrings) (61).

The hold-relax with agonist contraction is the most effective PNF stretching technique due to facilitation via both reciprocal and autogenic inhibition.

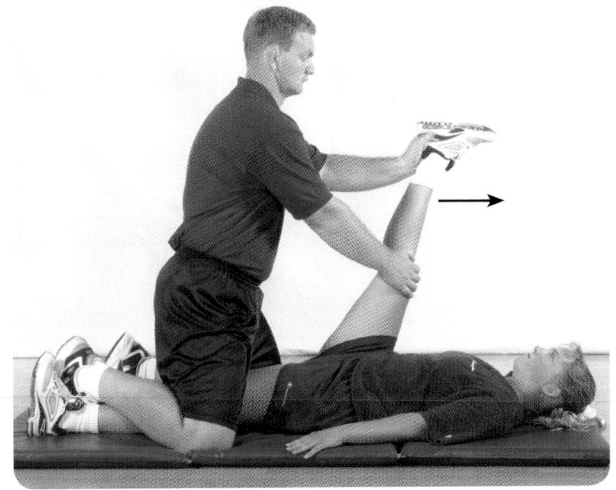

Figure 13.3 Passive prestretch of hamstrings during hold-relax PNF hamstring stretch.

Figure 13.4 Isometric action during hold-relax PNF hamstring stretch.

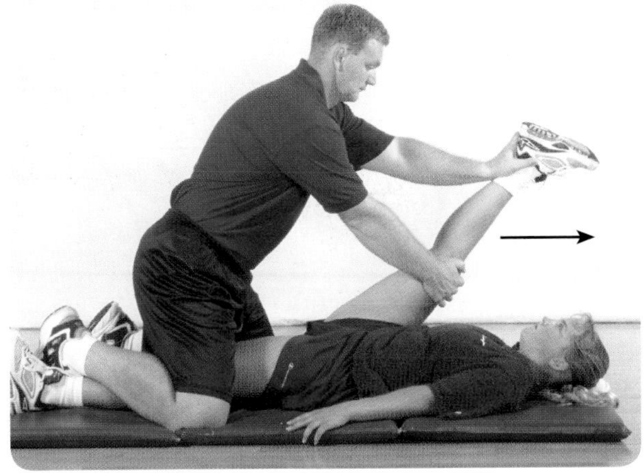

Figure 13.5 Increased ROM during passive stretch of hold-relax PNF hamstring stretch.

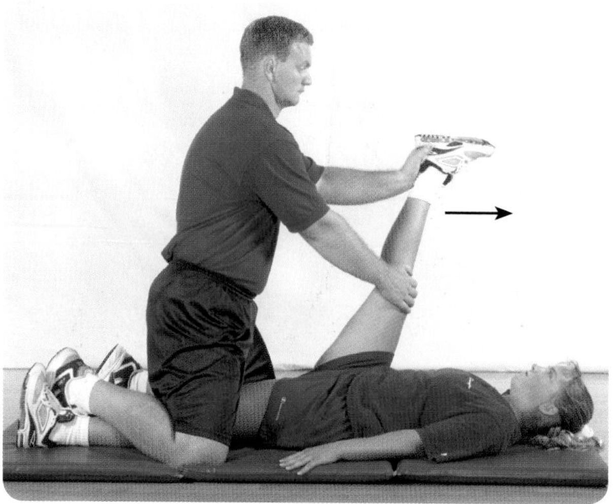

Figure 13.6 Passive prestretch of hamstrings during contract-relax PNF stretch.

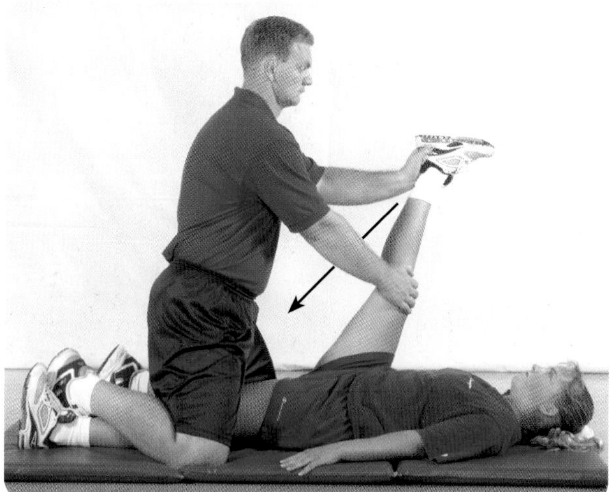

Figure 13.7 Concentric action of hip extensors during contract-relax PNF stretch.

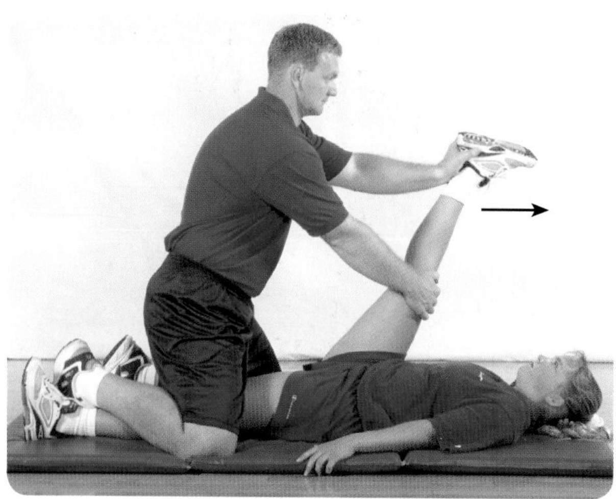

Figure 13.8 Increased ROM during passive stretch of contract-relax PNF stretch.

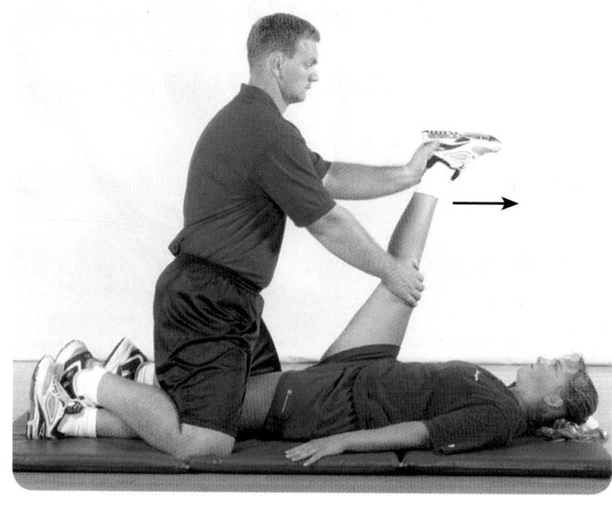

Figure 13.9 Passive prestretch during hold-relax with agonist contraction PNF hamstring stretch.

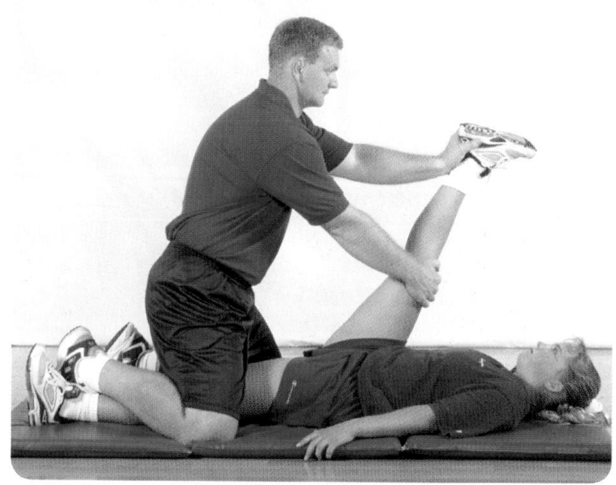

Figure 13.10 Isometric action of hamstrings during hold-relax with agonist contraction PNF hamstring stretch.

Figure 13.11 Concentric contraction of quadriceps during hold-relax with agonist contraction PNF hamstring stretch, creating increased ROM during passive stretch.

Common PNF Stretches With a Partner

The following are common PNF stretches performed with a partner. Each is illustrated with a photo.

- Calves and ankles (figure 13.12)
- Chest (figure 13.13)
- Groin (figure 13.14)
- Hamstrings and hip extensors (previously described)
- Quadriceps and hip flexors (figure 13.15)
- Shoulders (figure 13.16)

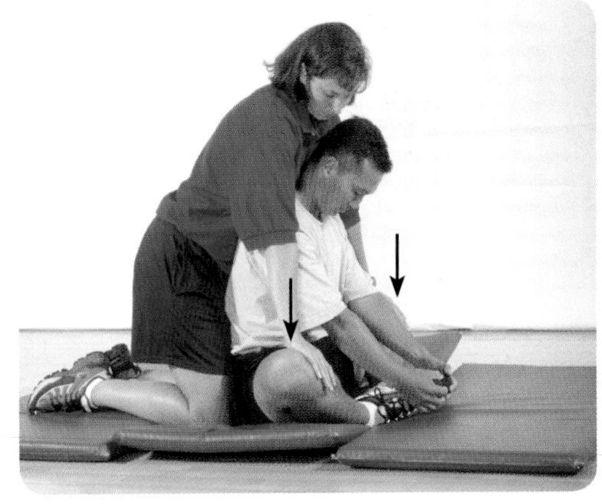

Figure 13.14 Partner PNF stretching for the groin.

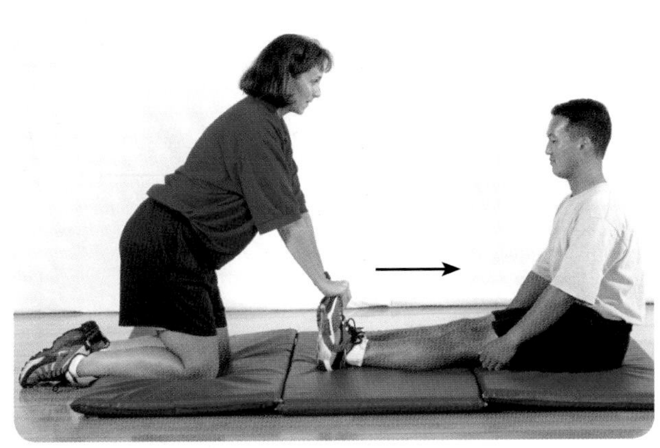

Figure 13.12 Partner PNF stretching for the calves.

Figure 13.15 Partner PNF stretching for the quadriceps and hip flexors.

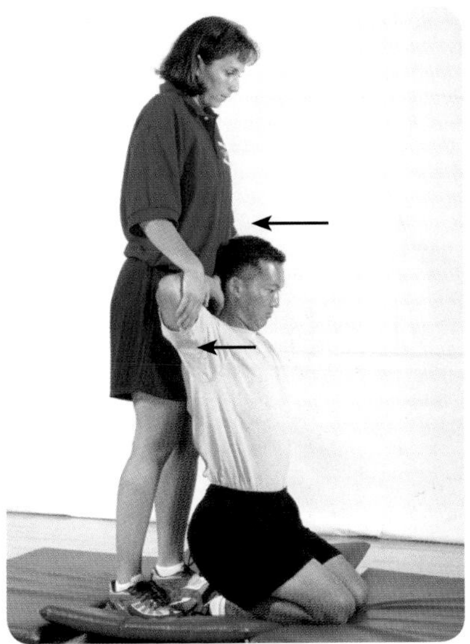

Figure 13.13 Partner PNF stretching for the chest.

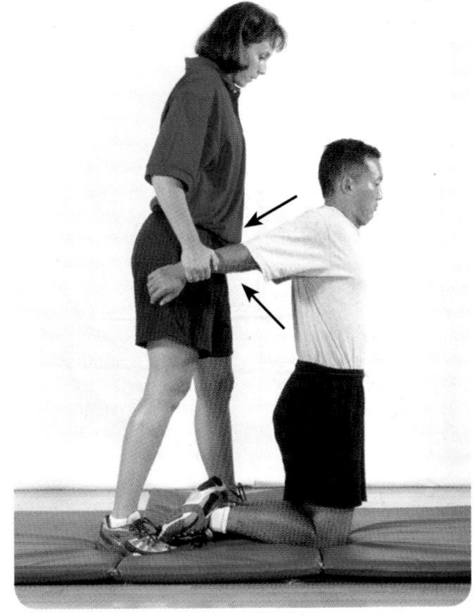

Figure 13.16 Partner PNF stretching for the shoulders.

CONCLUSION

A warm-up can provide benefits that enhance subsequent performance. Warm-up should be geared toward the particular sport or activity and should consist of both general and specific phases. During warm-up, dynamic stretching techniques are generally more appropriate than static stretching methods. The warm-up should prepare the athlete for the upcoming activity but should not induce undue fatigue. Strength and conditioning professionals should consider each athlete's unique combination of joint structure, age, sex, and sport requirements when recommending stretching protocols.

Optimal flexibility for performance varies from sport to sport. For athletes who need to increase flexibility, static and PNF stretching techniques will allow for an effective increase in ROM. These techniques are a key component of an extended training program.

STATIC STRETCHING TECHNIQUES

Guidelines for Static Stretching

- Get into a position that facilitates relaxation.
- Move to the point in the ROM where you experience a sensation of mild discomfort. If performing partner-assisted PNF stretching, communicate clearly with your partner.
- Hold stretches for 30 seconds.
- Repeat unilateral stretches on both sides.

Precautions for Static Stretching

- Decrease stretch intensity if you experience pain, radiating symptoms, or loss of sensation.
- Use caution when stretching a hypermobile joint.
- Avoid combination movements that involve the spine (e.g., extension and lateral flexion).
- Stabilizing muscles should be active to protect other joints and prevent unwanted movements.

LOOK RIGHT AND LEFT

1. Stand or sit with the head and neck upright.
2. Turn the head to the right using a submaximal concentric muscle action.
3. Turn the head to the left using a submaximal concentric muscle action.

Muscle Affected
Sternocleidomastoid

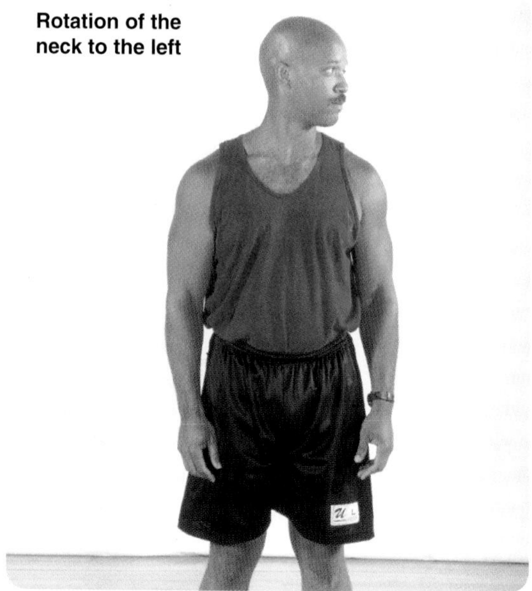

FLEXION AND EXTENSION

1. Standing or sitting with head and neck upright, flex the neck by tucking the chin toward the chest.
2. If the chin touches the chest, try to touch the chin lower on the chest.
3. Extend the neck by trying to come as close as possible to touching the head to the back.

Muscles Affected
Sternocleidomastoid, suboccipitals, splenae

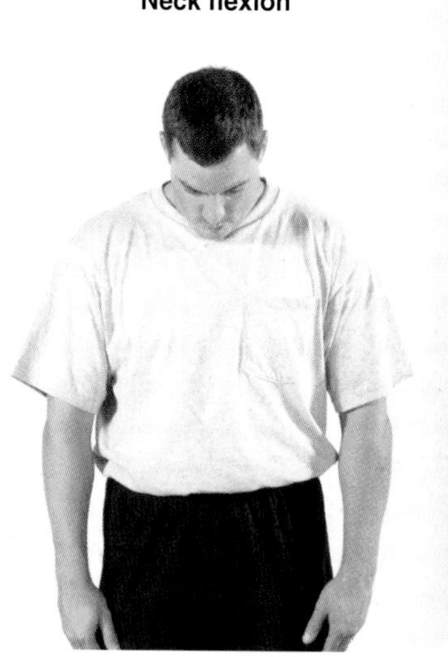

STRAIGHT ARMS BEHIND BACK

1. Standing, place both arms behind the back.
2. Interlock fingers with palms facing each other.
3. Straighten the elbows fully.
4. Slowly raise the arms, keeping the elbows straight.
5. Keep head upright and neck relaxed.

Muscles Affected
Anterior deltoid, pectoralis major

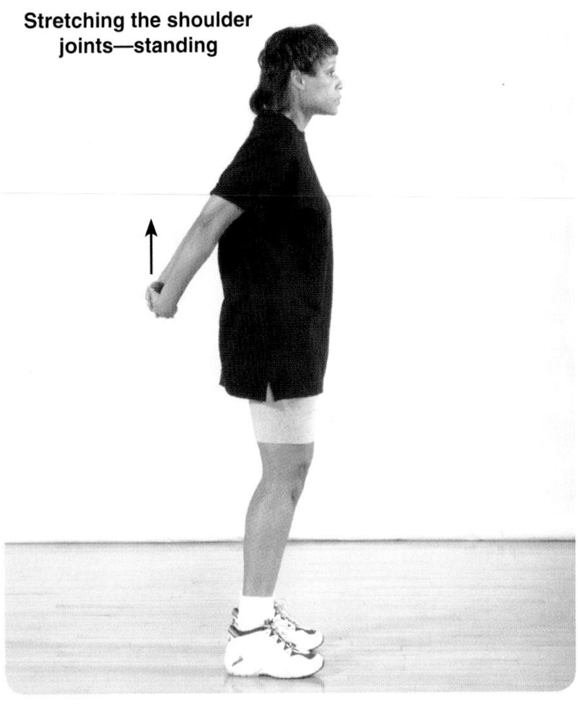
Stretching the shoulder joints—standing

SEATED LEAN-BACK

1. Sitting with the legs straight and arms extended, place palms on the floor about 12 inches (30 cm) behind the hips.
2. Point the fingers away from the body (backward).
3. Slide the hands backward and lean backward.

Muscles Affected
Deltoids, pectoralis major

Stretching the shoulder joints—seated

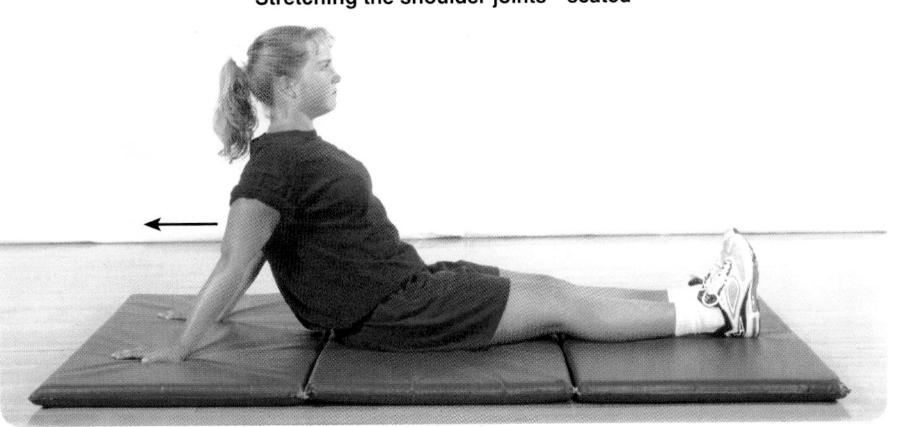

BEHIND-NECK STRETCH (CHICKEN WING)

1. Standing or sitting, abduct the right shoulder and flex the elbow.
2. Reach the right hand down toward the left scapula.
3. Grasp the right elbow with the left hand.
4. Pull the elbow behind the head with the left hand to increase shoulder abduction.

Muscles Affected
Triceps brachii, latissimus dorsi

CROSS ARM IN FRONT OF CHEST

1. Stand or sit with the left elbow slightly flexed (15°-30°) and the arm across the body (i.e., shoulder in horizontal adduction).
2. Grasp the upper arm just above the elbow, placing the right hand on the posterior side of the upper arm.
3. Pull the left arm across the chest (toward the right) with the right hand.

Muscles Affected
Posterior deltoid, rhomboids, middle trapezius

Stretching the upper back

ARMS STRAIGHT UP ABOVE HEAD (PILLAR)

1. Stand with the arms in front of the torso, fingers interlocked with palms facing out.
2. Slowly straighten the arms above the head with the palms up.
3. Continue to reach upward with the hands and arms.
4. While continuing to reach upward, slowly reach slightly backward.

Muscles Affected
Latissimus dorsi

Stretching the upper back and forearms

SPINAL TWIST (PRETZEL)

1. Sitting with the legs straight and the upper body nearly vertical, place the right foot to the left side of the left knee.
2. Place the back of the left elbow on the right side of the right knee, which is now bent.
3. Place the right palm on the floor 12 to 16 inches (30-40 cm) behind the hips.
4. Push the right knee to the left with the left elbow while turning the shoulders and head to the right as far as possible. Try to look behind the back.

Muscles Affected
Internal oblique, external oblique, piriformis, erector spinae

Stretching the low back and sides

SEMI–LEG STRADDLE

1. Sit with knees flexed 30° to 50°; let the legs totally relax.
2. Point the knees outward; the sides of the knees may or may not touch the floor.
3. Lean forward from the waist and reach forward with extended arms.

Note: Bending the knees and relaxing the legs decreases hamstring involvement and increases lower back stretch.

Muscles Affected
Erector spinae

Stretching the low back from a seated position

FORWARD LUNGE (FENCER)

1. Standing, take a long step forward with the right leg and flex the right knee until it is directly over the right foot (as in the free weight lunge exercise).
2. Keep the right foot flat on the floor.
3. Keep the back leg straight.
4. Keep the back foot pointed in the same direction as the front foot; it is not necessary to have the heel on the floor.
5. Keep the torso upright and rest the hands on the hips or the front leg.
6. Slowly lower the hips forward and downward.

Muscles Affected
Iliopsoas, rectus femoris

Stretching the hip flexors

SUPINE KNEE FLEX

1. Lie on the back with legs straight.
2. Flex the right knee and hip, bringing the thigh toward the chest.
3. Place both hands behind the thigh and continue to pull the thigh toward the chest.

Muscles Affected
Hip extensors (gluteus maximus and hamstrings)

Stretching the gluteals and hamstrings

SIDE BEND WITH STRAIGHT ARMS

1. Stand with feet approximately 16 inches (40 cm) apart.
2. Interlace the fingers with the palms away from the torso and facing outward.
3. Reach upward with straight arms.
4. Keeping the arms straight, lean from the waist to the left side. Do not bend the knees.

Muscles Affected
External oblique, latissimus dorsi, serratus anterior

Stretching the sides and upper back

SIDE BEND WITH BENT ARM

1. Stand with feet approximately 16 inches (40 cm) apart.
2. Flex the right elbow and raise the elbow above the head.
3. Reach the right hand down toward the left shoulder.
4. Grasp the right elbow with the left hand.
5. Pull the elbow behind the head.
6. Keeping the arm bent, lean from the waist to the left side.
7. Do not bend the knees.

Muscles Affected
External oblique, latissimus dorsi, serratus anterior, triceps brachii

Stretching the sides, triceps, and upper back

SIDE QUADRICEPS STRETCH

1. Lie on the left side with both legs straight.
2. Place the left forearm flat on the floor and the upper arm perpendicular to the floor.
3. Place the left forearm at a 45° angle to the torso.
4. Flex the right leg (knee), with the heel of the right foot moving toward the buttocks.
5. Grasp the front of the ankle with the right hand and pull toward the buttocks.

Note: The stretch occurs as a result of knee flexion and hip extension.

Muscles Affected
Quadriceps, iliopsoas

Stretching the quadriceps

SITTING TOE TOUCH

1. Sit with the upper body nearly vertical and legs straight.
2. Lean forward using hip flexion and grasp the toes with each hand. Slightly pull the toes toward the upper body and pull the chest toward the legs. If you have limited flexibility, try to grasp the ankles.

Muscles Affected
Hamstrings, erector spinae, gastrocnemius

Stretching the hamstrings and lower back

SEMISTRADDLE (FIGURE FOUR)

1. Sit with the upper body nearly vertical and legs straight.
2. Place the sole of the left foot on the inner side of the right knee. The outer side of the left leg should be resting on the floor.
3. Lean forward using hip flexion and grasp the toes of the right foot with the right hand. Slightly pull the toes toward the upper body as the chest is also pulled toward the right leg.

Muscles Affected
Gastrocnemius, hamstrings, erector spinae

Stretching the hamstrings and lower back

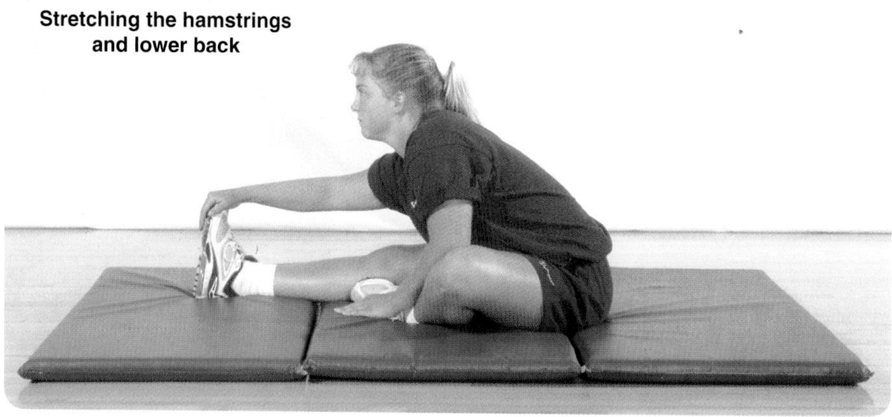

STRADDLE (SPREAD EAGLE)

1. Sit with the upper body nearly vertical and legs straight. Abduct the hips, spreading the legs as far as possible.
2. With both hands, grasp the toes of the right foot and pull on the toes slightly while pulling the chest toward the right leg.
3. Repeat toward the center by grasping the right toes with the right hand and the left toes with the left hand. Pull the torso forward and toward the ground.

Muscles Affected
Gastrocnemius, hamstrings, erector spinae, hip adductors, sartorius

Stretching the hamstrings and hip adductors

Stretching the hamstrings, hip adductors, and lower back

BUTTERFLY

1. Sitting with the upper body nearly vertical and legs straight, flex both knees, bringing the soles of the feet together.
2. Pull the feet toward the body.
3. Place the hands on the feet and the elbows on the legs.
4. Pull the torso slightly forward as the elbows push down, causing hip abduction.

Muscles Affected
Hip adductors, sartorius

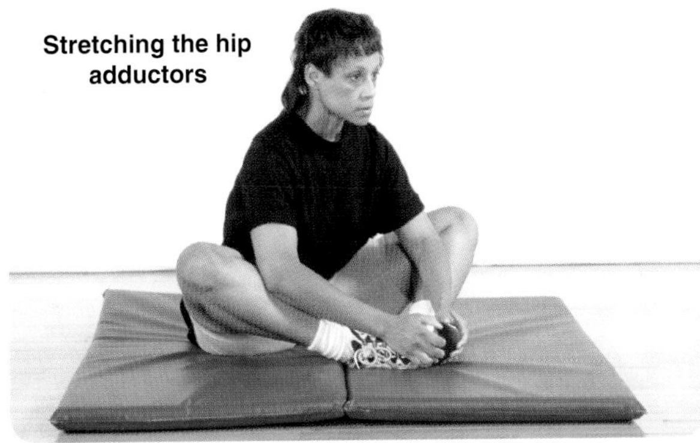

Stretching the hip adductors

WALL STRETCH

1. Stand facing the wall with feet shoulder-width apart and toes approximately 2 feet (0.6 m) from the wall.
2. Lean forward, placing the hands on the wall.
3. Step back approximately 2 feet (0.6 m) with the stretch leg while flexing the opposite knee.
4. Extend the knee of the stretch leg and lower the heel to the floor to apply the stretch.

Muscles Affected
Gastrocnemius, soleus; Achilles tendon

Stretching the calves

STEP STRETCH

1. Place the ball of one foot on the edge of a step or board 3 to 4 inches (8-10 cm) high, with the other foot flat on the step.
2. With straight legs, lower the heel of the foot on the edge of the step as far as possible.
3. Repeat with the other leg.

Note: To stretch the Achilles tendon, complete the same stretch with 10° of knee flexion.

Muscles Affected
Gastrocnemius, soleus; Achilles tendon

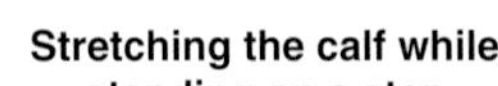

Stretching the calf while standing on a step

Preparing to stretch the Achilles tendon by slightly bending the knee

Stretching the Achilles tendon by lowering the heel

DYNAMIC STRETCHING TECHNIQUES

Guidelines for Dynamic Stretching

- Carry out 5 to 10 repetitions for each movement, either in place or over a given distance.
- Progressively increase the ROM on each repetition.
- Increase the speed of motion on subsequent sets where appropriate.
- Contract the muscles as you move through the ROM.

Precautions for Dynamic Stretching

- Move progressively through the ROM.
- Move deliberately but without bouncing (movement must be controlled at all times).
- Do not forsake good technique for additional ROM.

ARM SWINGS

1. Stand erect and raise the arms in front of the body until they are parallel to the floor.
2. While walking over a prescribed distance, swing the arms in unison to the right so the left arm is in front of the chest, the fingers of the left hand are pointing directly lateral to the left shoulder, and the right arm is behind the body.
3. Immediately reverse the direction of movement to swing the arms in unison to the left.
4. Movement should occur only at the shoulder joints (i.e., keep torso and head facing forward).
5. Alternate swinging the arms in unison to the right and left.

Muscles Affected
Latissimus dorsi, teres major, anterior and posterior deltoids, pectoralis major

INCHWORM

1. Stand erect with the feet placed shoulder-width apart.
2. While slightly flexing the knees, bend forward at the waist and place hands shoulder-width apart flat on the floor.
3. The weight of the body should be shifted back (i.e., not directly over the hands), with the buttocks high in the air—imagine making an inverted V with the body.
4. Move the hands alternately forward, as if taking short steps with the hands, until the body is in the push-up position.
5. Walk the legs to the hands using small steps while keeping the knees slightly flexed.
6. Repeat the motion over a prescribed distance.

Muscles Affected
Erector spinae, gastrocnemius, gluteus maximus, hamstrings, soleus, anterior tibialis

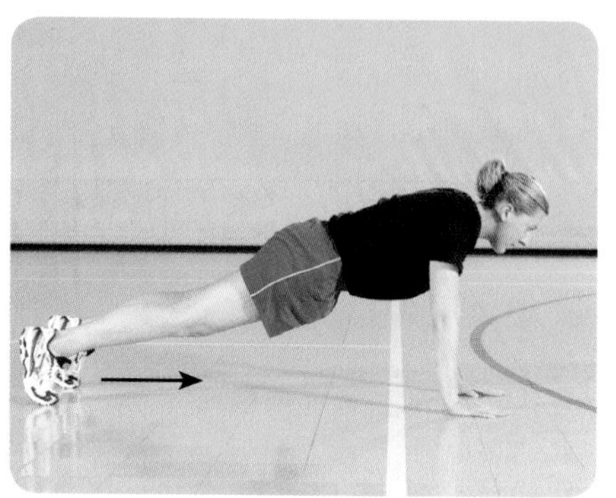

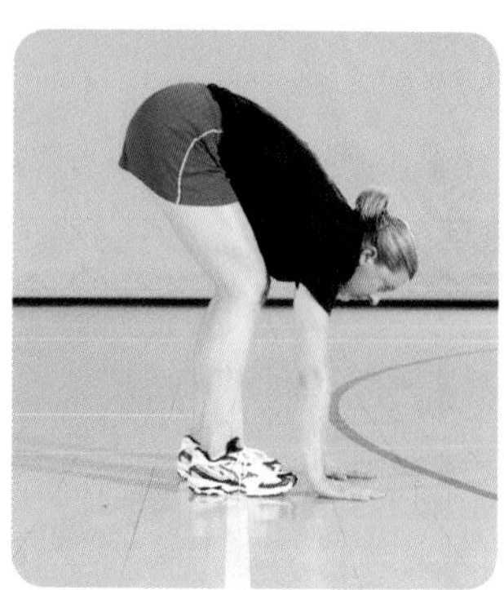

LUNGE WALK

1. Stand erect with the feet parallel to each other and shoulder-width apart.
2. Take an exaggerated step directly forward with the left leg, planting the left foot flat on the floor pointing straight ahead.
3. Allow the left hip and knee to slowly flex, keeping the left knee directly over the left foot.
4. Slightly flex the right knee and lower it until it is 1 to 2 inches (3-5 cm) above the floor; the right foot should be pointed straight ahead.
5. Balance the weight evenly between the ball of the right foot and the entire left foot.
6. Keep the torso perpendicular to the floor by "sitting back" on the right leg.
7. Forcefully push off of the floor by extending the left hip and knee.
8. Pick up the right foot and place it next to the left foot; do not stutter-step forward.
9. Stand erect, pause, and then step forward with the right leg, progressing forward with each step.

Muscles Affected
Gluteus maximus, hamstrings, iliopsoas, quadriceps

LUNGE WITH TWIST

1. Stand erect with the feet parallel to each other and shoulder-width apart.
2. Take an exaggerated step directly forward with the right leg, planting the right foot flat on the floor pointing straight ahead.
3. Allow the right hip and knee to slowly flex, keeping the right knee directly over the right foot.
4. Slightly flex the left knee and lower it until it is 1 to 2 inches (3-5 cm) above the floor; the left foot should be pointed straight ahead.
5. Reach up high with the left arm and bend the torso laterally toward the right leg.
6. Return to an erect torso position, and then forcefully push off the floor by extending the right hip and knee.
7. Pick up the left foot and place it next to the right foot; do not stutter-step forward.
8. Stand erect, pause, and then step forward with the left leg, progressing forward with each step.

Muscles Affected
Gluteus maximus, hamstrings, iliopsoas, latissimus dorsi, internal and external oblique, rectus femoris

WALKING KNEE LIFT

1. Stand erect with the feet parallel to each other and shoulder-width apart.
2. Step forward with the left leg and flex the right hip and knee to move the right thigh upward toward the chest.
3. Grasp the front of the right knee/upper shin and use the arms to pull the right knee up further and to squeeze the thigh against the chest.
4. Dorsiflex the left foot as the right hip and knee are flexed.
5. Keeping the torso erect, pause for a moment, then proceed to step down with the right leg.
6. Shift the body weight to the right leg and repeat the motion with the left leg.
7. Progress forward with each step, increasing the ROM and speed on subsequent steps.

Muscles Affected
Gluteus maximus, hamstrings

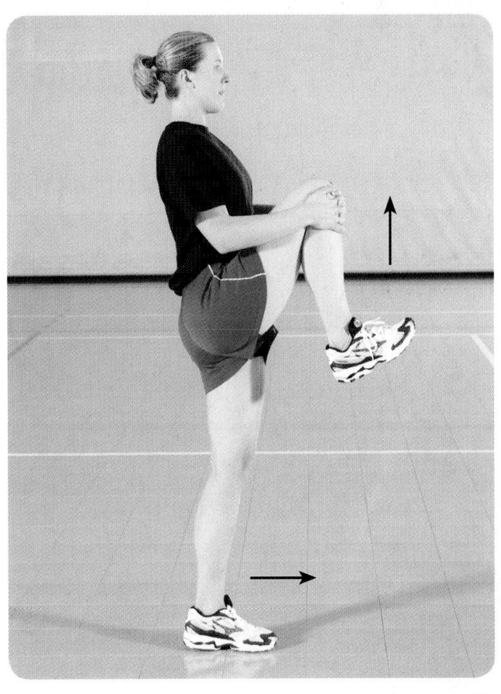

FORWARD LUNGE WITH ELBOW TO INSTEP

1. Stand erect with the feet parallel to each other and shoulder-width apart.
2. Take an exaggerated step directly forward with the left leg, planting the left foot flat on the floor pointing straight ahead.
3. Allow the left hip and knee to slowly flex, keeping the left knee directly over the left foot.
4. Slightly flex the right knee and lower it until it is 1 to 2 inches (3-5 cm) above the floor; the right foot should be pointed straight ahead.
5. Lean forward, bringing the left arm forward and touching the left elbow to the instep of the left foot; the right hand may be placed on the floor to maintain balance.
6. Lean back to return to an erect torso position, and then forcefully push off the floor by extending the left hip and knee.
7. Pick up the right foot and place it next to the left foot; do not stutter-step forward.
8. Stand erect, pause, and then step forward with the right leg, progressing forward with each step.

Muscles Affected
Biceps femoris, erector spinae, gastrocnemius, gluteus maximus, hamstrings, iliopsoas, latissimus dorsi, internal and external oblique, quadriceps, rectus femoris, soleus

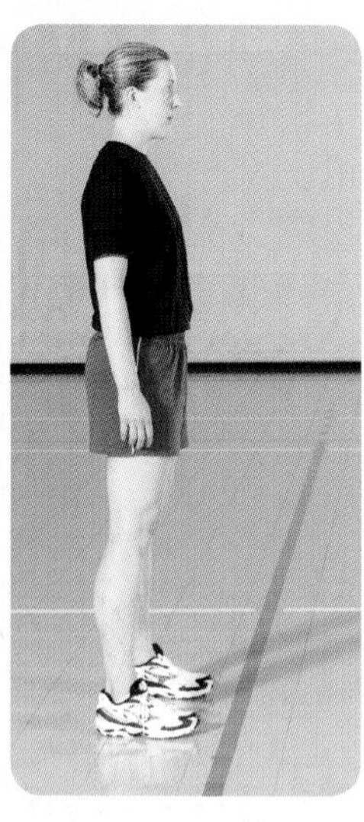

HEEL-TO-TOE WALK

1. Stand erect with the feet parallel to each other and shoulder-width apart.
2. Take a small step forward with the right leg; place the heel of the right foot on the ground first and then continue to dorsiflex the foot.
3. Immediately roll forward and rise up as high as possible onto the ball of the right foot.
4. Swing the left leg forward in order to take another small step.
5. Repeat with the left leg, progressing forward with each step.

Muscles Affected
Gastrocnemius, soleus, anterior tibialis

WALKING OVER AND UNDER

This exercise mimics the motion of trying to step laterally over and then under a hurdle.

1. Stand erect with the feet parallel to each other and shoulder-width apart.
2. Flex the left hip and knee and then abduct the left thigh until it is parallel to the floor.
3. Step laterally to the left as if stepping laterally over an imaginary hurdle.
4. Place the left foot firmly on the ground, shift the body weight to the left leg, and then proceed to lift the right leg over the imaginary hurdle.
5. After lifting the right leg over the hurdle and placing the right foot firmly on the ground, stand erect, pause, and then flex the hips and knees and dorsiflex the ankles to assume a full squat position.
6. Extend the left leg laterally, as if performing a lateral lunge.
7. Keeping the body weight low, move the body laterally as if ducking under an imaginary hurdle.
8. Stand erect, pause, and repeat the motion in the opposite direction.

Muscles Affected
Hip abductors, hip adductors, gastrocnemius, gluteus maximus, hamstrings, iliopsoas, rectus femoris, soleus

KEY TERMS

active stretch 300
agonist contraction 301
autogenic inhibition 299
ball-and-socket joint 298
ballistic stretch 300
contract-relax 303
dynamic flexibility 297
dynamic stretch 300
elasticity 298
ellipsoidal joint 298
fibrosis 298
flexibility 297
general warm-up 297
Golgi tendon organ (GTO) 299
hinge joint 298
hold-relax 303
hold-relax with agonist contraction 303
mechanoreceptor 299
mobility drills 300
muscle spindle 299
passive stretch 300
plasticity 298
proprioceptive neuromuscular facilitation (PNF) 301
range of motion (ROM) 297
reciprocal inhibition 299
specific warm-up 297
static flexibility 297
static stretch 300
stretch reflex 299

STUDY QUESTIONS

1. When stimulated during PNF stretching, Golgi tendon organs allow the relaxation of the

a. stretched muscle by contracting the reciprocal muscle.
b. reciprocal muscle by contracting the stretched muscle.
c. reciprocal muscle by its own contraction.
d. stretched muscle by its own contraction.

2. Which of the following stretching techniques decreases muscle spindle stimulation?

a. dynamic
b. ballistic
c. static
d. passive

3. Dynamic stretching is the MOST similar to which of the following?

a. specific warm-up
b. general warm-up
c. low-intensity stretch
d. static stretch

4. Stimulation of muscle spindles induces a

a. relaxation of GTOs.
b. relaxation of the stretched muscle.
c. contraction of the stretched muscle.
d. contraction of the reciprocal muscle.

5. After performing the "hold-relax with agonist contraction" PNF stretch for the hamstrings, which of the following explains the resulting increase in flexibility?

I. autogenic inhibition
II. stretch inhibition
III. reciprocal inhibition
IV. crossed-extensor inhibition

a. I and III only
b. II and IV only
c. I, II, and III only
d. II, III, and IV only

CHAPTER 14

Resistance Training and Spotting Techniques

Roger W. Earle, MA, and Thomas R. Baechle, EdD

After completing this chapter, you will be able to

- understand the general techniques involved in properly performing resistance training exercises,
- provide breathing guidelines,
- determine the appropriateness of wearing a weight belt,
- provide recommendations for spotting free weight exercises, and
- teach proper resistance training exercise and spotting techniques.

This chapter provides guidelines and strategies for performing and teaching safe and effective lifting and spotting techniques. At the core of safe and effective resistance training is proper exercise execution. Exercises that are performed and spotted correctly promote injury-free results and do so in a time-efficient manner.

The first half of this chapter summarizes the fundamental techniques involved in properly performing and spotting exercises and using a weight belt during lifting. The last section provides checklists and photographs depicting proper resistance training exercise and spotting techniques. It is assumed that the reader is familiar with these exercises. Therefore, the techniques presented are simply guidelines that represent the most commonly accepted method of performing the exercises. No attempt has been made to describe all variations for properly executing and spotting the exercises included in this chapter.

EXERCISE TECHNIQUE FUNDAMENTALS

There are several commonalities among resistance training exercise techniques. Most free weight and machine exercises involve some sort of handgrip on a bar, dumbbell, or handle, and absolutely all exercises require an optimal body or limb position, movement range and speed, and method of breathing. Additionally, some exercises may also warrant the use of a weight belt and certain procedures for lifting a bar off the floor.

Handgrips

Two common grips are used in resistance training exercises: (a) the **pronated grip**, with palms down and knuckles up, also called the **overhand grip**; and (b) the **supinated grip**, with palms up and knuckles down, also known as the **underhand grip** (figure 14.1). (A variation of either grip is the **neutral grip** in which the knuckles point laterally—as in a handshake.) Two less common grips are the **alternated grip**, in which one hand is in a pronated grip and the other is in a supinated grip, and the **hook grip**, which is similar to the pronated grip except that the thumb is positioned under the index and middle fingers. The hook grip is typically used for performing exercises that require a stronger grip (power exercises, e.g., snatch). Note that the thumb is wrapped around the bar in all of the grips shown; this positioning is called a **closed grip**. When the thumb does not wrap around the bar, the grip is called an **open** or **false grip**.

Establishing the proper grip in an exercise involves placing the hands at the correct distance from each other (referred to as the **grip width**). The three grip widths (shown in figure 14.2) are common, wide, and narrow. For most exercises, the hands are placed approximately shoulder-width apart. The hand positioning for all exercises should result in a balanced, even bar.

Stable Body and Limb Positioning

Whether an exercise requires lifting a barbell or dumbbell from the floor or pushing and pulling while one is positioned in or on a machine, establishing a stable position is critical. A stable position enables the athlete to maintain proper body alignment during an exercise, which in turn places an appropriate stress on muscles and joints.

Exercises performed while standing typically require that the feet be positioned slightly wider than hip-width with the heels and balls of the feet in contact with the floor. Establishing a stable position in or on machines sometimes requires

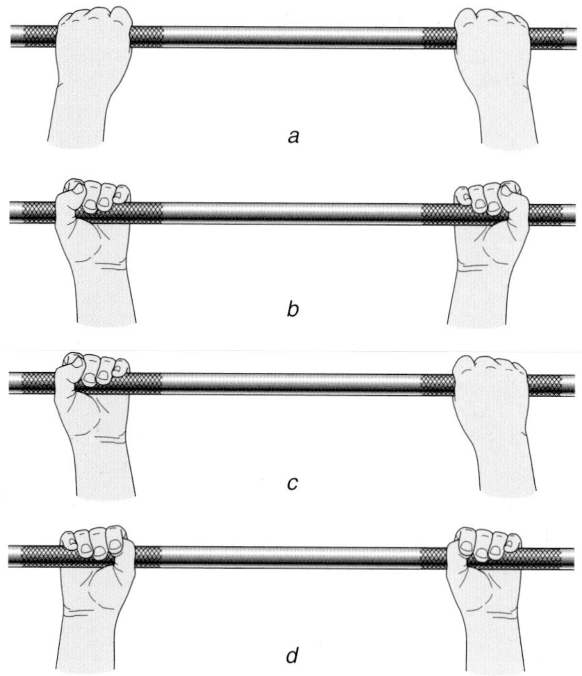

Figure 14.1 Bar grips: *(a)* pronated, *(b)* supinated, *(c)* alternated, *(d)* hook (posterior view).

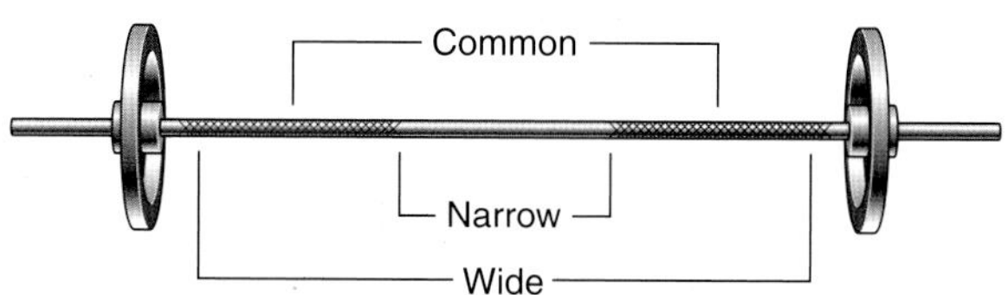

Figure 14.2 Grip widths.

adjusting the seat or resistance arm and fastening belts snugly.

Seated or **supine** (lying face up) exercises performed on a bench require a specific posture. The athlete should position the body to achieve a five-point body contact position:

1. Head is placed firmly on the bench or back pad.
2. Shoulders and upper back are placed firmly and evenly on the bench or back pad.
3. Buttocks are placed evenly on the bench or seat.
4. Right foot is flat on the floor.
5. Left foot is flat on the floor.

Establishing and maintaining this **five-point body contact position** at the beginning and throughout the movement phases promotes maximal stability and spinal support.

Exercises performed while standing typically require that the feet be positioned slightly wider than hip-width with the heels and balls of the feet in contact with the floor. Seated or supine exercises performed on a bench usually require a five-point body contact position.

Cam-, pulley-, or lever-based exercise machines that have an axis of rotation require specific positioning of the athlete's body, arms, or legs for reasons of safety and optimal execution. To align the primary joint of the body involved in the exercise with the axis of the machine, it may be necessary to move the seat; the ankle or arm roller pad; or the thigh, chest, or back pad. For example, adjust the ankle roller pad (up or down) and the back pad (forward or backward) to line up the knee joint with the machine axis before performing the leg (knee) extension exercise.

Before performing machine exercises, adjust seat and pads to position the body joint primarily involved in the exercise in alignment with the machine's axis of rotation.

Range of Motion and Speed

When the entire range of motion (ROM) is covered during an exercise, the value of the exercise is maximized and flexibility is maintained or improved. Ideally, an exercise's full ROM should mimic the full ROM of the involved joint or joints in order for the greatest improvements to occur, but sometimes this is not possible (trailing leg knee joint during a lunge) or recommended (using intervertebral joints during a squat).

Repetitions performed in a slow, controlled manner increase the likelihood that full ROM can be reached. However, when power or quick-lift exercises (e.g., power clean, push jerk, and snatch) are performed, an effort should be made to accelerate the bar to a maximal speed while still maintaining control.

Breathing Considerations

The most strenuous movement of a repetition—typically soon after the transition from the eccentric phase to the concentric phase—is referred to as the **sticking point**. Strength and conditioning professionals should typically instruct athletes to exhale *through* the sticking point and to inhale during the less stressful phase of the repetition. For example, since the sticking point of the biceps curl exercise occurs about midway through the upward movement phase (concentric elbow flexion), the athlete should exhale during this portion. Inhalation, then, should occur as the bar is lowered back to the starting position. This breathing strategy applies to most resistance training exercises.

There are some situations in which breath holding may be suggested, however. For experienced and well-resistance-trained athletes performing **structural exercises** (those that load the vertebral column and therefore place stress on it) with high loads, the **Valsalva maneuver** can be helpful for maintaining proper vertebral alignment and support. As explained in chapter 4, the Valsalva maneuver involves expiring against a closed glottis, which, when combined with contracting the abdomen and rib cage muscles, creates rigid compartments of fluid in the lower torso and air in the upper torso (i.e., the "fluid ball"). The advantage of the Valsalva maneuver is that it increases the rigidity of the entire torso to aid in supporting the vertebral column, which in turn reduces the associated compressive forces on the disks during lifting. It also helps to establish the "flat-back" and erect upper torso position described in the technique checklists for certain exercises. Be aware, however, that the resulting increase in intra-abdominal pressure has potentially detrimental side effects, such as dizziness, disorientation, excessively high blood pressure, and blackouts. This is why the breath-holding phase is—and should be—quite transient, only about 1 to 2 seconds (at most). Even a very well-trained individual should not extend the length of the breath-holding phase, as blood pressure can quickly rise to triple resting levels.

Strength and conditioning professionals involved in conducting 1-repetition maximum (1RM) tests in, for example, the squat, deadlift, hip sled, leg press, shoulder press, or power clean, need to be aware of the advantages and disadvantages of coaching athletes in the Valsalva maneuver. While it is obviously important that the vertebral column be internally supported during these movements for safety and technique reasons, it is recommended that an athlete not extend the breath-holding period.

For most exercises, exhale through the sticking point of the concentric phase and inhale during the eccentric phase. Experienced and well-trained athletes may want to use the Valsalva maneuver when performing structural exercises to assist in maintaining proper vertebral alignment and support.

Weight Belts

The use of a weight belt can contribute to injury-free training. Its appropriateness depends on the type of exercise performed and the relative load lifted. It is recommended that a weight belt be worn for exercises that place stress on the lower back and during sets that use near-maximal or maximal loads. Adopting this strategy may reduce the risk of lower back injury when combined with proper lifting and spotting techniques. A drawback to weight belt use is that wearing a belt too often reduces opportunities

Figure 14.3 Correct technique for lifting a bar off the floor.

for the abdominal muscles to be trained. Furthermore, no weight belt is needed for exercises that do not stress the lower back (e.g., biceps curl, lat pulldown), or for exercises that do stress the lower back (e.g., back squat or deadlift) but involve the use of light loads.

Typically an athlete should wear a weight belt when performing exercises that place stress on the lower back and during sets that involve near-maximal or maximal loads. A weight belt is not needed for exercises that do not stress the lower back or for those that do stress the lower back but involve light loads.

Lifting a Bar off the Floor

Often an athlete needs to lift a barbell or dumbbells off the floor, either while performing an exercise or in order to move the bar to a different location in the strength and conditioning facility. The position of the feet and back shown in figure 14.3 enables the leg muscles to make a major contribution as the bar is lifted off the floor. Keeping the bar close to the body and the back flat during the upward pull of the bar helps avoid excessive strain on the lower back. A more detailed explanation of this technique is presented within the exercise checklist section later in this chapter (deadlift and power clean exercises on pp. 359 and 372-373, respectively).

SPOTTING FREE WEIGHT EXERCISES

A **spotter** is someone who assists in the execution of an exercise to help protect the athlete from injury. A spotter may also serve to motivate the athlete and help in the completion of **forced repetitions** (also referred to as **partner-assisted reps**), but the spotter's primary responsibility is the safety of the athlete being spotted. The spotter must realize that poor execution of this responsibility may result in serious injury, not only to the athlete being spotted, but also to the spotter. Although partner-assisted actions are valuable in helping an athlete benefit from training, the importance of promoting safety cannot be overemphasized.

The remainder of this section offers additional insight on when and how to spot free weight exercises. This information provides a foundation for strength and conditioning professionals to apply to their specific training environment.

Types of Exercises Performed and Equipment Involved

Free weight exercises performed over the head (e.g., barbell shoulder press) or with the bar on the back (e.g., back squat), racked anteriorly on the shoulders or on the clavicles (e.g., front squat), or over

3

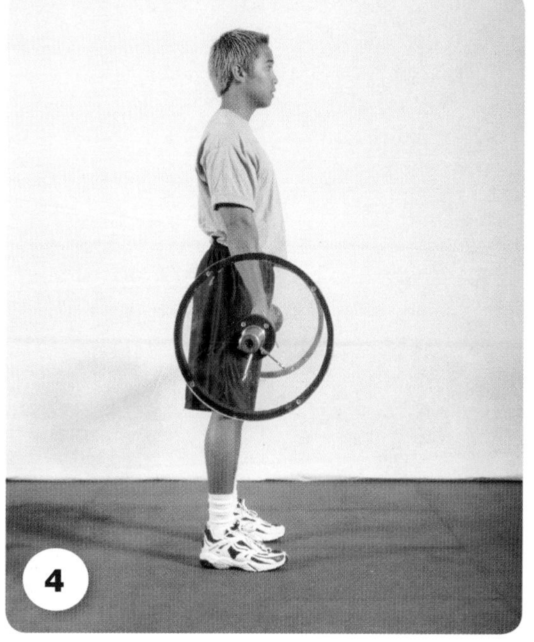

4

the face (e.g., bench press, lying triceps extension) are more challenging for the athlete to correctly execute than those in which the bar or dumbbells are held or raised at the sides or in front (e.g., lateral shoulder raise or barbell biceps curl, respectively) and therefore should involve one or more spotters. The overhead, bar-on-the-back or bar-on-the-front-shoulders, and over-the-face exercises (especially using dumbbells) also require more skill on the part of the spotter and are potentially the most dangerous to the athlete. Spotting dumbbell exercises typically requires more skill than spotting barbell exercises because there is an additional piece of equipment to observe and spot. Power exercises should not be spotted.

With the exception of power exercises, free weight exercises performed with a bar moving over the head, positioned on the back, racked on the front of the shoulders, or passing over the face typically require one or more spotters.

Spotting Overhead Exercises and Those With the Bar on the Back or Front Shoulders

Ideally, to promote the safety of the lifter, the spotters, and others nearby, overhead exercises and those involving the bar on the back or front shoulders should be performed inside a power rack with the crossbars in place at an appropriate height. All plates, bars, locks, and weight-plate trees must be cleared from the lifting area so that they cannot be tripped over or run into. Athletes who are not lifting should be instructed to stay clear of the lifting area. Since the loads lifted in these exercises can be considerable, to exert sufficient leverage the spotter or spotters should be at least as strong and at least as tall as the athlete who is lifting. Out-of-the-rack exercises (e.g., forward step lunge or step-up) with heavy weights can result in serious injury. These exercises should be executed only by well-trained and skilled athletes and spotted by experienced professionals.

Spotting Over-the-Face Exercises

When spotting over-the-face barbell exercises, it is important for the spotter to grasp the bar with an alternated grip, usually narrower than the athlete's grip. Because of the bar's curved trajectory in some exercises (e.g. lying triceps extension, barbell pull-over), the spotter will use an alternated grip to pick up the bar and return it to the floor but a supinated grip to spot the bar. This helps ensure that the bar does not roll out of the spotter's hands and onto the athlete's face or neck. Since the spotter may be called upon to catch the bar or assist in lifting moderate to heavy loads (usually from a higher vantage point), establishing a solid base of support and a flat-back position is critically important.

For dumbbell exercises, it is important to spot as close to the dumbbells as possible or, in a few exercises, to spot the dumbbell itself. Although some individuals advocate spotting dumbbell movements by placing the hands on the athlete's upper arms or elbows (figure 14.4*a*), this technique may lead to injury. If the athlete's elbows "collapse" (i.e., flex), the spotter will not be in a position to stop the dumbbells from striking the athlete's face or chest. Spotting at the forearms near the wrists (figure 14.4*b*) provides a safer technique. Note that for some exercises (e.g., dumbbell pullover and overhead dumbbell triceps extension), it is necessary to spot with hands on the dumbbell itself.

Figure 14.4 *(a)* Incorrect dumbbell spotting location. *(b)* Correct spotting location. (Arrows indicate the spotter's hand placement on the athlete's arms.)

Do Not Spot Power Exercises

Whereas spotting is recommended in the types of exercises previously described, it is not advised in power exercises. Instead of spotting these exercises, the strength and conditioning professional needs to teach athletes how to get away from a bar that is unmanageable. Spotting these types of exercises is too dangerous to both the spotter and athlete. Athletes should be instructed that when they miss the bar in front, they should push the bar away or simply drop it. They should be taught that if they lose the bar behind the head, they should release it and jump forward. For these reasons, the surrounding area or platform should be cleared of other athletes and equipment before such exercises are performed.

Number of Spotters

The number of spotters needed is largely determined by the load being lifted, the experience and ability of the athlete and spotters, and the physical strength of the spotters. Obviously, with heavier loads the likelihood of injury increases, as does the severity of the injury should an accident occur. Once the load exceeds the spotter's ability to effectively protect the athlete (and him- or herself), another spotter must become involved. On the other hand, one spotter is preferred if he or she can easily handle the load, because two or more spotters must coordinate their actions with those of the athlete. As the number of spotters increases, so does the chance that an error in timing or technique may occur.

Communication Between Athlete and Spotter

Communication is the responsibility of both the spotter and the athlete. Before beginning a set, the athlete should tell the spotter how the bar will initially be handled, how many repetitions will be performed, and when he or she is ready to move the bar into position. If spotters do not have this information they may take control of the bar improperly, too soon, or too late and consequently disrupt the exercise or injure the athlete.

Use of a Liftoff

The term **liftoff** refers to moving the bar from the upright supports to a position in which the athlete can begin the exercise. Usually the spotter helps place the barbell or dumbbells into the athlete's hands while the elbows are extended and helps to move the barbell or dumbbells to the proper starting position. Some athletes want the spotter to provide a liftoff; others do not. If a liftoff is needed or requested, the athlete and spotter need to agree in advance on a verbal signal (e.g., the command "up" or "I will give it to you on the count of three"). Typically, the athlete signals that he or she is ready; the spotter says, "One, two, three," and on "three" the bar is moved into position. Liftoffs are normally used in the bench press (off the supports), shoulder press (off the supports or the shoulders), and squatting exercises if the supports are too low and nonadjustable. When two spotters are involved and the athlete wants a liftoff, as with a bench press, one spotter should assist with the liftoff and then quickly move to the end of the bar to spot (the other spotter is already at the other end). The spotter providing the liftoff must be sure that the athlete has complete control of the bar at the conclusion of the liftoff. If two spotters are used, both should help the athlete place the bar back onto the supports on completion of the exercise.

Amount and Timing of Spotting Assistance

Knowing how much and when to help an athlete is an important aspect of spotting and requires experience. Most athletes typically need just enough help to successfully complete a repetition (i.e., a partner-assisted action); other times they might need the spotter to handle the entire load. At the first indication that a repetition will be missed, the athlete should quickly ask or signal the spotter (sometimes with just a grunt or sound) for help, and the spotter needs to immediately attempt to provide the amount of assistance needed. If the athlete cannot contribute anything to the completion of the repetition, the athlete should immediately tell the spotter to "take it" or use some other phrase agreed upon before the lift. Regardless of when or why the spotter is needed to assist, he or she should take the bar—if possible—from the athlete quickly and smoothly, trying to avoid abrupt changes in the amount of load being handled by the athlete. The athlete should try to stay with the bar until it is racked or placed safely on the floor. This helps to protect both the spotter and athlete from injury.

The spotting guidelines provided in the exercise technique checklists are appropriate for a typical training environment. Spotting procedures may vary when excessively heavy loads are being used—such as 1RM attempts—because more spotters are typically needed.

CONCLUSION

It is critically important that the strength and conditioning professional provide athletes with proper instruction in resistance training exercise technique, including the fundamentals of breathing and weight belt use. In addition, the strength and conditioning professional needs to teach athletes how and when exercises should be spotted. Combined with quality supervision and ongoing feedback, this attention to proper instruction results in a safe training environment and an effective and appropriate training stimulus.

RESISTANCE TRAINING EXERCISES

BENT-KNEE SIT-UP

Starting Position

- Lie in a supine position on a floor mat.
- Flex the knees to bring the heels close to the buttocks.
- Fold the arms across the chest or abdomen.
- All repetitions begin from this position.

Upward Movement Phase

- Flex the neck to move the chin toward the chest.
- Keeping the feet, buttocks, and lower back flat and stationary on the mat, curl the torso toward the thighs until the upper back is off the mat.

Downward Movement Phase

- Uncurl the torso back to the starting position.
- Keep the feet, buttocks, lower back, and arms in the same position.

Major Muscle Involved
Rectus abdominis

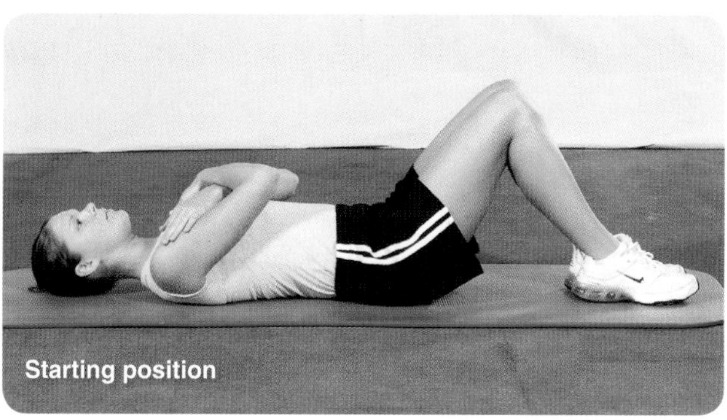
Starting position

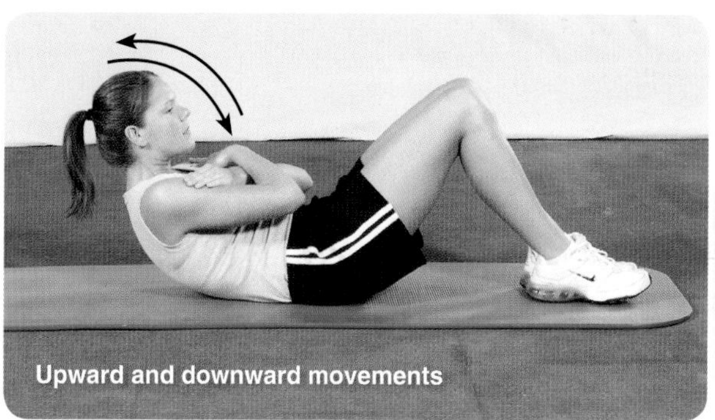
Upward and downward movements

ABDOMINAL CRUNCH

Starting Position

- Lie in a supine position on a floor mat.
- Place the calves and ankles on a bench with the hips and knees flexed to about 90°.
- Fold the arms across the chest or abdomen.
- All repetitions begin from this position.

Upward Movement Phase

- Flex the neck to move the chin toward the chest.
- Keeping the buttocks and lower back flat and stationary on the mat, curl the torso toward the thighs until the upper back is off the mat.

Downward Movement Phase

- Uncurl the torso back to the starting position.
- Keep the feet, buttocks, lower back, and arms in the same position.

Major Muscle Involved
Rectus abdominis

Starting position

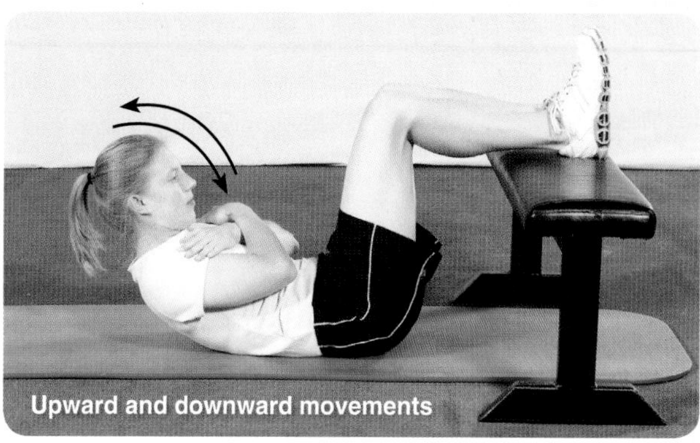
Upward and downward movements

BENT-OVER ROW

Before Beginning

- Grasp the bar with a closed, pronated grip.
- Grip should be wider than shoulder-width.
- Lift the bar from the floor as described for the deadlift exercise (p. 359), but use a pronated grip, not an alternated grip.

Starting Position

- Position the feet in a shoulder-width stance with the knees slightly flexed.
- Flex the torso forward so that it is slightly above parallel to the floor.
- Create a flat-back torso position.
- Focus the eyes a short distance ahead of the feet.
- Allow the bar to hang with the elbows fully extended.
- All repetitions begin from this position.

Upward Movement Phase

- Pull the bar toward the torso.
- Keep the torso rigid, back flat, and knees slightly flexed.
- Do not jerk the torso upward.
- Touch the bar to the lower chest or upper abdomen.

Downward Movement Phase

- Lower the bar back to the starting position.
- Maintain the flat-back and stationary torso and knee positions.
- At the end of the set, flex the hips and knees to place the bar on the floor and stand up.

Major Muscles Involved
Latissimus dorsi, teres major, middle trapezius, rhomboids, posterior deltoids

Starting position

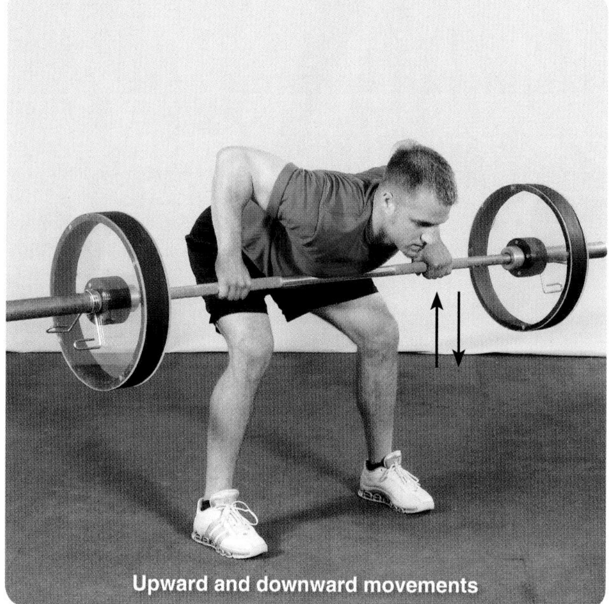
Upward and downward movements

LAT PULLDOWN (MACHINE)

Starting Position

- Grasp the bar with a closed, pronated grip.
- Grip should be wider than shoulder-width.
- Sit down on the seat facing the machine.
- Position the thighs under the pads with the feet flat on the floor. If necessary, adjust the seat and thigh pad.
- Lean the torso slightly backward.
- Extend the elbows fully.
- All repetitions begin from this position.

Downward Movement Phase

- Pull the bar down and toward the upper chest.
- Maintain the slight torso backward lean; do not jerk the torso backward.
- Touch the bar to the clavicle and upper-chest area.

Upward Movement Phase

- Allow the elbows to slowly extend back to the starting position.
- Keep the torso in the same position.
- At the end of the set, stand up and return the bar to its resting position.

Major Muscles Involved
Latissimus dorsi, teres major, middle trapezius, rhomboids, posterior deltoids

Starting position

Downward and upward movements

SEATED ROW (MACHINE)

Starting Position

- Sit erect with the feet flat on the floor and press the torso against the chest pad.
- Grasp the handles with a closed grip, either pronated or neutral. If necessary, adjust the seat height to position the arms approximately parallel to the floor.
- Allow the elbows to extend fully.
- All repetitions begin from this position.

Backward Movement Phase

- Pull the handles toward the chest or upper abdomen.
- Maintain an erect torso position and keep the elbows next to the torso.
- Pull the handles as far back as possible.
- Do not jerk the torso backward.

Forward Movement Phase

- Allow the handles to move forward, back to the starting position.
- Keep the torso in the same position.

Major Muscles Involved
Latissimus dorsi, teres major, middle trapezius, rhomboids, posterior deltoids

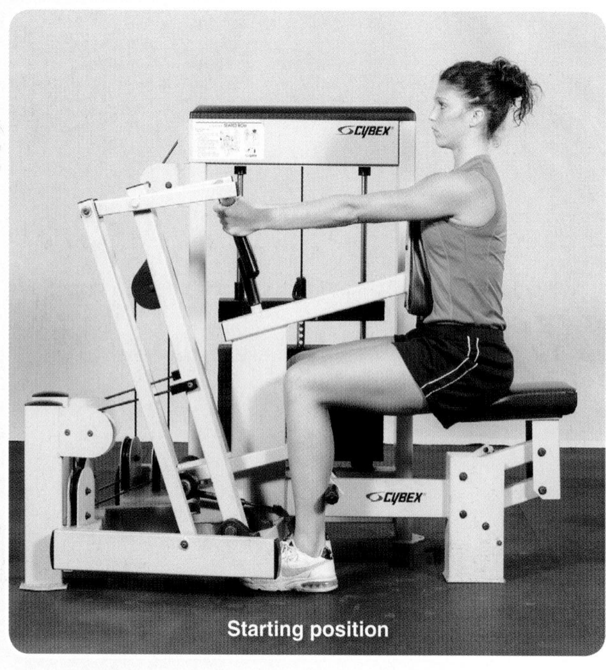

Starting position

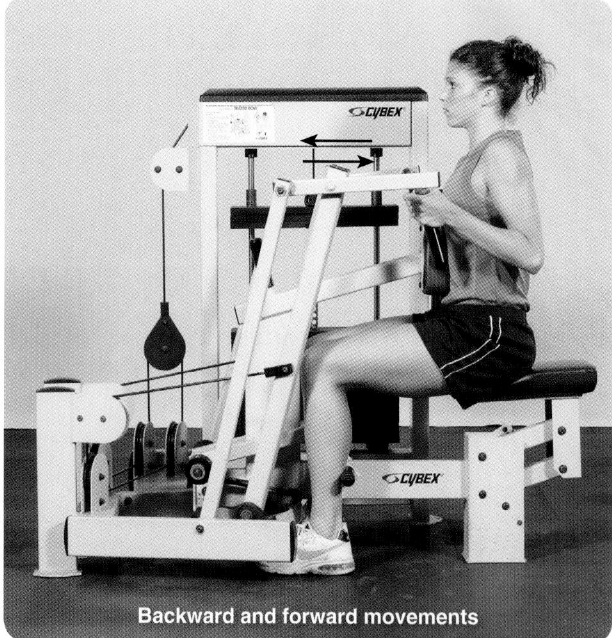

Backward and forward movements

LOW-PULLEY SEATED ROW (MACHINE)

Starting Position

- Sit on the floor (or on the long seat pad, if available) and place the feet on the machine frame or foot supports.
- Grasp the handles with a closed grip, either neutral or pronated.
- Sit in an erect position with the torso perpendicular to the floor, knees slightly flexed, and the feet and legs parallel to each other.
- Allow the elbows to fully extend with the arms approximately parallel to the floor.
- All repetitions begin from this position.

Backward Movement Phase

- Pull the handles toward the abdomen.
- Maintain an erect torso position with the knees in the same slightly flexed position. Do not jerk the upper body or lean back.
- Continue pulling until the handles touch the abdomen.

Forward Movement Phase

- Allow the elbows to slowly extend back to the starting position.
- Maintain an erect torso position with the knees in the same slightly flexed position.
- At the end of the set, flex the knees and hips to return the weight to its resting position.

Major Muscles Involved
Latissimus dorsi, teres major, middle trapezius, rhomboids, posterior deltoids

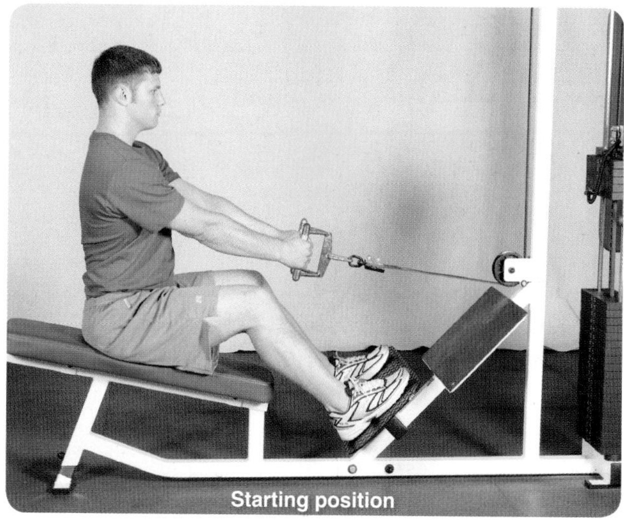

Starting position

Backward and forward movements

BARBELL BICEPS CURL

Starting Position

- Grasp the bar with a closed, supinated grip.
- Grip should be shoulder-width so the arms touch the sides of the torso.
- Stand erect with the feet shoulder-width apart and the knees slightly flexed.
- Rest the bar on the front of the thighs with the elbows fully extended.
- All repetitions begin from this position.

Upward Movement Phase

- Flex the elbows until the bar is near the anterior deltoids.
- Keep the torso erect and the upper arms stationary.
- Do not jerk the body or swing the bar upward.

Downward Movement Phase

- Lower the bar until the elbows are fully extended.
- Keep the torso and knees in the same position.
- Do not bounce the bar on the thighs between repetitions.

Major Muscles Involved
Biceps brachii, brachialis, brachioradialis

Starting position

Upward and downward movements

HAMMER CURL

Starting Position

- Grasp two dumbbells using a closed, neutral grip.
- Stand erect with the feet shoulder-width apart and the knees slightly flexed.
- Position the dumbbells alongside the thighs with the elbows fully extended.
- All repetitions begin from this position.

Upward Movement Phase

- Keeping the dumbbell in a neutral grip, flex the elbow of one arm until the dumbbell is near the anterior deltoid. The other arm should be kept stationary at the side of the thigh.
- Keep the torso erect and the upper arm stationary.
- Do not jerk the body or swing the dumbbell upward.

Downward Movement Phase

- Lower the dumbbell until the elbow is fully extended.
- Keep the dumbbell in a neutral grip position.
- Keep the torso and knees in the same position.
- Repeat the upward and downward movement phases with the other arm (alternate arms).

Major Muscles Involved
Brachialis, biceps brachii, brachioradialis

Starting position

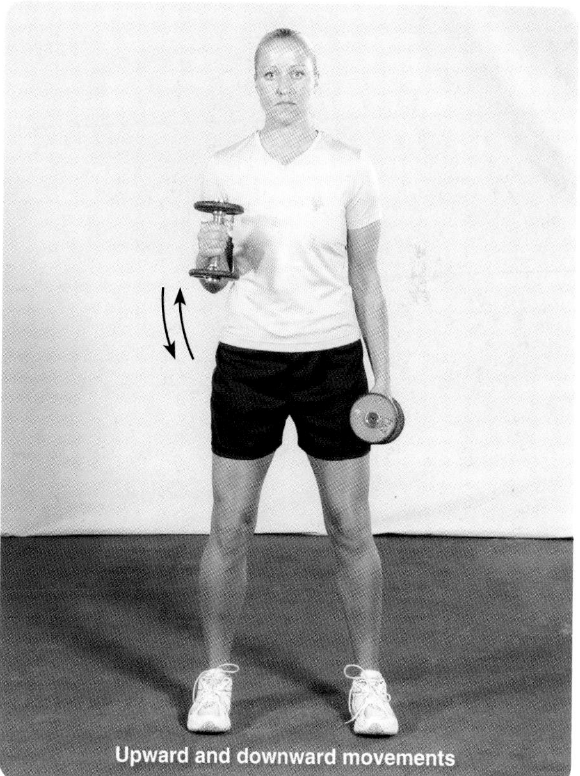
Upward and downward movements

STANDING CALF (HEEL) RAISE (MACHINE)

Starting Position

- Position the body evenly under the shoulder pads.
- Grasp the handles and place the balls of the feet on the nearest edge of the step with the legs and feet hip-width apart and parallel to each other.
- Stand erect with the knees fully extended but not forcefully locked out.
- Allow the heels to lower to a comfortable, stretched position.
- All repetitions begin from this position.

Upward Movement Phase

- Keeping the torso erect and the legs and feet parallel, push up as high as possible on the toes.
- Push up off the step; do not invert or evert the ankles.
- Keep the knees extended but not locked out.

Downward Movement Phase

- Allow the heels to lower slowly back to the starting position.
- Maintain the same body position.

Major Muscles Involved
Gastrocnemius, soleus

Starting position

Upward and downward movements

SEATED CALF (HEEL) RAISE (MACHINE)

Starting Position

- Sit erect on the seat and place the balls of the feet on the nearest edge of the step with the legs and feet hip-width apart and parallel to each other.
- Lower the thigh/knee pad so it firmly presses against the knees and front of the lower-thigh area.
- Plantar-flex the ankles to remove the supports.
- Allow the heels to lower to a comfortable, stretched position.
- All repetitions begin from this position.

Upward Movement Phase

- Keeping the torso erect and the legs and feet parallel, push up on the toes as high as possible.
- Push up off the step; do not invert or evert the ankles.

Downward Movement Phase

- Allow the heels to lower slowly back to the starting position.
- Maintain the same body position.
- At the end of the set, re-place the supports and remove the feet.

Major Muscles Involved
Soleus, gastrocnemius

Starting position

Upward and downward movements

FLAT BARBELL BENCH PRESS (AND DUMBBELL VARIATION)

This exercise can also be performed with two dumbbells, using a closed, pronated grip. The spotter assists by spotting the athlete's forearms near the wrists instead of the bar.

Liftoff

Starting positions

Starting Position: Athlete

- Lie in a supine position on a bench in the five-point body contact position.
- Place the body on the bench so that the eyes are below the racked bar.
- Grasp the bar with a closed, pronated grip slightly wider than shoulder-width apart.
- Signal the spotter for assistance in moving the bar off the supports.
- Position the bar over the chest with the elbows fully extended.
- All repetitions begin from this position.

Starting Position: Spotter

- Stand erect and very close to the head of the bench (but do not distract the athlete).
- Place the feet shoulder-width apart with the knees slightly flexed.
- Grasp the bar with a closed, alternated grip inside the athlete's hands.
- At athlete's signal, assist with moving the bar off the supports.
- Guide the bar to a position over the athlete's chest.
- Release the bar smoothly.

Downward Movement Phase: Athlete

- Lower the bar to touch the chest at approximately nipple level.
- Keep the wrists stiff and the forearms perpendicular to the floor and parallel to each other.
- Maintain the five-point body contact position.

Downward Movement Phase: Spotter

- Keep the hands in the alternated grip position close to—but not touching—the bar as it descends.
- Slightly flex the knees, hips, and torso and keep the back flat when following the bar.

Upward Movement Phase: Athlete

- Push the bar upward until the elbows are fully extended.
- Keep the wrists stiff and the forearms perpendicular to the floor and parallel to each other.
- Maintain the five-point body contact position.
- Do not arch the back or raise the chest to meet the bar.
- At the end of the set, signal the spotter for assistance in racking the bar.
- Keep a grip on the bar until it is racked.

Upward Movement Phase: Spotter

- Keep the hands in the alternated grip position close to—but not touching—the bar as it ascends.
- Slightly extend the knees, hips, and torso and keep the back flat when following the bar.
- At the athlete's signal, grasp the bar with an alternated grip inside the athlete's hands.
- Guide the bar back onto the supports.
- Keep a grip on the bar until it is racked.

Major Muscles Involved
Pectoralis major, anterior deltoids, triceps brachii

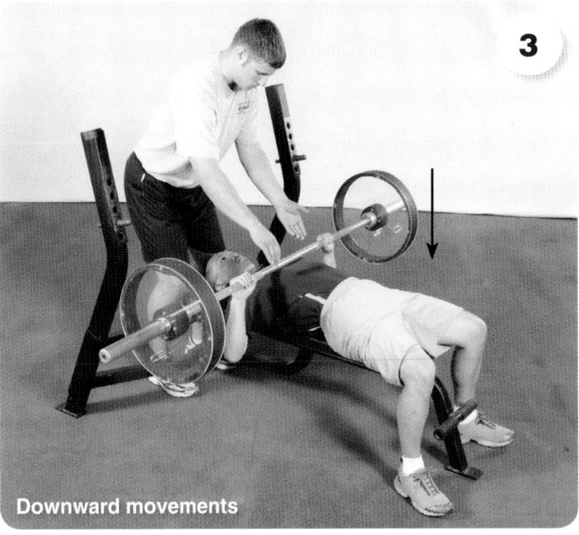

Downward movements

Upward movements

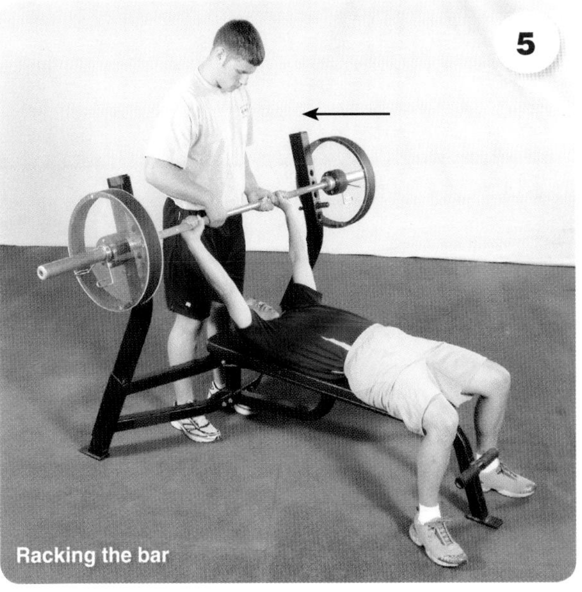

Racking the bar

INCLINE DUMBBELL BENCH PRESS (AND BARBELL VARIATION)

This exercise can also be performed with a barbell, using a closed, pronated grip slightly wider than shoulder-width. The spotter assists by spotting the bar instead of the athlete's forearms.

Starting Position: Athlete

- Grasp two dumbbells using a closed, pronated grip.
- Lie in a supine position on an inclined bench in the five-point body contact position.
- Signal the spotter for assistance in moving the dumbbells into the starting position.
- Press the dumbbells in unison to an extended-elbow, parallel-arm position above the head and face.
- All repetitions begin from this position.

Starting Position: Spotter

- Stand erect and very close to the head of the bench (but do not distract the athlete).
- Place the feet shoulder-width apart with the knees slightly flexed.
- Grasp the athlete's forearms near the wrists.
- At athlete's signal, assist with moving the dumbbells to a position over the athlete's head and face.
- Release the athlete's forearms smoothly.

Downward Movement Phase: Athlete

- Lower the dumbbells in unison alongside the chest near the armpits and aligned with the nipples.
- Keep the wrists stiff and directly above the elbows, with the dumbbell handles aligned with each other.
- Lower the dumbbells down and slightly out to be near the armpits and in line with the upper one-third area of the chest (between the clavicles and the nipples).
- Maintain the five-point body contact position.
- Do not arch the back or raise the chest to meet the dumbbells.

Downward Movement Phase: Spotter

- Keep the hands near—but not touching—the athlete's forearms as the dumbbells descend.
- Slightly flex the knees, hips, and torso and keep the back flat when following the dumbbells.

Upward Movement Phase: Athlete

- Push the dumbbells upward until the elbows are fully extended.
- Keep the wrists stiff and directly above the elbows, with the dumbbell handles aligned with each other.
- Maintain the five-point body contact position.

Upward Movement Phase: Spotter

- Keep the hands near—but not touching—the athlete's forearms as the dumbbells ascend.
- Slightly extend the knees, hips, and torso and keep the back flat when following the dumbbells.

Major Muscles Involved
Pectoralis major, anterior deltoids, triceps brachii

Starting positions

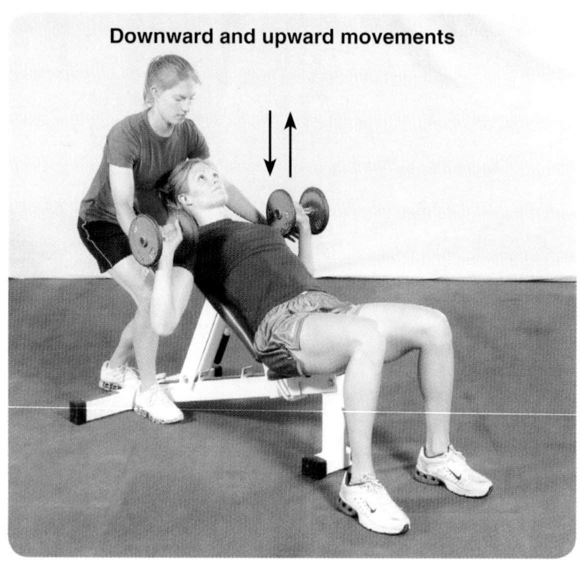

Downward and upward movements

FLAT DUMBBELL FLY (AND INCLINE VARIATION)

This exercise can also be performed on an incline bench. Begin by positioning the dumbbells over the head and face instead of over the chest.

Starting Position: Athlete

- Grasp two dumbbells using a closed, neutral grip.
- Lie in a supine position on a bench in the five-point body contact position.
- Signal the spotter for assistance in moving the dumbbells into the starting position.
- Press the dumbbells in unison to an extended-elbow position above the chest.
- Slightly flex the elbows and point them out to the sides.
- All repetitions begin from this position.

Starting Position: Spotter

- Position one knee on the floor with the foot of the other leg forward and flat on the floor (or kneel on both knees).
- Grasp the athlete's forearms near the wrists.
- At athlete's signal, assist with moving the dumbbells to a position over the athlete's chest.
- Release the athlete's forearms smoothly.

Downward Movement Phase: Athlete

- Lower the dumbbells in a wide arc until they are level with the shoulders or chest.
- Keep the dumbbell handles parallel to each other as the elbows move downward.
- Keep the wrists stiff and the elbows held in a slightly flexed position.
- Keep the hands, wrists, forearms, elbows, upper arms, and shoulders in the same vertical plane.
- Maintain the five-point body contact position.

Downward Movement Phase: Spotter

- Keep the hands near—but not touching—the athlete's forearms as the dumbbells descend.

Upward Movement Phase: Athlete

- Raise the dumbbells up toward each other in a wide arc back to the starting position.
- Keep the wrists stiff and the elbows held in a slightly flexed position.
- Keep the hands, wrists, forearms, elbows, upper arms, and shoulders in the same vertical plane.
- Maintain the five-point body contact position.

Upward Movement Phase: Spotter

- Keep the hands near—but not touching—the athlete's forearms as the dumbbells ascend.

Major Muscles Involved
Pectoralis major, anterior deltoids

Starting positions

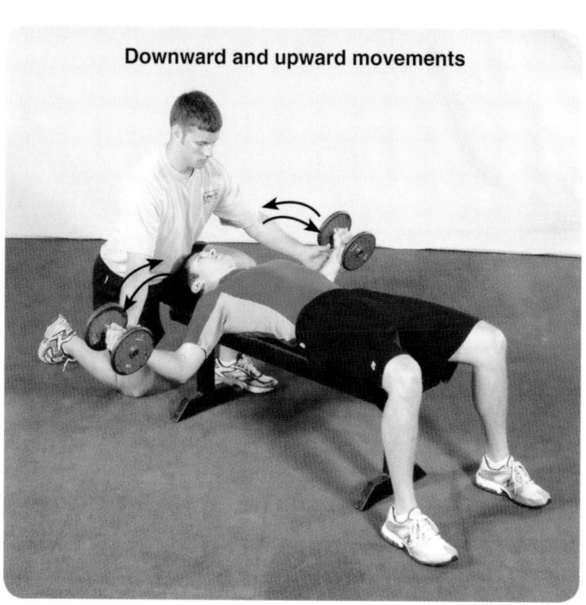
Downward and upward movements

VERTICAL CHEST PRESS (MACHINE)

Starting Position

- Sit down and lean back on the seat in the five-point body contact position.
- Grasp the handles with a closed, pronated grip.
- Align handles with the nipples. If necessary, adjust the seat height to correctly position the handles.
- Push the handles away from the chest to a fully extended elbow position.
- All repetitions begin from this position.

Backward Movement Phase

- Allow the handles to slowly move backward so that they are level with the chest.
- Maintain the five-point body contact position.

Forward Movement Phase

- Push the handles away from the chest back to the starting position.
- Maintain the five-point body contact position.
- Do not arch the lower back or forcefully lock out the elbows.

Major Muscles Involved
Pectoralis major, anterior deltoids, triceps brachii

Starting position

Backward and forward movements

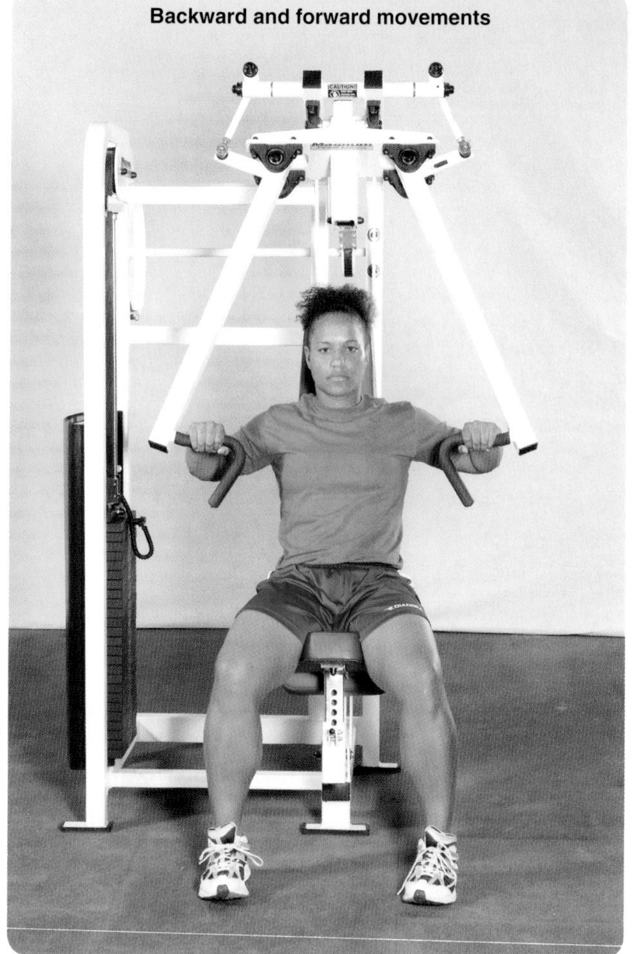

WRIST CURL

Starting Position

- Sit on the end of a bench.
- Grasp the bar with a closed, supinated grip 8 to 12 inches (20-30 cm) wide.
- Position the feet and legs parallel to each other with the toes pointing straight ahead.
- Lean the torso forward and place the elbows and forearms on the top of the thighs.
- Move the wrists forward until they extend slightly beyond the patellae.
- Allow the wrists to extend and the hands to open so that the fingertips hold the bar.

Upward Movement Phase

- Raise the bar by flexing the fingers and then the wrists.
- Flex the wrists as far as possible without moving the elbows or forearms.
- Do not jerk the shoulders backward or swing the bar upward.

Downward Movement Phase

- Allow the wrists and fingers to slowly extend back to the starting position.
- Keep the torso and arms in the same position.

Major Muscles Involved
Flexor carpi ulnaris, flexor carpi radialis, palmaris longus

Starting position

Upward and downward movements

WRIST EXTENSION

Starting Position

- Sit on the end of a bench.
- Grasp the bar with a closed, pronated grip 8 to 12 inches (20-30 cm) wide.
- Position the feet and legs parallel to each other with the toes pointing straight ahead.
- Lean the torso forward and place the elbows and forearms on the top of the thighs.
- Move the wrists forward until they extend slightly beyond the patellae.
- Keep a closed grip on the bar but allow the wrists to flex toward the floor.

Upward Movement Phase

- Raise the bar by extending the wrists.
- Extend the wrists as far as possible without moving the elbows or forearms.
- Do not jerk the body backward or swing the bar upward.

Downward Movement Phase

- Allow the wrists to slowly flex back to the starting position.
- Keep the torso and arms in the same position.
- Maintain a closed grip.

Major Muscles Involved
Extensor carpi ulnaris, extensor carpi radialis brevis (and longus)

Starting position

Upward and downward movements

HIP SLED (MACHINE)

Starting position

Starting Position

- Sit in the machine with the lower back, hips, and buttocks pressed against their pads.
- Place the feet flat on the platform hip-width apart with the toes slightly angled out.
- Position the legs parallel to each other.
- Grasp the handles or the sides of the seat and move the hips and knees to a fully extended position, but do not forcefully lock the knees.
- Keep the hips on the seat and the back against the back pad.
- Remove the support mechanism from the foot platform and grasp the handles or the seat again.
- All repetitions begin from this position.

Downward Movement Phase

- Allow the hips and knees to slowly flex to lower the platform.
- Do not allow the platform to lower rapidly.
- Keep the hips and buttocks on the seat and the back flat against the back pad.
- Keep the knees aligned over the feet as they flex.
- Allow the hips and knees to flex until the thighs are parallel to the foot platform, the buttocks lose contact with the seat, the hips roll off of the back pad, or the heels rise off the foot platform.

Downward and upward movements

Upward Movement Phase

- Push the platform up by extending the hips and knees.
- Push to a fully extended position, but do not forcefully lock out the knees.
- Maintain the same hip and back position; do not allow the buttocks to rise.
- Keep the knees aligned over the feet as they extend.
- At the end of the set, re-place the supports, remove the feet, and exit the machine.

Major Muscles Involved
Gluteus maximus, semimembranosus, semitendinosus, biceps femoris, vastus lateralis, vastus intermedius, vastus medialis, rectus femoris

BACK SQUAT

Starting Position: Athlete

- Grasp the bar with a closed, pronated grip (actual width depends on the bar position).
- Step under the bar and position the feet parallel to each other.
- Place the bar in a balanced position on the upper back and shoulders in one of two locations:
  1. *Low bar position*—across the posterior deltoids at the middle of the trapezius (using a handgrip wider than shoulder-width)
  2. *High bar position*—above the posterior deltoids at the base of the neck (using a handgrip only slightly wider than shoulder-width)
- Lift the elbows up to create a "shelf" for the bar using the upper back and shoulder muscles.
- Hold the chest up and out.
- Tilt the head slightly up.
- Once in position, signal the spotters for assistance in moving the bar off the supports.
- Extend the hips and knees to lift the bar.
- Take one or two steps backward.
- Position the feet shoulder-width apart (or wider), even with each other, with the toes pointed slightly outward.
- All repetitions begin from this position.

Starting Position: Two Spotters

- Stand erect at opposite ends of the bar with the feet shoulder-width apart and the knees slightly flexed.
- Grasp the end of the bar by cupping the hands together with the palms facing upward.

Lowest squat position

Low bar position

High bar position

Starting positions with high bar position

Downward movement positions

- At athlete's signal, assist with lifting and balancing the bar as it is moved off the supports.
- Release the bar smoothly.
- Hold the hands 2 to 3 inches (5-8 cm) below the ends of the bar.
- Move sideways in unison with the athlete as the athlete moves backward.
- Once the athlete is in position, get into a hip-width stance with the knees slightly flexed and the torso erect.

Downward Movement Phase: Athlete

- Maintain a position with the back flat, elbows high, and the chest up and out.
- Allow the hips and knees to slowly flex while keeping the torso-to-floor angle relatively constant.
- Keep the heels on the floor and the knees aligned over the feet.
- Continue flexing the hips and knees until the thighs are parallel to the floor, the trunk begins to round or flex forward, or the heels rise off the floor.

Downward Movement Phase: Two Spotters

- Keep the cupped hands close to—but not touching—the bar as it descends.
- Slightly flex the knees, hips, and torso to keep a flat-back position when following the bar.

Upward Movement Phase: Athlete

- Maintain a position with flat back, high elbows, and the chest up and out.
- Extend the hips and knees at the same rate (to keep the torso-to-floor angle constant).
- Keep the heels on the floor and the knees aligned over the feet.
- Do not flex the torso forward or round the back.
- Continue extending the hips and knees to reach the starting position.
- At the end of the set, step forward toward the rack.
- Squat down until the bar rests on the supports.

Upward Movement Phase: Two Spotters

- Keep the cupped hands close to—but not touching—the bar as it ascends.
- Slightly extend the knees, hips, and torso and keep the back flat when following the bar.
- At the end of the set, move sideways in unison with the athlete back to the rack.
- Simultaneously grasp the bar and assist with balancing the bar as it is racked.
- Release the bar smoothly.

Major Muscles Involved
Gluteus maximus, semimembranosus, semitendinosus, biceps femoris, vastus lateralis, vastus intermedius, vastus medialis, rectus femoris

Upward movement positions

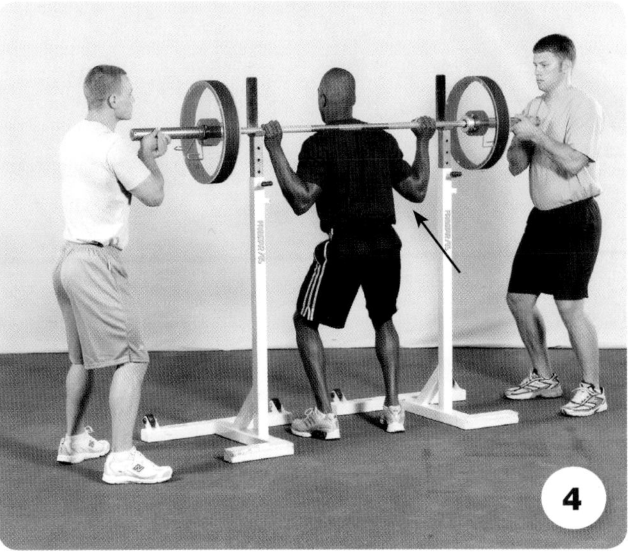

Racking the bar

FRONT SQUAT

Starting Position: Athlete

- Step under the bar and position the feet parallel to each other.
- Place the hands on the bar in one of two arm positions:
  1. Parallel arm position
     - Grasp the bar with a closed, pronated grip.
     - Grip should be slightly wider than shoulder-width.
     - Move up to the bar to place it on top of the anterior deltoids and clavicles.
     - Fully flex the elbows to position the upper arms parallel to the floor.
  2. Crossed-arm position
     - Flex the elbows and cross the arms in front of the chest.
     - Move up to the bar to place it on top of the anterior deltoids.
     - Use an open grip with the hands on top of the bar and the fingers holding it in place.
     - Lift the elbows to position the arms parallel to the floor.
- Hold the chest up and out.
- Tilt the head slightly up.
- Once in position, signal the spotter for assistance in moving the bar off the supports.
- Extend the hips and knees to lift the bar.
- Take one or two steps backward.
- Position the feet shoulder-width apart (or wider), even with each other, with the toes pointed slightly outward.
- All repetitions begin from this position.

Starting Position: Two Spotters

- Stand erect at opposite ends of the bar with the feet shoulder-width apart and the knees slightly flexed.
- Grasp the end of the bar by cupping the hands together with the palms facing upward.

Lowest squat position

Parallel arm position

Crossed-arm position

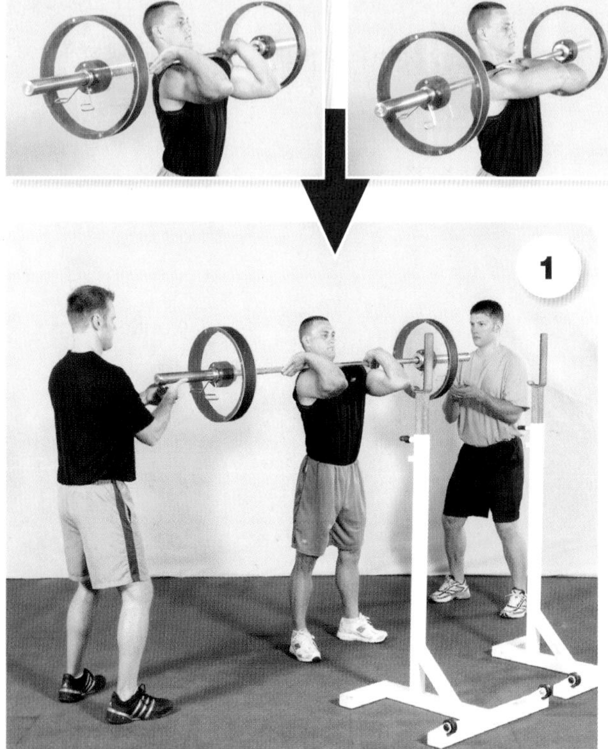

Starting positions with parallel arm position

Downward movement positions

- At athlete's signal, assist with lifting and balancing the bar as it is moved off the supports.
- Release the bar smoothly.
- Hold the hands 2 to 3 inches (5-8 cm) below the ends of the bar.
- Move sideways in unison with the athlete as the athlete moves backward.
- Once the athlete is in position, get into a hip-width stance with the knees slightly flexed and the torso erect.

Downward Movement Phase: Athlete

- Maintain a position with the back flat, elbows high, and the chest up and out.
- Allow the hips and knees to slowly flex while keeping the torso-to-floor angle relatively constant.
- Keep the heels on the floor and the knees aligned over the feet.
- Do not flex the torso forward or round the back.
- Continue flexing the hips and knees until the thighs are parallel to the floor, the trunk begins to round or flex forward, or the heels rise off the floor.

Downward Movement Phase: Two Spotters

- Keep the cupped hands close to—but not touching—the bar as it descends.
- Slightly flex the knees, hips, and torso and keep the back flat when following the bar.

Upward Movement Phase: Athlete

- Maintain a position with the back flat, elbows high, and the chest up and out.
- Extend the hips and knees at the same rate (to keep the torso-to-floor angle constant).
- Keep the heels on the floor and the knees aligned over the feet.
- Do not flex the torso forward or round the back.
- Continue extending the hips and knees to reach the starting position.
- At the end of the set, step forward toward the rack.
- Squat down until the bar rests on the supports.

Upward Movement Phase: Two Spotters

- Keep the cupped hands close to—but not touching—the bar as it ascends.
- Slightly extend the knees, hips, and torso and keep the back flat when following the bar.
- At the end of the set, move sideways in unison with the athlete back to the rack.
- Simultaneously grasp the bar and assist with balancing the bar as it is placed back on the supports.
- Release the bar smoothly.

Major Muscles Involved
Gluteus maximus, semimembranosus, semitendinosus, biceps femoris, vastus lateralis, vastus intermedius, vastus medialis, rectus femoris

Upward movement positions

Racking the bar

FORWARD STEP LUNGE

This exercise can also be performed with two dumbbells, using a closed, neutral grip. The athlete allows the dumbbells to hang at arm's length alongside the body throughout the exercise. The spotter assists the athlete in the same manner as in the barbell version, although the task of helping the athlete rack the bar is not applicable. *Note*: This exercise cannot be performed inside a typical power rack. The use of a tiered squat rack or a power rack that has supports on the outside is recommended. To allow an optimal view of the exercise technique, a rack is not shown in the photos.

Starting Position: Athlete

- Step under the bar and position the feet parallel to each other.
- Grasp the bar with a closed, pronated grip.
- Place the bar in a balanced position on the upper back and shoulders above the posterior deltoids at the base of the neck (using a handgrip only slightly wider than shoulder-width).
- Lift the elbows up to create a "shelf" for the bar using the upper back and shoulder muscles.
- Hold the chest up and out.
- Tilt the head slightly up.
- Once in position, signal the spotter for assistance in moving the bar off the supports.
- Extend the hips and knees to lift the bar.
- Take two or three steps backward.
- All repetitions begin from this position.

Starting Position: Spotter

- Stand erect and very close to the athlete (but do not distract the athlete).
- Place the feet shoulder-width apart with the knees slightly flexed.
- At athlete's signal, assist with lifting and balancing the bar as it is moved out of the rack.
- Move in unison with the athlete as the athlete moves backward to the starting position.
- Once the athlete is in position, get into a hip-width stance with the knees slightly flexed and the torso erect.
- Position the hands near the athlete's hips, waist, or torso.

Forward Movement Phase: Athlete

- Take one exaggerated step directly forward with one leg (the lead leg).
- Keep the torso erect as the lead foot moves forward and contacts the floor.
- Keep the trailing foot in the starting position, but allow the trailing knee to slightly flex.

Starting positions

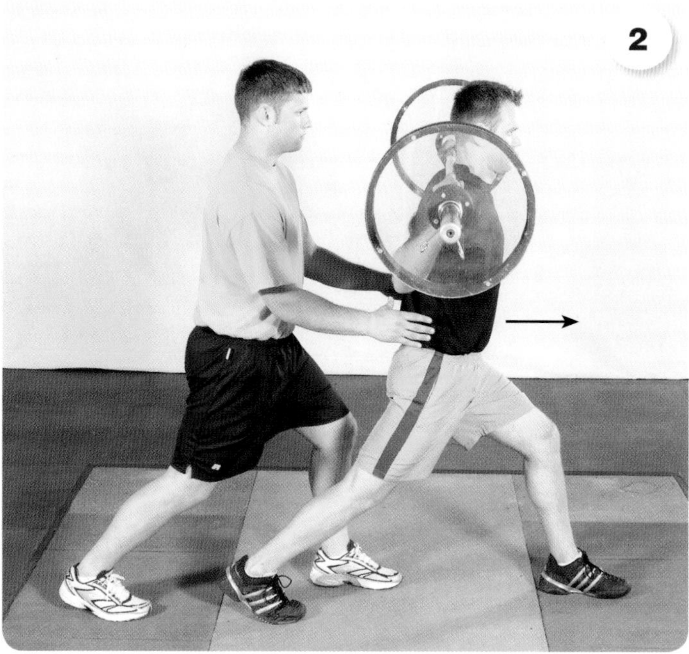

Beginning of forward movement positions

- Plant the lead foot flat on the floor pointing straight ahead or slightly inward.
- Allow the lead hip and knee to slowly flex.
- Keep the lead knee directly over the lead foot.
- Continue to flex the trailing knee until it is 1 to 2 inches (3-5 cm) above the floor.
- Balance the weight evenly between the ball of the trailing foot and the whole lead foot.
- Keep the torso perpendicular to the floor by "sitting back" on the trailing leg.

Forward Movement Phase: Spotter

- Step forward with the same foot as the athlete.
- Keep the lead knee and foot aligned with the athlete's lead foot.
- Plant the foot 12 to 18 inches (30-46 cm) behind the athlete's foot.
- Flex the lead knee as the athlete's lead knee flexes.
- Keep the torso erect.
- Keep the hands near the athlete's hips, waist, or torso.
- Assist only when necessary to keep the athlete balanced.

Backward Movement Phase: Athlete

- Forcefully push off the floor by extending the lead hip and knee.
- Maintain the same erect torso position; do not jerk the upper body backward.
- Bring the lead foot back to a position next to the trailing foot; do not stutter-step backward.
- Stand erect in the starting position, pause, and then alternate lead legs.
- At the end of the set, step toward the rack and place the bar in the supports.

Backward Movement Phase: Spotter

- Push backward with the lead leg in unison with the athlete.
- Bring the lead foot back to a position next to the trailing foot; do not stutter-step backward.
- Keep hands near the athlete's hips, waist, or torso.
- Stand erect in the starting position, pause to wait for the athlete, and alternate lead legs.
- Assist only when necessary to keep the athlete balanced.
- At the end of the set, help the athlete rack the bar.

Major Muscles Involved
Gluteus maximus, semimembranosus, semitendinosus, biceps femoris, vastus lateralis, vastus intermedius, vastus medialis, rectus femoris, iliopsoas

Completion of forward movement positions

Backward movement positions

STEP-UP

Note: The box used should be 12 to 18 inches (30-46 cm) high, or high enough to create a 90° angle at the knee joint when the foot is on the box. To allow an optimal view of the exercise technique, a rack is not shown in the photos.

Starting Position: Athlete

- Grasp the bar with a closed, pronated grip.
- Step under the bar and position the feet parallel to each other.
- Place the bar in a balanced position on the upper back and shoulders above the posterior deltoids at the base of the neck (using a handgrip only slightly wider than shoulder-width).
- Lift the elbows up to create a "shelf" for the bar using the upper back and shoulder muscles.
- Hold the chest up and out.
- Tilt the head slightly up.
- Once in position, signal the spotter for assistance in moving the bar off the supports.
- Extend the hips and knees to lift the bar.
- Walk toward the box and stand in a position near the box that is as far away from the box as the box is tall.
- All repetitions begin from this position.

Starting Position: Spotter

- Stand erect and very close to the athlete (but do not distract the athlete).
- Place the feet shoulder-width apart with the knees slightly flexed.
- At athlete's signal, assist with lifting and balancing the bar as it is moved out of the rack.
- Move in unison with the athlete as the athlete moves to the starting position.
- Once the athlete is in position, get into a hip-width stance with the knees slightly flexed and the torso erect.
- Position the hands near the athlete's hips, waist, or torso.

Upward Movement Phase: Athlete

- Step up with one leg (the lead leg) to place the entire foot on the top of the box.
- Keep the torso erect; do not lean forward.
- Keep the trailing foot in the starting position, but shift the body weight to the lead leg.
- Forcefully extend the lead hip and knee to move the body to a standing position on top of the box.

Starting positions

Initial contact of lead foot with top of box

- Do not push off or hop up with the trailing leg or foot.
- At the highest position, stand erect and pause before beginning the downward movement phase.

Upward Movement Phase: Spotter

- Lean the torso forward and reach with the arms (but do not take a step) toward the athlete as the athlete steps up on the box.
- Keep the hands as near as possible to the athlete's hips, waist, or torso (since the athlete is stepping away).
- Assist only when necessary to keep the athlete balanced.

Downward Movement Phase: Athlete

- Shift the body weight to the same lead leg.
- Step off the box with the same trailing leg.
- Maintain an erect torso position.
- Place the trailing foot on the floor 12 to 18 inches (30-46 cm) away from the box.
- When the trailing foot is in full contact with the floor, shift the body weight to the trailing leg.
- Step off the box with the lead leg.
- Bring the lead foot back to a position next to the trailing foot.
- Stand erect in the starting position, pause, and then alternate lead legs.
- At the end of the set, step toward the rack and place the bar in the supports.

Downward Movement Phase: Spotter

- Follow the athlete with the arms as the athlete steps back down to the floor.
- Keep the hands near the athlete's hips, waist, or torso.
- Stand erect in the starting position and pause to wait for the athlete.
- Assist only when necessary to keep the athlete balanced.
- At the end of the set, help the athlete rack the bar.

Major Muscles Involved
Gluteus maximus, semimembranosus, semitendinosus, biceps femoris, vastus lateralis, vastus intermedius, vastus medialis, rectus femoris

Beginning of upward movement positions

Completion of upward movement positions

GOOD MORNING

Note: To allow an optimal view of the exercise technique, a rack is not shown in the photos.

Starting Position

- Grasp the bar with a closed, pronated grip.
- Step under the bar and position the feet parallel to each other.
- Place the bar in a balanced position on the upper back and shoulders above the posterior deltoids at the base of the neck (using a handgrip only slightly wider than shoulder-width).
- Lift the elbows up to create a "shelf" for the bar using the upper back and shoulder muscles.
- Hold the chest up and out.
- Tilt the head slightly up.
- Position the feet shoulder-width apart (or wider), even with each other, with the toes pointed slightly outward.
- All repetitions begin from this position.

Downward Movement Phase

- Begin the exercise by slowly permitting the hips to flex. The buttocks should move straight back during the descent.
- Maintain a flat back and high elbow position; do not round the upper back during the descent.
- The bar should be slightly behind the toes; do not allow the heels to rise off the floor.
- Keep the knees slightly flexed during the descent.
- Continue the downward movement until the torso is approximately parallel to the floor.

Upward Movement Phase

- Raise the bar by extending the hips.
- Keep the back flat and the knees slightly flexed during the ascent.
- Continue extending the hips to reach the starting position.

Major Muscles Involved
Gluteus maximus, semimembranosus, semitendinosus, biceps femoris, erector spinae

Starting position

Downward and upward movements

DEADLIFT

Starting Position

- Stand with the feet flat and placed between hip- and shoulder-width apart with the toes pointed slightly outward.
- Squat down with the hips lower than the shoulders, and grasp the bar with a closed, alternated grip.
- Place the hands on the bar slightly wider than shoulder-width apart, outside of the knees, with the elbows fully extended.
- Place the feet flat on the floor and position the bar approximately 1 inch (3 cm) in front of the shins and over the balls of the feet.
- Position the body with the
  - back flat or slightly arched,
  - trapezius relaxed and slightly stretched,
  - chest held up and out,
  - head in line with the vertebral column or slightly hyperextended,
  - heels in contact with the floor,
  - shoulders over or slightly in front of the bar, and
  - eyes focused straight ahead or slightly upward.
- All repetitions begin from this position.

Upward Movement Phase

- Lift the bar off the floor by extending the hips and knees.
- Keep the torso-to-floor angle constant; do not let the hips rise before the shoulders.
- Maintain a flat-back position.
- Keep the elbows fully extended and the shoulders over or slightly ahead of the bar.
- As the bar is raised, keep it as close to the shins as possible.
- As the bar rises just above the knees, move the hips forward to move the thighs against and the knees under the bar.
- Continue to extend the hips and knees until the body reaches a fully erect torso position.

Downward Movement Phase

- Allow the hips and knees to flex to slowly lower the bar to the floor.
- Maintain the flat-back body position; do not flex the torso forward.

Major Muscles Involved
Gluteus maximus, semimembranosus, semitendinosus, biceps femoris, vastus lateralis, vastus intermedius, vastus medialis, rectus femoris

Starting position

Middle position

End position

STIFF-LEG DEADLIFT

Starting Position

- After performing the deadlift exercise to lift the bar off the floor, slightly to moderately flex the knees and keep them in this position throughout this exercise.
- All repetitions begin from this position.

Downward Movement Phase

- Begin the exercise by forming a flat back, then flex the torso forward at the hips slowly and under full control toward the floor.
- Keep the knees in the same slightly or moderately flexed position with the back flat or slightly arched and the elbows fully extended during the descent.
- Lower the bar until the plates touch the floor, the back cannot be held in the flat position, the knees fully extend, or the heels rise off of the floor.

Upward Movement Phase

- Extend the torso at the hips back to the standing starting position.
- Keep the knees slightly flexed and the torso in a flat-back position.
- Do not jerk the torso backward or flex the elbows.

Major Muscles Involved
Gluteus maximus, semimembranosus, semitendinosus, biceps femoris, erector spinae

Starting position

Downward and upward movements

LEG (KNEE) EXTENSION (MACHINE)

Starting Position

- Sit down in the machine and press the back firmly against the back pad.
- Place the feet behind and in contact with the roller pad.
- Position the legs parallel to each other.
- Align the knees with the axis of the machine. If necessary, adjust the back pad or the roller pad to position the legs correctly.
- Grasp the handles or the sides of the seat.
- All repetitions begin from this position.

Upward Movement Phase

- Raise the roller pad by fully extending the knees.
- Keep the torso erect and the back firmly pressed against the back pad.
- Keep the thighs, lower legs, and feet parallel to each other.
- Maintain a tight grip on the handles or the sides of the seat.
- Do not forcefully lock out the knees.

Downward Movement Phase

- Allow the knees to slowly flex back to the starting position.
- Keep the torso erect and the back firmly pressed against the back pad.
- Keep the thighs, lower legs, and feet parallel to each other
- Do not allow the buttocks to lift off the seat.
- Maintain a tight grip on the handles or the sides of the seat.

Major Muscles Involved
Vastus lateralis, vastus intermedius, vastus medialis, rectus femoris

Starting position

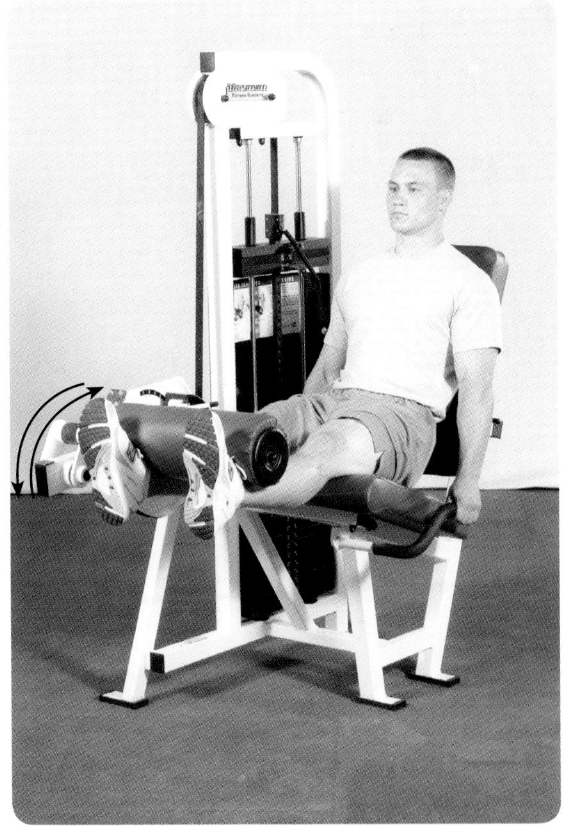

Upward and downward movements

LEG (KNEE) CURL (MACHINE)

Starting Position

- Lie in a prone position on the machine and press the hips and torso firmly against the pads.
- Place the ankles behind and in contact with the roller pad.
- Position the legs parallel to each other.
- Position the knees slightly off the bottom edge of the thigh pad.
- Align the knees with the axis of the machine. If necessary, adjust the roller pad to position the legs correctly.
- Grasp the handles or the sides of the chest pad.
- All repetitions begin from this position.

Upward Movement Phase

- Raise the roller pad by fully flexing the knees.
- Keep the torso stationary and the hips and torso firmly pressed against the pads.
- Do not allow the hips or thighs to lift off the thigh pad.
- Maintain a tight grip on the handles or the sides of the chest pad.

Downward Movement Phase

- Allow the knees to slowly extend back to the starting position.
- Keep the torso stationary and the hips and torso firmly pressed against the pads.
- Maintain a tight grip on the handles or the sides of the chest pad.
- Do not forcefully lock out the knees.

Major Muscles Involved
Semimembranosus, semitendinosus, biceps femoris

Starting position

Upward and downward movements

SHOULDER PRESS (MACHINE)

Starting Position

- Sit down and lean back to place the body in the five-point body contact position.
- Grasp the handles with a closed, pronated grip.
- Align handles with the top of the shoulders. If necessary, adjust the seat height to position the handles correctly.

Upward Movement Phase

- Push the handles upward until the elbows are fully extended.
- Maintain the five-point body contact position.
- Do not arch the lower back or forcefully lock out the elbows.

Downward Movement Phase

- Allow the elbows to slowly flex to lower the handles to the starting position.
- Maintain the five-point body contact position.

Major Muscles Involved
Anterior and medial deltoids, triceps brachii

Starting position

Upward and downward movements

SEATED BARBELL SHOULDER PRESS (AND DUMBBELL VARIATION)

This exercise can also be performed with two dumbbells, using a closed, pronated grip. The spotter assists by spotting the athlete's forearms near the wrists instead of the bar.

Starting Position: Athlete

- Sit down on a vertical shoulder press bench and lean back to place the body in the five-point body contact position.
- Grasp the bar with a closed, pronated grip.
- Grip should be slightly wider than shoulder-width.
- Signal the spotter for assistance in moving the bar off the supports.
- Press the bar over the head until the elbows are fully extended.
- All repetitions begin from this position.

Starting Position: Spotter

- Stand erect behind the bench with the feet shoulder-width apart and the knees slightly flexed.
- Grasp the bar with a closed, alternated grip inside the athlete's hands.
- At athlete's signal, assist with moving the bar off the supports.
- Guide the bar to a position over the athlete's head.
- Release the bar smoothly.

Downward Movement Phase: Athlete

- Allow the elbows to slowly flex to lower the bar.
- Keep the wrists stiff and the forearms parallel to each other.
- Extend the neck slightly to allow the bar to pass by the face as it is lowered to touch the clavicles and anterior deltoids.
- Maintain the five-point body contact position.

Downward Movement Phase: Spotter

- Keep the hands in the alternated grip position close to—but not touching—the bar as it descends.
- Keep the knees slightly flexed and the back flat when following the bar.

Upward Movement Phase: Athlete

- Push the bar upward until the elbows are fully extended.
- Extend the neck slightly to allow the bar to pass by the face as it is raised.
- Keep the wrists stiff and the forearms parallel to each other.
- Maintain the five-point body contact position.
- Do not arch the back or rise off the seat.
- At the end of the set, signal the spotter for assistance in racking the bar.
- Keep a grip on the bar until it is racked.

Upward Movement Phase: Spotter

- Keep the hands in the alternated grip position close to—but not touching—the bar as it ascends.
- Slightly extend the knees, hips, and torso and keep the back flat when following the bar.
- At the athlete's signal after the set is completed, grasp the bar with an alternated grip inside the athlete's hands.
- Guide the bar back onto the supports.
- Keep a grip on the bar until it is racked.

Major Muscles Involved
Anterior and medial deltoids, triceps brachii

Starting positions

Downward and upward movements

UPRIGHT ROW

Starting Position

- Grasp the bar with a closed, pronated grip approximately shoulder-width apart or narrower.
- Stand erect with feet shoulder-width apart, knees slightly flexed.
- Rest the bar on the front of the thighs with the elbows fully extended and pointing out to the sides.

Upward Movement Phase

- Pull the bar up along the abdomen and chest toward the chin.
- Keep the elbows pointed out to the sides as the bar brushes against the body.
- Keep the torso and knees in the same position.
- Do not rise up on the toes or swing the bar upward.
- At the highest bar position, the elbows should be level with or slightly higher than the shoulders and wrists.

Downward Movement Phase

- Allow the bar to slowly descend back to the starting position.
- Keep the torso and knees in the same position.

Major Muscles Involved
Deltoids, upper trapezius

Starting position

Upward and downward movements

LATERAL SHOULDER RAISE

Starting Position

- Grasp two dumbbells with a closed, neutral grip.
- Position the feet shoulder- or hip-width apart, with the knees slightly flexed, torso erect, shoulders back, and eyes focused ahead.
- Move the dumbbells to the front of the thighs, positioning them with the palms facing each other.
- Slightly flex the elbows and hold this flexed position throughout the exercise.

Upward Movement Phase

- Raise the dumbbells up and out to the sides; the elbows and upper arms should rise together and ahead of the forearms and hands and dumbbells.
- Maintain an erect upper body position with the knees slightly flexed and feet flat.
- Do not jerk the body or swing the dumbbells upward.
- Continue raising the dumbbells until the arms are approximately parallel to the floor or nearly level with the shoulders.

Downward Movement Phase

- Allow the dumbbells to descend slowly back to the starting position.
- Keep the torso and knees in the same position.

Major Muscles Involved
Deltoids

Starting position

Upward and downward movements

LYING BARBELL TRICEPS EXTENSION

Starting Position: Athlete

- Lie in a supine position on a bench in the five-point body contact position.
- Grasp the bar from the spotter with a closed, pronated grip about 12 inches (30 cm) wide.
- Position the bar over the chest with the elbows fully extended and the arms parallel.
- Point the elbows toward the knees (not out to the sides).
- All repetitions begin from this position.

Starting Position: Spotter

- Stand erect and very close to the head of the bench (but do not distract the athlete).
- Place the feet shoulder-width apart with the knees slightly flexed.
- Grasp the bar with a closed, alternated grip.
- Hand the bar to the athlete.
- Guide the bar to a position over the athlete's chest.
- Release the bar smoothly.

Downward Movement Phase: Athlete

- Keeping the upper arms stationary, allow the elbows to slowly flex to lower the bar toward the face.
- Keep the wrists stiff and the upper arms perpendicular to the floor and parallel to each other.
- Lower the bar until it almost touches the head or face.
- Maintain the five-point body contact position.

Downward Movement Phase: Spotter

- Keep the hands in a supinated grip position close to—but not touching—the bar as it descends.
- Slightly flex the knees, hips, and torso and keep the back flat when following the bar.

Upward Movement Phase: Athlete

- Push the bar upward by extending the elbows back to the starting position.
- Keep the wrists stiff and the elbows pointed toward the knees.
- Keep the upper arms parallel to each other and perpendicular to the floor.
- Maintain the five-point body contact position.

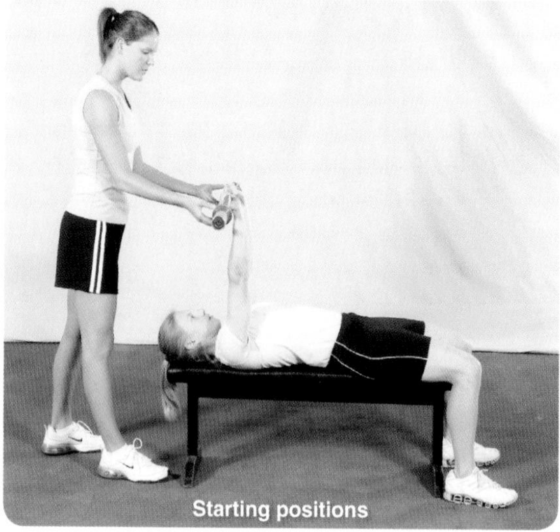
Starting positions

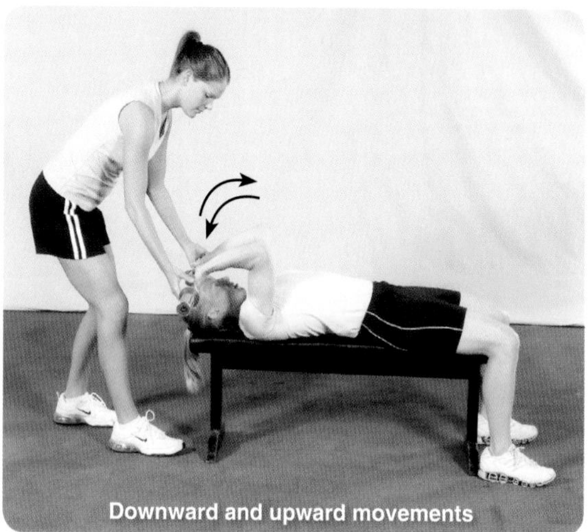
Downward and upward movements

- At the end of the set, signal the spotter to take the bar.
- Keep a grip on the bar until the spotter removes it.

Upward Movement Phase: Spotter

- Keep the hands in a supinated grip position close to—but not touching—the bar as it ascends.
- Slightly extend the knees, hips, and torso and keep the back flat when following the bar.
- At the athlete's signal after the set is completed, grasp the bar with an alternated grip, take it from the athlete, and set it on the floor.

Major Muscles Involved
Triceps brachii

TRICEPS PUSHDOWN (MACHINE)

Starting Position

- Grasp the bar with a closed, pronated grip 6 to 12 inches (15-30 cm) wide.
- Stand erect with feet shoulder-width apart, knees slightly flexed. Place the body close enough to the machine to allow the cable to hang straight down when it is held in the starting position.
- Pull the bar down to position the upper arms against the sides of the torso.
- Flex the elbows to position the forearms parallel to the floor or slightly above.
- All repetitions begin from this position.

Downward Movement Phase

- Push the bar down until the elbows are fully extended.
- Keep the torso erect and the upper arms stationary.
- Do not forcefully lock out the elbows.

Upward Movement Phase

- Allow the elbows to slowly flex back to the starting position.
- Keep the torso, arms, and knees in the same position.
- At the end of the set, return the bar to its resting position.

Major Muscles Involved
Triceps brachii

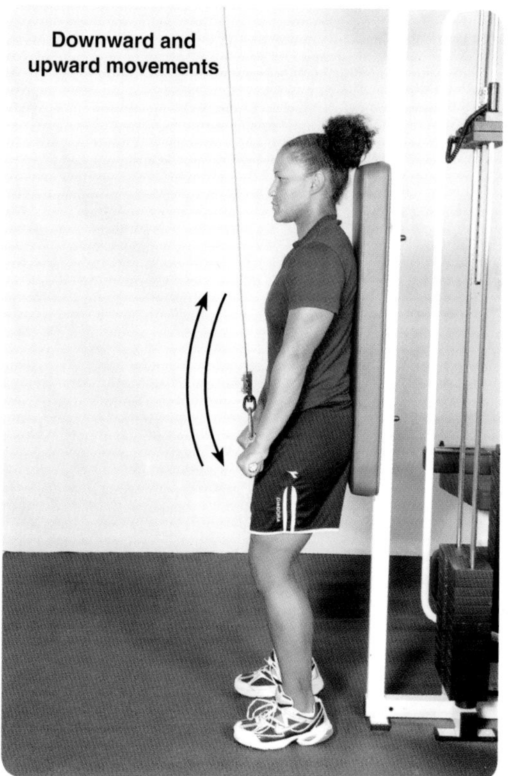

PUSH PRESS (AND PUSH JERK VARIATION)

This exercise consists of quickly and forcefully pushing the bar from the shoulders to over the head. Although the ascent consists of two phases, the upward movement of the bar occurs in one continuous motion without interruption.

Both the push press and the push jerk exercises involve a rapid hip and knee extension that accelerates the bar off the shoulders, followed immediately by movements that position the bar overhead. The technique used to attain this final bar position varies, however. In the push press, the hip and knee extension thrust is only forceful enough to drive the bar one-half to one-third the distance overhead. From this height, the bar is "pressed out" to the overhead position, with the hips and knees remaining fully extended after the thrust. The push jerk involves a more forceful hip and knee thrust so that the bar is actually "thrown" upward and caught with extended elbows in the overhead position with the hips and knees slightly flexed.

For either exercise, the athlete can begin with a bar taken from shoulder-height supports outside a power rack or by lifting a bar from the floor to the shoulders (via a repetition of the power clean exercise).

The following checklist describes the exercises using a power rack (although the rack is not shown).

Starting Position

- Grasp the bar with a closed, pronated grip.
- Grip should be slightly wider than shoulder-width.
- Step under the bar and position the feet hip-width apart and parallel to each other.
- Move up to the bar to place it on top of the anterior deltoids and clavicles.
- Extend the hips and knees to lift the bar off the supports.
- Stand in the middle of the lifting platform.
- Position the feet shoulder-width apart (or wider) and even with each other with the toes pointed slightly outward.
- All repetitions begin from this position.

Preparation Phase: Dip

- Flex the hips and knees at a slow to moderate speed to move the bar in a straight path downward.

Starting position

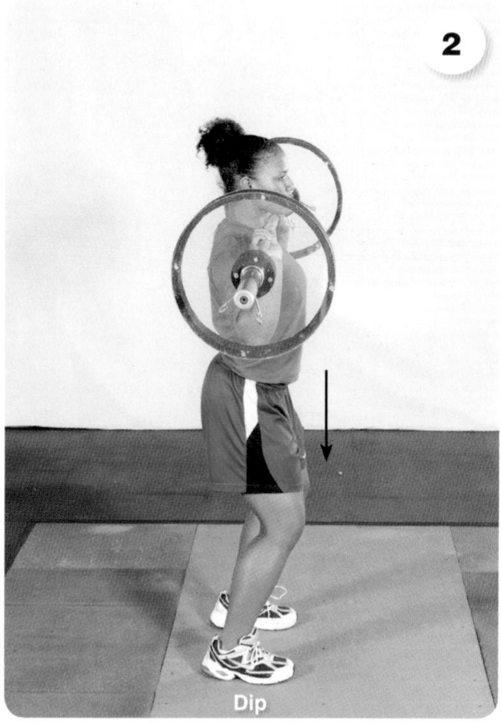

Dip

- Continue the dip to a depth not to exceed a quarter-squat, the catch position of the power clean, or 10% of the athlete's height.
- Keep the feet flat on the floor, the torso erect, and the upper arms parallel to the floor.

Upward Movement Phase: Drive

- Immediately upon reaching the lowest position of the dip, reverse the movement by forcefully and quickly extending the hips and knees and then the elbows to move the bar overhead.

Catch (for the Push Press)

- After the hips and knees are fully extended and the bar is overhead from the drive phase, press it up the rest of the way until the elbows are fully extended.
- In this position the torso is erect, the head is in a neutral position, the feet are flat on the floor, and the bar is slightly behind the head.

Catch (for the Push Jerk)

- After the hips and knees are fully extended and the bar is overhead from the drive phase, quickly re-flex the hips and knees to approximately a quarter-squat position and simultaneously extend the elbows fully to catch the bar overhead at the same moment as the bar reaches its highest position.
- Catch the bar with the torso erect, the head in a neutral position, the feet flat on the floor, and the bar slightly behind the head.

Downward Movement Phase

- Lower the bar by gradually reducing the muscular tension of the arms to allow a controlled descent of the bar to the shoulders.
- Simultaneously flex the hips and knees to cushion the impact of the bar on the shoulders.
- At the end of the set, step toward the rack and place the bar in the supports.

Major Muscles Involved
Gluteus maximus, semimembranosus, semitendinosus, biceps femoris, vastus lateralis, vastus intermedius, vastus medialis, rectus femoris, soleus, gastrocnemius, deltoids, trapezius

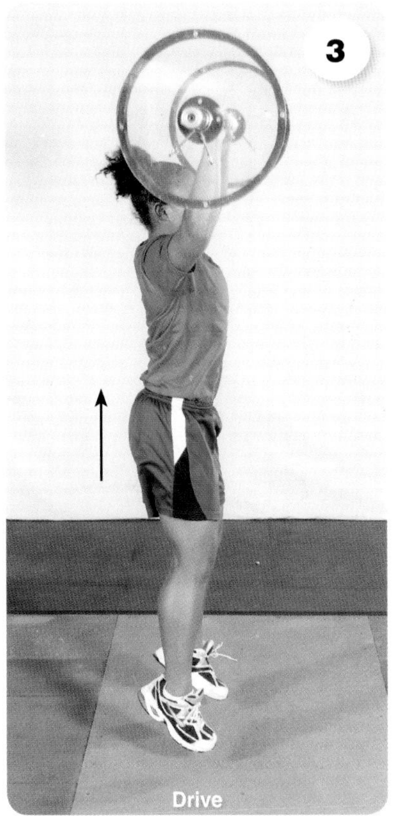

Drive

Catch (for the push press)

Catch (for the push jerk)

POWER CLEAN (AND HANG CLEAN VARIATION)

This exercise consists of quickly and forcefully pulling the bar from the floor to the front of the shoulders—all in one movement. Although the ascent consists of four phases, the upward movement of the bar occurs in one continuous motion without interruption. The hang clean is similar to the power clean exercise, except that the bar *begins* positioned at the thighs just above the knees, not on the floor, and it does *not* return to the floor between repetitions.

Starting Position

- Stand with the feet placed between hip- and shoulder-width apart with the toes pointed slightly outward.
- Squat down with the hips lower than the shoulders and grasp the bar with a closed, pronated grip.
- Place the hands on the bar slightly wider than shoulder-width apart, outside of the knees, with the elbows fully extended.
- Place the feet flat on the floor and position the bar approximately 1 inch (3 cm) in front of the shins and over the balls of the feet.
- Position the body with the
  - back flat or slightly arched,
  - trapezius relaxed and slightly stretched,
  - chest held up and out,
  - head in line with the vertebral column or slightly hyperextended,
  - shoulders over or slightly in front of the bar, and
  - eyes focused straight ahead or slightly upward.
- All repetitions begin from this position.

Upward Movement Phase: First Pull

- Lift the bar off the floor by forcefully extending the hips and knees.
- Keep the torso-to-floor angle constant; do not let the hips rise before the shoulders.
- Maintain a flat-back position.
- Keep the elbows fully extended and the shoulders over or slightly ahead of the bar.
- As the bar is raised, keep it as close to the shins as possible.

Upward Movement Phase: Transition (Scoop)

- As the bar rises just above the knees, thrust the hips forward and slightly re-flex the knees to move the thighs against and the knees under the bar.
- Keep the back flat or slightly arched and the elbows fully extended and pointing out to the sides.

1 Starting position

2 First pull

3 Scoop

Upward Movement Phase: Second Pull

- Forcefully jump upward by quickly extending the hips and knees and plantar-flexing the ankles.
- Keep the bar as close to the body as possible.
- Keep the back flat and the elbows pointing out to the sides.
- Keep the shoulders over the bar and the elbows extended as long as possible.
- When the lower body joints reach full extension, rapidly shrug the shoulders upward with the elbows still fully extended.
- As the shoulders reach their highest elevation, flex the elbows to begin pulling the body under the bar.
- Continue to pull with the arms as high and as long as possible.
- Due to the explosive nature of this phase, the torso is erect or slightly hyperextended, the head is tilted slightly back, and the feet may lose contact with the floor.

Upward Movement Phase: Catch

- After the lower body has fully extended, pull the body under the bar and rotate the arms around and under the bar.
- Simultaneously, flex the hips and knees to a quarter-squat position.
- Once the arms are under the bar, lift the elbows to position the upper arms parallel to the floor.
- Rack the bar across the front of the clavicles and anterior deltoids.
- Catch the bar with
  - a nearly erect torso,
  - the shoulders slightly ahead of the buttocks,
  - a neutral head position, and
  - flat feet.
- After gaining control and balance, stand up by extending the hips and knees to a fully erect position.

Downward Movement Phase

- Lower the elbows to unrack the bar from the anterior deltoids and clavicles then slowly lower the bar down to the thighs.
- Simultaneously flex the hips and knees to cushion the impact of the bar on the thighs.
- Squat down with the elbows fully extended until the bar touches the floor.

Major Muscles Involved
Gluteus maximus, semimembranosus, semitendinosus, biceps femoris, vastus lateralis, vastus intermedius, vastus medialis, rectus femoris, soleus, gastrocnemius, deltoids, trapezius

4

Middle of the second pull

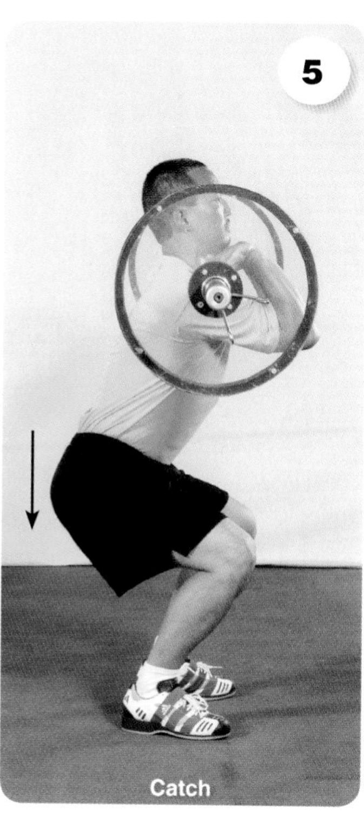

5

Catch

SNATCH

This exercise consists of quickly and forcefully pulling the bar from the floor to over the head with the elbows fully extended—all in one movement. Although the ascent consists of multiple phases, the upward movement of the bar occurs in one continuous motion without interruption.

Starting Position

- Stand with the feet placed between hip- and shoulder-width apart with the toes pointed slightly outward.
- Squat down with the hips lower than the shoulders and grasp the bar with a closed, pronated grip.
- The grip width is wider than for other exercises; a way to estimate it is to measure and use one of these distances for spacing the hands:
  - Distance from the edge of the clenched fist of one hand to the opposite shoulder when the arm is straight out at the side
  - Elbow-to-elbow distance when the arms are straight out at the sides
- Extend the elbows fully.
- Place the feet flat on the floor and position the bar approximately 1 inch (3 cm) in front of the shins and over the balls of the feet.
- Position the body with the
  - back flat or slightly arched,
  - trapezius relaxed and slightly stretched,
  - chest held up and out,
  - head in line with the vertebral column or slightly hyperextended,
  - heels in contact with the floor,
  - shoulders over or slightly in front of the bar, and
  - eyes focused straight ahead or slightly upward.
- All repetitions begin from this position.

Upward Movement Phase: First Pull

- Lift the bar off the floor by forcefully extending the hips and knees.
- Keep the torso-to-floor angle constant; do not let the hips rise before the shoulders.
- Maintain the flat-back position.
- Keep the elbows fully extended and the shoulders over or slightly ahead of the bar.
- As the bar is raised, keep it as close to the shins as possible.

Upward Movement Phase: Transition (Scoop)

- As the bar rises just above the knees, thrust the hips forward and slightly re-flex the knees to move the thighs against and the knees under the bar.
- Keep the back flat or slightly arched and the elbows fully extended and pointing out to the sides.

Upward Movement Phase: Second Pull

- Forcefully jump upward by quickly extending the hips and knees and plantar-flexing the ankles.
- Keep the bar as close to the body as possible.
- Keep the back flat and the elbows pointing out to the sides.
- Keep the shoulders over the bar and the elbows extended as long as possible.
- When the lower body joints reach full extension, rapidly shrug the shoulders upward with the elbows still fully extended.
- As the shoulders reach their highest elevation, flex the elbows to begin pulling the body under the bar.
- Continue to pull with the arms as high and as long as possible.
- Due to the explosive nature of this phase, the torso is erect or slightly hyperextended, the head is tilted slightly back, and the feet may lose contact with the floor.

Upward Movement Phase: Catch

- After the lower body has fully extended, pull the body under the bar and rotate the hands around and under the bar.
- Simultaneously, flex the hips and knees to a quarter-squat position.
- Once the body is under the bar, catch the bar over and slightly behind the head with
  - fully extended elbows,
  - a neutral head position, and
  - flat feet.
- After gaining control and balance, stand up by extending the hips and knees to a fully erect position.
- Stabilize the bar overhead.

Downward Movement Phase

- Lower the bar from the overhead position by gradually reducing the muscular tension of the shoulders to allow a controlled descent of the bar to the thighs.
- Simultaneously flex the hips and knees to cushion the impact of the bar on the thighs.
- Squat down with the elbows fully extended until the bar touches the floor.

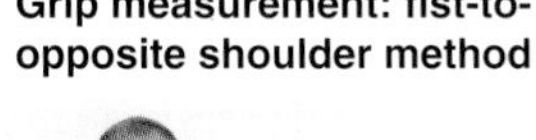

Grip measurement: fist-to-opposite shoulder method

Grip measurement: elbow-to-elbow

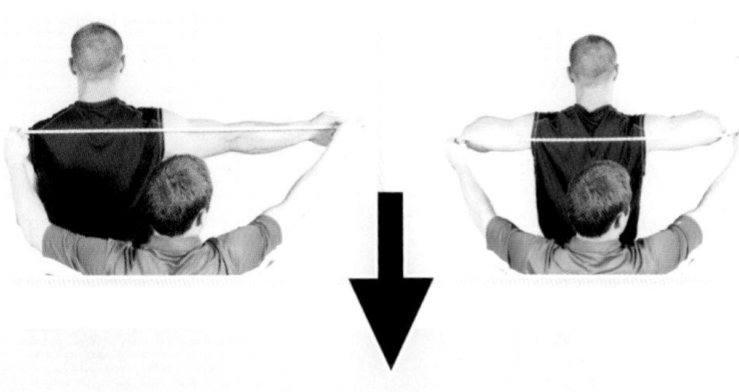

Starting position

First pull

Major Muscles Involved
Gluteus maximus, semimembranosus, semitendinosus, biceps femoris, vastus lateralis, vastus intermedius, vastus medialis, rectus femoris, soleus, gastrocnemius, deltoids, trapezius

Scoop

End of the second pull

Catch

KEY TERMS

alternated grip 326
closed grip 326
false grip 326
five-point body contact position 327
forced repetition 329
grip width 326
hook grip 326
liftoff 331
neutral grip 326
open grip 326
overhand grip 326
partner-assisted reps 329
pronated grip 326
spotter 329
sticking point 327
structural exercise 328
supinated grip 326
supine 327
underhand grip 326
Valsalva maneuver 328

STUDY QUESTIONS

1. All of the following exercises require a spotter EXCEPT the

a. flat dumbbell fly.
b. overhead triceps extension.
c. forward step lunge.
d. lat pulldown.

2. During which of the following exercises should a spotter's hands be placed on the athlete's wrists?

a. bench press
b. incline dumbbell bench press
c. upright row
d. lying barbell triceps extension

3. Which of the following grips should be used during the deadlift exercise?

I. overhand
II. closed
III. pronated
IV. alternated

a. I and III only
b. II and IV only
c. I, II, and III only
d. II, III, and IV only

4. Which of the following is the correct foot pattern in the step-up exercise?

a. step up LEFT foot, step up RIGHT foot, step down LEFT foot, step down RIGHT foot
b. step up RIGHT foot, step up LEFT foot, step down LEFT foot, step down RIGHT foot
c. step up LEFT foot, step down LEFT foot, step up RIGHT foot, step down RIGHT foot
d. step up RIGHT foot, step up LEFT foot, step down RIGHT foot, step down LEFT foot

5. The primary movement during the second pull phase of the power clean exercise is

a. hip flexion.
b. hip extension.
c. knee flexion.
d. dorsiflexion.

SECTION 4

Program Design

PART I

Anaerobic Exercise Prescription

Well-constructed strength and conditioning programs are based on the application of sound principles during each step of a process called *program design*. This section discusses those training principles, highlights pertinent recent research, and provides recommendations on how to design different types of training programs. The information in part I of this section is grouped into three content areas:

- Resistance training (chapter 15)
- Plyometric training (chapter 16)
- Speed, agility, and speed-endurance development (chapter 17)

The application of training principles is presented in each chapter; the most comprehensive discussion occurs in chapter 15, where the seven steps or variables involved in designing safe and effective resistance training programs are presented in detail (shown in the sidebar on p. 382). A unique feature of this chapter is the use of scenarios to illustrate how the variables can be manipulated to develop resistance training programs.

Regardless of the type of training program (resistance, plyometric, speed, etc.), there are three foundational principles that always apply: specificity, overload, and progression. A lack of attention to any of these principles often produces less than desirable training outcomes and sometimes injury.

SPECIFICITY

One of the most basic concepts to incorporate in all training programs is *specificity*. The term, first suggested by DeLorme in 1945 (3), refers to the method whereby an athlete is trained in a specific manner to produce a specific adaptation or training outcome. For example, to design a resistance training program that is specific to strengthening the chest muscles, the strength and conditioning professional must give an athlete an exercise like the bench press that recruits the pectoralis major. Sometimes used interchangeably with specificity is the acronym *SAID*, which stands for *specific adaptation to imposed demands*. The underlying principle is that the type of demand placed on the body dictates the type of adaptation that will occur. For instance, athletes training for power in high-speed movements (e.g., baseball pitch, tennis serve) should attempt to activate or recruit the same motor units required by their sport at the highest velocity possible (5). Incorporating resistance training exercises that mimic the movement patterns of the athlete's sport increases the likelihood that muscles involved in the sport will be recruited. For instance, if a high jumper performs depth jumps as part of a plyometric exercise program, he or she should experience an improvement in performance in high jumping because the force production and muscular recruitment at the ankle, knee, and hip are similar to those with the high jump.

Specificity also relates to the athlete's sport season. As an athlete progresses through the preseason, in-season, and postseason, all forms of training should gradually progress in an organized manner from generalized to sport specific (1, 2, 4, 5). Although participation in the sport itself provides the greatest opportunity to improve performance in the sport, the proper application of the specificity principle certainly increases the likelihood that other training will also positively contribute to performance.

OVERLOAD

Overload refers to assigning a workout or training regime of greater intensity than the athlete is accustomed to. Without the stimulus of overload, even an otherwise well-designed program greatly limits an athlete's ability to make improvements.

The obvious application of this principle in the design of resistance training programs involves increasing the loads assigned in the exercises. Other more subtle changes include increasing the number of sessions per week (or per day in some instances), adding exercises or sets, emphasizing complex over simple exercises, decreasing the length of the rest periods between sets and exercises, or any combination of these or other changes. Applying the overload principle, for instance, in a sprint training program may be accomplished through the use of gravity-assisted and wind-resisted training (e.g., downhill running and parachute sprinting, respectively). Another application is to advance an athlete's plyometric program from single- to multiple-jump drills or to raise the box height for depth jumps. The intent is to stress the body at a higher level than it is used to. When the overload principle is properly applied, overtraining is avoided and the desired training adaptation will occur.

PROGRESSION

If a training program is to continue producing higher levels of performance, the intensity of the training must become progressively greater. *Progression*, when applied properly, promotes long-term training benefits. Although it is customary to focus only on the resistance used, one can progressively increase training intensity by raising the number of weekly training sessions, adding more drills or exercises to each session, changing the type or difficulty of the drills or exercises, or increasing the training stimulus. The issue of importance is that progression is based on the athlete's training status and is introduced systematically and gradually.

CONCLUSION

The use of the specificity and overload training principles ensures that the muscles involved in the selected exercises are those relied on in the sport and that the loads assigned are sufficient to challenge the athlete to become stronger, sometimes larger, faster, and more resistant to fatigue. The rate at which sport performance improves depends largely on the manner in which overload is imposed. A progressive and methodical application of overload in an athlete's program over time provides the stimulus and the needed recovery to produce optimal results.

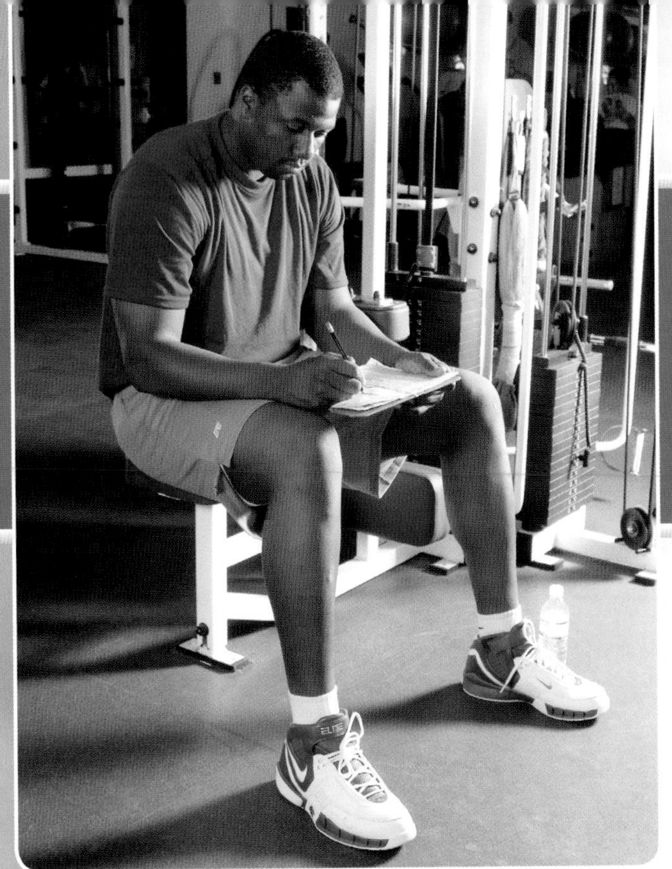

CHAPTER 15

Resistance Training

Thomas R. Baechle, EdD, Roger W. Earle, MA, and Dan Wathen, MS

After completing this chapter, you will be able to

- evaluate the requirements and characteristics of a sport and assess an athlete for the purpose of designing a resistance training program;
- select exercises based on type, sport specificity, technique experience, equipment availability, and time availability;
- determine training frequency based on training status, sport season, load, exercise type, and other concurrent exercise;
- arrange exercises in a training session according to their type;
- determine 1-repetition maximum (1RM), predicted 1RM from a multiple RM, and RM loads;
- assign load and repetitions based on the training goal;
- know when and by how much an exercise load should be increased;
- assign training volumes according to the athlete's training status and the training goal; and
- determine rest period lengths based on the training goal.

Designing a resistance training program is a complex process that requires the recognition and manipulation of seven **program design** variables (referred to in this chapter as steps 1 through 7). This chapter discusses each variable, shown in the sidebar, in the context of three scenarios that enable the strength and conditioning professional to see how training principles and program design guidelines can be integrated into an overall program.

The three scenarios include a basketball center (scenario A) in her preseason, an American football offensive lineman (scenario B) during his offseason, and a cross-country runner (scenario C) during his season (see the scenarios on p. 383). It is understood that, in each scenario, the athlete is well conditioned for his or her sport, has no musculoskeletal dysfunction, and has been cleared for training and competition by the sports medicine staff. The athletes in scenarios A (basketball center) and B (American football lineman) have been resistance training since high school, are accustomed to lifting heavy loads, and are skilled in machine and free weight exercises. The high school cross-country runner in scenario C, in contrast, began a resistance training program in the preseason only four weeks ago, so his training is limited and his exercise technique skills are not well developed.

Resistance Training Program Design Variables

1. Needs analysis
2. Exercise selection
3. Training frequency
4. Exercise order
5. Training load and repetitions
6. Volume
7. Rest periods

STEP 1: NEEDS ANALYSIS

The strength and conditioning professional's initial task is to perform a **needs analysis**, a two-stage process that includes an evaluation of the requirements and characteristics of the sport and an assessment of the athlete.

Evaluation of the Sport

The first task in a needs analysis is to determine the unique characteristics of the sport. This information enables the strength and conditioning professional to design a program specific to those requirements and characteristics. Although this task can be approached in several ways (40, 78, 102), it should at least include consideration of the following attributes of the sport (27, 56):

- Body and limb movement patterns and muscular involvement (**movement analysis**)

Athlete Scenarios

Scenario A		Scenario B		Scenario C	
Sex:	Female	Sex:	Male	Sex:	Male
Age:	20 years old	Age:	28 years old	Age:	17 years old
Sport:	Collegiate basketball	Sport:	Professional American football	Sport:	High school cross-country running
Position:	Center	Position:	Offensive lineman	Position:	(Not applicable)
Season:	Beginning of the preseason	Season:	Beginning of the off-season	Season:	Beginning of the in-season

- Strength, power, hypertrophy, and muscular endurance priorities (**physiological analysis**)
- Common sites for joint and muscle injury and causative factors (**injury analysis**)

Other characteristics of a sport—such as cardiovascular endurance, speed, agility, and flexibility requirements—should also be evaluated. This chapter, however, focuses only on the physiological outcomes that specifically relate to resistance training program design: strength, power, hypertrophy, and muscular endurance.

For example, a movement analysis of the shot put field event reveals that it is an all-body movement that begins with the athlete in a semicrouched stance, with many joints flexed and adducted, and culminates in an upright stance with many joints extended and abducted. The most heavily recruited muscles (not in order) are the elbow extensors (triceps brachii), shoulder abductors (deltoids), hip extensors (gluteals, hamstrings), knee extensors (quadriceps), and ankle plantarflexors (soleus, gastrocnemius). Physiologically, shot putting requires high levels of strength and power for a successful performance. Also, enhanced muscular hypertrophy is advantageous since the muscle's ability to produce force increases as its cross-sectional area becomes greater (51). The muscular endurance requirement is minimal, however. Reports from the sports medicine community indicate that the muscles and tendons surrounding the shoulder and elbow joints tend to be injured due to overuse. (Refer to chapter 20 for information about injuries.)

Assessment of the Athlete

The second task is to **profile** the athlete's needs and goals by evaluating training (and injury) status, conducting a variety of tests (e.g., maximum strength testing), evaluating the results, and determining the primary goal of training. The more individualized the assessment process, the more specific the resistance training program for each athlete can be.

Training Status

An athlete's current condition or level of preparedness to begin a new or revised program (**training status**) is an important consideration when designing training programs. This includes an evaluation by a sports medicine professional of any current or previous injuries that may affect training. Also important is the athlete's **training background** or **exercise history** (training that occurred *before* he or she began a new or revised program), because this information will help the strength and conditioning professional better understand the athlete's training capabilities. An assessment of the athlete's training background should examine the

- type of training program (sprint, plyometric, resistance, etc.),
- length of recent regular participation in previous training program(s),
- level of intensity involved in previous training program(s), and
- degree of **exercise technique experience** (i.e., the knowledge and skill to perform resistance training exercises properly).

Table 15.1 provides an example of how such information might be used to classify athletes' training status as beginner, intermediate, or advanced. The strength and conditioning professional should realize that the three classifications exist on a continuum and cannot be definitively described.

Physical Testing and Evaluation

Physical evaluation involves conducting assessments of the athlete's strength, flexibility, power, speed, muscular endurance, body composition, cardiovascular endurance, and so on. In this chapter, the needs analysis focuses on assessing maximal muscular strength. Strength and conditioning professionals should refer to step 5 (training load and repetitions), page 392 and chapters 11 and 12 for a complete discussion of these procedures.

To yield pertinent and reliable data that can be used effectively to develop a resistance training program, the tests selected should be related to the athlete's sport, consistent with the athlete's level of skill, and realistically based on the equipment available. The result of the movement analysis discussed previously provides direction in selecting tests. Typically, major upper body exercises (e.g., bench press and shoulder press) and exercises that mimic jumping movements in varying degrees (e.g., power clean, squat, hip sled) are used in testing batteries. Refer to step 2, page 386, for a discussion of exercise selection.

After testing is completed, the results should be compared with normative or descriptive data (refer to chapter 12) to determine the athlete's strengths and weaknesses. Based on this evaluation and the needs analysis of the sport, a training program can be developed to improve deficiencies, maintain strengths, or further develop physiological qualities that will enable the athlete to better meet the demands of the sport.

Primary Resistance Training Goal

The athlete's test results, the movement and physiological analysis of the sport, and the priorities of the athlete's sport season determine the primary goal or outcome for the resistance training program. Typically, this goal is to improve strength, power, hypertrophy, or muscular endurance. Despite a potential desire or need to make improvements in two different areas (e.g., strength *and* muscular endurance), an effort should be made to concentrate on only one training outcome per season. An example of how the strength and conditioning professional may prioritize the resistance training emphases during the four main sport seasons is shown in table 15.2.

TABLE 15.1

Example of Classifying Resistance Training Status

	RESISTANCE TRAINING BACKGROUND				
Resistance training status	**Current program**	**Training age**	**Frequency (per week)**	**Training stress***	**Technique experience and skill**
Beginner (untrained)	Not training or just began training	<2 months	≤1-2	None or low	None or minimal
Intermediate (moderately resistance-trained)	Currently training	2-6 months	≤2-3	Medium	Basic
Advanced (well resistance-trained)	Currently training	≥1 years	≥3-4	High	High

*In this example, "training stress" refers to the degree of physical demand or stimulus of the resistance training program.

TABLE 15.2

Example of General Training Priorities by Sport Season

	PRIORITY GIVEN TO		
Sport season	**Sport practice**	**Resistance training**	**Resistance training goal***
Off-season	Low	High	Hypertrophy and muscular endurance (initially); strength and power (later)
Preseason	Medium	Medium	Sport and movement specific (i.e., strength, power, or muscular endurance, depending on the sport)
In-season	High	Low	Maintenance of preseason training goal
Postseason (active rest)	Variable	Variable	Not specific (may include activities other than sport skill or resistance training)

*The actual training goals and priorities are based on the specific sport or activity and may differ from the goals listed here.

Application of the Needs Analysis

(Refer to p. 383 for a description of the scenario athletes.)

 **Scenario A** **Female collegiate basketball player** **Preseason**	 **Scenario B** **Male professional American football lineman** **Off-season**	 **Scenario C** **Male high school cross-country runner** **In-season**
Sport evaluation **Movement analysis** *Sport:* Running and jumping, ball handling, shooting, blocking, and rebounding *Muscular involvement:* All major muscle areas, especially the hips, thighs, and shoulders **Physiological analysis (primary requirement)** Strength/power	***Sport evaluation*** **Movement analysis** *Sport:* Grabbing, pushing, repelling, and deflecting opponents *Muscular involvement:* All major muscle areas, especially the hips, thighs, chest, arms, and low back **Physiological analysis (primary requirement)** Hypertrophy	***Sport evaluation*** **Movement analysis** *Sport:* Running, repetitive leg and arm movements *Muscular involvement:* All lower body muscle areas, postural muscles, shoulders and arms **Physiological analysis (primary requirement)** Muscular endurance
Athlete's profile **Training background** ▪ Has resistance trained regularly since high school ▪ Possesses excellent skill in performing free weight and machine exercises ▪ Just completed a 4×/week resistance training program in the off-season consisting of: *Upper body exercises* (2×/week): 6 exercises (2 core, 4 assistance), 3 sets of 10RM-12RM loads *Lower body exercises* (2×/week): 6 exercises (2 core, 4 assistance), 3 sets of 10RM-12RM loads	***Athlete's profile*** **Training background** ▪ Has resistance trained regularly throughout high school, college, and his professional career ▪ Possesses excellent skill in performing free weight and machine exercises ▪ Just completed a 2×/week resistance training program in the postseason[b] consisting of: *All exercises performed in each session:* 8 exercises (3 core, 5 assistance; 2 lower body, 6 upper body), 2-3 sets of 12RM-15RM loads	***Athlete's profile*** **Training background** ▪ Just began resistance training in preseason ▪ Has only limited skill in performing free weight and machine exercises ▪ Just completed a 2×/week resistance training program in the preseason[c] consisting of: *All exercises performed in each session:* 7 exercises (3 core, 4 assistance; 3 lower body, 4 upper body), 1-2 sets of 15RM loads
Classification of resistance training status Advanced	***Classification of resistance training status*** Advanced	***Classification of resistance training status*** Beginner
Primary preseason resistance training goal Strength/power[a]	***Primary off-season resistance training goal*** Hypertrophy	***Primary in-season resistance training goal*** Muscular endurance
COMMENTS [a]The preseason will address both of these goals through a combination of appropriate exercise selection and volume load assignments.	**COMMENTS** [b]Due to the extreme physical demands of American football, this athlete's postseason training volume was greater than is often assigned for the active rest phase of a typical program (see chapter 19).	**COMMENTS** [c]Because this athlete just began his resistance training program, his frequency was limited to only 2×/week in the preseason rather than the three to four sessions/week typically completed by better-trained individuals.

The information in this table reflects one approach to evaluating the requirements of a sport and profiling an athlete.

STEP 2: EXERCISE SELECTION

Exercise selection involves choosing exercises for a resistance training program. To make informed exercise selections, the strength and conditioning professional must understand the nature of various types of resistance training exercises, the movement and muscular requirements of the sport, the athlete's exercise technique experience, the equipment available, and the amount of training time available.

Exercise Type

Although there are literally hundreds of resistance training exercises to select from when one is designing a program, most involve primary muscle groups or body areas and fall into categories based on their relative importance to the athlete's sport.

Core and Assistance Exercises

Exercises can be classified as either core or assistance based on the size of the muscle areas involved and their level of contribution to a particular sport movement. **Core exercises** recruit one or more large muscle areas (i.e., chest, shoulder, back, hip, or thigh), involve two or more primary joints (**multijoint exercises**), and receive priority when one is selecting exercises because of their direct application to the sport. **Assistance exercises** usually recruit smaller muscle areas (i.e., upper arm, abdominals, calf, neck, forearm, lower back, or anterior lower leg), involve only one primary joint (**single-joint exercises**), and are considered less important to improving sport performance. Generally, all the joints at the shoulder—the glenohumeral and shoulder girdle articulations—are considered one *primary* joint when resistance training exercises are categorized as core or assistance. The spine is similarly considered a single primary joint (as in the abdominal crunch and back extension exercises).

A common application of assistance exercises is for injury prevention and rehabilitation, as these exercises often isolate a specific muscle or muscle group. The muscles that are predisposed to injury from the unique demands of a sport skill (e.g., the shoulder external rotators for overhand pitching) or those that require reconditioning after an injury (e.g., a quadriceps contusion) can be specifically conditioned by an assistance exercise.

Structural and Power Exercises

A core exercise that emphasizes loading the spine directly (e.g., back squat) or indirectly (e.g., power clean) can be further described as a **structural exercise**. More specifically, a structural exercise involves muscular stabilization of posture during performance of the lifting movement (e.g., maintaining a rigid torso and a flat back during the back squat). A structural exercise that is performed very quickly or explosively is considered a **power exercise** (see pp. 370-375 in chapter 14). Typically, power exercises are assigned to athletes when they are appropriate for the athlete's sport-specific training priorities (58).

Movement Analysis of the Sport

In the needs analysis step (step 1), the strength and conditioning professional has identified the unique requirements and characteristics of the sport. The exercises selected for a resistance training program that focus on conditioning for a particular sport need to be similar to the activities of that sport in their body and limb movement patterns, joint ranges of motion, and muscular involvement. The exercises should also create muscular balance to reduce risk of injury from disproportionate training.

Sport-Specific Exercises

The more similar the training activity is to the actual sport movement, the greater the likelihood that there will be a positive transfer to that sport (13, 24, 27, 30, 55, 78, 81, 99, 107). This is the **specificity** concept, also called the **specific adaptation to imposed demands (SAID) principle**. Table 15.3 provides examples of resistance training exercises that relate in varying degrees to the movement patterns of various sports. The strength and conditioning professional should find this table helpful when trying to identify sport-specific exercises. For example, the primary muscles involved in jumping for basketball are the hip and knee extensors. An athlete can exercise these muscles by performing the hip sled or back squat, but which exercise is preferable? Certainly both exercises strengthen the hip and knee extensors, but because jumping is performed from an erect body position with balance and weight-bearing forces as considerations, the back squat is more specific to jumping and is therefore preferred over the hip sled (115). The power clean is even more specific to jumping because of its quick movement characteristics and is preferred

TABLE 15.3

Examples of Movement-Related Resistance Training Exercises

Movement pattern	Related exercises
Ball dribbling and passing	Close-grip bench press, dumbbell bench press, triceps pushdown, reverse curl, hammer curl
Ball kicking	Unilateral hip adduction and abduction, forward step lunge, leg (knee) extension, leg raise
Freestyle swimming	Lat pulldown, lateral shoulder raise, forward step lunge, upright row, barbell pullover
Jumping	Power clean, push jerk, back squat, front squat, standing calf (heel) raise
Racket stroke	Flat dumbbell fly, bent-over lateral raise, wrist curl, wrist extension
Rowing	Power clean, bent-over row, seated row, hip sled, horizontal leg press, deadlift, good morning
Running, sprinting	Forward step lunge, step-up, leg (knee) extension, leg (knee) curl, toe raise (dorsiflexion)
Throwing, pitching	Barbell pullover, overhead triceps extension, shoulder internal and external rotation

over the back squat (especially if the back squat is performed slowly) if time constraints require choosing only one of the two exercises.

Muscle Balance

Exercises selected for the specific demands of the sport should maintain a balance of muscular strength across joints and between opposing muscle groups (e.g., biceps brachii and triceps brachii). Avoid designing a resistance training program that increases the risk of injury due to a disparity between the strength of the **agonist**, the muscle or muscle group actively causing the movement (e.g., the quadriceps in the leg [knee] extension exercise), and the **antagonist**, the sometimes passive (i.e., not concentrically involved) muscle or muscle group located on the opposite side of the limb (e.g., the hamstrings in the leg [knee] extension exercise). If an imbalance is created or discovered, exercises to restore an appropriate strength balance need to be selected. For example, if isokinetic testing reveals that the hamstrings are extremely weak compared with the quadriceps, additional hamstring exercises could be added to compensate for the imbalance (27, 30, 78, 81, 99, 107, 114). Note that **muscle balance** does not always mean equal strength, just a proper ratio of strength, power, or muscular endurance of one muscle or muscle group relative to another muscle or muscle group.

Exercise Technique Experience

An important part of the needs analysis described earlier is evaluating the athlete's training status and exercise technique experience. If there is any question whether an athlete can perform an exercise with proper technique, the strength and conditioning professional should ask the athlete to demonstrate the exercise. If the athlete uses incorrect technique, the strength and conditioning professional should provide complete instruction. Often, unskilled individuals are introduced to machines and free weight assistance exercises (27, 30, 114) because these are considered easier to perform than free weight core exercises due to their lower balance and coordination requirements (27, 30, 99, 114). Despite this, one should not assume that the athlete will perform exercises correctly, even those that are relatively easy to perform.

Availability of Resistance Training Equipment

The availability of training equipment must be considered in the selection of exercises. A lack of certain equipment may necessitate selecting exercises that are not as sport specific. For example, the absence of Olympic-type barbells with revolving sleeves would preclude exercises such as the power clean, and an insufficient supply of barbell plates may result in substituting exercises that do not require as much resistance; for example, the back squat could be replaced by the front squat.

Available Training Time per Session

The strength and conditioning professional should weigh the value of certain exercises against the time it takes to perform them. Some exercises take longer to complete than others. If time for a training session is limited, exercises that are more time efficient may need to be given priority over others. For example, the machine leg press could be selected instead of the free weight lunge to train the hips and thighs of a 100 m sprinter. The time required to move the machine pin to the correct slot in a weight stack and perform 10 repetitions of a machine leg press is much less than the time required for the lunge exercise, for which the athlete has to load both ends of a bar, attach the locks, back out of the power rack, establish a stable starting position, perform 10 repetitions of *each* leg, and rerack the bar. Although the machine leg press is less sport specific, the time saved may permit including other exercises or performing more sets. The benefit of including the more sport-specific lunge exercise, on the other hand, may be worth the additional time needed, although this depends on the goals of the training season and time available.

Application of the Exercise Selection Guidelines

(Refer to p. 383 for a description of the scenario athletes. Exercises are not shown in order of execution.)

Scenario A
Female collegiate basketball player
Preseason

Core

Hang clean (all body, power)[a]
Push jerk (all body, power)[a]
Front squat (hip and thigh)
Incline bench press (chest)

Assistance

Abdominal crunch (abdomen)
Seated row (upper back)
Dumbbell alternating curl (anterior upper arm)[b]
Triceps pushdown (posterior upper arm)[b]

COMMENTS

[a]These exercises are included to maximize power and match the jumping movements of basketball.

[b]These exercises involve motions similar to dribbling the ball.

Scenario B
Male professional American football lineman
Off-season

Core[c]

Back squat (hip and thigh)
Deadlift (hip and thigh)[d]
Bench press (chest)
Shoulder press (shoulders)

Assistance

Abdominal crunch (abdomen)
Step-up (hip and thigh)
Leg (knee) curl (posterior thigh)
Bent-over row (upper back)
Shoulder shrug (upper back and neck)
Barbell biceps curl (anterior upper arm)
Lying triceps extension (posterior upper arm)
Seated calf (heel) raise (posterior lower leg)

COMMENTS

This athlete has extra time available to perform more resistance training exercises because sport skill practice is not the first priority in the off-season.

[c]Greater training frequency allows more core exercises to be included (see step 3).

[d]The deadlift is a nonpower core exercise that is foundational for the power clean, an exercise that could be added in the next season (the preseason) or cycle.

Scenario C
Male high school cross-country runner
In-season

Core

Lunge (hip and thigh)[e]
Vertical chest press (chest)[f]

Assistance

Abdominal crunch (abdomen)
Leg (knee) curl (posterior thigh)
Lateral shoulder raise (shoulders)
One-arm dumbbell row (upper back)[g]
Toe raise (dorsiflexion) (anterior lower leg)
Machine back extension (lower back)

COMMENTS

[e]Although not always considered a core exercise, the lunge recruits muscles and joints that have direct application to running.

[f]This exercise also involves the triceps brachii muscle, so an assistance exercise to isolate the triceps is not needed. This reduces the time devoted to the resistance training portion of the in-season program.

[g]This exercise also involves the biceps brachii muscle, so an assistance exercise to isolate the biceps is not needed. This reduces the time devoted to the resistance training portion of the in-season program.

STEP 3: TRAINING FREQUENCY

Training frequency refers to the number of training sessions completed in a given time period. For a resistance training program, a common time period is one week. When determining training frequency, the strength and conditioning professional should consider the athlete's training status, sport season, projected exercise loads, types of exercises, and other concurrent training or activities.

Training Status

The athlete's level of preparedness for training, which was determined during the needs analysis (step 1), is an influential factor in determining training frequency because it affects the number of rest days needed between training sessions. Traditionally, three workouts per week are recommended for many athletes, as the intervening days allow sufficient recovery between sessions (4, 12). As an athlete adapts to training and becomes better conditioned, it is appropriate to consider increasing the number of training days to four and, with additional training, maybe five, six, or seven (see table 15.4). The general guideline is to schedule training sessions so that there is at least one rest or recovery day—but not more than three—between sessions that stress the same muscle groups (4, 49). For example, if a strength and conditioning professional wants a beginner athlete to perform a total body resistance training program two times per week, the sessions should be spaced out evenly (e.g., Monday and Thursday or Tuesday and Friday). If the athlete trains only on Monday and Wednesday, the absence of a training stimulus between Wednesday and the following Monday may result in a *decrease* in the athlete's training status (21, 34, 49), although, for a short time in well-trained athletes, one session a week can maintain strength (21, 34).

TABLE 15.4

Resistance Training Frequency Based on Training Status

Training status	Frequency guidelines (sessions per week)
Beginner	2-3
Intermediate	3-4
Advanced	4-7

Data from references 4, 34, 36, 37, 38, 48, and 60.

More highly resistance-trained (intermediate or advanced) athletes can augment their training by using a **split routine** in which different muscle groups are trained on different days. Training nearly every day may seem to violate the recommended guidelines for recovery, but grouping exercises that train a portion of the body (e.g., upper body or lower body) or certain muscle areas (e.g., chest, shoulder, and triceps) gives the trained athlete an opportunity to adequately recover between similar training sessions (see table 15.5). For instance, a common lower body–upper body regime includes four training sessions per week: lower body on Monday and Thursday and upper body on Tuesday and Friday (or vice versa). This way, there are two or three days of rest between each upper or lower body training session, even though the athlete trains on two consecutive days twice a week (50). For split routines with three distinct training days, the rest days are not on the same day each week.

Sport Season

Another influence on resistance training frequency is the sport season. For example, the increased emphasis on practicing the sport skill during the in-season necessitates a decrease in the time spent in the weight room and, consequently, reduces the frequency of resistance training (see tables 15.2 and 15.6). The problem is that there simply is not enough time to fit all the desired modes of training into each day. So, even though a well-trained athlete may be capable of completing four or more resistance training sessions per week, the other time demands of the sport may not permit this.

Training Load and Exercise Type

Athletes who train with maximal or near-maximal loads require more recovery time prior to their next training session (27, 30, 65, 83, 97, 99). The ability to train more frequently may be enhanced by alternating lighter and heavier training days (27, 30, 65, 99). This concept of training variation is discussed in chapter 19. There is also evidence that upper body muscles can recover more quickly from heavy loading sessions than lower body muscles (48). The same is true regarding an athlete's ability to recover faster from single-joint exercises compared to multijoint exercises (98). These research findings may explain why, for example, powerlifters may schedule only one very heavy deadlift or squat training session per week.

TABLE 15.5

Examples of Common Split Routines

		SAMPLE TRAINING WEEK							
Training day	Body parts or muscle groups trained	Su	M	Tu	W	Th	F	Sa	Resulting training frequency
1 2	Lower body Upper body	***Rest***	Lower body	Upper body	***Rest***	Lower body	Upper body	***Rest***	4 times per week
1 2 3	Chest, shoulders, triceps Lower body Back, trapezius, biceps	***Rest***	Chest, shoulders, triceps	Lower body	Back, trapezius, biceps	***Rest***	Chest, shoulders, triceps	Lower body	5 times per week*
1 2 3	Chest and back Lower body Shoulders and arms	Chest and back	Lower body	Shoulders and arms	***Rest***	Chest and back	Lower body	Shoulders and arms	6 times per week*

*Frequency varies between 5 times per week and 6 times per week, depending on the day of the week that is the first training day.

TABLE 15.6

Resistance Training Frequency Based on the Sport Season (for a Trained Athlete)

Sport season	Frequency guidelines (sessions per week)
Off-season	4-6
Preseason	3-4
In-season	1-3
Postseason (active rest)	0-3

Data from references 27, 100, and 104.

Other Training

Exercise frequency is also influenced by the overall amount of physical stress, so the strength and conditioning professional must consider the effects of all forms of exercise. If the athlete's program already includes aerobic or anaerobic (e.g., sprinting, agility, speed-endurance, plyometric) training, sport skill practice, or any combination of these components, the frequency of resistance training may need to be reduced (18). Additionally, the effects of a physically demanding occupation may be relevant. Athletes who work in manual labor jobs, instruct or assist others in physical activities, or are on their feet all day may not be able to withstand the same training frequency as athletes who are less active outside of their sport-related pursuits.

STEP 4: EXERCISE ORDER

Exercise order refers to a sequence of resistance exercises performed during one training session. Although there are many ways to arrange exercises, decisions are invariably based on how one exercise affects the quality of effort or the technique of another exercise. Usually exercises are arranged so that an athlete's maximal force capabilities are available (from a sufficient rest or recovery period) to complete a set with proper exercise technique. Four of the most common methods of ordering resistance exercises are described in the following paragraphs. Strength and conditioning professionals may consult the work of Fleck and Kraemer (27) for detailed information on other exercise arrangement strategies.

Application of the Training Frequency Guidelines

(Refer to p. 383 for a description of the scenario athletes.)

 **Scenario A** **Female collegiate basketball player** **Preseason**	**Scenario B** **Male professional American football lineman** **Off-season**	 **Scenario C** **Male high school cross-country runner** **In-season**
Advanced training status allows 4-7×/week	***Advanced training status allows*** 4-7×/week	***Beginner training status allows*** 2-3×/week
Frequency guideline based on the sport season 3-4×/week	***Frequency guideline based on the sport season*** 4-6×/week	***Frequency guideline based on the sport season*** 1-3×/week
Assigned resistance training frequency 3×/week[a] ▪ Monday, Wednesday, and Friday ▪ All exercises performed each session	***Assigned resistance training frequency*** 4×/week (split routine[b]) ▪ Monday and Thursday (lower body exercises) ▪ Tuesday and Friday (upper body exercises)	***Assigned resistance training frequency*** 2×/week[c] ▪ Wednesday and Saturday ▪ All exercises performed each session
COMMENTS [a]Training frequency is decreased from the previous season (off-season) to allow for more time and physical resources to apply to basketball-specific sport skill training.	**COMMENTS** [b]A split routine allows for more overall exercises to be performed without an excessive increase in training time (per session) because the exercises are divided over more training days.	**COMMENTS** [c]The assigned training days need to be planned so that they do not affect the athlete's performance on the scheduled days for cross-country meets.

Power, Other Core, Then Assistance Exercises

Power exercises such as the snatch, hang clean, power clean, and push jerk *should be performed first* in a training session, followed by other nonpower core exercises, and then assistance exercises (27, 93, 101). The literature also refers to this arrangement as *multijoint exercises and then single-joint exercises* or *large muscle areas and then small muscle areas* (6, 23, 27, 81, 99, 104). Power exercises require the highest level of skill and concentration of all the exercises and are most affected by fatigue (27). Athletes who become fatigued are prone to using poor technique and consequently are at higher risk of injury. The explosive movements and extensive muscular involvement of power exercises also result in a significant energy expenditure (99). This is another reason to have athletes perform such exercises first, while they are still metabolically fresh. If power exercises are not selected in step 2 (exercise selection), then the recommended order of exercises is *core exercises and then assistance exercises.*

The "reverse" exercise arrangement, called **preexhaustion**, is a viable ordering method that purposely fatigues a large muscle group as a result of performance of a single-joint exercise prior to a multijoint exercise involving the same muscle (110). For example, athletes can perform the leg (knee) curl exercise before the back squat exercise to preexhaust the hamstring muscle group.

Upper and Lower Body Exercises (Alternated)

One method of providing the opportunity for athletes to recover more fully between exercises is to alternate upper body exercises with lower body exercises. This arrangement is especially helpful for untrained individuals who find that completing several upper or lower body exercises in succession is too strenuous (27, 81). Also, if training time is limited, this method of arranging exercises minimizes the length of the rest periods required between exercises and maximizes the rest between body areas. The result is a decrease in overall training time, because the athlete can perform an upper body exercise and then immediately go to a lower body exercise without having to wait for the upper body to rest. If the exercises are performed with minimal rest periods (20-30 seconds), this method is also referred to as **circuit training**, a method sometimes also used to improve cardiorespiratory endurance (33), although to a lesser extent than conventional aerobic exercise training.

"Push" and "Pull" Exercises (Alternated)

Another method of improving recovery and recruitment between exercises is to alternate pushing exercises (e.g., bench press, shoulder press, and triceps extension) with pulling exercises (e.g., lat pulldown, bent-over row, biceps curl) (6). This push-pull arrangement ensures that the same muscle group will not be used in two exercises (or sets, in some cases) in succession, thus reducing fatigue in the involved muscles. In contrast, arranging several pulling exercises (e.g., pull-up, seated row, hammer curl) one after the other, even with a rest period between each, will compromise the number of repetitions performed because the biceps brachii muscle (involved in all three exercises) will become less responsive due to fatigue. The same result would occur if several pushing exercises (e.g., incline bench press, shoulder press, triceps pushdown) were sequentially arranged (all three engage the triceps brachii) (93). There are also push-pull arrangements for the lower body—for example, hip sled and back squat as "push" and stiff-leg deadlift and leg (knee) curl as "pull"—but the classification of some exercises as "push" or "pull" is not as clear (e.g., leg [knee] extension). The alternation of push and pull exercises is also used in circuit training programs and is an ideal arrangement for athletes beginning or returning to a resistance training program (6, 7, 27).

Supersets and Compound Sets

Other methods of arranging exercises involve having athletes perform one set of a pair of exercises with little to no rest between them. Two common examples are referred to as supersets and compound sets. A **superset** involves two sequentially performed exercises that stress two opposing muscles or muscle areas (i.e., an agonist and its antagonist) (6, 99). For example, an athlete performs 10 repetitions of the barbell biceps curl exercise, sets the bar down, then goes over to the triceps pushdown station and performs 10 repetitions. A **compound set** involves sequentially performing two different exercises for the same muscle group (6). For instance, an athlete completes a set of the barbell biceps curl exercise, then switches to dumbbells and immediately performs a set of the hammer curl exercise. In this case, the stress on the same muscle is compounded because both exercises recruit the same muscle area. Both methods of arranging and performing pairs of exercises are time efficient and purposely more demanding—and consequently may not be appropriate for unconditioned athletes. Note, however, that sometimes the meanings of *superset* and *compound set* are interchanged (27).

STEP 5: TRAINING LOAD AND REPETITIONS

Load is most simply referred to as the amount of weight assigned to an exercise set and is often characterized as the most critical aspect of a resistance training program (27, 30, 71, 82, 99).

Terminology Used to Quantify and Qualify Mechanical Work

Mechanical work can be defined as the product of force and displacement (sometimes labeled *distance*). An athlete can perform (external) mechanical work via "demands" made upon the body to generate (internal) metabolic energy. Thus, it is important to quantify the amount of mechanical work or degree of metabolic demand in order to plan variation in the training program and to avoid the exhaustion phase of Selye's General Adaptation Syndrome (see chapter 19) associated with overtraining (see chapters 5 and 6).

A quantity measure for resistance training "work" is needed. Traditionally, at least in the sport of Olympic weightlifting, this "work" is called the "load" and it can be calculated by multiplying each weight lifted by the number of times it is lifted and summing all such values over a training session.

However, **load-volume** (29) or **volume-load** (61, 87) may be a better term than just "load." This quantity is highly related to mechanical work and the associated metabolic energy demands and physiological stress, and also is distinguished from **repetition- (rep-) volume** (i.e., the total number of

The authors want to publicly recognize the insightful and critically important contribution of John Garhammer, PhD, CSCS, in providing and explaining the concepts of mechanical work, load-volume, repetition-volume, and intensity.

Application of the Exercise Order Guidelines

(Refer to p. 383 for a description of the scenario athletes.)

Scenario A
Female collegiate basketball player
Preseason

Assigned exercise order strategies

- Power, other core, then assistance exercises
- "Push" and "pull" exercises (alternated)

Monday, Wednesday, and Friday

Hang clean[a]
Push jerk[b]
Front squat[a]
Incline bench press[b]
Seated row
Dumbbell alternating curl
Triceps pushdown
Abdominal crunch

COMMENTS

[a,b]These exercises are alternated to provide relative rest between their similar movement patterns while still following the "power, other core, then assistance" exercise order strategy.

Scenario B
Male professional American football lineman
Off-season

Assigned exercise order strategies

- Core and then assistance exercises
- "Push" and "pull" exercises (alternated)

Lower body (Monday and Thursday)

Deadlift[c]
Back squat[c]
Step-up[c]
Leg (knee) curl
Seated calf (heel) raise

Upper body (Tuesday and Friday)

Bench press
Bent-over row
Shoulder press
Barbell biceps curl[d]
Shoulder shrug
Lying triceps extension
Abdominal crunch

COMMENTS

[c]These exercises do not follow the "push" and "pull" (alternated) exercise arrangement and could be performed in a variety of sequences (e.g., back squat, deadlift, step-up).

[d]Although the barbell biceps curl exercise is a "pulling" movement and occurs before another "pull" exercise (shoulder shrug), it does not affect the athlete's ability to perform the shoulder shrug exercise.

Scenario C
Male high school cross-country runner
In-season

Assigned exercise order strategies

- Core and then assistance exercises
- Upper and lower body exercises (alternated), circuit training

Wednesday and Saturday

Lunge
Vertical chest press
Leg (knee) curl
One-arm dumbbell row
Toe raise (dorsiflexion)
Lateral shoulder raise
Machine back extension[e]
Abdominal crunch

Complete one set of each exercise, then repeat.[f]

COMMENTS

[e]Exercises that concentrically train the lower back muscles should be performed after exercises that require an erect torso or a flat-back position (e.g., lunge and lateral shoulder raise). Fatigue of the lower back muscles can result in incorrect and potentially injurious exercise technique in structural or standing exercises.

[f]The eight exercises are performed one set at a time, one immediately after the other (i.e., in a "circuit").

repetitions; see "Step 6: Volume," p. 405, for more explanation).

To explain load-volume further (29), if a barbell that weighs 100 "weight units" is lifted 2 vertical "distance units" for 15 repetitions, the total concentric mechanical work is 3,000 "work units" (100 × 2 × 15). However, load-volume (1,500 units) does not include the distance value but is still directly related to the amount of mechanical work performed and the extent of the metabolic demand the athlete experiences to lift the weight for the required repetitions. Note that the load-volume is not affected by the rep and set scheme (i.e., 15 sets of 1 repetition, 5 sets of 3 repetitions, 3 sets of 5 repetitions, or 1 set of 15 repetitions). Various repetition and set schemes affect the true **intensity** value for resistance exercise and indicate the *quality* of work performed. Instead of using time to calculate mechanical or metabolic power or intensity, it is more practical to use a value that is proportional to time, namely, rep-volume (29). The more repetitions performed, the longer the training session (rest period lengths are an additional consideration and are not directly accounted for). Dividing load-volume by rep-volume results in the average weight lifted per repetition per workout session. This is a good approximation for mechanical and metabolic power output, which are true intensity or quality of work parameters (29).

Relationship Between Load and Repetitions

The number of times an exercise can be performed (**repetitions**) is inversely related to the load lifted; the heavier the load, the lower the number of repetitions that can be performed. Therefore, focusing on one training goal automatically implies the use of a certain load and repetition regime (e.g., training for muscular strength involves lifting heavy loads for few repetitions).

Before assigning training loads, the strength and conditioning professional should understand this relationship between loads and repetitions. Load is commonly described as either a certain percentage of a **1-repetition maximum (1RM)**—the greatest amount of weight that can be lifted with proper technique for only one repetition—or the most weight lifted for a specified number of repetitions, a **repetition maximum (RM)** (19). For instance, if an athlete can perform 10 repetitions with 60 kg in the back squat exercise, her 10RM is 60 kg. It is assumed that the athlete provided a *maximal effort*; if she had stopped at nine repetitions but could have performed one more, she would not have achieved a 10RM. Likewise, if she lifted 55 kg for 10 repetitions (but could have performed more), her true 10RM was not accurately assessed because she possibly could have lifted 60 kg for 10 repetitions.

Table 15.7 shows the relationship between a submaximal load—calculated as a percentage of the 1RM—and the number of repetitions that can be performed at that load. By definition, 100% of the 1RM allows the athlete to perform one repetition. As the percentage of the 1RM (i.e., the load lifted) decreases, the athlete will be able to successfully complete more repetitions. Other %1RM–repetition tables with slightly different %1RM values can be found in the literature (5, 15, 16, 25, 62, 68, 73, 110), but they vary by only about 0.5 to 2 percentage points from those provided in table 15.7.

Although %1RM–repetition tables provide helpful guidelines for assigning an athlete's training loads, research to date does not support the widespread use of such tables for establishing training loads for every exercise assigned to athletes, for the following reasons:

TABLE 15.7

Percent of the 1RM and Repetitions Allowed (%1RM–Repetition Relationship)

%1RM	Number of repetitions allowed
100	1
95	2
93	3
90	4
87	5
85	6
83	7
80	8
77	9
75	10
70	11
67	12
65	15

Data from references 5, 15, 16, 25, 62, 68, 73, and 110.

- Table 15.7 assumes there is a linear association between the loads lifted and the repetitions performed; however, several studies have reported a curvilinear relationship (64, 68, 70).
- Resistance-trained athletes may be able to exceed the number of repetitions listed in the table at any given percentage of their 1RM, especially in lower body core exercises (46, 47).
- The number of repetitions that can be performed at a certain percent of the 1RM is based on a single set. When an athlete performs multiple sets, the loads may need to be reduced so that the desired number of repetitions can be completed in all of the sets (110).
- Despite the prevalence of 1RM research, athletes may not always perform the predicted number of repetitions at a specified percentage of a 1RM (reviews in 27, 104). For instance, studies conducted by Hoeger and colleagues (46, 47) showed that subjects were able to perform two to three *times* more repetitions than are listed in table 15.7.

- A certain percentage of the 1RM assigned to a machine exercise can result in more repetitions at the same percentage of the 1RM than with a similar free weight exercise (46, 47).
- Exercises involving smaller muscle areas may not produce as many repetitions as seen in table 15.7, and exercises recruiting large muscle areas are likely to result in more repetitions performed (85, 104).
- The most accurate relationship between percentages of the 1RM and the maximum repetitions possible is for loads ≥75% of the 1RM and ≤10 repetitions (3, 15, 16, 96, 109). Empirical evidence further suggests that as the percentage of the 1RM decreases, the variability in the number of repetitions that can be completed increases.

Therefore, loads calculated from the %1RM in table 15.7 should be used only as a guideline for estimating a particular RM load for a resistance training exercise. Even with the inherent weaknesses just explained, it appears that it is still more accurate to assign loads based on a percentage of a test-established 1RM than it is to estimate a 1RM from a submaximal load (45, 46, 78, 94).

1RM and Multiple-RM Testing Options

To gather information needed to assign a training load, the strength and conditioning professional has the option of determining the athlete's

- actual 1RM (directly tested),
- estimated 1RM from a multiple-RM test (e.g., a 10RM), or
- multiple RM based on the number of repetitions planned for that exercise (the "goal" repetitions; e.g., five repetitions per set).

Once the actual 1RM is measured or estimated, the athlete's training load is calculated as a percentage of the 1RM. Alternatively, a multiple-RM test may be performed based on goal repetitions, thereby eliminating computations or estimations. In many cases, the strength and conditioning professional will use a variety of testing options depending on the exercises selected and the athlete's training background. A common strategy for testing sufficiently conditioned athletes is to conduct a 1RM test in several core exercises and use multiple-RM testing for assistance exercises.

Testing the 1RM

To assign training loads based on a percentage of the 1RM, the strength and conditioning professional must first determine the athlete's 1RM. This method of assessment is typically reserved for resistance-trained athletes who are classified as intermediate or advanced and have exercise technique experience in the exercises being tested. Individuals who are untrained, inexperienced, injured, or medically supervised may not be appropriate participants for 1RM testing. 1RM testing requires an adequate training status and lifting experience, as the assessment of maximal strength places significant stress on the involved muscles, connective tissues, and joints. Thus, it has been suggested that a 3RM test could be used instead of a maximal 1RM test (104). Ignoring an athlete's training status and exercise technique experience will diminish the safety and accuracy of 1RM test results.

When selecting exercises for 1RM testing, the strength and conditioning professional should choose core exercises because the large muscle groups and multiple joints are better able to handle the heavy loads. Despite this guideline, an exercise should not be selected for 1RM testing if it cannot provide valid and reliable data (i.e., does not accurately and consistently assess maximal muscular strength). For instance, the large upper back musculature and multiple joints involved in the bent-over row exercise can probably tolerate the loads from a 1RM test, but maintaining a correct body position throughout testing would be extremely difficult. The weaker stabilizing muscles of the lower back might become very fatigued after several testing sets, resulting in a loss of proper exercise technique and invalid and potentially unreliable test data.

A variety of procedures can be used to accurately determine a 1RM; one method is described in figure 15.1. (Refer to chapters 11 and 12 for administrative guidelines and test protocol explanations.) Despite an orderly testing sequence, variations in training status and exercise type will affect the absolute load increases in sequential testing sets. For example, the gradual load increase for 1RM attempts for an athlete who can back squat 495 pounds (225 kg) may be 20 to 30 pounds (9-14 kg) per testing set. For a weaker athlete with a back squat 1RM of 100 pounds (45 kg), a 20- or 30-pound testing load increment is too aggressive and is not precise enough to yield an accurate 1RM value. To improve the appropriateness and accuracy of the sequential testing sets, figure

1RM TESTING PROTOCOL

1. Instruct the athlete to warm up with a light resistance that easily allows 5 to 10 repetitions.
2. Provide a 1-minute rest period.
3. Estimate a warm-up load that will allow the athlete to complete three to five repetitions by adding
   - 10 to 20 pounds (4-9 kg) or 5% to 10% for upper body exercise or
   - 30 to 40 pounds (14-18 kg) or 10% to 20% for lower body exercise.
4. Provide a 2-minute rest period.
5. Estimate a conservative, near-maximal load that will allow the athlete to complete two to three repetitions by adding
   - 10 to 20 pounds (4-9 kg) or 5% to 10% for upper body exercise or
   - 30 to 40 pounds (14-18 kg) or 10% to 20% for lower body exercise.
6. Provide a 2- to 4-minute rest period.
7. Make a load increase:
   - 10 to 20 pounds (4-9 kg) or 5% to 10% for upper body exercise or
   - 30 to 40 pounds (14-18 kg) or 10% to 20% for lower body exercise.
8. Instruct the athlete to attempt a 1RM.
9. If the athlete was successful, provide a 2- to 4-minute rest period and go back to step 7.

If the athlete failed, provide a 2- to 4-minute rest period, then decrease the load by subtracting

- 5 to 10 pounds (2-4 kg) or 2.5% to 5% for upper body exercise or
- 15 to 20 pounds (7-9 kg) or 5% to 10% for lower body exercise

AND then go back to step 8.

Continue increasing or decreasing the load until the athlete can complete one repetition with proper exercise technique. Ideally, the athlete's 1RM will be measured within three to five testing sets.

Figure 15.1 A 1RM testing protocol.

Reprinted, by permission, from Earle, 2006 (23).

15.1 also includes relative percentages that can be used instead of the absolute load adjustments.

Estimating a 1RM

When maximal strength testing is not warranted, testing with a 10RM load (and then estimating or predicting the 1RM) can be a suitable secondary option. This approach is appropriate for nearly all athletes, provided they can demonstrate the proper technique in the exercise tested. Core and assistance exercises can be selected for 10RM testing, but excessive warm-up and testing sets may fatigue the athlete and compromise the accuracy of the test. Additionally, power exercises do not lend themselves well to multiple-RM testing above five repetitions for repeated testing sets because technique can deteriorate rapidly (99, 110). Lower (and more accurate) multiple-RM determinations using heavier loads can be made once the athlete has sufficient training and technique experience.

The protocol for 10RM testing is similar to that for 1RM testing, but each set requires 10 repetitions, not one. After the completion of warm-up sets, the athlete's sequential load changes for the 10RM test are smaller than those listed in figure 15.1 (approximately one-half). Continue the process of testing until a load allowing only 10 repetitions is determined. An experienced strength and conditioning professional will be able to adjust the loads so that the 10RM can be measured within three to five testing sets.

Using a 1RM Table To estimate the athlete's 1RM, consult table 15.8. In the "Max reps (RM) = 10" (%1RM = 75) column, first find the tested 10RM load; then read across the row to the "Max reps (RM) = 1" (%1RM = 100) column to discover the athlete's projected 1RM. For example, if an athlete's 10RM is 300 pounds, the estimated 1RM is 400 pounds. As noted in connection with table 15.7, the %1RM–repetition associations vary in the literature. This table is intended for use as a guide until the

TABLE 15.8

Estimating 1RM and Training Loads

Max reps (RM)	1	2	3	4	5	6	7	8	9	10	12	15
%1RM	100	95	93	90	87	85	83	80	77	75	67	65
Load (pounds or kg)	10	10	9	9	9	9	8	8	8	8	7	7
	20	19	19	18	17	17	17	16	15	15	13	13
	30	29	28	27	26	26	25	24	23	23	20	20
	40	38	37	36	35	34	33	32	31	30	27	26
	50	48	47	45	44	43	42	40	39	38	34	33
	60	57	56	54	52	51	50	48	46	45	40	39
	70	67	65	63	61	60	58	56	54	53	47	46
	80	76	74	72	70	68	66	64	62	60	54	52
	90	86	84	81	78	77	75	72	69	68	60	59
	100	95	93	90	87	85	83	80	77	75	67	65
	110	105	102	99	96	94	91	88	85	83	74	72
	120	114	112	108	104	102	100	96	92	90	80	78
	130	124	121	117	113	111	108	104	100	98	87	85
	140	133	130	126	122	119	116	112	108	105	94	91
	150	143	140	135	131	128	125	120	116	113	101	98
	160	152	149	144	139	136	133	128	123	120	107	104
	170	162	158	153	148	145	141	136	131	128	114	111
	180	171	167	162	157	153	149	144	139	135	121	117
	190	181	177	171	165	162	158	152	146	143	127	124
	200	190	186	180	174	170	166	160	154	150	134	130
	210	200	195	189	183	179	174	168	162	158	141	137
	220	209	205	198	191	187	183	176	169	165	147	143
	230	219	214	207	200	196	191	184	177	173	154	150
	240	228	223	216	209	204	199	192	185	180	161	156
	250	238	233	225	218	213	208	200	193	188	168	163

(continued)

TABLE 15.8 *(continued)*

Max reps (RM)	1	2	3	4	5	6	7	8	9	10	12	15
%1RM	100	95	93	90	87	85	83	80	77	75	67	65
Load (pounds or kg)	260	247	242	234	226	221	206	208	200	195	174	169
	270	257	251	243	235	230	224	216	208	203	181	176
	280	266	260	252	244	238	232	224	216	210	188	182
	290	276	270	261	252	247	241	232	223	218	194	189
	300	285	279	270	261	255	249	240	231	225	201	195
	310	295	288	279	270	264	257	248	239	233	208	202
	320	304	298	288	278	272	266	256	246	240	214	208
	330	314	307	297	287	281	274	264	254	248	221	215
	340	323	316	306	296	289	282	272	262	255	228	221
	350	333	326	315	305	298	291	280	270	263	235	228
	360	342	335	324	313	306	299	288	277	270	241	234
	370	352	344	333	322	315	307	296	285	278	248	241
	380	361	353	342	331	323	315	304	293	285	255	247
	390	371	363	351	339	332	324	312	300	293	261	254
	400	380	372	360	348	340	332	320	308	300	268	260
	410	390	381	369	357	349	340	328	316	308	274	267
	420	399	391	378	365	357	349	336	323	315	281	273
	430	409	400	387	374	366	357	344	331	323	288	280
	440	418	409	396	383	374	365	352	339	330	295	286
	450	428	419	405	392	383	374	360	347	338	302	293
	460	437	428	414	400	391	382	368	354	345	308	299
	470	447	437	423	409	400	390	376	362	353	315	306
	480	456	446	432	418	408	398	384	370	360	322	312
	490	466	456	441	426	417	407	392	377	368	328	319
	500	475	465	450	435	425	415	400	385	375	335	325
	510	485	474	459	444	434	423	408	393	383	342	332
	520	494	484	468	452	442	432	416	400	390	348	338
	530	504	493	477	461	451	440	424	408	398	355	345
	540	513	502	486	470	459	448	432	416	405	362	351
	550	523	512	495	479	468	457	440	424	413	369	358
	560	532	521	504	487	476	465	448	431	420	375	364
	570	542	530	513	496	485	473	456	439	428	382	371
	580	551	539	522	505	493	481	464	447	435	389	377
	590	561	549	531	513	502	490	472	454	443	395	384
	600	570	558	540	522	510	498	480	462	450	402	390

Data from references 5, 15, 16, 25, 62, 68, 73, and 110.

athlete has developed the neuromuscular attributes that will make testing with heavier loads (e.g., 1RM-5RM) safe and effective (27, 65, 99).

Using Prediction Equations Equations are also available to predict the 1RM from multiple-RM loads (15, 16, 25, 68). Researchers who have reviewed such equations report that as the loads used in multiple-RM testing become heavier (i.e., bringing the loads closer to the actual 1RM), the accuracy of the 1RM estimation increases. Likewise, predictions are more accurate when the equations are based on loads equal to or less than a 10RM (3, 15, 16, 69, 96, 99, 109). Furthermore, the results obtained from lower multiple-RM testing (and subsequent predictions of the 1RM) are generally more accurate when an athlete has been consistently training with low multiple-RM resistances (i.e., heavy loads) for a few months prior to testing (110).

Multiple-RM Testing Based on Goal Repetitions

A third option for determining training loads requires the strength and conditioning professional to first decide the number of repetitions (i.e., the **goal repetitions**) the athlete will perform in the actual program for the exercise being tested. For example, if the strength and conditioning professional decides that the athlete should perform six repetitions for the bench press exercise in the training program, the multiple-RM testing protocol should have the athlete perform the exercise with a load that will result in six repetitions (6RM). Core and assistance exercises can be selected for multiple-RM testing, but, as previously mentioned, high-repetition testing sets can create significant fatigue and may compromise the accuracy of the tested multiple RM. This effect seems to be more problematic for exercises that involve multiple joints and large muscle areas due to their high metabolic demand (99). Further, multiple-RM testing (and subsequent load assignments) for assistance exercises should be at or above an 8RM to minimize the isolative stress on the involved joint and connective tissue (6, 23). In other words, even if an athlete is following a muscular strength training program that involves 2RM loads for the core exercises, the heaviest load the assistance exercises should be assigned is an 8RM.

Assigning Load and Repetitions Based on the Training Goal

During the *needs analysis* (step 1, p. 382), the strength and conditioning professional is challenged to choose the primary goal of the resistance training program based on the athlete's testing results, the movement and physiological analysis of the sport, and the priorities of the athlete's sport season. Once decided on, the training goal can be applied to determine specific load and repetition assignments via the RM continuum, a percentage of the 1RM (either directly tested or estimated), or the results of multiple-RM testing. As explained previously, the testing methods determine how the loads and repetitions are assigned for each exercise (i.e., loads are *calculated* as a percentage of a tested or estimated 1RM; training loads are *specifically determined* from multiple-RM testing). The options for testing and assigning training loads and repetitions are summarized in figure 15.2.

Repetition Maximum Continuum

Figure 15.3 shows how RM ranges are associated with training goals; relatively heavy loads should be used if the goal is strength or power, moderate loads for hypertrophy, and light loads for muscular endurance (as indicated by the larger font sizes). To state this another way, low multiple RMs appear to have the greatest effect on strength and maximum power training, and high multiple RMs seem to result in better muscular endurance improvements (2, 4, 17, 26, 71, 104). The continuum concept effectively illustrates that a certain RM *emphasizes* a specific outcome, but the training benefits are blended at any given RM.

Percentage of the 1RM

Despite the physiological blend of training effects, the specificity principle still dictates the dominant outcome that is attained and enhanced with a particular training load. The relationship between the percentage of the 1RM and the estimated number of repetitions that can be performed at that load (table 15.7) allows the strength and conditioning professional to assign a specific resistance to be used for an exercise in a training session. In other words, the training goal is attained when the athlete lifts a load of a certain percentage of the 1RM for a specific number of repetitions (table 15.9).

How to Calculate a Training Load For example, suppose an athlete's training goal is muscular strength and the tested 1RM in the bench press exercise is 220 pounds (100 kg). To increase strength, the athlete needs to handle loads of at least 85% of the 1RM (after warm-up) that typically allow performance of up to six repetitions per set

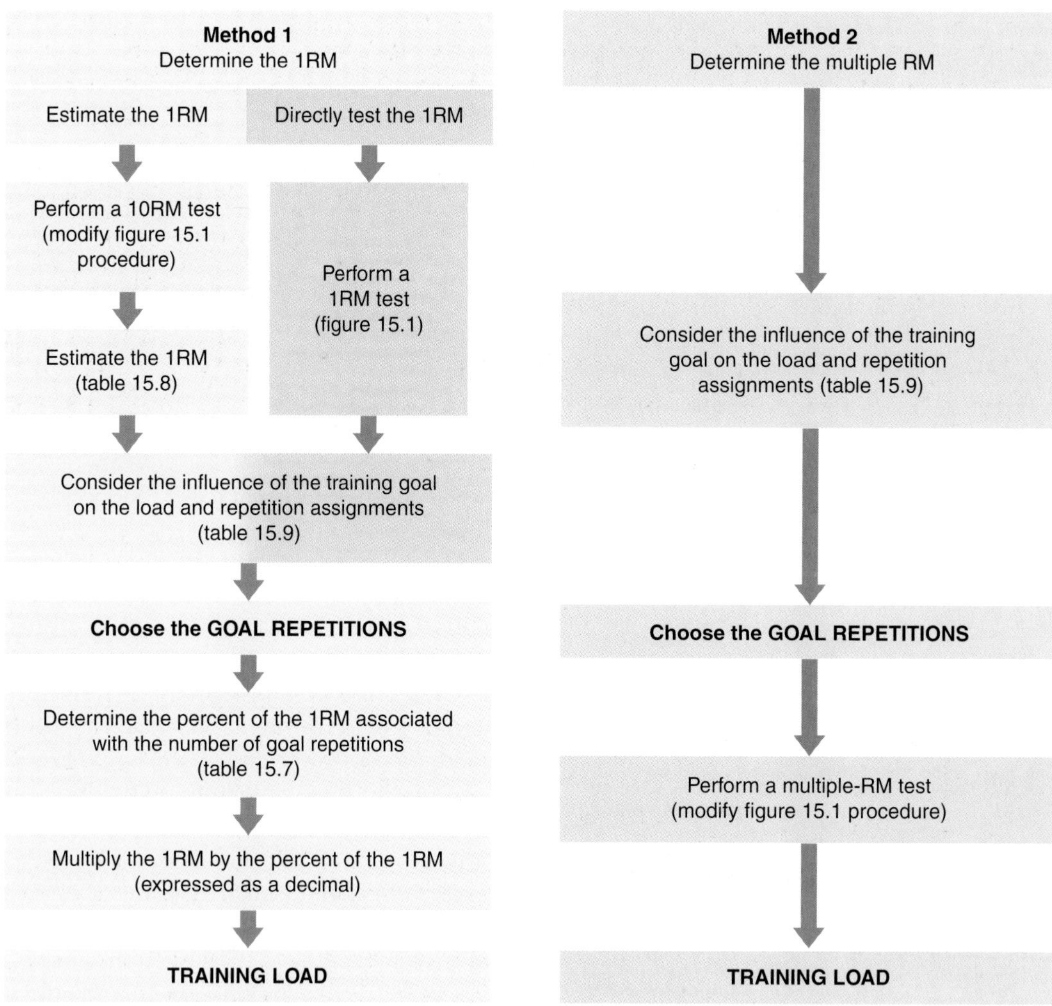

Figure 15.2 Summary of testing and assigning training loads and repetitions.

Reprinted, by permission, from Earle, 2006 (23).

(table 15.9). More specifically, if the strength and conditioning professional assigns four repetitions per set for this exercise, the corresponding load will be approximately 90% of the 1RM (table 15.7), or approximately 200 pounds (90 kg). Note that the strength and conditioning professional should make adjustments to assigned loads based on observation of the ease or difficulty an athlete experiences in lifting the load for the required repetitions.

Assigning Percentages for Power Training

The force–velocity curve (discussed in chapter 4) illustrates that the greater the amount of concentric muscular force generated, the slower the muscle shortening and corresponding movement velocity (and vice versa). Maximal power, in contrast, is produced at intermediate velocities (53) with the lifting of moderate, not maximal, loads (76). Performing a 1RM involves slower movement velocities; maximum force is generated, but with reduced power output (27, 28, 117). Seldom is an athlete required to demonstrate a singular, maximal, slow-speed muscular strength effort in a sport (except in powerlifting, for example). Most sport movements are faster (75) and involve higher power outputs (54) than those produced during a 1RM test. This does not mean that an athlete's power capabilities are unaffected by maximal muscular strength training, however. Because speed- or power-related sport movements often begin from zero or near-zero velocities, slow-velocity strength gains have direct application to power production (27). For these reasons, the load and repetition assignments for power training overlap the guidelines for strength training (table 15.9).

Single-joint muscle action data reveal that peak power is reached with the lifting of very light loads—30% of the 1RM (28, 53). With such a light

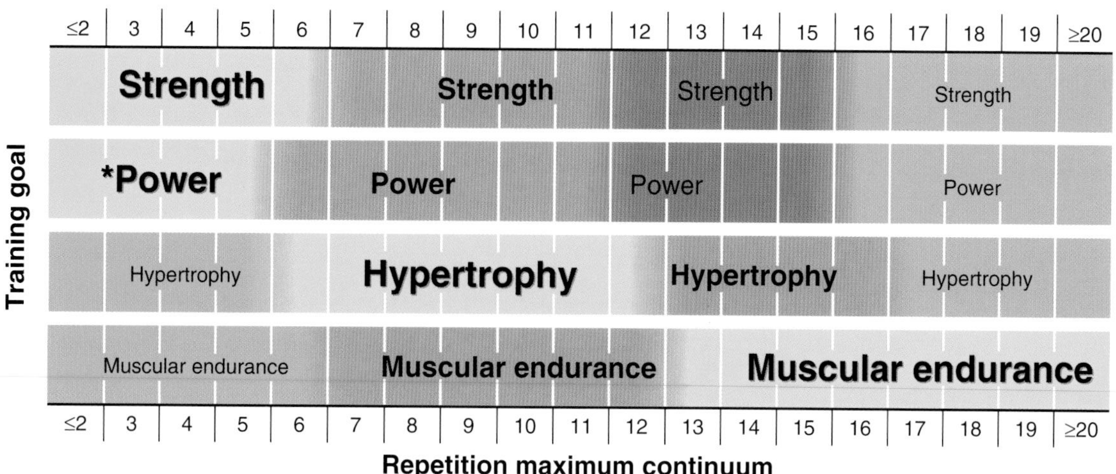

Figure 15.3 This continuum shows how RM ranges are associated with various training goals.

*The repetition ranges shown for power in this figure are *not consistent* with the %1RM–repetition relationship. On average, loads equaling about 80% of the 1RM apply to the two- to five-repetition range. Refer to the discussion of assigning percentages for power training on page 400 for further explanation.

Adapted from references 27 and 100.

TABLE 15.9

Load and Repetition Assignments Based on the Training Goal

Training goal	Load (%1RM)	Goal repetitions
*Strength	≥85	≤6
†Power:		
Single-effort event	80-90	1-2
Multiple-effort event	75-85	3-5
Hypertrophy	67-85	6-12
Muscular endurance	≤67	≥12

*These RM loading assignments for muscular strength training apply only to core exercises; assistance exercises should be limited to loads not heavier than an 8RM (6).

†The load and repetition assignments shown for power in this table are *not consistent* with the %1RM–repetition relationship. On average, loads equaling about 80% of the 1RM apply to the two- to five-repetition range. Refer to the discussion of assigning percentages of the 1RM for power training on page 400 for further explanation.

Data from references 11, 26, 27, 30, 42, 44, 58, 65, 78, 99, 105, 106, and 107.

weight, however, multijoint power exercises are difficult to execute properly (29) with typical resistance training equipment because the athlete cannot sufficiently overload the muscles and still control the bar's deceleration at the end of the exercise range of motion (74). On the other end of the load continuum, data from multiple national- and world-level weightlifting and powerlifting championships clearly indicate that power output increases as the weight lifted decreases from 100% of the 1RM (i.e., the 1RM) to 90% of the 1RM (28, 29, 31, 32, 91). In fact, for the back squat and deadlift exercises, power output for a load at 90% of the 1RM may be *twice* as high as with the 1RM load due to a large decrease in the time required to complete the exercise with the lighter load (32). Even for the already "fast" power exercises, there is still a 5% to 10% increase in power output as the load decreases from the 1RM to 90% of the 1RM (32). Considering these issues, the most effective and practical application is to assign loads that are about 80% of the 1RM for resistance training exercises designed to improve maximal power production (28, 58, 74).

To promote program specificity, particular load and repetition assignments are indicated for athletes training for *single-effort power events* (e.g., shot put, high jump, weightlifting) and for *multiple-effort power events* (e.g., basketball, volleyball). Garhammer (29) suggests that single-effort event athletes be assigned sets of one to two repetitions using loads that equal 80% to 90% of the 1RM, especially on heavy training days. For sports with multiple maximum power efforts (e.g., the frequent maximum vertical jumping motions of a volleyball blocker), three to five repetitions per set with loads at 75% to 85% of the 1RM are recommended (29).

On the basis of the %1RM–repetition relationships shown in table 15.7, the strength and conditioning professional may question the load assignments for power training in table 15.9. The %1RM loads may appear to be too low compared to the goal number

Application of the Training Load and Repetition Guidelines

(Refer to page 383 for a description of the scenario athletes.)

Scenario A
Female collegiate basketball player
Preseason

Primary preseason resistance training goal

Strength/power

Testing and assigning loads and repetitions

Influence of the training goals

Power exercises: 75-85% of the 1RM; 3-5 repetitions[a]

Other core exercises: ≥85% of the 1RM; ≤6 repetitions

Assistance exercises: limited to loads not heavier than an 8RM

Number of goal repetitions

Power exercises: 5
Core exercises: 6
Assistance exercises: 10

Testing methods

3RM testing for power exercises[b]

- Hang clean
- Push jerk

1RM testing for other core exercises[c]

- Front squat
- Incline bench press

10RM testing for assistance exercises[d]

- Seated row
- Dumbbell alternating curl
- Triceps pushdown

Testing results

3RM hang clean	115 lb (53 kg)
Estimated 1RM[e]	*124 lb (56 kg)*
3RM push jerk	110 lb (50 kg)
Estimated 1RM[e]	*118 lb (54 kg)*
1RM front squat	185 lb (84 kg)
1RM incline bench press	100 lb (45 kg)
10RM seated row	90 lb (41 kg)
10RM dumbbell alternating curl	20 lb (9 kg)
10RM triceps pushdown	40 lb (18 kg)

Training loads

For power exercises:

- Assign 75% of the estimated 1RM

Hang clean	95 lb (43 kg)
Push jerk	90 lb (41 kg)

(All loads are rounded off to the nearest 5 lb.)

For other core exercises:

- Assign 85% of the tested 1RM

Front squat	155 lb (70 kg)
Incline bench press	85 lb (39 kg)

(All loads are rounded off to the nearest 5 lb.)

For assistance exercises:

- Assign loads equal to the loads from 10RM testing

Scenario B
Male professional American football lineman
Off-season

Primary off-season resistance training goal

Hypertrophy

Testing and assigning loads and repetitions

Influence of the training goals

67-85% of the 1RM; 6-12 repetitions

Number of goal repetitions

Core exercises: 10
Assistance exercises: 10

Testing methods

1RM testing for core exercises

- Deadlift
- Back squat[i]
- Bench press[i]
- Shoulder press[i]

10RM testing for new assistance exercises[j]

- Step-up
- Seated calf (heel) raise
- Bent-over row
- Shoulder shrug

Testing results

1RM deadlift	650 lb (295 kg)
1RM back squat	675 lb (307 kg)
1RM bench press	425 lb (193 kg)
1RM shoulder press	255 lb (116 kg)
10RM step-up	205 lb (93 kg)
10RM seated calf (heel) raise	155 lb (70 kg)
10RM bent-over row	215 lb (98 kg)
10RM shoulder shrug	405 lb (184 kg)

Training loads

For core exercises:

- Assign 75% of the tested 1RM

Deadlift	490 lb (223 kg)
Back squat	505 lb (230 kg)
Bench press	320 lb (145 kg)
Shoulder press	190 lb (86 kg)

(All loads are rounded off to the nearest 5 lb.)

For assistance exercises:

- Assign loads equal to the loads from the 10RM testing ***OR***
- Equal to the loads used in the postseason

Leg (knee) curl	190 lb (86 kg)
Barbell biceps curl	115 lb (52 kg)
Lying triceps extension	125 lb (57 kg)

Scenario C
Male high school cross-country runner
In-season

Primary in-season resistance training goal

Muscular endurance

Testing and assigning loads and repetitions

Influence of the training goals

≤67% of the 1RM; ≤12 repetitions

Number of goal repetitions

Core exercises: 12
Assistance exercises: 15

Testing methods

12RM testing for core exercises[k]

- Lunge
- Vertical chest press

15RM testing for new assistance exercises[k]

- One-arm dumbbell row
- Lateral shoulder raise

Testing results

12RM lunge	45 lb (20 kg)
12RM vertical chest press	70 lb (32 kg)
15RM one-arm dumbbell row	25 lb (11 kg)
15RM lateral shoulder raise	10 lb (5 kg)

Training loads

For all exercises:

- Equal to the loads from 12 (or 15) RM testing ***OR***
- Equal to the loads used in the preseason

Leg (knee) curl	65 lb (30 kg)
Toe raise (dorsiflexion)	20 lb (9 kg)
Machine back extension	50 lb (23 kg)

Application of the Training Load and Repetition Guidelines (continued)

 Scenario A Female collegiate basketball player Preseason	 Scenario B Male professional American football lineman Off-season	 Scenario C Male high school cross-country runner In-season
Weekly loading regime (power/core exercises)[f] *Mondays ("heavy" day)* ▪ Assign the full load assignments (calculated under "Training loads") *Wednesdays ("light" day)* ▪ Assign only 80% of Monday's "heavy day" loads[g] *Fridays ("medium" day)* ▪ Assign only 90% of Monday's "heavy day" loads[h]		
COMMENTS [a] The load and repetition assignments shown for power exercises are based on basketball, a multiple-effort event, and are not consistent with the %1RM–repetition relationship. [b] To test for power, a multiple-RM (3RM) protocol is used. From the result, the 1RM is estimated and load assignments are made by calculating a percent of the estimated 1RM. [c] The athlete did perform these exercises in the off-season, but to raise the accuracy of the load assignments for the preseason, the athlete will be tested to determine the current 1RM. [d] Even though some of these exercises were part of the off-season program, they all require multiple-RM testing because the preseason goal repetitions for these exercises is 10, rather than 12 from the previous season. [e] Estimate the 1RM using table 15.8, pages 397-398. [f] The loads for the assistance exercises remain constant throughout the week; only the loads for the power and other core exercises change. [g] Calculate 80% of the loads lifted in Monday's training session and perform the same number of goal repetitions. Even if the athlete is able to, do not allow more repetitions than the designated goal number (power–5; other core–6). [h] Calculate 90% of the loads lifted in Monday's training session and perform the same number of goal repetitions. Even if the athlete is able to, do not allow more repetitions than the designated goal number (power–5; other core–6).	**COMMENTS** [i] The athlete did perform these exercises in the postseason, but to raise the accuracy of the load assignments for the off-season, the athlete will be tested to determine the current 1RM. [j] The exercises shown here were selected as new exercises for the off-season program and therefore require 10RM testing. The other assistance exercises were carried over from the postseason and do not require testing because the load and repetition assignments will be identical.	**COMMENTS** [k] The exercises shown here were selected as new exercises for the in-season program and therefore require 12RM or 15RM testing. The other assistance exercises were carried over from the preseason and do not require testing because the load and repetition assignments will be identical.

of repetitions. For example, according to table 15.7, three to five repetitions are typically associated with loads 93% to 87% of the 1RM, not 75% to 85% of the 1RM as table 15.9 indicates. Power exercises cannot be maximally loaded at any repetition scheme because the quality of the movement technique will decline before momentary muscle fatigue defines a true multiple-RM set (27). Therefore, slightly lighter loads allow the athlete to complete repetitions with maximum speed to promote maximum power development. For example, power exercises are usually limited to five repetitions per set, but with loads up to and equal to a 10RM (i.e., approximately 75% of the 1RM) (58). This load adjustment to promote peak power output also applies to the RM continuum (figure 15.3). Power training can be emphasized across the range of five repetitions or fewer, but the strength and conditioning professional should realize that these loads are not true repetition *maximums*.

Variation of the Training Load

Training for muscular strength and power places a high physiological stress on an athlete's body. Intermediate and advanced resistance-trained athletes are accustomed to lifting heavy loads and possess the experience and motivation to make nearly every set an RM set. Despite this high training status, this degree of training demand typically cannot be tolerated very long without contributing to an overtrained state. For example, an athlete may resistance train three days a week with muscular strength as the goal (e.g., Mondays, Wednesdays, and Fridays). It would be difficult for the athlete to perform the same high-load, low-volume regime—especially in the power and other core exercises—with only one to two days of rest between sessions.

One strategy to counterbalance the overtraining associated with the heavy loads is to alter the loads (%1RMs) for the power and other core exercises so that only one training day each week (e.g., Monday) is a heavy day. These "heavy day" loads are designed to be full repetition maximums, the greatest resistance that can be successfully lifted for the goal number of repetitions. The loads for the other training days are reduced (intentionally) to provide recovery after the heavy day while still maintaining sufficient training frequency and volume. In the example of the three-days-a-week program, Wednesdays and Fridays are "light" and "medium" training days (respectively). For the light day, calculate 80% of the loads lifted in the power and other core exercises on the heavy day (Monday) and instruct the athlete to complete the same number of goal repetitions. Even if the athlete is able to perform more repetitions than the designated goal number, he or she should not do so. Similarly, calculate 90% of the loads lifted in the power and other core exercises from Monday's training session for the "medium" day and instruct the athlete to perform only the assigned number of goal repetitions (5, 6, 99, 110). This approach can be used for any training frequency. For instance, a two-days-a-week program could have a heavy day and a light day, or an upper body–lower body split routine could consist of two heavy days (one upper body day and one lower body day) followed by two light days. Varying the training loads also works well with an athlete's other training, in that heavy lifting days can fall on light sport conditioning days, and light lifting days on heavy sport conditioning days (110). The strength and conditioning professional needs to monitor this schedule, so that it does not lead to heavy training *every* day (99).

Progression of the Training Load

As the athlete adapts to the training stimulus, the strength and conditioning professional needs to have a strategy for advancing exercise loads so that improvements will continue over time (**progression**). Monitoring each athlete's training and charting his or her response to the prescribed workouts enable the strength and conditioning professional to know when and to what extent the loads should be increased.

Timing Load Increases

A conservative method that can be used to increase an athlete's training loads is called the **2-for-2 rule** (6). If the athlete can perform two or more repetitions over his or her assigned repetition goal for a given exercise in the last set in two consecutive workouts, weight should be added to that exercise for the next training session. For example, a strength and conditioning professional assigns three sets of 10 repetitions in the bench press exercise, and the athlete performs all 10 repetitions in all sets. After several workout sessions (the specific number depends on many factors), the athlete is able to complete 12 repetitions in the third (last) set for two consecutive workouts. In the following training session, the load for that exercise should be increased.

Quantity of Load Increases

The decision as to the size of the load increase can be difficult to make, but table 15.10 provides general recommendations based on the athlete's condition (stronger or weaker) and body area (upper or lower body). Despite these guidelines, the significant variation in training status, load-volumes, and exercises (type and muscular involvement) greatly influences the appropriate load increases. To contend with this variability, relative load increases of 2.5% to 10% can be used instead of the absolute values shown in table 15.10.

STEP 6: VOLUME

Volume relates to the total amount of weight lifted in a training session (27, 77, 110), and a **set** is a group of repetitions sequentially performed before the athlete stops to rest (27). Repetition-volume is the total number of repetitions performed during a workout session (8, 27, 84, 99), and load-volume is the total number of sets multiplied by the number of repetitions per set then multiplied by the weight lifted per repetition. For example, the load-volume for two sets of 10 repetitions with 50 pounds would be expressed as 2 × 10 × 50 pounds or 1,000 pounds. (If different sets are performed with different amounts of weight, the volumes per set are calculated and then added to obtain the total training session volume.)

In the example just given (a load-volume of 1,000 pounds), multiplying each repetition by the additional factor of vertical displacement of the weight during that repetition would yield the concentric work performed. The displacement factor is fairly constant for a given athlete, so it is not used, but the resulting load-volume is still directly proportional to concentric work. As previously stated, load-volume divided by repetition-volume results in the average weight lifted per repetition, which is related to intensity or the quality of work. In running exercise, the common (rep) volume measure is distance. If an intensity value is known or measured (such as running pace, which relates to percent $\dot{V}O_2max$), then total metabolic energy cost (which is proportional to mechanical work done) can be calculated. This value is comparable to load-volume in resistance exercise. The same concepts are applicable to the number of foot or hand contacts (volume) in plyometric exercise, the number of strokes (volume) in swimming or rowing, or the number of throws or jumps (volume) for various sport activities.

TABLE 15.10

Examples of Load Increases

Description of the athlete*	Body area exercise	Estimated load increase†
Smaller, weaker, less trained	Upper body	2.5-5 pounds (1-2 kg)
	Lower body	5-10 pounds (2-4 kg)
Larger, stronger, more trained	Upper body	5-10+ pounds (2-4+ kg)
	Lower body	10-15+ pounds (4-7+ kg)

*The strength and conditioning professional will need to determine which of these two subjective categories applies to a specific athlete.

†These load increases are appropriate for training programs with load-volumes of approximately three sets of 5 to 10 repetitions. Note that the goal repetitions per set remain constant as the loads are increased.

Multiple Versus Single Sets

Some have advocated that one set of 8 to 12 repetitions (after warm-up) performed to volitional muscular failure is sufficient to maximize gains in muscular strength and hypertrophy (14, 52, 113). Additionally, others have reported increases in maximum strength after the performance of only one set per exercise per session (1, 34, 66, 67).

Single-set training may be appropriate for untrained individuals (27) or during the first several months of training (34), but many studies indicate that higher volumes are necessary to promote further gains in strength, especially for intermediate and advanced resistance-trained athletes (57, 72, 103, 116). Further, the musculoskeletal system will eventually adapt to the stimulus of one set to failure and require the added stimulus of multiple sets for continued strength gains (27). Moreover, performing three sets of 10 repetitions *without going to failure* enhances strength better than one set to failure in 8 to 12 repetitions (59, 61), although the higher training volume with use of three sets is a contributing factor (8, 26, 99). Therefore, an athlete who performs multiple sets from the initiation of his or her resistance training program will increase muscular strength faster than with single-set training (61, 71). The strength and conditioning professional cannot expect, however, that an athlete will be able to successfully complete multiple sets with full RM loads at fixed repetition schemes for every exercise in each training session. Fatigue will affect the number of repetitions that can be performed in later sets.

Training Status

The training status of athletes affects the volume they will be able to tolerate. It is appropriate for an athlete to perform only one or two sets as a beginner and to add sets as he or she becomes better trained. As the athlete adapts to a consistent and well-designed program, more sets can gradually be added to match the guidelines associated with the given training goal.

Primary Resistance Training Goal

Training volume is directly based on the athlete's resistance training goal. Table 15.11 provides a summary of the guidelines for the number of repetitions and sets commonly associated with strength, power, hypertrophy, and muscular endurance training programs.

TABLE 15.11

Volume Assignments Based on the Training Goal

Training goal	Goal repetitions	Sets*
Strength	≤6	2-6
†Power:		
Single-effort event	1-2	3-5
Multiple-effort event	3-5	3-5
Hypertrophy	6-12	3-6
Muscular endurance	≥12	2-3

*These assignments do not include warm-up sets and typically apply to core exercises only (6, 58).

†The repetition assignments shown for power in this table are *not consistent* with the %1RM–repetition relationship. On average, loads equaling about 80% of the 1RM apply to the two- to five-repetition range. Refer to the discussion of assigning percentages of the 1RM for power training on page 400 for further explanation.

Data from references 12, 27, 29, 30, 42, 65, 78, 99, 105, 106, and 107.

Strength and Power

In classic research, DeLorme (19) and DeLorme and Watkins (20) recommended sets of 10 repetitions as ideal to increase muscular strength, although the regime was originally developed for injury rehabilitation. Later, Berger (10, 11) determined that three sets of six repetitions created maximal strength gains, at least in the bench press and back squat exercises. Although Berger's work seemed to be conclusive, his subsequent research (9) showed no significant difference among six sets of a 2RM load, three sets of a 6RM load, and three sets of a 10RM load despite the differences in volume. Since then, many other studies have also been unable to support an exact set and repetition scheme to promote maximal increases in strength (22, 34, 35, 43, 79, 90, 98, 118). An important qualifier regarding these inconclusive reports is that most involved relatively untrained subjects, thus implying that nearly *any* type of program will cause improvements in strength for these individuals.

When training an athlete for strength, assigning volume begins with an examination of the optimal number of repetitions for maximal strength gains. As discussed earlier (and shown in figure 15.3 and table 15.9), this appears to be sets of six or fewer repetitions (at the corresponding RM load) for core exercises (12, 26, 27, 30, 42, 44, 58, 65, 78, 99, 100, 105, 106, 107). Comprehensive reviews of the literature by Fleck and Kraemer (27) and Tan (104) conclude that a range of two to five sets or three to six sets (respectively) promotes the greatest increases in strength. Specific set guidelines based on exercise type suggest that only one to three sets may be appropriate or necessary for assistance exercises (6, 58).

Volume assignments for power training are typically lower than those for strength training in order to maximize the quality of exercise. This reduction in volume results from fewer goal repetitions and lighter loads (figure 15.3 and table 15.9) rather than the recommended number of sets (29, 58). The common guideline is three to five sets (after warm-up) for power exercises included in a trained athlete's program (29, 44, 99, 100).

Hypertrophy

It is generally accepted that higher training volumes are associated with increases in muscular size (41, 71). This is the result of both a moderate to higher number of repetitions per set (6 to 12; see figure 15.3 and table 15.9) and the commonly recommended three to six sets per exercise (26, 42, 44, 80, 105). Additionally, although research studies usually only focus on one or two exercises (total or per muscle group), empirical observations, interviews with elite bodybuilders (95), and more exhaustive prescriptive guidelines (26, 58) suggest that performing three or more exercises per muscle group is the most effective strategy for increasing muscle size (42). The effect on training volume from these assignments can be quite substantial.

Muscular Endurance

Resistance training programs that emphasize muscular endurance involve performing many repetitions—12 or more—per set (12, 26, 27, 30, 58, 65, 78, 100, 105, 106, 107). Despite this relatively high repetition assignment, the overall volume-load is not necessarily overly inflated since the loads lifted are lighter and fewer sets are performed, commonly two to three per exercise (58).

Application of the Volume Guidelines

(Refer to p. 383 for a description of the scenario athletes.)

Scenario A Female collegiate basketball player Preseason		Scenario B Male professional American football lineman Off-season		Scenario C Male high school cross-country runner In-season	
Power exercises	4 sets of 5 repetitions	Core exercises	4 sets of 10 repetitions	Core exercises	3 sets of 12 repetitions
Other core exercises	3 sets of 6 repetitions	Assistance exercises	3 sets of 10 repetitions	Assistance exercises	2 sets of 15 repetitions
Assistance exercises	2 sets of 10 repetitions	(The number of sets does not include warm-ups.)		(The number of sets does not include warm-ups.)	
(The number of sets does not include warm-ups.)					
Monday, Wednesday, and Friday		***Lower body (Monday and Thursday)***		***Wednesday and Saturday***	
Hang clean	4 × 5[a]	Deadlift	4 × 10	Lunge	3 × 12
Push jerk	4 × 5	Back squat	4 × 10	Vertical chest press	3 × 12
Front squat	3 × 6	Step-up	3 × 10	Leg (knee) curl	2 × 15
Incline bench press	3 × 6	Leg (knee) curl	3 × 10	One-arm dumbbell row	2 × 15
Seated row	2 × 10	Seated calf (heel) raise	3 × 10	Toe raise (dorsiflexion)	2 × 15
Dumbbell alternating curl	2 × 10	***Upper body (Tuesday and Friday)***		Machine back extension	2 × 15
Triceps pushdown	2 × 10	Bench press	4 × 10	Abdominal crunch	3 × 20
Abdominal crunch	3 × 20	Bent-over row	3 × 10		
		Shoulder press	4 × 10	Complete one set of each exercise, then repeat.[b]	
		Barbell biceps curl	3 × 10		
		Shoulder shrug	3 × 10		
		Lying triceps extension	3 × 10		
		Abdominal crunch	3 × 20		
COMMENTS [a]Represented as sets × repetitions here and in scenarios B and C.				**COMMENTS** [b]The eight exercises are performed one set at a time, one immediately after the other (i.e., in a "circuit"). Once two sets/circuits are completed, the athlete performs the final sets of the lunge, vertical chest press, and abdominal crunch exercises in that order.	

STEP 7: REST PERIODS

The time dedicated to recovery between sets and exercises is called the **rest period** or **interset rest**. The length of the rest period between sets and exercises is highly dependent on the goal of training, the relative load lifted, and the athlete's training status (if the athlete is not in good physical condition, rest periods initially may need to be longer than typically assigned).

The amount of rest between sets is strongly related to load; the heavier the loads lifted, the longer the rest periods the athlete will need between sets. For example, training for muscular strength with 4RM loads requires significantly longer rest periods between sets than training for muscular endurance in which lighter 15RM loads are lifted (27, 30, 65, 83, 99, 114). Despite the relationship between training goals and the length of rest periods (e.g., long rest periods for muscular strength training programs), not all exercises in a resistance training program should be assigned the same rest periods. It is important that the strength and conditioning professional allocate rest periods based on the relative load lifted and the amount of muscle mass involved in each exercise. An example of this specificity is for an assistance exercise as part of a muscular strength training program. Whereas a core exercise such as the bench press may involve a 4RM load and a 4-minute rest period, an assistance exercise such as the lateral shoulder raise may be performed with a 12RM load and therefore require only a 1-minute rest period (even though 1-minute rest periods generally apply to a hypertrophy training program). The recommended rest period lengths for strength, power, hypertrophy, and muscular endurance programs are shown in table 15.12.

Strength and Power

Training may enhance an athlete's ability to exercise with less rest (27, 65, 97, 99, 114), but athletes who seek to perform maximal or near-maximal repetitions with a heavy load usually need long rest periods, especially for lower body or all-body structural exercises (111). For example, Robinson and colleagues (87) observed that, in the back squat exercise, 3 minutes of interset rest resulted in greater strength gains than a 30-second rest period. Common guidelines for rest period length are at least 2 minutes (58, 92, 108) or a range of 2 to 5 minutes (60, 63) or 3 to 5 minutes (27, 65, 97, 99, 112, 114). These recovery intervals appear to apply equally to resistance training programs designed to improve maximal strength and those that focus on muscular power (58).

TABLE 15.12

Rest Period Length Assignments Based on the Training Goal

Training goal*	Rest period length
Strength	2-5 minutes
Power: Single-effort event Multiple-effort event	2-5 minutes
Hypertrophy	30 seconds-1.5 minutes
Muscular endurance	≤30 seconds

*Because there are occasions when the prescribed percentage of the 1RM for assistance exercises falls outside the range associated with the training goal (e.g., ≥8RM loads are recommended for assistance exercises as part of a muscular strength training program [6]), the strength and conditioning professional should examine the loads used for each exercise when assigning rest periods rather than generally applying the guidelines for a training goal.

Data from references 27, 60, 63, 65, 97, 99, 112, and 114.

Hypertrophy

Athletes who are interested in gaining muscular size often use a short to moderate interset rest period (27, 30, 58, 60, 83, 99). Some reviews of hypertrophy training programs support a limited rest period because they recommend that the athlete begin the next set before full recovery has been achieved (42, 105). Despite this, the high metabolic demand of exercises involving large muscle groups merits consideration (i.e., extra recovery time) when rest period lengths are being assigned (99). Typical strategies for the length of rest periods are less than 1.5 minutes (58) or a span of 30 seconds to 1 minute (60, 63, 106) or 30 seconds to 1.5 minutes (42, 105).

Muscular Endurance

A muscular endurance training program has very short rest periods, often less than 30 seconds. This restriction of the recovery time is purposeful; only a minimal amount of rest is allowed when light loads are being lifted for many repetitions. This type of program is designed to meet the guideline of the specificity principle for muscular endurance (6). Short rest periods are characteristic of circuit training programs (33, 39) in which it is common to alternate exercises and limit rest period lengths to 30 seconds or less (86, 88, 89).

Application of the Rest Period Guidelines

(Refer to p. 383 for a description of the scenario athletes.)

Scenario A
Female collegiate basketball player
Preseason

Power and core exercises	3 minutes
Assistance exercises	60 seconds-1.5 minutes

Monday, Wednesday, and Friday

Hang clean	3 minutes
Push jerk	3 minutes
Front squat	3 minutes
Incline bench press	3 minutes
Seated row	1.5 minutes[a]
Dumbbell alternating curl	60 seconds[a]
Triceps pushdown	60 seconds[a]
Abdominal crunch	20 seconds[b]

COMMENTS

[a]Despite following a muscular strength training program, the athlete is performing sets of 10 repetitions in this exercise, a volume assignment for hypertrophy training. Therefore, the length of the rest period should be 30 seconds to 1.5 minutes. The rest period for the single-joint exercises is slightly shorter because fewer muscles are involved.

[b]Again, although this athlete is training for muscular strength, she is performing sets of 20 repetitions in this exercise, a volume assignment for muscular endurance. Therefore, the length of the rest period should be ≤30 seconds.

Scenario B
Male professional American football lineman
Off-season

Core exercises	1.5 minutes
Assistance exercises	60 seconds

Lower body (Monday and Thursday)

Deadlift	1.5 minutes
Back squat	1.5 minutes
Step-up	1.5 minutes[c]
Leg (knee) curl	60 seconds
Seated calf (heel) raise	60 seconds

Upper body (Tuesday and Friday)

Bench press	1.5 minutes
Bent-over row	60 seconds
Shoulder press	1.5 minutes
Barbell biceps curl	60 seconds
Shoulder shrug	60 seconds
Lying triceps extension	60 seconds
Abdominal crunch	20 seconds[d]

COMMENTS

[c]This exercise is classified as an assistance exercise and, like the others, could be assigned a 60-second rest period. Despite this, the step-up is a unilateral exercise that requires more time for completion of each set. Therefore, a longer rest period is provided.

[d]Although this athlete is training for hypertrophy, he is performing sets of 20 repetitions in this exercise, a volume assignment for muscular endurance. Therefore, the length of the rest period should be ≤30 seconds.

Scenario C
Male high school cross-country runner
In-season

Core exercises	30 seconds[e]
Assistance exercises	20 seconds[e]

Wednesday and Saturday

Lunge	30 seconds
Vertical chest press	30 seconds
Leg (knee) curl	20 seconds
One-arm dumbbell row	20 seconds
Toe raise (dorsiflexion)	20 seconds
Lateral shoulder raise	20 seconds
Machine back extension	20 seconds
Abdominal crunch	20 seconds

Complete one set of each exercise, then repeat.[f]

COMMENTS

[e]Both of these rest period assignments fall within the guidelines for muscular endurance training. Due to the higher goal repetitions and lighter loads for assistance exercises, the rest period length was slightly shortened.

[f]The eight exercises are performed one set at a time, one immediately after the other (i.e., in a "circuit"). Once two sets/circuits are completed, the athlete performs the final sets of the lunge, vertical chest press, and abdominal crunch exercises in that order.

CONCLUSION

Well-designed programs are based on the application of sound principles during each step of a process referred to as *program design*. The process begins with a needs analysis to determine the specific demands of the sport and the training status of the athlete. With this knowledge, appropriate exercises are selected and training frequency is established. The order of exercises in the workout is considered next, followed by load assignments and training volume choices based on desired training outcomes. Deciding on the length of the rest periods is the last step leading to the design of a sport-specific resistance training program. A composite view that includes all of the program design variables (steps 1-7) for the three scenarios is shown on page 410.

Application of All Program Design Variables (Steps 1-7)

(Refer to p. 383 for a description of the scenario athletes.)

Scenario A
Female collegiate basketball player
Preseason

Monday ("heavy" day)

Exercise	Sets × reps @ load
Hang clean[a]	4 × 5 @ 95 lb (43 kg)
Push jerk[a]	4 × 5 @ 90 lb (41 kg)
Front squat[a]	3 × 6 @ 155 lb (70 kg)
Incline bench press[a]	3 × 6 @ 85 lb (39 kg)
Seated row[b]	2 × 10 @ 90 lb (41 kg)
Dumbbell alternating curl[d]	2 × 10 @ 20 lb (9 kg)
Triceps pushdown[d]	2 × 10 @ 40 lb (18 kg)
Abdominal crunch[c]	3 × 20

Wednesday ("light" day)

80% of Monday's load in power/core exercises

Exercise	Sets × reps @ load
Hang clean[a]	4 × 5 @ 75 lb (34 kg)
Push jerk[a]	4 × 5 @ 70 lb (32 kg)
Front squat[a]	3 × 6 @ 125 lb (57 kg)
Incline bench press[a]	3 × 6 @ 70 lb (32 kg)
Seated row	2 × 10 @ 90 lb (41 kg)
Dumbbell alternating curl[d]	2 × 10 @ 20 lb (9 kg)
Triceps pushdown [d]	2 × 10 @ 40 lb (18 kg)
Abdominal crunch	3 × 20

Friday ("medium" day)

90% of Monday's load in power/core exercises

Exercise	Sets × reps @ load
Hang clean[a]	4 × 5 @ 85 lb (39 kg)
Push jerk[a]	4 × 5 @ 80 lb (36 kg)
Front squat[a]	3 × 6 @ 140 lb (64 kg)
Incline bench[a] press	3 × 6 @ 75 lb (34 kg)
Seated row[b]	2 × 10 @ 90 lb (41 kg)
Dumbbell alternating curl[d]	2 × 10 @ 20 lb (9 kg)
Triceps pushdown[d]	2 × 10 @ 40 lb (18 kg)
Abdominal crunch	3 × 20

Scenario B
Male professional American football lineman
Off-season

Lower body (Monday and Thursday[g])

Exercise	Sets × reps @ load
Deadlift[b]	4 × 10 @ 490 lb (223 kg)
Back squat[b]	4 × 10 @ 505 lb (230 kg)
Step-up[b]	3 × 10 @ 205 lb (93 kg)
Leg (knee) curl[d]	3 × 10 @ 190 lb (86 kg)
Seated calf raise[d]	3 × 10 @ 155 lb (70 kg)

Upper body (Tuesday and Friday[g])

Exercise	Sets × reps @ load
Bench press[b]	4 × 10 @ 320 lb (145 kg)
Bent-over row[d]	3 × 10 @ 215 lb (98 kg)
Shoulder press[b]	4 × 10 @ 190 lb (86 kg)
Barbell biceps curl[d]	3 × 10 @ 115 lb (52 kg)
Shoulder shrug[d]	3 × 10 @ 405 lb (184 kg)
Lying triceps extension[d]	3 × 10 @ 125 lb (57 kg)
Abdominal crunch[c]	3 × 20

Scenario C
Male high school cross-country runner
In-season

Wednesday and Saturday

Exercise	Sets × reps @ load
Lunge[e]	3 × 12 @ 45 lb (20 kg)
Vertical chest press[e]	3 × 12 @ 70 lb (32 kg)
Leg (knee) curl[c]	2 × 15 @ 65 lb (30 kg)
One-arm dumbbell row[c]	2 × 15 @ 25 lb (11 kg)
Toe raise[c]	2 × 15 @ 20 lb (9 kg)
Lateral shoulder raise[c]	2 × 15 @ 10 lb (5 kg)
Machine back extension[c]	2 × 15 @ 50 lb (23 kg)
Abdominal crunch[c]	3 × 20

Complete one set of each exercise, then repeat.[f]

COMMENTS

Rest period lengths:

[a]3 minutes

[b]1.5 minutes

[c]20 seconds

[d]60 seconds

[e]30 seconds

[f]The eight exercises are performed one set at a time, one immediately after the other (i.e., in a "circuit"). Once two sets/circuits are completed, the athlete performs the final sets of the lunge, vertical chest press, and abdominal crunch exercises in that order.

[g]Reduce the loads on Thursday and Friday by 5% to 10%.

KEY TERMS

STUDY QUESTIONS

1. When determining a baseball player's resistance training program needs, all of the following factors should be considered EXCEPT
   a. programs of other players.
   b. past medical history.
   c. training status.
   d. position on the field.

2. The basketball coach says his starting center needs to jump higher. In addition to beginning a plyometric program, which of the following resistance training exercises are MOST specific to this goal?
   I. power clean
   II. leg (knee) curl
   III. front squat
   IV. seated calf (heel) raise

   a. I and III only
   b. II and IV only
   c. I, II, and III only
   d. II, III, and IV only

3. The soccer team is transitioning from off-season to preseason training. How should the team's resistance training frequency be altered?
   a. Increase frequency to improve muscular endurance.
   b. Do not change frequency and add plyometrics.
   c. Decrease frequency to allow increased sport skill practice.
   d. Design a split routine with three days on and one day off.

4. An American football lineman has difficulty driving into defensive linemen and believes he has lost his explosive ability. Which of the following is the BEST exercise order to help this athlete improve his performance?
   a. back squat, hip sled, leg (knee) curl, power clean
   b. power clean, back squat, hip sled, leg (knee) curl
   c. leg (knee) curl, back squat, power clean, hip sled
   d. hip sled, power clean, leg (knee) curl, back squat

5. What percentage of the 1RM typically allows an individual to perform 6 repetitions with that load?
   a. 92
   b. 90
   c. 85
   d. 80

6. Which of the following volumes has the potential to increase muscular strength the MOST?
   a. 5 sets of 5 repetitions
   b. 1 set of 5 repetitions
   c. 5 sets of 15 repetitions
   d. 1 set of 15 repetitions

7. A female triathlete needs to improve the muscular endurance of her upper body. Using 3 sets of 15 repetitions per exercise, which of the following rest period lengths will MAXIMIZE her goal?
   a. 3 minutes
   b. 1.5 minutes
   c. 45 seconds
   d. 30 seconds

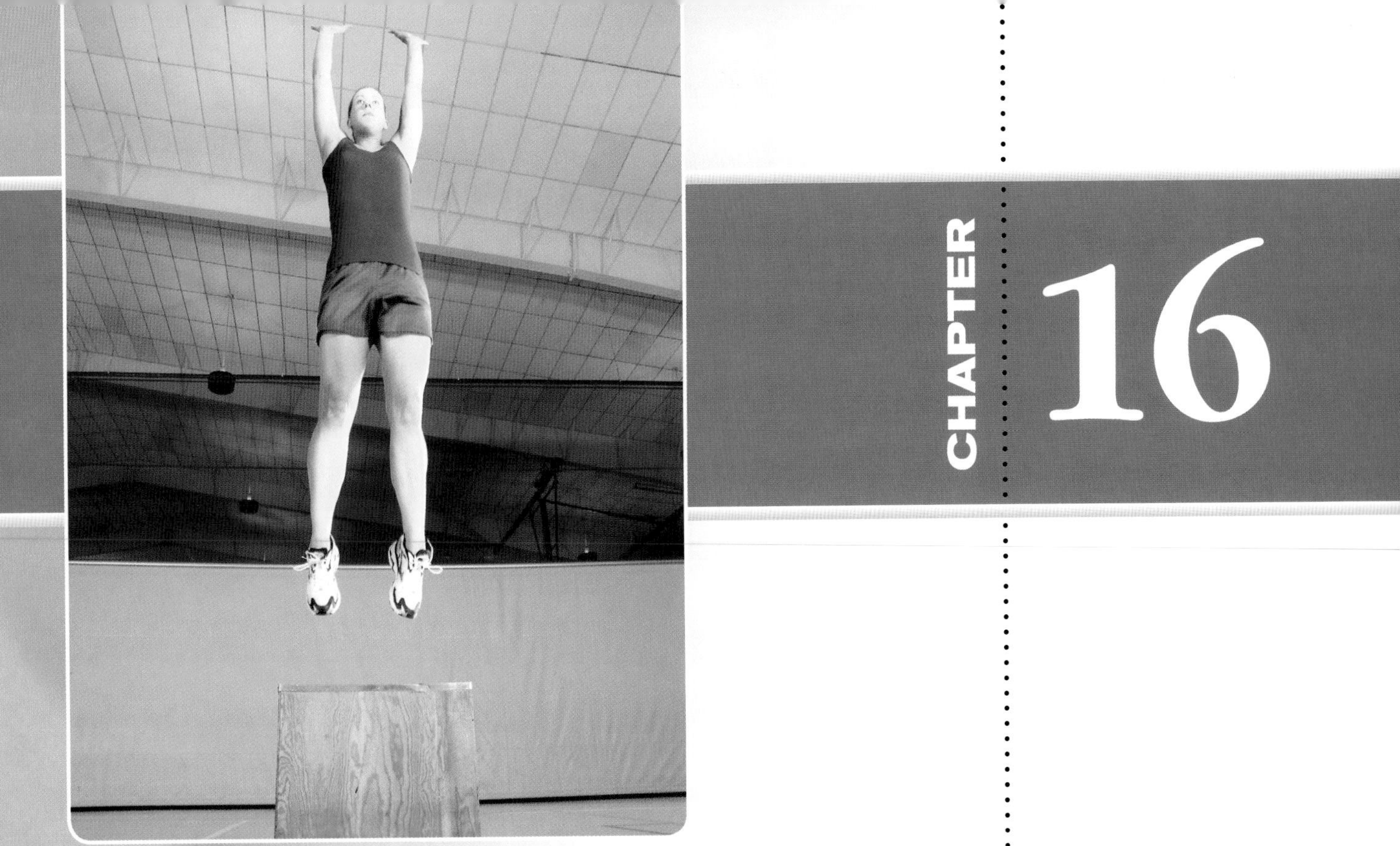

CHAPTER 16

Plyometric Training

David H. Potach, PT, and Donald A. Chu, PhD, PT

After completing this chapter, you will be able to

- explain the physiology of plyometric exercise,
- identify the phases of the stretch-shortening cycle,
- identify the components of a plyometric training program,
- design a safe and effective plyometric training program,
- recommend proper equipment for use during plyometric exercise, and
- teach correct execution of lower and upper body plyometric exercises.

Plyometric exercise refers to those activities that enable a muscle to reach maximal force in the shortest possible time. "Plyometric" is a combination of Greek words that literally means to increase measurement (*plio* = more; *metric* = measure) (55). Practically defined, plyometric exercise is a quick, powerful movement using a prestretch, or countermovement, that involves the **stretch-shortening cycle (SSC)** (52). The purpose of plyometric exercise is to increase the power of subsequent movements by using both the natural elastic components of muscle and tendon and the stretch reflex. To effectively use plyometrics as part of a training program, it is important to understand: (1) the mechanics and physiology of plyometric exercise, (2) principles of plyometric program design, and (3) methods of safely and effectively performing specific plyometric exercises.

PLYOMETRIC MECHANICS AND PHYSIOLOGY

Functional movements and athletic success depend on both the proper function of all active muscles and the speed at which these muscular forces are used. The term used to define this force–speed relationship is **power**. When used correctly, plyometric training has consistently been shown to improve the production of muscle force and power (30, 49). This increased production of power is best explained by two proposed models: mechanical and neurophysiological (52).

Mechanical Model of Plyometric Exercise

In the *mechanical model*, elastic energy in the musculotendinous components is increased with a rapid stretch and then stored (3, 14, 31). When this movement is immediately followed by a concentric muscle action, the stored elastic energy is released, increasing the total force production (3, 14, 31). Hill (31) provides an excellent description (illustrated in figure 16.1) that helps with understanding the behavior of skeletal muscle. Of the mechanical model's many elements, it is the **series elastic component (SEC)** that is the workhorse of plyometric exercise. While the SEC includes some muscular components, it is the tendons that constitute the majority of the SEC. When the musculotendinous unit is stretched, as in an eccentric muscle action, the SEC acts as a spring and is lengthened; as it lengthens, elastic energy is stored. If the muscle begins a concentric action immediately after the eccentric action, the stored energy is released, allowing the SEC to contribute to the total force production by naturally returning the muscles and tendons to their unstretched configuration. If a concentric muscle action does not occur immediately following the eccentric action, or if the eccentric phase is too long or requires too great a motion about the given joint, the stored energy dissipates and is lost as heat.

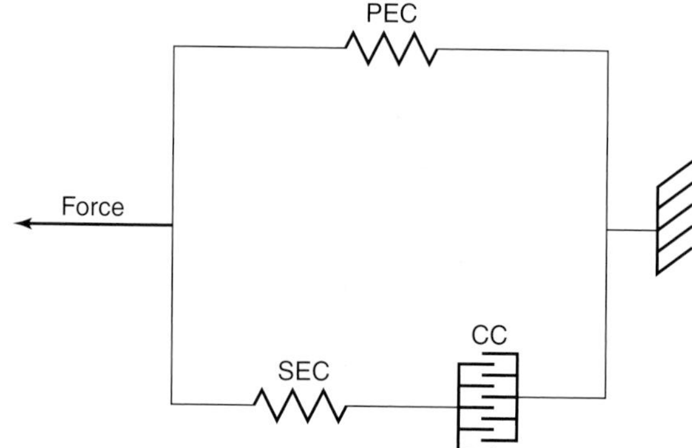

Figure 16.1 Mechanical model of skeletal muscle function. The series elastic component (SEC), when stretched, stores elastic energy that increases the force produced. The contractile component (CC) (i.e., actin, myosin, and cross-bridges) is the primary source of muscle force during concentric muscle action. The parallel elastic component (PEC) (i.e., epimysium, perimysium, endomysium, and sarcolemma) exerts a passive force with unstimulated muscle stretch.

Reprinted, by permission, from Albert, 1995 (1).

Neurophysiological Model of Plyometric Exercise

The neurophysiological model involves the **potentiation** (change in the force–velocity characteristics of the muscle's contractile components caused by stretch [21]) of the concentric muscle action by use of the stretch reflex (figure 16.2) (8, 9, 10, 11). The **stretch reflex** is the body's involuntary response to an external stimulus that stretches the muscles (27, 42). This reflexive component of plyometric exercise is primarily composed of muscle spindle activity. **Muscle spindles** are proprioceptive organs that are sensitive to the rate and magnitude of a stretch; when a quick stretch is detected, muscular activity reflexively increases (27, 42). During plyometric exercises, the muscle spindles are stimulated by a rapid stretch, causing a reflexive muscle action. This reflexive response potentiates, or increases, the activity in the agonist muscle, thereby increasing the force the muscle produces (8, 9, 10, 11, 35). As in the mechanical model, if a concentric muscle action does not immediately follow a stretch (i.e., there is too long a time between stretch and concentric action or movement over too large a range), the potentiating ability of the stretch reflex is negated.

While it is likely that both the mechanical and neurophysiological models contribute to the increased production of force seen during plyometric exercise (3, 8, 9, 10, 11, 14, 31, 35), the degree to which each model contributes remains uncertain. Further research is needed to improve our understanding of both models and their respective roles in plyometric exercise.

Stretch-Shortening Cycle

The SSC employs the energy storage capabilities of the SEC and stimulation of the stretch reflex to facilitate a maximal increase in muscle recruitment over a minimal amount of time. The SSC involves three distinct phases as shown in table 16.1. While the table delineates the SSC's individual mechanical and neurophysiological events during each phase, it is important to remember that all of the events listed do not necessarily occur within the given phase. That is, some of the events may last longer or may require less time than allowed in the given phase. Phase I is the **eccentric phase**, which involves preloading the agonist muscle group(s). During this phase, the SEC stores elastic energy, and the muscle spindles are stimulated. As the muscle spindles are stretched, they send a signal to the ventral root of the spinal cord via the Type Ia afferent nerve fibers (see figure 16.2). To visualize the eccentric phase, consider the long jump. The time from touchdown of the foot to the bottom of the movement is the eccentric phase (figure 16.3*a*).

Phase II is the time between the eccentric and concentric phases and is termed the **amortization**—or transition—**phase**. This is the time from the end of the eccentric phase to the initiation of the concentric muscle action. There is a delay between the eccentric and concentric muscle actions during

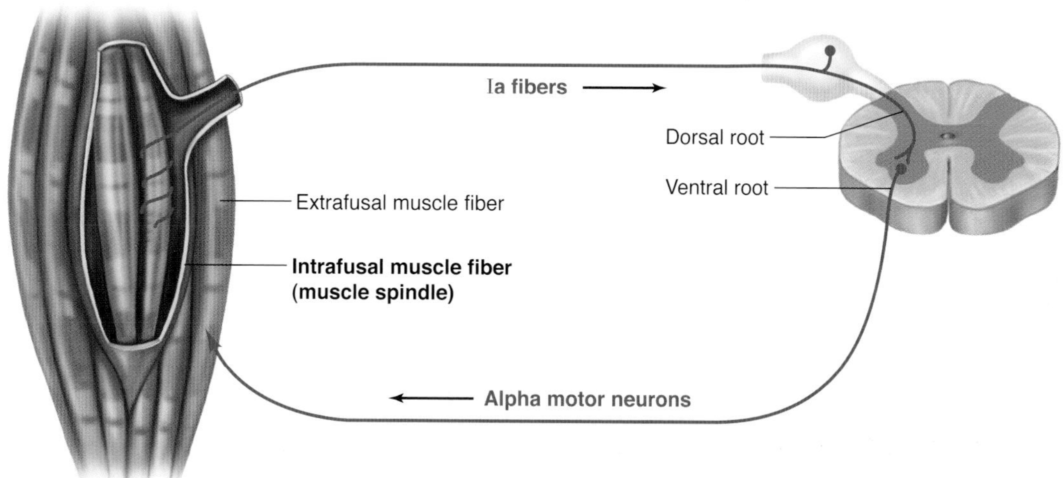

Figure 16.2 Illustration of the stretch reflex. When muscle spindles are stimulated, the stretch reflex is stimulated, sending input to the spinal cord via Type Ia nerve fibers. After synapsing with the alpha motor neurons in the spinal cord, impulses travel to the agonist extrafusal fibers, causing a reflexive muscle action.

Adapted, by permission, from Wilk et al., 1993 (52).

TABLE 16.1

Stretch-Shortening Cycle

Phase	Action	Physiological event
I—Eccentric	Stretch of the agonist muscle	▪ Elastic energy is stored in the series elastic component. ▪ Muscle spindles are stimulated.
II—Amortization	Pause between phases I and III	▪ Type Ia afferent nerves synapse with alpha motor neurons. ▪ Alpha motor neurons transmit signals to agonist muscle group.
III—Concentric	Shortening of agonist muscle fibers	▪ Elastic energy is released from the series elastic component. ▪ Alpha motor neurons stimulate the agonist muscle group.

Figure 16.3 The long jump and stretch-shortening cycle. *(a)* The eccentric phase begins at touchdown and continues until the movement ends. *(b)* The amortization phase is the transition from eccentric to concentric phases; it is quick and without movement. *(c)* The concentric phase follows the amortization phase and comprises the entire push-off time, until the athlete's foot leaves the surface.

which Type Ia afferent nerves synapse with the alpha motor neurons in the ventral root of the spinal cord (see figure 16.2). The alpha motor neurons then transmit signals to the agonist muscle group. This phase of the SSC is perhaps the most crucial in allowing greater power production; its duration must be kept short. If the amortization phase lasts too long, the energy stored during the eccentric phase dissipates as heat, and the stretch reflex will not increase muscle activity during the concentric phase (12). Consider the long jumper mentioned earlier. Once the jumper has touched down and movement has stopped, the amortization phase has begun. As soon as movement begins again, the amortization phase has ended (figure 16.3*b*).

The **concentric phase**, phase III, is the body's response to the eccentric and amortization phases. During this phase, the energy stored in the SEC during the eccentric phase either is used to increase the force of the subsequent movement or is dissipated as heat. This stored elastic energy increases the force produced during the concentric phase movement beyond that of an isolated concentric muscle action (13, 49). In addition, the alpha motor neurons stimulate the agonist muscle group, resulting in a reflexive concentric muscle action (i.e., the stretch reflex). The efficiency of these subsystems is essential to the proper performance of plyometric exercises. Again, visualize the long jumper. As soon as movement begins in an upward direction, the concentric phase of the SSC has begun and the amortization phase has ended (figure 16.3*c*). In this example, one of the agonist muscles is the gastrocnemius. Upon touchdown, the gastrocnemius undergoes a rapid stretch (eccentric phase), there is a delay in movement (amortization phase), and then the muscle concentrically plantarflexes the ankle, allowing the athlete to push off the ground (concentric phase).

The rate of musculotendinous stretch is vital to plyometric exercise (35). A high stretch rate results in greater muscle recruitment and activity during the SSC concentric phase. The importance of the stretch rate may be illustrated by three different vertical jump tests: a static squat jump, a countermovement jump, and an approach jump with several steps. As the rate of stretch increases, an athlete's absolute performance in these tests improves; the static squat jump results in the lowest jump height, and the approach jump in the highest. The static squat jump requires the athlete to get into a squatting position (i.e., 90° hip flexion and 90° knee flexion) followed by a jump up. This jump does not use stored elastic energy and is too slow to allow potentiation from the stretch reflex because there is essentially no eccentric phase. The countermovement jump uses a rapid eccentric element (i.e., partial squat) followed immediately by rapid concentric muscle activity (i.e., jump up). The rapid eccentric phase allows the athlete to store (and use) elastic energy in the stretched musculotendinous unit and stimulates the stretch reflex, thereby potentiating muscle activity (6, 29). The approach jump uses an even quicker, more forceful eccentric phase than the countermovement jump; the increased rate of stretch during the eccentric phase allows a further increase in vertical jump height (4, 5, 7, 25).

The stretch-shortening cycle combines mechanical and neurophysiological mechanisms and is the basis of plyometric exercise. A rapid eccentric muscle action stimulates the stretch reflex and storage of elastic energy, which increase the force produced during the subsequent concentric action.

PLYOMETRIC PROGRAM DESIGN

Plyometric exercise prescription is similar to resistance and aerobic exercise prescriptions—mode, intensity, frequency, duration, recovery, progression, and a warm-up period must all be included in the design of a sound plyometric training program. Unfortunately, there is little research demarcating optimal program variables for the design of plyometric exercise programs. Therefore, when prescribing plyometric exercise, practitioners must rely on the available research, practical experience, and the methodology used for designing resistance and aerobic training programs. The guidelines that follow are largely based on Chu's work (16, 18) and the National Strength and Conditioning Association's position statement (43).

Mode

The mode of plyometric training is determined by the body region performing the given exercise. For example, a single-leg hop is a lower body plyometric exercise, while a two-hand medicine ball throw is an upper body exercise. Modes of plyometric exercise are discussed in the paragraphs that follow.

Lower Body Plyometrics

Lower body plyometrics are appropriate for virtually any athlete and any sport, including track and field throwing and sprinting, soccer, volleyball, basketball, American football, and baseball. These sports require athletes to produce a maximal amount of muscular force in a short amount of time. American football, baseball, and sprinting generally require horizontal or lateral movement during competition, while volleyball involves primarily horizontal and vertical movements. Soccer and basketball players must make quick, powerful movements and changes of direction in all planes to compete successfully. A basketball center is an example of an athlete who would benefit greatly from a plyometric training program, as the center is required to jump repeatedly for rebounds. To be successful, the center must be able to outjump the opposing center in order to rebound more loose balls. Lower body plyometric training allows the player the ability to produce more force in a shorter amount of time, thereby allowing a higher jump.

There are a wide variety of lower body plyometric drills with various intensity levels and directional movements. Types of lower body plyometric drills include **jumps in place**, **standing jumps**, **multiple hops and jumps**, **bounds**, **box drills**, and **depth jumps**. See table 16.2 for descriptions of these drills.

Upper Body Plyometrics

Rapid, powerful upper body movements are requisites for several sports and activities, including baseball, softball, tennis, golf, and throws in track and field (i.e., the shot put, discus, and javelin). As an example, a baseball pitcher routinely throws a baseball at 80 to 100 miles per hour (129-161 km/hour). To reach velocities of this magnitude, the pitcher's shoulder joint must move at more than 6,000°/s (19, 22, 23, 45). Plyometric training of the shoulder joint would not only increase pitching velocity, it may also prevent injury to the shoulder and elbow joints, although further research is needed to substantiate the role of plyometrics in injury prevention.

Plyometric drills for the upper body are not used as often as those for the lower body and have been studied less extensively, but they are nonetheless essential to athletes who require upper body power (44). Plyometrics for the upper body include medicine ball **throws**, catches, and several types of **push-ups**.

Trunk Plyometrics

In general, it is difficult to perform true plyometric drills that directly target trunk musculature because all the requisite plyometric elements may not be present. Plyometric exercise uses stored elastic energy (mechanical model) and potentiates muscle activity through stimulation of the stretch reflex (neurophysiological model). Following the eccentric phase of the SSC, there is likely some storage of elastic energy during "plyometric" trunk drills. However, research supports the notion that the stretch reflex is not sufficiently involved during many trunk exercises to potentiate muscle activity. Stretch reflex latencies (time from reflex stimulation to the beginning of agonist muscle activity) largely depend on nerve conduction velocities and therefore increase with greater distances from the spinal cord (i.e., longer nerves) (34, 36, 38, 46). Quadriceps and gastrocnemius stretch reflexes typically range from 20 to 30 ms and from 30 to 45 ms, respectively (34, 46). Although no research has addressed abdominal stretch reflexes, it may be assumed that

TABLE 16.2

Lower Body Plyometric Drills

Type of drill	Rationale
Jumps in place	These drills involve jumping and landing in the same spot. Jumps in place emphasize the vertical component of jumping and are performed repeatedly, without rest between jumps; the time between jumps is the stretch-shortening cycle's amortization phase. Examples of jumps in place include the squat jump and tuck jump.
Standing jumps	These emphasize either horizontal or vertical components. Standing jumps are maximal efforts with recovery between repetitions. The vertical jump and jumps over barriers are examples of standing jumps.
Multiple hops and jumps	Multiple hops and jumps involve repeated movement and may be viewed as a combination of jumps in place and standing jumps. One example of a multiple jump is the zigzag hop.
Bounds	Bounding drills involve exaggerated movements with greater horizontal speed than other drills. Volume for bounding is typically measured by distance but may be measured by the number of repetitions performed. Bounding drills normally cover distances greater than 98 feet (30 m) and may include single- and double-leg bounds in addition to the alternate-leg bounds illustrated in this chapter.
Box drills	These drills increase the intensity of multiple hops and jumps by using a box. The box may be used to jump on or off. The height of the box depends on the size of the athlete, the landing surface, and the goals of the program. Box drills may involve one, both, or alternating legs.
Depth jumps	Depth jumps use gravity and the athlete's weight to increase exercise intensity. The athlete assumes a position on a box, steps off, lands, and immediately jumps vertically, horizontally, or to another box. The height of the box depends on the size of the athlete, the landing surface, and the goals of the program. Depth jumps may involve one or both legs.

the latencies are shorter, as the muscles are closer to the spinal cord.

Exercises for the trunk may be performed "plyometrically" provided that movement modifications are made. Specifically, the exercise movements must be shorter and quicker to allow stimulation and use of the stretch reflex. Figure 16.4 depicts a typical medicine ball sit-up. Its relatively large range of motion and the time needed to complete the movement do not permit reflexive potentiation of the abdominal muscles. The exercise can be modified to decrease both the range of motion and time, thereby allowing the agonist muscles to be potentiated (figure 16.5) and making the exercise more like a plyometric exercise.

Intensity

Plyometric intensity refers to the amount of stress placed on involved muscles, connective tissues, and joints and is controlled primarily by the type of drill performed. The intensity of plyometric drills covers a large range; skipping is relatively low in intensity, while depth jumps place high stress on the muscles and joints. In addition to the type of drill, several other factors also affect plyometric intensity (table 16.3). Generally, as intensity increases, volume should decrease (48). Because the intensity of plyometric exercise can vary significantly, careful consideration must be given to choosing proper drills during a specific training cycle.

Figure 16.4 Medicine ball sit-up. The large range of motion and time needed to complete this exercise negate abdominal muscle potentiation by the stretch reflex.

Figure 16.5 Plyometric sit-up. The relatively small range of motion and quick movement in this exercise may increase abdominal muscle activity through use of the stretch reflex.

TABLE 16.3

Factors Affecting the Intensity of Lower Body Plyometric Drills

Factor	Effect
Points of contact	The ground reaction force during single-leg lower body plyometric drills places more stress on an extremity's muscles, connective tissues, and joints than during double-leg plyometric drills.
Speed	Greater speed increases the intensity of the drill.
Height of the drill	The higher the body's center of gravity, the greater the force on landing.
Body weight	The greater the athlete's body weight, the more stress is placed on muscles, connective tissues, and joints. External weight (in the form of weight vests, ankle weights, and wrist weights) can be added to the body to increase a drill's intensity.

Frequency

Frequency is the number of plyometric training sessions per week and typically ranges from one to three, depending on the sport and the time of year. As with other program variables, research is limited on the optimal frequency for training plyometrically. Because the literature is sparse, strength and conditioning professionals often rely on practical experience when determining the frequency with which athletes train with plyometric exercise. Rather than concentrating on the frequency, many authors suggest relying more on the recovery time between plyometric training sessions (16). Forty-eight to 72 hours between plyometric sessions is a typical recovery time guideline for prescribing plyometrics (16); using these typical recovery times, athletes commonly perform two to four plyometric sessions per week.

As previously mentioned, plyometric frequency may vary depending on the demands of the given sport, intensity and volume of daily workouts (e.g., practice, resistance training, running, and plyometrics), and time of the training cycle. For example, during the season, one session per week is appropriate for American football players, while two or three sessions per week are common for track and field athletes (2). During the off-season, plyometric training frequency may increase to two or three sessions per week for American football players and to three to four sessions per week for track and field athletes (2). Because research thus far is unfortunately insufficient to provide appropriate guidelines for plyometric training frequency, the use of proper recovery times between sessions and practical experience may be the best determinants of frequency.

Recovery

Because plyometric drills involve maximal efforts to improve anaerobic power, complete and adequate recovery (the time between repetitions, sets, and workouts) is required (43). Recovery for depth jumps may consist of 5 to 10 seconds of rest between repetitions and 2 to 3 minutes between sets. The time between sets is determined by a proper work-to-rest ratio (i.e., 1:5 to 1:10) and is specific to the volume and type of drill being performed. Drills should not be thought of as cardiorespiratory conditioning exercises but as power training. As with resistance training, recovery between workouts must be adequate to prevent overtraining (two to four days of recovery, depending on the sport and time of year). Furthermore, drills for a given body area should not be performed two days in succession (43). Although new research tangentially addresses recovery and training frequency (46), manipulation of recovery time between repetitions, exercises, and workouts has yet to be adequately explored in plyometric research; further work must be done in this area to provide more concrete times for recovery.

Volume

Plyometric volume is typically expressed as the number of repetitions and sets performed during a given training session. Lower body plyometric volume is normally given as the number of foot contacts (each time a foot, or the feet together, contact the surface) per workout (2, 16) but may also be expressed as distance, as with plyometric bounding. For example, an athlete beginning a plyometric training program may start with a single-leg bound for 98 feet (30 m) per repetition but may progress to 328 feet (100 m) per repetition for the same drill. Recommended lower body plyometric volumes vary for athletes of different levels of experience; suggested volumes are provided in table 16.4. Upper body plyometric volume is typically expressed as the number of throws or catches per workout.

Program Length

Research has yet to determine an optimal plyometric training program length. Currently, most programs range from 6 to 10 weeks (2, 30); however, vertical jump height improves as quickly as four weeks after the start of a plyometric training program (46). In general, plyometric training should be prescribed similarly to both resistance and aerobic training. For those sports requiring quick, powerful movements, it is beneficial to perform plyometric exercise throughout the training cycle (macrocycle). The intensity and volume of the chosen drills should vary with the sport and the season (i.e., off-season, preseason, or in-season).

Progression

Plyometrics is a form of resistance training and thus must follow the principles of progressive overload. *Progressive overload* is the systematic increase in training frequency, volume, and intensity in various combinations. Typically, as intensity increases, volume decreases. The sport, training phase, and design of the strength and conditioning program (resistance training, running, plyometrics, and time of year) determine the training schedule and method of progressive overload. An off-season plyometric program for American football, for example, may be performed twice a week. The program's intensity should progress from low to moderate volumes of low-intensity plyometrics, to low to moderate volumes of moderate intensity, to low to moderate volumes of moderate to high intensity.

Warm-Up

As in any training program, the plyometric exercise session must begin with a general warm-up, stretching, and a specific warm-up (refer to chapter 13 for a discussion of warming up). The specific warm-up for plyometric training should consist of low-intensity, dynamic movements. Refer to table 16.5 for a list and explanation of types of specific warm-up drills.

Effective plyometric programs include the same variables that are essential to any training program design: mode, intensity, frequency, recovery, volume, program length, progression, and warm-up.

TABLE 16.4

Appropriate Plyometric Volumes

Plyometric experience	Beginning volume*
Beginner (no experience)	80 to 100
Intermediate (some experience)	100 to 120
Advanced (considerable experience)	120 to 140

*Volume is given in contacts per session.

TABLE 16.5

Plyometric Warm-Up Drills

Drill	Explanation
Marching	Mimics running movements Emphasizes posture and movement technique Enhances proper lower body movements for running
Jogging	Prepares for impact and high-intensity plyometric drills ▪ Toe jogging—not allowing heel to touch the ground (emphasizes quick reaction) ▪ Straight-leg jogging—not allowing or minimizing leg flexion in preparation for impact of plyometric drills ▪ "Butt-kickers"—flexing knee to allow heel to touch the buttocks
Skipping	Exaggerated form of reciprocal upper and lower extremity movements Emphasis on quick takeoff and landing, mimics plyometric activities
Footwork	Drills that target changes of direction Preparation for changes of direction during plyometric drills Examples: shuttle, shuffle, pattern, and stride drills
Lunging	Based on the forward step lunge exercise (see pp. 354-355) May be multidirectional (e.g., forward, side, backward)

AGE CONSIDERATIONS

It is becoming more common for younger and older individuals to want to augment the training programs for their sport with plyometric exercise. When these exercises are applied appropriately, these populations can experience the same positive outcomes with minimal risk of injury.

Adolescents

Although plyometrics have commonly been viewed as appropriate only for conditioning elite adult athletes, prepubescent and adolescent children may also benefit from training with plyometric and plyometric-like exercises. Besides providing the well-documented muscular power and bone strength adaptations, regular participation in an appropriately designed plyometric training program can better prepare young athletes for the demands of sport practice and competition (17) by enhancing neuromuscular control and performance. Research has yet to determine a universal age at which people are physically able to begin participating in a plyometric training program. An analysis of the body's development provides some insight into the issue. Because the epiphyseal plates of the bones of prepubescent children have yet to close (33, 40), depth jumps and other high-intensity lower body drills are contraindicated (2, 32, 39). While the growth plates are open, highly intense activity and injury may cause them to close prematurely, resulting in limb length discrepancies (32). Further, and as with all forms of exercise, boys and girls should have the emotional maturity to accept and follow directions and should be able to appreciate the benefits and concerns associated with this method of training. Empirically, 7- and 8-year-olds have been trained in progressive plyometric programs, and they continue to lead active lives as teenagers and adults (17).

Plyometric exercise programs for children should be used to develop the neuromuscular control and the anaerobic skills that will carry over to participation in sport and athletics, both during childhood and as they advance to higher levels of competition. For these reasons, it is extremely important to gradually progress from relatively simple to more complex drills. It is important to focus on the quality of the movements (e.g., proper body alignment and speed of movement) to develop techniques that will be essential for more advanced exercises.

As with adults, recovery between workouts must be adequate to prevent overtraining. While the optimal amount of recovery needed between plyometric workouts is unknown, it should vary based on the intensity of the training program and the athlete's skills, abilities, and tolerances as well as on the time of year (i.e., off-season, preseason, or in-season). Therefore, a minimum of two to three days between plyometric workouts should be considered essential to optimize adaptations to the training program and minimize the athlete's risk of injury (17).

Under proper supervision and with an appropriate program, prepubescent and adolescent children may perform plyometric exercises. Depth jumps and high-intensity lower body plyometrics are contraindicated for this population.

Masters

Masters athletes are finding that they can maintain their physical capabilities late into life and are looking for additional training insights. When designing a plyometric training program for a masters athlete, the strength and conditioning professional needs to be specific in deciding on the goal or goals of the program. Some primary issues to consider are any preexisting orthopedic conditions (such as osteoarthritis or any sort of surgical joint intervention) or joint degeneration. These call for even greater caution and a more careful use of plyometric exercise. For example, a healthy masters athlete without surgical history who wants to improve his or her running performance should use depth jumps and single-leg exercises cautiously, so alternate-leg bounding and the double-leg hop would be better choices. Similarly, a masters runner with a history of knee surgery such as partial meniscus removal, or with significant joint degeneration, should consider depth jumps and single-leg plyometric exercises contraindicated and should use other forms of plyometrics cautiously.

After consideration of the predispositions of the masters athlete's physical condition, a plyometric program should be designed according to the same guidelines as outlined for adult athletes, with the following changes. The plyometric program should include no more than five low- to moderate-intensity exercises; the volume should be lower, that is, should include fewer total foot contacts than a standard plyometric training program; and the recovery time between plyometric workouts should be three to four days. With these guidelines in place—and as with all athletes—it is important to note how the masters athlete feels after training and recovery. Soreness may occur, but the program should be modified if chronic or excessive pain or discomfort is present.

TABLE 16.6

Sample Schedule for Integrating Resistance Training and Plyometrics

Day	Resistance training	Plyometrics
Monday	High-intensity upper body	Low-intensity lower body
Tuesday	Low-intensity lower body	High-intensity upper body
Thursday	Low-intensity upper body	High-intensity lower body
Friday	High-intensity lower body	Low-intensity upper body

PLYOMETRICS AND OTHER FORMS OF EXERCISE

Plyometric exercise is only one part of an athlete's overall training program. Many sports and activities use multiple energy systems or require other forms of exercise to properly prepare athletes for competition. Each energy system and sport-specific need must be included in a well-designed training program.

Plyometric Exercise and Resistance Training

A combination of plyometrics and resistance training during a training cycle should be structured to allow maximal efficiency and physical improvement. The following list and table 16.6 provide guidelines for developing a combined program:

- Combine lower body resistance training with upper body plyometrics, and upper body resistance training with lower body plyometrics.
- Performing heavy resistance training and plyometrics on the same day is not usually recommended (15, 20). However, some athletes may benefit from **complex training**, a combination of high-intensity resistance training followed by plyometrics. If athletes perform this type of training, adequate recovery is needed between plyometrics and other high-intensity training.
- Traditional resistance training exercises may be combined with plyometric movements to further enhance gains in muscular power (53, 54). For example, performing a squat jump with approximately 30% of one's squat 1-repetition maximum (1RM) as an external resistance further increases performance (53, 54). This is an advanced form of complex training that is appropriate only for athletes who have previously participated in high-intensity plyometric training programs.

Plyometric and Aerobic Exercise

Many sports—such as basketball and soccer—have both an anaerobic (i.e., power) and an aerobic component. Therefore, multiple types of training must be combined to best prepare athletes for these types of sports. Because aerobic exercise may have a negative effect on power production (15), it is advisable to perform plyometric exercise before aerobic endurance training. The design variables do not change and should complement each other to most effectively train these athletes for competition.

SAFETY CONSIDERATIONS

Plyometric exercise is not inherently dangerous; however, as with all modes of exercise, the risk of injury exists. Injuries can occur simply due to an accident, but they more typically occur when proper training procedures are violated and may be the result of an insufficient strength and conditioning base, inadequate warm-up, improper progression of lead-up drills, inappropriate volume or intensity for the phase of training, poor shoes or surface, or a simple lack of skill. The following sections identify and address these and other risk factors. Knowledge of risk factors can improve the safety of athletes performing plyometric exercise.

Pretraining Evaluation of the Athlete

To reduce the risk of injury and facilitate the performance of plyometric exercises, the athlete must understand proper plyometric technique and possess a sufficient base of strength, speed, and balance. In addition, the athlete must be sufficiently mature, both physically and psychologically, to participate in a plyometric training program. The following evaluative items can help determine whether an athlete meets these conditions.

Technique

Before adding any drill to an athlete's plyometric program, the strength and conditioning professional must demonstrate proper technique to the athlete in order to maximize the drill's effectiveness and minimize the risk of injury. For lower body plyometrics, proper landing technique is essential, particularly for depth jumps. If the center of gravity is offset from the base of support, performance is hindered and injury may occur. The shoulders should be over the knees during the landing, which the jumper accomplishes through flexion of the ankles, knees, and hips (figure 16.6).

Strength

Consideration of the athlete's level of strength is necessary before he or she performs plyometrics.

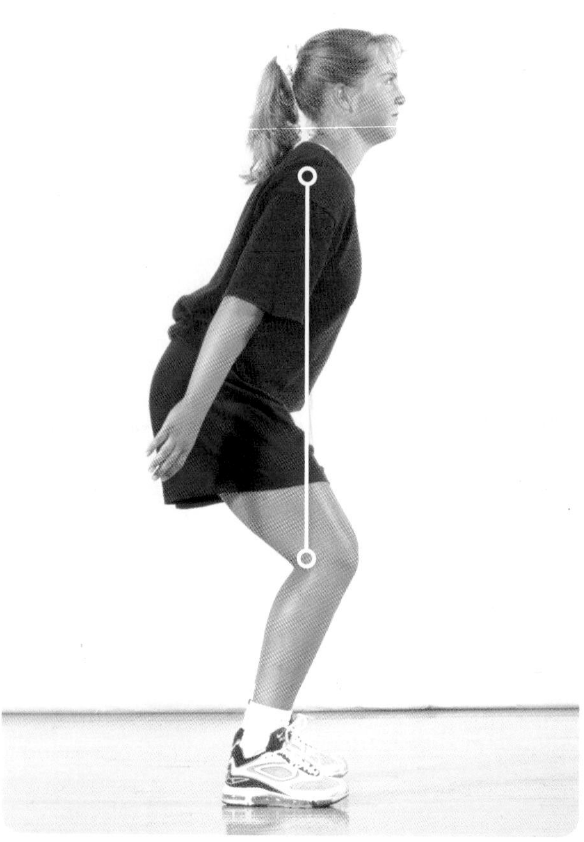

Figure 16.6 Proper plyometric landing position. The shoulders are in line with the knees, which helps to place the center of gravity over the body's base of support.

For lower body plyometrics, the athlete's 1RM squat should be at least 1.5 times his or her body weight (15, 20, 32, 43, 51). For upper body plyometrics, the bench press 1RM should be at least the athlete's body weight for larger athletes (those weighing over 220 pounds, or 100 kg) and at least 1.5 times the body weight for smaller athletes (those weighing less than 220 pounds) (32, 51). An alternative measure of prerequisite upper body strength is the ability to perform five clap push-ups in a row (51). These should be considered minimal standards for performing high-intensity plyometrics. For athletes who do not possess sufficient muscular strength or a sufficient fitness level, plyometrics should be delayed until they meet minimum standards.

Speed

Because plyometric exercise involves quick movements, the ability to move rapidly is essential before one begins a plyometric program. For lower body plyometrics, the athlete should be able to perform five repetitions of the squat with 60% body weight in 5 seconds or less (51). To meet this speed prerequisite, participation in sprint training and speed-specific resistance training programs is helpful. To satisfy the speed requirement for upper body plyometrics, the athlete should be able to perform five repetitions of the bench press with 60% body weight in 5 seconds or less.

Balance

A less obvious lower body plyometric requirement is balance. **Balance** is the maintenance of a position without moving for a given period of time. Many lower body plyometric drills require the athlete to move in nontraditional patterns (e.g., double-leg zigzag hop and backward skip) or on a single leg (e.g., single-leg tuck jump and single-leg hop). These types of drills necessitate a solid, stable base of support upon which the athlete can safely and correctly perform the exercises. Three balance tests are provided in table 16.7, listed in order of difficulty; each test position must be held for 30 seconds (50). For example, an athlete beginning plyometric training for the first time would be required to stand on one leg for 30 seconds without falling. An experienced athlete beginning an advanced plyometric training program must maintain a single-leg half squat for 30 seconds without falling. The surface on which the balance testing is performed must be the same as that used in the plyometric drills.

TABLE 16.7

Balance Tests

Test	Variations
Standing	Double leg
	Single leg
Quarter squat	Double leg
	Single leg
Half squat	Double leg
	Single leg

Physical Characteristics

Athletes who weigh more than 220 pounds (100 kg) may be at an increased risk for injury when performing plyometric exercises (43, 51). Greater weight increases the compressive force on joints during the exercises, thereby predisposing these joints to injury. Therefore, athletes weighing over 220 pounds (100 kg) should avoid high-volume, high-intensity plyometric exercises. Further, athletes weighing over 220 pounds should not perform depth jumps from heights greater than 18 inches (46 cm) (43, 51). As with other forms of exercise, an athlete's joint structure and previous injuries must also be examined before he or she begins a plyometric training program. Previous injuries or abnormalities of the spine, lower extremities, or upper extremities may increase an athlete's risk of injury during plyometric exercise. Specifically, athletes with a history of muscle strains, pathological joint laxity, or spinal dysfunction—including vertebral disk dysfunction or compression—should use caution when beginning a plyometric training program (24, 25, 32, 47).

Equipment and Facilities

In addition to participants' fitness and health, the area and equipment used for plyometric drills may significantly affect their safety.

Landing Surface

To prevent injuries, the landing surface used for lower body plyometrics must possess adequate shock-absorbing properties. A grass field, suspended floor, or rubber mat is a good surface choice (32). Surfaces such as concrete, tile, and hardwood are not recommended because they lack effective shock-absorbing properties (32). Excessively thick exercise mats (6 inches [15 cm] or thicker) may extend the amortization phase and thus not allow efficient use of the stretch reflex. Mini-trampolines are commonly used for beginning plyometric and balance training in rehabilitation (28). While these devices may provide a necessary introduction to plyometrics, especially for those recovering from musculoskeletal injury, mini-trampolines, like thick exercise mats, are not effective for plyometric training of uninjured athletes because the amortization phase is extended while the athlete is in contact with the elastic surface.

Training Area

The amount of space needed depends on the drill. Most bounding and running drills require at least 30 m (33 yards) of straightaway, though some drills may require a straightaway of 100 m (109 yards). For most standing, box, and depth jumps, only a minimal surface area is needed, but the ceiling height must be 3 to 4 m (9.8-13.1 feet) in order to be adequate.

Equipment

Boxes used for box jumps and depth jumps must be sturdy and should have a nonslip top. Boxes should range in height from 6 to 42 inches (15 to 107 cm) and should have landing surfaces of at least 18 by 24 inches (46 by 61 cm) (16). The box should be constructed of sturdy wood (e.g., 3/4-inch [1.9 cm] plywood) or heavy-gauge metal. To further reduce injury risk, there are several ways of making the landing surface nonslip: adding nonslip treads, mixing sand into the paint used to cover the box, or affixing rubberized flooring to the top (16).

Proper Footwear

Participants must use footwear with good ankle and foot support; good lateral stability; and a wide, nonslip sole (43). Shoes with a narrow sole and poor upper support (e.g., running shoes) may invite ankle problems, especially with lateral movements. Shoes with insufficient foot support may lead to arch and/or lower leg injuries, while footwear without enough cushioning might lead to damage of more proximal joints (e.g., knee and hip joints).

Supervision

In addition to the safety considerations already outlined, close monitoring of athletes is necessary to ensure proper technique. Plyometric exercise is not intrinsically dangerous when performed correctly; but as with other forms of training, poor technique may unnecessarily predispose an athlete to injury.

Depth Jumping

There is a limit to the maximal height at which a depth jump can be effectively and safely performed. A height of 48 inches (1.2 m) would provide a significant overload on the muscles, but the resistance may be too great for many athletes to overcome while maintaining correct technique (40). Jumping from such a height increases the possibility of injury; furthermore, the amount of force to be overcome is so great that the amortization phase is extended and thus the purpose of the exercise defeated. The recommended height for depth jumps ranges from 16 to 42 inches (41 to 107 cm), with 30 to 32 inches (76 to 81 cm) being the norm (4, 18, 26, 37, 38, 41). Depth jump box height for athletes who weigh over 220 pounds (100 kg) should be 18 inches (46 cm) or less.

What Are the Steps for Implementing a Plyometric Program?

1. Evaluate the athlete.
2. Ensure that facilities and equipment are safe.
3. Establish sport-specific goals.
4. Determine program design variables.
5. Teach the athlete proper technique.
6. Properly progress the program.

CONCLUSION

The major goal of plyometric training is to rapidly apply force to provide an overload to the agonist muscles. Although it has been repeatedly shown that plyometric exercise increases muscular power for participants in a formal training program (30, 46, 53, 54), research has yet to determine whether mechanical or neurophysiological adaptations account for the improvement. Plyometrics should be considered not an end in itself, but part of an overall program that includes strength, speed, aerobic and flexibility training, and proper nutrition. After the athlete has begun a proper strength and conditioning program, plyometric training may be used to further develop power.

PLYOMETRIC DRILLS

Lower Body Plyometric Drills

JUMPS IN PLACE

STANDING JUMPS

MULTIPLE HOPS AND JUMPS

BOUNDS

BOX DRILLS

DEPTH JUMPS

Upper Body Plyometric Drills

THROWS

PLYOMETRIC PUSH-UPS

Trunk Plyometrics

Jumps in Place

TWO-FOOT ANKLE HOP

Intensity level: Low

Direction of jump: Vertical

Starting position: Get into a comfortable, upright stance with feet shoulder-width apart.

Arm action: None or double arm

Preparatory movement: Begin with a slight countermovement.

Upward movement: Hop up, with primary motion at the ankle joint.

Downward movement: Land in the starting position and immediately repeat hop.

Note: This drill should be performed with little horizontal (forward or backward) or lateral movement.

SQUAT JUMP

Intensity level: Low

Direction of jump: Vertical

Starting position: Get into a squat position (thighs slightly above parallel with the ground) with feet shoulder-width apart. Interlock fingers and place hands behind head.

Arm action: None

Preparatory movement: None

Upward movement: Explosively jump up to a maximum height.

Downward movement: Land in the squat position and immediately repeat the jump.

JUMP AND REACH

Intensity level: Low

Direction of jump: Vertical

Starting position: Get into a comfortable, upright stance with feet shoulder-width apart.

Arm action: Double arm with reach at top of jump

Preparatory movement: Begin with a countermovement.

Upward movement: Explosively jump up and reach for an object or target.

Downward movement: Land in starting position and immediately repeat jump.

Note: Emphasis is on vertical height with minimal delay between jumps.

Note: This drill should be performed with little horizontal (forward or backward) or lateral movement.

DOUBLE-LEG TUCK JUMP

Intensity level: Medium

Direction of jump: Vertical

Starting position: Get into a comfortable, upright stance with feet shoulder-width apart.

Arm action: Double arm

Preparatory movement: Begin with a countermovement.

Upward movement: Explosively jump up. Pull the knees to the chest, quickly grasp the knees with both hands, and release before landing.

Downward movement: Land in the starting position and immediately repeat the jump.

SPLIT SQUAT JUMP

Intensity level: Medium

Direction of jump: Vertical

Starting position: Get into a lunge position with one leg forward (hip and knee joints flexed approximately 90°) and the other behind the midline of the body.

Arm action: Double arm or none

Preparatory movement: Begin with a countermovement.

Upward movement: Explosively jump up, using the arms to assist as needed. Maximum height and power should be emphasized.

Downward movement: When landing, maintain the lunge position (same leg forward) and immediately repeat the jump.

Note: After completing a set, rest and switch front legs.

CYCLED SPLIT SQUAT JUMP

Intensity level: High

Direction of jump: Vertical

Starting position: Get into a lunge position with one leg forward (hip and knee joints flexed approximately 90°) and the other behind the midline of the body.

Arm action: Double arm or none

Preparatory movement: Begin with a countermovement.

Upward movement: Explosively jump up, using the arms to assist as needed. While off the ground, switch the position of the legs. Maximum height and power should be emphasized.

Downward movement: When landing, maintain the lunge position (opposite leg forward) and immediately repeat the jump.

Note: Be sure the lunge is not too deep (as in the far right photo), as the SSC may not be able to effectively contribute to subsequent jumps.

SINGLE-LEG TUCK JUMP

Intensity level: High

Direction of jump: Vertical

Starting position: Get into a comfortable, upright stance on one foot. The nonjumping leg is held in a stationary position with the knee flexed during the exercise.

Arm action: Double arm

Preparatory movement: Begin with a countermovement.

Upward movement: Explosively jump up. Pull the knee of the jumping leg to the chest, grasp the knee with both hands, and release before landing.

Downward movement: Land in the starting position and immediately repeat the jump using the same leg.

Repeat with the opposite leg after a brief rest.

PIKE JUMP

Intensity level: High

Direction of jump: Vertical

Starting position: Get into a comfortable, upright stance with feet shoulder-width apart.

Arm action: Double arm

Preparatory movement: Begin with a countermovement.

Upward movement: Explosively jump up. Keeping the legs straight and together, try to lift them to the front and try to touch the toes with the hands.

Downward movement: Land in the starting position and immediately repeat the jump.

DOUBLE-LEG VERTICAL JUMP

Intensity level: Low

Direction of jump: Vertical

Starting position: Get into a comfortable, upright stance with feet shoulder-width apart.

Arm action: Double arm

Preparatory movement: Begin with a countermovement.

Upward movement: Explosively jump up, using both arms to assist, and reach for a target.

Downward movement: Land in the starting position and repeat the jump. Allow recovery time between jumps.

JUMP OVER BARRIER

Intensity level: Medium

Direction of jump: Horizontal and vertical

Equipment: A barrier such as a cone or hurdle

Starting position: Get into a comfortable, upright stance with feet shoulder-width apart.

Arm action: Double arm

Preparatory movement: Begin with a countermovement.

Upward movement: Jump over a barrier with both legs, using primarily hip and knee flexion to clear the barrier. Keep the knees and feet together without lateral deviation.

Downward movement: Land in the starting position and repeat the jump. Allow recovery time between jumps.

Note: The height of the barrier should be progressively increased (e.g., from a cone to a hurdle).

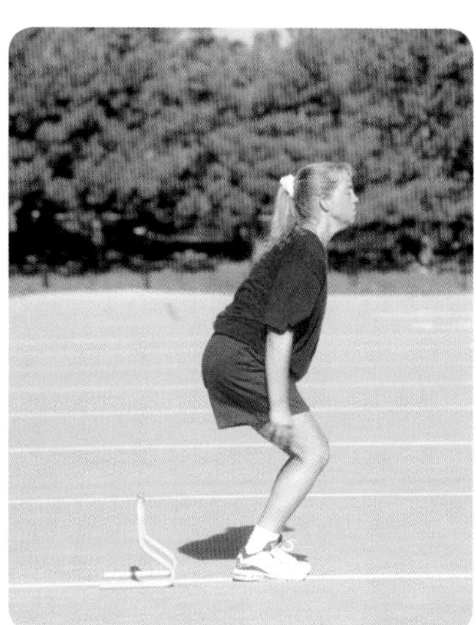

SINGLE-LEG VERTICAL JUMP

Intensity level: High

Direction of jump: Vertical

Starting position: Get into a comfortable, upright stance on one foot. The nonjumping leg is held in a stationary position with the knee flexed during the exercise.

Arm action: Double arm

Preparatory movement: Begin with a countermovement.

Upward movement: Explosively jump up, using both arms to assist, and reach for a target.

Downward movement: Land in the starting position and repeat the jump using the same leg. Allow recovery time between jumps.

Repeat with the opposite leg after a brief rest.

DOUBLE-LEG HOP

Intensity level: Medium

Direction of jump: Horizontal and vertical

Starting position: Get into a comfortable, upright stance with feet shoulder-width apart.

Arm action: Double arm

Preparatory movement: Begin with a countermovement.

Upward movement: Jump as far forward as possible.

Downward movement: Land in the starting position and immediately repeat the hop.

DOUBLE-LEG ZIGZAG HOP

Intensity level: High

Direction of jump: Diagonal

Equipment: Place about 10 hurdles 18 to 24 inches (45-60 cm) apart in a zigzag pattern.

Starting position: Get into a comfortable, upright stance with feet shoulder-width apart. Stand on the outside of the first hurdle. Elbows should be flexed at 90° and held at the sides of the body.

Arm action: Double arm

Preparatory movement: Begin with a countermovement.

Upward movement: Jump from the outside of the first hurdle to the outside of the second hurdle, keeping the shoulders perpendicular to an imaginary line through the center of all hurdles.

Downward movement: Immediately upon landing on the outside of the second hurdle, change direction and jump diagonally over the second hurdle to the outside of the third hurdle.

Continue hopping over all the hurdles.

Note: For a less intense version of this drill, set the hurdles in a straight line and hop over one hurdle at a time. Intensity of the zigzag hop can be increased by performing the hops with one leg only.

SINGLE-LEG HOP

Intensity level: High

Direction of jump: Horizontal and vertical

Starting position: Get into a comfortable, upright stance on one foot. The nonjumping leg is held in a stationary position with the knee flexed during the exercise.

Arm action: Double arm

Preparatory movement: Begin with a countermovement.

Upward movement: Explosively jump forward, using both arms to assist.

Downward movement: Land in the starting position and immediately repeat the hop using the same leg.

Repeat with the opposite leg after a brief rest.

FRONT BARRIER HOP

Intensity level: Medium

Direction of jump: Horizontal and vertical

Equipment: Two barriers such as two cones or two hurdles

Starting position: Facing the first barrier, get into a comfortable, upright stance with feet shoulder-width apart.

Arm action: Double arm

Preparatory movement: Begin with a countermovement.

Upward movement: Jump over the first barrier with both legs, using primarily hip and knee flexion to clear the barrier. Keep the knees and feet together without lateral deviation.

Downward movement: Land in the starting position and immediately repeat the jump over a second barrier.

Note: Intensity level of the front barrier hop can be increased from medium to high by progressively increasing the height of the barrier (e.g., from a cone to a hurdle) or by performing the hops with one leg only.

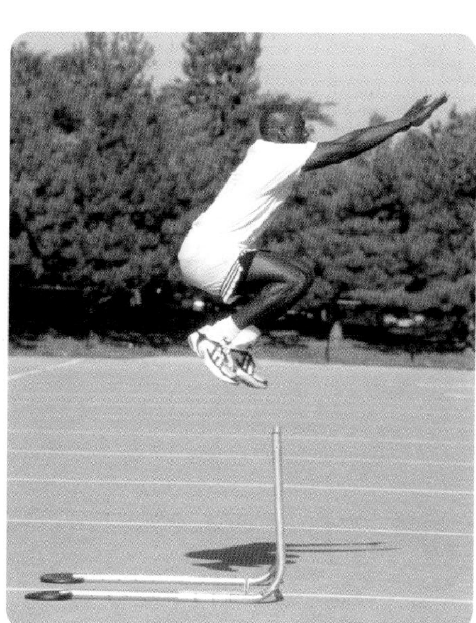

LATERAL BARRIER HOP

Intensity level: Medium

Direction of jump: Lateral and vertical

Equipment: A barrier such as a cone or hurdle

Starting position: With the barrier to one side, get into a comfortable, upright stance with feet shoulder-width apart.

Arm action: Double arm

Preparatory movement: Begin with a countermovement.

Upward movement: Jump over the barrier with both legs, using primarily hip and knee flexion to clear the barrier. Keep the knees and feet together.

Downward movement: Land on the opposite side of the barrier and immediately repeat the jump to the starting side.

Note: Intensity level of the lateral barrier hop can be increased from medium to high by progressively increasing the height of the barrier (e.g., from a cone to a hurdle) or by performing the hops with one leg only.

SKIP

Intensity level: Low

Direction of jump: Horizontal and vertical

Starting position: One leg is lifted to approximately 90° of hip and knee flexion.

Arm action: Reciprocal (as one leg is lifted, the opposite arm is lifted)

Preparatory movement: Begin with a countermovement on one leg.

Upward movement: Jump up and forward on one leg. The opposite leg should remain in the starting flexed position until landing.

Downward movement: Land in the starting position on the same leg. Immediately repeat the skip with the opposite leg.

POWER SKIP

Intensity level: Low

Direction of jump: Vertical and horizontal

Starting position: One leg is lifted to approximately 90° of hip and knee flexion.

Arm action: Double arm

Preparatory movement: Begin with a countermovement on one leg.

Upward movement: Jump up and forward on one leg. Move the flexed, nonjumping leg up and into greater hip and knee flexion while jumping. Both arms should be used to assist with the upward movement.

Downward movement: Land in the starting position on the same leg. Immediately repeat the skip with the opposite leg.

Note: Emphasis is on the effectiveness of the skip.

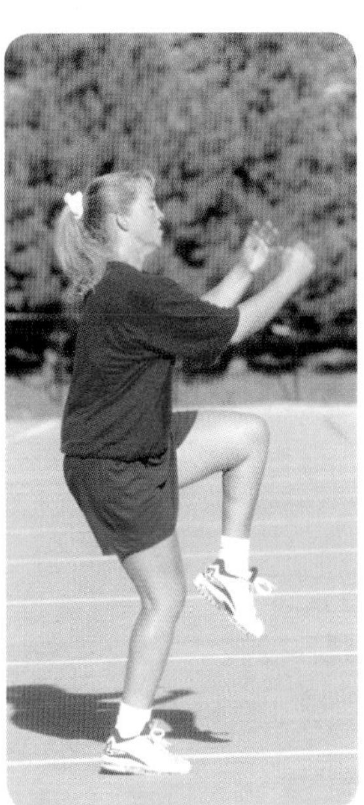

BACKWARD SKIP

Intensity level: Low

Direction of jump: Backward, horizontal, and vertical

Starting position: One leg is lifted to approximately 90° of hip and knee flexion.

Arm action: Double arm

Preparatory movement: Begin with a countermovement on one leg.

Upward movement: Jump backward with one leg and flex the hip and knee of the nonskipping leg to approximately 90°. Both arms should be used to assist with the movement.

Downward movement: Land in the starting position on the same leg. Immediately repeat the skip with the opposite leg.

SINGLE-ARM ALTERNATE-LEG BOUND

Intensity level: Medium

Direction of jump: Horizontal and vertical

Starting position: Get into a comfortable, upright stance with feet shoulder-width apart.

Arm action: Single arm

Preparatory movement: Jog at a comfortable pace; begin the drill with the left foot forward.

Upward movement: Push off with the left foot as it contacts the ground. During push-off, bring the right leg forward by flexing the thigh to a position approximately parallel with the ground and the knee at 90°.

During this flight phase of the drill, reach forward with the left arm.

Downward movement: Land on the right leg and immediately repeat the sequence on the opposite side upon landing.

Note: A bound is an exaggeration of the running gait; the goal is to cover as great a distance as possible during each stride.

DOUBLE-ARM ALTERNATE-LEG BOUND

Intensity level: Medium

Direction of jump: Horizontal and vertical

Starting position: Get into a comfortable, upright stance with feet shoulder-width apart.

Arm action: Double arm

Preparatory movement: Jog at a comfortable pace; begin the drill with the left foot forward.

Upward movement: Push off with the left foot as it contacts the ground. During push-off, bring the right leg forward by flexing the thigh to a position approximately parallel with the ground and with the knee at 90°.

During this flight phase of the drill, reach forward with both arms.

Downward movement: Land on the right leg and immediately repeat the sequence on the opposite side upon landing.

Note: A bound is an exaggeration of the running gait; the goal is to cover as great a distance as possible during each stride.

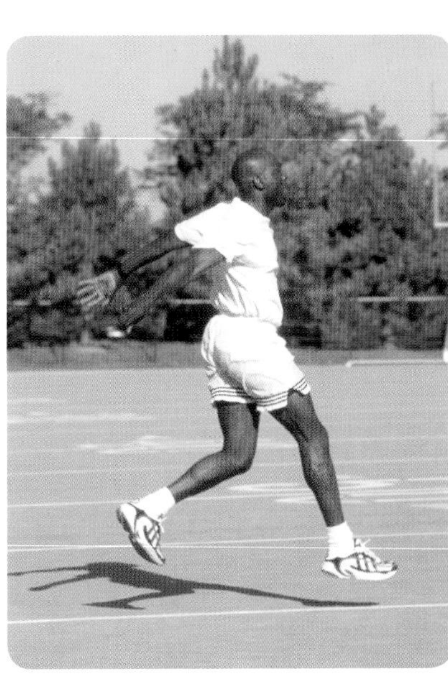

SINGLE-LEG PUSH-OFF

Intensity level: Low

Direction of jump: Vertical

Equipment: Plyometric box, 6 to 18 inches (15-46 cm) high

Starting position: Stand facing the plyometric box with one foot on the ground and one foot on the box. The heel of the foot on the box should be near the box's closest edge.

Arm action: Double arm

Preparatory movement: None

Upward movement: Jump up using the foot on the box to push off.

Downward movement: Land with the same foot on the box; this foot should land just before the ground foot. Immediately repeat the movement.

Note: Intensity may be increased by increasing the height of the box. Begin with a height of 6 inches (15 cm).

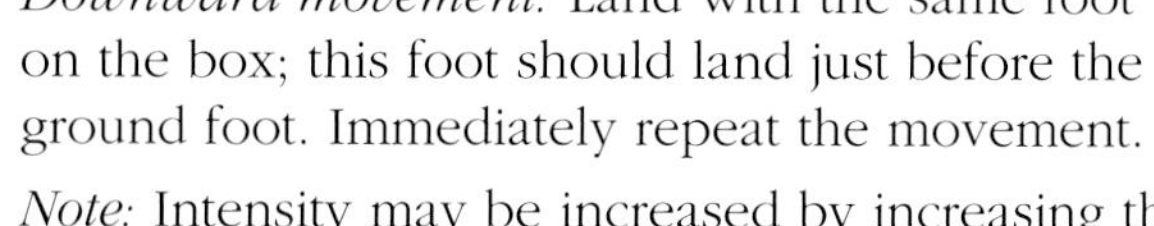

ALTERNATE-LEG PUSH-OFF

Intensity level: Low

Direction of jump: Vertical

Equipment: Plyometric box, 6 to 18 inches (15-46 cm) high

Starting position: Stand facing the plyometric box with one foot on the ground and one foot on the box. The heel of the foot on the box should be near the box's closest edge.

Arm action: Double arm

Preparatory movement: None

Upward movement: Jump up using the foot on the box to push off.

Downward movement: Land with the opposite foot on the box; this foot should land just before the ground foot. Immediately repeat the movement, reversing the feet each repetition.

Note: Intensity may be increased by increasing the height of the box. Begin with a height of 6 inches (15 cm).

LATERAL PUSH-OFF

Intensity level: Low

Direction of jump: Vertical

Equipment: Plyometric box, 6 to 18 inches (15-46 cm) high

Starting position: Stand to one side of the plyometric box with one foot on the ground and one foot on the box. The inside of the foot on the box should be near the box's closest edge.

Arm action: Double arm

Preparatory movement: None

Upward movement: Jump up using the foot on the box to push off.

Downward movement: Land with the same foot on the box; this foot should land just before the ground foot. Immediately repeat the movement.

Note: Intensity may be increased by increasing the height of the box. Begin with a height of 6 inches (15 cm).

SIDE-TO-SIDE PUSH-OFF

Intensity level: Medium

Direction of jump: Vertical

Equipment: Plyometric box, 6 to 18 inches (15-46 cm) high

Starting position: Stand to one side of the plyometric box with one foot on the ground and one foot on the box. The inside of the foot on the box should be near the box's closest edge.

Arm action: Double arm

Preparatory movement: None

Upward movement: Jump up and over the box using the foot on the box to push off.

Downward movement: Land with the opposite foot on the opposite side of the top of the box; this foot should land just before the ground foot. Immediately repeat the movement to the opposite side.

Note: Intensity may be increased by increasing the height of the box. Begin with a height of 6 inches (15 cm).

JUMP TO BOX

Intensity level: Low

Direction of jump: Vertical and slightly horizontal

Equipment: Plyometric box, 6 to 42 inches (15-107 cm) high

Starting position: Facing the plyometric box, get into a comfortable, upright stance with feet shoulder-width apart.

Arm action: Double arm

Preparatory movement: Begin with a countermovement.

Upward movement: Jump onto the top of the box using both legs.

Downward movement: Land on both feet in a half squat position, step down from the box, and repeat.

Note: Intensity may be increased by increasing the height of the box. Begin with a height of 6 inches (15 cm).

SQUAT BOX JUMP

Intensity level: Medium

Direction of jump: Vertical and slightly horizontal

Equipment: Plyometric box, 6 to 42 inches (15-107 cm) high

Starting position: Facing the plyometric box with hands clasped behind head, get into a comfortable, upright stance with feet shoulder-width apart.

Arm action: None

Preparatory movement: Begin with a countermovement.

Upward movement: Jump onto the top of the box using both legs.

Downward movement: Land on both feet in a half squat position, step down from the box, and repeat.

Note: Intensity may be increased by increasing the height of the box. Begin with a height of 6 inches (15 cm).

LATERAL BOX JUMP

Intensity level: Medium

Direction of jump: Vertical and slightly horizontal

Equipment: Plyometric box, 6 to 42 inches (15-107 cm) high

Starting position: Stand to one side of the plyometric box; get into a comfortable, upright stance with feet shoulder-width apart.

Arm action: Double arm

Preparatory movement: Begin with a countermovement.

Upward movement: Jump onto the top of the box using both legs.

Downward movement: Land on both feet in a half squat position, step down from the box, and repeat in the opposite direction.

Note: Intensity may be increased by increasing the height of the box. Begin with a height of 6 inches (15 cm).

JUMP FROM BOX

Intensity level: Medium

Direction of jump: Vertical

Equipment: Plyometric box, 12 to 42 inches (30-107 cm) high

Starting position: Get into a comfortable, upright stance with feet shoulder-width apart on the plyometric box; toes should be near the edge of the box.

Arm action: None

Preparatory movement: Step from box.

Downward movement: Land on the floor with both feet, quickly absorbing the impact upon landing.

Step back onto the box and repeat.

Note: Intensity may be increased by increasing the height of the box. Begin with a height of 12 inches (30 cm).

DEPTH JUMP

Intensity level: High

Direction of jump: Vertical

Equipment: Plyometric box, 12 to 42 inches (30-107 cm) high

Starting position: Get into a comfortable, upright stance with feet shoulder-width apart on the plyometric box; toes should be near the edge of the box.

Arm action: Double arm

Preparatory movement: Step from box.

Downward movement: Land on the floor with both feet.

Upward movement: Upon landing, immediately jump up as high as possible.

Note: When stepping from the box, step straight out. Do not first jump up or lower your center of gravity as you step down, as these adjustments will change the height from which the exercise is performed.

Note: Time on the ground should be kept to a minimum. Intensity may be increased by increasing the height of the box. Begin with a height of 12 inches (30 cm).

Note: Upon landing, emphasis should be on jumping up, with minimal horizontal movement. The far right photo shows too much forward movement.

DEPTH JUMP TO SECOND BOX

Intensity level: High

Direction of jump: Vertical and horizontal

Equipment: Two plyometric boxes, 12 to 42 inches (30-107 cm) high

Starting position: Get into a comfortable, upright stance with feet shoulder-width apart on the plyometric box, facing the second box; toes should be near the edge of the box.

Arm action: Double arm

Preparatory movement: Step from box.

Downward movement: Land on the floor with both feet.

Upward movement: Upon landing, immediately jump onto the second box.

Note: When stepping from the box, step straight out. Do not first jump up or lower your center of gravity as you step down, as these adjustments will change the height from which the exercise is performed.

Note: Time on the ground should be kept to a minimum. Intensity may be increased by increasing the height of the box. Begin with a height of 12 inches (30 cm).

Note: The distance between boxes depends on experience and ability; the greater the distance between boxes, the higher the intensity of the jump. Begin with the boxes placed 24 inches (61 cm) apart.

SQUAT DEPTH JUMP

Intensity level: High

Direction of jump: Vertical

Equipment: Plyometric box, 12 to 42 inches (30-107 cm) high

Starting position: Get into a comfortable, upright stance with feet shoulder-width apart on the plyometric box; toes should be near the edge of the box.

Arm action: Double arm or none

Preparatory movement: Step from box.

Downward movement: Land on the floor in a squat position (90° of hip and knee flexion) with both feet. (The subject in the center photo should have greater hip and knee flexion.)

Upward movement: Upon landing, immediately jump up as high as possible; land in the same squat position.

Note: When stepping from the box, step straight out. Do not first jump up or lower your center of gravity as you step down, as these adjustments will change the height from which the exercise is performed.

Note: Time on the ground should be kept to a minimum. Intensity may be increased by increasing the height of the box. Begin with a height of 12 inches (30 cm).

Note: Upon landing, emphasis should be on jumping up, with minimal horizontal movement.

DEPTH JUMP WITH LATERAL MOVEMENT

Intensity level: High

Direction of jump: Vertical and lateral

Equipment: Plyometric box, 12 to 42 inches (30-107 cm) high; a partner

Starting position: Get into a comfortable, upright stance with feet shoulder-width apart on the plyometric box; toes should be near the edge of the box.

Arm action: Double arm

Preparatory movement: Step from box.

Downward movement: Land on the floor with both feet. Have a partner point to the right or left just before you land.

Upward movement: Upon landing, immediately sprint in the direction determined by your partner.

Note: When stepping from the box, step straight out. Do not first jump up or lower your center of gravity as you step down, as these adjustments will change the height from which the exercise is performed.

Note: Time on the ground should be kept to a minimum. Intensity may be increased by increasing the height of the box. Begin with a height of 12 inches (30 cm).

DEPTH JUMP WITH STANDING LONG JUMP

Intensity level: High

Direction of jump: Vertical and horizontal

Equipment: Plyometric box, 12 to 42 inches (30-107 cm) high

Starting position: Get into a comfortable, upright stance with feet shoulder-width apart on the plyometric box; toes should be near the edge of the box.

Arm action: Double arm

Preparatory movement: Step from box.

Downward movement: Land on the floor with both feet.

Upward movement: Upon landing, immediately jump forward as far as possible with both feet.

Note: When stepping from the box, step straight out. Do not first jump up or lower your center of gravity as you step down, as these adjustments will change the height from which the exercise is performed.

Note: Time on the ground should be kept to a minimum. Intensity may be increased by increasing the height of the box. Begin with a height of 12 inches (30 cm).

SINGLE-LEG DEPTH JUMP

Intensity level: High

Direction of jump: Vertical

Equipment: Plyometric box, 12 to 42 inches (30-107 cm) high

Starting position: Get into a comfortable, upright stance with feet shoulder-width apart on the plyometric box; toes should be near the edge of the box.

Arm action: Double arm

Preparatory movement: Step from box.

Downward movement: Land on the floor with one foot.

Upward movement: Upon landing, immediately jump up as high as possible with the landing foot.

Note: When stepping from the box, step straight out. Do not first jump up or lower your center of gravity as you step down, as these adjustments will change the height from which the exercise is performed.

Note: Time on the ground should be kept to a minimum. Intensity may be increased by increasing the height of the box. Begin with a height of 12 inches (30 cm).

Note: This is a very advanced form of the depth jump and should be performed only by those with adequate experience and ability as demonstrated in other versions of the depth jump.

CHEST PASS

Intensity level: Low

Direction of throw: Forward

Equipment: Medicine or plyometric ball weighing 2 to 8 pounds (0.9-3.6 kg); rebounder or partner

Starting position: Get into a comfortable, upright stance with feet shoulder-width apart; face the rebounder or partner approximately 10 feet (3 m) away. Raise the ball to chest level with the elbows flexed.

Preparatory movement: Begin with a countermovement. (A countermovement for plyometric throws requires cocking the arms, that is, moving the arms slightly backward before the actual throw.)

Arm action: Using both arms, throw the ball to the rebounder or partner by extending the elbows. When the rebounder or partner returns the ball, catch it, return to the starting position, and immediately repeat the movement.

Note: Intensity may be increased by increasing the weight of the medicine ball. Begin with a 2-pound (0.9 kg) ball.

TWO-HAND OVERHEAD THROW

Intensity level: Low

Direction of throw: Forward

Equipment: Medicine or plyometric ball weighing 2 to 8 pounds (0.9-3.6 kg); rebounder or partner

Starting position: Get into a comfortable, upright stance with feet shoulder-width apart; face the rebounder or partner approximately 10 feet (3 m) away. Raise the ball overhead.

Preparatory movement: Begin with a countermovement. (A countermovement for plyometric throws requires cocking the arms, that is, moving the arms slightly backward before the actual throw.)

Arm action: Using both arms, throw the ball to the rebounder or partner, keeping the elbows extended. When the rebounder or partner returns the ball, catch the ball overhead and immediately repeat the throw.

Note: Intensity may be increased by increasing the weight of the medicine ball. Begin with a 2-pound (0.9 kg) ball.

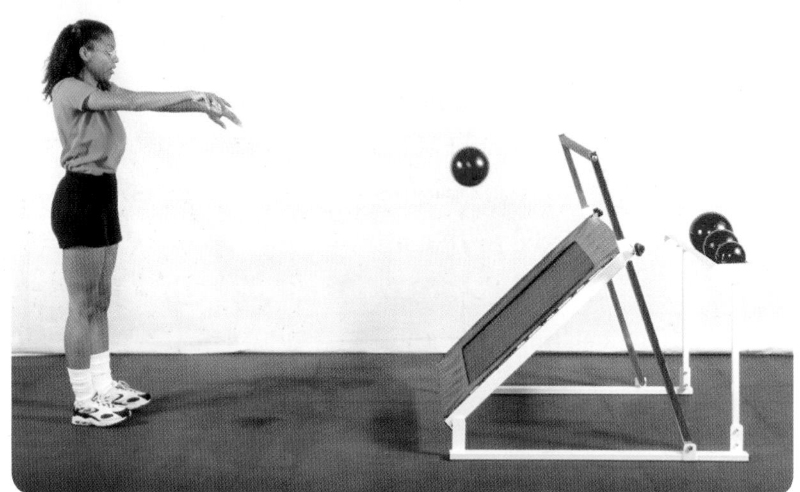

TWO-HAND SIDE-TO-SIDE THROW

Intensity level: Low

Direction of throw: Forward and diagonal

Equipment: Medicine or plyometric ball weighing 2 to 8 pounds (0.9-3.6 kg); rebounder or partner

Starting position: Get into a comfortable, upright stance with feet shoulder-width apart; face the rebounder or partner approximately 10 feet (3 m) away. Raise the ball in both hands to a position over one shoulder with the elbows flexed.

Preparatory movement: Begin with a countermovement. (A countermovement for plyometric throws requires cocking the arms, that is, moving the arms slightly backward before the actual throw.)

Arm action: Using both arms, throw the ball to the rebounder or partner by extending the elbows. When the rebounder or partner returns the ball, catch the ball over the opposite shoulder and immediately repeat the throw.

Note: Intensity may be increased by increasing the weight of the medicine ball. Begin with a 2-pound (0.9 kg) ball.

SINGLE-ARM THROW

Intensity level: Medium

Direction of throw: Forward

Equipment: Medicine or plyometric ball weighing 1 to 5 pounds (0.5-2.3 kg); rebounder or partner

Starting position: Get into a comfortable, upright stance with feet shoulder-width apart; face the rebounder or partner approximately 10 feet (3 m) away. Raise the ball in one hand to a position of 90° of shoulder abduction and 90° of elbow flexion, with arm rotated so the forearm is perpendicular to the floor.

Preparatory movement: Begin with a countermovement. (A countermovement for plyometric throws requires cocking the arm, that is, moving the arm slightly backward before the actual throw.)

Arm action: Using one arm, throw the ball to the rebounder or partner. When the rebounder or partner returns the ball, catch the ball in the starting position, allow the shoulder to externally rotate slightly, and immediately repeat the throw.

Note: Intensity may be increased by increasing the weight of the medicine ball. Begin with a 1-pound (0.5 kg) ball.

Note: This drill may also be performed using a natural throwing motion.

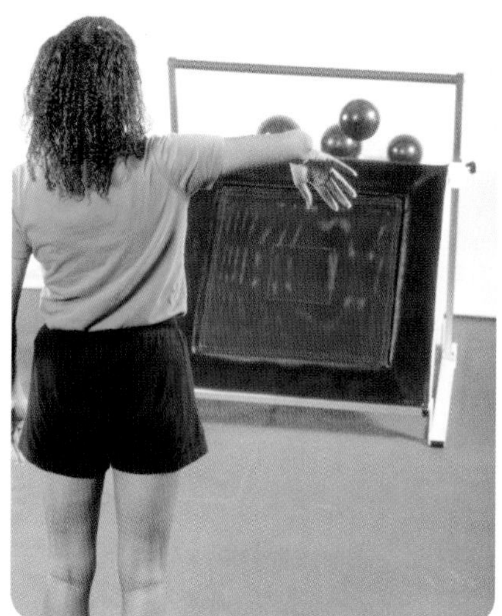

POWER DROP

Intensity level: High

Direction of throw: Upward

Equipment: Medicine or plyometric ball weighing 2 to 8 pounds (0.9-3.6 kg); partner; plyometric box 12 to 42 inches (30-107 cm) high

Starting position: Lie supine on the ground with elbows extended and both shoulders in approximately 90° of flexion; head should be near the base of the box. The partner should be on a box with the medicine ball held above the athlete's arms.

Preparatory movement: None

Arm action: When the partner drops the ball, catch it using both arms and immediately throw the ball back up to the partner.

Note: Intensity may be increased by increasing the weight of the medicine ball or by increasing the height of the box. Begin with a 2-pound (0.9 kg) ball and a height of 12 inches (30 cm).

DEPTH PUSH-UP

Intensity level: Medium

Direction of movement: Vertical

Equipment: Medicine or plyometric ball weighing 5 to 8 pounds (2.3-3.6 kg)

Starting position: Lie in a push-up position, with the hands on the medicine ball and elbows extended.

Preparatory movement: None

Downward movement: Quickly remove the hands from the medicine ball and drop down. Contact the ground with hands slightly wider than shoulder-width apart and elbows slightly flexed. Allow the chest to almost touch the medicine ball by letting the elbows flex.

Upward movement: Immediately and explosively push up by fully extending the elbows. Quickly place the palms on the medicine ball and repeat the exercise.

Note: When the upper body is at maximal height during the upward movement, the hands should be higher than the medicine ball.

Note: Intensity may be increased by increasing the size of the medicine ball. Begin with a 5-pound (2.3 kg) ball.

45° SIT-UP

Intensity level: Medium

Equipment: Medicine or plyometric ball weighing 2 to 8 pounds (0.9-3.6 kg); a partner

Starting position: Sit on the ground with the trunk at an approximately 45° angle. The partner should be in front with the medicine ball.

Preparatory movement: The partner throws the ball to your outstretched hands.

Downward action: Once the partner throws the ball, catch it using both arms, allow minimal trunk extension, and immediately return the ball to the partner.

Note: Intensity may be increased by increasing the weight of the medicine ball. Begin with a 2-pound (0.9 kg) ball.

Note: The force used to return the ball to the partner should come predominantly from the abdominal muscles.

KEY TERMS

amortization phase 415
balance 424
bound 418
box drill 418
complex training 423
concentric phase 416
depth jump 418
eccentric phase 415
jumps in place 418
multiple hops and jumps 418
muscle spindle 415
potentiation 415
power 414
push-up 418
series elastic component (SEC) 414
standing jump 418
stretch reflex 415
stretch-shortening cycle (SSC) 414
throw 418

STUDY QUESTIONS

1. All of the following are phases of the stretch-shortening cycle EXCEPT
   a. amortization.
   b. concentric.
   c. eccentric.
   d. isometric.

2. Which of the following structures detects rapid movement and initiates the stretch reflex?
   a. Golgi tendon organ
   b. muscle spindle
   c. extrafusal muscle fiber
   d. Pacinian corpuscle

3. Which of the following is a primary component of the series elastic component?
   a. tendon
   b. muscle fiber
   c. actin
   d. ligament

4. Which of the following is the BEST surface on which to perform lower body plyometric drills?
   a. trampoline
   b. exercise mat
   c. asphalt
   d. suspended wood floor

5. Which of the following should be assessed before beginning a lower body plyometric training program?
   I. balance
   II. strength
   III. speed
   IV. lean body mass
   a. I and III only
   b. II and IV only
   c. I, II, and III only
   d. I, II, III, and IV

6. Which of the following types of plyometric drills is generally considered to be the MOST intense?
   a. jumps in place
   b. bounds
   c. depth jumps
   d. box jumps

7. Which of the following work-to-rest ratios is the MOST appropriate to assign to a plyometric training workout?
   a. 1:5
   b. 1:4
   c. 1:3
   d. 1:2

CHAPTER 17

Speed, Agility, and Speed-Endurance Development

Steven S. Plisk, MS

After completing this chapter, you will be able to

- apply sound movement principles to locomotion modes and techniques and teach their correct execution;
- analyze the abilities and skills needed in specific movement tasks;
- apply sound means and methods for developing speed, agility, and speed-endurance; and
- design and implement training programs to maximize athletic performance.

This chapter addresses the issue of speed development on three fronts:

- **Speed**—the skills and abilities needed to achieve high movement velocities
- **Agility**—the skills and abilities needed to explosively change movement velocities or modes
- **Speed-endurance**—the ability to maintain maximal movement velocities or repeatedly achieve maximal accelerations and velocities

When athletes are performing functional tasks, their technique—including its speed of execution—is a skillful expression of their abilities. There is a common misconception that skills and abilities are unrelated, when in fact they are interrelated. Strength and conditioning professionals should analyze the skills and abilities needed in a target activity and specifically develop them in training.

In simple terms, functional movement speed is a manifestation of an athlete's strength. Forces are expressed in terms of acceleration, time or rate of application, and velocity. Movement techniques involve skillful application of these forces to specific motor tasks. The greater the mass being accelerated, the briefer the time of execution, or the higher the velocity of movement, the more explosively an athlete must apply forces in order to execute a technique. Running is the technical example used throughout this chapter because it is a fundamental motor skill and means of locomotion in many sports. It also has an explosive, ballistic quality common to other movements. For these reasons, the training methods and principles presented here are applicable to many athletic activities.

The term *agility* is commonly used in two contexts: changing movement velocity and performing locomotion modes other than linear sprinting. Velocity is a vector quantity characterized by speed and direction, so in a broad sense there is an agility component to any task involving changes in either parameter. Variable, rather than constant, movement velocities and modes are the rule rather than the exception in many sports. There is a corresponding need to address specific acceleration, maximum-velocity, and multidirectional skills in training. The ability to explosively decelerate and reaccelerate is especially important because of the extreme forces involved in such tasks.

Speed-endurance provides the metabolic conditioning needed to support the maintenance of running speed and agility over an extended period (6+ seconds) or to achieve maximum acceleration or speed during repetitive sprints. Relatively few athletic activities involve a single, brief effort. Many sports consist of ongoing submaximal activity with intense, intermittent bursts in effort. Even in brief, discrete activities, specific endurance qualities are necessary to achieve certain volume-loads in training. It is therefore important to develop athletes' **special endurance**—the ability to repeatedly perform maximal or near-maximal efforts in competition-specific **exercise: relief patterns** (commonly called **work:rest ratios**). This is a variation on the speed-endurance concept and requires two qualities: the metabolic power to execute specific techniques at the targeted effort level, and the metabolic capacity to do so repetitively.

*Thanks to Aaron Dragone, MSPT, CSCS; John Gray, MS, CSCS; G. Gregory Haff, PhD; CSCS,*D; FNSCA; Everett Harman, PhD, CSCS, NSCA-CPT; William Kraemer, PhD, CSCS, FACSM, FNSCA; Robert Newton, PhD; CSCS,*D; David Pendergast, EdD (for the metabolic conditioning guidelines provided in the Training Plan); Jason Perrone, BS, CSCS; James Radcliffe, MS, CSCS; Raoul F. Reiser II, PhD, CSCS, FACSM; Dietmar Schmidtbleicher, PhD; Loren Seagrave, BS; Michael Stone, PhD, FNSCA; John Taylor, MS; CSCS,*D; CP; FNSCA; Vladimir Zatsiorsky, PhD; and Erin Zietz, BS, CSCS.

Movement techniques involve task-specific application of forces that are manifested in terms of acceleration, time or rate of application, and velocity. Strength and conditioning professionals should identify the target activity's requisite skills and abilities via task analysis and specifically address them in training.

MOVEMENT MECHANICS

In order to execute movement techniques, athletes must skillfully apply **force**—the product of mass and acceleration. Due to the time and velocity constraints imposed by functional activities, task-specific force application can also be expressed in terms of two other parameters:

Impulse—the change in momentum resulting from a force, measured as the product of force and time (figure 17.1)

Power—the rate of doing work, measured as the product of force and velocity (figure 17.2)

When the mechanics of explosive activities like running are analyzed, each of these variables influences performance. For example, more *force* is needed to accelerate a predetermined mass at a greater rate, or greater mass at a predetermined rate. More *impulse* is needed to achieve a predetermined momentum in less time, or greater momentum in a predetermined time. More *power* is needed to achieve a predetermined velocity with higher resistance, or higher velocity with a predetermined resistance.

Impulse

The brief execution times of most athletic tasks require high rates of force development (RFD). For example, force is applied for 0.1 to 0.2 seconds during the ground support phase of running, whereas absolute maximum force development may require 0.6 to 0.8 seconds (figure 17.1) (30, 50, 53, 61, 62, 63, 104, 105, 109, 124, 142). Even in nonballistic modes of locomotion such as cycling, rowing, or swimming, performance is influenced by the ability to generate force quickly and thereby achieve a desired impulse.

In practice, the rate, amplitude, and direction of force application are equally significant in the performance of functional tasks. The issue is one of specificity to the demands of the target task(s). Thus, a basic objective of training is to improve RFD, effectively moving the force–time curve up and to the left, in turn generating greater impulse

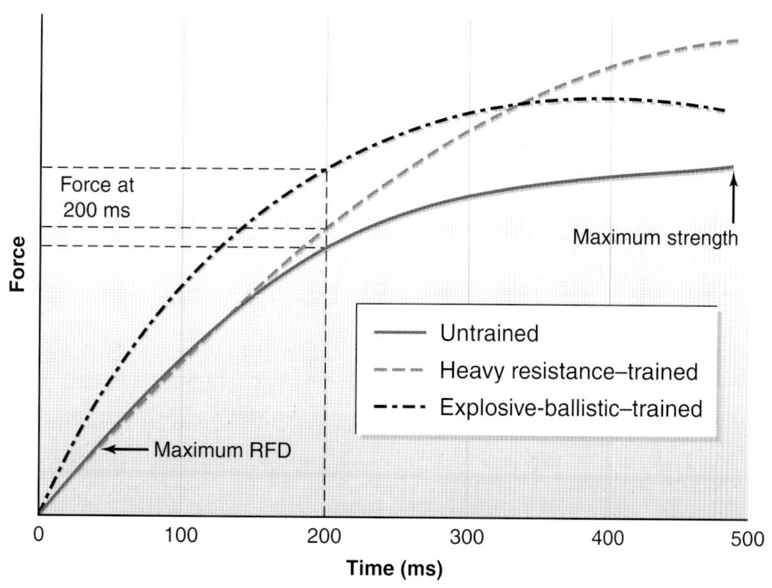

Figure 17.1 Force as a function of time, indicating maximum strength, rate of force development (RFD), and force at 0.2 seconds for untrained (solid blue line), heavy resistance–trained (dashed purple line), and explosive-ballistic–trained (dotted black line) subjects. Impulse is the change in momentum resulting from a force, measured as the product of force and time (represented by the area under each curve), and is increased by improving RFD. When functional movements are performed, force is typically applied very briefly, that is, often for 0.1 to 0.2 seconds, whereas absolute maximum force development may require 0.6 to 0.8 seconds.

Reprinted, by permission, from Häkkinen and Komi, 1985 (46).

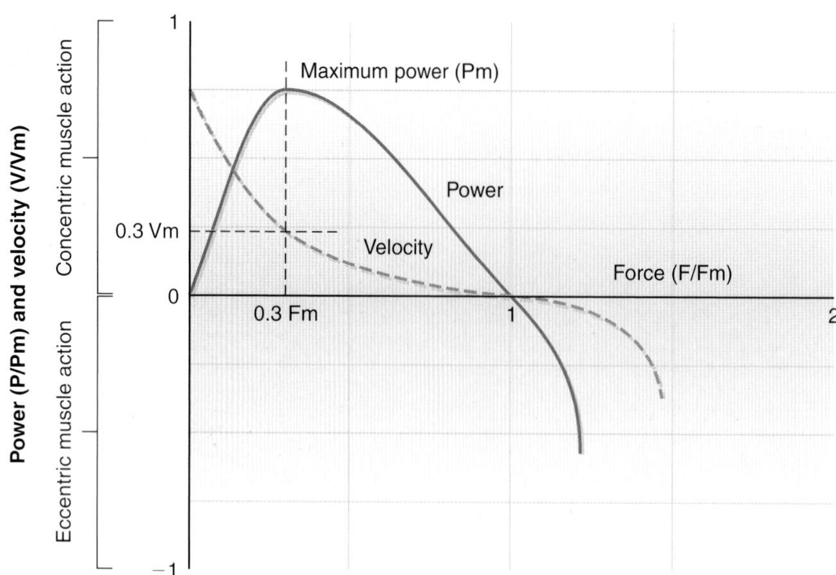

Figure 17.2 Velocity as a function of force (dashed purple line) and resulting power production/absorption (solid blue line) in concentric and eccentric muscle actions. The greatest forces occur during explosive eccentric (lengthening) actions. Depending on the movement, maximum power (Pm) is usually produced at 30% to 50% of maximum force (Fm) and velocity (Vm).

Adapted, by permission, from Faulkner, Clafin, and McCully, 1986 (34).

and momentum during the limited time in which force is applied.

Power

The ability to achieve high movement velocities requires skillful force application across a spectrum of power outputs and muscle actions (figure 17.2). For this reason, resistance training should involve a variety of concentric and eccentric loads and velocities. Training programs that are restricted to narrow force–velocity ranges may have limited transfer to athleticism.

Achievable movement speed for a particular task is load dependent, so it is rather meaningless to consider either variable independently (20, 60, 61, 62, 63, 104, 105, 109, 129, 131, 142). Simply put, as resistance increases, so does the role of strength in determining movement velocity and acceleration. In this sense, **velocity specificity** is really the final movement velocity targeted when a mass is being accelerated.

In terrestrial movements such as running or jumping, resistance usually includes the athlete's body mass and possibly equipment (in contact or collision activities, the opponent's body mass is a significant factor as well). For this reason, it is difficult to find examples of sports in which high power outputs are not required to rapidly accelerate, decelerate, or achieve high velocities. The athlete's percentage of fast-twitch motor units and the ability to optimally activate and coordinate them primarily determine these capabilities (64, 120, 122, 132). In contrast, isometric or low-velocity strength is a function of muscle cross-sectional area, that is, the number of active sarcomeres in parallel. Once the upper limit for specific muscle tension has been developed (40-45 N/cm^2 in trained athletes), hypertrophy is required—especially in fast-twitch fibers—in order to further increase force and speed production (30, 109).

The peak force and power levels absorbed by the tissues during active lengthening can be significantly greater than those produced during shortening (figure 17.2) (50, 53, 61, 62, 63, 91, 109, 116, 142). For example, the eccentric ground reaction force (GRF) during sprinting can approach four times an athlete's body weight, and Achilles tendon forces can be severalfold higher (61, 62, 63, 79). These forces are transmitted through a single leg and may limit an athlete's technical proficiency or cause noncontact injury if not adequately addressed in training. Thus the demands of athletic movements dictate two more training objectives in addition to improving concentric power production capability: developing the eccentric strength needed to tolerate extreme force and power absorption during eccentric (braking) actions and the reactive strength needed to rapidly recoil into concentric (propulsive) actions.

Athletes skillfully apply forces when executing movement techniques. Because of time and velocity constraints, a technique can be characterized in terms of task-specific impulse and power. The ability to achieve high movement velocities and accelerations involves high RFD as well as force application across a range of power outputs and muscle actions.

Practical Implications

While the concepts just described are valid as general principles, it is important to recognize how athletes' mechanics change as they move (73). For example, leverage changes with varying limb positions and joint angles. The force–velocity relationship changes as athletes accelerate and decelerate. The length–force relationship changes and elastic structures are loaded or unloaded as muscles lengthen and shorten. These factors feed back to the neuromuscular system through reflexes that compensate for load and stretch, and in turn modify motor behavior via stiffness regulation (1, 2, 10, 15, 24, 30, 52, 55, 85). Collectively, these dynamic relationships emphasize the need for task specificity in training.

Functional Versus Simple Movements

Speed of execution in complex, multijoint movements is determined by an interplay of neuromuscular, mechanical, and energetic factors (22, 49, 53, 61, 70, 102, 103, 109, 114, 129). Explosiveness in such tasks can be expressed in terms of acceleration, momentum, or velocity. These, in turn, are load-dependent functions of force, impulse, and power, respectively. Speed in complex movements tends to correlate poorly with that in unresisted, elementary actions (109, 114, 129, 131), in which it is usually expressed in terms of reaction time, movement frequency or time, and ability to quickly initiate movement. The peak rate of intrinsic muscle shortening in such unloaded conditions (~15 μm/s) depends on several factors (5, 14, 30, 61, 109, 129):

- Contractility and excitability of the athlete's neuromuscular system
- Muscle architecture, that is, fiber and fascicle lengths and number of active sarcomeres in series
- Motor unit composition and maximal cross-bridge cycling rates in respective fiber types (determined by the specific constellation of protein isoforms and adenosine triphosphatase [ATPase] activities, as well as volume and density of the sarcoplasmic reticulum and resulting calcium transients)

Many functional tasks begin with preparatory countermovements involving springlike actions referred to as the **stretch-shortening cycle (SSC)**—an eccentric-concentric coupling phenomenon in which muscle-tendon complexes are rapidly and forcibly lengthened, or stretch loaded, and immediately shortened in a reactive or elastic manner. Graphically, the SSC can be illustrated as a rapid transition from eccentric action in the lower right part of the force–velocity curve to concentric action in the upper left (figure 17.2). Stretch-shortening cycle actions are particularly prevalent in sports involving running, jumping, and other explosive changes in momentum or velocity. Their performance is a distinct capability that is independent of maximal strength in elite athletes (50, 61, 62, 63, 104, 105, 109, 116, 142).

Stretch-shortening actions exploit two phenomena: (1) intrinsic muscle-tendon behavior and (2) force and length reflex feedback to the motoneural system (1, 2, 10, 15, 24, 30, 52, 55, 61, 62, 63, 85). Acutely, SSC actions tend to increase mechanical efficiency, impulse, and power via elastic energy recovery, whereas chronically, they upregulate muscle stiffness and enhance neuromuscular activation (50, 62, 63, 104, 105, 109, 116, 142).

Training activities aimed at improving SSC performance should fulfill two criteria (51, 104, 105, 109, 116, 142):

- They should involve skillful, multijoint movements that transmit forces through the kinetic chain and exploit elastic-reflexive mechanisms.
- In order to manage fatigue and emphasize work quality and technique, they should be structured around brief work bouts or clusters separated by frequent rest pauses.

In practice, a combination of progressive plyometric and heavy resistance methods can accomplish these objectives. An intriguing example of this strategy is **complex training**, in which alternating SSC tasks with heavy resistance exercises within the same session enhances their working effect. The basis of this method is an acute aftereffect phenomenon referred to as postactivation potentiation (54, 96, 100). It is becoming increasingly popular as a means of enhancing advanced athletes' performance, but may be inappropriate for novices or youths.

It is important to distinguish **reactive ability** from **reaction time**. The former is a characteristic of explosive strength exhibited in SSC actions that can be improved through reactive-explosive training; in contrast, the latter is relatively untrainable and correlates poorly with movement action time or performance in many explosive events. For example, an elite sprinter's auditory reaction time typically ranges from 0.12 to 0.18 seconds but is not significantly related to his or her 100 m results (23, 47, 79, 81, 83, 84). Other factors such as acceleration, speed-endurance, and, to a lesser extent, maximum speed are more closely associated with overall sprint times (23, 57, 79, 106, 114). Reaction time is, however, an important determinant of performance in quick timing tasks (e.g., a batter hitting a baseball) and defensive types of stimulus-response actions (e.g., a goaltender making a save).

Aerobic Endurance Versus Power Sports

It is generally understood that explosive strength qualities are important in power sports involving running, jumping, and other changes in speed or direction. There is a common misconception, however, that their role in aerobic endurance activities is minor. For example, since elite marathoners' running velocities are about half those achieved by sprinters (51, 92, 106, 136, 137), explosive force output is often mistakenly believed to be insignificant. Ground contact times at intermediate running speeds tend to be longer than those at top speeds (~0.2 seconds at 5-6 m/s) (51, 53, 92, 106, 114, 124) but are significantly shorter than required for maximal force development (figure 17.1).

Because running is an inherently ballistic activity, power, impulse, and reactive ability are important determinants of performance over any distance or duration. The value of explosive strength for long-distance aerobic endurance events becomes apparent when one considers the improvements that are achievable with modest increases in stride frequency, length, or efficiency (51, 59, 101). It is also important to consider the potential benefits in terms of injury prevention.

As emphasized previously, the ability to apply force rapidly—as well as to accelerate and decelerate one's body mass—is the rule rather than the exception in athletics. Running is an explosive activity requiring high RFD and power output at all velocities. Indeed, even during prolonged steady-state running, athletes apply GRFs in a series of brief spikes (33, 51, 92, 101, 106, 124). It is simplistic, therefore, to categorize any sport on a physiologic basis without giving equal attention to task-specific mechanics.

Stretch-shortening cycle actions are especially prevalent in athletic tasks. The target activity's movement mechanics have important implications in training and should be addressed in the task analysis.

RUNNING SPEED

Bipedal running is a ballistic mode of locomotion with an alternating **flight phase** and single-leg **support phase** (by comparison, walking is nonballistic; there is no flight phase, and the stance alternates between double and single support phases). Sprinting is a series of running strides that repeatedly launch the athlete's body as a projectile at maximal acceleration or velocity (or both), usually over brief distances and durations. Running speed is the interaction of **stride frequency** and **stride length** (figure 17.3).

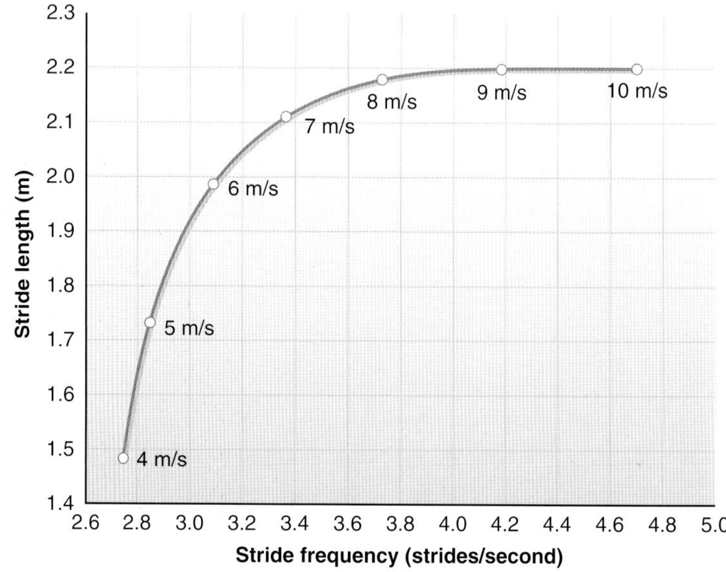

Figure 17.3 Stride length–frequency interaction as a function of running velocity.

m/s = meters per second

Adapted, by permission, from Dillman, 1975 (25).

It is instructive to compare running speed, stride frequency, and stride length in elite and novice athletes (13, 23, 39, 47, 57, 79, 81, 83, 84, 92, 106, 139):

- Elite sprinters achieve greater stride length and are capable of increasing it up to ~45 m from a static start, whereas novices achieve their maximum stride length at ~25 m (figure 17.4*a*).
- Elite sprinters achieve greater stride frequency (~5 strides per second) and are capable of increasing it up to ~25 m from a static start, whereas novices achieve their maximum stride frequency at ~10 to 15 m (figure 17.4*b*).
- Elite sprinters produce greater initial forces and velocities at the start, achieve much greater rates of acceleration, and reach maximal velocities of up to 12 m/s after ~5 to 6 seconds (45-55 m); novices reach their top speed at 20 to 30 m (figure 17.4*c*).

Figure 17.3 illustrates the stride length–frequency relationship at different running velocities. As speed approaches maximum, frequency changes more than length and is thereby more important in determining final velocity (79, 83, 84, 106, 139). Effective stride length refers to horizontal projection of the athlete's center of mass rather than foot-to-foot touchdown distance. This has important implications regarding foot placement at ground strike, as discussed later. Stride

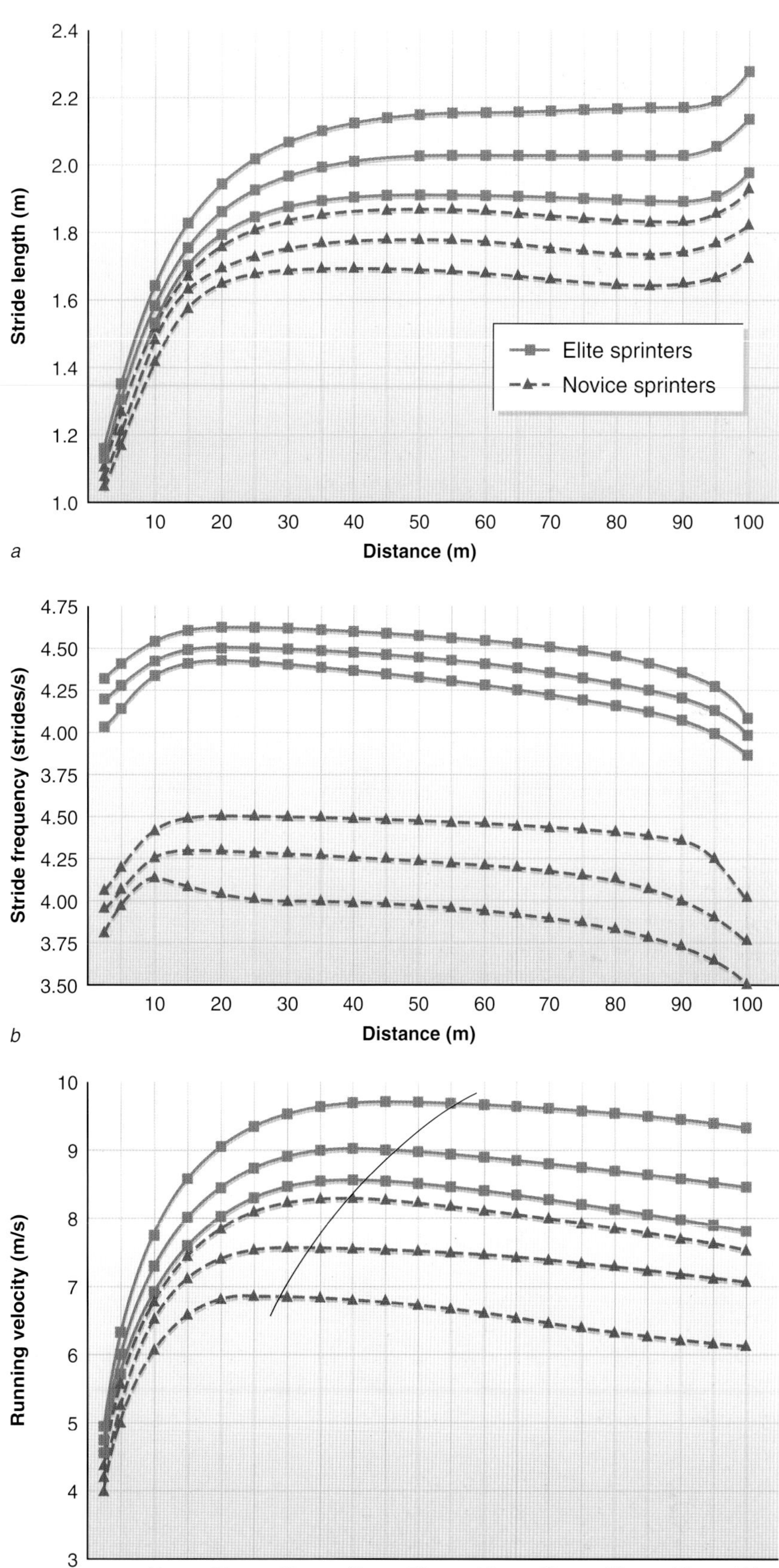

Figure 17.4 *(a)* Stride length, *(b)* stride frequency, and *(c)* running velocity in 100 m sprinters of varying qualification.

Reprinted, by permission, from Schmolinsky, 2000 (106).

length is related to body height and leg length, making it unique for each individual (79, 81), and is influenced by the impulse applied during ground contact and the resulting trajectory.

Stride frequency also tends to vary among individuals and generally seems to be more trainable than stride length. As the athlete accelerates to his or her maximum stride rate, ground contact time decreases from ≤0.2 seconds during acceleration to ≤0.1 seconds at top speed; and impulse production becomes increasingly dependent on the ability to generate explosive GRFs (20, 23, 39, 47, 57, 69, 79, 81, 83, 84, 92, 106, 139).

Sprinting Performance and Stride Analysis

Linear sprinting involves a series of subtasks: the start and acceleration (figure 17.5) and maximum velocity (figure 17.6). Although the respective movement mechanics are distinct, acceleration and maximum-velocity running are both characterized by two phases: flight, which includes **recovery** and **ground preparation**; and support, which includes eccentric **braking** and concentric **propulsion**.

Figure 17.7 is a sprint technique checklist that accompanies figures 17.5 and 17.6. These guidelines are based on linear running and are useful for teaching as well as evaluation purposes. In some cases, they can also be adapted to multidirectional tasks, as discussed in the section on agility.

Running is a ballistic mode of locomotion with alternating phases of flight (composed of recovery and ground preparation) and single-leg support (composed of eccentric braking and concentric propulsion).

Figure 17.5 Sprinting technique during the start and acceleration.

Reprinted, by permission, from Schmolinsky, 2000 (106).

Figure 17.6 Sprinting technique at maximum velocity: *(i)* early flight; *(ii)* midflight; *(iii)* late flight; *(iv)* early support; *(v)* late support.

Reprinted, by permission, from Schmolinsky, 2000 (106).

SPRINTING TECHNIQUE CHECKLIST: START, ACCELERATION, AND MAXIMUM VELOCITY

Start *(Figure 17.5)*

Even distribution of body weight in a medium heel-to-toe three- or four-point staggered stance

- ☐ Front knee angle is ~90°; rear knee angle ranges from ~110° to 130°
- ☐ In elite sprinters: Front hip angle is ~40°; rear hip angle is ~80°
- ☐ In subelite sprinters: Front hip angle is ~50°; rear hip angle is ~90°

Explosive push-off with both legs

- ☐ Starting torso angle is ~42° to 45° from horizontal (in elite and subelite sprinters)
- ☐ Rear leg produces greater initial force, but lifts off earlier (force is applied for ≤0.18 seconds in elite sprinters)
- ☐ Front leg has a greater influence on starting velocity and must exert force longer (force is applied for ≤0.37 seconds in elite sprinters)
- ☐ Peak starting force and impulse can exceed 1,500 newtons and 230 newton-seconds, respectively

Front leg completes its extension as the rear leg swings forward

Arm action has important functions

- ☐ As rear foot lifts up and swings forward, the opposite arm swings forward and up; elbow flexes ~90° as hand swings toward the forehead to enhance momentum and overcome inertia
- ☐ Forward leg swing requires a backward arm countermovement

Acceleration *(Figure 17.5)*

First two strides (in elite sprinters)

- ☐ Support phases are ≤0.20 and 0.18 seconds, respectively (includes eccentric braking and concentric propulsion)
- ☐ Flight phases are ≤0.70 and 0.90 seconds, respectively

Every athlete has an optimal stride rate:length ratio; both increase for the first 15 to 20 m, or 8 to 10 strides, from a static start

- ☐ Stride length and frequency gradually increase, up to ~45 m and ~25 m, respectively
- ☐ After the first two strides off the line, foot touches down in front of the center of gravity
- ☐ Forward body lean progressively decreases from ≤45° to ≤5° with increasing stride rate and length; an upright sprinting position is achieved by ~20 m
- ☐ Acceleration rates can approach 11.8 m/s^2
- ☐ Peak GRFs can exceed 3,000 watts

(CONTINUED)

Figure 17.7 A checklist for sprinting technique at start, acceleration, and maximum velocity.

From NSCA, 2008, *Essentials of Strength Training and Conditioning*, 3rd ed., T.R. Baechle and R.W. Earle (eds.), (Champaign, IL: Human Kinetics). Data from Schmolinsky, 1993 (106).

Head is in a relaxed, neutral position

- ☐ Eyes are focused straight ahead

Extended leg and trunk form a "power line" position along the long axis

- ☐ Thigh of the swing leg is perpendicular (with lower leg parallel) to the trunk

Maximum Velocity *(Figure 17.6)*

Flight (nonsupport) phase

- ☐ Push-off leg folds tightly toward the hip in a relaxed "heeling" motion
- ☐ Flexed leg functions as a pendulum and thrusts forward at maximum speed (~20 m/s in elite sprinters), assisting push-off leg power
- ☐ Smallest knee angle occurs when the thigh is vertical
- ☐ When the thigh reaches maximum possible knee lift, lower leg swings forward in a relaxed movement
- ☐ Thigh begins to move down, sweeping the lower leg backward and down with a "pawing" action
- ☐ "Cocked" foot lightly meets the ground directly under or a minimal distance in front of the center of gravity

Forward support phase

- ☐ Body weight is balanced such that only the ball of the foot touches the ground
- ☐ Trunk is virtually erect (<5° forward lean)
- ☐ Horizontal braking forces and vertical displacement are minimized
- ☐ Peak GRFs are generated within 0.04 seconds (in elite sprinters)

Rear support phase

- ☐ Propulsion velocity depends on the push-off impulse and direction
- ☐ "Triple extension" (hip-knee-ankle) is important; push-off angle from the surface is ~50° to 55°

Leg drive is facilitated by explosive arm action

- ☐ Shoulders are kept steady; elbows are flexed at ~90° and kept close to the body; hands are loosely cupped
- ☐ In an explosive "hammering" motion, hands swing forward and up above shoulder height (upper arm is perpendicular to trunk), then down and backward through the pocket and past the hips

Relaxed carriage of head prevents facial and neck muscle tightening

- ☐ Natural alignment with the trunk and shoulders
- ☐ Mouth is open and jaw is allowed to sag

At maximum velocity

- ☐ Flight phase duration is 0.12 to 0.14 seconds
- ☐ Support phase duration is 0.08 to 0.10 seconds; up to 1,800 newtons (GRFs)

Figure 17.7 *(continued)*

From NSCA, 2008, *Essentials of Strength Training and Conditioning*, 3rd ed., T.R. Baechle and R.W. Earle (eds.), (Champaign, IL: Human Kinetics). Data from Schmolinsky, 1993 (106).

Figure 17.8 itemizes the fundamental movements occurring in maximum-velocity sprinting. Following is a summary of the key muscular requirements (65, 92, 135, 139):

- As the recovery leg swings forward, eccentric knee flexor activity controls its forward momentum and helps prepare for efficient touchdown. Consequently, this muscle group achieves maximum muscle lengths and extremely high stretching rates. Its activity then switches from eccentric to concentric action and continues briefly into the support phase, facilitating power transfer to the leg.
- During ground support, the high moment at the ankle joint indicates the importance of the plantarflexors. Elastic strain energy is stored and recovered via SSC action in this muscle group. Eccentric knee extensor activity also allows the quadriceps femoris to store and recover elastic energy, again helping transfer power to the leg.
- According to the available evidence, effort during the late support phase neither is essential to sprinting efficiency nor poses a high risk for injury. This suggests that the purpose of "triple extension" of the hip, knee, and ankle

FUNDAMENTAL MOVEMENTS OCCURRING IN MAXIMUM-VELOCITY SPRINTING

Early Flight *(Figure 17.6i)*

- *Eccentric hip flexion:* decelerates backward rotation of thigh
- *Eccentric knee extension:* decelerates backward rotation of leg/foot

Midflight *(Figure 17.6ii)*

- *Concentric hip flexion:* accelerates thigh forward
- *Eccentric knee extension → eccentric knee flexion*

Late Flight *(Figure 17.6iii)*

- *Concentric hip extension:* rotates thigh backward in preparation for foot contact
- *Eccentric knee flexion:* accelerates leg backward, limiting knee extension; stops before foot strike (aided by concentric knee flexion to minimize braking at touchdown)

Early Support *(Figure 17.6iv)*

- *Continued concentric hip extension:* minimizes braking effect of foot strike
- *Brief concentric knee flexion followed by eccentric hip extension:* resists tendency of hip/ankle extension to hyperextend knee; absorbs landing shock
- *Eccentric plantarflexion:* helps absorb shock and control forward rotation of tibia over ankle

Late Support *(Figure 17.6v)*

- *Eccentric hip flexion:* decelerates backward thigh rotation; rotates trunk in preparation for forward takeoff
- *Concentric knee extension:* propels center of gravity forward
- *Concentric plantarflexion:* aids in propulsion

Figure 17.8 This list describes the fundamental movements of the flight and support phases in maximum velocity sprinting.

Sources: Putnam & Kozey (92), Wood (139).

during ground support is to generate propulsive force as early as possible, that is, once the foot touches down from the front side of the body, rather than to push from the backside. Thus, optimal recovery mechanics are another important determinant of sprinting speed and efficiency because the athlete must properly position his or her leg for ground contact as it swings forward. The role of explosive strength and the problems associated with overstriding—that is, counterproductive braking forces and increased ground contact times—then become apparent.

Technical Errors and Fatigue Effects

Table 17.1 itemizes common sprinting mistakes, as well as accompanying causes and corrections. Mistakes are usually associated with fatigue, deficient coordinative or physical abilities (or both), improper coaching, or simple misunderstanding. Unfortunately, some athletes have learned unsound mechanics. In some cases, these may be due to incorrect coaching guidelines—for example, trying to stay low or lean forward at maximum velocity, minimizing foot lift during recovery in order to have quicker feet, or overstriding in an attempt to pull

TABLE 17.1

Sprinting Technique Errors, Causes, and Corrections

Error	Cause	Correction
Start and acceleration		
Hands too wide apart in four-point stance	Misunderstanding of movement	Placing arms at shoulder-width
90° knee angle of front leg not achieved	Hips too high or low	Adjusting hip height
Excessive weight distributed to arms	Improper weight distribution	Raising hips upward more than forward; straightening arms and distributing weight evenly
Unnecessary tension in dorsal muscles; neck hyperextension	Misunderstanding of movement	Normal head alignment; eyes focused on ground
"Jumped" first stride	Push-off angle too high; upward thrust too steep	Increasing forward lean; maintaining proper head alignment; accelerating rear leg action
Premature upright posture	Inadequate push-off force; improper carriage of head	Increasing push-off force; maintaining forward trunk lean; keeping eyes focused on ground without lifting head
Maximum velocity		
Insufficient leg extension at push-off—that is, the athlete "sits"	Inadequate power transmission; push-off not powerful enough and too hasty	Ankle joint work in forward movement, running and hopping, running and jumping, bouncing, special strengthening
Feet turned excessively outward	Faulty running form	Running in lane; walking, jogging, and slow running with feet turned slightly inward
"Bouncing" with marked vertical swaying	Push-off force directed too vertically	Longer push-off; hitting chalk marks at regular intervals; starting exercises; increased stride rate
Forward swing of lead leg too wide; flat foot plant	Trunk/thigh weakness; fatigue	Snatching thigh in diagonal support (with and without additional load); high knee lift under difficult conditions, for example in deep snow, sand, uphill, or with weighted footwear; strengthening exercises
Ineffective arm movements—that is, transverse movement, excessive backward swing, hunched shoulders	Excessive shoulder movement; insufficient shoulder joint flexibility	Practicing proper movements during easy stride, side-straddle position, or jogging
Head and neck hyperextended or hyperflexed	Fatigue; misunderstanding of movement	Normal erect head carriage, eyes focused ahead

Data from Schmolinsky (106).

the ground under the body. Likewise, some athletes' prior speed training experience consists of fatiguing sprint conditioning, which can reinforce unsound mechanics. While such problems are often beyond the strength and conditioning professional's influence, it is important not to repeat these mistakes and to take corrective measures when possible.

Training Goals

The bottom-line goal of sprinting is to achieve high stride frequency and optimal stride length, with a trajectory characterized by explosive horizontal push-off and minimal vertical impulse. This involves reflexive ground contact and brief application of very high GRFs, with limited range of motion (ROM) at the ankle (by virtue of high stiffness regulation) during the support phase.

The following are some fundamental training objectives regarding performance enhancement and injury prevention (92, 139):

- *Minimize braking forces at ground contact* by maximizing the backward velocity of the leg and foot at touchdown and by planting the foot directly beneath the center of gravity.
- *Emphasize brief ground support times as a means of achieving rapid stride rate.* As previously mentioned, this requires a high level of explosive strength.
- *Emphasize functional training of the hamstring muscle group* with respect to its biarticular structure and dual role (simultaneous concentric hip extension and eccentric knee flexion) during late recovery. Eccentric knee flexor strength is the most important aspect limiting recovery of the leg as it swings forward.

Running speed is the interaction of stride frequency and stride length. The goal of sprinting is to achieve high stride frequency and optimal stride length, with explosive horizontal push-off and minimal vertical impulse.

AGILITY

Agility effectively comprises an athlete's entire movement skill set, with linear running being one component of overall maneuverability. In the international community, agility is often broadly defined as an athlete's collective **coordinative abilities** (28, 49, 125). These are the basic elements of technical skills used to perform motor tasks spanning the power spectrum from dynamic, gross activities to fine motor control tasks:

- *Adaptive ability*—modification of action sequence upon observation or anticipation of novel or changing conditions and situations
- *Balance*—static and dynamic equilibrium
- *Combinatory ability*—coordination of body movements into a given action
- *Differentiation*—accurate, economical adjustment of body movements and mechanics
- *Orientation*—spatial and temporal control of body movements
- *Reactiveness*—quick, well-directed response to stimuli
- *Rhythm*—observation and implementation of dynamic motion pattern, timing, and variation

Coordinative abilities are believed to be most trainable in preadolescence, which is considered a critical or sensitive period for skill development (6, 9, 22, 28, 49, 72, 125, 132). This window of opportunity begins to close during adolescence, during which the focus should progress from basic movement competencies and fitness qualities to specific skills and abilities—that is, from general to special preparation.

An agility needs analysis seems like a daunting challenge, considering the range of movement tasks involved in many sports. Athletes must skillfully perform different modes of locomotion (e.g., running forward, backward, and laterally) and efficiently transition from one mode to another. They must manage momentum while maneuvering and changing velocities. They regularly support their bodies on a single limb, with the center of mass frequently outside its base of support. External forces—especially gravity—confront them and constantly disturb their balance. In many cases, athletes perform these tasks while manipulating objects and deploying complex strategies.

Current lines of evidence on athletes' agility performance deal with cornering techniques (2, 18, 43, 44, 127), backward running performance (4, 21, 36, 123), the mechanics of certain maneuvers (e.g., crossover or sidestep cutting) with regard to mechanisms of injury (37, 56, 75, 89, 90, 110), and the specificity of certain agility skills in relation to linear running (16, 29, 68, 74, 140, 141). To date, however, there are few comprehensive resources on this issue. One can simplify an agility needs analysis by categorizing skills rationally and addressing task specificity on two fronts: change in velocity and mode of locomotion.

Agility is an expression of an athlete's coordinative abilities, which are the basis of acceleration, maximum-velocity, and multidirectional skills.

Skill Classification

Movement skills can be classified according to three basic motor behavior criteria (70, 102, 103): general versus special tasks, closed versus open tasks, and continuous versus discrete versus serial tasks. These schemes are not mutually exclusive, so it is useful in practice to categorize tasks according to each set of criteria.

General Versus Special Skills

General agility tasks target the development of one or more basic coordinative abilities, whereas special tasks unify them in a skill-specific manner. The basis of this concept is the motor learning principle of **practice specificity** with respect to sensorimotor, processing, and contextual effects on acquisition, retention, and transfer (70, 102, 103).

Closed Versus Open Skills

Closed agility skills have programmed assignments and predictable or stable environments. The athlete rather than the context determines where, when, and how to begin the action, with the objective of optimizing motor patterns and achieving consistent performances (70, 102, 103). Examples include preplanned tasks such as the pro agility drill and the T-test.

Open skills have nonprogrammed assignments and unpredictable or unstable environments. The context changes during performance, and the training objective is to rapidly respond and adapt to new or unforeseen stimuli and situations (70, 102, 103). Examples include unanticipated tasks with no predetermined structure (e.g., open-field dodging in team games) in which perceptual skills and feedback adjustments play more prominent roles than premovement planning. Some tasks are performed in semipredictable circumstances (e.g., the assignment or environment is variable, but can be anticipated to some extent with experience and practice).

Continuous Versus Discrete Versus Serial Skills

Continuous tasks have no identifiable start or finish, with activity beginning and ending arbitrarily. They are usually performed at low or intermediate speeds due to their ongoing, cyclical nature. From a motor control standpoint, premovement planning tends to be limited, and feedback and error detection and correction significantly influence performance (70, 102, 103).

In contrast, discrete tasks have a definite start and finish. Their brief, acyclical nature often—but not always—allows them to be performed at high speeds, with motor programs tending to play a more dominant role than they do in continuous tasks (70, 102, 103).

Serial tasks are composed of discrete skills performed in sequence, with successful execution of each subtask determining the overall outcome (70, 102, 103). Most athletic skills belong in this category, whereas pure examples of continuous or discrete tasks are rare. For example, continuous cyclic events such as a marathon, while prolonged, usually have a clearly defined beginning and end. Discrete acyclic activities such as a 100 m sprint, although brief, often consist of serial subtasks.

Change in Velocity

For most land sports, linear running mechanics are part of a larger skill set involving acceleration, maximum-velocity, and multidirectional movements. A growing body of evidence demonstrates limited transfer between linear sprinting and agility skills, even when locomotion modes and distances are identical (16, 29, 68, 74, 140, 141). Thus, task specificity is an important consideration in training.

Agility tasks involving changes in velocity can be characterized by several criteria:

- Initial speed and direction
- Decrease or increase in speed (or both) and redirection of movement
- Final speed and direction

Changing velocities involves more than performing stop and go activities. Athletes tend to use various techniques as they move through a spectrum of speeds and directions. For example, certain tasks may require a power cut in which the athlete decelerates significantly and redirects sharply (>90° from the original path); others require a speed cut involving subtler deceleration and redirection (<90°) (93).

Athletes often use cornering techniques when accelerating through a radial or hyperbolic path. These can involve longer routes than cutting maneuvers, but are often faster because they enable athletes to maintain or increase speed as they redirect (2). The smaller the radius, the lower the cornering speed, and the longer the support phase duration tends to be, partly due to the coefficient of friction between the athlete's foot and the ground (2, 43, 44, 127). Athletes generally need less body lean for stability when running larger radii, in which case GRFs—especially with the inside leg—tend to determine cornering speed (2, 18).

Athletes' acceleration and deceleration patterns can differ widely between sports, regardless of apparent similarities in playing surface areas, number of players per team, and so on. Even within a sport, athletes' respective abilities and responsibilities influence their movements. Novice and intermediate athletes cannot achieve the same maximal running velocities or rates of acceleration as advanced athletes—that is, novice athletes reach lower top speeds, and reach them sooner, possibly within 3 to 4 seconds (20-30 m) as compared with 5 to 6 seconds (50-60 m) for elite athletes. Furthermore, initial and final movement velocities, as well as their rate and amplitude of change, can vary significantly. Thus, strength and conditioning professionals should use discretion when generalizing the results of task analysis for a given sport, position, or level of competition.

Locomotion Mode

Any method of locomotion, including running, involves a distinct skill set. Even within a given method, different modes of movement—forward, backward, diagonal, lateral, or any combination of these—may be required depending on the situation or assignment. In addition to skillfully performing each mode in discrete fashion, athletes must efficiently transition between the modes in serial fashion. Agility tasks involving changes in locomotion mode can therefore be characterized by the following criteria:

- The specific locomotion mode(s) performed and the movement technique(s) used to execute them discretely
- The specific sequence(s) in which they are performed and the technique(s) used to transition between them serially

The available evidence suggests that backpedal running is a distinct technique rather than a simple reversal of forward running. The anatomical and functional asymmetry of the leg imposes different mechanical constraints on the respective movements, as is evident in terms of movement kinetics and kinematics (4, 21, 123) as well as muscle actions and firing patterns (36).

Athletes' maximal backward running velocities tend to be ~60% to 80% of their forward velocities (4). High-speed backpedal running is characterized by shorter stride length; greater stride frequency; longer support time; later application of peak GRF; greater hip angular velocity; and smaller ROM at the hip, knee, and ankle joints (4). Hip moment and power patterns are similar in magnitude, but opposite in direction, to those occurring during forward running (21). Backward running also tends to result in significantly lower peak GRF and impulse (123) and less power or work at the knee and ankle (21, 36).

The situations in which backpedaling occurs in a particular sport—and sequences in which it is coupled with other modes of movement—tend to vary according to positional assignments or responsibilities. Once again, this supports the need for task analysis and training specificity.

Strength and conditioning professionals can simplify the agility needs analysis by addressing task specificity on two fronts (change in velocity, mode of locomotion) and classifying motor skills according to basic schemes (general vs. special tasks, closed vs. open tasks, continuous vs. discrete vs. serial tasks).

Technical Considerations

Using the criteria outlined previously, linear sprinting can be described as a closed, serial task with the following characteristics:

- *Velocity:* The athlete starts with an initial speed of zero, maximally accelerates forward, and achieves maximum speed over a specified distance (e.g., 100 m) with minimal deceleration or redirection.
- *Mode:* The athlete runs forward by executing a series of discrete subtasks (start, acceleration, maximum velocity) without transitioning to another mode of locomotion.

Using this as a starting point, it is possible to adapt certain sprinting mechanics to various multidirectional tasks. Considering the forces involved when the athlete explosively decelerates, as well as the role of SSC actions when the athlete redirects, some basic principles of plyometric training are also applicable.

Body Position

As is the case during acceleration, an athlete's body lean must increase as the rate of deceleration increases; that is, the base of support must move farther from the center of gravity in order to maintain dynamic stability. During reacceleration, the athlete's posture should progressively climb toward vertical, approaching ≤5° as maximal velocity is reacquired.

To the extent that it is practical, athletes should strive to achieve a power line position when redirecting (similar to the sprint start and acceleration; figure 17.5), especially as they fully extend the support leg and drive off the ground. It can be tempting to cue athletes to align the horizontal axis of this position in the direction of intended movement, but this may not be appropriate due to inertial and centripetal forces.

Visual Focus

The key role of visual focus during sprinting has important implications in multidirectional tasks also (86). In general, the athlete should carry the head in a neutral position and focus the eyes directly ahead. When running forward or backward, the athlete should focus on the point he or she is moving toward or away from and should use peripheral vision when moving laterally. Exceptions to this guideline are appropriate when one is focusing on a projectile, teammate, opponent, or other visual target or for tactical reasons (e.g., using the eyes for deception when "looking off" an opponent).

When the athlete is executing directional changes (e.g., cutting left or right) and transitions (e.g., a turn-and-run maneuver from a backpedal into a forward sprint in the same direction), specific footwork techniques such as an open or crossover step can be accompanied by quick redirection of focus to a new visual target. An error in either action can result in rounding off a turn or weaving outside of a desired movement path, with subsequent loss of time or efficiency.

Leg Action

In general, the greater the deceleration during execution of multidirectional tasks, the greater the need to subsequently reacquire high stride rate and stride length during reacceleration. As is the case with linear acceleration, the athlete's body lean is likely to limit the cyclical action of the leg compared with that in maximum-velocity running.

Arm Action

Multidirectional tasks also require effective arm action (86). The athlete must rapidly accelerate into a new path or mode (or both) when redirecting or when performing transitions and turns. As is the case when the athlete drives out of the sprint start, powerful arm action should be used to facilitate leg drive and in turn reacquire high stride rate and stride length; an example is during transitioning from a backpedal into a forward sprint in the opposite direction or vice versa. Inadequate or improper arm action may result in a loss of speed or efficiency.

Braking Mechanics

The more explosively athletes change velocities, the greater the need for eccentric strength and reactive ability. In addition to enabling athletes to decelerate, braking forces may help control rotation about the long axis of the body during maneuvering (58, 91).

Some basic guidelines for safe and effective plyometric training can be adapted to agility tasks (50, 104, 105, 109, 116, 142). Perhaps most importantly, the capability to decelerate from a given velocity is requisite to changing directions—just as the athlete must be able to land safely and efficiently from a given drop height before attempting depth or rebound jumps from that height. The following is an example of how to progressively develop and evaluate this capability (86).

1. Instruct the athlete to run forward and achieve second gear (1/2 speed), and then decelerate and stop within three steps.
2. Instruct the athlete to run forward and achieve third gear (3/4 speed), and then decelerate and stop within five steps.
3. Instruct the athlete to run forward and achieve fourth gear (full speed), and then decelerate and stop within seven steps.

A similar approach is useful with backward and lateral movements as well. While the choice of velocities and braking distances is somewhat arbitrary, athletes should progressively develop the ability to decelerate from different speeds before attempting to redirect explosively.

Athletes should learn proper braking mechanics, especially regarding initial foot contact during the support phase. Due to the anatomy of the ankle and the placement of the athlete's foot relative to the center of mass, it is common for the heel to strike the ground first and the forefoot to subsequently "crash" when decelerating explosively. Besides limiting traction by reducing the surface area that contacts the ground, this may be problematic in terms of orthopedic stresses and muscle activation patterns. A preferred technique is to position the ankle such that contact occurs on a full foot, thereby maximizing the interface with the ground and engaging the entire lower extremity in eccentric force reduction.

METHODS OF DEVELOPING SPEED AND AGILITY

From a hierarchical standpoint, the methods for developing speed and agility can be categorized as primary, secondary, or tertiary. This scheme is largely a matter of practicality and is based on a continuum of skills and abilities ranging from special to general. The key to applying these methods lies in their skillful combination rather than exclusive or disproportionate use of any one of them.

Primary Method

The primary method for speed and agility development is execution of sound movement technique in a specific task. Initially, athletes should perform tasks at submaximal learning speeds to establish proper mechanics. As they progress toward mastery, task performance can approach or exceed full competition speed (23, 39, 57, 106). For execution of specific techniques, an athlete's mechanics should target the performance criteria discussed in the previous sections.

In contrast to some skills, running is a natural activity that most athletes have experience with—correct or otherwise. On the one hand, children usually learn the rough technique of running at an early age (9, 72). To some extent, technique training can focus on perfecting form and correcting faults more than on teaching novel mechanics. On the other hand, many athletes acquire inefficient movement habits due to incorrect coaching or unfamiliarity with the advanced technique. This presents a challenge in terms of skill acquisition because it involves revising established motor programs (guidelines for teaching movement skills are presented in the "Program Design" section, p. 476).

Secondary Methods

Secondary methods of speed and agility training include **sprint resistance** and **sprint assistance**. These target the development of special skills in modified performance conditions.

Sprint Resistance

This method includes gravity-resisted running (e.g., upgrade or upstair sprinting) or other means of achieving an overload effect (e.g., harness, parachute, sled, or weighted vest). The objective is to provide resistance without arresting the athlete's movement mechanics, primarily as a means of improving explosive strength and stride length (23, 32, 39, 57, 65, 66, 97). In general, ≥10% changes in movement resistance have detrimental effects on technique (e.g., arresting the athlete's arm and leg action in an attempt to muscle through each stride). Thus, strength and conditioning professionals should apply overload conservatively.

Sprint Assistance

Sprint assistance includes gravity-assisted running (e.g., downgrade sprinting on a shallow [3-7°] slope), high-speed towing (e.g., harness and stretch cord), or other means of achieving an overspeed effect. The objective is to provide assistance without significantly altering the athlete's movement mechanics, primarily as a means of improving stride rate (23, 31, 39, 57, 65, 66, 79, 97, 114, 130). Regardless of whether the athlete actually achieves overspeed, this method may also improve quality of effort during normal maximum-velocity sprinting by reducing the time and energy needed to accelerate. In general, apply assistance conservatively, exceeding maximum velocity by ≤10% (~1 m/s). Beyond this threshold, the athlete may tend to lean back and overstride in an attempt to brake and protect him- or herself.

Tertiary Methods

Tertiary methods of speed and agility training include **mobility**, **strength**, and **endurance training**. These target the development of general skills and abilities.

Mobility

It is important to view functional flexibility in the context of the optimal ROMs needed to perform specific tasks. During running, the hip and knee joints move through relatively larger ROMs than the ankle, which acts almost isometrically during the support phase by virtue of reflex stiffness and SSC action (1, 2, 10, 33, 38, 62, 63). The ability to fully retract the leg during recovery is requisite to achieving proper ground preparation position and subsequent ground strike. Inadequate mobility can therefore result in improper foot placement (e.g., overstriding), with longer ground contact times and higher braking forces.

If an athlete has sufficient mobility, the forces occurring within normal ROMs—rather than his or her flexibility—may determine performance or predisposition to injury. Therefore, it is simplistic to apply the notion of full range of motion to all tasks or joint actions.

Athletes can develop mobility restrictions because of imbalanced training or adaptive shortening, for example, due to inactivity or immobilization. Strength and conditioning professionals should identify such limitations and specifically address them in training. Regular flexibility training generally seems to have beneficial effects on athletic performance (77, 108) and equivocal effects in terms of injury prevention (121). Given the task-specific functions of multiarticular muscles (135, 138), it is important to assess flexibility with valid means and to use discretion when generalizing isolated joint actions to multijoint tasks.

Strength

Athletes must develop explosive strength qualities in order to maximize their speed and agility performance. This does not imply, however, that they should perform only low-resistance, high-speed movements in training. The ability to achieve high movement velocities requires skillful force application across a range of power outputs and muscle actions. For maximal transfer to athleticism, resistance training programs should progressively address the entire force–velocity spectrum (figure 17.2). This is achievable with mixed methods training strategies (22, 49, 50, 88, 109, 116, 128, 132, 142).

Strength and conditioning professionals should select and prioritize strength training tasks according to their **dynamic correspondence** with the target activity (109, 129, 131). Rate and time of peak force production (impulse; figure 17.1) and dynamics of effort (power; figure 17.2) are especially important criteria. Other considerations include amplitude and direction of movement, accentuated region of force application, and regime of muscular work. The keys to optimal transfer are threefold: identify the target activity's mechanics via task-specific needs analysis, choose training movements accordingly, and distinguish between specificity and simulation of a task's outward appearance.

Stretch-shortening cycle actions fulfill most or all of these criteria and usually deserve high priority in speed and agility training. The following is a simple classification scheme for plyometric tasks associated with SSC actions (104, 105):

- *Long response*—ground contact >0.25 second, large angular displacement
- *Short response*—ground contact <0.25 second, small angular displacement

This scheme is useful in selecting tasks to improve specific running mechanics. For example, long-response plyometrics such as countermovement or squat jumps transfer most directly to start and acceleration performance, whereas short-response plyometrics such as depth or drop jumps have more transfer to maximum-velocity running.

Further, athletic movements like running and jumping involve force transmission and summation through the kinetic chain, rather than isolation within body segments (3, 10, 53, 109, 116, 124, 135, 138, 142). For example, since the primary propulsive forces occur during ground contact, closed chain movements of the lower limb would be a logical starting point in selecting exercises to improve sprinting performance. The strength and conditioning professional might assign open chain exercises to a secondary, but still important, role. Indeed, braking the forward swing of the recovery leg in preparation for ground strike beneath the body is an open chain movement that athletes must execute properly in order to efficiently apply GRFs during the support phase.

Speed-Endurance

The concept of speed-endurance originated in racing events (23, 39, 48, 49, 57, 106, 107, 115, 133, 136, 137) and is the basis of the special endurance paradigm discussed next. Figure 17.9 summarizes traditional methods for developing this quality. The athlete's training status and the demands of his or her sport should determine the respective role of each method.

CLASSIC METHODS FOR SPEED-ENDURANCE DEVELOPMENT

Competitive-Trial Methods

- Supramaximal training
  - *Intensity:* greater than competition
  - *Duration/distance:* less than competition
- Maximal training
  - *Intensity:* equal to or less than competition
  - *Duration/distance:* equal to competition
- Submaximal training
  - *Intensity:* less than competition
  - *Duration/distance:* greater than competition

Distance-Duration Methods

- Continuous training (70-95% competitive speed/power)
- Variable training (structured changes in intensity, duration, volume, and density)
- Fartlek training (unstructured changes in intensity, duration, volume, and density)

Interval Methods

- Extensive training
  - *Intensity:* low-medium (60-80% competitive speed/power)
  - *Duration/distance:* short-medium; for example 14 to 180 seconds at 100 to 1,000 m running distance (advanced athletes), 17 to 100 seconds at 100 to 400 m running distance (beginners)
  - *Volume:* large; for example 8 to 40 reps (advanced athletes), 5 to 12 reps (beginners)
  - *Density:* high; short incomplete relief interval allowing heart rate to recover to 125 to 130 beats/min (advanced athletes) or 110 to 120 beats/min (beginners) (<1/3 the time needed for complete recovery); for example 45 to 90 seconds or 60 to 120 seconds for advanced and beginner athletes, respectively
- Intensive training
  - *Intensity:* high (80-90% competitive speed/power)
  - *Duration/distance:* short; for example 13 to 180 seconds at 100 to 1,000 m running distance (advanced athletes), 14 to 95 seconds at 100 to 400 m running distance (beginners)
  - *Volume:* small; for example 4 to 12 reps (advanced athletes) or 4 to 8 reps (beginners)
  - *Density:* medium; longer but still incomplete relief interval allowing heart rate to recover to 110 to 120 beats/min, for example 90 to 180 seconds (advanced athletes) and 120 to 240 seconds (beginners)

Repetition Methods

- *Intensity:* very high (90-100% competitive speed/power)
- *Duration/distance:* very short–medium; for example 2 to 3 seconds up to several minutes
- *Volume:* very small; for example three to six reps
- *Density:* low; long near-complete rest interval allowing heart rate to recover to ≤100 beats/min; for example 3 to 5 minutes

Figure 17.9 Repetition methods are appropriate for speed and agility training. Competitive-trial and interval methods are appropriate for speed-endurance training.

Sources: Harre (48, 49); Schmolinsky (106); Steinhofer (115); Viru, Korge, and Parnet (133); Viru (132).

The objective of the competitive-trial method of training is to develop an athlete's special endurance—the specific metabolic conditioning needed to perform his or her movement skills in competition or practice (22, 23, 48, 49, 109). The underlying strategy is to develop the ability to achieve a predetermined effort distribution, or a target pace or series of target paces, in training and competition. This method can be adapted to sports other than race events (87, 95, 117, 118).

Figure 17.10 outlines a procedure for establishing special endurance training criteria according to competitive exercise:relief patterns in various sports (87). This **tactical metabolic training** concept offers certain advantages. It economizes training time and effort by optimizing athletes' arousal, attention, and motivation through sport skill–based metabolic conditioning drills—for example, performing a series of playbook assignments in competition-specific workloads.

It is equally important to understand the limitations of this method. Unless accompanied by telemetry data, tactical modeling does not provide a direct measure of workload intensity. The strength and conditioning professional must therefore establish target training pace(s) for the observed interval duration(s). For activities in which resistance is limited to the athlete's body mass, one can estimate this by reversing an established method of projecting running time as a function of distance (23, 106, 136, 137)—that is, projecting running distance as a function of time, and then making empirical adjustments according to an athlete's developmental status and workload tolerance. The energy cost can be estimated as a function of movement velocity for a variety of locomotion modes (27), thereby establishing equivalent workloads for different modalities.

Another limitation of this procedure is that tactical models based on play start-stoppage patterns may not account for the total volume of work performed in competition, especially if activity continues when play is suspended (e.g., after a score, penalty, or time-out). In general, however, this method is a pragmatic way to model special endurance training tasks on the underlying tempo of competition.

The primary method for speed and agility development is execution of sound movement technique in a specific task. Secondary methods include sprint resistance and sprint assistance training. Tertiary methods include mobility, strength, and speed-endurance training.

PROGRAM DESIGN

Program design involves planning at several levels, each with its own set of considerations: microcycles (short-term), mesocycles (medium-term), and macrocycles (long-term). This process is referred to as **periodization**—the planned distribution or variation in training means and methods on a periodic or cyclic basis (22, 49, 50, 88, 109, 116, 132, 142).

At each level of planning, strength and conditioning professionals must rationally manipulate the following variables. While these are useful in quantifying workloads, it is important to accompany them with qualitative criteria regarding task-specific learning and training goals:

- *Exercise (or work) interval*—the duration (e.g., in seconds) or distance (e.g., in meters) over which a repetition is executed
- *Exercise order*—the sequence in which a set of repetitions is executed
- *Exercise:relief*—the relative density of exercise and relief intervals in a set, expressed as a ratio (also called *work:rest ratio*)
- *Frequency*—the number of training sessions performed in a given time period (e.g., day or week)
- *Intensity*—the effort with which a repetition is executed
- *Relief or recovery (or rest) interval*—the time period between repetitions and sets
- *Repetition*—the execution of a specific workload assignment or movement technique
- *Series*—a group of sets and recovery intervals
- *Set*—a group of repetitions and relief intervals
- *Volume*—the amount of work (repetitions × sets) performed in a given training session or time period

Short-Term Planning

Fatigue management and task specificity are the driving forces in short-range planning of speed and agility development. Fatigue is a progressive process that begins at the onset of work and affects task execution well before failure occurs (5, 14, 35, 40, 99, 119). It is a normal result of intense activity, but tends to interfere with skill acquisition and performance (70, 102, 103).

TACTICAL MODELING PROCEDURE FOR ESTABLISHING SPECIAL ENDURANCE TRAINING CRITERIA

1. Identify competition model with respect to (examples are provided):
   - Level
     - Professional, collegiate, high school, club
     - Conference, division, league
   - Scheme, style, system
     - Offensive
     - Defensive
   - Time period
     - Contest, game, match
     - Half, period, quarter
   - Personnel
     - Team
     - Platoon, shift
     - Position
2. Identify nature and scope of tactical events:
   - Intensity level(s)
     - Subjective
     - Objective
   - Outcomes, goals, objectives
     - "Settled" events, such as attack, possession, rally, series
     - "Unsettled/transitional" events, such as clear, fast break, special teams, turnover
     - Power play, extra-man or man-down situation
3. Video record specific competition(s) or segment(s) with respect to selected tactical events and assignments.
4. Evaluate the following:
   - Fundamental exercise:relief pattern
     - Frequency distribution
     - Central tendency versus variability
   - Subdivisions
     - One or more sprints or transitional events (or both) superimposed on continuous activity
   - Set-groupings as a function of extended-recovery intervals consequent to
     - Injuries
     - Penalties
     - Scores
     - Media, official, tactical time-outs
5. Select core training and testing task(s):
   - Workload intensity and duration
   - Position- and situation-specific assignment(s) and technique(s)

Figure 17.10 This procedure can be used to establish special endurance training criteria for a sport.

Reprinted, by permission, from Plisk and Gambetta, 1997 (87).

The intent of speed-endurance training, to enhance fatigue resistance and tolerance, is somewhat different from that of speed and agility training. For this reason, it involves tactics that purposefully stress the metabolic systems. Training tasks in both cases are technical in nature. Strength and conditioning professionals should therefore apply sound motor learning strategies when teaching movement skills.

Speed and Agility Sessions

Maximum running velocity has been directly related to muscle myokinase (MK) and creatine phosphokinase (CPK) activities and inversely related to total lactate dehydrogenase (LDH) activity (64, 120). Thus, enzymes associated with adenosine triphosphate (ATP) resynthesis capacity and pyruvate-lactate interconversion are key determinants of sprinting speed. Sprint-type training has its greatest effects on the phosphagen pathways, with lesser but significant effects on glycolytic or oxidative metabolism (5, 7, 14, 42, 98, 111, 112, 132).

Intense, brief activities engage the phosphagen pathway, especially in fast-twitch muscle fibers (5, 7, 14, 26, 41, 45, 79, 94, 112). Likewise, these pathways account for much of the energy yield during the transition from rest to exercise, or from one workload to another, in all fiber types. Although intramuscular ATP levels rarely drop more than 40% to 60%, several seconds of intense activity can virtually deplete creatine phosphate (CP); this is highly correlated with sprinting fatigue (5, 14, 26, 76, 112, 132).

Creatine phosphate repletion is achieved oxidatively, with a biphasic time course characterized by initial rapid (half-time 20-22 seconds) and subsequent slow (half-time ~170 seconds) components (5, 14, 17, 26, 71, 76, 112, 134). Adenosine diphosphate levels modulate the initial phase, which seems to be unaffected by intracellular pH, whereas the latter phase is depressed at low pH (5, 14, 76). This has important implications with respect to fatigue during repeated efforts.

Sprint training tends to modify muscle contractile characteristics via at least three mechanisms: hypertrophy, especially in fast-twitch fibers; increased development of the sarcoplasmic reticulum; and shifts in myosin heavy-chain isoforms, with both Types I and IIx fibers shifting toward IIa (98). There is also limited evidence suggesting that sprint training enhances muscle Na^+/K^+ pump activity (114) and nerve conduction velocity (99).

Although much of the evidence on fatigue addresses peripheral factors in working muscle tissue (5, 14, 35), there is also a central component involving the motoneural system (40, 99, 119). Acute performance impairment is usually the combined result of several mechanisms, with their relative contributions varying according to the nature of the task. Collectively, there are several practical implications for conducting training sessions (12, 22, 23, 42, 48, 49, 78, 94, 98, 99, 106, 111, 114, 115, 132, 133):

- Because of their high neuromuscular and motor coordination demands, athletes should conduct speed and agility tasks early in a training session, before other fatiguing activities.
- Structure training sessions around brief work bouts and frequent 2- to 3-minute rest periods in order to maximize the quality of learning and training effects. Repetition methods are an ideal choice in this case, whereas competitive-trial and interval methods are generally better suited for speed-endurance training, as discussed later (figure 17.9).
- Where feasible, it can be beneficial to distribute daily sessions into modules separated by recovery breaks, or to subdivide workloads into brief clusters separated by frequent rest pauses, or both.

When one is prescribing training stimuli, the challenge is to strike a balance between opposing fitness and fatigue responses (8, 142). For this reason, sound strategies usually have two basic features: a fairly stable menu of training tasks over any given micro- or mesocycle, and regular variation in workload and technique targets, for example on a daily or weekly basis (or both).

Decisions regarding intensity and volume prescriptions are required on a day-to-day as well as an individual session basis. In fact, the interaction of these variables drives much of the program design process—hence the value of a practical indicator of training stress like **volume-load**, the product of work volume and intensity (116). When conducting speed and agility sessions, the strength and conditioning professional can quantify volume-load in terms of running speeds and distances. At the lower end is the stimulus threshold required to trigger desired effects, whereas at the upper end is a point of diminishing returns, beyond which further application yields no beneficial—or possibly detrimental—effects. These tend to be moving targets as an athlete's fitness and adaptivity improve with long-term development (22, 49, 50, 109, 116, 132, 142).

Volume-load progression is a central issue at all levels of planning. Variable rather than linear strategies tend to yield superior results (22, 49, 50, 88, 109, 116, 132, 142) and can be achieved through various methods. A basic tactic at the microcyclic level is to establish a fixed training frequency, for example one day on, one day off or two on, two off, and manipulate simple workload parameters such as intensity (movement speed) and volume (repetition distance and number).

Speed-Endurance Sessions

As workload duration or repetition progresses, glycolytic activity can exceed mitochondrial capacity to oxidize the resulting end products—especially if recovery periods are limited. Acid–base balance in the tissues is disturbed because of coupling between ATPase and glycolysis, not just H^+ production via the glycolytic pathway (5, 14, 35, 41, 45, 76, 80, 112). The resulting disturbances in excitation-contraction coupling and cross-bridge formation impair the muscle's mechanical properties and energetic efficiency via depressed RFD, peak force, velocity, power, and CP repletion, as well as prolonged relaxation time (5, 14, 35, 76).

Pyruvate-lactate clearance is achieved oxidatively and is facilitated by shuttling of lactate between sites of production (in both fiber types) and consumption (especially in Type I fibers) (5, 7, 14, 41, 45, 80, 126). This mechanism allows oxidative metabolism to buffer glycolysis to some extent while increasing energy yield. Oxidative and nonoxidative pathways work interdependently during and after intense activity (5, 7, 11, 12, 14, 41, 45, 80, 112, 126). A simplistic interpretation of this is that distance-duration training methods are useful when athletes are preparing for intensive sports. Indeed, submaximal exercise can be appropriate for acute priming and recovery activities. In terms of chronic training effects, however, interval methods tend to increase glycolytic as well as oxidative enzyme activities, acid–base buffering capability, and various indices of lactic power and capacity (5, 11, 12, 14, 42, 98, 111); low-intensity speed-endurance training does not, and in fact may reduce nonoxidative enzyme activities (5, 14). Although mitochondrial adaptations to interval methods are modest by comparison, the functional benefits may offset the drawbacks. Depending on the nature of the sport, therefore, strength and conditioning professionals should use low-intensity speed-endurance training with discretion.

A practical solution is to subdivide a given volume of preparatory speed-endurance work into segments, effectively rest-pausing as needed to achieve the targeted objectives for power output and task performance. For example, rather than middle- or long-duration activities, total distance can be structured into sets of shuttles or striders with workloads at or above $\dot{V}O_2$max and exercise:relief ratios adjusted accordingly. This approach exploits the advantages of intensive, low- or moderate-volume intermittent training while emphasizing task execution rather than just exertion.

Even during off-season periods, workloads need not be limited to submaximal levels. A superior method of speed-endurance training for many sports is to maximally engage the oxidative pathways in intermittent tasks instead of continuous, submaximal workloads (figure 17.9) (5, 11, 12, 14). During preseason periods, speed-endurance training can then progress to competitive-trial methods. The tactical metabolic training procedure outlined previously is a pragmatic way to model these sessions on competition-specific criteria (figure 17.10).

Motor Learning Guidelines

Certain strategies for teaching motor skills yield superior results. Some are straightforward, whereas others may seem counterintuitive. For example, according to the principle of practice specificity, the sensorimotor, processing, and contextual demands of training tasks should correspond to the target activity in order to maximize the acquisition, retention, and transfer of motor skills (70, 102, 103). However, an optimal level of contextual interference in the form of varied or random practice will enhance learning, although at the expense of short-term performance (70, 102, 103).

Following is a summary of evidence-based guidelines for teaching movement skills (70, 102, 103):

- *Physical versus mental practice.* Active physical practice is generally superior to mental practice. The strength and conditioning professional can usually achieve optimal learning effects by skillfully combining the two; however, mental practice is especially useful for preperformance preparation. Purposeful, structured practice activities can be supplemented with off-task imaging and cognitive rehearsal. Regardless of how dynamic a task is, the key objectives are information processing, decision making, and problem solving. Optimal arousal, motivation, and focused attention are necessary to achieve the desired learning and performance goals.

- *Amount of practice.* The benefits of overlearning skills are well documented. A substantial body of evidence supports the 10-year rule for achieving mastery (19, 113). The acquisition of expertise in a wide range of performance domains, including sport, involves up to 10 years—or 10,000 hours—of regular, guided, deliberate preparation. More practice is generally better, but its content and structure are also vital.
- *Whole versus part practice.* Two criteria should form the basis for this choice: (1) number and interdependence of skill parts and (2) athlete's developmental status. Part practice is preferable for tasks that are highly complex but low in organization. Whole practice is preferable for tasks that are low in complexity but highly organized. There are advantages to each method because functional tasks tend to reside in the middle of this continuum, and skill acquisition involves learning the parts as well as uniting them into a cohesive whole. Given the limits on athletes' attentional capacity, it is usually appropriate to use variants of part practice such as task segmentation or simplification. If this is impractical, cue athletes' attention to one or more specific parts during practice of whole skills.
- *Augmented feedback and instruction.* Extrinsic feedback is beneficial when a skill is complex or the athlete is a novice, and essential when intrinsic feedback is limited or difficult to interpret. Frequent feedback is important during the early stage of learning, but can be detrimental if the athlete becomes dependent on it. The verbal instructions should combine demonstration-modeling and verbal instruction, focus on (but not be redundant with) intrinsic feedback, provide information on proper performance as well as error correction, progress from qualitative to quantitative information, and gradually decrease in frequency.
- *Practice distribution.* Motor skill learning generally improves with shorter, more frequent practice sessions. There are practical considerations, however, in terms of limited time and possible trade-offs with the amount of practice. Distributed practice tends to improve long-term acquisition and transfer of continuous skills, as well as acute performance. Massed practice tends to improve acquisition and transfer of discrete skills but can reduce acute performance.
- *Practice variation.* It may be advantageous for novice athletes to begin with blocked practice involving one version of a task until they master the basic technique. The strength and conditioning professional should then introduce varied practice—that is, changing task order or conditions—to help athletes develop specific schemas. This may seem paradoxical because blocked practice usually improves acute performance but reduces learning, retention, and transfer. Varied practice can reduce acute performance but significantly improves long-term skill acquisition.

Medium-Term Planning

The basic objectives of medium-range planning are to exploit complementary training effects at optimal times and minimize the compatibility problems associated with concurrent training. Certain types of training can interfere with one another when performed in parallel, at least in previously untrained subjects (67, 109, 116, 132, 142). This creates a dual problem. On one hand, athletes must develop high levels of specific fitness qualities in order to optimize athleticism; on the other hand, cumulative fatigue can be problematic when athletes are trying to develop these two simultaneously. Advanced athletes can tolerate greater training stress but are typically closer to an overtraining threshold than novices.

Sequenced training strategies are based on the premise that the delayed effects of certain training stimuli can alter the responses to others (47, 109, 116, 128, 131, 132, 142). The rate of involution, or decay, of training effects is a central consideration in exploiting this phenomenon (132). Acutely, involution is a function of the half-life of the tissues that are synthesized during adaptive remodeling—for example, the half-life of glycolytic enzymes is relatively brief, ranging from ~1 1/2 hours to a few days, whereas oxidative enzymes turn over more slowly and myofibrillar proteins have a comparatively greater life span. Chronically, the longer the training cycle, the more stable its residual effect.

This allows athletes to maintain the performance gains acquired during one training cycle with relatively small volume-loads during the next training cycle, thus creating an opportunity to strive toward a new training goal. A general rule is to organize training into approximately four-week periods (88, 132, 142), which seem to represent an optimal biological window for integrating responses over the intermediate term.

Sequenced training involves alternating blocks of accumulation and restitution, each with essentially one objective (50, 109, 116, 128, 131, 132, 142). For example, the accumulation block emphasizes strength development while allocating minimal, that is, maintenance-type, workloads to speed and agility training. The restitution block reverses the emphasis, reducing strength workloads while targeting speed and agility development. A sample outline of a sequenced preseason program is presented in the "Training Plan" section.

Sequenced training is a significant departure from the concurrent strategies commonly used in basic and intermediate applications. Much of the literature describing this method addresses it in theoretical terms but offers limited supporting evidence or practical guidelines. In any case, the following things are clear (88, 109, 116, 132, 142): Such strategies are appropriate for experienced athletes, not youths or novices. The duration of the off-season period must be long enough to permit deployment of a series of blocks, which may not be the case in sports with long competitive seasons. Appropriate ordering can potentiate the effect of one block on the next, whereas inappropriate ordering may have a negative effect. It is important to understand the principle of dynamic correspondence, as well as the nature of residual or delayed training responses, in order to get the desired effect. Strength and conditioning professionals should use discretion in prescribing workloads during the accumulation blocks, limit their duration to about four weeks, and consider using various fatigue management tactics.

Long-Term Planning

An athlete's developmental status becomes a dominant consideration at the long-range level of planning (6, 9, 22, 28, 49, 50, 72, 109, 116, 132, 142). This process is analogous to curriculum design, with the subject matter consisting of movement skills and progression in learning and training objectives, which occurs on two fronts: means, that is, general to special tasks; and methods, that is, extensive to intensive workloads.

Following is an example of how to plan long-term training in a series of progressive stages (6, 19, 113):

- *Years 1-2: Fundamental.* Training tasks involve deliberate play rather than performance-oriented activity while emphasizing basic movement competencies and fun. The skills introduced in this stage should be simple but challenging for youth athletes.
- *Years 3-4: Novice (learning to train).* Training begins to involve structured practice. The program continues to emphasize basic movement competencies and mechanics while starting to target the development of motor abilities.
- *Years 5-6: Intermediate (training to train).* Training begins to involve deliberate practice, with balanced emphasis on competency-based and performance-based tasks. The program continues targeting the development of movement techniques and motor abilities.
- *Years 7-8: Advanced (training to compete).* Development of specific techniques and abilities gets high priority, and these techniques and abilities are applied in complex tactics and competitive situations.
- *Years 9-10: Elite (training to win).* Mastery of specific strategies, skills, and abilities gets top priority. The program focuses on achieving sport performance expertise.

Movement mechanics and techniques, as well as basic fitness qualities—that is, general preparation tasks—are priorities during the early stages. The intent is to automate these so that the athlete can progressively focus on tactical and strategic targets—that is, special preparation tasks—as he or she advances toward the elite level. The strength and conditioning professional should introduce age-appropriate movement skills such that athletes can practice them at each level with the expectation of achieving proficiency at others (9, 28, 72). As athletes master each skill, they should review and maintain it while progressing to newer, more complex tasks.

Program design involves multiple levels of planning: microcycles (short-term), mesocycles (medium-term), and macrocycles (long-term).

Training Plan

In the sidebar titled "Tactical Modeling and Special Endurance Training Example for American Football" is a sample outline of a 14-week preseason macrocycle for collegiate or professional American football, organized into four successive blocks each three to four weeks in length. This scheme is modifiable for different situations. The premise of this sample outline is threefold. First, ATP resynthesis during plays is initially achieved via the phosphagen pathways, but lactic and oxidative mechanisms are maximally engaged over a series of downs. Second, CP repletion during recovery is $\dot{V}O_2$ dependent. Third, pyruvate-lactate removal is achieved largely by oxidation in Type I muscle fibers. Each of these factors is a function of $\dot{V}O_2$max; thus increasing oxidative power is critical for rapidly resynthesizing CP, oxidizing pyruvate-lactate, minimizing glycogen depletion, and thereby sustaining power output with minimal fatigue over the course of the game.

1. *Accumulation (three weeks):* 12 resistance training sessions distributed over this period on a four-days-per-week schedule; six speed, agility, and speed-endurance sessions distributed on a two-days-per-week schedule. The objective of metabolic conditioning is to maximize oxidative capacity and pyruvate-lactate consumption via three to four repetitive exercise bouts of ≤10-minute duration.
2. *Restitution (four weeks):* 12 resistance training sessions distributed over this period on a three-days-per-week schedule; 12 speed, agility, and speed-endurance sessions distributed on a three-days-per-week schedule. The objective of speed and agility training is to execute sound movement mechanics at submaximal speeds. The objectives of metabolic conditioning are to enhance pyruvate-lactate tolerance via 2- to 3-minute all-out exercise intervals with 8 to 10 minutes of recovery and to maintain $\dot{V}O_2$max.
3. *Accumulation (three weeks):* 12 resistance training sessions distributed over this period on a four-days-per-week schedule; six speed, agility, and speed-endurance sessions distributed on a two-days-per-week schedule. The objective of speed and agility training is to execute sound movement mechanics at full speed, and in assisted and resisted conditions. $\dot{V}O_2$max maintenance training continues in this phase. The objective of special endurance training is to maximally stress the metabolic systems via specific phosphagen-lactic-oxidative interaction, assuming that the athlete trains all-out in each exercise bout and that training continues only as long as the athlete can achieve the desired power output. As illustrated in the sidebar, there are two viable choices for each team's offense: an ideal approach based on how many plays it takes to successfully reach the end zone, or a real approach based on combined successful and unsuccessful possessions. Since success is the objective of each possession, the ideal model may be a better alternative:
   - *Ideal.* One training session simulates one quarter consisting of three successful touchdown drives. In this example, each Washington Redskins (WR) possession consists of 10 plays whereas each Buffalo Bills (BB) possession consists of 16 plays. Exercise:relief ratios for each team are the same (figure 17.11).
   - *Real.* One training session simulates a series of quarters, each consisting of 16 total plays for the WR offense (that is, three sets of five to six plays) or 19 total plays for the BB offense (that is, three sets of six to seven plays). Respective exercise: relief ratios for the two teams are 5:36 seconds and 5:27 seconds (figure 17.11). Initially, training simulates one quarter of combined successful and unsuccessful touchdown drives; the equivalent of an entire game can be completed in one session with progressive addition of the second, third and fourth quarters.
4. *Restitution (four weeks):* 12 resistance training sessions distributed over this period on a three-days-per-week schedule; 12 speed, agility, and speed-endurance sessions distributed on a three-days-per-week schedule. Objectives for speed, agility, and speed-endurance training are the same as in the previous block, but the frequencies have changed.

In this example, each block allocates significantly different training frequencies and densities to the respective qualities. Even greater contrast is achievable during the restitution periods, for example through distribution of eight resistance training sessions on a two-days-per week schedule. Of course, the strength and conditioning professional can also manipulate basic intensity and volume parameters.

Tactical Modeling and Special Endurance Training Example for American Football

Once the strength and conditioning professional identifies a competition model (**step 1**) according to the criteria in figure 17.10, he or she must make some important decisions regarding the nature and scope of tactical events to simulate in training (**step 2**). Video analysis (**step 3**) of the Buffalo Bills' and Washington Redskins' offenses during the 1991-1992 National Football League playoffs—that is, two American Football Conference and National Football Conference playoff contests each and Super Bowl XXVI—yields the following evaluation (**step 4**) (87):

Washington Redskins' Offense

Number of series	12.3 per game (3.1 per quarter)
Field position	–44-yard line
Yardage achieved	5.5 net yards per play
Number of plays	64.7 per game (16.2 per quarter); 10.2 per ideal series; 5.3 per real series
Exercise:relief	5.0 ± 1.5 seconds:36.4 ± 6.6 seconds (figure 17.11)
Step 5:	
Ideal drill/test:	Simulate successful series, for example two to three sets of 10 sprints
Real drill/test:	Simulate one quarter of combined successful and unsuccessful series, for example three sets of five to six sprints

Buffalo Bills' Offense

Number of series	13.3 per game (3.3 per quarter)
Field position	–30-yard line
Yardage achieved	4.3 net yards per play
Number of plays	74.7 per game (18.7 per quarter); 16.3 per ideal series; 5.6 per real series
Exercise:relief	5.0 ± 1.6 seconds:26.9 ± 6.9 seconds (figure 17.11)
Step 5:	
Ideal drill/test:	Simulate successful series, for example two to three sets of 16 sprints
Real drill/test:	Simulate one quarter of combined successful and unsuccessful series, for example three sets of six to seven sprints

Sidebar and figure reprinted, by permission, from Plisk and Gambetta, 1997 (87).

When determining how much of an actual contest to simulate in one conditioning session, the choice between ideal and real criteria is a key decision. If one quarter of play is selected, there are two options for each team according to where possession is obtained, what plays are selected, and how much yardage is gained. In this example, the options are: an idealistic quarter consisting of 10- or 16-play series based on how many plays it takes WR or BB, respectively, to reach the end zone; or a realistic quarter consisting of 16 or 19 total plays based on combined (successful and unsuccessful) drives. Since scoring a touchdown is the primary objective of each series, the ideal option is perhaps the more viable one.

The strength and conditioning professional can then select core training and testing tasks (**step 5**). General examples include sprint or agility drills that fit the observed exercise:relief pattern—for example, repeated 40-yard (37 m) sprints or pro agility shuttles. More specialized examples include positional playbook assignments mixed according to play selection—for example, blocking drills, pass routes, and running paths for offensive players or coverage, pursuit, and stunt drills for defensive players.

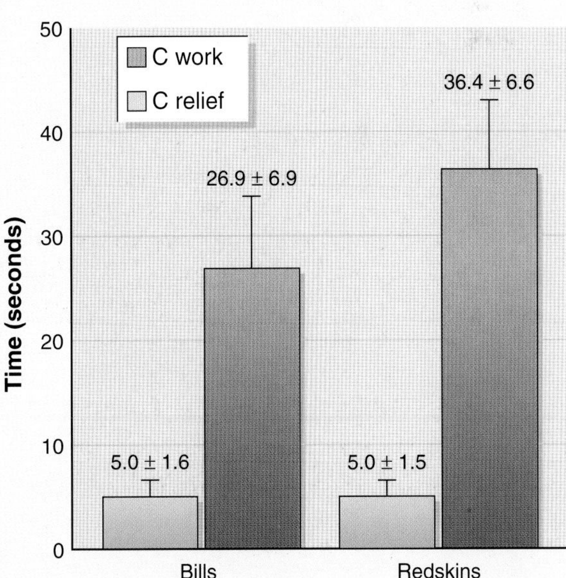

Figure 17.11 Comparison of play durations and relief intervals during the 1991-1992 National Football League playoffs: C work = combined rushing and passing play exercise interval; C relief = combined postplay relief interval.

CONCLUSION

Strength and conditioning professionals need an integrated plan of action when developing athletes' speed, agility, and speed-endurance. They should analyze target activities and specifically address the requisite skills and abilities in training.

Functional movements involve task-specific force application. These forces are expressed in terms of acceleration, time or rate of application, and velocity. Acceleration, maximum-velocity, and multidirectional skills involve distinct movement mechanics. Collectively, these comprise the skill set that an athlete uses to perform a wide range of tasks and maneuvers. Athletes should also develop the special endurance needed to achieve specific performance objectives in competition and training.

Running speed is the interaction of stride frequency and length. The goal of sprinting is to achieve high stride frequency and optimal stride length, with explosive horizontal push-off and minimal vertical impulse. Agility is an expression of an athlete's coordinative abilities. Strength and conditioning professionals should classify motor skills rationally and analyze task-specific modes of locomotion and changes in velocity.

Strength and conditioning professionals should also prioritize training methods for speed and agility development according to a hierarchy—from the execution of sound movement technique in a specific task, to the development of special skills and abilities in modified conditions, to the development of general skills and abilities.

Combining various means and methods of training into a sound program involves planning on multiple levels, from task specificity and fatigue management over the short term to the prescription of developmentally appropriate targets over the long term. These considerations present certain program design challenges that can be resolved with periodization strategies.

KEY TERMS

agility 458
braking 464
complex training 461
coordinative abilities 469
dynamic correspondence 474
endurance training 473
exercise:relief pattern 458
flight phase 462
force 459
ground preparation 464
impulse 459
mobility training 473
periodization 476
power 459
practice specificity 470
propulsion 464
reaction time 462
reactive ability 462
recovery 464
sequenced training 480
special endurance 458
speed 458
speed-endurance 458
sprint assistance 473
sprint resistance 473
strength training 473
stretch-shortening cycle (SSC) 461
stride frequency 462
stride length 462
support phase 462
tactical metabolic training 476
velocity specificity 460
volume-load 478
work:rest ratio 458

STUDY QUESTIONS

1. The ability to maintain maximal velocity for longer than 6 seconds is referred to as which of the following types of endurance?
   a. special
   b. speed
   c. strength
   d. cardiovascular

2. Which of the following is the MOST influential factor to determine a sprinter's maximum velocity?
   a. reaction time
   b. stride length
   c. leg length
   d. stride frequency

3. During the ground support phase of linear sprinting, which of the following muscles are responsible for storing and recovering elastic energy?
   I. gastrocnemius
   II. hamstrings
   III. quadriceps
   IV. anterior tibialis
   a. I and III only
   b. II and IV only
   c. I, II, and III only
   d. II, III, and IV only

4. All of the following actions during the ground support phase contribute to optimal stride length and frequency EXCEPT
   a. minimizing the horizontal braking force
   b. contacting the ground ahead of the center of gravity
   c. maximizing the backward velocity of the leg
   d. limiting the range of motion at the ankle

5. An athlete just completed a training cycle that focused on speed training. When applying the sequenced training strategy, which of the following training goals or exercise modes is the MOST appropriate to choose or prioritize for the NEXT training cycle?
   a. agility
   b. plyometrics
   c. SSC
   d. strength

6. Which of the following describe how maximal backward sprinting is different from maximal forward sprinting?
   I. shorter stride length
   II. greater stride frequency
   III. longer ground support time
   IV. earlier application of peak GRFs
   a. I and III only
   b. II and IV only
   c. I, II, and III only
   d. II, III, and IV only

7. Which of the following elements of agility technical skills requires spatial and temporal control of body movements?
   a. differentiation
   b. rhythm
   c. balance
   d. orientation

PART II

Aerobic Exercise Prescription

Part II of section 4, "Program Design," discusses the steps or variables involved in designing an aerobic endurance training program (listed on p. 492). There are many similarities to anaerobic exercise prescription. This part includes a discussion of the general principles as they apply to aerobic endurance training and the stepwise approach to designing a safe and effective program.

Improvements in aerobic endurance performance can be derived only when sound principles are applied during training. Although the fundamental mechanisms responsible for inducing adaptations during training are undefined, it is clear that in order to adapt, the various systems of the body must be challenged by an exercise stimulus (e.g., specificity and overload). The physiological systems that are not involved during the training session or not stressed sufficiently by exercise will not adapt to the training program (1, 2).

Training specificity refers to the distinct adaptations to the physiological systems that arise from the training program. A training effect is limited to the physiological systems used and overloaded during training (2, 4). Unless training programs are strictly designed to involve and stress a physiological system, there will be very limited or possibly no adaptations in that system. To improve aerobic endurance performance, training programs must be designed to enhance the function of the respiratory, cardiovascular, and musculoskeletal systems.

For a training adaptation to occur, a physiological system must be exercised at a level beyond that to which it is presently accustomed (3). During continued overload, the physiological systems of the body will adapt to the exercise stress. Adaptations within the physiological systems will occur until the tissues are no longer overloaded. This necessitates use of a greater overload. Exercise frequency, duration, and intensity are the variables most often manipulated to provide overload to the systems of the body.

CHAPTER 18

Aerobic Endurance Exercise Training

Benjamin H. Reuter, PhD, and Patrick S. Hagerman, EdD

After completing this chapter, you will be able to

- discuss the factors related to aerobic endurance performance;
- select the mode of aerobic endurance training;
- set aerobic endurance training frequency based on training status, sport season, and recovery requirements;
- assign aerobic endurance training duration and understand its interaction with training intensity;
- assign aerobic endurance exercise intensity and understand the various methods used to monitor intensity;
- describe the various types of aerobic endurance programs;
- apply the program design variables based on the sport season; and
- address the issues of cross-training, detraining, tapering, and supplemental resistance training when designing an aerobic endurance training program.

Successful performance in aerobic endurance competitions involving running, cycling, and swimming is dependent on the athlete's ability to cover a fixed distance in the shortest time possible. This requires athletes to be in peak physical condition for the competition. To reach this level of performance, athletes must train hard, yet intelligently, to maximize the physiological adaptations derived from training. In fact, the physical condition of the aerobic endurance athlete is of primary importance if that athlete is to perform at optimal levels during competition (16, 25, 50, 68, 72). A common trend with many aerobic endurance athletes is to adopt and embrace the training practices of other highly successful or well-known aerobic endurance athletes. Although this strategy may be effective for a few, most aerobic endurance athletes would likely be better served by constructing their own training regimen based on a good working knowledge of sound training principles and an understanding of their own physical limitations and needs.

Numerous types of training programs have been designed for aerobic endurance athletes. These training programs vary in the mode, frequency, duration, and intensity of the activity. What successful aerobic endurance athletes have in common is a training program designed to enhance their strengths and improve their weaknesses. This chapter is designed to provide the strength and conditioning professional with a good working knowledge of the scientific principles of aerobic endurance training and conditioning. Specifically, the chapter includes information about the factors related to performance, aerobic endurance training program design variables, and the various types of programs. Additional discussion focuses on sport season training and special issues related to aerobic endurance training. As it would be exhausting to review relevant information about training for all possible aerobic endurance sports, only basic aerobic endurance training topics are presented, with specific examples as they relate to running, cycling, and swimming.

FACTORS RELATED TO AEROBIC ENDURANCE PERFORMANCE

When designing aerobic endurance training programs, it is important to understand those factors that influence and play a significant role in successful aerobic endurance performance. This allows for the development of sound training programs while minimizing unnecessary training that may lead to counterproductive adaptations, fatigue, overwork, or overtraining.

Maximal Aerobic Power

As the duration of the aerobic endurance event increases, so does the proportion of the total energy demand that must be met by aerobic metabolism. Therefore, high **maximal aerobic power ($\dot{V}O_2$max)** is necessary for success in aerobic endurance events (54). A high correlation has been shown to exist between $\dot{V}O_2$max and performance in aerobic endurance events (2, 20, 32, 54, 55). Consequently, aerobic endurance training programs should be designed to improve $\dot{V}O_2$max. However, although a high $\dot{V}O_2$max is important for successful performance, other factors may be equally or even more important. These factors include a high lactate threshold, good exercise economy, a high ability to use fat as a fuel source, and a high percentage of Type I muscle fibers. Fuel utilization and fiber type characteristics were discussed in chapter 6.

Lactate Threshold

In aerobic endurance events, the best competitor among athletes with similar $\dot{V}O_2$max values is typically the person who can sustain aerobic energy production at the highest percentage of his or her $\dot{V}O_2$max without accumulating large amounts of lactic acid in the muscle and blood (50). Although numerous terms have been used to describe this phenomenon, **lactate threshold** is the one most commonly employed in the literature. The lactate threshold is that speed of movement or percentage of $\dot{V}O_2$max at which a specific blood lactate concentration is observed or the point at which blood lactate concentration begins to increase above resting levels (72). Several studies have shown that an athlete's lactate threshold appears to be a better indicator of his or her aerobic endurance performance than $\dot{V}O_2$max (22, 23). The **maximal lactate steady state** is another term that often appears in the aerobic endurance training literature (4). The maximal lactate steady state is defined as the exercise intensity at which maximal lactate production is equal to maximal lactate clearance within the body (4). The maximal lactate steady state is considered by many to be a better indicator of aerobic endurance performance than either $\dot{V}O_2$max or the lactate threshold (4, 34). What is clear from this information is that aerobic endurance athletes must improve their lactate threshold or maximal lactate steady state. This requires athletes to conduct some training at elevated levels of blood and muscle lactate to maximize training improvements.

Exercise Economy

A measure of the energy cost of activity at a given exercise velocity is referred to as the **exercise economy**. Athletes with a high exercise economy expend less energy during exercise to maintain a given exercise velocity (e.g., running speed). Several investigators have suggested that exercise economy is an important factor in successful performance in running events (15, 31), with better performers having a slightly shorter stride length and greater stride frequency compared to less successful performers (13). During cycling, exercise economy can be affected by body mass size, cycling velocity, and aerodynamic positioning (23, 56, 69). For cyclists, an increase in body mass and cycling velocity and an inefficient body position generate greater wind resistance, resulting in a decrease in exercise economy. It has been demonstrated that elite swimmers are much more economical than nonelite swimmers (71) and use less oxygen at any given swimming velocity. The most profound impact on exercise economy during swimming can be observed when swimming technique becomes more efficient. As improvements in stroke mechanics occur, energy demand for a given swimming velocity is reduced (70). Training to improve exercise economy is critical for aerobic endurance athletes.

An improvement in exercise economy can enhance maximal aerobic power ($\dot{V}O_2$max) and lactate threshold.

DESIGNING AN AEROBIC ENDURANCE PROGRAM

An effective aerobic endurance training program must include an exercise prescription specifically developed for the individual athlete. This requires manipulation of the four primary program design variables. The sidebar lists the design variables as steps 1 through 5. Unfortunately, many coaches and athletes often use the training practices or programs of current successful coaches or athletes in their sport. This does not carefully consider the strengths and weaknesses of the athlete and may lead to development of an ineffective or potentially harmful training program. The optimal way to develop a sound training program is to have the factors related to aerobic endurance performance evaluated and then use that information to generate a training program specific to the athlete. For example, an athlete with poor exercise economy should place emphasis on training to improve exercise economy. This might include interval training with a focus on technique, as well as using long rest

Aerobic Endurance Training Program Design Variables

Step 1: Exercise mode
Step 2: Training frequency
Step 3: Training intensity
Step 4: Exercise duration
Step 5: Exercise progression

periods. Conversely, athletes who need to increase lactate threshold might consider performing more high-intensity training.

Training programs for female athletes do not have to be different from those used to train male athletes; evidence indicates that males and females respond similarly to training programs (11, 55, 59). Refer to chapter 7 for a discussion on sex-related differences and their implications for exercise.

Step 1: Exercise Mode

The exercise **mode** refers to the specific activity performed by the athlete: cycling, running, swimming, and so on. When training to improve aerobic endurance performance, the athlete should select activities that mimic as closely as possible the movement pattern employed in competition. This will effectively cause positive adaptations in specific physiological systems of the body. For example, the recruitment of specific muscle fibers and the adaptation of the energy systems within those fibers must be challenged during aerobic endurance training. Selecting the appropriate exercise mode during training ensures that the systems used in competition are challenged to improve. Remember that the more specific the training mode is to the sport, the greater the improvement in performance (13, 16, 23, 33, 36, 45, 49, 50, 68, 72). For an athlete involved in multiple aerobic endurance sports, or one who is interested in a general aerobic endurance fitness program, cross-training or participation in multiple aerobic endurance activities may be warranted (1).

Step 2: Training Frequency

Training **frequency** refers to the number of training sessions conducted per day or per week. The frequency of training sessions will depend on an interaction of exercise intensity and duration, the training status of the athlete, and the specific sport season. Higher exercise intensity and longer duration may necessitate less frequent training to allow sufficient recovery from exercise sessions. The training status of the athlete can influence training frequency, with lesser-trained athletes requiring more recovery days at the initiation of a training period than more highly trained athletes. The sport season that the athlete is currently in can also influence training frequency; an off-season program may include five training days per week, but training frequency may progress to daily workouts (or even multiple workouts per day for a triathlete) in the preseason. Additionally, fewer training sessions may be required to maintain an achieved level of physiological function or performance than to attain that level initially (68). Appropriate training frequency is important for the aerobic endurance athlete, as too much training may increase the risk of injury, illness, or overtraining. A number of studies have shown increased injury rates with training sessions more frequent than five times per week (46, 61); however, these studies used active individuals in a wide age range, not only young and healthy athletes, as subjects. Conversely, too little training will not result in positive adaptations to the various systems of the body. Research has shown that it is necessary to train more than twice per week in order to increase $\dot{V}O_2max$ (37, 73).

Recovery from individual training sessions is essential if the athlete is to derive maximum benefits from the subsequent training session. Exercise performance has been shown to improve following relative rest from difficult training sessions (3). Obtaining sufficient rest, becoming rehydrated, and restoring fuel sources are critical issues for the athlete during recovery. Relaxation and avoidance of strenuous physical activity are particularly important following days of high-intensity or long-duration training. Postexercise ingestion of adequate fluids is important for replacing the fluid lost during training. If the training session was especially long or intense, then postexercise carbohydrate intake is important for replacing the muscle and liver glycogen stores that were likely depleted.

Step 3: Training Intensity

Central to causing training adaptations in the body is the interaction of training intensity and duration. Generally, the higher the exercise intensity, the shorter the exercise duration. Adaptations in the body are specific to the **intensity**, or effort expended during a training session. High-intensity aerobic exercise increases cardiovascular and respiratory function and allows for improved oxygen delivery to the working muscles (64). Increasing exercise intensity may also benefit skeletal muscle adaptations by affecting muscle fiber recruitment (29). As exercise intensity is increased, greater recruitment of Type II muscle fibers occurs to meet the increased power needs. This training stimulus allows those fibers to become more aerobically trained, thereby possibly improving overall aerobic performance.

The regulation of exercise intensity is critical to the success of each training session and ultimately the entire program. An exercise intensity that is too low does not **overload** the body's systems and induce the desired physiological adaptations, whereas an intensity that is too high results in fatigue and a premature end to the training session (62). In either instance, the training session will be poor and ineffective.

The most accurate methods for regulating exercise intensity are to monitor oxygen consumption during exercise to determine its percentage of $\dot{V}O_2$max or to periodically measure the blood lactate concentration to determine the relationship to the lactate threshold. Until recently, obtaining accurate maximal oxygen uptake values required access to a laboratory. At least one company has now introduced a gas analyzer system designed for fitness facilities. To date, the system has not been tested for validity or reliability, but the concept is promising. If $\dot{V}O_2$max testing is not available, exercise prescriptions can use heart rate, ratings of perceived exertion, metabolic equivalents, or exercise velocity to monitor exercise intensity. Cycling power–measuring devices are frequently used by professional and top-level amateur competitors.

Heart Rate

Heart rate is likely the most frequently used method for prescribing aerobic exercise intensity. The reason is the close relationship between heart rate and oxygen consumption, especially when the intensity is between 50% and 90% of **functional capacity** ($\dot{V}O_2$max), also called **heart rate reserve (HRR)**, which is the difference between an athlete's maximal heart rate and his or her resting heart rate (8). The most accurate means of regulating intensity using this method is to determine the specific heart rate associated with the desired percentage of $\dot{V}O_2$max or the heart rate associated with the lactate threshold. For the greatest precision, this necessitates laboratory testing to identify these exercise intensities. If laboratory testing is unavailable, then the individual's **age-predicted** (estimated) **maximal heart rate (APMHR)** can be used as the basis for determining exercise intensity. Refer to the sidebar on page 494 for formulas and sample calculations for determining aerobic endurance exercise heart rate ranges using the **Karvonen method** and the **percentage of maximal heart rate (MHR) method**. The relationship between $\dot{V}O_2$max, HRR, and MHR is shown in table 18.1.

Although the Karvonen and percentage of maximal heart rate formulas provide practical intensity assignments, basing them on age-predicted maximal heart rates may entail some inaccuracies (vs. laboratory-tested maximal heart rates) when exercise intensity is being monitored during cycling or running (58). It has been determined that age contributes 75% of the variability of heart rate; the effects of other factors such as mode of exercise and fitness level must also be considered with the use of heart rate to monitor intensity (58). Additionally, using estimations of exercise intensity via estimated maximal heart rate equations provides no information about the intensity associated with the lactate threshold. Without some knowledge of an athlete's lactate threshold, a highly effective aerobic endurance training program cannot be developed.

TABLE 18.1

Relationship Between $\dot{V}O_2$max, HRR, and MHR

% $\dot{V}O_2$max	% HRR	% MHR
50	50	66
55	55	70
60	60	74
65	65	77
70	70	81
75	75	85
80	80	88
85	85	92
90	90	96
95	95	98
100	100	100

HRR = heart rate reserve; MHR = percentage of maximal heart rate.

Target Heart Rate Calculations

Karvonen Method

Formula:

- Age-predicted maximum heart rate (APMHR) = 220 – age
- Heart rate reserve (HRR) = APMHR – resting heart rate (RHR)
- Target heart rate (THR) = (HRR × exercise intensity) + RHR

Do this calculation twice to determine the target heart rate range (THRR).

Example:

A 30-year-old athlete with an RHR of 60 beats/min is assigned an exercise intensity of 60% to 70% of functional capacity:

- APMHR = 220 – 30 = 190 beats/min
- RHR = 60 beats/min
- HRR = 190 – 60 = 130 beats/min
- Lowest number of the athlete's THRR = (130 × 0.60) + 60 = 78 + 60 = 138 beats/min
- Highest number of the athlete's THRR = (130 × 0.70) + 60 = 91 + 60 = 151 beats/min

When monitoring heart rate during exercise, divide the THRR by 6 to yield the athlete's THRR in number of beats for a 10-second interval:

138 ÷ 6 = 23   151 ÷ 6 = 25

The athlete's THRR is 23-25 beats per 10 seconds.

Percentage of Maximal Heart Rate Method

Formula:

- Age-predicted maximum heart rate (APMHR) = 220 – age
- Target heart rate (THR) = (APMHR × exercise intensity)

Do this calculation twice to determine the target heart rate range (THRR).

Example:

A 20-year-old athlete is assigned an exercise intensity of 70% to 85% of maximal heart rate:

- APMHR = 220 – 20 = 200 beats/min
- Lowest number of the athlete's THRR = 200 × 0.70 = 140 beats/min
- Highest number of the athlete's THRR = 200 × 0.85 = 170 beats/min

When monitoring heart rate during exercise, divide the THRR by 6 to yield the athlete's THRR in number of beats for a 10-second interval:

140 ÷ 6 = 23   170 ÷ 6 = 28

The athlete's THRR is 23-28 beats per 10 seconds.

Ratings of Perceived Exertion

Ratings of perceived exertion (RPE) can also be used to regulate intensity during aerobic endurance training (27, 38). Typically, the 15-point Borg scale (6) is used, although the category-ratio scale could be used as well (7) (table 18.2). Once again, laboratory testing is required to ensure accuracy between specific exercise intensities and an RPE scale. It appears that RPE can be used to accurately regulate intensity when there are changes in fitness level (9); however, researchers have demonstrated that the RPE–intensity relationship can be influenced by various external environmental factors such as passive distracters and environmental temperature (14, 63).

Metabolic Equivalents

Metabolic equivalents (METs) may also be used to prescribe exercise intensity. One MET is equal to $3.5 \text{ ml} \cdot \text{kg}^{-1} \cdot \text{min}^{-1}$ of oxygen consumption and is considered the amount of oxygen required by the body at rest (75). Metabolic equivalent values have been determined for a variety of physical activities; a brief list is shown in table 18.3. For example, an activity with a MET value of 10.0 requires 10 times the oxygen uptake that is required by an individual at rest. Assigning MET values as part of an aerobic exercise prescription requires the strength and conditioning professional to know (or estimate) an athlete's maximal oxygen uptake in order to be able to calculate an exercise MET level (40).

Power Measurement

Cyclists may use power-measuring cranks and hubs to monitor exercise intensity (26). Due to cost, these devices are probably suitable only for professionals and top-level amateurs. Research studies have

TABLE 18.2

Ratings of Perceived Exertion (RPE) Scales

15-point Borg scale		Category-ratio scale	
6	No exertion at all	0	Nothing at all
7		0.3	
	Extremely light	0.5	Extremely weak
8		1	Very weak
9	Very light	1.5	
10		2	Weak
11	Light	2.5	
12		3	Moderate
13	Somewhat hard	4	
14		5	Strong
15	Hard (heavy)	6	
16		7	Very strong
17	Very hard	8	
18		9	
19	Extremely hard	10	Extremely strong
20	Maximal exertion	11	
		*	Absolute maximum

The scales shown here are the most recent versions from Borg, 1998 (5).

indicated that at least two of the devices provide valid and reliable power measures (35, 52). Using power to monitor intensity in cycling has an advantage over other measures because metabolic rate is closely related to mechanical power production (26). Using power as an intensity measure also allows reproducible intensity efforts regardless of environmental conditions, which may influence other measurements of intensity such as heart rate and training velocity (26).

Step 4: Exercise Duration

Exercise **duration** refers to the length of time of the training session. The duration of a training session is often influenced by the exercise intensity: the longer the exercise duration, the lower the exercise intensity (66). For example, exercise that is conducted at an intensity above the maximal lactate steady state (e.g., 85% of $\dot{V}O_2max$) will have a relatively short duration (20-30 minutes) because the accumulation of lactate within the muscle will contribute to fatigue. Conversely, exercise that is performed at a much lower intensity (e.g., 70% of $\dot{V}O_2max$) may be performed for several hours before the athlete experiences fatigue.

The duration of a training session is often influenced by the exercise intensity: the longer the exercise duration, the lower the exercise intensity.

TABLE 18.3

Metabolic Equivalents for Physical Activities

METs	Activity
1.0	Lying or sitting quietly, doing nothing, lying in bed awake
2.0	Walking, <2 miles per hour (<3.2 km/h), level surface
2.5	Walking, 2 miles per hour (3.2 km/h), level surface
3.0	Resistance training (free weight, Nautilus or Universal type), light or moderate effort
3.0	Stationary cycling, 50 W, very light effort
3.0	Walking, 2.5 miles per hour (4 km/h)
3.3	Walking, 3 miles per hour (4.8 km/h), level surface
3.5	Calisthenics, home exercise, light or moderate effort
3.5	Stair stepping (with a 4-inch [10 cm] step height), 20 steps per minute
3.8	Walking, 3.5 miles per hour (5.6 km/h), level surface
4.0	Water aerobics, water calisthenics

(continued)

TABLE 18.3 *(continued)*

METs	Activity
4.8	Stair stepping (with a 4-inch [10 cm] step height), 30 steps per minute
5.0	Aerobic dance, low impact
5.0	Walking, 4 miles per hour (6.4 km/h), level surface
5.5	Stationary cycling, 100 W, light effort
6.0	Outdoor cycling, 10 to 11.9 miles per hour (16.1-19.2 km/h)
6.0	Resistance training (free weight, Nautilus or Universal type), vigorous effort
6.3	Stair stepping (with a 12-inch [31 cm] step height), 20 steps per minute
6.3	Walking, 4.5 miles per hour (7.2 km/h), level surface
6.9	Stair stepping (with an 8-inch [20 cm] step height), 30 steps per minute
7.0	Aerobic dance, high impact
7.0	Stationary cycling, 150 W, moderate effort
7.0	Swimming laps, freestyle, slow, moderate or light effort
8.0	Calisthenics (e.g., push-ups, sit-ups, pull-ups, jumping jacks), vigorous effort
8.0	Circuit training, including some aerobic stations, with minimal rest
8.0	Outdoor cycling, 12 to 13.9 miles per hour (19.3-22.4 km/h)
8.0	Walking, 5 miles per hour (8.0 km/h)
8.5	Step aerobics (with a 6- to 8-inch [15-20 cm] step)
9.0	Running, 5.2 miles per hour (8.4 km/h) (11.5 minutes per mile)
9.0	Stair stepping (with a 12-inch [31 cm] step height), 30 steps per minute
10.0	Outdoor cycling, 14 to 15.9 miles per hour (22.5-25.6 km/h)
10.0	Running, 6 miles per hour (9.7 km/h) (10 minutes per mile)
10.0	Step aerobics (with a 10- to 12-inch [25-31 cm] step)
10.0	Swimming laps, freestyle, fast, vigorous effort
10.5	Stationary cycling, 200 W, vigorous effort
11.0	Running, 6.7 miles per hour (10.8 km/h) (9 minutes per mile)
11.5	Running, 7 miles per hour (11.3 km/h) (8.5 minutes per mile)
12.0	Outdoor cycling, 16 to 19 miles per hour (25.7-30.6 km/h)
12.5	Running, 7.5 miles per hour (12.1 km/h) (8 minutes per mile)
12.5	Stationary cycling, 250 W, very vigorous effort
13.5	Running, 8 miles per hour (12.9 km/h) (7.5 minutes per mile)
14.0	Running, 8.5 miles per hour (13.7 km/h) (7 minutes per mile)
15.0	Running, 9 miles per hour (14.5 km/h) (6 minutes, 40 seconds per mile)
16.0	Outdoor cycling, >20 miles per hour (>32.2 km/h)
16.0	Running, 10 miles per hour (16.1 km/h) (6 minutes per mile)

Step 5: Exercise Progression

Once athletes begin an aerobic endurance exercise program, they need to continue the program to either maintain or advance their aerobic fitness level. Research seems to indicate that aerobic fitness does not decrease for up to five weeks when intensity of training is maintained and frequency decreases to as few as two times per week (43).

Depending on the goals of the athlete, progression of an aerobic endurance exercise program initially involves increasing the frequency, intensity, and duration of exercise. General recommendations are that individuals always include at least one recovery or active rest day in each week of training. Most athletes have the goal of attempting to increase rather than just maintain aerobic fitness. This requires regular progression of the training program. Typically, exercise frequency, intensity, or duration should not increase more than 10% each week (40). At higher levels of fitness, athletes will reach a point where it is not feasible to increase either the frequency or the duration of exercise. When this occurs, progressions in training will occur only through exercise intensity manipulation (40).

As shown by the sidebar "Examples of Aerobic Exercise Progression," exercise progression can manipulate combinations of frequency, intensity, and duration. Progression of training frequency may be limited by constraints such as school and work. It may not be possible for the athlete to incorporate more than one training session each day. Training intensity measurement should use the same methods as used in the original exercise intensity prescription. The best method is determined by the equipment available to monitor intensity (heart rate monitor, RPE charts, or machines that provide MET workloads). Progression of training intensity should be monitored very carefully to avoid overtraining. The duration of each training session will be limited by the same constraints as training frequency. Athletes who train predominantly outdoors will also be limited by the number of daylight hours, especially in the late fall, winter, and early spring.

TYPES OF AEROBIC ENDURANCE TRAINING PROGRAMS

There are several types of aerobic endurance training programs, each with varying frequency, intensity, duration, and progression parameters. Each type incorporates the five design variables and results in regimens created for specific outcomes. Table 18.4 summarizes the types of aerobic endurance training and their common prescriptive guidelines. Sample training programs for each type of aerobic endurance training are included in the following sections, with the specific training mode being discussed highlighted in blue.

Long, Slow Distance Training

The intensity for **long, slow distance training (LSD)** is equivalent to approximately 70% of

Examples of Aerobic Exercise Progression

Example A

Week 1: four times per week at an intensity of 70% to 85% THR for 40 minutes

Week 2: five times per week at an intensity of 70% to 85% THR for 45 minutes

Week 3: three times per week at an intensity of 70% to 85% THR for 40 minutes, one time per week for 50 minutes at 60% to 75% THR

Week 4: four times per week at an intensity of 70% to 85% THR for 45 minutes, one time per week for 50 minutes at 60% to 75% THR

Week 5: four times per week at an intensity of 70% to 85% THR for 45 minutes, one time per week for 55 minutes at 60% to 75% THR

Example B

Week 1: three times per week at an intensity of 60% to 70% THR for 30 minutes

Week 2: four times per week at an intensity of 60% to 70% THR for 35 minutes

Week 3: three times per week at an intensity of 65% to 75% THR for 30 minutes

Week 4: four times per week at an intensity of 65% to 70% THR for 35 minutes

Week 5: three times per week at an intensity of 70% to 75% THR for 30 minutes

TABLE 18.4

Types of Aerobic Endurance Training

Training type	Frequency per week*	Duration (work bout portion)	Intensity
Long, slow distance (LSD)	1-2	Race distance or longer (~30-120 minutes)	~70% of $\dot{V}O_2$max
Pace/tempo	1-2	~20-30 minutes	At the lactate threshold; at or slightly above race pace
Interval	1-2	3-5 minutes (with a work:rest ratio of 1:1)	Close to $\dot{V}O_2$max
Repetition	1	30-90 seconds (with a work:rest ratio of 1:5)	Greater than $\dot{V}O_2$max
Fartlek	1	~20-60 minutes	Varies between LSD and pace/tempo training intensities

*The other days of the week are composed of other training types and rest/recovery days.

Data from references 16, 25, 50, 68, and 72.

$\dot{V}O_2$max (or about 80% of maximum heart rate). The training distance should be greater than race distance, or the duration should be at least as long as 30 minutes to 2 hours (25). This intensity and duration is typically characterized as "conversation" exercise, with the athlete able to talk without undue respiratory distress. The physiological benefits derived from LSD training primarily include enhanced cardiovascular and thermoregulatory function, improved mitochondrial energy production and oxidative capacity of skeletal muscle, and increased utilization of fat as a fuel (10, 12, 17, 19, 29, 33, 39, 44, 45, 48, 65, 72). These changes are likely to improve the lactate threshold intensity by enhancing the body's ability to clear lactate. Chronic use of this type of training also causes a change in the metabolic characteristics of the involved muscles (39, 47) and an eventual shift of Type IIx fibers to Type I fibers (60, 67).

The increase in fat utilization may also cause a sparing of muscle glycogen (21, 24, 41, 45, 48, 53, 72). The intensity during LSD training is lower than the intensity used during competition, and this may be a disadvantage if too much of this type of training is performed. Additionally, LSD training does not stimulate the neurological patterns of muscle fiber recruitment that are required during a race (72), and this may result in adaptations in muscle fibers that are not used during competition.

Pace/Tempo Training

Pace/tempo training employs an intensity at or slightly higher than race competition intensity. The intensity corresponds to the lactate threshold; therefore, this type of training is also often called *threshold training* (25) or *aerobic/anaerobic interval training* (16). There are two ways to conduct

Sample LSD Training Program for a Marathon Runner

Sunday	Monday	Tuesday	Wednesday	Thursday	Friday	Saturday
Rest day	45-minute Fartlek run	**60-minute LSD run**	45-minute interval run	60-minute run at race pace over hills and flats	45-minute repetition run	**120-minute LSD run**

COMMENTS

- Frequency: To help combat overtraining or overuse, the two LSD training days should be spread out evenly during the week to allow recovery between sessions.
- Duration: Since the athlete's race distance is a marathon (26.2 miles, 42 km), the duration or running distance of the LSD training sessions should approach those of the marathon (for a trained athlete), at least for one of the two LSD sessions.
- Intensity: To complete the extended LSD sessions, the athlete should run at a lower intensity or training pace (minutes per mile or per km); high respiratory stress is not required.

pace/tempo training: steady and intermittent (25). Steady pace/tempo training is continuous training conducted at an intensity equal to the lactate threshold for durations of approximately 20 to 30 minutes. The purpose of pace/tempo training is to stress the athlete at a specific intensity and improve energy production from both aerobic and anaerobic metabolism. Intermittent pace/tempo training is also referred to as *tempo intervals*, *cruise intervals*, or *threshold training* (25). During intermittent pace/tempo training, the intensity is the same as for a steady threshold workout, but the training session consists of a series of shorter intervals with brief recovery periods between work intervals. During pace/tempo training, it is important to avoid exercising at a higher intensity than the prescribed pace. If the workout seems relatively easy, it is better to increase the distance than to increase the intensity. The primary objective for this type of training is to develop a sense of race pace and enhance the body systems' ability to sustain exercise at that pace. Pace/tempo training involves the same pattern of muscle fiber recruitment as is required in competition. The benefits derived from this type of training include improved running economy and increased lactate threshold.

Interval Training

Interval training involves exercise at an intensity close to $\dot{V}O_2$max. The work intervals should last between 3 and 5 minutes, although they can be as short as 30 seconds (2). The rest intervals for 3- to 5-minute work intervals should be equal to the work interval, thereby keeping the work:rest ratio (W:R) at 1:1. Interval training permits the athlete to train at intensities close to $\dot{V}O_2$max for a greater amount of time than would be possible in a single exercise session at a continuous high intensity. This type of training should not be performed until a firm base of aerobic endurance training has been attained (50). Interval training is very stressful on the athlete and should be used sparingly. The benefits derived from interval training include an increased $\dot{V}O_2$max and enhanced anaerobic metabolism.

Repetition Training

Repetition training, or REPS, is conducted at intensities greater than $\dot{V}O_2$max, with the work intervals typically lasting between 30 and 90 seconds. Due to the high reliance on anaerobic metabolism, long recovery periods are needed between similar

Sample Pace/Tempo Training Program for a 50 km Cyclist

Sunday	Monday	Tuesday	Wednesday	Thursday	Friday	Saturday
Rest day	60-minute LSD ride	**30-minute pace/tempo ride**	45-minute Fartlek ride	45-minute easy ride	**30-minute pace/tempo ride**	90-minute LSD ride

COMMENTS

- Frequency: Because the pace/tempo rides are stressful, the two training days should be spread out during the week to allow recovery between sessions.
- Duration: For *steady* pace/tempo training, exercise duration is shorter than race distance or duration to allow for a higher training intensity.
- Intensity: The athlete should cycle at a high intensity or training pace (minutes per mile or per km); high respiratory stress is required to simulate race pace.

Sample Interval Training Program for a 10 km Runner

Sunday	Monday	Tuesday	Wednesday	Thursday	Friday	Saturday
Rest day	**10 reps of 0.5 km intervals at race pace with a 1:1 W:R ratio**	10 km easy run	45-minute LSD run	**5 reps of 1 km intervals at race pace with a 1:1 W:R ratio**	45-minute LSD run	45-minute Fartlek run on flat course

COMMENTS

- Frequency: Because the interval runs are stressful, the two training days should be spread out during the week to allow recovery between sessions.
- Duration: The total distance or duration of the training portion of the session (i.e., the sum of the interval work bouts) should approach the competition distances as the athlete becomes more highly trained.
- Intensity: The athlete should run at an intensity (pace) close to $\dot{V}O_2$max when completing the work bout portions of the interval training sessions.

sessions. The recovery periods are approximately four to six times as long as the work intervals, resulting in a work:rest ratio of approximately 1:5 (25). The benefits of REPS training include improved running speed, enhanced running economy, and an increased capacity for and tolerance of anaerobic metabolism. This type of training is also beneficial for the final kick or push of an aerobic endurance race.

Fartlek Training

Fartlek training is a combination of several of the previously mentioned types of training. Although Fartlek training is generally associated with running, it can also be used for cycling and swimming. A sample Fartlek run involves easy running (~70% $\dot{V}O_2max$) combined with either hill work or short, fast bursts of running (~85-90% $\dot{V}O_2max$) for short time periods. Athletes can apply this basic format to cycling and swimming by simply combining long, slow distance training, pace/tempo training, and interval training. A Fartlek training workout challenges all systems of the body and may help reduce the boredom and monotony associated with daily training. This type of training is likely to enhance $\dot{V}O_2max$, increase the lactate threshold, and improve running economy and fuel utilization.

The various types of training induce different physiological responses. A sound program should incorporate all types of training into the athlete's weekly, monthly, and yearly training schedule.

APPLICATION OF PROGRAM DESIGN TO TRAINING SEASONS

The program design variables and the various types of aerobic endurance training are often applied to athletes' sport seasons to create a yearly training program. Typically, the training year is divided into phases that include the off-season (sometimes

Sample Repetition Training Program for a Triathlete

(Swim training portion; the race distance is 2.4 miles)

Sunday	Monday	Tuesday	Wednesday	Thursday	Friday	Saturday
Rest day	60-minute LSD swim	**50-minute repetition training using 60-second work bouts with 5-minute recovery periods of easy swimming**	45-minute LSD swim	"Rest" day (no swim workout)	1-mile swim at race pace	60-minute LSD swim

COMMENTS

- Frequency: Because the REPS workouts are stressful, only one training day should occur during the week.
- Duration: The total distance or duration of the training portion of the session (i.e., the sum of the interval work bouts) should approach the competition distance as the athlete becomes more highly trained.
- Intensity: The athlete should swim at an intensity (pace) higher than $\dot{V}O_2max$ when completing the work bout portions of the REPS training sessions.

Sample Fartlek Training Program for a Collegiate Cross-Country Runner

Sunday	Monday	Tuesday	Wednesday	Thursday	Friday	Saturday
Rest or easy run	60-minute LSD run	**45-minute Fartlek run of hard/easy work on hills and flats**	25-minute pace/tempo run	45-minute LSD run	25-minute LSD run	Competition

COMMENTS

- Frequency: Because the Fartlek runs are stressful, only one training day should occur during the week.
- Duration: The total distance or duration of the training portion of the session (i.e., the sum of the interval work bouts) should approach the competition distance as the athlete becomes more highly trained.
- Intensity: The athlete should run at an intensity (pace) close to $\dot{V}O_2max$ when completing the work bout portions of the Fartlek training sessions.

TABLE 18.5

Sport Season Objectives and Program Design Assignments

Sport season	Objective	Frequency per week	Duration	Intensity
Off-season (base training)	Develop sound conditioning base	5-6	Long	Low to moderate
Preseason	Improve factors important to aerobic endurance performance	6-7	Moderate to long	Moderate to high
In-season (competition)	Maintain factors important to aerobic endurance performance	5-6 (training and racing)	Short (training)	Low (training)
			Race distance	High (racing)
Postseason (active rest)	Recovery from competitive season	3-5	Short	Low

Data from references 16, 25, 50, 68, and 72.

called **base training**), preseason, in-season (sport competition), and postseason (active rest). Table 18.5 summarizes the main objectives and the typical program design assignments for each training season.

Off-Season (Base Training)

The priority in off-season training is to develop a base of cardiorespiratory fitness. Initially, the training program should be composed of long-duration and low-intensity workouts. As the off-season continues, intensity and, to a lesser extent, duration are increased; however, the increase in training duration should not be more than 5% to 10% per week (76). Increasing the training duration too much can actually lead to decreases in aerobic endurance performance (19). Periodic increases in exercise intensity occur when an athlete has adapted to the training stimulus and requires additional overload for continued improvements.

Preseason

During the preseason, the athlete should focus on increasing intensity, maintaining or reducing duration, and incorporating all types of training into the program. The strengths and weaknesses of the individual athlete should determine the amount and frequency of each type of training.

In-Season (Competition)

The in-season training program needs to be designed to include competition or race days in the training schedule. Low-intensity and short-duration training days should precede scheduled competitions so that the athlete is fully recovered and rested. The types of training employed during the in-season are based on the continued goal of improving weaknesses and maintaining strengths of the athlete.

Postseason (Active Rest)

During the postseason, the main focus should be on recovering from the previous competitive season. Low training duration and intensity are typical for this active rest phase, but enough overall exercise or activity should be performed to maintain a sufficient level of cardiorespiratory fitness, muscular strength, and lean body mass. During the postseason, the aerobic endurance athlete should focus on rehabilitating injuries incurred during the competitive season and improving the strength of weak or underconditioned muscle groups.

A sound year-round aerobic endurance training program should be divided into sport seasons with specific goals and objectives designed to improve performance gradually and progressively.

SPECIAL ISSUES RELATED TO AEROBIC ENDURANCE TRAINING

In addition to the program design variables, it is important to consider other related issues when developing an aerobic endurance training program.

These include cross-training, detraining, tapering, and supplemental resistance training. The strength and conditioning professional should contemplate these issues when adapting the types of aerobic endurance training programs to an individual athlete or developing an aerobic endurance program based on the sport season.

Cross-Training

Cross-training is a mode of training that can be used to maintain general conditioning in athletes during periods of reduced training due to injury or during recovery from a training cycle (33). Cross-training may reduce the likelihood of overuse injuries because it distributes the physical stress of training to different muscle groups than those used during training (76). Multiple-event athletes also use cross-training to maximize performance in swimming, cycling, and running. The benefits derived from cross-training include adaptations of the respiratory, cardiovascular, and musculoskeletal systems (49, 57, 76). It seems reasonable to expect that cross-training would maintain some level of conditioning in single-event athletes who perform another mode of training (e.g., runners who perform cycling or swimming). To be effective in maintaining $\dot{V}O_2max$, cross-training must be equal in intensity and duration to the athlete's primary mode of exercise (36, 51, 74); however, cross-training will not improve single-event performance to the same magnitude as mode-specific training only (33).

Detraining

Detraining occurs when the athlete reduces the training duration or intensity or stops training altogether due to a break in the training program, injury, or illness. In the absence of an appropriate training stimulus, the athlete experiences a loss of the physiological adaptations brought about by training. It has been demonstrated that most of the physiological adaptations attained with training regress rapidly toward pretraining levels when the training stimulus is removed (28, 30, 48). To avoid some of the effects of detraining, the use of other training modes may be beneficial; however, cross-training may only attenuate some of the loss of physiological adaptation normally seen during complete cessation of training. Aerobic endurance athletes can minimize the effects of detraining by continuing to use their primary mode of exercise at reduced frequency and intensity, if possible (72).

Tapering

Tapering is an important component of the training program as aerobic endurance athletes prepare for major competition. Tapering involves the systematic reduction of training duration and intensity, combined with an increased emphasis on technique work and nutritional intervention. The objective of tapering the training regimen is to attain peak performance at the time of competition. Although most of the available research on tapering has been conducted on swimmers (18, 43), the use of tapering is not limited solely to these aerobic endurance athletes. Runners and cyclists would likely benefit from some type of tapering regimen prior to competition to allow for achieving adequate recovery, rehydration, and increased muscle and liver glycogen stores.

Resistance Training

Resistance training is an important but often overlooked factor in improving performance in aerobic endurance athletes. Overall, research on the effects of resistance training on performance in trained aerobic endurance athletes is limited; however, there are some data to suggest that benefits can be derived from performing resistance training during aerobic endurance training. Of particular importance, Hickson and colleagues (42) demonstrated that although the $\dot{V}O_2max$ of highly trained aerobic athletes did not improve from resistance training, there was an improvement in short-term exercise performance during both cycling and running. Benefits that aerobic endurance athletes may obtain from performing resistance training include faster recovery from injuries, prevention of overuse injuries, and reduction of muscle imbalances. Increased strength is important for various aspects of aerobic endurance competition, including hill climbing, bridging gaps between competitors during breakaways from groups, and the final sprint (76). Chapter 15 provides guidelines for designing resistance training programs that can apply to aerobic endurance athletes; refer to scenario C for a sample program that focuses on a high school cross-country runner.

CONCLUSION

Training to improve aerobic endurance performance requires a well-developed and scientifically based program. The training program should be developed in conjunction with periodic performance assessment and should be structured to enhance the strengths and improve the weaknesses of the athlete. A combination of a variety of the training types described in this chapter should be used so that all physiological systems involved in successful performance are overloaded and challenged to respond with positive adaptations.

Training programs should be developed far enough in advance and with enough structure to ensure enhancement of performance, but with enough flexibility to avoid overuse injuries and overtraining. Although other forms of training can be employed to avoid boredom and overtraining, activity-specific training results in the best adaptations to training and ultimately the most improvement in performance.

KEY TERMS

age-predicted maximal heart rate (APMHR) 493
base training 501
cross-training 502
detraining 502
duration 495
exercise economy 491
Fartlek training 500
frequency 492
functional capacity 493
heart rate reserve (HRR) 493
intensity 492
interval training 499
Karvonen method 493
lactate threshold 491
long, slow distance training (LSD) 497
maximal aerobic power ($\dot{V}O_2$max) 490
maximal lactate steady state 491
mode 492
overload 493
pace/tempo training 498
percentage of maximal heart rate (MHR) method 493
ratings of perceived exertion (RPE) 494
recovery 492
repetition training 499
tapering 502

STUDY QUESTIONS

1. Which of the following adaptations occur as an outcome of an aerobic endurance training program?

   I. increased oxygen delivery to working tissues
   II. higher rate of aerobic energy production
   III. greater utilization of fat as a fuel source
   IV. increased disturbance of the acid-base balance

   a. I and III only
   b. II and IV only
   c. I, II, and III only
   d. II, III, and IV only

2. Which of the following types of training is conducted at an intensity equal to the lactate threshold?

   a. pace/tempo
   b. interval
   c. repetition
   d. Fartlek

3. Which of the following is the method most commonly used to assign and regulate exercise intensity?

   a. oxygen consumption
   b. heart rate
   c. ratings of perceived exertion
   d. race pace

4. The loss of physiological adaptations upon the cessation of training is an example of

   a. specificity of training.
   b. cross-training.
   c. detraining.
   d. tapering.

5. The longest aerobic endurance training sessions should be performed during which of the following sport seasons?

   a. postseason
   b. preseason
   c. in-season
   d. off-season

PART III

Applying Exercise Prescription Principles

Effective program design involves the use of periodization, which is the varying or cycling of training specificity, intensity, and volume to achieve peak levels of conditioning. Planned variations of the program design variables associated with exercise help athletes avoid staleness and overtraining while encouraging continuous adaptations to progressively more demanding training stimuli. These scheduled modifications apply to all types of training, although they are frequently associated with resistance training programs.

Part III of section 4, "Program Design," addresses how to design a periodization program using the training principles defined and discussed in the previous program design chapters. An element of chapter 19, "Periodization," is the comprehensive example of an overall strength and conditioning program based on a scenario from chapter 15, "Resistance Training." More specifically, the preseason training program described in scenario A of chapter 15 is the starting point for the in-season, postseason, and off-season programs discussed in chapter 19. Combined with components of other types of training, this periodized program is an example of a complete strength and conditioning program.

In addition, chapter 20 discusses rehabilitation and reconditioning. Although these concepts are often not thought of as relating to program design principles in the strictest sense, the strength and conditioning professional must use and apply a sound knowledge of the development of exercise programs in order to effectively integrate them into the rehabilitation and reconditioning of athletes.

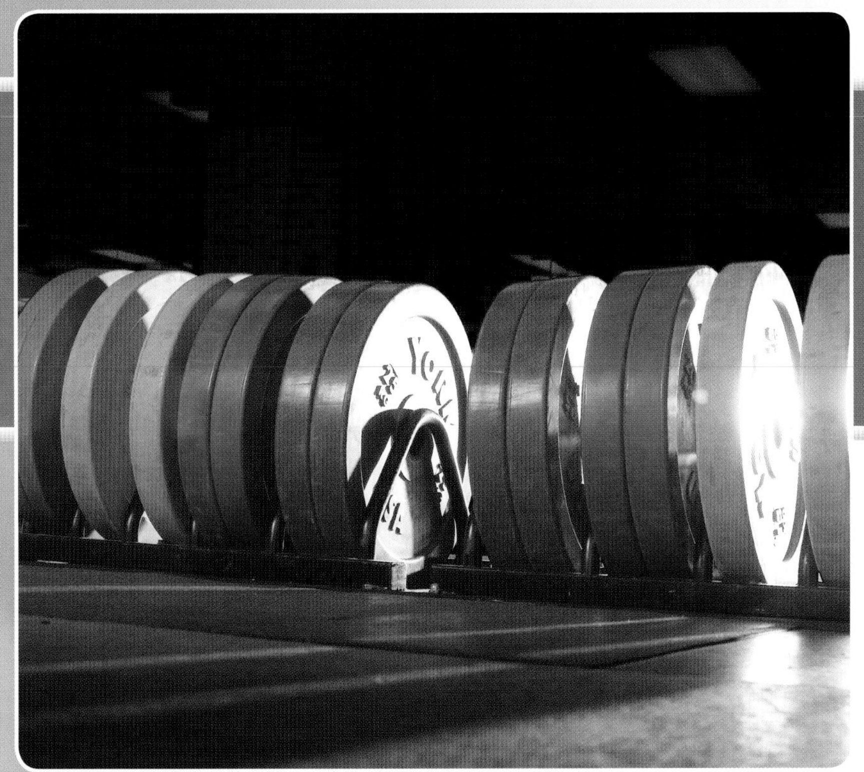

CHAPTER 19

Periodization

Dan Wathen, MS, Thomas R. Baechle, EdD, and Roger W. Earle, MA

After completing this chapter, you will be able to

- understand the value, role, and application of periodization in strength and conditioning programs;
- describe the four periods of the traditional periodization model;
- describe the three phases of the preparatory period of the traditional periodization model;
- relate the four sport seasons to the four periods of the traditional periodization model; and
- apply the program design variables to create a periodized training program.

While strength and conditioning programs bring about significant improvements in strength, eventually physical adaptations and psychological adjustments will occur less frequently, and the athlete will experience performance plateaus or decrements. There may also be an increased risk of injury and other symptoms associated with overtraining. To promote long-term training and performance improvements, the strength and conditioning professional should include preplanned, systematic variations in training specificity, intensity, and volume organized in periods or cycles within an overall program. This program design strategy is called **periodization**. The concept of periodization was proposed in the 1960s by Russian physiologist Leo Matveyev (15). Later, American exercise scientists modified Matveyev's work with special application to training strength and power athletes (10, 20, 22).

This chapter discusses the concept of periodization as it applies to a strength and conditioning program. A periodized training year can be divided into smaller blocks of time, each with its own goals and priorities. This overall schedule can encompass all aspects of an athlete's program, including general conditioning, sport-specific activities, and resistance training. The second half of this chapter presents a detailed example of a year-long periodized strength and conditioning program. To understand the intricacies of that program, the reader is encouraged to first read chapter 15.

RESPONSES TO TRAINING STRESS

The manner in which the human body reacts to stress was described by Canadian biologist and endocrinologist Hans Selye as the **General Adaptation Syndrome** (GAS) (19). Selye delineated a three-stage response to stress (alarm, resistance, and exhaustion). Later, Garhammer (10) applied Selye's GAS concept to resistance training and exercise conditioning. When the body experiences a new stress or a more intense stress than previously applied (e.g., lifting heavier resistance training loads or a greater load-volume; see chapter 15), the first response is the *shock* or *alarm phase*. This phase may last several days or several weeks, during which the athlete may experience excessive soreness, stiffness, and a temporary drop in performance. Next is the *resistance phase*, one in which the body adapts to the stimulus and returns to more normal functioning. In this phase, the body is able to demonstrate its ability to withstand the stress, an attribute that may manifest itself for an extended period depending on the health and training status of the athlete. Here, the athlete relies on neurological adaptations to continue training while the muscle tissue adapts by making various biochemical, structural, and mechanical adjustments that lead to increased performance (22). This phase of adaptation is sometimes called **supercompensation**.

However, if the stress persists for an extended time, the *exhaustion phase* is reached. Some of the same symptoms experienced during the alarm phase reappear (fatigue, soreness, etc.), and the athlete loses the ability to adapt to the stressor. Staleness, overtraining, and other maladaptations may occur when there is no training variety or when the training stress is too great. In addition, non-training-related stress (e.g., occupational issues, insufficient sleep, poor diet) can contribute to the overall stress level and lead to the exhaustion phase. It is this phase that the strength and conditioning professional should strive to avoid. Although the actual dimensions (i.e., slope, magnitude, and timing) of the curve shown in figure 19.1 vary based on the individual athlete, the figure illustrates the three distinct phases of the body's response to training stress.

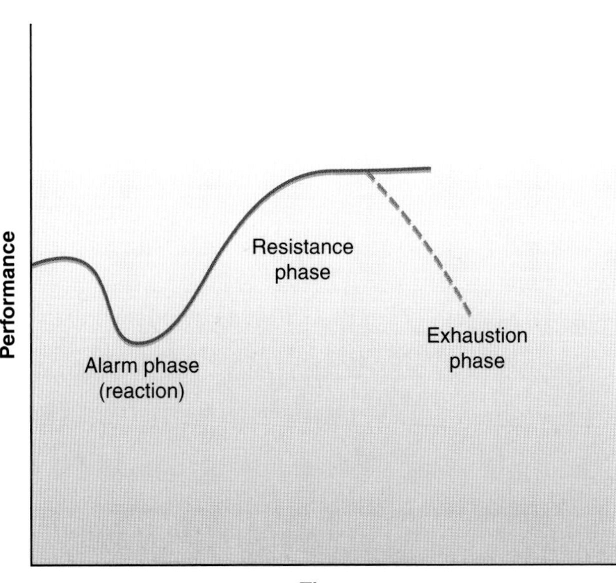

Figure 19.1 The General Adaptation Syndrome (GAS).

Reprinted, by permission, from Selye, 1956 (19).

PERIODIZATION CYCLES

The traditional periodization model partitions the overall program into specific time periods. The largest division is a **macrocycle**, which typically constitutes an entire training year but may also be a period of many months up to four years (for Olympic athletes). Within the macrocycle are two or more **mesocycles**, each lasting several weeks to several months. The number depends on the goals of the athlete and, if applicable, the number of sport competitions contained within the period. Each mesocycle is divided into two or more **microcycles** that are typically one week long but could last for up to four weeks, depending on the program (4, 5, 6, 8, 9, 20, 22). This short cycle focuses on daily and weekly training variations.

PERIODIZATION PERIODS

The planned implementation of the meso- and microcycles within an overall macrocycle is the basis for changing (varying) the program design variables. Predominantly, it is the intensity and volume assignments of the training and conditioning programs that are manipulated to the greatest extent. Sport-specific training also involves acquiring and perfecting skill-related techniques, but attention (time) dedicated to these outcomes varies based on their relative importance to the match or game schedule. Therefore, periodization involves shifting training priorities *from* non-sport-specific activities of high volume and low intensity *to* sport-specific activities of low volume and high intensity over a period of many weeks to prevent overtraining and optimize performance.

The periodization model and the process of moving through the periodization cycles or phases can also be likened to the sequence and evolution of learning academic concepts and skills from simple to complex (see chapter 17 for a detailed explanation and application).

According to Matveyev (15), the major divisions of training are the preparatory, competition, and transition periods. Later, Stone, O'Bryant, and Garhammer (21) added a "first transition" between the preparatory and competitive periods. Thus, the conventional periodization model includes four distinct periods: preparatory, first transition, competition, and second transition. Figure 19.2 illustrates the periodization model that can be applied to athletes with a novice or lower training status. Intensity begins lower and gradually increases, and volume starts higher and slowly decreases as the athlete becomes conditioned. Not all novice athletes, however, are able to tolerate large changes in these variables (15, 22, 24). Also, because advanced athletes invariably train closer to their abilities and have smaller adaptational windows, their volume and intensity assignments are consistently higher, as seen in figure 19.3 (7, 11, 20, 22). This modification of Matveyev's model reveals a shift from lower intensities and higher volumes earlier in the preparation period to higher intensities and lower volumes in the competition period, but the fluctuations are smaller and occur in the upper end of their values.

Preparatory Period

The initial **preparatory period** is usually the longest and occurs during the time of the year

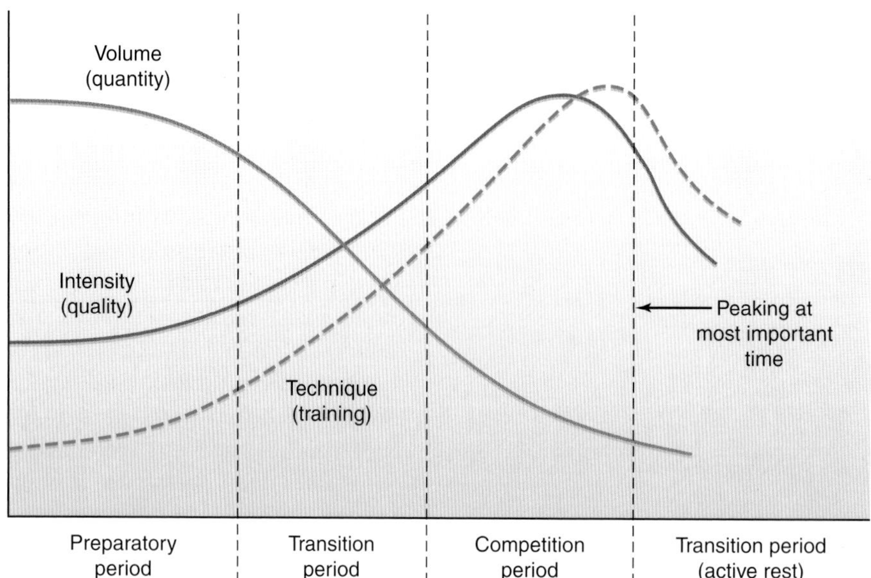

Figure 19.2 Matveyev's model of periodization (appropriate for novice athletes).

Adapted, by permission, from Stone and O'Bryant, 1987 (20).

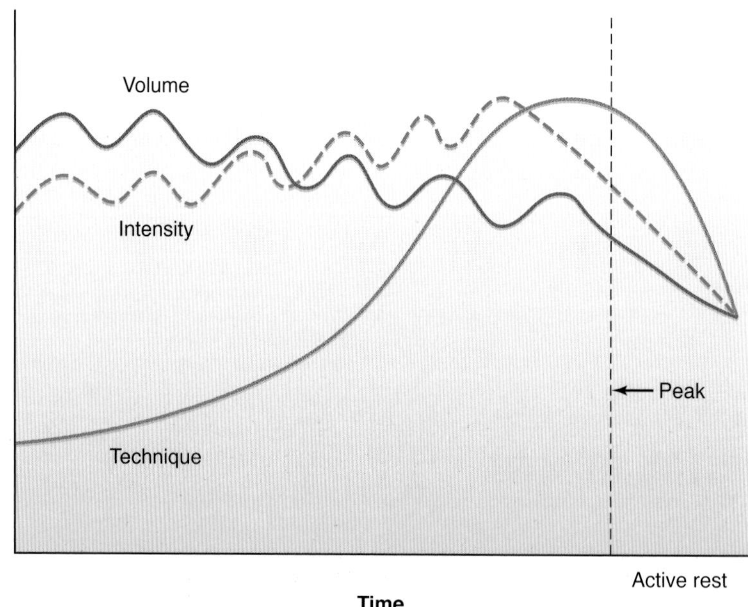

Figure 19.3 A modification of Matveyev's model of periodization (tailored for advanced athletes).

Adapted, by permission, from Stone and O'Bryant, 1987 (20).

when there are no competitions and only a limited number of sport-specific skill practices or game strategy sessions. The major emphasis of this period is establishing a base level of conditioning to increase the athlete's tolerance for more intense training. Conditioning activities begin at relatively low intensities and high volumes: long, slow distance running or swimming; low-intensity plyometrics; and high-repetition resistance training with light to moderate resistances. Because high-volume training causes significant fatigue and can involve large time commitments, the athlete is not exposed to optimal conditions (i.e., does not have enough time or energy) for improving sport-specific technique. As a result, technique training is not a high priority during this period (4, 5, 6). As the preparatory period unfolds, however, microcycles are designed to gradually increase resistance training loads and sport conditioning intensity, decrease training volume, and give more attention to sport technique training.

A further modification of Matveyev's original model was the creation of three phases within the preparatory period that delineate more refined differences in training intensity and volume, especially for the resistance training component. In order, these are the hypertrophy/endurance phase, the basic strength phase, and the strength/power phase (20, 22).

Hypertrophy/Endurance Phase

The **hypertrophy/endurance phase** occurs during the early stages of the preparatory period and may last from one to six weeks (8). During this phase, training begins at a very low intensity with very high volume. The goals for this phase are to increase lean body mass or develop an endurance (muscular and metabolic) base, or both, for more intense training in later phases and periods (4, 5, 6). Initially, the sport conditioning activities may not be specific to the athletic event. However, as the preparatory period continues over several weeks, the training activities become more specific to the sport. For example, a sprinter may begin the preparatory period with longer-distance runs (longer than his or her competition distance) at slower speeds, lower-intensity plyometrics such as double-leg bounding and hopping, and resistance training exercises that are not necessarily biomechanically or structurally similar to running (hip sled, leg curl, etc.). The athlete may also handle very low to moderate loads for many repetitions in a resistance training program (table 19.1). This phase may be followed by an intermediate recovery week or microcycle of low-intensity, low-volume training prior to the beginning of the next phase.

The hypertrophy/endurance phase involves very low to moderate intensity (50-75% of the 1-repetition maximum [1RM]) and very high to moderate volume (three to six sets of 10-20 repetitions).

Basic Strength Phase

Later in the preparatory period, the aim of the **basic strength phase** is to increase the strength of the muscles essential to the primary sport movements (4, 5, 6). For example, the sprinter's running program progresses to include interval sprints of

TABLE 19.1

A Periodization Model for Resistance Training

Period	Preparation ⟶		First transition	Competition			
Phase / Variable	Hypertrophy and endurance	Basic strength	Strength/ power	Peaking	OR	Maintenance	Second transition (active rest)
Intensity	Low to moderate	High	High	Very high		Moderate	Recreational activity (may not involve resistance training)
	50-75% 1RM	80-90% 1RM	87-95% 1RM[†] 75-90% 1RM[‡]	≥93% 1RM		≈80-85% 1RM	
Volume[#]	High to moderate	Moderate	Low	Very low		Moderate	
	3-6 sets	3-5 sets	3-5 sets	1-3 sets		≈2-3 sets	
	10-20 repetitions	4-8 repetitions	2-5 repetitions	1-3 repetitions		≈6-8 repetitions	

[#]These assignments do not include warm-up sets and typically apply to core exercises only (1, 14).

[†]These percentages of the 1RM and the repetition ranges apply to nonpower core exercises only.

[‡]These percentages of the 1RM and the repetition ranges apply to power exercises only and are *not consistent* with the typical %1RM–repetition relationship described in chapter 15. Refer to the section "Assigning Percentages for Power Training" on page 400 for further explanation.

Adapted from references 10, 20, 21, and 22.

moderate distances and more complex and specialized plyometric drills. Similarly, the resistance training program becomes more specific to the sport (e.g., squats and lunges with free weights) and involves heavier loads for fewer repetitions than the hypertrophy/endurance phase (table 19.1).

The basic strength phase involves high intensity (80-90% of the 1RM) and moderate volume (three to five sets of four to eight repetitions).

Strength/Power Phase

The last stage of the preparatory period is the **strength/power phase**. Here, the sprinter's interval and speed training intensifies to near competitive pace, speed training drills are performed (e.g., sled towing, sprints against resistance, and uphill and downhill sprints), plyometric drills mimic sprinting, and the resistance training program involves performing power/explosive exercises at high loads and low volumes. As explained in chapter 15, the load assignments for power exercises do not follow the typical %1RM–repetition relationship, but their relative intensities are still elevated during this phase (table 19.1).

The strength/power phase involves high intensity (75-95% of the 1RM, depending on the exercise) and low volume (three to five sets of two to five repetitions).

First Transition Period

As mentioned earlier, Stone, O'Bryant, and Garhammer (21) modified Matveyev's original model by inserting the **first transition period** between the preparatory and competitive periods to denote the break between high-volume training and high-intensity training (4, 5, 6). Often, this period provides one week of lower intensity, lower volume, or a combination of both before the beginning of the competition period.

Competition Period

The goal for the **competition period** is to peak strength and power through further increases in training intensity with additional decreases in training volume. Also, practice in skill technique and game strategy increases dramatically as time spent in physical conditioning decreases proportionately. For example, a sprinter places even more emphasis on speed, reaction time, sprinting-specific plyometric drills, and technique training, much of which is gained through actual competitions. The competition period may last from one to three weeks; but for most organized sports, this period spans the entire competitive season and may last for many months. This prolonged time requires some manipulation of the intensity on a weekly or microcycle basis, but in general the period is characterized by very high-intensity and very low-volume training activities (table 19.1). Typically, this mesocycle will place the athlete in peak condition for only about three weeks; trying to overextend this will inevitably result in overtraining (3, 4, 5, 6). For sports with multiple major contests spread across multiple weeks or months, the goal is to preserve strength, power, and performance levels by following a maintenance program of moderate intensities and moderate volumes (table 19.1) (4, 5, 6, 16).

The competition period includes peaking and maintenance. For peaking, athletes use very high intensity (≥93% of the 1RM) and very low volume (one to three sets of one to three repetitions). For maintenance, athletes use moderate intensity (≈80-85% of the 1RM) and moderate volume (about two to three sets of about six to eight repetitions).

Second Transition Period (Active Rest)

Between the competitive season and the next macrocycle's preparatory period is the **second transition period**. This period, commonly referred to as **active rest** or **restoration**, lasts one to four weeks and focuses on unstructured, non-sport-specific recreational activities performed at low intensities with low volumes (table 19.1). Care should be taken to avoid excessively aggressive training immediately after peaking or after a prolonged competitive season. It is important to the athlete's long-term progress to allow time to rehabilitate any injuries and to rest, physically and mentally (4, 5, 6). For example, a sprinter may engage in recreational activities such as volleyball, racket sports, and swimming in a leisurely manner and perform low-volume, non-sport-specific resistance training with light loads. A secondary use of the active rest concept is the practice of inserting a one-week break between long phases (three weeks) or periods. The purpose of this **unloading week** is to prepare the body for the increased demand of the next phase or period. Plus, many strength and conditioning professionals believe that significantly reducing the volume and load assignments will make the athlete less susceptible to overtraining symptoms.

The second transition (active rest) period consists of recreational activity that may not involve resistance training.

APPLYING SPORT SEASONS TO THE PERIODIZATION PERIODS

In practical terms, periodization involves manipulating training intensity and volume while being respectful of the seasonal demands of a particular sport and athlete. This necessitates regular variations in training to provide sufficient intensity and volume while also avoiding or minimizing training monotony and staleness. Most scholastic, intercollegiate, and professional sports have an annual schedule that consists of off-season, preseason, in-season, and postseason mesocycles. These seasons typically relate to the periods of periodization as described in the following paragraphs (although there can be considerable variation in season lengths).

Off-Season

The off-season is the period between the postseason and six weeks (although this varies greatly) prior to the first contest of the next year's season. This season includes most of the preparatory period and can be divided into multiple shorter mesocycles if it is overly long (e.g., 16 to 24 weeks). In that case, the athlete may complete two or more rotations through the hypertrophy/endurance and basic strength phases, possibly including even the strength/power phase, depending on the sport (see figures 19.4 and 19.5).

Preseason

The preseason period occurs next, leads up to the first contest, and commonly contains the late stages of the preparatory period and the first transition period.

In-Season

The competition, or in-season period, contains all the contests scheduled for that year, including any tournament games. Most sports have long in-seasons

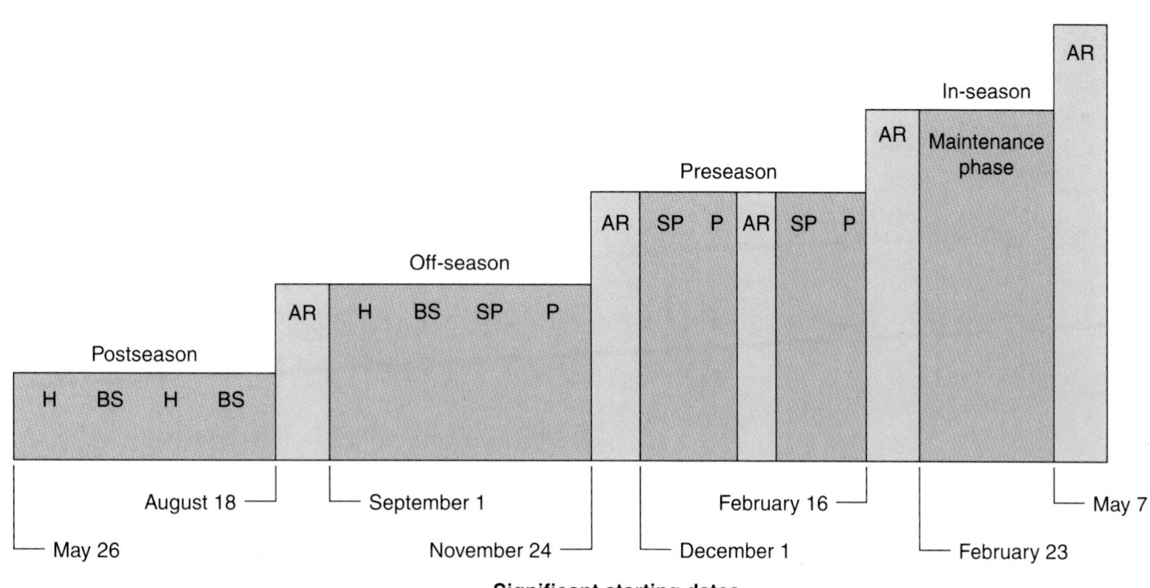

Figure 19.4 Macrocycle for tennis. H = hypertrophy/endurance; BS = basic strength; AR = active rest; SP = strength/power; P = peaking.

Adapted, by permission, from Chargina et al., 1983 (4).

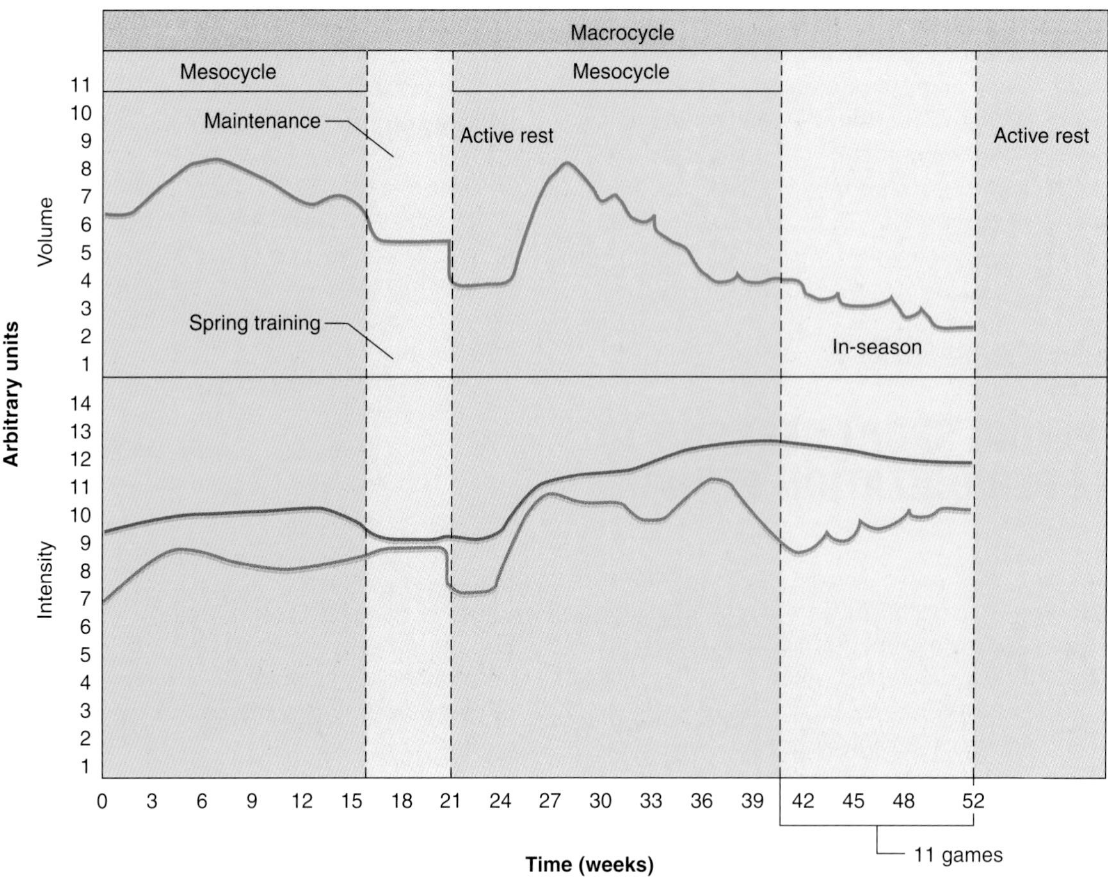

Figure 19.5 Macrocycle for a team sport. Blue line = emphasis on sport technique training or practice.

that may necessitate multiple mesocycles arranged around the most important contests. Thus, a long competition period (12-16+ weeks) presents some unique challenges in terms of designing a training program. One solution is to divide the competitive period into multiple three- or four-week mesocycles that peak the athlete's performance for the most critical contests (see figure 19.5). This does not mean that the athlete will be in poor condition for the other contests, but the training program is adjusted to assign greater intensities and lower volumes only when the athlete is peaking for the most important competitions. The other approach, as previously mentioned, is to design a maintenance program consisting of moderate intensities and low-to-moderate volumes (see figure 19.4).

Postseason

After the final contest, the postseason or second transition period provides active or relative rest for the athlete before the start of the next year's off-season or preparatory period. In addition, shorter active rest periods could be used throughout the training macrocycle, not just during the postseason. After each mesocycle, week-long microcycles of relative rest (i.e., low-intensity and low-volume training) can be scheduled prior to the beginning of the next mesocycle (see figure 19.4).

UNDULATING (NONLINEAR) VERSUS LINEAR PERIODIZATION MODELS

The traditional resistance training periodization model is often referred to as **linear** due to the gradual, progressive mesocycle increases in intensity over time. An alternative to this model involves large daily (i.e., within the week or microcycle) fluctuations in the load and volume assignments for core exercises. This type of periodization model is termed **undulating** or **nonlinear** (2, 8, 18). As an example, an undulating program may require an athlete to perform four sets with a 6RM load on the first training day of the week (e.g., Tuesday), three sets with a 10RM load on the next training day (Thursday), and five sets with a 3RM load on the last training day (Saturday). In this case, both the load and volume are modified. These variations are in contrast to the linear model, which may have the athlete perform four sets with a 6RM load on the heavy training day with fluctuations in the loads on the other training days (i.e., a "heavy-light-medium" approach), but with no changes in training volume (i.e., four sets of six repetitions are performed each training day).

Some research studies have shown that the undulating model is more effective in improving strength than the linear model (13, 18, 23), although other evidence suggests that there is no difference (2). An underlying factor that appears to support the undulating model is the absence of accumulated neural fatigue caused by the extended, ever-increasing training intensities common to the linear model (12). Additionally, undulating periodization programs have application to sports that have many in-season contests and therefore do not train to peak strength and power. A concern, however, is that the high relative levels of daily intensity in undulating models would more quickly result in an overtrained state in an athlete with a higher training status. While the terms *linear* and *undulating* have, for better or worse, become part of the periodization landscape, it should be noted that periodization by its very nature should be undulating with respect to regular fluctuations in microcycle volume and load and linear with respect to the long-term nature of fitness goals (17).

EXAMPLE OF A MACROCYCLE

An example of one approach to designing a full macrocycle spanning all four sport seasons is described on pages 515 through 521. The program is based on the preseason resistance training program for scenario A from chapter 15, "Resistance Training," which focuses on a female college basketball center. Background and initial testing information about this athlete is provided on pages 383 and 385. Additional examples of periodized programs have been described in the literature (8, 20, 25).

The macrocycle example provided in this chapter begins where the preseason program from chapter 15 left off and shows a continuation of the training program through the in-season, postseason, and the following year's off-season. The primary focus of the macrocycle example is the resistance training component of scenario A. Although other modes of training are described briefly (e.g., plyometrics, anaerobic conditioning, aerobic endurance), this macrocycle example is not intended to illustrate every aspect or variation of a strength and conditioning program for basketball. Also, although this macrocycle example is divided into four sport seasons (each one is a mesocycle) that are made up of many two- to four-week microcycles, an alternative, valid periodization model denotes each season as a macrocycle that is divided into multiple mesocycles.

Preseason Mesocycle

After one or two unloading weeks following the off-season, the athlete begins the preseason period of training. For this example, this period covers about 3 1/2 months (mid-August until the first game, possibly mid-November). The goals of the preseason are to increase the intensity of sport-specific training and the attention given to basketball drills and skills. The resistance training portion is planned for three times per week and focuses primarily on strength and power outcomes. Other training modes (e.g., plyometrics and anaerobic conditioning) hold high priority, especially if they directly contribute to basketball training. Although chapter 15 does not show microcycle progression, it does describe the resistance training portion of this season in detail; therefore, please refer to page 410 for the preseason program example. The same method of applying the periodization concepts described in this chapter can be used to design the remainder of the preseason mesocycle.

In-Season Mesocycle (Competition Period)

After an unloading week following the preseason, the athlete is ready to begin the competition period of training. The in-season period typically spans November to April, about 20 weeks (including a four-week tournament period, although it could last longer). The goals for the in-season are to maintain and possibly improve strength, power, flexibility, and anaerobic conditioning. The time constraints of games, skill and strategy practice, and travel result in a lower volume of off-court training activities. Due to multiple games each week, resistance training may be limited to 30 minutes, one to three times per week, consisting of an undulating regime of varying volumes of relatively high intensities. Power and basketball-specific nonpower core exercises predominate, with assistance exercises added for balance. See the sample in-season program on page 517. Plyometric sessions should be alternated with resistance training and conducted once or twice weekly, depending on the number of games.

On days when no resistance training is scheduled, 15 to 20 minutes of various short sprint intervals could be performed once or twice weekly during practice. Speed, agility, and other running conditioning can be incorporated into practice time, and flexibility training can be part of the practice and game warm-up and cool-down. Two to three days of rest should be afforded between resistance training, plyometrics, and sprint interval sessions, depending on the game schedule. Similar to the previous mesocycle, the majority of the athlete's time is spent on skill and strategy development, with the remainder devoted to conditioning.

The athlete is in good condition from the previous microcycles, so she should be able not only to maintain that condition, but also to peak again if the team continues in the conference tournament. In that case, she would revert back to microcycle 2 and progress to microcycle 3 if the team qualifies for a tournament to be held after the conference tournament. If the tournament game schedules do not allow for more than one resistance training workout a week, the athlete should perform all of the week's power and core exercises (if time allows) and omit the assistance exercises. Two examples of specific weekly tournament schedules are shown on page 518.

Postseason Mesocycle (Active Rest Period)

After completion of the competitive season, there is a (second) transition period of active rest with no formal or structured workouts. For this example, the transition period lasts a month (from April 4 until May 1). The goal of this mesocycle is for the athlete to recuperate physically and psychologically from the long in-season. Recreational games and fitness activities include swimming, jogging, circuit weight training, volleyball, racquetball, and informal basketball. All activities are performed at low intensities with low volumes.

Off-Season Mesocycle

Following the off-season active rest period, the athlete should be rested enough to begin off-season training. For this example, this preparatory period lasts about 14 weeks, from the beginning of May to the beginning of August. The goal of the off-season is to establish a base level of conditioning to increase the athlete's tolerance for more intense training in later phases and periods. During the first week, testing should be performed so the strength and conditioning professional can determine initial training loads for the exercises in the first microcycle. In later microcycles, when more or other exercises are added, the training loads can be estimated from loads used in similar exercises or can be determined directly from RM testing. For example, the strength and conditioning professional can reasonably predict a training load for the hang clean from loads used for the power clean, or the actual RM load could be measured. Other performance tests related to basketball are shoulder and trunk and hip flexibility tests, 12-minute run, 300-yard (274 m) shuttle run, line drill, T-test, vertical jump, and skinfold measurements (see chapter 12 for testing protocols). Testing should also be performed at the end of the off-season to evaluate the program, to chart improvements, to discern areas requiring additional training and attention, and to provide foundational information for designing the preseason program.

The resistance training component holds higher priority in the off-season, and an athlete may follow a split routine of four or more training days per week. In this example, the basketball player begins the off-season with an all-body, three-times-per-week regime but soon progresses to an upper body–lower body split program consisting of four training days per week (two heavy and two light) (see pp. 519 to 521). These advancements also involve a gradual increase in loading, with an associated decrease in training volume. Other training includes aerobic endurance exercise to maintain or improve body composition and cardiovascular fitness. These conditioning workouts are scheduled on non-resistance training days, and flexibility training can be emphasized in the warm-up and cool-down portions of each training session.

In-Season Mesocycle (Competition Period)

Female college basketball center
5 months (20 weeks): November 21 - April 3 (including tournament play)
(Beginning after an unloading week November 15 - 21)

MICROCYCLE 1 4 WEEKS: NOVEMBER 22 - DECEMBER 19 • UNLOADING WEEK: DECEMBER 20 - 26			
Weekly workout #1		***Weekly workout #2***	
High pull	1 × 4 @ 80% 1RM	Push press	1 × 6 @ 75% 1RM
Back squat	1 × 6RM	Hip sled	1 × 10RM
Incline bench press	1 × 6RM	Close-grip decline bench press	1 × 12RM
Lateral shoulder raise	1 × 10RM	Seated low-pulley row	1 × 12RM
Abdominal crunch	Max in 60 seconds	Supine leg raise	Max in 60 seconds
MICROCYCLE 2 4 WEEKS: DECEMBER 27 - JANUARY 23 • UNLOADING WEEK: JANUARY 24 - 30			
Weekly workout #1		***Weekly workout #2***	
Hang clean	1 × 3 @ 85% 1RM	Push jerk	1 × 5 @ 77% 1 RM
Front squat	1 × 5RM	Step-up	1 × 8RM
Standing shoulder press	1 × 5RM	Close-grip bench press	1 × 12RM
Lying triceps extension	1 × 10RM	Lat pulldown	1 × 12RM
Abdominal crunch	Max in 60 seconds	Supine leg raise	Max in 60 seconds
MICROCYCLE 3 4 WEEKS: JANUARY 31 - FEBRUARY 27 • UNLOADING WEEK: FEBRUARY 28 - MARCH 6			
Weekly workout #1		***Weekly workout #2***	
Power clean	1 × 2 @ 90% 1RM	Hang snatch	1 × 4 @ 80% 1RM
Back squat	1 × 4RM	Forward step lunge	1 × 6RM
Bench press	1 × 4RM	Close-grip decline bench press	1 × 10RM
Barbell biceps curl	1 × 8RM	Upright row	1 × 10RM
Abdominal crunch	Max in 60 seconds	Supine leg raise	Max in 60 seconds
TOURNAMENT MICROCYCLE 4 WEEKS: MARCH 7 - APRIL 3			
Go back to microcycle 2; progress again to microcycle 3 if tournament play extends beyond four weeks.			

COMMENTS

- Although this sport season is labeled as a mesocycle and made up of four 4-week microcycles, an alternative, valid periodization model could consider each microcycle as a mesocycle (so the in-season would be a macrocycle that is composed of four mesocycles).
- The in-season program incorporates an undulating, nonlinear periodization regime—weekly workout #1 involves heavier loads for fewer repetitions, and weekly workout #2 involves lighter loads for more repetitions, but all are performed at their respective repetition maximums where indicated.
- The volume assignments are represented as sets × repetitions.
- The athlete's training loads are determined from testing at the end of the preseason or estimated from previous training cycles.
- For each workout shown, the number of sets does not include warm-up sets.
- Refer to table 15.7 on page 394 for the relationship between the %1RM and the number of repetitions allowed (i.e., the RM load).
- Refer to table 15.12 on page 408 for the rest period length assignments based on the training goal.

Tournament Week A (Two Games)

Sunday	Monday	Tuesday	Wednesday	Thursday	Friday	Saturday
Practice (or rest)	Practice and resistance training workout	Practice	Practice and plyometric workout	Game	Practice and interval sprints	Game

Tournament Week B (Three Games)

Sunday	Monday	Tuesday	Wednesday	Thursday	Friday	Saturday
Game	Practice (or rest)	Practice and resistance training workout	Practice	Game	Practice and interval sprints	Game

Reviewing the Macrocycle Example

For a model such as the one presented here to function optimally, the sport coach and the strength and conditioning professional must plan the program together and share goals and strategies. Without the cooperation of all involved professionals, optimal performance cannot be fully achieved.

The macrocycle illustrated in this chapter is one model for implementing the periodization principle of cycling training volume and intensity. Other athletes and events will require subtle to radical variations from the example.

CONCLUSION

Periodization, based on Selye's General Adaptation Syndrome, organizes an athlete's training into cycles to promote peak condition for the most important competitions. The year's training cycle, or macrocycle, is divided into two or more mesocycles that contain preparatory, competition, and two transition periods. Each period has two or more microcycles that are often divided into heavy, medium, and light training days. The mesocycles begin with high-volume and low-intensity training and progress to low-volume and high-intensity training just prior to the competition period. Transition periods of active rest follow each competition period and may be interspersed between phases or periods as unloading weeks. The nature of the sporting season dictates the length and number of mesocycles during the training year.

Off-Season Mesocycle

Female college basketball center
3½ months (14 weeks): May 2 - August 7

INITIAL PRETESTING (FOR MICROCYCLE 1) • 1 WEEK: MAY 2 - 8

5RM for power exercises

Power clean

10RM for nonpower core exercises

Hip sled
Bench press

12-15RM for assistance exercises

Leg (knee) curl
Lat pulldown
Lying triceps extension
Upright row

Other testing

Sit-and-reach test
Shoulder elevation
1.5-mile (2.4 km) run
300-yard (274 m) shuttle run
Line drill
T-test
Vertical jump
Body composition (skinfolds)

MICROCYCLE 1 — 2 WEEKS: MAY 9 - 22 • HYPERTROPHY/ENDURANCE PHASE 1

Week 1: 3×/week (Monday/Wednesday/Friday)

Exercise	Sets × reps
Power clean	2 × 5 @ 80% 5RM
Hip sled	2 × 10 @ 90% 10RM
Leg (knee) curl	2 × 12-15RM
Bench press	2 × 10 @ 90% 10RM
Lat pulldown	2 × 12-15RM
Lying triceps extension	2 × 12-15RM
Upright row	2 × 12-15RM
Abdominal crunch	2 × 20

Week 2: 3×/week (Monday/Wednesday/Friday)

Exercise	Sets × reps
Power clean	3 × 5 @ 85% 5RM
Hip sled	3 × 10RM
Leg (knee) curl	3 × 12-15RM
Bench press	3 × 1RM
Lat pulldown	2 × 12-15RM
Lying triceps extension	2 × 12-15RM
Upright row	2 × 12-15RM
Abdominal crunch	2 × 20

MICROCYCLE 2 — 2 WEEKS: MAY 23 - JUNE 5 • BASIC STRENGTH PHASE 1

Week 1: 3×/week (Monday/Wednesday/Friday)

Heavy day (Monday):

Exercise	Sets × reps
Power clean	3 × 5 @ 95% 5RM
Hip sled	3 × 6 @ 90% 6RM
Leg (knee) curl	3 × 10RM
Bench press	3 × 6 @ 90% 6RM
Lat pulldown	2 × 10RM
Lying triceps extension	2 × 10RM
Upright row	2 × 10RM
Abdominal crunch	2 × 20
Light day (Wednesday):	80% of Monday's load for power/core exercises
Medium day (Friday):	90% of Monday's load for power/core exercises

Week 2: 3×/week (Monday/Wednesday/Friday)

Heavy day (Monday):

Exercise	Sets × reps
Power clean	3 × 5RM
Hip sled	3 × 6RM
Leg (knee) curl	3 × 10RM
Bench press	3 × 6RM
Lat pulldown	3 × 10RM
Lying triceps extension	3 × 10RM
Upright row	3 × 10RM
Abdominal crunch	2 × 20
Light day (Wednesday):	80% of Monday's load for power/core exercises
Medium day (Friday):	90% of Monday's load for power/core exercises

UNLOADING WEEK — 1 WEEK: JUNE 6 - 12

Week 1: 3×/week (Monday/Wednesday/Friday)

Exercise	Sets × reps
Power clean	3 × 5 @ 70% 5RM
Hip sled	2 × 6 @ 70% 6RM
Bench press	2 × 6 @ 70% 6RM
Abdominal crunch	3 × 20

(continued)

MICROCYCLE 3
2 WEEKS: JUNE 13 - 26 • HYPERTROPHY/ENDURANCE PHASE 2

Week 1: 4×/week

Lower body: 2×/week (Monday/Thursday)

Heavy day (Monday):	
Hang snatch	3 × 5 @ 95% 5RM
Back squat	3 × 10RM
Lunge	3 × 12RM
Leg (knee) curl	3 × 12RM
Seated calf (heel) raise	3 × 12RM
Light day (Thursday):	85% of Monday's load for power/core exercises

Upper body: 2×/week (Tuesday/Friday)

Heavy day (Tuesday):	
Push jerk	3 × 5 @ 95% 5RM
Incline bench press	3 × 10RM
Bent-over row	3 × 12RM
Shoulder press	3 × 10RM
Barbell biceps curl	2 × 12RM
Triceps pushdown	2 × 12RM
Abdominal crunch	3 × 20
Light day (Friday):	85% of Tuesday's load for power/core exercises

Week 2: 4×/week

Lower body: 2×/week (Monday/Thursday)

Heavy day (Monday):	
Hang snatch	3 × 5RM
Back squat	4 × 10RM
Lunge	3 × 12RM
Leg (knee) curl	3 × 12RM
Seated calf (heel) raise	3 × 12RM
Light day (Thursday):	85% of Monday's load for power/core exercises

Upper body: 2×/week (Tuesday/Friday)

Heavy day (Tuesday):	
Push jerk	3 × 5RM
Incline bench press	4 × 10RM
Bent-over row	3 × 12RM
Shoulder press	4 × 10RM
Barbell biceps curl	2 × 12RM
Triceps pushdown	2 × 12RM
Abdominal crunch	3 × 20
Light day (Friday):	85% of Tuesday's load for power/core exercises

MICROCYCLE 4
2 WEEKS: JUNE 27 - JULY 10 • BASIC STRENGTH PHASE 2

Week 1: 4×/week

Lower body: 2×/week (Monday/Thursday)

Heavy day (Monday):	
Hang snatch	4 × 5RM
Back squat	3 × 6 @ 90% 6RM
Lunge	3 × 8RM
Leg (knee) curl	3 × 8RM
Seated calf (heel) raise	3 × 8RM
Light day (Thursday):	85% of Monday's load for power/core exercises

Upper body: 2×/week (Tuesday/Friday)

Heavy Day (Tuesday):	
Push jerk	4 × 5RM
Incline bench press	3 × 6 @ 90% 6RM
Bent-over row	3 × 8RM
Shoulder press	3 × 6 @ 90% 6RM
Barbell biceps curl	2 × 8RM
Triceps pushdown	2 × 8RM
Abdominal crunch	3 × 20
Light day (Friday):	85% of Tuesday's load for power/core exercises

Week 2: 4×/week

Lower body: 2×/week (Monday/Thursday)

Heavy day (Monday):	
Hang snatch	4 × 5RM
Back squat	3 × 6RM
Lunge	3 × 8RM
Leg (knee) curl	3 × 8RM
Seated calf (heel) raise	3 × 8RM
Light day (Thursday):	85% of Monday's load for power/core exercises

Upper body: 2×/week (Tuesday/Friday)

Heavy day (Tuesday):	
Push jerk	4 × 5RM
Incline bench press	3 × 6RM
Bent-over row	3 × 8RM
Shoulder press	3 × 6RM
Barbell biceps curl	3 × 8RM
Triceps pushdown	3 × 8RM
Abdominal crunch	3 × 20
Light day (Friday):	85% of Tuesday's load for power/core exercises

UNLOADING WEEK
1 WEEK: JULY 11 - 17

Week 1: 4×/week

Lower body: 2×/week (Monday/Thursday)

Hang snatch	4 × 5 @ 70% 5RM
Back squat	3 × 6 @ 70% 6RM
Abdominal crunch	3 × 20

Upper body: 2×/week (Tuesday/Friday)

Push jerk	4 × 5 @ 70% 5RM
Incline bench press	3 × 6 @ 70% 6RM
Shoulder press	3 × 6 @ 70% 6RM

MICROCYCLE 5
2 WEEKS: JULY 18 - 31 • STRENGTH/POWER PHASE 1

Week 1: 4×/week		***Week 2: 4×/week***	
Lower body: 2×/week (Monday/Thursday)		**Lower body: 2×/week (Monday/Thursday)**	
Heavy day (Monday):		*Heavy day (Monday):*	
Power clean	4 × 3 @ 90% 3RM	Power clean	5 × 3RM
Hang snatch	5 × 3 @ 90% 3RM	Hang snatch	5 × 3RM
Front squat	4 × 4 @ 90% 4RM	Front squat	4 × 4RM
Leg (knee) curl	3 × 8RM	Leg (knee) curl	3 × 8RM
Seated calf (heel) raise	3 × 8RM	Standing calf (heel) raise	3 × 8RM
Light day (Thursday):	85% of Monday's load for power/core exercises	*Light day (Thursday):*	85% of Monday's load for power/core exercises
Upper body: 2×/week (Tuesday/Friday)		**Upper body: 2×/week (Tuesday/Friday)**	
Heavy day (Tuesday):		*Heavy day (Tuesday):*	
Push jerk	4 × 3 @ 90% 3RM	Push jerk	5 × 3RM
Push press	4 × 3 @ 90% 3RM	Push press	5 × 3RM
Bench press	4 × 4 @ 90% 4RM	Bench press	4 × 4RM
Seated row	3 × 8RM	Seated row	3 × 8RM
Lying triceps extension	2 × 8RM	Lying triceps extension	2 × 8RM
Hammer curl	2 × 8RM	Hammer curl	2 × 8RM
Abdominal crunch	3 × 20	Abdominal crunch	3 × 20
Light day (Friday):	85% of Tuesday's load for power/core exercises	*Light day (Friday):*	85% of Tuesday's load for power/core exercises

UNLOADING WEEK
1 WEEK: AUGUST 1 - 7

Week 1: 4×/week

Lower body: 2×/week (Monday/Thursday)		**Upper body: 2×/week (Tuesday/Friday)**	
Power clean	4 × 3 @ 70% 3RM	Push jerk	4 × 3 @ 70% 3RM
Hang snatch	4 × 3 @ 70% 3RM	Push press	4 × 3 @ 70% 3RM
Front squat	3 × 4 @ 70% 4RM	Bench press	3 × 4 @ 70% 4RM
		Abdominal crunch	3 × 20

POSTTESTING
(PRIOR TO IN-SEASON) • 1 WEEK: AUGUST 8 - 14

1RM for power exercises

Power clean
Hang snatch
Push jerk
Push press

1RM for nonpower core exercises

Front squat
Bench press

(Other exercises to test are based on the in-season program)

Other testing

Sit-and-reach test
Shoulder elevation
1.5-mile (2.4 km) run
300-yard (274 m) shuttle run
Line drill
T-test
Vertical jump
Body composition (skinfolds)

COMMENTS

- Although this sport season is labeled as a mesocycle and made up of four 4-week microcycles, an alternative, valid periodization model could consider each microcycle as a mesocycle (so the off-season would be a macrocycle that is comprised of four mesocycles).
- The off-season program consists of two rotations of the hypertrophy/endurance and basic strength phases, followed by the strength/power phase. Training frequency begins with an all-body, three-times-per-week regime but progresses to an upper-body, lower-body split program consisting of four training days per week (two heavy and two light).
- The volume assignments are represented as "sets × repetitions."
- Training loads can be estimated from loads used in similar exercises in previous cycles or determined directly from RM testing.
- For each workout shown, the number of sets does not include warm-up sets.
- Refer to table 15.7 on page 394 for the relationship between the %1RM and the number of repetitions allowed (i.e., the RM load).
- Refer to table 15.12 on page 408 for the rest period length assignments based on the training goal.

KEY TERMS

active rest 512
basic strength phase 511
competition period 512
first transition period 512
General Adaptation Syndrome 508
hypertrophy/endurance phase 511
linear periodization 514
macrocycle 509
mesocycle 509
microcycle 509
nonlinear periodization 515
periodization 508
preparatory period 509
restoration 512
second transition period 512
strength/power phase 512
supercompensation 508
undulating periodization 515
unloading week 513

STUDY QUESTIONS

1. During which stage of the General Adaptation Syndrome does the body physiologically adapt to heavier training loads?
   a. alarm
   b. resistance
   c. exhaustion
   d. restoration

2. For a basketball guard, which of the following BEST describes the relationship between resistance exercise volume and resistance exercise intensity at the beginning of the preparatory period?
   a. high volume, low intensity
   b. high volume, high intensity
   c. low volume, high intensity
   d. low volume, low intensity

3. During which of the following periods are sport-specific activities performed in the greatest volume?
   a. preparatory
   b. first transition
   c. competition
   d. second transition

4. Which of the following BEST describes appropriate activity during the second transition period for a college soccer player?
   a. low-intensity recreational exercise
   b. high-intensity aerobic exercise
   c. sport-specific exercise
   d. high-volume plyometric exercise

5. Which of the following phases are commonly used to vary workouts during the preparatory period?
   I. hypertrophy
   II. cardiovascular
   III. basic strength
   IV. supercompensation
   a. I and III only
   b. II and IV only
   c. I, II, and III only
   d. II, III, and IV only

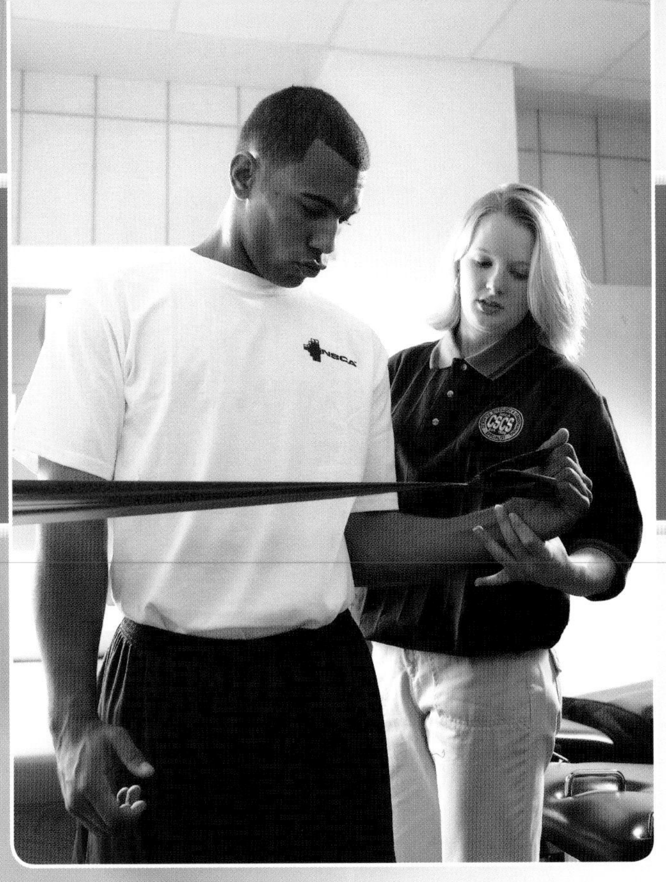

CHAPTER 20

Rehabilitation and Reconditioning

David H. Potach, PT, and Terry L. Grindstaff, DPT

After completing this chapter, you will be able to

- identify the members of the sports medicine team and their responsibilities during the rehabilitation and reconditioning of injured athletes,
- recognize the types of injuries athletes sustain,
- comprehend the timing and events of tissue healing,
- understand the goals of each tissue healing phase, and
- describe the strength and conditioning professional's role during injury rehabilitation and reconditioning.

As the employment of strength and conditioning professionals continues to increase, their role will expand to allow more active participation in the rehabilitation and reconditioning of injured athletes. The strength and conditioning professional has unique knowledge and insight regarding optimal athletic function and can serve a vital role during the final stages of an advanced rehabilitation program by preparing the athlete for a return to competition. These abilities give the strength and conditioning professional distinct responsibilities during rehabilitation from athletic injury. To fully understand how the strength and conditioning professional can best augment the rehabilitation of injured athletes, one must first recognize the role of each member of the sports medicine team. Furthermore, an understanding of different types of injury and the physiological healing process is essential to hastening the recovery from injury.

This chapter is not intended to provide the reader with rehabilitation protocols for specific injuries. Rather, the aim is to explain the physiological events that follow a musculoskeletal injury, thereby allowing optimal goal setting by the strength and conditioning professional to improve injury outcomes. The information contained in this chapter should ultimately be used to maximize function of the injured athlete. The rehabilitation and reconditioning approach follows five basic principles as outlined in the sidebar (44, 45).

Principles of Rehabilitation and Reconditioning

- Healing tissues must not be overstressed.
- The athlete must fulfill specific criteria to progress from one phase to another during the rehabilitative process.
- The rehabilitation program must be based on current clinical and scientific research.
- The program must be adaptable to each individual and his or her specific requirements and goals.
- Rehabilitation is a team-oriented process requiring all the members of the sports medicine team to work together toward a common goal of returning the athlete to unrestricted competition as quickly and safely as possible.

SPORTS MEDICINE TEAM

All members of the sports medicine team are responsible for educating coaches and athletes regarding injury risks, precautions, and treatments; they must also prevent injuries and rehabilitate those athletes who have sustained injury. Several different professionals play important roles in assisting the injured athlete's return to the playing field, necessitating effective communication.

Sports Medicine Team Members

The **team physician** provides medical care to an organization, school, or team. He or she may specialize in a variety of fields, including family medicine, pediatrics, and orthopedics (33, 40). Specific responsibilities of the team physician may include injury prevention, supervision of athletes during games, injury and illness evaluation and diagnosis, and referral to other professionals as needed (33). Although not responsible for daily rehabilitation, the team physician makes the final determination of an athlete's readiness for return to competition (33). Another important role of the team physician is the prescription of medications as needed, including anti-inflammatory, pain, and cold and flu medications.

The person typically responsible for the day-to-day physical health of the athlete is the **athletic trainer** or athletic therapist. In the United States, an athletic trainer is certified by the National Athletic Trainers' Association Board of Certification as a *Certified Athletic Trainer* (ATC). The athletic trainer works under the supervision of the team physician and is employed primarily by secondary schools, colleges, or professional teams but may also work in a sports medicine clinic. Primary responsibilities of this individual include management and rehabilitation of injuries resulting from physical activity and prevention of injuries with the prescription of sport-specific exercise and the application of prophylactic equipment (e.g., tape and braces). Specifically, the athletic trainer evaluates acute injuries, provides the injured athlete with therapeutic exercise to hasten the rehabilitation process, treats injuries with **therapeutic modalities**, and serves as an administrator for the sports medicine team (2). Because the athletic trainer has a significant amount of contact with the athlete, he or she plays a key role in promoting communication among members of the sports medicine team, the coach, and the athlete.

A **physical therapist** (or **physiotherapist**) with a background in orthopedics or sports medicine can play a valuable role in reducing pain and restoring function to the injured athlete. Physical therapists are typically based in rehabilitation clinics and have a close working relationship with a variety of medical specialists. A physical therapist may be consulted for specific treatment strategies or may supervise long-term rehabilitation. In the United States, physical therapists with expertise in sport injury management may become board certified through the American Board of Physical Therapy Specialties (ABPTS) and obtain the *Sports Certified Specialist* (SCS) credential. These board-certified specialists are becoming more common participants in the evaluation, treatment, and rehabilitation of acutely injured athletes and often serve in the dual capacity of team athletic trainer and sports physical therapist.

The **strength and conditioning professional** plays a valuable role within the sports medicine team and is an integral part of the rehabilitation and reconditioning process. Ideally, this person should be certified by the National Strength and Conditioning Association Certification Commission as a *Certified Strength and Conditioning Specialist* (CSCS) to ensure that he or she has the knowledge and background to contribute to the rehabilitation process. In consultation with the athletic trainer or sports physical therapist, this professional uses an understanding of the proper technique and application of several types of exercise (e.g., resistance, plyometric, and aerobic exercise) to develop a reconditioning program to ready the injured athlete for return to competition. Furthermore, he or she possesses an extensive understanding of the role that biomechanics play in a wide variety of sports and activities, which may allow him or her to suggest exercises for advanced rehabilitation and reconditioning of many injuries.

Additionally, the sports medicine team often includes specialized members who assist with the postacute rehabilitation and reconditioning of injured athletes. An **exercise physiologist** has a formal background in the study of the exercise sciences and uses his or her expertise to assist with the design of a conditioning program that carefully considers the body's metabolic response to exercise and the ways in which that reaction aids the healing process. Because proper nutrition is crucial in recovery from injury, a **nutritionist** with a background in sport nutrition may provide guidelines regarding proper food choices to optimize tissue recovery. Ideally, the nutritionist has been formally trained in food and nutrition sciences and is a *Registered Dietitian* (RD) recognized by the American Dietetic Association's Commission on Dietetic Registration. Finally, recovering from an injury is often mentally traumatic for an athlete; a licensed **psychologist** or **psychiatrist** with a background in sport may provide strategies that help the injured athlete better cope with the mental stress accompanying an injury.

Communication

Communication among members of the sports medicine team is essential (43). Because the strength and conditioning professional deals primarily with the athletic trainer, this section addresses communication between these two members of the sports medicine team.

To most effectively train injured athletes, the strength and conditioning professional must understand the diagnosis of the given injury and its exercise indications and contraindications. An **indication** is a form of treatment required by the rehabilitating athlete. For example, a softball outfielder with shoulder impingement must maintain lower extremity function, so the athletic trainer may request that the athlete continue to perform lower extremity strength, speed, agility, and power exercises during the shoulder rehabilitation. Therefore, lower body exercise is indicated. A **contraindication** is an activity or practice that is inadvisable or prohibited due to the given injury. For example, during the later phases of rehabilitation from an anterior shoulder dislocation, an American football player may require upper body strengthening before being cleared to play. The athletic trainer requests that the athlete initiate upper body strengthening, but the bench press exercise may be contraindicated because it can place the injured shoulder in a vulnerable position. To clarify the strength and conditioning professional's role during this process, it may be beneficial to have the sports medicine team use a form that specifies the indications and contraindications, providing for safe and efficient conditioning (figure 20.1).

The strength and conditioning professional must also communicate efficiently and effectively with other members of the sports medicine team. Specifically, other members should be aware of the strength and conditioning exercises that the injured athlete is performing, responses to the exercises, and any additional information deemed important by the strength and conditioning professional. In other words, the strength and conditioning professional should answer the following questions: What is the athlete doing? How is the athlete progressing? Do any program changes need to be made? Figure 20.2 is a sample form that the strength and conditioning professional can use to communicate a given program's components and the athlete's subjective and objective responses to those components.

The sports medicine team includes a large number of professionals working together to provide an optimal rehabilitation and reconditioning environment. The relationship among members requires thoughtful communication to ensure a safe, harmonious climate for the injured athlete.

TYPES OF INJURY

Macrotrauma is a specific, sudden episode of overload injury to a given tissue, resulting in disrupted tissue integrity. Trauma to the bone can lead to either a contusion or a fracture. Skeletal fractures can result from a direct blow to a bone and can be given a variety of classifications (e.g., closed, open, avulsed, incomplete). Joint trauma is manifested as either a **dislocation** (complete displacement of the joint surfaces) or a **subluxation** (partial displacement of the joint surfaces) and may result in joint laxity or instability. Ligamentous trauma is termed a **sprain** and is assigned a classification of *first degree* (partial tear of the ligament without increased joint instability), *second degree* (partial tear with minor joint instability), or *third degree* (complete tear with full joint instability).

Musculotendinous trauma is classified as either a **contusion** (if the trauma was direct) or a strain (if the trauma was indirect). A muscle contusion is an area of excess accumulation of blood and fluid in the tissues surrounding the injured muscle; it may severely limit the injured muscle's movement. Muscle **strains** are tears of muscle fibers and are further assigned grades, or degrees. A *first-degree* strain is a partial tear of individual fibers and is characterized by strong but painful muscle activity. A *second-degree* strain is a partial tear with weak, painful muscle activity. A *third-degree* muscle strain is a complete tear of the fibers and is manifested by very weak, painless muscle activity. A tendon, like a muscle, can also rupture if the tensile load applied to it exceeds its limit. Typically, the tendon's collagen fibers are significantly stronger than the muscle fibers to which they attach, so failure is more likely to occur within the muscle belly, at the musculotendinous junction, or at the tendon's attachment to the bone than within the substance of the tendon.

Microtrauma, or overuse injury, results from repeated, abnormal stress applied to a tissue by continuous training or training with too little recovery time. Overuse injuries may be due to training errors (e.g., poor program design), suboptimal training surfaces (e.g., too hard or uneven), faulty biomechanics or technique during performance, insufficient motor control, decreased flexibility, or skeletal malalignment and predisposition (17). Two common overuse injuries involve bone and tendon.

REHABILITATION REFERRAL

Date: *January 2, 2009*

Name: *Allison Janssen*

Sport and position: *Volleyball setter*

Injury date: *November 22, 2008*

Surgery date: *December 3, 2008*

Diagnosis: *Left ACL reconstruction*

Indications

Stationary bicycle *Progress gradually up to 60 minutes*

No running at this time

Single-leg hip sled *Less than 90° left knee flexion, begin without resistance, progress only after consultation with athletic training staff*

Upper extremity resistance exercises

Contraindications

Leg extension exercise
Full squats
Plyometrics
Running

Jonah Christopher, ATC *January 2, 2009*

Figure 20.1 A sample rehabilitation referral form, which communicates indications and contraindications to sports medicine team members.

The most common overuse injury to bone is a stress fracture, and although anthropomorphism (i.e., body type and structure) plays a large role (17), stress fractures are often the result of a rapid increase in training volume (18, 36) or excessive training volume on hard training surfaces (11, 13, 37). **Tendinitis** is an inflammation of a tendon (20); and if the cause of the inflammation is left uncorrected, chronic tendinitis or tendinopathy may develop.

Macrotrauma is a specific, sudden episode of overload injury to a tissue, resulting in disrupted tissue integrity. Microtrauma results from repeated, abnormal stresses applied to a tissue by continuous training or training with too little recovery time. Each injury requires specific rehabilitation strategies to allow return to function.

STRENGTH AND CONDITIONING SUMMARY

Date: *October 22, 2009*

Name: *Molly Eliza*

Sport: *Soccer*

Position: *Midfield*

Diagnosis: *Grade II right MCL sprain*

Injury date: *October 8, 2009*

ACTIVITY SUMMARY

Number of sessions: *7*

Date begun: *October 15, 2009*

Current Activities

Activity	Sets	Reps	Resistance
½ squats	3	10	115
Leg extension	3	10	60
Leg flexion	3	10	50
Heel raise	3	15	95
	Time		**Speed**
Stationary bicycle	20 minutes		80 rpm
Stair-stepper	20 minutes		70 feet per minute
Jogging	10 minutes		5.0 mph

Assessment

No difficulty with ½ squats, may increase squat depth to ¾.

Suggestions

Increase squat depth, increase jogging speed and time.

Jill Michaels, CSCS *October 22, 2009*

Figure 20.2 A sample strength and conditioning summary form, which records the athlete's current activities and responses to those activities.

TISSUE HEALING

The process of returning to competition following injury involves the healing of the injured tissues and the preparation of these tissues for the return to function. To better understand the strength and conditioning professional's role during rehabilitation and reconditioning, it is necessary to review the general phases of tissue healing following musculoskeletal injury. The timing of the events occurring within each phase differs for each tissue type and is affected by a variety of systemic and local factors, including age, lifestyle, degree of injury, and the structure that has been damaged. However, all tissues follow the same basic pattern of healing (table 20.1).

Inflammation Phase

Inflammation is the body's initial reaction to injury and is necessary for normal healing to occur. Both local and systematic inflammatory responses take place during this phase, allowing the eventual healing and replacement of damaged tissue. During the inflammatory phase, several events transpire that contribute to both tissue healing and an initial decrease in function. The injured area becomes red and swollen due to changes in vascularity, blood flow, and capillary permeability. After tissues are damaged, a locally hypoxic environment leads to tissue death that allows the release of several chemical mediators, including histamine and bradykinin. These substances further increase blood flow and capillary permeability, thereby allowing **edema**, the escape of fluid into the surrounding tissues. Edema inhibits contractile tissues and can significantly limit the injured athlete's function. Tissue debris and pathogens are removed from the injured area by increased blood flow and a process called *phagocytosis*; phagocytosis allows the release of macrophages, which search for and remove cellular debris that may slow healing.

The inflammatory substances present during this phase may noxiously stimulate sensory nerve fibers, causing the injured athlete to sense pain that may further contribute to the decrease in function. This phase typically lasts two to three days following an acute injury but may last longer with a compromised blood supply and more severe structural damage. Though the inflammatory phase is critical to tissue healing, if it does not end within a reasonable amount of time, the phases that follow may not occur, thereby delaying the rehabilitation process.

TABLE 20.1

Tissue Healing

Phase	Events
Inflammation	■ Pain, swelling, and redness
↓	■ Decreased collagen synthesis
	■ Increased number of inflammatory cells
Repair	■ Collagen fiber production
↓	■ Decreased collagen fiber organization
	■ Decreased number of inflammatory cells
Remodeling	■ Proper collagen fiber alignment
	■ Increased tissue strength

Repair Phase

Once the inflammatory phase has ended, tissue **repair** begins; this phase allows the replacement of tissues that are no longer viable following injury. In an attempt to improve tissue integrity, the original, damaged tissue is regenerated (i.e., tissue identical to the injured tissue is produced), and scar tissue is formed. New capillaries and connective tissue form in the area, and collagen fibers (see figure 5.5, p. 106) are randomly laid down to serve as the framework upon which the repair takes place. Because the collagen fibers are positioned somewhat haphazardly, however, the alignment is such that optimal strength of the new tissue is not yet achieved. Collagen fibers are strongest when they lie longitudinally to the primary line of stress, yet many of the new fibers are positioned transversely, which limits their ability to transmit force. This phase of tissue healing begins as early as two days after injury and may last up to two months.

Remodeling Phase

The weakened tissue produced during the repair phase is strengthened during the **remodeling** phase of healing. Production of collagen fibers has now decreased significantly, allowing the newly formed tissue the opportunity to improve its structure, strength, and function. With increased loading, the collagen fibers of the newly formed scar tissue begin to hypertrophy and align themselves along the lines of stress (20). The thicker and more optimally aligned collagen fibers become stronger, which allows the injured athlete's return to function. Although strength of the collagen fibers improves significantly, the new tissue will likely never be as strong as the tissue it has replaced (1, 6, 14, 16). Tissue remodeling can last up to two to four months after injury (29).

Following injury, all damaged tissues go through the same general phases of healing: inflammation, repair, and remodeling. Characteristic events define each phase and separate one phase from another.

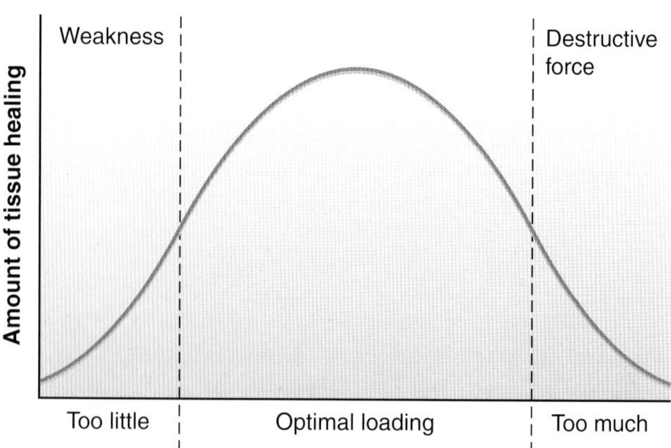

Figure 20.3 Loading during rehabilitation.

REHABILITATION AND RECONDITIONING STRATEGIES

The strength and conditioning professional must consider both the athlete's subjective response to injury and the physiological mechanisms of tissue healing; both are essential in relation to an athlete's return to optimal performance. The process of returning to competition following injury involves healing of the injured tissues, preparation of these tissues for the return to function, and use of proper techniques to maximize rehabilitation and reconditioning. While the goal is a rapid resumption of activity, it is important to remember that each athlete responds differently to injury and thus progresses uniquely during rehabilitation.

Goals of Rehabilitation and Reconditioning

As a preface to discussion of the goals of treatment during injury rehabilitation, two points must be made. First, healing tissue must not be overstressed (44, 45). During tissue healing, controlled therapeutic stress is necessary to optimize collagen matrix formation (1, 4, 6, 16, 20), but too much stress can damage new structures and significantly slow the athlete's return to competition. This means choosing a level of loading that neither overloads nor underloads the athlete's healing tissue (figure 20.3). It should be obvious that when one is choosing the load, it is necessary to consider the phase of healing and athlete type. For example, a stress that underloads a tissue during remodeling probably overloads it during inflammation. Further, a stress that underloads a professional basketball center probably overloads an amateur cross-country runner. The plane of movement is another necessary consideration. As an example, the medial collateral ligament of the knee is most loaded in the frontal plane during terminal knee extension. Therefore, frontal plane movements should be avoided during early healing phases. However, those frontal plane movements should probably be included in some form during the later phases.

Second, the athlete must meet specific objectives to progress from one phase of healing to the next (44, 45). These objectives may depend on range of motion, strength, or activity. It is the responsibility of the team physician, athletic trainer, physical therapist, or a combination of these professionals to establish these guidelines, which assist the entire team with the athlete's rehabilitation.

Inflammation Phase

The body's first response to an injury is inflammation, a reaction that is essential for subsequent healing but also important to manage properly so as to not retard the rehabilitation process.

Treatment Goal The goal for treatment during the inflammatory phase is to prevent disruption of new tissue. A healthy environment for new tissue regeneration and formation is essential for preventing prolonged inflammation and disruption of new blood vessel and collagen production. To achieve these goals, relative rest, ice, compression, and elevation are the primary treatment options. Passive modalities that help reduce inflammation (e.g., ice, ultrasound, and electrical stimulation) are common treatment choices. The athletic trainer provides the majority of passive treatment for the athlete during this acute phase.

It is also important to realize that a quick return to function relies on the health of other body tissues.

Therefore, the power, strength, and endurance of the musculoskeletal tissues and the function of the cardiorespiratory system must be maintained. The strength and conditioning professional can provide significant knowledge and expertise in this area. To accomplish these tasks, the strength and conditioning professional should consult with the athletic trainer to determine which types of exercises are indicated and contraindicated for the specific injury. Maximal protection of the injured structures is the primary goal during this phase. Assuming that this requirement is fulfilled, exercises may include general aerobic and anaerobic training and resistance training of the uninjured extremities. If movement of the injured limb is not contraindicated, isolated exercises that target areas proximal and distal to the injured area may also be permissible provided that they do not stress the injured area. Examples include hip abduction and rotation exercises following knee injury (22, 24, 31) or scapula stabilizing exercises following glenohumeral joint injury (25, 42).

Exercise Strategies Although a rapid return to competition is crucial, rest is necessary to protect the damaged tissue from additional injury. Therefore, exercise involving the injured area is not recommended during this phase.

Repair Phase

After the inflammatory phase, the body begins to repair the damaged tissue with similar tissue, but the resiliency of the new tissue is low. Repair of the weakened injury site can take up to eight weeks if the proper amount of restorative stress is applied, or longer if too much or too little stress is applied.

Treatment Goal The treatment goal during the repair phase is to prevent excessive muscle atrophy and joint deterioration of the injured area. In addition, a precarious balance must be maintained in which disruption of the newly formed collagen fibers is avoided but low-load stresses are gradually introduced to allow increased collagen synthesis and prevent loss of joint motion. To protect the new, relatively weak collagen fibers, the athlete should avoid active resistive exercise involving the damaged tissue. Too little activity, though, can also have a deleterious effect, as newly formed fibers will not optimally align and may form adhesions, thereby preventing full motion. Early protected motion hastens the optimal alignment of collagen fibers and promotes improved tissue mobility. As in the inflammatory phase, therapeutic modalities are permissible, but their goal during repair is to promote collagen synthesis. Ultrasound, electrical stimulation, and ice are continued in order to support and hasten new tissue formation (5, 23, 34). Again, the maintenance of muscular and cardiorespiratory function remains essential for the uninjured areas of the body. The strength and conditioning professional has considerable expertise to offer the other members of the sports medicine team regarding selection of the appropriate activities. Possible exercise forms during the repair phase include strengthening of the uninjured extremities and areas proximal and distal to the injury, aerobic and anaerobic exercise, and improving strength and neuromuscular control of the involved areas.

Exercise Strategies The following exercises should be used during the repair phase *only* after consultation with the team physician, athletic trainer, or physical therapist. Isometric exercise may be performed provided that it is pain free and otherwise indicated. Submaximal isometric exercise allows the athlete to maintain neuromuscular function and improve strength with movements performed at an intensity low enough that the newly formed collagen fibers are not disrupted. Unfortunately, isometric strengthening is joint angle specific; that is, strength gains occur only at the angles used (26). Therefore, if indicated, it may be appropriate for the athlete to perform isometric exercises at multiple angles (26).

Resistance training is velocity specific (26); therefore, isokinetic exercise can be an important aspect of strengthening following injury. Isokinetic exercise uses equipment that provides resistance to movement at a given speed (e.g., 60°/s or 120°/s). Because no sport is performed at one speed, however, isokinetic exercise is somewhat limited in its real-world application. Furthermore, most isokinetic equipment allows single-joint exercise only, which permits concentration on a specific muscle or joint but is not always the most functional method of strengthening.

While isotonic exercise involves movements with constant external resistance, the amount of force required to move the resistance varies, depending primarily on joint angle and the length of each agonist muscle. Isotonic exercise uses several different forms of resistance, including gravity (i.e., exercises performed without equipment, with gravitational effects as the only source of resistance), dumbbells, barbells, and weight-stack machines. The speed at which the movement occurs is controlled by the athlete; movement speed can be a program design variable, with more acute injuries calling for slower movement and the later phases of healing amenable to faster, more sport-specific movement.

Proprioception is an afferent response to stimulation of sensory receptors in skin, muscles, tendons, ligaments, and the joint capsule. Proprioception contributes to the conscious and unconscious control of posture, balance, stability, and sense of position (35).

Neuromuscular control, on the other hand, is the ability of muscle to respond to afferent proprioceptive information to maintain joint stability (35). For example, when running on an uneven surface, cross-country runners require their lower extremities—especially their ankles—to adjust to the ground to prevent falls and injuries; that ability to adjust is neuromuscular control. After an injury, neuromuscular control, like strength and flexibility, is usually impaired (12). Specific types of exercises exist to improve neuromuscular control following injury and can be manipulated through alterations in surface stability, vision, and speed. Mini-trampolines, balance boards, and stability balls can be used to create unstable surfaces for upper and lower extremity training. Athletes can perform common activities such as squats and push-ups on uneven surfaces to improve neuromuscular control. Exercises may also be performed with eyes closed, thus removing visual input, to further challenge balance. Finally, increasing the speed at which exercises are performed provides additional challenges to the system. Specifically controlling these variables within a controlled environment will allow the athlete to progress to more challenging exercises in the next stage of healing.

Remodeling Phase

The outcome of the repair phase is the replacement of damaged tissue with collagen fibers. After those fibers are laid down, the body can begin to remodel and strengthen the new tissue, allowing the athlete to gradually return to full activity.

Treatment Goal Optimizing tissue function is the primary goal during the final phase of healing. Athletes improve function by continuing and progressing the exercises performed during the repair phase and by adding more advanced, sport-specific exercises that allow progressive stresses to be applied to the injured tissue. The athlete can be tempted to do "too much too soon," which may further damage the injured tissues. It is important to remember that, while there may be less pain with activity at this point, the injured tissues have not fully healed and require further attention to achieve complete recovery (figure 20.4). Progressive tissue loading allows improved collagen fiber alignment and fiber hypertrophy.

Exercise Strategies Ultimately, rehabilitation and reconditioning exercises must be functional to facilitate a return to competition. Examples of functional training include joint angle–specific strengthening, velocity-specific muscle activity, closed kinetic chain

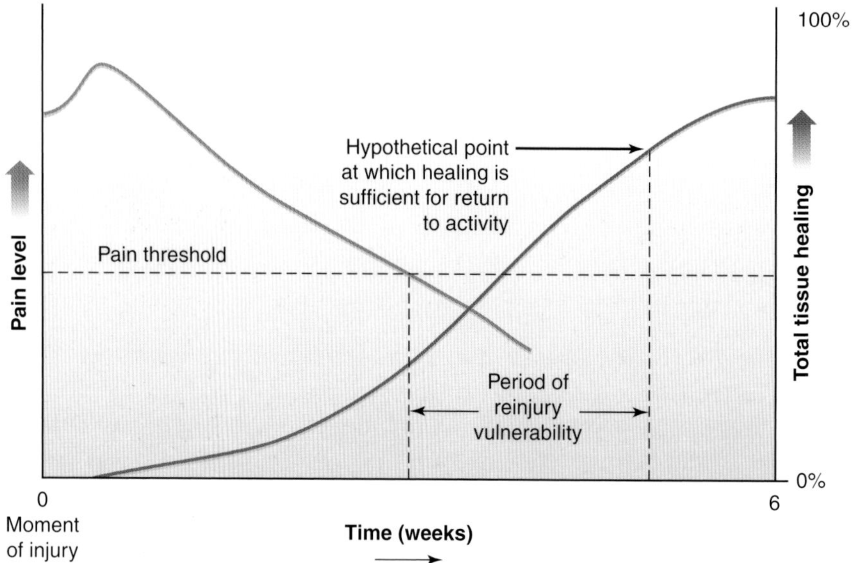

Figure 20.4 Profile of a typical soft tissue injury response. Pain is often used as a guide for tissue health. Pain levels (purple line) often decrease well before tissue healing (blue line) is complete, which may lead athletes to believe they can return to competition before the body is actually ready.

Reprinted, by permission, from Leadbetter, 1992 (29).

exercises, and exercises designed to further enhance neuromuscular control. Strengthening should transition from general exercises to *sport-specific exercises* designed to replicate movements common in given sports. For example, for a basketball guard who has rotator cuff tendinitis, rotator cuff strengthening may progress from a specific rotator cuff exercise to lateral dumbbell raises to machine seated shoulder presses to push-press exercises (figure 20.5). *Specificity of movement speed* is another important program design variable. Strengthening exercises are velocity specific; that is, the speed at which an athlete trains is directly related to the speed at which strength increases. Consider a sprinter with a hamstring muscle strain. Whereas initial reconditioning may concentrate on the recovery of flexibility and strength of the injured muscles, the nature of this athlete's sport necessitates exercises performed at rapid speeds during the later phases of rehabilitation and reconditioning. Exercise selection for a sprinter with an improving hamstring muscle strain might progress from hamstring flexibility to eccentric strength to concentric strength to dynamic stretching and finally to rapid isotonic strengthening. Examples of velocity-specific exercise include isokinetic, plyometric, and speed training. Please refer to chapters

Figure 20.5 Progression of rotator cuff rehabilitation. Exercises generally transition from *(a, b)* isolation exercises to *(c, d)* multijoint, sport-specific exercises.

16 and 17 for a thorough discussion of plyometric and speed training, respectively.

The kinetic chain is the collective effort or involvement of two or more sequential joints to create movement (38). A **closed kinetic chain** exercise is one in which the terminal joint meets with considerable resistance that prohibits or restrains its free motion (38); that is, the distal joint segment is stationary. Lower extremity closed kinetic chain exercises have often been classified as a more functional form of exercise compared with open kinetic chain exercises (7, 21, 41) because most sport-related activities are performed with the feet "fixed" to the surface. For example, during the closed kinetic chain squat exercise, the feet are "fixed" to the floor and essentially do not move, providing a base upon which movement occurs (figure 20.6*a*). Closed kinetic chain exercises have several advantages, including increased joint stability and functional movement patterns; during sport activity, joints are not typically used in isolation but rather work in concert with the adjacent joints and surrounding musculature. Although closed kinetic chain exercises are commonly viewed as lower extremity exercises, closed chain upper extremity exercises exist as well (figure 20.6*b*) (3).

An **open kinetic chain** exercise uses a combination of successively arranged joints in which the terminal joint is free to move; open kinetic chain exercises allow for greater concentration on an isolated joint or muscle (21). An example is the leg (knee) extension exercise, during which the feet and lower legs are allowed to move freely (figure 20.7). The leg extension allows greater concentration on the quadriceps at the knee joint; in comparison, the squat, which also uses the quadriceps muscles and knee joint, relies on muscle activity at both the hip and ankle joints as well (figure 20.6*a*). Although closed kinetic chain exercises are often viewed as more functional, most activities involve both closed and open kinetic chain movements. In sprinting, for example, while one lower extremity is on the ground (closed kinetic chain), the other is in the air (open kinetic chain), which means that both types of movements can occur simultaneously (figure 20.8). In some situations, an open chain exercise may therefore be an equally appropriate choice.

Exercises designed to improve neuromuscular control, which were introduced during the repair phase, should be continued and progressed as appropriate during the remodeling phase.

Program Design

The area in which strength and conditioning professionals can best contribute to the rehabilitation and reconditioning process is the provision of resistance and aerobic training programs designed for the injured athlete. Their experience in prescribing exercise for uninjured athletes gives strength and conditioning professionals the ability to properly adapt training programs for those recovering from injury. Although protocols do exist for exercise prescription following injury, many do not incorporate sport-specific program design variables; the same principles used to design resistance and aerobic

Figure 20.6 Closed kinetic chain exercises: *(a)* squat exercise, and *(b)* push-up exercise.

Rehabilitation and Reconditioning Goals and Strategies

Although rehabilitation and reconditioning programs must be individualized, the following are lists of general goals and approaches for each phase.

Inflammation

- Prevention of new tissue disruption and prolonged inflammation with the use of relative rest and passive modalities
- Maintenance of function of the cardiorespiratory and surrounding neuromusculoskeletal systems
- No active exercise for the injured area

Repair

- Prevention of excessive muscle atrophy and joint deterioration of the injured area
- Maintenance of function of the neuromusculoskeletal and cardiorespiratory systems
- Possible exercise options:
  - Submaximal isometric, isokinetic, and isotonic exercise
  - Balance and proprioceptive training activities

Remodeling

- Optimization of tissue function
- Progressive loading of the neuromusculoskeletal and cardiorespiratory systems as indicated
- Possible exercise options:
  - Joint angle–specific strengthening
  - Velocity-specific muscle activity
  - Closed and open kinetic chain exercises
  - Proprioceptive training activities

Figure 20.7 Example of an open kinetic chain exercise—leg (knee) extension exercise.

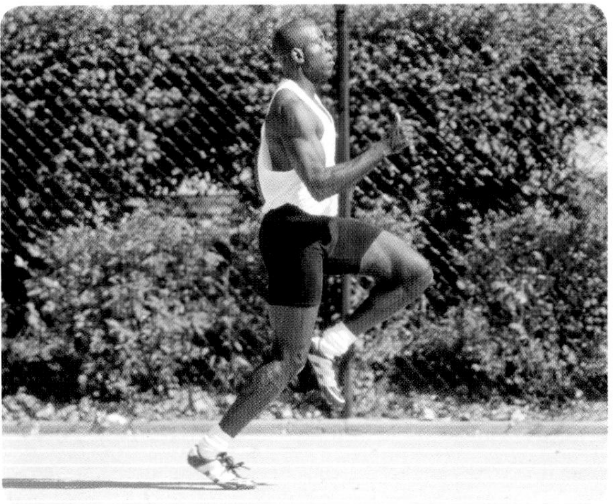

Figure 20.8 Sprinting offers an example of open and closed kinetic chain movements occurring together.

training programs for uninjured athletes should be applied during rehabilitation and reconditioning.

Resistance Training

Several programs have been developed to assist with the design of resistance training programs (8, 10, 15, 27, 39, 46), and many of these programs have been advocated for use in the rehabilitation setting (8, 27, 30, 32, 46). Both the De Lorme (8) and Oxford (46) programs use three sets of 10 repetitions with a pyramid-type design. De Lorme's program progresses from light to heavy resistance. The initial set involves 10 repetitions of 50% of the athlete's 10-repetition maximum (10RM); the second set increases the resistance to 75% of the 10RM; and the final set requires 100% of the 10RM (8, 9). The Oxford system (46) is the reverse of De Lorme's system; that is, it progresses from heavy to light resistance. The first set performed is 100% of the athlete's 10RM; the second is 75% of the 10RM; and the third is 50% of the 10RM (46).

Knight's (28) **daily adjustable progressive resistive exercise (DAPRE)** system requires and allows more manipulation of intensity and volume than either the De Lorme or the Oxford system (8, 9, 46); DAPRE involves four sets, with repetitions ranging from 10 to possibly one during the final set. The first set requires 10 repetitions of 50% of the estimated 1RM, and the second set requires six repetitions of 75% of the estimated 1RM. The third set in the DAPRE requires the maximum number of repetitions of 100% of the estimated 1RM; the number of repetitions performed during the third set determines the adjustment to be made in resistance for the fourth set (table 20.2). The De Lorme, Oxford, and Knight systems are protocols that have demonstrated the ability to increase muscle strength (9, 28, 30, 32, 46) and may be appropriate when one is designing rehabilitation resistance training programs. However, athletes require rehabilitation and reconditioning programs tailored to the demands of their respective sports. Although these protocols (9, 28, 46) are established strengthening programs, they may be too strict to allow individualization for athletes of different sports.

Programs for both the healthy and the damaged tissues of an injured athlete require the same basic design principles provided in chapter 15. According to the specific adaptation to imposed demands (SAID) principle, the system will adapt to the demands placed on it. Therefore, the goal of training (specific adaptation) should dictate the design of the resistance training program (imposed demands). For example, during the remodeling phase of an injured marathoner's patellofemoral rehabilitation, his or her quadriceps muscles must be trained for maximal muscular endurance. Therefore, the athlete should perform many repetitions of the rehabilitation exercises to prepare the muscles for the demands of long-distance running. Conversely, an Olympic weightlifter rehabilitating from the same injury requires fewer repetitions of high-intensity rehabilitation and reconditioning exercises during the later portions of the remodeling phase to prepare the muscles for the power demands of this sport. Refer to page 537 for a comparative example of the rehabilitation strategies for these two athletes.

Aerobic and Anaerobic Training

Although research has yet to determine an optimal aerobic training program for use in the rehabilitation setting, the program should mimic specific sport and metabolic demands. The strength and conditioning professional, having a background in designing and implementing conditioning exercises for healthy athletes, is the ideal member of the sports medicine team to prescribe and supervise the aerobic training portion of the injured athlete's reconditioning program. As with the resistance training program, the strength and conditioning professional must consider the demands that the given sport places on the injured athlete. Keeping these demands and the contraindications of the injury in mind, the strength and conditioning professional can use the prescription guidelines in chapter 18 to create an appropriate training program to allow an uncomplicated return to competition.

Again consider rehabilitation from a patellofemoral injury for a marathon runner, a wrestler, and an Olympic lifter; the metabolic energy demands of

TABLE 20.2

Resistance Adjustments for DAPRE Protocol

Number of repetitions performed during set 3	Adjusted resistance for set 4	Resistance for next exercise session
0-2	–5-10 pounds (–2.3-4.5 kg)	–5-10 pounds (–2.3-4.5 kg)
3-4	–0-5 pounds (–0-2.3 kg)	Same resistance
5-6	Same resistance	+5-10 pounds (+2.3-4.5 kg)
7-10	+5-10 pounds (+2.3-4.5 kg)	+5-15 pounds (+2.3-6.8 kg)
11	+10-15 pounds (+4.5-6.8 kg)	+10-20 pounds (+4.5-9 kg)

Application of Design Principles for Resistance Training Programs During Rehabilitation and Reconditioning From Patellofemoral Injury

		ATHLETE	
Phase of healing	**Design variable**	**Marathon runner**	**Olympic lifter**
Inflammatory	Goals and exercises	▪ None that require quadriceps activity—relative rest of this area needed to reduce inflammation ▪ Maintenance of muscular strength and endurance of adjacent areas (i.e., hip extensors, knee flexors, and plantar flexors) ▪ Maintenance of cardiorespiratory fitness	▪ None that require quadriceps activity—relative rest of this area needed to reduce inflammation ▪ Maintenance of muscular strength and power of adjacent areas (i.e., hip extensors, knee flexors, and plantar flexors) ▪ Maintenance of upper-body muscular strength and power
Repair	Goals and exercises	▪ Isometric quadriceps strengthening at full knee extension (progressing to multiple angles) ▪ Progress to pain-free isotonic quadriceps strengthening (following consultation with sports medicine team) ▪ Continue exercise of adjacent areas ▪ Continue aerobic exercise; may begin stationary bicycle or stair-stepper (per recommendation of sports medicine team)	▪ Isometric quadriceps strengthening at full knee extension (progressing to multiple angles) ▪ Progress to pain-free isotonic quadriceps strengthening (following consultation with sports medicine team) ▪ Continue exercise of adjacent areas ▪ Continue upper-body muscular strength and power exercises
	Sets × repetitions	2-3 × 15-20	3-4 × 8-10
	Intensity	Submaximal (≤50% 1RM)	Submaximal (≥50% 1RM)
Remodeling	Goals and exercises	▪ Begin more sport-specific activities, movements, and speeds ▪ Return to running, gradually increasing distance and speed as tolerated ▪ Add lunge and squat (increase knee range of motion as able)	▪ Begin more sport-specific activities, movements, and speeds ▪ Increase movement speeds to those similar to competition ▪ Add Romanian deadlift and squat (increase knee range of motion as able)
	Sets × repetitions	2-3 × 15-20	4-5 × 3-8
	Intensity	Progress to maximal intensity (50%-75% 1RM)	Progress to maximal intensity (>75% 1RM)

their rehabilitation and reconditioning are markedly different. For the marathon runner's goals, aerobic fitness is of much greater concern and must be addressed immediately. The metabolic demands for the wrestler involve a combination of aerobic and anaerobic systems; therefore interval training is more appropriate (19). In contrast, the Olympic lifter's program would focus on maintaining anaerobic fitness. Selecting the appropriate training device depends on the region of the body that is injured. A variety of options exist to modify aerobic and anaerobic training. These include, but are not limited to, the upper body ergometer, deep water running, biking, and elliptical machines. Strategies to maintain cardiorespiratory fitness must be implemented even during the inflammatory phase. And, as already emphasized, it is important to remember that to allow optimal healing, these athletes' injured tissues (i.e., knee extensor muscles and structures) must not be overstressed.

Designing strength and conditioning programs for injured athletes requires the strength and conditioning professional to examine the rehabilitation and reconditioning goals to determine what type of program will allow the quickest return to competition.

CONCLUSION

Effective athletic injury rehabilitation and reconditioning require efficient communication among the members of the sports medicine team. Each member plays a distinct role in ensuring the injured athlete's return to function; although the job of each professional is different, the tasks of each complement those of the others on the team. Goals are established for each athlete, and therapeutic exercise programs must be designed, administered, and progressed according to the tissue healing sequence. The program must be individualized to effectively return the athlete to normal function and competitive athletics. Early rehabilitation for initial tissue protection and strengthening is more structured than later rehabilitation phases; the latter allow for progression to functional activities that are specific to the athlete's sport and position. Designing reconditioning programs for injured athletes necessitates a careful examination of the sport requirements and a thorough understanding of both the healing process and therapeutic exercise.

KEY TERMS

athletic trainer 525
closed kinetic chain 534
contraindication 526
contusion 526
daily adjustable progressive resistive exercise (DAPRE) 536
dislocation 526
edema 529
exercise physiologist 525
indication 526
inflammation 529
macrotrauma 526
microtrauma 526
neuromuscular control 532
nutritionist 525
open kinetic chain 534
physical therapist 525
physiotherapist 525
proprioception 532
psychiatrist 525
psychologist 525
remodeling 529
repair 529
sprain 526
strain 526
strength and conditioning professional 525
subluxation 526
team physician 524
tendinitis 527
therapeutic modality 525

STUDY QUESTIONS

1. All of the following individuals can provide medical supervision during a college soccer match EXCEPT the
   a. athletic trainer.
   b. team physician.
   c. Certified Strength and Conditioning Specialist.
   d. Sports Certified Physical Therapist.

2. All of the following are typically the result of overuse EXCEPT
   a. stress fracture.
   b. grade III joint sprain.
   c. tendinitis.
   d. microtraumatic injury.

3. All of the following are phases of healing following an injury EXCEPT
   a. inflammation.
   b. reconditioning.
   c. remodeling.
   d. repair.

4. Which of the following types of activity is inappropriate during the inflammatory phase of a medial collateral ligament sprain?
   a. lower extremity plyometrics
   b. submaximal isometric quadriceps strengthening
   c. hip joint stretching
   d. upper extremity ergometry

5. Which of the following are closed kinetic chain exercises?

   I. back squat
   II. leg (knee) extension
   III. pull-up
   IV. bench press

   a. I and III only
   b. II and IV only
   c. I, II, and III only
   d. II, III, and IV only

6. The rotator cuff muscles act as stabilizers to the shoulder joint. During the remodeling phase of rotator cuff (supraspinatus muscle) tendinitis rehabilitation of a basketball player, what exercise repetition range is MOST appropriate for improving the muscular endurance of the rotator cuff muscles?

   a. 3-5
   b. 5-8
   c. 8-12
   d. 12-20

SECTION 5

Organization and Administration

CHAPTER 21

Facility Organization and Risk Management

Michael Greenwood, PhD, and Lori Greenwood, PhD

After completing this chapter, you will be able to

- identify the four phases and specific components of planning and designing a strength and conditioning facility,
- identify specific program needs of athletic groups that use the strength and conditioning facility,
- identify key elements for assessing space requirements and equipment needs in the strength and conditioning facility,
- explain various strategies for effectively scheduling the strength and conditioning facility,
- identify key aspects of facility and equipment maintenance and cleaning, and implement appropriate maintenance and cleaning schedules,
- identify tools and supplies necessary for maintaining the strength and conditioning facility and equipment, and
- identify common areas of potential litigation in the strength and conditioning facility.

Insufficient time, facility space, equipment, and qualified supervisory staff are often major concerns for the strength and conditioning professional. It is a challenge to effectively and safely use the space and time allotted to properly administer strength and conditioning programs. The strength and conditioning professional is responsible not only for knowing how to organize groups of athletes effectively for resistance training and conditioning activities, but also for understanding effective facility and equipment maintenance and the safe arrangement of equipment.

In some cases the strength and conditioning professional might be responsible for developing a facility with limited space and resources or designing a new facility from the ground up. Both situations present unique challenges for meeting the strength and conditioning needs of every athlete and team. Another responsibility of strength and conditioning professionals must be to implement consistent inspection, maintenance, and cleaning schedules to ensure a safe and functional training environment for every athlete. In addition, the strength and conditioning staff must be familiar with aspects of professional and **product liability** to safeguard athletes against injury and strength and conditioning professionals against **litigation**.

This chapter discusses the steps necessary in designing a new facility, the differences between modifying an existing facility and designing a new one, and the critical aspects applicable to the design of all facilities. It also addresses the need for knowledge concerning the function, proper use, maintenance, and cleaning of equipment, as well as knowledge of product liability and litigation.

GENERAL ASPECTS OF NEW FACILITY DESIGN

Designing and building a new facility takes a great deal of time—up to two years in many cases. This section provides a thumbnail sketch of all that is involved in directing this type of project.

The first step in planning and designing a new strength and conditioning facility is to form a committee of professionals who represent various areas of expertise. Such a committee can consist of an administrator, architect, contractor, lawyer, student-athlete, sport coach, instructors who will use the facility, various sport conditioning experts, and other professionals who can give valuable input regarding facility design. When implementing the planning and designing phases, the committee needs to keep in mind that the strength and conditioning facility must be economical to operate and maintain.

Forming a committee of professionals is the first step in planning and designing a new strength and conditioning facility.

The planning and designing of a new strength and conditioning facility is usually a two-year process that can be separated into four phases: the

predesign phase, **design phase**, **construction phase**, and **preoperation phase** (18). A checklist for the facility design process is presented in figure 21.1 on page 559.

Predesign Phase

The predesign phase usually requires 25% of the total project time (about six months) and includes the following components (18):

- A predesign or planning committee analyzes the programs and services that will be provided to athletes so that the facility is built to meet program needs; otherwise it will be necessary to attempt to fit programs into a potentially inadequate space. The planning committee will work with the architect to develop the design of the new facility (23). There is no greater priority when designing a facility than completing a **needs analysis** or **assessment**. The needs assessment can be based on internal demand as highlighted by future facility users or by industry-driven needs (8). As a means of accomplishing this important step, the committee should answer the questions included in the section "Assessing Athletic Program Needs" (p. 546). All subsequent decisions are based on the outcome of evaluating the facility's projected programs and services for future growth patterns (23).
- A **feasibility study** is conducted to determine costs, facility location, programs of interest to each athletic group, and projected usage. An analysis of strengths, weaknesses, opportunities, and threats ("SWOT") is often a primary task of a feasibility study (8).
- A master plan that details project goals and the procedures for meeting those goals is developed and referred to by all contributing experts throughout the project. In the master plan, attention must be paid not only to present needs but also to future needs as the interest in strength and conditioning continues to grow. A common mistake made in the predesign phase is planning for today and not 10 years from now.
- Architect selection begins with the acceptance of a number of bids from professionals who are credentialed in their field (e.g., the American Institute of Architects) and who have positive references from previous work.

Design Phase

The design phase may require about 10% of the total project time (approximately three months) and includes the following elements (18):

- The design and planning committee comprising a variety of qualified professionals is finalized.
- The planning committee works with the architect to finalize facility blueprints.
- Equipment specifications for allocated facility spaces are included in the project design.
- Facility spacing is designed to be user friendly, taking into consideration health codes, safety codes, legal codes, and traffic flow while maintaining an aesthetically pleasing environment.
- The facility is designed to provide easy access to all athletes who may use it (e.g., both those with and those without disabilities).

A quick reference checklist regarding general components of facility design is presented in figure 21.2 on pages 560-562.

Construction Phase

The construction phase takes up the greatest percentage of the project time. The construction phase is normally 50% of the total project time (about 12 months) and involves the following tasks (18):

- Construction of the building is begun and completed.
- The master plan must be continuously consulted to ensure that the project goals and objectives set in the predesign phase are achieved.
- Deadlines must be set and adhered to, or a default penalty may have to be paid by the architect or contractors.
- The strength and conditioning professional and the planning committee should be present on the job site as often as possible during the construction phase to make sure the design features are being adhered to (23).

Preoperation Phase

The preoperation phase (start-up phase) requires about 15% of the total project time (approximately three to four months) and focuses on staffing considerations (18).

- A process for selecting staff that meets standard hiring guidelines is created.
- Qualified staff are hired.
- For each position, the staff should have an appropriate level of education, employment experience, and certification (see chapter 22 for more detail).
- A plan for continued staff development, including continuing education, in-service training, and advanced credentialing, is developed.

EXISTING STRENGTH AND CONDITIONING FACILITIES

Strength and conditioning professionals often assume responsibility for an existing facility. The phases of planning and design for an existing facility are similar to those for a new one except that they apply to renovation or modification rather than building from scratch. The focus is on improving and reorganizing the strength and conditioning area to meet current athletic program needs.

There are several primary differences between modifying an existing facility and designing a new one. First, the composition of the committee of professionals is likely to be different. For example, legal aid and contractor expertise may not be necessary with an existing facility, but the current facility director (if there is one) will need to be involved. Second, there may be no construction phase. If construction is needed, it will be less extensive—for example, reconfiguring walls to provide more appropriate office space, rewiring for different lighting requirements, or improving the heating and cooling system. Other common modifications of existing facilities include extending pathways and hallways, adding or adapting mirrors, bringing the facility into compliance with laws that protect people with disabilities (e.g., the Americans with Disabilities Act [ADA] in the United States), upgrading toilets and showers, adapting or adding public address and sound systems, improving lighting and adding natural lighting where possible, replacing subflooring, and renovating floor surfaces. Third, the strength and conditioning professional may not have as active a role (or any role at all) in hiring facility staff. Nevertheless, it is critical that the qualifications of the current staff, including education, experience, and professional certification, be evaluated by the strength and conditioning professional. (Enforcing staff requirements may necessitate the assistance of the current facility director and upper administration.) Other aspects of renovating an existing facility, such as rearranging equipment to meet recommended safety guidelines and creating or updating facility policies and procedures (discussed later in this chapter and also in chapter 22), are integral duties of the strength and conditioning professional.

The remainder of this chapter deals with topics that all strength and conditioning professionals should be aware of, whether they are building a facility from the ground up or managing an existing facility.

The strength and conditioning professional should assess existing equipment based on the needs of all athletes and teams that use the facility.

ASSESSING ATHLETIC PROGRAM NEEDS

After determining specific program needs, the strength and conditioning professional should assess existing equipment on the basis of the needs of all athletes and teams that plan to use the facility. The strength and conditioning professional needs to answer the following questions:

How many athletes will use the facility? Information regarding the number of athletes using the facility simultaneously and overall is important for establishing equipment needs and placement. Knowing the number of athletes also helps the strength and conditioning professional to schedule and design appropriate training programs to meet the needs of all athletic groups.

What types of specific strength and conditioning training does each athletic group require (e.g., circuits, machines, free weights, Olympic lifts, plyometrics, agility)? Knowledge of the training goals of each athletic group is essential for determining equipment needs and the amount of time required by each group using the facility. The seasonal periodization cycle of each group determines the amount of time needed in the facility, and knowing these cycles allows the strength and conditioning professional to organize training times to eliminate scheduling conflicts.

What are the age groups of the athletes using the strength and conditioning facility (e.g., youth, adult)? The time allotted per session and the number of days per week for youth resistance training are typically less than for older, more physically mature athletes. This is particularly true for younger athletes who are starting a new resistance training program. In addition, younger athletes have different equipment needs than adults because of their smaller size and lower strength levels. Special equipment for youth resistance training can be found on the market. It is always a challenge to find equipment that fits younger athletes, however, because the majority of resistance machines are designed for adults. Caution is necessary in adapting resistance equipment, particularly if it places the athletes at risk for injury.

What is the training experience of the athletes using the facility (e.g., novice, intermediate, advanced)? Novice athletes typically spend more time learning resistance training exercises and techniques than intermediate or advanced athletes. Therefore, novice athletes need more one-on-one instruction and supervision than athletes with more resistance training experience. The training experience of an athlete does not refer to age or overall resistance training experience; it refers to an individual's knowledge of a specific exercise and his or her ability to perform that exercise correctly. An athlete may be advanced on one exercise (e.g., bench press) but a novice on another (e.g., power clean) and so may require more teaching and supervision for that exercise. A sensible progression should be used at all experience levels to enhance training adaptations and meet sport-specific training needs.

When will resistance training fit into each athletic team's schedule (e.g., early morning, late afternoon, early evening)? Secondary school athletes normally resistance train before or after school because of their fixed academic schedules. In some circumstances, these athletes are allowed to resistance train during an off period, a physical education class, or a study hall. The strength and conditioning professional must be present to supervise these athletes whenever they train, even if they are with a partner. Collegiate athletes may have more flexibility for scheduling their resistance training times.

What repairs and adaptations to equipment must be made to meet the athletes' needs? Existing equipment may be sufficient provided that it is maintained properly; if not, it may require refurbishing or modification. Resistance training equipment and accessories such as cables, belts, and pulleys should be checked on a regular basis and maintained according to manufacturers' guidelines. Often, worn cables or belts are the result of misaligned or damaged pulleys. Cables with a protective plastic coating should be used to avoid fraying. Replacements for worn or damaged parts should be kept in stock so that training is not hindered while equipment repairs are in progress. Even with proper seat adjustments, some resistance machines place athletes into positions and angles that are not conducive to proper or beneficial lifting technique. Purchasing adjustable resistance training equipment that can accommodate a wide spectrum of shapes and sizes is one solution to this problem.

DESIGNING THE STRENGTH AND CONDITIONING FACILITY

Before arranging and positioning existing equipment, one must consider the design of the strength and conditioning facility, whether new or existing. To determine space requirements, the strength and conditioning professional must consider the number of athletes who will use the facility. Published guidelines for strength and conditioning facilities range from as low as 40 square feet (3.7 m^2) (18) to as high as 50 square feet (4.6 m^2) (24) per athlete. Kroll (16) bases area-to-athlete ratios on specific resistance training areas and exercises that the athlete performs. For example, more space per athlete is required for free weight exercises than for resistance training machines. Specific information regarding space requirements per athlete is given later in this chapter (see "Arranging Equipment in the Strength and Conditioning Facility" on p. 550). In addition, the strength and conditioning professional should pay particular attention to facility location and access, structural and functional considerations, environmental factors, and safety and supervision.

Location

- Strength and conditioning rooms ideally should be located on the ground floor with accessible service entrances for moving heavy and bulky equipment in and out of the facility.
- If strength and conditioning rooms are not located on the ground floor, the flooring must be stable enough (with load-bearing capacity of 100 pounds per square foot, or 488 kg/m^2) to avoid any structural damage from dropped heavy equipment (18). In addition, the weight room should not be placed above

areas sensitive to sound or vibration, such as classrooms, office areas, or meeting rooms (17). The weight room should be designed and built with sound absorption in mind (21).

Supervision Location

- The strength and conditioning professional's office ideally should be centrally located and should have larger than average windows on all sides to allow a clear view of all areas in the facility (17).

Access

- The facility must provide free and unobstructed access—including all entrances, exits, and walkways inside and outside the facility—to all athletes (e.g., with or without disabilities). In the United States, the ADA outlines specific requirements for making facilities accessible for people with disabilities (24).
- The minimum width for doors should be 36 inches (91 cm) to accommodate wheelchairs.
- Hallways and circulation passages must have a width of at least 60 inches (152 cm).
- All thresholds should be flush. If not, any change in elevation in excess of 0.5 inches (1.3 cm) must have a ramp or lift with a slope of 1 foot (30 cm) for every inch (2.5 cm) of elevation change. Mechanical lifts or elevators can be used as an alternative to ramps where there are severe changes in height.
- The facility should have a set of double doors with a removable middle post to allow passage of large equipment. Hallways must also be wide enough to accommodate the same equipment (17).
- Emergency exits must be clearly visible and provide essential signage to those with visual impairments.
- Emergency exits must remain free of obstructions and be well lit at all times.

Ceiling Height

- The ceiling height, especially in lifting platform areas, should have 12 to 14 feet (3.7-4.3 m) of clearance from low-hanging items such as ceiling fans, beams, pipes, lighting, and signs (17). When the strength and conditioning facility is being built from scratch, higher ceilings may be needed if low-hanging items are used.

Flooring

- The two most commonly used types of flooring are carpet and a resilient, rubberized surface. Carpet has the advantages of being fairly inexpensive and allowing wide color choices (6). Carpet in cardiovascular fitness and stretching areas should be treated with antiseptic, antifungal, and antibacterial agents (24).
- Rubberized flooring can be purchased as interlocking rubber mats that form a wall-to-wall grid. Although initially more expensive than carpet, this type of flooring provides a better shock-absorbing cushion than carpet and is more durable (21). Carpet is typically used under resistance training machines. If the room is equipped predominately with free weights, then rubberized flooring should be used (18).
- A poured rubber surface is the most expensive choice. However, a poured rubber floor is very durable, does not have seams as interlocking mats do into which dirt and water can settle, and provides a stable surface for plyometric drills (6, 15).
- Wood is the best flooring for Olympic platforms because, if well maintained, it provides a smooth, flat surface with excellent footing (20).

Environmental Factors

- Proper lighting of the facility is important for safety and motivation. The weight room should be lit to 75 to 100 foot-candles (807-1,076 lux), a standard measure of light intensity (17). Another recommendation is for illumination of at least 50 foot-candles (538 lux) at floor level (24). Metal-halide incandescent lighting is suggested because of the high intensity of light it projects. Windows can be included in the resistance training facility design to provide additional lighting and ventilation. Windows should be placed a minimum of 20 inches (51 cm) above the floor to protect them from rolling items. Do not arrange the floor plan so that spotters or lifters are likely to come in contact with windows. High windows or skylights can be used, but to avoid glare and potential injury, supine exercise areas should not be placed directly under this natural lighting.
- A recommended temperature range for the strength and conditioning facility is 72 °F to

78 °F (22-26 °C) (2). Other temperature recommendations range between 68 °F and 72 °F (20-22 °C) (24). Zone heating and cooling systems are recommended because these units effectively regulate room temperature based on the number of athletes training at one time. If the room temperature is too hot or cold, the quality of strength and conditioning sessions is reduced. In addition, care should be taken to maintain constant facility temperatures because drastic fluctuations can increase humidity and condensation, which results in damp floors and equipment corrosion (17).

- Relative humidity should be 60% or less (24). Dehumidifiers may be required to control excess humidity levels and should have proper drainage capabilities to avoid water damage (17).
- Air circulation should be at least 8 to 12 air exchanges per hour; the optimal level is 12 to 15 exchanges per hour (17). Air exchange must have the appropriate mix of inside and outside air. Local engineering codes govern the exact mix (24). In a 1,200-square-foot (111 m^2) facility, two to four ceiling fans can aid in the circulation of air (18). The combination of proper air exchange and ceiling fans helps eliminate strong odors common to strength and conditioning facilities.
- Sound levels should not exceed 90 decibels (24). Music can be a form of motivation for many, but it can also pose a problem if the stereo system is not properly managed. Volume should be low enough to allow for clear communication at all times between spotters, strength and conditioning professionals, and athletes. The stereo system should be controlled by the strength and conditioning professional, not the athletes (2). To provide equal sound distribution in the strength and conditioning facility, speakers should be placed high in all corners of the room (18).

Electrical Service

- Grounded electrical outlets should be installed. Some cardiovascular machines (e.g., stationary cycles, treadmills, stair climbers) require a higher voltage outlet.
- The number of electrical outlets needed in a strength and conditioning facility exceeds the number needed for a conventional room. Outlets must accommodate all electrical training equipment (if applicable) and should be located throughout the facility to allow use of vacuum cleaners and electric tools.
- Ground-fault circuit interrupters are necessary safety devices for automatically shutting down power in the event of an electrical short due to water or insulation problems (24).

Mirrors

- Mirrors are an important design consideration in any strength and conditioning facility. Lifting technique is enhanced by strategic placement of mirrors throughout the facility so that athletes and strength and conditioning professionals can benefit from the immediate feedback. For safety, mirrors give the strength and conditioning professional effective vantage points from which to monitor large groups of athletes training at the same time.
- Mirrors also enhance the aesthetic appearance of the strength and conditioning facility.
- Mirrors should be placed at least 20 inches (51 cm) above the floor so that they cannot be broken by rolling equipment. Since the diameter of a weight plate is 18 inches (46 cm), a height of 20 inches (51 cm) provides a 2-inch (5 cm) safety margin (17).
- Bumper rails or special padding can be anchored to the base of the wall to help protect the mirrors and walls from the strength and conditioning equipment.
- When a mirror is cracked or broken, it should be replaced immediately.

Other Considerations

- Drinking fountains should be easily accessible to athletes but should be placed where they do not hinder traffic flow or cause a distraction to training. Locating drinking fountains close to entrances of the facility enhances availability without impeding traffic flow.
- Rest rooms for male and female athletes should be clearly marked and should be adjacent to the strength and conditioning area.
- Telephones should be located in the strength and conditioning professional's office and must be available to staff for emergency use. Additional telephones may be placed at the front entranceway and mounted at a maximum height of 4 feet (1.2 m) to accommodate athletes with disabilities (24).

- Signage should be used to display operational policies, facility rules, and safety guidelines and to clearly mark entrances, exits, and rest rooms. Rules and safety guidelines should be displayed in numerous locations throughout the facility to increase the likelihood that athletes will read them. Signage can also be used to identify the relevant credentials of strength and conditioning staff (24).
- Bulletin boards are used for communication—to display announcements, educational information, and motivational items such as facility strength records. Bulletin boards should be located either at the front entrance of the facility or next to the strength and conditioning professional's office. Athletes and visitors should be able to clearly see them without having to enter a training area (17).
- In many strength and conditioning facilities, a storage room is not included in the design plan due to the limited amount of space available. If included, the storage space should optimally be 100 to 300 square feet (9-28 m^2) (18). This space can be used to store an array of cleaning equipment, resistance training accessories, and tools.

ARRANGING EQUIPMENT IN THE STRENGTH AND CONDITIONING FACILITY

It is essential to consider equipment needs when placing equipment in the available space. A floor plan can be drawn to enable visualization of the present and potential locations of all equipment. In addition, it is important to determine the athletic groups that will use the strength and conditioning facility and to establish a list of existing equipment. When equipment is arranged, apparatus should be placed so as to use the space most safely and efficiently. Safety should always be the top priority when one is determining equipment placement (1). These are two generally accepted methods for organizing the strength and conditioning facility:

1. Creating resistance training areas that emphasize different body parts (e.g., shoulder area, leg area, back area)
2. Creating training areas according to types of equipment (e.g., free weights, resistance machines, stretching mats, aerobic machines)

Organizing the resistance training areas by equipment type is usually the preferred method for functionality and appearance, but the organization generally depends on the needs of a specific athletic program (16).

Safety and function are top priorities when one is deciding on placement of equipment.

Equipment Placement

- All power exercises should be placed away from windows, mirrors, exits, and entrances to avoid breakage of glass, distraction, or collision with equipment or other athletes. The equipment for these exercises should be placed in areas that are readily supervised to ensure safety and proper lifting technique.
- The tallest machines or pieces of equipment (e.g., squat racks, power racks, lat pulldown machines, Smith machines) should be arranged along the walls. Dumbbell racks are also traditionally placed against the walls, with shorter, smaller pieces of equipment placed in the middle of the room to improve visibility (as well as appearance) and maximize use of space.
- Barbells and dumbbells should be placed a minimum of 36 inches (91 cm) between bar ends and spotter areas for ease of movement without obstruction.
- Weight trees should be placed in close proximity to plate-loaded equipment while a distance of 36 inches (91 cm) is maintained between lifting equipment and trees.
- Tall pieces of equipment, such as squat racks, may need to be bolted to the walls or floors for increased stability and safety.
- Equipment should be placed at least 6 inches (15 cm) from mirrors.

Traffic Flow

- Traffic should flow around the perimeter of each exercise area such that people do not need to enter designated exercise areas in order to gain access to another exercise area. Carpet can be used to designate walkways and to separate resistance training areas that have rubberized flooring.

- There should be at least one walkway that bisects the strength and conditioning facility so that traffic flow does not hinder the training process. This type of walkway also provides quick and easy access in and out of the facility in emergency situations.
- An unobstructed pathway 36 inches (91 cm) wide should be maintained in the facility at all times as stipulated by applicable laws. Doors should not open into pathways and hallways. Machines and equipment must not block or hinder traffic flow (24).

Stretching and Warm-Up Area

- A 49-square-foot (4.6 m^2) area per athlete should be allotted for stretching and warm-up activities (16). A larger warm-up area per person can be assigned if partner stretching is emphasized in the program design.

Circuit Training Area

- All resistance training machines and equipment must be spaced at least 24 inches (61 cm) and preferably 36 inches (91 cm) apart. A path of at least 36 inches is needed to accommodate athletes in lightweight sport wheelchairs.
- When a free weight station is used in the circuit, the area per athlete needs to include a 36-inch (91 cm) **safety space cushion** to allow sufficient room between the bar tips of adjacent stations. See table 21.1 for specific space needs for free weight exercises within a circuit training area.

TABLE 21.1

Calculations for Space Needs

Area	Examples	Formula
Prone and supine exercises	Bench press Lying triceps extension	**Formula**: Actual weight bench length (6-8 feet [1.8-2.4 m]) + safety space cushion of 3 feet (0.9 m) *multiplied by* a suggested user space for a weight bench "width" of 7 feet (2.1 m) + a safety space cushion of 3 feet (0.9 m) **Example 1**: If using a 6-foot-long weight bench for the bench press exercise, (6 feet + 3 feet) × (7 feet + 3 feet) = 90 square feet **Example 2 (metric approximations)**: If using a 2-meter-long weight bench for the bench press exercise, (2 meters [bench] + 1 meter [safety space]) × (2 meters [user space] + 1 meter [safety space]) = 9 square meters
Standing exercises	Biceps curl Upright row	**Formula**: Actual bar length (4-7 feet [1.2-2.1 m]) + a double-wide safety space cushion of 6 feet (1.8 m) *multiplied by* a suggested user space for a standing exercise "width" of 4 feet (1.2 m) **Example 1**: If using a 4-foot curl bar for the biceps curl exercise, (4 feet + 6 feet) × (4 feet) = 40 square feet **Example 2 (metric approximations)**: If using a 1-meter curl bar for the biceps curl exercise, (1 meter [bar] + 2 meters [safety space]) × (1 meter [user space]) = 3 square meters
Standing exercises in a rack	Back squat Shoulder press	**Formula**: Actual bar length (5-7 feet [1.5-2.1 m]) + a double-wide safety space cushion of 6 feet (1.8 m) *multiplied by* a suggested user space for a standing exercise (from a rack) "width" of 8 to 10 feet (2.4-3 m) **Example 1**: If using a 7-foot Olympic bar for the back squat exercise, (7 feet + 6 feet) × (10 feet) = 130 square feet **Example 2 (metric approximations)**: If using a 2-meter Olympic bar for the back squat exercise, (2 meters [bar] + 2 meters [safety space]) × (3 meters [safety space]) = 12 square meters
Olympic lifting area	Power clean	**Formula**: Lifting platform height (typically 8 feet [2.4 m]) + a perimeter walkway safety space cushion of 4 feet (1.2 m) *multiplied by* a lifting platform width (typically 8 feet [2.4 m]) + perimeter walkway safety space cushion of 4 feet (1.2 m) **Example 1**: (8 feet + 4 feet) × (8 feet + 4 feet) = 144 square feet **Example 2 (metric approximations)**: (2.5 meters [platform] + 1 meter [safety space]) × (2.5 meters [platform] + 1 meter [safety space]) = 12.25 square meters

- Multistation machines can also be used for circuit training but require more space than single-station machines. If possible, allow for more than the recommended 36-inch (91 cm) spacing between multistation machines and single-station machines.

Free Weights

- Olympic bars should be spaced 36 inches (91 cm) between ends.
- The area for one free weight station should accommodate three to four people.
- See table 21.1 for space needs for prone and supine exercises, standing exercises, and standing exercises in a rack (16).

Olympic Lifting Area

- The Olympic lifting area should accommodate three to four people (although only one athlete at a time should perform a power exercise).
- Perimeter walkways around the platform area should be 3 to 4 feet (0.9-1.2 m) wide.
- **Olympic standards** (portable and adjustable walk-in racks) should be secured into the platform (19) rather than resting on top of the platform (19, 20).
- If the Olympic standards are moveable, they should be stored out of the way when not in use.
- See table 21.1 for space needs for an Olympic lifting area (16).

Aerobic Area

- The aerobic equipment area requires 24 square feet (2.2 m^2) for bikes and stair machines, 6 square feet (0.6 m^2) for skiing machines, 40 square feet (3.7 m^2) for rowers, and 45 square feet (4.2 m^2) for treadmills (16). These numbers include the needed space between the machines.

The strength and conditioning professional may wish to make several blank copies of the facility floor plan and fill in various equipment placement and spacing possibilities to meet the needs of the athletes and program requirements. The floor plans shown in figures 21.3 and 21.4 (pp. 563 and 564) are examples of strength and conditioning facilities for a secondary school and university setting, respectively. These examples show reasonable traffic flow without obstruction; high-risk training areas positioned away from traffic; efficient use of space; and equipment placement for safety, functionality, and ease of supervision around the entire strength and conditioning facility.

MAINTAINING AND CLEANING SURFACES

Maintaining and cleaning the strength and conditioning facility begin with assessment of the types of surfaces that exist in the facility and the maintenance difficulties that could arise in each area. The strength and conditioning professional should frequently assess the facility's overall design; the condition of walls, floors, and ceilings; environmental factors (e.g., wear, tears, holes, leaks, excess humidity); and the accessibility and safe placement of equipment. Cleaning the facility is handled not only by the custodial staff, but also by the strength and conditioning staff. Therefore, the strength and conditioning professional must be aware of proper procedures for maintaining and cleaning the facility on a regular basis. Scheduling frequent maintenance and cleaning ensures safe training, protects investments, and maintains the strength and conditioning facility's appearance.

The safety checklist of the National Strength and Conditioning Association (NSCA) (figure 21.5, pp. 565-567) lists general maintenance and cleaning tasks by area (flooring, walls, etc.). It also incorporates facility layout issues, especially those relating to safety. In addition the checklist specifies tasks by frequency, showing what should be done daily, weekly, and so on. The general guidelines can be modified and made more specific for a particular facility.

Scheduling frequent maintenance and cleaning ensures safe training, protects investments, and maintains the strength and conditioning facility's appearance.

MAINTAINING AND CLEANING EQUIPMENT

Maintaining a facility also involves making sure equipment is functional, clean, and safe to use. Equipment that is constantly used (or abused) and not consistently cleaned or maintained is unsafe, can present health hazards, and must be repaired or replaced frequently. Nonfunctional or broken equipment should bear "out of order" signs; or, if a long delay before repair is expected, such equipment should be removed from the area or locked out of service. Improper maintenance and cleaning procedures devour funds from already limited budgets—funds that could be used to improve the strength and conditioning facility. Therefore, the strength and conditioning professional should clean and maintain equipment on a regular basis. In a large facility, the strength and conditioning professional can assign staff members to cleaning and maintenance according to specific training areas. This method is useful even in smaller facilities with limited staff. Again, the NSCA's safety checklist (figure 21.5, pp. 565-567) can be useful for organizing an inspection and maintenance schedule.

Maintenance equipment should be kept in a toolbox located in a locked cabinet or supply closet. Cleaning supplies should be kept in a locked supply cabinet located near the office or supervisor station. Supplies should be inventoried and restocked twice a week. Items that should be on hand for equipment maintenance and cleaning are listed in figure 21.6 (p. 568).

SCHEDULING THE STRENGTH AND CONDITIONING FACILITY

The ideal scheduling situation is to have more than one strength and conditioning facility that is properly equipped and monitored. However, few organizations are fortunate enough to have multiple facilities to consistently accommodate the training times and needs of every athletic team. Therefore, when organizing groups of athletes, the strength and conditioning professional should consider the following guidelines, taking into account the size of the facility, the amount and type of available equipment, the number of athletes per team, the number of athletic teams to be served simultaneously, and the needs of each team.

Seasonal Priority and Peak Hours

Athletic teams that are in-season normally have priority over off-season teams in the facility schedule. Usually two or more athletic teams have overlapping competitive seasons, which requires organizing the facility schedule to accommodate all in-season practice and game schedules. Off-season teams may have to be scheduled in the early morning hours or when the in-season teams are not using the facility (e.g., on game days, during practice times). Depending on the total number of athletes, in-season and off-season teams can be scheduled together, since the seasonal periodization cycles, and therefore training programs and equipment usage, typically differ.

Less time is allotted for in-season strength and conditioning programs than for off-season programs. Off-season programs may require 1 1/2 to 2 hours of training three days per week, with the majority of the training spent performing free weight exercises. In-season programs may require only 20 to 30 minutes of training two to three days per week, with the exception of those teams that have a larger number of athletes performing free weight exercises (16).

The strength and conditioning professional should attempt to schedule the facility so that there is an even flow of athletes throughout the day. To promote an optimal training environment for the athletes and proper supervision ratios, one should avoid overscheduling the facility. Even with careful planning, 2:00 to 6:00 p.m. is usually peak time in the strength and conditioning facility, especially for in-season teams. Another popular time block for facility usage at universities is 6:30 to 8:00 a.m., before athletes attend morning classes (16). Since this is not a preferred time, off-season teams are normally scheduled during these early morning hours. In secondary schools and professional sport clubs, facility use needs to be scheduled around school activities and off-court or off-field team events.

Athletes who use the strength and conditioning facility for rehabilitation usually are assigned times that avoid peak hours and other priorities such as athletic practice or class. To accommodate greater numbers of athletes and teams, a facility schedule can be created that places athletic teams on a rotation of alternating days (Monday, Wednesday, Friday or Tuesday, Thursday, Saturday). Refer to figure 22.7 on page 580 for a sample form to send to sport coaches to ask for their desired use of the strength and conditioning facility.

Staff-to-Athlete Ratio

Athletes in a strength and conditioning facility must be properly supervised to ensure health, safety, and optimal instruction at all times. *Supervision* refers to the actual physical presence of the strength and conditioning professional and should adhere to recommended guidelines for staff-to-athlete ratios. Recommended **staff-to-athlete ratios** are based on the age and experience level of the athletes. Younger athletes and those with less experience require more supervision than older or more experienced athletes. It is recommended that middle school strength and conditioning facilities not exceed a 1:10 staff-to-athlete ratio, secondary school facilities should not exceed a 1:15 ratio, and facilities that serve athletes older than secondary school should not exceed a 1:20 ratio (2, 12, 13). Another recommendation is that facilities not exceed a 1:50 staff-to-athlete ratio (24).

Another consideration in the determination of staff-to-athlete ratios should be the type of strength and conditioning program that is being conducted. Athletes engaged in circuit training with resistance training machines do not require as much supervision as athletes who are performing power exercises.

Before scheduling the facility, the strength and conditioning professional should consider seasonal athletic priorities, group size, equipment availability, and staff-to-athlete ratios.

LITIGATION ISSUES

Everyone involved in athletic activities must be concerned with legal liability, including the strength and conditioning professional. The risk of injury cannot be totally eliminated, but it can be effectively managed by the strength and conditioning professional. **Risk management** is the employment of strategies to decrease and control the risk of injury from athletic participation and therefore the risk of liability exposure. The first steps in risk management are to understand integral key terms and identify the areas of potential liability exposure that could cause injuries and lead to litigation. Although each facility is unique, there are recognizable areas of potential liability that are present in all strength and conditioning facilities. The following sections discuss these risk areas and the need for an emergency care plan, reliable record keeping, and liability insurance.

Common Legal Terminology

To understand the potential legal ramifications of running a strength and conditioning facility, the strength and conditioning professional must first understand the following common legal terms.

liability—A legal responsibility, duty, or obligation. Strength and conditioning professionals have a duty to the athletes they serve by virtue of their employment not only to act when an injury occurs, but to prevent injury (4).

standard of care—What a reasonable and prudent person would do under similar circumstances. A strength and conditioning professional is expected to act according to his or her education, level of training, and certification status (e.g., CSCS, NSCA-CPT, EMT, CPR, AED, First Aid).

negligence—Failure to act as a reasonable and prudent person would under similar circumstances. Four elements must exist in order for a strength and conditioning professional to be found negligent: **duty**, **breach of duty**, **proximate cause**, and **damages** (22). The strength and conditioning professional must be found to have had a duty to act and to have failed to act (a breach) with the appropriate standard of care, resulting in damages (physical or economic injury) to another person because of the natural and continuous sequence of reasonably foreseeable events (proximate cause). For example, a strength and conditioning professional sees that a cable is excessively worn on a resistance training machine, notes it, but does not post an "out of order" sign. An athlete uses that machine and incurs an injury. In this case, the strength and conditioning professional could be found negligent: His or her duty was to fix the cable or post a sign, but he or she failed to act, and an athlete sustained an injury because of the potentially injurious situation of a cable that was ready to break.

assumption of risk—Knowing that an inherent risk exists with participation in an activity and voluntarily deciding to participate anyway (9). All athletic activities, including strength and conditioning, involve a certain level of risk; athletes must be thoroughly informed of the risk and should sign a statement to that effect.

Supervision

It has been estimated that 80% of all court cases concerning athletic injuries deal with some aspect of supervision (4). All athletes should be constantly supervised, which requires the actual physical presence of a qualified strength and conditioning professional for overseeing all activities (10, 11, 14). To provide proper supervision, supervisor stations need to be located where a clear view of the facility and athletes is possible (17). Suggested staff-to-athlete ratios should be adhered to.

Instruction

A qualified strength and conditioning professional must properly instruct athletes in safe and effective strength and conditioning techniques. Instruction involves teaching an athlete a skill in a safe manner and correcting the athlete if necessary. Emphasizing safety and proper technique for resistance training rather than the amount of weight lifted helps reduce the incidence of injury and therefore liability exposure. Instructional methods, procedures, and progressions that are consistent with professional guidelines and standards should be used (4).

Medical Clearance

Before any athlete begins a strength and conditioning program, it is vital that he or she receive a preparticipation physical examination by a licensed physician. The strength and conditioning professional does not need a copy of the physical examination but should require a signed statement to show proof of medical clearance to participate. Athletes who are returning from an injury or illness or who have special needs (e.g., have diabetes, asthma, epilepsy, hypertension) should also be required to show proof of medical clearance before beginning or returning to a strength and conditioning program.

Note, however, that it is the responsibility of the sports medicine staff (e.g., the team or program's certified athletic trainer, physician, or physical therapist) to allow an athlete to begin formal involvement in the strength and conditioning program. This applies to both athletes who are new to the school or program and athletes who are just recovering from an injury or illness. This stipulation is important because it is not in the strength and conditioning professional's **scope of practice** (i.e., proper legal parameters and professional duties) to diagnose or evaluate an individual's medical or health condition. Therefore, only the sports medicine staff can provide medical clearance (and proof thereof) and answer any questions about participation.

Emergency Care Plan

An **emergency care plan** is a written document that details the proper procedures for caring for injuries. All personnel in the strength and conditioning facility must know the emergency care plan and the proper procedures for dealing with emergencies. The following are the typical items included or described in an emergency plan:

- EMS (emergency medical services) activation procedures
- Names and telephone numbers of primary, secondary, and tertiary individuals to contact
- Specific address of the strength and conditioning facility (to give directions to EMS)
- Location of the telephones
- Location of nearest exits
- Designated personnel qualified to care for injuries (i.e., sports medicine staff)
- Ambulance access
- Location of emergency supplies and first aid kit
- Plan of action in case of fire, tornado, life-threatening injury, crime, terrorism, and so forth

In addition to posting the emergency care plan in a clearly visible location, it is critical that all strength and conditioning professionals maintain current first aid and cardiopulmonary resuscitation (CPR) certification and practice the emergency care plan at least quarterly.

Record Keeping

Documentation is fundamental to the management of a strength and conditioning facility. Records should be kept on file of cleaning and maintenance, safety procedures, manufacturer's warranties and guidelines, assumption-of-risk forms, medical waivers and clearance forms, personnel credentials, professional guidelines and recommendations (e.g., use of weight belts, resistance training techniques), and injury report forms (4). Injury report forms should be maintained as long as possible in case an injury suit is filed. The time during which individuals can file a lawsuit (i.e., the **statute of limitations**) varies (from state to state in the United States as well as throughout the world), so it is a good practice to maintain files indefinitely or to check with a legal authority (10).

Liability Insurance

Because of the potential for injury in athletic participation, it is a good idea for strength and conditioning staff members to purchase professional liability insurance, especially if they are not covered under the facility policy. Strength and conditioning professionals should consult their human resource manager, legal consultant, or professional organization (e.g., NSCA) for further information.

The risk of injury cannot be totally eliminated, but it can be effectively managed by the strength and conditioning professional.

Product Liability

Product liability refers to the legal responsibilities of those who manufacture or sell products if a person sustains injury or damage as a result of using the product (3). Although strength and conditioning professionals may not manufacture or sell a product, they can be named as codefendants in product liability suits. Therefore, it is important for strength and conditioning professionals to understand the concept of product liability and actions that could place them at risk for litigation. Although product liability applies only to those who are in the business of manufacturing or selling products, there are behaviors that can void liability of the manufacturer or seller and place responsibility in the hands of the strength and conditioning professional. Two key considerations that determine whether the manufacturer or seller is liable are whether the product has been changed from the condition in which it was originally sold and whether the product is used as intended by the manufacturer (5). To avoid injury to athletes caused by strength and conditioning equipment, the following steps should be taken:

- Use equipment only for the purpose intended by the manufacturer. Refer to the manufacturer's instructional materials that accompany the equipment, including user age and size specifications.
- Be certain that equipment meets existing professional standards and guidelines. Do not purchase and use equipment that has been deemed unsafe or ineffective by professional organizations and experts. Be aware of equipment recalls, and return such equipment to the manufacturer immediately.
- Buy only from reputable manufacturers. Strength and conditioning professionals must do their homework to check on the safety record of a manufacturer or seller and any claims that may have been filed against that manufacturer or seller. Organizations such as the Better Business Bureau in the United States, other strength and conditioning colleagues, and professional organizations are good resources for this information.
- Do not modify equipment unless such adaptations are clearly designated and instructions for doing so are included in the product information. Some equipment is designed to be modified for specific needs, such as fitting, but directions for modifying the product must be followed exactly.
- Apply all warning labels that accompany a new equipment purchase. If such labels are not placed on the machine in plain view and an individual is injured (and the injury relates to what the warning label addresses), the strength and conditioning professional can be held liable.
- Continually inspect equipment for damage and wear that may place an athlete at risk for injury. To recognize potential problems, the strength and conditioning professional must understand the purpose, capabilities, and limitations of equipment and how equipment can cause injury. Always inspect newly purchased equipment prior to use. If new equipment arrives damaged, immediately notify the manufacturer or seller and have it replaced. If currently owned equipment becomes damaged, remove it for repair or replacement. If equipment is too large to remove or no storage space exists, clearly affix a sign on the equipment stating that it should not be used.
- Do not allow unsupervised athletes to use equipment. Constant supervision of the athletes by the strength and conditioning professional ensures that equipment is used for its intended purpose and with proper technique (4, 5).

Strength and conditioning professionals should understand the concept of product liability and the actions that could place them at risk for litigation.

CONCLUSION

Designing the strength and conditioning facility for safety and for effective use of equipment, time, and space can be a challenging task. Planning and designing a new strength and conditioning facility is a complicated venture; but with a committee of professionals who represent various areas of expertise and knowledge of the design and construction process, it can be accomplished. In most situations, however, the strength and conditioning professional inherits an existing facility and therefore must assess the needed modifications to accommodate all athletes. Once the facility is in place, the strength and conditioning professional can study floor plans to determine proper placement of equipment and to enhance safety and functionality in the facility. Proper maintenance and cleaning of the equipment and facility on a regular schedule will extend the life span of the facility and its equipment. If the strength and conditioning facility and its equipment are not properly maintained and cleaned, injuries can occur. Claims of negligence may be made if injuries occur and appropriate precautions have not been taken. Strength and conditioning professionals must also be aware of the proper function and repair of all equipment to reduce the possibility of product liability.

KEY TERMS

assumption of risk 554
breach of duty 554
construction phase 545
damages 554
design phase 545
duty 554
emergency care plan 555
feasibility study 545
liability 554
litigation 544
needs analysis 545
needs assessment 545
negligence 554
Olympic standards 552
predesign phase 545
preoperation phase 545
product liability 544
proximate cause 554
risk management 554
safety space cushion 551
scope of practice 555
staff-to-athlete ratio 554
standard of care 554
statute of limitations 555

STUDY QUESTIONS

1. When planning and designing a new strength and conditioning facility, a feasibility study should occur during which phase?

a. predesign
b. design
c. construction
d. preoperation

2. Which of the following must be considered when determining the space requirements of a college strength and conditioning facility?

I. accessibility for the athletes
II. amount and type of equipment
III. number of athletes using the facility
IV. number of athletic teams desiring to use the facility

a. I and III only
b. II and IV only
c. I, II, and III only
d. II, III, and IV only

3. What staff-to-athlete ratio is recommended for a college strength and conditioning facility?

a. 1:10
b. 1:15
c. 1:20
d. 1:50

4. What temperature range is recommended for a strength and conditioning facility?

a. 72-78 °F (22-26 °C)
b. 70-78 °F (21-26 °C)
c. 65-75 °F (18-24 °C)
d. 68-78 °F (20-26 °C)

5. A strength and conditioning facility's tallest pieces of equipment should be placed along the perimeter walls to

I. prevent equipment from tipping over.
II. improve facility visibility.
III. anchor them to the walls.
IV. allow proper lifting technique.

a. I and IV only
b. II and III only
c. II, III, and IV only
d. I, II, and III only

6. Routine maintenance and cleaning of a strength and conditioning facility and its equipment provide for

I. safe participation.
II. protection of investments.
III. enhanced facility appearance.
IV. improved athletic performance.

a. I and IV only
b. II and IV only
c. I, II, and III only
d. II, III, and IV only

7. What is the recommended minimum distance between the floor and the bottom of the mirrors on the walls?

a. 16 inches (41 centimeters)
b. 18 inches (46 centimeters)
c. 20 inches (51 centimeters)
d. 22 inches (56 centimeters)

8. Which of the following may compromise safety in the lifting platform area?

I. splinters in the platform
II. misplaced bumper plates
III. chalk buildup
IV. a wooden surface

a. I and III only
b. II and IV only
c. I, II, and III only
d. II, III, and IV only

CHECKLIST FOR THE FACILITY DESIGN PROCESS

- ☐ Involve and organize all the individuals who will have a role in planning the facility. This might include the head strength and conditioning director, athletic director, athletic consultants, financiers, and people who will be operating and using the facility.
- ☐ Conduct a comprehensive program analysis to determine present and future needs; then realize that the need for future facilities may fluctuate based on the expansion of existing activities or the creation of new ones, and determine how you will proceed.
- ☐ Conduct a feasibility study.
- ☐ Write a comprehensive facility plan, including information concerning space needs, programming trends, existing facilities, modern facility innovation, and available equipment.
- ☐ Write a detailed description of the services to be provided, their associated needs, and their manner of functioning. This can be an extended part of the facility plan.
- ☐ Select and hire a well-qualified planning team.
- ☐ Write down the detailed qualitative and quantitative space requirements necessary to accommodate the proposed services.
- ☐ Develop a well-defined and realistic project completion schedule.
- ☐ Review carefully the architectural drawings and specifications at each stage.
- ☐ Select and hire reputable contractors for the construction of the facility.
- ☐ Complete the facility under the control of a well-qualified project supervisor.
- ☐ Hire well-qualified and competent staff.
- ☐ Formally inspect the facility, install the fixed and movable equipment, and orient the staff.
- ☐ Occupy the facility and initiate the service.

Figure 21.1 Use a checklist such as this one to ensure that you cover all of the steps necessary for designing a strength and conditioning facility.

From NSCA, 2008, *Essentials of Strength Training and Conditioning*, 3rd ed., T.R. Baechle and R.W. Earle (eds.), (Champaign, IL: Human Kinetics). Reprinted, by permission, from R.W. Patton et al. 1989, *Developing and managing health fitness facilities* (Champaign, IL: Human Kinetics), 161(18).

COMMON DESIGN AND SPECIFICATIONS OF A STRENGTH AND CONDITIONING FACILITY

General Features

It is assumed that the facility design process has been carried out as described and that these checklists will serve to verify that appropriate procedures have been followed. These lists will also help to prevent costly design mistakes.

- ☐ A comprehensive master plan has been prepared on the nature and scope of the program, and the special requirements for space, equipment, fixtures, and facilities have been dictated by the activities to be conducted (form follows function).
- ☐ The facility has been planned to meet the total requirements of the program, both present and future, as well as the special needs of those who are to be served. Any possible future additions or expansions are included in the present plans to permit economy of construction and costs.
- ☐ The plans and specifications meet the codes of all governmental agencies whose approval is required by law.
- ☐ The plans of the facility conform to accepted standards and practices.
- ☐ The following factors have been considered for the proposed facility and site:
    - Feeder streets (new or existing)
    - Parking areas
    - Electrical supplies
    - Water supplies
    - Sewage lines
    - Gas lines
    - Storm drainage
    - Soil topography
- ☐ The selection of equipment and supplies has been based on a cost-per-use ratio, as well as on ongoing maintenance costs.
- ☐ Sufficient attention has been given to fire codes, fire and security systems, and emergency escape routes.
- ☐ Window heights are appropriate for privacy, safety, maintenance, and use of natural light.
- ☐ Floor and wall surfaces have been selected according to the following criteria: year-round usage, dust and moisture resistance, stainlessness, inflammability, nonabrasiveness, durability, resiliency, safety, maintenance, and cost per use.

Indoor Facilities (General)

- ☐ All passageways are free of obstruction so two-way traffic can occur. Every effort has been made to eliminate hazards.
- ☐ Buildings, specialty areas, and facilities are clearly identified.
- ☐ Administrative offices, workout areas, and service facilities are properly interrelated; the same is true for medical, first aid, and emergency rooms.
- ☐ Special needs of people with physical disabilities have been met, including installation of a ramp into the building at a major entrance.
- ☐ Storage rooms are of adequate size and are accessible to appropriate areas. All dead space is used, such as areas under stairwells.
- ☐ Low-cost maintenance features have been considered.
- ☐ All areas, courts, facilities, equipment, climate control, security, and the like conform rigidly to detailed standards and specifications.

Figure 21.2 Common design and specifications of a strength and conditioning facility.

From NSCA, 2008, *Essentials of Strength Training and Conditioning*, 3rd ed., T.R. Baechle and R.W. Earle (eds.), (Champaign, IL: Human Kinetics). Reprinted, by permission, from R.W. Patton et al. 1989, *Developing and managing health fitness facilities* (Champaign, IL: Human Kinetics), 162-167(18).

- ☐ Drinking fountains are conveniently placed in the locker rooms and workout areas or immediately adjacent to them.
- ☐ Provision is made for repair, maintenance, replacement, and storage of equipment.
- ☐ Antipanic hardware is used on doors as required by fire regulations.
- ☐ Space relationships and equipment are planned in accordance with the type and number of users.
- ☐ Warning signals—both visible and audible—are included in the plans.
- ☐ Ramps have a slope equal to or less than a 1-foot (30 cm) vertical rise for every 12 linear feet (3.6 m). Alternatively, the maximum slope can be described as 1 foot (30 cm) for every inch (2.5 cm) of elevation change.
- ☐ Minimum landings for ramps are 5 feet by 5 feet (1.5 m by 1.5 m); they extend at least 1 foot (30 cm) beyond the swinging arc of a door and have at least a 6-foot (1.8 m) clearance at the bottom.

Climate Control

- ☐ The building has climate control throughout (i.e., heating, ventilation, and air-conditioning, or HVAC).
- ☐ HVAC systems are on both a zone control and an individual room control system.
- ☐ Temperature and humidity are specific to a particular area.

Electrical

- ☐ Lighting intensity meets approved standards.
- ☐ An adequate number of electrical outlets are appropriately placed throughout the facility. They should be 3 feet (0.9 m) above the floor unless otherwise specified.
- ☐ Service area lights are controlled by dimmer units.
- ☐ Natural light, when used, is controlled properly to reduce glare.

Walls

- ☐ Electrical wall plates are located within the wall where needed and are firmly attached.
- ☐ Materials that clean easily and are impervious to moisture are used where moisture is prevalent.
- ☐ Drinking fountains are provided in adequate number and are properly recessed in the wall.
- ☐ One wall (at least) of the aerobics room has full-length mirrors.
- ☐ Wall coverings are aesthetically pleasing and match the overall decor of the facility.

Ceilings

- ☐ The ceiling height is adequate for the activities to be performed in a given area.
- ☐ Ceiling support beams are designed and engineered to withstand stress.
- ☐ Acoustical materials impervious to moisture are used in moisture-prevalent areas.
- ☐ All ceilings except those in storage areas are acoustically treated with sound-absorbent materials.
- ☐ Skylights in exercise rooms are impractical and therefore are seldom used because of problems in waterproofing roofs and controlling sun rays.
- ☐ Ceiling and crawl spaces are easily accessible for maintenance and repair purposes.

(CONTINUED)

Figure 21.2 *(continued)*

From NSCA, 2008, *Essentials of Strength Training and Conditioning*, 3rd ed., T.R. Baechle and R.W. Earle (eds.), (Champaign, IL: Human Kinetics). Reprinted, by permission, from R.W. Patton et al. 1989, *Developing and managing health fitness facilities* (Champaign, IL: Human Kinetics), 162-167(18).

Floors

- ☐ Floor plates, where needed, are flush mounted.

Storage and Issuance Rooms

- ☐ The storage areas conform to fire laws.
- ☐ The storage and issue areas are centrally located and are of sufficient number to handle peak periods effectively.
- ☐ The doors to storage areas are wide and do not have a riser.
- ☐ The storage areas have appropriate security.
- ☐ Storage areas have adequate ventilation.

Activity Areas Checklist

- ☐ The floor area and dimensions have been determined by the activities to be conducted.
- ☐ Adequate space or buffer zones are provided between activity areas.
- ☐ Wall surfaces were selected to allow their use for activities, cleaning, and maintenance.
- ☐ The floor surface material has been selected to allow for a maximum variety of uses.
- ☐ Adequate storage rooms are conveniently located near activity areas.
- ☐ Acoustical standards are met for all rooms.
- ☐ Lighting quality meets all standards.
- ☐ Provisions are included for an emergency safety lighting system.
- ☐ There is a properly installed, high-quality public address system.
- ☐ There are provisions for an intercom system that may be connected with the public address system.
- ☐ Climate control systems are adequate.
- ☐ Floor plates have been installed.
- ☐ Provisions have been included for repair, maintenance, and installation of ceiling fixtures.
- ☐ Provisions have been included for proper and necessary signs, both illuminated and nonilluminated, pertaining to areas, exits, and participants.
- ☐ There is a suitable lock-and-key system for doors, storage rooms, light controls, sound system controls, intercom controls, climate controls, and public address systems.

Provisions for People With Disabilities

- ☐ Necessary provisions are present for parking, loading, and unloading areas, and ramps are provided wherever necessary. (Elevators should also be considered.)
- ☐ All doorways and passageways are of sufficient width to accommodate wheelchairs. The feasibility of electrically operated doors has been considered.
- ☐ All thresholds are flush.
- ☐ All doorways or entryways to toilets, telephone areas, food and refreshment areas, locker rooms, and special rooms are sufficient to accommodate wheelchairs.
- ☐ Rest room facilities are provided for people with disabilities.

Figure 21.2 *(continued)*

From NSCA, 2008, *Essentials of Strength Training and Conditioning*, 3rd ed., T.R. Baechle and R.W. Earle (eds.), (Champaign, IL: Human Kinetics). Reprinted, by permission, from R.W. Patton et al. 1989, *Developing and managing health fitness facilities* (Champaign, IL: Human Kinetics), 162-167(18).

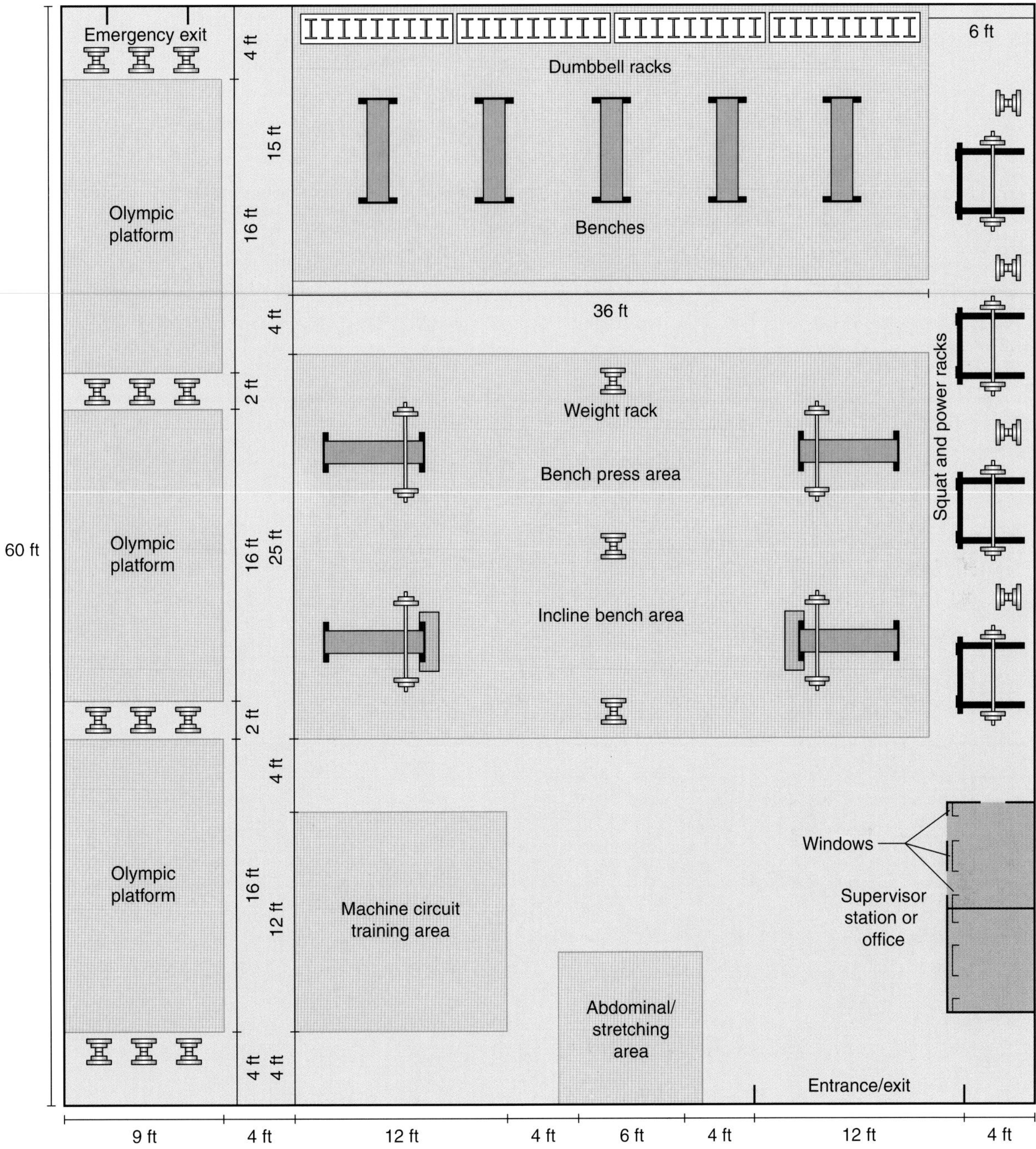

Figure 21.3 Example of a secondary school strength and conditioning facility floor plan.

3 feet (ft) ≈ 1 m

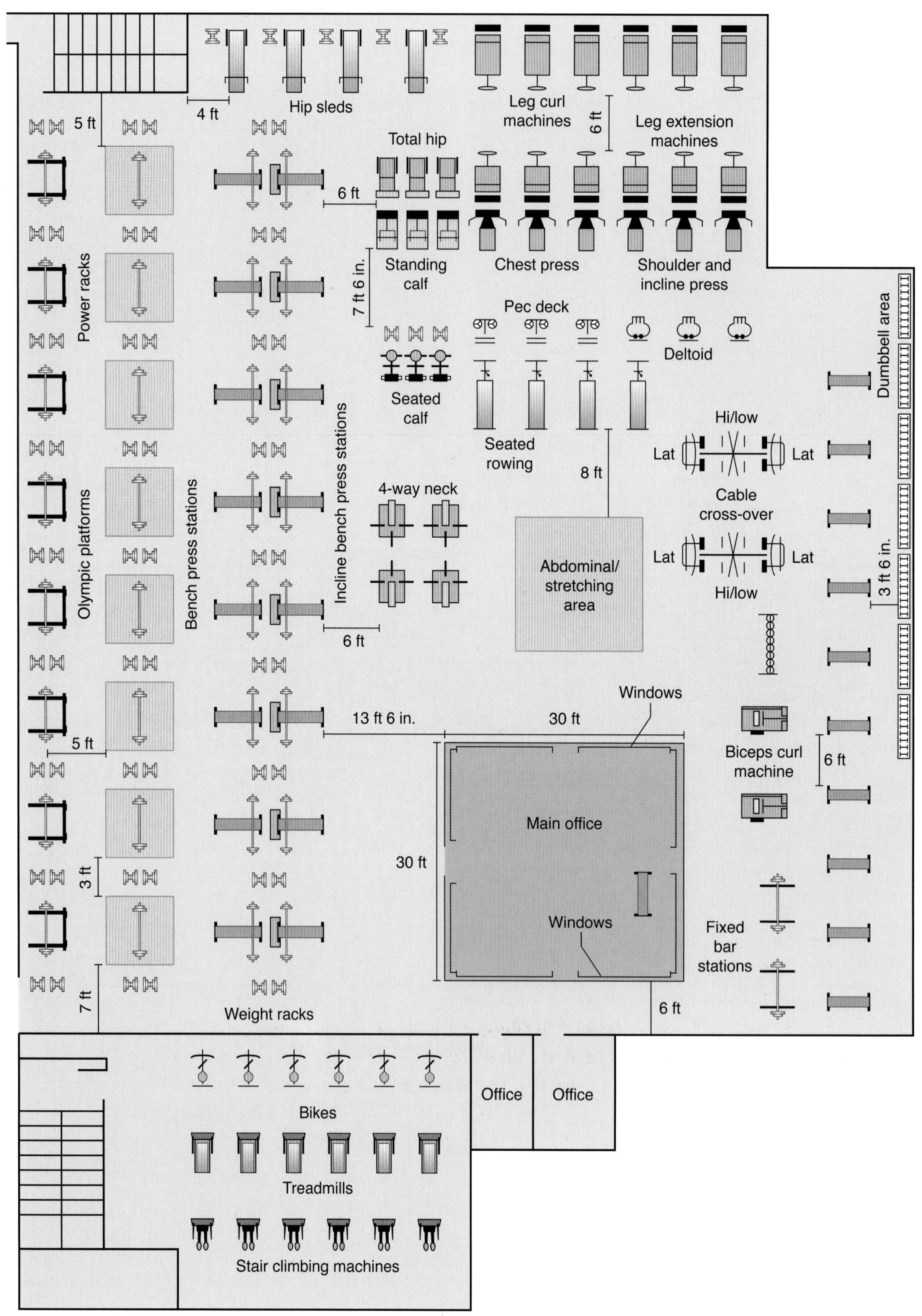

Figure 21.4 Example of a university strength and conditioning facility floor plan.

3 feet (ft) ≈ 1 m

NSCA'S SAFETY CHECKLIST FOR EXERCISE FACILITY AND EQUIPMENT MAINTENANCE

Exercise Facility

Floor

- ☐ Inspected and cleaned daily
- ☐ Wooden flooring free of splinters, holes, protruding nails, and loose screws
- ☐ Tile flooring resistant to slipping; no moisture or chalk accumulation
- ☐ Rubber flooring free of cuts, slits, and large gaps between pieces
- ☐ Interlocking mats secure and arranged with no protruding tabs
- ☐ Nonabsorbent carpet free of tears; wear areas protected by throw mats
- ☐ Area swept and vacuumed or mopped on a regular basis
- ☐ Flooring glued or fastened down properly

Walls

- ☐ Wall surfaces cleaned two to three times a week (or more often if needed)
- ☐ Walls in high-activity areas free of protruding appliances, equipment, or wall hangings
- ☐ Mirrors and shelves securely fixed to walls
- ☐ Mirrors and windows cleaned regularly (especially in high-activity areas, such as around drinking fountains and in doorways)
- ☐ Mirrors placed a minimum of 20 inches (51 cm) off the floor in all areas
- ☐ Mirrors not cracked or distorted (replace immediately if damaged)

Ceiling

- ☐ All ceiling fixtures and attachments dusted regularly
- ☐ Ceiling tile kept clean
- ☐ Damaged or missing ceiling tile replaced as needed
- ☐ Open ceilings with exposed pipes and ducts cleaned as needed

Exercise Equipment

Stretching and Body Weight Exercise Area

- ☐ Mat area free of weight benches and equipment
- ☐ Mats and bench upholstery free of cracks and tears
- ☐ No large gaps between stretching mats
- ☐ Area swept and disinfected daily
- ☐ Equipment properly stored after use
- ☐ Elastic cords secured to base with safety knot and checked for wear
- ☐ Surfaces that contact skin treated with antifungal and antibacterial agents daily
- ☐ Nonslip material on the top surface and bottom or base of plyometric boxes
- ☐ Ceiling height sufficient for overhead exercises (12 feet [3.7 m] minimum) and free of low-hanging apparatus (beams, pipes, lighting, signs, etc.)

Resistance Training Machine Area

- ☐ Easy access to each station (a minimum of 2 feet [61 cm] between machines; 3 feet [91 cm] is optimal)

(CONTINUED)

Figure 21.5 NSCA's Safety Checklist for Exercise Facility and Equipment Maintenance.

From NSCA, 2008, *Essentials of Strength Training and Conditioning*, 3rd ed., T.R. Baechle and R.W. Earle (eds.), (Champaign, IL: Human Kinetics). Reprinted, by permission, from National Strength and Conditioning Association, 2004, *NSCA's Essentials of Personal Training*, edited by R.W. Earle and T.R. Baechle (Champaign, IL: Human Kinetics), 604-606.

- ☐ Area free of loose bolts, screws, cables, and chains
- ☐ Proper selectorized pins used
- ☐ Securing straps functional
- ☐ Parts and surfaces properly lubricated and cleaned
- ☐ Protective padding free of cracks and tears
- ☐ Surfaces that contact skin treated with antifungal and antibacterial agents daily
- ☐ No protruding screws or parts that need tightening or removal
- ☐ Belts, chains, and cables aligned with machine parts
- ☐ No worn parts (frayed cable, loose chains, worn bolts, cracked joints, etc.)

Resistance Training Free Weight Area

- ☐ Easy access to each bench or area (a minimum of 2 feet [61 cm] between machines; 3 feet [91 cm] is optimal)
- ☐ Olympic bars properly spaced (3 feet [91 cm]) between ends
- ☐ All equipment returned after use to avoid obstruction of pathway
- ☐ Safety equipment (belts, collars, safety bars) used and returned
- ☐ Protective padding free of cracks and tears
- ☐ Surfaces that contact skin treated with antifungal and antibacterial agents daily
- ☐ Securing bolts and apparatus parts (collars, curl bars) tightly fastened
- ☐ Nonslip mats on squat rack floor area
- ☐ Olympic bars turn properly and are properly lubricated and tightened
- ☐ Benches, weight racks, standards, and the like secured to the floor or wall
- ☐ Nonfunctional or broken equipment removed from area or locked out of service
- ☐ Ceiling height sufficient for overhead exercises (12 feet [3.7 m] minimum) and free of low-hanging apparatus (beams, pipes, lighting, signs, etc.)

Olympic Lifting Platform Area

- ☐ Olympic bars properly spaced (3 feet [91 cm]) between ends
- ☐ All equipment returned after use to avoid obstruction of lifting area
- ☐ Olympic bars rotate properly and are properly lubricated and tightened
- ☐ Bent Olympic bars replaced; knurling clear of debris
- ☐ Collars functioning
- ☐ Sufficient chalk available
- ☐ Wrist straps, belts, and knee wraps available, functioning, and stored properly
- ☐ Benches, chairs, boxes kept at a distance from lifting area
- ☐ No gaps, cuts, slits, splinters in mat
- ☐ Area properly swept and mopped to remove splinters and chalk
- ☐ Ceiling height sufficient for overhead exercises (12 feet [3.7 m] minimum) and free of low-hanging apparatus (beams, pipes, lighting, signs, etc.)

Aerobic Exercise Area

- ☐ Easy access to each station (minimum of 2 feet [61 cm] between machines; 3 feet [91 cm] is optimal)
- ☐ Bolts and screws tight

Figure 21.5 *(continued)*

From NSCA, 2008, *Essentials of Strength Training and Conditioning,* 3rd ed., T.R. Baechle and R.W. Earle (eds.), (Champaign, IL: Human Kinetics). Reprinted, by permission, from National Strength and Conditioning Association, 2004, *NSCA's Essentials of Personal Training,* edited by R.W. Earle and T.R. Baechle (Champaign, IL: Human Kinetics), 604-606.

- ☐ Functioning parts easily adjustable
- ☐ Parts and surfaces properly lubricated and cleaned
- ☐ Foot and body straps secure and not ripped
- ☐ Measurement devices for tension, time, and rpms properly functioning
- ☐ Surfaces that contact skin treated with antifungal and antibacterial agents daily

Frequency of Maintenance and Cleaning Tasks

Daily

- ☐ Inspect all flooring for damage or wear
- ☐ Clean (sweep, vacuum, or mop and disinfect) all flooring
- ☐ Clean and disinfect upholstery
- ☐ Clean and disinfect drinking fountain
- ☐ Inspect fixed equipment's connection with floor
- ☐ Clean and disinfect equipment surfaces that contact skin
- ☐ Clean mirrors
- ☐ Clean windows
- ☐ Inspect mirrors for damage
- ☐ Inspect all equipment for damage; wear; loose or protruding belts, screws, cables, or chains; insecure or nonfunctioning foot and body straps; improper functioning or improper use of attachments, pins, or other devices
- ☐ Clean and lubricate moving parts of equipment
- ☐ Inspect all protective padding for cracks and tears
- ☐ Inspect nonslip material and mats for proper placement, damage, and wear
- ☐ Remove trash and garbage
- ☐ Clean light covers, fans, air vents, clocks, and speakers
- ☐ Ensure that equipment is returned and stored properly after use

Two to Three Times per Week

- ☐ Clean and lubricate aerobic machines and the guide rods on selectorized resistance training machines

Once per Week

- ☐ Clean (dust) ceiling fixtures and attachments
- ☐ Clean ceiling tile

As Needed

- ☐ Replace light bulbs
- ☐ Clean walls
- ☐ Replace damaged or missing ceiling tiles
- ☐ Clean open ceilings with exposed pipes or ducts
- ☐ Remove (or place sign on) broken equipment
- ☐ Fill chalk boxes
- ☐ Clean bar knurling
- ☐ Clean rust from floor, plates, bars, and equipment with a rust-removing solution

Figure 21.5 *(continued)*

From NSCA, 2008, *Essentials of Strength Training and Conditioning,* 3rd ed., T.R. Baechle and R.W. Earle (eds.), (Champaign, IL: Human Kinetics). Reprinted, by permission, from National Strength and Conditioning Association, 2004, *NSCA's Essentials of Personal Training,* edited by R.W. Earle and T.R. Baechle (Champaign, IL: Human Kinetics), 604-606.

CHECKLIST OF COMMON MAINTENANCE EQUIPMENT AND CLEANING SUPPLIES

Place a "✓" next to items in toolbox.

Maintenance Equipment

- ☐ File
- ☐ Hammer
- ☐ Pliers (standard and needle-nose)
- ☐ Screwdrivers (standard and Phillips)
- ☐ Allen wrench set
- ☐ Crescent wrench
- ☐ Mallet
- ☐ Carpet knife
- ☐ Heavy-duty stapler
- ☐ Nuts, bolts, washers, nails, and screws in various sizes
- ☐ Heavy-duty glue
- ☐ Transparent tape
- ☐ Masking tape
- ☐ Duct tape
- ☐ Drill and drill bit set
- ☐ Lubricant spray
- ☐ Socket set
- ☐ Vise grips

Place a "✓" next to items in supply closet.

Cleaning Supplies

- ☐ Disinfectant (germicide)
- ☐ Specialty cleaners (wood, wall surfaces, upholstery, etc.)
- ☐ Window and mirror cleaner
- ☐ Lubrication sprays
- ☐ Spray bottles (4)
- ☐ Paper towels
- ☐ Cloth towels and hand rags (12 or more)
- ☐ Sponges
- ☐ Broom and dustpan
- ☐ Small vacuum cleaner
- ☐ Vacuum cleaner bags
- ☐ Whisk broom
- ☐ Mop and bucket
- ☐ Gum and stain remover (for carpet and upholstery)

Figure 21.6 These items should be kept in a cabinet or supply closet.

From NSCA, 2008, *Essentials of Strength Training and Conditioning*, 3rd ed., T.R. Baechle and R.W. Earle (eds.), (Champaign, IL: Human Kinetics).

CHAPTER 22

Developing a Policies and Procedures Manual

Boyd Epley, MEd, and John Taylor, MS

After completing this chapter, you will be able to

- develop or clarify the goals and objectives of a strength and conditioning program,
- clearly define and distinguish job duties of various strength and conditioning positions,
- understand the many policies and activities of a strength and conditioning facility that help to achieve the goals and objectives,
- understand appropriate administrative decisions that lead to a safe and effective program, and
- ultimately create a policies and procedures manual for a strength and conditioning facility.

Written policies and procedures are important for a strength and conditioning program, much as having a business plan is important for a business professional. Communicating a plan of action to the strength and conditioning staff and having the plan correctly implemented establish a standard of excellence and help ensure athlete safety. With more athletic teams and Olympic sport programs added to the list of duties of the traditional strength and conditioning professional, a larger, well-qualified staff is essential for getting the job done right. Plus, because legal liability is a common concern to all people responsible for sport activities, there is a heightened need for quality instruction and supervision as well as continual inspection and maintenance of a training facility.

Policies and procedures concern both athletes (and other users) and strength and conditioning staff members. **Policies** are essentially a facility's rules and regulations; they reflect the goals and objectives of the program. **Procedures** describe how policies are met or carried out. Before detailing specific policies and procedures, it is necessary to examine program goals and objectives, because they are the basis on which policies and procedures are created. The goal of this chapter is to guide the strength and conditioning professional in creating a policies and procedures manual that establishes and improves the standard of care and excellence of his or her program.

MISSION STATEMENT AND PROGRAM GOALS

A mission statement is vital to the success of any organization; it is the foundation of effective administration. Creating a mission statement requires forward thinking with the end result in mind. A good mission statement provides focus, direction, and a sense of purpose. According to the Drucker Foundation (7), the following are suggested criteria for an effective mission statement (p. 136):

- Is short and sharply focused
- Is clear and easily understood
- Defines why we do what we do; why the organization exists
- Does not prescribe means
- Is sufficiently broad
- Provides direction for doing the right things
- Addresses our opportunities
- Matches our competence
- Inspires our commitment
- Says what, in the end, we want to be remembered for

The following is an example of a holistic mission statement of a strength and conditioning program:

> To provide to athletes the means by which they can train consistently, sensibly, and systematically over designated periods of time in a safe, clean, and professional environment to help prevent injury and improve athletic performance.

Program goals are the desired end products of a strength and conditioning program. The most foundational goal of a strength and conditioning program is to improve athletic performance. This alone could serve as the mission statement for the program; however, strength and conditioning professionals in whose programs injuries have occurred realize that injury prevention should also be a goal.

Developing a mission statement and a list of program objectives (see the following section) should involve not only the entire strength and conditioning department, but also the athletic administration and sports medicine departments. For larger institutions, other support staff (e.g., graduate assistants, interns, secretaries, volunteers, and student-athlete representatives) may also be contributory resources. The more people participating, the better, so that all involved groups and individuals take ownership and commit to achieving the strength and conditioning program's mission, goals, and objectives.

A mission statement provides focus, direction, and a sense of purpose for a strength and conditioning program.

PROGRAM OBJECTIVES

Program objectives are specific means of attaining program goals. If program goals are stated but the ways in which these goals might be attained are not specified, the result may be that athletes never achieve them. Program objectives should encompass all areas of the program to ensure that the goals are attained. Following is a sample list of objectives that can lead to reaching program goals and prepare a strength and conditioning professional to handle the job requirements.

- Design and administer strength, flexibility, aerobic, plyometric, and other training programs that reduce the likelihood of injuries and improve athletic performance. More precisely, design training programs that create the desired results in body composition, hypertrophy, strength, muscular endurance, cardiovascular endurance, speed, agility, coordination, balance, and power.
- Develop training programs to account for biomechanical and physiological differences among individual athletes, taking into consideration their ages, sex, training status, physical limitations, and injury status.
- Recognize acute and chronic physiological responses and adaptations to training and their implications for the design of sport-specific training programs.
- Educate athletes on the importance of good nutrition and its role in health and performance.
- Educate athletes about the effects of performance-enhancing substances and their abuse, relevant school policy, legislation, and safe and viable alternatives.

To work toward creating a strength and conditioning program that meets the preceding objectives, the strength and conditioning professional in charge of a facility needs to establish written job (position) descriptions, policies, and procedures and to familiarize both staff and participants with the established goals, objectives, responsibilities, and procedures.

JOB TITLES, DESCRIPTIONS, AND DUTIES OF THE STRENGTH AND CONDITIONING STAFF

In order for a facility to achieve a high standard of excellence, it is imperative that the roles and duties of each staff member be distinct and be clearly delineated. Figure 22.1 provides an overview of the preparedness required of each staff member. The title and responsibilities of the strength and conditioning professional are continually changing as the field grows and becomes better recognized. Although job responsibilities vary according to institution, it would be prudent to consult *Strength and Conditioning Professionals Standards and Guidelines* (6) when one is developing job descriptions and responsibilities.

Guideline 2.2 of this document states the following:

> The Strength and Conditioning practitioner should achieve and maintain professional certification(s) with continuing education requirements and a code of ethics, such as the CSCS credential offered through the NSCA Certification Commission. (p. 16)

Appendix A of the same document defines the strength and conditioning professional:

> Certified Strength and Conditioning Specialists are professionals who practically apply foundational knowledge to assess, motivate, educate, and train athletes for the primary goal of improving sports performance. They conduct sport-specific testing sessions, design and implement safe and effective strength training and conditioning programs, and provide guidance for athletes in nutrition and injury prevention. Recognizing their area of expertise is

STAFF PREPAREDNESS

1. Maintenance of professional certification
2. Maintenance of standard first aid certification, CPR, and AED
3. Review of emergency response procedures
   a. Rudimentary first aid procedures annually
   b. Common training facility injuries and their prevention
   c. Building evacuation plan
4. Knowledge and understanding of program policies and procedures
   a. Review of room capacity and safe supervision ratios
   b. Review of preparticipation screening and clearance procedure
   c. Review of personal and professional liability, negligence, and insurance coverage issues
5. Knowledge and understanding of governing body rules and regulations
   a. Review of general knowledge of regulations
   b. Review of rules specific to administering the strength and conditioning program
6. Knowledge and understanding of cleaning and maintenance issues and needs
7. Knowledge and understanding of program philosophy and instruction methods
   a. Technique and drill instruction
   b. Body composition guidelines and nutritional consultation
   c. Motivational issues
      - Pushing athletes beyond physical limits
      - Athletes who overtrain
      - Athletes who refuse to follow program recommendations

Figure 22.1 Points of preparedness required of each staff member.

Adapted, by permission, from Taylor, 2006 (8).

> separate and distinct from the medical, dietetic, athletic training, and sport coaching fields, Certified Strength and Conditioning Specialists consult with and refer athletes to these professionals when appropriate. (p. 24)

The following sections present three hierarchical levels of strength and conditioning staff; however, in many smaller (and even moderate-sized) institutions, there may be only one or two individuals who must handle all aspects of a strength and conditioning program without the benefit or support of a staff. A high school may have one coach who oversees the weight room while sport coaches and physical education teachers run the classes. The person in charge of the weight room should be considered the director and should carry out the duties required of the head strength and conditioning professional.

Strength and Conditioning Director (Head Strength and Conditioning Professional)

A strength and conditioning director (referred to hereafter as *director*)—also commonly referred to as the head strength and conditioning professional—is both a practitioner and an administrator. This person is responsible for the overall strength and conditioning program, facility, equipment, staff, and such administrative tasks as preparing a budget, purchasing equipment, preparing proposals, and working with the school administration and media. Typically, the director is paid a salary by the institution as an athletic department staff member. Figure 22.2 shows a sample job listing for such a position (adapted from a listing in the *NCAA News*). Figure 22.3 provides a general job

STRENGTH AND CONDITIONING PROFESSIONAL JOB LISTING

Responsibilities include developing and monitoring performance training programs for athletic teams, instructing proper resistance training exercise technique and speed development, testing and evaluating physical performance, and overseeing operation and general maintenance of the performance training program as assigned by the director of athletics. A Bachelor's degree is required but a Master's degree is preferred (with emphasis in exercise science, exercise physiology, or physical education). Two years' experience is required in progressively responsible positions involving development and management of sport-specific individual and group performance training programs. Excellent communication, supervisory, and management skills are required. Position also requires the individual to hold the CSCS certification. Salary commensurate with experience.

Figure 22.2 A job announcement similar to this can be used to attract quality applicants.

description for the strength and conditioning director.

The director is also responsible for developing, presenting, and enforcing the written policies and procedures of the staff and participants in the program. He or she achieves this by having staff and student-athlete orientation meetings and by periodically evaluating the staff's professional performance. A sample form for the evaluation of student staff members is provided in figure 22.4. This form could be adapted to apply more specifically and effectively to the assistant strength and conditioning coach, the facility supervisor (if he or she is not a student), or any other professional staff position.

Assistant Strength and Conditioning Professional

The assistant strength and conditioning professional is responsible for many of the same duties as the director but is usually only *directly* responsible for a limited number of teams, not the whole program. *Strength and Conditioning Professional Standards and Guidelines* does not differentiate between head and assistant strength and conditioning professionals regarding certification. Thus, assistant strength and conditioning professionals should also achieve and maintain a professional certification (6). An assistant strength coach could have either a full- or part-time salary or, in some cases, could serve as a volunteer, depending on the size of the institution. (See figure 22.5 for a general job description.) A high school sport coach who oversees his or her team's strength training program would be considered an assistant strength and conditioning professional and therefore should follow the duties described in figure 22.5.

Facility Supervisor

The facility supervisor is usually a part-time staff member, often an exercise science student, who is responsible for observing activities within the strength and conditioning facility and cleaning and maintaining its equipment. The facility supervisor also assists the director and the assistant strength coaches when necessary. Typically, he or she is an unpaid volunteer who specifically works in the strength and conditioning facility to gain valuable experience in the field. (See figure 22.6 for a general job description.)

When combined with a well-designed policies and procedures manual, these three levels of staffing foster a learning, supportive, and cooperative work environment. The following excerpt from Epley (3) illustrates this concept:

> If you wanted to become a pilot, you would first study the rules and regulations in an official flight manual before ever getting in the cockpit of an airplane. Eventually, new pilots learn procedures to fly alongside a certified pilot. They only fly solo after the instructor believes they are ready to fly solo. This model also applies for the strength and conditioning profession. In order to maintain a standard of excellence in a program, there should be a balanced mix of student strength professionals learning the procedures from the strength and conditioning "flight manual" (i.e., the facility's Policies

RESPONSIBILITIES OF THE STRENGTH AND CONDITIONING DIRECTOR

- Direct all facets of staff, program, and facility operations.
- Design (or have final review of) all training programs.
- Oversee the athletic performance operation to ensure compliance with institutional, conference, and governing bodies' rules and regulations.
- Develop and submit the annual budget and ensure budgetary compliance through efficient financial management.
- Generate income and budget available funds for maintenance and improvement of the facility.
- Oversee the selection, installation, and maintenance of performance equipment including cleaning and repair.
- Conduct orientation meetings for student-athletes on such issues as facility rules, the value of proper training and nutrition, and the dangers of banned substances.
- Develop staff work and supervision schedules, assign duties, and evaluate performance.
- Coordinate time schedules for use of the facility by each sport team and individual student-athletes.
- Assist with on-campus recruiting activities for prospective student-athletes.
- Serve on various departmental, institutional, conference, governing body, and professional committees and task forces.
- Work and communicate with coaches in the athletic department.
- Travel with sport teams (if applicable) and provide remote-site performance training programs, including pregame warm-up.
- Maintain a performance training library for professional development.
- Achieve and maintain professional certification(s) with continuing education requirements and a code of ethics, such as the CSCS credential offered through the NSCA Certification Commission. Depending on the professional's scope of activities, responsibilities, and knowledge requirements, relevant certifications offered by other governing bodies may also be appropriate (5).
- Perform other duties and special projects as requested by supervisor.
- Perform the duties of the assistant strength and conditioning professional and facility supervisor as needed.

Figure 22.3 A sample job description for a strength and conditioning director.

Adapted from Earle, 1993 (2) and Epley, 1998 (3).

and Procedures Manual) and graduate assistants or interns working alongside the certified head strength and conditioning professional learning how to be experienced professionals. (p. 6)

The roles and responsibilities of strength and conditioning staff members should be distinct and clearly communicated.

STAFF POLICIES AND ACTIVITIES

The strength and conditioning professional—more specifically, the director—is responsible for instructing and educating assistants and supervisors about the facility's written policies and procedures. Each staff member needs to understand the strength

STUDENT STAFF EVALUATION

Evaluation of staff member: ____

For period: ___________ to ___________

The evaluation process is a method of assessing individual performance. It is an opportunity to bring to light any outstanding contributions or deficiencies among student staff members, improve individual job performance, determine appropriate personnel actions, and stimulate individual development.

Communication

Has the respect of the athletes while maintaining discipline	1	2	3	4	5	N/A
Teaches proper resistance training exercise technique	1	2	3	4	5	N/A
Has the ability to motivate athletes and elicit team unity	1	2	3	4	5	N/A
Enforces the weight room rules	1	2	3	4	5	N/A
Exhibits courtesy to athletes of both genders	1	2	3	4	5	N/A
Does not subject athletes to verbal or physical abuse	1	2	3	4	5	N/A

Assumes Responsibility and Leadership

Follows instructions	1	2	3	4	5	N/A
Is adaptable to new ideas	1	2	3	4	5	N/A
Is always trying to learn	1	2	3	4	5	N/A
Does not delegate authority without permission	1	2	3	4	5	N/A
Demonstrates a high level of integrity	1	2	3	4	5	N/A
Adjusts training activity to fit skill or age level of the athlete	1	2	3	4	5	N/A
Demonstrates good judgment	1	2	3	4	5	N/A
Demonstrates consistent attendance and promptness	1	2	3	4	5	N/A
Submits paperwork on time as requested	1	2	3	4	5	N/A
Possesses the ability to get the project done, large or small	1	2	3	4	5	N/A
Submits high-quality work	1	2	3	4	5	N/A
Possesses an appropriate appearance	1	2	3	4	5	N/A

Attitude

Functions compatibly with all staff, athletes, and other departments	1	2	3	4	5	N/A
Is trustworthy with sensitive information	1	2	3	4	5	N/A
Does not gossip about coaches, athletic trainers, or athletes	1	2	3	4	5	N/A
Strives for objectives as stated in department's role and mission statement	1	2	3	4	5	N/A

Key

1 = Significantly below performance expectations

2 = Minimally acceptable performance

3 = Meets performance expectations

4 = Exceeds performance expectations

5 = Clearly exceptional performance

Figure 22.4 This sample student staff evaluation form can be used to assess staff competencies.

From NSCA, 2008, *Essentials of Strength Training and Conditioning,* 3rd ed., T.R. Baechle and R.W. Earle (eds.), (Champaign, IL: Human Kinetics). Reprinted, by permission, from B.D. Epley, 1998, *Flight manual* (Lincoln, NE: University of Nebraska Printing).

RESPONSIBILITIES OF THE ASSISTANT STRENGTH AND CONDITIONING PROFESSIONAL

- Develop and monitor strength and conditioning programs for assigned athletic teams.
- Assist in fitness testing, computation of results, and evaluation of individual athletes.
- Teach proper resistance training exercise technique and assist in spotting when necessary.
- Assist in the general maintenance and cleaning of the facility and its equipment.
- Anticipate potential risks of injury, take measures to remove them, and, in the event of an injury, have the ability to implement emergency medical procedures.
- Assist the director with all tasks for which he or she is responsible, and manage general operation of the facility in the director's absence.
- Effectively and properly motivate athletes to achieve maximum potential in all areas of performance.
- Work and communicate with coaches in the athletic department.
- Prepare the workout sheets for assigned sports.
- Assist in the training of student assistants.
- Keep updated on current strength and conditioning research.
- Achieve and maintain professional certification(s) with continuing education requirements and a code of ethics, such as the CSCS credential offered through the NSCA Certification Commission. Depending on the professional's scope of activities, responsibilities, and knowledge requirements, relevant certifications offered by other governing bodies may also be appropriate (5).
- Perform other duties as assigned by the director.
- Perform the duties of the facility supervisor as needed.

Figure 22.5 A sample job description for an assistant strength and conditioning professional.

Adapted from Earle, 1993 (2) and Epley, 1998 (3).

and conditioning program's goals and objectives, cooperatively work with others' responsibilities and schedules, and maintain a professional code of conduct. It is the responsibility of the strength and conditioning director to ensure that staff are properly trained and prepared.

Discussed here are various policies typically established and activities typically observed in a strength and conditioning facility. This information is provided for reference only; each strength and conditioning facility is unique and may have certain characteristics that dictate the specific application of these policies and activities.

Orientation Meeting

Typically, at the beginning of the school year or sport season, an orientation meeting is held for the athletes and sport coaches before their first use of the strength and conditioning facility. At this meeting the director provides the phone numbers of the facility and staff and explains the services of the staff, the training schedule and program, facility rules, disciplinary actions, the award system, and emergency procedures.

Annual Plan

An annual plan or project list allows the strength and conditioning staff to foresee upcoming projects before it is too late to meet demands. Although such a plan can be time-consuming and difficult to keep up with, once the cycle repeats itself the plan's benefits become apparent. The following is an approach to creating the first annual plan:

- List projects in advance for all 12 months.
- Include special events and a list of "to dos" for each month.

RESPONSIBILITIES OF THE FACILITY SUPERVISOR

- Supervise the facility during assigned times.
- Enforce facility policies and rules.
- Maintain, check, and clean the facility and its equipment.
- Anticipate potential risks of injury, take measures to eliminate or reduce them, and alert participants to these risks.
- Assist in spotting and teaching proper resistance training exercise technique when necessary.
- Monitor equipment checkout.
- Assist in testing of athletes.
- Attend all required staff meetings.
- Effectively and properly motivate athletes to achieve their maximum potential in all areas of performance.
- Wear proper uniform when working in the facility.
- Make sure all the weights are in proper place when opening, throughout the day, and before closing.
- Check whether first aid kit is stocked with necessary supplies.
- Learn to teach technique of each exercise correctly.
- Make sure bars are evenly loaded and collars are securely fastened.
- In the event of an injury, be capable of implementing an emergency medical procedure.
- Be involved with professional activities (e.g., be an NSCA member).
- Perform other duties as assigned by the director and assistant strength and conditioning professional.

Figure 22.6 General job description for a facility supervisor.

Adapted from Earle, 1993 (2) and Epley, 1998 (3).

- Identify which staff member should handle which project.
- Prioritize the list.
- Discuss or cover the list with the staff.
- Review the month when it is over.
- Update the list for next year.

Budgetary Issues

When the athletic director asks for the annual strength and conditioning budget, the strength and conditioning director should be prepared to provide a complete list of new equipment that will be needed for the entire year. In some cases, it is a good idea to include a **capital outlay** category for new construction or new purchases. But more typically, only a few categories in a budget have discretionary funds that allow freedom to buy new items. Some expenses, such as facility utilities (e.g., electricity, water, heating) and custodial services, may not be the financial responsibility of the strength and conditioning department. Common categories that can be controlled are telephone, publicity or printing, postage, clerical supplies, computers, travel to professional conventions, and equipment rental. The director should make sure there is money available in the budget *before* requesting a purchase.

Staff Facility Use

The director and the assistant strength and conditioning professionals usually have full access to the facility within their professional and ethical discretion. Facility supervisors typically have access to the facility only during normal operational hours if they have been performing their duties and responsibilities to the satisfaction of the director.

Staff Workout Times

Staff members should be strongly encouraged to follow a personal resistance training and fitness program. Their training preferably occurs at a time when sport teams are not in the facility. The earlier hours of weekdays (i.e., before athletes arrive) are usually the best time for staff to work out. If an athlete is also present, the staff member is expected to help monitor the facility and provide spotting assistance when necessary. A staff member should *not* be permitted to work out when the team for which he or she is responsible is training.

Relationships With Athletes and Other Staff Members

To uphold ethics and professionalism, all staff members should refrain from having personal relationships of any type with any of the athletes or other staff members. If a relationship existed prior to an individual's becoming a staff member, a professionally objective attitude should be maintained while both parties are present in the facility. Program policies should include a clear description of acceptable coach–athlete interaction. The strength and conditioning professional may be faced with an athlete who is distressed due to personal reasons. Possible areas of concern might include family and personal relationships, drug use, sexual harassment, and academic demands. Strength and conditioning professionals should not attempt to provide counseling. They are not to give advice, but to listen to athletes, mirror what they say, and then refer them to an appropriate professional. All such incidents or meetings should be well documented (8).

Staff Professional Goals

All staff members should make a daily effort to increase their knowledge of scientific and practical applications of strength and conditioning concepts, whether through active involvement in a professional organization like the National Strength and Conditioning Association (NSCA) or an academic institution, continual personal development (attending conferences and clinics, studying professional journals, giving presentations, asking questions, etc.), or simply playing an active role in the day-to-day activities of the facility. Continuing education is a necessary part of maintaining a professional certification and reducing liability exposure, especially in the area of supervision and instruction. Litigation issues in this area often involve questions of "professional instructor qualifications," which include continuing education (6).

Posted Messages and Signs

It is helpful to have a centralized bulletin board where notices, staff messages, facility hours of operation, evacuation procedures, and other vital information can be posted. When a staff member or athlete first arrives at the strength and conditioning facility each day, he or she should check the bulletin board for new messages. Signage, including safety and usage instructions as well as warnings and notices, should be posted so as to be seen by users prior to their use of the facility (6).

Touring the Strength and Conditioning Facility

There are generally three types of outside groups that may come into the strength and conditioning facility. Large groups and the general public should not be allowed inside the facility when athletes are training. A viewing area should be provided so that visitors can see into the facility without disturbing the athletes. The second type of group is guests of the athletic director or a sport coach, who may tour the inside of the strength and conditioning facility. A path should be created to allow them to see the activity up close without interfering with the action. The third type of group comprises recruits or other special guests who receive a customized one-on-one tour.

Approved Exercises, Techniques, Spotting Guidelines, and Safety Equipment

For each exercise that is included on the sport teams' workout sheets, including plyometric, agility, and speed development drills, the director needs to inform the staff regarding how the exercise technique should be taught to athletes and also provide demonstrations and instruction. A copy of all programs designed by staff (i.e., the list of exercises to be performed) should be on file in the director's office before a team begins their program.

From a safety standpoint, spotting, in conjunction with the use of appropriate safety equipment, is critical (6). All staff members should be willing to spot when necessary. Staff should effectively communicate with the lifter to ensure safe, proper, and effective spotting (refer to chapter 14 for more information about spotting techniques).

Testing Procedures and Schedule

At the beginning of each school semester or sport season, the strength and conditioning director needs to meet with each head sport coach to determine the initial physical testing schedule and, depending on the strength and conditioning professional's background and experience, which tests to perform. It can be a challenge to figure out how to test all the athletes from the different sports, however. At the very least, the strength and conditioning staff needs to

- determine the overall testing schedule based on number of athletes and available staff;
- reserve the facility (if applicable);
- notify the athletes and coaches of the dates and times of testing;
- notify the school sports information department of dates, times, location, and so on, so that video or photos can be taken of new records or selected performers (if applicable);
- prepare the facility and equipment for testing;
- develop data collection sheets for each athlete; and
- explain to the athletes any safety tips, scoring methods for tests, traffic flow procedures, and practice opportunities.

In addition to a testing schedule, a regular training schedule for each team should be established. Ensuring that established supervision and instruction guidelines are followed (6) requires effective scheduling. Training sessions must be scheduled at specific times to ensure that recommended staff-to-athlete ratios are maintained (refer to chapter 21 for staff-to-athlete ratios) and to ensure proper management of users during peak usage times (6). A policy should be developed that designates how priority is assigned in the scheduling process. This is especially important for institutions with smaller facilities, those lacking adequate human resources, and those that have multiple facilities. A sample form to send to sport coaches to ascertain their desired training schedule is shown in figure 22.7.

Workout Sheet

The process of generating a workout sheet (sometimes called a *progress card*) is different for each strength and conditioning program. All staff members must be familiar with every exercise on each athlete's workout sheet and should not advise an athlete to perform exercises that are not listed on the workout sheet unless this has been suggested by the director or the sports medicine staff. A strong commitment to follow the recommended program is required.

Records and Awards

Providing and promoting a motivational atmosphere is critical to a successful strength and conditioning program. The strength and conditioning staff needs to develop a strategy of encouraging an athlete to optimal performance and rewarding accomplishment and outstanding effort. Some of the more obvious facets of this effort include planning the purchase of awards in advance, choosing how and when the awards will be presented, creating mini-goals and mini-awards as stepping-stones to larger goals, giving equal awards to men and women, posting new school records immediately after they are set, and having reasonable expectations of each individual athlete's abilities. Remember, an award can be motivational, but sometimes only one athlete out of the entire team is the winner, or awards may go to only a few. This type of award is acceptable if it is balanced with ways in which other athletes are rewarded. For example, a weekly newsletter that highlights performance accomplishments is a good way to motivate and reward multiple athletes for a job well done (1, 3).

Adherence to a facility's written policies and procedures is integral to the achievement of the strength and conditioning program's goals and objectives.

FACILITY ADMINISTRATION

Proper administration of the facility helps to maintain a safe and effective program—one that achieves the program's goals and objectives. The director is ultimately responsible for facility administration. Several details of facility administration are discussed here, though other administrative issues

TRAINING SCHEDULE REQUEST

Sport: ____________

Semester: ____________ Year: ____________

Number of athletes: ____________

Contact person: ________________________

Office phone: ____________ Cell phone: ____________

Weight Training Sessions

First choice

Weekday (M-F) training *days* (circle): M Tu W Th F

Weekday (M-F) training *times* for the days circled above: ____________

Weekend (Sat-Sun) training *days* (circle): Sat Sun

Weekend (Sat-Sun) training *times* for the days circled above: _________

Second choice

Weekday (M-F) training *days* (circle): M Tu W Th F

Weekday (M-F) training *times* for the days circled above: ____________

Weekend (Sat-Sun) training *days* (circle): Sat Sun

Weekend (Sat-Sun) training *times* for the days circled above: _________

Running/Conditioning Sessions

First choice

Weekday (M-F) training *days* (circle): M Tu W Th F

Weekday (M-F) training *times* for the days circled above: ____________

Weekend (Sat-Sun) training *days* (circle): Sat Sun

Weekend (Sat-Sun) training *times* for the days circled above: _________

Second choice

Weekday (M-F) training *days* (circle): M Tu W Th F

Weekday (M-F) training *times* for the days circled above: ____________

Weekend (Sat-Sun) training *days* (circle): Sat Sun

Weekend (Sat-Sun) training *times* for the days circled above: _________

Other needs or concerns:

____

____

____

Figure 22.7 The best way to satisfy the scheduling needs of all teams without conflicts in facility usage is to survey teams to determine their preferred training times.

From NSCA, 2008, *Essentials of Strength Training and Conditioning*, 3rd ed., T.R. Baechle and R.W. Earle (eds.), (Champaign, IL: Human Kinetics). Reprinted, by permission, from R.W. Earle, 1993, *Staff and facility policies and procedures manual.* (Omaha, NE: Creighton University Press), 6 (2).

are discussed in chapter 21. All these areas need to be addressed in the facility's policies and procedures manual.

Access to and Supervision of the Facility

Two key issues in facility administration are access—who should be allowed to be in the facility and when—and supervision. Here we discuss preparticipation exams, the establishment of eligibility criteria, and what to do if an ineligible person enters the facility. In all situations, it is ultimately the professional and legal responsibility of the institution to ensure that the strength and conditioning facility is supervised whenever it is occupied.

Preparticipation Requirement for Student-Athletes

Before an athlete is allowed access to the strength and conditioning facility, preparticipation screening and clearance must be required. This requirement is established under Section 1 of *Strength and Conditioning Professional Standards and Guidelines* (6). Standard 1.1 "requires athletes to undergo health care provider screening and clearance prior to participation." Procedures should be in place to ensure that documentation of screening and clearance of each athlete is on record in the main office of the strength and conditioning program before athletes are allowed to participate.

Eligibility Criteria

To focus the attention and efforts of the strength and conditioning staff on a target training population, certain eligibility requirements should be established. The following is a list of typical individuals or groups who are allowed to use the strength and conditioning facility at an institution:

- Full- or part-time student-athletes participating in an athletic department-sponsored sport
- Newly incoming and just-transferred student-athletes who have registered for school and have confirmation of team status as designated by the head sport coach
- Students in physical education classes
- All athletic department coaching and administrative staff
- All sports medicine department staff
- Alumni athletes who participated in an athletic department-sponsored sport and completed their eligibility
- Individuals and groups approved by the athletic director or strength and conditioning director

Other individuals or groups may request access to the strength and conditioning facility. These persons or groups must receive prior approval by the athletic director or strength and conditioning director and should have a prearranged schedule that specifies when they will use the facility so proper supervision can be provided. To be consistent and objective, it is advantageous to have a policy in place to refer to rather than having to decide on a case-by-case basis. This policy is especially important as it relates to the facility fee, if any. The following are examples of common criteria by which to determine whether outside organizations can use a strength and conditioning facility:

- Use must be preapproved by the athletic director.
- Use must be preapproved by the strength and conditioning director.
- The program or session must be supervised by strength and conditioning department staff.
- The program or session must be scheduled during off-hours when athletes are not present.
- The individual or organization must supply written proof of additional liability insurance.
- All participants must sign a release agreement form. Figure 22.8 shows a sample release of liability form. Check any such form for compliance with current local and national laws before it is used.
- All participants must follow the rules and regulations of the strength and conditioning facility.
- The athletic director and the strength and conditioning director have the right to limit an individual's or group's access, if warranted.

Action for an Ineligible Person

If a person who has not been approved for access is in the facility, it is the staff's duty to explain the eligibility criteria to that person. (Student facility supervisors should not attempt to deal with this situation themselves; instead, they should inform another staff member about it.) The individual should then be asked to leave the facility. If the person refuses to leave, the staff should contact the

SAMPLE RELEASE AGREEMENT FORM FOR FACILITY USE BY AN OUTSIDE INDIVIDUAL OR GROUP

(School Name)

Release Agreement

I, the undersigned, do hereby acknowledge and understand that I will be using the *(school name)* strength and conditioning facility.

I further acknowledge that I have been advised of the risks involved in the use of the strength and conditioning facility and its equipment, and I further acknowledge that I have been warned that my use of the strength and conditioning facility and its equipment could result in injury or harm to myself.

I acknowledge and assume any such risk to my person should I use the strength and conditioning facility and its equipment.

In the event that I should sustain injury to myself as a result of my use of the strength and conditioning facility and its equipment, I hereby agree to hold harmless the *(school name)*, the coaches, athletic trainers, supervisors, or any other employees.

I have read and fully understand the contents of this "hold harmless" agreement and execute same as my own voluntary act.

I agree to modify my workout to conform to the recommendations of the *(school name)* strength and conditioning staff if asked to do so, and I agree to leave the strength and conditioning facility if asked to do so by a member of the *(school name)* strength and conditioning staff.

Signature:______________________ Date:______________________

Name (printed):______________________________________

Figure 22.8 All participants must sign a liability waiver, which should be modified as needed to comply with local and national laws. Reducing liability for on-premise injuries during use of the facility is critical in any risk management strategy.

Adapted from Earle, 1993 (2) and Epley, 1998 (3).

strength and conditioning director, who should in turn discuss the situation with the individual. If the person still does not agree to leave, the campus or local authorities should be notified so that they can escort the individual from the facility.

Telephone and Music System Use

The telephone is to be used only by the strength and conditioning staff and should remain in the office unless all the staff members are on the floor, at which time it can be moved outside the office if necessary and possible. Personal calls by the staff should be kept to a minimum. Other individuals should not be allowed to use the telephone unless they receive permission from a staff member. Rules and regulations of certain governing bodies, like the National Collegiate Athletic Association, may restrict or prevent student-athletes from using departmental telephones. To answer the telephone, the staff member should answer with a friendly "Training facility; this is [staff member's name]" or "Good morning/afternoon/evening; [name of program or facility]."

The music system (and the office computer) is to be operated and used by the staff only. Typically, if only one team is present, the athletes can request particular music, but when more than one team are training simultaneously, the staff should control the music selection unless a consensus about the type of music played can be reached. Despite these guidelines, the strength and conditioning staff has the final decision in this matter. The volume should be at a reasonable level so that it does not interfere with announcements, technique instruction, and spotting communications, although with more individuals present in the facility the volume can be higher.

Facility Rules and Guidelines

Strength and conditioning facility policies and rules are important for providing participants with guidelines for conduct and behavior, keeping order, and keeping the program on course toward the goal of providing a safe, clean, and professional training environment. Refer to figure 22.9 for a list of common facility rules and policies. These should be posted in the training area where they can be easily seen.

To ensure that athletes adhere to the facility rules, the strength and conditioning director may want to require them to sign and date a copy of the facility rules and guidelines to acknowledge that they understand and will adhere to all rules prior to facility use. This process will reduce the possibility of claims that they did not know the repercussions of aberrant behavior. The facility rules need to be enforced, with possible disciplinary actions posted, documented, and levied in proportion to the offense. Following is an example of a tiered penalty system applied to a repeated violation (2). (Note that this type of policy must be established with full support and involvement of the athletic director and all sport coaches. Typically, the strength and conditioning staff does not have to pursue disciplinary actions past the first or second offense because most sport coaches want to handle the situation.)

- *First offense:* A verbal warning by a staff member, an explanation of the nature and importance of the rule or guideline that was broken, and a reminder of the disciplinary action that will result from a second offense.
- *Second offense:* Dismissal from the facility for one day, documentation of the offense by the staff member, correspondence with the athlete's sport coach, and a reminder of the disciplinary action that will result from a third offense.
- *Third offense:* Dismissal from the facility for one week, documentation of the offense by the staff member, correspondence with the athlete's sport coach, and a reminder of the disciplinary action that will result from a fourth offense.
- *Fourth offense:* Dismissal from the facility for the remainder of the year, documentation of the offense by the staff member, correspondence with the athlete's sport coach and the athletic director, and a reminder of the disciplinary action that will result from a fifth offense.
- *Fifth offense:* Permanent dismissal from the facility, documentation of the offense by the staff member, and correspondence with the athlete's sport coach and the athletic director.

Emergency Procedures

The strength and conditioning staff should try to foresee potential emergency situations, if possible. Obviously, most emergencies occur without warning, so an emergency plan needs to be in place (see chapter 21 for details on risk management). An emergency plan should list strategies for handling emergency situations; provide names, titles, and telephone numbers of important individuals to contact; and identify which rooms are lockdown rooms. All staff members should be familiar with the emergency plan so that they can respond appropriately. Also, the emergency plan should be in writing and posted for easy reference in several prominent locations in the facility. See figure 22.10 for an example of posted emergency procedures.

Every exit in the weight training facility should be marked and should be familiar to all staff members and athletes. To allow continual monitoring of who is entering and leaving the facility, there should be only one main entrance and exit. Any other exits are to be used only in an emergency or if facility occupants are so instructed by the strength and conditioning staff. Appendix G of *Strength and Conditioning Professional Standards and Guidelines* provides details on emergency care and planning (6). The appendix discusses components of emergency care and provides an emergency plan template. It is recommended that professionals consult *Strength and Conditioning Professional Standards and Guidelines* when developing an emergency plan specific to their own setting.

FACILITY RULES AND GUIDELINES

- Prior to participation, athletes must go through a preparticipation screening and clearance procedure (5).
- Prior to participation, all athletes must attend an orientation on common risks involved in resistance training, the proper execution of various exercises, and the possible consequences if proper technique is not used.
- Athletes must have a workout sheet, follow it, and record workout contents.
- If an athlete has an injury that inhibits a portion of the workout, the athlete must receive a modified program from the athletic medicine department that describes which exercises should be avoided and which ones may be substituted.
- Athletes are required to use locks on the ends of all barbells.
- No one should squat outside the squat or power rack.
- Bumper plates are required on the platforms for all power exercises.
- Athletes must not wear weight belts when the belts could contact equipment upholstery.
- Athletes should move weights from the racks to the bar only. They should never set plates on the floor or lean them against equipment or walls. Athletes should return dumbbells to the rack in the proper order. Athletes should not drop or throw weights or dumbbells.
- Athletes should show respect for equipment and facilities at all times; spitting in or defacing the facility is not tolerated and will result in immediate expulsion.
- The weight room requires concentration. Horseplay, loud or offensive language, or temper tantrums are not permitted.
- The staff offices and telephones are off limits to athletes unless permission to use them is given.
- Athletes should wear proper training attire, particularly shirts and athletic shoes, at all times.
- Athletes should use spotters for exercises that place the bar on the back or front shoulders and exercises that involve a bar or dumbbells moving over the face or above the head. Power exercises are *not* spotted.
- Athletes should immediately report any facility-related injury or facility or equipment irregularity to the supervisor on duty.
- Tobacco, food, chewing gum, glass bottles, cans, alcohol, drugs, and banned substances are not allowed in the strength and conditioning facility; plastic water bottles are acceptable.
- Supervisors are not responsible for users' personal belongings or lost or stolen items.
- Jewelry such as loose necklaces, bracelets, hanging earrings, and watches should not be worn.
- Athletes should keep feet off the walls.
- Athletes should minimize chalk and powder on the floor.
- All guests and visitors must report to the office for signing of the waiver form.
- Former athletes must have their programs preapproved by a staff supervisor and must sign a waiver form.

Figure 22.9 A list of rules and policies should be posted in the training area where it can be easily seen.

Adapted from Earle, 1993 (2); Epley, 1998 (3); and Epley, 1998 (4).

- Athletic department personnel can use these facilities for personal workouts if they do not interfere with the needs of the athletes.
- Non–athletic department personnel are allowed to use the facilities with permission of the athletic director after signing a waiver form. Recognized users may include athletes, students, guests, staff, faculty with permission, former athletes, family members, and visiting teams.
- Equipment leaving the weight room shall be checked out by the supervisor and recorded at the supervisor's desk.
- The on-duty supervisors have authority over all weight room conduct and use of equipment and may expel an athlete from the facility for failure to follow instructions.

Figure 22.9 *(continued)*

Adapted from Earle 1993 (2), Epley 1998 (3), and Epley 1998 (4).

EXAMPLE OF POSTED EMERGENCY PROCEDURES

Accidents or Injuries

Non-life-threatening situations

Step 1 Contact the athletic medicine department; if there is no answer, contact Campus Security.

Step 2 Provide all requested information.

Step 3 Follow all given instructions.

Life-threatening situations

Step 1 Call 911 or other emergency response number.

Step 2 Send someone to contact Campus Security.

Step 3 Send someone to contact the athletic medicine department.

Step 4 Do not attempt to move victim unless absolutely necessary.

Step 5 If victim is not breathing, administer CPR if you are trained.

Step 6 Stay with victim and administer any necessary first aid until help arrives.

Building Evacuation

Step 1 Follow posted evacuation corridors and move to assigned evacuation area.

Step 2 Primary and secondary plan coordinators should ensure that all individuals have been evacuated.

Step 3 Call 911 for any individuals who are disabled and cannot be evacuated.

Step 4 Primary and secondary plan coordinators should account for all individuals at the assigned evacuation area.

(CONTINUED)

Figure 22.10 Staff review of posted emergency procedures is imperative in risk management.

Adapted from Earle, 1993 (2); Epley, 1998 (3); and Taylor, 2006 (8).

FIGURE 22.10 (CONTINUED)

Fire

Step 1 If smoke or flame is detected, activate fire alarm.

Step 2 Evacuate building through emergency fire doors.

Step 3 Contact Campus Security.

Tornado

Under "Watch" conditions

Step 1 Understand that conditions are such that a tornado could develop.

Step 2 Turn off any recorded music, and turn on the radio to monitor weather.

Under "Warning" conditions

Step 1 Understand that a tornado has been sighted or detected by radar; the local civil defense sirens will sound.

Step 2 Guide athletes to seek shelter in locker rooms or corridors as directed by Campus Security or an Athletic Department staff member.

Step 3 Remain in the shelter until an all-clear signal is given.

Crime in Progress

Step 1 If you observe a suspicious person or activity, contact Campus Security.

Step 2 If possible, give a complete description of the person or activity.

Step 3 Do not attempt to foil the suspicious activity or crime.

Important Telephone Numbers

Emergency: ______________________

Campus Security: ______________________

Athletic medicine department: ______________

Athletic department: ____________________

Student health center: __________________

Team physician: ______________________

Figure 22.10 *(continued)*

Adapted from Earle, 1993 (2); Epley, 1998 (3); and Taylor, 2006 (8).

Emergency plans should be rehearsed and discussed on a regular basis to ensure the safety of strength and conditioning staff members and all users of the strength and conditioning facility.

Building Evacuation Plan

A building evacuation plan should be developed. This plan should be readily available, should be posted or kept in several conspicuous places, should include emergency escape route maps, and should be reviewed annually by department personnel. In the event of an evacuation, an area away from the facility should be designated where the staff and student-athletes are to gather. The primary and secondary plan coordinators are responsible for accounting for all employees and student-athletes after an emergency evacuation has been completed. If individuals in the area need assistance for evacuation and the assistance cannot easily be provided due to the nature of the situation, activate the emergency medical system by calling the emergency response number (e.g., 911 in the United States) (8).

Accidents and Injuries

It is the staff's duty to promote a safe and accident-free environment. If an accident does occur, it is important to notify the strength and conditioning director, the sports medicine department, and campus security (if applicable), depending on the situation. If there is any question about the severity of the injury, staff should not hesitate to activate the emergency medical system by calling the emergency response number. The strength and conditioning staff must fill out an injury report form whenever an accident occurs in the facility.

Fire

In the case of a small, contained fire, staff should be familiar with the location of the fire extinguisher and use it to try to put out the fire. If extinguishing the fire is unsuccessful or in the case of a larger, unconfined fire, staff should pull the fire alarm and warn others in the building. A building evacuation plan should be followed. It is the strength and conditioning staff's responsibility to make sure that all facility occupants escape safely. At least one strength and conditioning staff member must stay at the scene to answer any questions that the fire department might have.

Tornadoes and Severe Weather

In the event of a tornado or severe weather, safety is the most important concern of the strength and conditioning staff. It is important that no athlete or staff member leave the facility during severe weather. It is the staff's responsibility, with direction from campus security, to determine what to do and where to go during severe weather.

First Aid Kit

Everyone in the weight training facility should know the location of the first aid kit. It should be kept in the office and should be opened only by a staff member. It is the strength and conditioning staff's responsibility to ensure that the first aid kit has all materials necessary to deal with all types of injuries. The staff should make routine checks of the first aid kit to ensure that it contains all necessary supplies.

CONCLUSION

Program goals give a strength and conditioning program direction and purpose, and program objectives help keep the program on task by providing steps toward these goals. Based on goals and objectives, policies and procedures are developed to guide participant and staff conduct and to ensure a safe training environment. Strength and conditioning professionals have a variety of responsibilities in the day-to-day operation of a strength and conditioning facility. Those duties are specific to their hierarchical position and are critical to the effectiveness of the program. To provide direction to athletes and strength and conditioning staff, each facility should have its own unique policies and procedures manual, with guidelines included for each topic covered in this chapter.

KEY TERMS

capital outlay 577
policies 570
procedures 570
program goals 570
program objectives 571

STUDY QUESTIONS

1. The primary goals of a strength and conditioning program are to
   a. lower the potential for injury and improve performance.
   b. produce winning teams and develop an individual's potential.
   c. attract recruits and improve participation.
   d. improve quickness and flexibility.

2. Of the following people, who is MOST responsible for determining the equipment needs for a strength and conditioning facility?
   a. strength and conditioning director
   b. assistant strength and conditioning professional
   c. facility supervisor
   d. individual sport coach

3. Which of the following should be required of the assistant strength and conditioning professional?
   a. certification
   b. responsibility for all of the sport teams
   c. budget preparation
   d. staff supervision

4. When deciding which nonuniversity individuals and groups can use the university strength and conditioning facility, which of the following individuals should provide approval?
   I. team doctor
   II. athletic director
   III. athletic trainer
   IV. strength and conditioning director
   a. I and III only
   b. I and IV only
   c. II and III only
   d. II and IV only

5. For the third day in a row, a member of the crew team has worn sandals to the strength and conditioning facility to work out. He has been reminded of the guidelines in response to each of the previous two incidents. What are examples of appropriate actions for the strength and conditioning director to take at this time?
   I. permanent dismissal from the facility
   II. documentation of the offense
   III. explanation of the importance of wearing proper footwear
   IV. dismissal from the facility for one week
   a. I and III only
   b. III and IV only
   c. I, II, and III only
   d. II, III, and IV only

Answers to Study Questions

Chapter 1

1. a, 2. b, 3. a, 4. c, 5. b, 6. b, 7. b

Chapter 2

1. d, 2. b, 3. a, 4. c, 5. a, 6. c, 7. b, 8. a

Chapter 3

1. d, 2. a, 3. b, 4. b, 5. d, 6. a

Chapter 4

1. b, 2. c, 3. d, 4. a, 5. a, 6. c

Chapter 5

1. b, 2. a, 3. a, 4. a, 5. a, 6. d

Chapter 6

1. d, 2. d, 3. d, 4. a, 5. c, 6. c

Chapter 7

1. c, 2. c, 3. d, 4. a, 5. c, 6. c, 7. d, 8. b

Chapter 8

1. b, 2. a, 3. a, 4. d, 5. c, 6. b, 7. b

Chapter 9

1. c, 2. d, 3. a, 4. b, 5. b

Chapter 10

1. b, 2. b, 3. c, 4. c, 5. c, 6. c

Chapter 11

1. a, 2. c, 3. b, 4. d, 5. b

Chapter 12

1. b, 2. c, 3. c, 4. c, 5. c, 6. d, 7. b

Chapter 13

1. d, 2. c, 3. a, 4. c, 5. a

Chapter 14

1. d, 2. b, 3. b, 4. b, 5. b

Chapter 15

1. a, 2. a, 3. c, 4. b, 5. c, 6. a, 7. d

Chapter 16

1. d, 2. b, 3. a, 4. d, 5. c, 6. c, 7. a

Chapter 17

1. b, 2. d, 3. a, 4. b, 5. d, 6. c, 7. d

Chapter 18

1. c, 2. a, 3. b, 4. c, 5. d

Chapter 19

1. b, 2. a, 3. c, 4. a, 5. a

Chapter 20

1. c, 2. b, 3. b, 4. a, 5. a, 6. d

Chapter 21

1. a, 2. c, 3. c, 4. a, 5. d, 6. c, 7. c, 8. c

Chapter 22

1. a, 2. a, 3. b, 4. d, 5. d

References

Chapter 1 Structure and Function of the Muscular, Neuromuscular, Cardiovascular, and Respiratory Systems

1. Beck, K.C., and B.D. Johnson. Pulmonary adaptations to dynamic exercise. In: *American College of Sports Medicine Resource Manual for Guidelines for Exercise Testing and Prescription,* 3rd ed., J.L. Roitman, ed. Baltimore: Williams & Wilkins. 1998. pp. 305-313.
2. Bergman, R.A., and A.K. Afifi. *Atlas of Microscopic Anatomy.* Philadelphia: Saunders. 1974.
3. Billeter, R., and H. Hoppeler. Muscular basis of strength. In: *Strength and Power in Sport,* P.V. Komi, ed. Boston: Blackwell Scientific. 1992. pp. 39-63.
4. Castro, M.J., D.F. Apple Jr., R.S. Staron, G.E.R. Campos, and G.A. Dudley. Influence of complete spinal cord injury on skeletal muscle within six months of injury. *J Appl Physiol* 86:350-358. 1999.
5. Castro, M.J., J.A. Kent-Braun, A.V. Ng, R.G. Miller, and G.A. Dudley. Fiber-type specific Ca^{2+} actomyosin ATPase activity in multiple sclerosis. *Muscle Nerve* 21:547-549. 1998.
6. Dudley, G.A., J. Czerkawski, A. Meinrod, G. Gillis, A. Baldwin, and M. Scarpone. Efficacy of naproxen sodium for exercise-induced dysfunction, muscle injury and soreness. *Clin J Sport Med* 7:3-10. 1997.
7. Dudley, G.A., R.T. Harris, M.R. Duvoisin, B.M. Hather, and P. Buchanan. Effect of voluntary versus artificial activation on the relation of muscle torque to speed. *J Appl Physiol* 69:2215-2221. 1990.
8. Durstine, J.L., and P.G. Davis. Specificity of exercise training and testing. In: *American College of Sports Medicine Resource Manual for Guidelines for Exercise Testing and Prescription,* 3rd ed., J.L. Roitman, ed. Baltimore: Williams & Wilkins. 1998. pp. 472-479.
9. Guyton, A.C., and J.E. Hall. *Textbook of Medical Physiology,* 10th ed. Philadelphia: Saunders. 2000.
10. Harris, R.T., and G.A. Dudley. Factors limiting force during slow, shortening muscle actions in vivo. *Acta Physiol Scand* 152:63-71. 1994.
11. Hather, B.M., P.A. Tesch, P. Buchanan, and G.A. Dudley. Influence of eccentric actions on skeletal muscle adaptations to resistance. *Acta Physiol Scand* 143:177-185. 1991.
12. Hunter, G.R., M.M. Bamman, D.E. Larson-Meyer, D.R. Joanisse, J.P. McCarthy, T.E. Blaudeau, and B.R. Newcomer. Inverse relationship between exercise economy and oxidative capacity in muscle. *Eur J Appl Physiol* 94:558-568. 2005.
13. Hunter, G.R., and M.I. Culpepper. Joint angle specificity of fixed mass versus hydraulic resistance knee flexion training. *J Strength Cond Res* 9(1):13-16. 1995.
14. Hunter, G.R., and M.I. Culpepper. Knee extension torque joint position relationships following isotonic fixed resistance and hydraulic resistance training. *Athl Training* 23(1):16-20. 1988.
15. Hunter, G.R., J.P. McCarthy, and M.M. Bamman. Effects of resistance training on older adults. *Sports Medicine* 34(5):329-348. 2003.
16. Hunter, G.R., B.R. Newcomer, R.L. Weinsier, D.L. Karapondo, D.E. Larson-Meyer, D.R. Joanisse, and M.M. Bamman. Age is independently related to muscle metabolic capacity in premenopausal women. *J Appl Physiol* 93:70-76. 2002.
17. Kent-Braun, J.A., A.V. Ng, M.J. Castro, M.W. Weiner, G.A. Dudley, and R.G. Miller. Strength, skeletal muscle size and enzyme activity in multiple sclerosis. *J Appl Physiol* 83:1998-2004. 1997.
18. Klug, G.A., and G.F. Tibbits. The effect of activity on calcium mediated events in striated muscle. In: *Exercise and Sport Science Reviews,* vol. 16, K.B. Pandolf, ed. New York: Macmillan. 1988. pp. 1-60.
19. Kovaleski, J.E., R.H. Heitman, T.L. Trundle, and W.F. Gilley. Isometric preload versus isokinetic knee extension resistance training. *Med Sci Sports Exerc* 27(6):895-899. 1995.
20. Larry, J.A., and S.F. Schaal. Normal electrocardiograms. In: *American College of Sports Medicine Resource Manual for Guidelines for Exercise Testing and Prescription,* 3rd ed., J.L. Roitman, ed. Baltimore: Williams & Wilkins. 1998. pp. 397-401.
21. Mahler, D.A. Respiratory anatomy. In: *American College of Sports Medicine Resource Manual for Guidelines for Exercise Testing and Prescription,* 3rd ed., J.L. Roitman, ed. Baltimore: Williams & Wilkins. 1998. pp. 70-77.
22. McArdle, W.D., F.I. Katch, and V.I. Katch. *Exercise Physiology,* 6th ed. Philadelphia: Williams & Wilkins. 2007.
23. McComas, A.J. *Skeletal Muscle: Form and Function.* Champaign, IL: Human Kinetics. 1996.
24. Murray, T.D., and J.M. Murray. Cardiovascular anatomy. In: *American College of Sports Medicine Resource Manual for Guidelines for Exercise Testing and Prescription,* 3rd ed., J.L. Roitman, ed. Baltimore: Williams & Wilkins. 1998. pp. 61-69.
25. Ploutz, L.L., R.L. Biro, P.A. Tesch, and G.A. Dudley. Effect of resistance training on muscle mass involvement in exercise. *J Appl Physiol* 76:1675-1681. 1994.
26. Smerdu, V., I. Karsch-Mizrachi, M. Campione, L. Leinwand, and S. Schiaffino. Type IIx myosin heavy chain transcripts are expressed in type IIb fibers of human skeletal muscle. *J Appl Physiol* 267(6 Pt 1):C1723-1728. 1994.
27. Stone, M., and H. O'Bryant. *Weight Training: A Scientific Approach.* Minneapolis: Burgess International. 1987.
28. Witherspoon, J.D. *Human Physiology.* New York: Harper & Row. 1984.

Chapter 2 Bioenergetics of Exercise and Training

1. Ahlborg, G., and P. Felig. Influence of glucose ingestion on the fuel-hormone response during prolonged exercise. *J Appl Physiol* 41:683-688. 1967.
2. Ahlborg, G., and P. Felig. Lactate and glucose exchange across the forearm, legs and splanchnic bed during and after prolonged leg exercise. *J Clin Invest* 69:45-54. 1982.
3. Åstrand, P., K. Rodahl, H.A. Dahl, and S.B. Strømme. *Textbook of Work Physiology,* 4th ed. Champaign, IL: Human Kinetics. 2003.
4. Barany, M., and C. Arus. Lactic acid production in intact muscle, as followed by ^{13}C and ^{1}H nuclear magnetic resonance. In: *Human Muscle Power,* N.L. Jones, N. McCartney, and A.J. McComas, eds. Champaign, IL: Human Kinetics. 1990. pp. 153-164.
5. Barnard, R.J., V.R. Edgerton, T. Furakawa, and J.B. Peter. Histochemical, biochemical and contractile properties of red, white and intermediate fibers. *Am J Physiol* 220:410-441. 1971.
6. Berg, W.E. Individual differences in respiratory gas exchange during recovery from moderate exercise. *Am J Physiol* 149:507-530. 1947.
7. Boobis, I., C. Williams, and S.N. Wooten. Influence of sprint training on muscle metabolism during brief maximal exercise in man. *J Physiol* 342:36P-37P. 1983.
8. Bridges, C.R., B.J. Clark, III, R.L. Hammond, and L.W. Stephenson. Skeletal muscle bioenergetics during frequency-dependent fatigue. *Am J Physiol* 29:C643-C651. 1991.
9. Brooks, G.A. Amino acid and protein metabolism during exercise and recovery. *Med Sci Sports Exerc* 19:S150-S156. 1987.
10. Brooks, G.A. The lactate shuttle during exercise and recovery. *Med Sci Sports Exerc* 18:360-368. 1986.
11. Brooks, G.A., K.E. Brauner, and R.G. Cassens. Glycogen synthesis and metabolism of lactic acid after exercise. *Am J Physiol* 224:1162-1186. 1973.

12. Brooks, G.A., T.D. Fahey, and K.M. Baldwin. *Exercise Physiology: Human Bioenergetics and Its Application,* 4th ed. New York: McGraw-Hill. 2005.
13. Burgomaster, K.A., G.J.F. Heigenhauser, and M.J. Gibala. Effect of short-term sprint interval training on human skeletal muscle carbohydrate metabolism during exercise and time-trial performance. *J Appl Physiol* 100:2041-2047. 2006.
14. Burgomaster, K.A., S.C. Hughes, G.J.F. Heigenhauser, S.N. Bradwell, and M.J. Gibala. Six sessions of sprint interval training increases muscle oxidative potential and cycle endurance capacity in humans. *J Appl Physiol* 98:1985-1990. 2005.
15. Carling, D. AMP-activated protein kinase: Balancing the scales. *Biochimie* 87(1):87-91. 2005.
16. Cerretelli, P., G. Ambrosoli, and M. Fumagalli. Anaerobic recovery in man. *Eur J Appl Physiol* 34:141-148. 1975.
17. Cerretelli, P., D. Rennie, and D. Pendergast. Kinetics of metabolic transients during exercise. *Int J Sports Med* 55:178-180. 1980.
18. Christensen, E.H., R. Hedman, and B. Saltin. Intermittent and continuous running. (A further contribution to the physiology of intermittent work.) *Acta Physiol Scand* 50:269-286. 1960.
19. Coggan, A.R., and E.F. Coyle. Reversal of fatigue during prolonged exercise by carbohydrate infusion or ingestion. *J Appl Physiol* 63:2388-2395. 1987.
20. Constable, S.H., R.J. Favier, J.A. McLane, R.D. Feil, and M. Chen. Energy metabolism in contracting rat skeletal muscle: Adaptation to exercise training. *Am J Physiol* 253:316-322. 1987.
21. Constantin-Teodosiu, D., P.L. Greenhaff, D.B. McIntyre, J.M. Round, and D.A. Jones. Anaerobic energy production in human skeletal muscle in intense contraction: A comparison of 31P magnetic resonance spectroscopy and biochemical techniques. *Exp Physiol* 82:593-601. 1997.
22. Coyle, E.F., J.M. Hagberg, B.F. Hurley, W.H. Martin, III, A.A. Ehsani, and J.O. Holloszy. Carbohydrate feeding during prolonged strenuous exercise can delay fatigue. *J Appl Physiol* 55:230-235. 1983.
23. Craig, B.W., J. Lucas, R. Pohlman, and H. Stelling. The effects of running, weightlifting and a combination of both on growth hormone release. *J Appl Sport Sci Res* 5(4):198-203. 1991.
24. Cramer, J.T. Creatine supplementation in endurance sports. In: *Essentials of Creatine in Sports,* J. Stout, J. Antonio, and D. Kalman, eds. New York: Springer. 2007.
25. Creer, A.R., M.D. Ricard, R.K. Conlee, G.L. Hoyt, and A.C. Parcell. Neural, metabolic, and performance adaptations to four weeks of high intensity sprint-interval training in trained cyclists. *Int J Sports Med* 25:92-98. 2004.
26. Davis, J.A., M.H. Frank, B.J. Whipp, and K. Wasserman. Anaerobic threshold alterations caused by endurance training in middle-aged men. *J Appl Physiol* 46:1039-1046. 1979.
27. diPrampero, P.E., L. Peeters, and R. Margaria. Alactic O_2 debt and lactic acid production after exhausting exercise in man. *J Appl Physiol* 34:628-632. 1973.
28. Dohm, G.L., R.T. Williams, G.J. Kasperek, and R.J. VanRij. Increased excretion of urea and N-methylhistidine by rats and humans after a bout of exercise. *J Appl Physiol* 52:27-33. 1982.
29. Donovan, C.M., and G.A. Brooks. Endurance training affects lactate clearance, not lactate production. *Am J Physiol* 244:E83-E92. 1983.
30. Dudley, G.A., and R. Djamil. Incompatibility of endurance- and strength-training modes of exercise. *J Appl Physiol* 59(5):1446-1451. 1985.
31. Dudley, G.A., and T.F. Murray. Energy for sport. *NSCA J* 3(3):14-15. 1982.
32. Dudley, G.A., and R. Terjung. Influence of aerobic metabolism on IMP accumulation in fast-twitch muscle. *Am J Physiol* 248:C37-C42. 1985.
33. DuFax, B., G. Assmann, and W. Hollman. Plasma lipoproteins and physical activity: A review. *Int J Sports Med* 3:123-136. 1982.
34. Edington, D.E., and V.R. Edgerton. *The Biology of Physical Activity.* Boston: Houghton Mifflin. 1976.
35. Ericksson, B.O., P.D. Gollnick, and B. Saltin. Muscle metabolism and enzyme activities after training in boys 11-13 years old. *Acta Physiol Scand* 87:485-497. 1973.
36. Essen, B. Glycogen depletion of different fiber types in man during intermittent and continuous exercise. *Acta Physiol Scand* 103:446-455. 1978.
37. Fabiato, A., and F. Fabiato. Effects of pH on the myofilaments and sarcoplasmic reticulum of skinned cells from cardiac and skeletal muscle. *J Physiol* 276:233-255. 1978.
38. Farrel, P.A., J.H. Wilmore, E.F. Coyle, J.E. Billing, and D.L. Costill. Plasma lactate accumulation and distance running performance. *Med Sci Sports* 11(4):338-344. 1979.
39. Fleck, S.J., and W.J. Kraemer. *Designing Resistance Training Programs,* 3rd ed. Champaign, IL: Human Kinetics. 2003.
40. Freund, H., and P. Gendry. Lactate kinetics after short strenuous exercise in man. *Eur J Appl Physiol* 39:123-135. 1978.
41. Friedman, J.E., P.D. Neufer, and L.G. Dohm. Regulation of glycogen synthesis following exercise. *Sports Med* 11(4):232-243. 1991.
42. Fuchs, F., Y. Reddy, and F.N. Briggs. The interaction of cations with calcium binding site of troponin. *Biochim Biophys Acta* 221:407-409. 1970.
43. Ganong, W.F. *Review of Medical Physiology,* 22nd ed. New York: McGraw-Hill Medical. 2005.
44. Garrett, R.H., and C.M. Grisham. *Biochemistry,* 2nd ed. Fort Worth: Saunders College Publishing. 1999.
45. Gastin, P.B. Energy system interaction and relative contribution during maximal exercise. *Sports Med* 31(10):725-741. 2001.
46. Gibala, M.J., J.P. Little, M.V. Essen, G.P. Wilkin, K.A. Burgomaster, A. Safdar, S. Raha, and M.A. Tarnopolsky. Short-term sprint interval versus traditional endurance training: Similar initial adaptations in human skeletal muscle and exercise performance. *J Physiol* 575:901-911. 2006.
47. Gollnick, P.D., R.B. Armstrong, B. Saltin, W. Saubert, and W.L. Sembrowich. Effect of training on enzyme activity and fiber composition of human muscle. *J Appl Physiol* 34:107-111. 1973.
48. Gollnick, P.D., R.B. Armstrong, W. Saubert, K. Piel, and B. Saltin. Enzyme activity and fibre composition in skeletal muscle of untrained and trained men. *J Appl Physiol* 33:312-319. 1972.
49. Gollnick, P.D., and W.M. Bayly. Biochemical training adaptations and maximal power. In: *Human Muscle Power,* N.L. Jones, N. McCartney, and A.J. McComas, eds. Champaign, IL: Human Kinetics. 1986. pp. 255-267.
50. Gollnick, P.D., W.M. Bayly, and D.R. Hodgson. Exercise intensity, training diet and lactate concentration in muscle and blood. *Med Sci Sports Exerc* 18:334-340. 1986.
51. Gollnick, P.D., and L. Hermansen. Significance of skeletal muscle oxidative enzyme enhancement with endurance training. *Clin Physiol* 2:1-12. 1982.
52. Graham, T.E., J.W.E. Rush, and D.A. MacLean. Skeletal muscle amino acid metabolism and ammonia production during exercise. In: *Exercise Metabolism,* M. Hargreaves, ed. Champaign, IL: Human Kinetics. 2006. pp. 41-72.
53. Grassi, B. Delayed metabolic activation of oxidative phosphorylation in skeletal muscle at exercise onset. *Med Sci Sports Exerc* 37(9):1567-1573. 2005.
54. Hadmann, R. The available glycogen in man and the connection between rate of oxygen intake and carbohydrate usage. *Acta Physiol Scand* 40:305-330. 1957.
55. Harris, R.C., R.H.T. Edwards, E. Hultman, L.O. Nordesjo, B. Nylind, and K. Sahlin. The time course of phosphocreatinine resynthesis during recovery of the quadriceps muscle in man. *Pflugers Arch* 97:392-397. 1976.
56. Henry, F.M. Aerobic oxygen consumption and alactic debt in muscular work. *J Appl Physiol* 3:427-450. 1957.
57. Hermansen, L. Effect of metabolic changes on force generation in skeletal muscle during maximal exercise. In: *Human Muscle Fatigue,* R. Porter and J. Whelan, eds. London: Pittman Medical. 1981.
58. Hermansen, L., and I. Stenvold. Production and removal of lactate in man. *Acta Physiol Scand* 86:191-201. 1972.
59. Hickson, R.C. Interference of strength development by simultaneously training for strength and endurance. *Eur J Appl Physiol* 215:255-263. 1980.

60. Hickson, R.C., B.A. Dvorak, E.M. Gorostiaga, T.T. Kurowski, and C. Foster. Potential for strength and endurance training to amplify endurance performance. *J Appl Physiol* 65(5):2285-2290. 1988.
61. Hickson, R.C., M.A. Rosenkoetter, and M.M. Brown. Strength training effects on aerobic power and short-term endurance. *Med Sci Sports Exerc* 12:336-339. 1980.
62. Hill, A.V. Muscular exercise, lactic acid and the supply and utilization of oxygen. *Proc Roy Soc Lond (Biol)* 96:438. 1924.
63. Hirvonen, J., S. Ruhunen, H. Rusko, and M. Harkonen. Breakdown of high-energy phosphate compounds and lactate accumulation during short submaximal exercise. *Eur J Appl Physiol* 56:253-259. 1987.
64. Housh, T.J., D.J. Housh, and H.A. deVries. *Applied Exercise and Sport Physiology,* 2nd ed. Scottsdale, AZ: Holcomb Hathaway. 2006.
65. Hultman, E., and H. Sjoholm. Biochemical causes of fatigue. In: *Human Muscle Power,* N.L. Jones, N. McCartney, and A.J. McComas, eds. Champaign, IL: Human Kinetics. 1986. pp. 215-235.
66. Hultsmann, W.C. On the regulation of the supply of substrates for muscular activity. *Bibl Nutr Diet* 27:11-15. 1979.
67. Hurley, B.F., D.R. Seals, J.M. Hagberg, A.C. Goldberg, S.M. Ostrove, J.O. Holloszy, W.G. Wiest, and A.P. Goldberg. Strength training and lipoprotein lipid profiles: Increased HDL cholesterol in body builders versus powerlifters and effects of androgen use. *JAMA* 252:507-513. 1984.
68. Jacobs, I. Blood lactate: Implications for training and sports performance. *Sports Med* 3:10-25. 1986.
69. Jacobs, I., P. Kaiser, and P. Tesch. Muscle strength and fatigue after selective glycogen depletion in human skeletal muscle fibers. *Eur J Appl Physiol* 46:47-53. 1981.
70. Jacobs, I., P.A. Tesch, O. Bar-Or, J. Karlsson, and R. Dotow. Lactate in human skeletal muscle after 10 and 30 s of supramaximal exercise. *J Appl Physiol* 55:365-367. 1983.
71. Jones, N., and R. Ehrsam. The anaerobic threshold. In: *Exercise and Sport Sciences Review,* vol. 10, R.L. Terjung, ed. Philadelphia: Franklin Press. 1982. pp. 49-83.
72. Juel, C. Intracellular pH recovery and lactate efflux in mouse soleus muscles stimulated in vitro: The involvement of sodium/proton exchange and a lactate carrier. *Acta Physiol Scand* 132:363-371. 1988.
73. Karatzaferi, C., A. de Haan, R. Ferguson, W. van Mechelen, and A. Sargeant. Phosphocreatine and ATP content in human single muscle fibers before and after maximum dynamic exercise. *Pflugers Arch* 442:467-474. 2001.
74. Karlsson, J. Lactate and phosphagen concentrations in working muscle of man. *Acta Physiol Scand* 485:358-365. 1971.
75. Karlsson, J., L.O. Nordesjo, L. Jorfeldt, and B. Saltin. Muscle lactate, ATP and CP levels during exercise and after physical training in man. *J Appl Physiol* 33(2):194-203. 1972.
76. Kindermann, W., G. Simon, and J. Keul. The significance of the aerobic-anaerobic transition for the determination of work load intensities during endurance training. *Eur J Appl Physiol* 42:25-34. 1979.
77. Knuttgen, H.G., and P.V. Komi. Basic definitions for exercise. In: *Strength and Power in Sport,* P.V. Komi, ed. Oxford: Blackwell Scientific. 1992. pp. 3-8.
78. Lambert, C.P., M.G. Flynn, J.B. Boone, T.J. Michaud, and J. Rodriguez-Zayas. Effects of carbohydrate feeding on multiple-bout resistance exercise. *J Appl Sport Sci Res* 5(4):192-197. 1991.
79. Lehmann, M., and J. Keul. Free plasma catecholamines, heart rates, lactate levels, and oxygen uptake in competition weightlifters, cyclists, and untrained control subjects. *Int J Sports Med* 7:18-21. 1986.
80. Lemon, P.W., and J.P. Mullin. Effect of initial muscle glycogen levels on protein catabolism during exercise. *J Appl Physiol Respir Env Exerc Physiol* 48:624-629. 1980.
81. MacDougall, J.D. Morphological changes in human skeletal muscle following strength training and immobilization. In: *Human Muscle Power,* N.L. Jones, N. McCartney, and A.J. McComas, eds. Champaign, IL: Human Kinetics. 1986. pp. 269-288.
82. MacDougall, J.D., G.R. Ward, D.G. Sale, and J.R. Sutton. Biochemical adaptations of human skeletal muscle to heavy resistance training and immobilization. *J Appl Physiol* 43:700-703. 1977.
83. Mainwood, G., and J. Renaud. The effect of acid-base on fatigue of skeletal muscle. *Can J Physiol Pharmacol* 63:403-416. 1985.
84. Mazzeo, R.S., G.A. Brooks, D.A. Schoeller, and T.F. Budinger. Disposal of blood [1-13C] lactate in humans during rest and exercise. *J Appl Physiol* 60(10):232-241. 1986.
85. McArdle, W.D., F.I. Katch, and V.L. Katch. *Exercise Physiology: Energy, Nutrition, and Human Performance,* 6th ed. Philadelphia: Lippincott, Williams & Wilkins. 2007.
86. McCartney, N., L.L. Spriet, G.J.F. Heigenhauser, J.M. Kowalchuk, J.R. Sutton, and N.L. Jones. Muscle power and metabolism in maximal intermittent exercise. *J Appl Physiol* 60:1164-1169. 1986.
87. Medboe, J.I., and S. Burgers. Effect of training on the anaerobic capacity. *Med Sci Sports Exerc* 22(4):501-507. 1991.
88. Meyer, R.A., and R.L. Terjung. Differences in ammonia and adenylate metabolism in contracting fast and slow muscle. *Am J Physiol* 237: C111-C118. 1979.
89. Nakamura, Y., and A. Schwartz. The influence of hydrogen ion concentration on calcium binding and release by skeletal muscle sarcoplasmic reticulum. *J Gen Physiol* 59:22-32. 1972.
90. Opie, L.J., and E.A. Newsholme. The activities of fructose-1,6-diphosphate, phosphofructokinase, and phosphoenolpyruvate carboxykinase in white and red muscle. *Biochem J* 103:391-399. 1967.
91. Pike, R.L., and M. Brown. *Nutrition: An Integrated Approach,* 2nd ed. New York: Wiley. 1984.
92. Poortmans, J.R. Protein turnover and amino acid oxidation during and after exercise. *Med Sports Sci* 17:130-147. 1984.
93. Robergs, R.A., F. Ghiasvand, and D. Parker. Biochemistry of exercise-induced metabolic acidosis. *Am J Physiol Regul Integr Comp Physiol* 287:R502-R516. 2004.
94. Robergs, R.A., D.R. Pearson, D.L. Costill, W.J. Fink, D.D. Pascoe, M.A. Benedict, C.P. Lambert, and J.J. Zachweija. Muscle glycogenolysis during differing intensities of weight-resistance exercise. *J Appl Physiol* 70(4):1700-1706. 1991.
95. Roberts, A.D., R. Billeter, and H. Howald. Anaerobic muscle enzyme changes after interval training. *Int J Sports Med* 3:18-21. 1982.
96. Rozenek, R., L. Rosenau, P. Rosenau, and M.H. Stone. The effect of intensity on heart rate and blood lactate response to resistance exercise. *J Strength Cond Res* 7(1):51-54. 1993.
97. Sahlin, K., M. Tonkonogy, and K. Soderlund. Energy supply and muscle fatigue in humans. *Acta Physiol Scand* 162:261-266. 1998.
98. Saltin, B., and P.D. Gollnick. Skeletal muscle adaptability: Significance for metabolism and performance. In: *Handbook of Physiology,* L.D. Peachey, R.H. Adrian, and S.R. Geiger, eds. Baltimore: Williams & Wilkins. 1983. pp. 540-555.
99. Saltin, B., and J. Karlsson. Muscle glycogen utilization during work of different intensities. In: *Muscle Metabolism During Exercise,* B. Pernow and B. Saltin, eds. New York: Plenum Press. 1971. pp. 289-300.
100. Sant'Ana Pereira, J.A., A.J. Sargeant, A.C. Rademaker, A. de Haan, and W. van Mechelen. Myosin heavy chain isoform expression and high energy phosphate content in human muscle fibres at rest and post-exercise. *J Physiol* 496(Pt 2):583-588. 1996.
101. Scala, D., J. McMillan, D. Blessing, R. Rozenek, and M.H. Stone. Metabolic cost of a preparatory phase of training in weightlifting: A practical observation. *J Appl Sport Sci Res* 1(3):48-52. 1987.
102. Sherman, W.M., and G.S. Wimer. Insufficient carbohydrate during training: Does it impair performance? *Sports Nutr* 1(1):28-44. 1991.
103. Sjodin, B., and I. Jacobs. Onset of blood lactate accumulation and marathon running performance. *Int J Sports Med* 2:23-26. 1981.
104. Smith, S.A., S.J. Montain, R.P. Matott, G.P. Zientara, F.A. Jolesz, and R.A. Fielding. Creatine supplementation and age influence muscle metabolism during exercise. *J Appl Physiol* 85:1349-1356. 1998.
105. Stainsby, W.M., and J.K. Barclay. Exercise metabolism: O_2 deficit, steady level O_2 uptake and O_2 uptake in recovery. *Med Sci Sports* 2:177-195. 1970.

106. Sugden, P.H., and E.A. Newsholme. The effects of ammonium, inorganic phosphate and potassium ions on the activity of phosphofructokinase from muscle and nervous tissues of vertebrates and invertebrates. *Biochem J* 150:113-122. 1975.
107. Sutton, J. Hormonal and metabolic responses to exercise in subjects of high and low work capacities. *Med Sci Sports* 10:1-6. 1978.
108. Tanaka, K., Y. Matsuura, S. Kumagai, A. Matsuzuka, K. Hirakoba, and K. Asano. Relationships of anaerobic threshold and onset of blood lactate accumulation with endurance performance. *Eur J Appl Physiol* 52:51-56. 1983.
109. Taylor, D.J., P. Styles, P.M. Matthews, D.A. Arnold, D.G. Gadian, P. Bore, and G.K. Radda. Energetics of human muscle: Exercise-induced ATP depletion. *Magn Reson Med* 3(1):44-54. 1986.
110. Tesch, P. Muscle fatigue in man, with special reference to lactate accumulation during short intense exercise. *Acta Physiol Scand* 480:1-40. 1980.
111. Tesch, P.A., L.L. Ploutz-Snyder, L. Ystrom, M.J. Castro, and G.A. Dudley. Skeletal muscle glycogen loss evoked by resistance exercise. *J Strength Cond Res* 12:67-73. 1998.
112. Thorstensson, P. Muscle strength, fiber types and enzymes in man. *Acta Physiol Scand* 102:443. 1976.
113. Thorstensson, P., B. Sjodin, and J. Karlsson. Actinomyosin ATPase, myokinase, CPK and LDH in human fast and slow twitch muscle fibres. *Acta Physiol Scand* 99:225-229. 1975.
114. Vandewalle, H., G. Peres, and H. Monod. Standard anaerobic exercise tests. *Sports Med* 4:268-289. 1987.
115. VanHelder, W., M. Radomski, R. Goode, and K. Casey. Hormonal and metabolic response to three types of exercise of equal duration and external work output. *Eur J Appl Physiol* 54:337-342. 1985.
116. Vihko, V., A. Salmons, and J. Rontumaki. Oxidative and lysomal capacity in skeletal muscle. *Acta Physiol Scand* 104:74-81. 1978.
117. Walsh, B., M. Tonkonogi, K. Soderlund, E. Hultman, V. Saks, and K. Sahlin. The role of phosphorylcreatine and creatine in the regulation of mitochondrial respiration in human skeletal muscle. *J Physiol* 537(Pt 3):971-978. 2001.
118. Weir, J.P., T.W. Beck, J.T. Cramer, and T.J. Housh. Is fatigue all in your head? A critical review of the central governor model. *Br J Sports Med* 40:573-586. 2006.
119. Weir, J.P., and J.T. Cramer. Principles of musculoskeletal exercise programming. In: *ACSM Resource Manual for Exercise Testing and Prescription,* 5th ed., L.A. Kaminsky (senior ed.), S. Glass (section ed.). American College of Sports Medicine. Philadelphia: Lippincott, Williams & Wilkins. 2005. pp. 350-365.
120. Wells, J., B. Balke, and D. Van Fossan. Lactic acid accumulation during work. A suggested standardization of work classification. *J Appl Physiol* 10:51-55. 1957.
121. Whipp, B.J., C. Scard, and K. Wasserman. O_2 deficit-O_2 debt relationship and efficiency of aerobic work. *J Appl Physiol* 28:452-458. 1970.
122. Williams, J.H., and G.A. Klug. Calcium exchange hypothesis of skeletal muscle: A brief review. *Muscle Nerve* 18:421-434. 1995.
123. Withers, R.T., W.M. Sherman, D.G. Clark, P.C. Esselbach, S.R. Nolan, M.H. Mackay, and M. Brinkman. Muscle metabolism during 30, 60 and 90 s of maximal cycling on an airbraked ergometer. *Eur J Appl Physiol* 63:354-362. 1991.
124. York, J., L.B. Oscai, and D.G. Penny. Alterations in skeletal muscle lactate dehydrogenase isozymes following exercise training. *Biochem Biophys Res Commun* 61:1387-1393. 1974.
125. Yoshida, I. Effect of dietary modifications on lactate threshold and onset of blood lactate accumulation during incremental exercise. *Eur J Appl Physiol* 53:200-205. 1984.

Chapter 3 Endocrine Responses to Resistance Exercise

1. Adem, A., S.S. Jossan, R. D'Argy, P.G. Gillberg, A. Nordberg, B. Windbald, and V. Sara. Insulin-like growth factor I (IGF-1) receptors in the human brain: Quantitative autoradiographic localization. *Brain Res* 503(2):299-303. 1989.
2. Allen, R.E., and L.K. Boxhorn. Regulation of skeletal muscle satellite cell proliferation and differentiation by transforming growth factor-beta, insulin-like growth factor I, and fibroblast growth factor. *J Cell Physiol* 138(2):311-315. 1988.
3. Allen, R.E., R.A. Merkel, and R.B. Young. Cellular aspects of muscle growth: Myogenic cell proliferation. *J Anim Sci* 49(1):115-127. 1979.
4. Atha, J. Strengthening muscle. In: *Exercise and Sport Sciences Reviews,* D.I. Miller, ed. Philadelphia: Franklin Institute Press. 1981. pp. 1-73.
5. Bartalena, L. Recent achievements in studies on thyroid hormone binding proteins. *Endocr Rev* 11:47-64. 1990.
6. Baxter, R.C., and J.L. Martin. Structure of the Mr 140000 growth hormone-dependent insulin-like growth factor binding protein complex: Determination by reconstitution affinity-labeling. *Proc Nat Acad Sci USA* 86(18):6898-6902. 1989.
7. Baxter, R.C., J.L. Martin, and V.A. Beniac. High molecular weight insulin-like growth factor binding protein complex: Purification and properties of the acid-labile subunit from human serum. *J Biol Chem* 264(20):11843-11848. 1989.
8. Ben-Ezra, V., R.G. McMurray, and A. Smith. Effects of exercise or diet on plasma somatomedin-C [abstract]. *Med Sci Sports Exerc* 17(2):209. 1985.
9. Biro, J., and E. Endroczi. Nuclear RNA content and synthesis in anterior pituitary in intact, castrated and androgen sterilized rats. *Endocrinol Exp* 11:164-168. 1977.
10. Bleisch, W., V.N. Lunie, and F. Nottebohm. Modification of synapses in androgen-sensitive muscle. Hormonal regulation of acetylcholine receptor number in the songbird *Syrinx J Neurosci* 4:786-792. 1984.
11. Blum, W.F., E.W. Jenne, F. Reppin, K. Kietzmann, M.B. Ranke, and J.R. Bierich. Insulin-like growth factor I (IGF-I)-binding protein complex is a better mitogen than free IGF-I. *Endocrinology* 125:766-772. 1989.
12. Borer, K.T., D.R. Nicoski, and V. Owens. Alteration of pulsatile growth hormone secretion by growth-inducing exercise: Involvement of endogenous opiates and somatostatin. *Endocrinology* 118:844-850. 1986.
13. Boule, N.G., S.J. Weisnagel, T.A. Lakka, A. Tremblay, R.N. Bergman, T. Rankinen, A.S. Leon, J.S. Skinner, J.H. Wilmore, D.C. Rao, and C. Bouchard. Effects of exercise training on glucose homeostasis: The HERITAGE Family Study. *Diabetes Care* 28:108-114. 2005.
14. Buckler, J.M. The effect of age, sex, and exercise on the secretion of growth hormone. *Clin Sci* 37:765-774. 1969.
15. Buckler, J.M.H. The relationship between exercise, body temperature and plasma growth hormone levels in a human subject. *J Physiol* 214:25-26. 1971.
16. Chang, F., W. Dodds, M. Sullivan, M. Kim, and W. Malarkey. The acute effects of exercise on prolactin and growth hormone secretion: Comparison between sedentary women and women runners with normal and abnormal menstrual cycles. *J Clin Endocrinol Metab* 62:551-556. 1985.
17. Clarkson, P., and I. Tremblay. Exercise-induced muscle damage, repair, and adaptation in humans. *J Appl Physiol* 65(1):1-6. 1988.
18. Clemmons, D.R., H.W. Busby, and L.E. Underwood. Mediation of the growth promoting actions of growth hormone by somatomedin-C/insulin-like growth factor I and its binding protein. In: *The Physiology of Human Growth,* J.M. Tanner and M.A. Preece, eds. Cambridge: Cambridge University Press. 1989. pp. 111-128.
19. Clemmons, D.R., J.P. Thissen, M. Maes, J.M. Ketelslegers, and L.E. Underwood. Insulin-like growth factor-I (IGF-I) infusion into hypophysectomized or protein-deprived rats induces specific IGF-binding proteins in serum. *Endocrinology* 125(6):2967-2972. 1989.
20. Cumming, D.C., S.R. Wall, M.A. Galbraith, and A.N. Belcastro. Reproductive hormone responses to resistance exercise. *Med Sci Sports Exerc* 19:234-238. 1987.
21. Czech, M.P. Signal transmission by the insulin-like growth factors. *Cell* 59:235-238. 1989.

22. Daughaday, W.H., and P. Rotwein. Insulin-like growth factors I and II. Peptide, messenger ribonucleic acid and gene structures, serum and tissue concentrations. *Endocr Rev* 10:68-91. 1989.
23. Deschenes, M.R., W.J. Kraemer, J.A. Bush, T.A. Doughty, D. Kim, K.M. Mullen, and K. Ramsey. Biorhythmic influences on functional capacity of human muscle and physiological responses. *Med Sci Sports Exerc* 30(9):1399-1407. 1998.
24. Deschenes, M.R., C.M. Maresh, L.E. Armstrong, J.M. Covault, W.J. Kraemer, and J.F. Crivello. Endurance and resistance exercise induce muscle fiber type specific responses in androgen binding capacity. *J Steroid Biochem Mol Biol* 50(3/4):175-179. 1994.
25. DeSouza, M.J., M.S. Maguire, C.M. Maresh, W.J. Kraemer, K. Ruben, and A.B. Loucks. Adrenal activation and the prolactin response to exercise in eumenorrheic and amenorrheic runners. *J Appl Physiol* 70(6):2378-2387. 1991.
26. Djarova, T., A. Ilkov, A. Varbanova, A. Nikiforova, and G. Mateev. Human growth hormone, cortisol, and acid-base balance changes after hyperventilation and breath-holding. *Int J Sports Med* 7:311-315. 1986.
27. Ekins, R. Measurement of free hormones in blood. *Endocr Rev* 11:5-45. 1990.
28. Elliot, D., L. Goldberg, and W. Watts. Resistance exercise and plasma beta-endorphin/beta-lipotrophin immunoreactivity. *Life Sci* 35:515-518. 1984.
29. Estrada, M., A. Espinosa, M. Muller, and E. Jaimovich. Testosterone stimulates intracellular calcium release and mitogen-activated protein kinases via a G protein-coupled receptor in skeletal muscle cells. *Endocrinology* 144:3586-3597. 2003.
30. Fagin, J.A., C. Fernandez-Mejia, and S. Melmed. Pituitary insulin-like growth factor-I gene expression: Regulation by triodothyronine and growth hormone. *Endocrinology* 125(5):2385-2391. 1989.
31. Fahey, T.D., R. Rolph, P. Moungmee, J. Nagel, and S. Mortar. Serum testosterone, body composition, and strength of young adults. *Med Sci Sports Exerc* 8:31-34. 1976.
32. Faria, A.C.S., J.D. Veldhuis, M.O. Thorner, and M.L. Vance. Half-time of endogenous growth hormone (GH) disappearance in normal man after stimulation of GH secretion by GH-releasing hormone and suppression with somatostatin. *J Clin Endocrinol Metab* 68(3):535-541. 1989.
33. Finkelstein, J.W., H.P. Roffwarg, R.M. Boyar, J. Kream, and L. Hellman. Age-related change in the twenty-four hour spontaneous secretion of growth hormone. *J Clin Endocrinol Metab* 35:665-670. 1972.
34. Fleck, S.J. *Successful Long-Term Weight Training*. Indianapolis: Masters Press. 1999.
35. Fleck, S.J., and W.J. Kraemer. *Designing Resistance Training Programs,* 3rd ed. Champaign, IL: Human Kinetics. 2003.
36. Fleck, S.J., and W.J. Kraemer. *Periodization Breakthrough*. Ronkonkoma, NY: Advanced Research Press. 1996.
37. Florini, J.R. Hormonal control of muscle cell growth. *J Anim Sci* 61:21-37. 1985.
38. Florini, J.R. Hormonal control of muscle growth. *Muscle Nerve* 10:577-598. 1987.
39. Florini, J.R., P.N. Prinz, M.V. Vitiello, and R.L. Hintz. Somatomedin-C levels in healthy young and old men: Relationship of peak and 24 hour integrated levels of growth hormone. *J Gerontol* 40:2-7. 1985.
40. Fluckey, J.D., W.J. Kraemer, and P.A. Farrell. Arginine-stimulated insulin secretion from isolated rat pancreatic islets is increased following acute resistance exercise. *J Appl Physiol* 79(4):1100-1105. 1995.
41. Forbes, B., L. Szabo, R.C. Baxter, F.J. Ballard, and J.C. Wallace. Classification of the insulin-like growth factor binding proteins into three distinct categories according to their binding specificities. *Biochem Biophys Res Commun* 157:196-202. 1988.
42. French, D.N., W.J. Kraemer, J.S. Volek, B.A. Spiering, D.A. Judelson, J.R. Hoffman, and C.M. Maresh. Anticipatory responses of catecholamines on muscle force production. *J Appl Physiol* 102(1):94-102. 2007.
43. Fry, A.C., W.J. Kraemer, J.M. Lynch, N.T. Triplett, and L.P. Koziris. Does short-term near maximal intensity machine resistance training induce overtraining? *J Strength Cond Res* 8(3):188-191. 1994.
44. Fry, A.C., W.J. Kraemer, and L.T. Ramsey. Pituitary-adrenal-gonadal responses to high-intensity resistance exercise overtraining. *J Appl Physiol* 85(6):2352-2359. 1998.
45. Fry, A.C., W.J. Kraemer, M.H. Stone, B.J. Warren, S.J. Fleck, J.T. Kearney, and S.E. Gordon. Endocrine responses to over-reaching before and after 1 year of weightlifting training. *Can J Appl Physiol* 19(4):400-410. 1994.
46. Fry, A.C., W.J. Kraemer, M.H. Stone, B.J. Warren, J.T. Kearney, C.M. Maresh, C.A. Weseman, and S.J. Fleck. Endocrine and performance responses to high volume training and amino acid supplementation in elite junior weightlifters. *Int J Sports Nutr* 3(3):306-322. 1993.
47. Fry, A.C., W.J. Kraemer, F. van Borselen, J.M. Lynch, J.L. Marsit, E.P. Roy, N.T. Triplett, and H.G. Knuttgen. Performance decrements with high-intensity resistance exercise overtraining. *Med Sci Sports Exerc* 26(9):1165-1173. 1994.
48. Fry, A.C., W.J. Kraemer, F. van Borselen, J.M. Lynch, J.L. Marsit, N.T. Triplett, and L.P. Koziris. Catecholamine responses to short-term, high intensity resistance exercise overtraining. *J Appl Physiol* 77(2):941-946. 1994.
49. Galbo, H. *Hormonal and Metabolic Adaptation to Exercise*. Stuttgart: Georg Thieme Verlay. 1983.
50. Gharib, S.D., M.E. Wioerman, M.A. Shupnik, and W.W. Chin. Molecular biology of the pituitary gonadotropins. *Endocr Rev* 71:177-199. 1990.
51. Goldberg, A.L., and H. Goodman. Relationship between growth hormone and muscular work in determining muscle size. *J Appl Physiol* 200:655-666. 1969.
52. Goldspink, G. Changes in muscle mass and phenotype and the expression of autocrine and systemic growth factors by muscle in response to stretch and overload. *J Anat* 194(Pt 3):323-334. 1999.
53. Gordon, S.E., W.J. Kraemer, N.H. Vos, J.M. Lynch, and H.G. Knuttgen. Effect of acid-base balance on the growth hormone response to acute, high-intensity cycle exercise. *J Appl Physiol* 76(2):821-829. 1994.
54. Gotshalk, L.A., C.C. Loebel, B.C. Nindl, M. Putukian, W.J. Sebastianelli, R.U. Newton, K. Häkkinen, and W J. Kraemer. Hormonal responses of multiset versus single-set heavy resistance exercise protocols. *Can J Appl Physiol* 22(3):244-255. 1997.
55. Griggs, R.C., D. Halliday, W. Kingston, and R.T. Moxley, III. Effect of testosterone on muscle protein synthesis in myotonic dystrophy. *Ann Neurol* 20:590-596. 1986.
56. Guezennec, Y., L. Leger, F. Lhoste, M. Aymonod, and P.C. Pesquies. Hormone and metabolite response to weight-lifting training sessions. *Int J Sports Med* 7:100-105. 1986.
57. Guma, A., J.R. Zierath, H. Wallberg-Henriksson, and A. Klip. Insulin induces translocation of GLUT-4 glucose transporters in human skeletal muscle. *Am J Physiol* 268:E613-622. 1995.
58. Häkkinen, K. Neuromuscular and hormonal adaptations during strength and power training. *J Sports Med Phys Fitness* 29:9-24. 1989.
59. Häkkinen, K., P.V. Komi, M. Alén, and H. Kauhanen. EMG, muscle fibre and force production characteristics during a one year training period in elite weightlifters. *Eur J Appl Physiol* 56:419-427. 1987.
60. Häkkinen, K., A. Pakarinen, M. Alén, H. Kauhanen, and P.V. Komi. Daily hormonal and neuromuscular responses to intensive strength training in 1 week. *Int J Sports Med* 9:422-428. 1988.
61. Häkkinen, K., A. Pakarinen, M. Alén, H. Kauhanen, and P.V. Komi. Neuromuscular and hormonal adaptations in athletes to strength training in two years. *J Appl Physiol* 65(6):2406-2412. 1988.
62. Häkkinen, K., A. Pakarinen, M. Alén, H. Kauhanen, and P.V. Komi. Relationships between training volume, physical performance capacity, and serum hormone concentrations during prolonged training in elite weight lifters. *Int J Sports Med* 8:61-65. 1987.
63. Häkkinen, K., A. Pakarinen, M. Alén, and P.V. Komi. Serum hormones during prolonged training of neuromuscular performance. *Eur J Appl Physiol* 53:287-293. 1985.

64. Häkkinen, K., A. Pakarinen, H. Kyrolainen, S. Cheng, D.H. Kim, and P.V. Komi. Neuromuscular adaptations and serum hormones in females during prolonged power training. *Int J Sports Med* 11:91-98. 1990.
65. Han, V.K.M., A.J. D'Ercole, and P.K. Lund. Cellular localization of somatomedin (insulin-like growth factor) messenger RNA in the human fetus. *Science* 236:193-196. 1987.
66. Hansson, H.A., C. Brandsten, C. Lossing, and K. Petruson. Transient expression of insulin-like growth factor I immunoreactivity by vascular cells during angiogenesis. *Exp Mol Pathol* 50(1):125-138. 1989.
67. Hetrick, G.A., and J.H. Wilmore. Androgen levels and muscle hypertrophy during an eight-week training program for men/women [abstract]. *Med Sci Sports Exerc* 11:102. 1979.
68. Hill, D.J., C. Camacho-Hubner, P. Rashid, A.J. Strain, and D.R. Clemmons. Insulin-like growth factor (IGF)-binding protein release by human fetal fibroblasts: Dependency on cell density and IGF peptides. *J Endocrinol* 122(1):87-98. 1989.
69. Horikawa, R., K. Asakawa, N. Hizuka, K. Takano, and K. Shizume. Growth hormone and insulin-like growth factor I stimulate Leydig cell steroidogenesis. *Eur J Pharmacol* 166(1):87-93. 1989.
70. Housley, P.R., E.R. Sanchez, and J.F. Grippo. Phosphorylation and reduction of glucocorticoid components. In: *Receptor Phosphorylation,* V.M. Moudgil, ed. Boca Raton, FL: CRC Press. 1989. pp. 289-314.
71. Ikeda, T., K. Fujiyama, T. Takeuchi, M. Honda, O. Mokuda, M. Tominaga, and H. Mashiba. Effect of thyroid hormone on somatomedin-C release from perfused rat liver. *Experientia* 45(2):170-171. 1989.
72. Ishii, D.N. Relationship of insulin-like growth factor II gene expression in muscle to synaptogenesis. *Proc Nat Acad Sci USA* 86(8):2898-2902. 1989.
73. Jahreis, G., V. Hesse, H.E. Schmidt, and J. Scheibe. Effect of endurance exercise on somatomedin-C/insulin-like growth factor I concentration in male and female runners. *Exp Clin Endocrinol* 94:89-96. 1989.
74. Kelly, A., G. Lyongs, B. Gambki, and N. Robinstein. Influences of testosterone on contractile proteins of the guinea pig temporalis muscle. *Adv Exp Med Biol* 182:155-168. 1985.
75. Kjaer, M., and G. Henrik. Effect of physical training on the capacity to secrete epinephrine. *J Appl Physiol* 64:11-16. 1988.
76. Kraemer, W.J. Endocrine responses and adaptations to strength training. In: *The Encyclopedia of Sports Medicine: Strength and Power,* P.V. Komi, ed. Oxford: Blackwell Scientific. 1992. pp. 291-304.
77. Kraemer, W.J. Endocrine responses to resistance exercise. *Med Sci Sports Exerc* 20(suppl.):S152-S157. 1988.
78. Kraemer, W.J. Hormonal mechanisms related to the expression of muscular strength and power. In: *The Encyclopedia of Sports Medicine: Strength and Power,* P.V. Komi, ed. Oxford: Blackwell Scientific. 1992. pp. 64-76.
79. Kraemer, W.J. Physiological and cellular effects of exercise training. In: *Sports-Induced Inflammation,* W.B. Leadbetter, J.A. Buckwalter, and S.L. Gordon, eds. Park Ridge, IL: American Academy of Orthopaedic Surgeons. 1990. pp. 659-676.
80. Kraemer, W.J. The physiological basis for strength training in mid-life. In: *Sports and Exercise in Midlife,* S.L. Gordon, ed. Park Ridge, IL: American Academy of Orthopaedic Surgeons. 1994. pp. 413-433.
81. Kraemer, W.J. A series of studies: The physiological basis for strength training in American football: Fact over philosophy. *J Strength Cond Res* 11(3):131-142. 1997.
82. Kraemer, W.J., L.E. Armstrong, P. Rock, R.W. Hubbard, L.J. Marchitelli, N. Leva, and J.E. Dziados. Responses of human atrial natriuretic factor to high intensity submaximal exercise in the heat. *Eur J Appl Physiol* 57:399-403. 1988.
83. Kraemer, W.J., B.A. Augilera, M. Terada, R.U. Newton, J.M. Lynch, G. Rosendaal, J.M. McBride, S.E. Gordon, and K. Häkkinen. Responses of insulin-like growth factor-I to endogenous increases in growth hormone after heavy-resistance exercise. *J Appl Physiol* 79(4):1310-1315. 1995.
84. Kraemer, W.J., and T.R. Baechle. Development of a strength training program. In: *Sports Medicine,* 2nd ed., A.J. Ryan and F.L. Allman, eds. San Diego: Academic Press. 1989. pp. 113-127.
85. Kraemer, W.J., A. Clemson, N.T. Triplett, J.A. Bush, R.U. Newton, and J.M. Lynch. The effects of plasma cortisol elevation on total and differential leukocyte counts in response to heavy resistance exercise. *Eur J Appl Physiol* 73(1-2):93-97. 1996.
86. Kraemer, W.J., M.R. Deschenes, and S.J. Fleck. Physiological adaptations to resistance exercise: Implications for athletic conditioning. *Sports Med* 6:246-256. 1988.
87. Kraemer, W.J., J.E. Dziados, S.E. Gordon, L.J. Marchitelli, A.C. Fry, J. Hoffman, and K. Reynolds. The effects of graded exercise on plasma catecholamines and proenkephalin peptide F responses at sea level. *Eur J Appl Physiol* 61:214-217. 1990.
88. Kraemer, W.J., J.E. Dziados, L.J. Marchitelli, S.E. Gordon, E.A. Harman, R. Mello, S.J. Fleck, P.N. Frykman, and N.T. Triplett. Effects of different heavy-resistance exercise protocols on plasma B-endorphin concentrations. *J Appl Physiol* 74(1):450-459. 1993.
89. Kraemer, W.J., and S.J. Fleck. Resistance training: Exercise prescription. *Phys Sportsmed* 16(6):69-81. 1988.
90. Kraemer, W.J., S.J. Fleck, R. Callister, M. Shealy, G. Dudley, C.M. Maresh, L. Marchitelli, C. Cruthirds, T. Murray, and J.E. Falkel. Training responses of plasma beta-endorphin, adrenocorticotropin and cortisol. *Med Sci Sports Exerc* 21(2):146-153. 1989.
91. Kraemer, W.J., S.J. Fleck, and M. Deschenes. A review: Factors in exercise prescription of resistance training. *NSCA J* 10(5):36-41. 1988.
92. Kraemer, W.J., S.J. Fleck, J.E. Dziados, E.A. Harman, L.J. Marchitelli, S.E. Gordon, R. Mello, P.N. Frykman, L.P. Koziris, and N.T. Triplett. Changes in hormonal concentrations following different heavy resistance exercise protocols in women. *J Appl Physiol* 75(2):594-604. 1993.
93. Kraemer, W.J., S.J. Fleck, and W.J. Evans. Strength and power training: Physiological mechanisms of adaptation. In: *Exercise and Sport Sciences Reviews,* vol. 24, J.O. Holloszy, ed. Baltimore: Williams & Wilkins. 1996. pp. 363-397.
94. Kraemer, W.J., A.C. Fry, P.N. Frykman, B. Conroy, and J. Hoffman. Resistance training and youth. *Pediatr Exerc Sci* 1:336-350. 1989.
95. Kraemer, W.J., A.C. Fry, B.J. Warren, M.H. Stone, S.J. Fleck, J.T. Kearney, B.P. Conroy, C.M. Maresh, C.A. Weseman, N.T. Triplett, and S.E. Gordon. Acute hormonal responses in elite junior weightlifters. *Int J Sports Med* 13(2):103-109. 1992.
96. Kraemer, W.J., S.E. Gordon, S.J. Fleck, L.J. Marchitelli, R. Mello, J.E. Dziados, K. Friedl, E. Harman, C. Maresh, and A.C. Fry. Endogenous anabolic hormonal and growth factor responses to heavy resistance exercise in males and females. *Int J Sports Med* 12(2):228-235. 1991.
97. Kraemer, W.J., K. Häkkinen, R.U. Newton, M. McCormick, B.C. Nindl, J.S. Volek, L.A. Gotshalk, S.J. Fleck, W.W. Campbell, S.E. Gordon, P.A. Farrell, and W.J. Evans. Acute hormonal responses to heavy resistance exercise in younger and older men. *Eur J Appl Physiol* 77:206-211. 1998.
98. Kraemer, W.J., and L.P. Koziris. Olympic weightlifting and power lifting. In: *Physiology and Nutrition for Competitive Sport,* D.R. Lamb, H.G. Knuttgen, and R. Murray, eds. Carmel, IN: Cooper. 1994. pp. 1-54.
99. Kraemer, W.J., L. Marchitelli, D. McCurry, R. Mello, J.E. Dziados, E. Harman, P. Frykman, S.E. Gordon, and S.J. Fleck. Hormonal and growth factor responses to heavy resistance exercise. *J Appl Physiol* 69(4):1442-1450. 1990.
100. Kraemer, W.J., and B.C. Nindl. Factors involved with overtraining for strength and power. In: *Overtraining in Sport,* R.B. Kreider, A.C. Fry, and M.L. O'Toole, eds. Champaign, IL: Human Kinetics. 1998. pp. 69-86.
101. Kraemer, W.J., B.J. Noble, M.J. Clark, and B.W. Culver. Physiologic responses to heavy-resistance exercise with very short rest periods. *Int J Sports Med* 8:247-252. 1987.
102. Kraemer, W.J., B.J. Noble, B. Culver, and R.V. Lewis. Changes in plasma proenkephalin peptide F and catecholamine levels during

graded exercise in men. *Proc Nat Acad Sci USA* 82:6349-6351. 1985.

103. Kraemer, W.J., J. Patton, S.E. Gordon, E.A. Harman, M.R. Deschenes, K. Reynolds, R.U. Newton, N.T. Triplett, and J.E. Dziados. Compatibility of high intensity strength and endurance training on hormonal and skeletal muscle adaptations. *J Appl Physiol* 78(3):976-989. 1995.
104. Kraemer, W.J., J.F. Patton, H.G. Knuttgen, C.J. Hannan, T. Kittler, S. Gordon, J.E. Dziados, A.C. Fry, P.N. Frykman, and E.A. Harman. The effects of high intensity cycle exercise on sympatho-adrenal medullary response patterns. *J Appl Physiol* 70:8-14. 1991.
105. Kraemer, W.J., J.F. Patton, H.G. Knuttgen, L.J. Marchitelli, C. Cruthirds, A. Damokosh, E. Harman, P. Frykman, and J.E. Dziados. Hypothalamic-pituitary-adrenal responses to short duration high-intensity cycle exercise. *J Appl Physiol* 66:161-166. 1989.
106. Kraemer, W.J., P.B. Rock, C.S. Fulco, S.E. Gordon, J.P. Bonner, C.D. Cruthirds, L.J. Marchitelli, L. Trad, and A. Cymerman. Influence of altitude and caffeine during rest and exercise on plasma levels of proenkephalin peptide F. *Peptides* 9:1115-1119. 1988.
107. Kraemer, W.J., B.A. Spiering, J.S. Volek, N.A. Ratamess, M.J. Sharman, M.R. Rubin, D.N. French, R. Silvestre, D.L. Hatfield, J.L. Van Heest, J.L. Vingren, D.A. Judelson, M.R. Deschenes, and C.M. Maresh. Androgenic responses to resistance exercise: Effects of feeding and L-carnitine. *Med Sci Sports Exerc* 38:1288-1296. 2006.
108. Kraemer, W.J., R.S. Staron, D. Karapondo, A.C. Fry, S.E. Gordon, J.S. Volek, B. Nindl, L. Gotshalk, R.U. Newton, and K. Häkkinen. The effects of short-term resistance training on endocrine function in men and women. *Eur J Appl Physiol* 78(1):69-76. 1998.
109. Kraemer, W.J., J.S. Volek, J.A. Bush, M. Putukian, and W.J. Sebastianelli. Hormonal responses to consecutive days of heavy-resistance exercise with or without nutritional supplementation. *J Appl Physiol* 85(4):1544-1555. 1998.
110. Kuoppasalmi, K., and H. Adlercreutz. Interaction between catabolic and anabolic steroid hormones in muscular exercise. In: *Exercise Endocrinology,* K. Fotherby and S.B. Pal, eds. Berlin: Walter de Gruyter. 1985. pp. 65-98.
111. Lukaszewska, J., B. Biczowa, D. Bobilewixz, M. Wilk, and B. Bouchowixz-Fidelus. Effect of physical exercise on plasma cortisol and growth hormone levels in young weight lifters. *Endokrynol Pol* 2:149-158. 1976.
112. MacDougall, J. Morphological changes in human skeletal muscle following strength training and immobilization. In: *Human Muscle Power,* N.L. Jones, N. McCartney, and A.J. McComas, eds. Champaign, IL: Human Kinetics. 1986. pp. 269-284.
113. Mahler, D.A., L.N. Cunningham, G.S. Skrinar, W.J. Kraemer, and G.L. Colice. Beta-endorphin activity and hypercapnic ventilatory responsiveness after marathon running. *J Appl Physiol* 66(5):2431-2436. 1989.
114. Martin, J.B. Growth hormone releasing factor. In: *Brain Peptides,* D.T. Krieger, J.J. Brownstein, and J.B. Martin, eds. New York: Wiley. 1983. pp. 976-980.
115. McCall, G.E., W.C. Byrnes, S.J. Fleck, A. Dickinson, and W.J. Kraemer. Acute and chronic hormonal responses to resistance training designed to promote muscle hypertrophy. *Can J Appl Physiol* 24(1):96-107. 1999.
116. McCusker, R.H., C. Camacho-Hubner, and D.R. Clemmons. Identification of the types of insulin-like growth factor-binding proteins that are secreted by muscle cells in vitro. *J Biol Chem* 264(14):7795-7800. 1989.
117. McKoy, G., W. Ashley, J. Mander, S.Y. Yang, N. Williams, B. Russell, and G. Goldspink. Expression of insulin growth factor-1 splice variants and structural genes in rabbit skeletal muscle induced by stretch and stimulation. *J Physiol* 516(Pt 2):583-592. 1999.
118. Michel, G., and E. Baulieu. Androgen receptor in rat skeletal muscle: Characterization and physiological variations. *Endocrinology* 107:2088-2097. 1980.
119. Mulligan, S.E., S.J. Fleck, S.E. Gordon, L.P. Koziris, N.T. Triplett-McBride, and W.J. Kraemer. Influence of resistance exercise volume on serum growth hormone and cortisol concentrations in women. *J Strength Cond Res* 10(4):256-262. 1996.
120. Okayama, T. Factors which regulate growth hormone secretion. *Med J* 17(1):13-19. 1972.
121. Pakarinen, A., K. Häkkinen, and P. Komi. Serum thyroid hormones thyrotropin and thyroxine binding globulin during prolonged strength training. *Eur J Appl Physiol* 57:394-398. 1988.
122. Rance, N.E., and S.R. Max. Modulation of the cytosolic androgen receptor in striated muscle by sex steroids. *Endocrinology* 115(3):862-866. 1984.
123. Ratamess, N.A., W.J. Kraemer, J.S. Volek, C.M. Maresh, J.L. Van Heest, M.J. Sharman, M.R. Rubin, D.N. French, J.D. Vescovi, R. Silvestre, D.L. Hatfield, S.J. Fleck, and M.R. Deschenes. Androgen receptor content following heavy resistance exercise in men. *J Steroid Biochem Mol Biol* 93:35-42. 2005.
124. Riss, T., J. Novakofski, and P. Bechtel. Skeletal muscle hypertrophy in rats having growth hormone-secreting tumor. *J Appl Physiol* 61(5):1732-1735. 1986.
125. Rogol, A.D. Growth hormone: Physiology, therapeutic use, and potential for abuse. In: *Exercise and Sport Sciences Reviews,* K.B. Pandolf, ed. Baltimore: Williams & Wilkins. 1989. pp. 353-377.
126. Rosner, W. The functions of corticosteroid-binding globulin and sex-hormone-binding globulin: Recent advances. *Endocr Rev* 11:80-91. 1990.
127. Sale, D.G. Neural adaptation to resistance training. *Med Sci Sport Exerc* 20:135-145. 1988.
128. Skierska, E., J. Ustupska, B. Biczowa, and J. Lukaszewska. Effect of physical exercise on plasma cortisol, testosterone and growth hormone levels in weight lifters. *Endokrynol Pol* 2:159-165. 1976.
129. Skottner, A., M. Kanie, E. Jennische, J. Sjogren, and L. Fryklund. Tissue repair and IGF-1. *Acta Paediatr Scand* 347:110-112. 1988.
130. Sonntag, W.E., L.J. Forman, N. Miki, and J. Meiters. Growth hormone secretion and neuroendocrine regulation. In: *Handbook of Endocrinology,* G.H. Gass and H.M. Kaplan, eds. Boca Raton, FL: CRC Press. 1982. pp. 35-39.
131. Staron, R.S., D.L. Karapondo, W.J. Kraemer, A.C. Fry, S.E. Gordon, J.E. Falkel, F.C. Hagerman, and R.S. Hikida. Skeletal muscle adaptations during the early phase of heavy-resistance training in men and women. *J Appl Physiol* 76(3):1247-1255. 1994.
132. Stone, M.H., R. Byrd, and C. Johnson. Observations on serum androgen response to short term resistive training in middle age sedentary males. *NSCA J* 5:40-65. 1984.
133. Stone, M., and H. O'Bryant. *Weight Training, Scientific Approach.* Minneapolis: Burgess. 1987.
134. Suikkari, A.-M., V.A. Koivisto, R. Koistinen, M. Seppala, and H. Yki-Jarvinen. Dose-response characteristics for suppression of low molecular weight plasma insulin-like growth factor-binding protein by insulin. *J Clin Endocrinol Metab* 68(1):135-140. 1989.
135. Suikkari, A.-M., V.A. Koivisto, R. Koistinen, M. Seppala, and H. Yki-Jarvinen. Prolonged exercise increases serum insulin-like growth factor-binding protein concentrations. *J Clin Endocrinol Metab* 68(1):141-144. 1989.
136. Sutton, J.R. Effect of acute hypoxia on the hormonal response to exercise. *J Appl Physiol Respir Env Exerc Physiol* 39:587-592. 1977.
137. Tapperman, J. *Metabolic and Endocrine Physiology.* Chicago: Year Book Medical. 1980.
138. Terjung, R. Endocrine response to exercise. In: *Exercise and Sport Sciences Reviews,* vol. 6, R.S. Hutton and D.I. Miller, eds. Lexington, MA: Collamore. 1979. pp. 153-180.
139. Triplett-McBride, N.T., A.M. Andrea, M. Mastro, J.M. McBride, J.A. Bush, M. Putukian, W.J. Sebastianelli, and W.J. Kraemer. Plasma proenkephalin peptide F and human B cell responses to exercise stress in fit and unfit women. *Peptides* 19(4):731-738. 1998.
140. Turner, J.D., P. Rotwein, J. Novakofski, and P.J. Bechtel. Induction of messenger RNA for IGF-I and -II during growth hormone-stimulated muscle hypertrophy. *Am J Physiol* 255(4):E513-E517. 1988.
141. VanHelder, W.P., R.C. Goode, and M.W. Radomski. Effect of anaerobic and aerobic exercise of equal duration and work expenditure on plasma growth hormone levels. *Eur J Appl Physiol* 52:255-257. 1984.

142. VanHelder, W.P., M.W. Radomski, and R.C. Goode. Growth hormone responses during intermittent weight lifting exercise in men. *Eur J Appl Physiol* 53:31-34. 1984.
143. Vermeulen, A. Physiology of the testosterone-binding globulin in man. In: *Steroid-Protein Interactions: Basic and Clinical Aspects,* R. Frairia, H.L. Bradlow, and G. Gaidano, eds. New York: New York Academy of Sciences. 1988. pp. 103-111.
144. Vicencio, J.M., C. Ibarra, M. Estrada, M. Chiong, D. Soto, V. Parra, G. Diaz-Araya, E. Jaimovich, and S. Lavandero. Testosterone induces an intracellular calcium increase by a nongenomic mechanism in cultured rat cardiac myocytes. *Endocrinology* 147:1386-1395. 2006.
145. Vingren, J.L., L.P. Koziris, S.E. Gordon, W.J. Kraemer, R.T. Turner, and K.C. Westerlind. Chronic alcohol intake, resistance training, and muscle androgen receptor content. *Med Sci Sports Exerc* 37:1842-1848. 2005.
146. Weiss, L.W., K.J. Cureton, and F.N. Thompson. Comparison of serum testosterone and androstenedione responses to weight lifting in men and women. *Eur J Appl Physiol* 50(3):413-419. 1983.
147. Westerlind, K.C., W.C. Byrnes, P.S. Freedson, and F.I. Katch. Exercise and serum androgens in women. *Phys Sportsmed* 15:87-94. 1987.
148. Willoughby, D.S., and L. Taylor. Effects of sequential bouts of resistance exercise on androgen receptor expression. *Med Sci Sports Exerc* 36:1499-1506. 2004.
149. Wolf, M., S.H. Ingbar, and A.C. Moses. Thyroid hormone and growth hormone interact to regulate insulin-like growth factor-I messenger RNA and circulating levels in the rat. *Endocrinology* 125(6):2905-2914. 1989.
150. Yeoh, S.I., and R.C. Baxter. Metabolic regulation of the growth hormone-independent insulin-like growth factor binding protein in human plasma. *Acta Endocrinol* 119:465-473. 1988.
151. Young, I.R., S. Mesiano, R. Hintz, D.J. Caddy, M.M. Ralph, C.A. Browne, and G.D. Thorburn. Growth hormone and testosterone can independently stimulate the growth of hypophysectomized prepubertal lambs without any alteration in circulating concentrations of insulin-like growth factors. *J Endocrinol* 121(3):563-570. 1989.
152. Zorzano, A., D.E. James, N.B. Ruderman, and P.F. Pilch. Insulin-like growth factor I binding and receptor kinase red and white muscle. *Fed Eur Biochem Soc* 234(2):257-262. 1988.

Chapter 4 Biomechanics of Resistance Exercise

1. Alexander, R., and A. Vernon. The dimensions of the knee and ankle muscles and the forces they exert. *J Human Mvmt Studies* 1:115-123. 1975.
2. Anderson, C.K., and D.B. Chaffin. A biomechanical evaluation of five lifting techniques. *Appl Ergon* (March):2-7. 1986.
3. Åstrand, P., K. Rodahl, H.A. Dahl, and S.B. Strømme. *Textbook of Work Physiology: Physiological Basis of Exercise,* 4th ed. Champaign, IL: Human Kinetics. 2003.
4. Bartelink, D.L. The role of abdominal pressure in relieving the pressure on the lumbar intervertebral discs. *J Bone Joint Surg* 39B(4):718-725. 1957.
5. Chaffin, D.B., G.B.J. Andersson, and B.J. Martin. *Occupational Biomechanics,* 3rd ed. New York: Wiley. 1999.
6. Curl, L.A., and R.F. Warren. Glenohumeral joint stability. *Clin Orthop Rel Res* 330:54-65. 1999.
7. Ellison, A.E., A.L. Boland, P. Grace, and H. Calehuff, eds. *Athletic Training and Sports Medicine.* Chicago: American Academy of Orthopaedic Surgeons. 1986.
8. Enoka, R.M. *Neuromechanics of Human Movement.* Champaign, IL: Human Kinetics. 2001.
9. Fleck, S.J., and W.J. Kraemer. *Designing Resistance Training Programs,* 3rd ed. Champaign, IL: Human Kinetics. 2003.
10. Garhammer, J. Weight lifting and training. In: *Biomechanics of Sport,* C. Vaughn, ed. Boca Raton, FL: CRC Press. 1989. pp. 169-211.
11. Gowitzke, B.A., and M. Milner. *Scientific Bases of Human Movement,* 3rd ed. Baltimore: Williams & Wilkins. 1988.
12. Gray, H. *Anatomy of the Human Body,* 28th ed. Philadelphia: Lea & Febiger. 1966.
13. Gregor, R.J. The structure and function of skeletal muscle. In: *Kinesiology and Applied Anatomy,* 7th ed., P.J. Rasch, ed. Philadelphia: Lea & Febiger. 1989. pp. 34-35.
14. Harman, E. Resistive torque analysis of 5 Nautilus exercise machines. *Med Sci Sports Exerc* 15(2):113. 1983.
15. Harman, E., and P. Frykman. The effects of knee wraps on weightlifting performance and injury. *NSCA J* 12(5):30-35. 1990.
16. Harman, E.A., M. Johnson, and P.N. Frykman. A movement-oriented approach to exercise prescription. *NSCA J* 14(1):47-54. 1992.
17. Harman, E.A., R.M. Rosenstein, P.N. Frykman, and G.A. Nigro. Effects of a belt on intra-abdominal pressure during weight lifting. *Med Sci Sports Exerc* 21(2):186-190. 1989.
18. Haxton, H.A. Absolute muscle force in the ankle flexors of man. *J Physiol* 103:267-273. 1944.
19. Hay, J.G., and J.G. Reid. *The Anatomical and Mechanical Bases of Human Motion.* Englewood Cliffs, NJ: Prentice Hall. 1982.
20. Herbert, L., and G. Miller. Newer heavy load lifting methods help firms reduce back injuries. *Occup Health Saf* (February):57-60. 1987.
21. Hester, D., G. Hunter, K. Shuleva, and T. Kekes-Sabo. Review and evaluation of relative strength-handicapping models. *NSCA J* 12(1):54-57. 1990.
22. Higdon, A., W.B. Stiles, A.W. Davis, and C.R. Evces. *Engineering Mechanics.* Englewood Cliffs, NJ: Prentice Hall. 1976.
23. Hill, A.V. *First and Last Experiments in Muscle Mechanics.* London: Cambridge University Press. 1970.
24. Hole, J.W. *Human anatomy and physiology,* 4th ed. Dubuque, IA: Brown. 1987.
25. Ikai, M., and T. Fukunaga. Calculation of muscle strength per unit cross-sectional area of human muscle by means of ultrasonic measurement. *Int Z Angew Physiol Arbeitphysiol* 26:26-32. 1968.
26. Johnson, J.H., S. Colodny, and D. Jackson. Human torque capability versus machine resistive torque for four Eagle resistance machines. *J Appl Sport Sci Res* 4(3):83-87. 1990.
27. Jorgensen, K. Force-velocity relationship in human elbow flexors and extensors. In: *Biomechanics A-V,* P.V. Komi, ed. Baltimore: University Park Press. 1976.
28. Knapik, J.J., J.E. Wright, R.H. Mawdsley, and J. Braun. Isometric, isotonic, and isokinetic torque variations in four muscle groups through a range of joint motion. *J Am Phys Ther Assoc* 63(6):938-947. 1983.
29. Knuttgen, H., and W. Kraemer. Terminology and measurement in exercise performance. *J Appl Sport Sci Res* 1(1):1-10. 1987.
30. Lander, J.E., B.T. Bates, J.A. Sawhill, and J. Hamill. A comparison between free-weight and isokinetic bench pressing. *Med Sci Sports Exerc* 17(3):344-353. 1985.
31. Lander, J.E., J.R. Hundley, and R.L. Simonton. The effectiveness of weight-belts during multiple repetitions of the squat exercise. *Med Sci Sports Exerc* 24(5):603-609. 1990.
32. Lander, J.E., R.L. Simonton, and J.K.F. Giacobbe. The effectiveness of weight-belts during the squat exercise. *Med Sci Sports Exerc* 22(1):117-126. 1990.
33. McDonagh, M.J.N., and C.T.M. Davies. Adaptive response of mammalian skeletal muscle to exercise with high loads. *Eur J Appl Physiol* 52:139-155. 1984.
34. Meriam, J.L., and L.G. Kraige. *Engineering Mechanics: Dynamics,* 5th ed. New York: Wiley. 2002.
35. Moore, J.R., and G. Wade. Prevention of anterior cruciate ligament injuries. *NSCA J* 11(3):35-40. 1989.
36. Moore, K.L., A.F. Dalley, and A.M.R. Agur. *Clinically Oriented Anatomy,* 5th ed. Philadelphia: Lippincott, Williams & Wilkins. 2005.
37. Moritani, T., and H.A. deVries. Neural factors versus hypertrophy in the time course of muscle strength gain. *Am J Phys Med* 58(3):115-130. 1979.
38. Morris, J.M., D.B. Lucas, and B. Bresler. Role of the trunk in stability of the spine. *J Bone Joint Surg* 43A:327-351. 1961.

39. Pappas, A.M., T.P. Goss, and P.K. Kleinman. Symptomatic shoulder instability due to lesions of the glenoid labrum. *Am J Sports Med* 11(5):279-288. 1983.
40. Perrine, J.J., and V.R. Edgerton. Muscle force-velocity and power-velocity relationships under isokinetic loading. *Med Sci Sports* 10(3):159-166. 1978.
41. Practical considerations for utilizing plyometrics, part 2. *NSCA J* 8(4):14-24. 1986.
42. Requa, R.K., and J.G. Garrick. Adult recreational fitness. In: *Epidemiology of Sports Injuries,* C.G. Caine, D.J. Caine, and K.L. Lindener, eds. Champaign, IL: Human Kinetics. 1996. pp. 14-28.
43. Scott, S.H., and D.A. Winter. A comparison of three muscle pennation assumptions and their effect on isometric and isotonic force. *J Biomech* 24(2):163-167. 1991.
44. Smith, E.L. Exercise for the prevention of osteoporosis: A review. *Phys Sportsmed* 10:72-83. 1982.
45. Stauber, W.T. Eccentric action of muscles: Physiology, injury, and adaptation. In: *Exercise and Sports Sciences Reviews,* vol. 17, K.B. Pandolf, ed. Baltimore: Williams & Wilkins. 1989. pp. 157-185.
46. Stone, M. Explosive exercises/explosive training: NSCA position paper. *NSCA J* 15(3):7-15. 1993.
47. Taylor, B.N., ed. *The International System of Units (SI).* Gaithersburg, MD: National Institute of Standards and Technology. 2001.
48. Totten, L. Knee wraps. *NSCA J* 12(5):36-38. 1990.
49. *Webster's Encyclopedic Unabridged Dictionary of the English Language.* San Diego: Thunder Bay. 1996.
50. Zemper, E.D. Four year study of weight room injuries in a national sample of college football teams. *NSCA J* 12:32-34. 1990.

Chapter 5 Adaptations to Anaerobic Training Programs

1. Aagaard, P. Training-induced changes in neural function. *Exerc Sports Sci Rev* 31:61-67. 2003.
2. Aagaard, P., J.L. Andersen, P. Dyhre-Poulsen, A. Leffers, A. Wagner, P. Magnusson, J. Halkjær-Kristensen, and E.B. Simonsen. A mechanism for increased contractile strength of human pennate muscle in response to strength training: Changes in muscle architecture. *J Physiol* 534:613-623. 2001.
3. Aagaard, P., E.B. Simonsen, J.L. Andersen, P. Magnusson, and P. Dyhre-Poulsen. Increased rate of force development and neural drive of human skeletal muscle following resistance training. *J Appl Physiol* 93:1318-1326. 2002.
4. Aagaard, P., E.B. Simonsen, J.L. Andersen, P. Magnusson, and P. Dyhre-Poulsen. Neural adaptation to resistance training: Changes in evoked V-wave and H-reflex responses. *J Appl Physiol* 92:2309-2318. 2002.
5. Abe, T., K. Kumagai, and W.F. Brechue. Fascicle length of leg muscles is greater in sprinters than distance runners. *Med Sci Sports Exerc* 32:1125-1129. 2000.
6. Adams, A. Effect of exercise upon ligament strength. *Res Q* 37:163-176. 1976.
7. Adams, G.R., R.T. Harris, D. Woodard, and G. Dudley. Mapping of electrical muscle stimulation using MRI. *J Appl Physiol* 74:532-537. 1993.
8. Alway, S.E., J.D. MacDougall, and D.G. Sale. Contractile adaptations in the human triceps surae after isometric exercise. *J Appl Physiol* 66:2725-2732. 1989.
9. American College of Sports Medicine. Progression models in resistance training for healthy adults. *Med Sci Sports Exerc* 34:364-380. 2002.
10. Andersen, J.L., and P. Aagaard. Myosin heavy chain IIX overshoot in human skeletal muscle. *Muscle Nerve* 23:1095-1104. 2000.
11. Andersen, P., and J. Henriksson. Capillary supply of the quadriceps femoris muscle of man: Adaptive response to exercise. *J Physiol* 270:677-690. 1977.
12. Baker, D., S. Nance, and M. Moore. The load that maximizes the average mechanical power output during explosive bench press throws in highly trained athletes. *J Strength Cond Res* 15:20-24. 2001.
13. Baker, D., S. Nance, and M. Moore. The load that maximizes the average mechanical power output during jump squats in power trained athletes. *J Strength Cond Res* 15:92-97. 2001.
14. Bamman, M.M., J.R. Shipp, J. Jiang, B.A. Gower, G.R. Hunter, A. Goodman, C.L. McLafferty, and R.J. Urban. Mechanical load increases muscle IGF-1 and androgen receptor mRNA concentrations in humans. *Am J Physiol* 280:E383-E390. 2001.
15. Beck, K.C., and B.D. Johnson. Pulmonary adaptations to dynamic exercise. In: *American College of Sports Medicine Resource Manual for Guidelines for Exercise Testing and Prescription,* 3rd ed., J.L. Roitman, ed. Baltimore: Williams & Wilkins. 1998. pp. 305-313.
16. Bell, G.J., D. Syrotuik, T.P. Martin, R. Burnham, and H.A. Quinney. Effect of concurrent strength and endurance training on skeletal muscle properties and hormone concentrations in humans. *Eur J Appl Physiol* 81:418-427. 2000.
17. Bell, G.J., and H.A. Wenger. The effect of one-legged sprint training on intramuscular pH and nonbicarbonate buffering capacity. *Eur J Appl Physiol* 58:158-164. 1988.
18. Bickel, C.S., J. Slade, E. Mahoney, F. Haddad, G.A. Dudley, and G.R. Adams. Time course of molecular responses of human skeletal muscle to acute bouts of resistance exercise. *J Appl Physiol* 98:482-488. 2005.
19. Biolo, G., S.P. Maggi, B.D. Williams, K.D. Tipton, and R.R. Wolfe. Increased rates of muscle protein turnover and amino acid transport after resistance exercise in humans. *Am J Physiol* 268:E514-E520. 1995.
20. Blazevich, A.J., N.D. Gill, R. Bronks, and R.U. Newton. Training-specific muscle architecture adaptations after 5-wk training in athletes. *Med Sci Sports Exerc* 35:2013-2022. 2003.
21. Blazevich, A.J., and A. Giorgi. Effect of testosterone administration and weight training on muscle architecture. *Med Sci Sports Exerc* 33:1688-1693. 2001.
22. Brahm, H., H. Mallmin, K. Michaelsson, H. Strom, and S. Ljunghall. Relationship between bone mass measurements and lifetime physical activity in a Swedish population. *Calcif Tiss Int* 62:400-412. 1998.
23. Budgett, R. Overtraining syndrome. *Br J Sports Med* 24(4):231-236. 1990.
24. Bush, J.A., W.J. Kraemer, A.M. Mastro, T. Triplett-McBride, J.S. Volek, M. Putukian, W.J. Sebastianelli, and H.G. Knuttgen. Exercise and recovery responses of adrenal medullary neurohormones to heavy resistance exercise. *Med Sci Sports Exerc* 31:554-559. 1999.
25. Callister, R., R.J. Callister, S.J. Fleck, and G.A. Dudley. Physiological and performance responses to overtraining in elite judo athletes. *Med Sci Sports Exerc* 22:816-824. 1990.
26. Callister, R., M.J. Shealy, S.J. Fleck, and G.A. Dudley. Performance adaptations to sprint, endurance and both modes of training. *J Appl Sport Sci Res* 2:46-51. 1988.
27. Campos, G.E., T.J. Luecke, H.K. Wendeln, K. Toma, F.C. Hagerman, T.F. Murray, K.E. Ragg, N.A. Ratamess, W.J. Kraemer, and R.S. Staron. Muscular adaptations in response to three different resistance-training regimens: Specificity of repetition maximum training zones. *Eur J Appl Physiol* 88:50-602. 2002.
28. Carolan, B., and E. Cafarelli. Adaptations in coactivation after isometric resistance training. *J Appl Physiol* 73:911-917. 1992.
29. Carter, D.R., M.C.H. Van der Meulen, and G.S. Beaupre. Mechanical factors in bone growth and development. *Bone* 18(1 suppl.):5S-10S. 1996.
30. Chilibeck, P.D., A. Calder, D.G. Sale, and C.E. Webber. Twenty weeks of weight training increases lean tissue mass but not bone mineral mass or density in healthy, active young women. *Can J Physiol Pharmacol* 74:1180-1185. 1996.
31. Colletti, L.A., J. Edwards, L. Gordon, J. Shary, and N.H. Bell. The effects of muscle-building exercise on bone mineral density of the radius, spine, and hip in young men. *Calcif Tissue Int* 45:12-14. 1989.

32. Conroy, B.P., W.J. Kraemer, C.M. Maresh, and G.P. Dalsky. Adaptive responses of bone to physical activity. *Med Exerc Nutr Health* 1:64-74. 1992.
33. Conroy, B.P., W.J. Kraemer, C.M. Maresh, S.J. Fleck, M.H. Stone, A.C. Fry, P.D. Miller, and G.P. Dalsky. Bone mineral density in elite junior Olympic weightlifters. *Med Sci Sports Exerc* 25:1103-1109. 1993.
34. Conwall, M.W., and B.F. Leveau. The effect of physical activity on ligamentous strength: An overview. *J Orthop Sports Phys Ther* 5:275-277. 1984.
35. Costill, D.L., A. Barnett, R. Sharp, W.J. Fink, and A. Katz. Leg muscle pH following sprint running. *Med Sci Sports Exerc* 15:325-329. 1983.
36. Craig, B.W., R. Brown, and J. Everhart. Effects of progressive resistance training on growth hormone and testosterone levels in young and elderly subjects. *Mech Ageing Dev* 49:159-169. 1989.
37. Cussler, E.C., T.G. Lohman, S.B. Going, L.B. Houtkooper, L.L. Metcalfe, H.G. Flint-Wagner, R.B. Harris, and P.J. Teixeira. Weight lifted in strength training predicts bone change in postmenopausal women. *Med Sci Sports Exerc* 35:10-17. 2003.
38. Deligiannis, A., E. Zahopoulou, and K. Mandroukas. Echocardiographic study of cardiac dimensions and function in weight lifters and body builders. *Int J Sports Cardiol* 5:24-32. 1988.
39. Deschenes, M.R., J. Covault, W.J. Kraemer, and C.M. Maresh. The neuromuscular junction: Muscle fibre type differences, plasticity and adaptability to increased and decreased activity. *Sports Med* 17:358-372. 1994.
40. Deschenes, M.R., D.A. Judelson, W.J. Kraemer, V.J. Meskaitis, J.S. Volek, B.C. Nindl, F.S. Harman, and D.R. Deaver. Effects of resistance training on neuromuscular junction morphology. *Muscle Nerve* 23:1576-1581. 2000.
41. Deschenes, M.R., C.M. Maresh, J.F. Crivello, L.E. Armstrong, W.J. Kraemer, and J. Covault. The effects of exercise training of different intensities on neuromuscular junction morphology. *J Neurocytol* 22:603-615. 1993.
42. Deschenes, M.R., C.M. Maresh, and W.J. Kraemer. The neuromuscular junction: Structure, function, and its role in the excitation of muscle. *J Strength Cond Res* 8:103-109. 1994.
43. Dettmers, C., M.C. Ridding, K.M. Stephan, R.N. Lemon, J.C. Rothwell and R.S. Frackowiak. Comparison of regional cerebral blood flow with transcranial magnetic stimulation at different forces. *J Appl Physiol* 81:596-603. 1996.
44. Dook, J.E., J.C. Henderson, and R.I. Price. Exercise and bone mineral density in mature female athletes. *Med Sci Sports Exerc* 29:291-296. 1997.
45. Dudley, G.A. Metabolic consequences of resistive-type exercise. *Med Sci Sports Exerc* 20(suppl.):S158-S161. 1988.
46. Dudley, G.A., and R. Djamil. Incompatibility of endurance- and strength-training modes of exercise. *J Appl Physiol* 59:1446-1451. 1985.
47. Dudley, G.A., and S.J. Fleck. Strength and endurance training: Are they mutually exclusive? *Sports Med* 4:79-85. 1987.
48. Dudley, G.A., P.A. Tesch, B.J. Miller, and M.D. Buchanan. Importance of eccentric actions in performance adaptations to resistance training. *Aviat Space Environ Med* 62:543-550. 1991.
49. Durstine, J.L., and P.G. Davis. Specificity of exercise training and testing. In: *American College of Sports Medicine Resource Manual for Guidelines for Exercise Testing and Prescription,* 3rd ed., J.L. Roitman, ed. Baltimore: Williams & Wilkins. 1998. pp. 472-479.
50. Edge, J., D. Bishop, and C. Goodman. The effects of training intensity on muscle buffer capacity in females. *Eur J Appl Physiol* 96:97-105. 2006.
51. Edge, J., D. Bishop, S. Hill-Haas, B. Dawson, and C. Goodman. Comparison of muscle buffer capacity and repeated-sprint ability of untrained, endurance-trained and team-sport athletes. *Eur J Appl Physiol* 96:225-234. 2006.
52. Enoka, R.M. Neural adaptations with chronic physical activity. *J Biomech* 30:447-455. 1997.
53. Falkel, J.E., S.J. Fleck, and T.F. Murray. Comparison of central hemodynamics between power lifters and bodybuilders during exercise. *J Appl Sport Sci Res* 6:24-35. 1992.
54. Felici, F., A. Rosponi, P. Sbriccoli, C. Filligoi, L. Fattorini, and M. Marchetti. Linear and non-linear analysis of surface electromyograms in weightlifters. *Eur J Appl Physiol* 84:337-342. 2001.
55. Fisher, A.G., T.D. Adams, F.G. Yanowitz, J.D. Ridges, G. Orsmond, and A.G. Nelson. Noninvasive evaluation of world class athletes engaged in different modes of training. *Am J Cardiol* 63:337-341. 1989.
56. Fleck, S.J. Cardiovascular adaptations to resistance training. *Med Sci Sports Exerc* 20(suppl.):S146-S151 1988.
57. Fleck, S.J. Cardiovascular responses to strength training. In: *The Encyclopedia of Sports Medicine: Strength and Power in Sport,* 2nd ed., P.V. Komi, ed. Malden, MA: Blackwell Scientific. 2003. pp. 387-406.
58. Fleck, S.J., and L.S. Dean. Resistance-training experience and the pressor response during resistance exercise. *J Appl Physiol* 63:116-120. 1987.
59. Fleck, S.J., and W.J. Kraemer. *Designing Resistance Training Programs,* 3rd ed. Champaign, IL: Human Kinetics. 2003.
60. Fleck, S.J., and W.J. Kraemer. Hyperplasia vs. hypertrophy. *NSCA J* 5:62-63. 1983.
61. Fleck, S.J., and W.J. Kraemer. *Periodization Breakthrough: The Ultimate Training System.* Ronkonkoma, NY: Advanced Research Press. 1996.
62. Fleck, S.J., C. Henke, and W. Wilson. Cardiac MRI of elite junior Olympic weight lifters. *Int J Sports Med* 10:329-333. 1989.
63. Frost, H.M. Why do marathon runners have less bone than weight lifters? A vital-biomechanical view and explanation. *Bone* 20:183-189. 1997.
64. Fry, A.C. *Physiological responses to short-term high intensity resistance exercise overtraining.* PhD dissertation, The Pennsylvania State University. 1993.
65. Fry, A.C., and W.J. Kraemer. Resistance exercise overtraining and overreaching. *Sports Med* 23:106-129. 1997.
66. Fry, A.C., W.J. Kraemer, J.M. Lynch, N.T. Triplett, and L.P. Koziris. Does short-term near maximal intensity machine resistance training induce overtraining? *J Strength Cond Res* 8:188-191. 1994.
67. Fry, A.C., W.J. Kraemer, and L.T. Ramsey. Pituitary-adrenal-gonadal responses to high-intensity resistance exercise overtraining. *J Appl Physiol* 85:2352-2359. 1998.
68. Fry, A.C., W.J. Kraemer, M.H. Stone, B.J. Warren, S.J. Fleck, J.T. Kearney, and S.E. Gordon. Endocrine responses to over-reaching before and after 1 year of weightlifting training. *Can J Appl Physiol* 19:400-410. 1994.
69. Fry, A.C., W.J. Kraemer, F. van Borselen, J.M. Lynch, J.L. Marsit, E.P. Roy, N.T. Triplett, and H.G. Knuttgen. Performance decrements with high-intensity resistance exercise overtraining. *Med Sci Sports Exerc* 26:1165-1173. 1994.
70. Gabriel, D.A., G. Kamen, and G. Frost. Neural adaptations to resistive exercise: Mechanisms and recommendations for training practices. *Sports Med* 36:133-149. 2006.
71. Gettman, L.R., L.A. Culter, and T. Strathman. Physiological changes after 20 weeks of isotonic vs isokinetic circuit training. *J Sports Med Phys Fitness* 20:265-274. 1980.
72. Glowacki, S.P., S.E. Martin, A. Maurer, W. Back, J.S. Green, and S.F. Crouse. Effects of resistance, endurance, and concurrent exercise on training outcomes in men. *Med Sci Sports Exerc* 36:2119-2127. 2004.
73. Goldberg, A.L., J.D. Etlinger, L.F. Goldspink, and C. Jablecki. Mechanism of work-induced hypertrophy of skeletal muscle. *Med Sci Sports Exerc* 7:248-261. 1975.
74. Goldspink, G. Changes in muscle mass and phenotype and the expression of autocrine and systemic growth factors by muscle in response to stretch and overload. *J Anat* 194:323-334. 1999.
75. Goldspink, G., and S.Y. Yang. Effects of activity on growth factor expression. *Int J Sports Nutr Exerc Metab* 11:S21-S27. 2001.
76. Gonyea, W.J. The role of exercise in inducing skeletal muscle fiber number. *J Appl Physiol* 48:421-426. 1980.

77. Gonyea, W.J., G.C. Erikson, and F. Bonde-Petersen. Skeletal muscle fiber splitting induced by weightlifting exercise in cats. *Acta Physiol Scand* 99:105-109. 1977.
78. Gorassini, M., J.F. Yang, M. Siu, and D.J. Bennett. Intrinsic activation of human motor units: Reduction of motor unit recruitment thresholds by repeated contractions. *J Neurophysiol* 87:1859-1866. 2002.
79. Granhed, H., R. Jonson, and T. Hansson. The loads on the lumbar spine during extreme weight lifting. *Spine* 12:146-149. 1987.
80. Green, H., A. Dahly, K. Shoemaker, C. Goreham, E. Bombardier, and M. Ball-Burnett. Serial effects of high-resistance and prolonged endurance training on Na+-K+ pump concentration and enzymatic activities in human vastus lateralis. *Acta Physiol Scand* 165:177-184. 1999.
81. Häkkinen, K., M. Alén, M. Kallinen, M. Izquierdo, K. Jokelainen, H. Lassila, E. Maikia, W.J. Kraemer, and R.U. Newton. Muscle CSA, force production and activation of leg extensor during isometric and dynamic actions in middle-aged and elderly men and women. *J Aging Phys Activity* 6:232-247. 1998.
82. Häkkinen, K., M. Alén, W.J. Kraemer, E. Gorostiaga, M. Izquierdo, H. Rusko, J. Mikkola, A. Häkkinen, H. Valkeinen, E. Kaarakainen, S. Romu, V. Erola, J. Ahtiainen, and L. Paavolainen. Neuromuscular adaptations during concurrent strength and endurance training versus strength training. *Eur J Appl Physiol* 89:42-52. 2003.
83. Häkkinen, K., M. Izquierdo, X. Aguado, R.U. Newton, and W.J. Kraemer. Isometric and dynamic explosive force production of leg extensor muscles in men at different ages. *J Human Mvmt Studies* 31:105-121. 1996.
84. Häkkinen, K., M. Kallinen, M. Izquierdo, K. Joelainen, H. Lassila, E. Maikia, W.J. Kraemer, R.U. Newton, and M. Alén. Changes in agonist-antagonist EMG, muscle CSA and force during strength training in middle-aged and older people. *J Appl Physiol* 84:1341-1349. 1998.
85. Häkkinen, K., P.V. Komi, and M. Alén. Effect of explosive type strength training on isometric force- and relaxation-time, electromyographic and muscle fibre characteristics of leg extensor muscles. *Acta Physiol Scand* 125:587-600. 1985.
86. Häkkinen, K., R.U. Newton, S.E. Gordon, M. McCormick, J.S. Volek, B.C. Nindl, L.A. Gotshalk, W.W. Campbell, W.J. Evans, A. Häkkinen, B. Humphries, and W.J. Kraemer. Changes in muscle morphology, electromyographic activity, and force production characteristics during progressive strength training in young and older men. *J Gerontol Biol Sci* 53:415-423. 1998.
87. Häkkinen, K., and A. Pakarinen. Acute hormonal responses to two different fatiguing heavy-resistance protocols in male athletes. *J Appl Physiol* 74:882-887. 1993.
88. Häkkinen, K., A. Pakarinen, M. Alén, H. Kauhanen, and P.V. Komi. Daily hormonal and neuromuscular responses to intensive strength training in 1 week. *Int J Sports Med* 9:422-428. 1988.
89. Häkkinen, K., A. Pakarinen, M. Alén, H. Kauhanen, and P.V. Komi. Neuromuscular and hormonal adaptations in athletes to strength training in two years. *J Appl Physiol* 65:2406-2412. 1988.
90. Häkkinen, K., A. Pakarinen, M. Alén, H. Kauhanen, and P.V. Komi. Relationships between training volume, physical performance capacity, and serum hormone concentrations during prolonged training in elite weight lifters. *Int J Sports Med* 8(suppl.):61-65. 1987.
91. Hansen, S., T. Kvorning, M. Kjaer, and G. Szogaard. The effect of short-term strength training on human skeletal muscle: The importance of physiologically elevated hormone levels. *Scand J Med Sci Sports* 11:347-354. 2001.
92. Hather, B.M., P.A. Tesch, P. Buchanan, and G.A. Dudley. Influence of eccentric actions on skeletal muscle adaptations to resistance. *Acta Physiol Scand* 143:177-185. 1991.
93. Henderson, N.K., C.P. White, and J.A. Eisman. The role of exercise and fall risk reduction in prevention of osteoporosis. *Endocrin Metab Clin N Am* 27:369-387. 1998.
94. Hickson, R.C. Interference of strength development by simultaneously training for strength and endurance. *Eur J Appl Physiol* 45:255-263. 1980.
95. Ho, K., R. Roy, J. Taylor, W. Heusner, W. Van Huss, and R. Carrow. Muscle fiber splitting with weightlifting exercise. *Med Sci Sports Exerc* 9:65. 1977.
96. Hurley, B.F. Effects of resistance training on lipoprotein-lipid profiles: A comparison to aerobic exercise training. *Med Sci Sports Exerc* 21:689-693. 1989.
97. Hutton, R.S., and R.M. Enoka. Kinematic assessment of a functional role for recurrent inhibition and selective recruitment. *Exp Neurol* 93:369-379. 1986.
98. Jablecki, C.K., J.E. Heuser, and S. Kaufman. Autoradiographic localization of new RNA synthesis in hypertrophying skeletal muscles. *J Cell Biol* 57:743-759. 1973.
99. Kannus, P., L. Jozsa, A. Natri, and M. Jarvinen. Effects of training, immobilization and remobilization on tendons. *Scand J Med Sci Sports* 7:67-71. 1997.
100. Karlsson, T.S., O. Johnell, and K.J. Obrandt. Is bone mineral advantage maintained long-term in previous weightlifters? *Calcif Tiss Int* 57:325-328. 1995.
101. Kawakami, Y., T. Abe, S.Y. Kuno, and T. Fukunaga. Training-induced changes in muscle architecture and specific tension. *Eur J Appl Physiol* 72:37-43. 1995.
102. Kearns, C.F., T. Abe, and W.F. Brechue. Muscle enlargement in sumo wrestlers includes increased muscle fascicle length. *Eur J Appl Physiol* 83:289-296. 2000.
103. Kelley, G.A., and K.S. Kelley. Progressive resistance exercise and resting blood pressure: A meta-analysis of randomized controlled trials. *Hypertension* 35:838-843. 2000.
104. Kellis, E., F. Arabatzi, and C. Papadopoulos. Muscle co-activation around the knee in drop jumping using the co-contraction index. *J Electromyogr Kines* 13:229-238. 2003.
105. Kemp, T.J., T.J. Sadusky, F. Saltisi, N. Carey, J. Moss, S.Y. Yang, D.A. Sassoon, G. Goldspink, and G.R. Coulton. Identification of Ankrd2, a novel skeletal muscle gene coding for a stretch-responsive ankyrin-repeat protein. *Genomics* 66:229-241. 2000.
106. Kim, J.S., J.M. Cross, and M.M. Bamman. Impact of resistance loading on myostatin expression and cell cycle regulation in young and older men and women. *Am J Physiol Endocrinol Metab* 288: E1110-1119. 2005.
107. Kjaer, M.J. Role of extracellular matrix in adaptation of tendon and skeletal muscle to mechanical loading. *Physiol Rev* 84:649-698. 2004.
108. Klitgaard, H., and T. Clausen. Increased total concentration of Na-K pumps in vastus lateralis muscle of old trained human subjects. *J Appl Physiol* 67:2491-2494. 1989.
109. Kojic, S., E. Medeot, E. Guccione, H. Krmac, I. Zara, V. Martinelli, G. Valle, and G. Faulkner. The ankrd2 protein, a link between the sarcomere and the nucleus in skeletal muscle. *J Mol Biol* 339:313-325. 2004.
110. Konig, D., M. Huonker, A. Schmid, M. Halle, A. Berg, and J. Keul. Cardiovascular, metabolic, and hormonal parameters in professional tennis players. *Med Sci Sports Exerc* 33:654-658. 2001.
111. Kosek, D.J., J.S. Kim, J.K. Petrella, J.M. Cross, and M.M. Bamman. Efficacy of 3 days/wk resistance training on myofiber hypertrophy and myogenic mechanisms in young vs. older adults. *J Appl Physiol* 101:531-544. 2006.
112. Kraemer, W.J. Endocrine responses and adaptations to strength training. In: *The Encyclopedia of Sports Medicine: Strength and Power in Sport,* 1st ed., P.V. Komi, ed. Malden, MA: Blackwell Scientific. 1992. pp. 291-304.
113. Kraemer, W.J. Endocrine responses to resistance exercise. *Med Sci Sports Exerc* 20(suppl.):152-157. 1988.
114. Kraemer, W.J., S.J. Fleck, R. Callister, M. Shealy, G. Dudley, C.M. Maresh, L. Marchitelli, C. Cruthirds, T. Murray, and J.E. Falkel. Training responses of plasma beta-endorphin, adrenocorticotropin and cortisol. *Med Sci Sports Exerc* 21:146-153. 1989.
115. Kraemer, W.J., S.J. Fleck, J.E. Dziados, E.A. Harman, L.J. Marchitelli, S.E. Gordon, R. Mello, P.N. Frykman, L.P. Koziris, and N.T. Triplett. Changes in hormonal concentrations after different heavy-resistance exercise protocols in women. *J Appl Physiol* 75:594-604. 1993.

116. Kraemer, W.J., S.J. Fleck, C.M. Maresh, N.A Ratamess, S.E. Gordon, K.L. Goetz, E.A. Harman, P.N. Frykman, J.S. Volek, S.A. Mazzetti, A.C. Fry, L.J. Marchitelli, and J.F. Patton. Acute hormonal responses to a single bout of heavy resistance exercise in trained power lifters and untrained men. *Can J Appl Physiol* 24:524-537. 1999.
117. Kraemer, W.J., S.E. Gordon, S.J. Fleck, L.J. Marchitelli, R. Mello, J.E. Dziados, K. Friedl, E. Harman, C. Maresh, and A.C. Fry. Endogenous anabolic hormonal and growth factor responses to heavy resistance exercise in males and females. *Int J Sports Med* 12:228-235. 1991.
118. Kraemer, W.J., and L.A. Gotshalk. Physiology of American football. In: *Exercise and Sport Science,* W.E. Garrett and D.T. Kirkendall, eds. Philadelphia: Lippincott, Williams & Wilkins. 2000. pp. 795-813.
119. Kraemer, W.J., and L.P. Koziris. Olympic weightlifting and power lifting. In: *Physiology and Nutrition for Competitive Sport,* D.R. Lamb, H.G. Knuttgen, and R. Murray, eds. Carmel, IN: Cooper. 1994. pp. 1-54.
120. Kraemer, W.J., L.P. Koziris, N.A. Ratamess, K.Häkkinen, N.T. Triplett-McBride, A.C. Fry, S.E. Gordon, J.S. Volek, D.N. French, M.R. Rubin, A.L. Gómez, M.J. Sharman, J.M. Lynch, M. Izquierdo, R.U. Newton, and S.J. Fleck. Detraining produces minimal changes in physical performance and hormonal variables in recreationally strength-trained men. *J Strength Cond Res* 16:373-382. 2002.
121. Kraemer, W.J., L. Marchitelli, D. McCurry, R. Mello, J.E. Dziados, E. Harman, P. Frykman, S.E. Gordon, and S.J. Fleck. Hormonal and growth factor responses to heavy resistance exercise. *J Appl Physiol* 69:1442-1450. 1990.
122. Kraemer, W.J., and B.C. Nindl. Factors involved with overtraining for strength and power. In: *Overtraining in Sport,* R.B. Kreider, A.C. Fry, and M.L. O'Toole, eds. Champaign, IL: Human Kinetics. 1998. pp. 69-86.
123. Kraemer, W.J., B.C. Nindl, N.A. Ratamess, L.A. Gotshalk, J.S. Volek, S.J. Fleck, R.U. Newton, and K. Häkkinen. Changes in muscle hypertrophy in women with periodized resistance training. *Med Sci Sports Exerc* 36:697-708. 2004.
124. Kraemer, W.J., B.J. Noble, B.W. Culver, and M.J. Clark. Physiologic responses to heavy-resistance exercise with very short rest periods. *Int J Sports Med* 8:247-252. 1987.
125. Kraemer, W.J., J. Patton, S.E. Gordon, E.A. Harman, M.R. Deschenes, K. Reynolds, R.U. Newton, N.T. Triplett, and J.E. Dziados. Compatibility of high intensity strength and endurance training on hormonal and skeletal muscle adaptations. *J Appl Physiol* 78:976-989. 1995.
126. Kraemer, W.J., and N.A. Ratamess. Endocrine responses and adaptations to strength and power training. In: *The Encyclopedia of Sports Medicine: Strength and Power in Sport,* 2nd ed., P.V. Komi, ed. Malden, MA: Blackwell Scientific. 2003. pp. 387-406.
127. Kraemer, W.J., and N.A. Ratamess. Fundamentals of resistance training: Progression and exercise prescription. *Med Sci Sport Exerc* 36:674-678. 2004.
128. Kraemer, W.J., and N.A. Ratamess. Hormonal responses and adaptations to resistance exercise and training. *Sports Med* 35:339-361. 2005.
129. Kraemer, W.J., and N.A. Ratamess. Physiology of resistance training: Current issues. *Orthop Phys Ther Clin N Am: Exerc Tech* 4:467-513. 2000.
130. Kraemer, W.J., N.A. Ratamess, and D.N. French. Resistance training for health and performance. *Curr Sports Med Rep* 1:165-171. 2002.
131. Kraemer, W.J., N. Ratamess, A.C. Fry, T. Triplett-McBride, L.P. Koziris, J.A. Bauer, J.M. Lynch, and S.J. Fleck. Influence of resistance training volume and periodization on physiological and performance adaptations in college women tennis players. *Am J Sports Med* 28:626-633. 2000.
132. Kraemer, W.J., M.R. Rubin, K. Häkkinen, B.C. Nindl, J.O. Marx, J.S. Volek, D.N. French, A.L. Gómez, M.J. Sharman, T. Scheett, N.A. Ratamess, M.P. Miles, A.M. Mastro, J.L. Van Heest, C.M. Maresh, J.R. Welsch, and W.C. Hymer. Influence of muscle strength and total work on exercise-induced plasma growth hormone isoforms in women. *J Sci Med Sport* 6:295-306. 2003.
133. Kraemer, W.J., B.A. Spiering, J.S. Volek, N.A. Ratamess, M.J. Sharman, M.R. Rubin, D.N. French, R. Silvestre, D.L. Hatfield, J.L. Van Heest, J.L. Vingren, D.A. Judelson, M.R. Deschenes, and C.M. Maresh. Androgenic responses to resistance exercise: Effects of feeding and L-carnitine. *Med Sci Sports Exerc* 38:1288-1296. 2006.
134. Kraemer, W.J., R.S. Staron, D. Karapondo, A.C. Fry, S.E. Gordon, J.S. Volek, B. Nindl, L. Gotshalk, R.U. Newton, and K. Häkkinen. The effects of short-term resistance training on endocrine function in men and women. *Eur J Appl Physiol* 78:69-76. 1998.
135. Kraemer, W.J., J.S. Volek, K.L. Clark, S.E. Gordon, T. Incledon, S.M. Puhl, N.T. Triplett-McBride, J.M. McBride, M. Putukian, and W.J. Sebastianelli. Physiological adaptations to a weight-loss dietary regimen and exercise programs in women. *J Appl Physiol* 83:270-279. 1997.
136. Kubo, K., H. Kanehisa, and T. Fukunaga. Effects of resistance and stretching training programmes on the viscoelastic properties of human tendon structures in vivo. *J Physiol* 538:219-226. 2002.
137. Kubo, K., T. Komuro, N. Ishiguro, N. Tsunoda, and Y. Sato. Effects of low-load resistance training with vascular occlusion on the mechanical properties of muscle and tendon. *J Appl Biomech* 22:112-119. 2006.
138. Kubo, K., H. Yata, H. Kanehisa, and T. Fukunaga. Effects of isometric squat training on the tendon stiffness and jump performance. *Eur J Appl Physiol* 96:305-314. 2006.
139. Kuipers, H., and H.A. Keizer. Overtraining in elite athletes: Review and directions for the future. *Sports Med* 6:79-92. 1988.
140. Langberg, H., L. Rosendal, and M. Kjaer. Training-induced changes in peritendinous type I collagen turnover determined by microdialysis in humans. *J Physiol* 534:297-302. 2001.
141. Leveritt, M., and P.J. Abernethy. Acute effects of high-intensity endurance exercise on subsequent resistance activity. *J Strength Cond Res* 13:47-51. 1999.
142. Leveritt, M., P.J. Abernethy, B. Barry, and P.A. Logan. Concurrent strength and endurance training: The influence of dependent variable selection. *J Strength Cond Res* 17:503-508. 2003.
143. Luthi, J.M., H. Howald, H. Claassen, K. Rosler, P. Vock, and H. Hoppeler. Structural changes in skeletal muscle tissue with heavy-resistance exercise. *Int J Sports Med* 7:123-127. 1986.
144. MacDougall, J.D. Adaptability of muscle to strength training—a cellular approach. In: *Biochemistry of Exercise VI.* Champaign, IL: Human Kinetics. 1986. pp. 501-513.
145. MacDougall, J.D., G.C.B. Elder, D.G. Sale, and J.R. Sutton. Effects of strength training and immobilization on human muscle fibers. *Eur J Appl Physiol* 43:25-34. 1980.
146. MacDougall, J.D., M.J. Gibala, M.A. Tarnopolsky, J.R. MacDonald, S.A. Interisano, and K.E. Yarasheski. The time course for elevated muscle protein synthesis following heavy resistance exercise. *Can J Appl Physiol* 20:480-486. 1995.
147. MacDougall, J.D., D.G. Sale, S.E. Alway, and J.R. Sutton. Muscle fiber number in biceps brachii in bodybuilders and control subjects. *J Appl Physiol* 57:1399-1403. 1984.
148. MacDougall, J.D., D.G. Sale, G.C. Elder, and J.R. Sutton. Muscle ultrastructural characteristics of elite powerlifters and bodybuilders. *Eur J Appl Physiol* 48:117-126. 1982.
149. MacDougall, J.D., D.G. Sale, G.C.B. Elder, and J.R. Sutton. Muscle ultrastructural characteristics of elite powerlifters and bodybuilders. *Med Sci Sports Exerc* 2:131. 1980.
150. MacDougall, J.D., D.G. Sale, G. Elder, and J.R. Sutton. Ultrastructural properties of human skeletal muscle following heavy resistance exercise and immobilization. *Med Sci Sports Exerc* 8:72. 1976.
151. MacDougall, J.D., D.G. Sale, J.R. Moroz, G.C.B. Elder, J.R. Sutton, and H. Howald. Mitochondrial volume density in human skeletal muscle following heavy resistance training. *Med Sci Sports Exerc* 11:164-166. 1979.
152. MacDougall, J.D., D. Tuxen, D.G. Sale, J.R. Moroz, and J.R. Sutton. Arterial blood pressure response to heavy resistance exercise. *J Appl Physiol* 58:785-790. 1985.
153. MacDougall, J.D., G.R. Ward, D.G. Sale, and J.R. Sutton. Biochemical adaptation of human skeletal muscle to heavy resistance training and immobilization. *J Appl Physiol* 43:700-703. 1977.
154. McArdle, W.D., F.I. Katch, and V.I. Katch. *Exercise Physiology,* 4th ed. Philadelphia: Lea & Febiger. 1994.

155. McCall, G.E., W.C. Byrnes, A. Dickinson, P.M. Pattany, and S.J. Fleck. Muscle fiber hypertrophy, hyperplasia, and capillary density in college men after resistance training. *J Appl Physiol* 81:2004-2012. 1996.
156. McCall, G.E., W.C. Byrnes, S.J. Fleck, A. Dickinson, and W.J. Kraemer. Acute and chronic hormonal responses to resistance training designed to promote muscle hypertrophy. *Can J Appl Physiol* 24:96-107. 1999.
157. McCarthy, J.P., J.C. Agre, B.K. Graf, M.A. Pozniak, and A.C. Vailas. Compatibility of adaptive responses with combining strength and endurance training. *Med Sci Sports Exerc* 27:429-436. 1995.
158. McCarthy, J.P., M.A. Pozniak, and J.C. Agre. Neuromuscular adaptations to concurrent strength and endurance training. *Med Sci Sports Exerc* 34:511-519. 2002.
159. McCartney, N., R.S. McKelvie, J. Martin, D.G. Sale, and J.D. MacDougall. Weight-training induced attenuation of the circulatory response of older males to weight lifting. *J Appl Physiol* 74:1056-1060. 1993.
160. Milner-Brown, H.S., R.B. Stein, and R.G. Lee. Synchronization of human motor units: Possible roles of exercise and supraspinal reflexes. *Electroenceph Clin Neurophysiol* 38:245-254. 1975.
161. Minchna, H., and G. Hantmann. Adaptation of tendon collagen to exercise. *Int Orthop* 13:161-165. 1989.
162. Moritani, T., and H.A. deVries. Neural factors versus hypertrophy in the time course of muscle strength gain. *Am J Phys Med* 58:115-130. 1979.
163. Munn, J., R.D. Herbert, and S.C. Gandevia. Contralateral effects of unilateral resistance training: A meta-analysis. *J Appl Physiol* 96:1861-1866. 2004.
164. Nardone, A., C. Romano, and M. Schieppati. Selective recruitment of high-threshold human motor units during voluntary isotonic lengthening of active muscles. *J Physiol* 409:451-471. 1989.
165. Newton, R.U., W.J. Kraemer, K. Häkkinen, B.J. Humphries, and A.J. Murphy. Kinematics, kinetics, and muscle activation during explosive upper body movements: Implications for power development. *J Appl Biomech* 12:31-43. 1996.
166. Nilsson, B.E., and N.E. Westlin. Bone density in athletics. *Clin Orthop* 77:179-182. 1971.
167. Nindl, B.C., W.C. Hymer, D.R. Deaver, and W.J. Kraemer. Growth hormone pulsatility profile characteristics following acute heavy resistance exercise. *J Appl Physiol* 91:163-172. 2001.
168. Oda, S., and T. Moritani. Maximal isometric force and neural activity during bilateral and unilateral elbow flexion in humans. *Eur J Appl Physiol* 69:240-243. 1994.
169. Oettmeier, R., J. Arokoski, A.J. Roth, A.J. Helminen, M. Tammi, and K. Abendroth. Quantitative study of articular cartilage and subchondral bone remodeling in the knee joint of dogs after strenuous running training. *J Bone Min Res* 7:5419-5423. 1992.
170. Ortenblad, N., P.K. Lunde, K. Levin, J.L. Andersen, and P.K. Pedersen. Enhanced sarcoplasmic reticulum Ca(2+) release following intermittent sprint training. *Am J Physiol* 279:R152-R160. 2000.
171. Pensini, M., A. Martin, and M.A. Maffiuletti. Central versus peripheral adaptations following eccentric resistance training. *Int J Sports Med* 23:567-574. 2002.
172. Pette, D., and R.S. Staron. Mammalian skeletal muscle fiber type transitions. *Int Rev Cytol* 170:143-223. 1997.
173. Phillips, S., K. Tipton, A. Aarsland, S. Wolf, and R. Wolfe. Mixed muscle protein synthesis and breakdown after resistance exercise in humans. *Am J Physiol* 273:E99-E107. 1997.
174. Ploutz, L.L., P.A. Tesch, R.L. Biro, and G.A. Dudley. Effect of resistance training on muscle use during exercise. *J Appl Physiol* 76:1675-1681. 1994.
175. Pocock, N.A., J. Eisman, T. Gwinn, P. Sambrook, P. Kelley, J. Freund, and M. Yeates. Muscle strength, physical fitness, and weight but not age to predict femoral neck bone mass. *J Bone Min Res* 4(3):441-448. 1989.
176. Raastad, T., T. Glomsheller, T. Bjoro, and J. Hallen. Changes in human skeletal muscle contractility and hormone status during 2 weeks of heavy strength training. *Eur J Appl Physiol* 84:54-63. 2001.
177. Ratamess, N.A., M.J. Falvo, G.T. Mangine, J.R. Hoffman, A.D. Faigenbaum, and J. Kang. The effect of rest interval length on metabolic responses to the bench press exercise. *Eur J Appl Physiol.* 100(1): 1-17, 2007.
178. Ratamess, N.A., and M. Izquierdo. Forthcoming. Neuromuscular adaptations to training. In: *The Olympic Textbook of Medicine in Sport*, ed. M. Schwellnus. Hoboken, NJ: John Wiley and Sons, Inc.
179. Ratamess, N.A., W.J. Kraemer, J.S. Volek, C.M. Maresh, J.L. Van Heest, M.S. Sharman, M.R. Rubin, D.N. French, J.D. Vescovi, R. Silvestre, D.L. Hatfield, S.J. Fleck, and M.R. Deschenes. Effects of heavy resistance exercise volume on post-exercise androgen receptor content in resistance-trained men. *J Steroid Biochem Mol Biol* 93:35-42. 2005.
180. Ratamess, N.A., W.J. Kraemer, J.S. Volek, M.R. Rubin, A.L. Gómez, D.N. French, M.J. Sharman, M.M. McGuigan, T.P. Scheett, K. Häkkinen, and F. Dioguardi. The effects of amino acid supplementation on muscular performance during resistance training overreaching: Evidence of an effective overreaching protocol. *J Strength Cond Res* 17:250-258. 2003.
181. Roth, S.M., R.E. Ferrell, D.G. Peters, E.J. Metter, B.F. Hurley, and M.A. Rogers. Influence of age, sex, and strength training on human muscle gene expression determined by microarray. *Physiol Genomics* 10:181-190. 2002.
182. Roth, S.M., G.F. Martel, R.E. Ferrell, E.J. Metter, B.F. Hurley, and M.A. Rogers. Myostatin gene expression is reduced in humans with heavy-resistance strength training: A brief communication. *Exp Biol Med* 228:706-709. 2003.
183. Rutherford, O.M., and D.A. Jones. The role of learning and coordination in strength training. *Eur J Appl Physiol* 55:100-105. 1986.
184. Saaf, R.B. Effect of exercise on adult cartilage. *Acta Orthop Scand Suppl* 7:1-83. 1950.
185. Sabo, D., L. Bernd, J. Pfeil, and A. Reiter. Bone quality in the lumbar spine in high-performance athletes. *Eur Spine J* 5:258-263. 1996.
186. Sadusky, T.J., T.J. Kemp, M. Simon, N. Carey, and G.R. Coulton. Identification of Serhl, a new member of the serine hydrolase family induced by passive stretch of skeletal muscle in vivo. *Genomics* 73:38-49. 2001.
187. Sale, D.G. Influence of exercise and training on motor unit activation. *Exerc Sport Sci Rev* 15:95-151. 1987.
188. Sale, D.G. Neural adaptation in strength and power training. In: *Human Muscle Power*, N.L. Jones, N. McCartney, and A.J. McComas, eds. Champaign, IL: Human Kinetics. 1986. pp. 289-307.
189. Sale, D.G. Neural adaptations to strength training. In: *The Encyclopedia of Sports Medicine: Strength and Power in Sport,* 2nd ed., P.V. Komi, ed. Malden, MA: Blackwell Scientific. 2003. pp. 281-314.
190. Sale, D.G., I. Jacobs, J.D. MacDougall, and S. Garner. Comparison of two regimens of concurrent strength and endurance training. *Med Sci Sports Exerc* 22:348-356. 1990.
191. Sale, D.G., D.E. Moroz, R.S. McKelvie, J.D. MacDougall, and N. McCartney. Effect of training on the blood pressure response to weight lifting. *Can J Appl Physiol* 19:60-74. 1994.
192. Sale, D.G., A.R.M. Upton, A.J. McComas, and J.D. MacDougall. Neuromuscular functions in weight-trainers. *Exp Neurol* 82:521-531. 1983.
193. Seger, J.Y., and A. Thorstensson. Effects of eccentric versus concentric training on thigh muscle strength and EMG. *Int J Sports Med* 26:45-52. 2005.
194. Semmler, J.G., M.V. Sale, F.G. Meyer, and M.A. Nordstrom. Motor-unit coherence and its relation with synchrony are influenced by training. *J Neurophysiol* 92:3320-3331. 2004.
195. Sharp, R.L., D.L. Costill, W.J. Fink, and D.S. King. Effects of eight weeks of bicycle ergometer sprint training on human muscle buffer capacity. *Int J Sports Med* 7:13-17. 1986.
196. Shima, S.N., K. Ishida, K. Katayama, Y. Morotome, Y. Sato, and M. Miyamura. Cross education of muscular strength during unilateral resistance training and detraining. *Eur J Appl Physiol* 86:287-294. 2002.

197. Shinohara, M., M. Kouzaki, T. Yoshihisa, and T. Fukunaga. Efficacy of tourniquet ischemia for strength training with low resistance. *Eur J Appl Physiol* 77:189-191. 1998.
198. Skerry, T.M. Mechanical loading and bone: What sort of exercise is beneficial to the skeleton? *Bone* 20:179-181. 1997.
199. Staff, P.H. The effects of physical activity on joints, cartilage, tendons, and ligaments. *Scand J Med* 29(suppl.):59-63. 1982.
200. Staron, R.S. The classification of human skeletal muscle fiber types. *J Strength Cond Res* 11:67. 1997.
201. Staron, R.S., D.L. Karapondo, W.J. Kraemer, A.C. Fry, S.E. Gordon, J.E. Falkel, F.C. Hagerman, and R.S. Hikida. Skeletal muscle adaptations during the early phase of heavy-resistance training in men and women. *J Appl Physiol* 76:1247-1255. 1994.
202. Staron, R.S., E.S. Malicky, M.J. Leonardi, J.E. Falkel, F.C. Hagerman, and G.A. Dudley. Muscle hypertrophy and fast fiber type conversions in heavy resistance-trained women. *Eur J Appl Physiol* 60:71-79. 1989.
203. Stone, M.H., R.E. Keith, J.T. Kearney, S.J. Fleck, G.D. Wilson, and N.T. Triplett. Overtraining: A review of the signs, symptoms and possible causes. *J Appl Sport Sci Res* 5:35-50. 1991.
204. Taaffe, D.R., T.L. Robinson, C.M. Snow, and R. Marcus. High impact exercise promotes bone gain in well-trained female athletes. *J Bone Min Res* 12:255-260. 1997.
205. Takarada, Y., Y. Sato, and N. Ishii. Effects of resistance exercise combined with vascular occlusion on muscle function in athletes. *Eur J Appl Physiol* 86:308-314. 2002.
206. Ter Haar Romeny, B.M., J.J. Dernier Van Der Goen, and C.C.A.M. Gielen. Changes in recruitment order of motor units in the human biceps muscle. *Exp Neurol* 78:360-368. 1982.
207. Tesch, P.A. Acute and long-term metabolic changes consequent to heavy-resistance exercise. In: *Muscular Function in Exercise and Training,* P. Marconnet and P.V. Komi, eds. Basel: Karger. 1987. pp. 67-89.
208. Tesch, P.A. Skeletal muscle adaptations consequent to long-term heavy-resistance exercise. *Med Sci Sports Exerc* 20(suppl.):S124-S132. 1988.
209. Tesch, P.A., and L. Larsson. Muscle hypertrophy in bodybuilders. *Eur J Appl Physiol* 49:310. 1982.
210. Tipton, C.M., R.D. Matthes, J.A. Maynard, and R.A. Carey. The influence of physical activity on ligaments and tendons. *Med Sci Sports Exerc* 7:165-175. 1975.
211. Tremblay, M.S., J.L. Copeland, and W. Van Helder. Effect of training status and exercise mode on endogenous steroid hormones in men. *J Appl Physiol* 96:531-539. 2003.
212. Turto, H., S. Lindy, and J. Halme. Procollagen proline hydroxylase activity in work-induced hypertrophy of rat muscle. *Am J Physiol* 226:63-65. 1974.
213. Van Custem, M., J. Duchateau, and K. Hainut. Changes in single motor unit behaviour contribute to the increase in contraction speed after dynamic training in humans. *J Physiol* 513:295-305. 1998.
214. Virvidakis, K., E. Georgion, A. Konkotsidis, K. Ntalles, and C. Proukasis. Bone mineral content of junior competitive weightlifters. *Int J Sports Med* 11:214-246. 1990.
215. Wang, N., R.S. Hikida, R.S. Staron, and J.A. Simoneau. Muscle fiber types of women after resistance training—quantitative ultrastructure and enzyme activity. *Pflugers Arch* 424:494-502. 1993.
216. Wilson, G.J., R.U. Newton, A.J. Murphy, and B.J. Humphries. The optimal training load for the development of dynamic athletic performance. *Med Sci Sports Exerc* 25:1279-1286. 1993.
217. Wittich, A., C.A. Mautalen, M.B. Oliveri, A. Bagur, F. Somoza, and E. Rotemberg. Professional football (soccer) players have a markedly greater skeletal mineral content, density, and size than age- and BMI-matched controls. *Calcif Tiss Int* 63:112-117. 1998.
218. Woo, S.L.-Y., K. An, S.P. Arnoczky, J.S. Wayne, D.C. Fithian, and B.S. Myers. Anatomy, biology, and biomechanics of tendon, ligament, and meniscus. In: *Orthopaedic Basic Science,* S.R. Simon, ed. Rosemont, IL: American Academy of Orthopaedic Surgeons. 1994. pp. 1-184.

Chapter 6: Adaptations to Aerobic Endurance Training Programs

1. Andersen, P., and J. Henriksson. Training induced changes in the subgroups of human Type II skeletal muscle fibers. *Acta Physiol Scand* 99:123-125. 1975.
2. Åstrand, P.O. Physical performance as a function of age. *JAMA* 205:729-733. 1968.
3. Åstrand, P.O., K. Rodahl, H.A. Dahl, and S.B. Strømme. *Textbook of Work Physiology: Physiological Basis of Exercise,* 4th ed. Champaign, IL: Human Kinetics. 2003.
4. Atha, J. Strengthening muscle. *Exerc Sport Sci Rev* 9:1-73. 1981.
5. Beck, K.C., and B.D. Johnson. Pulmonary adaptations to dynamic exercise. In: *American College of Sports Medicine Resource Manual for Guidelines for Exercise Testing and Prescription,* 3rd ed., J.L. Roitman, ed. Baltimore: Williams & Wilkins. 1998. pp. 305-313.
6. Bevegard, B.S., and J.R. Shepherd. Regulation of the circulation during exercise in man. *Physiol Rev* 47:178-213. 1967.
7. Brooks, G.A., T.D. Fahey, and T.P. White. *Exercise Physiology: Human Bioenergetics and Its Applications,* 2nd ed. Mountain View, CA: Mayfield. 1996.
8. Brynteson, P., and W.E. Sinning. The effects of training frequencies on the retention of cardiovascular fitness. *Med Sci Sports Exerc* 5:20-33. 1973.
9. Buckwalter, J.A. Osteoarthritis and articular cartilage use, disuse, and abuse: Experimental studies. *J Rheum* 22(suppl. 43):13-15. 1995.
10. Budgett, R. Overtraining syndrome. *Br J Sports Med* 24(4):231-236. 1990.
11. Callister, R., R.J. Callister, S.J. Fleck, and G.A. Dudley. Physiological and performance responses to overtraining in elite judo athletes. *Med Sci Sports Exerc* 22(6):816-824. 1990.
12. Callister, R., M.J. Shealy, S.J. Fleck, and G.A. Dudley. Performance adaptations to sprint, endurance and both modes of training. *J Appl Sport Sci Res* 2:46-51. 1988.
13. Clausen, J.P. Effect of physical training on cardiovascular adjustments to exercise in man. *Physiol Rev* 57:779-815. 1977.
14. Costill, D.L., J. Daniels, W. Evans, W. Fink, G. Krahenbuhl, and B. Saltin. Skeletal muscle enzymes and fiber composition in male and female track athletes. *J Appl Physiol* 40(2):149-154. 1976.
15. Dalsky, G.P., K.S. Stocke, A.A. Ehsani, E. Slatopolsky, W.C. Lee, and S.J. Birge. Weight-bearing exercise training and lumbar bone mineral content in postmenopausal women. *Ann Intern Med* 108:824-828. 1988.
16. Deschenes, M.R., W.J. Kraemer, J.F. Crivello, C.M. Maresh, L.E. Armstrong, and J. Covault. The effects of different treadmill running programs on the muscle morphology of adult rats. *Int J Sports Med* 16:273-277. 1995.
17. Durstine, J.L., and P.G. Davis. Specificity of exercise training and testing. In: *American College of Sports Medicine Resource Manual for Guidelines for Exercise Testing and Prescription,* 3rd ed. J.L. Roitman, ed. Baltimore: Williams & Wilkins. 1998. pp. 472-479.
18. Fardy, P.S. Training for aerobic power. In: *Toward an Understanding of Human Performance,* E.J. Burke, ed. Ithaca, NY: Mouvement. 1977. pp. 10-14.
19. Fleck, S.J., and W.J. Kraemer. The overtraining syndrome. *NSCA J* 4(4):50-51. 1982.
20. Fleck, S.J., and W.J. Kraemer. *Periodization Breakthrough: The Ultimate Training System.* Ronkonkoma, NY: Advanced Research Press. 1996.
21. Fox, E.L., R.W. Bowers, and M.L. Foss. *The Physiological Basis of Physical Education and Athletics,* 5th ed. Dubuque, IA: Brown. 1993.
22. Franklin, B.A. Normal cardiorespiratory responses to acute exercise. In: *American College of Sports Medicine Resource Manual for Guidelines for Exercise Testing and Prescription,* 3rd ed., J.L. Roitman, ed. Baltimore: Williams & Wilkins. 1998. pp. 137-145.
23. Franklin, B.A., and J.L. Roitman. Cardiorespiratory adaptations to exercise. In: *American College of Sports Medicine Resource Manual*

for Guidelines for Exercise Testing and Prescription, 3rd ed., J.L. Roitman, ed. Baltimore: Williams & Wilkins. 1998. pp. 146-155.

24. Frost, H.M. Why do marathon runners have less bone than weight lifters? A vital-biomechanical view and explanation. *Bone* 20(3):183-189. 1997.
25. Fry, A.C., and W.J. Kraemer. Resistance exercise overtraining and overreaching. *Sports Med* 23(2):106-129. 1997.
26. Fry, A.C., W.J. Kraemer, and L.T. Ramsey. Pituitary-adrenal-gonadal responses to high-intensity resistance exercise overtraining. *J Appl Physiol* 85(6):2352-2359. 1998.
27. Gaesser, G.A., and L.A. Wilson. Effects of continuous and interval training on the parameters of the power-endurance time relationship for high-intensity exercise. *Int J Sports Med* 9:417-421. 1988.
28. Galbo, H. Endocrinology and metabolism in exercise. *Int J Sports Med* 2:203-211. 1981.
29. Galbo, H. *Hormonal and Metabolic Adaptation to Exercise.* New York: Thieme-Stratton. 1983.
30. Gollnick, P.D. Relationship of strength and endurance with skeletal muscle structure and metabolic potential. *Int J Sports Med* 3(suppl. 1):26-32. 1982.
31. Gollnick, P.D., R. Armstrong, B. Saltin, C. Saubert, W. Sembrowich, and R. Shepard. Effects of training on enzyme activity and fiber composition of human skeletal muscle. *J Appl Physiol* 34(1):107-111. 1973.
32. Gollnick, P.D., R. Armstrong, K.P. Saubert, and B. Saltin. Enzyme activity and fiber composition in skeletal muscle of untrained and trained men. *J Appl Physiol* 33(3):312-319. 1972.
33. Guyton, A.C. *Textbook of Medical Physiology,* 10th ed. Philadelphia: Saunders. 2000.
34. Havenith, G., and M. Holewijn. Environmental considerations: Altitude and air pollution. In: *American College of Sports Medicine Resource Manual for Guidelines for Exercise Testing and Prescription,* 3rd ed., J.L. Roitman, ed. Baltimore: Williams & Wilkins. 1998. pp. 215-222.
35. Hickson, R.C., H.A. Bomze, and J.O. Holloszy. Linear increase in aerobic power induced by a strenuous program of endurance exercise. *J Appl Physiol* 42:372-376. 1977.
36. Hickson, R.C., B.A. Dvorak, E.M. Gorostiaga, T.T. Kurowski, and C. Foster. Potential for strength and endurance training to amplify endurance performance. *J Appl Physiol* 65:2285-2290. 1988.
37. Hoffman, M.D., L.M. Sheldahl, and W.J. Kraemer. Therapeutic exercise. In: *Rehabilitation Medicine: Principles and Practice,* 3rd ed., J.A. DeLisa and B.M. Gans, eds. Philadelphia: Lippincott-Raven. 1998. pp. 697-743.
38. Holloszy, J.O. Effects of exercise on mitochondrial oxygen uptake and respiratory enzyme activity in skeletal muscle. *J Biol Chem* 242:2278-2282. 1967.
39. Holloszy, J.O. The regulation of carbohydrate and fat metabolism during and after exercise. *Front Biosci* 3:D1011-1027. 1998.
40. Howald, H. Training-induced morphological and functional changes in skeletal muscle. *Int J Sports Med* 3:1-12. 1982.
41. Jansson, E., B. Sjodin, and P. Tesch. Changes in muscle fibre type distribution in man after physical training: A sign of fibre transformation? *Acta Physiol Scand* 104:235-237. 1978.
42. Karvonen, M.J., E. Kentala, and O. Mustala. The effects of training on heart rate: A longitudinal study. *Ann Med Exp Biol Fenn* 35:307-315. 1957.
43. Kraemer, W.J. Endocrine responses and adaptations to strength training. In: *The Encyclopedia of Sports Medicine: Strength and Power in Sport,* 1st ed., ed. P.V. Komi. Malden, MA: Blackwell Scientific. 1992. pp. 291-304.
44. Kraemer, W.J. Endocrine responses to resistance exercise. *Med Sci Sports Exerc* 20(suppl.):152-157. 1988.
45. Kraemer, W.J. Exercise prescription in weight training: A needs analysis. *NSCA J* 5(1):64-65. 1983.
46. Kraemer, W.J. Exercise prescription in weight training: Manipulating program variables. *NSCA J* 5(3):58-59. 1983.
47. Kraemer, W.J. The physiological basis for conditioning in wrestling. *NSCA J* 4(3):49. 1982.
48. Kraemer, W.J. Programming: Variables in successful program design. *NSCA J* 6(2):54-55. 1984.
49. Kraemer, W.J., and T.R. Baechle. Development of a strength training program. In: *Sports Medicine,* 2nd ed., F.L. Allman and A.J. Ryan, eds. Orlando, FL: Academic Press. 1989. pp. 113-127.
50. Kraemer, W.J., N.D. Duncan, and J.S. Volek. Resistance training and elite athletes: Adaptations and program considerations. *J Orthop Sports Phys Ther* 28(2):110-119. 1998.
51. Kraemer, W.J., and S.J. Fleck. Aerobic metabolism, training, and evaluation. *NSCA J* 5(5):52-54. 1982.
52. Kraemer, W.J., A.C. Fry, B.J. Warren, M.H. Stone, S.J. Fleck, J.T. Kearney, B.P. Conroy, C.M. Maresh, C.A. Weseman, N.T. Triplett, and S.E. Gordon. Acute hormonal responses in elite junior weightlifters. *Int J Sports Med* 13(2):103-109. 1992.
53. Kraemer, W.J., L. Marchitelli, D. McCurry, R. Mello, J.E. Dziados, E. Harman, P. Frykman, S.E. Gordon, and S.J. Fleck. Hormonal and growth factor responses to heavy resistance exercise. *J Appl Physiol* 69(4):1442-1450. 1990.
54. Kraemer, W.J., and B.C. Nindl. Factors involved with overtraining for strength and power. In: *Overtraining in Sport,* R.B. Kreider, A.C. Fry, and M.L. O'Toole, eds. Champaign, IL: Human Kinetics. 1998. pp. 69-86.
55. Kraemer, W.J., B.J. Noble, B. Culver, and R.V. Lewis. Changes in plasma proenkephalin peptide F and catecholamine levels during graded exercise in men. *Proc Nat Acad Sci USA* 82:6349-6351. 1985.
56. Kraemer, W.J., J.F. Patton, H.G. Knuttgen, L.J. Marchitelli, C. Cruthirds, A. Damokosh, E. Harman, P. Frykman, and J.E. Dziados. Hypothalamic-pituitary-adrenal responses to short duration high-intensity cycle exercise. *J Appl Physiol* 66:161-166. 1989.
57. Kraemer, W.J., J.S. Volek, and S.J. Fleck. Chronic musculoskeletal adaptations to resistance training. In: *American College of Sports Medicine Resource Manual for Guidelines for Exercise Testing and Prescription,* 3rd ed., J.L. Roitman, ed. Baltimore: Williams & Wilkins. 1998. pp. 174-181.
58. Kuipers, H., and H.A. Keizer. Overtraining in elite athletes: Review and directions for the future. *Sports Med* 6:79-92. 1988.
59. Lemon, W.R., and F.J. Nagle. Effects of exercise on protein and amino acid metabolism. *Med Sci Sports Exerc* 13:141-149. 1981.
60. Lesmes, G.R., E.L. Fox, C. Stevens, and R. Otto. Metabolic responses of females to high-intensity interval training of different frequencies. *Med Sci Sports Exerc* 10:229-232. 1978.
61. Lortie, G., J.A. Simoneau, P. Hamel, M.R. Boulag, F. Landry, and C. Bouchard. Responses of maximal aerobic power and capacity to aerobic training. *Int J Sports Med* 5:232-236. 1984.
62. McArdle, W.D., F.I. Katch, and V.I. Katch. *Exercise Physiology,* 6th ed. Philadelphia: Lea & Febiger. 2007.
63. Moody, D.L., J.H. Wilmore, R.N. Girandola, and J.P. Royce. The effects of a jogging program on the body composition of normal and obese high school girls. *Med Sci Sports Exerc* 4:210-213. 1972.
64. Morgan, T., L. Cobb, F. Short, R. Ross, and D. Gunn. Effects of long-term exercise on human muscle mitochondria. In: *Muscle Metabolism During Exercise,* B. Pernow and B. Saltin, eds. New York: Plenum Press. 1971. pp. 87-95.
65. Noble, B.J. *Physiology of Exercise and Sport.* St. Louis: Times Mirror/Mosby. 1986.
66. Oettmeier, R., J. Arokoski, A.J. Roth, A.J. Helminen, M. Tammi, and K. Abendroth. Quantitative study of articular cartilage and subchondral bone remodeling in the knee joint of dogs after strenuous running training. *J Bone Min Res* 7:S419-S423. 1992.
67. Ploutz-Snyder, L.L., J.A. Simoneau, R.M. Gilders, R.S. Staron, and F.C. Hagerman. Cardiorespiratory metabolic adaptations to hyperoxic training. *Eur J Appl Physiol* 73:38-48. 1996.
68. Pollock, M.L., and A. Jackson. Body composition: Measurement and changes resulting from physical training. In: *Toward an Understanding of Human Performance,* E.J. Burke, ed. Ithaca, NY: Mouvement. 1977. pp. 21-36.
69. Saaf, R.B. Effect of exercise on adult cartilage. *Acta Orthop Scand Suppl* 7(1):1-83. 1950.

70. Sale, D.G. Influence of exercise and training on motor unit activation. *Exerc Sport Sci Rev* 15:95-151. 1987.
71. Sawka, M.N., M.J. Joyner, D.S. Miles, R.J. Robertson, L.L. Spriet, and A.J. Young. American College of Sports Medicine position stand. The use of blood doping as an ergogenic aid. *Med Sci Sports Exerc* 28(6):i-viii. 1996.
72. Scheuer, J., and C.M. Tipton. Cardiovascular adaptations to physical training. *Annu Rev Physiol* 39:221-251. 1977.
73. Staff, P.H. The effects of physical activity on joints, cartilage, tendons, and ligaments. *Scand J Med* 29(suppl.):59-63. 1982.
74. Stone, M.H., S.J. Fleck, N.T. Triplett, and W.J. Kraemer. Health- and performance-related potential of resistance training. *Sports Med* 11(4):210-231. 1991.
75. Stone, M.H., R.E. Keith, J.T. Kearney, S.J. Fleck, G.D. Wilson, and N.T. Triplett. Overtraining: A review of the signs, symptoms and possible causes. *J Appl Sport Sci Res* 5(1):35-50. 1991.
76. Triplett-McBride, N.T., A.M. Andrea, M. Mastro, J.M. McBride, J.A. Bush, M. Putukian, W.J. Sebastianelli, and W.J. Kraemer. Plasma proenkephalin peptide F and human B cell responses to exercise stress in fit and unfit women. *Peptides* 19(4):731-738. 1998.
77. Vogel, J.A., J.F. Patton, R.P. Mello, and W.L. Daniels. An analysis of aerobic capacity in a large United States population. *J Appl Physiol* 60:494-500. 1986.
78. Wilt, F. Training for competitive running. In: *Exercise Physiology,* H.B. Falls, ed. New York: Academic Press. 1968. pp. 395-414.
79. Wittich, A., C.A. Mautalen, M.B. Oliveri, A. Bagur, F. Somoza, and E. Rotemberg. Professional football (soccer) players have a markedly greater skeletal mineral content, density, and size than age- and BMI-matched controls. *Calcif Tiss Int* 63(2):112-117. 1998.

Chapter 7 Age- and Sex-Related Differences and Their Implications for Resistance Exercise

1. American Academy of Pediatrics. Intensive training and sports specialization in young athletes. *Pediatrics* 106:154-157. 2000.
2. American Academy of Pediatrics. Strength training by children and adolescents. *Pediatrics* 107:1470-1472. 2001.
3. American College of Sports Medicine. *ACSM's Guidelines for Exercise Testing and Prescription,* 7th ed. Baltimore: Williams & Wilkins. 2006.
4. American College of Sports Medicine. Exercise and physical activity for older adults. *Med Sci Sports Exerc* 30:992-1008. 1998.
5. American Orthopaedic Society for Sports Medicine. *Proceedings of the Conference on Strength Training and the Prepubescent.* Chicago: Author. 1988.
6. Arendt, E., and R. Dick. Knee injury patterns among men and women in collegiate basketball and soccer: NCAA data and review of literature. *Am J Sports Med* 23:694-701. 1995.
7. Bailey, D., and A. Martin. Physical activity and skeletal health in adolescents. *Pediatr Exerc Sci* 6:330-347. 1994.
8. Bassey, E., M. Fiatarone, E. O'Neill, M. Kelly, W. Evans, and L. Lipsitz. Leg extensor power and functional performance in very old men and women. *Clin Sci (Colch)* 82:321-327. 1992.
9. Blanksby, B., and J. Gregor. Anthropometric, strength, and physiological changes in male and female swimmers with progressive resistance training. *Aust J Sport Sci* 1:3-6. 1981.
10. Blimkie, C. Benefits and risks of resistance training in youth. In: *Intensive Participation in Children's Sports,* B. Cahill and A. Pearl, eds. Champaign, IL: Human Kinetics. 1993. pp. 133-167.
11. Boden, B.P., G.S. Dean, J.A. Feagin, and W.E. Garrett. Mechanisms of anterior cruciate ligament injury. *Orthopedics* 23:573-578. 2000.
12. Brady, T., B. Cahill, and L. Bodnar. Weight training related injuries in the high school athlete. *Am J Sports Med* 10:1-5. 1982.
13. British Association of Exercise and Sport Sciences. BASES position statement on guidelines for resistance exercise in young people. *J Sport Sci* 22:383-390. 2004.
14. Brown, E., and R. Kimball. Medical history associated with adolescent power lifting. *Pediatrics* 72:636-644. 1983.
15. Buenen, G., and R. Malina. Growth and physical performance relative to the timing of the adolescent growth spurt. In: *Exercise and Sport Science Reviews,* K. Pandolf, ed. New York: Macmillan. 1988. pp. 503-540.
16. Bulgakova, N., A. Vorontsov, and T. Fomichenko. Improving the technical preparedness of young swimmers by using strength training. *Soviet Sports Rev* 25:102-104. 1990.
17. Byrd, R., K. Pierce, L. Rielly, and J. Brady. Young weightlifters' performance across time. *Sports Biomechanics* 2:133-140. 2003.
18. Campbell, W., M. Crim, V. Young, and W. Evans. Increased energy requirements and changes in body composition with resistance training in older adults. *Am J Clin Nutr* 60:167-175. 1994.
19. Campbell, W., M. Crim, V. Young, J. Joseph, and W. Evans. Effects of resistance training and dietary protein intake on protein metabolism in older adults. *Am J Appl Physiol* 268:E1143-E1153. 1995.
20. Carnethon, M., M. Gulati, and P. Greenland. Prevalence and cardiovascular disease correlates of low cardiorespiratory fitness in adolescents and adults. *JAMA* 294:2981-2988. 2005.
21. Castro, M., D. McCann, J. Shaffrath, and W. Adams. Peak torque per unit cross-sectional area differs between strength-training and untrained adults. *Med Sci Sports Exerc* 27:397-403. 1995.
22. Centers for Disease Control and Prevention. Strength training among adults ≥65 years—United States, 2001. *MMWR* 53:1-4. 2004.
23. Charette, S., L. McEvoy, G. Pyka, C. Snow-Harter, D. Guido, R. Wiswell, and R. Marcus. Muscle hypertrophy response to resistance training in older women. *J Appl Physiol* 70:1912-1916. 1991.
24. Chilibeck, P., A. Calder, D. Sale, and C. Webber. A comparison of strength and muscle mass increases during resistance training in young women. *Eur J Appl Physiol* 77:170-175. 1998.
25. Christmas, C., and R. Andersen. Exercise and older patients. Guidelines for the clinician. *J Am Geriatr Soc* 48:318-324. 2000.
26. Chu, D., A. Faigenbaum, and J. Falkel. *Progressive Plyometrics for Kids.* Monterey, CA: Healthy Learning. 2006.
27. Colliander, E., and P. Tesch. Bilateral eccentric and concentric torque of quadriceps and hamstrings in females and males. *Eur J Appl Physiol* 59:227-232. 1989.
28. Colliander, E., and P. Tesch. Responses to eccentric and concentric resistance training in females and males. *Acta Physiol Scand* 141:149-156. 1990.
29. Conroy, B., W. Kraemer, C. Maresh, S. Fleck, M. Stone, A. Fry, P. Miller, and G. Dalsky. Bone mineral density in elite junior Olympic weightlifters. *Med Sci Sports Exerc* 25:1103-1109. 1993.
30. Cumming, D., S. Wall, M. Galbraith, and A. Belcastro. Reproductive hormone responses to resistance exercise. *Med Sci Sports Exerc* 19:234-238. 1987.
31. Cureton, K., M. Collins, D. Hill, and F. McElhannon. Muscle hypertrophy in men and women. *Med Sci Sports Exerc* 20:338-344. 1988.
32. Dalsky, G., K. Stocke, A. Ehasani, E. Slatopolsky, W. Lee, and S. Birge. Weight-bearing exercise training and lumbar bone mineral content in post menopausal women. *Ann Intern Med* 108:824-828. 1988.
33. Davies, B., E. Greenwood, and S. Jones. Gender differences in the relationship of performance in the handgrip and standing long jump tests to lean limb volume in young athletes. *Eur J Appl Physiol* 58:315-320. 1988.
34. De Loes, M., L. Dahlstedt, and R. Thomeé. A 7-year study on risks and costs of knee injuries in male and female youth participants in 12 sports. *Scand J Med Sci Sports* 10:90-97. 2000.
35. De Vos, N., N. Singh, D. Ross, T. Stavrinos, R. Orr, and M. Singh. Optimal load for increasing muscle power during explosive resistance training in older adults. *J Gerontol A Biol Sci Med Sci* 60:638-647. 2005.
36. Docherty, D., H. Wenger, M. Collis, and H. Quinney. The effects of variable speed resistance training on strength development in prepubertal boys. *J Human Mvmt Studies* 13:377-382. 1987.
37. Drinkwater, B. Weight-bearing exercise and bone mass. *Phys Med Rehabil Clin N Am* 6:567-578. 1995.
38. Emery, C. Injury prevention and future research. *Med Sci Sports Exerc* 48:179-200. 2005.

39. Evans, W. Exercise training guidelines for the elderly. *Med Sci Sports Exerc* 31:12-17. 1999.
40. Evans, W. What is sarcopenia? *J Gerontol* 50A:5-8. 1995.
41. Faigenbaum, A. Strength training for children and adolescents. *Clin Sports Med* 19:593-619. 2000.
42. Faigenbaum, A., W. Kraemer, B. Cahill, J. Chandler, J. Dziados, L. Elfrink, E. Forman, M. Gaudiose, L. Micheli, M. Nitka, and S. Roberts. Youth resistance training: Position statement paper and literature review. *Strength Cond* 18:62-75. 1996.
43. Faigenbaum, A., and P. Mediate. The effects of medicine ball training on fitness performance of high school physical education students. *Physical Educator* 63(3):160-167. 2006.
44. Faigenbaum, A., L. Milliken, R. LaRosa Loud, B. Burak, C. Doherty, and W. Westcott. Comparison of 1 and 2 days per week of strength training in children. *Res Q Exerc Sport* 73:416-424. 2002.
45. Faigenbaum, A., L. Milliken, L. Moulton, and W. Westcott. Early muscular fitness adaptations in children in response to two different resistance training regimens. *Pediatr Exerc Sci* 17:237-248. 2005.
46. Faigenbaum, A., L. Milliken, and W. Westcott. Maximal strength testing in healthy children. *J Strength Cond Res* 17:162-166. 2003.
47. Faigenbaum, A., and C. Polakowski. Olympic-style weightlifting, kid style. *Strength Cond J* 21:73-76. 1999.
48. Faigenbaum, A., and J. Schram. Can resistance training reduce injuries in youth sports? *Strength Cond J* 26:16-21. 2004.
49. Faigenbaum, A., and W. Westcott. *Strength and Power for Young Athletes*. Champaign, IL: Human Kinetics. 2000.
50. Faigenbaum, A., W. Westcott, R. LaRosa Loud, and C. Long. The effects of different resistance training protocols on muscular strength and endurance development in children. *Pediatrics* 104:E5. 1999.
51. Faigenbaum, A., W. Westcott, C. Long, R. LaRosa-Loud, M. Delmonico, and L. Micheli. Relationship between repetitions and selected percentages of the one repetition maximum in healthy children. *Pediatr Phys Ther* 10:110-113. 1998.
52. Faigenbaum, A., W. Westcott, L. Micheli, A. Outerbridge, C. Long, R. LaRosa Loud, and L. Zaichkowsky. The effects of strength training and detraining on children. *J Strength Cond Res* 10:109-114. 1996.
53. Faigenbaum, A., L. Zaichkowsky, W. Westcott, L. Micheli, and A. Fehlandt. The effects of a twice per week strength training program on children. *Pediatr Exerc Sci* 5:339-346. 1993.
54. Falk, B., and A. Eliakim. Resistance training, skeletal muscle and growth. *Pediatr Endocrinol Rev* 1:120-127. 2003.
55. Falk, B., and G. Mor. The effects of resistance and martial arts training in 6 to 8 year old boys. *Pediatr Exerc Sci* 8:48-56. 1996.
56. Falk, B., and G. Tenenbaum. The effectiveness of resistance training in children. A meta-analysis. *Sports Med* 22:176-186. 1996.
57. Fiatarone, M., E. Marks, N. Ryan, C. Meredith, L. Lipsitz, and W. Evans. High-intensity strength training in nonagenarians: Effects on skeletal muscle. *JAMA* 263:3029-3034. 1990.
58. Fiatarone, M., E. O'Neill, N. Ryan, K. Clements, G. Solares, M. Nelson, S. Roberts, J. Kehayias, L. Lipsitz, and W. Evans. Exercise training and nutritional supplementation for physical frailty in very elderly people. *N Engl J Med* 330:1769-1775. 1994.
59. Ford, H., and J. Puckett. Comparative effects of prescribed weight training and basketball programs on basketball test scores of ninth grade boys. *Percept Mot Skills* 56:23-26. 1983.
60. Frontera, W., C. Meredith, K. O'Reilly, H. Knuttgen, and W. Evans. Strength conditioning of older men: Skeletal muscle hypertrophy and improved function. *J Appl Physiol* 42:1038-1044. 1988.
61. Fukunga, T., K. Funato, and S. Ikegawa. The effects of resistance training on muscle area and strength in prepubescent age. *Ann Physiol Anthrop* 11:357-364. 1992.
62. Galvao, D., and D. Taaffe. Resistance training for the older adult.: Manipulating training variables to enhance muscle strength. *J Strength Cond Res* 27:48-54. 2005.
63. Garhammer, J. A comparison of maximal power outputs between elite male and female weightlifters in competition. *Int J Sport Biomech* 7:3-11. 1991.
64. Garhammer, J. A review of power output studies of Olympic and powerlifting: Methodology, performance prediction and evaluation tests. *J Strength Cond Res* 7:76-89. 1993.
65. George, D., K. Stakiw, and C. Wright. Fatal accident with weightlifting equipment: Implications for safety standards. *Can Med Assoc J* 140:925-926. 1989.
66. Gumbs, V., D. Segal, J. Halligan, and G. Lower. Bilateral distal radius and ulnar fractures in adolescent weight lifters. *Am J Sports Med* 10:375-379. 1982.
67. Häkkinen, K., and A. Häkkinen. Muscle cross-sectional area, force production and relaxation characteristics in women at different ages. *Eur J Appl Physiol* 62:410-414. 1991.
68. Häkkinen, K., A. Pakarinen, and M. Kallinen. Neuromuscular adaptations and serum hormones in women during short-term intensive strength training. *Eur J Appl Physiol* 64:106-111. 1992.
69. Häkkinen, K., A. Pakarinen, H. Kyrolainen, S. Cheng, D. Kim, and P. Komi. Neuromuscular adaptations and serum hormones in females during prolonged power training. *Int J Sports Med* 11:91-98. 1990.
70. Hamill, B. Relative safety of weight lifting and weight training. *J Strength Cond Res* 8:53-57. 1994.
71. Henwood, T., and D. Taaffe. Improved physical performance in older adults undertaking a short-term programme of high-velocity resistance training. *Gerontology* 51:108-115. 2005.
72. Hetherington, M. Effect of isometric training on the elbow flexion force torque of grade five boys. *Res Q* 47:41-47. 1976.
73. Hewett, T. Neuromuscular and hormonal factors associated with knee injuries in female athletes: Strategies for intervention. *Sports Med* 29:313-327. 2000.
74. Hewett, T., G. Myer, and K. Ford. Reducing knee and anterior cruciate ligament injuries among female athletes. *J Knee Surg* 18:82-88. 2005.
75. Holloway, J. A summary chart: Age related changes in women and men and their possible improvement with training. *J Strength Cond Res* 12:126-128. 1998.
76. Hurley, B., and J. Hagberg. Optimizing health in older persons: Aerobic or strength training? In: *Exercise and Sport Sciences Reviews*, J. Holloszy, ed. Philadelphia: Wilkins & Wilkins. 1998. pp. 61-89.
77. Imamura, K., H. Ashida, T. Ishikawa, and M. Fujii. Human major psoas muscle and sacrospinalis muscle in relation to age: A study by computed tomography. *J Gerontol* 38:678-681. 1983.
78. Ingle, L., M. Sleap, and K. Tolfrey. The effect of a complex training and detraining programme on selected strength and power variables in early pubertal boys. *J Sports Sci* 24:987-997. 2006.
79. Iwamoto, J., T. Takeda, and S. Ichimura. Effect of exercise training and detraining on bone mineral density in postmenopausal women with osteoporosis. *J Orthop Sci* 6:128-132. 2001.
80. Jette, A., and L. Branch. The Framingham disability study: II. Physical disability among the aging. *Am J Public Health* 71:1211-1216. 1981.
81. Kanis, J., L. Melton, C. Christiansen, C. Johnson, and N. Khaltaev. The diagnosis of osteoporosis. *J Bone Min Res* 9:1137-1141. 1994.
82. Katzmarzyk, P., R. Malina, and G. Beunen. The contribution of biologic maturation to the strength and motor fitness of children. *Ann Human Biol* 24:493-505. 1997.
83. Komi, P., and J. Karlsson. Skeletal muscle fibre types, enzyme activities and physical performance in young males and females. *Acta Physiol Scand* 103:210-218. 1978.
84. Kraemer, W. Endocrine responses to resistance exercise. *Med Sci Sports Exerc* 20(suppl.):152-157. 1988.
85. Kraemer, W., K. Adams, E. Cafarelli, G. Didley, C. Dooly, M. Feigenbaum, S. Fleck, B. Franklin, R. Newtown, J. Potteiger, M. Stone, N. Ratamess, and T. Triplet-McBride. Progression models in resistance training for healthy adults. *Med Sci Sports Exerc* 34:364-380. 2002.
86. Kraemer, W., A. Fry, P. Frykman, B. Conroy, and J. Hoffman. Resistance training and youth. *Pediatr Exerc Sci* 1:336-350. 1989.
87. Kraemer, W., S. Mazzetti, B. Nindl, L. Gotshalk, J. Bush, J. Marx, K. Dohi, A. Gomez, M. Miles, S. Fleck, R. Newton, and K. Häkkinen. Effect of resistance training on women's strength/power and occupational performances. *Med Sci Sports Exerc* 33:1011-1025. 2001.
88. Lauback, L. Comparative muscle strength of men and women: A review of the literature. *Aviat Space Environ Med* 47:534-542. 1976.

89. Layne, J., and M. Nelson. The effects of progressive resistance training on bone density: A review. *Med Sci Sports Exerc* 31:25-30. 1999.
90. Lexell, J., and D. Downham. What is the effect of ageing on Type II muscle fibers? *J Neurol Sci* 107:250-251. 1992.
91. Lillegard, W., E. Brown, D. Wilson, R. Henderson, and E. Lewis. Efficacy of strength training in prepubescent to early postpubescent males and females: Effects of gender and maturity. *Pediatr Rehabil* 1:147-157. 1997.
92. Lopopolo, R., M. Greco, D. Sullivan, R. Craik, and K. Mangione. Effect of therapeutic exercise on gait speed in community-dwelling elderly people: A meta analysis. *Phys Ther* 86:520-540. 2006.
93. Magill, R., and D. Anderson. Critical periods as optimal readiness for learning sports skills. In: *Children and Youth in Sport: A Biopsychosocial Perspective,* F. Smoll and R. Smith, eds. Madison, WI: Brown & Benchmark. 1995. pp. 57-72.
94. Malina, R. Physical activity and training: Effects on stature and the adolescent growth spurt. *Med Sci Sports Exerc* 26:759-766. 1994.
95. Malina, R., C. Bouchard, and O. Bar-Or. *Growth, Maturation, and Physical Activity.* Champaign, IL: Human Kinetics. 2004.
96. Mayhew, J., and P. Salm. Gender differences in anaerobic power tests. *Eur J Appl Physiol* 60:133-138. 1990.
97. McCartney, N. Acute responses to resistance training and safety. *Med Sci Sports Exerc* 31:31-37. 1999.
98. McKay, H., L. MacLean, M. Petit, K. MacKelvie-O'Brien, P. Janssen, T. Beck, and K. Khan. "Bounce at the Bell": A novel program of short bursts of exercise improves proximal femur bone mass in early pubertal children. *Br J Sports Med* 39:521-526. 2005.
99. Meltzer, D. Age dependence of Olympic weightlifting ability. *Med Sci Sports Exerc* 26:1053-1067. 1994.
100. Meredith, C., W. Frontera, and W. Evans. Body composition in elderly men: Effect of dietary modification during strength training. *J Am Geriatr Soc* 40:155-162. 1992.
101. Metter, E., R. Conwit, J. Tobin, and J. Fozard. Age-associated loss of power and strength in the upper extremities in women and men. *J Gerontol Biol Sci Med* 52:B267-276. 1997.
102. Micheli, L. The child athlete. In: *ACSM's Guidelines for the Team Physician,* R. Cantu and L. Micheli, eds. Philadelphia: Lea & Febiger. 1991. pp. 228-241.
103. Micheli, L. Overuse injuries in children's sports: The growth factor. *Orthop Clin N Am* 14:337-360. 1983.
104. Micheli, L. Preventing injuries in sports: What the team physician needs to know. In: *F.I.M.S. Team Physician Manual,* 2nd ed., K. Chan, L. Micheli, A. Smith, C. Rolf, N. Bachl, W. Frontera, and T. Alenabi, eds. Hong Kong: CD Concept. 2006. pp. 555-572.
105. Micheli, L. Strength training in the young athlete. In: *Competitive Sports for Children and Youth,* E. Brown and C. Branta, eds. Champaign, IL: Human Kinetics. 1988. pp. 99-105.
106. Micheli, L., R. Glassman, and M. Klein. The prevention of sports injuries in children. *Clin Sports Med* 19:821-834. 2000.
107. Miller, A., J. MacDougall, M. Tarnopolsky, and D. Sale. Gender differences in strength and muscle fiber characteristics. *Eur J Appl Physiol* 66:254-262. 1992.
108. Moeller, J., and M. Lamb. Anterior cruciate ligament injuries in female athletes. *Phys Sportsmed* 25:31-48. 1997.
109. Morris, F., G. Naughton, J. Gibbs, J. Carlson, and J. Wark. Prospective ten-month exercise intervention in premenarcheal girls: Positive effects on bone and lean mass. *J Bone Min Res* 12:1453-1462. 1997.
110. National Association for Sport and Physical Education. *Physical Education for Lifelong Fitness,* 2nd ed. Champaign, IL: Human Kinetics. 2004. pp. 3-12.
111. National Collegiate Athletic Association. Injury rate for women's basketball increases sharply. *NCAA News* 31(May 11):9, 13. 1994.
112. National Strength and Conditioning Association. Strength training for female athletes. *NSCA J* 11:43-55, 29-36. 1989.
113. Nelson, M., M. Fiatarone, C. Morganti, I. Trice, R. Greenberg, and W. Evans. Effects of high intensity strength training on multiple risk factors for osteoporotic fractures. *JAMA* 272:1909-1914. 1994.
114. Newcomer, K., and M. Sinaki. Low back pain and its relationship to back strength and physical activity in children. *Acta Paediatr* 85:1433-1439. 1996.
115. Nichols, D., C. Sanborn, and A. Love. Resistance training and bone mineral density in adolescent females. *J Pediatr* 139:494-500. 2001.
116. Nielsen, B., K. Nielsen, M. Behrendt-Hansen, and E. Asmussen. Training of "functional muscular strength" in girls 7-19 years old. In: *Children and Exercise IX,* K. Berg and B. Eriksson, eds. Baltimore: University Park Press. 1980. pp. 69-77.
117. Ogden, C., M. Carroll, L. Curtin, M. McDowell, C. Tabak, and K. Flegal. Prevalence of overweight and obesity in the United States, 1999-2004. *JAMA* 295:1549-1555. 2006.
118. Orr, R., N. de Vos, N. Singh, D. Ross, T. Stavrinos, and M. Fiatarone-Singh. Power training improves balance in healthy older adults. *J Gerontol A Biol Sci Med Sci* 61:78-85. 2006.
119. Otis, C., B. Drinkwater, and M. Johnson. American College of Sports Medicine: Position stand: The female athlete triad. *Med Sci Sports Exerc* 29:i-ix. 1997.
120. Ozmun, J., A. Mikesky, and P. Surburg. Neuromuscular adaptations following prepubescent strength training. *Med Sci Sports Exerc* 26:510-514. 1994.
121. Pfeiffer, R., and R. Francis. Effects of strength training on muscle development in prepubescent, pubescent and postpubescent males. *Phys Sportsmed* 14:134-143. 1986.
122. Ramsay, J., C. Blimkie, K. Smith, S. Garner, and J. MacDougall. Strength training effects in prepubescent boys. *Med Sci Sports Exerc* 22:605-614. 1990.
123. Rians, C., A. Weltman, B. Cahill, C. Janney, S. Tippet, and F. Katch. Strength training for prepubescent males: Is it safe? *Am J Sports Med* 15:483-489. 1987.
124. Risser, W. Weight training injuries in children and adolescents. *Am Fam Physician* 44:2104-2110. 1991.
125. Rowe, P. Cartilage fracture due to weight lifting. *Br J Sports Med* 13:130-131. 1979.
126. Ryan, J., and G. Salciccioli. Fractures of the distal radial epiphysis in adolescent weight lifters. *Am J Sports Med* 4:26-27. 1976.
127. Ryushi, T., K. Häkkinen, H. Kauhanen, and P. Komi. Muscle fiber characteristics, muscle cross sectional area and force production in strength athletes, physically active males and females. *Scand J Sports Sci* 10:7-15. 1988.
128. Shambaugh, J., A. Klein, and J. Herbert. Structural measures as predictors of injury in basketball players. *Med Sci Sports Exerc* 23:522-527. 1991.
129. Shaw, C., K. McCully, and J. Posner. Injuries during the one repetition maximum assessment in the elderly. *J Cardiopulm* 15:283-287. 1995.
130. Shephard, R. Exercise and training in women, part 1: Influence of gender on exercise and training response. *Can J Appl Physiol* 25:19-34. 2000.
131. Strong, W., R. Malina, C. Blimkie, S. Daniels, R. Dishman, B. Gutin, A. Hergenroeder, A. Must, P. Nixon, J. Pivarnik, T. Rowland, S. Trost, and F. Trudeau. Evidence based physical activity for school-age youth. *J Pediatr* 46:732-737. 2005.
132. Tanner, J. *Growth at Adolescence.* Oxford: Blackwell Scientific. 1962.
133. Telama, R., X. Yang, J. Viikari, I. Valimaki, O. Wanne, and O. Raitakari. Physical activity from childhood to adulthood: A 21 year tracking study. *Am J Prev Med* 28:267-273. 2005.
134. Tsolakis, C., G. Vagenas, and A. Dessypris. Strength adaptations and hormonal responses to resistance training and detraining in preadolescent males. *J Strength Cond Res* 18:625-629. 2004.
135. Vandervoot, A., and A. McComas. Contractile changes in opposing muscle of the human ankle joint with aging. *J Appl Physiol* 61:361-367. 1986.
136. Vicente-Rodriguez, G. How does exercise affect bone development during growth? *Sports Med* 36:561-569. 2006.
137. Virvidakis, K., E. Georgiu, A. Korkotsidis, K. Ntalles, and C. Proukakis. Bone mineral content of junior competitive weightlifters. *Int J Sports Med* 11:244-246. 1990.

138. Volek, J., C. Forsythe, and W. Kraemer. Nutritional aspects of women strength athletes. *Br J Sports Med* 40:742-748. 2006.
139. Watts, K., T. Jones, E. Davis, and D. Green. Exercise training in obese children and adolescents. *Sports Med* 35:375-392. 2005.
140. Weltman, A., C. Janney, C. Rians, K. Strand, B. Berg, S. Tippet, J. Wise, B. Cahill, and F. Katch. The effects of hydraulic resistance strength training in pre-pubertal males. *Med Sci Sports Exerc* 18:629-638. 1986.
141. West, R. The female athlete: The triad of disordered eating, amenorrhoea and osteoporosis. *Sports Med* 26:63-71. 1998.
142. Westcott, W., and T. Baechle. *Strength Training for Seniors*. Champaign, IL: Human Kinetics. 1999.
143. Wojtys, E., L. Huston, T. Lindenfeld, T. Hewett, and M. Greenfield. Association between the menstrual cycle and anterior cruciate injuries in female athletes. *Am J Sports Med* 26:614-619. 1998.
144. Yarasheski, K., J. Zachwieja, and D. Bier. Acute effects of resistance exercise on muscle protein synthesis in young and elderly men and women. *Am J Appl Physiol* 265:210-214. 1993.

Chapter 8 Psychology of Athletic Preparation and Performance

1. Attner, P. Payton vs. Harris vs. Brown. *Sporting News* (Oct. 1):2-3. 1984.
2. Bandura, A. Self-efficacy: Toward a unifying theory of behavior change. *Psychol Rev* 84(2):191-215. 1977.
3. Costello, F. Personal communication. 1993.
4. Cox, R.H. *Sport Psychology: Concepts and Applications*. Dubuque, IA: Brown & Benchmark. 1994.
5. Daniels, J.T. A physiologist's view of running economy. *Med Sci Sports Exerc* 17:332-338. 1985.
6. Deci, E.L. Intrinsic motivation: Theory and application. In: *Psychology of Motor Behavior and Sport 1977,* D.M. Landers and R.W. Christina, eds. Champaign, IL: Human Kinetics. 1978. pp. 388-396.
7. Easterbrook, J.A. The effect of emotion on cue utilization and the organization of behavior. *Psychol Rev* 66:183-201. 1959.
8. Eysenck, H.J. *The Biological Basis of Personality*. Springfield, IL: Charles C Thomas. 1967.
9. Fazey, J., and L. Hardy. *The Inverted-U Hypothesis: A Catastrophe for Sport Psychology?* British Association of Sport Sciences Monograph No. I. Leeds: National Coaching Foundation. 1988.
10. Feltz, D.L., and D.M. Landers. The effects of mental practice on motor skill learning and performance: A meta-analysis. *J Sport Psychol* 5:25-57. 1983.
11. Fitts, D.M., and M.I. Posner. *Human Performance*. Belmont, CA: Brooks/Cole. 1967.
12. Gould, D. Goal setting for peak performance. In: *Applied Sport Psychology: Personal Growth to Peak Performance,* J.M. Williams, ed. Mountain View, CA: Mayfield. 1998. pp. 182-196.
13. Gould, D., K. Hodge, K. Peterson, and J. Giannini. An exploratory examination of strategies used by elite coaches to enhance self-efficacy in athletes. *J Sport Exerc Psychol* 11(2):128-140. 1989.
14. Hanin, Y.L. Interpersonal and intragroup anxiety in sports. In: *Anxiety in Sports: An International Perspective,* D. Hackfort and C.D. Spielberger, eds. New York: Hemisphere. 1989. pp. 19-28.
15. Harris, D.V. *Involvement in Sport: A Somatopsychic Rationale for Physical Activity*. Philadelphia: Lea & Febiger. 1973.
16. Harris, D.V., and B.L. Harris. *The Athlete's Guide to Sports Psychology: Mental Skills for Physical People*. New York: Leisure Press. 1984.
17. Hatfield, B.D., and F.S. Daniels. The use of hypnosis as a stress management technique. *Mot Skills Theory Pract* 5(1):62-68. 1981.
18. Hatfield, B.D., D.M. Landers, and W.J. Ray. Cognitive processes during self-paced motor performance: An electroencephalographic profile of skilled marksmen. *J Sport Psychol* 6:42. 1984.
19. Hatfield, B.D., T.W. Spalding, A.D. Mahon, B.A. Slater, E.B. Brody, and P. Vaccaro. The effect of psychological strategies upon cardiorespiratory and muscular activity during treadmill running. *Med Sci Sports Exerc* 24(2):218-225. 1992.
20. Hatfield, B.D., and G.A. Walford. Understanding anxiety: Implications for sport performance. *NSCA J* 9(2):60-61. 1987.
21. Hillyard, S.A., and L. Anilo-Vento. Event-related brain potentials in the study of visual selective attention. *Proc Nat Acad Sci* 95:781-787. 1998.
22. Jacobson, E. *Progressive Relaxation,* 1st ed. Chicago: University of Chicago Press. 1929.
23. Johnson, W.R., and G.F. Kramer. Effects of different types of hypnotic suggestions upon physical performance. *Res Q* 31:469-473. 1960.
24. Kandel, E.R., and J.H. Schwartz. *Principles of Neural Science*. New York: Elsevier. 1985.
25. Lamb, D.R. The sports medicine umbrella. *Sport Med Bull* 19(4):8-9. 1984.
26. Landers, D.M. The arousal–performance relationship revisited. *Res Q Exerc Sport* 51(1): 77-90. 1980.
27. Locke, E.A., and G.P. Latham. The application of goal setting to sports. *J Sport Psychol* 7:205-222. 1985.
28. Martens, R. *Coaches Guide to Sport Psychology*. Champaign, IL: Human Kinetics. 1987.
29. Martens, R. *Social Psychology and Physical Activity*. New York: Harper & Row. 1975.
30. Martin, G., and D. Hrycaiko. Effective behavioral coaching: What's it all about? *J Sport Psychol* 5(1):8-20. 1983.
31. McClelland, D.C., J.W. Atkinson, R.W. Clark, and E.L. Lowell. *The Achievement Motive*. New York: Appleton-Century-Crofts. 1953.
32. Morgan, W.P., and M.L. Pollock. Psychologic characterization of the elite distance runner. *Ann NY Acad Sci* 301:482-503. 1977.
33. Nideffer, R. Test of attentional and interpersonal style. *J Pers Soc Psychol* 34:394-404. 1976.
34. Oxendine, J.B. Emotional arousal and motor performance. *Quest* 13:23-30. 1970.
35. Porges, S.W., P.M. McCabe, and B.C. Yongue. Respiratory-heart rate interaction: Psychophysiological implications for pathophysiology and behavior. In: *Perspectives in Cardiovascular Psychophysiology,* J.T. Caccioppo and R.E. Petty, eds. New York: Guilford. 1982. pp. 223-264.
36. Schwartz, G.E., R.J. Davidson, and D.J. Goleman. Patterning of cognitive and somatic processes in the self-regulation of anxiety: Effects of meditation versus exercise. *Psychosom Med* 40:321-328. 1978.
37. Spielberger, C.D. *Understanding Stress and Anxiety*. London: Harper & Row. 1979.
38. Spielberger, C.D., R.L. Gorsuch, and R.F. Lushene. *Manual for the State-Trait Anxiety Inventory*. Palo Alto, CA: Consulting Psychologists Press. 1970.
39. Thayer, R.E. Measurement through self-report. *Psychol Rep* 20:663-678. 1967.
40. Tichy, N.M., and S. Stratford. *Control Your Destiny or Someone Else Will*. New York: Doubleday. 1993.
41. Weinberg, R.S. The effects of success and failure on the patterning of neuromuscular energy. *J Mot Behav* 10:53-61. 1978.
42. Weinberg, R.S., L.D. Bruya, H. Garland, and A. Jackson. Effect of goal difficulty and positive reinforcement on endurance performance. *J Sport Exerc Psychol* 12:144-156. 1990.
43. Weinberg, R.S., C. Fowler, A. Jackson, J. Bagnall, and L. Bruya. Effect of goal difficulty on motor performance: A replication across tasks and subjects. *J Sport Exerc Psychol* 13:160-173. 1991.
44. Williams, J.M., and V. Krane. Psychological characteristics of peak performance. In: *Applied Sport Psychology: Personal Growth to Peak Performance,* J.M. Williams, ed. Mountain View, CA: Mayfield. 1998. pp. 158-170.
45. Wolpe, J. *Psychotherapy by Reciprocal Inhibition*. Stanford, CA: Stanford University Press. 1958.
46. Yerkes, R.M., and J.D. Dodson. The relationship of strength of stimulus to rapidity of habit formation. *J Comp Neurol Psychol* 18:459-482. 1908.

Chapter 9 Performance-Enhancing Substances

1. Abrahamsen, B., T.L. Nielsen, J. Hangaard, G. Gregerson, N. Vahl, L. Korsholm, T.B. Hansen, M. Andersen, and C. Hagen. Dose-, IGF-1- and sex-dependent changes in lipid profile and body composition during GH replacement therapy in adult onset GH deficiency. *Eur J Endocrinol* 150:671-679. 2004.
2. Adamson, J.W., and D. Vapnek. Recombinant erythropoietin to improve athletic performance. *N Engl J Med* 324:698-699. 1991.
3. Alén, M., and K. Häkkinen. Physical health and fitness of an elite bodybuilder during 1 year of self-administration of testosterone and anabolic steroids: A case study. *Int J Sports Med* 6:24-29. 1985.
4. Alén, M., K. Häkkinen, and P.V. Komi. Changes in neuromuscular performance and muscle fibre characteristics of elite power athletes self-administering androgenic and anabolic steroids. *Acta Physiol Scand* 122:535-544. 1984.
5. Anderson, W.A., M.A. Albrecht, and D.B. McKeag. Second replication of a national study of the substance use/abuse habits of college student athletes. Final report. *NCAA News*. 1993.
6. Anderson, W.A., M.A. Albrecht, D.B. McKeag, D.O. Hough, and C.A. McGrew. A national survey of alcohol and drug use by college athletes. *Phys Sportsmed* 19:91-104. 1991.
7. Anderson, W.A., and D.B. McKeag. *The Substance Use and Abuse Habits of College Student Athletes*. Research Paper No. 2. Mission, KS: NCAA. 1985.
8. Anselme, F., K. Collump, B. Mercier, S. Ahmaidi, and C. Prefaut. Caffeine increases maximal anaerobic power and blood lactate concentrations. *Eur J Appl Physiol* 65:188-191. 1992.
9. Antal, L., and C. Good. Effects of oxprenolol on pistol shooting under stress. *Practitioner* 224:755-760. 1980.
10. Aoki, M.S., A.L.R.A. Almeida, F. Navarro, L.F.B.P. Costa-Rosa, and R.F.P. Bacurau. Carnitine supplementation fails to maximize fat mass loss induced by endurance training in rats. *Ann Nutr Metab* 48:90-94. 2004.
11. Arenas, J., J.R. Ricoy, A.R. Encinas, P. Pola, S. D'Iddio, M. Zeviani, S. Didonato, and M. Corsi. Carnitine in muscle, serum, and urine of nonprofessional athletes: Effects of physical exercise, training, and L-carnitine administration. *Muscle Nerve* 14:598-604. 1991.
12. Bacurau, R.F.P., F. Navarro, R.A. Bassit, M.O. Meneguello, R.V.T. Santos, A.L.R. Almeida, and L.F.B.P. Costa Rosa. Does exercise training interfere with the effects of L-carnitine supplementation? *Nutrition* 19:337-341. 2003.
13. Ball, D., and R.J. Maughan. The effect of sodium citrate ingestion on the metabolic response to intense exercise following diet manipulation in man. *Exp Physiol* 82:1041-1056. 1997.
14. Balsom, P.D., B. Ekblom, K. Soderlund, B. Sjoden, and E. Hultman. Creatine supplementation and dynamic high-intensity intermittent exercise. *Scand J Med Sci Sports* 3:143-149. 1993.
15. Balsom, P.D., K. Soderlund, and B. Ekblom. Creatine in humans with special reference to creatine supplementation. *Sports Med* 3:143-149. 1994.
16. Barnett, C., D.L. Costill, M.D. Vukovich, K.J. Cole, B.H. Goodpaster, S.W. Trappe, and W.J. Fink. Effect of L-carnitine supplementation on muscle and blood carnitine content and lactate accumulation during high intensity sprint cycling. *Int J Sport Nutr* 4:280-288. 1994.
17. Behre, H.M., and E. Nieschlag. Testosterone buciclate (20 Aet-1) in hypogonadal men: Pharmacokinetics and pharmacodynamics of the new long-acting androgen ester. *J Clin Endocrinol Metab* 75:1204-1210. 1992.
18. Bell, D.G., and I. Jacobs. Combined caffeine and ephedrine ingestion improves run times of Canadian forces warrior test. *Aviat Space Environ Med* 70:325-329. 1999.
19. Bell, D.G., I. Jacobs, T.M. McLellan, and J. Zamecnik. Reducing the dose of combined caffeine and ephedrine preserves the ergogenic effect. *Aviat Space Environ Med* 71:415-419. 2000.
20. Bell, D.G., I. Jacobs, and J. Zamecnik. Effects of caffeine, ephedrine and their combination on time to exhaustion during high-intensity exercise. *Eur J Appl Physiol Occup Physiol* 77:427-433. 1998.
21. Bell, G.J., and H.A. Wenger. The effect of one-legged sprint training on intramuscular pH and non-bicarbonate buffering capacity. *Eur J Appl Physiol* 58:158-164. 1988.
22. Bemben, M.G., D.A. Bemben, D.D. Loftiss, and A.W. Khehans. Creatine supplementation during resistance training in college football athletes. *Med Sci Sports Exerc* 33:1667-1673. 2001.
23. Bergen, W.G., and R.A. Merkel. Body composition of animals treated with partitioning agents: Implications for human health. *FASEB J* 5:2951-2957. 1991.
24. Berglund, B., and B. Ekblom. Effect of recombinant human erythropoietin treatment on blood pressure and some haematological parameters in healthy men. *J Intern Med* 229:125-130. 1991.
25. Berning, J.M., K.J. Adams, and B.A. Stamford. Anabolic steroid usage in athletics: Facts, fiction, and public relations. *J Strength Cond Res* 18:908-917. 2004.
26. Bessman, S.P., and F. Savabi. The role of the phosphocreatine energy shuttle in exercise and muscle hypertrophy. In: *Biochemistry of Exercise VII*, A.W. Taylor, P.D. Gollnick, H.J. Green, C.D. Ianuzzo, E.G. Noble, G. Metivier, and J.R. Sutton, eds. Champaign, IL: Human Kinetics. 1990. pp. 167-177.
27. Bhasin, S., T.W. Storer, N. Berman, C. Callegari, B. Clevenger, J. Phillips, T.J. Bunnell, R. Tricker, A. Shirazi, and R. Casaburi. The effects of supraphysiological doses of testosterone on muscle size and strength in normal men. *N Engl J Med* 335:1-7. 1996.
28. Bhasin, S., L. Woodhouse, and T.W. Storer. Proof of the effect of testosterone on skeletal muscle. *J Endocrinol* 170:27-38. 2001.
29. Bird, S., K. Tarpenning, and K. Marino. Independent and combined effects of liquid carbohydrate/essential amino acid ingestion on hormonal and muscular adaptations following resistance training in untrained men. *Eur J Appl Physiol* 3:1-14. 2006.
30. Bishop, D., and M. Spencer. Determinants of repeated-sprint ability in elite female hockey players. *J Sci Med Sport* 6:199-209. 2004.
31. Bogdanis, G.C., M.E. Nevill, L.H. Boobis, and H.K.A. Lakomy. Contribution of phosphocreatine and aerobic metabolism to energy supply during repeated sprint exercise. *J Appl Physiol* 80:876-884. 1996.
32. Boje, O. Doping. *Bulletin of the Health Organization of the League of Nations* 8:439-469. 1939.
33. Boobis, L.H. Metabolic aspects of fatigue during sprinting. In: *Exercise: Benefits, Limitations and Adaptations*, D. Macleod, R. Maughan, M. Nimmo, T. Reilly, and C. Williams, eds. London: Spon. 1987. pp. 116-143.
34. Brandsch, C., and K. Eder. Effect of L-carnitine on weight loss and body composition of rats fed a hypocaloric diet. *Ann Nutr Metab* 46:205-210. 2002.
35. Brenner, M., J. Walberg-Rankin, and D. Sebolt. The effect of creatine supplementation during resistance training in women. *J Strength Cond Res* 14:207-213. 2000.
36. Brown, C.M., J.C. McGrath, J.M. Midgley, A.G. Muir, J.W. O'Brien, C.M. Thonoor, C.M. Williams, and V.G. Wilson. Activities of octopamine and synephrine stereoisomers on alpha-adrenoceptors. *Br J Pharmacol* 93:417-429. 1988.
37. Brown, G.A., M. Vukovich, and D.S. King. Testosterone prohormone supplements. *Med Sci Sports Exerc* 38:1451-1461. 2006.
38. Brown, G.A., M.D. Vukovich, R.L. Sharp, T.A. Reifenrath, K.A. Parsons, and D.S. King. Effect of oral DHEA on serum testosterone and adaptations to resistance training in young men. *J Appl Physiol* 87:2274-2283. 1999.
39. Bruce, C.R., M.E. Anderson, S.F. Fraser, N.K. Stepto, R. Klein, W.G. Hopkins, and J.A. Hawley. Enhancement of 2000-m rowing performance after caffeine ingestion. *Med Sci Sports Exerc* 32:1958-1963. 2000.
40. Buckley, W.E., C.E. Yesalis, K.E. Friedl, W.A. Anderson, A.L. Streit, and J.E. Wright. Estimated prevalence of anabolic steroid use among male high school seniors. *JAMA* 260:3441-3445. 1988.
41. Burke, D.G., S. Silver, L.E. Holt, T. Smith-Palmer, C.J. Culligan, and P.D. Chilibeck. The effect of continuous low dose creatine supplementation on force, power, and total work. *Int J Sport Nutr Exerc Metab* 10:235-244. 2000.
42. Carpene, C., J. Galitzky, E. Fontana, C. Atgie, M. Lafontan, and M. Berlan. Selective activation of beta3-adrenoreceptors by octopamine: Comparative studies in mammalian fat cells. *Naunyn Schmiedebergs Arch Pharmacol* 359:310-321. 1999.

43. Casal, D.C., and A.S. Leon. Failure of caffeine to affect substrate utilization during prolonged running. *Med Sci Sports Exerc* 17:174-179. 1985.
44. Cheetham, M.E., L.H. Boobis, S. Brooks, and C. Williams. Human muscle metabolism during sprint running. *J Appl Physiol* 61:54-60. 1986.
45. Collomp, K., S. Ahmaidi, M. Audran, J.L. Chanal, and C. Prefaut. Effects of caffeine ingestion on performance and anaerobic metabolism during the Wingate test. *Int J Sports Med* 12:439-443. 1991.
46. Collomp, K., S. Ahmaidi, J.C. Chatard, M. Audran, and C. Prefaut. Benefits of caffeine ingestion on sprint performance in trained and untrained swimmers. *Eur J Appl Physiol* 64:377-380. 1992.
47. Cooke, R.R., R.P. McIntosh, J.G.A. McIntosh, and J.W. Delahunt. Serum forms of testosterone in men after an HCG stimulation: Relative increase in non-protein bound forms. *Clin Endocrinol* 32:165-175. 1990.
48. Cooke, W.H., P.W. Grandjean, and W.S. Barnes. Effect of oral creatine supplementation on power output and fatigue during bicycle ergometry. *J Appl Physiol* 78:670-673. 1995.
49. Coombes, J., and L. McNaughton. Effects of bicarbonate ingestion on leg strength and power during isokinetic knee flexion and extension. *J Strength Cond Res* 7:241-249. 1993.
50. Costill, D.L., G.P. Dalsky, and W.J. Fink. Effects of caffeine ingestion on metabolism and exercise performance. *Med Sci Sports* 10:155-158. 1978.
51. Cottrell, G.T., J.R. Coast, and R.A. Herb. Effect of recovery interval on multiple-bout sprint cycling performance after acute creatine supplementation. *J Strength Cond Res* 16:109-116. 2002.
52. Cox, G., and D.G. Jenkins. The physiological and ventilatory responses to repeated 60s sprints following sodium citrate ingestion. *J Sports Sci* 12:469-475. 1994.
53. Cox, G., I. Mujika, D. Tumilty, and L. Burke. Acute creatine supplementation and performance during a field test simulating match play in elite female soccer players. *Int J Sport Nutr Exerc Metab* 12:33-46. 2002.
54. Crist, D.M., G.T. Peake, R.B. Loftfield, J.C. Kroner, and P.A. Egan. Supplemental growth hormone alters body composition, muscle protein metabolism and serum lipids in fit adults: Characterization of dose-dependent and response-recovery effects. *Mech Ageing Dev* 58:191-205. 1991.
55. Dawson, B., M. Cutler, A. Moody, S. Lawrence, C. Goodman, and N. Randall. Effects of oral creatine loading on single and repeated maximal short sprints. *Austr J Sci Med Sport* 27:56-61. 1995.
56. Dickman, S. East Germany: Science in the disservice of the state. *Science* 254:26-27. 1991.
57. Di Pasquali, M. Clenbuterol: A new anabolic drug. *Drugs Sport* 1:8-11. 1992.
58. Dubin, C. *Commission of Inquiry into the Use of Drugs and Banned Practices Intended to Increase Athletic Performance*. Ottawa, ON: Canadian Government Publishing Center. 1990.
59. Dunnett, M., and R.C. Harris. Influence of oral beta-alanine and L-histidine supplementation on the carnosine content of the gluteus medius. *Equine Vet J* 30(suppl.):499-504. 1999.
60. DuRant, R.H., L.G. Escobedo, and G.W. Heath. Anabolic-steroid use, strength training, and multiple drug use among adolescents in the United States. *Pediatrics* 96:23-28. 1995.
61. Eckerson, J.M., J.R. Stout, G.A. Moore, N.J. Stone, K. Nishimura, and K. Tamura. Effect of two and five days of creatine loading on anaerobic working capacity in women. *J Strength Cond Res* 18:168-172. 2004.
62. Edge, J., D. Bishop, and C. Goodman. The effects of training intensity on muscle buffer capacity in females. *Eur J Appl Physiol* 96:97-105. 2006.
63. Edge, J., D. Bishop, C. Goodman, and B. Dawson. Effects of high- and moderate-intensity training on metabolism and repeated sprints. *Med Sci Sports Exerc* 37:1975-1982. 2005.
64. Ekblom, B., and B. Berglund. Effect of erythropoietin administration on maximal aerobic power. *Scand J Med Sci Sports* 1:88-93. 1991.
65. Essig, D., D.L. Costill, and P.J. Van Handel. Effects of caffeine ingestion on utilization of muscle glycogen and lipid during leg ergometer cycling. *Int J Sports Med* 1:86-90. 1980.
66. Fahey, T.D., and C.H. Brown. The effects of an anabolic steroid on the strength, body composition, and endurance of college males when accompanied by a weight training program. *Med Sci Sports* 5:272-276. 1973.
67. Febbraio, M.A., T.R. Flanagan, R.J. Snow, S. Zhao, and M.F. Carey. Effect of creatine supplementation on intramuscular TCr, metabolism and performance during intermittent, supramaximal exercise in humans. *Acta Physiol Scand* 155:387-395. 1995.
68. Forbes, G.B. The effect of anabolic steroids on lean body mass: The dose-response curve. *Metabolism* 34:571-573. 1985.
69. Forbes, G.B., C.R. Porta, B.E. Herr, and R.C. Griggs. Sequence of changes in body composition induced by testosterone and reversal of changes after drug is stopped. *JAMA* 267:397-399. 1992.
70. Fowler, W.M., Jr., G.W. Gardner, and G.H. Egstrom. Effect of an anabolic steroid on physical performance in young men. *J Appl Physiol* 20:1038-1040. 1965.
71. Friedl, K.E., J.R. Dettori, C.J. Hannan, Jr., T.H. Patience, and S.R. Plymate. Comparison of the effects of high dose testosterone and 19-nortestosterone to a replacement dose of testosterone on strength and body composition in normal men. *J Steroid Biochem Mol Biol* 40:607-612. 1991.
72. Friedl, K.E., and R.J. Moore. Ergogenic aids: Clenbuterol, mahuang, caffeine, L-carnitine and growth hormone releasers. *NSCA J* 14(4):35-44. 1992.
73. Fudula, P.J., R.M. Weinrieb, J.S. Calarco, K.M. Kampman, and C. Boardman. An evaluation of anabolic-androgenic steroid abusers over a period of 1 year: Seven case studies. *Ann Clin Psychiatry* 15:121-130. 2003.
74. Fugh-Berman, A., and A. Myers. Citrus aurantium, an ingredient of dietary supplements marketed for weight loss: Current status of clinical and basic research. *Exp Biol Med* 229:698-704. 2004.
75. Gaitanos, G., M. Nevill, S. Brooks, and C. Williams. Repeated bouts of sprint running after induced alkalosis. *J Sports Sci* 9:355-370. 1991.
76. Gaitanos, G.C., C. Williams, L. Boobis, and S. Brooks. Human muscle metabolism during intermittent maximal exercise. *J Appl Physiol* 75:712-719. 1993.
77. Gallagher, P.M., J.A. Carrithers, M.P. Godard, K.E. Schulze, and S. Trappe. β-hydroxy-β-methylbutyrate ingestion, part I: Effects on strength and fat free mass. *Med Sci Sports Exerc* 32:2109-2115. 2000.
78. Gallagher, P.M., J.A. Carrithers, M.P. Godard, K.E. Schulze, and S. Trappe. β-hydroxy-β-methylbutyrate ingestion, part II: Effects on hematology, hepatic and renal function. *Med Sci Sports Exerc* 32:2116-2119. 2000.
79. Gareau, R., M. Audran, R.D. Baynes, C.H. Flowers, A. Duvallet, L. Senecal, and G.R. Brisson. Erythropoietin abuse in athletes. *Nature* 380:113. 1996.
80. Giamberardino, M.A., L. Dragani, R. Valente, F. Di Lias, R. Saggini, and L. Vecchiet. Effects of prolonged L-carnitine administration on delayed muscle pain and CK release after eccentric effort. *Int J Sports Med* 17:320-324. 1996.
81. Golding, L.A., J.E. Freydinger, and S.S. Fishel. The effect of an androgenic-anabolic steroid and a protein supplement on size, strength, weight and body composition in athletes. *Phys Sportsmed* 2:39-45. 1974.
82. Graham, T.E., E. Hibbert, and P. Sathasivam. Metabolic and exercise endurance effects of coffee and caffeine ingestion. *J Appl Physiol* 85:883-889. 1998.
83. Graham, T.E., and L.L. Spriet. Metabolic, catecholamine and exercise performance responses to varying doses of caffeine. *J Appl Physiol* 78:867-874. 1995.
84. Greenhaff, P.L. Creatine and its application as an ergogenic aid. *Int J Sport Nutr* 5:S100-110. 1995.
85. Greer, F., C. McLean, and T.E. Graham. Caffeine, performance, and metabolism during repeated Wingate exercise tests. *J Appl Physiol* 85:1502-1508. 1998.

86. Griggs, R.C., W. Kingston, R.F. Jozefowicz, B.E. Herr, G. Forbes, and D. Halliday. Effect of testosterone on muscle mass and muscle protein synthesis. *J Appl Physiol* 66:498-503. 1989.

87. Gruber, A.J., and H.G. Pope. Ephedrine abuse among 36 female weightlifters. *Am J Addict* 7:256-261. 1998.

88. Haff, G.G., K.B. Kirksey, M.H. Stone, B.J. Warren, R.L. Johnson, M. Stone, H. O'Bryant, and C. Proulx. The effect of 6 weeks of creatine monohydrate supplementation on dynamic rate of force development. *J Strength Cond Res* 14:426-433. 2000.

89. Haller, C.A., N.L. Benowitz, and P. Jacob. Hemodynamic effects of ephedra-free weight-loss supplements in humans. *Am J Med* 118:998-1003. 2005.

90. Harris, R.C., K. Soderlund, and E. Hultman. Elevation of creatine in resting and exercised muscle of normal subjects by creatine supplementation. *Clin Sci* 83:367-374. 1992.

91. Harris, R.C., M.J. Tallon, M. Dunnett, L. Boobis, J. Coakley, H.J. Kim, J.L. Fallowfield, C.A. Hill, C. Sale, and J.A. Wise. The absorption of orally supplied β-alanine and its effect on muscle carnosine synthesis in human vastus lateralis. *Amino Acids* 30:279-289. 2006.

92. Hausswirth, C., A.X. Bigard, R. Lepers, M. Berthelot, and C.Y. Gunzennec. Sodium citrate ingestion and muscle performance in acute hypobaric hypoxia. *Eur J Appl Physiol* 71:362-368. 1995.

93. Hervey, G.R., A.V. Knibbs, L. Burkinshaw, D.B. Morgan, P.R. Jones, D.R. Chettle, and D. Vartsky. Effects of methandienone on the performance and body composition of men undergoing athletic training. *Clin Sci* 60:457-461. 1981.

94. Hesse, D.G., D.E. Matthews, R.L. Leibel, J.M. Gertner, D.A. Fischman, and S.F. Lowry. Recombinant growth hormone enhances muscle myosin heavy-chain mRNA accumulation and amino acid accrual in humans. *Proc Nat Acad Sci USA* 86:3371-3374. 1989.

95. Heymsfield, S.B., C. Arteaga, C. McManus, J. Smith, and S. Moffitt. Measurement of muscle mass in humans: Validity of the 24-hour urinary creatinine method. *Am J Clin Nutr* 37:478-494. 1983.

96. Hill, C.A., R.C. Harris, H.J. Kim, B.D. Harris, C. Sale, L.H. Boobis, C.K. Kim, and J.A. Wise. Influence of β-alanine supplementation on skeletal muscle carnosine concentrations and high intensity cycling capacity. *Amino Acids* 32:225-233. 2007.

97. Hirvonen, J., A. Nummela, H. Rusko, S. Rehunen, and M. Harkonen. Fatigue and changes of ATP, creatine phosphate, and lactate during the 400-m sprint. *Can J Sport Sci* 17:141-144. 1992.

98. Hirvonen, J., S. Rehunen, H. Rusko, and M. Harkonen. Breakdown of high-energy phosphate compounds and lactate accumulation during short supramaximal exercise. *Eur J Appl Physiol* 56:253-259. 1987.

99. Hoffman, A.R., J.E. Kuntze, J. Baptista, H.B.A. Baum, G.P. Baumann, B.M.K. Biller, R.V. Clark, D. Cook, S.E. Inzucchi, D. Kleinberg, A. Klibanski, L.S. Phillips, E.C. Ridgeway, R.J. Robbins, J. Schlechte, M. Sharma, M.O. Thorner, and M.L. Vance. Growth hormone (GH) replacement therapy in adult-onset GH deficiency: Effects on body composition in men and women in a double-blind, randomized, placebo-controlled trial. *J Clin Endocrinol Metab* 89:2048-2056. 2004.

100. Hoffman, J.R. *Physiological Aspects of Sport Training and Performance*. Champaign, IL: Human Kinetics. 2002. pp. 15-26.

101. Hoffman, J.R., J. Cooper, M. Wendell, J. Im, and J. Kang. Effects of β-hydroxy β-methylbutyrate on power performance and indices of muscle damage and stress during high intensity training. *J Strength Cond Res* 18:747-752. 2004.

102. Hoffman, J.R., J. Kang, N.A. Ratamess, P.F. Jennings, G. Mangine, and A.D. Faigenbaum. Effect of nutritionally enriched coffee consumption on aerobic and anaerobic exercise performance. *J Strength Cond Res* 21(2):456-459. 2007.

103. Hoffman, J.R., J. Kang, N.A. Ratamess, P.F. Jennings, G. Mangine, and A.D. Faigenbaum. Thermogenic effect from nutritionally enriched coffee consumption. *J Int Soc Sports Nutr* 3:35-41. 2006.

104. Hoffman, J.R., and N.A. Ratamess. Medical issues associated with anabolic steroid use: Are they exaggerated? *J Sports Sci Med* 5:182-193. 2006.

105. Hoffman, J.R., N.A. Ratamess, J. Kang, G. Mangine, A.D. Faigenbaum, and J.R. Stout. Effect of creatine and β-alanine supplementation on performance and endocrine responses in strength/power athletes. *Int J Sport Nutr Exerc Metab* 16:430-446. 2006.

106. Hoffman, J.R., J.R. Stout, M. Falvo, J. Kang, and N. Ratamess. The effect of low-dose, short-duration creatine supplementation on anaerobic exercise performance. *J Strength Cond Res* 19:260-264. 2005.

107. Horswill, C., D. Costill, W. Fink, M. Flynn, J. Kirwan, J. Mitchell, and J. Houmard. Influence of sodium bicarbonate on sprint performance: Relationship to dosage. *Med Sci Sports Exerc* 20:566-569. 1988.

108. Hulsmann, W.C., and M.L. Dubelaar. Aspects of fatty acid metabolism in vascular endothelial cells. *Biochimie* 70:681-868. 1988.

109. Hulsmann, W.C., and M.L. Dubelaar. Carnitine requirement of vascular endothelial and smooth muscle cells in imminent ischemia. *Mol Cell Biochem* 116:125-129. 1992.

110. Hultman, E., G. Cederblad, and P. Harper. Carnitine administration as a tool to modify energy metabolism during exercise. *Eur J Appl Physiol* 62:450. 1991.

111. Hultman, E., K. Soderlund, J.A. Timmons, G. Cederblad, and P.L. Greenhaff. Muscle creatine loading in man. *J Appl Physiol* 81:232-237. 1996.

112. Ibanez, J., T. Pullinen, E. Gorostiaga, A. Postigo, and A. Mero. Blood lactate and ammonia in short-term anaerobic work following induced alkalosis. *J Sports Med Phys Fitness* 35:187-193. 1995.

113. Irving, L.M., M. Wall, D. Neumark-Sztainer, and M. Story. Steroid use among adolescents: Findings from project EAT. *J Adolesc Health* 30:243-252. 2002.

114. Ivy, J.L., D.L. Costill, W.J. Fink, and R.W. Lower. Influence of caffeine and carbohydrate feedings on endurance performance. *Med Sci Sports* 11:6-11. 1979.

115. Jackman, M., P. Wendling, D. Friars, and T.E. Graham. Metabolic, catecholamine, and endurance responses to caffeine during intense exercise. *J Appl Physiol* 81:1658-1663. 1996.

116. Jowko, E., P. Ostaszewski, M. Jank, J. Sacharuk, A. Zieniewicz, J. Wilczak, and S. Nissen. Creatine and β-hydroxy-β-methylbutyrate (HMB) additively increase lean body mass and muscle strength during a weight-training program. *Nutrition* 17:558-566. 2001.

117. Kerner, J., and C. Hoppel. Fatty acid import into mitochondria. *Biochim Biophys Acta* 1486:1-17. 2000.

118. Kessler, D.A. The Food and Drug Administration and its problems [letter reply]. *N Engl J Med* 326:70-71. 1992.

119. King, D.S., R.L. Sharp, M.D. Vukovich, G.A. Brown, T.A. Reifenrath, N.L. Uhi, and K.A. Parsons. Effect of oral androstenedione on serum testosterone and adaptations to resistance training in young men. *JAMA* 281:2020-2028. 1999.

120. Knitter, A.E., L. Panton, J.A. Rathmacher, A. Petersen, and R. Sharp. Effects of β-hydroxy-β-methylbutyrate on muscle damage after a prolonged run. *J Appl Physiol* 89:1340-1344. 2000.

121. Kraemer, W.J., B.A. Spiering, J.S. Volek, N.A. Ratamess, M.J. Sharman, M.R. Rubin, D.N. French, R. Silvestre, D.L. Hatfield, J.L. Van Heest, J.L. Vingren, D.A. Judelson, M.R. Deschenes, and C.M. Maresh. Androgenic responses to resistance exercise: Effects of feeding and L-carnitine. *Med Sci Sports Exerc* 38:1288-1296. 2006.

122. Kraemer, W.J., J.S. Volek, D.N. French, M.R. Rubin, M.J. Sharman, A.L. Gomez, N.A. Ratamess, R.U. Newton, B. Jemiolo, B.W. Craig, and K. Häkkinen. The effects of L-carnitine L-tartrate supplementation on hormonal responses to resistance exercise and recovery. *J Strength Cond Res* 17:455-462. 2003.

123. Kreider, R.B., M. Ferreira, M. Wilson, and A.L. Almada. Effects of calcium β-hydroxy-β-methylbutyrate (HMB) supplementation during resistance-training on markers of catabolism, body composition and strength. *Int J Sports Med* 20:503-509. 1999.

124. Kreider, R.B., M. Fereira, M. Wilson, P. Grindstaff, S. Plisk, J. Reinardy, E. Cantler, and A.L. Almada. Effects of creatine supplementation on body composition, strength and sprint performance. *Med Sci Sports Exerc* 30:73-82. 1998.

125. Kruse, P., J. Ladefoged, U. Nielsen, P. Paulev, and J.P. Sorensen. β-blockade used in precision sports: Effect on pistol shooting performance. *J Appl Physiol* 61:417-420. 1986.

126. LaBotz, M., and B.W. Smith. Creatine supplement use in an NCAA division I athletic program. *Clin J Sports Med* 9:167-169. 1999.

127. Leder, B.Z., C. Longcope, D.H. Catlin, B. Ahrens, D.A. Schoenfeld, and J.S. Finkelstein. Oral androstenedione administration and serum testosterone concentrations in young men. *JAMA* 283:779-782. 2000.
128. Lehmkuhl, M., M. Malone, B. Justice, G. Trone, E. Pistilli, D. Vinci, E. Haff, J.L. Kilgore, and G.G. Haff. The effects of 8-weeks of creatine monohydrate and glutamine supplementation on body composition and performance measures. *J Strength Cond Res* 17:425-438. 2003.
129. Linderman, J., and K. Gosselink. The effects of sodium bicarbonate ingestion on exercise performance. *Sports Med* 18:75-80. 1994.
130. Linossier, M.T., D. Dormis, P. Bregere, A. Geyssant, and C. Denis. Effect of sodium citrate on performance and metabolism of human skeletal muscle during supramaximal cycling exercise. *Eur J Appl Physiol* 76:48-54. 1997.
131. Loughton, S.J., and R.O. Ruhling. Human strength and endurance responses to anabolic steroids and training. *J Sports Med Phys Fitness* 17:285-296. 1977.
132. Lundby, C., J.J. Thomsen, R. Boushel, M. Koskolou, J. Warberg, J.A.L. Calbet, and P. Robach. Erythropoietin treatment elevates haemoglobin concentration by increasing red blood cell volume and depressing plasma volume. *J Physiol* 578:309-314. 2007.
133. MacRae, J.C., P.A. Skene, A. Connell, V. Buchan, and G.E. Lobley. The action of the β_2-agonist clenbuterol on protein and energy metabolism in fattening wether lambs. *Br J Nutr* 59:457-465. 1988.
134. Mahesh, V.B., and R.B. Greenblatt. The in vivo conversion of dehydroepiandrosterone and androstenedione to testosterone in the human. *Acta Endocrinol* 41:400-406. 1962.
135. Maltin, C.A., M.I. Delday, J.S. Watson, S.D. Heys, I.M. Nevison, I.K. Ritchie, and P.H. Gibson. Clenbuterol, a beta-adrenoceptor agonist, increases relative muscle strength in orthopaedic patients. *Clin Sci* 84:651-654. 1993.
136. Martineau, L., M.A. Horan, N.J. Rothwell, and R.A. Little. Salbutamol, a β_2-adrenoreceptor agonist, increases skeletal muscle strength in young men. *Clin Sci* 83:615-621. 1992.
137. McCartney, N., L.L. Spriet, G.J.F. Heigenhauser, J.M. Kowalchuk, J.R. Sutton, and N.L. Jones. Muscle power and metabolism in maximal intermittent exercise. *J Appl Physiol* 60:1164-1169. 1986.
138. McNaughton, L., K. Backx, G. Palmer, and N. Strange. Effects of chronic bicarbonate ingestion on the performance of high-intensity work. *Eur J Appl Physiol* 80:333-336. 1999.
139. McNaughton, L., S. Ford, and C. Newbold. Effect of sodium bicarbonate ingestion on high-intensity exercise in moderately trained women. *J Strength Cond Res* 11:98-102. 1997.
140. Migeon, C.J. Adrenal androgens in man. *Am J Med* 53:606-626. 1972.
141. Mujica, I., J.C. Chatard, L. Lacoste, F. Barale, and A. Geyssant. Creatine supplementation does not improve sprint performance in competitive swimmers. *Med Sci Sports Exerc* 28:1435-1441. 1996.
142. Mujika, I., S. Padilla, J. Ibanez, M. Iquierdo, and E. Gorostiaga. Creatine supplementation and sprint performance in soccer players. *Med Sci Sports Exerc* 32:518-525. 2000.
143. Nevill, M.E., L.S. Boobis, and C. Williams. Effect of training on muscle metabolism during treadmill sprinting. *J Appl Physiol* 67:2376-2382. 1989.
144. Nissen, S., R. Sharp, M. Ray, J.A. Rathmacher, D. Rice, J.C. Fuller, A.S. Connelly, and N. Abumrad. Effect of leucine metabolite β-hydroxy-β-methylbutyrate on muscle metabolism during resistance-exercise training. *J Appl Physiol* 81:2095-2104. 1996.
145. O'Connor, D.M., and M.J. Crowe. Effects of beta-hydroxy-beta-methylbutyrate and creatine monohydrate supplementation on the aerobic and anaerobic capacity of highly trained athletes. *J Sports Med Phys Fitness* 43:64-68. 2003.
146. Odland, L.M., J.D. MacDougall, M.A. Tarnopolsky, A. Elorriaga, and A. Borgmann. Effect of oral creatine supplementation on muscle [PCr] and short-term maximum power output. *Med Sci Sports Exerc* 29:216-219. 1997.
147. O'Shea, J.P. The effects of anabolic steroids on dynamic strength levels of weightlifters. *Nutr Rep Int* 4:363-370. 1971.
148. Pacy, P.J., G.M. Price, D. Halliday, M.R. Quevedo, and D.J. Millward. Nitrogen homeostasis in man: The diurnal responses of protein synthesis and degradation and amino acid oxidation to diets with increasing protein intakes. *Clin Sci (London)* 86(1):103-116. 1994.
149. Paddon-Jones, D., A. Keech, and D. Jenkins. Short-term beta-hydroxy-beta-methylbutyrate supplementation does not reduce symptoms of eccentric muscle damage. *Int J Sport Nutr Exerc Metab* 11:442-450. 2001.
150. Panton, L.B., J.A. Rathmacher, S. Baier, and S. Nissen. Nutritional supplementation of the leucine metabolite beta-hydroxy-beta-methylbutyrate (HMB) during resistance training. *Nutrition* 16:734-739. 2000.
151. Pearson, D.R., D.G. Hamby, W. Russel, and T. Harris. Long-term effects of creatine monohydrate on strength and power. *J Strength Cond Res* 13:187-192. 1999.
152. Perry, P.J., B.C. Lund, M.J. Deninger, E.C. Kutscher, and J. Schneider. Anabolic steroid use in weightlifters and bodybuilders. An internet survey of drug utilization. *Clin J Sport Med* 15:326-330. 2005.
153. Poortmans, J.R., H. Auquier, V. Renaut, A. Durussel, M. Saugy, and G.R. Brisson. Effect of short-term creatine supplementation on renal responses in men. *Eur J Appl Physiol* 76:566-567. 1997.
154. Poortmans, J.R., and M. Francaux. Long-term oral creatine supplementation does not impair renal function in healthy athletes. *Med Sci Sports Exerc* 31:1108-1110. 1999.
155. Pope, H.G., Jr., A.J. Gruber, P. Choi, R. Olivardia, and K.A. Phillips. Muscle dysmorphia: An underrecognized form of body dysmorphic disorder. *Psychosomatics* 38:548-557. 1997.
156. Pope, H.G., Jr., and D.L. Katz. Affective and psychotic symptoms associated with anabolic steroid use. *Am J Psychiatry* 145:487-490. 1988.
157. Pope, H.G., Jr., and D.L. Katz. Homicide and near-homicide by anabolic steroid users. *J Clin Psychiatry* 51:28-31. 1990.
158. Pope, H.G., and D.L. Katz. Psychiatric and medical effects of anabolic-androgenic steroid use. A controlled study of 160 athletes. *Arch Gen Psychiatry* 51:375-382. 1994.
159. Pope, H.G., Jr., D.L. Katz, and J.I. Hudson. Anorexia nervosa and "reverse anorexia" among 108 male bodybuilders. *Compr Psychiatry* 34:406-409. 1993.
160. Pope, H.G., E.M. Kouri, and J.I. Hudson. Effects of supraphysiologic doses of testosterone on mood and aggression in normal men. *Arch Gen Psychiatry* 57:133-140. 2000.
161. Prather, I.D., D.E. Brown, P. North, and J.R. Wilson. Clenbuterol: A substitute for anabolic steroids? *Med Sci Sports Exerc* 27:1118-1121. 1995.
162. Preen, D., B. Dawson, C. Goodman, S. Lawrence, J. Beilby, and S. Ching. Effect of creatine loading on long-term sprint exercise performance and metabolism. *Med Sci Sports Exerc* 33:814-821. 2001.
163. Ransone, J., K. Neighbors, R. Lefavi, and J. Chromiak. The effect of β-hydroxy-β-methylbutyrate on muscular strength and body composition in collegiate football players. *J Strength Cond Res* 17:34-39. 2003.
164. Rasmussen, B., K. Tipton, S. Miller, S. Wolf, and R. Wolfe. An oral essential amino acid-carbohydrate supplement enhances muscle protein anabolism after resistance exercise. *J Appl Physiol* 88:386-392. 2000.
165. Ratamess, N.A. *Coaches' Guide to Performance-Enhancing Supplements.* Monterey, CA: Coaches Choice Books. 2006.
166. Reeds, P.J., S.M. Hay, P.M. Dorwood, and R.M. Palmer. Stimulation of growth by clenbuterol: Lack of effect on muscle protein biosynthesis. *Br J Nutr* 56:249-258. 1986.
167. Robergs, R.A., F. Ghiasv, and D. Parker. Biochemistry of exercise-induced metabolic acidosis. *Am J Physiol Regul Integr Comp Physiol* 287:R502-R516. 2004.
168. Rozenek, R., C.H. Rahe, H.H. Kohl, D.N. Marple, G.D. Wilson, and M.H. Stone. Physiological responses to resistance-exercise in athletes self-administering anabolic steroids. *J Sports Med Phys Fitness* 30:354-360. 1990.
169. Rubin, M.R., J.S. Volek, A.L. Gomez, N.A. Ratamess, D.N. French, M.J. Sharman, and W.J. Kraemer. Safety measures of L-carnitine L-tartrate supplementation in healthy men. *J Strength Cond Res* 15:486-490. 2001.

170. Rudman, D., A.G. Feller, H.S. Nagraj, G.A. Gergans, P.Y. Lalitha, A.F. Goldberg, R.A. Schlenker, L. Cohn, I.W. Rudman, and D.E. Mattson. Effects of human growth hormone in men over 60 years old. *N Engl J Med* 323:1-6. 1990.
171. Salomon, F., R.C. Cuneo, R. Hesp, and P.H. Sonksen. The effects of treatment with recombinant human growth hormone on body composition and metabolism in adults with growth hormone deficiency. *N Engl J Med* 321:1797-1803. 1989.
172. Sapir, D.G., O.E. Owen, T. Pozefsky, and M. Walser. Nitrogen sparing induced by a mixture of essential amino acids given chiefly as their keto analogs during prolonged starvation in obese subjects. *J Clin Invest* 54:974-980. 1974.
173. Schilling, B.K., M.H. Stone, A. Utter, J.T. Kearney, M. Johnson, R. Coglianese, L. Smith, H.S. O'Bryant, A.C. Fry, M. Starks, R. Keith, and M.E. Stone. Creatine supplementation and health variables: A retrospective study. *Med Sci Sports Exerc* 33:183-188. 2001.
174. Schwandt, H.J., B. Heyduck, H.C. Gunga, and L. Rocker. Influence of prolonged physical exercise on the erythropoietin concentration in the blood. *Eur J Appl Physiol* 63:463-466. 1991.
175. Shekelle, P., M. Hardy, S. Morton, M. Maglione, M. Suttorp, E. Roth, and L. Jungvig. Ephedra and ephedrine for weight loss and athletic performance enhancement: clinical efficacy and side effects. *Evid Rep Technol Assess (Summ)* 76:1-4. 2003.
176. Silvester, L.J. Self-perceptions of the acute and long-range effects of anabolic-androgenic steroids. *J Strength Cond Res* 9:95-98. 1995.
177. Slater, G., D. Jenkins, P. Logan, H. Lee, M. Vukovich, J.A. Rathmacher, and AG Hahn. Beta-hydroxy-beta-methylbutyrate (HMB) supplementation does not affect changes in strength or body composition during resistance training in trained men. *Int J Sport Nutr Exerc Metab* 11:384-396. 2001.
178. Snow, R.J., M.J. McKenna, S.E. Selig, J. Kemp, C.G. Stathis, S. Zhao. Effect of creatine supplementation on sprint exercise performance and muscle metabolism. *J Appl Physiol* 84:1667-1673. 1998.
179. Spiering, B.A., W.J. Kraemer, J.L. Vingren, D.L. Hatfield, M.S. Fragala, J. Ho, C.M. Maresh, J.M. Anderson, and J.S. Volek. Responses of criterion variables to different supplemental doses of L-carnitine L-tartrate. *J Strength Cond Res* 21:259-264. 2007.
180. Spriet, L.L. Caffeine and performance. *Int J Sport Nutr* 5(suppl.): S84-S99. 1995.
181. Spriet, L.L., D.A. MacLean, D.J. Dyck, E. Hultman, G. Cederblad, and T.E. Graham. Caffeine ingestion and muscle metabolism during prolonged exercise in humans. *Am J Physiol* 262:E891-E898. 1992.
182. Stamford, B.A., and T. Moffatt. Anabolic steroid: Effectiveness as an ergogenic aid to experienced weight trainers. *J Sports Med Phys Fitness* 14:191-197. 1974.
183. Stout, J.R., J.T. Cramer, J. O'Kroy, M. Mielke, R. Zoeller, and D. Torok. Effects of β-alanine and creatine monohydrate supplementation on the physical working capacity at neuromuscular fatigue threshold. *J Strength Cond Res* 20:928-931. 2006.
184. Stout, J.R., J.T. Cramer, R.F. Zoeller, D. Torok, P. Costa, J.R. Hoffman, R.C. Harris, and J. O'Kroy. Effects of β-alanine supplementation on the onset of neuromuscular fatigue and ventilatory threshold in women. *Amino Acids* 32:381-386. 2007.
185. Stout, J.R., J. Eckerson, K. Ebersole, G. Moore, S. Perry, T. Housh, A. Bull, J. Cramer, and A. Batheja. Effect of creatine loading on neuromuscular fatigue threshold. *J Appl Physiol* 88:109-112. 2000.
186. Street, C., J. Antonio, and D. Cudlipp. Androgen use by athletes: A reevaluation of the health risks. *Can J Appl Physiol* 21:421-440. 1996.
187. Strømme, S.B., H.D. Meen, and A. Aakvaag. Effects of an androgenic-anabolic steroid on strength development and plasma testosterone levels in normal males. *Med Sci Sports* 6:203-208. 1974.
188. Suzuki, Y., I. Osamu, N. Mukai, H. Takahashi, and K. Takamatsu. High level of skeletal muscle carnosine contributes to the latter half of exercise performance during 30-s maximal cycle ergometer sprinting. *Jpn J Physiol* 52:199-200. 2002.
189. Swirzinski, L., R.W. Latin, K. Berg, and A. Grandjean. A survey of sport nutrition supplements in high school football players. *J Strength Cond Res* 14:464-469. 2000.
190. Tarnopolsky, M.A. Caffeine and endurance performance. *Sports Med* 18:109-125. 1994.
191. Tesch, P.A. Exercise performance and β-blockade. *Sports Med* 2:389-412. 1985.
192. Tipton, K.D., E. Borsheim, S.E. Wolf, A.P. Sanford, and R.R. Wolfe. Acute response of net muscle protein balance reflects 24-h balance after exercise and amino acid ingestion. *Am J Physiol Endocrinol Metab* 284:E76-E89. 2003.
193. Tipton, K.D., A.A. Ferrando, S.M. Phillips, D. Doyle, Jr., and R.R. Wolfe. Post-exercise net protein synthesis in human muscle from orally administered amino acids. *Am J Physiol Endocrinol Metab* 276: E628-E634. 1999.
194. Tipton, K.D., B.B. Rasmussen, S.L. Miller, S.E. Wolf, S.K. Owens-Stovall, B.E. Petrini, and R.R. Wolfe. Timing of amino acid-carbohydrate ingestion alters anabolic response of muscle to resistance exercise. *Am J Physiol Endocrinol Metab* 281: E197-E206. 2001.
195. Tiryaki, G.R., and H.A. Atterbom. The effects of sodium bicarbonate and sodium citrate on 600 m running time of trained females. *J Sports Med Phys Fitness* 35:194-198. 1995.
196. Tischler, M.E., M. Desautels, and A.L. Goldberg. Does leucine, leucyl-tRNA, or some metabolite of leucine regulate protein synthesis and degradation in skeletal and cardiac muscle? *J Biol Chem* 257:1613-1621. 1982.
197. Trice, I., and E.M. Haymes. Effects of caffeine ingestion on exercise-induced changes during high-intensity, intermittent exercise. *Int J Sport Nutr* 5:37-44. 1995.
198. Underwood, L.E., K.M. Attie, and J. Baptista. Growth hormone (GH) dose-response in young adults with childhood-onset GH deficiency: A two-year, multicenter, multiple dose, placebo-controlled study. *J Clin Endocrinol Metab* 88:5273-5280. 2003.
199. U.S. Food and Drug Administration, Center for Food Safety and Applied Nutrition. Information paper on Dietary Supplement Health and Education Act of 1994 [online]. http://vm.cfsan.fda.gov/~dms/dietsupp.html.
200. Van Marken Lichtenbelt, W.D., F. Hartgens, N.B.J. Vollaard, S. Ebbing, and H. Kuipers. Bodybuilders' body composition: Effect of nandrolone decanoate. *Med Sci Sports Exerc* 36:484-489. 2004.
201. Van Someren, K., K. Fulcher, J. McCarthy, J. Moore, G. Horgan, and R. Langford. An investigation into the effects of sodium citrate ingestion on high-intensity exercise performance. *Int J Sport Nutr* 8:357-363. 1998.
202. Volek, J.S., N.D. Duncan, S.A. Mazzetti, R.S. Staron, M. Putukian, A.L. Gomez, D.R. Pearson, W.J. Fink, and W.J. Kraemer. Performance and muscle fiber adaptations to creatine supplementation and heavy resistance training. *Med Sci Sports Exerc* 31:1147-1156. 1999.
203. Volek, J.S., and W.J. Kraemer. Creatine supplementation: Its effect on human muscular performance and body composition. *J Strength Cond Res* 10:200-210. 1996.
204. Volek, J.S., W.J. Kraemer, M.R. Rubin, A.L. Gomez, N.A. Ratamess, and P. Gaynor. L-carnitine, L-tartrate supplementation favorably affects markers of recovery from exercise stress. *Am J Physiol Endocrinol Metab* 282:E474-E482. 2002.
205. Wallace, M.B., J. Lim, A. Cutler, and L. Bucci. Effects of dehydroepiandrosterone vs androstenedione supplementation in men. *Med Sci Sports Exerc* 31:1788-1792. 1999.
206. Ward, P. The effect of an anabolic steroid on strength and lean body mass. *Med Sci Sports* 5:277-282. 1973.
207. Webster, M., M. Webster, R. Crawford, and L. Gladden. Effect of sodium bicarbonate ingestion on exhaustive resistance exercise performance. *Med Sci Sports Exerc* 25:960-965. 1993.
208. Welle, S., R. Jozefowicz, G. Forbes, and R.C. Griggs. Effect of testosterone on metabolic rate and body composition in normal men and men with muscular dystrophy. *J Clin Endocrinol Metab* 74:332-335. 1992.
209. Wiles, J.D., S.R. Bird, J. Hopkins, and M. Riley. Effect of caffeinated coffee on running speed, respiratory factors, blood lactate and perceived exertion during 1500-m treadmill running. *Br J Sports Med* 26:116-120. 1992.
210. Williams, M.H. Alcohol, marijuana, and beta blockers. In: *Perspec-*

tives in Exercise Science and Sports Medicine. Volume 4: Ergogenic, D.R. Lamb and M.H. Williams, eds. Carmel, IN: Benchmark Press. 1991. pp. 331-372.

211. Willoughby, D.S., J.R. Stout, and C.D. Wilborn. Effects of resistance training and protein plus amino acid supplementation on muscle anabolism, mass, and strength. *Amino Acids* 32(4):467-477. 2007.
212. Wilson, J.D. Androgen abuse by athletes. *Endocr Rev* 9:181-199. 1988.
213. Yesalis, C.E. Epidemiology and patterns of anabolic-androgenic steroid use. *Psychiatr Ann* 22:7-18. 1992.
214. Yesalis, C.E., S.P. Courson, and J. Wright. History of anabolic steroid use in sport and exercise. In: *Anabolic Steroids in Sport and Exercise,* 2nd ed., C.E. Yesalis, ed. Champaign, IL: Human Kinetics. 2000. pp. 51-71.

Chapter 10 Nutritional Factors in Health and Performance

1. Ahlborg, B., J. Bergstrom, J. Brohult, L. Ekelund, E. Hultman, and G. Maschio. Human muscle glycogen content and capacity for prolonged exercise after different diets. *Foersvarsmedicin* 3:85-99. 1967.
2. Akermark, C., I. Jacobs, M. Rasmusson, and J. Karlsson. Diet and muscle glycogen concentration in relation to physical performance in Swedish elite ice hockey players. *Int J Sport Nutr* 6:272-284. 1996.
3. American College of Sports Medicine Position Stand. Exercise and fluid replacement. *Med Sci Sports Exerc* 28:i-vii. 1996.
4. American Psychiatric Association. *Diagnostic and Statistical Manual of Mental Disorders,* 4th ed. Text Revision. Washington, DC. 2000.
5. Armstrong, L.W., C.M. Maresh, J.W. Castellani, M.F. Bergeron, R.W. Kenefick, K.E. LaGasse, and D. Riebe. Urinary indices of hydration status. *Int J Sport Nutr* 4:265-279. 1994.
6. Ashley, C.D., J.F. Smith, J.B. Robinson, and M.T. Richardson. Disordered eating in female collegiate athletes and collegiate females in an advanced program of study: A preliminary investigation. *Int J Sport Nutr* 6:391-401. 1996.
7. Balsom, P.D., K. Wood, P. Olsson, and B. Ekblom. Carbohydrate intake and multiple sprint sports: With special reference to football (soccer). *Int J Sports Med* 20:48-52. 1999.
8. Below, P.R., R. Mora-Rodriguez, J. Gonzalez-Alonso, and E.F. Coyle. Fluid and carbohydrate ingestion independently improve performance during 1 h of intense exercise. *Med Sci Sports Exerc* 27:200-210. 1995.
9. Benson, J.E., C.J. Geiger, P.A. Eiserman, and G.M. Wardlaw. Relationship between nutrient intake, body mass index, menstrual function, and ballet injury. *J Am Diet Assoc* 89:58-63. 1989.
10. Boskind-White, M., and W.C. White. Bulimarexia: A historical-sociocultural perspective. In: *Handbook of Eating Disorders,* K.D. Brownell and J.P. Foreyt, eds. New York: Basic Books. 1986. pp. 354-366.
11. Brown, R.C., and C.M. Cox. Effects of high fat versus high carbohydrate diets on plasma lipids and lipoproteins in endurance athletes. *Med Sci Sports Exerc* 30:1677-1683. 1998.
12. Burke, L.M., G.R. Collier, S.K. Beasley, P.G. Davis, P.A. Fricker, P. Heeley, K. Walder, and M. Hargreaves. Effect of coingestion of fat and protein with carbohydrate feedings on muscle glycogen storage. *J Appl Physiol* 78:2187-2192. 1995.
13. Burke, L.M., G.R. Collier, P.G. Davis, P.A. Fricker, A.J. Sanigorski, and M. Hargreaves. Muscle glycogen storage after prolonged exercise: Effect of the frequency of carbohydrate feedings. *Am J Clin Nutr* 64:115-119. 1996.
14. Burke, L.M., G.R. Collier, and M. Hargreaves. Glycemic index—a new tool in sport nutrition? *Int J Sport Nutr* 8:401-415. 1998.
15. Burke, L.M., G.R. Collier, and M. Hargreaves. Muscle glycogen storage after prolonged exercise: Effect of the glycemic index of carbohydrate feedings. *J Appl Physiol* 75:1019-1023. 1993.
16. Cater, N.B., H.J. Heller, and M.A. Denke. Comparison of the effects of medium-chain triacylglycerols, palm oil, and high oleic acid sunflower oil on plasma triacylglycerol fatty acids and lipid and lipoprotein concentrations in humans. *Am J Clin Nutr* 65:41-45. 1997.
17. Christensen, E., and O. Hansen. Arbeits fahigeit und ernahrung. *Scand Arch Physiol* 81:169. 1939.
18. Cohen, J.L., L. Potosnak, O. Frank, and H. Baker. A nutritional and hematologic assessment of elite ballet dancers. *Phys Sportsmed* 13:43-54. 1985.
19. Cole, K.J., D.L. Costill, R.D. Starling, B.H. Goodpaster, S.W. Trappe, and W.J. Fink. Effect of caffeine ingestion on perception of effort and subsequent work production. *Int J Sport Nutr* 6:14-23. 1996.
20. Costill, D.L., W.M. Sherman, W.J. Fink, C. Maresh, M. Witten, and J.M. Miller. The role of dietary carbohydrates in muscle glycogen resynthesis after strenuous running. *Am J Clin Nutr* 34:1831-1836. 1981.
21. Coyle, E.F. Timing and method of increased carbohydrate intake to cope with heavy training, competition, and recovery. *J Sports Sci* 9:29-52. 1991.
22. Davis, B. Essential fatty acids in vegetarian nutrition. *Vegetarian Diet* 7:5-7. 1998.
23. DeMarco, H.M., K.P. Sucher, C.J. Cisar, and G.E. Butterfield. Pre-exercise carbohydrate meals: Application of glycemic index. *Med Sci Sports Exerc* 31:164-170. 1999.
24. Dreon, D.M., H.A. Fernstrom, P.T. Williams, and R.M. Krauss. A very-low-fat diet is not associated with improved lipoprotein profiles in men with a predominance of large, low-density lipoproteins. *Am J Clin Nutr* 69:411-418. 1999.
25. Dummer, G.M., L.W. Rosen, W.W. Heuser, P.J. Roberts, and J.E. Counsilman. Pathogenic weight-control behaviors of young competitive swimmers. *Phys Sportsmed* 15:75-84. 1987.
26. Epstein, Y., and L.E. Armstrong. Fluid-electrolyte balance during labor and exercise: Concepts and misconceptions. *Int J Sport Nutr* 9:1-12. 1999.
27. Ernst, N.D., C.T. Sempos, R.R. Briefel, and M.B. Clark. Consistency between US dietary fat intake and serum total cholesterol concentrations: The National Health and Nutrition Examination Surveys. *Am J Clin Nutr* 66(suppl.):965S-972S. 1997.
28. Faigenbaum, A.D., J.S. Nye-McKeown, and C.R. Morilla. Coaching athletes with eating disorders. *Strength Cond* 18(2):22-30. 1996.
29. Fogelholm, G.M., R. Koskinen, J. Laakso, T. Rankinen, and I. Ruokonen. Gradual and rapid weight loss: Effects on nutrition and performance in male athletes. *Med Sci Sports Exerc* 25:371-373. 1993.
30. Foster-Powell, K., S. Holt, and J.C. Brand-Miller. International table of glycemic index and glycemic load values: 2002. *Am J Clin Nutr* 76:5-56. 2002.
31. Fujisawa, T., K. Mulligan, L. Wada, L. Schumacher, J. Riby, and N. Kretchmer. The effect of exercise on fructose absorption. *Am J Clin Nutr* 58:75-79. 1993.
32. Grandjean, A.C., K.J. Reimers, and J.S. Ruud. Dietary habits of Olympic athletes. In: *Nutrition in Exercise and Sport,* I. Wolinsky, ed. Boca Raton, FL: CRC Press. 1998. pp. 421-430.
33. Greenleaf, J.E., and M.H. Harrison. Water and electrolytes. In: *Nutrition and Aerobic Exercise,* D.K. Layman, ed. Washington, DC: American Chemical Society. 1986. pp. 107-124.
34. Hawley, J.A., E.J. Schabort, T.D. Noakes, and S.C. Dennis. Carbohydrate-loading and exercise performance: An update. *Sports Med* 24:73-81. 1997.
35. Helge, J.W., B. Wulff, and B. Kiens. Impact of a fat-rich diet on endurance in man: Role of the dietary period. *Med Sci Sports Exerc* 30:456-461. 1998.
36. Hill, J.O., H. Drougas, and J.C. Peters. Obesity treatment: Can diet composition play a role? *Ann Intern Med* 119(7 Pt 2):694-697. 1993.
37. Horswill, C.A. Effective fluid replacement. *Int J Sport Nutr* 8:175-195. 1998.
38. Horvath, P.J., R.G. Genovese, B. O'Reilly, R.A. Melton-Bork, L. Gilchrist, and J. Leddy. The effect of peanuts or carbohydrate-rich energy bars on performance of female collegiate soccer players. *FASEB Journal* 13(4 Pt):A542. 1999.

39. Howell, W.H., D.J. McNamara, M.A. Tosca, B.T. Smith, and J.A. Gaines. Plasma lipid and lipoprotein responses to dietary fat and cholesterol: A meta-analysis. *Am J Clin Nutr* 65:1747-1764. 1997.
40. Hubbard, K., A. O'Neill, and C. Cheakalos. Out of control: Weight-obsessed, stressed-out coeds are increasingly falling prey to eating disorders. *People* 51:52-72. 1999.
41. Jacobs, K.A., and W.M. Sherman. The efficacy of carbohydrate supplementation and chronic high-carbohydrate diets for improving endurance performance. *Int J Sport Nutr* 9:92-115. 1999.
42. Jenkins, D.J.A., T.M.S. Wolever, R.H. Taylor, H. Barker, H. Fielden, J.M. Baldwin, A.C. Bowling, H.C. Newman, A.L. Jenkins, and D.V. Goff. Glycemic index of foods: A physiological basis for carbohydrate exchange. *Am J Clin Nutr* 34:362-366. 1981.
43. Jeukendrup, A.E., J.J.H.C. Thielen, A.J.M. Wagenmakers, F. Brouns, and W.H.M. Saris. Effect of medium-chain triacylglycerol and carbohydrate ingestion during exercise on substrate utilization and subsequent cycling performance. *Am J Clin Nutr* 67:397-404. 1998.
44. Kochan, R.G., D.R. Lamb, S.A. Lutz, C.V. Perrill, E.M. Reimann, and K.K. Schlende. Glycogen synthase activation in human skeletal muscle: Effects of diet and exercise. *Am J Physiol* 236:E660-E666. 1979.
45. Leddy, J., P. Horvath, J. Rowland, and D. Pendergast. Effect of a high or a low fat diet on cardiovascular risk factors in male and female runners. *Med Sci Sports Exerc* 29:17-25. 1997.
46. Lemon, P.W.R. Effects of exercise on dietary protein requirements. *Int J Sports Nutr* 8:426-447. 1998.
47. Loosli, A.R., and J. Benson. Nutritional intake in adolescent athletes. *Pediatr Clin North Am* 37(5):1143-1152. 1990.
48. Lucas, A.R. The eating disorder "epidemic": More apparent than real? *Pediatr Ann* 21(11):746-751. 1992.
49. MacDougall, G.R., D.G. Ward, D.G. Sale, and J.R. Sutton. Muscle glycogen repletion after high intensity intermittent exercise. *J Appl Physiol* 42:129-132. 1977.
50. Maughan, R.J., P.L. Greenhaff, J.B. Leiper, D. Ball, C.P. Lambert, and M. Gleeson. Diet composition and the performance of high-intensity exercise. *J Sports Sci* 15:265-275. 1997.
51. Maughan, R.J., J.B. Leiper, and S.M. Shirreffs. Restoration of fluid balance after exercise-induced dehydration: Effects of food and fluid intake. *Eur J Appl Physiol* 73:317-325. 1996.
52. Maughan, R.J., J.H. Owen, S.M. Shirreffs, and J.B. Leiper. Post-exercise rehydration in man: Effects of electrolyte addition to ingested fluids. *Eur J Appl Physiol* 69:209-215. 1994.
53. Mitchell, J.B., P.C. DiLauro, F.X. Pizza, and D.L. Cavender. The effect of pre-exercise carbohydrate status on resistance exercise performance. *Int J Sports Nutr* 7:185-196. 1997.
54. Moffatt, R.J. Dietary status of elite female high school gymnasts: Inadequacy of vitamin and mineral intake. *J Am Diet Assoc* 84:1361-1363. 1984.
55. Muoio, D.M., J.J. Leddy, P.J. Horvath, A.B. Awad, and D.R. Pendergast. Effect of dietary fat on metabolic adjustments to maximal VO_2 and endurance in runners. *Med Sci Sports Exerc* 26:81-88. 1994.
56. National Academy of Sciences Institute of Medicine. *Dietary Reference Intakes for Energy, Carbohydrate, Fiber, Fat, Fatty Acids, Cholesterol, Protein, and Amino Acids (Macronutrients)*. Washington, DC: National Academy Press. 2005.
57. National Academy of Sciences Institute of Medicine. *Dietary Reference Intakes Set*. Washington, DC: National Academy Press. 1997-2004.
58. National Heart, Lung, and Blood Institute National Institutes of Health (NHLBI-NIH). Clinical guidelines of the identification, evaluation, and treatment of overweight and obesity in adults: Executive summary. *Am J Clin Nutr* 68:899-917. 1998.
59. National Heart, Lung, and Blood Institute National Institutes of Health (NHLBI-NIH). *Third Report of the Expert Panel on Detection, Evaluation, and Treatment of High Blood Cholesterol in Adults* (Adult Treatment Panel III). NIH Publication No. 01-3670. Bethesda, MD. 2001.
60. Okano, G., Y. Sato, and Y. Murata. Effect of elevated blood FFA levels on endurance performance after a single fat meal ingestion. *Med Sci Sports Exerc* 30:763-768. 1998.
61. Parkin, J.M., M.F. Carey, I.K. Martin, L. Stojanovska, and M.A. Febbraio. Muscle glycogen storage following prolonged exercise: Effect of timing of ingestion of high glycemic index food. *Med Sci Sports Exerc* 29:220-224. 1997.
62. Pendergast, D.R., P.J. Horvath, J.J. Leddy, and J.T. Venkatraman. The role of dietary fat on performance, metabolism, and health. *Am J Sports Med* 24:S53-S58. 1996.
63. Perron, M., and J. Endres. Knowledge, attitudes, and dietary practices of female athletes. *J Am Diet Assoc* 85:573-576. 1985.
64. Phinney, S.D., B.R. Bistrian, W.J. Evans, E. Gervino, and G.L. Blackburn. The human metabolic response to chronic ketosis without caloric restriction: Preservation of submaximal exercise capability with reduced carbohydrate oxidation. *Metabolism* 32:769-776. 1983.
65. Piehl, K.S., S. Adolfsson, and K. Nazar. Glycogen storage and glycogen synthase activity in trained and untrained muscle of man. *Acta Physiol Scand* 90:779-788. 1974.
66. Pizza, F.X., M.G. Flynn, B.D. Duscha, J. Holden, and E.R. Kubitz. A carbohydrate loading regimen improves high intensity, short duration exercise performance. *Int J Sport Nutr* 5:110-116. 1995.
67. Reimers, K.J. Evaluating a healthy, high performance diet. *Strength Cond* 16:28-30. 1994.
68. Rivlin, R.S., ed. Fats and oil consumption in health and disease. *Am J Clin Nutr* 66(4S). 1997.
69. Rolls, B.J., V.H. Castellanos, J.C. Halford, A. Kilara, D. Panyam, C.L. Pelkman, G.P. Smith, and M.L. Thorwart. Volume of food consumed affects satiety in men. *Am J Clin Nutr* 67:1170-1177. 1998.
70. Romijn, J.A., E.F. Coyle, L.S. Sidossis, A. Gastaldelli, J.F. Horowitz, E. Endert, and R.R. Wolfe. Regulation of endogenous fat and carbohydrate metabolism in relation to exercise intensity and duration. *Am J Physiol* 265:E380-E391. 1993.
71. Rosen, L.W., and D.O. Hough. Pathogenic weight-control behaviors of female college gymnasts. *Phys Sportsmed* 16(9):141-144. 1988.
72. Roy, B.D., and M.A. Tarnopolsky. Influence of differing macronutrient intakes on muscle glycogen resynthesis after resistance exercise. *J Appl Physiol* 84:890-896. 1998.
73. Roy, B.D., M.A. Tarnopolsky, J.D. MacDougall, J. Fowles, and K.E. Yarasheski. Effect of glucose supplement timing on protein metabolism after resistance training. *J Appl Physiol* 82:1882-1888. 1997.
74. Schlundt, D.G., J.O. Hill, J. Pope-Cordle, D. Arnold, K.L. Virts, and M. Katahn. Randomized evaluation of low fat ad libitum carbohydrate diet for weight reduction. *Int J Obes* 17:623-629. 1993.
75. Sherman, W.M. Metabolism of sugars and physical performance. *Am J Clin Nutr* 62(suppl.):228S-241S. 1995.
76. Sherman, W.M., J.A. Doyle, D.R. Lamb, and R.H. Strauss. Dietary carbohydrate, muscle glycogen, and exercise performance during 7 d of training. *Am J Clin Nutr* 57:27-31. 1993.
77. Sherman, W.M., and G.S. Wimer. Insufficient carbohydrate during training: Does it impair performance? *Sport Nutr* 1(1):28-44. 1991.
78. Shirreffs, S.M., A.J. Taylor, J.B. Leiper, and R.J. Maughan. Post-exercise rehydration in man: Effects of volume consumed and drink sodium content. *Med Sci Sports Exerc* 28:1260-1271. 1996.
79. Sparks, M.J., S.S. Selig, and M.A. Gebbraio. Pre-exercise carbohydrate ingestion: Effect of the glycemic index on endurance exercise performance. *Med Sci Sports Exerc* 30:844-849. 1998.
80. Spitzer, R.L., S. Yanovski, T. Wadden, R. Wing, M.D. Marcus, A. Stunkard, M. Devlin, J. Mitchell, D. Hasin, and R.L. Horne. Binge eating disorder: Its further validation in a multisite study. *Int J Eating Disord* 13(2):137-153. 1993.
81. Streit, K.J., N.H. Stevens, V.J. Stevens, and J. Rossner. Food records: A predictor and modifier of weight change in a long-term weight loss program. *J Am Diet Assoc* 91(2):213-216. 1991.
82. Strober, M. Anorexia nervosa: History and psychological concepts. In: *Handbook of Eating Disorders*, K.D. Brownell and J.P. Foreyt, eds. New York: Basic Books. 1986. pp. 231-246.
83. Sugiura, K., and K. Kobayashi. Effect of carbohydrate ingestion on sprint performance following continuous and intermittent exercise. *Med Sci Sports Exerc* 30:1624-1630. 1998.
84. Sundgot-Borgen, J. Eating disorders in female athletes. *Sports Med* 17(3):176-188. 1994.

85. Surwit, R.S., M.N. Feinglos, C.C. McCaskill, S.L. Clay, M.A. Babyak, B.S. Brownlow, C.S. Plaisted, and P.-H. Lin. Metabolic and behavior effects of a high-sucrose diet during weight loss. *Am J Clin Nutr* 65:908-915. 1997.
86. Symons, J.D., and I. Jacobs. High-intensity exercise performance is not impaired by low intramuscular glycogen. *Med Sci Sports Exerc* 21:550-557. 1989.
87. Tarnopolsky, M.A., M. Bosman, J.R. MacDonald, D. Vandeputte, J. Martin, and B.D. Roy. Postexercise protein-carbohydrate and carbohydrate supplements increase muscle glycogen in men and women. *J Appl Physiol* 83:1877-1883. 1997.
88. Thomas, D.E., J.R. Brotherhood, and J.C. Brand. Carbohydrate feeding before exercise: Effect of glycemic index. *Int J Sports Med* 12:180-186. 1991.
89. Thomas, D.E., J.R. Brotherhood, and J.B. Miller. Plasma glucose levels after prolonged strenuous exercise correlate inversely with glycemic response to food consumed before exercise. *Int J Sport Nutr* 4:361-373. 1994.
90. United States Department of Agriculture and Center for Nutrition Policy and Promotion. *MyPyramid*. Washington, DC: U.S. Government Printing Office. 2005.
91. Vandenberghe, K., P. Hespel, B.V. Eynde, R. Lysens, and E.A. Richter. No effect of glycogen level on glycogen metabolism during high intensity exercise. *Med Sci Sports Exerc* 27:1278-1283. 1995.
92. Vereeke West, R. The female athlete. The triad of disordered eating, amenorrhea and osteoporosis. *Sports Med* 26(2):63-71. 1998.
93. Volek, J.S., K. Houseknecht, and W.J. Kraemer. Nutritional strategies to enhance performance of high-intensity exercise. *Strength Cond* 19:11-17. 1997.
94. Volek, J.S., W.J. Kraemer, J.A. Bush, T. Incledon, and M. Boetes. Testosterone and cortisol in relationship to dietary nutrients and resistance exercise. *J Appl Physiol* 82:49-54. 1997.
95. Walberg, J.L., M.K. Leidy, D.J. Sturgill, D.E. Hinkle, S.J. Ritchey, and D.R. Sebolt. Macronutrient needs in weight lifters during caloric restriction. *Med Sci Sports Exerc* 19:S70. 1987.
96. Walsh, B.T., and M.J. Devlin. Eating disorders: Progress and problems. *Science* 280:1387-1390. 1998.
97. Wardlaw, G.M., and J. Hampl. *Perspectives in Nutrition,* 7th ed. Columbus, OH: McGraw-Hill. 2007.
98. Wee, S.L., C. Williams, S. Gray, and J. Horabin. Influence of high and low glycemic index meals on endurance running capacity. *Med Sci Sports Exerc* 31:393-399. 1999.
99. Wilmore, J.H., A.R. Morton, H.J. Gilbey, and R.J. Wood. Role of taste preference on fluid intake during and after 90 min of running at 60% of VO_2max in the heat. *Med Sci Sport Exerc* 30:587-595. 1998.
100. Young, K., and C.T.M. Davies. Effect of diet on human muscle weakness following prolonged exercise. *Eur J Appl Physiol* 53:81-85. 1984.
101. Young, V.R., and P.L. Pellett. Plant proteins in relation to human protein and amino acid nutrition. *Am J Clin Nutr* 59:1203S-1212S. 1994.
102. Zelitch Yanovski, S. Binge eating disorder: Current knowledge and future directions. *Obes Res* 1(4):306-324. 1993.
103. Zhu, Y.I., and J.E. Haas. Iron depletion without anemia and physical performance in young women. *Am J Clin Nutr* 66:334-341. 1997.
104. Ziegler, P., S. Hensley, J.B. Roepke, S.H. Whitaker, B.W. Craig, and A. Drewnowski. Eating attitudes and energy intakes of female skaters. *Med Sci Sports Exerc* 30:583-586. 1998.

Chapter 11: Principles of Test Selection and Administration

1. Allerheigen, B., J. Arce, M. Arthur, D. Chu, A. Vermeil, L. Lilja, D. Semenick, B. Ward, and M. Woicik. Testing for football. *NSCA J* 5(5):12-68. 1983.
2. Altug, Z., T. Altug, and A. Altug. A test selection guide for assessing and evaluating athletes. *NSCA J* 9(3):67-69. 1987.
3. American Alliance for Health, Physical Education, Recreation and Dance. *AAHPERD Health Related Fitness Test*. Reston, VA: Author. 1980.
4. Anastasi, A. *Psychological Testing,* 5th ed. New York: Macmillan. 1982.
5. Anderson, B. Flexibility testing. *NSCA J* 3(2):20-23. 1981.
6. Baumgartner, T., and A. Jackson. *Measurement for Evaluation in Physical Education and Exercise Science*. Dubuque, IA: Brown. 1987.
7. Brukner, P., and K. Khan. *Clinical Sports Medicine,* 3rd ed. New York: McGraw-Hill. 2006.
8. Chu, D., and A. Vermeil. The rationale for field testing. *NSCA J* 5(2):35-36. 1983.
9. Cooper, K. *The New Aerobics*. New York: Bantam. 1972.
10. Epley, B. The Nebraska timer: A simple, accurate way to measure the 40-yard dash. *NSCA J* 4(5):14-15. 1982.
11. Fleck, S., and M. Marks. Interval training. *NSCA J* 5(5):40-62. 1983.
12. Fox, E., and D. Mathews. *The Physiological Basis of Physical Education and Athletics*. Philadelphia: Saunders. 1981.
13. Garl, T., L. Rink, and B. Bomba. Evaluating basketball conditioning. *NSCA J* 10(4):46-47. 1988.
14. Gilliam, G. Basketball bioenergetics: Physiological basis. *NSCA J* 6(6):44-73. 1985.
15. Gilliam, G., and M. Marks. 300-yard shuttle run. *NSCA J* 5(5):46. 1983.
16. Hackney, A.C. Military operations at moderate altitude: Effects on physical performance. *Military Med* 157(12):625-629. 1992.
17. Hastad, D.N., and A.C. Lacy. *Measurement and Evaluation in Contemporary Physical Education*. Scottsdale, AZ: Gorsuch. 1989.
18. Hopkins, C. *Understanding Educational Research*. Columbus, OH: Merrill. 1980.
19. Johnson, B., and J. Nelson. *Practical Measurements for Evaluation in Physical Education,* 2nd ed. Minneapolis: Burgess. 1974.
20. Kinnear, T.C., and J.R. Taylor. *Marketing Research: An Applied Approach,* 2nd ed. New York: McGraw-Hill. 1983.
21. Kontor, K. Testing and evaluation. *NSCA J* 3(2):7. 1981.
22. Kontor, K. Truth in testing. *NSCA J* 3(6):11. 1982.
23. Kraemer, W., and S. Fleck. Anaerobic metabolism and its evaluation. *NSCA J* 4(2):20-21. 1982.
24. Kraning, K.K., and R.R. Gonzalez. A mechanistic computer simulation of human work in heat that accounts for physical and physiological effects of clothing, aerobic fitness, and progressive dehydration. *J Therm Biol* 22(4/5):331-342. 1997.
25. Margaria, R., P. Carretelli, P. diPrampero, C. Massori, and G. Torelli. Kinetics and mechanism of oxygen debt contraction in man. *J Appl Physiol* 18:371-377. 1963.
26. McArdle, W.D., F.I. Katch, and V.L. Katch. *Exercise Physiology: Energy, Nutrition, and Human Performance,* 6th ed. Baltimore: Williams & Wilkins. 2007.
27. Messick, S. Validity. In: *Educational Measurement,* 3rd ed., R. Linn, ed. New York: Macmillan. 1989.
28. Safrit, M. *Evaluation in Physical Education*. Englewood Cliffs, NJ: Prentice Hall. 1980.
29. Stone, M., H. Newton, and H. O'Bryant. Anaerobic capacity. *NSCA J* 5(6):40-41. 1984.
30. Stone, M., and H. O'Bryant. *Weight Training: A Scientific Approach*. Minneapolis: Burgess. 1987.
31. Tesch, P. Anaerobic testing: Practical applications. *NSCA J* 6(5):44-73. 1984.
32. Wade, G. Tests and measurements: Meeting the standards of professional football. *NSCA J* 4(3):23. 1982.

Chapter 12 Administration, Scoring, and Interpretation of Selected Tests

1. Adams, G.M. *Exercise Physiology Lab Manual,* 3rd ed. Dubuque, IA: McGraw-Hill. 1998.
2. Altug, Z., T. Altug, and A. Altug. A test selection guide for assessing and evaluating athletes. *NSCA J* 9(3):62-66. 1987.
3. American Alliance for Health, Physical Education, Recreation and Dance. *AAHPERD Health-Related Fitness Test*. Reston, VA: Author. 1980.

4. American College of Sports Medicine. *ACSM's Guidelines for Exercise Testing and Prescription,* 5th ed. Franklin, B.A., M.H. Whaley, E.T. Howley, and G.J. Balady, eds. Philadelphia: Lippincott, Williams & Wilkins. 1995.
5. American College of Sports Medicine. *ACSM's Guidelines for Exercise Testing and Prescription,* 6th ed. Franklin, B.A., M.H. Whaley, E.T. Howley, and G.J. Balady, eds. Philadelphia: Lippincott, Williams & Wilkins. 2000.
6. American College of Sports Medicine. *ACSM's Guidelines for Exercise Testing and Prescription,* 7th ed. Franklin, B.A., M.H. Whaley, E.T. Howley, and G.J. Balady, eds. Philadelphia: Lippincott, Williams & Wilkins. 2006.
7. Anderson, B. Flexibility testing. *NSCA J* 3(2):20-23. 1981.
8. Arthur, M., M.J. Arthur, and B.L. Bailey. *Complete Conditioning for Football.* Champaign, IL: Human Kinetics. 1998.
9. Bar-Or, O. The Wingate anaerobic test: An update on methodology, reliability and validity. *Sports Med* 4:381-391. 1987.
10. Baumgartner, T., and A. Jackson. *Measurement for Evaluation in Physical Education and Exercise Science.* Dubuque, IA: Brown. 1987.
11. Behnke, A., and J. Wilmore. *Evaluation and Regulation of Body Build and Composition.* Englewood Cliffs, NJ: Prentice Hall. 1974.
12. Berg, R., R.W. Latin, and T. Baechle. Survey of physical fitness of NCAA Division I football players. *NSCA J* 14(3):68-72. 1992.
13. Burke, E. *Toward an Understanding of Human Performance.* Ithaca, NY: Mouvement. 1980.
14. Canadian Society for Exercise Physiology. *The Canadian Physical Activity, Fitness and Lifestyle Approach: CSEP-Health and Fitness Program's Health-Related Appraisal and Counseling Strategy,* 3rd ed. Ottawa, ON: Canadian Society for Exercise Physiology. 2003.
15. Chu, D. *Explosive Power and Strength.* Champaign, IL: Human Kinetics. 1996.
16. Cooper, K. *The New Aerobics.* New York: Bantam Books. 1972.
17. Costill, D., S. Miller, W. Myers, F. Kehoe, and W. Hoffman. Relationships among selected tests of explosive leg strength and power. *Res Q* 39(3):785-787. 1968.
18. Department of the Army. *Physical Fitness Training: Field Manual No. 21-20.* Washington, DC: Headquarters, Department of the Army. 1998.
19. Edgren, H. An experiment in the testing ability and progress in basketball. *Res Q* 3(1):159-171. 1932.
20. Epley, B. *Husker Power.* Lincoln, NE: University of Nebraska Press. 1983.
21. Epley, B. The Nebraska Timer: A simple, accurate way to measure the 40 yard dash. *NSCA J* 4(5):14-15. 1982.
22. Fleck, S., and M. Marks. Interval training. *NSCA J* 5(5):40-62. 1983.
23. Fox, E.L., R.W. Bowers, and M.L. Foss. *The Physiological Basis for Exercise and Sport,* 5th ed. Dubuque, IA: Brown. 1993. pp. 674-676.
24. Gilliam, G.M., and M. Marks. 300 yard shuttle run. *NSCA J* 5(5):46. 1983.
25. Golding, L.A., C.R. Myers, and W.E. Sinning. *Y's Way to Physical Fitness,* 3rd ed. Champaign, IL: Human Kinetics. 1989.
26. Gotshalk, L. Discipline and strictness in testing and training. *NSCA J* 7(5):72-73. 1985.
27. Gould, D. Goal setting for peak performance. In: *Applied Sport Psychology,* 2nd ed., J.E. Williams, ed. Mountain View, CA: Mayfield. 1993. pp. 158-169.
28. Henschen, K.P. Athletic staleness and burnout: Diagnosis, prevention, and treatment. In: *Applied Sport Psychology,* 2nd ed., J.E. Williams, ed. Mountain View, CA: Mayfield. 1993. pp. 328-337.
29. Heyward, V.H. *Advanced Fitness Assessment and Exercise Prescription,* 4th ed. Champaign, IL: Human Kinetics. 2002.
30. Heyward, V. H., and L.M. Stolarczyk. *Applied Body Composition Assessment.* Champaign, IL: Human Kinetics. 1996.
31. Hitchcock, H., and B. Pauletto. Tennessee's championship preseason conditioning program. *Coaching Women's Basketball* 5:10-14. 1987.
32. Hoffman, J. *Norms for Fitness, Performance, and Health.* Champaign, IL: Human Kinetics. 2006.
33. Hopkins, C. *Understanding Educational Research.* Columbus, OH: Merrill. 1980.
34. Jackson, A., and M. Pollock. Generalized equations for predicting body density of men. *British Journal of Nutrition* 49:497-504. 1978.
35. Jackson, A., M. Pollock, and L. Gettman. Inter-tester reliability of selected skinfold and circumference measurements and percent fat estimates. *Res Q* 49:546-551. 1978.
36. Jackson, A., M. Pollock, and A. Ward. Generalized equations for predicting body density of women. *Medicine and Science in Sports and Exercise* 12:175-182. 1980.
37. Johnson, B., and J. Nelson. *Practical Measurements for Evaluation in Physical Education,* 2nd ed. Minneapolis: Burgess. 1974.
38. Katch, F., and W. McArdle. *Nutrition, Weight Control, and Exercise.* Boston: Houghton Mifflin. 1977.
39. Kontor, K. Editorial: Testing and evaluation. *NSCA J* 3(2):7. 1981.
40. Kordich, J. Evaluating your client: Fitness assessment protocols and norms. In: *NSCA Certification Commission Essentials of Personal Training Symposium Workbook Presentation 4,* 18-19. Lincoln, NE: NSCA Certification Commission. 2006.
41. Kraemer, W., and S. Fleck. Anaerobic metabolism and its evaluation. *NSCA J* 4(2):20-21. 1982.
42. Kurland, H. Isokinetic testing and training. *NSCA J* 2(2):34-35. 1980.
43. Lohman, T.G., L. Houtkooper, and S. Going. Body fat measurement goes high-tech: Not all are created equal. *ACSM's Health and Fitness J* 7:30-35. 1997.
44. Madole, K. Reliability and validity of the T-test for college-age males [abstract]. *J Strength Cond Res* 11(4):283. 1997.
45. Mayhew, J., B. Levy, T. McCormick, and G. Evans. Strength norms for NCAA Division II college football players. *NSCA J* 9(3):67-69. 1987.
46. McArdle, W., F. Katch, and V. Katch. *Essentials of Exercise Physiology,* 2nd ed., Philadelphia: Lea & Febiger. 2005.
47. Morrow, J.R., A.W. Jackson, J.G. Disch, and D.P. Mood. *Measurement and Evaluation in Human Performance,* 3rd ed., Champaign, IL: Human Kinetics. 2005.
48. Nieman, D.C. *Fitness and Sports Medicine,* 3rd ed. Palo Alto, CA: Bull. 1995.
49. Oborny, C. Personal correspondence. Creighton University, Omaha, NE. 1998.
50. Pauole, K. The T-test as a measure of speed, power, and agility for females [abstract]. *J Strength Cond Res* 11(4):283. 1997.
51. Pauole, K., K. Madole, J. Garhammer, M. Lacourse, and R. Rozenek. Reliability and validity of the T-test as a measure of agility, leg power, and leg speed in college age males and females. *J Strength Cond Res* 14:443-450. 2000.
52. Plisk, S. Personal correspondence. Yale University, New Haven, CT. 1998.
53. Pollock, M., J. Wilmore, and S. Fox. *Exercise in Health and Disease.* Philadelphia: Saunders. 1984.
54. Safrit, M. *Evaluation in Physical Education.* Englewood Cliffs, NJ: Prentice Hall. 1980.
55. Schweigert, D. Normative values for common preseason testing protocols: NCAA Division II women's basketball. *NSCA J* 18(6):7-10. 1996.
56. Semenick, D. Bridging the gap: Anaerobic testing. *NSCA J* 6(5):45, 70-73. 1984.
57. Semenick, D. Bridging the gap: Basketball bioenergetics. *NSCA J* 6(6):44-73. 1984.
58. Semenick, D. Conditioning program: Testing and evaluation. *NSCA J* 3(2):8-9. 1981.
59. Semenick, D. Tests and measurements: The T-test. *NSCA J* 12(1):36-37. 1990.
60. Semenick, D. Tests and measurements: The vertical jump. *NSCA J* 12(3):68-69. 1990.
61. Sifft, J. Statistics for sport performance. *NSCA J* 8(6):46-47. 1986.

62. Sifft, J. Using descriptive statistics in sport performance. *NSCA J* 5(5):26-28. 1983.
63. Slaughter, M.H., T.G. Lohman, R.A. Boileau, C.A. Horswill, R.J. Stillman, M.D. Van Loan, and D.A. Bemben. Skinfold equations for estimation of body fatness in children and youth. *Human Biology* 60:709-723. 1988
64. Sloan, A., and J. Weir. Nomograms for prediction of body density and total body fat from skinfold measurements. *J Appl Physiol* 28(2):221-222. 1970.
65. Stone, M., and H. O'Bryant. *Weight Training: A Scientific Approach*. Minneapolis: Burgess. 1987.
66. Taylor, J. Personal correspondence. New Mexico State University, Las Cruces. 1998.
67. Tesch, P. Bridging the gap: Anaerobic testing. *NSCA J* 6(5):44, 67. 1984.
68. Thomas, J., and K. Nelson. *Introduction to Research in Health, Physical Education, Recreation and Dance*. Champaign, IL: Human Kinetics. 1985.
69. Wathen, D. Personal correspondence. Youngstown State University, Youngstown, OH. 1998.
70. Wilkerson, G. Time expectations for a well-conditioned athlete in the 1 1/2 mile. *NSCA J* 5(5):44-45. 1983.
71. YMCA. *YMCA Fitness Testing and Assessment Manual*, 4th ed., L.A. Golding, ed. Champaign, IL: Human Kinetics. 2000.

Chapter 13 Warm-Up and Stretching

1. Andersen, J.C. Stretching before and after exercise: Effect on muscle soreness and injury risk. *J Athl Train* 40(3):218-220. 2005.
2. Anthony, C.P., and N.J. Kolthoff. *Textbook of Anatomy and Physiology*, 9th ed. St. Louis: Mosby. 1975.
3. Arthur, M., and B. Bailey. *Complete Conditioning for Football*. Champaign, IL:. Human Kinetics. 1998.
4. Asmussen, E., F. Bonde-Peterson, and K. Jorgenson. Mechano-elastic properties of human muscles at different temperatures. *Acta Physiol Scand* 96:86-93. 1976.
5. Bandy, W.D., and J.M. Irion. The effect of time on static stretch on the flexibility of the hamstring muscles. *Phys Ther* 74(9):845-850, discussion 850-852. 1994.
6. Bandy, W.D., J.M. Irion, and M. Briggler. The effect of static stretch and dynamic range of motion training on the flexibility of the hamstring muscles. *J Orthop Sports Phys Ther* 27(4):295-300. 1998.
7. Bandy, W.D., J.M. Irion, and M. Briggler. The effect of time and frequency of static stretching on flexibility of the hamstring muscles. *Phys Ther* 77(10):1090-1096. 1997.
8. Behm, D.G., A. Bambury, F. Cahill, and K. Power. Effect of acute static stretching on force, balance, reaction time, and movement time. *Med Sci Sports Exerc* 36(8):1397-1402. 2004.
9. Behm, D.G., D.C. Button, and J.C. Butt. Factors affecting force loss with prolonged stretching. *Can J Appl Physiol* 26(3):261-272. 2001.
10. Bergh, U., and B. Ekblom. Influence of muscle temperature on maximal strength and power output in human muscle. *Acta Physiol Scand* 107:332-337. 1979.
11. Brodowicz, G.R., R. Welsh, and J. Wallis. Comparison of stretching with ice, stretching with heat, or stretching alone on hamstring flexibility. *J Athl Train* 31:324-327. 1996.
12. Burkett, L.N., W.T. Phillips, and J. Ziuraitis. The best warm-up for the vertical jump in college-age athletic men. *J Strength Cond Res* 19(3):673-676. 2005.
13. Cherry, D.B. Review of physical therapy alternatives for reducing muscle contracture. *Phys Ther* 60:877-881. 1980.
14. Church, J.B., M.S. Wiggins, F.M. Moode, and R. Crist. Effect of warm-up and flexibility treatments on vertical jump performance. *J Strength Cond Res* 15(3):332-336. 2001.
15. Cipriani, D., B. Abel, and D. Pirrwitz. A comparison of two stretching protocols on hip range of motion: Implications for total daily stretch duration. *J Strength Cond Res* 17(2):274-278. 2003.
16. Condon, S.M., and R.S. Hutton. Soleus muscle electromyographic activity and ankle dorsiflexion range of motion during four stretching procedures. *Phys Ther* 67:24-30. 1987.
17. Corbin, C.B., L.J. Dowell, R. Lindsey, and H. Tolson. *Concepts in Physical Education*. Dubuque, IA: Brown. 1978.
18. Cornelius, W.J. The effective way. *NSCA J* 7(3):62-64. 1985.
19. Cornelius, W.J., and M.M. Hinson. The relationship between isometric contractions of hip extensors and subsequent flexibility in males. *Sports Med Phys Fitness* 20:75-80. 1980.
20. Cornwell, A., A.G. Nelson, and B. Sidaway. Acute effects of stretching on the neuromechanical properties of the triceps surae muscle complex. *Eur J Appl Physiol* 86(5):428-434. 2002.
21. Cramer, J.T., T.J. Housh, J.W. Coburn, T.W. Beck, and G.O. Johnson. Acute effects of static stretching on maximal eccentric torque production in women. *J Strength Cond Res* 20(2):354-358. 2006.
22. Cramer, J.T., T.J. Housh, G.O. Johnson, J.M. Miller, J.W. Coburn, and T.W. Beck. Acute effects of static stretching on peak torque in women. *J Strength Cond Res* 18(2):236-241. 2004.
23. Cramer, J.T., T.J. Housh, J.P. Weir, G.O. Johnson, J.W. Coburn, and T.W. Beck. The acute effects of static stretching on peak torque, mean power output, electromyography, and mechanomyography. *Eur J Appl Physiol* 93(5-6):530-539. 2005.
24. Davis, D.S., P.E. Ashby, K.L. McCale, J.A. McQuain, and J.M. Wine. The effectiveness of 3 stretching techniques on hamstring flexibility using consistent stretching parameters. *J Strength Cond Res* 19(1):27-32. 2005.
25. Depino, G.M., W.G. Webright, and B.L. Arnold. Duration of maintained hamstring flexibility after cessation of an acute static stretching protocol. *J Athl Train* 35(1):56-59. 2000.
26. deVries, H.A., T.J. Housh, and L.L. Weir. *Physiology of Exercise for Physical Education, Athletics and Exercise Science*, 5th ed. Dubuque, IA: Brown. 1995.
27. de Weijer, V.C., G.C. Gorniak, and E. Shamus. The effect of static stretch and warm-up exercise on hamstring length over the course of 24 hours. *J Orthop Sports Phys Ther* 33(12):727-733. 2003.
28. Earle, R.W., and T.R. Baechle, eds. *NSCA's Essentials of Personal Training*. Champaign, IL: Human Kinetics. 2004.
29. Enoka, R.M. *Neuromechanics of Human Movement*, 3rd ed. Champaign, IL: Human Kinetics. 2001.
30. Etnyre, B.R., and L.D. Abraham. Gains in range of ankle dorsiflexion using three popular stretching techniques. *Am J Phys Med* 65(4):189-196. 1986.
31. Evetovich, T.K., N.J. Nauman, D.S. Conley, and J.B. Todd. Effect of static stretching of the biceps brachii on torque, electromyography, and mechanomyography during concentric isokinetic muscle actions. *J Strength Cond Res* 17(3):484-488. 2003.
32. Faigenbaum, A.D., M. Bellucci, A. Bernieri, B. Bakker, and K. Hoorens. Acute effects of different warm-up protocols on fitness performance in children. *J Strength Cond Res* 19(2):376-381. 2005.
33. Fleck, S.J., and W.J. Kraemer. *Designing Resistance Training Programs*, 3rd ed. Champaign, IL: Human Kinetics. 2004.
34. Fletcher, I.M., and B. Jones. The effect of different warm-up stretch protocols on 20 meter sprint performance in trained rugby union players. *J Strength Cond Res* 18(4):885-888. 2004.
35. Flexibility: Roundtable. *NSCA J* 6(4):10-22, 71-73. 1984.
36. Fox, E.L. *Sports Physiology*. Philadelphia: Saunders. 1979.
37. Fradkin, A.J., B.J. Gabbe, and P.A. Cameron. Does warming up prevent injury in sport? The evidence from randomised controlled trials. *J Sci Med Sport* 9(3):214-220. 2006.
38. Funk, D.C., A.M. Swank, B.M. Mikla, T.A. Fagan, and B.K. Farr. Impact of prior exercise on hamstring flexibility: A comparison of proprioceptive neuromuscular facilitation and static stretching. *J Strength Cond Res* 17(3):489-492. 2003.
39. Getchell, B. *Physical Fitness: A Way of Life*. New York: Wiley. 1979.
40. Gleim, G.W., and M.P. McHugh. Flexibility and its effects on sports injury and performance [review]. *Sports Med* 24(5):289-299. 1997.
41. Gremion, G. Is stretching for sports performance still useful? A review of the literature. *Rev Med Suisse* 27:1(28):1830-1834. 2005.

42. Hedrick, A. Dynamic flexibility training. *Strength Cond J* 22(5):33-38. 2000.
43. Hedrick, A. Flexibility, body-weight and stability ball exercises. In: *NSCA's Essentials of Personal Training,* T.R. Baechle and R.W. Earle, eds. Champaign, IL: Human Kinetics. 2004.
44. Herbert, R.D., and M. Gabriel. Effects of stretching before and after exercise on muscle soreness and risk of injury: A systematic review. *Br Med J* 325:468-470. 2002.
45. Hoffman, J. *Physiological Aspects of Sports Performance and Training.* Champaign, IL: Human Kinetics. 2002.
46. Holland, G.J. The physiology of flexibility: A review of the literature. *Kinesthesiol Rev* 1:49-62. 1966.
47. Holt, L.E., T.M. Travis, and T. Okia. Comparative study of three stretching techniques. *Percept Mot Skills* 31:611-616. 1970.
48. Johansson, P.H., L. Lindstrom, G. Sundelin, and B. Lindstrom. The effects of pre-exercise stretching on muscular soreness, tenderness and force loss following heavy eccentric exercise. *Scand J Med Sci Sports* 9(4):219-225. 1999.
49. Knapik, J.J., C.L. Bauman, and B.H. Jones. Preseason strength and flexibility imbalances associated with athletic injuries in female collegiate athletes. *Am J Orthop Soc Sports Med* 19:76-81. 1991.
50. Knapik, J.J., B.H. Jones, C.L. Bauman, and J.M. Harris. Strength, flexibility and athletic injuries. *Sports Med* 14(5):277-288. 1992.
51. Knudson, D.V., P. Magnusson, and M. McHugh. Current issues in flexibility fitness. *Pres Council Phys Fitness Sports* 3:1-6. 2000.
52. Leighton, J.R. A study of the effect of progressive weight training on flexibility. *J Assoc Phys Ment Rehabil* 18:101. 1964.
53. Little, T., and A.G. Williams. Effects of differential stretching protocols during warm-ups on high-speed motor capacities in professional soccer players. *J Strength Cond Res* 20(1):203-207. 2006.
54. Lund, H., P. Vestergaard-Poulsen, I.L. Kanstrup, and P. Sejrsen. The effect of passive stretching on delayed onset muscle soreness, and other detrimental effects following eccentric exercise. *Scand J Med Sci Sports* 8(4):216-221. 1998.
55. Mann, D.P., and M.T. Jones. Guidelines to the implementation of a dynamic stretching program. *Strength Cond J* 21(6):53-55. 1999.
56. Marek, S.M., J.T. Cramer, A.L. Fincher, L.L. Massey, S.M. Dangelmaier, S. Purkayastha, K.A. Fitz, and J.Y. Culbertson. Acute effects of static and proprioceptive neuromuscular facilitation stretching on muscle strength and power output. *J Athl Train* 40(2):94-103. 2005.
57. Marshall, J.L., N. Johanson, T.L. Wickiewicz, H.M. Tishler, B.L. Koslin, S. Zeno, and A. Myers. Joint looseness: A function of the person and the joint. *Med Sci Sports Exerc* 12:189-194. 1980.
58. McArdle, W.D., F.I. Katch, and V.L. Katch. *Exercise Physiology: Energy, Nutrition and Human Performance,* 6th ed. Baltimore: Lippincott, Williams & Wilkins. 2007.
59. McAtee, R.E., and J. Charland. *Facilitated Stretching,* 3rd ed. Champaign, IL: Human Kinetics. 2007.
60. McFarland, B. Developing maximum running speed. *NSCA J* 6(5):24-28. 1984.
61. Moore, M.A., and R.S. Hutton. Electromyographic investigation of muscle stretching techniques. *Med Sci Sports Exerc* 12(5):322-329. 1980.
62. Nelson, A.G., and J. Kokkonen. Acute muscle stretching inhibits maximal strength performance. *Res Q Exerc Sport* 72(4):415-419. 2001.
63. Nelson, A.G., J. Kokkonen, and D.A. Arnall. Acute muscle stretching inhibits muscle strength endurance performance. *J Strength Cond Res* 19(2):338-343. 2005.
64. Nelson, R.T., and W.D. Bandy. Eccentric training and static stretching improve hamstring flexibility of high school males. *J Athl Train* 39(3):254-258. 2004.
65. Pope, R.P., R.D. Herbert, J.D. Kirwan, and B.J. Graham. A randomised trial of pre-exercise stretching for prevention of lower limb injury. *Med Sci Sports Exerc* 32:271-277. 2000.
66. Power, K., D. Behm, F. Cahill, M. Carroll, and W. Young. An acute bout of static stretching: Effects on force and jumping performance. *Med Sci Sports Exerc* 36(8):1389-1396. 2004.
67. Prentice, W.E. A comparison of static stretching and PNF stretching for improving hip joint flexibility. *Athl Training* 18(1):56-59. 1983.
68. Riewald, S. Stretching the limits of knowledge on stretching. *Strength Cond J* 26(5):58-59. 2004.
69. Roberts, J.M., and K. Wilson. Effect of stretching duration on active and passive range of motion in the lower extremity. *Br J Sports Med* 33(4):259-263. 1999.
70. Sady, S.P., M. Wortman, and D. Blanket. Flexibility training: Ballistic, static or proprioceptive neuromuscular facilitation? *Arch Phys Med Rehabil* 63(6):261-263. 1992.
71. Safran, M.R., W.E. Garrett, A.V. Seaber, R.R. Glisson, and B.M. Ribbeck. The role of warm-up in muscular injury prevention. *Am J Sports Med* 16(2):123:128. 1988.
72. Shrier, I. Does stretching improve performance? A systematic and critical review of the literature [review]. *Clin J Sport Med* 14(5):267-273. 2004.
73. Shrier, I. Meta-analysis on pre-exercise stretching. *Med Sci Sports Exerc* 36(10):1832. 2004.
74. Shrier, I. Stretching before exercise: An evidence based approach. *Br J Sports Med* 34(5):324-325. 2000.
75. Shrier, I. Stretching before exercise does not reduce the risk of local muscle injury: A critical review of the clinical and basic science literature. *Clin J Sport Med* 9(4):221-227. 1999.
76. Tanigawa, M.C. Comparison of the hold relax procedure and passive mobilization on increasing muscle length. *Phys Ther* 52:725-735. 1972.
77. Thacker, S.B., J. Gilchrist, D.F. Stroup, and C.D. Kimsey, Jr. The impact of stretching on sports injury risk: A systematic review of the literature. *Med Sci Sports Exerc* 36(3):371-378. 2004.
78. Todd, T. Historical perspective: The myth of the muscle-bound lifter. *NSCA J* 6(4):37-41. 1985.
79. Unick, J., H.S. Kieffer, W. Cheesman, and A. Feeney. The acute effects of static and ballistic stretching on vertical jump performance in trained women. *J Strength Cond Res* 19(1):206-212. 2005.
80. Voss, D.E., M.K. Ionta, and B.J. Myers. *Proprioceptive Neuromuscular Facilitation: Patterns and Techniques,* 3rd ed. Philadelphia: Harper & Row. 1985.
81. Wallmann, H.W., J.A. Mercer, and J.W. McWhorter. Surface electromyographic assessment of the effect of static stretching of the gastrocnemius on vertical jump performance. *J Strength Cond Res* 19(3):684-688. 2005.
82. Walter, S.D., S.F. Figoni, F.F. Andres, and E. Brown. Training intensity and duration in flexibility. *Clin Kinesthesiol* 50:40-45. 1996.
83. Weiss, L.W., K.J. Cureton, and F.N. Thompson. Comparison of serum testosterone and androstenedione responses to weight lifting in men and women. *Eur J Appl Physiol* 50:413-419. 1983.
84. Wilmore, J.H., R.B. Parr, R.N. Girandola, P. Ward, P.A. Vodak, T.J. Barstow, T.V. Pipes, G.T. Romero, and P. Leslie. Physiological alterations consequent to circuit weight training. *Med Sci Sports* 10:79-84. 1978.
85. Winters, M.V., C.G. Blake, J.S. Trost, T.B. Marcello-Brinker, L.M. Lowe, M.B. Garber, and R.S. Wainner. Passive versus active stretching of hip flexor muscles in subjects with limited hip extension: A randomized clinical trial. *Phys Ther* 84(9):800-807. 2004.
86. Witvrouw, E., N. Mahieu, L. Danneels, and P. McNair. Stretching and injury prevention: An obscure relationship. *Sports Med* 34(7):443-449. 2004.
87. Yamaguchi, T., and K. Ishii. Effects of static stretching for 30 seconds and dynamic stretching on leg extension power. *J Strength Cond Res* 19(3):677-683. 2005.
88. Young, W.B., and D.G. Behm. Effects of running, static stretching and practice jumps on explosive force production and jumping performance. *J Sports Med Phys Fitness* 43(1):21-27. 2003.
89. Young, W.B., and D.G. Behm. Should static stretching be used during a warm up for strength and power activities. *Strength Cond J* 24(6):33-37. 2002.

Section 4, Part I

1. Anderson, T., and J.T. Kearney. Muscular strength and absolute and relative endurance. *Res Q Exerc Sport* 53:1-7. 1982.
2. Bompa, T.A. *Theory and Methodology of Training*. Dubuque, IA: Kendall/Hunt. 1983.
3. DeLorme, T.L. Restoration of muscle power by heavy-resistance exercises. *J Bone Joint Surg* 27:645. 1945.
4. Edgerton, V.R. Neuromuscular adaptation to power and endurance work. *Can J Appl Sport Sci* 1:49-58. 1976.
5. Fleck, S.J., and W.J. Kraemer. *Designing Resistance Training Programs,* 2nd ed. Champaign, IL: Human Kinetics. 1997.

Chapter 15 Resistance Training

1. Alén, M., A. Pakarinen, K. Häkkinen, and P.V. Komi. Responses of serum androgenic-anabolic and catabolic hormones to prolonged strength training. *Int J Sports Med* 9:229-233. 1988.
2. Anderson, T., and J.T. Kearney. Muscular strength and absolute and relative endurance. *Res Q Exerc Sport* 53:1-7. 1982.
3. Arnold, M.D., J.L. Mayhew, D. LeSuer, and J. McCormick. Accuracy of predicting bench press and squat performance from repetitions at low and high intensity [abstract]. *J Strength Cond Res* 9:205-206. 1995.
4. Atha, J. Strengthening muscle. *Exerc Sport Sci Rev* 9:1-73. 1981.
5. Baechle, T.R., and R.W. Earle. *Weight Training: A Text Written for the College Student*. Omaha: Creighton University Press. 1989.
6. Baechle, T.R., and R.W. Earle. *Weight Training: Steps to Success,* 3rd ed. Champaign, IL: Human Kinetics. 2006.
7. Baker, D., and R.U. Newton. Acute effect of power output of alternating an agonist and antagonist muscle exercise during complex training. *J Strength Cond Res* 19(1):202-205. 2005.
8. Baker, D., G. Wilson, and R. Carlyon. Periodization: The effect on strength of manipulating volume and intensity. *J Strength Cond Res* 8:235-242. 1994.
9. Berger, R.A. Comparative effects of three weight training programs. *Res Q* 34:396-398. 1963.
10. Berger, R.A. Effect of varied weight training programs on strength. *Res Q* 33:168-181. 1962.
11. Berger, R.A. Optimum repetitions for the development of strength. *Res Q* 33:334-338. 1962.
12. Berger, R.A. Strength improvement. *Strength Health,* August. 1972.
13. Bompa, T.A. *Theory and Methodology of Training*. Kendall/Hunt: Dubuque, IA. 1983.
14. Brzycki, M. Accent on intensity. *Schol Coach* 97:82-83. 1988.
15. Brzycki, M. Strength testing: Predicting a one-rep max from reps-to-fatigue. *JOHPERD* 64:88-90. 1993.
16. Chapman, P.P., J.R. Whitehead, and R.H. Binkert. The 225-lb reps-to-fatigue test as a submaximal estimate of 1RM bench press performance in college football players. *J Strength Cond Res* 12(4):258-261. 1998.
17. Clarke, D.H. Adaptations in strength and muscular endurance resulting from exercise. *Exerc Sport Sci Rev* 1:73-102. 1973.
18. Craig, B.W., J. Lucas, R. Pohlman, and H. Schilling. The effect of running, weightlifting and a combination of both on growth hormone release. *J Appl Sport Sci Res* 5(4):198-203. 1991.
19. DeLorme, T.L. Restoration of muscle power by heavy-resistance exercises. *J Bone Joint Surg* 27:645. 1945.
20. DeLorme, T.L., and A.L. Watkins. Technics of progressive resistance exercise. *Arch Phys Med Rehabil* 29:263-273. 1948.
21. DeRenne, C., R.K. Hetzler, B.P. Buxton, and K.W. Ho. Effects of training frequency on strength maintenance in pubescent baseball players. *J Strength Cond Res* 10:8-14. 1996.
22. Dudley, G.A., P.A. Tesch, B.J. Miller, and P. Buchanan. Importance of eccentric actions in performance adaptations to resistance training. *Aviat Space Environ Med* 62:543-550. 1991.
23. Earle, R.W. Weight training exercise prescription. In: *Essentials of Personal Training Symposium Workbook*. Lincoln, NE: NSCA Certification Commission. 2006.
24. Edgerton, V.R. Neuromuscular adaptation to power and endurance work. *Can J Appl Sport Sci* 1:49-58. 1976.
25. Epley, B. Poundage chart. In: *Boyd Epley Workout*. Lincoln, NE: University of Nebraska. 1985.
26. Fleck, S.J., and W.J. Kraemer. *Designing Resistance Training Programs*. Champaign, IL: Human Kinetics. 1987.
27. Fleck, S.J., and W.J. Kraemer. *Designing Resistance Training Programs,* 3rd ed. Champaign, IL: Human Kinetics. 2003.
28. Garhammer, J. A review of power output studies of Olympic and powerlifting: Methodology, performance prediction and evaluation tests. *J Strength Cond Res* 7(2):76-89. 1993.
29. Garhammer, J. Personal communication. 2007.
30. Garhammer, J. *Sports Illustrated Strength Training*. New York: Harper & Row. 1986.
31. Garhammer, J. Weight lifting and training. In: *Biomechanics of Sport,* C.L. Vaughan, ed. Boca Raton, FL: CRC. 1989. pp. 169-211.
32. Garhammer, J., and T. McLaughlin. Power output as a function of load variation in Olympic and power lifting [abstract]. *J Biomech* 13(2):198. 1980.
33. Gettman, L.R., and M.J. Pollock. Circuit weight training: A critical review of its physiological benefits. *Phys Sportsmed* 9:44-60. 1981.
34. Graves, J.E., M.L. Pollock, S.H. Leggett, R.W. Braith, D.M. Carpenter, and L.E. Bishop. Effect of reduced training frequency on muscular strength. *Int J Sports Med* 9:316-319. 1988.
35. Häkkinen, K. Factors affecting trainability of muscular strength during short-term and prolonged training. *NSCA J* 7(2):32-37. 1985.
36. Häkkinen, K. Neuromuscular responses in male and female athletes to two successive strength training sessions in one day. *J Sports Med Phys Fitness* 32:234-242. 1992.
37. Häkkinen, K., A. Pakarinen, M. Alén, H. Kauhanen, and P.V. Komi. Daily hormonal and neuromuscular responses to intensive strength training in 1 week. *Int J Sports Med* 9:422-428. 1988.
38. Häkkinen, K., A. Pakarinen, M. Alén, H. Kauhanen, and P.V. Komi. Neuromuscular and hormonal responses in elite athletes to two successive strength training sessions in one day. *Eur J Appl Physiol* 57:133-139. 1988.
39. Harman, E., and P. Frykman. CSCS coaches' school: Order of exercise: The multiple mini-circuit weight-training program. *NSCA J* 14(1):57-61. 1992.
40. Harman, E., M. Johnson, and P. Frykman. CSCS coaches' school: Program design: A movement-oriented approach to exercise prescription. *NSCA J* 14(1):47-54. 1992.
41. Hather, B.M., P.A. Tesch, P. Buchanan, and G.A. Dudley. Influence of eccentric actions on skeletal muscle adaptations to resistance training. *Acta Physiol Scand* 143:177-185. 1992.
42. Hedrick, A. Training for hypertrophy. *Strength Cond* 17(3):22-29. 1995.
43. Henderson, J.M. The effects of weight loadings and repetitions, frequency of exercise and knowledge of theoretical principles of weight training on changes in muscular strength. *Diss Abstracts Int* 31A:3320. 1970.
44. Herrick, A.R., and M.H. Stone. The effects of periodization versus progressive resistance exercise on upper and lower body strength in women. *J Strength Cond Res* 10(2):72-76. 1996.
45. Hickson, R., M.A. Rosenkoetter, and M.M. Brown. Strength training effects on aerobic power and short-term endurance. *Med Sci Sports Exerc* 12:336-339. 1980.
46. Hoeger, W., S.L. Barette, D.F. Hale, and D.R. Hopkins. Relationship between repetitions and selected percentages of one repetition maximum. *J Appl Sport Sci Res* 1(1):11-13. 1987.
47. Hoeger, W., D.R. Hopkins, S.L. Barette, and D.F. Hale. Relationship between repetitions and selected percentages of one repetition maximum: A comparison between untrained and trained males and females. *J Appl Sport Sci Res* 4:47-54. 1990.

48. Hoffman, J.R., W.J. Kraemer, A.C. Fry, M. Deschenes, and M. Kemp. The effects of self-selection for frequency of training in a winter conditioning program for football. *J Appl Sport Sci Res* 4:76-82. 1990.
49. Hoffman, J.R., C.M. Maresh, L.E. Armstrong, and W.J. Kraemer. Effects of off-season and in-season resistance training programs on a collegiate male basketball team. *J Human Muscle Perform* 1:48-55. 1991.
50. Hunter, G.R. Changes in body composition, body build, and performance associated with different weight training frequencies in males and females. *NSCA J* 7(1):26-28. 1985.
51. Ikai, M., and T. Fukunaga. Calculation of muscle strength per unit cross-sectional area of human muscle by means of ultrasonic measurement. *Int Z Angew Physiol Arbeitphysiol* 26:26-32. 1968.
52. Jones, A. *Nautilus Training Principles*. Bulletin No. 2. Deland, FL: Nautilus. 1971.
53. Knuttgen, H.G., and W.J. Kraemer. Terminology and measurement in exercise performance. *J Appl Sport Sci Res* 1:1-10. 1987.
54. Komi, P.V. Neuromuscular performance: Factors influencing force and speed production. *Scand J Sports Sci* 1:2-15. 1979.
55. Kraemer, W.J. Endocrine responses and adaptations to strength training. In: *The Encyclopedia of Sports Medicine: Strength and Power in Sport,* 1st ed., P.V. Komi, ed. Malden, MA: Blackwell Scientific. 1992. pp. 291-304.
56. Kraemer, W.J. Exercise prescription in weight training: A needs analysis. *NSCA J* 5(1):64-65. 1983.
57. Kraemer, W.J. A series of studies: The physiological basis for strength training in American football: Fact over philosophy. *J Strength Cond Res* 11(3):131-142. 1997.
58. Kraemer, W.J., and L.P. Koziris. Muscle strength training: Techniques and considerations. *Phys Ther Pract* 2:54-68. 1992.
59. Kraemer, W.J., R.U. Newton, J. Bush, J. Volek, N.T. Triplett, and L.P. Koziris. Varied multiple set resistance training program produces greater gain than single set program. *Med Sci Sports Exerc* 27:S195. 1995.
60. Kraemer, W.J., B.J. Noble, M.J. Clark, and B.W. Culver. Physiologic responses to heavy resistance exercise with very short rest periods. *Int J Sports Med* 8:247-252. 1987.
61. Kramer, J.B., M.H. Stone, H.S. O'Bryant, M.S. Conley, R.L. Johnson, D.C. Nieman, D.R. Honeycutt, and T.P. Hoke. Effects of single vs. multiple sets of weight training: Impact of volume, intensity, and variation. *J Strength Cond Res* 11(3):143-147. 1997.
62. Lander, J. Maximum based on reps. *NSCA J* 6(6):60-61. 1984.
63. Larson, G.D., Jr., and J.A. Potteiger. A comparison of three different rest intervals between multiple squat bouts. *J Strength Cond Res* 11(2):115-118. 1997.
64. LeSuer, D.A., J.H. McCormick, J.L. Mayhew, R.L. Wasserstein, and M.D. Arnold. The accuracy of predicting equations for estimating 1RM performance in the bench press, squat, and deadlift. *J Strength Cond Res* 11(4):211-213. 1997.
65. Lombardi, V.P. *Beginning Weight Training*. Dubuque, IA: Brown. 1989.
66. Luthi, J.M., H. Howald, H. Claassen, K. Rosler, P. Vock, and H. Hoppler. Structural changes in skeletal muscle tissue with heavy-resistance exercise. *Int J Sports Med* 7:123-127. 1986.
67. Marcinik, E.J., J. Potts, G. Schlabach, S. Will, P. Dawson, and B.F. Hurley. Effects of strength training on lactate threshold and endurance performance. *Med Sci Sports Exerc* 23:739-743. 1991.
68. Mayhew, J.L., T.E. Ball, M.E. Arnold, and J.C. Bowen. Relative muscular endurance performance as a predictor of bench press strength in college men and women. *J Appl Sport Sci Res* 6(4):200-206. 1992.
69. Mayhew, J.L., J.S. Ware, M.G. Bemben, B. Wilt, T.E. Ward, B. Farris, J. Juraszek, and J.P. Slovak. The NFL-225 test as a measure of bench press strength in college football players. *J Strength Cond Res* 13(2):130-134. 1999.
70. Mayhew, J.L., J.S. Ware, and J.L. Prinster. Using lift repetitions to predict muscular strength in adolescent males. *NSCA J* 15(6):35-38. 1993.
71. McDonagh, M.J.N., and C.T.M. Davies. Adaptive response of mammalian skeletal muscle to exercise with high loads. *Eur J Appl Physiol* 52:139-155. 1984.
72. McGee, D., T.C. Jessee, M.H. Stone, and D. Blessing. Leg and hip endurance adaptations to three weight-training programs. *J Appl Sport Sci Res* 6:92-95. 1992.
73. Morales, J., and S. Sobonya. Use of submaximal repetition tests for predicting 1-RM strength in class athletes. *J Strength Cond Res* 10(3):186-189. 1996.
74. Newton, R.U., B. Humphries, A. Murphy, G.J. Wilson, and W.J. Kraemer. Biomechanics and neural activation during fast bench press movements: Implications for power training. Presented at the NSCA Conference. New Orleans, June 1994.
75. Newton, R.U., and W.J. Kraemer. Developing explosive muscular power: Implications for a mixed methods training strategy. *NSCA J* 16:(5):20-31. 1994.
76. Newton, R.U., W.J. Kraemer, K. Häkkinen, B.J. Humphries, and A.J. Murphy. Kinematics, kinetics, and muscle activation during explosive upper body movements: Implications for power development. *J Appl Biomech* 12:31-43. 1996.
77. O'Bryant, H.S., R. Byrd, and M.H. Stone. Cycle ergometer performance and maximum leg and hip strength adaptations to two different methods of weight training. *J Appl Sport Sci Res* 2:27-30. 1988.
78. O'Shea, P. *Scientific Principles and Methods of Strength Fitness*. Reading, MA: Addison-Wesley. 1976.
79. O'Shea, P. Effects of selected weight training programs on the development of strength and muscle hypertrophy. *Res Q* 37:95-102. 1966.
80. Ostrowski, K.J., G.J. Wilson, R. Weatherby, P.W. Murphy, and A.D. Lyttle. The effect of weight training volume on hormonal output and muscular size and function. *J Strength Cond Res* 11(3):148-154. 1997.
81. Pauletto, B. Choice and order of exercise. *NSCA J* 8(2):71-73. 1986.
82. Pauletto, B. Intensity. *NSCA J* 8(1):33-37. 1986.
83. Pauletto, B. Rest and recuperation. *NSCA J* 8(3):52-53. 1986.
84. Pauletto, B. Sets and repetitions. *NSCA J* 7(6):67-69. 1985.
85. Poliquin, C. Five steps to increasing the effectiveness of your strength training program. *NSCA J* 10(3):34-39. 1988.
86. Richardson, T. Program design: Circuit training with exercise machines. *NSCA J* 15(5):18-19. 1993.
87. Robinson, J.M., M.H. Stone, R.L. Johnson, C.M. Penland, B.J. Warren, and R.D. Lewis. Effects of different weight training exercise/rest intervals on strength, power, and high intensity exercise endurance. *J Strength Cond Res* 9(4):216-221. 1995.
88. Roundtable: Circuit training. *NSCA J* 12(2):16-27. 1990.
89. Roundtable: Circuit training—part II. *NSCA J* 12(3):10-21. 1990.
90. Sale, D.G., J.D. MacDougall, I. Jacobs, and S. Garner. Interaction between concurrent strength and endurance training. *J Appl Physiol* 68:260-270. 1990.
91. Santa Maria, D.L., P. Grzybinski, and B. Hatfield. Power as a function of load for a supine bench press exercise. *NSCA J* 6(6):58. 1984.
92. Sewall, L.P., and J.E. Lander. The effects of rest on maximal efforts in the squat and bench press. *J Appl Sport Sci Res* 5:96-99. 1991.
93. Sforzo, G.A., and P.R. Touey. Manipulating exercise order affects muscular performance during a resistance exercise training session. *J Strength Cond Res* 10(1):20-24. 1996.
94. Simmons, L. Training by percents. *Powerlifting USA* 12(2):21. 1988.
95. Snyder, G., and R. Wayne. *Posedown: Muscletalk with the Champs*. New York: Sterling. 1987.
96. Sobonya, S., and J. Morales. The use of maximal repetition test for prediction of 1 repetition maximum loads [abstract]. *Sports Med Train Rehabil* 4:154. 1993.
97. Spassov, A. Bulgarian training methods. Paper presented at the symposium of the National Strength and Conditioning Association. Denver, June 1989.
98. Staron, R.S., E.S. Malicky, M.J. Leonardi, J.E. Falkel, F.C. Hagerman, and G.A. Dudley. Muscle hypertrophy and fast fiber type conver-

sions in heavy resistance-trained women. *Eur J Appl Physiol Occ Physiol* 60:71-79. 1989.
99. Stone, M.H., and H.S. O'Bryant. *Weight Training: A Scientific Approach*. Minneapolis: Burgess. 1987.
100. Stone, M.H., H.S. O'Bryant, J. Garhammer, J. McMillan, and R. Rozenek. A theoretical model of strength training. *NSCA J* 4(4):36-40. 1982.
101. Stone, M.H., and D. Wilson. Resistive training and selected effects. *Med Clin North Am* 69:109-122. 1985.
102. Stone, W.J., and W.A. Kroll. *Sports Conditioning and Weight Training,* 2nd ed. Carmel, IN: Brown & Benchmark. 1986.
103. Stowers, T., J. McMillan, D. Scala, V. Davis, D. Wilson, and M.H. Stone. The short-term effects of three different strength-power training methods. *NSCA J* 5(3):24-27. 1983.
104. Tan, B. Manipulating resistance training program variables to optimize maximum strength in men. *J Strength Cond Res* 13(3):289-304. 1999.
105. Tesch, P.A. Training for bodybuilding. In: *The Encyclopedia of Sports Medicine: Strength and Power in Sport,* 1st ed., P.V. Komi, ed. Malden, MA: Blackwell Scientific. 1992. pp. 370-380.
106. Tesch, P.A., and L. Larson. Muscle hypertrophy in body builders. *Eur J Appl Physiol* 49:301-306. 1982.
107. Verhoshansky, Y. *Fundamentals of Special Strength Training in Sport*. Livonia, MI: Sportivny Press. 1976.
108. Wagner, L.L., S.A. Evans, J.P. Weir, T.J. Housh, and G.O. Johnson. The effect of grip width on bench press performance. *Int J Sport Biomech* 8:1-10. 1992.
109. Ware, J.S., C.T. Clemens, J.L. Mayhew, and T.J. Johnston. Muscular endurance repetitions to predict bench press and squat strength in college football players. *J Strength Cond Res* 9(2):99-103. 1995.
110. Wathen, D. Load assignment. In: *Essentials of Strength Training and Conditioning,* T.R. Baechle, ed. Champaign, IL: Human Kinetics. 1994.
111. Weir, J.P., L.L. Wagner, and T.J. Housh. The effect of rest interval length on repeated maximal bench presses. *J Strength Cond Res* 8(1):58-60. 1994.
112. Weiss, L. The obtuse nature of muscular strength: The contribution of rest to its development and expression. *J Appl Sport Sci Res* 5(4):219-227. 1991.
113. Westcott, W.L. Four key factors in building a strength program. *Schol Coach* 55:104-105. 1986.
114. Westcott, W.L. *Strength Fitness*. Boston: Allyn & Bacon. 1982.
115. Wilk, K.E., R.F. Escamilla, G.S. Fleisig, S.W. Barrentine, J.R. Andrews, and M.L. Boyd. A comparison of tibiofemoral joint forces and electromyographic activity during open and closed chain exercises. *Am J Sports Med* 24(4):518-527. 1996.
116. Willoughby, D.S. The effects of mesocycle-length weight training programs involving periodization and partially equated volumes on upper and lower body strength. *J Strength Cond Res* 7:2-8. 1993.
117. Wilson, G., B. Elliott, and G. Kerr. Bar path and force profile characteristics for maximal and submaximal loads in the bench press. *Int J Sport Biomech* 5:390-402. 1989.
118. Withers, R.T. Effect of varied weight-training loads on the strength of university freshmen. *Res Q* 41:110-114. 1970.

Chapter 16 Plyometric Training

1. Albert, M. *Eccentric Muscle Training in Sports and Orthopaedics*. New York: Churchill Livingstone. 1995.
2. Allerheilegen, B., and R. Rogers. Plyometrics program design. *Strength Cond* 17(4):26-31. 1995.
3. Asmussen, E., and F. Bonde-Peterson. Storage of elastic energy in skeletal muscles in man. *Acta Physiol Scand* 91:385-392. 1974.
4. Aura, O., and J.T. Viitasalo. Biomechanical characteristics of jumping. *Int J Sport Biomech* 5(1):89-97. 1989.
5. Bobbert, M.F. Drop jumping as a training method for jumping ability. *Sports Med* 9(1):7-22. 1990.
6. Bobbert, M.F., K.G.M. Gerritsen, M.C.A. Litjens, and A.J. Van Soest. Why is countermovement jump height greater than squat jump height? *Med Sci Sports Exerc* 28:1402-1412. 1996.
7. Borkowski, J. Prevention of pre-season muscle soreness: Plyometric exercise [abstract]. *Athl Training* 25(2):122. 1990.
8. Bosco, C., A. Ito, P.V. Komi, P. Luhtanen, P. Rahkila, H. Rusko, and J.T. Viitasalo. Neuromuscular function and mechanical efficiency of human leg extensor muscles during jumping exercises. *Acta Physiol Scand* 114:543-550. 1982.
9. Bosco, C., and P.V. Komi. Potentiation of the mechanical behavior of the human skeletal muscle through prestretching. *Acta Physiol Scand* 106:467-472. 1979.
10. Bosco, C., P.V. Komi, and A. Ito. Pre-stretch potentiation of human skeletal muscle during ballistic movement. *Acta Physiol Scand* 111:135-140. 1981.
11. Bosco, C., J.T. Viitasalo, P.V. Komi, and P. Luhtanen. Combined effect of elastic energy and myoelectrical potentiation during stretch shortening cycle exercise. *Acta Physiol Scand* 114:557-565. 1982.
12. Cavagna, G.A. Storage and utilization of elastic energy in skeletal muscle. In: *Exercise and Sport Science Reviews,* vol. 5, R.S. Hutton, ed. Santa Barbara, CA: Journal Affiliates. 1977. pp. 80-129.
13. Cavagna, G.A., B. Dusman, and R. Margaria. Positive work done by a previously stretched muscle. *J Appl Physiol* 24:21-32. 1968.
14. Cavagna, G.A., F.P. Saibere, and R. Margaria. Effect of negative work on the amount of positive work performed by an isolated muscle. *J Appl Physiol* 20:157-158. 1965.
15. Chambers, C., T.D. Noakes, E.V. Lambert, and M.I. Lambert. Time course of recovery of vertical jump height and heart rate versus running speed after a 90-km foot race. *J Sports Sci* 16:645-651. 1998.
16. Chu, D. *Jumping Into Plyometrics,* 2nd ed. Champaign, IL: Human Kinetics. 1998.
17. Chu, D., A. Faigenbaum, and J. Falkel. *Progressive Plyometrics for Kids*. Monterey, CA: Healthy Learning. 2006.
18. Chu, D., and L. Plummer. Jumping into plyometrics: The language of plyometrics. *NSCA J* 6(5):30-31. 1984.
19. Dillman, C.J., G.S. Fleisig, and J.R. Andrews. Biomechanics of pitching with emphasis upon shoulder kinematics. *J Orthop Sports Phys Ther* 18:402-408. 1993.
20. Dursenev, L., and L. Raeysky. Strength training for jumpers. *Soviet Sports Rev* 14(2):53-55. 1979.
21. Enoka, R.M. *Neuromechanical Basis of Kinesiology,* 2nd ed. Champaign, IL: Human Kinetics. 1994.
22. Escamilla, R.F., G.S. Fleisig, S.W. Barrentine, and J.R. Andrews. Kinematic comparisons of throwing different types of baseball pitches. *J Appl Biomech* 14(1):1-23. 1998.
23. Feltner, M., and J. Dapena. Dynamics of the shoulder and elbow joints of the throwing arm during a baseball pitch. *Int J Sport Biomech* 2:235. 1986.
24. Fowler, N.E., A. Lees, and T. Reilly. Changes in stature following plyometric drop-jump and pendulum exercises. *Ergonomics* 40:1279-1286. 1997.
25. Fowler, N.E., A. Lees, and T. Reilly. Spinal shrinkage in unloaded and loaded drop-jumping. *Ergonomics* 37:133-139. 1994.
26. Gambetta, V. Plyometric training. *Track Field Q Rev* 80(4):56-57. 1978.
27. Guyton, A.C., and J.E. Hall. *Textbook of Medical Physiology,* 10th ed. Philadelphia: Saunders. 2000.
28. Halling, A.H., M.E. Howard, and P.W. Cawley. Rehabilitation of anterior cruciate ligament injuries. *Clin Sports Med* 12:329-348. 1993.
29. Harman, E.A., M.T. Rosenstein, P.N. Frykman, and R.M. Rosenstein. The effects of arms and countermovement on vertical jumping. *Med Sci Sports Exerc* 22:825-833. 1990.
30. Hewett, T.E., A.L. Stroupe, T.A. Nance, and F.R. Noyes. Plyometric training in female athletes. *Am J Sports Med* 24:765-773. 1996.
31. Hill, A.V. *First and Last Experiments in Muscle Mechanics*. Cambridge: Cambridge University Press. 1970.
32. Holcomb, W.R., D.M. Kleiner, and D.A. Chu. Plyometrics: Considerations for safe and effective training. *Strength Cond* 20(3):36-39. 1998.
33. Kaeding, C.C., and R. Whitehead. Musculoskeletal injuries in adolescents. *Prim Care* 25(1):211-223. 1998.

34. Karst, G.M., and G.M. Willett. Onset timing of electromyographic activity in the vastus medialis oblique and vastus lateralis muscles in subjects with and without patellofemoral pain syndrome. *Phys Ther* 75:813-823. 1995.

35. Kilani, H.A., S.S. Palmer, M.J. Adrian, and J.J. Gapsis. Block of the stretch reflex of vastus lateralis during vertical jump. *Human Mvmt Sci* 8:247-269. 1989.

36. Knowlton, G.C., and L.P. Britt. Relation of height and age to reflex time [abstract]. *Am J Physiol* 159:576. 1949.

37. Korchemny, R. Evaluation of sprinters. *NSCA J* 7(4):38-42. 1985.

38. Kroll, W. Patellar reflex time and reflex latency under Jendrassik and crossed extensor facilitation. *Am J Phys Med* 47:292-301. 1968.

39. LaChance, P. Plyometric exercise. *Strength Cond* 17:16-23. 1995.

40. Lipp, E.J. Athletic physeal injury in children and adolescents. *Orthop Nurs* 17(2):17-22. 1998.

41. Luhtanen, P., and P. Komi. Mechanical factors influencing running speed. In: *Biomechanics VI-B*, E. Asmussen, ed. Baltimore: University Park Press. 1978. pp. 23-29.

42. Matthews, P.B.C. The knee jerk: Still an enigma? *Can J Physiol Pharmacol* 68:347-354. 1990.

43. National Strength and Conditioning Association. Position statement: Explosive/plyometric exercises. *NSCA J* 15(3):16. 1993.

44. Newton, R.U., A.J. Murphy, B.J. Humphries, G.J. Wilson, W.J. Kraemer, and K. Häkkinen. Influence of load and stretch shortening cycle on the kinematics, kinetics and muscle activation that occurs during explosive upper-body movements. *Eur J Appl Physiol* 75:333-342. 1997.

45. Pappas, A.M., R.M. Zawacki, and T.J. Sullivan. Biomechanics of baseball pitching: A preliminary report. *Am J Sports Med* 13:216-222. 1985.

46. Potach, D.H., G.M. Karst, N. Stergiou, and R.M. Latin. The effects of a plyometric training program on the stretch reflex latencies of quadriceps femoris and gastrocnemius. *Am J Sports Med*. Submitted.

47. Radcliffe, J.C., and L.R. Osternig. Effects on performance of variable eccentric loads during depth jumps. *J Sport Rehabil* 4:31-41. 1995.

48. Stone, M.H., and H.S. O'Bryant. *Weight Training: A Scientific Approach*. Edina, MN: Burgess International. 1987.

49. Svantesson, U., G. Grimby, and R. Thomeé. Potentiation of concentric plantar flexion torque following eccentric and isometric muscle actions. *Acta Physiol Scand* 152:287-293. 1994.

50. Voight, M.L., P. Draovitch, and S. Tippett. Plyometrics. In: *Eccentric Muscle Training in Sports and Orthopaedics*, M. Albert, ed. New York: Churchill Livingstone. 1995. pp. 61-88.

51. Wathen, D. Literature review: Plyometric exercise. *NSCA J* 15(3):17-19. 1993.

52. Wilk, K.E., M.L. Voight, M.A. Keirns, V. Gambetta, J.R. Andrews, and C.J. Dillman. Stretch-shortening drills for the upper extremities: Theory and clinical applications. *J Orthop Sports Phys Ther* 17:225-239. 1993.

53. Wilson, G.J., A.J. Murphy, and A. Giorgi. Weight and plyometric training: Effects on eccentric and concentric force production. *Can J Appl Physiol* 21:301-315. 1996.

54. Wilson, G.J., R.U. Newton, A.J. Murphy, and B.J. Humphries. The optimal training load for the development of dynamic athletic performance. *Med Sci Sports Exerc* 25:1279-1286. 1993.

55. Wilt, F. Plyometrics: What it is and how it works. *Athl J* 55(5):76, 89-90. 1975.

Chapter 17 Speed, Agility, and Speed-Endurance Development

1. Alexander, R.M. Mechanics of skeleton and tendons. In: *Handbook of Physiology*, section 1: *The Nervous System*, J.M. Brookhart, V.B. Mountcastle, V.B. Brooks, and S.R. Geiger, eds. Bethesda, MD: American Physiological Society. 1981. pp. 17-42.

2. Alexander, R.M. *Principles of Animal Locomotion*. Princeton, NJ: Princeton University Press. 2003.

3. Alexander, R.M. Stability and manoeuvrability of terrestrial vertebrates. *Integ Comp Biol* 42(1):158-164. 2002.

4. Arata, A.W. Kinematic and Kinetic Evaluation of High Speed Backward Running. PhD dissertation, University of Oregon, Eugene. 1999.

5. Åstrand, P.O., K. Rodahl, H.A. Dahl, and S.B. Strømme. *Textbook of Work Physiology*, 4th ed. Champaign, IL: Human Kinetics. 2003.

6. Balyi, I. Long-term athlete development: Trainability in childhood and adolescence. *Olympic Coach* 16(1):4-9. 2004.

7. Bangsbo, J. Physiology of intermittent exercise. In: *Exercise and Sport Science*, W.E. Garrett, Jr., and D.T. Kirkendall, eds. Philadelphia: Lippincott, Williams & Wilkins. 2000. pp. 53-65.

8. Banister, E.W. Modeling elite athletic performance. In: *Physiological Testing of the High-Performance Athlete*, J.D. MacDougall, H.A. Wenger, and H.J. Green, eds. Champaign, IL: Human Kinetics. 1991. pp. 403-424.

9. Bar-Or, O., ed. *The Child and Adolescent Athlete*. Oxford: Blackwell Science. 1995.

10. Biewener, A.A. *Animal Locomotion*. Oxford: Oxford University Press. 2003.

11. Billat, L.V. Interval training for performance: A scientific and empirical practice (part I: aerobic interval training). *Sports Medicine* 31(1): 13-31. 2001.

12. Billat, L.V. Interval training for performance: A scientific and empirical practice (part II: anaerobic interval training). *Sports Med* 31(2):75-90. 2001.

13. Bosco, C., and C. Vittori. Biomechanical characteristics of sprint running during maximal and supramaximal speed. *New Studies Athletics* 1(1):39-45. 1986.

14. Brooks, G.A., T.D. Fahey, and K.M. Baldwin. *Exercise Physiology: Human Bioenergetics and Its Applications*, 4th ed. New York: McGraw-Hill. 2005.

15. Burke, R.E. Motor units: Anatomy, physiology, and functional organization. In: *Handbook of Physiology*, section 1: *The Nervous System*, J.M. Brookhart, V.B. Mountcastle, V.B. Brooks, and S.R. Geiger, eds. Bethesda, MD: American Physiological Society. 1981. pp. 345-422.

16. Buttifant, D., K. Graham, and K. Cross. Agility and speed of soccer players are two different performance parameters [abstract]. *J Sports Sci* 17(10):809. 1999.

17. Cerretelli, P., and P.E. diPrampero. Gas exchange in exercise. In: *Handbook of Physiology*, section 3: *The Respiratory System*, vol. IV: *Gas Exchange*, A.P. Fishman, L.E. Farhi, S.M. Tenney, and S.R. Geiger, eds. Bethesda, MD: American Physiological Society. 1987. pp. 297-339.

18. Chang, Y.H., K. Campbell, and R. Kram. Running speed on curved paths is limited by inside leg [abstract]. *Proceedings of the 25th Annual Meeting of the American Society of Biomechanics*. 2001. pp. 435-436.

19. Charness, N., P.J. Feltovich, R.R. Hoffman, and K.A. Ericsson, eds. *The Cambridge Handbook of Expertise and Expert Performance*. New York: Cambridge University Press. 2006.

20. Delecluse, C. Influence of strength training on sprint running performance: Current findings and implications for training. *Sports Med* 24(3):147-156. 1997.

21. Devita, P., and J. Stribling. Lower extremity joint kinetics and energetics during backward running. *Med Sci Sports Exerc* 23(5):602-610. 1991.

22. Dick, F.W. *Sports Training Principles*, 5th ed. London: A&C Black. 2007.

23. Dick, F.W. *Sprints and Relays*. London: British Amateur Athletic Board. 1987.

24. Dietz, V. Neuronal control of functional movement. In: *The Encyclopedia of Sports Medicine: Strength and Power in Sport*, 2nd ed., P.V. Komi, ed. Oxford: Blackwell Science. 2003. pp. 11-26.

25. Dillman, C.J. Kinematic analyses of running. *Exercise and Sport Sciences Reviews* 3: 193-218. 1975.

26. diPrampero, P.E. Energetics of muscular exercise. *Rev Physiol Biochem Pharmacol* 89:143-222. 1981.

27. diPrampero, P.E. The energy cost of human locomotion on land and in water. *Int J Sports Med* 7(2):55-72. 1986.
28. Drabik, J. *Children and Sports Training*. Island Pond, VT: Stadion. 1996.
29. Draper, J.A., and M.G. Lancaster. The 505 test: A test for agility in the horizontal plane. *Aust J Sci Med Sport* 17(1):15-18. 1985.
30. Edman, K.A.P. Contractile performance of skeletal muscle fibres. In: *The Encyclopedia of Sports Medicine: Strength and Power in Sport,* 2nd ed., P.V. Komi, ed. Oxford: Blackwell Science. 2003. pp. 114-133.
31. Faccioni, A. Assisted and resisted methods for speed development (part I). *Mod Athlete Coach* 32(2):3-6. 1994.
32. Faccioni, A. Assisted and resisted methods for speed development (part II). *Mod Athlete Coach* 32(3):8-11. 1994.
33. Farley, C.T., and D.P. Ferris. Biomechanics of walking and running: Center of mass movements to muscle action. In: *Exercise and Sports Sciences Reviews,* vol. 26, J.O. Holloszy, ed. Baltimore: Williams & Wilkins. 1998. pp. 253-285.
34. Faulkner, J.A., D.R. Calflin, K.K. McCully. Power output of fast and slow fibers from human skeletal muscles. In *Human Muscle Power,* N.L. Jones, N. McCarney, and A.J. McComas, eds. Champaign, IL: Human Kinetics. 1986.
35. Fitts, R.H. Cellular, molecular, and metabolic basis of muscle fatigue. In: *Handbook of Physiology,* section 12: *Exercise: Regulation and Integration of Multiple Systems,* L.B. Rowell and J.T. Shepherd, eds. New York: American Physiological Society/Oxford University Press. 1996. pp. 1151-1183.
36. Flynn, T.W., and R.W. Soutas-Little. Mechanical power and muscle action during forward and backward running. *J Orthop Sports Phys Ther* 17(2):108-112. 1993.
37. Ford, K.R., G.D. Myer, H.E. Toms, and T.E. Hewett. Gender differences in the kinematics of unanticipated cutting in young athletes. *Med Sci Sports Exerc* 37(1):124-129. 2005.
38. Fukunaga, T., Y. Kawakami, K. Kubo, and H. Kanehisa. Muscle and tendon interaction during human movements. *Exerc Sport Sci Rev* 30(3):106-110. 2002.
39. Gambetta, V., G. Winckler, J. Rogers, J. Orognen, L. Seagrave, and S. Jolly. Sprints and relays. In: *TAC Track and Field Coaching Manual,* 2nd ed., V. Gambetta, ed., and TAC Development Committees. Champaign, IL: Leisure Press. 1989. pp. 55-70.
40. Gandevia, S.C. Spinal and supraspinal factors in human muscle fatigue. *Physiol Rev* 81(4):1725-1789. 2001.
41. Gastin, P.B. Energy system interaction and relative contribution during maximal exercise. *Sports Med* 31(10):725-741. 2001.
42. Glaister, M. Multiple sprint work: Physiological responses, mechanisms of fatigue and the influence of aerobic fitness. *Sports Med* 35(9):757-777. 2005.
43. Greene, P.R. Running on flat turns: Experiments, theory, and applications. *J Biomech Eng* 107(2):96-103. 1985.
44. Greene, P.R., and T.A. McMahon. Running in circles. *Physiologist* 22(6):S35-S36. 1979.
45. Greenhaff, P.L., and J.A. Timmons. Interaction between aerobic and anaerobic metabolism during intense muscle contraction. *Exerc Sport Sci Rev* 26(1):1-30. 1998.
46. Häkkinen, K. and P.V. Komi. The effect of explosive type strength training on electromyographic and force production characteristic of leg extensor muscles during concentric and various stretch-shortening cycle exercises. *Scand J Sports Sci* 7(2): 65-76. 1985.
47. Harland, M.J., and J.R. Steele. Biomechanics of the sprint start. *Sports Med* 23(1):11-20. 1997.
48. Harre, D. Endurance—classification and development. *Mod Athlete Coach* 16(4):19-21. 1978.
49. Harre, D., ed. *Principles of Sports Training*. Berlin: Sportverlag. 1982.
50. Hartmann, J., and H. Tünnemann. *Fitness and Strength Training*. Berlin: Sportverlag. 1989.
51. Hawley, J.A., ed. *Running*. Oxford: Blackwell Science. 2000.
52. Henneman, E. Functional organization of motoneuron pool and its inputs. In: *Handbook of Physiology,* section 1: *The Nervous System,* J.M. Brookhart, V.B. Mountcastle, V.B. Brooks, and S.R. Geiger, eds. Bethesda, MD: American Physiological Society. 1981. pp. 423-507.
53. Hochmuth, G. *Biomechanics of Athletic Movement,* 4th ed. Berlin: Sportverlag. 1984.
54. Hodgson, M., D. Docherty, and D. Robbins. Post-activation potentiation: Underlying physiology and implications for motor performance. *Sports Med* 35(7):585-595. 2005.
55. Houk, J.C., and W.Z. Rymer. Neural control of muscle length and tension. In: *Handbook of Physiology,* section 1: *The Nervous System,* J.M. Brookhart, V.B. Mountcastle, V.B. Brooks, and S.R. Geiger, eds. Bethesda, MD: American Physiological Society. 1981. pp. 257-323.
56. James, C.R., P.S. Sizer, D.W. Starch, T.E. Lockhart, and J. Slauterbeck. Gender differences among sagittal plane knee kinematic and ground reaction force characteristics during a rapid sprint and cut maneuver. *Res Q Exerc Sport* 75(1):31-38. 2004.
57. Jarver, J., ed. *Sprints and Relays,* 5th ed. Los Altos, CA: Tafnews Press. 2000.
58. Jindrich, D.L., T.F. Besier, and D.G. Lloyd. A hypothesis for the function of braking forces during running turns. *J Biomech* 39(9):1611-1620. 2006.
59. Jung, A.P. The impact of resistance training on distance running performance. *Sports Med* 33(7):539-552. 2003.
60. Kawamori, N., and G.G. Haff. The optimal training load for the development of muscular power. *J Strength Cond Res* 18(3):675-684. 2004.
61. Komi, P.V. Neuromuscular performance: Factors influencing force and speed production. *Scand J Sports Sci* 1(1):2-15. 1979.
62. Komi, P.V. Stretch-shortening cycle. In: *The Encyclopedia of Sports Medicine: Strength and Power in Sport,* 2nd ed., P.V. Komi, ed. Oxford: Blackwell Science. 2003. pp. 184-202.
63. Komi, P.V., and C. Nicol. Stretch-shortening cycle of muscle function. In: *Biomechanics in Sport,* V.M. Zatsiorsky, ed. Oxford: Blackwell Science. 2000. pp. 87-102.
64. Komi, P.V., H. Rusko, J. Vos, and V. Vihko. Anaerobic performance capacity in athletes. *Acta Physiol Scand* 100(1):107-114. 1977.
65. Kozlov, I., and V. Muravyev. Muscles and the sprint. *Sov Sports Rev* 27(6):192-195. 1992.
66. Lavrienko, A., J. Kravstev, and Z. Petrova. New approaches to sprint training. *Mod Athlete Coach* 28(3):3-5. 1990.
67. Leveritt, M., P.J. Abernethy, B.K. Barry, and P.A. Logan. Concurrent strength and endurance training. *Sports Med* 28(6):413-427. 1999.
68. Little, T., and A.G. Williams. Specificity of acceleration, maximum speed, and agility in professional soccer players. *J Strength Cond Res* 19(1):76-78. 2005.
69. Mach, G. The individual sprint events. In: *Athletes in Action,* H. Payne, ed., and International Amateur Athletic Federation. London: Pelham. 1985. pp. 12-34.
70. Magill, R.A. *Motor Learning and Control,* 8th ed. New York: McGraw-Hill. 2006.
71. Mahler, M. Kinetics and control of oxygen consumption in skeletal muscle. In: *Symposia of the Giovanni Lorenzini Foundation,* vol. 9: *Exercise Bioenergetics and Gas Exchange,* P. Cerretelli and B.J. Whipp, eds. Amsterdam: Elsevier/North-Holland Biomedical Press. 1980. pp. 53-66.
72. Malina, R.M., C. Bouchard, and O. Bar-Or. *Growth, Maturation, and Physical Activity,* 2nd ed. Champaign, IL: Human Kinetics. 2004.
73. Marsh, R.L. How muscles deal with real-world loads: The influence of length trajectory on muscle performance. *J Exp Biol* 202(23):3377-3385. 1999.
74. Mayhew, J.L., F.C. Piper, T.M. Schwegler, and T.E. Ball. Contributions of speed, agility and body composition to anaerobic power measurement in college football players. *J Appl Sport Sci Res* 3(4):101-106. 1989.
75. McLean, S.G., K.B. Walker, and A.J. van den Bogert. Effect of gender on lower extremity kinematics during rapid direction changes: An integrated analysis of three sports movements. *J Sci Med Sports* 8(4):411-422. 2005.

76. McMahon, S., and D. Jenkins. Factors affecting the rate of phosphocreatine resynthesis following intense exercise. *Sports Med* 32(12):761-784. 2002.
77. McNeal, J.R., and W.A. Sands. Stretching for performance enhancement. *Curr Sports Med Rep* 5(3):141-146. 2005.
78. Merlau, S. Recovery time optimization to facilitate motor learning during sprint intervals. *Strength Cond J* 27(2):68-74. 2005.
79. Mero, A., P.V. Komi, and R.J. Gregor. Biomechanics of sprint running. *Sports Med* 13(6):376-392. 1992.
80. Meyer, R.A., and J.M. Foley. Cellular processes integrating the metabolic response to exercise. In: *Handbook of Physiology,* section 12: *Exercise: Regulation and Integration of Multiple Systems,* L.B. Rowell and J.T. Shepherd, eds. New York: American Physiological Society/Oxford University Press. 1996. pp. 841-869.
81. Moravec, P., J. Ruzicka, P. Susanka, E. Dostal, M. Kodejs, and M. Nosek. The 1987 International Athletic Foundation/IAAF scientific project report: Time analysis of the 100 metres events at the II World Championships in athletics. *New Studies Athletics* 3(3):61-96. 1988.
82. Newton, R.U., and W.J. Kraemer. Developing explosive muscular power: implications for a mixed methods training strategy. *Strength Cond* 16(5):20-31. 1994.
83. Ozolin, E. Contemporary sprint technique (part 1). *Sov Sports Rev* 21(3):109-114. 1986.
84. Ozolin, E. Contemporary sprint technique (part 2). *Sov Sports Rev* 21(4):190-195. 1986.
85. Partridge, L.D., and L.A. Benton. Muscle, the motor. In: *Handbook of Physiology,* section 1: *The Nervous System,* J.M. Brookhart, V.B. Mountcastle, V.B. Brooks, and S.R. Geiger, eds. Bethesda, MD: American Physiological Society. 1981. pp. 43-106.
86. Plisk, S.S. The angle on agility. *Training Cond* 10(6):37-43. 2000.
87. Plisk, S.S., and V. Gambetta. Tactical metabolic training. *Strength Cond* 19(2):44-53. 1997.
88. Plisk, S.S., and M.H. Stone. Periodization strategies. *Strength Cond J* 25(6):19-37. 2003.
89. Pollard, C.D., I.M. Davis, and J. Hamill. Influence of gender on hip and knee mechanics during a randomly cued cutting maneuver. *Clin Biomech* 19(10):1022-2031. 2004.
90. Pollard, C.D., R.C. Heiderscheit, R.E. van Emmerik, and J. Hamill. Gender differences in lower extremity coupling variability during an unanticipated cutting maneuver. *J Appl Biomech* 21(2):143-152. 2005.
91. Prilutsky, B.I. Eccentric muscle action in sport and exercise. In: *Biomechanics in Sport,* V.M. Zatsiorsky, ed. Oxford: Blackwell Science. 2000. pp. 56-86.
92. Putnam, C.A., and J.W. Kozey. Substantive issues in running. In: *Biomechanics of Sport,* C.L. Vaughan, ed. Boca Raton, FL: CRC Press. 1989. pp. 1-33.
93. Radcliffe, J. Getting into position. *Training Cond* 9(3):38-47. 1999.
94. Reilly, T., and J. Bangsbo. Anaerobic and aerobic training. In: *Training in Sport,* B. Elliott, ed. Chichester: Wiley. 1998. pp. 351-409.
95. Rhea, M.R., R.L. Hunter, and T.J. Hunter. Competition modeling of American football: Observational data and implications for high school, collegiate, and professional player conditioning. *J Strength Cond Res* 20(1):58-61. 2006.
96. Robbins, D. Postactivation potentiation and its practical applicability: A brief review. *J Strength Cond Res* 19(2):453-458. 2005.
97. Romanova, N. The sprint: Nontraditional means of training. *Sov Sports Rev* 25(2):99-102. 1990.
98. Ross, A., and M. Leveritt. Long-term metabolic and skeletal muscle adaptations to short-sprint training: Implications for sprint training and tapering. *Sports Med* 31(15):1063-1082. 2001.
99. Ross, A., M. Leveritt, and S. Riek. Neural influences on sprint running: Training adaptations and acute responses. *Sports Med* 31(6):409-425. 2001.
100. Sale, D.G. Postactivation potentiation: Role in human performance. *Exerc Sport Sci Rev* 30(3):138-143. 2002.
101. Saunders, P.U., D.B. Pyne, R.D. Telford, and J.A. Hawley. Factors affecting running economy in trained distance runners. *Sports Med* 34(7):465-485. 2004.
102. Schmidt, R.A., and T.D. Lee. *Motor Control and Learning,* 4th ed. Champaign, IL: Human Kinetics. 2005.
103. Schmidt, R.A., and C.A. Wrisberg. *Motor Learning and Performance,* 4th ed. Champaign, IL: Human Kinetics. 2007.
104. Schmidtbleicher, D. Strength training (part 1): Classification of methods. *Sci Per Res Tech Sport: Phys Training/Strength* W-4:1-12. August 1985.
105. Schmidtbleicher, D. Strength training (part 2): Structural analysis of motor strength qualities and its application to training. *Sci Per Res Tech Sport: Phys Training/Strength* W-4:1-10. September 1985.
106. Schmolinsky, G., ed. *Track and Field: The East German Textbook of Athletics.* Toronto: Sport Books. 1993.
107. Seagrave, L. Introduction to sprinting. *New Studies Athletics* 11(2/3):93-113. 1996.
108. Shrier, I. Does stretching improve performance? *Clin J Sports Med* 14(5):267-273. 2004.
109. Siff, M.C. *Supertraining,* 6th ed. Denver: Supertraining Institute. 2003.
110. Sigward, S.M, and C.M. Powers. The influence of gender on knee kinematics, kinetics and muscle activation patterns during side-step cutting. *Clin Biomech* 21(1):41-48. 2006.
111. Spencer, M., D. Bishop, B. Dawson, and C. Goodman. Physiological and metabolic responses of repeated-sprint activities: Specific to field-based team sports. *Sports Med* 35(12):1025-1044. 2005.
112. Spriet, L.L. Anaerobic metabolism during high-intensity exercise. In: *Exercise Metabolism,* M. Hargreaves, ed. Champaign, IL: Human Kinetics. 1995. pp. 1-39.
113. Starkes, J.L., and K.A. Ericsson, eds. *Expert Performance in Sports.* Champaign, IL: Human Kinetics. 2003.
114. Stein, N. Speed training in sport. In: *Training in Sport,* B. Elliott, ed. Chichester: Wiley. 1998. pp. 287-349.
115. Steinhofer, D. Terminology and differentiation of training methods. *Mod Athlete Coach* 35(1):15-21. 1997.
116. Stone, M.H., M. Stone, and W.A. Sands. *Principles and Practice of Resistance Training.* Champaign, IL: Human Kinetics. 2007.
117. Taylor, J. Basketball: Applying time motion data to conditioning. *Strength Cond J* 25(2):57-64. 2003.
118. Taylor, J. A tactical metabolic training model for collegiate basketball. *Strength Cond J* 26(5):22-29. 2004.
119. Taylor, J.L., G. Todd, and S.C. Gandevia. Evidence for a supraspinal contribution to human muscle fatigue. *Clin Exp Pharmacol Physiol* 33(4):400-405. 2006.
120. Tesch, P.A., J.E. Wright, J.A. Vogel, W.L. Daniels, D.S. Sharp, and B. Sjodin. The influence of muscle metabolic characteristics on physical performance. *Eur J Appl Physiol* 54(3):237-243. 1985.
121. Thacker, S.B., J. Gilchrist, D.F. Stroup, and C.D. Kimsey, Jr. The impact of stretching on sports injury risk: A systematic review of the literature. *Med Sci Sports Exerc* 36(3):371-378. 2004.
122. Thorstensson, A. Speed and acceleration. In: *The Olympic Book of Sports Medicine,* A. Dirix, H.G. Knuttgen, and K. Tittel, eds. Oxford: Blackwell Scientific. 1991. pp. 218-229.
123. Threlkeld, A.J., T.S. Horn, G.M. Wojtowicz, J.G. Rooney, and R. Shapiro. Kinematics, ground reaction force, and muscle balance produced by backward running. *J Orthop Sports Phys Ther* 11(2):56-63. 1989.
124. Tidow, G. Aspects of strength training in athletics. *New Studies Athletics* 5(1):93-110. 1990.
125. Tittel, K. Coordination and balance. In: *The Olympic Book of Sports Medicine,* A. Dirix, H.G. Knuttgen, and K. Tittel, eds. Oxford: Blackwell Scientific. 1991. pp. 194-211.
126. Tomlin, D.L., and H.A. Wenger. The relationship between aerobic fitness and recovery from high intensity intermittent exercise. *Sports Med* 31(1):1-11. 2001.
127. Usherwood, J.R., and A.M. Wilson. Accounting for elite indoor 200m sprint results. *Biol Lett* 2(1):47-50. 2006.
128. Verkhoshansky, Y.V. Principles for a rational organization of the training process aimed at speed development. *New Studies Athletics* 11(2-3):155-160. 1996.
129. Verkhoshansky, Y.V. Quickness and velocity in sports movements. *New Studies Athletics* 11(2-3):29-37. 1996.

130. Verkhoshansky, Y.V. Speed training for high level athletes. *New Studies Athletics* 11(2-3):39-49. 1996.
131. Verkhoshansky, Y.V., and V.V. Lazarev. Principles of planning speed and strength/speed endurance training in sports. *NSCA J* 11(2):58-61. 1989.
132. Viru, A. *Adaptation in Sports Training*. Boca Raton, FL: CRC Press. 1995.
133. Viru, A., P. Korge, and J. Parnat. Classification of training methods. *Mod Athlete Coach* 14(5/6):31-33. 1976.
134. Whipp, B.J., and M. Mahler. Dynamics of pulmonary gas exchange during exercise. In: *Pulmonary Gas Exchange,* vol. II: *Organism and Environment,* J.B. West, ed. New York: Academic Press. 1980. pp. 33-96.
135. Wiemann, K., and G. Tidow. Relative activity of hip and knee extensors in sprinting — implications for training. *New Studies Athletics* 10(1):29-49. 1995.
136. Wilt, F. A logical basis for the training of runners. In: *How They Train,* vol 1: *Middle Distances,* 2nd ed., F. Wilt, ed. Los Altos, CA: Track & Field News. 1973. pp. 9-28.
137. Wilt, F. Training for competitive running. In: *Exercise Physiology,* H.B. Falls, ed. New York: Academic Press. 1968. pp. 395-414.
138. Winters, J.M., and S.L.Y. Woo, eds. *Multiple Muscle Systems*. New York: Springer-Verlag. 1990.
139. Wood, G.A. Biomechanical limitations to sprint running. In: *Medicine and Sport Science,* vol. 25: *Current Research in Sports Biomechanics,* M. Hebbelink, R.J. Shephard, B. Van Gheluwe, and J. Atha, eds. Basel: Karger. 1987. pp. 58-71.
140. Young, W., M. Hawken, and L. McDonald. Relationship between speed, agility and strength qualities in Australian Rules football. *Strength Cond Coach* 4(4):3-6. 1996.
141. Young, W.B., M.H. McDowell, and B.J. Scarlett. Specificity of sprint and agility training methods. *J Strength Cond Res* 15(3):315-319. 2001.
142. Zatsiorsky, V.M., and W.J. Kraemer. *Science and Practice of Strength Training,* 2nd ed. Champaign, IL: Human Kinetics. 2006.

Section 4, Part II

1. Holloszy, J.O., and F.W. Booth. Biochemical adaptations to endurance exercise in muscle. *Annu Rev Physiol* 38:273-291. 1976.
2. Holloszy, J.O., and E.F. Coyle. Adaptations of skeletal muscle to endurance exercise and their metabolic consequences. *J Appl Physiol* 56:831-838. 1984.
3. Powers, S.K., and E.T. Howley. *Exercise Physiology: Theory and Application to Fitness and Performance*. Dubuque, IA: Brown & Benchmark. 1997.
4. Saltin, B., J. Henriksson, E. Nygaard, and P. Andersen. Fiber types and metabolic potentials of skeletal muscles in sedentary man and endurance runners. In: *Marathon: Physiological, Medical, Epidemiological, and Psychological Studies,* P. Milvy, ed. New York: New York Academy of Sciences. 1977. pp. 3-29.

Chapter 18 Aerobic Endurance Exercise Training

1. American College of Sports Medicine. 1998. The recommended quantity and quality of exercise for developing and maintaining cardiorespiratory and muscular fitness, and flexibility in healthy adults. *Med Sci Sports Exerc* 30(6):975-991.
2. Åstrand, P.O., K. Rodahl, H.A. Dahl, and S.B. Strømme. *Textbook of Work Physiology,* 4th ed. Champaign, IL: Human Kinetics. 2003.
3. Banister, E.W. Modeling elite athletic performance. In: *Physiological Testing of the High-Performance Athlete,* J.D. MacDougall, H.A. Wenger, and H.J. Green, eds. Champaign, IL: Human Kinetics. 1991. pp. 403-424.
4. Beneke, R. Anaerobic threshold, individual anaerobic threshold, and maximal lactate steady state in rowing. *Med Sci Sports Exerc* 27:863-867. 1995.
5. Borg, G. *Borg's Perceived Exertion and Pain Scales*. Champaign, IL: Human Kinetics. 1998.
6. Borg, G.A.V. Perceived exertion as an indicator of somatic stress. *Scand J Rehabil Med* 2:92-98. 1970.
7. Borg, G.A.V. Psychophysical bases of perceived exertion. *Med Sci Sports Exerc* 14:377-381. 1982.
8. Boulay, M.R., J.A. Simoneau, G. Lortie, and C. Bouchard. Monitoring high-intensity endurance exercise with heart rate and thresholds. *Med Sci Sports Exerc* 29:125-132. 1997.
9. Boutcher, S.H., R.L. Seip, R.K. Hetzler, E.F. Pierce, D. Snead, and A. Weltman. The effects of specificity of training on ratings of perceived exertion at the lactate threshold. *Eur J Appl Physiol* 59:365-369. 1989.
10. Brooks, G.A., and J. Mercier. Balance of carbohydrate and lipid utilization during exercise: The "crossover" concept. *J Appl Physiol* 76:2253-2261. 1994.
11. Burke, E.R. Physiological similar effects of similar training programs in males and females. *Res Q* 48:510-517. 1977.
12. Burke, E.R., F. Cerny, D.L. Costill, and W.J. Fink. Characteristics of skeletal muscle in competitive cyclists. *Med Sci Sports* 9:109-112. 1977.
13. Cavanagh, P.R., M.L. Pollock, and J. Landa. Biomechanical comparison of elite and good distance runners. In: *Marathon: Physiological, Medical, Epidemiological, and Psychological Studies,* P. Milvy, ed. New York: New York Academy of Sciences. 1977. pp. 328-345.
14. Ceci, R., and P. Hassman. Self-monitored exercise at three different RPE intensities in treadmill vs. field running. *Med Sci Sports Exerc* 23:732-738. 1991.
15. Conley, D.L., and G.S. Krahenbuhl. Running economy and distance running performance of highly trained athletes. *Med Sci Sports Exerc* 12:357-360. 1980.
16. Costill, D.L. *Inside Running: Basics of Sports Physiology*. Indianapolis: Benchmark Press. 1986.
17. Costill, D.L., W.J. Fink, and M.L. Pollock. Muscle fiber composition and enzyme activities of elite distance runners. *Med Sci Sports* 8:96-102. 1976.
18. Costill, D.L., D.S. King, R. Thomas, and M. Hargreaves. Effects of reduced training on muscular power in swimmers. *Phys Sportsmed* 13:94-101. 1985.
19. Costill, D.L., R. Thomas, R.A. Robergs, D.D. Pascoe, C.P. Lambert, S.I. Barr, and W.J. Fink. Adaptations to swimming training: Influence of training volume. *Med Sci Sports Exerc* 23:371-377. 1991.
20. Costill, D.L., H. Thomason, and E. Roberts. Fractional utilization of the aerobic capacity during distance running. *Med Sci Sports* 5:248-252. 1973.
21. Coyle, E.F., A.R. Coggan, M.K. Hemmert, and J.L. Ivy. Muscle glycogen utilization during prolonged strenuous exercise when fed carbohydrates. *J Appl Physiol* 61:165-172. 1986.
22. Coyle, E.F., A.R. Coggan, M.K. Hopper, and T.J. Walters. Determinants of endurance in well-trained cyclists. *J Appl Physiol* 64:2622-2630. 1988.
23. Coyle, E.F., M.E. Feltner, S.A. Kautz, M.T. Hamilton, S.J. Montain, A.M. Baylor, L.D. Abraham, and G.W. Petrek. Physiological and biomechanical factors associated with endurance cycling performance. *Med Sci Sports Exerc* 23:93-107. 1991.
24. Coyle, E.F., J.M. Hagberg, B.F. Hurley, W.H. Martin, A.A. Ehsani, and J.O. Holloszy. Carbohydrate feedings during prolonged strenuous exercise can delay fatigue. *J Appl Physiol* 55:230-235. 1983.
25. Daniels, J. Training distance runners—primer. *Gatorade Sports Sci Exch* 1:1-5. 1989.
26. Davidson, C.J., E.R. Pardyjak, and J.C. Martin. Training with power measurement: A new era in cycling training. *Strength Cond J* 25(5):28-29. 2003.
27. Dishman, R.K., R.W. Patton, J. Smith, R. Weinberg, and A.W. Jackson. Using perceived exertion to prescribe and monitor exercise training heart rate. *Int J Sports Med* 8:208-213. 1987.
28. Drinkwater, B.L., and S.M. Horvath. Detraining effects on young women. *Med Sci Sports* 4:91-95. 1972.
29. Dudley, G.A., W.M. Abraham, and R.L. Terjung. Influence of exercise intensity and duration on biochemical adaptations in skeletal muscle. *J Appl Physiol* 53:844-850. 1982.

30. Ehsani, A.A., J.M. Hagberg, and R.C. Hickson. Rapid changes in left ventricular dimensions and mass in response to physical conditioning and deconditioning. *Am J Cardiol* 42:52-56. 1978.
31. Farrell, P.A., J.H. Wilmore, E.F. Coyle, J.E. Billing, and D.L. Costill. Plasma lactate accumulation and distance running performance. *Med Sci Sports* 11:338-344. 1979.
32. Foster, C., J.T. Daniels, and R.A. Yarbrough. Physiological and training correlates of marathon running performance. *Aust J Sports Med* 9:58-61. 1977.
33. Foster, C., L.L. Hector, R. Welsh, M. Schrager, M.A. Green, and A.C. Snyder. Effects of specific versus cross-training on running performance. *Eur J Appl Physiol* 70:367-372. 1995.
34. Foxdal, P., B. Sjodin, A. Sjodin, and B. Ostman. The validity and accuracy of blood lactate measurements for the prediction of maximal endurance capacity. *Int J Sports Med* 15(2):89-95. 1994.
35. Gardner, A.S., D.T. Stephens, E. Martin, H. Lawton, H. Lee, and D. Jenkins. Accuracy of SRM and Power Tap power monitoring systems for bicycling. *Med Sci Sports Exerc* 36(7):1252-1258. 2004.
36. Gergley, T.J., W.D. McArdle, P. DeJesus, M.M. Toner, S. Jacobowitz, and R.J. Spina. Specificity of arm training on aerobic power during swimming and running. *Med Sci Sports Exerc* 16:349-354. 1984.
37. Gettman, L.R., M.L. Pollock, J.L. Durstine, A. Ward, J. Ayres, and A.C. Linnerud. Physiological responses of men to 1, 3, and 5 d, and 5 day per week training programs. *Res Q* 47:638-646. 1976.
38. Glass, S.C., R.G. Knowlton, and M.D. Becque. Accuracy of RPE from graded exercise to established training intensity. *Med Sci Sports Exerc* 24:1303-1307. 1992.
39. Gollnick, P.D. Metabolism of substrates: Energy substrate metabolism during exercise and as modified by training. *Fed Proc* 44:353-356. 1985.
40. Hagerman, P.S. Aerobic endurance training design. In: *NSCA's Essentials of Personal Training,* R.W. Earle and T.R. Baechle, eds. Champaign, IL: Human Kinetics. 2004.
41. Hermansen, L., E. Hultman, and B. Saltin. Muscle glycogen during prolonged severe exercise. *Acta Physiol Scand* 71:129-139. 1967.
42. Hickson, R.C., B.A. Dvorak, E.M. Gorostiaga, T.T. Kurowski, and C. Foster. Potential for strength and endurance training to amplify endurance performance. *J Appl Physiol* 65:2285-2290. 1988.
43. Hickson, R.C., and M.A. Rosenkoetter. Reduced training frequencies and maintenance of increased aerobic power. *Med Sci Sports Exerc* 13:13-16. 1981.
44. Holloszy, J.O., and F.W. Booth. Biochemical adaptations to endurance exercise in muscle. *Annu Rev Physiol* 38:273-291. 1976.
45. Holloszy, J.O., and E.F. Coyle. Adaptations of skeletal muscle to endurance exercise and their metabolic consequences. *J Appl Physiol* 56:831-838. 1984.
46. Hootman, J.M., C.A. Macera, B.E. Ainsworth, M. Martin, C.L. Addy, and S.N. Blair. Association among physical activity level, cardiorespiratory fitness, and risk of musculoskeletal injury. *Am J Epidemiol* 154(3):251-258. 2001.
47. Hoppeler, H. Exercise-induced ultrastructure changes in skeletal muscle. *Int J Sports Med* 7:187-204. 1986.
48. Klausen, K., L.B. Andersen, and I. Pelle. Adaptive changes in work capacity, skeletal muscle capillarization and enzyme levels during training and detraining. *Acta Physiol Scand* 113:9-16. 1981.
49. Kohrt, W.M., D.W. Morgan, B. Bates, and J.S. Skinner. Physiological responses of triathletes to maximal swimming, cycling, and running. *Med Sci Sports Exerc* 19:51-55. 1987.
50. Lamb, D.R. Basic principles for improving sport performance. *Sports Sci Exch* 8:1-5. 1995.
51. Magel, J.R., G.F. Foglia, W.D. McArdle, B. Gutin, and G.S. Pechar. Specificity of swim training on maximal oxygen uptake. *J Appl Physiol* 38:151-155. 1975.
52. Martin, J.C., D.L. Milliken, J.E. Cobb, K.L. McFadden, and A.R. Coggan. Validation of a mathematical model for road cycling power. *J Appl Biomech* 14(3):276-291. 1998.
53. Matoba, H., and P.D. Gollnick. Response of skeletal muscle to training. *Sports Med* 1:240-251. 1984.
54. Maughan, R.J. Physiology and nutrition for middle distance and long distance running. In: *Perspectives in Exercise Science and Sports Medicine: Physiology and Nutrition for Competitive Sport,* D.L. Lamb, H.G. Knuttgen, and R. Murray, eds. Carmel, IN: Cooper Publishing Group. 1994. pp. 329-371.
55. Maughan, R.J., and J.B. Leiper. Aerobic capacity and fractional utilization of aerobic capacity on elite and non-elite male and female marathon runners. *Eur J Appl Physiol* 52:80-87. 1983.
56. McCole, S.D., K. Claney, J.C. Conte, R. Anderson, and J.M. Hagberg. Energy expenditure during bicycling. *J Appl Physiol* 68:748-753. 1990.
57. O'Toole, M.L., P.S. Douglas, and W.D.B. Hiller. Applied physiology of a triathlon. *Sports Med* 8:201-225. 1989.
58. O'Toole, M.L., P.S. Douglas, and W.D.B. Hiller. Use of heart rate monitors by endurance athletes: Lessons from triathletes. *J Sports Med Phys Fitness* 38:181-187. 1998.
59. Perrault, H. Cardiorespiratory function. In: *Exercise and the Female: A Life Span Approach,* O. Bar-Or, D.L. Lamb, and P.M. Clarkson, eds. Carmel, IN: Cooper Publishing Group. 1996. pp. 147-214.
60. Pette, D. Historical perspectives: Plasticity of mammalian skeletal muscle. *J Appl Physiol* 90(3):1119-1124. 2001.
61. Pollock, M.L., R. Gettman, C.A. Milesis, M.D. Bah, J.L. Durstine, and R.B. Johnson. Effects of frequency and duration of training on attrition and incidence of injury. *Med Sci Sports* 9:31-36. 1977.
62. Potteiger, J.A., and B.W. Evans. Using heart rate and ratings of perceived exertion to monitor intensity in runners. *J Sports Med Phys Fitness* 35:181-186. 1995.
63. Potteiger, J.A., and S.F. Weber. Ratings of perceived exertion and heart rate as indicators of exercise intensity in different environmental temperatures. *Med Sci Sports Exerc* 26:791-796. 1994.
64. Powers, S.K., and E.T. Howley. *Exercise Physiology: Theory and Application to Fitness and Performance,* 6th ed. New York: McGraw-Hill. 2006.
65. Saltin, B., J. Henriksson, E. Nygaard, and P. Andersen. Fiber types and metabolic potentials of skeletal muscles in sedentary man and endurance runners. In: *Marathon: Physiological, Medical, Epidemiological, and Psychological Studies,* P. Milvy, ed. New York: New York Academy of Sciences. 1977. pp. 3-29.
66. Sharkey, B.J. Intensity and duration of training and the development of cardiorespiratory fitness. *Med Sci Sports* 2:197-202. 1970.
67. Short, K.R., J.L. Vittone, M.L. Bigelow, D.N. Proctor, J.M. Coenen-Schimke, P. Rys, and K. Sreekumaran Nair. Changes in myosin heavy chain mRNA and protein expression in human skeletal muscle with age and endurance exercise training. *J Appl Physiol* 99(1):95-102. 2005.
68. Svedenhag, J. Endurance conditioning. In: *Endurance in Sport,* R.J. Shephard and P.O. Åstrand, eds. London: Blackwell Scientific. 1992. pp. 290-296.
69. Swain, D.P., J.R. Coast, P.S. Clifford, M.C. Milliken, and J. Stray-Gundersen. Influence of body size on oxygen consumption during cycling. *J Appl Physiol* 62:668-672. 1987.
70. Troup, J.P., D. Strass, and T.A. Trappe. Physiology and nutrition for competitive swimming. In: *Perspectives in Exercise Science and Sports Medicine: Physiology and Nutrition for Competitive Sport,* D.L. Lamb, H.G. Knuttgen, and R. Murray, eds. Carmel, IN: Cooper Publishing Group. 1994. pp. 99-129.
71. Van Handel, P.J., A. Katz, J.P. Troup, and P.W. Bradley. Aerobic economy and competitive swim performance of U.S. elite swimmers. In: *Swimming Science V,* B.E. Ungerechts, K. Wilke, and K. Reischle, eds. Champaign, IL: Human Kinetics. 1988. pp. 219-227.
72. Wells, C.L., and R.R. Pate. Training for performance of prolonged exercise. In: *Perspectives in Exercise Science and Sports Medicine,* D.L. Lamb and R. Murray, eds. Indianapolis: Benchmark Press. 1995. pp. 357-388.
73. Wenger, H.A., and G.J. Bell. The interactions of intensity, frequency, and duration of exercise training in altering cardiorespiratory fitness. *Sports Med* 3:346-356. 1986.
74. Wilber, R.L., R.J. Moffatt, B.E. Scott, D.T. Lee, and N.A. Cucuzzo. Influence of water run training on the maintenance of aerobic performance. *Med Sci Sports Exerc* 28:1056-1062. 1996.
75. Wilmore, J.H., and D.L. Costill. *Physiology of Sport and Exercise,* 3rd ed. Champaign, IL: Human Kinetics. 2005.

76. Zupan, M.F., and P.S. Petosa. Aerobic and resistance cross-training for peak triathlon performance. *Strength Cond* 17:7-12. 1995.

Chapter 19 Periodization

1. Baechle, T.R., and B.R. Groves. *Weight Training: Steps to Success,* 2nd ed. Champaign, IL: Human Kinetics. 1998.
2. Baker, D., G. Wilson, and R. Carlyon. Periodization: The effect on strength of manipulating volume and intensity. *J Strength Cond Res* 8:235-242. 1994.
3. Bompa, T.A. *Theory and Methodology of Training.* Dubuque, IA: Kendall/Hunt. 1983.
4. Chargina, A., M. Stone, J. Piedmonte, H. O'Bryant, W.J. Kraemer, V. Gambetta, H. Newton, G. Palmeri, and D. Pfoff. Periodization roundtable. *NSCA J* 8(5):12-23. 1986.
5. Chargina, A., M. Stone, J. Piedmonte, H. O'Bryant, W.J. Kraemer, V. Gambetta, H. Newton, G. Palmeri, and D. Pfoff. Periodization roundtable. *NSCA J* 8(6):17-25. 1987.
6. Chargina, A., M. Stone, J. Piedmonte, H. O'Bryant, W.J. Kraemer, V. Gambetta, H. Newton, G. Palmeri, and D. Pfoff. Periodization roundtable. *NSCA J* 9(1):16-27. 1987.
7. Fleck, S.J. Periodized strength training: A critical review. *J Strength Cond Res* 13(1):82-89. 1999.
8. Fleck, S.J., and W.J. Kraemer. *Designing Resistance Training Programs,* 3rd ed. Champaign, IL: Human Kinetics. 2004.
9. Fleck, S.J., and W.J. Kraemer. Resistance training: Exercise prescription. *Phys Sportsmed* 16:69-81. 1988.
10. Garhammer, J. Periodization of strength training for athletes. *Track Tech* 73:2398-2399. 1979.
11. Häkkinen, K., A. Pakarinen, P.V. Komi, T. Ryushi, and H. Kauhanen. Neuromuscular adaptations and hormone balance in strength athletes, physically active males and females during intensity strength training. In: *Proceedings of the XII International Congress of Biomechanics,* R.J. Gregor, R.F. Zernicke, and W. Whiting, eds. Champaign, IL: Human Kinetics. 1989. pp. 889-894.
12. Komi, P.V. Training of muscle strength and power: Interaction of neuromotoric, hypertrophic, and mechanical factors. *Int J Sports Med* 7(suppl.):101-105. 1986.
13. Kraemer, W.J. A series of studies: The physiological basis for strength training in American football: Fact over philosophy. *J Strength Cond Res* 11(3):131-142. 1997.
14. Kraemer, W.J., and L.P. Koziris. Muscle strength training: Techniques and considerations. *Phys Ther Pract* 2:54-68. 1992.
15. Matveyev, L.P. *Periodization of Sports Training.* Moscow: Fiscultura i Sport. 1966.
16. Pauletto, B. Periodization-peaking. *NSCA J* 8(4):30-31. 1986.
17. Plisk, S.S., and M.H. Stone. Periodization strategies. *NSCA J* 25(6):19-37. 2003
18. Poliquin, C. Five steps to increasing the effectiveness of your strength training program. *NSCA J* 10(3):34-39. 1988.
19. Selye, H. *The Stress of Life.* New York: McGraw-Hill. 1956.
20. Stone, M.H., and H.S. O'Bryant. *Weight Training: A Scientific Approach.* Minneapolis: Burgess. 1987.
21. Stone, M.H., H.S. O'Bryant, and J. Garhammer. A hypothetical model for strength training. *J Sports Med Phys Fitness* (21):336, 342-351. 1981.
22. Stone, M.H., H.S. O'Bryant, J. Garhammer, J. McMillan, and R. Rozenek. A theoretical model of strength training. *NSCA J* 4(4):36-40. 1982.
23. Stone, M.H., J. Potteiger, K.C. Pierce, C.M. Proulx, H.S. O'Bryant, and R.L. Johnson. Comparison of the effects of three different weight training programs on the 1RM squat: A preliminary study. Presented at National Strength and Conditioning Association Conference. Las Vegas, NV, June 1997.
24. Tschiene, P. The distinction of training structure in different stages of athlete's preparation. Paper presented at International Congress of Sport Sciences. Edmonton, AB, July 1979.
25. Wathen, D. Periodization: Concepts and applications. In: *Essentials of Strength Training and Conditioning,* T.R. Baechle, ed. Champaign, IL: Human Kinetics. 1994.

Chapter 20 Rehabilitation and Reconditioning

1. Amadio, P.C.. *Tendon and Ligament.* In: *Wound Healing: Biochemical and Clinical Aspects,* I.K. Cohen, R.F. Diegelmann, and W.J. Lindblad, eds. Philadelphia: Saunders. 1992. p. 384.
2. Anderson, M.K., and S.J. Hall, eds. *Fundamentals of Sports Injury Management.* Baltimore: Williams & Wilkins. 1997.
3. Borsa, P.A., S.M. Lephart, M.S. Kocher, and S.P. Lephart. Functional assessment and rehabilitation of shoulder proprioception for glenohumeral instability. *J Sport Rehabil* 3:84-104. 1994.
4. Burkhart, S.S., T.C. Johnson, M.A. Wirth, and K.A. Athanasiou. Cyclic loading of transosseous rotator cuff repairs: Tension overload as a possible cause of failure. *Arthroscopy* 13:172-176. 1997.
5. Byl, N.N., A.L. McKenzie, J.M. West, J.D. Whitney, T.K. Hunt, and H.A. Scheuenstuhl. Low-dose ultrasound effects on wound healing: A controlled study with Yucatan pigs. *Arch Phys Med Rehabil* 73:656-664. 1992.
6. Curwin, S., and W. Stanish. *Tendinitis: Its Etiology and Treatment.* Lexington, MA: Collamore Press. 1984.
7. Davies, G.J. The need for critical thinking in rehabilitation. *J Sport Rehabil* 4:1-22. 1995.
8. De Lorme, T.L. Restoration of muscle power by heavy resistance exercise. *J Bone Joint Surg* 27:645-667. 1945.
9. De Lorme, T.L., and A.L. Watkins. Technics of progressive resistance exercise. *Arch Phys Med* 29:263-273. 1948.
10. Fleck, S.J., and W.J. Kraemer. *Designing Resistance Training Programs,* 3rd ed. Champaign, IL: Human Kinetics. 2004.
11. Fredericson, M., A. Bergman, K. Hoffman, and M. Dillingham. Tibial stress fractures in runners. *Am J Sports Med* 23:472-481. 1995.
12. Freeman, M.A.R., and B. Wybe. Articular contributions to limb muscle reflexes: The effects of a partial neurectomy of the knee joint on postural reflexes. *Br J Surg* 53:61. 1966.
13. Frey, C.C., and M.J. Shereff. Tendon injuries about the ankle in athletes. *Clin Sports Med* 7:103-118. 1988.
14. Galin, J.I., I.M. Goldstein, and R. Snyderman. *Inflammation: Basic Principles and Clinical Correlates.* New York: Raven Press. 1988.
15. Garhammer, J. *Sports Illustrated Strength Training.* New York: Harper & Row. 1986.
16. Gelberman, R.H., V.M. Goldberg, A. Kai-An, and A. Baines. *Tendinitis.* In: *Injury and Repair of the Musculoskeletal Soft Tissue,* S.L.-Y. Woo and J.A. Buckwalter, eds. Park Ridge, IL: American Academy of Orthopaedic Surgeons. 1988. p. 5.
17. Giladi, M., C. Milgrom, A. Simkin, and Y. Danon. Stress fractures: Identifiable risk factors. *Am J Sports Med* 19:647-652. 1991.
18. Greaney, R.B., F.H. Gerber, R.L. Laughlin, J.P. Kmet, C.D. Metz, T.S. Kilcheski, B.R. Rao, and E.D. Silverman. Distribution and natural history of stress fractures in U.S. marine recruits. *Radiology* 146:339-346. 1983.
19. Grindstaff, T.L., and D.H. Potach. Prevention of common wrestling injuries. *Strength Cond J* 28:20-28. 2006.
20. Gross, M.T. Chronic tendinitis: Pathomechanics of injury, factors affecting the healing response, and treatment. *J Orthop Sports Phys Ther* 16:248-261. 1992.
21. Hillman, S. Principles and techniques of open kinetic chain rehabilitation: The upper extremity. *J Sport Rehabil* 3:319-330. 1994.
22. Ireland, M.L., J.D. Willson, B.T. Ballantyne, and I.M. Davis. Hip strength in females with and without patellofemoral pain. *J Orthop Sports Phys Ther* 33:671-676. 2003.
23. Jackson, B.A., J.A. Schwane, and B.C. Starcher. Effect of ultrasound therapy on the repair of Achilles tendon injuries in rats. *Med Sci Sports Exerc* 23:171-176. 1991.
24. Jaramillo, J., T.W. Worrell, and C.D. Ingersoll. Hip isometric strength following knee surgery. *J Orthop Sports Phys Ther* 20:160-165. 1994.
25. Kibler, W.B. The role of the scapula in athletic shoulder function. *Am J Sports Med* 26:325-337. 1998.
26. Knapik, J.J., R.H. Mawdsley, and M.U. Ramos. Angular specificity and test mode specificity of isometric and isokinetic strength training. *J Orthop Sports Phys Ther* 5:58-65. 1983.

27. Knight, K.L. Knee rehabilitation by the daily adjustable progressive resistive exercise technique. *Am J Sports Med* 7:336-337. 1979.
28. Knight, K.L. Quadriceps strengthening with the DAPRE technique: Case studies with neurological implications. *Med Sci Sports Exerc* 17:646-650. 1985.
29. Leadbetter, W.B. Cell-matrix response in tendon injury. *Clin Sports Med* 11:533-578. 1992.
30. Leighton, J.R., D. Holmes, J. Benson, B. Wooten, and R. Schmerer. A study of the effectiveness of ten different methods of progressive resistance exercise on the development of strength, flexibility, girth, and body weight. *J Assoc Phys Ment Rehabil* 21:78-81. 1967.
31. Mascal, C.L., R. Landel, and C. Powers. Management of patellofemoral pain targeting hip, pelvis, and trunk muscle function: 2 case reports. *J Orthop Sports Phys Ther* 33:647-660. 2003.
32. McMorris, R.O., and E.C. Elkins. A study of production and evaluation of muscular hypertrophy. *Arch Phys Med Rehabil* 35:420-426. 1954.
33. Mellion, M.B., W.M. Walsh, and G.L. Shelton. *The Team Physician's Handbook,* 2nd ed. Philadelphia: Hanley & Belfus. 1997.
34. Ramirez, A., J.A. Schwane, C. McFarland, and B.C. Starcher. The effect of ultrasound on collagen synthesis and fibroblast proliferation in vitro. *Med Sci Sports Exerc* 29:326-332. 1997.
35. Riemann, B.L., and S.M. Lephart. The sensorimotor system, part I: The physiologic basis of functional joint stability. *J Athl Train* 37:71-79. 2002.
36. Romani, W.A., J.H. Gieck, D.H. Perrin, E.N. Saliba, and D.M. Kahler. Mechanisms and management of stress fractures in physically active persons. *J Athl Train* 37:306-314. 2002.
37. Stanski, C., J. McMaster, and P. Scranton. On the nature of stress fractures. *Am J Sports Med* 6:391-396. 1978.
38. Steindler, A. *Kinesiology of the Human Body Under Normal and Pathological Conditions.* Springfield, IL: Charles C Thomas. 1955.
39. Stone, M., and H. O'Bryant. *Weight Training: A Scientific Approach.* Minneapolis: Burgess International. 1987.
40. Tippett, S.R. *Coaches Guide to Sport Rehabilitation.* Champaign, IL: Leisure Press. 1990.
41. Voight, M.L., and G. Cook. Clinical application of closed kinetic chain exercises. *J Sport Rehabil* 5:25-44. 1996.
42. Voight, M.L., and B.C. Thomson. The role of the scapula in the rehabilitation of shoulder injuries. *J Athl Train* 35:364-372. 2000.
43. Wathen, D. Communication: Athletic trainer/conditioning coach relations—communication is the key. *NSCA J* 6:32-33. 1984.
44. Wilk, K.E., and C.A. Arrigo. An integrated approach to upper extremity exercises. *Orthop Phys Ther Clin N Am* 1:337. 1992.
45. Wilk, K.E., C.A. Arrigo, and J.R. Andrews. The rehabilitation program of the thrower's elbow. *J Orthop Sports Phys Ther* 17:225-239. 1993.
46. Zinovieff, A.N. Heavy resistance exercise: The Oxford technique. *Br J Phys Med* 14:129. 1951.

Chapter 21 Facility Organization and Risk Management

1. Adams, S., M. Adrian, and M. Bayless. *Catastrophic Injuries in Sports: Avoidance Strategies.* Salinas, CA: Coyote Press. 1984.
2. Armitage-Johnson, S. Providing a safe training environment, part II. *Strength Cond* 16(2):34. 1994.
3. Baley, J.A., and D.L. Matthews. *Law and Liability in Athletics, Physical Education, and Recreation.* Boston: Allyn & Bacon. 1984.
4. Bucher, C.A., and M.L. Krotee. *Management of Physical Education and Sport,* 11th ed. Boston: McGraw-Hill. 1998.
5. Coalition of Americans to Protect Sports (CAPS). *Sports Injury Risk Management: The Keys to Safety,* 2nd ed. North Palm Beach, FL: CAPS. 1998.
6. Coker, E. Weightroom flooring. *NSCA J* 11(1):26-27. 1989.
7. Earle, R.W., and T.R. Baechle, eds. *NSCA's Essentials of Personal Training.* Champaign, IL: Human Kinetics. 2004.
8. Fried, G. *Managing Sport Facilities.* Champaign, IL: Human Kinetics. 2005.
9. Halling, D. Legal terminology for the strength and conditioning specialist. *NSCA J* 13(4):59-61. 1991.
10. Herbert, D.L. A good reason for keeping records. *Strength Cond* 16(3):64. 1994.
11. Herbert, D.L. Legal aspects of strength and conditioning. *NSCA J* 15(4):79. 1993.
12. Hillmann, A., and D.R. Pearson. Supervision: The key to strength training success. *Strength Cond* 17(5):67-71. 1995.
13. Jones, L., and U.S. Weightlifting Federation. *USWF coaching accreditation course: Club Coach Manual.* Colorado Springs, CO: USWF. 1991.
14. Kroll, B. Liability considerations for strength training facilities. *Strength Cond* 17(6):16-17. 1995.
15. Kroll, W. Selecting strength training equipment. *NSCA J* 12(5):65-70. 1990.
16. Kroll, W. Structural and functional considerations in designing the facility, part I. *NSCA J* 13(1):51-58. 1991.
17. Kroll, W. Structural and functional considerations in designing the facility, part II. *NSCA J* 13(3):51-57. 1991.
18. Patton, R.W., W.C. Grantham, R.F. Gerson, and L.R. Gettman. *Developing and Managing Health/Fitness Facilities.* Champaign, IL: Human Kinetics. 1989.
19. Plisk, S.S., R.J. DeRosa, and W.G. Hughan. The Brooks-Dwyer Varsity Strength and Conditioning Room at Yale University. *Strength Cond* 21(5):71-75. 1999.
20. Plisk, S.S., and R.A. Plisk. Cost-effective training platform design and construction. *NSCA J* 13(2):40-46. 1991.
21. Polson, G. Weight room safety strategic planning—part IV. *Strength Cond* 17(1):35-37. 1995.
22. Rabinoff, R. Weight room litigation: What's it all about. *Strength Cond* 16(2):10-12. 1994.
23. Ray, R. *Management Strategies in Athletic Training,* 2nd ed. Champaign, IL: Human Kinetics. 2000.
24. Tharrett, A.J., K.J. McInnis, and J.A. Peterson, J.A. *ACSM's Health/Fitness Facility Standards and Guidelines,* 3rd ed. Champaign, IL: Human Kinetics. 2007.

Chapter 22 Developing a Policies and Procedures Manual

1. Arthur, M.J., and B.L. Bailey. *Complete Conditioning for Football.* Champaign, IL: Human Kinetics. 1998.
2. Earle, R.W. *Staff and Facility Policies and Procedures Manual.* Omaha, NE: Creighton University. 1993.
3. Epley, B.D. *Flight Manual.* Lincoln, NE: University of Nebraska Printing. 1998.
4. Epley, B.D. *Make the Play.* Lincoln, NE: University of Nebraska Printing. 1998.
5. Marriott, J.W. *The Spirit to Serve.* New York: Harper Collins. 1997.
6. NSCA Professional Standards and Guidelines Task Force. *Strength and Conditioning Professional Standards and Guidelines.* Colorado Springs, CO: NSCA. 2001.
7. Stern, G.J. *The Drucker Foundation Self-Assessment Tool: Process Guide.* New York: Drucker Foundation; San Francisco: Jossey-Bass. 1999.
8. Taylor, J.H. *Performance Training Program Manual.* Las Cruces, NM: New Mexico State University. 2006.

Index

Note: Page numbers ending in an *f* or a *t* indicate a figure or a table, respectively.

About the Editors

Thomas R. Baechle, EdD; CSCS,*D; NSCA-CPT,*D, is chair of the exercise science and athletic training department at Creighton University in Omaha, Nebraska. In his career covering more than 35 years as a fitness professional and academician, Baechle has earned numerous certifications and awards, taught at various universities, held a variety of professional and civic offices, and volunteered for many national and international associations and organizations related to fitness and personal health.

Baechle is widely published and lectures frequently. His recent honors include receiving the Outstanding Writing Achievement Award from Human Kinetics in 2007, Merit for Excellence in Education and Development of Professional Standards from the International Fitness Institute in 2006, the Distinguished Faculty Service Award from Creighton University in 2002, and the Lifetime Achievement Award from the NSCA in 1998.

Baechle makes his home with his wife, Susan, in Omaha.

Roger W. Earle, MA; CSCS,*D; NSCA-CPT,*D, earned his master's degree from the University of Nebraska at Omaha in exercise science. He is the associate executive director for the National Strength and Conditioning Association (NSCA) Certification Commission, where he is responsible for developing the Certified Strength and Conditioning Specialist (CSCS) and the NSCA-Certified Personal Trainer (NSCA-CPT) certification exams. Previously Earle served as the head strength and conditioning coach and a faculty member of the exercise science and athletic training department at Creighton University in Omaha.

Earle has over 20 years of experience as a personal fitness trainer for people of all ages and fitness levels, and he frequently gives lectures at national and international conferences about designing personalized exercise and training programs. He coauthored the first and second editions of *Fitness Weight Training* and coedited both the *NSCA's Essentials of Personal Training* and the first and second editions of *Essentials of Strength Training and Conditioning*.

Earle enjoys spending time with his wife, Tonya, and their four daughters at their home in Glendale, Arizona.